Behavior in Organizations

EDITION 10

Behavior in Organizations

Jerald Greenberg

Prentice Hall

Boston   Columbus   Indianapolis   New York   San Francisco   Upper Saddle River
Amsterdam   Cape Town   Dubai   London   Madrid   Milan   Munich   Paris
Montreal   Toronto   Delhi   Mexico City   Sao Paulo   Sydney   Hong Kong
Seoul   Singapore   Taipei   Tokyo

Editorial Director: Sally Yagan
Editor-in-Chief: Eric Svendsen
Acquisitions Editor: Jennifer M. Collins
Editorial Project Manager: Susan Abraham
Director of Marketing: Patrice Lumumba Jones
Senior Marketing Manager: Nikki Ayana Jones
Senior Marketing Assistant: Ian Gold
Senior Managing Editor: Judy Leale
Production Project Manager: Kelly Warsak
Senior Operations Supervisor: Arnold Vila
Operations Specialist: Ilene Kahn
Creative Director: Christy Mahon
Senior Art Director/Design Supervisor: Janet Slowik
Senior Art Director: Steven Frim
Interior and Cover Design: Wee Design Group

Manager, Visual Research: Beth Brenzel
Photo Researcher: Sheila Norman
Manager, Rights and Permissions: Hessa Albader
Permissions Coordinator: Suzanne DeWorken
Manager, Cover Visual Research & Permissions: Karen Sanatar
Cover Image: Campbell Laird/Images.com/Corbis
Media Project Manager: Lisa Rinaldi
Media Editor: Denise Vaughn
Full-Service Project Management: Sharon Anderson/ BookMasters, Inc.
Composition: Integra Software Services
Printer/Binder: Quebecor World Color/Versailles
Cover Printer: Lehigh-Phoenix Color/Hagerstown
Text Font: 10/12 Times

Credits and acknowledgments borrowed from other sources and reproduced, with permission, in this textbook appear on appropriate page within text.

Library of Congress Cataloging-in-Publication Data
Greenberg, Jerald.
  Behavior in organizations / Jerald Greenberg.—10th ed.
    p. cm.
  Includes bibliographical references and index.
  ISBN-13: 978-0-13-609019-9
  ISBN-10: 0-13-609019-2
  1. Organizational behavior. I. Title.
  HD58.7.G7176 2011
  658.3—dc22
                                    2010011791

10 9 8 7 6 5 4 3 2 1

Prentice Hall
is an imprint of

www.pearsonhighered.com

ISBN 10:   0-13-609019-2
ISBN 13: 978-0-13-609019-9

To Carolyn,
For showing me what people mean when they say,
"I couldn't have done it without you."
J.G.

Brief Contents

Contents

Preface

Welcome to *Behavior in Organizations,* 10th Edition. As with the tenth iteration of anything, it's a milestone. And, by nature, milestones encourage us to look at where we've been. In this case, I see a book that is entering its fourth decade of publication. This edition hardly could be more different from the first edition—published in the early 1980s—in scope, style, and coverage. But, as the epigram goes, *plus ça change, plus c'est la même chose* ("the more things change, the more they remain the same"). For *Behavior in Organizations,* what remained the same is fundamental—the book's commitment to reflecting the nature of organizational behavior (OB). No matter where the field has been, *Behavior in Organizations* was there to capture its essence. This commitment remains as strong as ever in the current edition, but accomplishing this objective also has been more challenging.

For this I can thank the unprecedented speed with which contemporary organizations have been changing, making them moving targets for scientists intent on studying the behavior of people within them. And as they work to get a grip on the (sometime seismically) shifting terrain of the nature of organizations, so too have I endeavored to characterize what OB scientists and practitioners do. This challenge is one I approach with alacrity because the field's changes have kept it exciting and vibrant. In particular, they have reflected a new focus on issues that are not only scientifically important but that also have considerable practical value. It's science that's relevant to real-world issues, and this makes it incredibly valuable.

OB has positioned itself as the field that provides insight into the dynamic relationships between individuals, groups/teams, and entire organizations and, of course, their interrelationships with the economic, cultural, and social environment. We trade in research and theory, but these tools do not suffer from ivory tower elitism. Instead, the field of OB is focused on applying its highly developed analytical tools to understanding something very real and dynamic—the behavior of people in the workplace. Over the years, I've seen shifts in directions, but OB is now facing the issue of relevance instead of skirting it. Accordingly, this book now provides more insight into what actually is occurring in the workplace. In other words, as the field keeps apace with the workplace, I keep my fingers on its pulse. And those fingers are connected directly to the keyboard from which this book has emerged.

I became well aware of these changes as I researched this edition. Some of our concepts (e.g., justice, trust, diversity) have received more attention than in years past, earning them increased emphasis in this edition. On the other hand, some once-dominant conceptualizations (e.g., Maslow's need hierarchy theory, Herzberg's two-factor theory) have faded from our radar screens, leading me to remove them from the book. These topics are interesting and have had impact, but they are more yesterday than today. As such, they have limited value in a book I claim to be a snapshot of OB as we currently find it.

Perhaps what surprised me most was the huge number of changes in the businesses highlighted as examples in the previous edition. Many of these organizations no longer exist. Even more have been transformed in ways that now make them inappropriate as examples of the practice or phenomena I once associated with them. Inevitably, some of the companies described in this book will have altered their ways of operation still further by the time you read this, making some of my examples imperfect. Unfortunate as this is, it simply is a by product of studying a dynamic field.

Major Objective: To Spotlight Organizational Behavior

People enjoy learning about behavior in organizations. It gives us unique insight into everyday processes and phenomena we often take for granted, knowledge that helps us understand a key part of the world in which we live. For a book such as this, the implication is that the material must be accessible and relevant to readers. I have been very deliberate in my effort to incorporate these qualities into this book.

Accessibility to Readers

In preparing this edition, I have adopted a very simple assumption: Unless readers find the material accessible and engaging, they will fail to get anything out of it—if they even bother to read it at all. With this in mind, I have done several things that may be seen throughout this book.

- As always, I have gone out of my way to use a friendly and approachable writing style, speaking directly to readers in straightforward prose. At the same time, I have done my best to refrain from condescension (by speaking down to readers) and elitism (by going over their heads).
- By carefully selecting material to which students can relate—such as accounts of organizational practices in companies with which they may be familiar—they are likely to find the material engaging. In this edition, for example, organizations such as Facebook and Apple, and cross-functional teams such as the Dave Matthews Band, are mentioned.
- Key points are easy to find because of the way the book is designed and by features such as **key terms** appearing in margins and a **"Summary and Review of Learning Objectives"** appearing at the end of each chapter.
- Graphics are used to enhance explanations of material for visually oriented learners. For example, the **"talking graphics"** I've used for many editions help readers take away the key findings of research appearing in graphs. Using arrows to point directly to the important aspects of research findings is the next best thing to having an instructor present to point them out.

These are among the several key features that help bring the material to life for students by making a fascinating topic readily understandable.

Focusing on Relevance

The field of OB is *not* about curiosity for its own sake. Rather, it's about finding real, scientifically based answers to practical questions. Thus, relevance is vital. Theories and research are important, many students believe, so long as they offer insight into appropriate action—that is, what to do and why. In preparing this book, my mission was to spotlight this relevance in a form that would enlighten the target audience—college students at all levels who desire to learn about the complexities of human behavior in organizations. I do this in three ways.

First, in each chapter I provide concrete information on putting organizational behavior to practical use in special sections titled **"OB in Practice."** This feature describes current practices being used in companies or principles that readily lend themselves to application. Examples include:

- How the "Good Hands People" Use Diversity as a Competitive Weapon (Chapter 6)
- Organizational Design Strategies for the Information Age (Chapter 15)
- Making Changes Stick: Tips from Three Established Organizations (Chapter 16)

A second way in which I attempt to make the material relevant is by highlighting two significant realities of contemporary organizations—shifts in demographic diversity and rapid globalization of the business environment. I do this in sections titled, **"Today's Diverse and Global Organizations."** These sections highlight ways in which differences between individuals with respect to their race, gender, sexual preference, or nationality impact various OB phenomena. Some examples include the following:

- Do Men and Women Respond Differently to Stress? (Chapter 5)
- Inequity in Housework: Comparing Married Women and Men (Chapter 7)
- How Does National Culture Affect the Decision-Making Process? (Chapter 10)

The third way in which I focus on relevance is by highlighting a topic that has been occupying the popular press in recent years—ethics (or lack thereof). As ethics scandals proliferate, it is especially important to examine insight offered by the field of OB. I do this in the present book in a special feature called **"The Ethics Angle."** Several such sections are as follows:

- Making a Business Case for Ethical Behavior (Chapter 2)
- Should Doctors Be Paid for Their Performance? (Chapter 7)
- Why Do People Make Unethical Decisions? Bad Apples, Bad Cases, and Bad Barrels (Chapter 10)

A Careful Balancing Act

Throughout this book I found it necessary to balance coverage in two ways: (a) in striking a balance between discussions of basic science and practical application and (b) in presenting material designed to impart knowledge intended to develop skills.

Balancing Basic Science and Practical Application

Because the field of OB is a blend of research, theory, and practical application, so too, quite deliberately, is this book. Indeed, I have taken extensive steps to ensure that it is the best of these seemingly disparate worlds. Consider just a few examples:

- In Chapter 3, I cover theories of learning and how these are involved in such organizational practices as training, organizational behavior management, and discipline.
- In Chapter 6, specific ways in which the various theories of motivation can be put into practice are discussed.
- In Chapter 10, it is not only various scientific studies of decision making that are identified, but also various practices that can be, and are being, followed to enhance the effectiveness of group decisions.

Beyond simply indicating how various research findings and theories may be applied, I also focus on application by adopting a *hands-on approach.* This is done by offering concrete, "how to" suggestions for readers. These are not only useful by themselves, but because they are derived from OB research and theory, they also provide clear illustrations of the field's practical utility. By weaving such recommendations throughout this book, OB is brought to life for readers at every juncture. Just a few examples include how to:

- Properly use communication media (Chapter 9)
- Brainstorm effectively (Chapter 10)
- Promote trust in organizations (Chapter 11)

By focusing on how findings from OB research may be applied in organizations, I am taking what amounts to an *evidence-based approach.* In recent years, so-called "evidence-based" movements have emerged in such applied fields as medicine, nursing, education, and management. The idea underlying these approaches is that guidelines for practice should be based on research findings. Although this idea may be novel to some fields, using research to inform practice is inherent in the nature of OB. For this reason, the practice of applying research and theory to organizational issues (evidence-based practice) and relying on knowledge of practical problems as input into research and theory (practice-based evidence) is a hallmark of the field of OB—and for this reason, it is emphasized in this book.

Balancing Knowledge and Skills

Educators tell us that there is a fundamental distinction between teaching people about something—providing *knowledge*—and showing them how to do it—developing their *skills.* In the field of OB, this distinction becomes blurred. After all, to appreciate fully how to do something, you have to have the requisite knowledge. For this reason, I pay attention to both knowledge and skills in this book. Consider the following illustrations:

- Chapter 5 investigates ways in which stress operates in the workplace. Beyond this, I also present an exercise to help readers recognize how they can build resilience as a way of alleviating the adverse effects of stress.
- Chapter 9 discusses the nature of the communication process. In addition, to help readers become effective communicators I include an exercise designed to promote active listening skills.
- Chapter 13 describes the nature of leadership. With an eye toward helping readers develop their own skills, I present a section that allows people to assess their own styles as leaders.
- Chapter 16 explains not only the reasons underlying individuals' resistance to organizational change but also various ways in which this may be overcome. In addition, I give students an opportunity to practice overcoming resistance to change in an exercise.

By doing these things—not only in these examples, but throughout the book—I intend not only to help readers understand OB, but also to enable them to practice it in their own lives.

New Coverage

In revising this book, I made many changes. Some came in the process of seeking that balance to which I just referred, and others were necessitated by my ongoing commitment to highlighting the latest advances in the field and to updating examples. Many of the changes are subtle, referring only to how a topic is framed relative to others. A good many others are more noticeable and involve the shifting of major sections into new places and the addition of brand new ones.

Here are just a few of the new topics and the chapters in which they appear:

- Compressed workweeks (Chapter 1)
- Idiosyncratic work arrangements (i-deals) (Chapter 1)
- Multifoci approach to organizational justice (Chapter 2)
- Neurological bases of organizational justice (Chapter 2)
- Basking in reflected glory/cutting off reflected failure (Chapter 3)
- Active learning techniques (Chapter 3)
- Cascading model of emotional intelligence (Chapter 4)
- National differences in expressivity (Chapter 5)
- Effects of mood on memory (Chapter 5)
- Preferential and nonpreferential affirmative action (Chapter 6)
- Affinity groups (part of expanded coverage of diversity) (Chapter 6)
- Strongest motivators for people at different organizational levels (Chapter 7)
- Pay-for-performance among physicians (Chapter 7)
- Cross-training (Chapter 8)
- Shared mental models (Chapter 8)
- Role of media richness in recruitment ads (Chapter 9)
- Communicating layoffs via e-mail (Chapter 9)
- Why people make unethical decisions (Chapter 10)
- Indecisiveness (Chapter 10)
- Swift trust (Chapter 11)
- Developing trustworthiness (Chapter 11)
- Straightforwardness (Chapter 12)
- Political skill (Chapter 12)
- Assessment centers (Chapter 13)
- Promoting authentic leadership (Chapter 13)
- Ethical and customer-centered organizational culture (Chapter 14)
- Openness to experience and support for creativity (Chapter 14)
- Strategic approach to organizational design (Chapter 15)
- Communities of practice (Chapter 15)
- Product offshoring, services offshoring, and innovation offshoring (Chapter 16)

Pedagogical Features

Faculty members who have adopted the previous edition of this book have valued its many pedagogical features. They will be pleased to find that these have returned, although updated and revised, of course.

End-of-Chapter Pedagogical Features

Two groups of pedagogical features may be found at the end of each chapter. The first, named **"Points to Ponder,"** includes three types of questions:

- *Questions for Review.* These are designed to help students determine the extent to which they picked up the major points contained in each chapter.
- *Experiential Questions.* These questions get students to understand various OB phenomena by thinking about experiences in their work lives.

- *Questions to Analyze.* The questions in this category are designed to help readers think about the connections between various OB phenomena and/or how they may be applied in organizational situations.

The second category of end-of-chapter pedagogical features is referred to as **"Experiencing OB."** This includes the following three types of experiential exercises.

- *Individual Exercise.* Students can complete these exercises on their own to gain personal insight into various OB phenomena.
- *Group Exercise.* By working in small groups, students will be able to experience an important OB phenomenon or concept. The experience itself also will help them develop team-building skills.
- *Practicing OB.* This exercise is applications-based. It describes a hypothetical problem situation and challenges the reader to explain how various OB practices can be applied to solving it.

Case Features

Each chapter contains two cases. Positioned at the beginning of the chapter, a **Preview Case** is designed to set up the material that follows by putting it in the context of a real organizational event. These are either completely new to this edition or updated considerably. A few examples of new Preview Cases include the following:

- The Talented Chief of Taleo (Chapter 1)
- A Huge Day's Pay for a Seriously Bad Day's Work (Chapter 2)
- Madison Avenue Welcomes Disabled Athletes (Chapter 6)
- The Woman Who Saved the Chicken Fajitas (Chapter 13)
- Saving Campbell's from the Soup (Chapter 16)

The end-of-chapter case, **Case in Point,** is designed to review the material already covered and to bring it to life. Specific tie-ins are made by use of discussion questions appearing after each Case in Point feature. These also are new or updated for this edition. Several examples of new cases include the following:

- Floyd's Barbershop: A Cut Above the Rest (Chapter 1)
- HP = Hidden Pretexting? What Did In Dunn? (Chapter 2)
- Domino's Pizza Takes a Bite Out of Turnover (Chapter 6)
- Inside the Peloton: Social Dynamics of the Tour de France (Chapter 8)
- A New Era for Newark (Chapter 13)

Updated Supplements Packages

Updating the book has required revising the supplements packages. This was done both for supplements available to faculty members who adopt this book in their classes and for their students.

Supplements for Instructors

At www.pearsonhighered.com/irc, instructors can access a variety of print, digital, and presentation resources available with this text in downloadable format. Registration is simple and gives you immediate access to new titles and new editions. As a registered faculty member, you can download resource files and receive immediate access and instructions for installing course management content on your campus server.

If you need assistance, our dedicated technical support team is ready to help with the media supplements that accompany this text. Visit 247pearsoned.custhelp.com for answers to frequently asked questions and toll-free user support phone numbers.

The following supplements are available to adopting instructors (for detailed descriptions, please visit www.pearsonhighered.com/irc):

- Instructor's Manual. Materials designed to provide ideas and resources for classroom teaching have been updated and revised.
- Test Item File. Questions that require students to apply the information about which they've read in the text have been revised and updated to support changes in this edition. Questions are also tagged to reflect the AACSB Learning Standards.

- TestGen Test Generating Software. Test management software containing all the material from the Test Item File is available. This software is completely user friendly and allows instructors to view, edit, and add test questions with just a few mouse clicks.
- PowerPoint Presentation. A ready-to-use PowerPoint slideshow has been designed for classroom presentation. Use it as is, or edit content to fit your individual classroom needs.

Supplements for Students

Several supplemental materials are available to help students at this book's companion Web site, **http://www.pearsonhighered.com/greenberg.** These include the following:

- Learning Objectives. This is a list of the six major learning objectives for each chapter.
- Chapter Quizzes. These are 20-item quizzes that students can use to assess their own familiarity with the content of each chapter. As a helpful feature, online "hints" are provided.
- Internet Exercises. Each chapter contains three exercises that require students to tap resources found on the Internet to expand their understanding of the material in each chapter.
- Student PowerPoints. A set of PowerPoint slides is given for each chapter. These outline the major points covered.

Finally—and Most Importantly—Acknowledgments

Writing is a solitary task. In contrast, the process of turning the millions of bytes of information I generate as a content provider into this beautiful book is anything but solitary. To the contrary, it requires the highly coordinated efforts of a team of dedicated professionals in different professions, all of whom lend their considerable talents toward making this book a reality. In preparing this text, I have been fortunate to work with a variety of hardworking people whose efforts are reflected on every page. Although I cannot possibly thank all of them here, I wish to express my appreciation to those whose help has been most valuable.

To begin, I must thank to my former coauthor on this book, Robert A. Baron. His guidance has helped me develop as a textbook author and his friendship over many decades has given me the confidence to undertake the challenges of authoring.

Second, I acknowledge sincerely the numerous colleagues who read and commented on various portions of the manuscript for this and earlier editions. Their suggestions were invaluable and helped us in many ways. These include:

Royce L. Abrahamson, Southwest Texas State University

Carlos J. Alsua, University of Alaska Anchorage

Rabi S. Bhagat, Memphis State University

Ralph R. Braithwaite, University of Hartford

Stephen C. Buschardt, University of Southern Mississippi

Dawn Carlson, University of Utah

M. Suzzanne Clinton, Cameron University

Roy A. Cook, Fort Lewis College

Cynthis Cordes, State University of New York at Binghamton

Aleta L. Crawford, University of Mississippi Tupelo

Fred J. Dorn, University of Mississippi

Julie Dziekan, University of Michigan–Dearborn

Megan L. Endres, Eastern Michigan University

Janice Feldbauer, Austin Community College

Patricia Feltes, Southwest Missouri State University

Olene L. Fuller, San Jacinto College North

Richard Grover, University of Southern Maine

W. Lee Grubb III, East Carolina University

Courtney Hunt, University of Delaware

Ralph Katerberg, University of Cincinnati

Paul N. Keaton, University of Wisconsin at LaCrosse

Mary Kernan, University of Delaware

Daniel Levi, California Polytechnic State University

Jeffrey Lewis, Pitzer College

Michael P. Lillis, Medaille College

Rodney Lim, Tulane University

Charles W. Mattox, Jr., St. Mary's University

Daniel W. McAllister, University of Nevada–Las Vegas

James McElroy, Iowa State University

Richard McKinney, Southern Illinois University

Morgan R. Milner, Eastern Michigan University

Linda Morable, Richland College

Paula Morrow, Iowa State University

Audry Murrell, University of Pittsburgh

David Olsen, California State University–Bakersfield

William D. Patzig, James Madison University

Shirley Rickert, Indiana University-Purdue University at Fort Wayne

Roger A. Ritvo, Auburn University Montgomery

David W. Roach, Arkansas Tech University

Jane P. Rose, Hiram College

Dr. Meshack M. Sagini, Langston University

Terri A. Scandura, University of Miami, Coral Gables

Holly Schroth, University of California Berkeley

Marc Siegall, California State University, Chico

Taggart Smith, Purdue University

Patrick C. Stubbleine, Indiana University-Purdue University at Fort Wayne

Paul Sweeney, Marquette University

Craig A. Tunwall, SUNY Empire State College

Edward Ward, St. Cloud State University

Carol Watson, Rider University

Philip A. Weatherford, Embry-Riddle Aeronautical University

Richard M. Weiss, University of Delaware

Stan Williamson, University of Louisiana-Monroe

Third, I wish to express appreciation to my editor, Jennifer Collins, who saw me through this project. Sometimes, it required cajoling or even threatening, but mostly her calm encouragement and constant support and direction—not to mention the patience of Job—made it possible for me to prepare this book. Editorial project manager Susie Abraham was always there to help, as was editorial assistant Meg O'Rourke. And, of course, I would be remiss in not thanking Eric Svendsen and members of the Prentice Hall team for their steadfast support of this book over the years.

Finally, my sincere thanks go to Prentice Hall's top-notch production team for making this book so beautiful—Kelly Warsak, project manager; Janet Slowik, art director; Suzanne DeWorken, permissions coordinator; and Sheila Norman, photo researcher; as well as Sharon Anderson at BookMasters and the staff at Integra Software Services. Their diligence and skill with the many behind-the-scenes tasks required in a book such as this one—not to mention their constant refinements—helped me immeasurably throughout the process of preparing this work.

It was a pleasure to work with such kind and understanding professionals, and I am greatly indebted to them for their contributions.

To all these truly outstanding individuals, and to many others too, my warm personal regards.

In Conclusion: An Invitation for Feedback

I would appreciate hearing from you! Let me know what you think about this textbook by writing to me at the publisher's Web site, college_marketing@prenhall.com. Please include "Feedback about Greenberg 10e" in the subject line. Your comments will not fall on deaf ears, I can assure you. I have been most responsive to comments from colleagues and students over the years and I intend to continue to listen. Finally, if you have any questions related to this book, please contact our customer service department online at **http://www.247.prenhall.com.**

With all this behind us, now, welcome to the world of organizational behavior.

Jerald Greenberg

CHAPTER

1 The Field of Organizational Behavior

Learning Objectives

After reading this chapter, you should be able to:

1. Define the concepts of organization and organizational behavior.
2. Describe the field of organizational behavior's commitment to the scientific method and the three levels of analysis it uses.
3. Trace the historical developments and schools of thought leading up to the field of organizational behavior today.
4. Identify the fundamental characteristics of the field of organizational behavior.
5. Describe how the field of organizational behavior today is being shaped by the global economy, increasing racial and ethnic diversity in the workforce, and advances in technology.
6. Explain how people's changing expectations about the desire to be engaged in their work and the need for flexibility in work have influenced the field of organizational behavior.

Chapter Outline

- Organizational Behavior: Its Basic Nature
- What Are the Field's Fundamental Assumptions?
- OB Then and Now: A Capsule History
- OB Responds to the Rise of Globalization and Diversity
- OB Responds to Advances in Technology
- OB Is Responsive to People's Changing Expectations

Preview Case

■ *The Talented Chief of Taleo*

Ask any executive to identify his or her company's most important asset and chances are good that the response will be "people." It's people who keep businesses alive, making it critical for human assets to be managed as carefully as money, inventory, or any other assets. With this in mind, most companies rely on some type of software to assist in the process of hiring, managing, developing, and compensating their employees. Tracking employee data in this fashion helps organizations keep tabs on who's in their workforces, what they can do, and where they're going.

In the case of 46 of the *Fortune* 100 companies—and over 4,000 others—this process of "talent management" is entrusted to Taleo, a company of only 900 employees located in Burlingame, California. Since its inception in 1996, the company helped organizations select world-class talent by tapping into the power of the Internet. Although this hardly seems unique today, it certainly was revolutionary back then. In those high-tech boom years, Taleo grew quickly and acquired other companies, allowing it to expand its services and to gain an international presence. Not surprisingly, however, the company faced challenges at the end of the first decade of the twenty-first century. The economy was nowhere near as robust as it was just a few years earlier, in the late 1990s. If companies aren't hiring, the need to manage the hiring process online is limited, leading Taleo to face a period of uncertainty.

If you're in the business of helping companies manage people, however, then one would expect you to manage people pretty well yourself. Thanks to Taleo's talented chairman and CEO, Michael Gregoire, the company did in fact manage people effectively even during the depth of the recession in 2008. Gregoire has been credited for single-handedly getting the company through a period in which its employees felt uncertain about their futures, retaining employees and clients at a time when many normally would be inclined to abandon ship.

So, how exactly did Gregoire do it? Experts acknowledge that what saved the day was his keen understanding of the dynamics of people in organizations. He discouraged employees from dwelling on their personal uncertainties and encouraged them to focus on what the company does—service its customers by offering solid products that meet their needs. If clients inquired about the company's problems, the sales force was armed with answers. They were completely open about what was going on behind the scenes but reassured clients that the company would be around to help them in the future. With this in mind, sales reps made it clear what Taleo is all about, describing "our value, our culture, and how we could really help them improve their company, their value, and their customers." As Gregoire described clients, "They buy software based on the relationship you have." And Taleo maintains outstanding relationships with its clients.

The company's approach to doing this involves having its sales reps help customers realize that they have problems and that Taleo could offer solutions. Because most companies weren't hiring, it was essential for them to keep their most talented employees from going to work at one of the few other companies that were hiring and to get as much as possible from the employees they already have. Taleo's solution involved using the company's products to help clients identify the skills that employees had (and that they wished to develop) and then moving them into positions that capitalize on these skills. Underutilizing resources is something that no company can afford today, and Taleo's products help prevent this from happening.

It looks like Michael Gregoire's emphasis on transparency and emphasizing customer solutions has been successful. In the first three quarters of 2009, when most companies' bottom lines were hemorrhaging, Taleo's revenues grew by an eye-popping 31 percent. Gregoire believes that this is the beginning of even more impressive figures to come. We share this optimism, and not just because of the nature and quality of his company's products. There's something more fundamental involved—Gregoire's ability to read people. In fact, his sensitivity to the importance of building relationships with customers and employees is fundamental to Taleo's success.

Gregoire appears to be aware of a key fact: No matter how good a company's products may be, there can be no company without people. From the founder down to the lowest ranking employee, it's all about people. If you've ever run or managed a business, you know that "people problems" can bring an organization down very rapidly. Hence, it makes sense to realize that people are a critical element in the effective functioning—indeed, the basic existence—of organizations. This people-centered orientation is what the field of *organizational behavior* (*OB* for short)—hence, this book—is all about. Simply put, OB is the field specializing in the study of human behavior in organizations.

OB scientists and practitioners study and attempt to solve problems by using knowledge derived from research in the *behavioral sciences,* such as psychology and sociology. Because the field of OB is firmly rooted in science, it relies on research to derive valuable information about organizations and the complex processes operating within them. Such knowledge is used as the basis for helping to solve a wide range of organizational problems. For example, what can be done to make people more productive and more satisfied on the job? When and how should people be organized into teams? How should jobs and organizations be designed so that people best adapt to changes in the environment? These are just a few of the many important questions addressed by the field of organizational behavior.

As you read this text, it will become very clear that OB specialists have attempted to learn about a wide variety of issues involving people in organizations. In fact, over the past few decades, OB has developed into a field so diverse that just about any aspect of what people do in the workplace is likely to have been examined by OB scientists.[1] The fruits of this labor already have been enjoyed by people interested in making organizations not only more productive, but also more pleasant for the individuals working in them.

In the remainder of this chapter, we will give you the background information you will need to understand the scope of OB and its importance. With this in mind, this first chapter is designed to introduce you to the field of OB by focusing on its history and its fundamental characteristics. We will begin by formally defining OB, describing exactly what it is and what it seeks to accomplish. Following this, we will summarize the history of the field, tracing its roots from its origins to its emergence as a modern science. Then, in the final sections of the chapter, we will discuss the wide variety of factors that make the field of OB the vibrant, ever-changing field it is today. At this point, we will be ready to face the primary goal of this book: to enhance your understanding of the human side of work by giving you a comprehensive overview of the field of organizational behavior.

Organizational Behavior: Its Basic Nature

As the phrase implies, OB deals with organizations. Although you already know from experience what an organization is, a formal definition helps to avoid ambiguity. An **organization** is a structured social system consisting of groups and individuals working together to meet some agreed-upon objectives. In other words, organizations consist of people, who alone and together in work groups strive to attain common goals. Although this definition is rather abstract, it is sure to take on more meaning as you continue reading this book. We say this with confidence because the field of OB is concerned with organizations of all types, whether large or small in size, public or private in ownership (i.e., whether or not shares of stock are sold to the public), and whether they exist to earn a profit or to enhance the public good (i.e., *nonprofit organizations,* such as charities and civic groups). Regardless of the specific goals sought, the structured social units working together toward them may be considered organizations.

organization
A structured social system consisting of groups and individuals working together to meet some agreed-upon objectives.

To launch our journey through the world of OB, we will address two fundamental questions: (1) What is the field of organizational behavior all about? and (2) Why is it important to know about OB?

What Is the Field of Organizational Behavior All About?

The field of *organizational behavior* deals with human behavior in organizations. Formally defined, **organizational behavior** is the multidisciplinary field that seeks knowledge of behavior in organizational settings by systematically studying individual, group, and organizational processes. This knowledge is used both by scientists interested in understanding human behavior and by practitioners interested in enhancing organizational effectiveness and individual well-being. In this book we highlight both purposes by focusing on how scientific knowledge has been—or may be—used for these practical purposes.

organizational behavior
The field that seeks to understand individual, group, and organizational processes in the workplace.

Our definition of OB highlights four central characteristics of the field. First, OB is firmly grounded in the scientific method. Second, OB studies individuals, groups, and organizations. Third, OB is interdisciplinary in nature. And fourth, OB is used as the basis for enhancing organizational effectiveness and individual well-being. We will now take a closer look at these four characteristics of the field.

OB APPLIES THE SCIENTIFIC METHOD TO PRACTICAL MANAGERIAL PROBLEMS. In our definition of OB, we refer to seeking knowledge and to studying behavioral processes. This should not be surprising since, as we noted earlier, OB knowledge is based on the **behavioral sciences.** These are fields such as psychology and sociology that seek knowledge of human behavior and society through the use of the scientific method. Although not as sophisticated as many of the "hard sciences," such as physics or chemistry—nor as mature as them—OB's orientation is still scientific in nature. Thus, like other scientific fields, OB seeks to develop a base of knowledge by using an empirical, research-based approach. That is, it is based on systematic observation and measurement of the behavior or phenomenon of interest. As we will describe in Appendix 1, organizational research is neither easy nor foolproof. After all, both people and organizations are quite complex, making it challenging sometimes to get a handle on understanding them. It is widely agreed that the scientific method is the best way to learn about behavior in organizations. For this reason, the scientific orientation should be acknowledged as a hallmark of the field of OB.

As they seek to improve organizational functioning and the quality of life of people working in organizations, managers rely heavily on knowledge derived from OB research. For example, researchers have shed light on such practical questions as:

- How can goals be set to enhance people's job performance?
- How can jobs be designed to enhance employees' feelings of satisfaction?
- Under what conditions do individuals make better decisions than groups?
- What can be done to improve the quality of organizational communication?
- What steps can be taken to alleviate work-related stress?
- What do leaders do to enhance the effectiveness of their teams?
- How can organizations be designed to make people highly productive?

Throughout this book we will describe scientific research and theory bearing on the answers to these and dozens of other practical questions. It is safe to say that the scientific and applied facets of OB not only coexist, but complement one another. Indeed, just as knowledge about the properties of physics may be put to use by engineers, and engineering data can be used to test theories of basic physics, so too are knowledge and practical applications closely intertwined in the field of OB.

OB FOCUSES ON THREE LEVELS OF ANALYSIS—INDIVIDUALS, GROUPS, AND ORGANIZATIONS. To best appreciate behavior in organizations, OB specialists cannot focus exclusively on individuals acting alone. After all, in organizations people frequently work together in groups and teams. Furthermore, people—alone and in groups—both influence and are influenced by their work environments. Considering this, it should not be surprising to learn that the field of OB focuses on three distinct levels of analysis—*individuals, groups,* and *organizations* (see Figure 1.1).

The field of OB recognizes that all three levels of analysis must be considered to comprehend fully the complex dynamics of behavior in organizations. Careful attention to all three levels of analysis—and the relationships between them—is a central theme in modern OB, and this will be reflected fully throughout this text. For example, we will be describing how OB scientists are concerned with individual perceptions, attitudes, and motives. We also will be describing how people communicate with each other and coordinate their activities among themselves in work groups. Finally, we will examine organizations as a whole—the way they are structured and operate in their environments, and the effects of their operations on the individuals and groups within them.

OB IS MULTIDISCIPLINARY IN NATURE. When you consider the broad range of issues and approaches that the field of OB encompasses, it is easy to appreciate the fact that the field is multidisciplinary in nature. By this, we mean that it draws on a wide variety of social science disciplines. Rather than studying a topic from only one particular perspective, the field of OB is likely to consider a wide variety of approaches. These range from the highly individual-oriented approach of psychology, through the more group-oriented approach of sociology, to issues in organizational quality studied by management scientists.

For a summary of some of the key fields from which OB draws, see Table 1.1. If, as you read this book, you recognize some particular theory or approach as familiar, chances are good that you may have learned something about it in another class. What makes OB so special is that it combines these various orientations together into a single field, one that's very broad and exciting.

---

behavioral sciences
Fields such as psychology and sociology that seek knowledge of human behavior and society through the use of the scientific method.

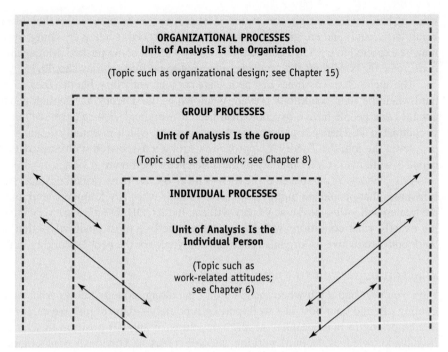

FIGURE 1.1

The Three Levels of Analysis Used in Organizational Behavior
To fully understand behavior in organizations, we must consider three levels of analysis: processes occurring within individuals, groups, and organizations.

OB SEEKS TO IMPROVE ORGANIZATIONAL EFFECTIVENESS AND THE QUALITY OF LIFE AT WORK. In the early part of the twentieth century, as railroads opened up the western portion of the United States and the nation's population grew rapidly (it doubled from 1880 to 1920!), the demand for manufactured products was great. New manufacturing plants were built, attracting waves of new immigrants in search of a living wage, and laborers were lured off farms by the employment prospects factory work offered. These men and women found that factories were gigantic, noisy, hot, and highly regimented—in short, brutal places in which to work. Bosses demanded more and more of their employees and treated them like disposable machines, replacing those who died from accidents or who quit with others who waited outside factory gates.

Clearly, the managers of a century ago held very negative views of employees. They assumed that people were basically lazy and irresponsible, and treated them with disrespect. This very negativistic approach, which has been with us for many years, reflects the traditional view of management, called a **Theory X** orientation. This philosophy of management assumes that people are basically lazy, dislike work, need direction, and will work hard only when they are pushed.

Today, however, if you asked corporate officials to describe their views of human nature, you'd probably find some more optimistic beliefs. Although some of today's managers still think that people are basically lazy, most would argue that the vast majority of people are capable of

Theory X
A traditional philosophy of management suggesting that most people are lazy and irresponsible, and will work hard only when forced to do so.

TABLE 1.1 The Multidisciplinary Roots of OB

Specialists in OB derive knowledge from a wide variety of social science disciplines to create a unique, multidisciplinary field. Some of the most important parent disciplines are listed here, along with some of the OB topics to which they are related (and the chapters in this book in which they are discussed).

Discipline	Relevant OB Topics
Psychology	Perception and learning (Chapter 3); personality (Chapter 4); emotion and stress (Chapter 5); attitudes (Chapter 6); motivation (Chapter 7); decision making (Chapter 10); creativity (Chapter 14)
Sociology	Group dynamics (Chapter 8); teamwork (Chapter 8); communication (Chapter 9)
Anthropology	Organizational culture (Chapter 14); leadership (Chapter 13)
Political science	Interpersonal conflict (Chapter 11); organizational power (Chapter 12)
Economics	Decision making (Chapter 10); negotiation (Chapter 11); organizational power (Chapter 12)
Management science	Organizational structure (Chapter 15); organizational change (Chapter 16)

working hard under the right conditions. If employees are recognized for their efforts (such as by being fairly paid) and are given an opportunity to succeed (such as by being well trained), they may be expected to put forth considerable effort without being pushed. Management's job, then, is to create the conditions that make people want to perform as they should.

The approach that assumes that people are not inherently lazy, but that they are willing to work hard when the right conditions prevail, is known as the **Theory Y** orientation. This philosophy assumes that people have a psychological need to work and seek achievement and responsibility. In contrast to the Theory X philosophy of management, which essentially demonstrates distrust for people on the job, the Theory Y approach is strongly associated with improving the quality of people's work lives (for a summary of the differences, see Figure 1.2).

The Theory Y perspective prevails within the field of organizational behavior today. It assumes that people are highly responsive to their work environments, and that the ways they are treated will influence the ways they will act. In fact, OB scientists are very interested in learning exactly what conditions will lead people to behave most positively—that is, what makes work both productive for organizations and enjoyable for the people working in them.

Why Is It Important to Know About OB?

Have you ever had a job where people don't get along, nobody knows what to do, everyone is goofing off, and your boss is—well, putting it politely—unpleasant? We can't imagine that you liked working in that company at all. Now, think of another position in which everyone was friendly, knowledgeable, hard working, and very pleasant. Obviously, that's more to your liking. Such a situation is one in which you are likely to be interested in going to work, doing your best, and taking pride in what you do. What lies at the heart of these differences are all issues that are of great concern to OB scientists and practitioners—and ones we will cover in this book.

The key reason to know about OB is simple—it matters. Indeed, OB makes a very big difference in the world of work. Not only does OB explain how people feel about their work, but importantly, how well they perform. In a survey of a wide range of professional workers, it was found that three factors were related to job performance: (1) management and organization, (2) information technology, and (3) workplace design.[2] Although the topics of information technology and workplace design are the primary focus of other fields, they also are related to OB. As a result, we discuss them both in this chapter and elsewhere in this book (e.g., Chapter 15). The first factor, management and organization, is precisely what OB is all about. Thus, studying OB provides important insight into work performance. And in today's competitive business world, overlooking this knowledge is a luxury no one can be without.

Theory Y
A philosophy of management suggesting that under the right circumstances, people are fully capable of working productively and accepting responsibility for their work.

FIGURE 1.2

Theory X Versus Theory Y: A Summary

The traditional, Theory X orientation toward people is far more negativistic than the more contemporary, Theory Y approach, which is widely accepted today. Some of the key differences between these management philosophies are summarized here.

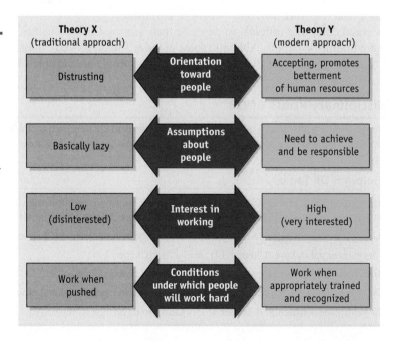

"Okay," you may be asking yourself, "in some companies things are nice and smooth, but in others, relationships are rocky—does it really matter?" As you will see throughout this book, the answer is a resounding *yes!* For now, here are just a few highlights of specific ways in which OB matters to people and the organizations in which they work.

- Companies whose managers accurately appraise the work of their subordinates enjoy lower costs and higher productivity than those that handle their appraisals less accurately.[3]
- People who are satisfied with the way they are treated on their jobs generally are more pleasant to their coworkers and bosses, and are less likely to quit than those who are dissatisfied with the way others treat them.[4]
- People who are trained carefully to work together in teams tend to be happier and more productive than those who simply are thrown together without any organizational support.[5]
- Employees who believe they have been treated unfairly on the job are more likely to steal from their employers and to reject the policies of their organizations than those who believe they have been treated fairly.[6]
- People who are mistreated by their supervisors on the job suffer more mental and physical illnesses than those who are treated with kindness, dignity, and respect.[7]
- Organizations that treat employees well with respect to pay/benefits, opportunities, job security, friendliness, fairness, and pride in the company are, on average, twice as profitable as the Standard & Poor's 500 companies.[8]
- Companies that offer good employee benefits and that have friendly working conditions are more profitable than those that are less people-oriented.[9]

By now, you might be asking yourself: Why, if OB is so important, is there no one person in charge of it in an organization? After all, companies tend to have officials who are responsible for other basic areas, such as finance, accounting, marketing, and production. Why not OB? That's a good question. If you've never heard of a vice president of OB or a manager of OB, it's because organizations do not have any such formal posts. So who is responsible for organizational behavior? In a sense, the answer is *everyone*!

Although OB is a separate area of study, it cuts across all areas of organizational functioning. Managers in all departments have to know such things as how to motivate employees, how to keep people satisfied with their jobs, how to communicate clearly, how to make teams function smoothly, and how to design jobs most effectively. In short, dealing with people at work is every-body's responsibility on the job. So, no matter what job you do in a company, knowing something about OB is sure to help you do it better. This is precisely why it's so vitally important for you to understand the material in this book. (However, many of the things people commonly think about behavior in organizations are untrue. That is, they are inconsistent with the findings of careful research on which the field is based. For a look at some such beliefs, please complete the Individual Exercise at the end of this chapter.)

What Are the Field's Fundamental Assumptions?

The field of OB is guided by two key assumptions—fundamental ideas that are widely accepted by everyone who does scientific research on OB or who puts these findings into practice in the workplace. First, OB recognizes that organizations are dynamic and always changing. Second, the field of OB assumes there is no one best way to behave in organizations, and that different approaches are called for in different situations. Because of their fundamental nature, let's examine these assumptions more closely.

OB Recognizes the Dynamic Nature of Organizations

Although OB scientists and practitioners are interested in the behavior of people, they also are concerned about the nature of organizations. Under what conditions will organizations change? How are organizations structured? How do organizations interact with their environments? These and related questions are of major interest to specialists in OB.

OB scientists recognize that organizations are not static, but dynamic and ever-changing enti-ties. In other words, they recognize that organizations are **open systems**—that is, self-sustaining connections between entities that use energy to transform resources from the environment (such as

open systems
Self-sustaining systems that transform input from the external environment into output, which the system then returns to the environment.

FIGURE 1.3

Organizations as Open Systems: Overview and Example

The open systems approach is characteristic of modern-day thinking in the field of OB. It assumes that organizations are self-sustaining—that is, within the environments in which they operate they transform inputs to outputs in a continuous fashion. This example illustrates the symphony orchestra as an open system, but the same concepts apply to all organizations.

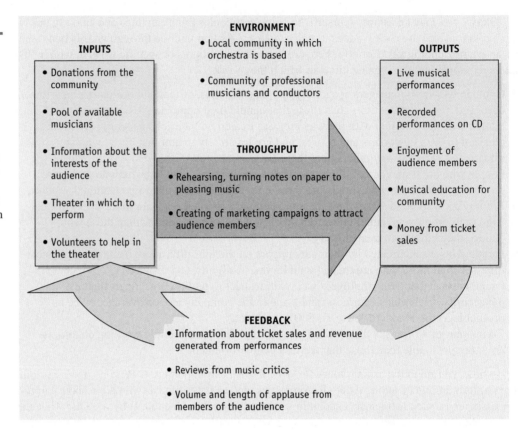

ENVIRONMENT
- Local community in which orchestra is based
- Community of professional musicians and conductors

INPUTS
- Donations from the community
- Pool of available musicians
- Information about the interests of the audience
- Theater in which to perform
- Volunteers to help in the theater

THROUGHPUT
- Rehearsing, turning notes on paper to pleasing music
- Creating of marketing campaigns to attract audience members

OUTPUTS
- Live musical performances
- Recorded performances on CD
- Enjoyment of audience members
- Musical education for community
- Money from ticket sales

FEEDBACK
- Information about ticket sales and revenue generated from performances
- Reviews from music critics
- Volume and length of applause from members of the audience

raw materials) into some form of output (for example, a finished product).[10] Figure 1.3 summarizes some of the key properties of open systems and provides an interesting example.

This diagram illustrates the open systems nature of symphony orchestras, but it applies to all types of organizations. They receive input from their environments and continuously transform it into output. This output gets transformed back to input, and the cyclical operation continues. Consider, for example, how organizations may tap the human resources of the community by hiring and training people to do jobs. These individuals may work to provide a product in exchange for wages. They then spend these wages, putting money back into the community, allowing more people to afford the company's products. This, in turn, creates the need for still more employees, and so on. If you think about it this way, it's easy to realize that organizations are dynamic and constantly changing.

The dynamic nature of organizations can be likened to the operations of the human body. As people breathe, they take in oxygen and transform it into carbon dioxide. This, in turn, sustains the life of green plants, which emit oxygen for people to breathe. The continuous nature of the open system characterizes not only human life, but the existence of organizations as well.

OB Assumes There Is No "One Best" Approach

What's the most effective way to motivate people? What style of leadership works best? Should groups of individuals be used to make important organizational decisions? Although these questions are quite reasonable, there is a basic problem with all of them. Namely, they all assume that there is a simple, unitary answer—that is, one best way to motivate, to lead, and to make decisions.

contingency approach
A perspective suggesting that organizational behavior is affected by a large number of interacting factors. How someone will behave is said to be contingent on many different variables at once.

Today's OB scientists agree that there really is no one best approach when it comes to such complex phenomena. To assume otherwise is not only overly simplistic but, as you will see, grossly inaccurate. When it comes to studying human behavior in organizations, there are no simple answers. For this reason, OB scholars embrace a **contingency approach**—an orientation that recognizes that behavior in work settings is the complex result of many interacting forces. This orientation is a hallmark of modern OB. Consider, for example, how an individual's personal characteristics (e.g., attitudes and beliefs) in conjunction with situational factors (e.g., relations between coworkers) may all work together when it comes to influencing how a particular individual is likely to behave on the job.

With this in mind, explaining OB phenomena often requires saying, "it depends." As our knowledge of work-related behavior becomes increasingly complex, it is difficult to give "straight answers." Rather, it is usually necessary to say that people will do certain things "under some conditions" or "when all other factors are equal." Such phrases provide a clear indication that the contingency approach is being used. In other words, a certain behavior occurs "contingent upon" the existence of certain conditions—hence, the name. We will come across this repeatedly throughout this book.

OB Then and Now: A Capsule History

Although today we take for granted the importance of understanding the functioning of organizations and the behavior of people at work, this was not always the case. In fact, it was only 100 years ago that people first became interested in studying behavior in organizations, and only during the last 50 years that it gained widespread acceptance.[11] To enable you to appreciate how the field of OB got to where it is today, we will outline its history and describe some of the most influential forces in its development.

The Early Days: Scientific Management and the Hawthorne Studies

The first attempts to study behavior in organizations came out of a desire by industrial efficiency experts to improve worker productivity. Their central question was straightforward: What could be done to get people to do more work in less time? This question was posed in a period of rapid industrialization and technological change in the United States. As engineers attempted to make machines more efficient, it was a natural extension of their efforts to work on the human side of the equation—making people more productive too.

SCIENTIFIC MANAGEMENT AND ITS DETRACTORS. Among the earliest pioneers in this area was Frederick Winslow Taylor, an engineer who noticed the inefficient practices of the employees in the steel mill in which he worked and attempted to change them.[12] This led Taylor to study the individual movements of laborers performing different jobs, searching for ways to do them that resulted in the fewest wasted movements. Research of this type was referred to as **time-and-motion studies.** In 1911, Taylor advanced the concept of **scientific management,** which not only identified ways to design manual labor jobs more efficiently, but also emphasized carefully selecting and training people to perform them. Although we take these ideas for granted today, Taylor is acknowledged to be the first person to carefully study human behavior at work.[13] Despite some successes, Taylor's approach was credited with destroying the soul of work and dehumanizing factories by transforming men into automatons. As he saw it, designing jobs to make people work more efficiently was just like designing machines to make them work more efficiently. The problem, of course, is that people are not machines.

Inspired by the prospects of scientific management, but taking a more humanistic approach, other work experts advanced the idea that social factors operating in the workplace are an important determinant of how effectively people work. At the forefront of this effort was Elton W. Mayo, an organizational scientist and consultant widely regarded as the founder of what is called the **human relations movement.**[14] This approach emphasized that the social conditions existing in organizations—the way employees are treated by management and the relationships they have with each other—influence job performance.[15]

THE HAWTHORNE STUDIES. Mayo's orientation was developed in the first investigations of organizational behavior, known as the **Hawthorne studies,** which began in 1927 at Western Electric's Hawthorne Works near Chicago (see Figure 1.4). Mayo and his associates were interested in determining, among other things, how to design work environments in ways that increased performance. With this objective in mind, they systematically altered key aspects of the work environment (e.g., illumination, the length of rest pauses, the duration of the workday and workweek) to see their effects on job performance. What they found was baffling: Productivity improved following almost every change in working conditions.[16] In fact, performance remained extremely high even when

---

time-and-motion study
A type of applied research designed to classify and streamline the individual movements needed to perform jobs with the intent of finding "the one best way" to perform them.

scientific management
An early approach to management and organizational behavior emphasizing the importance of designing jobs as efficiently as possible.

human relations movement
A perspective on organizational behavior that rejects the primarily economic orientation of scientific management and recognizes, instead, the importance of social processes in work settings.

Hawthorne studies
The earliest systematic research in the field of OB, this work was performed to determine how the design of work environments affected performance.

Baker Library/Harvard Business School.

FIGURE 1.4

The Hawthorne Studies

The earliest studies in the field of OB were conducted beginning in 1927 at Western Electric's Hawthorne Works, a factory outside of Chicago. What this research revealed about human nature on the job proved invaluable and stimulated the scientific study of behavior in organizations.

conditions returned to normal (i.e., the way they were before the study began). However, workers didn't always improve their performance. In another set of studies, workers sometimes restricted their output deliberately. Not only did they stop working long before quitting time, but in interviews, they admitted that they easily could have done more if they desired.

What accounts for these fascinating findings? Mayo recognized that the answer resided in the fact that how effectively people work depends not only on the physical characteristics of the work environment, but also the social conditions encountered. In the first set of studies, where productivity rose in all conditions, people simply were responding favorably to the special attention they received. It was these social factors more than the physical factors that had such positive effects on job performance. Knowing they were being studied made them feel special and motivated them to do their best. In reference to this phenomenon, the general tendency for people to behave differently than they normally would simply because they believe they are being studied has become known as the **Hawthorne effect.**

Hawthorne effect
The tendency for people being studied to behave differently than they ordinarily would.

The same explanation applies to the case in which people restricted their performance. Here, the employees feared that because they were being studied, the company was eventually going to raise the amount of work they were expected to do each day. So as to guard against the imposition of unreasonable standards (and, hopefully, to keep their jobs!), the workers agreed among themselves to keep their output low. In other words, informal rules (referred to as *norms*, which we will describe in Chapter 8) were established about what constituted acceptable levels of job performance. Anyone who violated these rules was pressured strongly by their coworkers to change their ways. Again, the social forces in this setting proved to be more potent determinants of job performance than the physical factors studied.

This conclusion, based on the surprising findings of the Hawthorne studies, is important because it ushered in a whole new way of thinking about behavior at work. It suggests that to understand the way people behave on the job, we must fully appreciate their attitudes and the processes by which they communicate with each other. This way of thinking, so fundamental to modern OB, may be traced back to Elton Mayo's pioneering Hawthorne studies.

Classical Organizational Theory

During the same time that proponents of scientific management got scientists thinking about the interrelationships between people and their jobs, another approach to managing people emerged.

This perspective, known as **classical organizational theory,** focused on the efficient structuring of overall organizations. The idea was that there is an efficient way to organize work in all organizations—much as proponents of scientific management searched for the ideal way to perform particular jobs.

One of the most influential classical organizational theorists was Henri Fayol, a French industrialist who pioneered various ideas about how organizations should be structured. For example, Fayol advocated that there should be a **division of labor,** the practice of dividing work into specialized tasks that enable people to specialize in what they do best. He also argued that in any organization it always should be clear to whom each worker is responsible—that is, which managers have authority over them. Although many of these ideas are regarded as simplistic today, they were considered quite pioneering more than 80 years ago.

Another well-known classical organizational theorist is the German sociologist Max Weber.[17] Among other things, Weber is well known for proposing the **bureaucracy**—a form of organization in which a set of rules are applied that keep higher-ranking organizational officials in charge of lower-ranking workers, who fulfill the duties assigned to them. As the description suggests, bureaucracies are organizations that carefully differentiate between those who give the orders and those who carry them out. A fan of bureaucracies, Henry Ford openly endorsed "the reduction of the necessity for thought on the part of the worker."[18] Making this possible are a set of rules such as those summarized in Table 1.2.

Given your own experiences with bureaucracies, you're probably not surprised to hear that this particular organizational form has not proven to be the perfect way to organize all work. Weber's universal view of bureaucratic structure contrasts with the more modern approaches to organizational design (see Chapter 15), which recognize that different forms of organizational structure may be more or less appropriate under different situations. (This is the contingency approach we described earlier.) Also, because bureaucracies draw sharp lines between the people who make decisions (managers) and those who carry them out (workers), they are not particularly popular today. After all, contemporary employees prefer to have more equal opportunities to make decisions than bureaucracies permit. Still, contemporary OB owes a great deal to Weber for his many pioneering ideas.

classical organizational theory
An early approach to the study of management that focused on the most efficient way of structuring organizations.

division of labor
The practice of dividing work into specialized tasks that enable people to specialize in what they do best.

bureaucracy
An organizational design developed by Max Weber that attempts to make organizations operate efficiently by having a clear hierarchy of authority in which people are required to perform well-defined jobs.

Late Twentieth Century: Organizational Behavior as a Social Science

Based on contributions noted thus far, the realization that behavior in work settings is shaped by a wide range of individual, group, and organizational factors set the stage for the emergence of the science of organizational behavior. By the 1940s, doctoral degrees were awarded in OB and the first textbooks were published, and by the late 1950s and early 1960s, OB was clearly a going concern.[19] In the 1970s, active programs of research were going on—investigations into such key processes motivation and leadership, and the impact of organizational structure.[20]

TABLE 1.2 Characteristics of an Ideal Bureaucracy

According to Max Weber, *bureaucracies* are the ideal organizational form. To function effectively, bureaucracies must possess the characteristics identified here.

Characteristic	Description
Formal rules and regulations	Written guidelines are used to control all employees' behaviors.
Impersonal treatment	Favoritism is to be avoided, and all work relationships are to be based on objective standards.
Division of labor	All duties are divided into specialized tasks and are performed by individuals with the appropriate skills.
Hierarchical structure	Positions are ranked by authority level in clear fashion from lower-level to upper-level.
Authority structure	The making of decisions is determined by one's position in the hierarchy; higher-ranking people have authority over those in lower-ranking positions.
Lifelong career commitment	Employment is viewed as a permanent, lifelong obligation on the part of the organization and its employees.
Rationality	The organization is committed to achieving its ends (e.g., profitability) in the most efficient manner possible. This is considered rational.

Unfortunately—but not unexpectedly for a new field—the development of scientific investigations into managerial and organizational issues was uneven and unsystematic in the middle part of the twentieth century. In response to this state of affairs, the Ford Foundation sponsored a project in which economists carefully analyzed the nature of business education in the United States. They published their findings in 1959 in what became a very influential work known as the *Gordon and Howell report*.[21] This work recommended that the field of management pay greater attention to basic academic disciplines, especially the social sciences. This advice had an enormous influence on business school curricula during the 1960s and promoted the development of the field of organizational behavior. After all, OB draws heavily on the basic social science disciplines that this report recommended for incorporation into business curricula.

It was precisely because of this work that the field of OB rapidly grew into one that borrows heavily from other disciplines (recall Table 1.1 on p. 5), making it the hybrid science that it is today. By the time the twentieth century drew to a close, OB clearly was a multidisciplinary field that was making important contributions to both science and practice.

OB in Today's Infotech Age

A century ago, when scientists first became aware of the importance of managing people, their primary challenge involved getting people to work efficiently, and they did so by treating people like the machines with which they worked—pushing them as hard as possible, sometimes until they broke down. Then, as we became more aware of the importance of the human element in the workplace, it became fashionable to treat people in a more humane fashion. Today, in what has been called *the infotech age,* computer technology has made it possible to eliminate vast amounts of grunt work that laborers used to have to perform. Much boring, monotonous, and dangerous physical labor has been eliminated by computer technology, and this has changed the way people work (see Figure 1.5).

Modern technology also has changed the way managers operate. Traditionally, low-level workers gathered information and fed it to higher-level workers, who carefully analyzed it all and made decisions for lower-level workers to carry out. Today, however, easy access to information in online databases has made it possible for almost any worker to gather the facts needed to

FIGURE 1.5

Technological Advances Affect (Almost) All Jobs

Technology has changed—and continues to change—the way many jobs are performed. We doubt that this will be one of them, but you never can tell.

Reprinted by permission of Dan Rosandich.

"Regular or digital?"

make his or her own decisions. And, although some managers still make decisions on behalf of their workers, today we are likely to see employees making many of their own decisions with the aid of information stored on computers. Because managers no longer have to be highly involved in their subordinates' work, they are freed to concentrate on the big picture, to come up with innovative ways to improve their whole organizations (see Chapter 14).

At the same time, the best managers have learned that they could use this opportunity, as one observer said, "to tap employees' most essential humanity, their ability to create, judge, imagine, and build relationships."[22] It is this focus that characterizes today's organizations—hence, the field of OB. Today, people are likely to care at least as much about the work they do as the money they make. They are likely to be deeply concerned about what their organization stands for and the extent to which they can make meaningful contributions to it. In short, contemporary OB recognizes that people care more than ever about the interpersonal side of work—recognition, relationships, and social interaction.

Despite the fact that technology has advanced, changing the way employees work, people have changed very little. Although they may take different forms, our needs and desires are pretty much the same. All of us are human, and just because we work differently than before, we should not discard the things about the behavior of people we have learned over the years.[23] Twenty-first-century OB scientists are busily at work cultivating that humanity by doing things that make it possible for people to do work that is more challenging, meaningful, and interesting to them than ever before. Although this focus is not entirely unique to the twenty-first century, it's safe to say that its sharp emphasis is indeed a key characteristic of modern OB.

To appreciate the nature of OB as a contemporary field, it is important to recognize its connection to the various economic, social, and cultural trends and forces that shape today's society. Specifically, these include three prominent trends: (1) the rise of global businesses with culturally diverse workforces, (2) rapid advances in technology, and (3) the rising expectations of people in general. We will discuss these forces in the remainder of this chapter.

OB Responds to the Rise of Globalization and Diversity

When your grandfather went to work, chances are good that he faced a world that was quite different from today. For one, the company he worked for was likely to be headquartered in the United States and faced competition from other U.S.-based organizations. He also was unlikely to find many women on the job—at least, not in high-ranking positions—nor was he likely to find many immigrants working with him. And, when he reached 65, in all likelihood, he retired. As we will describe here, this picture has all but disappeared. Today's organizations are global in nature and are populated by women and people of color, not to mention individuals who are working well into what would have been considered "retirement years." All of this, as we will note, has important implications for OB.

International Business and the Global Economy

To fully understand behavior in organizations, we must appreciate the fact that today's organizations operate within an economic system that is truly international in scope.[24] The nations of the world are not isolated from one another economically; what happens in one country has effects on other countries. As an illustration, consider that when a massive earthquake devastated the Caribbean island nation of Haiti in January 2010, its economic effects (although small because of the country's poor economic base) were felt beyond its borders. For example, the loss of Haiti's textile and apparel businesses have been felt by suppliers and customers throughout the world who counted on Haitian goods to sustain their own businesses.[25] This tendency for the world's countries to be influenced by one another is known as **globalization**—the process of interconnecting the world's people with respect to the cultural, economic, political, technological, and environmental aspects of their lives.[26]

The trend toward globalization, widespread in recent years, has been driven by three major forces. First, technology has been involved in several ways. Technology has drastically lowered the cost of transportation and communication, thereby enhancing opportunities for international

globalization
The process of interconnecting the world's people with respect to the cultural, economic, political, technological, and environmental aspects of their lives.

commerce. Technology also has helped companies bridge some of the inevitable cultural gaps (for an interesting example, see the section "Today's Diverse and Global Organizations" p. 16). Second, laws restricting trade generally have become liberalized throughout the world (e.g., in the United States and other heavily industrialized countries, free trade policies have been advocated). Third, developing nations have sought to expand their economies by promoting exports and opening their doors to foreign companies seeking investments.

If international trade is the major driver of globalization, then the primary vehicles are **multinational enterprises (MNEs)**—organizations that have significant operations (typically 25 percent or more of their output capacity) spread throughout various nations but are headquartered in a single nation. As of 2009, the top five largest MNEs in the world were Royal Dutch Shell, Exxon Mobil, Wal-Mart Stores, British Petroleum (BP), and Chevron.[27] Interestingly, not too many years ago, such lists also contained automakers (e.g., General Motors and Ford), but given their financial downturns in recent years, it's not surprising to find that they no longer appear. Still, the companies that sell oil and gasoline to fuel our cars dominate this list.

As you might imagine, the rise of MNEs has resulted in large numbers of people who are citizens of one country but who live and work in another country for some extended periods of time. Such individuals are known as **expatriates,** or **expats** for short (see Figure 1.6). Over the years, the number of expats throughout the world has risen, fallen, and shifted direction along with shifts in economic development throughout the world. As economies grow in various countries, MNEs establish offices there to capitalize on the boom. By the same token, shrinking economies sometimes leave expats without jobs in their newly adopted nations. In 2009 this occurred in Dubai on a very large scale as this once-booming Middle Eastern country went bust. Some 3.62 million expats had to return home after their formerly lucrative jobs dried up, making it impossible for them to maintain the lavish lifestyles they lived in Dubai during the good times.[28]

While working abroad, people are exposed to different **cultures**—the set of values, customs, and beliefs that people have in common with other members of a social unit (e.g., a nation).[29] And, when people are faced with new cultures, it is not unusual for them to become confused and disoriented—a phenomenon known as **culture shock.**[30] People also experience culture shock when they return to their native cultures after spending time away from it—a process of readjustment known as **repatriation.** In general, the phenomenon of culture shock results from people's recognition of the fact that others may be different from them in ways that they never imagined, and this takes some getting used to.

multinational enterprises (MNEs)
Organizations that have significant operations spread throughout various nations but are headquartered in a single nation.

expatriates (expats)
People who are citizens of one country, but who live and work in another country.

culture
The set of values, customs, and beliefs that people have in common with other members of a social unit (e.g., a nation).

culture shock
The tendency for people to become confused and disoriented as they attempt to adjust to a new culture.

repatriation
The process of readjusting to one's own culture after spending time away from it.

FIGURE 1.6

Expats: Away From Home But Right at Home

Although they work in London, these American expatriates felt right at home as they gathered to watch the returns of the 2008 presidential election on CNN. They seem to be quite excited about the results, too.

Richard Baker/Alamy Images.

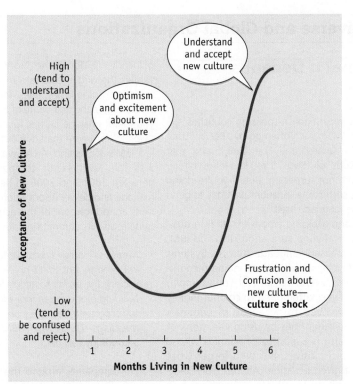

FIGURE 1.7

Adjusting to Foreign Culture: The General Stages
People's adjustment to new cultures generally follows the U-shaped curve illustrated here. After an initial period of excitement, culture shock often sets in. Then, after this period of adjustment (about 6 months), the more time spent in the new culture, the better it is accepted.

Scientists have observed that the process of adjusting to a foreign culture generally follows a U-shaped curve (see Figure 1.7).[31] That is, at first, people are optimistic and excited about learning a new culture. This usually lasts about a month or so. Then, for the next several months, they become frustrated and confused as they struggle to learn their new cultures (i.e., culture shock occurs). Finally, after about six months, people adjust to their new cultures and become more accepting of them and satisfied with them. These observations imply that feelings of culture shock are inevitable. Although some degree of frustration may be expected when you first enter a new country, the more time you spend learning its ways, the better you will come to understand and accept it.[32]

In general, culture shock results from the tendency for people to be highly *parochial* in their assumptions about others, taking a narrow view of the world by believing that there is one best way of doing things. They also tend to be highly *ethnocentric,* believing that their way of doing things is the best way. For example, Americans tend to be highly parochial by speaking only English (whereas most Europeans speak several languages), and ethnocentric by believing that everyone else in the world should learn their language. As we just explained, over time, exposure to other cultures teaches people that there may be many different ways of doing the same thing (making them less parochial), and that these ways may be equally good, if not better (making them less ethnocentric). Although these biases may have been reasonable for Americans over 50 years ago when the United States was the world's dominant economic power (producing three-quarters of its wealth), they would be extremely costly today. Indeed, because the world's economy is global in nature, suggesting that highly parochial and ethnocentric views have no place in contemporary organizations.

Analogously, highly narrow and biased views about the management of people in organizations may severely limit our understanding about behavior in organizations. During the 1950s and 1960s, management scholars tended to overlook the importance of cultural differences in organizations. They made two key assumptions: (1) that principles of good management are universal, and (2) that the best management practices are ones that work well in the United States.[33] This highly inflexible approach is known as the **convergence hypothesis.** Such a biased orientation reflects the fact that the study of behavior in organizations first emerged at a time in which the United States was the world's predominant economic power.

convergence hypothesis
A biased approach to the study of management, which assumes that principles of good management are universal, and that ones that work well in the United States will apply equally well in other nations.

Today's Diverse and Global Organizations

What's in a Name? It Depends Where You Live

In the United States and most English-speaking countries, we know that people named "Margaret" often go by "Peggy," that "Jack" may be "John," "James" may be "Jim," and that "Robert" may be called "Bob," or "Rob." If you know the culture, these alternative names are not surprising. But, if you're doing business on a global scale, such name variations are likely to be as foreign to you as the native language itself.

Besides being polite and avoiding embarrassment in business meetings, why might anyone care about this? To IBM, which in March 2006 purchased Language Analysis Systems (LAS), a company that develops multicultural name recognition technology, there are several reasons.[34] For example, banks and insurance companies attempting to combat money laundering and fraud may need to be aware of criminals attempting to disguise their identities by using variations of their names. The service also is useful to companies whose clients don't have nefarious motives, but who forget what nickname they used on a given occasion. Airlines, for example, find it useful to be able to search for reservations and other information provided using different names. Similarly, hospitals use the technology to avoid duplicating medical procedures administered to patients.

Although the exact way the LAS technology works is highly technical, what it does is straightforward. Drawing on a database of nearly a billion names from around the world, the software verifies the origin, cultural variations, and meaning of names. It focuses on nicknames, titles, format changes, and typographical errors. (Since the first name of the author of this book is "Jerald," you might imagine he has found his name listed as "Gerald" or "Gerold" on more than one occasion.)

IBM's acquisition of LAS was not an isolated move. Rather, it was the seventeenth company acquired in the five years between 2001 and 2006 to help customers use technology to manage and deliver information in today's global business world. In its announcement of this acquisition, IBM's official statement underscores its commitment to such technology:

Names are often times overlooked as miniature databases of knowledge, but that's precisely what they are. In our global society, the ability to accurately recognize and manage the building blocks of an individual's name can provide the key to recognizing identities across cultures, genders, and meanings. This is where IBM's global name recognition technology can help.[35]

To companies around the world, this represents a useful service. To readers of this book, however, the existence of this service reflects a key point: namely, that technology plays a central role in helping today's organizations address the challenges of globalization. Name recognition may seem minor to most of us, but on a global scale it's quite important—and as IBM officials surely hope, big business.

---

divergence hypothesis
The approach to the study of management which recognizes that knowing how to manage most effectively requires clear understanding of the culture in which people work.

With the ever-growing global economy, it has become clear that an American-oriented approach may be highly misleading when it comes to understanding the practices that work best in various countries. In fact, there may be many possible ways to manage effectively, and these will depend greatly on the individual culture in which people live. This alternative approach, which is widely accepted today, is known as the **divergence hypothesis.** Following this orientation, understanding the behavior of people at work requires carefully appreciating the cultural context within which they operate. For example, whereas American cultural norms suggest that it would not be inappropriate for an employee to question his or her superior, it would be taboo for a worker in Japan to do the same thing. Thus, today's organizational scholars are becoming increasingly sensitive to the ways in which culture influences organizational behavior (this point is illustrated in several places in every chapter of this book).

The Shifting Demographics of the Workforce: Trends Toward Diversity

Thus far, we have been discussing cultural differences between people from companies in different nations. However, widespread cultural differences also may be found *within* organizations in the United States. For example, the prevalence of women in the workforce, and the growing diversity of people from different races and ethnic groups, cannot be missed. Indeed, a broad range of people from both sexes as well as different races, ethnic groups, and nationalities can be found throughout U.S. organizations, and as summarized in Figure 1.8, their proportions have been changing.[36] Modern organizations have taken steps to accommodate—and capitalize on—growing levels of diversity within the workforce. It's also the case that Americans today are living longer, healthier lives than their parents and grandparents, keeping them in the workforce far longer than before. These trends take many forms, all of which have important implications for the field of OB.

FIGURE 1.8

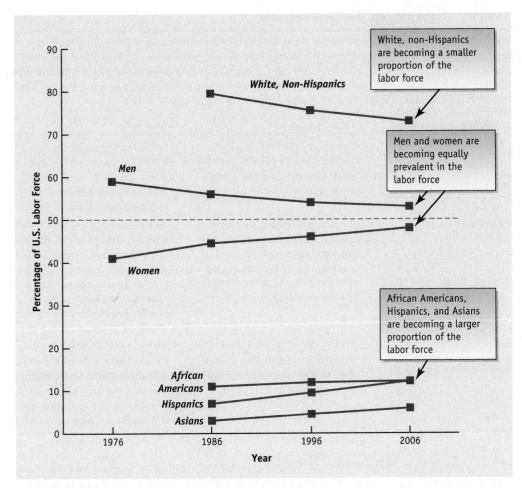

Demographic Shifts in the U.S. Labor Force

Although White people remain the largest portion of the U.S. labor force, they are becoming a smaller segment as people of other races and ethnic groups are growing in numbers. Additionally, although the numbers differ for various jobs, in 2009 the overall percentage of men and women in the workforce was reported to be equal. (Note that equality in numbers had not yet been reached when the statistics in this graph were reported only three years earlier.)

Source: U.S. Department of Labor, 2009; see Note 37.

MORE WOMEN ARE IN THE WORKFORCE THAN EVER BEFORE. In the 1950s, the "typical American family" was characterized by a man who went to work and his wife who stayed at home and watched the children. Although this profile still may be found, it is far from typical. In fact, women now comprise half of the workforce, a figure that has risen steadily over the years (see Figure 1.8).[37]

This trend stems not only from economic necessity but also from the growing social acceptance of women working outside the home. As women, who traditionally have worked inside the home, have moved to working outside the home, companies have found it beneficial—or even necessary, in some cases—to make accommodations that help make this possible. (For a look at some of the most popular practices in this regard, see Table 1.3.)

RACIAL AND ETHNIC DIVERSITY IS REALITY. Just as yesterday's workers were primarily males, they also were primarily white. However, just as growing numbers of women have made men less of a majority, so too has an influx of people from different racial and ethnic groups and differences in birth rates made white people a smaller majority. Specifically, the U.S. Census Bureau reported as follows:[38]

■ Between 1980 and 2000, the population of minority group members grew 11 times as rapidly as the White non-Hispanic population.
■ Currently, people of color comprise one-third of the U.S. population, but they are expected to be the majority by 2042.
■ By 2050, Hispanics will comprise 30 percent of the U.S. population.
■ The number of people in the U.S. who consider themselves to be multiracial is expected to triple from 5.2 million to 16.2 million by 2050.

It is apparent that the trend toward demographic diversity is in full swing today. In fact, so-called "minority" group members, as a whole, currently outnumber traditional majority group members in two U.S. states, California and New Mexico.[39] As these trends suggest, the meaning of the term minority is changing rapidly and is well on the way to becoming obsolete.[40]

TABLE 1.3 Employee Support Policies

With increasing frequency, companies are taking proactive steps to help men and women meet their personal needs and family obligations. In so doing, they make it possible for employees to satisfy the demands imposed by their nonwork lives. This allows companies to draw on the talents of a diverse group of prospective employees who otherwise might not be able to lend their talents to the organization. The three practices identified here have proven especially useful in this regard.

Practice	Description	Example
Child-care facilities	Sites at or near company locations where parents can leave their children while they are working.	At Toyota's Georgetown, Kentucky, plant, a child-care center is open 24 hours a day, offering outstanding services at very reasonable fees.
Elder-care facilities	Centers where aged parents of employees can stay and be cared for while their adult children are working. Given the rapid aging of the population, this benefit is growing in popularity.	At its Armonk, New York, head-quarters, IBM has been offering elder care to employees for over two decades. Recently, the company expanded this service by launching an online support group for individuals taking care of elderly parents.
Personal support policies	Widely varied practices that help employees meet the demands of their family lives, freeing them to concentrate on their work.	The Wilton Connor Packaging Co. in Charlotte, North Carolina, offers an on-site laundry, high school equivalency classes, door-to-door transportation, and a children's clothing swap center.

child-care facilities
Sites at or near company locations where parents can leave their children while they are working.

elder-care facilities
Facilities at which employees at work can leave elderly relatives for whom they are responsible (such as parents and grandparents).

personal support policies
Widely varied practices that help employees meet the demands of their family lives, freeing them to concentrate on their work.

PEOPLE ARE LIVING—AND WORKING—LONGER THAN EVER BEFORE. In the years after World War II, the peacetime economy flourished in the United States. With it came a large increase in population as soldiers returned from war and began families. The generation of children born during this period is referred to widely as the **baby boom generation.** Today, this large wave of individuals is approaching retirement age. But, because retirement is no longer automatic at age 65, aged baby boomers will comprise a growing part of the population in the next few years (see Figure 1.9). In fact, by 2030 almost 20 percent of the U.S. population will be at least 65. Already, people over 85 years old are the fastest-growing segment of the U.S. population.[41]

Two things occur as a result of this trend. First, older people in the workforce put more of a drain on the health-care system. As healthy as they may be thanks to modern medicine, it's a simple

baby boom generation
The generation of children born in the economic boom period following World War II.

FIGURE 1.9

People Are Living and Working Longer Than Ever

Don't tell Christy McDermott that the typical retirement age is 65. This 75-year old plans to continue working as a Wal-Mart greeter for as long as his health permits.

Zuma/Newscom.

truth that older bodies eventually wear out and require medical attention. And, of course, the physical prowess of older people surely isn't as great as it was when they were younger. This limits the physical nature of the work they can perform, which can be an issue for some manual labor jobs. But because technology has made physical labor less important than it was in years past, this is less of a problem today than it might have been a generation or so ago.

Second—and the other side of the coin—because older people are more experienced on the job, they offer skills that only time alone can provide. In fact, as such individuals retire, it is not unusual for them to leave gaps in the workplace that are difficult to fill. In many organizations, this creates serious problems. When older, top executives retire, for example, they take with them decades of experience that are almost impossible to replace. For this reason, many companies are instituting programs designed to help keep older employees working a little longer before ceasing employment completely. Among these are the following:

- *Phased-retirement.* These are plans in which individuals who are approaching the usual retirement age of 65 can make a transition to full retirement by continuing to work, usually with a reduced workload, as a transition to full-time retirement. This arrangement, which presumably allows the best of both work and retirement, can take the form of permitting part-time or seasonal work (in which employees work only on occasion), and offering extended leaves of absence (in which employees can take off time but can return to work when ready to do so).
- *Deferred retirement option plan (DROP).* This arrangement allows a person who has reached retirement age to continue working while depositing his or her retirement benefit into a separate account that he or she can claim as a lump sum when formally retired, usually one to five years later. This provides a tax incentive for people who want to extend their working years a bit beyond the usual retirement age.

It is important to recognize that such programs are important not only today, when there are many older individuals in the workplace, but they promise to be even more important when the next generation of workers approaches retirement age. We say this because there has been another recent wave of births: A record number of babies were born in the United States in 2007, over 4.31 million, the most since the middle of the baby boom in 1957.[42] As such, we can expect a large influx of Americans to enter the workplace in the next two decades.

IMPLICATIONS FOR OB.   That more women, people of color, and older workers are in the workforce than ever before is not merely an idle sociological curiosity. It also has important implications for OB—ones that we will examine more closely in this book. After all, the more people differ from each other, the more challenges they are likely to face when interacting with one another. How these interactions play out is likely to be seen on the job in important ways. For example, as we will describe, differences in age, gender, and ethnic group membership are likely to bring with them differences in communication style that must be addressed for organizations to function effectively (see Chapter 9). It also is the case that people at different stages of their lives are likely to be motivated by different things (see Chapter 7) and to be satisfied with different aspects of their jobs (see Chapter 7). And, as workers adjust to a wider variety of people in the workplace, issues about their norms and values (see Chapter 8) are likely to come up, as well as their willingness to accept others who are different from themselves (see Chapter 6). This can have important implications for potential stress and conflict in the workplace (see Chapters 5 and 11) and their career choices (see Appendix 2), which may be expected to influence their capacity to work effectively as members of the same work teams (see Chapter 8).

OB Responds to Advances in Technology

Since the Industrial Revolution in the nineteenth century, people have performed carefully prescribed sets of tasks—known as *jobs*—within large networks of workers who answered to those above them—hierarchical arrangements known as *organizations*. This picture, although highly simplistic, does a good job of characterizing the working arrangements that most people had during much of the twentieth century. Today, however, in the twenty-first century, the essential nature of jobs and organizations as we have known them has changed and continues to change all the time (a fact that we will chronicle in Chapter 16). Although many factors are responsible for this, experts agree that a major catalyst is rapidly advancing computer technology, especially the use of the Internet and wireless technology.[43]

As you might imagine, this state of affairs has important implications for organizations—and, hence, the field of OB. After all, as more work is shifted to digital brains, some work that once was performed by human brains becomes obsolete. At the same time, new opportunities arise as people scurry to find their footing amid the shifting terrain of the high-tech revolution. The implications of this for OB are considerable. We will now consider some of the most prominent trends in the world of work that have been identified in recent years. These involve how work is organized and performed, as well as the need for flexibility.

Leaner Organizations: Downsizing and Outsourcing

Technology has made it possible for fewer people to do more work than ever before. *Automation*, the process of replacing people with machines, is not new, of course; it has gone on, slowly and steadily, for decades. Today, however, because it is not large mechanical devices but digital data that are manipulated, scientists refer instead to the *informating* of the workplace.

informate
The process by which workers manipulate objects by "inserting data" between themselves and those objects.

The term **informate** describes the process by which workers use computer information technology to transform a once-physical task into one that involves manipulating a sequence of digital commands.[44] Thanks to this process, for example, today's auto workers can move around large hoods and trunk lids by pressing a few buttons on a keypad instead of physically manipulating them by hand. Likewise, the process of placing sales orders often is informated. Thanks to computer systems analysts, an order entered into a salesperson's laptop computer can trigger a chain of events involving everything associated with the job: placing a sales order, manufacturing the product to exact specifications, delivering the final product, sending out the bill, and even crediting the proper commission to the salesperson's payroll check.

Unlike the gradual process of automation, today's technology—and the process of informating—is occurring so rapidly that the very nature of work is changing as fast as we can keep up. With this, many jobs are disappearing, leaving organizations (at least the most successful ones!) smaller than before.[45] Indeed, organizations have been rapidly reducing the number of employees needed to operate effectively—a process known as **downsizing**.[46]

downsizing
The process of adjusting the number of employees needed to work in newly designed organizations (also known as *rightsizing*).

rightsizing
See *downsizing*.

Typically, this involves more than just laying off people in a move to save money. It is directed at adjusting the number of employees needed to work in newly designed organizations, and is therefore also known as **rightsizing**.[47] Whatever you call it, the bottom line is clear: Many organizations need fewer people to operate today than in the past—sometimes, far fewer. It's important to note that we're talking here not about jobs lost due to economic downturns but to changes in the way work is organized that no longer makes certain jobs necessary.

Another way organizations are restructuring is by completely eliminating those parts of themselves that focus on noncore sectors of the business (i.e., tasks that are peripheral to the organization) and hiring outside firms to perform these functions instead—a practice known as **outsourcing** (see Chapter 16).[48] By outsourcing secondary activities, an organization can focus on what it does best, its key capability—what is known as its **core competency.** Companies like ServiceMaster, which provides janitorial services, and ADP, which provides payroll processing services, make it possible for their client organizations to concentrate on the business functions most central to their missions. So for example, by outsourcing its maintenance work or its payroll processing, a manufacturing company may grow smaller and focus its resources on what it does best, producing goods.

outsourcing
The process of eliminating those parts of organizations that focus on noncore sectors of the business (i.e., tasks that are peripheral to the organization), and hiring outside firms to perform these functions instead.

core competency
An organization's key capability, what it does best.

Some critics fear that outsourcing represents a "hollowing out" of companies—a reduction of functions that weakens organizations by making them more dependent on others.[49] Others counter that outsourcing makes sense when the work that is outsourced is not highly critical to competitive success (e.g., janitorial services), or when it is so highly critical that it only can succeed by seeking outside assistance.[50] For example, it is a widespread practice for companies selling personal computers today to outsource the manufacturing of various components (e.g., hard drives, CD-ROMs, and chips) to other companies.[51] Although this practice may sound atypical compared to what occurs in most manufacturing companies, it isn't. In fact, one industry analyst has estimated that 30 percent of the largest American industrial firms outsource over half their manufacturing.[52]

The Virtual Organization

As more and more companies are outsourcing various organizational functions and are paring down to their core competencies, they might not be able to perform all the tasks required to complete a project. However, they certainly can perform their own highly specialized part of it very well. Now, if you put together several organizations whose competencies complement each other and have them work together on a special project, you'd have a very strong group of collaborators. This is the idea behind an organizational arrangement that is growing in popularity—the **virtual organization.** A virtual organization is a highly flexible, temporary organization formed by a group of companies that join forces to exploit a specific opportunity (we will describe them more thoroughly in Chapter 15).[53]

For example, various companies often come together to work on special projects in the entertainment industry (e.g., to produce a motion picture—see Figure 1.10) and in the field of construction (e.g., to build a shopping center). After all, technologies are changing so rapidly and skills are becoming so specialized these days that no one company can do everything by itself. And so, they join forces temporarily to form virtual organizations—not permanent organizations, but temporary ones without their own offices or organization charts. Although virtual organizations are not yet common, experts expect them to grow in popularity in the years ahead.[54] As one consultant put it, "It's not just a good idea; it's inevitable."[55]

virtual organization
A highly flexible, temporary organization formed by a group of companies that join forces to exploit a specific opportunity.

Telecommuting: Going to Work Without Leaving Home

In recent years, the practice of **telecommuting** (also known as **teleworking**) has been growing in popularity. This is the practice of using communications technology to enable work to be performed from remote locations, such as the home or anyplace with e-mail access. Although telecommuting was somewhat experimental at the end of the twentieth century, it's in full swing today. In fact, telecommuting currently is estimated to be used by approximately 14 million American workers on a regular basis.[56] Some companies, such as Booz Allen Hamilton, eBay, Goldman Sachs, the Principal Financial Group, S. C. Johnson & Son, and Yahoo! currently have the most active telecommuting programs.

telecommuting (teleworking)
The practice of using communications technology to perform work from remote locations, such as one's home.

UPI/Mark Hellman/Newscom.

FIGURE 1.10

Virtual Organizations in the Movie Business

Next time you exit the movie theater, take a close look at the credits. Not only are various actors and actresses listed along with technicians of all types, but also a number of different companies. The making of a modern motion picture, such as James Cameron's instant classic *Avatar*, is a good example of a so-called virtual organization. Various organizations with different areas of expertise (e.g., casting, sound recording, special effects, etc.) join forces long enough to bring a final product to fruition.

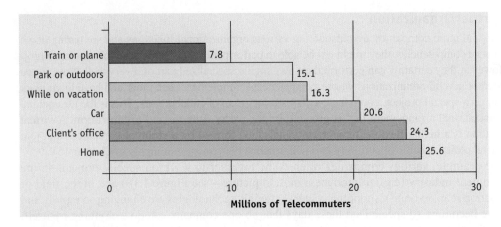

FIGURE 1.11

From Where Do People Telecommute?

Technology makes it possible for many of today's employees to do their work from locations other than their offices. As summarized here, several locations are particularly popular.

Source: IATC, 2009; see Note 57.

As shown in Figure 1.11, there are a wide variety of locations from which people telecommute.[57] Many people rely on more than just one, an average of 3.4 locations, in fact. For many, their local Starbucks represents "the third space" beyond office and home, wherever a notebook computer, a wireless network, and a latte may be found. But, with rapid increases in the availability of broadband connections in people's homes, the home is the fastest-growing location.

Both employees and employers enjoy the benefits of telecommuting. For example, telecommuting makes it possible for employees to avoid the hassle and expenses of daily commuting, which, in an era of congested roads and expensive fuel costs, can be dramatic. Employees working at home also enjoy saving money that they would have spent purchasing work clothing (unless you happen to wear ties or pantyhose around the house) and buying meals in restaurants and from vending machines. In fact, it has been estimated that each teleworker saves tens of thousands of dollars per year, taking into account all expenses.[58] Saving money is not the only reason why most telecommuters like the arrangement. They also enjoy the flexibility it gives them to balance work and family matters.[59]

Telecommuting also makes it possible for companies to save millions of dollars in expenses for office facilities.[60] At Hewlett-Packard, for example, about $230 million is being saved in annual office expenses. This occurs because companies are able to get more work done in the same space. Cisco Systems, for example, has so many teleworkers that it now takes only the physical space of 88 workers to do the work of 140 employees.[61] IBM also has been able to slash its office space by as much as 55 percent in some locations. As you might imagine, the savings are particularly important to small start-up companies, which can hire workforces without having to make large investments in office space.

Importantly, telecommuting allows companies to comply with governmental regulations (e.g., the Federal Clean Air Act of 1990) requiring them to reduce the number of trips made by their employees. In fact, the federal government is a major proponent of telecommuting. The Securities and Exchange Commission (SEC), the State Department, the Department of Justice, and four other large federal agencies now are required by law to offer all eligible workers the opportunity to telecommute.

A particularly interesting and all-too-real reason to use telecommuting is to help organizations get up and running after a disaster strikes. After all, if an organization's assets are spread out—as is the case if they are in the hands of employees who are geographically dispersed—they are less vulnerable to attacks by human threats (e.g., terrorist strikes, arsonists) and natural disasters (e.g., floods, hurricanes, and tornadoes). (For specific recommendations about how to incorporate telecommuting into a plan to prepare for disasters, see the "OB in Practice" section on p. 23.)

Despite these benefits, as you might imagine, telecommuting is not for everyone; it also has its limitations.[62] It works best on jobs that require concentration, have well-defined beginning

OB in Practice

Telecommuting as a Business Continuity Strategy

For the average person, poignant memories of the 9/11 terrorist attacks and Hurricane Katrina tragically linger on, but their toll on business adds another dimension of suffering among the untold thousands whose businesses and livelihoods either were disrupted or vanished in their wakes. As extreme as these acts were, they are but a few of the many disasters of one form or another that disrupt the operations of about one in five American businesses in an average year.[63] Other events—such as toxic spills, earthquakes, water main breaks, or communication cables severed by careless construction workers—also can disrupt business operations, underscoring the need for businesses to have sets of procedures in place to get up and running in the event of such disruptions.

business continuity plans
Systematic sets of plans designed to help organizations get up and running again in the event of a disruption of some sort.

Such preparations, known as **business continuity plans,** are in place in about only 40 percent of small organizations, leaving the others vulnerable in times of crisis. Specifically, these refer to systematic sets of plans designed to help organizations get up and running again in the event of a disruption of some sort. Indeed, although small businesses are the least prepared, they have the most to lose because their limited resources make it difficult, if not impossible, to sustain any disruption. Large organizations are somewhat better prepared, with plans in place in 80 percent. But, given that the average loss per hour of downtime in *Fortune* 1000 firms runs about $78,000, and that disruptions may last for days, weeks, or even months, no organization can afford to ignore preparing for the inevitable.

Telecommuting is a key part of any business continuity plan. The reasons are not hard to understand. Emergencies result in loss of workspace, loss of technology, and loss of staff. In each instance, telework helps reduce the risk because it allows organizations to disperse employees quickly and to set up offices elsewhere. Besides allowing for the speedy resumption of business, teleworking helps in emergencies because it allows employees to remain in the presence of their families, where they desire to be at such times.

Organizations should take the following steps to ensure that telecommuting provides the help needed in emergencies.

1. Keep company records, especially vital ones, on several backup servers. These should be geographically disbursed in the event that a disaster strikes a particular local area.
2. Ensure that workers have a list of locations where they can go to find access to electricity and the Internet. These should be both local and regional in nature.
3. Maintain databases of addresses, phone numbers, e-mail addresses, and emergency addresses (e.g., relatives living elsewhere) where everyone can be contacted.
4. Train all workers to be able to perform at least part of their jobs from distant locations, including how to use computers.
5. Keep training current and thorough. Just because someone once may have been computer-savvy does not ensure that he or she will continue to be so. Thorough training in distance collaboration and peer communication technology is key.
6. Emphasize the business necessity of such a plan so that everyone will take it seriously without being seen as alarmist.

Following these measures, of course, will not ward off disasters. They remain a real and unforeseen risk for all organizations. However, by using telecommuting, businesses will be better prepared to cope with their inevitable aftermath.

and end points, are easily portable, call for minimal amounts of special equipment, and can be done with little supervision.[64] Fortunately, at least some aspects of most sales and professional jobs meet these standards. Even so, making telecommuting work requires careful adjustments in the way work is done. Also, many people just don't have the kind of self-discipline needed to get work done without direct supervision. To see if you and your associates have what it takes to succeed at telecommuting, see the Group Exercise at the end of this chapter.

OB Is Responsive to People's Changing Expectations

OB scientists do not work in a vacuum. Instead, they are highly responsive to people's changing expectations with respect to various aspects of work. This is the case with respect to two particular areas of concern to the field of OB: (1) employees' and employers' desire for *engagement,* and (2) the flexibility employees expect from employers. We now discuss each of these forces and their impact on modern OB.

Employees and Employers Desire Engagement

When referring to people who are preparing to wed, we say that they are "engaged." Typically, such individuals believe in each other, they want to share a bright future together, they are respectful to each other, and they are willing to do what it takes to ensure the other's happiness and success. We also use the term *engagement* to refer to employers and employees who share similar commitments to one another.

engagement
A mutual commitment between employers and employees to do things to help one another achieve each other's goals and aspirations.

In the field of OB, **engagement** refers to a mutual commitment between employers and employees to do things to help one another achieve goals and aspirations.[65] Thus, engagement is a two-way process. Typically, it works like this: Organizations take steps to engage their employees, and employees, in turn, respond by engaging their organizations. This takes several forms, such as the following:

- High levels of pride in the organization
- Pride in the organizations' products and services
- Belief that the organization helps employees do their best
- Willingness to help others on the job
- Understanding "the big picture" and being willing to go beyond formal job requirements when necessary

Because engagement begins with employers, it's important to note what organizations can do to get the ball rolling. Organizations can do several specific things to promote feelings of engagement in their employees. Not surprisingly, these are practices that we will be describing (and recommending) in various places throughout this book. The four key drivers of engagement are as follows:

- Involving employees in making decisions (see Chapter 10)
- Giving employees opportunities to express their ideas and opinions (see Chapter 2)
- Providing opportunities for employees to develop their jobs (see Chapter 7)
- Showing concern for employees' well-being as individuals (see Chapter 6)

Considering this, we may ask, are today's employees engaged in their jobs? An extensive survey by the Gallup Organization revealed that the answer varies for different groups of employees.[66] Only 31 percent were classified as truly *engaged*. These individuals worked with passion and felt deep connections to their companies, helping to move them forward. The majority, however, 52 percent, were classified as *not engaged*. These people "checked out" of their jobs and only went through the motions. They put in time, but displayed very little energy or passion. Finally, 17 percent of the respondents were classified as being *actively disengaged*. Such individuals weren't only unhappy, but acted out their unhappiness on the job. Far too often, they undermined the accomplishments of their highly engaged counterparts (e.g., by sabotaging their work).

Generally, and this comes as no big surprise, people who are not engaged or who are actively disengaged do not enjoy their work experiences. At the same time, such individuals are not helping—and actively are hurting—their organizations. This comes at considerable cost to organizations, not only by making life miserable for everyone, but also financially. Specifically, the Gallup Organization's extensive, representative survey of U.S. workers age 18 and older revealed two disturbing findings (see summary in Figure 1.12): (1) The percentage of employees who are actively disengaged has not been dropping over the years, and (2) the cost of employing such individuals is dramatic—about $400 billion.

As alarming as these figures may be, there is good news: They can be lowered! And, although it's not always easy, the path to doing so is hardly a mystery. In fact, you hold the answer in your hands right now. Following the good management practices revealed by the field of organizational behavior is the key to promoting not only engagement, but a wealth of other beneficial outcomes both for organizations and the people who work in them.

In Search of Flexibility: Responding to Needs of Employees

Earlier, we mentioned that organizations are doing many different things to accommodate workers from two-income families, single-parent households, and people taking care of elderly relatives. Often, what's most needed is not a formal program, but greater flexibility. The diversity of lifestyles demands a diversity of working arrangements. Some organizations have proven to be so flexible that they even accommodate employees taking care of their dogs. Although Fido might not be a common sight in today's offices (even if, as some say, business has "gone to the dogs"), several practices have gained in popularity in recent years that provide the flexibility today's workers need.

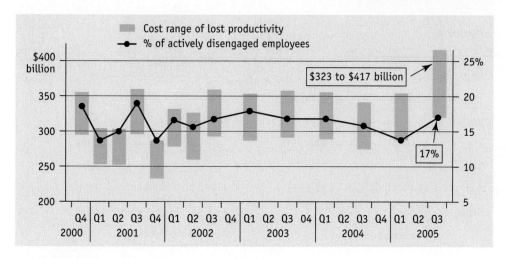

FIGURE 1.12

The High Cost of Active Disengagement

Employees who are actively disengaged at work comprise about 17 percent of the American workforce. These 23.3 million employees cost their organizations between $323 billion and $417 billion annually due to lost productivity.

Source: Copyright © 2006 The Gallup Organization, Princeton, NJ. All rights reserved. Reprinted with permission. Visit the *Gallup Management Journal* at http://gmj.gallup.com.

THE COMPRESSED WORKWEEK. The eight-hour/five-day workweek has been the traditional standard for many years. However, as employees have demanded more scheduling flexibility so as to have more personal time, companies have experimented with the **compressed workweek,** in which the time spent in a workweek is divided into fewer days. Three popular forms of the compressed workweek alternative schedule have been used (for a summary, see Figure 1.13).[67]

compressed workweek
The practice of working fewer days each week, but longer hours each day (e.g., four 10-hour days).

- *Four-day workweek.* Employees work 10 hours per day for four consecutive days, Monday through Thursday. The company is closed from Friday through Sunday. This gives employees three days off each week.
- *Three-day workweek.* Two groups of employees are formed, each of which works for three days of 13 hours and 20 minutes per day. One group works Monday through Wednesday, the other works Thursday through Saturday. The company is closed on Sunday. This gives employees four days off each week.
- *5/4-9 compressed plan.* Two groups of employees are formed. One works four 9-hour days plus one 8-hour day the first week. In week two, employees work four 9-hour days only. This order is reversed for the second group. The company is closed Saturday and Sunday. This arrangement gives employees two days off one week and three days off the next.

These alternative scheduling arrangements have been enjoyed by employees interested in improving the balance between their work lives and personal lives. They also have received a great deal of attention as a means of reducing the number of commutes to and from work. As gasoline prices have risen in recent years, many city and state governments in the United States have adopted four-day workweeks.[68] Not only does this reduce employees' travel expenses by 20 percent, but keeping buildings closed an extra day also saves energy costs within the facilities.

It is important to note, as you might imagine, that these alternative work schedules are not appropriate for all kinds of jobs. Obviously, such arrangements would not work in situations in which work must be performed only at certain times of day, such as when customers and suppliers are available to be contacted. Also, of course, we must consider fatigue. People may grow so tired working longer-than-usual days that their performance and safety may suffer. Under such conditions, lengthened days do not make good business sense. Finally, it's important to note that the benefit of improving balance between work and life schedules assumed to come from

FIGURE 1.13

The Compressed Workweek: Three Specific Schedules

The *compressed workweek* involves scheduling five standard days of work into four or fewer. Three particular schedules for accomplishing this, all used in various organizations, are summarized here.

Source: Adapted from U.S. Office of Personnel Management, 2008, see Note 67.

5/4–9 COMPRESSED PLAN

GROUP A

	WEEK 1		WEEK 2
MON	8 hrs		off
TUE	9 hrs		9 hrs
WED	9 hrs		9 hrs
THU	9 hrs		9 hrs
FRI	9 hrs		9 hrs
SAT	off		off
SUN	off		off

44 hrs worked week 1   36 hrs worked week 2

80 hrs worked over 2 weeks

GROUP B

MON	off		8 hrs
TUE	9 hrs		9 hrs
WED	9 hrs		9 hrs
THU	9 hrs		9 hrs
FRI	9 hrs		9 hrs
SAT	off		off
SUN	off		off

36 hrs worked week 1   44 hrs worked week 2

80 hrs worked over 2 weeks

FOUR-DAY WORK WEEK

MON	
TUE	10 hours/day
WED	× 4 days =
THU	40 hours/week
FRI	off
SAT	off
SUN	off

THREE-DAY WORK WEEK

	GROUP A		GROUP B
MON			off
TUE	13 hrs, 20 min/day × 3 days = 40 hrs/week		off
WED			off
THU	off		13 hrs, 20 min/day × 3 days = 40 hrs/week
FRI	off		
SAT	off		
SUN	off		off

compressed workweeks does not always occur. In particular, parents who have to pick up their children after school find it difficult to work too late into the day.

All things considered, although compressed workweeks are useful in some cases, they certainly are not desirable in all. Still, it's clear that they are not only a viable possibility, but a reality in many of today's organizations—and one that has clear implications for the study of behavior in organizations.

FLEXIBLE HOURS. If you take a look around your workplace, you'll find people at different stages of their lives. Some are single and just getting started in their careers, others may be raising families, and still others may have tried retirement but have chosen to return to work. These different individuals are likely to require different working hours. This has led contemporary organizations to put programs into place that allow for flexibility. One popular way of doing this is by implementing what are known as **flextime programs**—policies that give employees some discretion over when they can arrive at and leave work, thereby making it easier to adapt their work schedules to the demands of their personal lives.

Typically, flextime programs require employees to work a common core of hours, such as 9:00 A.M. to 12 noon and 1:00 P.M. to 3:00 P.M. Scheduling of the remaining hours, within certain spans (such as 6:00 A.M. to 9:00 A.M. and 3:00 P.M. to 6:00 P.M.), is then left up to the employees. (This stands in contrast to compressed workweeks, which do not offer any such options.) Generally, such programs have been well received and have been linked to improvements in performance and job satisfaction, as well as drops in employee turnover and absenteeism.[69] In recent years, many companies, both large and small, have found that flexible work scheduling has helped their employees meet the demands of juggling their work and family lives.[70]

THE CONTINGENT WORKFORCE: "PERMANENT TEMPORARY" EMPLOYEES. Recognizing that not all jobs are required to be performed all the time, many organizations are eliminating permanent jobs and hiring people to perform them whenever required. Such individuals comprise what has been referred to as the **contingent workforce**—people hired by organizations temporarily, to work as needed for finite periods of time.[71] This practice serves not only the needs of companies whose needs for employees grow and shrink over time and cannot afford to have full-time employees, but also individuals who are interested in working only occasionally.

The contingent workforce includes not only the traditional part-time employees, such as department store Santas, but also *freelancers* (i.e., independent contractors who are self employed), *on-call workers* (i.e., people who are called into work only when needed), and workers provided by *temporary help agencies*. As companies have sought to trim expenses in recent years (e.g., by not having fixed office expenses and not giving severance pay to laid off employees), the number of contingent workers has risen dramatically. In 2010, about one in four members of the American workforce was a contingent worker.[72] As shown in Figure 1.14, the specific jobs contingent workers do most frequently are in clerical fields.[73] Such highly flexible arrangements make it possible for organizations to grow or shrink as needed, and to have access to experts with specialized knowledge when these are required.

The current trend of trimming expenses has caused many companies to keep their staff sizes so small that they must frequently draw on the services of one of the nation's thousands of temporary-employment firms for help.[74] As a result, growing numbers of professionals, including lawyers and scientists (many of whom are paid over $250,000 per year), are working on a part-time or freelance basis these days. One temporary employment firm keeps a roster of 1,000 executives who fill in at different companies where needed.[75]

These arrangements come at a cost to employees and employers, however. Contingent employees generally do not receive such valuable fringe benefits as health insurance and contributions to retirement. Salaries take a hit too. People who work half time, for example, typically earn less than half of those who work full time. Managers who earn $3,200 per month working full time can expect to earn as little as $800 to $1,200 per month working half time.[76] On the other side of the coin, these figures represent considerable savings for companies. There is a downside to such arrangements for them as well. The lack of continuity and the time new employees spend "learning the ropes" only to leave shortly thereafter can put serious dents in

flextime programs
Policies that give employees some discretion over when they can arrive at and leave work, thereby making it easier to adapt their work schedules to the demands of their personal lives.

contingent workforce
People hired by organizations temporarily, to work as needed for finite periods of time.

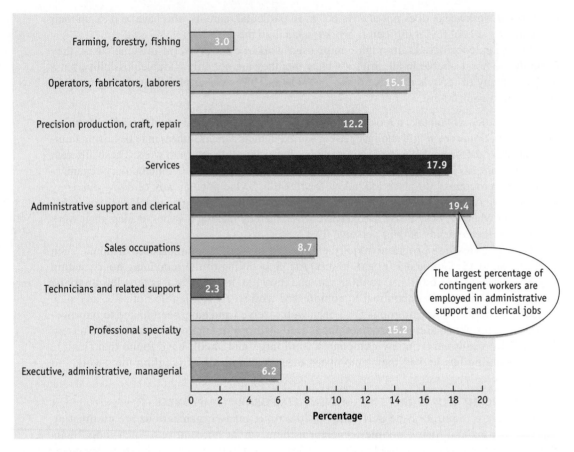

FIGURE 1.14

Contingent Workers: What Kinds of Jobs Do They Do?

As summarized here, contingent workers perform a wide variety of jobs. Most of these are in service businesses and in administrative support and clerical positions.

Source: Based on data from the Bureau of Labor Statistics, 2009; see Note 73.

efficiency. In short, contingent work arrangements have benefits and costs to all parties, and the opportunity to consider these trade-offs is a key characteristic of the contemporary workplace.

IDIOSYNCRATIC WORK ARRANGEMENTS. Traditionally, when new employees were hired, they were offered a standard set of benefits and working arrangements. People in various jobs were paid salaries and had work conditions that were predetermined based on their position. Of course, this still occurs most of the time. But, with increasing frequency, however, the arrangements between today's employers and employees are being negotiated to satisfy the unique interests of each. Such arrangements are known as **idiosyncratic work arrangements,** or more simply, **i-deals.** These are uniquely customized agreements negotiated between individual employees and their employers with respect to employment terms benefiting each party. I-deals may take two forms.

idiosyncratic work arrangements (i-deals)
Uniquely customized agreements negotiated between individual employees and their employers with respect to employment terms benefiting each party.

- *Ex ante i-deals* are negotiated before one begins a job, such as while negotiating the terms of employment (e.g., salary, fringe benefits, etc.).
- *Ex post i-deals* are arrangements about employment terms made once a person already is working in an organization.

Such arrangements are called i-deals because the deals are not only idiosyncratic in nature, but also reflect the fact that these arrangements are intended to be ideal for both employers and employees alike.[77] (Unless both parties benefit, of course, i-deals may not be considered fair. Even when they do, however, such arrangements may seem unfair to existing workers. For a discussion of this dynamic, see "The Ethics Angle" section on p. 29.)

The Ethics Angle

Are I-Deals Unfair?

By their nature, i-deals involve treating people differently. Suppose, for example, a law firm hires a highly regarded attorney who, for personal reasons (e.g., having to take children to school), is allowed to come to the office at 9:30 A.M., an hour after everyone else. Isn't this a form of favoritism, you may ask, because it treats one employee better than others?

Maybe, but not necessarily. To be an i-deal, such arrangements must help everyone. Admittedly, the arrangement might place a burden on paralegals (and possibly other attorneys) who may be called on to address pressing issues on the newly hired attorney's cases while he or she is away from the office. Still, the firm's partners might agree to the i-deal anyway on the grounds that over the long term everyone would benefit from the arrangement. The newly hired attorney benefits, of course, by being given hours that accommodate his or her personal needs. The firm benefits by allowing it to have the expert skills of this individual to service clients, such as by allowing it to broaden the range of cases it handles. Finally, because this individual is so highly regarded, other attorneys in the firm also stand to benefit. This new attorney's reputation may be expected to help attract new business that allows other attorneys to work on cases that are more desirable and/or lucrative. And of course, there's also the gain in prestige that comes from having this person on board. The spotlight on this highly regarded attorney stands to put a glow on everyone, thereby enhancing their own reputations ("She's in the same firm as X, so she must be pretty good"). As a result, everyone stands to benefit.

Although the i-deal need not be a cause for worry among the new person's colleagues, it still might arouse their concerns because they don't fully understand what's going on.[78] As you might imagine, when this special new attorney is initially hired, his or her colleagues are likely to suspect that this individual is being given favorable treatment. This makes sence since i-deals tend to be arranged in one-on-one discussions between employees (present or future) and one or more company officials. It's no wonder that employees may be suspicious about under-the-table deals made behind closed doors. So, given that the arrangement is meant to be beneficial to everyone, it's essential for both managers and the beneficiaries of the i-deals to explain this thoroughly to other employees, who are unlikely to be aware of this.

Managers need to make it clear precisely *why* they agreed to such nonstandard employment terms in the first place, explaining thoroughly how the arrangement stands to benefit everyone. They also should explain any special arrangements being made to minimize any possible burdens placed on other employees due to the i-deal (e.g., rescheduling paralegals). In other words, managers should help employees understand the personal benefits being realized and the personal costs being minimized that makes the i-deal work for all.

At the same time, the beneficiaries of i-deals should be careful about what they say. The fact that they are receiving special treatment is likely to make their colleagues feel jealous (if not also suspicious and insecure). Because of this, it's essential for recipients of i-deals to avoid bragging about their arrangements. They also should go out of their way to help their colleagues, making it clear that they are not prima donnas and that they still can be counted on to be good citizens of their companies.

JOB SHARING. Sometimes, two or more of employees assume the duties of a single job, splitting its responsibilities, salary, and some benefits in proportion to the time worked, a practice known as **job sharing.** Such arrangements are rapidly growing in popularity as people enjoy the kind of work that full-time jobs allow, but require the flexibility of part-time work.

It's not unusual for job sharing arrangements to be temporary, such as when people require time off for some personal reason for a fixed period of time. At Xerox, for example, several sets of employees share jobs, including two female employees who once were sales rivals, but who joined forces to share one job when they each faced the need to reduce their working hours so they could devote time to their new families.[79]

Pella (the Iowa-based manufacturer of windows) has found that job sharing is successful in reducing absenteeism among its production and clerical employees.[80] Not surprisingly, job sharing also can be effective in retaining employees who are looking for flexibility in their working hours and in attracting new employees for whom this is important.

Offsetting some of these benefits, two key drawbacks should be noted. First, of course, job sharing does not lend itself to all types of jobs. Unless two people can handle the job as effectively as one, without any problems in coordination, the practice should be avoided. Second, because people sharing jobs may not be counted as full-time employees, important fringe benefits (e.g., eligibility for health insurance) might not be available to them. As a result, although job sharing may be a useful option for many, it is not always a perfect solution to the need for flexibility.

VOLUNTARY REDUCED WORK TIME (V-TIME) PROGRAMS. Programs known as **voluntary reduced work time (V-time) programs** allow employees to reduce the amount of time they work by a certain amount (typically 10 or 20 percent), with a proportional reduction in pay. Over the past few years, these programs have become popular in various state agencies in the United

job sharing
A form of regular part-time work in which two or more employees assume the duties of a single job, splitting its responsibilities, salary, and benefits in proportion to the time worked.

voluntary reduced work time (V-time) programs
Programs that allow employees to reduce the amount of time they work by a certain amount (typically 10 or 20 percent), with a proportional reduction in pay.

States. For example, various employees of the New York State government have enjoyed having professional careers, but with hours that make it possible for them to also meet their family obligations. Not only does the state benefit from the money saved, but the employees also enjoy the extra time they gain for nonwork pursuits.

Summary and Review of Learning Objectives

1. **Define the concepts of organization and organizational behavior.**

   An organization is a structured social system consisting of groups and individuals working together to meet some agreed-upon objectives. Organizational behavior is the field that seeks knowledge of behavior in organizational settings by systematically studying individual, group, and organizational processes.

2. **Describe the field of organizational behavior's commitment to the scientific method and the three levels of analysis it uses.**

   The field of OB seeks to develop a base of knowledge about behavior in organizations by using an empirical, research-based approach. As such, it is based on systematic observation and measurement of the behavior or phenomenon of interest. The field of OB uses three levels of analysis—individuals, work groups, and entire organizations—all relying on the scientific method.

3. **Trace the historical developments and schools of thought leading up to the field of organizational behavior today.**

   The earliest approaches to organizational behavior relied on scientific management, an approach that essentially treated people like machines, emphasizing what it took to get the most out of them. For example, this approach relied on time-and-motion study, a type of applied research designed to find the most efficient way for people to perform their jobs. As this approach grew unpopular, it was supplanted by the human relations movement, which emphasized the importance of noneconomic, social forces in the workplace—an approach that remains popular to this day. Such factors were demonstrated in the Hawthorne studies, the first large-scale research project conducted in a work organization that demonstrated the importance of social forces in determining productivity. In contrast with scientific management's orientation toward organizing the work of individuals, proponents of classical organizational theory developed ways of efficiently structuring the way work is done. Weber's concept of bureaucracy is a prime example of this approach. Contemporary OB is characterized not by one best approach to management, but by systematic scientific research inspired from several social science disciplines. It takes a contingency approach to OB, recognizing that behavior may be influenced by a variety of different forces at once, thereby rejecting the idea that there is any single most effective approach to managing behavior in organizations.

4. **Identify the fundamental assumptions of the field of organizational behavior.**

   The field of OB assumes: (1) that organizations can be made more productive while also improving the quality of people's work life, (2) that there is no one best approach to studying behavior in organizations, and (3) that organizations are dynamic and ever-changing.

5. **Describe how the field of organizational behavior today is being shaped by the global economy, increasing racial and ethnic diversity in the workforce, and advances in technology.**

   The world's economy is becoming increasingly global, a trend that is affecting the field of OB in several distinct ways. For example, organizations are expanding overseas, requiring people to live and work in different countries, requiring considerable adjustment. As this occurs, much of what we thought we knew about managing people is proven to be limited by the culture in which that knowledge was developed (U.S. culture, in most cases). Racial and ethnic diversity in the workplace is in large part the result of shifting patterns of immigration that have brought more foreign nationals into the workforce. It also is the result of changes in social values and the economy that have made the presence of women common in today's workplace. Also, thanks to modern medicine, people are living longer, hence retiring from work later than ever before. Because technology has made it possible for fewer people to do more work, many organizations have been growing smaller, downsizing. Furthermore, as technology becomes increasingly specialized, organizations have found it useful to hire other companies to do nonessential aspects of their operations that they once performed themselves—a process known as outsourcing.

6. **Explain how people's changing expectations about the desire to be engaged in their work and the need for flexibility in work have influenced the field of organizational behavior.** Both employers and employees benefit when they are highly engaged with one another—that is, when they are highly committed to satisfying one another's interests. This drives organizations to follow various OB practices so as to avoid the extremely high costs of having actively disengaged workers. Today's employees also desire to have a high degree of flexibility in their work arrangements. This takes several forms: using idiosyncratic work arrangements, offering flexible hours, relying on contingent workers, using compressed workweeks, job sharing, and voluntary reduced work time programs.

Points to Ponder

Questions for Review

1. How can the field of organizational behavior contribute to both the effective functioning of organizations *and* to the well-being of individuals? Are these goals inconsistent? Why or why not?
2. What is the "contingency approach," and why is it so popular in the field of OB today?
3. Explain how the field of organizational behavior stands to benefit by taking a global perspective. What would you say are the major challenges associated with such a perspective?
4. How has the growing quest for quality products and services affected your own work?

Experiential Questions

1. Think about a person with whom you may have worked who happens to be very different from you, such as someone of the opposite sex who also is a member of a different racial group and/or from a different country. In what ways was this experience challenging for you? In what ways did these differences prove to be beneficial? What insight do you believe the field of OB can give you with respect to this experience?
2. How have your own life and the lives of your family members changed because of flexible new working arrangements that have become popular in recent years?
3. Describe some ways in which you may have been treated by your boss that helped you become an engaged employee, a not-engaged employee, or an actively disengaged employee. How did you respond as a result?

Questions to Analyze

1. Although only some people in an organization need to know about marketing or accounting or production, almost everyone benefits by knowing about organizational behavior. Do you agree with this statement? If not, why not? If so, exactly how can knowing OB help you in your own work?
2. The practice of engineering is constantly evolving, but the basic rules of physics on which it rests remain relatively unchanged. Do you think the same relationship exists between technology and OB? In other words, do the things that have made organizations and individuals successful in yesterday's low-tech era remain relevant today, or are they changing along with technology?
3. Although many employees enjoy the flexibility of working lots of part-time jobs or working for a series of employees on a temporary basis, it comes at a cost: Such employees often make low wages, have little security, and cannot count on having fringe benefits. How do you think this trend affects organizations? How are companies helped and how are they harmed by this trend? Do you think this trend has any adverse effects on a company's products?

Experiencing OB

Individual Exercise

How Much Do You Really Know About OB?

Because we've all done some kind of work and know other people who also work, it's not surprising that we assume various things about how people behave on the job. After all, it's something we experience all the time. However, the things we may believe to be true about behavior in organizations based on common sense or experience may be inconsistent with established research findings (many of which are noted in this book). Also, the things we think we know are unlikely to reflect all the complexities and subtle nuances of human behavior that only scientists are prepared to determine. This exercise will help you get a feel for this.

Directions

Answer each of the following questions by marking it either true or false. Please indicate what you really think and not what you suspect "the real" answer may be.

_____ 1. People who are satisfied with one job tend to be satisfied with other jobs too.

_____ 2. "Two heads are better than one," so groups make better decisions than individuals.

_____ 3. The best leaders always act the same, regardless of the situations they face.

_____ 4. Specific goals make people nervous; people work better when asked to do their best.

_____ 5. People get bored easily, leading them to welcome organizational change.

_____ 6. Money is the best motivator.

_____ 7. Today's organizations are more rigidly structured than ever before.

_____ 8. People generally shy away from challenges on the job.

_____ 9. Multiple channels of communication (e.g., written and spoken) tend to add confusion.

_____10. Conflict in organizations is always highly disruptive.

Scoring

Now, the moment of truth: The first statement is true; all the others are false. Give yourself one point for each question you answered correctly. Please note that when we refer to something as being "true," we mean that it has been supported by research. Here is where in this book you'll find information relevant to these statements: Question 1, Chapter 6; Question 2, Chapter 10; Question 3, Chapter 13; Question 4, Chapter 7; Question 5, Chapter 16; Question 6, Chapter 7; Question 7, Chapter 15; Question 8, Chapter 7; Question 9, Chapter 9; Question 10, Chapter 11.

Questions for Discussion

1. How did you score on this quiz? If you answered honestly, you probably didn't get them all correct. If so, don't be surprised. We're not. After all, many of the things people routinely believe about behavior in organizations are only partially true—that is, true under some conditions, but not always. In other words, this topic tends to be far more complex and nuanced than meets the eye. This is precisely why when it comes to studying OB we cannot rely on our common sense as a guide. Instead, we rely on scientific research (see Appendix 1 for a summary of how such research is conducted).

2. Are you surprised to learn of any of the answers we present as being correct? If so, keep in mind that although it's certainly not always perfect, the fact that research is carefully designed to describe and explain behavior in an unbiased fashion enhances our confidence in what it reveals. Indeed, OB is a science, and as such, the things we know about it are based not on what we think or hope or believe to be the case, but rather, on what research reveals. So, as you read this book you can be assured that the things we say are based on the results of careful scientific investigation—even (or especially) if it's not what you'd expect.

3. How did you score relative to your classmates? It may be interesting to see exactly what questions stumped the most people in your class. Then, you can look forward to learning about the topic associated with it later in this book.

Group Exercise

Is Your Team Ready for Telecommuting?

What happens when people who might ordinarily come into contact with one another on their jobs no longer have that social contact? Several things may happen. For example, when employees do not see each other on a regular basis, it is difficult to build the team spirit that is needed to establish quality goods and services in some organizations. As a result, telecommuting does not lend itself to all jobs and to all individuals. This exercise will help you determine if you and members of your work team are ready for telecommuting.

Directions

Working independently, each member of a work team should complete the following question-naire by indicating the extent to which each statement describes his or her own characteristics or current job situation.

1 = not at all

2 = slightly

3 = moderately

4 = somewhat

5 = greatly

Scale

To what extent . . .

1. Does your job allow you to work independently of others?
2. Is it important for you to see the people with whom you work face-to-face?
3. Are you able to complete jobs without being watched closely?
4. Are you comfortable using computers and high-tech equipment?
5. Is your company able to train you to use technology to do your job?
6. Are you able to manage your own time effectively?
7. Are you capable of finding a safe, secure, and nondistracting place to work?
8. Does your job performance depend on measurable aspects of your individual performance?
9. Would you miss the socializing that goes on in the office if you were away from it?
10. Is it possible for you to have access to the equipment and supplies needed to do your job while away from the office?

Scoring and Interpretation

1. Add together your scores for items 1, 3, 4, 5, 6, 7, 8, and 10.
2. Add together your scores for items 2 and 9. Subtract this sum from 12.
3. Add together the number from step 1 and the number from step 2. You will get a number from 10 to 50. This is your individual score.
4. Higher scores reflect higher degrees of individual readiness for telecommuting. Scores of 15 or lower reflect low degrees of readiness. Scores of 35 or higher reflect high degrees of readiness.
5. Add together the individual scores from all the members of your team. Then divide this number by the number of people in your team. This is your team's average readiness for telecommuting score.
6. Higher scores in step 5 reflect higher degrees of team readiness for telecommuting. Scores of 15 or lower reflect low degrees of team readiness. Scores of 35 or higher reflect high degrees of team readiness.

Questions for Discussion

1. In scoring the scale responses, why do you think questions 2 and 9 were treated differently from the others? How are they different?
2. Does your individual score (step 4) suggest that you are ready for telecommuting? Do you do so already? Might it be possible to telecommute some of the time if you are not doing so already?
3. Does your team score (step 6) suggest that your team is ready for telecommuting? Do some members of the team engage in telecommuting already? If so, how are the other members of the work team affected by this? If not, why do you think this is not already going on?

Practicing OB

When in Rome

You are the regional director of a large U.S.-based import-export company that is expanding international operations. This requires three of your top managers to move to Rome, Italy, for no less than two years, maybe longer. Given their lengthy stay, they will be moving their families along with them and setting up new households.

1. What problems would you anticipate these executives will have as they adjust to their new surroundings?

2. What specific measures could be taken to help these individuals avoid the symptoms of culture shock that are likely to arise?

3. What difficulties might these individuals have when they return to their own country at the end of their assignments? What could be done to minimize these problems?

Case in Point

■ *Floyd's Barbershop: A Cut Above the Rest*

In 2001, when the O'Brien brothers, Paul, Ron, and Bill, opened Floyd's 99 Barbershop in Denver, their only experience in the hair care business was as customers. Lacking tonsorial training, their particular skills, it seems, laid not in grooming hair but grooming loyal, creative, and hard-working employees.

Floyd's, named after the iconic barber from television's classic *Andy Griffith Show*, was conceived to be a friendly neighborhood place like the one owned by its namesake. But that's where the similarity ends. In the O'Briens' vision, Floyd's was not your father's traditional barbershop, nor was it a plush, unisex salon that smelled like hair chemicals. Instead, Floyd's was designed to be a hip and lively place for contemporary men. In many locations—there are now 27 Floyd's 99 Barbershops in six states—popular music is heard (played by live DJs on Saturdays), posters of rock stars adorn the walls, and sporting events are shown on plasma TV screens. The place is so hip that the Floyd's shop in Hollywood, California, was a location for an episode of the HBO series *Entourage*. It's no wonder that Bill O'Brien refers to Floyd's as "Hard Rock meets the barbershop."

Stylists at Floyd's know all the latest, contemporary cuts but also include old-fashioned services such as neck shaves with each haircut, and at reasonable prices ("less than twice the price of lunch" according to Rob O'Brien). Because it's impractical for today's highly mobile young men to commit to making appointments for haircuts, Floyd's doesn't take them. Yet, acknowledging the importance of timely service, customers can phone-in their place in line an hour or so ahead of arriving. But for anyone who does have to wait for his favorite barber (whose working hours be can checked online), it's not so bad because pool tables and computers with Internet access are available to help pass the time.

Not only are the O'Brien brothers attuned to what their customers want, they also are keenly sensitive to their employees. Illustrating this, consider how the O'Briens responded in March 2003 when a blizzard struck Denver. When the nightclub next door collapsed onto their shop, managers pleaded with firemen to rummage through the mounds of debris to retrieve their employees' tools and personal belongings. Unfortunately, the building housing Floyd's had to be demolished due to structural damage, leading to concerns about the business's future. Although the building was broken, the O'Briens' spirit was not broken—and employees came to appreciate this. Until a new shop could be built, complete with chrome and leather chairs and a barber pole out front, current employees were absorbed into other Floyd's locations and nobody lost a job. In fact, a billboard and the company's Web site made light of the events, adding to the belief that all would be well.

Although the O'Briens don't know how to cut hair, they surely know how to trim through layers of uncertainty to assuage their employees' fears. Employees and industry pundits would be hard pressed to challenge Bill's wife, Karen, who said that at Floyd's, "The founders' passion, personalities, and their constant desire to make a positive impact on people, along with the support of a qualified and professional management team, have poised the company for national and international expansion."

Questions for Discussion

1. Would you say that the O'Briens have adopted a Theory X or Theory Y approach to the management of their employees? On what do you base your answer?

2. Do the O'Briens appear to be doing anything to increase the feelings of engagement among their employees? If so, what are they? If not, what might they do?

3. How might Floyd's Barbershop: (a) use technology to enhance its business, and (b) respond to the need for flexibility among its employees?

2 Organizational Justice, Ethics, and Corporate Social Responsibility

Learning Objectives

After reading this chapter, you should be able to:

1. Identify four different forms of organizational justice and the organizational impact of each.

2. Describe strategies that can be used to promote organizational justice.

3. Explain what is meant by ethical behavior and describe its relation to the law.

4. Describe the individual and situational factors responsible for unethical behavior in organizations and methods for minimizing such behavior.

5. Explain ways of behaving ethically when conducting business internationally.

6. Explain what is meant by corporate social responsibility, describe the forms it takes, and characterize the relationship between responsible behavior and financial profitability.

Chapter Outline

- Organizational Justice: Fairness Matters
- Strategies for Promoting Organizational Justice
- Ethical Behavior in Organizations: Its Fundamental Nature
- Why Do Some People Behave Unethically, at Least Sometimes—and What Can Be Done About It?
- Using Corporate Ethics Programs to Promote Ethical Behavior
- Ethics in the International Arena
- Beyond Ethics: Corporate Social Responsibility

Preview Case

■ *A Huge Day's Pay for a Seriously Bad Day's Work*

For many years, banks and financial institutions had a good thing going—or so it seemed. They issued variable-rate mortgages to people with low income and poor credit, later packaging and reselling these "subprime" loans to unknowing investors as mortgage-backed securities. The profits were enormous, rewarding bank executives with salaries, bonuses, and stock options in the tens, if not hundreds, of millions of dollars. Despite alerts from some economists, greed apparently blinded the bankers. They convinced themselves that they could keep this up forever because home values would continue to rise, allowing consumers to refinance their loans.

The bankers were wrong. In fall 2008, many of the variable interest loans, with their initially low interest rates, which got borrowers in the door (literally), rose to levels that home owners could no longer afford, and they began defaulting. This led the value of the securities to nosedive, and soon the walls came tumbling down. Banks were losing money even faster than they had been making it, leading them to the brink of failure.

Recognizing that keeping the banks afloat was essential to preventing a major collapse of the financial system and a "Second Great Depression," the U.S. government intervened by launching the *Troubled Asset Relief Program (TARP)*. Through this initiative, the Treasury Department was able to purchase some $23 trillion in "troubled" assets and equity (e.g., losses stemming from home foreclosures) from financial institutions in an effort to stabilize them. As they regained health, the banks were to repay the government.

Although banks were being kept afloat by government bailouts, many executives continued to receive the same large paychecks that they were receiving before they took TARP funds. Some banks were spending millions of taxpayer dollars on bonuses for the very executives whose poor judgment created the problem in the first place. Instead of being forced to resign in disgrace for causing such serious problems, these top officials were, in essence, being rewarded by their victims, the American people.

Among the most egregious abusers was the large insurance company AIG. This firm's officials begged the government for a bailout and received $182.5 billion in return. Then, it used part of this money to pay tens of millions of dollars to its top executives. In March 2009, President Obama expressed his indignation. "People are rightly outraged about these particular bonuses," he said, adding, "But just as outrageous is the culture that these bonuses are a symptom of, that have existed for far too long—a situation where excess greed, excess compensation, excess risk-taking have all made us vulnerable and left us holding the bag."

Following the President's criticism, many AIG executives were shamed into returning their bonuses, although several explained that their particular work had nothing to do with the subprime mortgage crisis and that they deserved their bonuses. It also was explained that unless executives were rewarded with generous bonuses, they would go elsewhere, leaving these companies without competent leaders to get them out of trouble. Some agreed but others countered that the departure of the individuals who got into this mess would not be such a great loss.

From an economic and political standpoint, the situation with AIG is far more complex than depicted in this case. However, from the perspective of OB, the principle involved appears rather straightforward. "A fair day's work for a fair day's wages" is a cherished value in the workplace. Those who do well deserve to be rewarded for their accomplishments, but those who fail do not deserve to benefit. It sounds simple enough, at least in principle. However, the AIG scandal seems to suggest that when it comes to bank or insurance executives, different rules apply. And as President Obama suggested in no uncertain terms, this is unacceptable.

It's clear that people get upset when someone doesn't do the "right thing," although reasonable people don't always agree on precisely what this entails. Given that great philosophers over the years haven't reached consensus about what constitutes appropriate behavior, we shouldn't be too surprised that distinguishing between right and wrong in the workplace can be a complex undertaking.[1] Yet, it's clear from many of the cases that have been in the news at the beginning of the twenty-first century—the Enron scandal and the Bernard Madoff scandal being the most visible—that most people have a good sense of wrongdoing when they see it.[2] Still, whether it's cheating among athletes and sports officials, illicit behavior among politicians, or unabashed greed among corporate officers, recent headlines make it clear that people in organizations seem to face an unending array of ethical obstacles.[3] Not surprisingly, as we will describe in this chapter, the topic of *business ethics* is central to the study of OB. Specifically, OB provides a great deal of insight into why unethical behavior occurs and offers suggestions on how to curtail it.

As a natural outgrowth of the quest to behave ethically, many organizational leaders are going beyond merely doing what's right by proactively attempting to improve the communities in which they operate.[4] Indeed, many of today's organizations are demonstrating what is known as *corporate social responsibility*—not only attempting to meet prevailing legal and ethical standards but also exceeding them by embracing values that promote the greater welfare of society at large. Whether it involves donating money to charities, staffing community welfare projects, or taking steps to make our air and water clean, engaging in socially responsible behavior is of great concern to leaders of today's organizations. Here again, OB specialists have sought to explain this behavior, and their efforts will be outlined in this chapter.

Before focusing on ethics and corporate social responsibility, we begin this chapter by discussing a key concept that is central to understanding these themes—*organizational justice*.[5] People care a great deal about matters of justice on the job. Just ask any worker who feels that the small pay raise he received does not adequately reflect his important contributions, or someone who suspects that the boss is playing favorites by giving one of her coworkers more desirable work assignments. Workers in these cases are bound to cry foul, claiming that they have been treated unfairly. As these illustrations suggest, people are extremely sensitive to matters of justice and injustice in the workplace and are inclined to express their feelings in significant ways. Not surprisingly, when people are asked to describe what makes them angriest on the job, "being treated unfairly" tops the list.[6] Because of its importance, OB scientists have devoted a great deal of attention to studying organizational justice—the topic to which we now turn our attention.

Organizational Justice: Fairness Matters

Suppose you received a failing grade in a course. You don't like it, of course, but can you say that the grade is unfair? To answer this question, you would likely take several things into consideration. For example, does the grade accurately reflect how well you performed in the course? Were your exam scores added accurately and were they computed in an unbiased fashion? Has the professor treated you in a polite and professional fashion when addressing you? Finally, has the professor explained the grading process to you adequately? In judging how fairly you have been treated, questions such as these are likely to be raised—and your answers are likely to have a considerable impact on how you feel about your grade, the professor, and even the school as a whole. Moreover, they are likely to have a profound effect on how you respond, such as whether you quietly accept the grade, complain about it to someone, or even quit school entirely.

Although this example involves you as a student, the same considerations arise in the workplace. In that context, instead of talking about grades from professors, concerns about justice take analogous forms. Does your salary reflect your work accomplishments? How was your performance evaluation determined? Were you treated with dignity and respect by your boss? Were you given important job information in a thorough and timely manner? Matters such as these are relevant to **organizational justice**—the study of people's perceptions of fairness in organizations.

organizational justice
The study of people's perceptions of fairness in organizations.

Our discussion of organizational justice focuses on three key areas—the major forms of organizational justice, the relationships between these forms, and suggestions for promoting justice in organizations. Before we launch into our discussion of organizational justice, there are two important things about it you need to consider.

Two Important Points to Keep in Mind

Unlike philosophers, who attempt to make objective statements about *what justice really is*, OB scientists generally adopt the approach of psychologists, which focuses on *how justice is perceived*. After all, people respond to how they perceive things, which may or may not be based on objective truths. You will come to appreciate this more fully as you venture further into this book (and as we will explain in more detail in Chapter 3). For now, though, it's important to be aware that we are talking about people's perceptions.

Another thing to keep in mind about organizational justice is that it takes into account the particular focus or target of people's perceptions. So, when we speak about organizational justice, we must ask: to whom or what are judgments focused? For example, people may consider the

multifoci approach to justice
A conceptualization of organizational justice recognizing that people take into account both individuals and larger units when assessing fairness.

fairness of both individuals (e.g., specific managers) and larger units (e.g., their organizations as a whole), which may or may not be aligned. The notion that people may take into account different foci when assessing fairness is known as the **multifoci approach to justice.**[7]

Now that we've made these points explicit, let's begin. Our discussion of organizational justice will focus on three important considerations—the major forms of organizational justice, the relationships between these forms, and tips for promoting justice in organizations.

Forms of Organizational Justice and Their Effects

The complexity of the notion of organizational justice is reflected by the vast array of questions to which it is applicable. For example, justice is considered in everything from how decisions are made about who will make the office coffee and how much you get paid, to how well you are treated by your boss. Considering its complexity, OB scientists have recognized that organizational justice takes several different forms. These are known as *distributive justice, procedural justice, interpersonal justice,* and *informational justice* (for an overview, see Figure 2.1).[8]

distributive justice
The form of organizational justice that focuses on people's beliefs that they have received fair amounts of valued work-related outcomes (e.g., pay, recognition, etc.).

DISTRIBUTIVE JUSTICE. On the job, people are concerned with getting their "fair share" of resources. We all want to be paid fairly for the work we do, and we want to be adequately recognized for our efforts and any special contributions we bring to the job. **Distributive justice** is the form of organizational justice that focuses on people's beliefs that they have received fair amounts of valued work-related outcomes (e.g., pay, recognition, etc.). For example, workers in most Western nations believe that fairness demands getting paid in proportion to job performance, with better performers making more than poor performers. This is in keeping with the notion of "a fair day's wages for a fair day's work"—a cherished value in the United States. (It is the apparent violation of this principle by AIG executives—as described in this chapter's Preview Case on page 36—that triggered cries of injustice by President Obama and many others.)

People who believe that they have been dealt a distributive injustice on the job tend to experience high levels of stress (see Chapter 5) and also feel dissatisfied with their jobs and the companies in which they work. (Related to this, as you will see in the discussion of *equity theory* in Chapter 7, feelings of distributive justice can have a great impact on people's motivation to perform their jobs.) As an example of distributive injustice consider a situation that's been discussed in the press a great deal in recent years—the distribution of health-care services and costs. It has been

FIGURE 2.1

Forms of Organizational Justice and Their Effects

Organizational justice takes the four different forms identified here. Each of these forms of justice has been found to have different effects in organizations.

Source: Based on information in Greenberg, 2010; see Note 5.

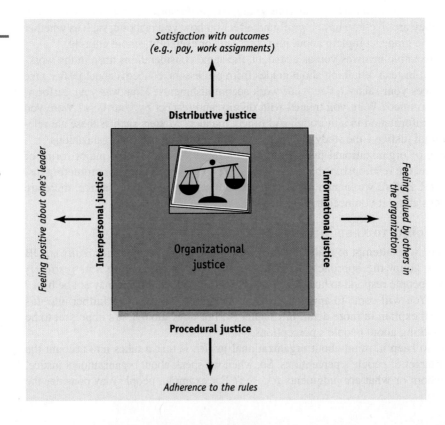

argued that one key problem with the health-care system in the United States is that people in lower-paying jobs pay proportionately more for their health insurance on an out-of-pocket basis, and use it less, than individuals in higher-paying jobs.[9] Whatever the reasons for this—and the way to fix it—may be (a complex topic that lies far beyond the scope of this book), it's clear that people seek a health-care system that is fair and, among other things, this requires *not* putting most of the burden on those who are least able to carry it.

PROCEDURAL JUSTICE. Assuming it's not too painful to do so, recall our example (on page 37) involving receipt of a failing grade. In assessing the fairness of this situation, you would want to know precisely *how* your grade was determined. After all, if the professor made an error in calculating your grade, it would be unfair for you to be penalized. In other words, fairness involves consideration of not only *how much* of various outcomes you receive (i.e., distributive justice) but also the process by which those outcomes are determined—that is, *procedural justice*. Specifically, **procedural justice** refers to people's perceptions of the fairness of the procedures used to determine the outcomes they receive.[10] When people judge procedural justice, they take into account a variety of different criteria. Among the most widely used are summarized in Table 2.1.

> **procedural justice**
> People's perceptions of the fairness of the procedures used to determine the outcomes they receive.

Let's consider an illustration. In the spring of 1998, New York City cab drivers went on strike to protest then–Mayor Giuliani's imposition of new safety rules.[11] As it worked out, the drivers had few gripes with the rules themselves. However, they felt it was unfair for the mayor to impose the rules without consulting them. In their eyes, fairness demanded having a voice in the decision-making process, and when they didn't get it they expressed their concerns by striking. How easily this could have been avoided! Clearly, giving people a voice is a major consideration when it comes to procedural justice, which is why it heads the list of criteria shown in Table 2.1.

Concerns about procedural justice are likely to take different forms in various settings. Consider these examples.[12]

- Formal performance appraisals—Workers consider their job performance ratings to be fair to the extent that certain procedures are followed, such as when raters are believed to be familiar with their work and when they believe that the standards used to judge them are applied to everyone equally and consistently (for an example, see Figure 2.2).[13]
- Classroom—As a student, you want to make sure your professor uses fair procedures when grading your exams, such as by applying the same criteria to everyone's exams while grading essays and by not making any arithmetic errors when scoring exams.
- Courtroom—In the United States, laws require that evidence be ignored in court if it has been mishandled or if the police violated established rules to gather it. Likewise, entire cases may be thrown out if certain procedural rules have been violated.

TABLE 2.1 Procedural Justice Criteria

In forming judgments of procedural justice, people take different factors into consideration. Some of the major ones are identified here, along with descriptions and examples of each.

Criterion	Description	Example
• Voice in the making of decisions	Perceptions of procedural justice are enhanced to the extent that people are given a say in the decisions affecting them.	Workers are given an opportunity to explain their feelings about their work to a supervisor who is evaluating their performance.
• Consistency in applying rules	To be fair, the rules used as the basis for making a decision about one person must be applied equally to making a decision about someone else.	A professor must use the same exact standards in evaluating the term papers of each student in the class.
• Accuracy in use of information	Fair decisions must be based on information that is accurate.	A manager calculating the amount of overtime pay a worker is to receive must add the numbers accurately.
• Opportunity to correct errors	Fair procedures are ones in which people have a readily available opportunity to correct any mistakes that have been made	Litigants have an opportunity to have a judge's decision reconsidered in the event that an error was made in legal proceedings.
• Safeguards against bias	A person making a decision must not have any opportunity to bias the results.	Lottery drawings are held in such a manner that each number is selected in a completely random, unbiased fashion.

Source: Based on information in Greenberg, 2010; see Note 5.

Jeff Greenberg/Alamy Images.

FIGURE 2.2

Performance Appraisals Are Now Sweeter at Jelly Belly

The family-owned Jelly Belly Candy Company, headquartered in Fairfield, California, has long been considered a fun place to work. The fun ended, however, when it came to formal performance appraisals. Workers complained that the system was unfair because different procedures were used throughout the company. Although there weren't quite as many procedures as the number of different flavors made, 50, the company's 600 employees were unclear about what was expected of them. This led the company to adopt a sweet new performance appraisal system that could be used for all employees in all three company locations. Shortly afterward, according to HR director Margie Poulos, staff members characterized the new, standardized system as "fair and realistic," a vast improvement over the former ad hoc systems that started from scratch each year.

- Professional football—To ensure that referees' calls are correct, the National Football League allows referees to review via videotape plays in which coaches believe that referees may have made an error.

It is important to note that following unfair procedures not only makes people dissatisfied with their outcomes (as in the case of distributive justice), but also leads them to reject the entire system as unfair.[14] Additionally, procedural justice affects people's tendencies to follow organizational rules: Workers are not inclined to follow an organization's rules when they have reason to believe that its procedures are inherently unfair. And, of course, when this occurs, serious problems are likely to arise. Accordingly, everyone in an organization—especially top officials—would be well advised to adhere to the criteria for promoting procedural justice summarized in Table 2.1.

INTERPERSONAL JUSTICE. Imagine that you were just laid off from your job. You're not happy about it, of course, but suppose that your boss explains this situation to you in a manner that takes some of the sting out of it. Although your boss cannot do anything about this high-level corporate decision, he or she is very sensitive to the harm this causes you and expresses concern for you in a highly sensitive and caring manner. Research has shown that people experiencing situations such as this tend to accept their layoffs as being fair and hold positive feelings about their supervisors (see Figure 2.1). Importantly, such individuals are less inclined to sue their former companies on the grounds of wrongful termination than those who believe they were treated in an opposite manner—that is, an insensitive and disrespectful fashion.[15]

The type of justice demonstrated in this example is known as **interpersonal justice.** This refers to people's perceptions of the fairness of the manner in which they are treated by others (typically, authority figures). You may be wondering what treating people with dignity and respect has to do with fairness. The answer is simple: People believe that they deserve to be treated in such a manner and that it is unfair for this not to happen.

interpersonal justice
People's perceptions of the fairness of the manner in which they are treated by others (typically, authority figures).

INFORMATIONAL JUSTICE. Imagine that you are a heavy smoker of cigarettes and learn that your company has just imposed a smoking ban. Although you may recognize that it's the right thing to do, you are unhappy about it because the ruling forces you to change your behavior and break an addictive habit. Will you accept the smoking ban as fair and do your best to go along with it? Research suggests that you will do so only under certain circumstances—if you are given clear and thorough information about the need for the smoking ban (e.g., the savings to the company and improvements to the health of employees).[16] The form of justice illustrated in this example is known as **informational justice.** This refers to people's perceptions of the fairness of the information used as the basis for making a decision. Because detailed information was provided about the basis for implementing the smoking ban, informational justice was high, leading people to accept the fairness of the smoking ban.

A key explanation for this phenomenon is that informational justice prompts feelings of being valued by others in an organization. This is known as the **group-value explanation** of organizational justice. The basic idea is that people believe they are considered an important part of the organization when an organizational official takes the time to explain thoroughly to them the rationale behind a decision. And people experiencing such feelings may be expected to believe that they are being treated in a fair manner.

informational justice
People's perceptions of the fairness of the information used as the basis for making a decision.

group-value explanation (of organizational justice)
The idea that people believe they are an important part of the organization when an organizational official takes the time to explain thoroughly to them the rationale behind a decision.

A Neurological Basis for Responses to Injustice

Typically, OB scientists focus only on people's perceptions and their behaviors, especially when it comes to organizational justice. Interestingly, however, a recent study found that people's reactions to distributive injustice and procedural injustice manifest themselves differently inside people's brains.[17]

To establish this, a group of scientists had students play a game that involved bargaining with others in the hope of winning a financial award. While completing the bargaining game, participants were lying down inside a machine that used functional magnetic resonance imaging (fMRI) to scan their brains. This equipment uses large magnets to determine activation in the brain in terms of the flow of blood to certain regions while people are engaged in various activities. Here, the researchers were looking to determine the regions of the brain that were activated when participants were victimized by the other players' acts of distributive injustice (taking too much money) and procedural injustice (violating established rules).

Based on previous research, it was expected that different regions of people's brains would respond to procedural injustice and distributive injustice. Procedural injustice, the scientists reasoned, is highly cognitive as people need to process information about what's going on to assess the extent to which various procedural rules have or have not been followed. As such, people experiencing violations of procedural justice were predicted to show signs of activation in the portions of their brains associated with cognition. By contrast, they noted that people respond to distributive injustice in highly emotional ways. For example, they get angry when they believe that someone has not given them what they deserve. Accordingly, the researchers predicted that the brains of people experiencing distributive injustice would show signs of activation in regions known to be associated with emotion. As summarized in Figure 2.3, this is precisely what they found.

These findings are important because they suggest that differences in reactions to distributive injustice and procedural injustice are "real" in the sense that they may be traced neurologically. It looks

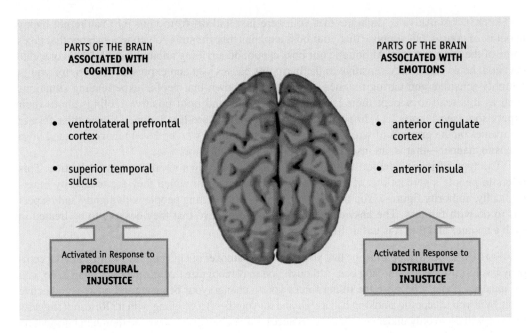

FIGURE 2.3

Neurological Reactions to Distributive Injustice and Procedural Injustice

Research using neurological imaging (fMRI) has found that people's brains respond differently when they are victims of distributive injustice and procedural injustice. As summarized here, different regions are activated in each case, suggesting that there are biological bases for reactions to unfairness.

Source: Based on suggestions by Dulebohn et al., 2009; see Note 17.

like there is an actual biological basis for people's reactions to injustice. Another intriguing suggestion from the findings is that as a species, people appear to be "hard wired" to be responsive to injustices.

Strategies for Promoting Organizational Justice

Treating people fairly on the job surely is a noble objective. Although many people are concerned about being fair for its own sake, of course, there's also a good practical reason for treating employees fairly. Specifically, individuals who believe they have been unfairly treated in any or all of the ways described respond quite negatively. We know, for example, that people who feel unfairly treated are likely to do such things as work less hard, steal from their employers, do poor-quality work, or even quit their jobs altogether—and then sue their former employers.[18]

Naturally, managers are likely to seek organizational justice to avoid these problems. In addition to minimizing such negative reactions, managers also are likely to seek the positive reactions associated with being perceived as fair. For example, fairness has been associated with such desirable behaviors as helping one's fellow workers and going along with organizational policies.[19]

As if these benefits aren't sufficiently convincing, think about what it would be like if entire departments or work groups were composed of employees who felt unfairly treated. The cumulative impact would be dramatic, and that is precisely what was found by scientists conducting a study in a hotel chain.[20] Analyzing 4,539 employees from 783 departments in 97 different hotels, they found that departments composed of employees who felt unfairly treated suffered significantly higher rates of turnover and lower levels of customer satisfaction than those composed of employees who felt fairly treated. And, of course, these factors have an enormous impact on a hotel's success. In view of these findings, there is good reason for managers to go out of their way to promote justice in the workplace. Fortunately, what we know about organizational justice points to some useful suggestions for doing so.

Pay Workers What They Deserve

The practices of saving a little money by underpaying employees, informally discouraging them from taking vacation days they are due, or asking them to work "off the clock" are doomed to fail.

Paying the "going wage" in your community for work of a certain type and not cheating workers out of what they have coming to them are far wiser investments. After all, workers who feel cheated out of their pay are unmotivated to perform at high levels (see Chapter 7). Fortunately, to help in this regard localized surveys are available that reveal the prevailing rates of pay for different jobs in various locations. For example, individual U.S. states maintain online databases that can be consulted to identify average wages and salaries for individuals performing various jobs in specific cities or counties. The U.S. Bureau of Labor Statistics maintains similar databases.

Our point is that determining and then paying prevailing wage rates with employees is a good way to promote justice. And so that employees understand the basis for their pay, it's useful to show them the statistics used for this purpose. A company paying below-market wages is likely to lose in the long run because the best workers will be disinclined to remain working there, or even to accept jobs there in the first place. Not giving workers what they have coming to them clearly is "penny wise and pound foolish," as the saying goes.

Offer Workers a Voice

One of the most strongly established principles of procedural justice is that people will better accept outcomes when they have had some input into determining them than when they are not involved.[21] This is known as the **fair process effect.** Often, promoting fairness in this manner is accomplished simply by conducting regular meetings with employees to hear what they have to say. The benefits of doing so result not only from making better-quality decisions (because it taps workers' expertise), but also from merely involving workers in the process. After all, workers whose input is solicited are inclined to feel better accepted as valued members of their organization than those who are ignored (this is the *group-value explanation* noted earlier). As shown in Figure 2.4, this leads them to perceive both that the resulting outcome is fair and that the procedure used to determine it is fair. And, as noted earlier, perceptions of distributive justice and procedural justice are quite beneficial to organizations.

fair process effect
The tendency for people to better accept outcomes into which they have had some input in determining than when they have no such involvement.

What can be done to promote voice in organizations? Although there are many good possibilities, here are some of the most widely used methods.

- *Meet regularly and invite input.* Discussing how to do things—especially things that affect the individuals involved—is one of the most effective ways to promote voice. This gives people input into the making of decisions, promoting the perceived fairness—and acceptance—of those decisions. With this in mind, many managers hold regular meetings in which they solicit input from everyone.

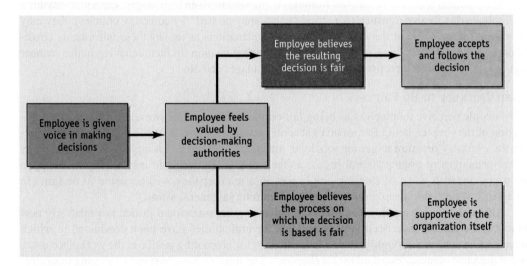

FIGURE 2.4

The Fair Process Effect: A Summary

According to the fair process effect, employees who are given a voice in the making of decisions affecting them will feel valued by the decision-making authorities (e.g., top company leaders). In turn, this leads employees to believe that both the decision-making procedure and the outcomes resulting from it are fair. As a result, employees will accept and follow the decision and be supportive of the organization itself.

- *Conduct employee surveys.* Companies conduct surveys among employees for many reasons. The most straightforward is to collect and systematically share employees' ideas about how to do things better. FedEx is one company that has made widespread use of this technique.
- *Keep an "open door policy."* Probably the easiest and most straightforward way to give employees voice is by letting them know that you are always available to talk. Managers who use such an "open door policy" send a strong message that they are interested in what their employees have to say. This not only results in good ideas but also makes it clear to employees that they are valued members of the workplace.
- *Use suggestion systems.* To encourage employees to share ideas, many companies and government agencies have online sites at which employees can share ideas. Frequently, an employee whose idea is implemented is given a reward that reflects the degree to which the suggestion led to savings for the company. Even paper-and-pencil "suggestion boxes" still are used for this purpose (for an example, see Figure 2.5).

Explain Decisions Thoroughly and in a Manner Demonstrating Dignity and Respect

To be fair, both interpersonally and informationally, it is essential for managers to take great care in presenting decisions to their employees. Specifically, fairness demands giving employees lots of information about how decisions were made and explaining those decisions in a manner that demonstrates dignity and respect for them. This is especially important when the decisions made have a negative impact on workers. After all, it's bad enough to learn something negative (e.g., a poor performance appraisal, a pay cut, or a layoff) without having a supervisor add insult to injury by not bothering to explain that decision thoroughly or by demonstrating a lack of concern for your feelings.[22]

Illustrating this point, consider what it's like to have to live through a long pay freeze. Although it's bound to be painful, people may be more accepting of a pay freeze, accepting it as fair, if the procedure used to determine the need for the pay freeze is believed to be thorough and careful—that is, if "a fair explanation" for it can be provided. This was precisely what was found in an interesting study of manufacturing workers' reactions to a pay freeze.[23] Specifically, the researchers made comparisons between two groups of workers: those who received a thorough explanation of the procedures necessitating the pay freeze (e.g., information about the organization's economic problems) and those who received no such information. Although all workers were adversely affected by the freeze, those receiving the explanation better accepted it. In particular, the explanation reduced their interest in looking for a new job.

The practical lesson to be learned from this is important: Even if managers cannot do anything to eliminate distributive injustice (e.g., their "hands may be tied" by company policies), they may be able to reduce some of the sting by providing explanations as to *why* these unfortunate conditions are necessary and doing so in a sensitive and caring fashion. In fact, behaving in this manner can be one of the most effective cost-free things a manager can do.

Train Workers to Be Fair

Most people perceive themselves as being fair on most occasions. However, as is clear from this section of the chapter, being fair involves several very specific forms of behavior. And, when facing the everyday pressure to get the job done, managers may not be taking into account as many of the principles of organizational justice as they should. With this in mind, it makes sense to train managers in ways of treating employees in a manner they will perceive to be fair. (In Chapter 3, we discuss the essential elements of training in general terms.)

Although training employees in ways of enhancing organizational justice is a relatively new practice, the results have been very promising. Several studies have been conducted in which managers have been thoroughly trained in techniques for promoting justice in the workplace using much the same content described in this chapter.[24] The training has consisted of sharing this information along with a series of case studies and exercises designed to increase managers' sensitivity to justice in the workplace. Managers who have been so trained reap several benefits compared to their untrained counterparts. Not only are the employees of the trained managers less inclined to respond in a negative fashion (e.g., by stealing from the company), but they also are more inclined to pitch in and help others in the organization (a phenomenon known as *organizational citizenship behavior,* which we will describe in Chapter 6).

Office of
Personnel Management

State of Arkansas
DEPARTMENT OF FINANCE AND ADMINISTRATION
P.O. Box 3278
LITTLE ROCK, ARKANSAS 72203–3278

PHONE (501) 682–1823
FAX (501) 682–5104

EMPLOYEE SUGGESTION FORM

Note: In accordance with Arkansas Code Annotated 21–11–101 the employee suggestion system is available to all full-time state employees of all departments, agencies, boards, commissions, or other agencies of the state supported by appropriation of state or federal funds.

MAIL TO:
 	
    Office of Personnel Management
    Employee Suggestion System
    Post Office Box 3278
    Little Rock, AR 72203
	DO NOT WRITE IN THIS SPACE	

	Employee Suggestion Number: _____	
	Accepted ❑	Unaccepted ❑

Please type or print your idea. Be sure to supply all information requested. You may attach additional sheets and examples if needed. READ INSTRUCTIONS CAREFULLY AND COMPLETELY.

WHAT IS THE PROBLEM AS YOU SEE IT?

WHAT IS YOUR SUGGESTION?

HOW WILL YOUR SUGGESTION IMPROVE THE PRESENT SITUATION OR BENEFIT THE AGENCY OR STATE? (BE SPECIFIC - IF MONEY WILL BE SAVED, STATE HOW MUCH AND SHOW HOW YOU FIGURED THE SAVINGS. ATTACH ADDITIONAL INFORMATION IF NEEDED)

FIGURE 2.5

Suggestion Systems: An Example

Although we tend to think of suggestion systems as popular in large companies, they also are used widely in the nonprofit sector. Here, for example, is the form used by employees of the state of Arkansas to identify suggestions that promise to make the state government "more efficient and more productive." Rewards equal to 10 percent of the first year's cost savings (up to $5,000) are given for money-saving suggestions. Certificates or rewards up to $100 are given to employees whose suggestions result in intangible benefits, such as ways of improving morale.

As a specific example of the effectiveness of training, consider a study that the author conducted in several hospitals.[25] Participants in the study were nurses at several hospitals and their immediate supervisors. The nurses in some of the hospitals experienced a change in their pay system that led them to suffer a pay cut of about 10 percent. Of course, they didn't like this distributive injustice. In fact, they suffered so much stress as a result (we will discuss this topic in detail in Chapter 5) that they reported symptoms of insomnia. In other words, they lost sleep over being treated unfairly.

As this was going on, the supervisors of the nurses were trained in ways to enhance interpersonal justice and informational justice among their subordinates. Specifically, in two 4-hour classroom sessions case studies and role-playing exercises were used to teach the supervisors specifically how to share information with employees in a manner that shows dignity and respect. As you can see from Figure 2.6, the results were interesting.

The nurses whose supervisors were trained in this manner reported significantly less insomnia after the training than before the training. However, the nurses whose supervisors were untrained failed to show any decrease in insomnia during this same period. Bottom line: The training worked. Training supervisors in interpersonal and informational justice (which managers generally have a chance to control on their own, unlike distributions and procedures, in many cases) helped buffer the negative effects of the distributive injustice. In other words, although managers who were trained to demonstrate high levels of informational and interpersonal justice toward their subordinates did not make their distributive injustices go away, they helped them to cope with them in a less stressful manner.

Our discussion of strategies for combating workplace injustice identifies two key issues worth highlighting. First, some sources of injustice stem from organization-wide policies involving

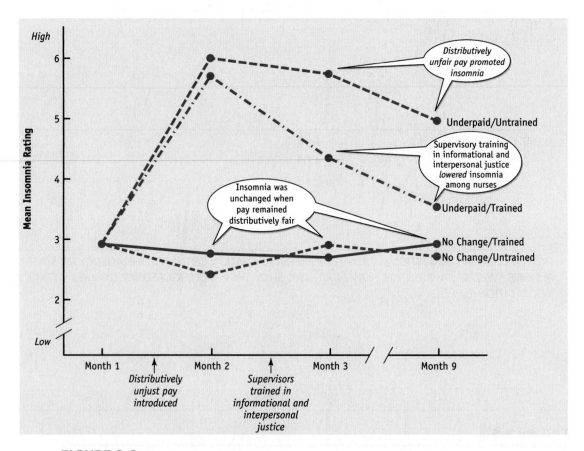

FIGURE 2.6

Losing Sleep over Injustice Can Be Overcome

A study by the author found that nurses suffered insomnia after their pay was changed in a manner that left them paid less than before (i.e., a distributive injustice). However, these insomnia reactions were reduced among nurses whose managers were trained in ways to promote interpersonal justice and informational justice.

Source: Adapted from Greenberg, 2006; see Note 25.

key practices, such as the determination of pay or the appraisal of performance, that are believed to be unfair. Changing such practices requires a commitment from top executives. However, by understanding the importance of organizational justice, all managers have at their disposal a set of tools for promoting fairness in the workplace. After all, there is generally nothing to stop anyone from sharing more information or from treating others with dignity and respect. And, as we have shown, such actions from individual managers go a long way toward reducing the harmful effects that may be caused by system-wide sources of injustice.

Ethical Behavior in Organizations: Its Fundamental Nature

When you think about Dutch tulips, your mind probably fills with images of their colorful beauty. Back in 1636–1637, however, Europeans were likely to think of a business scandal that became known as *tulip mania* or *tulipomania*. Although recent analyses discredit several aspects of the case, legend has it that speculators drove up the prices of some species of these highly valued flowers so that they could make an enormous profit.[26] Back then, one particular bulb, the Viceroy, sold for as much as 28 times the annual salary of a skilled craftsman.[27] Eventually, the economic bubble burst, causing many to lose lots of guilders.

Closer to American shores and featured prominently in our own history books, accounts of the early days of American business are riddled with sordid tales of magnates who would go to any lengths in their quest for success, destroying in the process not only the country's natural resources and the public's trust but also the hopes and dreams of millions of people. For example, legends abound of how John D. Rockefeller, founder of Standard Oil, regularly bribed politicians and stepped all over people in his quest to monopolize the oil industry.

We do not mean to imply that unsavory business practices are only a relic of the past. Far from it! As you know, they are all too common today—so much so that one newspaper reporter referred to ethical scandals as having reached "epidemic levels."[28] Just consider some of the major headlines from recent years:

- *New York Times* reporter Jayson Blair was caught plagiarizing and fabricating parts of his stories.[29]
- The two men who ran the wholesale telecommunications company Fortes Telecom charged business clients for Internet-based phone services, but obtained these services by hacking into the computers of 15 legitimate VoIP providers.[30]
- Preying on victims' desperation, a 42-year-old man was accused of felony home repair fraud for performing shoddy work or unfinished work on the homes of victims of Hurricane Katrina.[31]
- Indian children are alleged to have been sold to owners of sweatshops, where they work for 16 hours a day making clothing for Gap stores.[32]

And, of course, who can forget the now-classic scandals that emerged at the dawn of the new millennium?

- Martha Stewart served time in prison after being charged with obstruction of justice and lying to federal investigators in connection with a government probe of her alleged insider trading of ImClone stock.[33]
- Enron officers were cited for "cooking the books" to make millions for themselves.[34]
- Sears was found to use fraudulent practices in its auto-repair business.[35]
- Adelphia Communications officials were charged with using corporate funds to make exorbitant personal purchases.[36]

Clearly, human greed has not faded from the business scene since tulip mania. However, something *has* changed—namely, the public's acceptance of unethical behavior on the part of organizations. Consider this statement by a leading expert on business ethics.

Ethical standards, whether formal or informal, have changed tremendously in the last century. . . . Standards are considerably higher. Business-people themselves, as well as the public, expect more sensitive behavior in the conduct of economic enterprise. The issue is not just having the standards, however. It is living up to them.[37]

Not surprisingly—despite the spate of ethical crises that have captured the public's attention in recent years—growing intolerance of unethical business activity (and, cynically, fear of getting caught) has inspired business leaders to become more ethical. According to a survey conducted a few years ago, workers report that top managers are more inclined to keep their promises, less inclined to engage in misconduct, less likely to feel pressure to be unethical, and perceive greater attention paid to practicing honesty and respect for others. At the same time, whatever ethical misdeeds they do witness are much more likely to be reported to organizational authorities.[38]

To the extent that people are increasingly intolerant of unethical business activity, it should not be surprising to learn that OB scientists are interested in understanding unethical practices and developing strategies for combating them. We will consider these issues in this section and the next section of this chapter. First, however, to prepare you for understanding ethical behavior in organizations, it helps to begin by addressing a fundamental question: What is ethics?

What Do We Mean by Ethics?

Although people often talk about ethics, it's not always clear what the term means. With this in mind, let's define some key constructs. To understand what is meant by ethics, we first must understand the concept of *moral values*. When social scientists speak of **moral values,** they are referring to people's fundamental beliefs regarding what is right or wrong, good or bad. One of the most important sources of moral values is the religious background, beliefs, and training we receive. Although people's moral values may differ, several are widely accepted. For example, most people believe that helping someone in need (e.g., being charitable) is the right thing to do, whereas harming someone (e.g., killing) is wrong.

Based on these beliefs, people are guided in ways that influence the decisions they make and the actions in which they engage. These standards are what we mean by *ethics*. Thus, **ethics** refers to standards of conduct that guide people's decisions and behavior (e.g., not stealing from others is one such ethical standard).[39] With this in mind, organizational scientists acknowledge that it is not a company's place to teach employees values. After all, these come with people as they enter the workplace. However, it *is* a company's responsibility to set clear standards of behavior and to train employees in recognizing and following them.[40] (For a summary of the distinction between moral values and ethics, see Figure 2.7.)

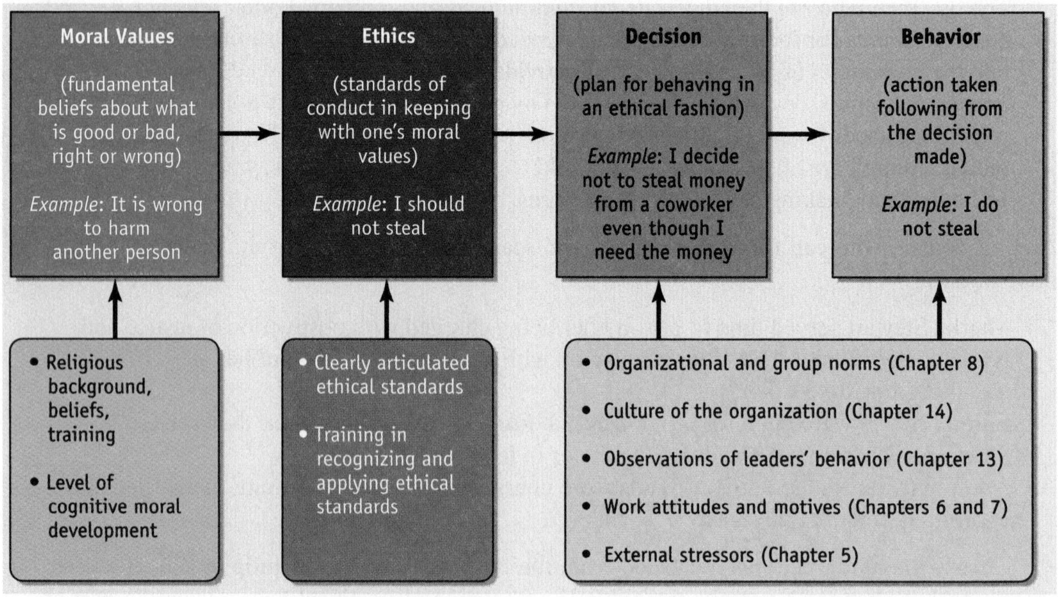

moral values (morals)
People's fundamental beliefs regarding what is right or wrong, good or bad.

ethics
Standards of conduct that guide people's decisions and behavior (e.g., not stealing from others).

Moral Values	Ethics	Decision	Behavior
(fundamental beliefs about what is good or bad, right or wrong) *Example*: It is wrong to harm another person	(standards of conduct in keeping with one's moral values) *Example*: I should not steal	(plan for behaving in an ethical fashion) *Example*: I decide not to steal money from a coworker even though I need the money	(action taken following from the decision made) *Example*: I do not steal
• Religious background, beliefs, training • Level of cognitive moral development	• Clearly articulated ethical standards • Training in recognizing and applying ethical standards	• Organizational and group norms (Chapter 8) • Culture of the organization (Chapter 14) • Observations of leaders' behavior (Chapter 13) • Work attitudes and motives (Chapters 6 and 7) • External stressors (Chapter 5)	

FIGURE 2.7

Moral Values Versus Ethics

As summarized here, moral values (which reside within an individual) provide the basis for ethics (which are standards of behavior that can be regulated by organizations). Ethical standards influence both decisions and behavior in the workplace, which also are affected by a host of other variables identified throughout this book.

Just as organizations prescribe other kinds of behavior that are expected in the workplace (e.g., when to arrive and leave), so too should they prescribe appropriate ethical behavior (e.g., how to complete expense reports and what precisely is considered a bribe). Not surprisingly, most top business leaders recognize that clearly prescribing ethical behavior is a fundamental part of good management. After all, says Kent Druyversteyn, former vice president of ethics at General Dynamics, "Ethics is about conduct."[41]

In looking at Figure 2.7, please note the row of rounded boxes at the bottom. These identify some of the factors affecting moral values, ethics, decisions, and behavior. The ones corresponding to ethics and values are described in this section of the chapter. However, as indicated in the box in the lower right corner, the decisions people make and the behaviors in which they engage are determined by a variety of considerations beyond ethics. Accordingly, these are discussed elsewhere throughout this book (note the references to other chapters in this book).

It's obvious that companies *should* do things to promote ethical behavior among employees simply because they are morally appropriate. At the same time, however, there's also a long-term financial incentive. As explained in "The Ethics Angle" section below, being ethical pays off on the bottom line.

The Ethics Angle

Making a Business Case for Ethical Behavior

It's easy to see how a company may reap short-term gains by being deceptive, such as by using lower quality ingredients or charging for services not performed. Over the long-term, however, such unethical practices are doomed to fail as customers will rebel against companies that deceive them. In fact, one can make a business case for long-term ethical behavior: It pays to be ethical because *good ethics is good business*. The evidence that being ethical pays off in the long run takes the following forms.[42]

- *Improved financial performance.* Companies that make a clear commitment to ethics outperform those that make no such commitment on standard measures of financial success. In fact, one study reported that companies that make an explicit commitment to ethical behavior returned twice the value to shareholders than those that were more casual about ethical issues.[43]
- *Reduced operating costs.* Many efforts to reduce waste and to save energy that protect the natural environment also help save money in the long run. For example, companies using environmentally sustainable energy sources (e.g., solar and wind power) are not only being good stewards of the environment but also stand to save on energy costs over time.[44]
- *Enhanced customer loyalty.* Customers are inclined to be loyal to companies that demonstrate a commitment to ethical behavior. Consider this tragic example. In 1982 several people in suburban Chicago died after taking Extra Strength Tylenol capsules. The manufacturer, Johnson & Johnson (J&J), immediately pulled all its Tylenol products off store shelves throughout the country.[45] J&J officials knew that although the company wasn't at fault they were willing to suffer huge losses so that they could do what was in the best interest of its customers. The company cooperated with officials and eventually it was established

that someone had laced the pills with cyanide while on store shelves. J&J's decisive actions and proactive efforts to help government agencies find the source of the problem led consumers to recognize J&J's commitment to them. Months later, Tylenol's share of the pain reliever market not only returned to where it was before this incident, but surpassed it, reflecting consumers' willingness to support a company that's committed to treating them ethically. This incident led to the development of the more expensive, but safer, tamper-resistant packaging in use today.

- *Increased ability to attract and retain employees.* People generally like working at companies of which they can be proud and that treat them well. When talented employees are difficult to find, companies with reputations for being ethical find it easier to attract good job candidates—and retain them.

Consider the other side of the coin. The evidence also is compelling that "bad ethics is bad business." Companies that survive ethical scandals do so under diminished capacity in large part because "the black eye" makes the public shy away from them—both as consumers and as stockholders—at least for a while.[46] Good examples from years past include Dow Corning (whose breast implants were found to be unsafe), BP (whose oil spill in the Gulf of Mexico created the worst environmental disaster in U.S. history), and the United Way (where a top official was accused of misusing agency funds). These misdeeds have cost their respective organizations dearly, and regaining the public's trust has proven to be a slow process. At United Way, for example, although only one person, the president of a single chapter, was involved in the ethical scandal, completely independent and scrupulously ethical chapters of the esteemed philanthropic organization suffered severe reductions in donations (one-fifth of former donors stopped giving altogether, and the remaining ones gave less) for at least five years.[47] The lesson is clear: Even if company executives do not recognize the benefits of behaving ethically, they surely cannot afford to ignore the costs of behaving unethically.

FIGURE 2.8

Ethical Versus Legal: Not Always Identical

It's important for today's business leaders to recognize that just because they might be able to "get away with" something that's legal doesn't mean that they should do it if it happens to be unethical. We suspect that this boy might have a hard time realizing this when he gets older.

www.CartoonStock.com/Jim Sizemore.

"And so the Little Corporate Raider grew to understand that 'unethical' was not the same as 'illegal,' and he lived happily ever after. The end."

Ethics and the Law

Being ethical is not the same as being legal (see Figure 2.8). In fact, a useful way to think of the law is as providing the minimum acceptable standard to which companies must adhere.

Being ethical typically involves following a higher standard. Vin Sarni, former CEO of PPG, put this well when he said, "It is not enough simply to say that our conduct is lawful. The law is the floor. Compliance with it will be the absolute minimum with respect to the PPG associate, no matter where he or she works. Our ethics go beyond the legal code."[48]

At the same time, it must be noted that the law plays a large role in governing ethical behavior within organizations. Some of the major laws enacted in the United States that influence ethical behavior in organizations are summarized in Table 2.2. Although all these laws are important when it comes to minimizing unethical behavior in organizations, two have proven to be especially influential.

Federal Sentencing Guidelines for Organizations
Guidelines for federal judges to follow when imposing penalties on organizations (e.g., restitution, fines, etc.) found guilty of breaking federal laws.

FEDERAL SENTENCING GUIDELINES FOR ORGANIZATIONS. Established in 1991, the **Federal Sentencing Guidelines for Organizations** provide guidelines for federal judges to follow when imposing penalties on organizations (e.g., restitution, fines, etc.) found guilty of breaking federal laws.

TABLE 2.2 Major U.S. Laws That Promote Ethical Behavior in Organizations

Businesses—and society at large—can be affected adversely by the unethical behavior of some people in organizations. As a safeguard, several laws have been enacted in the United States in recent decades. Some with the broadest impact are summarized here.

Year	Law	Description
1986	False Claims Act	Provides procedures for reporting fraudulent behavior against U.S. government agencies and protects whistle-blowers (see Chapter 11) who do so.
1988	Foreign Corrupt Practices Act (revised)	Prohibits organizations from paying bribes to foreign officials for purposes of getting business.
1991, amended in 2004	Federal Sentencing Guidelines for Organizations	Provides guidelines for federal judges to follow when imposing fines on organizations found guilty of committing federal crimes.
2002, revised in 2007	Sarbanes-Oxley Act	Enacted to guard against fraudulent accounting practices (such as occurred at Enron), this law initiates reforms in the standards by which public companies report accounting data.
2003	Federal Prosecution of Business Organizations	To protect investors against unscrupulous acts by top executives (also in response to the Enron scandal), these revisions to the Federal Sentencing Guidelines for Organizations now focus on the role of boards of directors—the only parties in organizations with sufficient clout to prevent wrongdoing by high-ranking officials.

These specify that judges should consider as mitigating factors any efforts on the part of companies to prevent and detect violations of the law (thereby going lighter on companies that have tried to avoid violations). The Guidelines specify the following things that companies can do in this regard.[49]

- Develop compliance standards and procedures designed to minimize criminal conduct.
- Make high-level personnel responsible for overseeing compliance with such standards and procedures.
- Avoid assigning to positions any employees they know (or should know) to be inclined to engage in illegal activities.
- Communicate ethical standards through training programs or by disseminating publications that explain appropriate behavior.
- Monitor behavior by having in place a system that employees can use to report criminal behavior without fear of retribution.
- Develop a system for enforcing standards, such as by disciplining employees appropriately.
- Respond appropriately to offenses by taking reasonable steps to ensure that they will not be repeated.

Because these guidelines are very explicit, it shouldn't be particularly surprising that they have played a huge role in putting into place various mechanisms to help promote ethical behavior in organizations.

THE SARBANES-OXLEY ACT. Widely referred to as **SOX**, the **Sarbanes-Oxley Act** was passed in an effort to avoid unscrupulous and fraudulent accounting practices (as occurred in the famous Enron scandal) by holding senior company officials personally accountable for their companies' accounting practices and reports. The rationale is simple: Instead of just signing off on reports whose veracity is questionable because they can do so with impunity, making executives personally liable for these documents will encourage them to ensure that they are accurate and that the practices used to create them meet proper standards.

> **SOX, Sarbanes-Oxley Act**
> A law enacted to guard against future accounting scandals (such as occurred at Enron), by initiating reforms in the standards by which public companies report accounting data.

This law has been somewhat controversial in recent years because of the enormous burdens it has placed on organizations by requiring them to submit various reports stipulating conformity with the law's various provisions.[50] SOX is very specific in places regarding precisely what must be done to avoid misreporting of financial information. Among other things, for example, it requires companies to do the following:[51]

- Perform a fraud risk assessment.
- Evaluate controls designed to prevent or detect fraud.
- Evaluate controls over the safeguarding of assets.

It's not too hard to realize that the complex and rapidly evolving nature of SOX has created a booming business in companies that specialize in helping organizations comply with it. In recent years, SOX has spawned dozens of books, software packages, and training programs aimed at company officials who want to ensure that their organizations are adhering to this law.[52] Make no mistake about it, complying with SOX is taken very seriously. If you have any doubts, consider the penalties stated in Section 802(a) of the law:[53]

> Whoever knowingly alters, destroys, mutilates, conceals, covers up, falsifies, or makes a false entry in any record, document, or tangible object with the intent to impede, obstruct, or influence the investigation or proper administration of any matter within the jurisdiction of any department or agency of the United States or any case filed under title 11, or in relation to or contemplation of any such matter or case, shall be fined under this title, imprisoned not more than 20 years, or both.

Why Do Some People Behave Unethically, at Least Sometimes—and What Can Be Done About It?

Management experts have long considered the matter of why some people behave unethically on at least some occasions. Put differently, is it a matter of good people who are led to behave unethically because of external forces acting on them (i.e., "good apples in bad barrels") or is it that bad people behave inappropriately in whatever setting they are in (i.e., "bad apples in good

cognitive moral development
Differences among people in the capacity to engage in the kind of reasoning that enables them to make moral judgments.

Kohlberg's theory of cognitive moral development
The theory based on the idea that people develop over the years in their capacity to understand what is right and wrong.

preconventional level of moral reasoning
In Kohlberg's theory of cognitive moral development, the level at which people (e.g., young children and some adults) haven't yet developed the capacity to assume the perspective of others, leading them to interpret what is right solely with respect to themselves.

barrels")? Acknowledging the key role of leaders in determining the ethical climate of an organization, some scientists have considered the possibility that because of their profound influence, some unethical leaders (so-called "bad apples") have made their companies unethical as well (turning "good barrels into bad"), or poisoning the whole barrel, so to speak.[54] Although the relative importance of "apples" and "barrels" has yet to be firmly decided, it is clear that ethical and unethical behavior is determined by *both* of these classes of factors—that is, individual factors (the person) and situational factors (the external forces people confront in the workplace). In this section of the chapter, we will consider both sets of factors.

Individual Differences in Cognitive Moral Development

As you know from experience, people appear to differ with respect to their adherence to moral considerations. Some individuals, for example, refrain from padding their expense accounts, even if they believe they will not get caught, solely because they believe it is the wrong thing to do. They strongly consider ethical factors when making decisions. However, this is not true of everyone. Still others, as you know, would not think twice about padding their expense accounts, often rationalizing that the amounts of money in question are small and that "the company expects me to do it." A key factor responsible for this difference is what psychologists refer to as **cognitive moral development**—that is, differences among people in their capacity to engage in the kind of reasoning that enables them to make moral judgments. (Scientists measure people's cognitive moral development by systematically analyzing how people say they would resolve various ethical dilemmas. For practice analyzing an ethical dilemma, complete this chapter's Group Exercise on page 68.)

The most well-known theory of cognitive moral development was introduced more than four decades ago by the psychologist Lawrence Kohlberg.[55] According to **Kohlberg's theory of cognitive moral development,** people develop over the years in their capacity to understand what is right. Specifically, the theory distinguishes among three levels of moral development (for a summary, see Figure 2.9). The first level is referred to as the **preconventional level of moral reasoning.**

FIGURE 2.9

Kohlberg's Theory of Cognitive Moral Development

This theory distinguishes among the three major levels of cognitive moral development summarized here. According to the theory, people at different levels define what is wrong in different ways, which are limited by their capacity for moral reasoning.

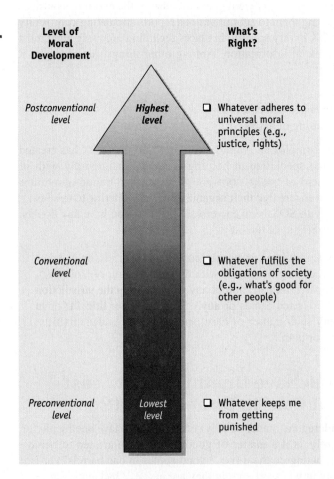

Level of Moral Development		What's Right?
Postconventional level	*Highest level*	❑ Whatever adheres to universal moral principles (e.g., justice, rights)
Conventional level		❑ Whatever fulfills the obligations of society (e.g., what's good for other people)
Preconventional level	*Lowest level*	❑ Whatever keeps me from getting punished

People at this level (children and about a quarter of all adults) haven't developed the capacity to assume the perspective of others. Accordingly, they interpret what is right solely with respect to themselves: It is wrong to do something if it leads one to be punished. Because their cognitive skills are not sufficiently advanced, such individuals generally cannot comprehend any argument one may make about something being wrong because it violates their social obligations to others.

As people interact with others over the years, most come to use higher-level cognitive processes to judge morality. In a more sophisticated fashion, they judge right and wrong in terms of what is good for the others around them and society as a whole. This second level is referred to as the **conventional level of moral reasoning.** Approximately two-thirds of adults fall into this category. What they do is governed strongly by what's expected of them by others, and they carefully scour the social environment for cues as to "what's right." People who engage in conventional moral reasoning obey the law not only because they fear the repercussions of not doing so, but also because they recognize that doing so is the right thing to do insofar as it promotes the safety and welfare of society as a whole.

Finally, Kohlberg's theory also identifies a third level of cognitive moral development, the **postconventional level of moral reasoning.** At this level, people judge what is right and wrong not solely in terms of their interpersonal and societal obligations but also in terms of complex philosophical principles of duty, justice, and rights. Very few people ever attain this level. Those who do, however, follow their own "moral compass," doing what they are convinced is truly right, even if others don't agree.

Research has found that people behave in very different ways as a function of the level of cognitive moral development they have attained. For example, as you might expect, people who are at higher levels of cognitive moral development (typically, conventional as opposed to preconventional) manifest their greater ethical behavior in several ways. Specifically, they are less inclined to harm others, less likely to misreport information even if it makes them look bad, and steal less from their employers.[56] Although efforts to raise people's levels of moral reasoning through training have been successful, few such efforts have been used in organizations.[57] This is in large part because most workers already function at the conventional level, making them sensitive to efforts to promote ethical behavior predicated on changing the social norms that exist within organizations. We now will consider some of the key social dynamics that influence ethical behavior.

Situational Determinants of Unethical Behavior

As you might imagine, many different situational factors can lead people to behave unethically on the job. Although the list may be long, it is not too difficult to identify some of the major organizational influences on unethical behavior. Here, we will consider three of the most important ones—managerial values that undermine integrity, organizational norms encouraging unethical behavior, and the impact of unethical behavior by leaders. Although these factors surely are interrelated, it is worth identifying them separately so as to highlight their important effects on ethical behavior.

SOME MANAGERIAL VALUES UNDERMINE INTEGRITY. Although most managers are inherently ethical, some have developed ways of thinking that lead them to make unethical decisions. Given how very influential top leaders are when it comes to influencing others in their organizations, it should not be surprising that unethical managerial values promote unethical organizational decisions.[58] Several well-known forms of unethical thinking are as follows:[59]

- **Bottom-line mentality.** This line of thinking supports financial success as the only value to be considered. It promotes short-term decisions that are immediately financially sound, despite the fact that they may cause long-term problems for the organization.
- **Exploitative mentality.** This view encourages "using" people in a way that promotes stereotypes and undermines empathy and compassion. This highly selfish perspective sacrifices concern for others in favor of benefits to one's own immediate interests (for an extreme example, see Figure 2.10).
- **Madison Avenue mentality.** This perspective suggests that anything is right if the public can be made to see it as right. The idea is that executives may be more concerned that their decisions appear to be right than about their legitimate morality. This kind of thinking leads some companies to hide their unethical behavior (e.g., dumping toxic waste under cover of night) or to otherwise justify them as acceptable.

conventional level of moral reasoning
In Kohlberg's theory of cognitive moral development, the level attained by most people, in which they judge right and wrong in terms of what is good for others and society as a whole.

postconventional level of moral reasoning
In Kohlberg's theory of cognitive moral development, the level at which people judge what is right and wrong not solely in terms of their interpersonal and societal obligations, but in terms of complex philosophical principles of duty, justice, and rights.

bottom-line mentality
The belief that an organization's financial success is the only thing that matters.

exploitative mentality
The belief that one's own immediate interests are more important than concern for others.

Madison Avenue mentality
A way of viewing the world according to which people are more concerned about how things appear to others than how they really are—that is, the appearance of doing the right thing matters more than the actual behavior.

Steven Hirsch/Splash News/Newscom.

FIGURE 2.10

An Exploitative Mentality Eventually Can Get You into Trouble

Bernard Madoff provides one of the most extreme examples of an exploitative mentality. After getting people to trust him, they invested their savings with Madoff's firm believing that they would enjoy high returns. In actuality, Madoff took $65 billion from thousands of clients without making any investments, fabricating documents to create the illusion that legitimate investments were being made all along. After carrying out this scam for many years, an investigation revealed that Madoff was running a huge Ponzi scheme in which new investors were used to pay off old investors. In June 2009, Madoff began serving a sentence of 150 years (the maximum allowed) for perjury, securities fraud, and related offenses.

Recognizing the problems associated with these various orientations is not difficult. Their overemphasis on short-term monetary gain may lead to decisions that not only hurt individuals in the long run but also threaten the very existence of organizations.

ORGANIZATIONS SOMETIMES ENCOURAGE BEHAVIOR THAT VIOLATES ETHICAL STANDARDS. It is easy to understand that people may behave unethically on the job to the extent that they are encouraged to do so. Consider, for example, how some business executives are expected to say nothing about ethically dubious behavior they've witnessed in the company. In fact, in many companies it is considered not only acceptable but also desirable to be secretive and deceitful. For example, the practice of **stonewalling**—willingly hiding relevant information—is quite common.

A major reason for this is that organizations may actually punish those who are too open and honest. As a case in point, consider the disclosure that in 1968 B.F. Goodrich allegedly rewarded employees who falsified and withheld data on the quality of aircraft brakes to meet safety certi-fication standards. This example illustrates how the *counternorms* of secrecy and deceitfulness were accepted and supported by the organization. **Counternorms** are accepted organizational practices that run contrary to society's prevailing ethical standards. For a summary of some of the most common counternorms found in organizations, see Figure 2.11.[60]

WORKERS EMULATE THE UNETHICAL BEHAVIOR OF THEIR SUPERIORS. Probably very few organizational leaders condone and actively promote unethical behavior. However, many promote unethical behavior unwittingly by way of the examples they set for their employees.

stonewalling
The practice of willingly hiding relevant information by being secretive and deceitful, which occurs when organizations punish individuals who are open and honest and reward those who go along with unethical behavior.

counternorms
Practices that are accepted within an organization despite the fact that they are contrary to the prevailing ethical standards of society at large.

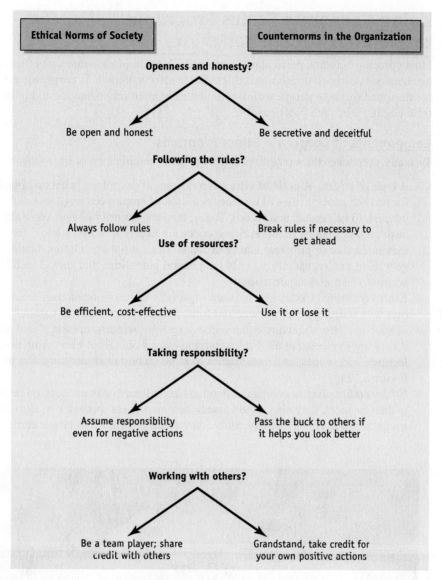

Ethical Norms of Society

Counternorms in the Organization

Openness and honesty?

Be open and honest

Be secretive and deceitful

Following the rules?

Always follow rules

Break rules if necessary to get ahead

Use of resources?

Be efficient, cost-effective

Use it or lose it

Taking responsibility?

Assume responsibility even for negative actions

Pass the buck to others if it helps you look better

Working with others?

Be a team player; share credit with others

Grandstand, take credit for your own positive actions

FIGURE 2.11

Ethical Norms Versus Organizational Counternorms

Although societal standards of ethics dictate the appropriateness of certain actions, counternorms that encourage and support opposite practices sometimes develop within organizations.

Source: Based on suggestions by Jansen & Von Glinow, 1985; see Note 60.

For example, suppose a manager submits an expense report to her administrative assistant to prepare for submission to the accounting office. Included on it are several items the assistant knows are not legitimate (e.g., lavish meals with clients). Although the manager might not be thinking about it, by padding her expense account she is sending a message to her administrative assistant that stealing from the company is an acceptable practice. Despite what she might say publicly about not stealing, her behind-the-scenes actions tell a different story. As a result, the administrative assistant might not think twice about taking a few dollars from the company's petty cash box to purchase her lunch. "After all," she may reason, "my boss takes a little extra money from the company, so it must be okay for me to do so too."

A survey of some 1,500 U.S. employees suggests that this is precisely what happens.[61] Specifically, employees who feel that the top managers in their organization act ethically themselves report seeing far less misconduct among their peers (15 percent) than those who feel that their top managers do not behave ethically themselves or who only talk about behaving ethically (56 percent). Obviously, when it comes to ethical conduct on the job, managers set an example by virtue of their own behavior, and their "actions speak louder than words." Putting it in the lingo of today's managers, to promote ethical behavior in their companies, it is essential for officials to "walk the talk."

Using Corporate Ethics Programs to Promote Ethical Behavior

corporate ethics programs
Formal, systematic efforts designed to promote ethics by making people sensitive to potentially unethical behavior and discouraging them from engaging in unethical acts.

Most companies today, particularly large ones, have in place some sort of formal, systematic mechanisms designed to promote ethics. These efforts, known as **corporate ethics programs,** are designed to make people aware of potentially unethical behavior and to discourage them from engaging in such practices.

Components of Corporate Ethics Programs

Typically, corporate ethics programs consist of some combination of the following components:[62]

code of ethics
A document describing what an organization stands for and the general rules of conduct expected of employees (e.g., to avoid conflicts of interest, to be honest, and so on).

- *A code of ethics.* A **code of ethics** is a document describing what an organization stands for and the general rules of conduct expected of employees (e.g., to avoid conflicts of interest, to be honest, and so on). Today, the vast majority of *Fortune* 1000 companies have codes of ethics in place. Some codes are highly specific, stating, for example, the maximum size of gifts that can be accepted from suppliers. Others, however, are more general in nature, specifying only the general guidelines that should be taken into account when making decisions.

ethics audit
The practice of assessing an organization's ethical practices by actively investigating and documenting incidents of dubious ethical value, discussing them in an open and honest fashion, and developing a concrete plan to avoid such actions in the future.

- *Ethics training.* Codes of ethics are especially effective when they are used in conjunction with training programs that reinforce the company's ethical values.[63] In the absence of such training, too many codes come across as "window dressing" and are ignored, if they are even read at all. Ethics training efforts consist of everything ranging from lectures, videotapes, and case studies to more elaborate simulations (for an example, see Figure 2.12).

- *Ethics audits.* Just as companies regularly audit their books to check on irregularities in their finances, they also should assess their employees' behavior so as to identify irregularities in ethical activity. Such assessments are known as **ethics audits.** These

NASA/JPL/UA/Lockheed/Martin/Rapport Press/Newscom.

FIGURE 2.12

Lockheed Martin Takes Ethics Training Seriously

As a manufacturer of high-tech equipment, often for the U.S. military, it's crucial that Lockheed Martin's 165,000 employees adhere to the highest ethical standards. To help ensure that this occurs, the company uses multiple methods of ethics training. These include live training sessions, self-paced interactive training sessions conducted online, and booklets explaining ways leaders can promote ethics in their teams.

require actively investigating and documenting incidents of dubious ethical value, discussing them in an open and honest fashion, and developing a concrete plan to avoid such actions in the future. Conducting an ethics audit can be quite revealing. For some useful guidelines on how to do so, see the OB in Practice section below.[64]

■ *An ethics committee.* An **ethics committee** is a group of senior-level managers from various areas of the organization who assist an organization's CEO in making ethical decisions. Members of the committee develop and evaluate company-wide ethics policies.

ethics committee
A group composed of senior-level managers from various areas of an organization who assist an organization's CEO in making ethical decisions by developing and evaluating company-wide ethics policies.

OB in Practice

Using Ethics Audits to Monitor the Triple Bottom Line

Historically, accountants have been called on to audit a company's financial records to ensure that its financial picture is accurate. These days, it's becoming increasingly common for companies to assess their officers' and employees' ethical behavior as well. That is, in addition to focusing exclusively on the financial picture, officials also are interested in assuring that their companies are doing well with respect to promoting environmental quality and social justice. With these three foci in mind, companies are said to be looking at not one, but three separate measures of success that also take into account the company's ethical performance. This is known as the **triple bottom-line.**

triple bottom-line
The contemporary notion that in addition to focusing on an organization's financial performance, officials also are interested in assuring that their companies are performing well with respect to promoting environmental quality and social justice.

With an eye toward assessing the environmental and social aspects of corporate performance, growing numbers of companies are taking steps to assess ethical lapses in their employees' behavior by conducting regular *ethics audits.* These consist of investigating and documenting ethically inappropriate behavior, analyzing the behavior thoroughly to find out why it occurred, and developing a plan to promote more ethical behavior in the future. Specifically, here are six guidelines that you can follow to conduct an ethics audit of your own workgroup.[65]

■ *Step 1: Obtain approval.* Instead of jumping right in, make sure that your own superiors and your company's top executives buy into your plan. It's important to gain assurance that they are not only committed to conducting the audit, but importantly, that they also are prepared to deal with whatever it reveals. This step should not be overlooked, no matter how certain you are that the audit should be performed. Simply "nosing around" without permission is sure to land you in trouble, so be sure to get clear approval from the highest levels before proceeding.

■ *Step 2: Plan and conduct a survey.* Putting together a team of employees at all levels and from various departments, draft a questionnaire assessing the company's ethical climate and the ethical behavior of its associates. The questions should look at what the company is doing (e.g., feelings about its treatment of employees) as well as current ethical problems (e.g., pressure to cheat customers). Using open-ended questions, the questionnaire also should examine people's ideas about why various unethical acts have occurred and what the company should be doing in the future. Administer this questionnaire broadly throughout the company in a manner that ensures complete anonymity (i.e., no identifying information should be provided).

■ *Step 3: Investigate company records.* In addition to what your colleagues tell you, it's also important to look at objective measures. As such, your audit should involve careful analyses of official documents, such as ethical mission statements and codes of ethics. You want to see how clear and thorough they are and what purpose they serve. Are people regularly trained in these standards or do they merely serve as "window dressing"?

■ *Step 4: Benchmark your results.* To interpret what your company is doing, it's useful to compare your company's ethical practices to those of other organizations in the same industry. Such information may be obtained from various sources such as the Internet, industry reports, trade publications, and informal information based on your past experiences.

■ *Step 5: Develop an action plan.* Now that you have a good sense of what the company is doing and how it may be improved, you should identify specific steps that can be taken to improve the situation. Be as clear as possible, identifying precisely who will do what and how things will improve as a result. To be effective, your plan must be practical and not overly grandiose. So, don't attempt too much. If you can address the major issues, that's a great beginning.

■ *Step 6: Prepare a written report.* You now are ready to draft a thorough report documenting your main findings along with your plans for addressing them. Before presenting this document to all concerned parties, it's a good idea to circulate it among all those who were involved in conducting the ethics audit. After all, you want to ensure that this important report is accurate and thorough before moving forward.

It's important to acknowledge that conducting an ethics audit is a major commitment and that its findings must be taken seriously. Because this process involves "stirring the pot," so to speak, it's not surprising that some companies are reluctant to initiate the process. Those that do, however, stand to benefit from following the steps outlined here.

ethics officer
A high-ranking organizational official (e.g., the general counsel or vice president of ethics) who is expected to provide strategies for ensuring ethical conduct throughout an organization.

ethics hotlines (ethics helplines)
Special telephone lines that employees can call to ask questions about ethical behavior and to report anonymously any ethical misdeeds they may have observed.

- *An ethics officer.* An **ethics officer** is a high-ranking organizational official (e.g., the general counsel or vice president of ethics) who is expected to provide strategies for ensuring ethical conduct throughout an organization. Because the Federal Sentencing Guidelines for Organizations specify that a specific, high-level individual should be responsible for ethical behavior, many companies have such an individual in place.
- *A mechanism for communicating ethical standards.* To be effective, ethics programs must clearly articulate—and reinforce—a company's ethical expectations to employees. With this in mind, growing numbers of companies are putting into place **ethics hotlines,** special phone lines that employees can call to ask questions about ethical behavior and to report anonymously any ethical misdeeds they may have observed.

The Effectiveness of Corporate Ethics Programs

By themselves, codes of ethics have only limited effectiveness in regulating ethical behavior in organizations.[66] However, an integrated ethics program that combines a code of ethics with additional components (e.g., an ethics officer, ethics training, etc.) can be quite effective. Specifically, it has been found that compared to companies that don't have ethics programs in place, within those that do, employees (a) are more likely to report ethical misconduct to company authorities, (b) are considered more accountable for ethics violations, and (c) face less pressure to compromise standards of business conduct.[67] Clearly, the ethics programs are being felt.

Ethics in the International Arena

Our discussion thus far suggests that figuring out how to behave ethically isn't always easy. If that's the case when conducting business at home, then imagine how much more complex things become when conducting business in other countries. After all, people in different cultures often have different ethical standards. Consider these examples:

- In China, using pirated software is considered acceptable.
- In Indonesia, bribing an official is considered an acceptable cost of doing business.
- In Japan, you cannot conduct business unless you give the other party a small gift.

In North America, of course, all such acts would be frowned on and considered illegal or at least ethically questionable. Clearly, the implications for conducting business globally are confusing. Given that a great deal of business conducted today is international in nature, it's important to consider the special ethical challenges this creates. Specifically, how does one behave ethically when conducting business abroad? The answer, as we now discuss, is complex and highly nuanced. However, problems may be avoided by adhering to several guiding principles that we will identify.

Ethical Relativism and Ethical Imperialism: Two Extreme Positions

Over the years, philosophers have approached international business ethics by distinguishing between two extreme approaches—*ethical relativism* and *ethical imperialism* (see Figure 2.13). As you will see, each of these viewpoints is problematic. However, understanding them is important because it will help you appreciate the most effective approach, which lies in between these two extremes.

ethical relativism
The belief that no culture's ethics are better than any other's and that there are no internationally acceptable standards of right and wrong (the opposite of *ethical imperialism*).

ETHICAL RELATIVISM: NOTHING IS SACRED. To some, the matter of how to conduct oneself when doing business abroad is as easy as "when in Rome, do what the Romans do." This calls for adopting the ethics of whatever country in which one does business—an approach known as **ethical relativism.** The rationale is that one culture's ethics are no better than any other's, and that there are no internationally acceptable standards of right and wrong.

The problem with this approach is that it may lead to condoning acts that violate one's own sense of morality.[68] Consider this example. Some time ago, several European pharmaceutical companies and tanneries were looking for places where they could dispose of toxic chemical waste. Government officials from most countries they approached said no, fearing the health risks to their people. Nigeria, however, agreed to the business even though local workers, who didn't have any protective clothing, had a good chance of coming into contact with deadly substances as they

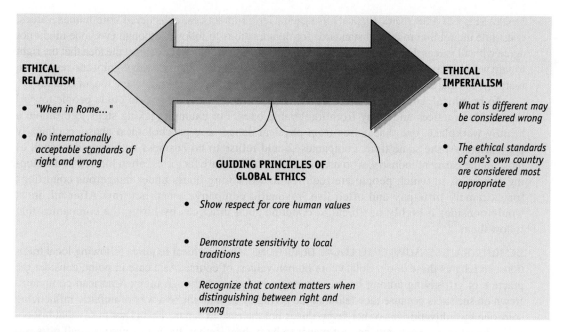

FIGURE 2.13

Approaches to Global Ethics: Two Extremes and a Middle Ground

Too often, people attempting to make ethical decisions in international settings follow one of the two ill-advised, extreme approaches identified here—*ethical relativism* and *ethical imperialism.* By adopting qualities of both approaches, a middle ground can be found in which people can be guided by three principles of global ethics.

Source: Based on suggestions by Donaldson, 1996; see Note 68.

moved the barrels that contained them. Despite the fact that the practice was permitted in Nigeria, it's easy to see how the risks to the workers make the practice ethically questionable.

ETHICAL IMPERIALISM: WHAT IS DIFFERENT MAY BE WRONG. Given that following ethical relativism may lead to moral transgressions, then how about the opposite approach? That is, what if, wherever they are, people use their own country's ethical standards? In other words, they do everywhere whatever they consider to be right while at home. This approach, which is the opposite of ethical relativism, is known as **ethical imperialism.**

It too has limitations. Highly absolute in its approach, ethical imperialism asserts that there is only a single set of rules regarding right and wrong—one's own. Thus, whatever is different is wrong. Obviously, this is very limiting because it fails to recognize cultural and situational differences that may influence ethical behavior. For example, North American–type training in avoiding sexual harassment (see Chapter 5) likely would be questioned in Middle Eastern countries, where the treatment of women is highly regulated by social and religious customs. Likewise, in parts of the world where people are dying from malnutrition, it may be ill-advised to impose standards for the use of agricultural chemicals that make sense in more developed countries, where lower crop yields are not problematic.

Given that the two extreme approaches to global business ethics are problematic, you may be thinking that the best approach lies somewhere in between. So too do most of today's experts in business ethics.

ethical imperialism
The belief that the ethical standards of one's own country should be imposed when doing business in other countries (the opposite of *ethical relativism*).

Three Guiding Principles of Global Ethics

It has been recommended that company officials doing business abroad should adopt a stance between the extremes of ethical relativism and ethical imperialism. In this connection, they may be guided by three key principles: (1) show respect for core human values, (2) demonstrate sensitivity to local traditions, and (3) recognize that context matters when distinguishing between right and wrong.[69]

SHOW RESPECT FOR CORE HUMAN VALUES. Certain practices, considered core human values, constitute the minimum ethical standards for organizations to follow. Although everyone might not agree with all values that might be included in this list, few would argue against the idea that the right to safe working conditions, the right to be free, and the right to be treated with dignity and respect are moral values that should guide all behavior in the business world (and elsewhere too, of course).

To be ethical, company officials must use their "moral compasses" to guide people toward acceptable practices and away from intolerable ones. For example, taking steps to promote a healthy workplace, one that is free from physical danger and psychological abuse, is ethically appropriate. At the same time, companies should refuse to do business with suppliers, such as those in the garment industry, who use *sweatshops*. These are factories, often located in developing countries, in which people are required to work long hours under dangerous conditions for extremely little pay and often live in squalid company-owned housing. After all, most would consider it highly unethical to condone such practices by hiring the companies that follow them.[70]

DEMONSTRATE SENSITIVITY TO LOCAL TRADITIONS. Being ethical requires following local traditions, so long as these don't violate core human values, of course. As a case in point, consider the practice of gift-giving among business partners in Japan. Although many American companies frown on such acts because they fear that the giving of gifts might be a way of unfairly influencing someone by cultivating his or her favor, this is not the case in Japan. This is not to say that bribery is condoned there. Such acts are not meant to be bribes. Rather, the act of giving small gifts is a customary ritual that connotes politeness and trust between the parties. To not accept a gift from a business partner would be considered highly impolite and insulting. These days, because American companies conduct so much business in Japan, officials are coming to accept this practice as acceptable. After all, when you understand precisely what the act means in Japanese culture, it hardly can be considered unethical.

It is important to note that demonstrating sensitivity to local traditions does *not* equate to moral relativism. A moral relativist would accept all actions as ethical in a country if those actions were deemed ethical there. The case of dumping hazardous waste in Nigeria, mentioned earlier, is a good illustration. Doing that surely violates core human values because it endangers people. Merely showing awareness of another country's cultural norms and adapting one's behavior accordingly, by contrast, may be a highly effective way of promoting ethical behavior.

RECOGNIZE THAT CONTEXT MATTERS WHEN DISTINGUISHING BETWEEN RIGHT AND WRONG. Ethical rules are not hard and fast. Sometimes what's right in one context may be considered wrong in another. Being ethical requires taking into account the nature of the setting in which acts occur.

In the United States, for example, it would be considered unethical (and potentially illegal) to hire one's own relatives instead of a more qualified nonfamily member. Such blatant nepotism is frowned on. By contrast, in India, such a practice makes sense. There, jobs are difficult to find, and some of the most successful companies offer as a perk to their employees the opportunity to hire their children once they graduate from school. This eases unemployment, thereby strengthening the economy. Additionally, Indians believe that keeping the family together is more important than pursuing economic opportunities. For these reasons, the practice of hiring relatives may be considered ethical—but only in India, where conditions are unique. That's our point: Different contexts may require different ethical guidelines.

If, upon reading this, you realize the complexities of attempting to behave ethically in international settings, then you have reached the same conclusion as many a seasoned businessperson. As one business expert put it, "Managers living and working abroad who are not prepared to grapple with moral ambiguity and tension should pack their bags and come home."[71]

Beyond Ethics: Corporate Social Responsibility

Usually, when we think of business organizations, we focus on their financial responsibilities to stockholders and investors—that is, to make money. Of course, this is not their only responsibility. To quote Henry Ford, "A business that makes nothing but money is a poor kind of business."[72] As we have been discussing, organizations also are responsible for obeying the law and answering to yet a higher standard, behaving ethically. In addition to these considerations, many of today's organizations are going beyond their ethical responsibilities by taking proactive steps to help society at large by virtue of their philanthropic (i.e., charitable) contributions.

Together, these four types of responsibilities—economic responsibilities, legal responsibilities, ethical responsibilities, and philanthropic responsibilities—reflect an organization's most fundamental forms of responsibility. Collectively, this is referred to as the **pyramid of corporate social responsibility** (see Figure 2.14).[73] The pyramid metaphor is used to reflect the fact that the most basic form of responsibility—financial responsibility—is at the base of the pyramid. After all, unless a company makes money, it will go out of business, making it impossible to attend to any responsibilities at all.

What Is Corporate Social Responsibility?

The term **corporate social responsibility** typically focuses at the top of the pyramid. It describes business practices that adhere to ethical values that comply with legal requirements, that demonstrate respect for individuals, and that promote the betterment of the community at large and the environment. It involves operating a business in a manner that meets or exceeds the ethical, legal, and public expectations that society has of businesses. Some examples of highly socially responsible actions from well-known companies are as follows:

- *Chiquita Brands International.* The world's top producer of bananas also is considered a leader in corporate social responsibility. The company has a corporate responsibility officer at the vice president level, avoids using toxic chemicals, and unlike some competitors, refrains from mistreating and underpaying its laborers.[74]
- *McDonald's.* So extensive is this international restaurant chain's commitment to social responsibility that it publishes online a very long *Worldwide Corporate Responsibility Report.* Among its many key activities is the Ronald McDonald House Charities, which works to improve the health and well-being of children and families around the world. The company also is engaged actively in protecting the environment by recycling and using innovative ways to conserve resources. An interesting feature of McDonald's 2009 report (published in January 2010) is that it rates the company's progress with respect to social responsibility goals set in previous years (e.g., having a sustainable supply chain, the community, and environmental responsibility).[75]
- *UPS.* For more than 50 years, this large package delivery firm has set up a separate nonprofit company, the UPS Foundation, to help the community. Recently, UPS has focused on sustaining the environment by deploying 245 new delivery trucks powered by compressed natural gas

pyramid of corporate social responsibility
The term used to describe an organization's four most basic forms of responsibility, in order from economic responsibility, to legal responsibility, to ethical responsibility, to philanthropic (i.e., charitable) responsibility.

corporate social responsibility
Business practices that adhere to ethical values that comply with legal requirements, that demonstrate respect for individuals, and that promote the betterment of the community at large and the environment.

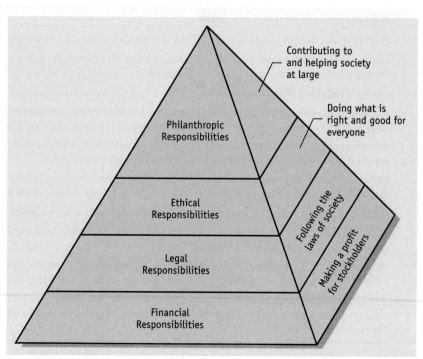

FIGURE 2.14

The Pyramid of Corporate Social Responsibility

To be socially responsible, companies must meet the four different types of responsibilities identified here. The most basic responsibilities, financial, are shown at the bottom because organizations would go out of business if they failed to meet their financial responsibilities.

Source: Based on suggestions by Carroll, 1991; see Note 73.

(CNG) to cities in Colorado and California. These so-called "green" trucks reflect the company's commitment to reducing emissions from fossil fuel and lowering its carbon footprint.

These three examples are noteworthy, but the companies are far from unique in their dedication to corporate social responsibility. In fact, many of the largest companies in the United States have been going out of their way to behave in a variety of socially responsible ways. For a small summary of what companies identified as being in the "top 10" most socially responsible firms are doing, see Table 2.3.[76]

Forms of Socially Responsible Behavior

Our examples make it clear that corporate social responsibility takes many different forms.[77] The major ones are as follows.

- *Helping the community by making charitable contributions.* One of the most popular ways for companies to be socially responsible is by giving donations back to the communities in which they operate. Such acts are not only helpful and generous, of course, but also stand to be good business practices insofar as helping the community promote business and helps develop future employees (for a good example, see Figure 2.15).
- *Preserving the environment.* Many companies are involved actively in efforts to preserve the natural environment. Chiquita Brands, McDonald's, and UPS described on the previous page provide good examples.[78] So interested are individuals in preserving the environment, that in 2010 the U.S. Securities and Exchange Commission (the SEC, which regulates standards for publicly traded companies) imposed a regulation that requires public companies to warn investors of any serious risks that global warming might pose to their businesses.[79]
- *Socially responsible investing.* Another popular form of being socially responsible involves being highly selective in making investments. This calls for making investments

TABLE 2.3 Top 10 Most Socially Responsible Companies in the United States

A research firm analyzed the level of corporate social responsibility among the largest companies in the United States in 2009. Basing its analysis on such key considerations as the companies' contributions to the community, attention to employees' needs, preservation of the environment, and advancement of minorities and women, the top 10 performers are listed here. As indicated, these companies excelled in different ways.

Rank	Company	Notable Socially Responsible Action
1	Bristol Myers-Squibb	Built hospitals to help people in communities that are underserved by medical professionals.
2	General Mills	Provided technical and financial support to develop irrigation systems, dig new wells, and establish a "village savings and loan" microfinancing organization to help African women start small businesses.
3	IBM	Saved 4.9 billion KWh of energy between 1990 and 2008 due to energy conservation programs.
4	Merck & Co.	Collaborated with community-based organizations and health-care providers in underserved communities to address the growing epidemics of pediatric asthma and type 2 diabetes.
5	HP	Helped establish technology centers at 12 Russian universities that are focused on building practical IT-related business skills (with 1,500 students admitted thus far).
6	Cisco Systems	Partnered with other companies to develop a scalable and sustainable communications platform that connects farmers in rural India with vital knowledge related to agriculture and livestock.
7	Mattel	Developed new packaging for products that minimizes waste and relies on biodegradable materials.
8	Abbott Laboratories	Improved HIV/AIDS services at more than 90 sites across Tanzania, including building a new treatment center at the country's largest hospital.
9	Kimberly Clark	Purchases virgin wood fiber from companies that use sustainable forest management practices thereby ensuring that the timber harvested does not exceed the rate at which forestlands can regenerate (protecting entire forest ecosystems as a result).
10	Entergy Corp.	Helped reduce home owners' energy costs by distributing weatherization kits and compact fluorescent lightbulbs.

Sources: Based on information reported by *The Corporate Responsibility Officer*, 2009, see Note 79; and the Web sites of the companies listed.

AFP Photo/Thony Belizaire/Newscom.

FIGURE 2.15

PepsiCo Helps Haitian Earthquake Victims

The earthquake that devastated Haiti in January 2010 inspired many companies to make generous donations to aid victims. PepsiCo was a leader in these efforts by donating $1 million. Half of this sum was directed toward immediate humanitarian relief (e.g., through allocations to the American Red Cross and other worthwhile charities), and the remaining half was aimed at long-term efforts to help rebuild Haiti's infrastructure and buildings so as to make them less vulnerable to any future natural disasters. The company also donated cases of its beverage products, Aquafina bottled water and Gatorade for victims and relief workers.

in companies that promote the well-being of society and refraining from investing in companies that may do harm.

- ■ *Promoting the welfare of employees.* One of the most fundamental ways a company has of being socially responsible is by promoting the welfare of its own employees. Several companies have gone out of their way to avoid abusive labor practices even if they prevail in the industry. As an illustration, the Brazilian cosmetics firm Natura Cosméticos shows its support for human rights by not using child labor. It also gives generously to educational programs and encourages its employees to do volunteer work for nonprofit organizations.

Do not be misled by these examples. Being socially responsible involves more than just a few isolated generous practices or occasional kind gestures. Moreover, it is not motivated by an interest in promoting a company's marketing or public relations efforts. It is far more integrative in nature and genuine in intent. Instead, corporate social responsibility is a comprehensive set of policies, practices, and programs that are integrated throughout business operations, and decision-making processes that are supported and rewarded by top management.

Profitability and Social Responsibility: The Virtuous Circle

Do socially responsible companies perform better financially than those that are less socially responsible? The answer is—generally, yes. A recent study compared the companies on the lists of the "100 Best Corporate Citizens" for the years 2001–2009 with a broad index of 1,000 companies with respect to total return on investments. The findings were impressive: Companies in the 100 Best lists outperformed the others by 26 percent.[80] Although there are many possible explanations for these results, and conditions may change in the future, what they suggest about the potential benefits of investing in socially responsible companies appears to be considered seriously—especially since similar findings have been reported by other scientists as well.[81]

Although there are surely many different reasons for this link between social responsibility and profitability, a key one, which we also mentioned in connection with ethics, is that people often support the socially responsible activities of organizations with their patronage and investments. With this in mind, there exist mutual funds that invest only in socially responsible companies (e.g., the ones described in the Today's Diverse and Global Organizations section below) and books that provide detailed information on the socially responsible (and irresponsible) behavior of companies that consumers and investors can use to guide their decisions.[82] Today, individuals who desire to support socially responsible companies by "voting with their dollars" can find it easy to get the information they need on the Internet. That this may contribute to the financial well-being of a company is important, of course, since financial considerations are an organization's most basic responsibility (which is why they are at the base of the corporate social responsibility pyramid shown in Figure 2.14). That said, it is important to keep in mind that most companies engaging in socially responsible behavior do so for its own sake, and not as a path to profitability.

Although profit may not be the primary objective for engaging in socially responsible behavior, it is clear that there is a strong link between the two. Moreover, this connection appears to be bidirectional in nature. The idea is straightforward: Companies that are successful financially invest in social causes because they can afford to do so (i.e., they "do good by doing well") and as we noted previously, socially responsible companies tend to perform well financially (i.e., they "do well by doing good"). This relationship, which has been referred to as the **virtuous circle,** is shown in Figure 2.16.[83]

With the virtuous circle in mind, it is not surprising to find that some of the world's most profitable organizations are also among the most philanthropic. As an example, let's consider ExxonMobil, which regularly is identified as one of the most profitable companies in the world. In 2008 alone, the Exxon Mobil Corporation, its divisions and affiliates, and the ExxonMobil Foundation donated $189 million in cash, goods, and services worldwide ($111 million in the

virtuous circle
The tendency for companies that are successful financially to invest in social causes because they can afford to do so (i.e., they "do good by doing well") and for socially responsible companies to perform well financially (i.e., they "do well by doing good").

Today's Diverse and Global Organizations

Starbucks and Dell Advance the Interests of Women

Although there's nothing particularly special about seeing a woman use a Dell notebook computer while sipping coffee at Starbucks, these two companies have done something very special to help that woman and others. They were the first global corporations to endorse the Calvert Women's Principles, the first global code of conduct designed to empower and advance the interests of women throughout the world.[85] Developed in 2004 by Calvert, the large family of mutual funds investing in socially responsible companies, the Principles are the first code of conduct to focus exclusively on women's rights. As described by Noeleen Heyzer, executive director of the United Nations Development Fund for Women, the Principles are "a concrete set of indicators for tracking the progress of gender justice in the corporate community."[86]

By endorsing the Principles, Dell and Starbucks are committing themselves to promoting proactively the interests of women in all their business practices. Specifically, these guidelines promote the interests of women in seven major ways.

1. Publicly disclosing the things they do to promote gender equality among employees.
2. Paying the legal wage to all women, giving men and women equal pay for equal work. This also includes failing to consider a woman's reproductive status as a basis for personnel decisions.
3. Protecting women against dangers of violence in the workplace, both physical and psychological.
4. Forbidding business activities or community practices that may exploit women in any way.
5. Being proactive in recruiting and appointing women to high-level company positions.
6. Promoting access to educational opportunities for women, such as those involving literacy, professional development, and the enhancement of vocational skills.
7. Publicly respecting the rights of women in advertising and promotion and ensuring that vendors and suppliers adhere to these principles as well.

While Dell and Starbucks go about their business, Calvert will be carefully monitoring their compliance with these Principles. The investment firm also hopes to pick up more major adopters of its Principles in the years ahead. Getting companies to endorse these Principles goes beyond being socially responsible. It also makes good business sense. Calvert's CEO Barbara Krumsiek put it well when she said, "No nation can achieve its full economic and human potential if half of its population remains marginalized and disempowered, and no corporation can meet the demands of sustainable development while ignoring the untapped potential of women."[87] We suspect that officials from Dell and Starbucks are thinking much the same.

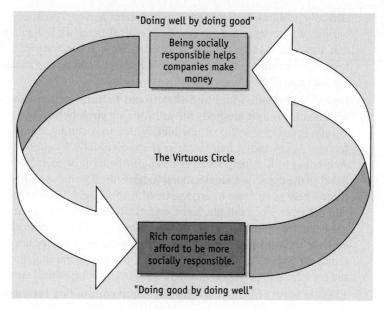

FIGURE 2.16

The Virtuous Circle

It has been suggested that socially responsible companies perform well financially because they are supported by customers and investors. As a result, they become wealthier, making it easier for them to become even more philanthropic. This is known as the *virtuous circle*.

Source: Based on suggestions by Treviño & Nelson, 2006; see Note 83.

United States and $78 million in other countries).[84] By making these donations, the company surely is promoting goodwill. That this results in increased profits is a distinct possibility. And as this occurs, it becomes possible for ExxonMobil to make still more generous charitable contributions. In this manner, the virtuous cycle continues.

Summary and Review of Learning Objectives

1. **Identify four different forms of organizational justice and the organizational impact of each.**

   Organizational justice, people's perceptions of fairness in organizations, takes four distinct forms. *Distributive justice* refers to the perceived fairness of rewards (e.g., pay) received. People who feel they have received fair amounts of reward feel satisfied with their jobs. *Procedural justice* refers to people's perceptions of the fairness of the procedures used to determine the outcomes they receive. When high levels of procedural justice are perceived, people are inclined to follow organizational rules and policies. *Interpersonal justice* refers to the fairness of interpersonal treatment by others. High levels of interpersonal justice are related to high levels of satisfaction with one's supervisor. Finally, *informational justice* refers to people's perceptions of the fairness of the information used as the basis for making a decision. People tend to be highly valued by organizations in which they perceive high levels of informational justice.

2. **Describe strategies that can be used to promote organizational justice.**

   Promoting organizational justice can be done in several ways. First, it is important to pay workers what they deserve—the "going rate" for the work done wherever they work. Underpaying workers promotes dissatisfaction, leading to turnover. Second, workers should be given a voice—that is, some input into decisions. This may involve such strategies as holding regular meetings, conducting employee surveys, keeping an "open door policy," and using suggestion systems. Third, follow openly fair procedures. Specifically, promote procedural fairness, such as by using unbiased, accurate information and applying decision rules consistently. Managers also should openly describe the fair procedures they are using. Fourth, managers should explain decisions thoroughly in a manner demonstrating dignity and respect. Fifth, workers should be trained to be fair, such as by adhering to the principles described in this chapter.

3. **Explain what is meant by ethical behavior and describe its relation to the law.**

   Whereas *moral values* are people's fundamental beliefs regarding what is right and wrong, *ethics* refers to standards of conduct that guide people's decisions and behavior. Organizations are concerned about promoting ethical behavior in organizations. Behaving ethically is highly desirable for two important reasons. First, good ethics is good business. In various ways, organizations in which ethical behavior prevails tend to be more successful than those marked by low levels of ethics. Second, behaving ethically is consistent with many legal requirements—most notably, the Federal Sentencing Guidelines for Organizations and the Sarbanes-Oxley Act.

4. **Describe the individual and situational factors responsible for unethical behavior in organizations and methods for minimizing such behavior.**
People behave ethically or unethically due to a combination of individual and situational factors. A key individual factor is the individual's level of *cognitive moral development.* According to Kohlberg's theory of cognitive level of moral development, over time people develop the capacity to make moral judgments. The more highly developed this capacity, the more likely people are to engage in ethical behavior. However, situational factors also dictate behavior. For example, some organizational norms (e.g., stonewalling) discourage ethical behavior, managerial values sometimes discourage ethical behavior, and subordinates emulate their manager's unethical acts. Unethical behavior may be minimized by corporate ethics programs that use codes of ethics, use ethics training, have bodies formally responsible for ethics, have a mechanism for communicating ethical standards, and use ethics audits.

5. **Explain ways of behaving ethically when conducting business internationally.**
Behaving ethically when conducting international business is challenging because different norms of ethics apply in different cultures. Managers should resist the temptation to engage in *ethical relativism* by blindly adopting whatever ethical norms prevail in a certain country and *ethical imperialism* by insisting on applying their own country's ethical standards wherever they do business. Instead, it is preferable to adopt a stance between these two extremes. This involves following the guiding principles of global ethics: (1) show respect for core human values, (2) demonstrate sensitivity to local traditions, and (3) recognize that context matters when distinguishing between right and wrong.

6. **Explain what is meant by corporate social responsibility, describe the forms it takes, and characterize the relationship between responsible behavior and financial profitability.**
Corporate social responsibility refers to business practices that adhere to ethical values, that comply with legal requirements, and that promote the betterment of individuals and the community at large. Its most popular forms include making charitable contributions to the community, preserving the environment, investing in a socially responsible manner, and promoting the welfare of employees. Generally, research shows that socially responsible companies tend to be more profitable than companies that are less socially responsible. This reflects the *virtuous circle,* the tendency for successful companies to be socially responsible because they can afford to do so, which in turn, helps their chances of being even more financially successful.

Points to Ponder

Questions for Review

1. What is organizational justice, and how are its four different types different from one another?
2. What specific things can managers do to help promote perceptions of fairness in their organizations?
3. What is the difference between ethics and moral values, and why should managers be concerned about promoting ethical behavior?
4. What special ethical challenges are created by doing business internationally?
5. What are the components of an ethics program, and how effective are such programs at promoting ethical behavior?
6. What is meant by corporate social responsibility, and why should organizations be concerned about being socially responsible?

Experiential Questions

1. Think about a time in which you were a victim of organizational injustice. What specific types of justice were violated? How did you feel, and how did you react? What could have been done to avoid these injustices?
2. What do you believe are the major ethical challenges faced by the employees of the company in which you work? What might be done to make people in your company behave more ethically?

3. How socially responsible is the company in which you work? What particular things does it do to enhance the community, the lives of its employees, and/or the environment? What else might it do to be more socially responsible?

Questions to Analyze

1. The people in a company believe that they are being unfairly treated. What forms might this take? Why is this problematic? What can be done to overcome this situation?

2. The people in your company are behaving unethically, making you feel uncomfortable. What might be responsible for this situation, and what might be done to overcome it?

3. A company desires to become more socially responsible. What particular things might it do to achieve this objective, and what benefits might be expected to result from these actions?

Experiencing OB

Individual Exercise

Assessing Organizational Justice Where You Work

To learn about how workers respond to various types of injustices they may experience in the workplace, scientists have found it useful to use rating scales like the one shown. By completing this scale, you will gain some useful insight into your own feelings about the fairness experienced in the organization in which you work.

Directions

1. Using the following scale, respond to each of the questionnaire items by selecting a number from 1 to 5 to indicate the extent to which it applies to you.
    1 = almost never
    2 = slightly
    3 = moderately
    4 = greatly
    5 = almost always
2. In responding to each item, think about a particular organization in which you work—or, if you are a student, think about a particular class.
3. Where you see the word "(outcome)," substitute a specific outcome that is relevant to you (e.g., for a worker, pay; for a student, a grade).
4. Where you see the word "(superior)," substitute a specific authority figure that is relevant to you (e.g., for a worker, one's supervisor; for a student, one's teacher).

Scale

To what extent . . .

1. _____ Is it possible for you to express your views about your (outcome)?
2. _____ Are your (outcomes) generally based on accurate information?
3. _____ Do you have an opportunity to correct decisions made about your (outcome)?
4. _____ Are you rewarded appropriately for the effort you put into your work?
5. _____ Do the (outcomes) you receive reflect the quality of your work?
6. _____ Is your (outcome) in keeping with your performance?
7. _____ Are you treated politely by your (superior)?
8. _____ Does your (superior) treat you with dignity and respect?
9. _____ Does your (superior) refrain from making inappropriate comments?
10. _____ Does your (superior) communicate openly with you?
11. _____ Does your (superior) tell you things in a timely fashion?
12. _____ Does your (superior) explain decisions to you in a thorough fashion?

Source: Adapted from Colquitt, 2001; see Note 5.

Scoring and Interpretation

1. Add your responses to questions 1, 2, and 3. This is your *distributive justice* score.
2. Add your responses to questions 4, 5, and 6. This is your *procedural justice* score.

3. Add your responses to questions 7, 8, and 9. This is your *interpersonal justice* score.
4. Add your responses to questions 10, 11, and 12. This is your *informational justice* score.
5. For each score, higher numbers (e.g., 12–15) reflect higher perceived amounts of the type of fairness in question, whereas lower scores (e.g., 3–6) reflect lower perceived amounts of that type of fairness.

Questions for Discussion

1. With respect to what particular type of fairness did you score highest? What specific experiences contributed to this assessment?
2. With respect to what particular type of fairness did you score lowest? What specific experiences contributed to this assessment?
3. What kinds of problems resulted from any violations of any type of organizational justice you may have experienced? What could have been done to avoid these violations?

Group Exercise

Taking Credit for Another Person's Ideas: Analyzing an Ethical Dilemma

More often than you might imagine, managers confront situations in which they have to decide the right thing to do. Such "ethical dilemmas," as they are known, are usually quite challenging. Discussing ethical dilemmas with others is often a useful way of shedding light on the ethical path by identifying ethical considerations that you may have overlooked on your own. This exercise will give you an opportunity to analyze an ethical dilemma.

Directions

1. Divide the class into multiple groups of three or four students.
2. Read the following ethical dilemma.
3. Working together with the others in your group, analyze the dilemma by answering the following questions:
   a. As the person in this situation, what do you think you would do? What factors enter into your decision?
   b. What do you think would be the *right thing* to do? Explain the basis for your answer.

Ethical Dilemma

You are a mechanical engineer working on developing new products for a large company. Your product-development team is composed of specialists in different fields from throughout the organization. Everyone shares ideas freely with one another, and the team as a whole shares credit for its accomplishments. At least, you think so. One day you learn that the team leader, an older gentleman who resents having to work with others, has been bad-mouthing several members of the team. Worse yet, he's also been taking credit for their ideas. Once, you even overheard him say, "Those guys can't do anything without me. I'm really the brains behind the operation. That idea for the new packaging design was all mine, but I let them take credit for it." Although you are not the direct victim of this assault—at least on this occasion—you are concerned about the effects on your team's morale and performance. You also fear that one day, it might be your ideas for which he is taking credit. You know this is wrong, but you don't know how best to handle the situation.

Questions for Discussion

1. Did the members of your group generally agree or disagree about what they would do in the situation described? What new viewpoints, if any, did you learn from others in your group?
2. Did the members of your group generally agree or disagree about what they thought was the right thing to do? What were the major points of agreement and disagreement?
3. Have you or members of your group ever been in similar situations? If so, how were they handled? From your own experiences and the experiences of others, what did you learn about handling an ethical dilemma of this nature?

Practicing OB

Employee Theft in Convenience Stores

The district manager of a chain of 24-hour convenience stores is very concerned about her stores' rate of employee theft, which is currently about twice the industry average and rising rapidly. Because this problem has arisen suddenly, you and she suspect that it is a response to some recently introduced changes in the company's overtime policy. Managers who used to be paid time-and-a-half for each hour they worked over 40 are now paid a flat salary that typically results in lower total wages for the same amount of work. Answer the following questions based on the information in this chapter.

1. What form of justice appears to have been violated by the new pay policy? Explain your answer.

2. In this case, the new pay policy was implemented without first discussing it with store managers. Do you think that the theft rate might have been lower had this been done? What else could be done to reduce the growing theft rate?

3. The company's code of ethics expressly prohibits theft, but other than being handed a copy along with other company documents and forms upon being hired, hardly anyone pays attention to it. What do you think could be done, if anything, to enhance the effectiveness of the code of ethics as a weapon for combating the theft problem?

■ HP = Hidden Pretexting? What Did in Dunn?

Case in Point

On January 23, 2006, CNET News.com quoted an anonymous source describing strategic plans made at a meeting of HP's board of directors. Because the meeting was held behind closed doors and with a history of similar media leaks occurring for about a year, HP's chairperson, Patricia Dunn, had enough. Frustrated, she wanted to get to the bottom of this and root out the mole before serious damage could be done. Although one can hardly blame Dunn for wanting to protect the interests of her company, her tactics may be considered questionable, at best.

Dunn was so angry that she authorized a private investigation firm to uncover the source of the leaks. But the firm she hired to conduct the probe, the data-brokering company Action Research Group, went a bit too far. Using a practice known as *pretexting*, the investigators obtained the telephone records of more than a dozen people—reporters, HP board members, and employees—by pretending to be them (i.e., contacting the telephone company under false pretexts). Believing that the practice already had been going on and that it seemed an appropriate means to expose the individuals who leaked vital information about the company, it went on with Dunn's full consent and knowledge for about a year.

There was only one problem with the plan: It was illegal. Almost a year to the day that the CNET story broke, a California Superior Court found that HP willingly and knowingly accessed telephone account information without the account holder's permission and that it violated an identity theft statute by obtaining personally identifying information and then using it for unlawful purposes. A settlement was agreed upon in which HP admitted no liability and no civil actions would be pursued against company

officers. In exchange, HP's attorneys agreed to take steps that would help ensure the company's ethical behavior in the future. Specifically, for five years, HP was required: (1) to appoint a chief ethics and compliance officer, (2) to retain an expert in the field of investigations to assist this individual in conducting proper investigations, (3) to expand the role of the company's chief privacy officer to review HP's investigation practices, and (4) to expand the codes of conduct followed by the company's employees and vendors so that they covered appropriate investigation procedures.

To insure that these practices were followed, HP was required to set aside $13.5 million (in addition to paying $1 million in statutory damages and reimbursement of costs borne by the California Attorney General's office). Unlike Enron, whose officials took steps to hide their guilt, Dunn cooperated fully with authorities although, of course, she stepped down as chairperson. Dunn explained that she was never aware that the tactics used in the probe were illegal, and regretted the use of "inappropriate techniques." Eager to put this distasteful chapter behind it, Dunn's replacement, HP chairman Mark Hurd, explained that he is "committed to ensuring that HP regains its standing as a global leader in corporate ethics and responsibility."

Questions for Discussion

1. What legal and ethical actions might Dunn have taken to prevent further leaks of sensitive information?

2. Of the four things that HP was required to do, which one do you believe will be most effective in avoiding future unethical behavior in the company? Why?

3. What aspects of the business environment might have put subtle pressures on Dunn to respond as she did?

■ Global Business at KPMG

International knowledge has become a top priority for managers at KPMG. KPMG provides audit, tax, and advisory services to clients located around the world. The company is an amalgam of firms located in approximately 180 countries; these businesses come together under the KPMG umbrella.

According to Aidan Walsh, head of KPMG's Global Mobility program, because today's clients are operating in foreign locations, KPMG must be prepared to provide the services they need in those markets. To that end, the company has implemented a program in which managers from one country are sent on assignments in another country.

The goal is to allow supervisors to gain business experience in foreign markets and languages; obtain cross-cultural experience; and possibly earn foreign certifications. Foreign assignments at KPMG last from three months to

five years. Walsh believes that because so many managers today want to acquire foreign experience, the program has given KPMG a competitive advantage when it comes to hiring.

Discussion Questions

1. Can KPMG be classified as a multinational enterprise? If so, how does this designation change the services KPMG offers?
2. How have the three major forces driving globalization (as discussed in Chapter 1) facilitated KPMG's global expansion, and what new challenges and opportunities do these forces bring to KPMG?
3. How does the Global Mobility program at KPMG help managers avoid both culture shock and the kind of ethnocentric behavior commonly found in managers initially exposed to new cultures?

■ Social Responsibility at Terra Cycle

Social responsibility is important at Terra Cycle, a company that makes consumer products from garbage. The company was founded by then–college student Tom Szaky, who initially developed his ideas for the company by entering and winning various business-plan competitions. However, it was not until he won a contest paying $1 million that Szaky's commitment to being an eco-capitalist solidified.

The contest rules required Szaky to change his focus from using waste materials to produce and package consumer products and to using more traditional inputs to produce an organic product. Szaky refused to compromise his ideals, rejected the prize money, and scraped together enough funds to start the business on his own. He claims that he is not an environmentalist; rather, he simply wants to do the right thing for society and the world.

Eco-friendly products usually are more expensive to produce than standard ones, keeping them from mainstream consumers. Szaky hopes to change this by showing how an eco-capitalist can make money while helping the environment simply by recognizing the value in waste.

Discussion Questions

1. How does Terra Cycle's business model reflect the basic elements of the pyramid of corporate social responsibility, as presented in Chapter 2?
2. Which of the forms of socially responsible behavior does Terra Cycle pursue?
3. How does the virtuous circle concept discussed in the text relate to Terra Cycle's approach to strategy and profitability?

■ Work/Life Balance

Providing a good balance between work and outside interests and responsibilities is important at Ernest & Young. In response to a survey indicating that employees valued flexibility in their jobs, the company has attempted to create an atmosphere in which people have the opportunity to achieve not only their career goals, but also their personal goals, whether these include family obligations or some other interest.

Ernest & Young has adopted what it refers to as its People First program, according to which the firm commits to doing right for employees, who in turn commit to doing right for the firm. Employee Maryella Goekel notes that the People First program enables workers to be 100 percent dedicated to whatever they are doing at a particular moment, whether it's outside or inside the firm. Goekel also notes that Ernest & Young tries to treat workers like adults rather than children, and makes the assumption that

once an employee knows what has to be accomplished, it will be done.

One person who has worked at Ernest & Young for more than a decade says that the firm's dedication to ensuring that workers have a balance between work and life through its flexible system gives the company a competitive advantage when it comes to employee retention.

Discussion Questions

1. Using the discussion of Theory X versus Theory Y in Chapter 1, explain why a work/life balance is important for employees at Ernest & Young.
2. How does Ernest & Young's People First program relate to the human relations movement described in Chapter 1?
3. How do the family friendly policies at Ernest & Young help the company meet the challenges associated with a demographically diverse workforce?

CHAPTER

3 Perception and Learning: Understanding and Adapting to the Work Environment

Learning Objectives

After reading this chapter, you should be able to:

1. Distinguish between the concepts of social perception and social identity.

2. Explain how the attribution process works, and describe the various sources of bias in social perception.

3. Understand how the process of social perception operates in the contexts of employment interviews and performance appraisals.

4. Define learning and describe the two types most applicable to OB: operant conditioning and observational learning.

5. Describe how principles of learning are involved in organizational training and innovative reward systems.

6. Compare the way organizations use reward in organizational behavior management programs, and how they can use punishment most effectively when administering discipline.

Chapter Outline

- Social Perception and Social Identity: Understanding Others and Ourselves
- The Attribution Process: Judging the Causes of Others' Behavior
- Perceptual Biases: Systematic Errors in Perceiving Others
- Stereotyping: Fitting People into Categories
- Perceiving Others: Organizational Applications
- Learning: Adapting to the World Around Us
- Training: Learning and Developing Job Skills
- Organizational Practices Using Reward and Punishment

Preview Case

■ A "Taylor-Made" Enterprise

In 1957, Jack Taylor, the sales manager of a Cadillac dealership in St. Louis, had an intriguing idea: Instead of selling cars outright, it might be more profitable to rent them repeatedly on a short-term basis. With a fleet of seven cars, and using the name of the aircraft carrier on which he served in World War II, Taylor launched Enterprise Rent-A-Car. Rather than competing with industry giants Hertz and Avis, who targeted business travelers by offering rentals at airports, Taylor sought a different market—individuals seeking temporary replacements for their damaged or stolen cars. From this modest start, Enterprise Rent-A-Car grew into the largest car rental company in the world, with more than 66,000 employees and 904,000 vehicles in operation.

As the business began to grow, Taylor's son, Andy, helped by working in rental branches, assisting customers, washing cars, and doing whatever was needed. Picking up all he could about the business, Andy Taylor worked his way up the ladder and now is chairman and CEO. Under his leadership, Enterprise quickly became a multibillion-dollar company (revenue of about $904 billion in 2009) that acquired former competitors National and Alamo, expanded into Europe (the United Kingdom, Germany, and Ireland), and developed spin-off businesses (e.g., corporate fleet services and truck rental).

To help ensure success, Taylor works tirelessly, acknowledging that "It doesn't matter how smart or talented you are if you are not willing to put in the work for future success." To ensure that employees do, he put a plan in place that rewards them for their performance. From the assistant manager level upward, Enterprise employees are paid a salary plus a percentage of their branch's profits. For the 7,000 U.S. office managers, compensation also takes into account customers' satisfaction ratings, assessed in monthly telephone surveys of thousands of recent customers. As a result, Enterprise employees benefit directly by running efficient operations and making customers happy.

Acknowledging the invaluable things he learned on the job, Taylor says, "Through my early experiences at Enterprise I was able to see firsthand the importance of customer service and employee development." So that today's employees can benefit from the same types of experiences, Enterprise promotes people from within the company. In fact, almost all of the company's senior managers started out staffing rental offices and worked their way up the corporate ladder as management trainees. In fact, Taylor believes that advancing in Enterprise's training program is like earning an MBA on the job—"an MBA without the IOU," as he puts it.

Andy Taylor emphasizes that Enterprise's success comes not from an overarching focus on profit, but from the fundamental belief that he and his father share—that profit follows naturally when you put people first. Indeed, making Enterprise a pleasant place for people to do business is the company's objective. One way Taylor does this is by visiting local offices so he can keep his finger on the pulse of the business, not passing up any opportunities to point out the good things that people are doing. As he put it, "It will be very satisfying if people say that, no matter how big our company got, we always stayed true to our goals of putting people first and always doing the right thing."

Based on recent indications, this is being recognized by others: Enterprise was named the best rental car company three years in a row (by *Entrepreneur* magazine), has been recognized as a Customer Service Champ (by *BusinessWeek*), and has been the recipient of numerous awards for its efforts to preserve the environment (e.g., Partners for Livable Communities awarded Enterprise its Bridge Builders Award to acknowledge its environmentally friendly programs and fuel-efficient vehicles). If there is any merit to these accolades, it's safe to say that Taylor's approach to business appears to be paying off.

There can be no doubt that Enterprise Rent-A-Car has been a major business success, and it is equally clear that OB appears to be involved in two ways. First, it's clear that Andy Taylor learned a great deal about what it took to succeed by observing his father. And *learning,* as you might imagine, is a vital process when it comes to performing effectively on the job, whether it's at the very top, as in this case, or learning lower-level skills. Second, Mr. Taylor demonstrated a keen sensitivity to his employees, recognizing how they felt and how they wished to be treated. At the same time, he also was concerned about the way other people perceived him, a key element of the process known as *social perception.*

Because social perception and learning are so fundamental to the way people behave in organizations, we devote this chapter to describing these topics in detail. Specifically, we begin by discussing the various processes that are responsible for social perception, and discuss the specific ways they operate in organizations. Then, we move to the topic of learning. Here, too, we cover both the basic principles that are responsible for successful learning and the specific applications of these principles on the job. After reading this chapter, you will come away with a good understanding of some of the basic psychological processes that occur not only at Enterprise, but in other organizations as well.

Social Perception and Social Identity: Understanding Others and Ourselves

When it comes to forming opinions about people, there is a subtle, yet powerful process going on—a process by which individuals come to judge and understand others with whom they come into contact. This process, known as *social perception,* will be described here. Then, after focusing on how we come to make judgments of others, we will examine the other side of the coin—namely, how we come to develop identities of ourselves. As you read about these phenomena, you will learn about processes that are so basic that you've probably never thought about them. As you will see, a great deal of insight can be derived by making explicit these important processes that we generally take for granted.

Social Perception: What Are Others Like?

Suppose you meet your new boss. You know her general reputation as a manager, you see the way she looks, hear the words she says, and read the memos she writes. In no time at all, you're trying to figure her out. Will she be easy to work with? Will she like you? Will she do a good job for the company? On the basis of whatever information you have available to you, even if it's very little, you will try to understand her and how you will be affected by her. Put differently, you will attempt to combine the various things you learn about her into a meaningful picture. This process is known as **social perception**—the process of combining, integrating, and interpreting information about others to gain an accurate understanding of them.

The social perception process is so automatic that we are almost never aware that it's happening. Yet it goes on all the time in organizations. Indeed, other people—whether they're bosses, coworkers, subordinates, family, or friends—can have profound effects on us. Understanding the people around us—to figure out who they are and why they do what they do—may be very helpful. After all, you wouldn't want to ask your boss for a raise when you believe he or she is in a bad mood! Clearly, social perception is very important in organizations, which is why we examine it so carefully in this chapter.[1]

Specifically, we explore various aspects of the social perception process in the sections that follow. To begin, we describe the **attribution** process—that is, the way people come to judge the underlying causes of others' behavior. Then we will note various imperfections of this process, errors and sources of bias that contribute to inaccurate judgments of others—as well as ways of overcoming them. Finally, we will highlight specific ways in which the attribution process is used in organizations. Before getting to this, however, we first turn our attention to an even more basic matter—understanding who we are.

Social Identity: Who Am I?

How would you answer if someone asked, "Who are you?" There are many things you could say. For example, you could focus on individual characteristics, such as your appearance, your personality, and your special skills and interests—that is, your **personal identity.** You also could answer in terms of the various groups to which you belong, saying, for example, that you are a student in a particular organizational behavior class, an employee of a certain company, or a citizen of a certain country—that is, your **social identity.** The conceptualization known as **social identity theory** recognizes that the way we perceive others and ourselves is based on both our unique characteristics (i.e., personal identity) and our membership in various groups (i.e., social identity).[2] For an overview of this approach, see Figure 3.1.

Social identity theory claims that the way we identify ourselves is likely to be based on our uniqueness in a group. Say, for example, that you are the only business major in an English class. In this situation, you will be likely to identify yourself as "the business major," and so too will

social perception
The process of combining, integrating, and interpreting information about others to gain an accurate understanding of them.

attribution
The process through which individuals attempt to determine the causes behind others' behavior.

personal identity
The characteristics that define a particular individual.

social identity
Who a person is, as defined in terms of his or her membership in various social groups.

social identity theory
A conceptualization recognizing that the way we perceive others and ourselves is based on both our unique characteristics (see *personal identity*) and our membership in various groups (see *social identity*).

FIGURE 3.1

Social Identity Theory: An Overview

According to *social identity theory,* people identify themselves in terms of their individual characteristics and their own group memberships. They then compare themselves to other individuals and groups to help define who they are, both to themselves and others.

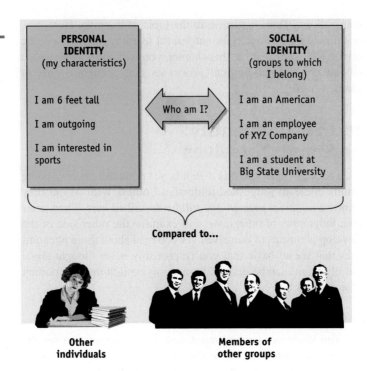

basking in reflected glory
The tendency for people to identify themselves with the successes of others such that those others' success becomes their own.

cutting off reflected failure
The tendency for people to avoid making failure part of their identities by dissociating themselves from individuals or teams that have lost.

others come to recognize you as such. In other words, that will become your identity in this particular situation. Because we belong to many groups, we are likely to have several unique aspects of ourselves to use as the basis for establishing our identities (e.g., you may be the only left-handed person, the only one to have graduated college, or even the only one to have sung in a rock band).

How do we know which particular bases for defining our personal identities people will choose? Given the natural desire to perceive ourselves positively and to get others to see us positively as well, we are likely to identify ourselves with groups we believe are perceived positively by others. We know, for example, that people in highly regarded professions, such as doctors, are more inclined to identify themselves with their professions than those who have lower-status jobs.[3] They enjoy the benefits of being associated with professions that are highly regarded because the esteem of being a member of that profession rubs off on them and those who associate with them. As a result, people who don't know someone but who know that he or she is a member of a positively regarded profession are likely to think positively of this individual. Not surprisingly, a friend introducing you to his or her spouse might be more inclined to indicate the person's profession when it is highly regarded but avoid mentioning it when it is not as impressive. For example, when introducing you to her spouse, the doctor, someone might say, "Meet Chris, the brain surgeon," but if the person is a janitor (an honest but less prestigious profession), she might just say, "Meet Chris," without mentioning his profession.

People also have a tendency to associate themselves with winning sports teams by wearing the colors and logos of those teams. In fact, the tendency to wear clothing that identifies oneself as a fan of a certain team depends on how successful that team has been: The better a team has performed, the more likely its fans are to sport apparel that publicly identifies them with that team, a phenomenon known as **basking in reflected glory**.[4] This refers to the tendency for people to identify themselves with the successes of others such that those others' successes becomes their own. By the same token, to avoid making failure a part of their identities, people do what they can to dissociate themselves with individuals or teams that have lost. This phenomenon is known as **cutting off reflected failure**.[5] For some interesting research findings illustrating these phenomena in a political context, see Figure 3.2.[6]

In addition to explaining how we perceive ourselves, social identity theory also explains how we come to perceive others. Specifically, the theory explains that we focus on the differences between ourselves and other individuals as well as members of other groups (see the lower portion of Figure 3.1). In so doing, we tend to simplify things by assuming that people in different groups share certain qualities that make them different from us—even if they really are not so different after all.

Chris Fitzgerald/Candidate/Photos/Newscom.

FIGURE 3.2

Basking in the Reflected Glory of a Newly Elected President

To support political candidates they favor, people often display signs on their property. Just how soon after an election they remove those signs depends on whether their preferred candidates won or lost. A study conducted immediately after the 2008 presidential election in the United States found that people continued to display signs for Barack Obama, the winner, significantly longer than signs for John McCain, the loser (an average of 4.87 days versus 2.97 days). This allowed Obama supporters to *bask in the reflected glory* of their candidate's historic victory, strengthening their identification with the president-elect.

Source: Data reported by Miller, 2009; see Note 5.

Not only do we perceive others as being different from ourselves, but we also perceive them as being different in negative ways. This is particularly so when we are competing against them (see Chapter 11). Take athletic competitions, for example. If you've ever heard the negative things that students from one college or university say about those from their archrivals in sports (or maybe even said them), then you know this phenomenon quite well. Although such statements are likely to be groundless, we generally find it comforting to believe them nonetheless. The explanation is simple. Making such categorizations helps bring order to the world. After all, distinguishing between "the good guys" and "the bad guys" makes otherwise complex judgments quite simple. And bringing simplicity to a complex world is what social perception is all about.

The Attribution Process: Judging the Causes of Others' Behavior

A question we often ask about others is "why?" Why did Kirsten not return my call? Why did Michael goof up the order? Why did the company president create the policy she did? When we ask such questions, we are attempting to get at two different types of information: (1) What is someone really like? (That is, what traits and characteristics does he or she possess?) (2) What made the person behave as he or she did? (That is, what accounted for his or her actions?) As we will see, people attempt to answer these questions in different ways.[7]

Making Correspondent Inferences: Using Acts to Judge Dispositions

Situations frequently arise in organizations in which we want to know what someone is like. Is your opponent a tough negotiator? Are your coworkers prone to be punctual? The more you know about what people are like, the better equipped you are to know what to expect and how to deal with them. How then, do we go about identifying another's traits?

The simple answer is that we learn about others by observing their behavior and then inferring their traits from this information. The judgments we make about what someone is like based on what we have observed about him or her are known as **correspondent inferences**.[8] Simply put, correspondent inferences are judgments about people's dispositions, their traits and characteristics, that correspond to what we have observed of their actions (see Figure 3.3).

correspondent inferences
Judgments about people's dispositions, their traits and characteristics, that correspond to what we have observed of their actions.

CHALLENGES IN JUDGING OTHERS ACCURATELY. At first blush, it would appear to be a simple matter to infer what people are like based on their behavior. A person with a disorganized desk may be perceived as sloppy. Someone who slips on the shop floor may be considered clumsy. Such judgments might be accurate, but not necessarily. After all, the messy desk actually may be the result of a coworker rummaging through it to find an important report. Similarly, the person who slipped could have encountered oily conditions under which anyone, even the least clumsy individual, would have fallen. In other words, it is important to recognize that the judgments we make about someone may be inaccurate because there are many possible causes of his or her behavior. Someone's underlying characteristics certainly may play a large role in determining what he or she does, but as we will explain in the next section, it also is possible for behavior to be shaped by external forces (in our examples, these would be the coworker's actions and the slippery floor.) For this reason, correspondent inferences may not always be accurate.

Correspondent inferences also might not be accurate because people on the job tend to conceal some of their traits—especially those likely to be viewed as negative. So, for example, a sloppy individual may work hard in public to appear to be organized. Likewise, the unprincipled person may talk a good show about the importance of being ethical. In other words, people often do their best to disguise some of their negative traits. In summary, because behavior is complex and has many different causes, and because people sometimes purposely disguise their true characteristics, correspondent inferences may not always be accurate.

MAKING ACCURATE INFERENCES ABOUT OTHERS. Despite such difficulties, we can use several techniques to help make more accurate correspondent inferences.

First, we can focus on others' behavior in situations in which they do not *have to* behave in a pleasant or socially acceptable manner. For example, anyone would behave in a courteous manner toward the president of the company, so when people do so, we don't learn too much about them.

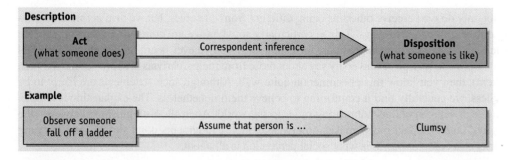

FIGURE 3.3

Correspondent Inferences: Judging Dispositions Based on Behavior

One of the ways in which we come to judge what others are like is by making inferences about them that follow from what we have observed of their behavior. Such judgments, known as *correspondent inferences,* are frequently misleading. How might the inference summarized here be inaccurate?

However, only those who are *really* courteous would be expected to behave politely toward someone of much lower rank—that is, someone toward whom they don't have to behave politely. In other words, someone who is polite toward the company president, but condescending toward a secretary, is probably really arrogant. The way people behave in situations in which a certain behavior is not clearly expected of them may reveal a great deal about their basic traits and motives.

Similarly, we can learn a great deal about someone by focusing on behavior for which there appears to be only a single logical explanation. For example, imagine finding out that your friend accepts a new job. Upon questioning him, you learn that the position is very high paying, involves interesting work, and is in a desirable location. What have you learned about what's important to your friend? Not too much. After all, any of these are good reasons to consider taking a position. Now, imagine finding out that the work is very demanding and that the job is in an undesirable location, but that it pays very well. In this case, you're more prone to learn something about your friend—namely, that he highly values money. Clearly, the opportunity to make accurate correspondent inferences about people is far greater in situations in which there is only one plausible explanation for their behavior than when there are several.

Causal Attribution of Responsibility: Answering the Question "Why?"

Imagine finding out that your boss just fired one of your fellow employees. Naturally, you'd ask yourself, "Why did he do that?" Was it because your coworker violated the company's code of conduct? Or was it because the boss is a cruel and heartless person? These two answers to the question "why?" represent two major classes of explanations for the causes of someone's behavior:

- **Internal causes of behavior**—explanations based on actions for which the individual is responsible
- **External causes of behavior**—explanations based on situations over which the individual has no control

In our example, the internal cause would be the person's violation of the rules, and the external cause would be the boss's cruel and arbitrary behavior.

Generally speaking, it is very important to be able to determine whether an internal or an external cause was responsible for someone's behavior. Knowing why something happened to someone else might help you prepare for something similar happening to you. For example, in this case, if you believe that your colleague was fired because of something for which she was responsible herself, such as violating a company rule, then you might not feel vulnerable because this is something you would not do. However, if you thought she was fired because of the arbitrary, spiteful nature of your boss then you might become the next victim. In this case, you might decide to take some precautionary actions, to do something to protect yourself from your boss, such as staying on his good side, or even giving up and finding a new job—before you are forced to do so.

KELLEY'S THEORY OF CAUSAL ATTRIBUTION. When it comes to social perception, the question of interest to social scientists is: How do people go about judging whether someone's actions were caused by internal or external causes? An answer to this question is provided by **Kelley's theory of causal attribution.** According to this conceptualization, we base our judgments of internal and external causality on observations we make with respect to three types of information.[9] These are as follows:

- **Consensus**—the extent to which other people behave in the same manner as the person we're judging. If others do behave similarly, consensus is considered high; if they do not, consensus is considered low.
- **Consistency**—the extent to which the person we're judging acts the same way at other times. If the person does act the same at other times, consistency is high; if he or she does not, then consistency is low.
- **Distinctiveness**—the extent to which a person behaves in the same manner in other contexts. If he or she behaves the same way in other situations, distinctiveness is low; if he or she behaves differently, distinctiveness is high.

According to the theory, after collecting this information, we combine what we have learned to make our attributions of causality. Here's how. If we learn that other people act like

---

internal causes of behavior
Explanations based on actions for which the individual is responsible.

external causes of behavior
Explanations based on situations over which the individual has no control.

Kelley's theory of causal attribution
The approach suggesting that people will believe others' actions to be caused by internal or external factors based on three types of information: *consensus, consistency,* and *distinctiveness.*

consensus
In *Kelley's theory of causal attribution,* information regarding the extent to which other people behave in the same manner as the person we're judging.

consistency
In *Kelley's theory of causal attribution,* information regarding the extent to which the person we're judging acts the same way at other times.

distinctiveness
In *Kelley's theory of causal attribution,* information regarding the extent to which a person behaves in the same manner in other contexts.

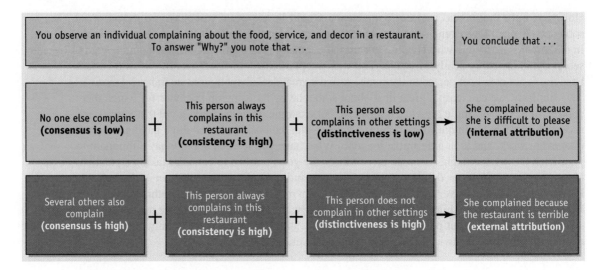

FIGURE 3.4

Kelley's Theory of Causal Attribution: An Example

In determining whether others' behavior stems mainly from internal or external causes, we focus on the three types of information illustrated here.

this one (consensus is high), this person behaves in the same manner at other times (consistency is high), and that this person does not act in the same manner in other situations (distinctiveness is high), we are likely to conclude that this person's behavior stemmed from *external* causes. In contrast, imagine learning that other people do not act like this one (consensus is low), this person behaves in the same manner at other times (consistency is high), and that this person acts in the same manner in other situations (distinctiveness is low). In this case, we would conclude that this person's behavior stemmed from *internal* causes.

AN EXAMPLE.   Because this explanation is highly abstract, let's consider an example to illustrate how the process works. Imagine that you're at a business lunch with several of your company's sales representatives when the sales manager makes some critical remarks about the restaurant's food and service. Further imagine that no one else in your party acts this way (consensus is low), you have heard the sales manager say the same things during other visits to the restaurant (consistency is high), and that you have seen her acting critically in other settings, such as the regional sales meeting (distinctiveness is low). What would you conclude in this situation? Probably that she is a "picky" person, someone who is difficult to please. In other words, her behavior stems from internal causes.

Now, imagine the same setting but with different observations. Suppose that several other members of your group also complain about the restaurant (consensus is high), that you have seen this person complain in the same restaurant at other times (consistency is high), but that you have never seen her complain about anything else before (distinctiveness is high). By contrast, in this case, you probably would conclude that the restaurant really *is* inferior. In this case, the sales manager's behavior stems from external causes. For a summary of these contrasting conclusions, see Figure 3.4.

Perceptual Biases: Systematic Errors in Perceiving Others

Computers may analyze information in an accurate, unbiased, tireless fashion, but the same cannot be said about human beings. We are far from perfect when it comes to gathering information about others and then making judgments about them. In fact, it is more likely to be the rule than the exception that our judgments of others will be imperfect. After all, we are not exactly unbiased in the judgments we make. As you might imagine, this can lead to serious problems for individuals and the organizations in which they work. In this section, we explore this state of affairs in some detail.

Researchers have noted that there are several systematic biases that interfere with making completely accurate judgments of others. These reflect systematic biases in the ways we think about others in general. Collectively, these biases are referred to as **perceptual biases.** We consider several such biases in this section of the chapter.

The Fundamental Attribution Error

Despite what Kelley's theory may imply, people are *not* equally predisposed to reach judgments regarding internal and external causality. Rather, they are more likely to explain others' actions in terms of internal causes rather than external causes. In other words, we are prone to assume that others' behavior is due to the way they are, their traits and dispositions (e.g., "she's just that kind of person"). So, for example, we are more likely to assume that someone who shows up for work late does so because she is lazy rather than because she got caught in traffic. This perceptual bias is so strong that it has been referred to as the **fundamental attribution error.**[10]

This particular bias stems from the fact that it is far simpler to explain someone's actions in terms of his or her traits than to recognize the complex pattern of situational factors that may have affected their actions. As you might imagine, this tendency can be quite damaging in organizations. Specifically, it leads us to assume prematurely that people are responsible for the negative things that happen to them (e.g., "he wrecked the company car because he is careless"), without considering external alternatives, ones that may be less damning (e.g., "another driver hit the car"). And this can lead to inaccurate judgments about people.

The Halo Effect: Keeping Perceptions Consistent

Have you ever heard someone say something like, "She's very smart, so she also must be hard-working"? Or, "He's not too bright, so I guess he's lazy"? If so, then you already are aware of a common perceptual bias known as the **halo effect.**[11] Once we form a positive impression of someone, we tend to view the things that person does in favorable terms—even things about which we have no knowledge. Similarly, a generally negative impression of someone is likely to be associated with negative evaluations of that person's behavior. Both of these tendencies are referred to as halo effects (even the negative case, despite the fact that the word *halo* has positive connotations).

In organizations, the halo effect often occurs when superiors rate subordinates using a formal performance appraisal form. In this context (which we will describe more fully later in this chapter), a manager evaluating one of his or her employees highly on some dimensions may assume that an individual who is so good at this particular thing also must be good at other things. The manager would then be likely to evaluate that person highly on other dimensions (see Figure 3.5). Put differently, the halo effect may be responsible for finding high correlations between the ratings given to people on various dimensions. When this occurs, the resulting evaluations are lacking in accuracy, and the quality of the resulting evaluations is compromised.

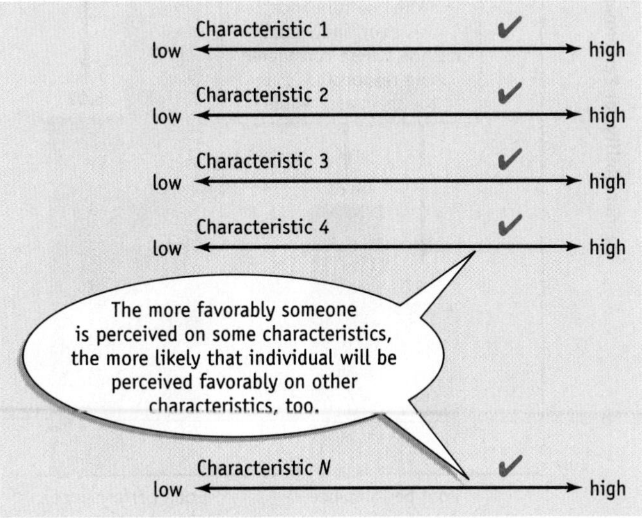

perceptual biases
Predispositions that people have to misperceive others in various ways.

fundamental attribution error
The tendency to attribute others' actions to internal causes (e.g., their traits) while largely ignoring external factors that also may have influenced behavior.

halo effect
The tendency for our overall impressions of others to affect objective evaluations of their specific traits; perceiving high correlations between characteristics that may be unrelated.

Characteristic 1   low ← ✔ → high
Characteristic 2   low ← ✔ → high
Characteristic 3   low ← ✔ → high
Characteristic 4   low ← ✔ → high

The more favorably someone is perceived on some characteristics, the more likely that individual will be perceived favorably on other characteristics, too.

Characteristic N   low ← ✔ → high

FIGURE 3.5

The Halo Effect: A Demonstration

One manifestation of the halo effect is the tendency for people rating others to give either consistently high ratings (if the individual is generally perceived in a positive manner) or low ratings (if the individual is generally perceived in a negative manner). Because each rating dimension is not considered independently, inaccurate evaluations may result.

The halo effect applies not only to individuals, but to work teams as well (a topic we will discuss in Chapter 8). Consider, for example, the way we tend to bias our perceptions of the teams for which we root as sports fans. Because we desire to see our team in a favorable light, we attribute positive characteristics to it when it wins ("This is the greatest team ever"). However, if our team loses, we tend to blame the loss on the mistakes or poor performance of one particular player ("The team is still good, but that one player ruined it for us"). This is known as the **team halo effect**—the tendency for people to credit teams for their successes but not to hold them accountable for their failures.

The team halo effect has been demonstrated clearly in an interesting study.[12] In this investigation, researchers asked college students to recall either a successful team experience or an unsuccessful team experience in which they had participated. They were then asked to complete a questionnaire indicating the extent to which they attributed that outcome to either the team as a whole or to the performance of a particular individual. The results, summarized in Figure 3.6, support the existence of the team halo effect. Specifically, whereas the team as a whole was believed to be much more responsible for good performance than for poor performance, specific team members were believed to be more responsible for poor performance than for good performance.

The Similar-to-Me Effect: "If You're Like Me, You Must Be Pretty Good"

Another common type of perceptual bias involves the tendency for people to perceive more favorably others who are like themselves than those who are dissimilar. This tendency, known as the **similar-to-me effect,** constitutes a potential source of bias when it comes to judging other people. In fact, research has shown that when superiors rate their subordinates, the more similar the parties are, the higher the rating the superior tends to give.[13] This tendency applies with respect to several different dimensions of similarity, such as similarity of work values and habits, similarity of beliefs about the way things should be at work, and similarity with respect to demographic variables (such as age, race, gender, and work experience).

This effect appears to be partly the result of the tendency for people to be able to empathize and relate better to similar others and to be more lenient toward them. However, it also appears

team halo effect
The tendency for people to credit teams for their successes but not to hold them accountable for their failures.

similar-to-me effect
The tendency for people to perceive in a positive light others who are believed to be similar to themselves in any of several different ways.

FIGURE 3.6

Evidence for the Team Halo Effect

According to the team halo effect, people tend to recognize teams more for their successes than for their failures. This effect was demonstrated in an experiment showing that people held teams much more responsible for good performance than for poor performance. When performance was poor, individual team members were considered more responsible than the team as a whole. This allowed people to continue feeling positive about the teams.

Source: Based on data reported by Naquin & Tynan, 2003; see Note 12.

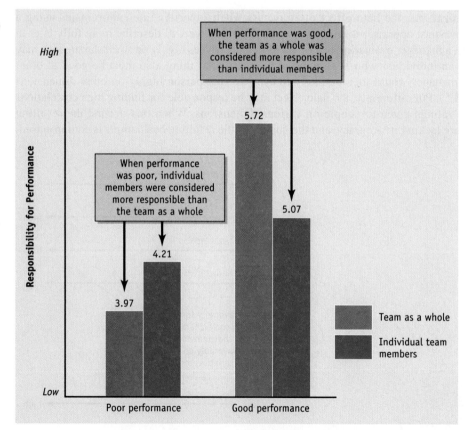

that subordinates tend to be more trusting and confident in supervisors who they perceive as being similar to themselves than those perceived as being dissimilar.[14] As a result, they may have a more positive relationship with such individuals, and this may lead superiors to judge similar subordinates more favorably.

Selective Perception: Focusing on Some Things While Ignoring Others

Another perceptual bias, known as **selective perception,** refers to the tendency for individuals to focus on certain aspects of the environment while ignoring others.[15] As people, we work in complex environments in which there are many stimuli that demand our attention; it makes sense that we tend to be selective, narrowing our perceptual fields. This constitutes a bias insofar as it limits our attention to some stimuli while heightening our attention to other stimuli.

As you might imagine, this process is likely to occur in organizations. In fact, research has shown that top executives asked to indicate the functions of their organizations that contribute most strongly to its effectiveness tend to cite functional areas that matched their backgrounds.[16] For example, executives whose backgrounds were in sales and marketing perceived changes in a company's line of products and services as being most important. Similarly, those who worked previously in research and development focused more on product designs than on other issues in their perceptions of the business environment. In other words, executives tend to be affected by selective perception. That is, they give greatest attention to those aspects of the business environments that match their background experiences. Keeping this tendency in mind, it is easy to understand why different people may perceive the same situations very differently.

selective perception
The tendency to focus on some aspects of the environment while ignoring others.

First-Impression Error: Confirming One's Expectations

Often, the way we judge someone is not based solely on how well that person performs now, but rather, on our initial judgments of that individual—that is, our *first impressions*. To the extent that our initial impressions guide our subsequent impressions, we have been victimized by **first-impression error.**

As you might imagine, this error can be especially problematic in organizations, where accurately judging others' performance is a crucial managerial task. When a subordinate's performance has improved, that needs to be recognized, but to the extent that current evaluations are based on poor first impressions, recognizing such improvement would be impossible. Likewise, inaccurate assessments of performance would result when initially good performers leave positive impressions that linger, even when confronted with evidence suggesting that one's performance has dropped (for a summary, see Figure 3.7).

Research suggests that the first-impression error may take very subtle forms.[17] For example, in one study, corporate interviewers evaluated prospective job applicants by viewing the application blanks and test scores of prospective employees. The more highly interviewers judged the applicants based on these two criteria alone, the more positively the applicants were treated subsequently during the interview process. In fact, candidates who made initially positive impressions were treated more positively during the interview (e.g., they were spoken to in a more pleasant interpersonal style). Thus, instead of using the interviews to gather additional unbiased information, as you would expect (and hope!), the recruiters studied appeared to use the interviews simply to confirm the first impressions they had already developed on the basis of the test scores and application blanks. This study provides clear evidence of the first-impression error in action.

Because the perceptual errors we've discussed thus far can lead to poor judgment on the job, it's important to consider some ways of overcoming them. For some recommendations in this regard, see the suggestions in Table 3.1. Although some of these guidelines may be difficult to follow, they can help the many forms of perceptual errors we've discussed thus far. As such, the effort required to put them into practice promises to be well worthwhile.

first-impression error
The tendency to base our judgments of others on our initial impressions of them.

Self-Fulfilling Prophecies: The Pygmalion Effect and the Golem Effect

In case it already isn't apparent just how important perceptions are in the workplace, consider the fact that the way we perceive others actually can dictate how effectively people will work. Put differently, perceptions can influence reality! This is the idea behind what is known as the **self-fulfilling prophecy**—the tendency for someone's expectations about another to cause that individual to behave in a manner consistent with those expectations.

self-fulfilling prophecy
The tendency for someone's expectations about another to cause that person to behave in a manner consistent with those expectations. This can be either positive (see the *Pygmalion effect*) or negative (see the *Golem effect*) in nature.

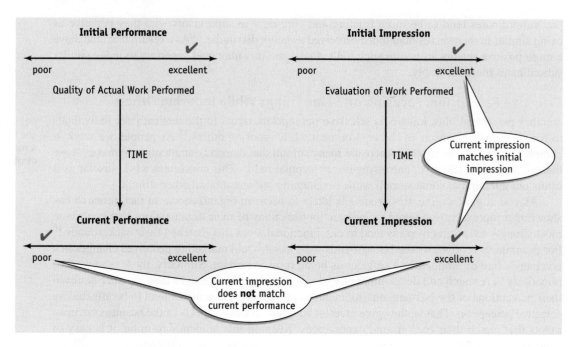

FIGURE 3.7

First-Impression Error: A Summary

When a first-impression error is made, the way we evaluate someone is more highly influenced by our initial impressions of that person than by his or her current performance. In this example, someone who was initially perceived as performing well continues to be rated highly despite a downturn in performance.

Pygmalion effect
A positive instance of the *self-fulfilling prophecy*, in which people holding high expectations of another tend to improve that individual's performance.

Self-fulfilling prophecies can take both positive and negative forms. In the positive case, holding high expectations of another tends to improve that individual's performance. This is known as the **Pygmalion effect.** This effect was demonstrated in a study of Israeli soldiers who were taking a combat command course.[18] The four instructors who taught the course were told that certain trainees had high potential for success, whereas the others had either normal potential

TABLE 3.1 Suggestions for Overcoming Bias in Social Perception

Biases in social perception are inevitable. Fortunately, however, there are things we can do to reduce their impact. Here are several guidelines to follow to help you perceive others more accurately in the workplace. We realize that many of these tactics are far easier to say than to do. However, to the extent that we conscientiously try to apply these suggestions to our everyday interactions with others in the workplace, we stand a good chance of perceiving people more accurately.

Suggestion	Explanation
Do not overlook the external causes of others' behavior.	The fundamental attribution error leads us to discount the possibility that people's poor performance may be due to conditions beyond their control. To combat this, ask yourself if anyone else might have performed just as poorly under the same conditions. If the answer is yes, then you should not automatically assume that the poor performer is to blame.
Evaluate people based on objective factors.	The more objective the information you use to judge others, the less your judgments will be subjected to perceptual distortion. So, whenever possible, judge work performance more on objective measures of quantity (e.g., sales volume) and quality (e.g., error rate) than on subjective, personal judgments.
Avoid making rash judgments.	It is human nature to jump to conclusions about people, but when you can, take the time to get to know people better before judging them. What you learn may make a big difference in your opinion.

or an unknown amount of potential. In reality, the trainees identified as belonging to each of these categories were assigned to that condition at random. Despite this, trainees who were believed to have high potential were found at the end of the training session to be more successful (e.g., they had higher test scores). This demonstrates the Pygmalion effect: Instructors who expected their trainees to do well found that the trainees actually did so.

Researchers also have found that the self-fulfilling prophecy works in the negative direction—that is, low expectations of success lead to poor performance. This is known as the **Golem effect.** Illustrating the Golem effect, researchers have found that Israeli paratroopers whose instructors expected them to perform poorly in their training class did, in fact, perform worse than those about whom instructors had no advance expectations.[19] Clearly, this effect can be quite devastating, but fortunately, it can be overcome.

A study compared the performance of two groups of female military recruits enrolled in a special training program for Israeli soldiers whose limited schooling and mental test scores made them unlikely to succeed in the military.[20] Platoon leaders in the experimental group were told, "You will be training recruits whose average ability is significantly higher than usual for special recruits" and "you can expect better than average achievement from the recruits in your platoon." Leaders of the control group were not given any such information, and their recruits performed poorly, as expected. However, the Pygmalion effect was found in the experimental group, suggesting that even those who are expected to perform poorly can be kept from doing so if their trainees are led to believe that success is possible.

Why do self-fulfilling prophecies, both the Pygmalion effect and the Golem effect, occur? Research into the underlying processes responsible for self-fulfilling prophecies suggests that both types of self-fulfilling prophecies operate according to the four steps summarized in Figure 3.8.[21]

The lesson to be learned from research on self-fulfilling prophecies is very clear: Managers should take concrete steps to promote the Pygmalion effect and to discourage the Golem effect. When leaders display enthusiasm toward people and express optimism about each person's potential, such positive expectations become contagious and spread throughout the organization. As a case in point, consider the great enthusiasm and support that Gordon Bethune showed toward employees of Continental Airlines in 1995, when he took over as that bankrupt company's CEO.[22] It would have been easy for him to be unsupportive and to show his disappointment with the workforce, but he did just the opposite. Only a few years after Bethune was at the helm, the airline turned around to become one of the most successful carriers in the sky (merging with United Airlines in 2010). Although the changes he made to the airline's systems and equipment helped,

Golem effect
A negative instance of the *self-fulfilling prophecy,* in which people holding low expectations of another tend to lower that individual's performance.

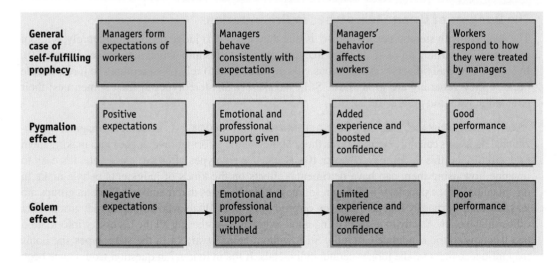

FIGURE 3.8

The Self-Fulfilling Prophecy: A Summary
The processes underlying the *self-fulfilling prophecy* are summarized here. As indicated, it may produce positive effects (known as the *Pygmalion effect*) or negative effects (known as the *Golem effect*).

these things alone would not have been enough if the employees felt like failures. Indeed, Bethune's acceptance and enthusiasm toward members of Continental's workforce contributed greatly to giving the encouragement needed to bring the airline "from worst to first."

Stereotyping: Fitting People into Categories

What comes to mind when you think about people who wear glasses? Are they studious? Eggheads? Although there is no evidence of such a connection, such images linger in many people's minds. Of course, this is only one example. You probably can think of many other commonly held beliefs about the characteristics of people belonging to specific groups. Such statements usually take the form: "People from group *X* possess characteristic *Y*." In most cases, the characteristics described tend to be negative. Assumptions of this type are referred to as **stereotypes**—beliefs that members of specific groups tend to share similar traits and are prone to behave identically.

Deep down inside many of us know, of course, that not all people belonging to a specific group possess the negative characteristics with which we associate them. In other words, most of us accept that the stereotypes we use are at least partially inaccurate. After all, not all *X*'s are *Y*'s; there are exceptions (maybe even quite a few!). If so, then why are stereotypes so prevalent? Why do we use them?

stereotype
A belief that all members of specific groups share similar traits and are prone to behave identically.

Why Do We Rely on Stereotypes?

To a great extent the answer resides in the fact that people tend to do as little cognitive work as possible when it comes to thinking about others.[23] That is, we tend to rely on mental shortcuts. If assigning people to groups allows us to assume that we know what they are like and how they may act, then we can save the tedious work of learning about them as individuals. After all, we come into contact with so many people that it's impractical, if not impossible, to learn everything about them we need to know. So, we rely on readily available information—such as someone's age, race, gender, or job type—as the basis for organizing our perceptions in a coherent way. It's simply efficient to do so.

So for example, if you believe that members of group *X* (those who wear glasses, for example) tend to possess trait *Y* (studiousness, in this case), then simply observing that someone falls into category *X* becomes the basis for believing that he or she possesses *Y*. To the extent that the stereotype applies in this case, then the perception will be accurate. However, such mental shorthand often leads us to make inaccurate judgments about people. This is the price we pay for using stereotypes.

The Dangers of Using Stereotypes in Organizations

The problem with stereotypes, of course, is that they lead us to judge people prematurely, without the benefit of learning more about them than just the categories into which they fit (see Figure 3.9). In today's ethnically diverse organizations, no one can afford to rely on stereotypes to judge people because they generally are groundless. Still, we all rely on stereotypes at least sometimes; their temptation is far too great to resist.

NEGATIVE ORGANIZATIONAL IMPACT: INACCURATE INFORMATION. As you might imagine, organizational decisions can only be as good as the accuracy of the information that goes into making them (we will discuss this in detail in Chapter 10). Because stereotypes often are inaccurate, it's easy to imagine how using them can have detrimental effects on the kinds of judgments people make in organizations. For example, if a human resources officer believes that members of certain groups are lazy, then she purposely may avoid hiring or promoting individuals who belong to that group. That officer may believe firmly that she is using good judgment—gathering all the necessary information and listening to the candidate carefully. Still, without being aware of it, the stereotypes she holds may influence the way she judges certain individuals. If the individual in question would have been a good hire, the company loses out—and of course, so too does the individual.

The result, of course, is that the fate of the individual in question is sealed in advance—not necessarily because of anything he or she may have done or said, but by the mere fact that he or she belongs to a certain group. In other words, even people who might not intend to act in a bigoted fashion still may be influenced by the stereotypes they hold.

Somos Images/Alamy Images.

FIGURE 3.9

What Are These People Like?

Although you don't know these people, you may be inclined to believe certain things about them simply because of their gender and the racial and ethnic groups to which they belong. Because such beliefs, known as *stereotypes*, are likely to be inaccurate, basing decisions on them can be problematic in the workplace.

NEGATIVE INDIVIDUAL IMPACT: STEREOTYPE THREATS. It is important to note that stereotypes don't influence only how people are perceived and treated by those who hold stereotypes, but also how members of stereotyped groups act as a result. Consider, for example, how people tend to live up to—or more properly, *down to*—the negative stereotypes that people hold about them. In an important study, African Americans and whites took a verbal ability test.[24] Consistent with the stereotype that they are intellectually inferior (although this actually is false), the African Americans performed more poorly than the whites. But, this occurred *only* when the test was described as a measure of intelligence. In other words, the African Americans conformed to the stereotype. Importantly, however, when the same test was given to a comparable group of African Americans and whites, but was described in ways that suggested nothing about intelligence, both groups performed equally well.

This idea—that stereotypes constrain behavior when a member of a stereotyped group is placed in a situation in which poor performance can be taken as an indication of the group's deficiency—is the basis of what is known as a *stereotype threat*.[25] Specifically, a **stereotype threat** is the uncomfortable feeling that people have when they run the risk of fulfilling a negative stereotype associated with a group to which they belong. Apparently, individuals facing situations in which they run the risk of substantiating a negative stereotype become so fearful of performing poorly in that situation that their performance actually suffers, making it possible for them to be taken as evidence of the very stereotype that they hoped to disprove (for a summary, see Figure 3.10).

Stereotype threats apply not only to African Americans, but to any group whose members are subjected to stereotypes—which, potentially, is anyone.[26] In one study, for example, a stereotype threat was created in a group of white male students by telling them that the research in which they were participating was designed to determine why Asian students perform better than Caucasians on tests of mathematical ability.[27] It was found that these participants performed significantly more poorly than a comparable group of white men who were not told anything about the reason for the test (i.e., a control group in which no stereotype threat was triggered). Here again, concern about substantiating the negative stereotype lowered task performance. Stereotype threats represent a key process by which stereotypes can exact stiff tolls on their victims.

In some cases, the negative effects of stereotyping go beyond hurt feelings, lowered performance, and lost opportunities. Stereotyping also can be very costly to its victims financially. A study by the National Bureau of Economic Research conducted over a 10-year period found that white women who were overweight by an average of 65 pounds earned hourly wages that were, on

stereotype threat
The uncomfortable feeling that people have when they run the risk of fulfilling a negative stereotype associated with a group to which they belong.

Stereotype Threat: An Overview

When members of a negatively stereotyped group are in a situation in which poor performance can be taken as an indication of their group's deficiency, they tend to substantiate the stereotype by performing poorly. The uncomfortable feeling experienced in this situation is known as a *stereotype threat.* Everyone is subject to experiencing stereotype threats.

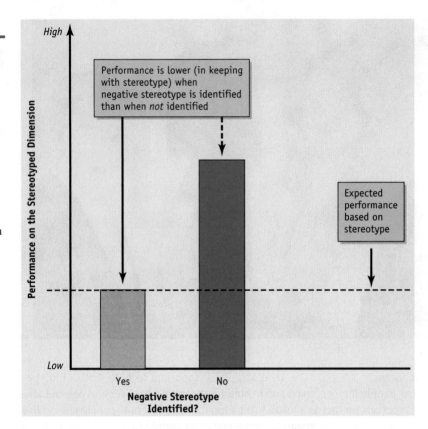

average, 7 percent lower than wages of their nonoverweight counterparts.[28] As the scientists noted, that's like losing the pay boost that would have been earned by a year of education or three years of work experience. Interestingly, both overweight and nonoverweight women held the same kinds of jobs and had the same levels of experience, suggesting that the lower pay of obese women reflects society's negative stereotypes toward them. It's fascinating to note that the same effects of weight on pay were *not* found among African American women. Although there may be several possible explanations for this racial difference, greater acceptance of different body types and fewer negative stereotypes about obese women among African Americans appears to be a key factor.

It's important to acknowledge that the effects of stereotyping others are not always as profound. Referring to accountants as "bean counters" and professors as "absent minded" are observations that also reflect stereotypes—ones that appear to be only mildly negative. Still, it must be cautioned that holding stereotypes of people in various groups run the risks of promoting unfair discrimination (Chapter 6), causing miscommunication (Chapter 9), and generating interpersonal conflict (Chapter 11). Given the problems associated with stereotyping, it is important to consider ways of combating it. (For a look into this issue, see the OB in Practice section on page 87.)

Perceiving Others: Organizational Applications

Thus far, we have identified some of the basic processes of social perception and have alluded to ways in which they are involved in organizational behavior. Now, in this section, we will make these connections more explicit. Specifically, we will describe the role of perception in two organizational activities: *employment interviews and performance appraisals.*

Employment Interviews: Managing Impressions to Prospective Employers

impression management
Efforts by individuals to improve how they appear to others.

The desire to make a favorable impression on others is universal. In one way or another, we all do things to attempt to control how other people see us, often attempting to get them to think of us in the best light possible. This process is known as **impression management.**[29] Generally,

OB in Practice

A Creative Approach to Avoiding Stereotyping

As you know from experience, it's hard to refrain from stereotyping. It comes to us automatically, and we do it unintentionally. If you have an image of a particular group in mind, you will be inclined to conjure it up whenever you encounter a member of that group. Accordingly, it would appear that stereotyping others is something about which we really cannot do too much.

Research has shown, however, that stereotyping might not be as inevitable as you think.[30] What, then, can be done to put the brakes on the stereotyping process? For one, this can occur when people are motivated to keep from stereotyping (e.g., because doing so threatens their images of themselves). In other words, those who really don't want to engage in stereotyping can keep themselves from doing so. More precisely, they can keep themselves from acting on whatever stereotypes they may have.

However, it's also possible to ensure that stereotypical images never enter your mind in the first place. Specifically, if your thinking takes different routes, it's possible to avoid activating stereotypes. The trick is to adopt a mind-set to "think differently." After all, if you avoid your typical associations between groups and their stereotypical characteristics, they are unlikely to come to mind.

You might think that you can do this simply by suppressing those thoughts from consciousness. This doesn't work, however. If you intentionally try to keep a thought out of your head, you actually are making yourself even *more* aware of it—what scientists refer to as making it *hyperaccessible*. To do this you would have to think about the very thing you want to avoid, which makes you think of it even more. This is known as the **rebound effect.** So, forcing stereotypes out of your mind isn't going to help.

rebound effect
The tendency to think about something when you try intentionally not to think about it.

There's another approach, however. Instead of intentionally trying to avoid stereotypes, actually thinking differently by attempting to be creative (see Chapter 14)—or even thinking about times you were creative—can eliminate triggers of the well-established connections on which stereotypical thoughts are based. Research has found that people who were asked to think of various creative things they did over the years were significantly less inclined to describe members of various groups in stereotypical ways than were others who were not asked to think about their own creativity.[31] Scientists take this as an indication that focusing on "thinking differently" helps people overcome the automatic activation of stereotypes. In other words, adopting the mind-set to "think differently" interferes with the kind of thinking required to trigger stereotypes (which, of course, tend to be well ingrained).

This raises an important and provocative question: What can be done to discourage stereotyping in the workplace? The answer isn't easy, of course. In keeping with the rebound effect, simply telling yourself *not* to engage in stereotyping isn't going to work. However, keeping yourself thinking creatively, taking different approaches to things in the work you do, *is* likely to keep your mind from letting those stereotypes come to awareness. This is a fragile process, as you might imagine, because—again, as per the rebound effect—as soon as you catch yourself thinking that you are fighting stereotypes, you are likely to become more aware of them.

Although this notion hasn't yet been tested in the workplace, it would seem that adopting the "think differently" mind-set on a regular basis might not be such a bad idea. For people whose jobs permit creative thinking, and for individuals who are capable of pulling it off, it just may keep stereotypes from entering into your mind. If your focus on thinking differently doesn't make you any more stereotype-resistant than those around you, then at least your efforts stand to make you more creative, and that can't hurt (again, see Chapter 14).

individuals devote considerable attention to the impressions they create in the eyes of others—especially when these others are important, such as prospective employers.

The impressions prospective employers form of us may be based on subtle behaviors, such as how we dress and speak, or more elaborate acts, such as announcing our accomplishments (see Figure 3.11).[32] They may be the result of calculated efforts to get others to think of us in a certain way, or they may be the passive, unintended effects of our actions.

When it comes to the employment interview, for example, there are several things job candidates commonly do to enhance the impressions they make. In an interesting study, researchers audiotaped interviews between college students looking for jobs and representatives of companies that posted openings at their campus' job placement centers.[33] The various statements made by the candidates were categorized with respect to the impression management techniques they used. Several tactics were commonly observed. Table 3.2 lists these specific tactics, gives an example of each, and shows the percentage of candidates who used these techniques. Interestingly, the most common technique was *self-promotion,* flatly asserting that one has certain desirable characteristics. In this case, candidates commonly described themselves as being hardworking, interpersonally skilled, goal-oriented, and effective as leaders.

Importantly, the study also found that candidates used these impression management techniques with great success. The more they relied on these tactics, the more positively they were viewed by

FIGURE 3.11

Dressing for Success Requires Dressing for the Job

It's important for employees to make favorable impressions on their coworkers by wearing the clothing expected of them on the job. At many offices today, this consists of "business casual" attire. But at most high-tech companies such as Google, dress is extremely casual. At the same time, a T-shirt and jeans would make an unfavorable impression in the executive suite, where the classic business suit remains standard attire. The most positive impressions may be made by dressing in the manner considered appropriate for the job.

TABLE 3.2 How Do Job Applicants Present Themselves Favorably?

Researchers have systematically recorded and categorized what job applicants say to present themselves favorably to recruiters interviewing them. Here is a list of techniques found during one study along with the percentages of participants using them. Descriptions and examples of each technique are given as well.

Impression Management Technique	Description	Percentage Using Technique
Self-promotion	Directly describing oneself in a positive manner for the situation at hand (e.g., "I am a hard worker").	100
Personal stories	Describing past events that make oneself look good (e.g., "In my old job, I worked late anytime it was needed").	96
Opinion conformity	Expressing beliefs that are assumed to be held by the target (e.g., agreeing with something the interviewer says).	54
Entitlements	Claiming responsibility for successful past events (e.g., "I was responsible for the 90 percent sales increase that resulted").	50
Other enhancement	Making statements that flatter, praise, or compliment the target (e.g., "I am very impressed with your company's growth in recent years").	46
Enhancements	Claiming that a positive event was more positive than it really was (e.g., "Not only did our department improve, it was the best in the entire company").	42
Overcoming obstacles	Describing how one succeeded despite obstacles that should have lowered performance (e.g., "I managed to get a 3.8 grade point average although I worked two part-time jobs").	33
Justifications	Accepting responsibility for one's poor performance but denying the negative implications of it (e.g., "Our team didn't win a lot, but it's just how you play the game that really matters").	17
Excuses	Denying responsibility for one's actions (e.g., "I didn't complete the application form because the placement center ran out of them").	13

Source: Based on information in Stevens & Kristof, 1995; see Note 33.

the interviewer along several important dimensions (e.g., fit with the organization). This study not only confirms that job candidates do indeed rely on impression management techniques during job interviews, but also that these cultivate the positive impressions desired. With this in mind, the job interview may be seen as an ongoing effort on behalf of candidates to present themselves favorably, and for interviewers to try to see through those attempts, trying to judge candidates accurately. As the evidence suggests, this task may not be as simple as it seems.

Performance Appraisal: Formal Judgments About Job Performance

One of the most obvious instances in which social perception occurs is when someone formally evaluates the job performance of another. This process, known as **performance appraisal,** may be defined as the process by which people (typically superiors) evaluate the performance of others (typically subordinates), often on an annual or semiannual basis, usually for purposes of determining raises, promotions, and training needs.[34]

performance appraisal
The process of evaluating employees on various work-related dimensions.

Ideally, this process should be completely rational, leading to unbiased and objective judgments about exactly how well each employee performed his or her job, focusing on both strengths and areas needing improvement (see Figure 3.12). However, based on what we have said about perception thus far, you're probably not surprised to learn that the performance evaluation process is far from objective. Indeed, people have a limited capacity to process, store, and retrieve information, making them prone to bias when it comes to evaluating others.[35]

Several such biases have been observed by researchers. For example, it has been found that people's ratings of others' performance depends on the extent to which that performance is consistent with the rater's initial expectations. Researchers in one study, for example, asked bank managers to indicate how well they expected their newest tellers to perform their jobs.[36] Then, four months later, they were asked to rate the tellers' actual job performance. It was found that managers gave higher ratings to those tellers whose performance matched their earlier expectations than to those who did either better or worse than predicted. These effects are unsettling because they suggest that the improved performance of some employees may go unrecognized—or, worse yet, be downgraded! Of course, to the extent that human resource management decisions are made on the basis of several sources of information, besides judgments by a single superior, it is unlikely that such biased judgments will go uncorrected. Nevertheless, these findings clearly underscore a key point: Perceptions are based not only on the characteristics of the person being perceived, but the perceiver as well.

This conclusion is supported by research showing several different attribution biases in evaluations of job performance. Consider, for example, research illustrating how the similar-to-me effect operates in a performance appraisal situation. A study conducted at a bank, for example, has shown that the more tellers do things to cultivate positive impressions on their superiors (e.g., do favors for them, agree with their opinions), the more the superiors view those tellers as being similar to themselves. And, the more similar they are believed to be, the more highly the superiors evaluated their work.[37]

FIGURE 3.12

A Performance Appraisal We Wouldn't Like to See

Performance appraisals are supposed to be unbiased, objective, and focused on both the positive and negative aspects of an employee's job performance. If this is the positive, we shudder to think what the negative might be.

Today's Diverse and Global Organizations

Performance Evaluations in the United States and Japan

Beyond individual biases that make the process of evaluating work performance inherently imprecise, widespread cultural differences also are likely to make a big difference when it comes to performance appraisal. In other words, the way people tend to evaluate others' work is likely to be influenced by the nations from which they come.[38] This shouldn't be too surprising if you consider that people from various countries differ with respect to several key variables involved in the performance appraisal process, such as how willing people are to be direct with others and how sensitive they are to differences in status. This point is illustrated clearly by comparing American and Japanese companies with respect to the performance appraisal practices they use.

Although direct supervisors are likely to conduct appraisals in both countries, the ways they go about doing so are very different in several key respects. For example, the American worker's job performance typically is appraised annually. However, in Japan, judgments of how effectively a worker is developing on the job usually occur monthly. Then, an overall evaluation of performance effectiveness is given only after a long time has passed—usually 12 years—making it possible for a highly meaningful assessment to occur. Although this may make little sense in the United States, where long-term commitments to companies are atypical, this approach is possible in Japan, where employees and companies tend to be highly loyal to each other, and where loyalty is rewarded by lifetime employment and regular promotion.[39]

(Recently, however, economic problems have been bringing this tradition to an end.)

The United States and Japan differ as well in terms of precisely how performance appraisals are conducted. In the United States, companies almost always rely on an official form to provide a precise written record of a supervisor's evaluation. In Japan, however, such directness would be considered inappropriate, and comments about performance are presented orally in a very subtle manner. In keeping with their bluntness, Americans generally are not reluctant to rebut (or, at least, to ask questions about) the judgments made about them. However, very few Japanese employees would consider challenging their supervisors so overtly, politely accepting their supervisors' judgments.

Finally, in the United States, it is almost always the individual worker who is evaluated. In Japan, however, the group or work team tends to be judged as a whole. This reflects the fact that Japanese society generally values collective efforts—people pitching in to work together is what matters most. Americans, by contrast, tend to be far more concerned about their individual performance and their individual rewards.[40]

Although you may find these differences to be interesting curiosities, Americans doing business in Japan and Japanese people doing business in the United States widely recognize the importance of such differences. Indeed, the willingness of American managers from American Airlines and Japanese managers from Japan Airlines to understand what it takes to appraise one another's work was considered a key factor in the 2010 decision of these airline giants to form a joint venture (we discuss joint ventures more fully in Chapter 16).[41]

As you might imagine, employees often attempt to make themselves look good to superiors by offering explanations of their work that focus on the internal reasons underlying their good performance and the external reasons underlying their poor performance. Indeed, two equally good performers are unlikely to receive the same performance ratings when different attributions are made about the underlying causes of their performance. Managers tend to give higher ratings to individuals whose poor performance is attributed to factors outside those individuals' control (e.g., someone who is trying hard, but is too inexperienced to succeed) than to those whose poor performance they attribute to internal factors (e.g., those who are believed to be capable, but who are just lazy and holding back). In other words, our evaluations of others' performance are qualified by the nature of the attributions we make about that performance.

Findings such as these illustrate our point that organizational performance evaluations are far from the unbiased, rational procedures one would hope to find. Instead, they represent a complex mix of perceptual biases—effects that must be appreciated and well understood if we are to have any chance of ultimately improving the accuracy of the performance evaluation process. As you will see in Today's Diverse and Global Organizations above, cultural differences in the performance appraisal process complicate things further.

Learning: Adapting to the World Around Us

Thus far in this chapter we have focused on perception, one of the basic human psychological processes most actively involved in explaining behavior in organizations. However, another process is equally important—*learning*. After all, learning is involved in a broad range of organizational behaviors, ranging from developing new vocational skills, through changing the way people do their jobs, to managing them in ways that foster the greatest productivity. Not surprisingly, the more a company fosters an environment in which employees are able to learn, the more productive and profitable that organization is likely to be.[42] Naturally, scientists in the field of OB are extremely interested in understanding the process of learning—both how it occurs and how it may be applied to the effective functioning of organizations.

Before turning attention to these matters, we first explain exactly what is meant by learning. Specifically, **learning** is defined as a relatively permanent change in behavior occurring as a result of experience.[43] Despite its simplicity, several aspects of this definition bear pointing out. First, it's clear that learning requires that some kind of change occur. Second, this change must be more than just temporary. Finally, it must be the result of experience—that is, continued contact with the world around us. Given this definition, we cannot say that short-lived performance changes on the job, such as those due to illness or fatigue, are the result of learning. Like so many concepts in the social sciences, learning is a difficult concept for scientists to understand because it cannot be observed directly. Instead, it must be inferred on the basis of behavioral changes.

Although there are several different types of learning, we will examine two that are most relevant in organizations. These are *operant conditioning* and *observational learning*.

Operant Conditioning: Learning Through Rewards and Punishments

Imagine you are a chef working at a catering company where you are planning a special menu for a fussy client. If your dinner menu is accepted and the meal is a hit, the company stands a good chance of picking up a huge new account. You work hard at doing the best job possible and present your culinary creation to the skeptical client. Now, how does the story end? If the client loves your meal, your grateful boss gives you a huge raise and a promotion. However, if the client hates it, your boss asks you to turn in your chef's hat. Regardless of which of these outcomes occur, one thing is certain: Whatever you did in this situation, you will be sure to do it again if it was successful, and to avoid doing it again if it failed.

This situation nicely illustrates an important principle of **operant conditioning** (also known as **instrumental conditioning**)—namely, that our behavior produces consequences and that how we behave in the future will depend on what those consequences are. If our actions have had pleasant effects, then we will be likely to repeat them in the future. If, however, our actions have unpleasant effects, we are less likely to repeat them in the future. This phenomenon, known as the **Law of Effect,** is fundamental to operant conditioning. Our knowledge of this phenomenon comes from the work of the famous social scientist B. F. Skinner.[44] Skinner's pioneering research has shown us that it is through the connections between our actions and their consequences that we learn to behave in certain ways. We summarize this process in Figure 3.13.

learning
A relatively permanent change in behavior occurring as a result of experience.

operant conditioning
The form of learning in which people associate the consequences of their actions with the actions themselves. Behaviors with positive consequences are repeated; behaviors with negative consequences are avoided.

instrumental conditioning
See *operant conditioning*.

Law of Effect
The tendency for behaviors leading to desirable consequences to be strengthened and those leading to undesirable consequences to be weakened.

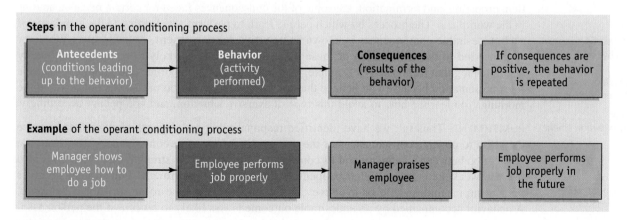

FIGURE 3.13

The Operant Conditioning Process: An Overview

The basic premise of operant conditioning is that people learn by connecting the consequences of their behavior with the behavior itself. In this example, the manager's praise increases the subordinate's tendency to perform the job properly in the future. Learning occurs by providing the appropriate antecedents and consequences.

TABLE 3.3 Contingencies of Reinforcement: A Summary

The four contingencies of reinforcement may be distinguished by the presentation or withdrawal of a pleasant or an unpleasant stimulus. Positively or negatively reinforced behaviors are strengthened, whereas punished or extinguished behaviors are weakened.

Stimulus Presented or Withdrawn	Desirability of Stimulus	Name of Contingency	Strength of Response	Example
Presented	Pleasant	Positive reinforcement	Increases	Praise from a supervisor encourages continuing the praised behavior.
	Unpleasant	Punishment	Decreases	Criticism from a supervisor discourages enacting the punished behavior.
Withdrawn	Pleasant	Extinction	Decreases	Failing to praise a helpful act reduces the odds of helping in the future.
	Unpleasant	Negative reinforcement	Increases	Future criticism is avoided by doing whatever the supervisor wants.

contingencies of reinforcement
The various relationships between one's behavior and the consequences of that behavior—*positive reinforcement, negative reinforcement, punishment,* and *extinction.*

The various relationships between a person's behavior and the consequences resulting from it are known collectively as **contingencies of reinforcement.** They represent the conditions under which rewards and punishments either will be given or taken away. Here, we describe the four contingencies of reinforcement—*positive reinforcement, negative reinforcement, punishment,* and *extinction*—and we summarize them in Table 3.3. As we will see later in this chapter, creating these conditions is an effective tool for managing behavior in organizations.

POSITIVE REINFORCEMENT. Operant conditioning is based on the idea that behavior is learned because of the pleasurable outcomes that we associate with it. In organizations, for example, people usually find it pleasant and desirable to receive monetary bonuses, paid vacations, and various forms of recognition. The process by which people learn to perform acts leading to such desirable outcomes is known as **positive reinforcement.** Whatever behavior led to the positive outcome is likely to occur again, thereby strengthening that behavior. For a reward to serve as a positive reinforcer, it must be made contingent on the specific behavior sought. So, for example, if a sales representative is given a bonus after landing a huge account, that bonus will only reinforce the person's actions *if* he or she associates it with the landing of the account. When this occurs, the individual will be more inclined in the future to do whatever helped get the account.

positive reinforcement
The process by which people learn to perform behaviors that lead to the presentation of desired outcomes.

NEGATIVE REINFORCEMENT (OR AVOIDANCE). Sometimes we also learn to perform acts because they permit us to avoid undesirable consequences. Unpleasant events, such as reprimands, rejection, probation, and termination, are some of the consequences faced for certain negative actions in the workplace. The process by which people learn to perform acts leading to the avoidance of such undesirable consequences is known as **negative reinforcement,** or **avoidance.** Whatever response led to the termination of these undesirable events is likely to occur again, thereby strengthening that response. For example, you may stay late at the office one evening to revise a sales presentation because you believe that the boss will "chew you out" if it's not ready in the morning. You learned how to avoid this type of aversive situation, and you behave accordingly.

negative reinforcement
The process by which people learn to perform acts that lead to the removal of undesired events.

avoidance
See *negative reinforcement.*

PUNISHMENT. Thus far, we have identified responses that are strengthened—either because they lead to positive consequences or the termination of negative consequences. However, the connection between a behavior and its consequences is not always strengthened; such links also may be weakened. This is what happens in the case of **punishment.** Punishment involves presenting an undesirable or aversive consequence in response to an unwanted behavior. A behavior accompanied by an undesirable outcome is less likely to reoccur if the person associates the negative consequences with the behavior. For example, if you are chastised by your boss for taking excessively long coffee breaks, you may be considered punished for this action. As a result, you will be less likely to take long breaks again in the future.

punishment
Decreasing undesirable behavior by following it with undesirable consequences.

EXTINCTION. The link between a behavior and its consequences also may be weakened by withholding reward—a process known as **extinction.** When a response that was once rewarded is no longer rewarded, it tends to weaken and eventually die out—or be *extinguished.* Let's consider an example. Suppose for many months you brought boxes of donuts to your weekly staff meetings.

extinction
The process through which responses that are no longer reinforced tend to gradually diminish in strength.

Your colleagues always thanked you as they gobbled them down. You were positively reinforced by their approval, so you continued bringing the donuts. Now, after several months of eating donuts, your colleagues' waists have begun to bulge, leading them to begin dieting. So, although tempting, your donuts go uneaten. After several months of no longer being praised for your generosity, you will be unlikely to continue bringing donuts. Your once-rewarded behavior will die out; it will be extinguished.

Observational Learning: Learning by Imitating Others

Although operant conditioning is based on the idea that we engage in behaviors for which we are directly reinforced, many of the things we learn on the job are *not* directly reinforced. Suppose, for example, on your new job you see one of your fellow sales representatives developing a potentially valuable sales lead by joining a local civic organization. Soon thereafter, talking to people around the office, you find out that yet another one of your colleagues has picked up a lucrative lead from a civic group to which he belongs. Chances are, after observing this several times, you too will eventually make the connection between joining such groups and getting sales leads. Although you may not have made useful contacts from such groups yourself, you would come to expect these leads to pan out on the basis of what you have observed from others. This is an example of a kind of learning known as **observational learning,** or **modeling.**[45] It occurs when someone acquires new knowledge *vicariously*—that is, by observing what happens to others. The person whose behavior is imitated is referred to as the *model*.

observational learning (modeling)
The form of learning in which people acquire new behaviors by systematically observing the rewards and punishments given to others.

STEPS IN THE OBSERVATIONAL LEARNING PROCESS. For people to learn by observing models, several processes must occur (for a summary of these, see Figure 3.14). These are as follows:

1. The learner must pay careful *attention* to the model; the greater the attention, the more effective the learning will be. To facilitate learning, models sometimes call attention to themselves. This is what happens when supervisors admonish their subordinates to "pay close attention" to what they're doing.
2. People must have good *retention* of the model's behavior. It helps to be able to develop a verbal description or a mental image of someone's actions to remember them. After all, we cannot learn from observing behavior we cannot remember.
3. There must be some *behavioral reproduction* of the model's behavior. Unless people are capable of doing exactly what the models do, they will not be able to learn from observing them. Naturally, this ability may be limited at first, but improve with practice.
4. Finally, people must have some *motivation* to learn from the model. Of course, we don't emulate every behavior we see, but we focus on those we have some reason or incentive to match—such as actions for which others are rewarded.

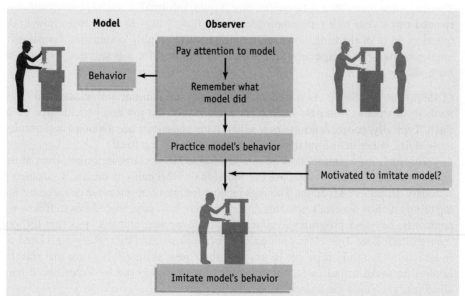

FIGURE 3.14

Observational Learning: An Overview

The process of *observational learning* requires that an observer pay attention to and remember a model's behavior. By observing what the model did and rehearsing those actions, the observer may learn to imitate the model, but only if the observer is motivated to do so (i.e., if the model was rewarded for behaving as observed).

EXAMPLES OF OBSERVATIONAL LEARNING IN ORGANIZATIONS. A great deal of what is learned about how to behave in organizations can be explained as the result of the process of observational learning.[46] For example, observational learning is a key part of many formal job instruction training programs.[47] As we will explain in the next section, trainees given a chance to observe experts doing their jobs, followed by an opportunity to practice the desired skills, and given feedback on their work, tend to learn new job skills quite effectively.

Observational learning also occurs in a very informal, uncalculated manner. For example, people who experience the norms and traditions of their organizations and who subsequently incorporate these into their own behavior may be recognized as having learned through observation. Indeed, people tend to learn the informal rules of their organizations through observational learning.

It is important to note that people learn not only what to do by observing others, but also what *not* to do. Specifically, research has shown that people observing their coworkers getting punished for behaving inappropriately on the job tend to refrain from engaging in those same actions themselves.[48] As you might imagine, this is a very effective way for people to learn how to behave—and without ever experiencing any displeasure themselves.

The principles of learning we have discussed thus far are used in organizations in many different ways. In the remaining part of this chapter, we discuss formal approaches to incorporating the various principles of learning in organizations—*training,* and practices involving the systematic use of rewards and punishments, such as *organizational behavior management* and *discipline.*

Training: Learning and Developing Job Skills

training
The process of systematically teaching employees to acquire and improve job-related skills and knowledge.

Probably the most obvious use to which principles of learning may be applied in organizations is **training**—the process through which people systematically acquire and improve the skills and knowledge needed to better their job performance. Just as students learn basic educational skills in the classroom, employees must learn job skills. Training is used not only to prepare new employees to meet the challenges of the jobs they will face, but also to upgrade and refine the skills of existing employees. The amount of money companies spend on training varies from industry to industry (most in finance and insurance, and least in retail), but averages over $1,200 per employee.[49] Although many companies trim their training budgets in financially difficult times, training is an excellent investment. It has been estimated that every $1 spent on training yields $4 in increased productivity and reduced turnover.[50] For an example of a company that is highly involved in training and highly successful at it, see Figure 3.15.

Varieties of Training Methods

Training takes many forms. Some training is quite informal in nature, consisting of having experienced employees take new employees under their wings to show them how to do the job in question. Most of the time, however, training involves highly systematic, formal efforts to teach employees how to do specific things that are required for job success. We now review these methods.

classroom training
The process of teaching people how to do their jobs by explaining various job requirements and how to meet them.

CLASSROOM TRAINING. As a student, you already are familiar with **classroom training.** In this method, instructors describe various requirements of the job and provide tips on how to meet them. Typically, people learning new skills in the classroom are given an opportunity to practice these skills, either in a simulated work setting or on the job itself.

Consider, for example, how people are trained as account representatives at the collection agency OSI. The account reps are the individuals who call consumers to arrange payment on seriously delinquent accounts. The reps receive four days of intensive classroom training, covering things such as approaches to take in getting people to pay, procedures to follow when sending payments, payment programs available to the consumer, and the laws that bill collectors are required to follow. This classroom training is supplemented by making simulated practice calls in which the budding reps get to practice their new skills. Following this training, they are allowed to make actual calls, but these are closely monitored by experienced personnel who stand ready to guide the trainee as needed.

AFP/Photos/Newscom.

FIGURE 3.15

And the Award for Training Goes to . . .

These employees of the large accounting firm PriceWaterhouse Coopers (PWC) are shown here preparing ballots to be sent to members of the Academy of Motion Picture Arts and Sciences, whose votes will determine Oscar winners. The firm's accountants are trained continuously to ensure they are kept abreast of changing standards and regulations as well as best practices in their industry. These efforts have been so extensive and successful that for three consecutive years (2008–2010) PWC has finished at the top of *Training* magazine's "Top 125" list of companies with the best training practices.

APPRENTICESHIP PROGRAMS. Growing in popularity today are formal **apprenticeship programs,** in which classroom training is systematically combined with on-the-job instruction over a long period (often several years in the case of skilled tradespeople such as carpenters, electricians, and masons). Recognizing the importance of such programs in developing human resources, the federal government has invested hundreds of millions of dollars in apprenticeship programs, encouraging training partnerships between government and private industry.[51] To ensure that people going into various trades are trained to appropriately high standards, many apprenticeship programs often are designed and regulated by professional trade associations. As just one example, the American Culinary Federation has long relied on a formal apprenticeship program to ensure the proper training of future chefs. This program specifies the nature and content of classroom experiences as well as the specific areas of competence that student chefs are expected to master while working under supervising chefs in restaurant kitchens.

apprenticeship programs
Formal training programs involving both on-the-job and classroom training usually over a long period, often used for training people in the skilled trades.

CROSS-CULTURAL TRAINING. Today, given the increasing globalization of the workplace, it is not surprising that many companies are sending their employees to work abroad. A growing number of companies are discovering that employees are more likely to succeed in their overseas assignments when they have been thoroughly trained in the culture of the country in which they will be living. Sure, it helps to know the language of the host country, but that's just the beginning. If you've ever lived in another country, or even visited one, for that matter, then you can appreciate how vital it would be to understand fully the culture of the people in any country in which you are doing business. With this in mind, many companies have been investing in **cross-cultural training (CCT),** a systematic way of preparing employees to live and work in another country.[52]

cross-cultural training (CCT)
A systematic way of preparing employees to live and work in another country.

TABLE 3.4 Summary of Techniques Used in Cross-Cultural Training (CCT)

People working overseas often are trained for their assignments using one or more of the techniques described here. Given the global nature of today's businesses, the importance of such training efforts cannot be overstated.

Technique	Description
Cultural briefings	Explain the major aspects of the host country culture, including customs, traditions, and everyday behaviors.
Area briefings	Explain the history, geography, economy, politics, and other general information about the host country and region.
Cases	Portray a real-life situation in business or personal life to illustrate some aspect of living or working in the host culture.
Role playing	Allows the trainee to act out a situation that he or she might face in living or working in the host country.
Culture assimilator	Provides a written set of situations that the trainee might encounter in living or working in the host country. Trainee selects from a set of responses to the situation and is given feedback as to whether it is appropriate and why.
Field experiences	Provide an opportunity for the trainee to go to the host country or another unfamiliar culture to experience living and working for a short time.

Source: Francesco, Anne Marie; Gold, Barry Allen, *International Organizational Behavior: Text Readings Cases,* 1st ed., © 1998. Electronically reproduced by permission of Pearson Education, Inc., Upper Saddle River, New Jersey. See Note 52.

Actually, CCT is not a single method, but a variety of specific training techniques that have proven effective. For a summary of some of the most effective CCT methods, see Table 3.4.

CORPORATE UNIVERSITIES. Many companies (e.g., Apple Computer, Motorola, and the Walt Disney Company, to name only a few) are so serious about training that they have developed their own **corporate universities**—facilities devoted to handling a company's training needs on a full-time basis.[53] Established in 1927, the "General Motors Institute," now known as "Kettering University," was the first corporate university. This Flint, Michigan, facility trains employees in almost every skill required by GM's worldwide employees. Among the best-known corporate universities is McDonald's "Hamburger University," in which McDonald's franchisees learn and/or polish the skills needed to successfully operate a McDonald's restaurant. Like several other companies, McDonald's has its own campus with full-time instructors.

Most corporate universities, however, offer less elaborate programs in more modest facilities run by either their human resources departments or a few top executives. Even very small start-up companies can have their own corporate universities by using any of a growing number of firms that provide customized educational services. Although their curricula vary widely, most corporate universities emphasize leadership development (which we will address in Chapter 13).

EXECUTIVE TRAINING PROGRAMS. Another popular form of training is **executive training programs**—sessions in which companies systematically attempt to develop the leadership skills of their top leaders.[54] In fact, the largest proportion of companies' training budgets, an average of 21 percent, falls into this category.[55] Executive training can be conducted by using in-house training staff, bringing in outside experts to train company personnel, sending trainees to specialized programs conducted by private consulting firms, or by registering them at continuing education programs offered at colleges and universities.[56] With respect to content, executive training programs cover a broad range of topics, and are often tailored to the specific needs of the companies that use them and the industries in which they operate. Topics frequently covered in such programs are methods for developing leadership skills and transforming organizations, both of which are addressed throughout this book (e.g., Chapters 13 and 16).

E-TRAINING. These days, because the investment in computer technology required to reach people in remote locations is so small, the vast majority of companies conducting training do at least some of it online. The term **e-training** is used to describe training based on

corporate universities
Centers devoted to handling a company's training needs on a full-time basis.

executive training programs
Sessions in which companies systematically attempt to develop their top leaders, either in specific skills or general managerial skills.

e-training
Training based on disseminating information online, such as through the Internet or a company's internal intranet network.

disseminating information online (e.g., through the Internet or a company's internal intranet network). Online training is so popular, in fact, that savvy investment companies (e.g., Chase Capital and Merrill Lynch) have been funneling tens of millions of dollars into companies such as Ninth House and Global Learning Systems, which provide multimedia employee training.[57]

In recent years, many companies have found it useful to use e-training. For example, the Buffalo, New York–based Delaware North, a contract food-service company, has used e-training as an efficient way to bring employees up to speed on new operations. According to Sherri Steinback, the company's manager of technical training and special projects, "We were rolling out a new financial application to over 125 units, and we needed an efficient way to train a diverse group scattered across the country."[58]

E-training also has been used in a wide variety of different industries.[59] Compared to traditional, classroom-based corporate training programs, the primary benefits of online training are (1) flexibility, (2) speed and efficiency, and (3) reduced cost. Given these considerations, it's not surprising that e-learning has been growing in popularity in recent years, comprising 20 percent of the time people spend in training activities.[60]

Despite these benefits, e-training is far from perfect. One problem that many companies are facing is that it is very costly for them to produce self-paced, online training materials (about six to eight times more, in many cases), which drastically cuts into any short-term savings that may result. Probably the most serious limitation of e-training is that many workers are uncomfortable with it. Even the most computer-savvy employees may find it deceptively easy to click ahead, thinking they know material that they really don't know that well. Others simply miss the social aspect of learning, the one-on-one experience they have in the classroom with their peers and the trainer (which, for some, may be a distraction). Indeed, some experts agree that one advantage of the traditional classroom experience is that it brought people together out of the office, a benefit that the more impersonal experience of sitting in front of a computer screen just cannot offer. In view of this, online technology may best be considered an adjunct to the total training package, a single tool rather than a replacement for the traditional, in-person training experience.

Principles of Learning: Keys to Effective Training

As you might imagine, no one approach to training is ideal. Some techniques are better suited to learning certain skills than are others. The reason for this is that various techniques incorporate different **principles of learning,** that is, the set of practices that make training effective. Not surprisingly, the best training programs often use many different approaches, thereby assuring that several different learning principles are incorporated into training.[61]

To appreciate what these particular principles are, just think about some of the ways you learned skills such as how to study, drive, or use a computer. Five particular principles are most relevant.

principles of learning
The set of practices that make training effective, such as participation, repetition, transfer of training, and feedback.

PROMOTE PARTICIPATION. People not only learn more quickly, but also retain the skills longer when they have been involved actively in the learning process. This is the practice of **participation.** The benefits of participation apply to the learning of both motor tasks as well as cognitive skills. For example, when learning to swim, there's no substitute for actually getting in the water and moving your arms and legs. In the classroom, students who listen attentively to lectures, think about the material, and get involved in discussions tend to learn more effectively than those who just sit passively.

participation
Active involvement in the process of learning; more active participation leads to more effective learning.

ENCOURAGE REPETITION. If you know the old adage "Practice makes perfect," you are already aware of the benefits of **repetition** on learning. Perhaps you learned the multiplication table, or a poem, or a foreign language phrase by going over it repeatedly. Indeed, mentally "rehearsing" such cognitive tasks has been shown to increase our effectiveness at performing them.[62] Scientists have established not only the benefits of repetition on learning, but also have shown that these effects are even greater when practice is spread over time than when it is lumped

repetition
The process of repeatedly performing a task so that it may be learned.

together. After all, when practice periods are too long, learning can suffer from fatigue, whereas learning a little bit at a time allows the material to sink in.

USE ACTIVE LEARNING.   For learning to be most effective, learners should be involved in an active manner (e.g., by completing some exercise), instead of a passive manner (e.g., by listening to lectures only). The term **active learning** is used to describe a collection of learner-centered techniques in which individuals are active participants in the learning process. In this way, it is akin to "learning by doing" but goes beyond it in several key ways. Specifically, active learning techniques give people control over their learning experience. They also require learners to explore and experiment with a task so they can figure out how to perform it themselves. Typically these techniques require learners to think carefully about the subject matter and to have emotional reactions to it. For an overview of the different techniques that fall into this category, see the summary in Table 3.5. Research has demonstrated that these techniques are quite effective in many different ways.[63]

CAPITALIZE ON TRANSFER OF TRAINING.   As you might imagine, for training to be most effective, what is learned during training sessions must be applied to the job. This is the idea of **transfer of training,** the degree to which training generalizes to actual work experiences. In general, the more closely a training program matches the demands and conditions faced on a job, the more effective that training will be. A good example is the elaborate simulation devices used to train pilots and astronauts. By closely simulating actual job conditions and equipment, the skills trained transfer to the job.[64]

GIVE FEEDBACK.   Regardless of the particular type of learning used, it is extremely difficult for learning to occur in the absence of **feedback**—that is, knowledge of the results of one's actions. Feedback provides information about the effectiveness of one's training, indicating improvements that need to be made.[65] For example, it is critical for people being trained as word processing operators to know exactly how many words they correctly entered per minute if they are to be able to gauge their improvement.

One type of feedback that has become popular in recent years is known as **360-degree feedback**—the process of using multiple sources from around the organization to evaluate the work of a single individual (see Figure 3.16). This goes beyond simply collecting feedback from superiors, as is customary, but extends the gathering of feedback from other sources, such as one's peers, direct reports (i.e., immediate subordinates), customers, and even oneself.[66] Many companies—including General Electric, AT&T, Monsanto, Florida Power and Light, DuPont, Westinghouse, Motorola, Fidelity Bank, FedEx, Nabisco, and Warner-Lambert, to name a few—have used 360-degree feedback to give more complete performance information to their employees, greatly improving not only their own work, but overall corporate productivity as well.[67]

active learning
A collection of learner-centered techniques in which individuals are active participants in the learning process.

transfer of training
The degree to which the skills learned during training sessions may be applied to performance of one's job.

feedback
Knowledge of the results of one's behavior.

360-degree feedback
The practice of collecting performance feedback from multiple sources at a variety of organizational levels.

TABLE 3.5 Active Learning Techniques

In contrast to traditional, passive learning, *active learning* gets people involved in the process of learning. The techniques summarized here are among the most widely used forms of active learning used today. As you can see, these differ with respect to the degree to which the trainer gets involved in guiding the trainee.

Technique	Description
Exploratory learning	Giving people opportunities to learn by exploring and experimenting with the task at hand so they can discover how to master it completely on their own
Guided exploration	Encouraging learners to explore things on their own but also helping by giving them directions to pursue that enable them to improve
Error framing	Instructing learners to make errors and to think about these as opportunities to learn
Mastery training	Encouraging learners to explore things on their own while also noting that errors are bound to occur and providing them with goals that help them master the skills involved

Source: Based on information in Bell & Kozlowski, 2008; see Note 68.

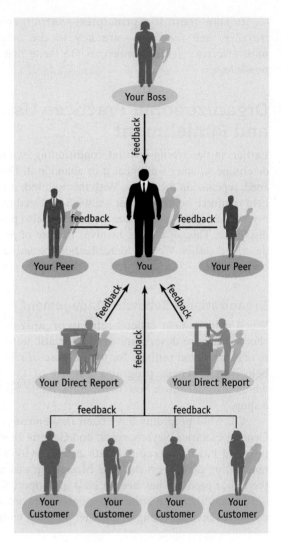

FIGURE 3.16

360-Degree Feedback: An Overview

Many companies rely on 360-degree feedback to provide valuable insight into how performance may be improved. As summarized here, this technique involves collecting performance feedback from multiple sources.

Despite its popularity, it's important to caution that 360-degree feedback isn't always successful; indeed, it sometimes is misused, resulting in more harm than good. This suggests that as a tool, 360-degree feedback should not be thrown into an organization with the blind hope that it will do some good. Instead, it's important to use this technique only under certain circumstances. For a summary of these conditions, see Table 3.6.[68]

TABLE 3.6 When Should 360-Degree Feedback Be Used?

For 360-degree feedback to be used successfully, it is essential that the following conditions be met. As outlined here, failure to adhere to these "four musts" may create problems that are likely to make the technique more of a liability than an asset.

For 360-Degree Feedback to Be Successful . . .	Or Else, the Following Problem May Occur . . .
Everyone involved must be trained carefully in how to give feedback.	People may be hurt by feedback that is destructive instead of constructive.
The consequences of engaging in poor performance must be spelled out clearly.	People may lack motivation to perform at a high level (see Chapter 7).
The behavior being measured must be essential to business success.	People may focus on improving their performance in ways that don't really matter.
The information collected must be used only for appropriate purposes, such as to improve performance.	People may believe that the information shared about them constitutes a violation of their privacy.

In sum, these five principles—*participation, repetition, active learning, transfer of training,* and *feedback*—are key to the effectiveness of any training program. The most effective training programs are those that incorporate as many of these principles as possible.

Organizational Practices Using Reward and Punishment

Earlier, in describing operant conditioning, we noted that the consequences of our behavior determine whether we repeat it or abandon it. Behaviors that are rewarded tend to be strengthened, repeated in the future. With this in mind, it is possible to administer rewards selectively to help reinforce behaviors that we wish repeated in the future. This is the basic principle behind *organizational behavior management.* It's also possible to influence workers' behavior by using discipline. This, of course, involves the use of *punishment,* a contingency of reinforcement we described earlier. We now describe both organizational behavior management and discipline in organizations.

Organizational Behavior Management

organizational behavior management (OB Mod)
The practice of altering behavior in organizations by systematically administering rewards.

When management experts refer to **organizational behavior management (OB Mod,** for short), they are describing the systematic application of positive reinforcement principles in organizational settings for the purpose of raising the incidence of desirable organizational behaviors.[69] These programs consist of the five general steps outlined in Table 3.7, which also describes how these steps might be followed in an effort to reduce accidents in a shop.

OB Mod programs have been implemented successfully at several companies, such as General Electric, Weyerhaeuser, and General Mills. At BFGoodrich, for example, an OB Mod program has been credited with productivity gains of 300 percent. However, it would be misleading to suggest that OB Mod programs are always successful. Where unsuccessful, the major problem has been a lack of support for rewarding desirable performance. This is unfortunate because some inexpensive rewards can go a long way toward bringing about desired behavioral changes. Another problem with OB Mod programs is that their effectiveness

TABLE 3.7 Steps for Creating an OB Mod Program

OB Mod programs involve following the five general steps listed on the left. To the right of each, an example is given of how each step might be applied to reducing accidents in a shop. Note how this involves the application of negative reinforcement.

Step	Example
1. Identify critical behaviors—that is, the particular behaviors you would like workers to perform.	You want to prevent workers from slipping on the shop floor.
2. For each critical behavior, obtain a baseline. This involves measuring how well people perform the desired task before anything is done to change it.	Count the number of times people slip on the shop floor over a typical month.
3. Analyze the behavior to determine the particular things that lead to it and that occur as a result.	After reviewing accident cases, you find that people are slipping because grease is dripping from parts being carried from place to place.
4. Using the information in step 3, develop an intervention—that is, an organizational program that seeks to raise the behavior in question by rewarding it when performed correctly.	Explain the dripping grease problem to workers and institute a program in which they are rewarded for being accident-free over certain periods of time. For example, after three accident-free months they might receive "I'm Safe" badges to affix to their shop coats. Larger gifts should be given in recognition of longer accident-free periods.
5. Assess how well the program is working. Repeat the process but implement changes designed to make it more effective.	Count accidents as done in step 2. If the rate has dropped, maintain the program. If not, revise it.

tends to be short term. As people get used to the rewards, they stop being special and need to be replaced by new ones. Ultimately, one would hope that employees would continue performing the desired behaviors in the absence of rewards, but as noted earlier, extinction is a potent phenomenon.

Discipline: Eliminating Undesirable Organizational Behaviors

Just as organizations systematically use rewards to encourage desirable behavior, they also use punishment to discourage undesirable behavior. Problems such as absenteeism, lateness, theft, and substance abuse cost companies vast sums of money, situations many companies attempt to manage by using **discipline**—the systematic administration of punishment. By administering an unpleasant outcome (e.g., suspension without pay) in response to an undesirable behavior (e.g., excessive tardiness), companies seek to minimize that behavior. In one form or another, using discipline is a relatively common practice. Most companies use some form of discipline, or at least the threat of discipline, in response to undesirable behaviors.[70]

discipline
The process of systematically administering punishments.

As you might imagine, disciplinary actions taken in organizations vary greatly. At one extreme, they may be very formal, such as written warnings that become part of the employee's permanent record. At the other extreme, they may be informal and low-key, such as friendly reminders and off-the-record discussions between supervisors and their problem subordinates.

In a survey, nursing supervisors were asked to list the disciplinary actions they most used and to rank them with respect to their severity.[71] The results, summarized in Figure 3.17, reveal that a broad range of disciplinary measures are used, ranging from most lenient to most harsh. Although this represents the responses of a limited sample, we suspect that these results are fairly typical of what would be found across a wide variety of jobs.

One very common practice involves using punishment *progressively*—that is, starting mildly, and then increasing in severity with each successive infraction. This is the idea behind **progressive discipline**—the practice of basing punishment on the frequency and severity of the infraction.[72] Let's consider an example of how progressive discipline might work for a

progressive discipline
The practice of gradually increasing the severity of punishments for employees who exhibit unacceptable job behavior.

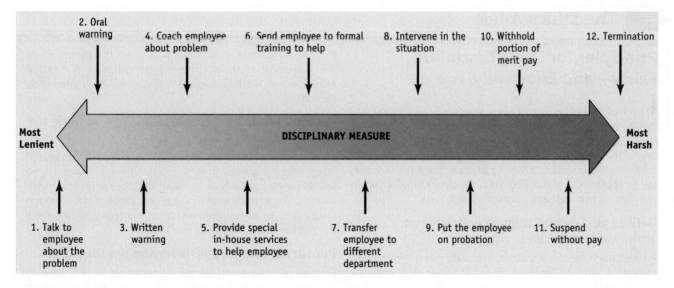

FIGURE 3.17

A Continuum of Disciplinary Measures

Ranked from mildest to most severe, these are the most commonly used disciplinary tactics used by nursing supervisors.

Source: Based on findings reported by Trahan & Steiner, 1994; see Note 71.

common problem such as chronic absenteeism or tardiness. First, the supervisor may give the employee an informal oral warning. Then, if the problem persists, there would be an official meeting with the supervisor, during which time a formal warning would be issued. The next offense would result in a formal written warning that becomes part of the employee's personnel record. Subsequent offenses would lead to suspension without pay. And finally, if all this failed, the employee would be terminated. In the case of more serious offenses—such as gambling, for example—some of the preliminary steps would be dropped, and a formal written warning would be given. For the most serious offenses, such as stealing or intentionally damaging company property, officials would move immediately to the most severe step, immediate dismissal.

Companies with the most effective disciplinary programs tend to *make the contingencies clear,* such as by specifying punishment rules in the company handbook. When this is done, employees know exactly what kind of behaviors the company will not tolerate, often minimizing the need to use discipline at all.

It probably comes as no surprise that supervisors do not always punish all inappropriate behaviors they encounter.[73] A key reason for this is that supervisors may feel constrained by limitations imposed by labor unions or by their own lack of formal authority. Also, in the absence of a clear company policy about how to use discipline, individuals may fear strong negative emotional reactions from the punished individual, if not also revenge and retaliation. As a result, many supervisors may turn the other way and simply do nothing when employees behave inappropriately. Although doing nothing may be easy in the long run, ignoring chronic problems is a way of informally approving of them, leading to increasingly serious problems in the future.

With this in mind, companies with the best disciplinary programs make it a practice to *take immediate action.* At Honda of America, for example, human resource specialist Tim Garrett notes that the company pays very close attention to all infractions of the rules, including ones "that other companies wouldn't think of paying attention to," adding, "If there's a problem, we'll pay attention to it right away."[74] (For a discussion of the principle underlying this practice and many others bearing on the use of discipline, see the The Ethics Angle section below.)

The Ethics Angle

Principles for Using Discipline Fairly—and Effectively, Too

It isn't easy to know exactly when and how to use discipline so that it can be done in a way that people consider fair and that has been shown to be effective. Fortunately, research has pointed to several principles that can be followed in this regard.[75] We now identify these, and using a running example, point out how they can be applied to a relatively common disciplinary situation: someone (let's call him Joe) being chronically late to work.

Deliver punishment immediately after an undesirable response occurs.

People's memories are imperfect, especially when they've done something wrong. The more time that passes after someone does something inappropriate, the less likely he or she is to remember the details of the act in question. As such, the connection between the particular negative behavior and the punishment will be weak. When this happens, the person being disciplined will be inclined to be unaware of what he or she did that requires punishment, leading that person to believe

that the punishment is unfair and to reject the person doing the punishing as mean. The recommendation is clear: If Joe arrives at work late, discuss this with him immediately thereafter.

Give moderate levels of punishment—nothing too high or too low.

If the consequences for performing an undesirable action are not very severe, it is unlikely to serve as a punishment. If they are too severe, people are likely to complain that they're unfairly harsh. Applying this to the late-arriving Joe, you should avoid being too lenient (e.g., by rolling your eyes) or too harsh (e.g., by firing him the first time he's a minute or two late).

Punish the undesirable behavior, not the person.

People's self-images are usually wrapped up in their jobs, so you don't want to lose those individuals by getting them to think negatively about themselves. Punishment should be impersonal in nature, focusing not on an individual's qualities, but on his or her actions. Make it clear that "it's not you" but "what you did." Applying this principle, you should refrain from calling Joe "lazy" but explain the problems that

(Continued)

result when he is not at his desk on time (e.g., customers cannot reach him).

Use punishment consistently across occasions.

If you sometimes fail to punish a wrongdoing, you may send the message that you sometimes can get away with breaking the rules. Then when you do issue a punishment, the wrongdoer is likely to think that it's unfair because you're enforcing the rule inconsistently (i.e., you're violating procedural justice; see Chapter 2). This would suggest that it's important to "write up" Joe (by putting a notation in his employee record) each and every time he is late.

Punish everyone equally for the same infraction.

If some people are punished while others are not, you will be accused of favoritism and will be considered unfair. After all, this inconsistency is a violation of procedural justice. It's critical to apply the rules evenly. Applying this to our example, it would be necessary to "write up" all employees whenever they are late, not just Joe.

Clearly communicate the reasons for the punishment given while showing dignity and respect.

Making clear exactly what behaviors lead to what disciplinary actions helps make punishment effective because it establishes those connections in the minds of the wrongdoers. Also, as suggested by the notion of informational justice, the explanation will help people perceive the punishment as fair, especially when it's made in a way that shows dignity and respect for the individual (i.e., when a high degree of interpersonal justice is shown). As for Joe, it's a good idea to explain that the punishment he receives is "nothing personal" and that you don't like having to do it, but company rules require you to take action. At this same time, it may be useful to work with Joe to figure out why he's chronically late and to find a way to avoid this.

Do not follow punishment with noncontingent rewards.

Managers sometimes attempt to minimize the pain of punishment by doing something nice to make up for it. This is a serious mistake because it reinforces bad behavior. For example, it may make everyone feel better if you were to send Joe home with pay so he could "think about the problem." However, this would send the message that "if you're late often enough you can get time off with pay," which would only make the problem worse. As a manager, then, you should resist the temptation to take away with one hand while giving with the other.

Managers should make every effort to follow these principles when disciplining employees. Not only do they represent the "right thing to do," but, at the same time, they also represent the "effective thing to do."

Summary and Review of Learning Objectives

1. **Distinguish between the concepts of social perception and social identity.**
   Social perception is the process through which people select, organize, and interpret the information around them as it pertains to other people. According to social identity theory, the way we perceive others and ourselves is based on both our own unique characteristics (known as personal identity) and our membership in various groups (known as social identity).

2. **Explain how the attribution process works and describe the various sources of bias in social perception.**
   The process of attribution involves judging the underlying reasons for people's behavior. Some of our judgments are based on inferences made on the basis of observing others' behavior. These judgments, known as correspondent inferences, are often inaccurate. Our search for explanations about the causes of others' behavior leads us to make either judgments of internal causality (the individual is responsible for his own actions) or external causality (someone or something else is responsible). Kelley's theory of causal attribution explains that such judgments will be based on three types of information: consensus (whether others act in a similar manner), consistency (whether the individual previously acted this way in the same situation), and distinctiveness (whether this person acted similarly in different situations).

   Several types of systematic errors, known as perceptual biases, limit the accuracy of social perception. These include the fundamental attribution error (the tendency to attribute others' actions to internal causes), the halo effect (the tendency to perceive others in either consistently positive or negative terms), the similar-to-me effect (the tendency to perceive similar others in a favorable light), first-impression error (the tendency for initial impressions to guide subsequent ones), and selective perception (the tendency for people to focus on only certain aspects of the environment). Perceptual inaccuracies also result from the tendency for people to rely on the use of stereotypes (the judgments of others based on the categories to which they belong).

Perceptual biases can result in self-fulfilling prophecies (the tendency for someone's expectations about another to cause that individual to behave in a manner consistent with those expectations). These can be positive in nature, such as when expecting someone's performance to be good actually makes it so (known as the Pygmalion effect). They also can be negative, such as when someone's performance is bad because it was expected to be bad (known as the Golem effect).

3. **Understand how the process of social perception operates in the contexts of employment interviews and performance appraisals.**

People are generally interested in getting others to perceive them favorably, and their efforts in this regard are referred to as impression management. This process is particularly important in employment interviews, although it sometimes interferes with the accuracy of information presented about individuals or companies. Biased judgments about others sometimes occur during the process of performance appraisal. In this context, people judge as superior those individuals whose performance matches their expectations, and those whose good performance is attributed to internal sources and whose poor performance is attributed to external sources.

4. **Define learning and describe the two types most applicable to OB: operant conditioning and observational learning.**

Learning refers to relative permanent changes in behavior occurring as a result of experience. In organizations, learning generally takes the form of *operant conditioning* and *observational learning.* In operant conditioning, individuals learn to behave certain ways based on the consequences of those actions. Stimuli that increase the probability of the behaviors preceding it are known as reinforcers. Reinforcement may be either *positive,* if it is based on the presentation of a desirable outcome, or *negative,* if it is based on the withdrawal of an unwanted outcome. The probability of certain responses can be decreased if an unpleasant outcome results (punishment), or if a pleasant outcome is withdrawn (extinction). Observational learning involves learning by modeling the behavior of others. By paying attention to and rehearsing the behavior of others, we can learn vicariously, that is, through the model's experiences.

5. **Describe how principles of learning are involved in organizational training and innovative reward systems.**

Learning is involved directly in efforts to teach people to acquire new job skills, the process known as training. Training is most effective when people can actively participate in the learning process, repeat the desired behaviors, receive feedback on their performance, and learn under conditions closely resembling those found on the job. Today, companies are experimenting with innovative reward systems that include skill-based pay (i.e., paying people for the various skills they have demonstrated on the job) and team-based rewards (i.e., paying people for their contributions to team performance).

6. **Compare the way organizations use reward in organizational behavior management programs and how they can use punishment most effectively when administering discipline.**

Organizational behavior management is a systematic attempt to apply principles of reinforcement to the workplace so as to improve organizational functioning. Reinforcing desired behaviors can improve organizational functioning greatly. In contrast to applications of reinforcement, discipline is the systematic application of punishments to minimize undesirable organizational behaviors. The effects of discipline are most effective when punishment is applied immediately after the undesirable activity, moderately severe, focused on the activity rather than the individual, applied consistently over time, and for all employees, clearly explained and communicated, and not weakened by the use of inadvertent rewards.

Points to Ponder

Questions for Review

1. What is social perception, and how is it applicable to the field of OB?
2. How do people come to make judgments about what others are like (known as the attribution process)?
3. In what ways is the attribution process biased, and what can be done about it?
4. How do operant conditioning and observational learning operate in the workplace?
5. What are the fundamental principles of learning, and how are they involved in organizations?
6. What should be done to ensure that efforts to punish employees are as effective as possible?

Experiential Questions

1. Think of a time when you made judgments about a new workmate as you got to know him or her. In what ways were these judgments biased? As you got to know this person better, did you change your mind? What lesson can you learn about reaching judgments about people prematurely?
2. As a manager, it's important not to judge employees based on your expectations. If you do, the Pygmalion effect or the Golem effect may occur. Think back at a situation on the job or at school in which either you or your supervisor/teacher had expectations that led to one of these self-fulfilling prophecies. Exactly what

happened? How was everyone involved affected, both positively and negatively? What could have been done to avoid this problem?

3. Think about any work-related training programs in which you may have been involved. In what ways were these efforts successful? What might have been done to make them even more effective?

Questions to Analyze

1. The attribution process is inherently inaccurate and subject to bias. In view of this, what chance do you think managers have of making accurate assessments of their subordinates' job performance? What could be done to combat these limitations, thereby making these important assessments more accurate?
2. E-learning is very popular today. What specific advice would you give anyone launching a corporate e-learning program who wants to make it as effective as possible? Do you think e-learning can ever be as effective as in-person training? In what ways might it be even more effective than in-person training?
3. Overall, do you think that managers will be able to more effectively change their subordinates' performance by using reward or by using punishment? However you answer, what specific steps would you take to make these efforts most effective? Explain your recommendations.

Experiencing OB

Individual Exercise

Identifying Occupational Stereotypes

Although we usually reserve our concern over stereotypes to those about women and members of racial and ethnic minorities, the simple truth is that people can hold stereotypes toward members of just about *any* group. And, in organizations, people are likely to hold stereotypes based on a variable whose importance cannot be downplayed—the occupational groups to which they belong. What we expect of people, and the way we treat them, is likely to be affected by stereotypes about their professions. This exercise will help you better understand this phenomenon.

Directions

Using the following scale, rate each of the following occupational groups with respect to how much of each characteristic people in these groups tend to show.

1 = not at all

2 = a slight amount

3 = a moderate amount

4 = a great amount

5 = an extreme amount

Accountants	Professors	Lawyers
——— interesting	——— interesting	——— interesting
——— generous	——— generous	——— generous
——— intelligent	——— intelligent	——— intelligent
——— conservative	——— conservative	——— conservative
——— shy	——— shy	——— shy
——— ambitious	——— ambitious	——— ambitious

Clergy	Physicians	Plumbers
——— interesting	——— interesting	——— interesting
——— generous	——— generous	——— generous
——— intelligent	——— intelligent	——— intelligent
——— conservative	——— conservative	——— conservative
——— shy	——— shy	——— shy
——— ambitious	——— ambitious	——— ambitious

Questions for Discussion

1. Did your ratings of the various groups differ? If so, which were perceived most positively and which were perceived most negatively?
2. On what characteristics, if any, did you find no differences with respect to the various groups? What do you think this means?
3. To what extent did your ratings agree with those of others? In other words, was there general agreement about the stereotypical nature of people in various occupational groups?
4. To what extent were your responses based on specific people you know? How did knowledge, or lack of knowledge, of members of the various occupational groups influence your ratings?
5. Do you believe that by becoming aware of these stereotypes you will perpetuate them in the future, or refrain from behaving in accord with them? Explain.

Group Exercise

Role Play: Conducting a Disciplinary Interview

Knowing how to discipline employees who behave inappropriately is an important managerial skill. The trick is to change the bad behavior into good behavior permanently, getting people to accept their mistakes and understand how to correct them. As you might imagine, this is often far more difficult than it sounds. After all, people are generally reluctant to admit their errors, and may have developed bad work habits that must be overcome. In addition, they tend to resist being chastised and don't like listening to criticism. With this in mind, disciplining others represents quite a challenge for managers, making it a skill worth developing.

Directions

1. Select four students from the class and divide them into two pairs. One person from each pair should read only the role sheet for Andy F., machine operator, and the other person from each pair should read only the role sheet for Barry B., his supervisor. Send both pairs outside the room until called on.
2. Members of the class will serve as observers and should read both role sheets.
3. Call in the first pair of role players and ask them to spend about 10 to 15 minutes playing their roles—that is, acting as they would if they were the characters about whom they just read in the role sheets. They should feel free to assume any additional facts not described in these sheets.

4. Members of the class should observe the role play, taking careful notes. The class should *not* get involved in what the actors are saying, but pay close attention to it.
5. Repeat steps 3 and 4 with the second pair of role players.

Role Sheets

Andy F., Machine Operator

You have worked at Acme Manufacturing for six years now and have had a good record. Because you do your job so well, you sometimes take liberties and horse around with your buddies. For example, one Friday afternoon you were caught dancing around the shop floor when a good song came on the radio. Barry B., your supervisor, called you on the carpet for leaving your station. You think he has it in for you and is trying to run you off the job. Although you were acting silly, you are convinced that it doesn't matter since you were getting your job done. Now, he has called you in to see him to discuss the situation.

Barry B., Supervisor

After several years of experience in other shops, you were hired by Acme Manufacturing to be its new shop supervisor, a job you've had for only four months. Things have gone well during that time, but you've been having trouble with one machine operator, Andy F. Andy seems to do an acceptable job, but is not giving it his all. Part of the problem is that he goofs around a lot. You have spoken to him about this informally a few times on the floor, but to no avail. One Friday afternoon you caught him away from his station, dancing around the shop floor. Not only wasn't he doing his own job, but he was distracting the others as well. You have just called Andy in to see you to discuss the situation.

Questions for Discussion

1. Did the supervisor, Barry B., define the problem in a nonthreatening way?
2. Did each party listen to the other, or did they shut each other out, merely explaining their own sides of the story?
3. Did Barry B. suggest specific things that Andy F. could do to improve? Were the specific punishments associated with future bad acts spelled out explicitly?
4. Were the discussions impersonal in nature, or did the parties focus on each other's personalities?
5. Considering all these questions, which supervisor would you say did a better job of administering discipline? What could be done to improve the way each supervisor conducted the disciplinary meeting?

Practicing OB

Managing People Who Are Goofing Off

Employees at a corporate call center have not been spending enough time at their cubicles answering phones, as required. Instead, they've been walking throughout the facility, talking to each other about personal matters. In other words, they're socializing and goofing off instead of working. Important calls have gone unanswered and customer service problems have arisen as a result.

1. What types of attributions would you be prone to make about these employees, and how would these be related to the performance evaluations you give them?
2. What types of errors would you be prone to make while making these judgments, and what might you do to overcome them so that you can make more accurate judgments?
3. How might you use training, innovative reward systems, organizational behavior management programs, and discipline to address the problem?

■ *Smiling Might Not Be Such a Safe Way to Treat Safeway Customers*

Any training course on the essentials of customer service will advise you always to smile at customers and to make eye contact with them. In fact, it seems so commonsensical as to not need repeating. Little would you imagine, therefore, that doing precisely this actually would cause problems for some supermarket clerks! Nonetheless, this is precisely what happened to a dozen female employees at a Safeway supermarket in Martinez, California. The women claimed that their eye contact and smiles elicited unwanted attention from some male shoppers who mistook these friendly gestures as acts of flirting. Some clerks even had to resort to hiding in the store to escape customers who were hungry for services that weren't for sale. A produce clerk at one northern California store was even followed to her car and propositioned by a supermarket shopper who got the wrong idea.

The root of the problem, argue the 12 clerks who filed grievances with the United Food and Commercial Workers Union, is Safeway's "Superior Service" policy, which explicitly requires them to smile at customers and to maintain three seconds of eye contact with each one. It also expects clerks to anticipate customers' needs, to help them find items for which they're looking, and to call them by name if paying by check or credit card.

This policy was in place for five years before Safeway officials started enforcing it by using undercover shoppers to spot violators, who were sent letters warning them of the negative evaluations and disciplinary measures (even firing!) that could result from failing to comply. Soon thereafter, the incidents of customer harassment began. The union is seeking a modified policy that gives workers some discretion in the matter, allowing them to choose whether or not to maintain eye contact or to refuse to carry a customer's bags to his car at night.

From its headquarters in Pleasanton, California, Safeway officials acknowledged that although some customers get out of hand, this is not the result of their policy. They add that not one of the store's employees, currently about 200,000, ever has been fired for failing to be friendly. However, 100 have been sent to a daylong remedial training class on friendliness, what they call "Smile School." This, says Safeway spokesperson Debra Lambert, "is not about discipline. It's about treating customers well and training employees to do that." Think about this when you complain about that surly clerk who doesn't even look up to acknowledge you the next time you're in your local supermarket looking for laundry detergent.

Questions for Discussion

1. How, specifically, is the process of attribution illustrated in this case?
2. What do you suppose is being done to help train people to be friendlier toward customers? In other words, what would you imagine goes on in Safeway's "Smile School"?
3. Describe what you believe might be the progressive discipline steps outlined in the warning letter sent to unfriendly Safeway clerks.

4 Individual Differences: Personality, Skills, and Abilities

Learning Objectives

After reading this chapter, you should be able to:

1. Define personality and describe its role in the study of organizational behavior.

2. Identify the Big Five dimensions of personality and elements of core self-evaluations, and describe how they are related to key aspects of organizational behavior.

3. Distinguish between positive and negative affectivity, and describe its effects on organizational behavior.

4. Describe achievement motivation, and distinguish among learning, performance, and avoidance goal orientations.

5. Describe Machiavellianism and the difference between morning and evening persons, and their role in work-related behavior.

6. Differentiate among cognitive intelligence, practical intelligence, and emotional intelligence and explain the influence of social skills on behavior in organizations.

Chapter Outline

- Personality: Its Basic Nature
- Major Work-Related Aspects of Personality: The "Big Five," Positive Versus Negative Affectivity, and Core Self-Evaluations
- Additional Work-Related Aspects of Personality
- Abilities and Skills: Having What It Takes to Succeed

Preview Case

■ *Kenneth Chenault: An American Success at American Express*

For American Express (AMEX), 2009 was a challenging year. Faced with a slumping economy, cardholders curbed their spending dramatically, and record numbers of even the wealthiest members had delinquent accounts. Despite this gloomy, recessionary profile, AMEX's chairman and CEO, Kenneth I. Chenault, vowed to turn things around—a proclamation that Wall Street would have dismissed as puffery had it come from an executive without a quarter-century of successes on his résumé.

Since joining AMEX in 1981, Chenault systematically worked his way to the top by masterminding a string of turnarounds in each unit he headed. In the mid-1980s, for example, he put himself on the map by reviving the once-struggling merchandise services unit. Partnering with Panasonic and Sharp (who were looking for markets for their new video recorders), he up-scaled the merchandise mix—which used to consist of only low-ticket items such as luggage tags and clocks—boosting annual sales from $100 million to $700 million in just a few years.

Basking in the glow of this accomplishment, Chenault earned a ticket to the company's more prestigious consumer-card division, where he transformed an admittedly uncompetitive niche company into a vast financial empire. One key to this success involved expanding the company's limited base of wealthy customers to less affluent people and signing on lower-level merchants who never took American Express cards, such as gas stations, discount stores, and supermarkets—eventually, even Wal-Mart. Aiding this effort, and in a move that raised more than a few eyebrows in the New York headquarters, Chenault slashed the fees that merchants were charged for processing customers' purchases (which, traditionally, were much higher than competitors MasterCard and Visa). Despite reduced individual-transaction revenue, the company more than made up the difference in increased volume. As Chenault transformed AMEX into a card for the masses, the company's income skyrocketed each year he was at the helm.

Behind Chenault's many accomplishments is a man who, since high school, has been exceptionally analytical in his approach to life. This comes across in his careful analyses of missteps (and there have been these as well) to ensure that they won't be repeated and by his penchant for encouraging his colleagues to question his ideas in a constructive manner. The more they challenge him, the more he thinks about the problem at hand. Given his highly analytical approach, it's not surprising that as a student at Bowdoin College and later at Harvard Law School, Chenault became known for debating important issues in a logical, unemotional and fact-driven style.

A proud African American, Chenault never let race serve as a basis for choosing sides of an issue. A colleague once noted that "Ken has the capacity to operate in the mainstream of both worlds" and is "never shunned by one group or the other." As Chenault rose through the ranks at AMEX based on his exceptional successes, people of all races were pulling for him—and were duly proud of him. Chenault is a leading figure in his field who just happens to be African American but whose winning appeal is universal.

Those who work with Chenault know him to be uncombative in style, but always honest and likable, a true gentleman. It would be a grievous error to take Chenault's quiet ways as a sign that he is anything less than a fierce competitor. Just as he wasn't afraid to take on the naysayers who were against the changes he brought about at AMEX, he also hasn't been afraid to take on competitors in the credit card business. In fact, over four years, Chenault ushered AMEX through a legal battle against Visa and MasterCard, claiming that these companies were guilty of restraint of trade by not allowing banks to issue American Express cards. In July 2008, just as bad financial news was released, AMEX won a $4 billion settlement—a tidy sum that will mitigate AMEX's financial losses during a difficult period. Chalk up another victory for Chenault.

If you were to describe Mr. Chenault, what terms would you use? Would you say he's dedicated? A visionary? A risk taker? Surely, he's all these things and more. No matter how you put it, Ken Chenault is quite special and a highly successful businessperson, to say the least. Many of us surely find it difficult to relate to such a unique individual. That makes sense. However, in our own ways—even if we aren't CEOs of giant financial services firms—we are each unique. After all, each of us has a one-of-a-kind mix of traits, characteristics, skills, and abilities—a combination that makes us different, in various ways, from every other human being on the planet.

individual differences
The many ways in which individuals differ from each other.

Scientists refer to the ways in which people differ from one another as **individual differences,** and such unique qualities can have major influences on our thinking and behavior as well as our lives and careers. Because such factors play a role in many aspects of behavior in work settings, they have long been of interest to experts in the field of organizational behavior. As such, in this chapter we provide a broad overview of this knowledge.

Our plan is as follows. First, we focus on *personality,* one very important aspect of individual differences. Here, we first consider the matter of how various facets of personality combine with elements of the work environment to influence behavior. This is important because according to the popular *interactionist perspective* to organizational behavior, how we behave is based on both who we are (i.e., individual influences) and the contexts in which we operate (i.e., situational influences).[1] Following this, we turn to the question of how personality can be measured. Since personality traits are not physical quantities that can be observed readily, measuring them can be challenging, but, as we will describe, researchers are able to assess personality quite effectively. Then, after describing these measurement methods, we discuss a variety of personality variables that have important effects in the workplace. Finally, in another major section, we will examine several *abilities* (mental and physical capacities to perform various tasks) and *skills* (proficiency at performing specific tasks acquired through training or experience) and their effects on various aspects of organizational behavior.

Personality: Its Basic Nature

How would you describe your own personality in a single sentence? Admittedly, that's a very difficult task, because what makes each of us unique is complex and hard to put into words. But personality involves more than just uniqueness. Since understanding the nature of personality is crucial to appreciating its potential role in organizational behavior, we begin by taking a closer look at this important concept.

What Is Personality?

As we noted earlier, we are all, in some ways, *unique*—that is, we all possess a distinct pattern of traits and characteristics not fully duplicated in any other person. Further, this pattern of traits tends to be stable over time.[2] Thus, if you know someone who is optimistic, confident, and friendly today, then chances are good that he or she also showed these same traits in the past and will continue to do so in the future. Together, these two features form the basis for a useful working definition of **personality**—the unique and relatively stable pattern of behavior, thoughts, and emotions shown by individuals (see Figure 4.1).[3] As we will describe in this chapter, personality plays an important role in organizational behavior.

personality
The unique and relatively stable pattern of behavior, thoughts, and emotions shown by individuals.

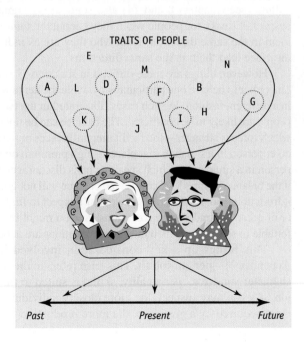

FIGURE 4.1

Personality: Defining Characteristics

When we speak of personality, we are referring to each individual's unique blend of traits that is relatively stable over time.

Personality and Situations: The Interactionist Approach

Earlier, we indicated that personality often combines with situational factors to influence behavior. Although people possess stable traits and characteristics that predispose them to behave in certain ways, these qualities by themselves do not completely determine how someone will behave in any given setting. Situations also introduce forces that affect how one is likely to behave. Together, both personal factors and situational factors combine to influence behavior. In other words, the way someone behaves is the result of both an individual's characteristics (e.g., his or her knowledge, abilities, skills, and personality) and the nature of the situation in which that person operates (e.g., the nature of the job and industry, the country in which the work is being performed, etc.). This approach, known as the **interactionist perspective,** is very popular in the field of OB today.[4]

interactionist perspective
The view that behavior is a result of a complex interplay between personality and situational factors.

Let's consider an example. Someone with a quick temper may be predisposed to act aggressively, but he or she may refrain from expressing anger (e.g., by screaming at a coworker) because of the negative consequences of doing so in that setting (e.g., losing a job, getting into legal trouble). In this case, the situation imposes demands to hold aggression in check. It's also possible, of course, that someone's aggressive tendencies are so strong that they override the demands of the situation, resulting in tragic consequences. It's useful to think of the interactionist perspective, as illustrated in Figure 4.2, as a combined set of forces—individual and situational—that can tip the balance so as to influence behavior in a certain way at any particular time.

In the field of organizational behavior, the question of whether various aspects of personality affect job performance has long been of interest.[5] As we will note later in this chapter, certain aspects of personality are indeed related to job performance. Although this is important, it doesn't tell the whole story, however. The strength of the effects of personality depends on many situational factors. These may include such factors as *job demands* (i.e., the set of tasks and duties associated with a specific job that motivates people to behave in certain ways; see Chapter 7) and *social norms* (i.e., pressures to go along with others in one's group; see Chapter 8). Overall, both personality and situational factors can serve as *facilitators*—factors that encourage certain behaviors, or *constraints*, factors that discourage certain behaviors.[6]

We present these in generic form in Figure 4.2, but let's now consider some specific scenarios. First, as depicted in *situation 1,* suppose you are a very quiet person, someone who is inclined to keep quiet most of the time. This would discourage you from saying anything, but you would be even more strongly disinclined from saying anything if you perceive the organization as discouraging people from speaking their minds (e.g., by punishing those who speak up at meetings). Now, consider *situation 2,* in which things are opposite. Here, suppose you are a very expressive person, someone who is inclined to speak up about things. This would facilitate voicing your opinions, but you would be especially likely to do so when organizational norms and culture (see Chapters 8 and 14) also send strong signals that this is encouraged. As you might suspect, it's easy for people when they encounter *situation 1* or *situation 2* because all forces lead them in the same direction. Both who they are as individuals and the demands of the situations they face lead them in the same directions.

However, things are more difficult in *situations 3 and 4.* Here, an individual's personality leads him or her to behave one particular way while the demands of the situation lead that person to behave in a different fashion. In such cases (illustrated in the two diagrams in the lower half of Figure 4.2), people are likely to be conflicted. The balance can be tipped slightly in either direction, depending on which force is stronger—the facilitating influences or the constraining influences. So, for example, a quiet person in a situation that places a high premium on speaking up (*situation 3*) and an expressive person in a situation in which speaking up is discouraged may go ever so slightly one way or another if the balance is tipped. Of course, the balance will not go too far because the opposite force will keep it from doing so. As a result, we wouldn't expect to find particularly high degrees of expressiveness or of quietness under such conditions. As you might imagine, people are likely to be quite uncomfortable in settings in which their predispositions are at odds with the demands of the situation.

person-job fit
The extent to which the traits and abilities of individuals match the requirements of the jobs they must perform.

This brings up a key consideration involved in selecting certain career options (see Appendix 2)—**person-job fit.** This term refers to the degree to which a person's unique blend of characteristics (e.g., personality, skills) is suited to the requirements for success on a particular job.[7] As you may suspect, the more closely individuals' personalities, traits, and abilities match those required by a given job, the more productive and satisfied they tend to be on those jobs.[8]

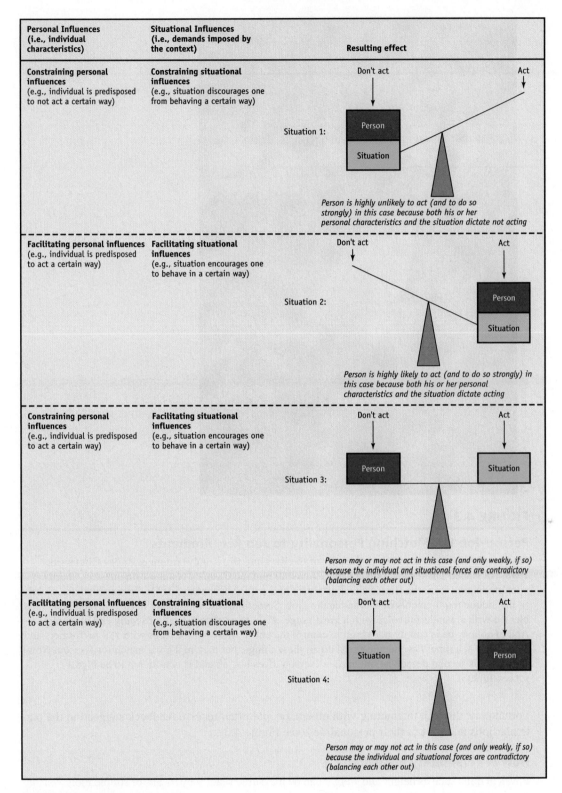

FIGURE 4.2

The Interactionist Perspective

This popular approach to the study of personality suggests that behavior in almost any context is a joint function of both characteristics of the individuals being considered and aspects of the specific context in which they are behaving. Various ways in which personalities and situations may either constrain or facilitate behavior are summarized here.

Zuma Wire West Photos/Newscom.

FIGURE 4.3

Person-Job Fit: Matching Personality to Job Requirements

Jonathan Lee Iverson has been ringmaster of the Ringling Bros. and Barnum & Bailey Circus since 1998. He landed this unusual job at age 22 (making him the Circus's youngest ringmaster), shortly after graduating from the Hartt School of Music in Hartford, Connecticut. Mr. Iverson's talents closely fit the unique requirements of this demanding job. Sometimes the ringmaster must sing, and Iverson is blessed with a wonderful voice with a great range. Also, he is exceptionally friendly and outgoing. And of course, he is simply not afraid to control the entire show—three rings with 180 performers and 80 animals at a time. Few people could do all these things, but they're a great match for Iverson. Now well into his second decade as ringmaster, Iverson loves his job and is considered to be highly successful at it.

Fortunately, through interacting with others, people often receive feedback suggesting the particular jobs that best fit their personalities (see Figure 4.3).

How Is Personality Measured?

Physical traits such as height and weight can be measured readily by means of simple tools. Various aspects of personality, however, cannot be assessed quite so simply. There are no rulers that we can put to the task. How, then, can we quantify differences between individuals with respect to their various personality characteristics? Several methods exist for accomplishing this task. In this section, we describe two of the most important techniques. Finally, we consider some of the essential requirements that all procedures for measuring individual differences must meet.

OBJECTIVE TESTS: PAPER-AND-PENCIL MEASURES OF WHO WE ARE. Have you ever completed a questionnaire in which you were asked to indicate whether each of a set of statements is true or false about yourself, the extent to which you agree or disagree with various sentences, or which of several pairs of activities you prefer (e.g., attending a football game versus reading a book)? If so, you appear to have completed what is known as an **objective test**—a paper-and-pencil inventory in which people are asked to respond to a series of questions designed to measure one or more aspects of their personalities. Objective tests are the most widely used method of measuring both personality and mental abilities (such as intelligence).

People's answers to the questions on objective tests are scored by comparing individuals' answers to special scoring keys. The score obtained by a specific person is then compared with those obtained by hundreds or even thousands of other people who have taken the test previously. In this way, an individual's relative standing on the trait or ability being measured can be determined. This can then be used to predict various aspects of behavior, such as success in specific kinds of jobs or training.

objective tests
Questionnaires and inventories designed to measure various aspects of personality.

PROJECTIVE TESTS. A very different approach to measuring personality is adopted in what are known as *projective tests*. These tests present individuals with ambiguous stimuli—for instance, a drawing of a scene in which it is not clear what the persons shown are doing. Individuals taking such tests then report what they perceive, and their answers are used as a basis for reaching conclusions about their personalities. Presumably, one reason why different people report "seeing" different things in the ambiguous stimuli they examine is that they differ with respect to personality; and such differences then, supposedly, become visible in their responses.

Do such tests really work—do they really provide insights into personality? There is considerable controversy over this issue so, except for a few widely used tests (e.g., one that measures the need for achievement), projective tests are not very popular among researchers in the field of OB. Instead, most prefer to use the objective tests described earlier. Now, let's turn to questions that relate to all measures of personality—questions about whether these measures really allow us to assess the variables we want to measure.

RELIABILITY AND VALIDITY: ESSENTIAL REQUIREMENTS OF PERSONALITY TESTS. Imagine that you weigh yourself on your bathroom scale every morning. One day, the weight reads "150 pounds." The next day, it reads "140 pounds." Although you may be happy with at least one of these results, you would probably suspect that something is wrong because you could not possibly have lost 10 pounds overnight. Instead, it is much more likely that there is something wrong with the scale. It is not recording your weight accurately. More formally, we would say that it is not measuring your weight in a *reliable* manner.

Clearly, to have confidence in something we measure—weight, various aspects of personality, or anything else—we must be able to measure it reliably. The **reliability** of a measure refers to the extent to which it is stable and consistent over time. As you might imagine, a measure of personality must have a high degree of reliability for it to be useful. Only those tests that show high degrees of reliability are used in research in the field of OB. After all, tests that do not yield reliable results may tell us little—or, even worse, they may be misleading.

reliability
The extent to which a test yields consistent scores on various occasions, and the extent to which all of its items measure the same underlying construct.

In addition to being reliable, a test must also be *valid*—that is, it must really measure what it claims to measure. To understand, think about those "tests" that often appear in popular magazines, such as ones with the provocative title, "Are You Compatible with Your Mate?" Considering that this is an interesting question, you go through the questions, check a few boxes, and then go to the scoring key to see if you'll be enjoying a life of bliss or if you'll end up in divorce court. Although you might find this exercise interesting and fun, and it might cause you to think about important things in your relationship, chances are good that this so-called test is not valid. In other words, such an exercise probably hasn't been tested by scientists to see if people's scores really do predict how their relationship ends up. In this case, we would say that the measure is low in *validity*. The term **validity** refers to the extent to which a test measures what it actually claims to measure. Naturally, we seek tests that have high degrees of validity because we can be confident of what their scores mean (for an example of the opposite of this, see Figure 4.4). Tests that are low in validity, however, are essentially useless. This is the case even if the test is reliable. After all, if a test reliably suggests inaccurate things, it certainly is without merit.

validity
The extent to which a test actually measures what it claims to measure.

How do we assess a test's validity? In actual practice, the process is complex, requiring many steps and sophisticated statistical procedures. In essence, though, a test's validity is established by demonstrating that scores on it are related to other aspects of behavior that already are known to reflect the trait being measured. In other words, a test of a personality trait is valid to the extent that what it measures is closely related to the "true" measure of that trait, as assessed by other established tests. For instance, a test of sales ability would be valid to the extent that successful

Evan Forsch/Evan Forsch Cartoon, Comics & Illustrations.

FIGURE 4.4

A Not-So-Valid Personality Test

It may be fun to think you can learn about people's personalities by how they squeeze tubes of toothpaste. However, because no scientific efforts have been made to determine if the squeezing of toothpaste tubes really means anything at all, such a "test" would have to be considered not valid. As such, it should not be used—except, of course, to get toothpaste out of a tube.

predictive validity
The extent to which the score achieved on a test administered to a person at one time predicts (i.e., is correlated with) some measure of his or her performance at some later time.

salespersons score high on it whereas those who are unsuccessful score low. Only to the extent that its validity has been so established would it be useful for selecting potential employees—ones likely to succeed at selling. Scientists refer to this type of validity as **predictive validity.** This term refers to the extent to which scores on a test administered at one time are correlated with scores on some performance measure assessed at a later time (see Figure 4.5).

Another example of predictive validity can be seen in the test you might have taken for admission into college, graduate school, or professional school. Such tests are considered valid because the individuals who score high on them tend to perform better in school than those who

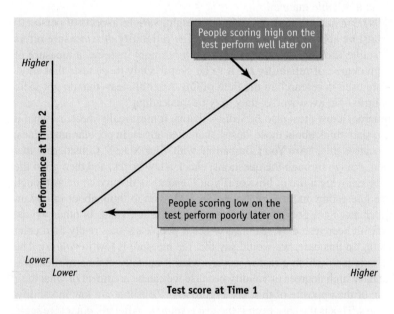

FIGURE 4.5

Predictive Validity

When a test has a high degree of predictive validity, it is able to predict performance assessed at some later point in time. The positive correlation between the test score and the measure of job performance shown here provides evidence of a high degree of predictive validity. This is desirable because it makes it possible to predict how someone will behave in the future based on tests administered in the present.

score lower. This positive correlation (see Appendix 1) between the test score and a measure of success (i.e., higher scores are associated with greater success) is an indication of its predictive validity. And this, of course, is precisely why colleges and universities rely on such tests. After all, if they didn't help predict success in their programs, there'd be no reason to use them.

At this point, we should note that all the traits and abilities considered in this chapter are measured by tests known to be both reliable and valid. Thus, you can have confidence in the findings we report concerning their relationships to important aspects of organizational behavior.

Do Organizations Have Personalities Too?

If you ask people what qualities come to mind when they think of Microsoft, chances are good that they'd say things like "arrogant" and "dominant." However, if you asked them about the Walt Disney Company, they'd likely say "family-oriented" and "friendly." Such responses seem to suggest that people think of organizations, much like people, as having certain traits—unique, stable characteristics that set them apart from other organizations—that is, distinct *personalities*. Can this be true? In one sense, it cannot. After all, organizations are not living entities and do not possess emotions, thoughts, or memories. In another sense, though, there is no doubt that we often *think about* organizations as though they do have distinct personalities (see Figure 4.6).

FIGURE 4.6

What Are These Organizations Like?

When asked to describe organizations, people tend to use qualities akin to human personality traits. For example, research has shown that although both Nike and Disney are considered to be highly innovative, Disney is seen as being a friendly, Boy Scout–type company, whereas Nike is considered a highly dominant and stylish company.

Source: Based on findings by Slaughter, Zickar, Highhouse, & Mohr, 2004; see Note 9.

If organizations have personalities, then what particular traits describe them? One team of researchers looked at this question.[9] Hundreds of business school students in the study were asked to rate several familiar companies (e.g., AT&T, Ford, McDonald's, Kroger, Wal-Mart, Subway, Bob Evans, JCPenney, Disney, Microsoft, Reebok, and Nike) on various traits. Interestingly, several distinct clusters emerged, with various companies rated highly on each. These clusters, traits describing them, and some of the companies rating highly on them are as follows:

- *Boy Scout:* friendly, attentive to people—Disney, Bob Evans
- *Innovative:* interesting, unique—Nike, Disney
- *Dominant:* successful, popular—Nike, Microsoft
- *Thrifty:* poor, sloppy—Bob Evans, JCPenney
- *Stylish:* modern, contemporary—Nike, Reebok

It's interesting that some companies rated highly on more than one cluster of characteristics. This shouldn't be too surprising because, just as some individuals possess high amounts of more than one personality characteristic, so too may organizations. For example, that Nike was perceived to be innovative, dominant, and stylish may square well with your own perception of this company.

Clearly, various companies are viewed as possessing different clusters of traits, but are these related to anything important? Do they really matter? The researchers who conducted this study predicted that organizational personalities would be linked to *organizational attractiveness*—the extent to which individuals perceive organizations as attractive places in which to work. To test this prediction, they prepared descriptions of a fictitious company that depicted it as possessing high amounts of the characteristics associated with each cluster. Participants were shown one of these descriptions and were asked to rate the company's personality and their attraction to it as a place in which to work. Results were clear: Ratings of the company's personality corresponded to the descriptions provided. Also, companies depicted as high on the Boy Scout, innovative, and stylish dimensions were rated as the best places in which to work.

What does this mean? It appears that we tend to think about organizations as having personalities, and that our perceptions in this regard influence our interest in working in such companies. Clearly, then, even if organizational personality does not exist in the same sense as individual personality, people do think of companies as having certain stable qualities. Savvy organizations certainly should take these into account when planning the nature of the recruitment ads they place in brochures and magazines.

Major Work-Related Aspects of Personality: The "Big Five," Positive Versus Negative Affectivity, and Core Self-Evaluations

Now that we have defined personality and described how it is measured, we will focus on several personality variables that have been linked closely to important aspects of organizational behavior. In this first section, we'll consider aspects of personality widely considered to be important because they influence many aspects of behavior in work settings. After that, we'll consider several additional aspects of personality that also have important implications for behavior in work settings, but whose effects are somewhat less general in scope.

The Big Five Dimensions of Personality: Our Most Fundamental Traits

How many different personality traits can you list? Some time ago, scientists searching an English language dictionary identified almost 18,000 traits.[10] Fortunately, we don't have to consider anywhere near this many. A good number of these traits are very similar, and only a handful have been found to play a role in organizational behavior. In fact, evidence suggests that there are a more manageable, five key dimensions to consider. Because these same five dimensions have emerged in so many different studies conducted in so many different ways, they are referred to as the **Big Five dimensions of personality.**[11] These are as follows:

- **Extraversion.** A tendency to seek stimulation and to enjoy the company of other people. This reflects a dimension ranging from energetic, enthusiastic, sociable, and talkative at the high end, to retiring, sober, reserved, silent, and cautious at the low end.
- **Agreeableness.** A tendency to be compassionate toward others. This dimension ranges from good-natured, cooperative, trusting, and helpful at the high end, to irritable, suspicious, and uncooperative at the low end.
- **Conscientiousness.** A tendency to show self-discipline, to strive for competence and achievement. This dimension ranges from well organized, careful, self-disciplined, responsible, and precise at the high end, to disorganized, impulsive, careless, and undependable at the low end.
- **Neuroticism.** A tendency to experience unpleasant emotions easily. This dimension ranges from poised, calm, composed, and not hypochondriacal at the low end, to nervous, anxious, high-strung, and hypochondriacal at the high end.
- **Openness to experience.** A tendency to enjoy new experiences and new ideas. This dimension ranges from imaginative, witty, and having broad interests at the high end, to down-to-earth, simple, and having narrow interests at the low end.

These five basic dimensions of personality are measured by means of questionnaires in which the people whose personalities are being assessed answer various questions about themselves. Some sample items similar to those on popular measures of the Big Five dimensions are shown in Table 4.1. By completing them, you gain a rough idea of where *you* stand on each of these dimensions.

Research on the relationship between various Big Five dimensions of personality and specific forms of behavior has established some important connections. Overall, the Big Five dimensions are related strongly to work performance.[12] This is the case across many different occupational groups (e.g., professionals, police, managers, salespersons, skilled laborers), and several kinds of performance measures (e.g., ratings of individuals' performance by managers or others, performance during training programs, personnel records). Of all the dimensions, however, *conscientiousness* shows the strongest association with task performance: The higher individuals are on this dimension, the higher their performance.[13] The next strongest connection to job performance is for *emotional stability:* The more emotionally stable someone is, the better his or her task performance tends to be.[14]

Big Five dimensions of personality
Five basic dimensions of personality that are related strongly to different forms of organizational behavior.

extraversion
A tendency to seek stimulation and to enjoy the company of other people; one of the Big Five personality dimensions.

agreeableness
A tendency to be compassionate toward others; one of the Big Five personality dimensions.

conscientiousness
A tendency to show self-discipline, to strive for competence and achievement; one of the Big Five personality dimensions.

neuroticism
A tendency to experience unpleasant emotions easily; one of the Big Five personality dimensions.

openness to experience
A tendency to enjoy new experiences and new ideas; one of the Big Five personality dimensions.

TABLE 4.1 The Big Five Dimensions of Personality

The items listed here are similar to ones used to measure each of the *Big Five dimensions of personality.* Answering them may give you some insight into these key aspects of your personality.

Directions: Indicate the extent to which you agree or disagree with each item by entering a number in the space beside it. Enter 5 if you agree strongly with the item, 4 if you agree, 3 if you neither agree nor disagree, 2 if you disagree, and 1 if you disagree strongly.

Conscientiousness

——— I keep my room neat and clean.
——— People generally find me to be extremely reliable.

Extraversion

——— I like lots of excitement in my life.
——— I usually am very cheerful.

Agreeableness

——— I generally am quite courteous to other people.
——— People never think I am cold and sly.

Emotional Stability

——— I often worry about things that are out of my control.
——— I usually feel sad or "down."

Openness to Experience

——— I have a lot of curiosity.
——— I enjoy the challenge of change.

Scoring: Add your scores for each item. Higher scores reflect greater degrees of the personality characteristic being measured.

Other dimensions of the Big Five also are linked to task performance, but in more specific ways. For instance, *agreeableness* is related positively to various interpersonal aspects of work (e.g., getting along well with others). And for some occupations—ones requiring individuals to interact with many other people during the course of the day (e.g., managers, police officers, salespeople)—*extraversion* is related positively to performance.

The Big Five dimensions also are related to team performance. Specifically, the higher the average scores of team members on conscientiousness, agreeableness, extraversion, and emotional stability, the higher their teams perform.[15] Overall, then, it appears that the Big Five dimensions are a key determinant of job performance for teams as well as individuals.

In addition, the Big Five traits also are linked to other important organizational processes.[16] For example, several of the Big Five dimensions play an important role in determining who becomes a leader (see Chapter 13).[17] People scoring high in extraversion, in openness to experience, and in agreeableness (e.g., the tendency to trust others, at least initially) are more likely to become leaders than others who score low on these dimensions.[18]

Research also has found that entrepreneurs—people who start their own businesses—possess higher or lower degrees of certain Big Five traits than managers in general.[19] Specifically, compared to managers in general, entrepreneurs score higher on conscientiousness and openness to experience, which makes sense since these qualities would appear to be quite important when starting a business. Entrepreneurs also score lower than managers on neuroticism (reflecting their tendency to be more poised and calm) and agreeableness (reflecting their tendency to be suspicious of others). Finally, entrepreneurs and managers are relatively equal with respect to extraversion. Of these variables, conscientiousness is particularly important because the higher entrepreneurs are in conscientiousness, the longer their new ventures tend to survive—and, the longer a new business exists, the more likely it is to be financially successful (see Figure 4.7).[20]

FIGURE 4.7

Eric Baird: One Conscientious Entrepreneur

The positive link between conscientiousness and entrepreneurial success is reflected in Eric Baird, the man behind MyUS.com, a fast-growing shipping and packaging company in Bradenton, Florida. Baird is a tireless worker whose discipline and hard work led the company to grow from sales of $10.147 million in 2006 to $26 million only two years later—a gain of 156 percent. In recognition of this staggering growth, Baird was named 2009 Entrepreneur of the Year by the *Gulf Coast Business Review*.

Mark Wemple/Mark Wemple Photography.

Positive and Negative Affectivity: Tendencies Toward Feeling Good or Bad

It is a basic fact of life that our moods fluctuate rapidly—and sometimes greatly—throughout the day. An e-mail message containing good news may leave us smiling, while an unpleasant conversation with a coworker may leave us feeling gloomy. Such temporary feelings are known as *mood states* and can strongly affect anyone at almost any time. However, mood states are only part of the total picture when considering how our feelings and emotions can affect our behavior at work.

As you probably know from experience, people differ not only in terms of their current moods—which can be affected by many different events—but also with respect to more stable tendencies to experience positive or negative feelings.[21] Some people tend to be "up" most of the time whereas others tend to be more subdued or even depressed; and these tendencies are apparent in a wide range of contexts. In other words, at any given moment people's *affective states* (their current feelings) are based both on temporary conditions (i.e., ever-changing moods) *and* relatively stable differences in lasting dispositions to experience positive or negative feelings (i.e., stable traits).

These differences in predisposition toward positive and negative moods are an important aspect of personality. In fact, such differences are related to the ways in which individuals approach many events and experiences on their jobs and in their lives in general. Some people, as you know, are generally energetic, exhilarated, and have a real zest for life. You know them to be "up" all the time. Such individuals may be said to be high in **positive affectivity.** They may be characterized as having an overall sense of well-being, seeing people and events in a positive light, and usually experiencing positive emotional states. By contrast, people who are low in positive affectivity are generally apathetic and listless.

Another dimension of mood is known as **negative affectivity.** It is characterized at the high end by people who are generally angry, nervous, and anxious, and at the low end by those who feel calm and relaxed most of the time.[22] As indicated in Figure 4.8, positive affectivity and negative affectivity are not the opposite of each other, but rather two separate dimensions.

As you might suspect, people who are high in positive affectivity behave differently from those who are high in negative affectivity with respect to several key aspects of organizational behavior. In fact, 42 percent of office workers responding to a survey indicated that they worked with people who could be described as "negative"—perpetual pessimists who think everything will turn out badly, criticizers who find fault with everything, and people who are just plain negative—they are simply "down" all the time.[23] Not only do such individuals perform poorly themselves, but their negativity also interferes with the performance of others. In other words,

positive affectivity
The tendency to experience positive moods and feelings in a wide range of settings and under many different conditions.

negative affectivity
The tendency to experience negative moods in a wide range of settings and under many different conditions.

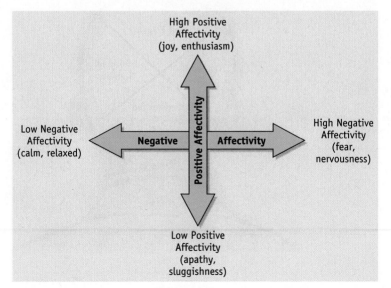

FIGURE 4.8

Positive and Negative Affectivity

Positive affectivity and negative affectivity are two independent dimensions. The mood states associated with high levels and low levels of each are shown here.

they create an atmosphere that reduces productivity and that, of course, can be costly. This comes across in terms of the following forms of behavior.

- *Decision making.* People with high levels of positive affectivity make superior decisions than those with high levels of negative affectivity.[24]
- *Team performance.* Work groups that have a positive affective tone (those in which the average level of positive affectivity is high) function more effectively than groups that have a negative affective tone (those in which the average level of negative affectivity is high).[25]
- *Aggressive behavior.* Because they tend to be very passive in nature, people who are high in negative affectivity are likely to be targets of aggression from others in their organizations.[26]

In view of these findings, it's little wonder that positive and negative affectivity are considered important personality traits when it comes to understanding organizational behavior.

Core Self-Evaluations: How Do We Think of Ourselves?

What is your image of yourself? To what extent is your self-concept positive or negative? Although most people view themselves in positive terms, not everybody does so to the same degree. Moreover, the particular way in which we view ourselves is not indicative of a single personality variable, but rather, four distinct elements of personality known as **core self-evaluations.** These refer to people's fundamental evaluations of themselves, their bottom-line conclusions about themselves.[27]

People's core self-evaluations are based on four particular personality traits (see Figure 4.9). These are as follows:

- **Self-esteem.** The overall value one places on oneself as a person
- **Generalized self-efficacy.** A person's beliefs about his or her capacity to perform specific tasks successfully
- **Locus of control.** The extent to which individuals feel that they are able to control things in a manner that affects them
- **Emotional stability.** The tendency to see oneself as confident, secure, and steady (this is the opposite of *neuroticism,* one of the Big Five personality variables)

Individually, each of the four dimensions of core self-evaluations has been researched extensively, and each is associated with beneficial organizational outcomes.[28] For example, take self-esteem. Individuals with high levels of self-esteem tend to welcome opportunities to perform

core self-evaluation
People's fundamental evaluations of themselves, their bottom-line conclusions about themselves.

self-esteem
The overall value one places on oneself as a person.

generalized self-efficacy
A person's beliefs about his or her capacity to perform specific tasks successfully.

locus of control
The extent to which individuals feel that they are able to control things in a manner that affects them.

emotional stability
The tendency to see oneself as confident, secure, and steady (the opposite of *neuroticism,* one of the Big Five personality variables).

FIGURE 4.9

Core Self-Evaluations

In assessing who we are as individuals, people rely on four aspects of personality, which together are known as *core self-evaluations.* These various components are shown here.

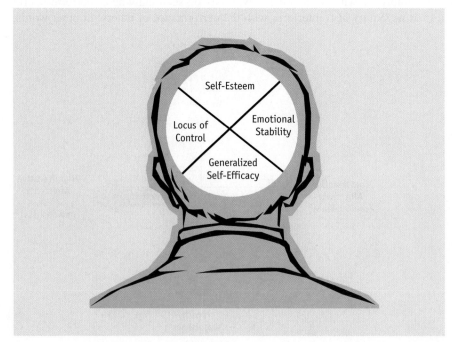

challenging jobs and enjoy rising to the occasion. Not surprisingly, they also put forth a great deal of effort and perform at high levels. By comparison, people who have low self-esteem perceive difficult work situations as threats and dislike them. As a result, they either try to avoid such tasks or don't give them their full effort because they expect to fail, and as a result, they tend to perform poorly.[29]

Now, let's consider generalized self-efficacy. Individuals who have high amounts of this trait are confident that they can do well at whatever they do. This, in turn, encourages them to take on such challenges; because they believe they will succeed, they are unlikely to give up when things get rough. As a result, they tend to be successful at these jobs. Then, because they associate the work with success, they are inclined to be satisfied with the jobs themselves. In view of this, it's important to consider how to raise self-efficacy on the job. For some suggestions in this regard, see the OB in Practice section below.

Locus of control also is related positively to job satisfaction and performance. Specifically, someone with a highly internal locus of control is likely to believe that he or she can do what it takes to influence any situation. He or she feels confident in being able to bring about change. As a result, individuals with high internal locus of control tend to be satisfied with their jobs because they strive to improve any undesirable conditions or seek new positions (not remaining in jobs in which they believe their fates are sealed). And as a result of making situations better, they tend to perform at high levels as well.

Finally, emotional stability also makes a difference. As we noted in conjunction with the Big Five dimensions of personality, emotional stability is the opposite of neuroticism (i.e., they are opposite ends of the same personality dimension). People scoring high on emotional stability generally feel confident and secure, which makes them willing to take on job challenges and to work hard to meet them. Not surprisingly, such individuals not only perform their jobs well but also enjoy high levels of satisfaction in doing them.

It's important to note that these individual effects tend to be particularly strong when taken together. In the aggregate, researchers consider core self-evaluations to be "among the

---

OB in Practice

Boosting Employees' Self-Efficacy

When people believe that they can do a job and do it well, the chances that they really *can* succeed often increase. Why? Because heightened feelings of self-efficacy (belief in one's ability to accomplish a specific task) have important benefits. They increase both motivation and persistence ("Why give up? I know I can make it!") and encourage individuals to set challenging goals ("I know I can do much better than before"). So, encouraging high levels of self-efficacy among employees is worthwhile. How can companies reach this objective? Here are three tips.

1. *Give Constructive—Not Destructive—Feedback.* Probably the most important reason to give people feedback on their work is to help them improve. Other motives certainly exist (e.g., some managers give employees negative feedback to "put them in their place" or "even the score"), but these reasons are *counterproductive* from the point of view of increasing self-efficacy. On the other hand, constructive feedback that focuses on how an employee can improve his or her performance can elevate self-efficacy because it helps reassure recipients that they *can* get there—that they have or can soon acquire the skills or strategies necessary for success.

2. *Expose Employees to Models of Good Performance—and Success.* How do people learn to do their jobs effectively? From direct practice, of course; but in addition, they acquire many skills and strategies from others. And the more of these they possess, the more likely they are to perform well—and so to experience increased self-efficacy. This suggests that companies that adopt carefully planned mentoring programs—programs in which inexperienced employees work closely with successful, experienced ones (see Appendix 2)—can help build self-efficacy among their employees.

3. *See Continuous Improvement.* Another technique for enhancing self-efficacy involves the quest for continuous improvement. GE's "Six Sigma" program, for instance, rests on the basic idea that "we can do it better—always!" The term *six sigma* is drawn from the field of statistics to refer to an outstanding level of performance, one that is far above average. Although some employees find this approach daunting at first, meetings and workshops soon convince them that they are part of a truly superb organization that will simply not settle for "average." The result? Employees come to view themselves as superior, leading both self-efficacy and performance to benefit as a result.

Through these and related steps, companies can boost the self-efficacy of their employees—and hence, their performance.

best dispositional predictors of job satisfaction and performance."[30] As a result, it's not surprising that OB scientists have paid a great deal of attention to core self-evaluations in recent years.[31]

Additional Work-Related Aspects of Personality

Although many experts on personality consider the dimensions we have discussed so far to be the most important, these are definitely not the only ones that have implications for organizational behavior. We'll now examine several others that also are related to important forms of behavior in work settings.

Machiavellianism: Using Others to Get Ahead

In 1513, the Italian philosopher Niccolò Machiavelli published a book titled *The Prince.* In it, he outlined a ruthless strategy for seizing and holding political power. The essence of his approach was *expediency:* Do whatever is required to defeat others or gain an advantage over them. Among the guiding principles he recommended were the following:

- Never show humility; arrogance is far more effective when dealing with others.
- Morality and ethics are for the weak; powerful people feel free to lie, cheat, and deceive whenever it suits their purpose.
- It is much better to be feared than loved.

In short, Machiavelli urged those who desired power to adopt a single-minded approach to success. To him, this involved rejecting such notions as friendship, loyalty, decency, and fair play. A truly successful leader, he suggested, should not be distracted by these factors, but be willing to do whatever it takes to win.

Fortunately, most people don't adopt Machiavelli's philosophy at extreme levels. However, as you may have experienced, some individuals do, in fact, embrace many of these principles. This observation has led some researchers to propose that acceptance of this ruthless creed reflects a dimension of personality—known, appropriately, as **Machiavellianism.** Persons high on this dimension (high Machs) accept Machiavelli's suggestions and seek to manipulate others in a ruthless manner.[32] In contrast, persons low on this dimension (low Machs) reject this approach and do, in fact, care about fair play, loyalty, and other principles Machiavelli rejected. Machiavellianism is measured by means of a questionnaire known as the *Mach scale,* which consists of items similar to the ones shown in Table 4.2.

Machiavellianism
A personality trait involving willingness to manipulate others for one's own purposes.

CHARACTERISTICS OF HIGH MACHS. As you might expect, the higher people score on the Mach scale, the lower they score on the Big Five dimensions of agreeableness and extraversion, suggesting that getting along with them is not particularly easy.[33] Such individuals are smooth and charming, they lie easily, and they have no qualms about manipulating or conning others. They also have little remorse or guilt over harming people, and are callous and show little empathy toward others. In addition, they also tend to be impulsive, irresponsible, and prone to feeling bored.

If this description sounds to you like the "con artists" we often read about in the news, you are correct: People scoring high in Machiavellianism show precisely these characteristics.[34] Although we don't know his score on the Mach scale, we expect fully that Bernard Madoff would be a high Mach. As we described in Chapter 2, Madoff coldly and deliberately swindled thousands of investors—many of whom he knew personally—out of tens of billions of dollars by leading them to believe that he was investing their money successfully. In reality, he was running a Ponzi scheme, in which later investors were used to pay early investors. Consistent with being Machiavellian, despite his heartless behavior, Madoff has been characterized as "an affable, charismatic man who moved comfortably among power brokers on Wall Street and in Washington" and whose "employees say he treated them like family."[35] Although Madoff expressed sorrow for his actions while imprisoned for his crimes (which, given what he's like, may or may not be genuine), he admitted to being insensitive to the harm he ultimately brought others.

MACHIAVELLIANISM AND SUCCESS. If high Machs are willing to do whatever it takes to succeed, you might expect that they would tend to be successful. Indeed, Madoff was wildly

TABLE 4.2 Measuring Machiavellianism

The items listed here are similar to those included in one of the most widely used measures of Machiavellianism. One's score on this scale reflects people's willingness to manipulate others in order to get ahead.

Directions: In the space next to each item, enter a number that characterizes your own feelings about that statement. If you disagree strongly, enter 1; if you disagree, enter 2; if you neither agree nor disagree, enter 3; if you agree, enter 4; if you strongly agree, enter 5.

———— 1. The best way to handle people is telling them what they want to hear.

———— 2. When you ask someone to do something for you, it is best to give the real reasons for wanting it rather than giving reasons that might carry more weight.

———— 3. Anyone who completely trusts anyone else is asking for trouble.

———— 4. It is hard to get ahead without cutting corners and bending the rules.

———— 5. It is safest to assume that all people have a vicious streak—and that it will come out when given a chance.

———— 6. It is never right to lie to someone else.

———— 7. Most people are basically good and kind.

———— 8. Most people work hard only when they are forced to do so.

Scoring: Add your responses to items 1, 3, 4, 5, and 8. To this number add the sum of 2, 6, and 7 after scoring them in reverse (so, if you responded with a 5, add 1 point; if you responded with a 4, add 2 points; if you responded with a 3, add 3 points; if you responded with a 2, add 4 points; and if you responded with a 1, add 5 points). Then, add your scores. The higher your score, the more Machiavellian you tend to be.

successful until he got caught. However, this is not always so. How well they do depends on two important factors—the kind of jobs they have, and the nature of the organizations in which they work.

First, research has shown that Machiavellianism is *not* closely related to success in the kinds of jobs in which people operate with a great deal of autonomy. These are jobs—such as salesperson, marketing executive, and university professor—in which employees have the freedom to act as they wish. This gives them good opportunities to free themselves from the clutches of high Machs or to avoid interacting with them altogether![36]

Second, as a general rule, high Machs tend to be quite successful in organizations that are *loosely structured* (i.e., ones in which there are few established rules) rather than those that are *tightly structured* (i.e., ones in which rules regarding expected behavior are clear and explicit).[37] Why? Because when rules are vague and unclear, it is easy for high Machs to "do their thing." When rules are clear and strict, in contrast, high Machs are far more limited in what they can do. (Obviously, given the high degree of regulation required in the investment business, it's clear that Madoff is an exception to this tendency, showing precisely just how audacious he was. As you may know, to prevent any such recurrence, regulations are even tighter today than they were when Madoff was at work.[38]) So while high Machs are always a danger, they are more likely to do harm under some conditions than others.

Achievement Motivation: The Quest for Excellence

Can you recall the person in your high school class who was named "most likely to succeed"? If so, you probably are thinking of someone who was truly competitive, an individual who wanted to win in every situation—or, at least, in all the important ones. Now, in contrast, can you think of someone you have known who was not at all competitive—who could not care less about winning? As you bring these people to mind, you are focusing on an important aspect of personality known as **achievement motivation (need for achievement)**. This personality characteristic refers to the strength of an individual's desire to excel at various tasks—to succeed and to do better than others.

achievement motivation (need for achievement)
The strength of an individual's desire to excel—to succeed at difficult tasks and to do them better than others.

NEED ACHIEVEMENT AND ATTRACTION TO EASY AND DIFFICULT TASKS. One of the most interesting differences between persons who are high and low in the need for achievement involves their preferences for tasks of varying difficulty.[39] Reflecting their strong desire for success, high need achievers avoid performing certain kinds of tasks. Understandably, because especially difficult tasks are likely to result in failure—an unacceptable result for high need achievers—they make an effort to steer clear of them. Interestingly, high need achievers also stay away from tasks that are very easy. Although high need achievers surely would succeed at simple tasks, these are not challenging enough to allow the people performing them to feel that they've accomplished much of anything. As a result, their needs to succeed would not be satisfied. So, what kinds of tasks attract high need achievers? The answer is: those falling between these extremes. High need achievers strongly prefer tasks of intermediate difficulty. Such tasks are easy enough to make success reasonable while at the same time sufficiently difficult to make it possible to dismiss any resulting failure on the basis of the task's difficulty.

By contrast, the opposite pattern occurs among people who are low in achievement motivation. In other words, such individuals prefer to perform tasks that are very easy and very difficult tasks to ones that are moderately difficult. The explanation relies on the same logic we used for people with high need for achievement. Specifically, because success is virtually certain, people who are low in achievement motivation like to perform easy tasks. Such individuals also prefer tasks that are very difficult even though they're likely to fail at them. This is because if a task is particularly difficult, anyone performing it would be expected to fail, suggesting that any failure is not the person's fault but merely a reflection of the task's inherent difficulty. And when failure is based on such external attributions (recall the process of attribution of causality discussed in Chapter 3), it does not pose a threat to an individual's self-esteem. In contrast, failure on a moderately difficult task may be a reasonable basis for making unflattering attributions about oneself (i.e., "I'm not very good at it"). As a result, low need achievers prefer to avoid such tasks (see Figure 4.10). Although these differences between persons high and low in need achievement are interesting by themselves, their real value becomes apparent when considering the role they play in managers' success.

FIGURE 4.10

Achievement Motivation and Attraction to Tasks

People who are high in achievement motivation are attracted to tasks of moderate difficulty, whereas people who are low in achievement motivation are attracted to tasks that are extremely easy or extremely difficult.

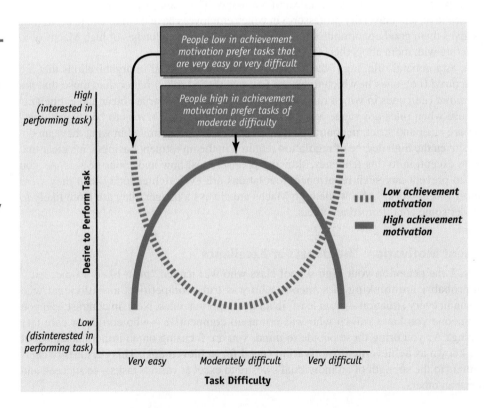

ARE HIGH NEED ACHIEVERS SUCCESSFUL MANAGERS? We have described people high in achievement motivation as having a highly task-oriented outlook. They are strongly concerned with getting things done, which encourages them to work hard and to strive for success. But do they always succeed, especially in managerial positions? As in the case of so many other questions in the field of OB, the answer is far from simple.

Given their intense desire to excel, it seems reasonable to expect that people high in achievement motivation will attain greater success in their careers than others. This is true to a limited extent. Research has shown that people high in achievement motivation tend to gain promotions more rapidly than those who are low in achievement motivation, at least early in their careers.[40] Their focus on attaining success "jump starts" their careers. However, as their careers progress, their unwillingness to tackle difficult challenges becomes a problem that interferes with their success. Further, they tend to be so highly focused on their own success that they sometimes are reluctant to delegate authority to others, thereby failing to get the help they often need from subordinates. Research has shown that CEOs who are high in achievement motivation tend to keep organizational power in the hands of just a few people, failing to empower their team members as needed (see Chapter 12). This is likely to interfere with their effectiveness as managers.[41]

At the same time, people who are high in achievement motivation benefit from the fact that they have a strong desire for feedback regarding their performance. In other words, because they want to succeed so badly, such individuals are keenly interested in knowing just how well they are doing. As a result, people who are high in need achievement have a strong preference for *merit-based pay systems*—that is, ones in which pay and other rewards are based on performance (see Chapter 7). This is so because such systems recognize people's individual achievements. In keeping with this, people who have high needs for achievement generally dislike seniority-based pay systems (i.e., those in which pay is based on how long one has worked in the company) because these fail to differentiate between employees with respect to their accomplishments on the job.[42]

ACHIEVEMENT MOTIVATION AND GOAL ORIENTATION: DO PEOPLE DIFFER IN THE KIND OF SUCCESS THEY SEEK? So far, our discussion has implied that the *degree* to which people desire to achieve is an important dimension along which people differ. But individuals also differ with respect to the *kind* of success they seek. In fact, individuals can have any one of three contrasting *goal orientations* when performing various tasks.[43] These are as follows.[44]

- **Learning goal orientation.** The desire to perform well because it satisfies an interest in meeting a challenge and learning new skills
- **Performance goal orientation.** The desire to perform well to demonstrate one's competence to others
- **Avoidance goal orientation.** The desire to achieve success to avoid appearing incompetent and to avoid receiving negative evaluations from others

The existence of these three different goal orientations—that is, various reasons for wanting to do well in various tasks—has important implications for performance in work settings. For instance, a learning goal orientation is related strongly to general self-efficacy, which we described earlier as a particular element of core self-evaluations.[45] The higher one's learning goal orientation, the greater is his or her general self-efficacy. Since self-efficacy exerts strong effects on performance, a learning goal orientation may be very helpful when it comes to performing many jobs.

Similarly, a learning goal orientation also may facilitate benefiting from on-the-job feedback. Specifically, people high in this orientation want to receive feedback and pay careful attention to it since it will help them to learn. In contrast, neither a performance goal orientation nor an avoidance goal orientation offers similar benefits.[46] So overall, organizations should strive to promote a learning goal orientation among their employees. How, exactly, can they do so? To a large extent, the answer lies in giving employees opportunities to acquire new job skills and then rewarding them for doing so (instead of just being competent at what they already know how to do). For an example of how one particular company goes about doing this, see Figure 4.11.

learning goal orientation
The desire to perform well because it satisfies an interest in meeting a challenge and learning new skills.

performance goal orientation
The desire to perform well to demonstrate one's competence to others.

avoidance goal orientation
The desire to achieve success to avoid appearing incompetent and to avoid receiving negative evaluation from others.

Feature Photo Service/Newscom.

FIGURE 4.11

Deloitte Consulting Promotes a Learning Goal Orientation

Considering that corporate consultants can be called on to do a wide variety of things, it's essential for them to have a broad array of skills on which to draw. To ensure that their employees are prepared to service the firm's clients, Deloitte Consulting goes out of its way to provide learning opportunities on an ongoing basis. Abandoning the traditional, one-size-fits-all approach to helping employees learn, Deloitte's professional development program, known as Mass Career Customization (MCC), allows employees to tailor their learning experiences to their own interests—and to adjust these when, and if, their life situations may change. This, together with liberal support for gaining various professional certifications (e.g., paying for training, providing time off work), helps promote a strong learning goal orientation at Deloitte.

That achievement motivation influences the success of individuals is far from surprising. But can it also contribute to the economic growth and well-being of entire societies? For information suggesting that it can, see the Today's Diverse and Global Organizations section on page 129.

Morning Persons and Evening Persons

According to the U.S. Department of Labor, about 15 percent of people in the U.S. labor force work at night or on rotating shifts.[47] Unfortunately, this can be costly given that the health and well-being of many individuals suffer when they work at night.[48] Yet, as you probably know from experience, there are some people who seem to thrive on "the graveyard shift" and actually prefer it. (In fact, if you are up late at night reading this, you may be one of them!)

The suggestion that there may be individual differences in the times of day at which people feel most alert and energetic is supported by evidence showing that such differences do, in fact, exist and that they are stable over time. Specifically, it appears that most people fall into one of

Today's Diverse and Global Organizations

Achievement Motivation and Economic Growth Around the World

Economists have demonstrated that a variety of factors—including the price and availability of natural resources, labor costs, and government policies that encourage or discourage growth—contribute to national differences in economic expansion. However, these factors do not tell the whole story. Indeed, it appears that one aspect of personality, too, may play a role: national differences in achievement motivation. Although achievement motivation, strictly speaking, relates to individuals, considerable evidence suggests that it also varies across different cultures. What's more, these differences are related to important economic variables.

This point is illustrated dramatically in a classic study in which researchers analyzed children's stories from 22 different cultures with respect to the degree to which they contained themes of achievement motivation (e.g., the story *The Little Engine That Could*, which was read by millions of children in the United States, expresses the value of achievement motivation).[49] The investigators then related the levels of achievement motivation indicated by these stories to key measures of economic development (e.g., per capita income and per capita electrical production). Their findings were impressive: The greater the emphasis placed on achievement in the children's stories in various nations, the more rapid was the economic growth in these nations as the children grew up!

Interestingly, these findings are not just a fluke; similar results have been reported in other research.[50] For example, a massive study involving more than 12,000 participants in 41 different countries has confirmed the idea that national differences in achievement motivation can be quite real and that they are related to differences in economic growth.[51] Specifically, it was found that various attitudes toward work, such as competitiveness, were different across countries, and that those countries whose citizens were most competitive tended to be those that had higher rates of economic growth.

---

two categories—they are either **morning persons,** who feel most energetic early in the day, or **evening persons,** who feel most energetic late in the day or at night.

Recently, a study was conducted involving 137 female nurses in Taipai, Republic of China, in which comparisons were made of their sleep quality as a function of the particular shifts in which they worked.[52] The day shift was from 7:30 A.M. to 3:30 P.M.; the evening shift was from 3:30 P.M. to 11:30 P.M.; and the night shift was from 11:30 P.M. to 7:30 A.M. Nurses completed two standardized scales, one assessing sleep quality and another assessing their morningness-eveningness (the reliability and validity of both had been established earlier, of course). It was found that the particular shifts the nurses worked were not related to the quality of their sleep, although whether they were morning persons or evening persons made a significant difference in this regard. Specifically, the sleep of evening people was significantly worse than that of morning people in two critical areas—subjective sleep quality and sleep duration.

The researchers explained that this was due to the fact that evening people kept significantly more variable schedules whereas morning people maintained more regular hours. In particular, morning persons slept on average 6 to 8 hours every day, regardless of when they worked or whether it was one of their days off. However, evening people slept between 5 to 8 hours on workdays but 10 to 12 hours on their days off. This suggests that evening persons were experiencing insufficient amounts of sleep on workdays and made up these sleep debts on their days off. When considered in light of the fact that people suffering insufficient amounts of sleep are prone to accidents and errors on the job, these findings for evening persons are of great concern (for an overview of the processes outlined here, see Figure 4.12 on page 130).[53]

It's clear that we cannot afford to have nurses making errors, so what can be done to avoid the obvious problems? As in the case of most personality variables, changing one's morningness-eveningness is not easy, so changing people to match their schedules isn't promising. Besides, changing people back after schedule changes are made would be impractical. Fortunately, it has been found that evening people can perform well when woking shifts that suit this aspect of their personality, such as evening shifts and night shifts. Evening persons are known to find it easier to work evening shifts and night shifts than morning persons since such schedules are in keeping with their predispositions.[54] Our recommendation, then, would be to match workers to schedules that suit their dispositions. Indeed, when this was done in research with students (i.e., when morning persons took early classes and evening persons took later classes), their grades were higher than when these variables were not matched.[55]

morning persons
Individuals who feel most energetic and alert early in the day.

evening persons
Individuals who feel most energetic and alert late in the day or at night.

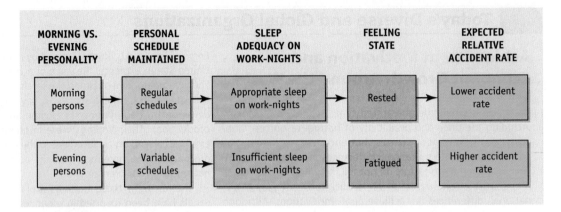

FIGURE 4.12

Morning Persons Versus Evening Persons: A Potentially Critical Difference

A recent study compared the sleep quality of a group of nurses who were identified as morning persons and evening persons. As summarized here, morning persons and evening persons were found to differ in several key ways. Ultimately, these may influence the capacity to perform the job safely.

Source: Based on suggestions from Chung et al., 2009; see Note 52.

These findings and those of several other studies suggest that individual differences in preferences for various times of day are not only real, but also that they are very important when it comes to job performance.[56] Ideally, only individuals who are at their best late in the day should be assigned to night work; this would constitute a good application of the principle of *person-job fit,* which we described earlier in this chapter. According to this principle, the closer the alignment between individuals' skills, abilities, and preferences and the requirements of their jobs, the more successful at these jobs they will be. The results of following such a policy might well be better performance, better health, and fewer accidents for employees—outcomes beneficial both to them and to their organizations.

Abilities and Skills: Having What It Takes to Succeed

abilities
Mental and physical capacities to perform various tasks.

skills
Dexterity at performing specific tasks, which has been acquired through training or experience.

As you know from experience, people differ greatly with respect to their **abilities**—the capacity to perform various tasks—and **skills**—dexterity at performing specific tasks, which has been acquired through training or experience.[57] For example, no matter how hard the author of this book might have tried, he never could have made it as a professional basketball player. He's neither sufficiently tall nor athletic to succeed. In other words, he lacks the basic physical abilities required by this sport. However, he has other abilities—at least, he likes to think that he does—that have allowed him to enjoy a fulfilling life outside of professional sports.

Both abilities and skills are important, of course, but since abilities are more general in nature and have implications for a broader range of organizational behavior, we'll pay a bit more attention to them in this section of the chapter. Our discussion of abilities will focus on two major types: *intellectual abilities* (or simply, *intelligence*), which involve the capacity to perform various cognitive tasks, and *physical abilities,* which refer to the capacity to perform various physical actions.

Intelligence: Three Major Types

When most people speak about intelligence or intellectual abilities, they generally are referring to one's capacity to understand complex ideas.[58] Of course, this is certainly very important. To succeed on a job, one must have the mental capacity to undertake the intellectual challenges associated with it. However, this kind of mental prowess is not the only kind of intelligence there is.[59] In fact, on the job, several distinct types of intelligence have proven to be very important. We now consider these.

COGNITIVE INTELLIGENCE. "Oh yes, Jennifer is very smart," someone might tell you in reference to the new person hired in your department. But what exactly is meant by "smart"? Traditionally, the term is used to refer to a specific kind of intellectual ability that psychologists term **cognitive intelligence.** This involves the ability to understand complex ideas, to adapt effectively to the environment, to learn from experience, to engage in various forms of reasoning, and to overcome obstacles by careful thought.[60]

As you know from discussions about intelligence (or IQ) tests in the media, people possess this type of intelligence to varying degrees. You also probably realize that different jobs require contrasting levels of cognitive intelligence for success. As you might suspect, the concept of cognitive intelligence is rather broad; it consists of a variety of different cognitive skills and abilities. Among these are abilities involving words, numbers, and visual images, including the following.

- *Verbal comprehension.* The ability to understand written material quickly and accurately
- *Verbal reasoning.* The ability to analyze verbal information so as to make valid judgments on the basis of logical implications of material
- *Word fluency.* The ability to express oneself rapidly, easily, and with flexibility
- *Numerical ability.* The ability to perform basic mathematical operations quickly and accurately
- *Numerical reasoning.* The ability to analyze logical relationships and to recognize the principles underlying them
- *Space visualization.* The ability to visualize three-dimensional forms in space and to be able to manipulate them mentally
- *Symbolic reasoning.* The ability to think and reason abstractly using symbols, rather than words or numbers, to manipulate abstract symbols mentally, and to make logically valid judgments based on them

It's probably no surprise that different jobs require various blends of these abilities. As some obvious examples, writers have to be adept at word fluency, statisticians have to be good at numerical ability and numerical reasoning, and architects have to be skilled at spatial visualization. As you read Appendix 2, you'll come to appreciate how various aspects of cognitive intelligence (and other types of intelligence too, as we will see) are involved in people's selections of various career alternatives. As practical as it may seem to assess people's cognitive intelligence, some have argued that doing so raises some ethical issues. For a discussion of these points, see "The Ethics Angle" section on page 132.

PRACTICAL INTELLIGENCE: SOLVING THE PROBLEMS OF EVERYDAY LIFE. Consider the following hypothetical incident.

> A business executive and a scientist are walking in the woods, when they spot a large grizzly bear. The bear starts running toward them, growling angrily, obviously intending to attack. Both the executive and the scientist start running, but after a few yards, the scientist stops, and calls to the executive: "There's no point in running. I have done the calculations, and there is no way we can outrun that bear." The executive shouts back over his shoulder: "I don't have to outrun the bear . . . I only have to outrun you!"

Although you may find this story a bit unsettling, it provides a clear illustration of individual differences in **practical intelligence**—the ability to devise effective ways of getting things done.[61] Growing evidence suggests that practical intelligence is indeed different from the kind of intelligence measured by IQ tests, and that it is especially important in business settings.[62] People with high amounts of practical intelligence are said to have "know-how." Although they might not be able to express very well exactly how they do something, the fact is that they actually can do it—and this, of course, is important. Often, the practical knowledge that people have is acquired informally on their own, largely because it goes unspoken. As such, people must recognize it, and its value, for themselves. For instance, although no one may ever tell an employee how to solve a problem that arises in the office, an individual with a high degree of practical intelligence would be likely to be able to figure out a solution on his or her own.

When thinking about practical intelligence, you shouldn't let the term *practical* mislead you. Practical is not only applicable to people who work with their hands, such as mechanics and

cognitive intelligence
The ability to understand complex ideas, to adapt effectively to the environment, to learn from experience, to engage in various forms of reasoning, and to overcome obstacles with careful thought.

practical intelligence
Adeptness at solving the practical problems of everyday life.

The Ethics Angle

Are IQ Tests Inherently Unethical?

The practice of testing people's cognitive intelligence dates back to the early 1900s when the French government hired psychologist Alfred Binet to develop a test to identify which particular school-children were likely to be in need of special attention in their classes.[63] Today, as you know, IQ tests are used widely in schools and also in some occupational settings. The National Football League, for example, routinely gives an intelligence test to prospective players so that any teams interested in drafting them can assess their mental capacity. This is important considering that players are required to understand many complex plays and that team owners naturally want to ensure that any players they draft (and pay astronomical salaries) are intellectually capable of learning their playbooks.

Although you may be well aware of the widespread use of intelligence tests, you may not realize that some people consider this practice to be unethical. Here, then, are some of the ethical concerns that have been raised.[64]

Considerations of privacy

Some believe that a person's innate abilities are his or her own business and that by assessing intelligence, people are being asked to reveal things that they might prefer to keep to themselves. With this in mind, it has been argued that anyone being given an IQ test should be made fully aware of the purposes for which it will be used—and that the people collecting this information should not stray from these. Confidentiality is important here because the potential to misuse information about a person's intelligence is a violation of privacy.

Unequal access to opportunities to develop intelligence

Intelligence is not fixed. People's cognitive capacities can grow and develop like their physical capacities. Just as people can exercise their bodies in gymnasiums, they also can exercise their minds, such as by attending school, by reading, by playing intellectually stimulating games (e.g., chess), and so on. Inherently, there's nothing unethical about this. However, some consider that because measures of IQ are likely to be correlated with having these intellectual opportunities and that these, in turn, are likely to differ based on people's socioeconomic status, that what we are measuring in the name of intelligence is nothing more than differential opportunities to develop cognitive intelligence skills. And with this in mind, it might be considered unfair to differentiate between people on this basis. Fortunately, scientists are capable of statistically controlling for socioeconomic factors when assessing IQ, and this clearly should be done whenever possible. Of course, the underlying problem can be countered by engaging in efforts to improve educational opportunities among those who are socioeconomically disadvantaged, thereby equalizing opportunities whenever possible.

People may misuse IQ tests for racist purposes

You've probably already heard about controversies surrounding the potentially racist nature of IQ tests, and this has made their use controversial in some situations. Unfortunately, some people have used IQ test scores to justify the mistreatment of individuals considered inferior, thereby advancing their racist agendas. This is certainly unethical, of course, and cannot be condoned. However, it's been countered that the misuse of IQ tests shouldn't lead to their elimination because the tests themselves are not at fault. The tests are tools that also can be put to good use. It also has been noted that studies administering **culture-free IQ tests**—that is, ones whose wording does not disadvantage any one group—to people from different racial and ethnic groups do *not* find that intelligence differs significantly between them.[65] In fact, there is a wider range of differences in IQ within people of any given race than there is between the races. Such findings challenge the underlying premise that IQ tests are tools that can be used to promote racism.

> **culture-free IQ tests**
> Tests that are unbiased because they do not give an advantage to members of any one particular group.

Obviously, the ethical issues outlined here are very important to consider. We presented both sides of the issue although, like most scientists, we believe that there's nothing inherently unethical about IQ tests, so long as they are used properly. Of course, we invite you to consider all sides before drawing your own conclusions.

---

plumbers. Clearly, such individuals *do* have to know how to perform certain physical actions, but they also have to have cognitive skills so they can assess problems they confront on the job. At the same time, people who perform jobs involving high degrees of cognitive intelligence also must have practical intelligence if they are to succeed. Take internal medicine physicians as an example. Yes, they certainly are likely to have vast amounts of cognitive knowledge about human physiology, diseases, and the efficacy of various drugs. At the same time, they also must have practical knowledge about the profession if they are to have successful practices. Such practical matters as how to run a medical office, how to satisfy insurance company regulations, and what continuing education seminars are most valuable all must be the focus of the doctor's attention. Attending to these practical matters while also staying abreast of the latest medical knowledge, although challenging, clearly is essential to the doctor's professional success.

> **emotional intelligence (EI)**
> The ability to make accurate judgments of emotions and to use such knowledge to enhance the quality of one's thinking; skills involved include the ability to recognize and regulate our own emotions, to influence those of others, and to facilitate performance.

EMOTIONAL INTELLIGENCE: MANAGING THE FEELING SIDE OF LIFE. A third important kind of intelligence that often plays key roles in organizations is known as *emotional intelligence*.[66] Formally, **emotional intelligence (EI)** refers to the ability to make accurate judgments of emotions and to use such knowledge to enhance the quality of one's thinking.[67] In other words,

EI refers to a cluster of abilities relating to the emotional or "feeling" side of life. Specifically, four different kinds of ability are involved.[68]

- *Appraisal and expression of emotions in oneself.* The individual's ability to understand his or her own emotions and to express these naturally
- *Appraisal and recognition of emotions in others.* The ability to perceive and understand others' emotions
- *Regulation of emotions in oneself.* The ability to regulate one's own emotions
- *Use of emotions to facilitate performance.* The ability to use emotions by directing them toward constructive activities and improved performance (e.g., by encouraging oneself to do better)

Much as tests of cognitive intelligence are used to derive intelligence quotient (IQ scores), tests of emotional intelligence are used to derive emotional quotient (EQ scores). One particular type of EQ test may be found in this chapter's Individual Exercise on pages 138–140. Completing this exercise will give you a good feel for the degree of emotional intelligence you possess.

EI is related to several key aspects of organizational behavior, such as job performance. Illustrating this, consider a study conducted at a large factory in China.[69] The employees who worked there were asked to rate the EI of their coworkers. Then, these ratings were compared to the performance ratings by the coworkers' supervisors. The results were clear: Individuals who had the highest levels of EI (as rated by their coworkers) had the highest levels of job performance (as assessed by their supervisors).

Knowing that such a relationship exists is one thing, but understanding precisely *why* is quite another. In other words, how can we explain this relationship? Recently, a conceptualization known as the *cascading model of emotional intelligence* has proposed an answer.[70] Specifically, the **cascading model of emotional intelligence** suggests that there's a progressive (i.e., cascading) pattern of emotion-related abilities involved: Emotions must be perceived, then understood, and then regulated before job performance is affected. The model specifies further that these are linked to key personality variables, such as conscientiousness, cognitive ability, and emotional stability. For an overview of this conceptualization, see Figure 4.13.

Although the diagram looks complicated, the model is really straightforward. Let's begin by looking at the horizontal row of boxes. The model begins at the left with perceiving emotions. That is, people must not only experience emotions but also be able to identify the emotions they feel. Although we don't always think of it, some people are more attuned to, and can better recognize, their emotions than others. After emotions are recognized, the next ability requires understanding emotion. This involves understanding how emotions differ from each other, and which particular emotion is most appropriate for a given context. At this point, it's important for people to regulate their emotional states. This may involve controlling their emotions so that they can maintain focus on their jobs. People who are grief-stricken (due to the loss of a family member) or extremely overjoyed (due to winning the lottery), for example, may find that their emotional states can adversely affect their job performance.

Not only does the cascading model specify that this series of abilities is involved but also that these are related to various emotions and other abilities. These are depicted in the column on the left side of the diagram (with arrows showing the interconnections between them). The top box represents conscientiousness. As we noted earlier, highly conscientious people display high levels of job performance. This is depicted by one of the arrows. The other arrow from the consciousness box leads to emotional perception. This reflects the tendency for highly conscientious people to be particularly adept at perceiving their emotions. It's almost as if they have developed a radar to help detect if they are aware of their emotions.[71]

The arrows from the cognitive ability box are easy to understand. The arrow from cognitive ability to emotion understanding reflects the fact that an individual's cognitive skills contribute to the ability to make sense of his or her emotions. And the other arrow, of course, simply reflects the fact that people who have high levels of cognitive ability are better prepared to succeed on their jobs than those who are less capable in this regard. Finally, let's consider the connections to emotional stability. The first arrow reflects the fact that people who are highly stable emotionally are particularly adept at regulating their emotions. Obviously, people who are emotionally unstable find it especially challenging to regulate their emotions, often demonstrating outbursts that

cascading model of emotional intelligence
Conceptualization proposing that emotional intelligence influences job performance through a succession of abilities: the ability to perceive emotions, then to understand them, and then to regulate them; these abilities, in turn, are linked to personality variables, such as conscientiousness and neuroticism, and also to cognitive ability.

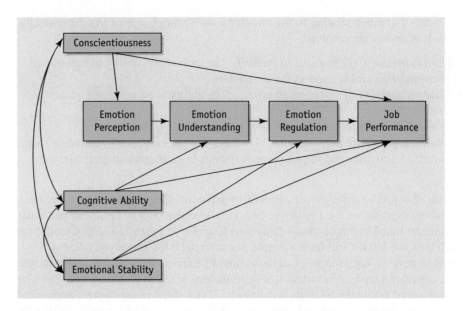

FIGURE 4.13

The Cascading Model of Emotional Intelligence

The *cascading model of emotional intelligence* sheds light on how emotional intelligence is related to job performance. Specifically, as suggested in the horizontal series of boxes, people must have the ability to perceive emotions, then they must have the ability to understand these emotions, and then the stage is set to regulate these emotions. In turn, how well someone can do this is likely to influence his or her job performance. The theory also proposes that these abilities are associated with certain personality variables, such as conscientiousness, cognitive ability, and emotional stability.

Source: Reproduced from Joseph, D. L., & Newman, D. A. (2010). Emotional intelligence: An integrative meta-analysis and cascading model. *Journal of Applied Psychology, 95,* 54–78.

may be quite embarrassing. Finally, the link from emotional stability to job performance reflects much the same idea. People who are emotionally unstable are not particularly adept at performing a wide variety of jobs, as you might imagine.

Concluding our discussion of the cascading model of emotional intelligence, it's important to note that this is a new conceptualization. Although it hasn't been in existence very long, it was developed as a result of thoroughly analyzing research findings bearing on the various links. As such, it's not merely a set of hypotheses requiring testing but rather the result of systematically summarizing dozens of existing research findings. With this in mind, it seems safe to consider the cascading model of emotional intelligence to be a very good explanation of the relationship between EI and job performance.

Physical Abilities: Capacity to Do the Job

physical abilities
People's capacities to engage in the physical tasks required to perform a job.

When we speak of **physical abilities,** we are referring to people's capacities to engage in the physical tasks required to perform a job. Although different jobs require different physical abilities, there are several types of physical abilities that are relevant to a variety of jobs. These include the following.

- *Strength.* The capacity to exert physical force against various objects
- *Flexibility.* The capacity to move one's body in an agile manner
- *Stamina.* The capacity to endure physical activity over prolonged periods
- *Speed.* The ability to move quickly

If we were to consider all jobs that people perform, it might be possible to identify those that require primarily intellectual abilities and those that require primarily physical abilities. For example, being a chemist in a research laboratory of a large company involves mainly intellectual abilities, whereas being a construction worker involves mainly physical abilities. However, such oversimplification can be misleading. Almost all jobs require *both* cognitive and physical abilities for success. For example, consider a firefighter. Obviously, such individuals must have high degrees of strength, flexibility, stamina, and speed to be able to perform their jobs well. At the same time, however, they also must possess appropriate cognitive abilities so they can assess the complex demands of the scene (e.g., wind velocity, structure of the building on fire, likely presence of victims, sources of oxygen, and so on). In sum, when it comes to assessing the physical demands of a job relative to the more cognitive demands, it's safest to consider this a matter not of "which?" but of "how much of each at any given time?"

Social Skills: Interacting Effectively with Others

In Chapter 3, we discussed various kinds of *employee training* and noted that many companies spend large sums of money training their employees. A major goal of such training is equipping employees with new *skills*—proficiencies in performing various tasks. Because skills are often linked closely to particular jobs or tasks, we cannot possibly examine even a tiny sample of them here. Instead, we'll focus on one particular cluster of skills that plays a key role in success in many different contexts: **social skills**—the capacity to interact effectively with others.[72]

social skills
The capacity to interact effectively with others.

TYPES OF SOCIAL SKILLS. What do social skills involve? Although there is far from total agreement on their precise nature, most researchers who have studied social skills and their role in organizational behavior would include the following:

- *Social perception.* Accuracy in perceiving others, including accurate perceptions of their traits, motives, and intentions (see Chapter 3)
- *Impression management.* Proficiency in the use of a wide range of techniques for inducing positive reactions in others (see Chapter 3)
- *Persuasion and social influence.* Skill at using various techniques for changing others' attitudes or behavior in desired directions (see Chapter 12)
- *Social adaptability.* The ability to adapt to a range of social situations and to interact effectively with people from many different backgrounds (see Chapter 6)
- *Emotional awareness/control.* Proficiency with respect to a cluster of skills relating to the emotional side of life (e.g., being able to regulate one's own emotions in various situations and being able to influence others' emotional reactions; see Chapter 5)

If these particular skills remind you of EI, that's not surprising; there is considerable overlap between EI and social skills. However, social skills are somewhat broader in scope. Social skills are important because they have considerable effects on behavior. For example, people with well-developed social skills tend to make good impressions on job interviews, receive positive evaluations of their performance, and perform well when negotiating with others.[73] In fact, a study of more than 1,400 employees found that social skills are the single best predictor of job performance ratings and assessments of potential for promotion for employees in a wide range of jobs.[74] In view of these benefits, it's reasonable to ask how to improve your own social skills. For some suggestions, see Table 4.3.

THE IMPORTANCE OF SOCIAL SKILLS: A DEMONSTRATION. Social skills have very broad and general effects, helping individuals to perform well in a wide range of contexts and on many different jobs. For instance, consider a particularly revealing study designed to investigate the joint effects of *conscientiousness,* one of the Big Five dimensions we discussed earlier, and social skills.[75] The researchers hypothesized that people with high levels of conscientiousness will perform well, but only when they have the requisite social skills to succeed.[76] The idea is that highly conscientiousness people who lack social skills may be seen as unreasonably demanding and inflexible by their coworkers. In other words, without social skills to soften the impact of their highly methodical and task-oriented behavior, they may be perceived negatively, as "driven drudges" rather than as valuable coworkers. And since cooperation and good relations with one's coworkers often is required for success on many tasks, such individuals may work at below average levels.

To test these predictions, the scientists measured the conscientiousness, social skills, and job performance of a variety of workers. As expected, the benefits of conscientiousness were greatest for people high in social skills, smaller for those with average social skills, and weakest for those who were low in social skills (see Figure 4.14). In other words, high levels of conscientiousness translated into excellent performance only for persons who were also socially skilled. For individuals who were low in social skills, in fact, high levels of conscientiousness actually reduced performance slightly. The conclusion is clear: The importance of social skills on the job cannot be overstated.

TABLE 4.3 The SOFTEN Approach to Improving Social Skills

Considering the benefits of having well-developed social skills, it's important to identify things you can do to improve your own ability to interact effectively with others. The following guidelines, following the acronym SOFTEN, generally prove helpful.

Suggestion	Explanation
Smile	Smiling at someone sends a very pleasant message. This is important because few of us want to interact with anyone having a sour disposition.
Open posture	By keeping your arms open (maintaining an open posture) when interacting with others, you send the message that you are welcoming the conversation. In contrast, covering yourself with your arms (maintaining a closed posture) sends the message that you are "closed for business," so to speak—uninterested in interacting with others.
Forward lean	Leaning forward while talking to others brings you closer to them. It speaks clearly of your engagement in the conversation. Leaning away, however, sends the message that you wish to escape them.
Touch	In some situations, and for some people, touching someone else is a sign that you are interested in what they have to say. You have to be careful about this, however, because some people may find it inappropriate or offensive, particularly in certain cultures. So, follow this suggestion with caution.
Eye contact	Looking someone in the eye when you speak to them or listen to them is an essential way to show that you are interested in the conversation. Looking away, however, makes it clear that you really don't want to be there.
Nod	As we note in Chapter 9, nodding is very helpful feedback for speakers because it shows that you are listening and understanding them. This keeps the conversation moving along, which, of course, is essential to ensuring a positive relationship.

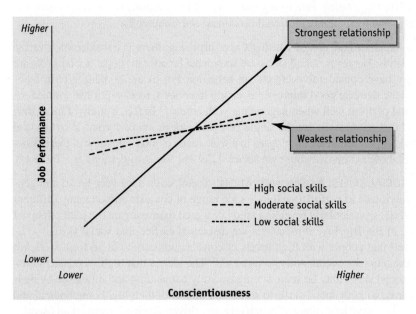

FIGURE 4.14

Social Skills, Conscientiousness, and Task Performance

As shown here, people who are highly conscientious show higher task performance than those who are low in conscientiousness, but only when they are also high in social skills. Individuals who are high in conscientiousness but low in social skills may come across as unreasonably demanding and inflexible, and this may lead other employees to avoid working with—or helping—them.

Source: Based on data from Witt & Ferris, 2003; see Note 76.

Summary and Review of Learning Objectives

1. **Define personality and describe its role in the study of organizational behavior.**
   Personality is the unique and relatively stable pattern of behavior, thoughts, and emotions shown by individuals. It, along with abilities (the capacity to perform various tasks) and various situational factors, determines behavior in organizations. This idea is reflected by the interactionist perspective, which is widely accepted in the field of organizational behavior today.

2. **Identify the Big Five dimensions of personality and elements of core self-evaluations, and describe how they are related to key aspects of organizational behavior.**
   The Big Five dimensions of personality—so named because they seem to be very basic aspects of personality—appear to play a role in the successful performance of many jobs. These are *conscientiousness, extraversion-introversion, agreeableness, neuroticism,* and *openness to experience.* Two of these dimensions, conscientiousness and neuroticism (emotional stability), have been found to be good predictors of success in many different jobs. This is especially true under conditions where job autonomy is high. Core self-evaluations are elements of personality reflecting people's fundamental evaluations of themselves, their bottom-line conclusions about themselves. These are self-esteem, generalized self-efficacy, locus of control, and emotional stability (opposite of the Big Five trait neuroticism). Each of the four dimensions of core self-evaluations is associated with beneficial organizational outcomes.

3. **Distinguish between positive and negative affectivity, and describe its effects on organizational behavior.**
   Positive affectivity and negative affectivity refer to stable tendencies for people to experience positive or negative moods at work, respectively. Compared to people scoring high in negative affectivity, those who are predisposed toward positive affectivity tend to make higher quality individual decisions and are more willing to help others. Negative affectivity on the part of customers can generate negative emotional reactions in service providers, and so reduce customers' satisfaction with the treatment they receive.

4. **Describe achievement motivation, and distinguish among learning, performance, and avoidance goal orientations.**
   Achievement motivation (or need for achievement) refers to the strength of an individual's desire to excel, to succeed at difficult tasks and to do them better than others. A learning goal orientation involves the desire to succeed in order to master new skills. A performance goal orientation involves the desire to succeed to demonstrate one's competence to others. An avoidance goal orientation involves the desire to succeed to avoid criticism from others or appearing to be incompetent.

5. **Describe Machiavellianism and the difference between morning and evening persons, and their role in work-related behavior.**
   People who adopt a manipulative approach to their relations with others are described as being high in Machiavellianism (known as high Machs). They are not influenced by considerations of loyalty, friendship, or ethics. Instead, they simply do whatever is needed to get their way. High Machs tend to be most successful in situations in which people cannot avoid them and in organizations in which there are few established rules. *Morning persons* are individuals who feel most energetic early in the day. *Evening persons* are those who feel most energetic at night. People tend to do their best work during that portion of the day that they prefer and during which they are most energetic.

6. **Differentiate among cognitive intelligence, practical intelligence, and emotional intelligence and explain the influence of social skills on behavior in organizations.**
   Cognitive intelligence is the ability to understand complex ideas, to adapt effectively to the environment, to learn from experience, to engage in various forms of reasoning, and to overcome obstacles by careful thought. Traditionally, this is what we have in mind when we refer to intelligence. However, other forms of intelligence play important roles in organizational functioning. These are practical intelligence, the ability to come up with effective ways of getting things done, and emotional intelligence, a cluster of abilities

relating to the emotional or "feeling" side of life. Social skills play an important role in success in many business contexts because getting along well with others is essential for obtaining positive outcomes, and may even influence the effects of key aspects of personality (e.g., conscientiousness) on performance.

Points to Ponder

Questions for Review

1. Why might two individuals whose personalities are very similar behave differently in a given situation?
2. What is the difference between being in a good mood and having the characteristic of *positive affectivity*?
3. Suppose you are considering jobs with two different companies. Would your perceptions of the "personalities" of those companies affect your decision? Should it?
4. How does having low *self-efficacy* interfere with task performance?
5. Would you prefer to hire employees who are high in learning goal orientation or performance goal orientation? Why?
6. Why are social skills so beneficial to many different kinds of careers?

Experiential Questions

1. Have you ever worked for an organization that selected future employees by means of psychological tests? If so, do you think the test made sense—for instance, did it really measure what it was supposed to measure?

2. Have you ever known someone who was high in conscientiousness but low in social skills? If so, was this individual successful in his or her career? Why or why not?
3. Where do you think *you* stand with respect to generalized self-efficacy? Are you fairly confident that you can accomplish most tasks you set out to do? Or do you have doubts about your ability to succeed in many situations?
4. Have you ever encountered someone who was very high in cognitive intelligence (the kind IQ tests measure), but low in practical intelligence? How could you tell?

Questions to Analyze

1. Suppose you had to choose an assistant. Would you prefer someone who is high in conscientiousness but low in agreeableness, or someone who is high in agreeableness but low in conscientiousness? Why?
2. Are you a morning or an evening person? When did you first decide that you were one or the other? Has the fact that you are a morning or an evening person affected your career decisions in any way?
3. Many persons who attain very high levels of business success were only below-average students in school. Why this might be so?

Experiencing OB

Individual Exercise

What Is Your EQ?

Various tests have been developed to measure the degree of emotional intelligence a person has, characterized as an emotional quotient (EQ score). The instrument presented here is similar to ones that some scientists have used to assess people's emotional intelligence. Although this contains just a sampling of items—and therefore, is not a definitive measure—completing this scale will give you a good sense of your own EQ.

Directions

The items on the following scale describe difficult situations that might be encountered on the job. For each, select the one response that best indicates what you would be most likely to do in that situation.

Scale

1. Someone with whom you work and who you consider to be a friend has borrowed one of your favorite screwdrivers. You asked him to return it to your toolbox, but so far he hasn't done so.
   _____ a. Who needs friends like this? I would end the friendship.
   _____ b. I'd ignore it. Keeping a friend is the most important thing.

_____ c. Until he returns the screwdriver, I'd act cool toward him and hope he gets the message.

_____ d. I'd explain to my friend why I really can use the screwdriver back and politely ask him to return it.

2. After several months on the job, your boss finally assigns you an important project. This is your chance to show him how good you are, but only if you succeed. If you blow it, your future with the company will be bleak.

_____ a. You spend several weeks working out the details of the project before telling anyone about this opportunity.

_____ b. You put the project aside for now, planning to return to it some other time.

_____ c. You get very nervous as you think about the implications.

_____ d. You relax, think about the project, and then bounce some of your ideas off one of your colleagues before pursuing what you believe is the best one.

3. One of your coworkers in an adjacent cubicle has an annoying habit of humming all the time, and it's really getting to you.

_____ a. You just put up with it because it's not really so bad.

_____ b. You explain to this person politely that his or her humming annoys you and explain the reasons why.

_____ c. You take an indirect approach by making a joke about his or her annoying humming and hope that this person will get the hint.

_____ d. You tell your boss that you'll quit your job if this person doesn't stop humming or if you aren't moved to a different cubicle.

4. You are in a business meeting with a client who, for no apparent reason, appears to be very uncomfortable talking to you.

_____ a. You do your best to involve the client in a conversation so that the two of you can learn about one another.

_____ b. You plan to schedule the next meeting at some other location.

_____ c. You begin to worry that you've done something to ruin the business deal.

_____ d. You assume that the client isn't interested in doing business with you so you don't pay much attention to the conversation and spend the time thinking about other things.

5. Walking through the office one day, you stumble and spill coffee all over the floor.

_____ a. You get angry and mutter something to yourself about being so clumsy.

_____ b. After cleaning up the mess you laugh at yourself and go about your business.

_____ c. You get extremely embarrassed and leave the office before anyone sees what you did.

_____ d. You give a dirty look to anyone who happened to see what you did.

6. For several months you were hoping to get an important promotion. You thought of yourself as an ideal candidate, but your boss apparently thought otherwise and recommended someone else instead.

_____ a. You forget about it and convince yourself that the promotion really wasn't that important to you.

_____ b. You keep on doing your best and realize that there will always be another opportunity to get promoted.

_____ c. You feel so upset that you hide in the restroom and cry.

_____ d. You keep thinking about what the promoted person has that you don't have and make yourself feel bad about what happened.

7. In the break room one day, one of your coworkers, Bob, began saying bad things about Cathy, a colleague you really admire but who wasn't there at the time.

_____ a. Although you don't mean them, you go along with Bob by adding a few negative remarks about Cathy yourself.

_____ b. You don't say anything to Bob at the time but later tell him in private how you feel about his remarks.

———— c. You interrupt Bob, saying that you're uncomfortable talking behind someone's back, and then change the subject.

———— d. You keep quiet but then feel bad about not stopping Bob from talking negatively about Cathy.

Scoring Procedure and Interpretation

1. One of the responses for each situation shows a higher degree of emotional intelligence than the others because it reveals empathy and respect for others. With this in mind, try to identify these "answers," that is, the responses that indicate the greatest amount of emotional intelligence.
2. Give yourself 1 point for answering the questions as follows. 1 = d, 2 = d, 3 = b, 4 = a, 5 = b, 6 = b, and 7 = c.
3. The higher your score, the higher your EQ.

Questions for Discussion

1. How successful were you at being able to predict the one response in each set of alternatives that reflected high emotional intelligence? (In other words, how closely did your responses to scoring point number 1 match the correct responses indicated in scoring point number 2?)
2. How did your EQ compare to what you thought it would be? How did it compare to those of other people in your class?
3. For item 7, why do you think the high EI answer was alternative "c" instead of "b"? What does this scoring reveal about standing up for others as an aspect of emotional intelligence?

Group Exercise

Machiavellianism in Action: The $10 Game

People who are high in Machiavellianism (high Machs) often come out ahead in dealing with others because they are true pragmatists. That is, they tend to be willing to do or say whatever it takes to win or to get their way. Several questionnaires exist for measuring Machiavellianism as a personality trait. However, tendencies in this direction also can be observed in many face-to-face situations. The following exercise offers one useful means for observing individual differences with respect to Machiavellianism.

Directions

1. Divide the class into groups of three.
2. Hand the three people in each group a sheet with the following instructions: Imagine that I have placed a stack of ten $1 bills on the table in front of you. This money will belong to *any two of you* who can decide how to divide it.
3. Allow groups up to 10 minutes to reach a decision on this task.
4. Ask each group whether they reached a decision, and what it was. In each group, you probably will find that two people agreed on how to divide the money, leaving the third "out in the cold."

Questions for Discussion

1. How did the two-person groups form? Was there a particular person in each group who was largely responsible for the formation of the winning coalition?
2. Why did the third person get left out of the agreement? What did this person say or do— or fail to say or do—that led to his or her being omitted from the two-person coalition that divided the money?
3. Do you think that actions in this situation are related to Machiavellianism? How? In other words, what particular things did anyone do that you took as an indicator of being a high Mach?

Practicing OB

Predicting Sales Success

A life insurance company has developed a test believed to measure success at personal face-to-face sales. It has used this test to choose new life insurance agents, believing that persons selected in this way will generate high levels of sales. Yet this has not happened. People who score very high on the test are not outselling the company's existing agents, who never took the test before they were hired. What's going on here?

1. Do you think the test of "selling ability" might be at fault? For instance, could it be that this test is not really valid? How would you find out if it is or is not?

2. What other factors might be involved? Assuming the test *is* valid, could the fact that the new agents lack experience be contributing to their relatively poor performance? If so, would you expect this will improve as they gain experience?

3. If you conclude that the test of selling ability is not really valid, how could you help the company develop a better test—one that really does measure this important ability?

■ *Howard Schultz: The Personality Behind Starbucks*

Case in Point

Contrary to popular belief, Howard Schultz was not the founder of Starbucks. Instead, Starbucks Coffee, Tea and Spice, as it was known, began in 1971 as a small coffeehouse in Seattle, the vision of three other men, Jerry Baldwin, Zev Siegel, and Gordon Bowker. A decade later, Schultz, who was selling kitchen equipment in New York City at the time, became curious when lots of coffee roasting equipment was being purchased by this small shop in Seattle. This led Schultz to Seattle to see what was going on. Excited by what he found in this fledgling business, Shultz envisioned having a chain of friendly, Italian-style espresso bars across the United States. At first, Baldwin, Siegel, and Bowker didn't share this image, but Schultz pushed to join the company so he could learn the business; the threesome eventually hired Schultz as Starbucks' marketing manager. After about a year, and the company now with four stores, Schultz convinced his bosses that thinking much larger might not be such a crazy idea. A few years later, Schultz raised $1.25 million and bought the franchise from its three owners. From 1987 to 1992 Schultz grew Starbucks to 150 stores, and by 1990 the company began turning a profit. The template for Starbucks as we know it today—serving 10 million customers a week from 3,300 stores around the world—was established.

Schultz is convinced that a huge part of the company's success rests on his commitment to detail, making sure that every little thing is done right, even the look and feel of the stores. As he put it, "We took things so fastidiously in terms of creating the visual, nonverbal cues of what it means to be in a Starbucks store." Not all CEOs maintain such a careful watch over such seemingly minor details, but Schultz has insisted over the years that nothing is too minor for his attention. This is not to say that he insists on having things his way. Far from it! Schultz always has been committed to gathering everyone's ideas and treating his employees fairly so that they are interested in sharing their ideas.

It cannot be said that Schultz's ego is as large as his ambitions or his successes, as often is found among successful entrepreneurs. Although every detail at Starbucks reflects Schultz's contributions, he always speaks of the company in collective terms, using *we, us,* and *our* instead of *I, me,* and *mine.* To him, it's all about a team of people who collectively buy into the idea of having a great company by serving exceptional products to people with outstanding customer service. After all, people can buy coffee anywhere, so keeping them coming back to Starbucks (which its average customer does 18 times per month) requires listening to people—customers and employees alike—and doing what it takes to keep them happy.

Years ago, for example, business at the typical Starbucks location slowed down later in the day, leading some stores to close around 7:30 P.M. In some locations, however, Schultz discovered that sales actually rose in the late afternoons and early evening hours. Visiting these stores, he discovered why. Apparently, customers started using the stores as meeting places. College students would assemble to study and businesspeople would gather for informal meetings there. Happy to accommodate them, these stores extended their hours and added food items, such as various pastries and now sandwiches, to the already

(Continued)

extensive list of beverage offerings on the menu. This kind of flexibility was in keeping with Schultz's interest in building the business by building successful relationships. To him, it's not about the coffee, but all about people.

Questions for Discussion

1. What particular Big Five personality traits and what elements of core self-evaluation appear to characterize Schultz?

2. What evidence, if any, points to the possibility that Schultz has a high level of achievement motivation?

3. How do you think Schultz's social skills may have contributed to the success of Starbucks? What other special skills and abilities do you think he has that have helped the company grow and prosper?

5 Coping with Organizational Life: Emotions and Stress

Learning Objectives

After reading this chapter, you should be able to:

1. Distinguish between emotions and moods.
2. Explain how emotions and moods influence behavior in organizations.
3. Describe ways in which people manage their emotions in organizations.
4. Identify the major causes of organizational stress.
5. Describe the adverse effects of organizational stress.
6. Identify various ways of reducing stress in the workplace.

Chapter Outline

- Understanding Emotions and Mood
- The Role of Emotions and Mood in Organizations
- Managing Emotions in Organizations
- The Basic Nature of Stress
- Major Causes of Stress in the Workplace
- Adverse Effects of Organizational Stress
- Reducing Stress: What Can Be Done?

Preview Case

■ *Stressing Stress-Free Jobs at Kaiser Permanente*

The expression "physician, heal thyself" suggests that doctors should take doses of their own medicine, so to speak, following their own advice to keep healthy. Kris Ludwigsen, a psychologist at a Kaiser Permanente medical facility in the San Francisco Bay Area, is one health-care professional who not only gets this point, but who acts on it.

In the course of counseling patients, Dr. Ludwigsen observed that many suffered physical maladies stemming from the stresses in their lives. But it was not only her patients who needed treatment, she noted; so too did the doctors and nurses with whom she worked. Since medical professionals often have to make life-and-death decisions and face considerable pressures to lower costs while raising service quality, Dr. Ludwigsen wasn't at all surprised that her colleagues showed signs of stress-related illnesses. Many were forgetful, irritable, quick to cry, easily distracted, and had difficulty concentrating. Unlike her patients, though, most of her colleagues didn't bother to seek treatment.

If they wouldn't come to her, she figured, she would reach out to them. With this in mind, Dr. Ludwigsen launched a comprehensive multistep work stress program for both Kaiser Permanente patients and employees. Since many people—even medical professionals—don't recognize their stress-related symptoms, she began by building awareness. Group sessions were held (strictly confidential, of course) in which people were made aware of some of the signs of stress they were exhibiting. Fatigue, migraines, hypertension, stomach problems, and even panic attacks are indications that it's time to take action.

Since some of the most effective things to do involve getting the stress "out of your system," Dr. Ludwigsen enlisted Kaiser Permanente's help. For example, the company sponsors programs to improve employees' experiences off the job. These include fitness and health classes, seminars to enrich personal relationships, and even training to show expectant mothers how to manage pregnancy in the workplace. On the more active side, the company also has extensive new exercise facilities and sponsors a half-marathon in San Francisco (which in 2010 timed runners by using a disposable computer chip). And to help people relax, it offers massages and yoga classes. In the words of one employee who has taken advantage of these opportunities, "It's really been helpful. My stomach's been fine and I'm sleeping better at night."

Interestingly, one of Dr. Ludwigsen's most important bits of advice was to get people to avoid working long hours so they could rest and spend more time with their families. Although hospital officials might have been concerned that this would cut into the productivity of doctors and nurses, who routinely work long shifts, it wasn't a problem. Gains in productivity resulting from good health more than offset any increased costs linked to shorter shifts, creating benefits for everyone.

These various efforts suggest that Dr. Ludwigsen's message came across loud and clear: Efforts at preventive health care are, in the long run, less expensive and more effective than treating disease. Although Kaiser Permanente may be said to be in the "pound of cure" business, it's also clear that it is committed strongly to offering far more than "an ounce of prevention."

There's no mistaking the wisdom of Kaiser Permanente's efforts to preserve the health and well-being of its employees and of Dr. Ludwigsen's commitment to bringing this about. If you have any doubt about the value of such efforts, consider this: The workplace is the single greatest source of *stress* in people's lives. And annual cost to American organizations is a staggering $300 billion annually, roughly $7,500 per employee.[1] Stress makes a difference in how well people perform, the number of errors they make, and even whether or not they show up for work or remain on their jobs at all. Given that stress plays such an important role in the behavior of people in organizations, it clearly warrants the attention we devote to it in this chapter.

To understand stress fully, it helps to look more broadly at the wide range of emotions that people feel in everyday work situations and their reactions to them. Whether your experiences are positive (e.g., getting a raise), negative (e.g., receiving a poor performance appraisal), or neutral (e.g., doing your job as usual), these everyday feelings—*emotions* and *moods*—play an important role in how we think and act. If emotions and moods seem to be trivial, it's simply because their effects are so widespread that we take them for granted. However, their impact on the way we work can be considerable.[2] Accordingly, we will examine them in this chapter as well.

We begin this chapter with an overview of emotions and mood in organizations, describing their basic nature and the important roles they play in organizations. Following this, we examine the nature of stress on the job, focusing closely on specific steps that can be taken to minimize its often harmful effects.

Understanding Emotions and Mood

Consider, for a moment, the following situations. Put yourself in the places of these characters, imagining how you would feel if you were them.

■ After a gloomy winter, a beautiful, sunny day finally arrived, making Maria happy. She was inspired to come up with lots of new ideas for her clients.

■ Hector was so upset about not making any progress on his sales report that he couldn't take it anymore. He left the work piled up on his desk and went to the gym to work out.

■ It was a special day for Patricia. She was so excited that Demond had asked her to marry him that she made her way through her delivery route in half the usual time—and with a lively spring in her step.

There's nothing special, here, right? Maria is happy, Hector is upset, and Patricia is excited. These are everyday situations to which people have typical reactions. You have them all the time yourself. But don't let these rather ordinary feelings mislead you into thinking that they are unimportant, especially on the job. Indeed, scientists acknowledge that people's feelings at any given time are quite important. They also recognize that two different kinds of feelings are involved—*emotions* and *moods*. These states, as you will see, have far broader consequences than you might imagine, and they operate in highly complex ways.

Properties of Emotions

By definition, **emotions** are overt reactions that express feelings about events. You get angry when a colleague takes advantage of you. You become sad when your best friend leaves to take a new job. And you become afraid of what the future holds when a larger firm merges with the company in which you've worked for the last 15 years. These are all examples of emotional reactions. To understand them, we now consider the various properties of emotions and the different forms they take.

emotions
Overt reactions that express feelings about events.

EMOTIONS ALWAYS HAVE AN OBJECT. Something or someone triggers emotions. For example, your boss may make you angry when she falsely accuses you of making a mistake or a change in company policy that prohibits overtime may leave you feeling worried. In each case, there is someone or something that caused your emotional reaction.

THE SPREAD OF EMOTIONS IS CONTAGIOUS. A key trigger of emotions in people is the emotions of others with whom we interact. This is described using the term **emotional contagion,** defined as the tendency to mimic others' emotional expressions, converging with them emotionally.[3] You may think of it as "catching" the emotions of others. This phenomenon is prevalent on the job, where workers frequently display the same emotional responses of the higher-ranking others with whom they interact (see Figure 5.1).[4]

emotional contagion
The tendency to mimic the emotional expressions of others, converging with them emotionally.

EXPRESSION OF EMOTIONS IS UNIVERSAL. People throughout the world generally portray particular emotions by using the same facial expressions. In fact, even people living in remote parts of the planet tend to express the same emotions in the same manner.[5] As a result, we can do a pretty good (but not perfect) job of recognizing the emotional states of others if we pay attention to their facial expressions. We have to be careful, however, because as we will point out later, people do not always express the emotions they really feel. When they do, however, we are fairly good at recognizing them.

CULTURE DETERMINES HOW AND WHEN PEOPLE EXPRESS EMOTIONS. Although people throughout the world generally express their emotions in the same manner, informal standards govern the degree to which it is acceptable for them to do so.[6] These expectations are known as **display rules.** For example, Italian cultural norms accept public displays of emotion (e.g., hugging good-bye at the airport, or yelling at one another in public), whereas cultural norms frown on such public displays in Great Britain, encouraging people there to "tone down" their emotional displays. For some interesting national differences in willingness to express emotions, see Table 5.1.[7]

display rules
Cultural norms about the appropriate ways to express emotions.

Types of Emotions

Despite what you might think, people do not have an infinite (or even a very large) number of unrelated emotions. Rather, people's emotions may be categorized in a few different ways. Depending on how you categorize them, different features of emotion are highlighted. We now describe two such ways of categorizing emotions.

Fancy/Alamy Images.

FIGURE 5.1

Emotional Contagion in the Workplace

The emotions we display tend to be picked up by others, resulting in a convergence of emotions. This so-called *emotional contagion* occurs regularly in the workplace, where emotions are easily spread from person to person. Can you think of situations on the job in which you "caught" the emotions of others with whom you came into contact? How about occasions in which you "spread" your emotions to others?

self-conscious emotions
Feelings that stem from within, such as shame, guilt, embarrassment, and pride.

SELF-CONSCIOUS EMOTIONS VERSUS SOCIAL EMOTIONS. A useful way of distinguishing between emotions is by comparing those that come from internal sources with those that come from external sources. This is the essence of the distinction between so-called *self-conscious emotions* and *social emotions* (for a summary, see Figure 5.2).

Self-conscious emotions refer to feelings that stem from within. Examples include *shame, guilt, embarrassment,* and *pride.*[8] Scientists believe that self-conscious emotions developed within

TABLE 5.1 National Differences in Expressivity

In a survey of more than 5,000 people in 32 nations, researchers found that people in some countries are more inclined to express their emotions than those in other countries. Listed in order from most expressive (rank 1) to least expressive (rank 32), the findings are summarized here. The scores shown are an index created by the scientists to reflect each country's level of expressivity (higher scores reflect higher degrees of expressivity).

Rank	Nation	Score	Rank	Nation	Score	Rank	Nation	Score
1	Zimbabwe	523	10 tied	India	495	22	Greece	452
2	Canada	520	13	Mexico	485	23 tied	Italy	451
3	United States	519	14	Georgia	478	23 tied	Croatia	451
4	Australia	510	15 tied	Poland	477	25	South Korea	449
5	Nigeria	506	15 tied	Portugal	477	26 tied	Switzerland	446
6	Denmark	505	17	People's Republic		26 tied	Malaysia	446
7	New Zealand	502		of China	471	28	Israel	442
8	Belgium	498	18	Czech Republic	468	29	Russia	432
9	Netherlands	496	19	Turkey	467	30	Bangladesh	422
10 tied	Brazil	495	20	Japan	464	31	Indonesia	420
10 tied	Hungary	495	21	Germany	455	32	Hong Kong	399

Source: Based on data reported by Matsumoto et al., 2008; see Note 7.

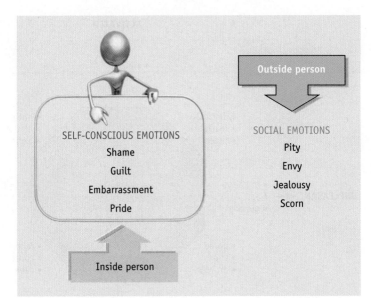

FIGURE 5.2

Self-Conscious Emotions Versus Social Emotions: A Summary
As indicated here, *self-conscious emotions* stem from within individuals, and *social emotions* refer to feelings stemming from outside individuals. Note the four examples in each category.

people to help them stay aware of and regulate their relationships with others. For example, we feel shame when we believe we have failed to meet expectations, and in such cases we are likely to humble ourselves to others, allowing them to have the upper hand. So, if we have done something to harm a coworker, we are likely to demonstrate—and express—feelings of embarrassment and shame, which help appease the relationship with that individual.[9] Interestingly, research has shown that our brains are involved closely in this process: People who have suffered damage to the orbitofrontal portions of their brains tend to be less effective at experiencing self-conscious emotions and at regulating the behaviors they guide than those whose brains are intact.[10]

Social emotions refer to people's feelings based on information external to themselves. Examples include *pity, envy, jealousy,* and *scorn*. For example, a worker may experience envy if she covets something that another has (e.g., a better work assignment) or pity if she feels sorry for someone else (e.g., someone who was hurt in an accident). These are all emotions likely to be experienced in the workplace.[11]

social emotions
People's feelings based on information external to themselves, such as pity, envy, jealousy, and scorn.

THE CIRCUMPLEX MODEL OF AFFECT. A popular way for scientists to differentiate between emotions has been by combining two different dimensions—the degree to which emotions are pleasant or unpleasant, and the degree to which they make one feel alert and engaged (a variable known as *activation*). This two-dimensional perspective is known as the **circumplex model of affect** (see Figure 5.3).[12] This diagram illustrates how various emotions are interrelated with respect to these two dimensions. Four major categories result.

To understand how to read this diagram (hence, to understand the circumplex model of affect), look, for example, at the upper right portion of Figure 5.3. It shows that being elated is a pleasant emotion (because it makes us feel good) and that it also is a highly activated emotion (because it encourages us to take action). They fall into the activated positive affect category. The same applies to the two other emotions in that part of the diagram (enthusiastic and excited). Within the diagram, any emotions that lie directly opposite each other are characterized in the opposite manner. So, following through on our example, being bored, tired, and drowsy are emotions considered opposite to enthusiastic, elated, and excited. They are at the opposite ends of the two main dimensions—that is, they generate unactivated negative affect.

circumplex model of affect
A theory of emotional behavior based on the degree to which emotions are pleasant or unpleasant and the degree to which they make one feel activated (i.e., feeling alert and engaged).

The Basic Nature of Mood

In contrast to emotions, which are highly specific and intense, we also have feelings that are more diffuse in scope, known as *moods*. Scientists define **mood** as an unfocused, relatively mild feeling that exists as background to our daily experiences. Whereas we are inclined to recognize the emotions we are feeling, moods are more subtle and difficult to detect. For example, you may say that you are in a good mood or a bad mood, but this isn't as focused as saying that you are experiencing a certain emotion, such as anger or sadness.

mood
An unfocused, relatively mild feeling that exists as background to our daily experiences.

FIGURE 5.3

The Circumplex Model of Affect

This conceptualization summarizes emotions in terms of two key dimensions: activated–unactivated and pleasant–unpleasant. The emotions within each grouping are similar to one another. Those across from one another in this diagram are considered opposite emotions.

Source: Based on Huelsman et al., 2003; see Note 12.

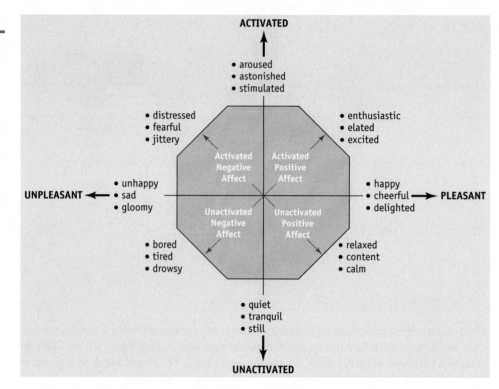

Moods fluctuate rapidly, sometimes widely, during the course of a day. Whereas favorable feedback from the boss may make us feel good, harsh criticism may put us in a bad mood. Such temporary shifts in feeling *states*—short-term differences in the way we feel—are only partly responsible for the moods that people demonstrate. Superimposed over these passing conditions are also more stable personality *traits*—consistent differences between people's predispositions toward experiencing positive or negative affect, as we discussed in Chapter 4. Mood, in other words, is a combination of both who we are, personality-wise, and the conditions we face (see Figure 5.4).[13]

Not surprisingly, then, the moods we experience can be based on our individual qualities (e.g., being depressed), as well as the general characteristics of our work groups or organizations (e.g., the extent to which they are upbeat, energetic, and enthusiastic). With this in mind, many companies today, including most of those appearing regularly on *Fortune* magazine's list of the "100 Best Companies to Work For," go out of their way to ensure that their employees have fun while on the job.[14]

FIGURE 5.4

Moods Matter Greatly

Being predisposed toward negative affect is only one determinant of people's moods. In addition to this stable trait, mood also is determined by more variable states, temporary conditions experienced that leave us feeling certain ways.

"You tested positive for being negative."

The Role of Emotions and Mood in Organizations

American statesman and inventor Benjamin Franklin is said to have observed that, "The Declaration of Independence only guarantees the American people the right to pursue happiness. You have to catch it yourself." This raises a question: What happens when people do, in fact, "catch" happiness? We certainly enjoy being happy, of course, but does this have any effect on work performance? We now consider these questions.

Are Happier People More Successful on Their Jobs?

To appreciate the answer to this question, let's clarify what we mean by *happy*. To most social scientists, individuals considered happy are those who frequently experience positive emotions in their lives. With this in mind, can it be said that people do better on their jobs when they are happy? The answer is yes—happy workers do indeed enjoy several advantages over their less happy counterparts.[15] Research shows that this takes two major forms.

JOB PERFORMANCE. Happier people tend to outperform less happy people in several different ways. To begin, they tend to get better jobs—that is, ones that give them higher levels of autonomy, meaning, and variety.[16] Then, once on their jobs, they perform them more successfully.[17] This has been found to occur among people in jobs ranging from dormitory resident advisor to cricket player.[18] Interestingly, this same effect also occurs at the highest echelons of organizations. Happier CEOs of companies tend to have happier employees working for them. And, importantly (as we will describe in Chapter 6), happy employees are inclined to remain on their jobs and not to seek new positions elsewhere.[19] In part because of this, organizations populated by happy individuals tend to be more profitable than those consisting of less happy people.[20] Obviously, the importance of happiness cannot be overstated when it comes to job performance.

INCOME. Do happier people earn higher incomes? Yes, they do. Research has found this to be the case in countries throughout the world. For example, high correlations between happiness and income were found among people in Germany and Russia.[21] This same relationship was found even among indigenous Malaysian farmers whose only income was the value of their property and belongings.[22] In these cases, because the relationships are correlational, it's unclear whether people make more money because they're happy or people become happy because they make more money (see Appendix 1). In either case, this connection is worth noting because it is quite strong.

Why Are Happier Workers More Successful?

What is behind these strong connections between happiness and work success? As in most OB phenomena, there are several answers.

DECISION QUALITY. Research has found that people showing high positive affectivity do a better job of making decisions than those showing high negative affectivity.[23] Specifically, people make decisions that are more accurate and more important to the group's effectiveness, and they have greater managerial potential. This ability to make better decisions is a particularly good reason why happy people tend to be successful.

EVALUATION. Mood also biases the way we evaluate people and things. For example, people report greater satisfaction with their jobs while they are in good moods than while they are in bad moods.[24] Being in a good mood also leads people to perceive (and admit to perceiving) the positive side of others' work. Because being in a good mood keeps managers from perceiving their subordinates' good behavior as bad (as might occur if they are biased or extremely tough), it leads them to offer the kind of encouraging feedback likely to help subordinates to improve (see Chapter 7). By contrast, managers whose bad moods lead them to evaluate their subordinates in an inappropriately negatively fashion are unable to help those subordinates improve their work. This, of course, interferes with the performance of those workers and the effectiveness of their managers.

MEMORY: ACCURACY OF SHORT-TERM RECALL. Mood is related to memory in an interesting manner. Although the effects of mood on memory tend to be subtle, the form of this relationship is somewhat counterintuitive. Specifically, people who are in negative moods have better *short-term memories* (i.e., capacity to recall information that was encountered recently) than those who are in positive moods.

Evidence to this effect was reported in a recent experiment conducted on days that were either cloudy and rainy (assumed to create negative moods) or sunny (assumed to create positive moods).[25] Participants in the study were randomly selected shoppers who made purchases at a convenience store where 10 assorted small toys were displayed at the checkout counter. After leaving the store, these individuals were approached by a research assistant who invited them to complete a questionnaire. Responses to this instrument confirmed that people tested on sunny days were, in fact, in better moods than those tested on cloudy, rainy days. The questionnaire also assessed shoppers' memories for the items at the checkout counter by giving them a list of 10 items that were present and another 10 items that were not present. The results summarized in Figure 5.5 reveal the negative effect of mood on memory. Specifically, compared to shoppers in positive moods, those in negative moods recalled more of the correct items and indicated seeing fewer of the incorrect items.

Why did this occur? One explanation is that people who are in good moods want to preserve them, and can do so by investing fewer of their cognitive resources on attending to the world around them. And because they are less observant, they cannot recall the things they see particularly well.[26] Another interesting explanation is that as a species, people have evolved in a manner that helps us adapt to negative moods in an unconscious manner that is adaptive. Specifically, we may have learned to respond to negative moods by interacting with our environments carefully by observing what's there so that we can respond to situations appropriately. This type of thinking, referred to as **accommodative processing (bottom-up processing)**, would account for the superior memory of people in bad moods. In contrast, people in good moods have less need to be especially attentive to their environments and therefore process information in a less effortful manner by merely using the knowledge they already have at their disposal instead of taking in new information. This type of thinking, referred to as **assimilative processing (top-down processing)**, would account for why people in good moods would not remember things they just saw and believe they saw things they didn't really see.

Before moving on, a word of caution is in order. It would be a serious mistake to take these findings as evidence that we should avoid putting people in good moods so as to guard against failing memories. Keep in mind that these effects reflect what occurs only when people are not trying to commit things to memory, in contrast to conditions on most jobs, where people go out of their way to focus on what's important. Under such circumstances, the subtle effects of mood demonstrated in this study are likely to be overridden by conscious efforts to process information appropriately. Would such deliberate effects also be influenced by mood? Surely, the minor mood changes induced by natural variation in weather would not make a difference here. However, major changes in mood, such as those induced by the death of a loved one or by winning large awards in the lottery, surely might impose sufficient distractions as to interfere with memory. In conclusion, the relationship between mood and memory is a complex one that is of considerable importance to understanding the behavior of people in organizations.

accommodative processing (bottom-up processing) A way of processing information in which people carefully observe what's going on around them so that they can respond to situations appropriately.

assimilative processing (top-down processing) A way of processing information in which people rely on the knowledge already at their disposal instead of taking in new information.

FIGURE 5.5

The Negative Impact of Mood on Memory

An experiment found that people in negative moods (due to cloudy, rainy weather) demonstrated better short-term recall than people in positive moods (due to sunny weather).

Source: Based on data reported by Forgas et al., 2009; see Note 25.

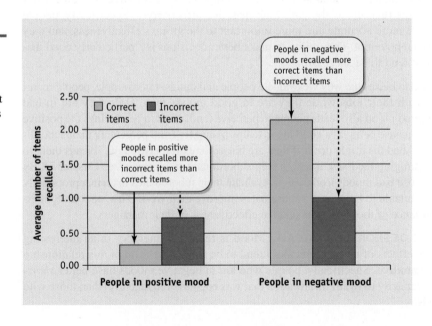

MEMORY: WHAT WE RECALL? Thus far, we've focused on the extent to which mood influences the *accuracy* of what is recalled. It's also important to note that mood impacts the *nature* of what is recalled as well. Specifically, it has been established that being in a positive mood helps people recall positive things, whereas being in a negative mood helps people recall negative things.[27] This idea is known as **mood congruence.**

As an example of mood congruence on the job, suppose you go to work while you're in a particularly good mood. This is likely to lead you to recall things that happened on the job that put you in a good mood there (e.g., the friendly relationships you have with your coworkers). Likewise, someone who is in a bad mood is likely to recall any negative things associated with work, such as a recent fight with the boss. This is important because of its potential effects on job performance. To the extent that focusing on positive things encourages people to put forth extra effort (which they would be unlikely to do when focusing primarily on how bad things are), they would be inclined to perform at higher levels than those focusing on negative aspects of the job (see Figure 5.6).

COOPERATION. Mood strongly affects the extent to which people help each other, cooperate with each other, and refrain from behaving aggressively (forms of behavior we will discuss in more detail in Chapter 11). People who are in good moods also tend to be highly generous and are inclined to help fellow workers who need their assistance. People who are in good moods also are inclined to work carefully with others to resolve conflicts with them, whereas people in bad moods are likely to keep those conflicts brewing. This is yet another reason why being in a good mood enhances job performance.

Clearly, people's moods and emotions have profound effects on their performance in organizations, and for a variety of reasons. Given this importance, it's not surprising that today's organizational scientists have been devoting a great deal of attention to this topic.[28] One way they do this is by developing theories to help explain the nature of moods and emotions. We now consider one particularly influential theory in this regard.

Affective Events Theory

In recent years, one of the guiding forces in the study of emotions in organizations has been **affective events theory (AET).**[29] This theory identifies various factors that lead to people's emotional reactions on the job and how these reactions affect those individuals (see Figure 5.7).[30]

mood congruence
The tendency to recall positive things when you are in a good mood and to recall negative things when you are in a bad mood.

affective events theory (AET)
The theory that identifies various factors that lead to people's emotional reactions on the job and how these reactions affect those individuals.

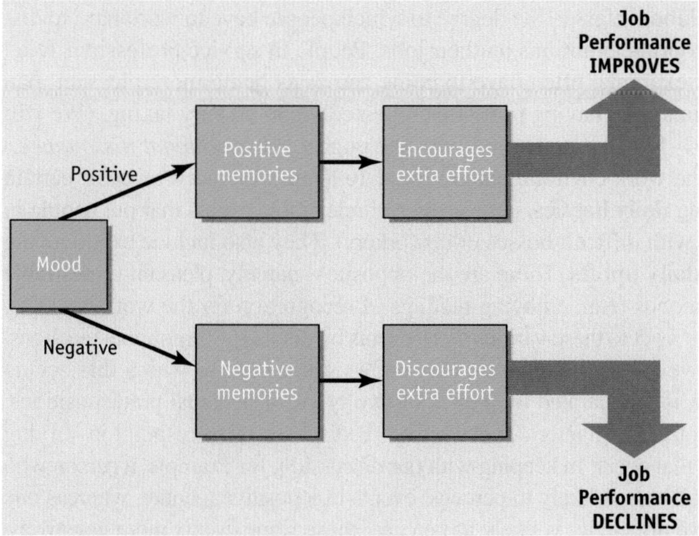

FIGURE 5.6

The Effects of Mood Congruence

The concept of *mood congruence* suggests that people's memories match their emotions. For example, people experiencing positive moods are inclined to have positive memories. This, in turn, encourages people to put forth extra effort, thereby improving their job performance. Just the opposite occurs in the case of negative moods.

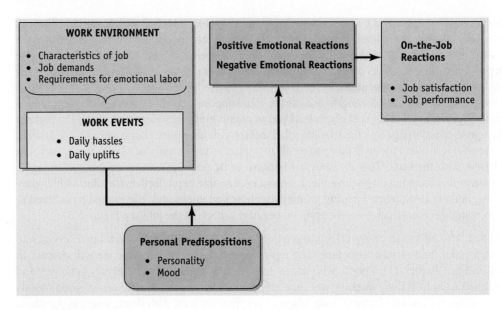

FIGURE 5.7

Affective Events Theory

According to affective events theory, people's job performance and job satisfaction are influenced by their positive and negative emotional reactions to events on the job. These events, in turn, are influenced by aspects of the work environment and various events that occur on the job. People's emotional reactions to these events depend on such individual characteristics as their moods and aspects of their personalities.

Source: Based on suggestions by Ashkanasy & Daus, 2002; see Note 28.

Beginning on the left side of Figure 5.7, AET recognizes that people's emotions are determined, in part, by various features of the work environment. For example, the way we feel is likely to be determined by various characteristics of the jobs we do (e.g., we are likely to feel good about jobs that are interesting and exciting), the demands we face (e.g., how pressured we are to meet deadlines), and by requirements for *emotional labor.*

emotional labor
The psychological effort involved in holding back one's true emotions.

The concept of **emotional labor** refers to the degree to which people have to work hard to display what they believe are appropriate emotions on their jobs. People in service professions (e.g., waitresses and salesclerks), for example, often have to come across as being more pleasant than they really feel. As you might imagine, having to do this repeatedly can be very taxing. (We will return to this idea on pages 153–154, in connection with the concept of *emotional dissonance.*)

These various features of the work environment are likely to lead to the occurrence of certain events. These include confronting **daily hassles,** unpleasant or undesirable events that put people in bad moods (e.g., having to deal with difficult bosses or coworkers). They also include experiencing more positive events known as **daily uplifts.** These are the opposite—namely, pleasant or desirable events that put people in good moods (e.g., enjoying feelings of recognition for the work they do).

daily hassles
Unpleasant or undesirable events that put people in bad moods.

daily uplifts
Pleasant or desirable events that put people in good moods.

As Figure 5.7 reveals, people react to these various work events by displaying emotional reactions, both positive and negative. However, as the diagram also shows, the extent to which this occurs depends on (or, as scientists say, is "moderated by") each of two types of personal predispositions: personality and mood. As we noted in Chapter 4, personality predisposes us to respond in varying degrees of intensity to the events that occur. In keeping with our discussion, for example, a person who has a high degree of positive affectivity is likely to perceive events in a positive manner, whereas one who has a high degree of negative affectivity is likely to perceive those same events more negatively.

Mood also influences the nature of the relationship between work events and emotional reactions, as Figure 5.7 suggests. This is in keeping with the point we made earlier—that the mood we are in at any given time can exaggerate the nature of the emotions we experience in response to an event. So, for example, an event that leads a person to experience a negative emotional reaction (e.g., having a fight with a coworker) is likely to make that individual feel even worse if he or she is in a bad mood at the time.

Finally, as the theory notes, these affective reactions have two important effects. First, they promote high levels of job performance. This should not be surprising, given that we already noted that happy people perform their jobs at high levels. Second, AET also notes that affective reactions are responsible for people's job performance and *job satisfaction*—that is, the extent to which they hold positive attitudes toward their jobs (we will discuss this in detail in Chapter 6). Indeed, research has established very strongly that people who are inclined to experience positive emotions are likely to be satisfied with their jobs.[31]

Putting this all together, consider the following example. You have been employed happily as a software engineer at a high-tech firm for about a year. You find the work pleasantly challenging and in line with your talents. Over the course of your workdays, you experience many enjoyable encounters with others. On this particular occasion, your boss just gave you a big pat on the back in recognition of your latest revenue-generating suggestion. And, because you have a high degree of positive affect and you are already in a good mood when this happened, you experience a very positive reaction to this event. As a result, you are strongly motivated to perform your job at a high level and you very much enjoy your work, taking pride in it as well.

Although AET contains many individual ideas, and it is relatively new, it already has received considerable support from researchers.[32] Its importance rests on two key ideas—one for scientists and one for practicing managers.[33] First, unlike many other theories of OB (such as the others described in this book), this approach recognizes the important role of emotions. Second, AET sends a strong message to managers: Do not overlook the emotional reactions of your employees. They may be more important than you think. In fact, when they accumulate over time, their impact can be considerable. Thus, it is clear that anyone in a supervisory capacity has to pay attention to managing emotions in the workplace. We now turn to this topic.

Managing Emotions in Organizations

As we discussed in Chapter 4 when describing *emotional intelligence,* emotions are important on the job. People who are good at "reading" and understanding emotions in others, and who are able to regulate their own emotional reactions, tend to have an edge when it comes to dealing with others.[34] As we now will describe, this is only one possible way in which people manage their emotions in organizations.

Emotional Dissonance

Imagine that you are a flight attendant for a major airline. After a cross-country flight with rude passengers, you finally reach your destination. You feel tired and annoyed, but you do not have the option of expressing how you really feel. You don't even have the luxury of acting neutrally and expressing nothing at all. Instead, you are expected to act peppy and cheerful, smiling and thanking the passengers for choosing your airline and cheerfully saying good-bye (more like "b'bye") to them as they exit the plane (see Figure 5.8). The conflict between the emotion you feel (anger) and the one you are required to express (happiness) may take its toll on your well-being. This example illustrates a kind of situation that is all too typical—one in which you are required to display emotions on the job that are inconsistent with how you actually feel.

This phenomenon, known as **emotional dissonance,** can be a significant source of work-related stress (the major topic that we will discuss in the second half of this chapter).[35] Emotional dissonance is likely to occur in situations in which there are strong expectations regarding the emotions a person is expected to display by virtue of his or her job requirements. Our flight attendant example illustrates this point. The same applies to customer service representatives, bank tellers, entertainers—just about anyone who provides services to the public.

When emotional dissonance occurs, people often have to try very hard to ensure that they display the appropriate emotions. As we noted earlier, the psychological effort involved in doing this is referred to as *emotional labor.* If you ever find yourself "biting your tongue"—that is, holding back from saying what you want to say—then you are expending a great deal of emotional labor. Actually, not saying what you really think is only part of the situation. Emotional labor also is invested in saying things you don't really feel. For example, you would have to invest a great deal of emotional labor when confronting a coworker who comes to you asking you how you feel about her awful new hairdo. You don't like it at all, but you struggle to keep your feelings to yourself (and not even to "leak" them nonverbally; see Chapter 9). When pressed to say something, you engage in "a little white lie" by telling her how very flattering it is.

emotional dissonance
Inconsistencies between the emotions we feel and the emotions we express.

Vario Images GmbH & Co. KG/Alamy Images.

FIGURE 5.8

Emotional Labor and Emotional Dissonance in Action

When people make an effort to display emotions they don't really feel, they are likely to be engaging in *emotional labor*. The more these displayed emotions differ from the ones someone actually feels, the more he or she is said to experience *emotional dissonance*. It's not uncommon for people who deal with the public, such as this flight attendant, to expend high amounts of emotional labor to cover up feeling grumpy and fatigued after a long flight and with uncooperative passengers.

felt emotions
The emotions people actually feel (which may differ from *displayed emotions*).

displayed emotions
Emotions that people show others, which may or may not be in line with their *felt emotions*.

Although this is a form of dishonesty, it is considered widely appropriate to keep from hurting people's feelings by saying the polite thing.

This discussion underscores an important point: The emotions people actually experience, known as **felt emotions,** may be discrepant from the emotions they show others, known as **displayed emotions.** This is not at all surprising. After all, our jobs do not always give us the luxury of expressing how we truly feel. To do so, such as by expressing the anger you feel toward your boss, is likely to lead to problems. As sociologists tell us, social pressure compels people to conform to expectations about which particular emotions are appropriate to show in public and which are not. As we noted earlier, such *display rules* vary among cultures. But they also appear to differ as a function of people's occupational positions.

It is an unspoken rule, for example, that an athletic coach is not supposed to be openly hostile and negative when speaking about an opponent (at least, when doing so in public). It also is expected that people considered "professionals," such as doctors and lawyers, demonstrate appropriate decorum and seriousness when interacting with their patients and clients. Should your own doctor or lawyer respond to your difficult situation by saying, "Wow, I sure wouldn't want to be in your shoes," you may find yourself looking for someone else to help you.

Controlling Anger (Before It Controls You)

anger
A heightened state of emotional arousal (e.g., increased heart rate, rapid breathing, flushed face, sweaty palms, etc.) fueled by cognitive interpretations of situations.

Quite often, behaving appropriately in business situations requires controlling negative emotions, particularly anger. After all, to be successful we cannot let the situations we face get the better of us. It's perfectly natural for anyone to get angry, particularly on the job, where there may be a great deal to anger us. We can be made angry, for example, by feeling unfairly treated (see Chapter 2), by believing that we are disrespected by others, by feeling that we are being attacked or threatened in some way, and the like.

Although we all know what *anger* is, and we have experienced it many times (perhaps too many), a precise definition is in order. By **anger,** scientists are referring to a heightened state of emotional

OB in Practice

Managing Anger in the Workplace

People often say that "it's good to let it all hang out" by expressing one's anger fully. The American Psychological Association advises, however, that this is a dangerous myth because people sometimes use this belief to grant themselves license to explode and take things too far.[36] And this, of course, does nothing to alleviate the source of your anger. In fact, excessive displays of anger are likely to make things worse.

This raises a critical question: What, precisely, can we do to control our anger? Although it's not always easy to keep our anger in check—and indeed, there are professionals who often are hired to help people do this (although rarely in the form taken in the 2003 Adam Sandler and Jack Nicholson film, *Anger Management*)—we all can do various things to control ourselves. Some of the key ones are as follows.

1. *Practice relaxation.* People who display dangerous amounts of anger often find it difficult to relax. As a result, they get frustrated easily and are inclined to "fly off the handle." By learning to relax, however, such individuals are better able to take control of their emotions. So, how can we do this? As we mention later in this chapter, *meditation* is especially helpful for getting people to keep their anger in check.
2. *Change the way you think.* When we get angry, we tend to think irrationally, making things worse than they really are—and this, of course, will not help. Being logical about the source of your anger is what's needed, and this involves getting clear facts and thinking things through. So, instead of screaming your head off the next time you're angry, try to figure out exactly what's going on. And if you cannot do so yourself, get someone to help you—a friend, for example, can be useful in pointing out any irrational thoughts you may have.
3. *Use humor.* There's nothing like humor to take the edge off your fury. Being silly can diffuse anger, keeping it in check. So, the next time you find yourself thinking that someone is a "dirtbag," don't come out and say so. Instead, think about exactly what a bag of dirt looks like. Imagining that person's head atop a burlap sack of topsoil may give you pause, making you chuckle. And this momentary relief may help you regain your composure.
4. *Leave the room.* When you feel anger welling up inside, move to another room or even leave the building. Changing your surroundings may help you escape whatever or whoever is causing you to be so angry. Even such temporary avoidance may be enough to keep you from saying or doing something that might make you sorry. Additionally, the time spent moving elsewhere also can help by distracting you from the immediacy of the situation.

If there ever was a time to refer to something as "easier said than done," this is it. However, if there ever was something that "must be done, or else," this also is it. Because so much is riding on the proper management of anger, efforts to put this advice to work for you are sure to pay off in the long run.

---

arousal (e.g., increased heart rate, rapid breathing, flushed face, sweaty palms, etc.) fueled by cognitive interpretations of situations. Anger reactions can run the gamut from irritation to outrage and fury.

Importantly, there are situations in which displaying anger can be purposeful and constructive. For example, to get a subordinate to take immediate action in a dangerous situation, a supervisor may express anger by raising her voice and looking that person straight in the eye. This would be the case should a military officer display her anger purposely to express urgency when ordering a soldier under her command to move immediately out of a combat zone. Because of its constructive and highly controlled nature, anger of this type is not problematic. In fact, it can be quite valuable. Where anger can be dangerous, however, is when it erupts violently and is out of control. We need to be concerned about this because aggression is a natural reaction to anger.

The challenge people face is to control their anger appropriately. This is the idea behind the practice of **anger management**—systematic efforts to reduce people's emotional feelings of anger and the physiological arousal it causes. Because we often cannot eliminate, avoid, or alter the things that anger us, it's important to learn to control our reactions. For some suggestions as to how to go about doing so, see the OB in Practice section above.

anger management
Systematic efforts to reduce people's emotional feelings of anger and the physiological arousal it causes.

The Basic Nature of Stress

Stress is an unavoidable fact of organizational life today, taking its toll on both individuals and organizations. According to one survey, 90 percent of American workers report feeling stressed at least once a week, and 40 percent describe their jobs as very stressful most of the time.[37] What stresses them? Lots of things, but having too much work to do and fear of being laid off are among people's most common concerns. As you might imagine, these sources of stress are both harmful to individual workers and costly to their organizations. In fact, about half of all American workers report that stress has adversely affected their health.[38] Not surprisingly, stress on the job has been linked to increases

stress
The pattern of emotional and physiological reactions occurring in response to demands from within or outside an organization. See *stressor.*

in accidents, lost productivity, and of course, phenomenal boosts in medical insurance. Overall, work-related stress has been estimated to cost American companies $300 billion annually.[39]

Considering these sobering statistics, it is clearly important to understand the nature of organizational stress. Formally, scientists define **stress** as the pattern of emotional and physiological reactions occurring in response to demands from within or outside organizations. In this portion of the chapter, we will review the major causes and effects of stress. Importantly, we also will describe various ways of effectively managing stress so as to reduce its negative impact. Before doing this, however, we will describe the basic nature of stress in more detail, beginning with an overview of stressors.

Stressors in Organizations

What do each of the following situations have in common?

- You are fired the day before you become eligible to receive your retirement pension.
- You find out that your company is about to eliminate your department.
- Your boss tells you that you will not be getting a raise this year.
- Your spouse is diagnosed with a serious illness.

stressor
Any demands, either physical or psychological in nature, encountered during the course of living.

The answer, besides that they are all awful situations, is that each situation involves external events (i.e., ones beyond your own control) that create extreme demands on you. Stimuli of this type are known as **stressors,** formally defined as any demands, either physical or psychological in nature, encountered during the course of living.

Scientists often find it useful to distinguish stressors in terms of how long-lasting they are. This results in the following three major categories (see Figure 5.9):

acute stressor
Stressors that bring some form of sudden change that threatens us either physically or psychologically, requiring people to make unwanted adjustments.

- **Acute stressors** are those that bring some form of sudden change that threatens us either physically or psychologically, requiring people to make unwanted adjustments. For example, you may be assigned to a different shift at work, requiring you to get up earlier in the morning and to eat meals at different times. As your body's equilibrium is disrupted, you respond physiologically (e.g., by being tired) and emotionally (e.g., by being grouchy).

episodic stressor
The result of experiencing several acute stressors in a short period of time.

- **Episodic stressors** are the result of experiencing several acute stressors in a short period of time, such as when you "have one of those days" in which everything goes wrong. In other words, you are experiencing particularly stressful episodes in life. This would be the case, for example, if within the course of a week you have a serious disagreement with one of your subordinates, you lose a major sales account, and then, to top it off, the pipes burst in your office, causing water to ruin your important papers and your computer. For a list of some of the most common episodic stressors, see Table 5.2.

chronic stressor
The most extreme type of stressor, constant and unrelenting in nature, and having a long-term effect on the body, mind, and spirit.

- **Chronic stressors** are the most extreme type of stressor because they are constant and unrelenting in nature, having a long-term effect on the body, mind, and spirit. For example, a person experiences chronic stressors if he or she is in a long-term abusive relationship with a boss or spouse or has a debilitating disease (e.g., arthritis or migraine headaches) that adversely affects his or her ability to work. In recent years, in which layoffs have been common, people have suffered stress due to considerable uncertainties about their future.

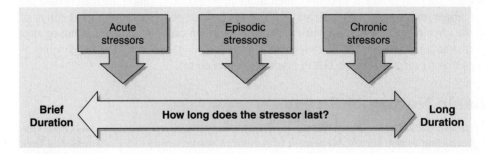

FIGURE 5.9

Different Types of Stressors

Whereas *acute stressors* tend to be of brief duration, *chronic stressors* endure for a long period of time. *Episodic stressors* generally last for intermediate periods of time.

TABLE 5.2 Common Episodic Stressors in the Workplace

Many of the most commonly encountered stressors in organizations are episodic in nature. If you think about these, it's not difficult to recognize how they actually are composed of several different acute stressors. For example, fear of losing one's job includes concerns over money, threats to self-esteem, embarrassment, and other acute stressors.

- Lack of involvement in making organizational decisions
- Unrelenting and unreasonable expectations for performance
- Poor communication with coworkers
- Fear of losing one's job
- Spending long amounts of time away from home
- Office politics and conflict
- Not being paid enough given one's level of responsibility and performance

The Cognitive Appraisal Process

The Roman emperor and philosopher Marcus Aurelius Antonius (A.D. 121–180) is quoted as saying, "If you are distressed by anything external, the pain is not due to the thing itself, but to your estimate of it; and this you have the power to revoke at any moment." This observation is as true today as it was some 2,000 years ago, when first spoken. The basic idea is that the mere presence of potentially harmful events or conditions in the environment is not enough for them to be stressors. For an event to become a stressor to someone, he or she must think of it as a stressor and acknowledge the danger and the difficulty of coping with it. As you think about the events or conditions you encounter, some may be considered especially threatening (warranting your concern), whereas others pose less of a problem to you (and can be ignored safely). Your assessment of the dangers associated with any potential stressor is based on **cognitive appraisal**—the process of judging the extent to which an environmental event is a potential source of stress. Let's consider this process more closely.

On some occasions, people appraise conditions instantly. Suppose, for example, you are camping in the woods when a bear looks like it's going to attack. You immediately assess that you are in danger and run away as fast as you can. This is a natural reaction, which biologists call a **flight response**. Indeed, making a rapid escape from a dangerous situation occurs automatically. So, without giving the matter much thought, you immediately flee from a burning office building because you judge the situation to be life-threatening. The situation is extreme, so you appraised it as dangerous automatically. In the blink of an eye, you recognized the danger and sought to escape. Although you may not have deliberated all the pros and cons of the situation, you did engage in a cognitive appraisal process: You recognized the situation as dangerous and took action instantly.

Most of the situations managers face are neither as extreme nor as clear-cut. In fact, the vast majority of would-be stressors become stressors only if people perceive them as such. For example, if you are an expert at writing sales reports and really enjoy doing them, the prospect of having to work extra hours on preparing one is not likely to be a stressor for you. However, for someone else who finds the same task to be an obnoxious chore, confronting it may well be a stressor. Likewise, the deadline might not be a stressor if you perceive that it is highly flexible and that nobody takes it seriously or if you believe you can get an extension simply by asking. The point is simple: Whether or not an environmental event is a stressor depends on how it is perceived. What might be a stressor for you under some circumstances might not be at other times or even for someone else under the same conditions. Remember, it's all just a matter of how things are appraised cognitively.

As you might imagine, it is important to appraise potential threats as accurately as possible. For example, to think that everyone in your department is happy when, in fact, they are all planning to quit surely would be a serious mistake. Likewise, interpreting a small dip in sales as a sign of economic collapse would cause you needless worry and may spark panic in others. As such, it is important to recognize what you can do as a manager to ensure that you and those

cognitive appraisal
A judgment about the stressfulness of a situation based on the extent to which someone perceives a stressor as threatening and is capable of coping with its demands.

flight response
An automatic rapid escape from a dangerous situation.

TABLE 5.3 Tips for Assessing Potential Stressors Accurately

It is important to recognize potential stressors and to take appropriate action. However, it can be very disruptive to assume mistakenly that something is a stressor when, in reality, nothing is wrong. With this in mind, here are some useful guidelines for appraising potential stressors accurately.

Suggestion	Explanation
Check with others.	Ask around. If others are not concerned about a situation, then maybe neither should you be concerned. Discussing the situation with people either may alleviate any feelings of stress you may have had or it may verify that something should, in fact, be done (perhaps even more than you planned).
Look to the past.	Your best bet for deciding what to do may be to consider what has happened over the years. You may want to be concerned about something that has caused problems in the past, but worrying about conditions that haven't been problems before might only make things worse by distracting your attention from what really matters.
Gather all the facts.	It's too easy to jump to conclusions, seeing problems as situations that really aren't so bad. Instead of sensing a problem and assuming the worst, look for more objective information about the situation.
Avoid negative mental monologues.	Too often, people talk themselves into perceiving situations as being worse than they really are, thereby adding to stress levels. You should avoid such negative mental monologues, focusing instead on the positive aspects of the situations you confront.

around you are assessing potential stressors accurately. For some recommendations in this regard, see Table 5.3.

Bodily Responses to Stressors

When we encounter stressors, our bodies (in particular, our sympathetic nervous systems and endocrine systems) are mobilized into action, such as through elevated heart rate, blood pressure, and respiration.[40] Arousal rises quickly to high levels, and many physiological changes take place. If the stressors persist, the body's resources eventually may become depleted, at which point people's ability to cope (at least physically) decreases sharply, and severe biological damage may result. These are the patterns of responses that we have in mind when we talk about stress.

To illustrate this, imagine that you are in an office building when you suddenly see a fire raging. How does your body react? As a natural, biological response, your body responds in several ways—including immediately after experiencing the stressor, a few minutes later, and after repeated exposure (see Figure 5.10).

For example, certain chemicals are released that make it possible for us to respond. Adrenaline boosts our metabolism, causing us to breathe faster, taking in more oxygen to help us be stronger and run faster. Aiding in this process, blood flows more rapidly (up to four times faster than normal) to prime the muscles, and other fluids are diverted from less essential parts of the body. As a result, people experiencing stressful conditions tend to experience dry mouths as well as cool, clammy, and sweaty skin. Other chemicals are activated that suppress the parts of the brain that control concentration, inhibition, and rational thought. (By the way, this is why people in emergency situations don't always think rationally or act politely.) In short, when exposed to stressors the body kicks into a self-protective mode, marshalling all its resources to preserve life. However, when this happens frequently, the chronic responses can be dangerous.

To the extent that people appraise various situations as stressors, they are likely to have stress reactions. And often these can have damaging behavioral, psychological, and/or medical effects. Indeed, physiological and psychological stress reactions can be so great that eventually they take their toll on the body and mind, resulting in such maladies as insomnia, cardiovascular disease, and depression. Such reactions are referred to as **strain,** defined as deviations from normal states of human function resulting from prolonged exposure to stressful events.

By nature, some people are less likely to be affected adversely by strain. Such persons are said to be highly *resilient.* The quality of **resiliency** refers to the extent to which one is able to "bounce back" from potentially stressful situations without being harmed by them. As you probably have seen in dealing with different people in your own lives, some individuals are far more resilient than others. To see how you fare in this regard, complete the Individual Exercise on page 172.

strain
Deviations from normal states of human functioning resulting from prolonged exposure to stressful events.

resiliency
The extent to which one is able to "bounce back" from potentially stressful situations without being harmed by them.

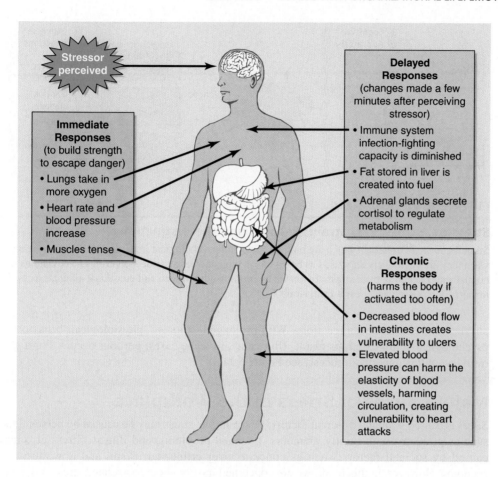

FIGURE 5.10

The Body's Reactions to Stress

As summarized here, the human body responds to stress in various ways involving several different physiological mechanisms. These responses differ based on whether they occur immediately after perceiving a stressor, a few minutes later, or after repeated exposure to stressors.

Sometimes people find themselves worn down by chronic levels of stress. Such people are often described as suffering from **burnout**—a syndrome of emotional, physical, and mental exhaustion coupled with feelings of low self-esteem or low self-efficacy, resulting from prolonged exposure to intense stress and the strain reactions following from them.[41] Fortunately, some of the signs of burnout are clear, if you know what to look for. The distinct characteristics of burnout are summarized in Table 5.4.[42]

Let's summarize where we have been thus far. We have identified physical and psychological causes of stress known as stressors. Through the cognitive appraisal process, these lead to various

burnout
A syndrome of emotional, physical, and mental exhaustion coupled with feelings of low self-esteem or low self-efficacy, resulting from prolonged exposure to intense stress, and the strain reactions following from them.

TABLE 5.4 Symptoms of Burnout

Burnout is a serious condition resulting from exposure to chronic levels of stress. The symptoms of burnout, summarized here, are important to recognize so as to avoid making an already bad state of affairs even worse. Anyone experiencing these symptoms should seek medical attention.

Symptom	Description
Physical exhaustion	Victims of burnout have low energy and feel tired much of the time. They also report many symptoms of physical strain, such as frequent headaches, nausea, poor sleep, and changes in eating habits (e.g., loss of appetite).
Emotional exhaustion	Depression, feelings of helplessness, and feelings of being trapped in one's job are all part of burnout.
Depersonalization	People suffering from burnout often demonstrate a pattern of attitudinal exhaustion known as *depersonalization*. That is, they become cynical, derogating others and themselves, including their jobs, their organizations, and even life in general.
Feelings of low personal accomplishment	People suffering from burnout conclude that they haven't been able to accomplish much in the past and assume that they probably won't succeed in the future.

Source: Based on information in Bakker et al., 2000; see Note 40.

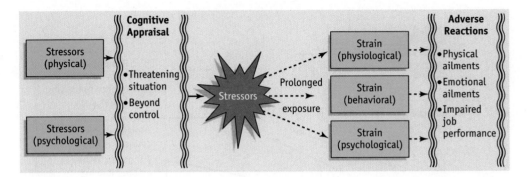

FIGURE 5.11

Stressors, Stress, and Strain: Recognizing the Distinctions

Stimuli known as *stressors* (which are both physical and psychological in nature) lead to stress reactions when they are cognitively appraised as being threatening and beyond one's control. The deviations from normal states resulting from stress are known as *strain*. Both physical and emotional ailments as well as impaired job performance result from strain.

physical and mental stress reactions. With prolonged exposure, physiological, behavioral, and psychological strain reactions result. Ultimately, in some cases, burnout occurs. For a graphic overview of this important process, see Figure 5.11.

Major Causes of Stress in the Workplace

Stress is caused by many different factors. For example, stress may be caused by personal factors such as problems with family members, financial problems, and illness. Stress also may be caused by societal factors, such as concerns over crime, terrorism, and downturns in the economy. However, in this book, we are concerned mostly about job-related stress. What causes stress in work settings? Unfortunately, as you will see, the list is quite long. Many different factors play a role in creating stress in the workplace.

Occupational Demands

Some jobs, such as emergency room physician, police officer, firefighter, and airline pilot, expose the people who hold them to high levels of stress. Others, such as college professor, janitor, and librarian, do not. This basic fact—that some jobs are generally (but not always) much more stressful than others—has been confirmed by the results of a survey involving more than 130 different occupations.[43] For a listing of some of the most and least stressful jobs, see Table 5.5.

What, precisely, makes some jobs more stressful than others? Research has shown that several features of jobs determine the levels of stress they generate. Specifically, people experience greater stress the more their jobs require:

- making decisions
- constantly monitoring devices or materials
- repeatedly exchanging information with others
- working in unpleasant physical conditions
- performing unstructured rather than structured tasks

The greater the extent to which a job possesses these characteristics, the higher the level of stress that job produces among individuals holding it. Nurses and long-distance bus drivers perform jobs that match this profile—and, not surprisingly, people in these occupations tend to show many of the adverse signs of stress. This is not to imply that people do not experience stress in every job. In fact, as you can see from Table 5.5, a variety of sources of stress can be found in different types of jobs.[44]

Conflict Between Work and Nonwork

If you've ever had to face the demands of working while at the same time trying to raise a family (or if you know someone who has been in this situation), you are probably well aware of how very stressful this can be. Not only must you confront the usual pressures to spend time at

TABLE 5.5 Top Ten Most Stressful and Least Stressful Jobs In America

Although very stressful situations can be found on just about any job, the ones shown here tend to have the highest and lowest overall levels of stress associated with them. As you review this list, you're likely to notice that the most stressful jobs contain high levels of the stress-inducing characteristics indicated in the bullet list on page 160. For example, air traffic controllers have to monitor devices, and police officers have to make decisions in unpleasant working conditions. (These are generalizations, of course; in some cases conditions may vary, making particular jobs more stressful or less stressful.)

Top 10 Most Stressful Jobs	Top 10 Least Stressful Jobs
1. Inner-city high school teacher	1. Forester
2. Police officer	2. Bookbinder
3. Miner	3. Telephone line worker
4. Air traffic controller	4. Toolmaker
5. Medical intern	5. Millwright
6. Stockbroker	6. Repair person
7. Journalist	7. Civil engineer
8. Customer service worker	8. Therapist
9. Secretary	9. Natural scientist
10. Waiter	10. Sales representative

Source: Health Magazine.

work while concentrating on what you're doing, but you also must attend to the demands placed on you by members of your family (e.g., to spend time with them). When people confront such incompatibilities in the various sets of obligations they have, they are said to experience **role conflict** (see Chapter 11). As you might expect, when we experience conflicts between our work and nonwork lives, something has to give. Not surprisingly, the more time people devote to their jobs, the more events in their nonwork lives (e.g., personal errands) adversely affect their work lives (e.g., not being able to complete assignments on time).

role conflict
Incompatibilities between the various sets of obligations people face.

The stressful nature of role conflicts is particularly apparent in one group whose members are often expected to rapidly switch back and forth between the demands of work and family—a source of stress known as **role juggling.** This is an especially potent source of stress in one very large segment of the population—working parents.[45] Indeed, the more people, such as working mothers and fathers, are forced to juggle the various roles in their lives, the less fulfilling they find those roles to be, and the more stress they suffer in their lives. (To see what one company is doing to minimize this problem, see Figure 5.12.)

role juggling
The need to switch back and forth between the demands of work and family.

Sexual Harassment: A Pervasive Problem in Work Settings

There can be no doubt that a particularly troublesome source of stress in today's workplace is **sexual harassment**—unwanted contact or communication of a sexual nature, usually against women. The stressful effects of sexual harassment stem from both the direct affront to the victim's personal dignity and the harasser's interference with that employee's capacity to do the job. After all, it's certainly difficult to pay attention to what you're doing on your job when you have to concentrate on ways to ward off someone's unwanted attentions! Not surprisingly, sexual harassment has led to voluntary turnover, but it also has caused some people to experience many severe symptoms of illness, including various forms of physical illness.[46]

sexual harassment
Unwanted contact or communication of a sexual nature, usually against women.

Unfortunately, this particular source of work-related stress is shockingly common. Indeed, when asked in a *New York Times*/CBS News poll whether they had ever been the object of unwanted sexual advances, propositions, or sexual discussions from men who supervise them, 30 percent of the women surveyed answered yes. And this is not a one-sided perception: When asked if they had ever said or done something at work that could be construed by a female colleague as harassment, 50 percent of the men polled admitted that they had, in fact, done so.[47]

There's good news, however. These days, many companies are training employees in ways to avoid sexual harassment. In fact, beginning in 2006, California law required employers to provide two hours of sexual harassment training and education to all supervisory employees.

FIGURE 5.12

Aflac's Effort to Reduce Role Juggling

You probably know Aflac's talking duck commercials, but you might not realize that this Columbus, Georgia–based insurance company runs two on-site child-care centers serving 523 children, more than any other such corporate facility in Georgia. These facilities are welcomed by the company's many employees who are parents, who otherwise would have difficulties managing their time—contributing to stress stemming from the demands of having to juggle their roles as parents and employees.

Jim West/Alamy Images.

At least 14 other states either require or strongly encourage employers to provide some type of sexual harassment training. Efforts of this type (whether or not mandated by law) are helping people become aware of ways they are behaving that may be considered inappropriate. What's more, this seems to be having a beneficial effect on the numbers of sexual harassment cases. U.S. government figures have shown a steady decline in the number of sexual harassment cases reported since 1997. Whereas 15,887 sexual harassment cases were filed in 1997, that figure dropped to 12,696 in 2009.[48] Despite this improvement, the number is 12,696 too high as each case reflects individuals who are being harmed.

Although the reduction is an encouraging sign that this important source of stress may be on the decline as today's employees become more enlightened, it's important to note that sexual harassment is far from gone. When you consider that the number of cases filed reflects only a small proportion of incidents of harassment that actually occur, it is apparent that sexual harassment remains a prevalent source of stress in today's workplace, one that should be taken seriously.

Role Ambiguity: Stress from Uncertainty

role ambiguity
Uncertainty about what one is expected to do on a job.

Even if individuals are able to avoid the stress associated with role conflict, they still may encounter an even more common source of job-related stress: **role ambiguity.** This occurs when people are uncertain about several aspects of their jobs (e.g., the scope of their responsibilities, what's expected of them, how to divide their time among various duties). Most people dislike such uncertainty and find it quite stressful, but it is difficult to avoid. In fact, role ambiguity is quite common: 35 to 60 percent of employees surveyed report experiencing it to some degree.[49] Clearly, managers who are interested in promoting a stress-free workplace should go out of their ways to help employees understand precisely what they are expected to do. As obvious as this may sound, such advice is all too frequently ignored in actual practice.

Overload and Underload

When the term *work-related stress* is mentioned, most people envision scenes in which employees are asked to do more work than they possibly can handle. Such an image is indeed quite legitimate, for such *overload* is an important cause of stress in many work settings. Findings of a recent study support this image.[50] Half of the 1,300 Americans who completed a survey about their work lives indicated that they routinely skip lunch to complete the day's work. And 52 percent reported that they often had to work more than 12 hours a day to get their jobs done.

If you think about it, this isn't particularly surprising. In today's business environment, where many companies are trimming staff size (the phenomenon known as *downsizing,* which we will discuss in Chapter 16), fewer employees are being asked to do more work. Not only does this cause overload, but so too does the proliferation of information with which people are bombarded today as life involves communication via more sources than ever before. Scientists use the term **information anxiety** to refer to pressure to store and process great deals of information in our heads and to keep up constantly with gathering it. This constitutes an all-too real source of overload today.

Overload is only part of the total picture when it comes to stress. Although being asked to do too much can be stressful, so too can being asked to do too little. In fact, there seems to be considerable truth in the following statement: "The hardest job in the world is doing nothing—you can't take a break." *Underload* leads to boredom and monotony. Since these reactions are quite unpleasant, underload, too, can be stressful.

information anxiety
Pressure to store and process a great deal of information in our head and to keep up constantly with gathering it.

Responsibility for Others: A Heavy Burden

By virtue of differences in their jobs, some individuals, such as managers, tend to deal more with people than others. And people, as you probably suspect, can be a major source of stress. In general, individuals who are responsible for other people experience higher levels of stress than those who have no such responsibility (see Figure 5.13). Such individuals are more likely to report feelings of tension and anxiety and are more likely to show overt symptoms of stress, such as ulcers or hypertension, than their counterparts in nonsupervisory positions.

This probably isn't too surprising if you think about it. After all, managers are often caught between the need to satisfy their staff members (e.g., giving them raises) while simultaneously meeting the demands of their own superiors (e.g., maintaining budgets). They also are often faced with meeting a variety of demands, creating responsibilities that weigh heavily on them. Not surprisingly, many managers think of stress as a normal, everyday part of their jobs.

Importantly, managers who deal with people ineffectively—such as those who communicate poorly and who treat people unfairly—add stress to the lives of the people they supervise. As you surely know from your own experiences, a poor manager can be quite a significant source of stress. That said, it is clear that knowing and effectively practicing what you have learned about OB in this book can help alleviate stress among others in the workplace.

Lack of Social Support: The Costs of Isolation

According to an old saying, "misery loves company." With respect to stress, this statement implies that if we have to face stressful conditions, it's better to do so along with others (and with their support) rather than alone. Does this strategy actually work? In general, the answer is yes. Research has shown that when individuals believe they enjoy the friendship and support of others at work—that is, when they have **social support**—their ability to resist the adverse effects of stress increases. For example, research has found that police officers who feel they can talk to their colleagues about their reactions to a traumatic event (such as a shooting) experience less stressful reactions than those who lack such support.[51] Clearly, social support can be an important buffer against the effects of stress.[52]

Social support can come from many different sources. One of these is cultural norms (e.g., caring for the elderly is valued among the Japanese, thereby reducing the social isolation many elderly people otherwise experience). Another source of social support is social institutions (e.g., counseling from the church or school officials, help from the Red Cross). And, of course, probably the most important and valuable source of support comes from

social support
The friendship and support of others, which help minimize reactions to stress.

FIGURE 5.13

Responsibility for Others: A Common Stressor

As this manager can probably tell you, one of the greatest ongoing sources of stress on the job stems from the fact that he has responsibility over others. Even when there are no problems, simply knowing that one's decisions can have a major impact on others has the potential to trigger stress in many people.

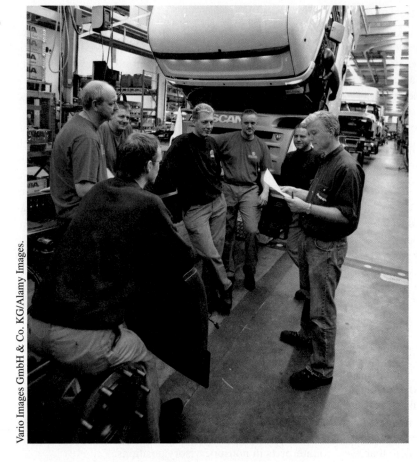

Vario Images GmbH & Co. KG/Alamy Images.

one's own friends and family members. These various sources help in several different ways.[53] These are as follows:

- *Boosting self-esteem.* Others can help make us feel better about ourselves.
- *Sharing information.* Talking to other people can help us learn about ways of coping with problems and give us a new perspective on things.
- *Providing diversion.* Spending time with others can be a friendly diversion from life's stressors, taking your mind off them.
- *Giving needed resources.* Time spent with others can result in their offering to help by giving money, advice, or other recourses needed to alleviate stress.

As we have shown here, not only does misery love company, but company also can help alleviate misery. This is something worth remembering the next time you feel stressed. Remember, don't go it alone. Friends can help, so seek them out.

Adverse Effects of Organizational Stress

By now, you probably are convinced that stress stems from many sources, and that it has important effects on the people who experience it. What may not yet be apparent, though, is just how powerful and far-reaching such effects can be. In fact, so widespread are the detrimental effects of stress (i.e., strain) that it has been estimated that their annual costs exceed 10 percent of the U.S. gross national product![54] Let's now examine some of the specific problems linked to stress.

Lowered Task Performance—But Only Sometimes

The most current evidence available suggests that stress exerts mainly negative effects on task performance. For the most part, the greater the stress people encounter on the job, the more adversely affected their job performance tends to be.[55] In some cases, this is particularly serious. For example, one study reported that people who are experiencing higher levels of stress have significantly higher chances of having an auto accident than those experiencing lower levels of stress.[56]

It is important to note, however, that the adverse relationship between stress and job performance does not always occur. Specifically, some people seem to "rise to the occasion" and turn in exceptional performances when confronted with what appear to be stressors. There appear to be two reasons for this. First, because some people are expert in the tasks being performed they are highly confident in what they are doing. This leads them to appraise a potentially stressful situation as challenging (and not stressful) rather than threatening (and therefore, stressful). Second, some people are by nature high sensation-seekers and thrive on stress. These individuals find stress exhilarating and thrilling and are highly motivated to perform well under such conditions. Most people, however, are just the opposite. They find high levels of stress upsetting, which interferes with their job performance.

Desk Rage

A particularly unsettling manifestation of stress on the job that has become all too prevalent in recent years is known as **desk rage**—the lashing out at others in response to stressful encounters on the job. Just as angered drivers have been known to express their negative reactions to others in dangerous ways (commonly referred to as *road rage*), so too have office workers been known to behave violently toward others when feeling stress from long hours and difficult working conditions. What makes desk rage so frightening is how extremely widespread it is and. For some suggestions that managers may follow to address the problem of desk rage, see Table 5.6.[57]

desk rage
Lashing out at others in response to stressful encounters on the job.

Stress and Health: The Silent Killer

How strong is the link between stress and personal health? The answer, say medical experts, is "very strong, indeed." In other words, physiological strain reactions can be quite severe. Some experts estimate that stress plays a role in anywhere from 50 to 70 percent of all forms of physical illness.[58] Included in these figures are some of the most serious and life-threatening ailments known to medical science. A list of some of the more common ones is shown in Table 5.7.[59] Even the most cursory look at this list reveals that the health-related effects of stress are not only

TABLE 5.6 Addressing Desk Rage: Useful Tips for Managers

Because desk rage is all too prevalent, it's important for managers to recognize how to address it. Experts have offered the following tips.

Tip	Comment
Take control of your emotions whenever an employee seems to lose control.	Don't do anything that might keep the argument going or make it worse.
Carefully consider what led the person to be so angry.	By identifying the trigger, you are in a good position to straighten things out, such as by offering an explanation about something.
Immediately encourage everyone involved to take a deep breath.	Breathing deeply helps people calm down; doing so will help you to discuss the situation calmly.
Take the feud outside the workplace.	Discussing heated personal issues in the workplace may involve others, but going outside—to lunch, say—moves the discussion to neutral territory where calm heads may prevail.
If someone seems to be having a particularly bad day, ask if there's anything you can do to help.	By intervening, you may be able to help with problems (e.g., overload), thereby eliminating conditions that promote anger.
Stay physically clear of someone who may be losing control.	By keeping an angry individual at arm's length, you may avoid a physical confrontation.
If you witness someone yelling at a coworker, intervene directly only if you are a supervisor. If you are a colleague, report this to your supervisor.	Direct intervention by a colleague may only make things worse by getting him or her involved as well. However, anyone witnessing acts of desk rage should report them at once to someone who has the authority to intervene.

Source: Lorenz, 2004; see Note 57.

TABLE 5.7 Health-Related Consequences of Stress

Stress causes a variety of different health problems, including medical, behavioral, and psychological problems. Listed here are some of the major consequences within each category.

Medical Consequences	Behavioral Consequences	Psychological Consequences
Heart disease and stroke	Smoking	Family conflict
Backache and arthritis	Drug and alcohol abuse	Sleep disturbances
Ulcers	Accident proneness	Sexual dysfunction
Headaches	Violence	Depression
Cancer	Appetite disorders	
Diabetes		
Cirrhosis of the liver		
Lung disease		

Source: Based on material reported by Quick et al., 2008; see Note 59.

quite widespread but also extremely serious. With this in mind, it's not surprising that many of today's companies are taking steps to keep stress in check. We examine these in the next section of this chapter. (Might you find differences between women and men with respect to their responses to stress, such as their likelihoods of showing signs of burnout? For a look at this question, see the Today's Diverse and Global Organizations section below.)

Today's Diverse and Global Organizations

Do Women and Men Respond Differently to Stress?

Although anyone's life can be stressful, it seems that women generally face more stressors than men. If nothing else, women are more likely than men to carry the primary responsibility for raising children at home while also facing responsibilities on the job. Women also are more likely than men to be victims of sexual harassment on the job. And women are more likely than men to confront discriminatory practices that keep them from advancing as rapidly on the job. Considering these things, it is not surprising that surveys have found that women face more stressors and are affected more adversely by them than men.[60]

Women and men differ not only with respect to the overall amounts of stress they face, but also with respect to its various forms. In fact, compared to men, women confront stress from a wider variety of sources. Women encounter more changes and greater pressure to perform well on the job. For them, signs of stress are most likely to be found whenever their jobs are chaotic or demanding. For men, however, work is most likely to be stressful when facing ambiguous demands about what to do or when working in a highly competitive atmosphere.

Interestingly, both men and women seek relief from stress by engaging in some of the same leisure-time activities. For example, both groups do things that make them laugh and also seek to reduce stress by attending religious services. However, research shows that men and women also differ in their particular choices of leisure activities to help cope with stress.[61] For example, whereas men are inclined to play hard by engaging in strenuous sports, women are more likely to engage in artistic and cultural activities to relax. Women also are more likely than men to respond to stress by maintaining healthy habits (e.g., eating properly and exercising regularly) and by seeking social support (e.g., talking to their friends about their problems).

Although both women and men take steps to cope with stress, woman generally have a harder time of it. Overall, women cope less effectively with the stress they face. They suffer more physical symptoms (e.g., elevated blood pressure), behavioral symptoms (e.g., sleeplessness), and emotional symptoms (e.g., anxiety and depression).

Why is this? There are several possibilities.

1. **Volume of stressors.** One possibility is that women cope less effectively because the overall levels of stress they face are so much higher than those faced by men.
2. **Coping.** Another possibility is that what women are doing to cope with the stressors they face is less effective than what men do to cope with their stressors.
3. **Physiological predisposition.** Another possibility is that the generally greater physical strength and stamina of men predisposes them to respond less adversely to whatever stressors they encounter.

Of course, various combinations of these explanations may be involved, as well as numerous other factors. Regardless of the reason, one thing is sure: When attempting to get employees to be affected less adversely to work stress, managers need to focus especially carefully on women. Going out of the way to include women in stress management programs appears to be a wise investment.

Reducing Stress: What Can Be Done?

Stress stems from so many different factors and conditions that to eliminate it entirely from our lives is impossible. However, there still are many things that both companies and individuals can do to reduce stress and to minimize its harmful effects.[62] To ensure that these tactics are followed, many companies have introduced systematic programs designed to help employees reduce and/or prevent stress. The underlying assumption of these programs is that by minimizing employees' adverse reactions to stress, they will be healthier, less likely to be absent, and, consequently, more productive on the job. This, in turn, is not only likely to have beneficial effects on the bottom lines of companies but also on the individual well-being of the employees who work in them.

Employee Assistance Programs and Stress Management Programs

About two-thirds of today's companies have some kind of formal program in place to help employees with various problems they may face in their personal lives (e.g., substance abuse, career planning, financial and legal problems).[63] Such efforts are known as **employee assistance programs (EAPs).** Sometimes, such programs are sponsored by trade unions, in which case, they are known as **member assistance programs (MAPs).**

Interest in offering systematic ways of promoting the welfare of employees has grown so great that many companies today are seeking the assistance of specialized organizations with whom they can contract to offer assistance programs for their employees. By outsourcing these services to firms that are expert in this area, companies are free to focus on their usual business while ensuring that they are taking care of their employees as needed. Privacy also is enhanced since using outsourced EAP services also helps ensure that personal information about employees is kept from their employers. Importantly, EAPs are paying off. According to the Employee Assistance Professionals Association, a trade group for companies offering professional EAP services to organizations, employee work loss is avoided in 60 percent of the cases in which EAP services are provided.[64]

Another systematic approach to addressing the stress problem comes in the form of **stress management programs.** These involve training employees in a variety of techniques (e.g., meditation and relaxation) that they can use to become less adversely affected by stress (we will describe several of these techniques on pages 168–170). About a quarter of all large companies have stress management programs in place.

Wellness Programs

Beyond helping employees reduce stress-related problems, about half of today's larger companies have **wellness programs** in place to keep them healthy. These are systematic efforts to train employees in a variety of things they can do to promote healthy lifestyles. Very broad-based, wellness programs usually consist of workshops in which employees can learn many things to reduce stress and maintain their health. Exercise, nutrition, and weight-management counseling are among the most popular areas covered.

As an interesting example, Blue Cross Blue Shield of Oklahoma built a financial incentive into the wellness program it uses for its 1,300 employees.[65] The company offers "Weight Watchers at Work" meetings. Employees have to pay to participate in the 16-week program—but as an incentive, if they attend at least 14 weekly sessions, they are reimbursed. In a recent five-year period, Blue Cross Blue Shield employees collectively have lost nearly 10 tons of excess weight.

As you might imagine, companies that have used such programs have found that they pay off handsomely. For example, at its industrial sites that offer wellness programs, DuPont has found that absenteeism is less than half of what it is at sites that do not offer such programs. Organizations such as The Travelers Companies and Union Pacific Railroad have enjoyed consistently high returns on each dollar they invest in employee wellness. And when it comes to saving money by promoting employee health, there is a lot at stake. Consider, for example, that annual health insurance costs in the United States due to obesity alone is $7.7 billion.[66]

As you might imagine, wellness programs help not only by reducing insurance costs, but also by reducing absenteeism due to illness. There's yet another way in which stress management efforts promise to help companies' bottom lines, and one of which most people are unaware. We are referring to the problem of **presenteeism**—the practice of showing up for work but being too sick to be able to work effectively. Paying workers who are not performing well is not only costly on its

employee assistance programs (EAPs)
Plans offered by employers that provide their employees with assistance for various personal problems (e.g., substance abuse, career planning, financial and legal problems).

member assistance programs (MAPs)
Plans offered by trade unions that provide their members with assistance for various personal problems (e.g., substance abuse, career planning, financial and legal problems).

stress management programs
Systematic efforts to train employees in a variety of techniques that they can use to become less adversely affected by stress.

wellness programs
Company-wide programs in which employees receive training regarding things they can do to promote healthy lifestyles.

presenteeism
The practice of showing up for work but being too sick to be able to work effectively.

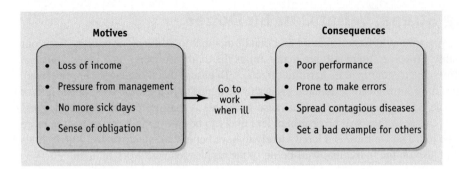

FIGURE 5.14

Presenteeism: Motives and Consequences

The opposite of absenteeism, *presenteeism* also can be problematic for organizations. Some of the motives that people might have for going to work when ill are summarized here, along with the consequences.

own, but also indirectly, given that it may lower morale by sending the message that it's important to show up even if you're sick. And, of course, depending on the particular illness people have, it may spread disease throughout a workplace, compounding the problem (for an overview of some possible motives for presenteeism and its results, see Figure 5.14). This practice is especially problematic in view of estimates that about one in four employees engage in presenteeism.[67] Given that stress is one of the leading causes of illness, it follows that reducing stress can help minimize the problem of presenteeism (and many others too, of course). (Although it would seem that wellness programs are beneficial for all, some concerns have been raised about the extent to which they are inherently ethical. For an overview of these considerations, see The Ethics Angle section on page 169.)

Managing Your Own Stress

Even if the company at which you work does not have a formal program in place to help you manage stress, there still are several things you can do by yourself to help control the stress in your life. We now describe several such tactics.

MANAGE YOUR TIME WISELY. People who don't use their time effectively find themselves easily overwhelmed, falling behind, not getting important things done, and having to work longer hours as a result. Not surprisingly, **time management**, the practice of taking control over how we spend time, is a valuable skill for reducing time pressure, which is a particularly widespread stressor. Some of the most effective time management practices are summarized in Table 5.8.

time management
The practice of taking control over how we spend time.

EAT A HEALTHY DIET AND BE PHYSICALLY FIT. Growing evidence indicates that reduced intake of salt and saturated fats, and increased consumption of fiber- and vitamin-rich fruits and vegetables, are steps that can greatly increase the body's ability to cope with the physiological effects of stress.[68] Regular exercise also helps. People who exercise regularly obtain many benefits closely related to resistance of the adverse effects of stress. For example, fitness reduces both the incidence of cardiovascular illness and the death rate from such diseases. Similarly, physical fitness lowers blood pressure, an important factor in many aspects of personal health.

With this in mind, it is not surprising that growing numbers of companies are taking steps to ensure that their employees maintain proper weight by eating properly and exercising regularly. Some even offer monetary incentives for doing so.[69]

meditation
The process of learning to clear one's mind of external thoughts, often by repeating slowly and rhythmically a single syllable (known as a *mantra*).

RELAX AND MEDITATE. Many people find that it helps to relieve stress by engaging in **meditation**, the process of learning to clear one's mind of external thoughts, often by repeating slowly and rhythmically a single syllable (known as a *mantra*). Those who follow this systematic way of relaxing claim that it helps to relieve the many sources of stress in their lives. For an overview of general steps to follow while meditating, see Table 5.9.[70]

GET A GOOD NIGHT'S SLEEP. One of the most effective ways to alleviate stress-related problems is one of the simplest—if you can do it—sleeping. We all need a certain amount of sleep to allow

The Ethics Angle

Companies and Employee Health: An Invitation for Big Brother?

At first blush, it would seem to be evident that wellness programs cannot help but benefit employees and employers alike. Although this is probably true on most occasions, it has been noted that wellness programs run the risk of being unethical because they enable companies to be too intrusive in their employees' lives. The seriousness of this risk will depend on the exact practices companies follow, but let's examine the general issues.

Some concerns have been raised that when companies have any connection to their employees' health and wellness, the potential exists for employers to use this information against their employees. This concern is especially relevant when companies have on-site medical clinics.

You might not realize it, but in the 1800s, most large companies had doctors on the premises that serviced the health-care needs of employees. By the 1940s, however, most of these medical clinics began closing in the wake of criticism that the doctors were more attuned to the financial needs of the companies that paid them than to the patients they saw.[71] Even today, might doctors who are paid by a company think twice about recommending time off for key employees whose services are especially vital? Even more seriously, might a company doctor share private information about the serious illness an employee might have so that he or she could be terminated before the company is forced to pay exorbitant medical bills, raising insurance premiums for everyone? Or, even if a doctor is not so blatant in disregarding a patient's privacy, might company officials be tempted to snoop around the clinic to see what information of interest they might find?

To avoid such problems, most organizations (which are not qualified to run medical clinics in the first place) outsource their on-site facilities to specialized companies that are qualified to operate them. One such company is Take Care Health Services (owned by Walgreens), whose employees design, staff, and run many in-house clinics. From an ethical perspective, this is intended to maintain a vital privacy buffer that keeps companies from prying into their employees' medical records. Taking the absence of any reports of breeches in security as evidence, they seem to be quite successful. Still, some especially cautious individuals may be reluctant to have their medical records housed under the same roofs as their companies.

Another concern has to do with the difference between "encouraging" employee health and "mandating" it. Consider this example. One company used to have a program in which employees were given opportunities to get complete physicals and then, if they were found to be healthy in key ways (e.g., appropriate weight, normal blood pressure, not smoking, etc.), they were awarded a $500 bonus. Then, one day in an effort to control rising health-care costs, the company moved from a voluntary program to a mandatory program.[72] Among other things, this included prohibiting employees from smoking, even off the job. Although not smoking surely is prudent, some employees complained that the practice of outlawing it is unethical because it violates their individual rights. Furthermore, several states have laws that prohibit companies from restricting the things employees can do while not on the job, making the practice illegal in some places as well.

What do you think? Are you concerned about the potential for a corporate Big Brother to interfere with private matters, such as personal health, or do you believe that proper safeguards can be implemented to avoid ethical conflicts of interest? Do you believe that those who harbor such concerns are being appropriately cautious or merely paranoid?

TABLE 5.8 Three Key Suggestions for Managing Your Time

Managing time well can be an effective means of reducing stress because it allows people to avoid last-minute crises and because it permits work to flow in a regular manner. Although these three suggestions may be easier said than done, following them can be very helpful.

Tip	Explanation
Prioritize your activities.	Distinguish between tasks that are urgent (ones that must be performed right away) and important (ones that must be done, but can wait). When determining how to spend your time, assign the greatest priority to tasks that are both important and urgent, a lower priority to tasks that are important but less urgent, and the lowest priority of all to tasks that are neither important nor urgent.
Allocate your time realistically—do not overcommit.	When planning, accurately assess how much time needs to be spent on each of the various tasks you perform. Budgeting too much time can lead to underload, and too little time can lead to overload. It also helps to build in buffers, some extra time to handle unexpected issues that might arise.
Take control of your time.	Make a "to do" list and carefully keep track of what you have to accomplish. Unless an urgent situation comes up, stay focused and don't allow others to derail you. The more you allow other people to interfere with your time, the less you will have accomplished at the end of the day.

TABLE 5.9 How to Meditate by Relaxing

Meditation can help people gain better control of negative emotions, such as anger, and it also can help lessen negative reactions to stress. For these reasons, learning to meditate can be very useful. Although there are several different types of meditation, the relaxation approach outlined here is both easiest to learn and among the most effective. Give it a try.

1. Go to a quiet, dark place where you will not be disturbed. Sit in a comfortable position. Let your mind go blank and slowly relax your muscles.

2. Focus into space, slowly letting everything out of your mind. Do not let thoughts intrude. If they do, work at pushing them away.

3. Breathe slowly and in a regular rhythm. As you breathe in, slowly make the sound "haaah" as you would when slipping into a hot bath. Then, as you exhale, slowly produce the sound "saaah," sounding and feeling like a sigh.

4. Repeat this process, breathing slowly and naturally. When you do, inhale through your nose and pause for a few seconds. Then exhale through your mouth, again pausing for a few seconds.

5. Should thoughts enter your mind while attempting this process, don't feel badly about it. Instead, realize that this is natural and pick up the process once again. This will take time to master, so be patient. With practice, you will be able to do this more quickly.

6. Continue this process for what feels like about 20 minutes. Don't look at the clock, though. As the time draws to a close, maintain awareness of your breathing and sit quietly. Then, slowly becoming aware of where you are, open your eyes and get up gradually.

Sources: Based on various sources in Note 70.

our bodies to recharge and function effectively. Eight hours per day is average, although some need more and others can function just fine on fewer. Although a restful night's sleep can help people ward off the harmful effects of stress, the problem for many is that they are so stressed that they have difficulty getting to sleep or maintaining their sleep, a widespread stress reaction known as *insomnia*.

AVOID INAPPROPRIATE SELF-TALK. This involves repeatedly telling ourselves how horrible and unbearable it will be if we fail, if we are not perfect, or if everyone we meet does not like us. Such thoughts seem ludicrous when spelled out in the pages of a book, but the fact is that most people entertain them at least occasionally. Unfortunately, such thoughts can add to personal levels of stress, as individuals *awfulize* or *catastrophize* in their own minds the horrors of not being successful, perfect, or loved. Fortunately, such thinking can be readily modified. For many people, merely recognizing that they have implicitly accepted such irrational and self-defeating beliefs is sufficient to produce beneficial change and increased resistance to stress.

time-out
A brief delay in activities designed to reduce mounting tension.

TAKE A TIME-OUT. When confronted with rising tension, people may find it useful to choose to insert a brief period of delay known as a **time-out.** This can involve taking a short break, going to the nearest restroom to splash cold water on one's face, or any other action that yields a few moments of breathing space. Such actions interrupt the cycle of ever-rising tension that accompanies stress and can help to restore equilibrium and the feeling of being at least partly in control of ongoing events.

Summary and Review of Learning Objectives

1. **Distinguish between emotions and moods.**
   Whereas *emotions* are overt reactions that express people's feelings about a specific event, moods are more general. Specifically, *moods* are unfocused, relatively mild feelings that exist as background to our daily experiences.

2. **Explain how emotions and mood influence behavior in organizations.**
   Emotions and mood affect behavior in organizations in various ways. Generally, happier people are more successful on their jobs; they perform at higher levels, and they make higher incomes. One reason for this is that people who are very upset tend to neither listen to nor understand the performance feedback they receive. Furthermore, happier people tend to make better decisions, remember positive events, give positive evaluations when appropriate, and cooperate with others.

3. **Describe ways in which people manage their emotions in organizations.**

   One way people manage their emotions is by keeping their negative feelings to themselves. Rather than offending another with our actual negative feelings, we may engage in the *emotional labor* of disguising our true feelings. The inconsistency between the emotions we express and the emotions we feel is known as *emotional dissonance.* People in organizations also manage their emotions by managing their anger and by displaying *compassion* for others when needed. This is especially important during major crises and emergencies.

4. **Identify the major causes of organizational stress.**

   Stress is caused by many different factors, including occupational demands, conflicts between the work and nonwork aspects of one's life (i.e., *role conflict*), not knowing what one is expected to do on the job (i.e., *role ambiguity*), overload and underload, having responsibility for other people, and experiencing sexual harassment.

5. **Describe the adverse effects of organizational stress.**

   Experiencing high levels of organizational stress has negative effects on task performance. It also adversely affects people's physical and mental health in a variety of ways. Stress also is a major cause of such serious problems as desk rage and burnout.

6. **Identify various ways of reducing stress in the workplace.**

   To help reduce employees' stress, companies are doing such things as using *employee assistance programs, wellness programs, absence control programs,* and *stress management programs.* As individuals, we can control the stress we face in our lives by following good *time management* techniques, eating a healthy diet and being physically fit, relaxing and meditating, avoiding inappropriate self-talk, and taking control over our reactions.

Points to Ponder

Questions for Review

1. What are *emotions* and *moods,* and how do they influence people's behavior in organizations?
2. What does affective events theory say about the effects of people's emotions on their behavior in organizations?
3. What advice would you give to leaders of a company who are interested in managing their employees' emotions?
4. What are the differences among *stressors, stress,* and *strain?*
5. What are the primary causes and consequences of stress on the job?
6. What steps can be taken to minimize the potentially harmful effects of stress on the job?

Experiential Questions

1. Think of a time when it was necessary for you to express compassion on the job in response to a traumatic situation. What were the circumstances? What did you do that was effective? What steps might you take to become even more effective the next time it is necessary to express compassion on the job?
2. What was the most stressful situation you ever encountered on the job? What were the stressors, and how did you react, both physically and psychologically? What role did social support play in helping you manage this stress?
3. What experiences have you had using stress management techniques—either formally or informally? For example, do you meditate? Do you find that physical exercise helps you relieve stress? Does talking to others help at all? Of the various techniques described in this chapter, which one do you think you would find most beneficial?

Questions to Analyze

1. We all experience emotions, but some people disguise their true feelings better than others. Do you think this is a helpful or harmful thing to do? Under what conditions do you think it would be most useful to express your true feelings? Likewise, when do you think it would be best to keep your feelings to yourself?
2. Social support can be a very helpful means of reducing stress. However, do you think it's wise to seek social support on the job, where you stand to make yourself vulnerable by talking about your work-related stressors (e.g., by showing your weaknesses or by speaking negatively about your bosses)? Or do you think that only your coworkers are in a good position to understand your work-related stressors, suggesting that you should talk to them about the work-related stress you are experiencing?
3. Stress management programs generally work well, but they are not always as effective as hoped. What problems and limitations do you believe may interfere with the effectiveness of stress management programs? How can these problems and limitations be overcome?

Experiencing OB

Individual Exercise

How Resilient Are You?

This questionnaire is designed to help you discover how resilient you are. People who are more resilient are less inclined to suffer problems associated with stress because they simply "bounce back" from them without experiencing harm.

Directions

Using the following scale, respond to each of the items by indicating how often you do what is indicated.

1 = never

2 = sometimes

3 = half the time

4 = usually

5 = always

_____ 1. I am able to "forgive and forget" whenever someone has hurt me.

_____ 2. Overall, I am more of an optimist than a pessimist.

_____ 3. I take some time out each day for quiet rest.

_____ 4. I am satisfied with the amount of time I spend having fun.

_____ 5. I find it easy to keep everything in my life organized and under control.

_____ 6. If I'm upset about something, I am able to speak about it openly.

_____ 7. I can confide in friends whenever something troubles me.

_____ 8. I usually get enough sleep to feel fully rested.

_____ 9. I make it a point to exercise regularly.

_____ 10. I eat a well-balanced diet most of the time.

Scoring and Interpretation

1. Add your points for all 10 items. These can range from 10 to 50.
2. Higher scores reflect a higher degree of resiliency.

Questions for Discussion

1. How does the score you earned compare to what you would have imagined before you took this test? Was it higher or lower? Are you surprised?
2. What do these items reveal about the factors that contribute to resiliency? Did you notice that this is essentially a checklist of things to do to reduce or avoid stress?
3. What did completing this questionnaire show you about what you might be able to do to become more resilient and, therefore, harmed less by stressors?

Group Exercise

Is Your Team Tough Enough to Endure Stress?

A test known as the Test of Attentional and Interpersonal Style (TAIS) (see Note 42) has been used in recent years to identify the extent to which a person can stay focused and keep his or her emotions under control—the core elements of performing well under high-pressure conditions. Completing this exercise (which is based on questions similar to those actually used by such groups as Olympic athletes and U.S. Navy Seals) will help you understand your own strengths and limitations in this regard. And, by discussing these scores with your teammates, you will come away with a good feel for the extent to which those with whom you work differ along this dimension as well.

Directions

1. Form groups of three or four people whom you know fairly well. If you are part of an intact group, such as a work team or a team of students working on a class project, meet with your fellow group members.

2. Individually, complete the following questionnaire by responding to each question as follows: "never," "rarely," "sometimes," "frequently," or "always."

    1. _____ When time is running out on an important project, I am the person who should be called on to take control of things.
    2. _____ When listening to a piece of music, I can pick out a specific voice or instrument.
    3. _____ The people who know me think of me as being "serious."
    4. _____ It is important to me to get a job completely right in every detail, even if it means being late.
    5. _____ When approaching a busy intersection, I easily get confused.
    6. _____ Just by looking at someone, I can figure out what he or she is like.
    7. _____ I am comfortable arguing with people.
    8. _____ At a cocktail party, I have no difficulty keeping track of several different conversations at once.

3. Discuss your answers with everyone else in your group. Item by item, consider what each person's response to each question indicates about his or her ability to focus.

Questions for Discussion

1. What questions were easiest to interpret? Which were most difficult?
2. How did each individual's responses compare with the way you would assess his or her ability to focus under stress?
3. For what jobs is the ability to concentrate under stress particularly important? For what jobs is it not especially important? How important is this ability for the work you do?

Practicing OB

Stressed-Out Employees Are Resigning

As the managing director of a large e-tail sales company, you are becoming alarmed about the growing levels of turnover your company has been experiencing lately. It already has passed the industry average, and you are growing concerned about the company's capacity to staff the call center and the warehouse during the busy holiday period. In conducting exit interviews, you learned that the employees who are leaving generally like their work and the pay they are receiving. However, they are displeased with the way their managers are treating them, and this is creating stress in their lives. They are quitting so they can take less stressful positions in other companies. Answer the following questions based on the material in this chapter.

1. Assuming that the employees' emotions and moods are negative, what problems would you expect to find in the way they are working?
2. How should the company's supervisors behave differently so as to get their subordinates to experience less stress on the job (or, at least, get them to react less negatively)?
3. What could the individual employees do to help manage their own stress more effectively?

Case in Point

■ A Basketball Court Judge Faces a Federal Court Judge

"**I**'ve brought shame on myself, my family and the profession" were the words of Tim Donaghy, as a federal district judge sentenced him to 15 months behind bars in July 2008. Formally, the charges against him were conspiracy to engage in wire fraud and transmitting betting information through interstate commerce. In plain English, the 41-year-old Donaghy, a 13-year veteran National Basketball Association (NBA) referee, admitted to taking thousands of dollars in payoffs from a professional gambler in exchange for giving inside tips on games he officiated.

Upon sentencing Donaghy, U.S. District Judge Carol Amon gave him credit for cooperating with the court but explained that a jail term was justified since, "The NBA, the players and the fans relied upon him to perform his job in an honest, reliable and non-conflicted manner." Instead, she said, he was "compromised by a financial interest in the game he was refereeing." The contrite Donaghy stood with his arms folded and showed no emotion. When

(Continued)

invited to speak, he told the judge, "I'm very sorry for the acts for which I stand before you."

Although sportswriters and NBA officials roundly criticized Donaghy for his actions, they also acknowledge the intensely stressful nature of the referee's job. Living out of a suitcase for over half a year, they log thousands of miles on the road during the season and face extreme pressure. Not only do they have to make split-second decisions, but they also have to do it in the shadow of giant players and coaches who are not exactly reticent about sharing their opinions about the nature of their calls.

Although Donaghy can serve his sentence and put the ordeal behind him, some believe that the problems for the NBA may be just beginning. In the course of defending himself, Donaghy revealed that NBA officials told referees to go easy on calling technical fouls against certain star players, who fans wanted to see on the court, and to make calls that extended playoffs to seven games so as to boost income for the league. NBA Commissioner David Stern has repeatedly denied that corruption went beyond Donaghy, explaining that Donaghy fabricated the claims to create the appearance that he was sharing

information in the hope of getting a lighter sentence. Although the court announced that Donaghy's claims of widespread game manipulation were unsubstantiated, the NBA recognizes the serious public relations nightmare it has on its hands.

Unless the game can be played with integrity on a level playing field (or, court, in this case), it has no future. To ensure the quality of officiating from now on, Commissioner Stern created a new position, senior vice president of referee operations, staffed by retired U.S. Army General Ronald Johnson. If you think being a referee on the court is stressful, imagine what it's like to be in charge of all of them from behind a desk in a New York office.

Questions for Discussion

1. What particular emotions do you believe Donaghy experienced as this situation unfolded?
2. What sources of stress did Donaghy encounter, and how did he respond to them?
3. Considering the stressful nature of his ordeal, what would you recommend to Donaghy that he do to alleviate some of the stress he encountered?

Part 2 Video Cases

■ Training and Development

Employee training is a major responsibility for most human resource departments. These programs provide employees with the tools they need to accomplish their job duties successfully. Developing a good plan begins with clearly identifying what needs to be achieved and then determining which kind of training is most appropriate. Once the answers to these questions have been identified, firms can ascertain who should conduct the training and how its effectiveness will be measured.

According to Jenny Herman of Lowes Hotels, for a training program to be effective, it should incorporate input from people in the field and be used on a pilot basis to work out any kinks before being rolled out to the entire firm. Various tools, including one-on-one relationships, mentoring programs, interactive training, and computer training, can be used. Training is not a one-time event, but an ongoing process. Companies also should implement management development programs

to help employees improve their skills and advance their careers.

Although an annual review can provide employees with some feedback, Martin Buckingham of Hot Jobs says that he prefers ongoing feedback. Herman claims that at her organization, the management development program focuses on the career plans of employees and the steps managers should take to move toward achieving their goals.

Discussion Questions

1. Which of the different types of training presented in Chapter 3 would be most effective for companies like Lowes Hotels?
2. Why are the keys to effective training presented in Chapter 3 so important to companies like those shown in the video?
3. Explain how 360-degree feedback can be used improve the effectiveness of training in situations like the one at Lowes Hotels.

■ Managing Stress

Stress in the workplace is all-too-commonplace. Some individuals, like Student Advantage's Vinnie Russo, feel pressured because they cannot say "no," even when they are already overscheduled. Other employees, like Heidi Vanvliet, feel stressed when they are faced with impossible

deadlines. People experience this pressure in different ways. Things that might cause strain in one person may be of little importance to another. An individual's experience also plays a role: An employee who has already put in an 18-hour day, for example, may feel bothered when facing a situation that on any other day would cause little problem.

(Continued)

Because high levels of stress can have a negative impact on performance, some companies have implemented programs designed to help workers deal with it. At Student Advantage, Kevin Roach shows employees how to integrate personal and professional goals. Roach points out that planning and prioritizing are important to managing stress, and that individuals need to be able to identify what adds value and what can be ignored.

Stressors can vary over time as circumstances change. When Student Advantage initially was founded, for example, most employees were relatively young and single. Today, however, many have families, and this change has introduced new stressors as managers strive to find a good balance between their family lives and professional lives. Similarly, as the company has grown and added more layers of management, more policies, and new procedures, additional stressors have been introduced for long-time employees who now must adapt to the more structured environment. As part of its effort to assist workers, Student Advantage takes special care to hire individuals who not only have the right technical skills, but who also will fit well with the corporate culture.

Discussion Questions

1. How can time-management tactics such as those in Table 5.8 (on page 169) help employees at Student Advantage lower their stress levels?

2. In the video clip, Amy Geeler claims she feels stressed when doing payroll. What are the major causes of organizational stress (as described in Chapter 5) and which of these does Amy appear to be experiencing?

3. In what ways does Student Advantage benefit from offering employee assistance programs?

CHAPTER

6 Work-Related Attitudes: Prejudice, Job Satisfaction, and Organizational Commitment

Learning Objectives

After reading this chapter, you should be able to:

1. Define attitudes and work-related attitudes, and describe the basic components of attitudes.
2. Distinguish between prejudice and discrimination, and identify various victims of prejudice in organizations.
3. Describe some of the things being done by today's organizations to manage diversity in their workforces and the effectiveness of these practices.
4. Explain the concept of job satisfaction, and summarize three major theories of job satisfaction.
5. Describe the consequences of job dissatisfaction and ways to promote job satisfaction.
6. Describe the concept of organizational commitment, its major forms, the consequences of low levels of organizational commitment, and how to overcome them.

Chapter Outline

- Attitudes: What Are They?
- Prejudice and Discrimination: Negative Attitudes and Behavior Toward Others
- Strategies for Overcoming Workplace Prejudice: Managing a Diverse Workforce
- Job Satisfaction: Its Nature and Major Theories
- Consequences of Job Dissatisfaction—and Ways to Reduce Them
- Organizational Commitment: Attitudes Toward Companies

Preview Case

■ *Madison Avenue Welcomes Disabled Athletes*

When we watch TV, we're inundated with images of athletes, and with increasing frequency, it's not unusual to see people with disabilities. However, athletes with physical disabilities remain a rare sight in the media. Although this might suggest that there aren't many disabled athletes out there, Cheri Blauwet would claim otherwise.

Cheri and about 4,000 other disabled athletes from 145 different countries participated in the 2008 Paralympic Games in Beijing, China. These elite athletes competed in a variety of sports (e.g., rowing, sailing, wheelchair rugby, and cycling, among many others) within categories based on their disability: spinal injury, amputee, visual impairment, cerebral palsy, and "les autres" (a category consisting of people with various locomotor conditions, such as multiple sclerosis and muscular dystrophy). A winner of several wheelchair races, Cheri also is an advanced medical student at Stanford University.

The thing that makes Cheri proudest, however, is the fact that she is the first female American Paralympian to be featured in a national television ad. First airing on May 29, 2008, the dramatic Visa spot shows her flying down a mountain road in her wheelchair as the rich voice of Morgan Freeman refers to her as a "heat-seeking, coming-through, get-out-of-the-way . . . world-class athlete." Visa officials like the fact that Cheri is "an incredible role model," and Cheri likes the fact that she paved the way for other disabled athletes to get endorsement deals.

Today, several disabled athletes are appearing in major media marketing efforts. A picture of Marlon Shirley, a below-the-knee amputee who is one of the world's fastest disabled sprinters, appears on McDonald's beverage cups, for example. And Tatyana McFadden, a medal-winning wheelchair racer who was born with spina bifida, may be seen discussing her sport at the Hilton Hotel's Web site. Although these athletes aren't making Michael Phelps or Peyton Manning kind of money, the endorsements are helping to defray their costs of competing, which is greatly welcomed. Although the money is nice, of course, most disabled athletes believe that the exposure helps send their message to the public: "Disabled does *not* mean unable."

It certainly must be gratifying for Cheri Blauwet and her fellow Paralympians to have an opportunity to participate in this event. The joy of competing, along with the notoriety of winning medals is surely thrilling. Still, once this special event is over, these talented athletes return to a world in which able-bodied people predominate and people with disabilities sometimes confront barriers that they, even with their athletic prowess, cannot readily overcome. We are referring here to our feelings about people and things, known as *attitudes*.

As you might imagine, attitudes are an important part of people's lives, particularly in the workplace. Indeed, people tend to have definite feelings about everything related to their jobs, whether it's the work itself, superiors, coworkers, subordinates, or even such mundane things as the food in the company cafeteria. Feelings such as these are referred to as *work-related attitudes*, the topic of this chapter. As you might imagine, not only may our attitudes toward our jobs or organizations have profound effects on the way we perform, but also on the quality of life we experience while at work.

In view of their importance, we will examine these effects closely in this chapter. Specifically, our discussion of work-related attitudes has three major areas of focus. First, we will consider attitudes toward others, including that special—and problematic—kind of negative attitude known as *prejudice*. Second, we will look at attitudes toward the job, known as *job satisfaction*. Third, we will conclude this chapter by focusing on people's attitudes toward the organizations in which they work, known as *organizational commitment*. Before getting to these specific work-related attitudes and to help you appreciate them fully, however, we begin by outlining the nature of attitudes in general.

Attitudes: What Are They?

If we asked you how you feel about your job, we'd probably find you to be very opinionated. You might say, for example, that you really like it and think it's very interesting. Or perhaps you may complain about it bitterly, noting that it makes you bored out of your mind. Maybe you'd hold views that are more complex, liking some things (e.g., "my boss is great") and disliking others (e.g., "the pay is terrible"). These feelings reflect the attitudes we hold. With this in mind, we now take a closer look at the nature of attitudes.

Basic Definitions

attitudes
Relatively stable clusters of feelings, beliefs, and behavioral intentions toward a specific object, person, or institution.

Formally, we define **attitudes** as relatively stable clusters of feelings, beliefs, and behavioral predispositions (i.e., intentions) toward some specific object, person, or institution. By including the phrase *relatively stable* in the definition, we are referring to feelings that are not fleeting and that, once formed, tends to persist. Indeed, as we will explain throughout this chapter (and again in Chapter 16), changing attitudes may require considerable effort.

work-related attitudes
Attitudes relating to any aspect of work or work settings.

When we speak of **work-related attitudes,** we are talking about those lasting feelings, beliefs, and behavioral tendencies toward various aspects of the job itself, the setting in which the work is conducted, the people involved and/or the organization as a whole. As you will discover as you read this chapter, work-related attitudes are associated with many important aspects of organizational behavior, including job performance, absence from work, and voluntary turnover.

Three Essential Components of Attitudes

Regardless of exactly what they may be, the attitudes you express consist of three major components: an *evaluative component,* a *cognitive component,* and a *behavioral component.*[1] Because these represent the basic building blocks of our definition of attitudes, we now examine them more closely (for an overview and example, see Figure 6.1).

evaluative component (of attitudes)
Our liking or disliking of any particular person, item, or event.

So far, we've been suggesting that attitudes have a great deal to do with how we feel about something. Indeed, this essential aspect of an attitude, its **evaluative component,** refers to our liking or disliking of any particular person, item, or event (what might be called the *attitude object,* the focus of our attitude). You may, for example, feel positively or negatively toward your boss, the sculpture in the lobby, or the fact that your company just landed a large contract.

cognitive component (of attitudes)
The things we believe about an attitude object, whether they are true or false.

Attitudes involve more than feelings; they also involve knowledge—that is, what you believe to be the case about an attitude object. For example, you might believe that one of your coworkers is paid much more than you, that the company is going to merge with another, or that your supervisor doesn't know as much as she should about her job. These beliefs, whether they're accurate or even totally false, comprise the **cognitive component** of attitudes.

FIGURE 6.1

Three Basic Components of Attitudes

People's *attitudes* toward specific objects (the focus of attitudes) are composed of the three fundamental components shown here: the evaluative component, the cognitive component, and the behavioral component. This example illustrates how someone might have a negative attitude toward his or her boss.

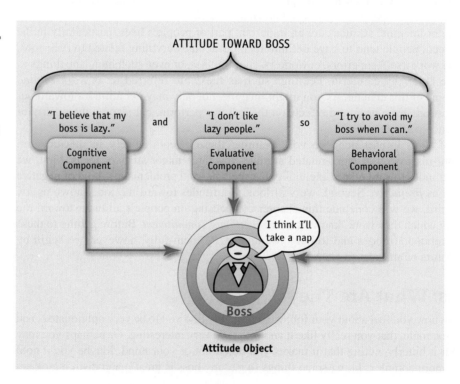

As you might imagine, the things you believe about something (e.g., "my boss is embezzling company funds") and the way you feel about it (e.g., "I can't stand working for him") may have effects on the way you are predisposed to behave (e.g., "I'm going to look for a new job"). In other words, attitudes also have a **behavioral component**—a predisposition to act in a certain way. It is important to note that such a predisposition may not be perfectly predictive of one's behavior. For example, although you may be interested in finding a new job, you might not actually bother to look for one if you suspect that a better position isn't available, or if there are other aspects of the job you like enough to compensate for your negative feelings. In other words, your intention to behave a certain way may or may not dictate how you actually will behave. It's important to keep this in mind as you come to understand the various attitudes described in this chapter.

Now that we have examined the basic nature of attitudes, we turn our attention to specific work-related attitudes. We begin by describing a crucial work-related attitude—*prejudice,* negative attitudes toward other people.

behavioral component (of attitudes)
Our predisposition to behave in a way consistent with our beliefs and feelings about an attitude object.

Prejudice and Discrimination: Negative Attitudes and Behavior Toward Others

How do you feel about your associate in the next cubicle? How about your boss, or accountants in general? Our attitudes toward other people are obviously very important when it comes to understanding behavior in organizations. Such attitudes are highly problematic—when they are negative—especially when these feelings are based on misguided beliefs that prompt harmful behavior. *Prejudice* is the term used to refer to attitudes of this type.

Specifically, **prejudice** is defined as negative feelings about people belonging to certain groups. Members of racial or ethnic groups, for example, are victims of prejudice when they are believed to be disinterested in working, unprincipled, or inferior in one way or another. Prejudicial attitudes, as you know, often hold people back, creating barriers to their success. Because of its considerable importance in organizations, we closely examine the nature of prejudice in this section of the chapter.

prejudice
Negative attitudes toward the members of specific groups, based solely on the fact that they are members of those groups (e.g., based on age, race, ethnicity, sexual orientation).

The Challenges of Organizational Demography

At the root of prejudicial feelings is the basic fact that people tend to be uncomfortable with others who are different from them. Today, as we chronicled in Chapter 1, demographic differences between people in the workplace are not the exception, but the rule. For example, not so long ago the American workforce was composed predominantly of white males. But that is no longer the case. In fact, white men now represent less than half of the current American workforce, and most new entrants to the workforce are expected to be women and people of color.[2] This is the result of three major trends.[3]

- Birth rates of nonwhites is higher than those of whites.
- Growing numbers of foreign nationals are entering the American workforce, making it more racially and ethnically diverse than ever.
- We now have equal proportions of men and women in the workforce overall (although these figures vary considerably for different jobs).

The study of the composition of a workforce with respect to various characteristics (e.g., age, gender, ethnic makeup, etc.) is known as **organizational demography.**[4] As demographic characteristics change, challenges often result. Among white men, for example, there's the growing recognition that their era of dominance in the workplace is over, which many find threatening.[5] Not only white men, but everyone in the workplace must become aware that stereotypes and prejudicial attitudes (which we will examine in the next sections of this chapter) impose potential barriers to success that must be eliminated. This is made difficult by the tendency for employees to feel uncomfortable working with others from whom they differ in key ways. When this occurs, disruptive interpersonal conflict sometimes results (see Chapter 11), potentially interfering with performance within work groups and teams.

Another likely reaction is that employees will distance themselves from those considered "different," triggering potentially serious disruptions to effective organizational communication

organizational demography
The nature of the composition of a workforce with respect to various characteristics (e.g., age, gender, ethnic makeup, etc.).

(see Chapter 9). In some cases, as shown in research on top management teams, people even resign when they feel sufficiently uncomfortable as members of demographically diverse teams.[6] As some researchers have concluded, "the greater the dissimilarity (between group members), the more negative outcomes, such as conflicts, divisiveness, or turnover are likely to occur."[7]

When viewed in light of the fact that demographic diversity is the rule rather than the exception in contemporary organizations, it's imperative for everyone in the workplace to accept everybody else. Doing so helps avoid the costly problems of disharmony and communication failure just noted. But that's just the beginning. By going a step further—not just accepting people in the workplace, but *valuing* them and *embracing* their differences—organizations stand to benefit greatly. Specifically, as we will describe later in this section of the chapter, important benefits are likely to result when working with people who bring different perspectives to the jobs they perform.[8] This is not surprising, given that people with diverse backgrounds have different experiences, and as a result, they can be expected to look at the world differently. Through these different lenses ideas may emerge that might never have materialized in more homogeneous groups. And in today's highly competitive business environment, no organizations can afford to overlook leveraging these vital human resources.

With this background in mind, we examine closely the nature of prejudicial attitudes in this section of the chapter. To provide a feel for how serious prejudices can be, we describe specific targets of prejudice in the workplace and the special nature of the problems these individuals confront. Following this, we then discuss various strategies that have been used to overcome prejudice in the workplace. Before turning to these topics, we begin by taking a closer look at the concept of prejudice and distinguish it from related concepts. This is critical because if we are to have any chance of reducing prejudice in the workplace, we must fully appreciate its basic nature.

Anatomy of Prejudice: Some Fundamental Distinctions

When people are prejudiced, they judge members of a group based on the qualities they attribute to that group. So, to the extent we believe that members of a certain group have various characteristics, learning that someone belongs to that group will lead us to believe that he or she also possesses those qualities. *Stereotype* is the term used to identify such beliefs.

stereotypes
Beliefs that individuals possess certain characteristics because of their membership in certain groups.

STEREOTYPES. Formally, a **stereotype** is a belief about someone based on the group to which that person belongs. As you probably realize, stereotypes, whether positive or negative, are generally inaccurate. If we knew more about someone than simply whatever we assume based on his or her membership in various groups, we are likely to make far more accurate judgments about that individual. However, to the extent that we often find it difficult or inconvenient to learn everything we need to know about someone, we frequently rely on stereotypes as mental shortcuts. So, for example, if you believe that individuals belonging to group X are not particularly bright, and you meet person A, who happens to belong to group X, you likely would assume that he or she is inclined to be unintelligent.

Although this may seem logical enough, by engaging in such stereotyping you run the risk of misjudging person A. After all, you don't know this individual (although you made an assumption based on his or her group membership). The person in question actually might be quite brilliant, despite presuming just the opposite. However, by drawing on the stereotype, you presupposed that person A wasn't too smart. Would you be willing to hire such an individual for a key post in your company? Probably not. Your predisposition against hiring A (a behavioral predisposition) in this situation reflects your prejudicial attitude. It also illustrates a potential cost of engaging in stereotyping.

discrimination
The behavior consistent with a prejudicial attitude; the act of treating someone negatively because of his or her membership in a specific group.

DISCRIMINATION. Prejudicial attitudes are particularly harmful when they translate into actual behaviors. In such instances, people become the victims of others' prejudices—that is, **discrimination** occurs. In other words, as summarized in Figure 6.2, prejudice is an attitude, whereas discrimination is a form of behavior following from that attitude.

Completing our example, you would refrain from hiring person A, thereby behaving consistently with your attitude. This would be neither in your best interest nor that of the victim of your prejudicial attitudes and discriminatory behavior. For this reason, it is important to identify ways of overcoming the natural tendency to base our attitudes on stereotypes and to discriminate unfairly among people on this basis. Later in this chapter, we will outline some strategies that are

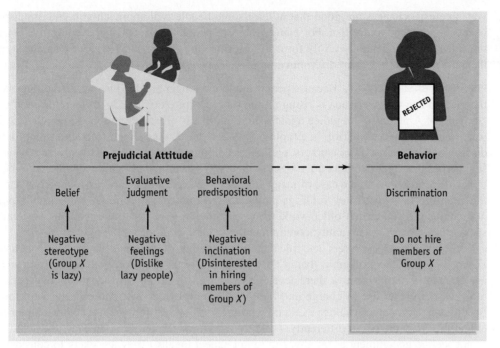

FIGURE 6.2

Prejudice Versus Discrimination: A Key Distinction

Prejudice is an attitude, and as such, it consists of the three basic components shown here. Discrimination refers to behavior based on that attitude. The example presented here illustrates this important distinction.

effective in this regard. Before doing so, however, it's important to highlight the adverse effects of prejudice in organizations today.

Everyone Can Be a Victim of Prejudice and Discrimination!

Unfortunate as it may be, this section's heading is painfully accurate: All of us are indeed potential victims of prejudice and discrimination. No matter what personal characteristics we may have, there very well may be people out there who harbor prejudice against us and who discriminate against us as a result (see Figure 6.3). This is not surprising if you consider that people hold stereotypes about many different things. Whatever you look like, wherever you're from, whatever

FIGURE 6.3

If Bob Can Be a Target of Discrimination, So Can You

As unlikely as we may be to come across this store, its existence (here, at least) illustrates a sobering fact: People discriminate against others based on just about anything, making everyone potential victims. It might be useful to keep this in mind before discriminating against someone on the basis of your own prejudices.

© Mike Baldwin / Cornered www.cartoonstock.com/Mike Baldwin.

your interests, chances are good that at least some people will approach you with predisposed beliefs about what you're like. For many groups of people, these beliefs have negative connotations, leading to potentially costly forms of discriminatory behavior. Here, we describe some of the most prevalent targets of discrimination in American society today.

PREJUDICE BASED ON AGE. Because people are living longer and the birth rate is holding steady, the median age of Americans is rising all the time. Despite this trend—often referred to as the "graying of America"—prejudice against older people is all too common. Although U.S. laws (e.g., the Age Discrimination in Employment Act) have done much to counter employment discrimination against older workers, prejudices continue to exist.[9] Part of the problem resides in stereotypes that older workers are too set in their ways to train and that they will tend to be sick or accident-prone. As in the case of many attitudes, these prejudices are not founded on accurate information. In fact, survey findings paint just the opposite picture: A Yankelovich poll of 400 companies found that older workers are considered very good or excellent, especially in such critical areas as punctuality, commitment to quality, and practical knowledge.

It is not just older workers who find themselves victims of prejudice but younger ones as well. For them, part of the problem is that as the average age of the workforce advances (from an average age of 29 in 1976 to 39 today), there develops a gap in expectations between the more experienced older workers who are in charge and the younger employees just entering the workforce.[10] Specifically, compared to older workers, who grew up in a different time, today's under-thirty employees view the world differently. They are more prone to question the way things are done, to not see the government as an ally, and to not expect loyalty. They are likely to consider self-development to be their main interest and are willing to learn whatever skills are necessary to make them marketable. (In describing these characteristics, we do not mean to draw on stereotypes. Instead, we are attempting to depict reliable intergenerational differences that follow from shifting societal norms.[11]) These differing perspectives may lead older employees, who are likely to be their superiors, to feel uncomfortable with their younger colleagues and vice versa. With this in mind, it's important to ask: What can be done to help bridge the generational communication gap at work? For some recommendations, see Table 6.1.[12]

TABLE 6.1 How to Bridge Generational Communication Gaps at Work

As people continue to work later into their lives, it's not unusual to find younger and older people working alongside one another. Because people are affected by the experiences they've had over the years, and these vary from one generation to the next, it follows that people of widely different ages will differ in values, expectations, and the way they think about things. Such factors conspire to make communication difficult. But to work effectively with one another, we all have to invest in learning to overcome the challenges. The following suggestions are designed to help bridge these communication gaps.

Recommendation	Description and Example
Have a discussion about the important events that influenced one another's lives.	When you come to appreciate the major factors that shaped another's thinking, you can better understand the perspectives they bring to things. A Vietnam veteran who was a prisoner of war may be greatly affected by this experience, even today.
Suspend your assumptions about people of different ages.	As we noted earlier, stereotypes can be misleading. Communication improves when you refrain from assuming things and make an effort to find out what the other person is like. Who knows, if you do this you might find an 80-year-old computer geek who likes rap music.
Don't treat others the way you want to be treated, but the way *they* want to be treated.	It's very easy to assume that you're treating someone politely, but it may be a good idea to discuss this with the other person to make sure. For example, although a younger person may think it's best to call an older person by his or her first name, that individual may be more comfortable if you used his or her last name.
Instead of ignoring age differences, discuss them openly.	There's a lot you can learn by talking to people of different ages and really taking in what they're saying. Doing this may help you learn more about the other person, helping you communicate more effectively with him or her. Such conversations may lead you to learn that you share some common interests, such as being fans of the same sports team.

Source: Based on suggestions by Lieberman et al., 2009; see Note 12.

PREJUDICE BASED ON PHYSICAL CONDITION. There are currently some 41 million Americans with disabilities, 13.6 million of whom are of working age, between 16 and 64. However, only a minority of these individuals hold jobs—and, among these, most work only part-time or irregularly.[13] Clearly, there exist barriers that are keeping millions of potentially productive people from gainful employment (and we're not even talking about being Paralympians like the ones featured in this chapter's Preview Case on page 177). The most formidable barriers are not physical but attitudinal. Most people who are not physically challenged don't know how to treat and what to expect from those who are. Experts advise that people with disabilities don't want to be pitied; they want to be respected for the skills and commitment to work they bring to their jobs. That is, they wish to be recognized as whole people who just happen to have disabling conditions. In other words, you should think of individuals with disabilities not as "handicapped people" but as people who just happen to have handicaps. Grammatically these terms may be identical, but their implications are worlds apart.

Legal remedies have been enacted to help break down these barriers. For example, in the early 1990s, legislation known as the Americans with Disabilities Act (ADA) was enacted in the United States to protect the rights of people with physical and mental disabilities. Its rationale is straightforward: Simply because an employee is limited in some way does not mean that accommodations cannot be made to help that individual perform his or her job.[14] Companies that do not comply are subject to legal damages, and some violators have paid dearly. However, the most important reason to refrain from discriminating against people with disabilities is not simply to avoid fines, but to tap into a pool of talented people who are capable of making valuable contributions if given an opportunity.

PREJUDICE AGAINST WOMEN. The number of women in the U.S. workforce has risen steadily in the past few decades and now equals the number of men. Despite this equality in numbers of workers, women as a whole occupy lower-level positions and, as a result, earn only 77.5 cents for every dollar earned by men.[15] In fact, the U.S. Bureau of Labor Statistics reports that women comprise only one-third of all the people considered managerial and professional employees.[16] Although women have been rising to higher-level positions in recent years, such changes at the top have come about very slowly. For example, in 2008 only 24 women were CEOs of *Fortune* 1000 companies and only 4 more were added to this number in 2009.[17] Thus, despite finding some women in high-profile positions (for an example, see Figure 6.4), their presence at the top of the corporate world remains the exception rather than the rule.

Why is this the case? One explanation that has been advanced is that because women are relative newcomers to their chosen fields, sufficient time may not have elapsed to allow more of them to have worked their way into the top echelons of organizations. As reasonable as this may be, however, women are not being promoted as quickly as men, and as a result, there's little reason to expect to see many more at the tops of organizations in the near future. Apparently, something else seems to be involved—and, unfortunately, it's more troublesome. We speak here of the persistence of powerful **sex-role stereotypes.** These are narrow-minded beliefs about the qualities of women and men and the kinds of tasks for which each is most appropriately suited.[18] For example, old-fashioned—and inaccurate—though it may be, some people like to believe that females are not sufficiently aggressive or determined to make it to the top.[19] (Recall our discussion of stereotypes earlier in this chapter.)

Sex-role stereotypes are problematic because they contribute to invisible barriers, known as the **glass ceiling,** that keep women from advancing as rapidly as men in certain fields.[20] The metaphor, unfortunately, is all too accurate. Because nothing formally is ever said or written about what women are considered to be like or capable of doing, the barrier is invisible, like glass. And because it imposes a restriction on the level of an organization to which women may rise, it also acts as a ceiling. Although we often speak of glass ceilings as sources of discrimination against women in the workplace, the term also is used sometimes to identify similar invisible barriers imposed on other groups as well.

PREJUDICE BASED ON SEXUAL ORIENTATION. Unlike people with physical disabilities, who are protected from discrimination by federal law, not much protection exists for another group whose members are frequently victims of prejudice—lesbian women, gay men, bisexuals and

sex-role stereotypes
Narrow-minded beliefs about the qualities of women and men and the kinds of tasks for which each is most appropriately suited.

glass ceiling
Invisible barriers that keep women from advancing as rapidly as men in certain fields.

FIGURE 6.4

Anne Mulcahy: A CEO Worth Copying

After 30 years at Xerox, Anne Mulcahy worked her way to the top, where she's chair and CEO. Under her leadership, Xerox has maintained its position as a market leader despite a weak economy that has slowed technology spending in recent years. A well-respected member of the business community, Mulcahy served as a member of President Obama's transition team in 2009. She appears here to the right of the president, along with Eric Schidt, CEO of Google, and David Barger, CEO of JetBlue (pictured to the president's left).

transgendered people (collectively referred to as the *LGBT community*). Existing protection comes at the local level, as several states and many municipalities have enacted laws to protect the rights of individuals in the workplace based on their sexual orientations. Unfortunately, although more people than ever are tolerant of nontraditional sexual orientations, antihomosexual prejudice still exists in the workplace.[21] Indeed, about two-thirds of CEOs from major companies admit their reluctance to put a homosexual on a top management committee. Not surprisingly, without the law to protect them and with prejudices being widespread, many members of the LGBT community are reluctant to make their sexual orientations openly known.

Fears of being "discovered," exposed as someone with a nontraditional sexual orientation, represents a considerable source of stress among such individuals. For example, a gay vice president of a large office-equipment manufacturer admitted in a magazine interview that he'd like to become the company's CEO but fears that his chances would be ruined if his sexual orientation were to become known. If the pressure of going through working life with a disguised identity is disruptive, imagine the cumulative effects on organizations in which several employees are in this situation. Such misdirections of energy can become quite a serious threat to productivity. In the words of consultant Mark Kaplan, "Gay and lesbian employees use a lot of time and stress trying to conceal a big part of their identity."[22] To work in an organization with a homophobic culture, to have to endure jokes slurring gays and lesbians, can easily distract even the most highly focused employees.

Fortunately, many companies are taking steps to reduce this problem.[23] As a beginning, some 10,000 employers in the United States offer domestic partner health benefits for their employees. Of these, 95 percent offer the benefits to both same-sex and different-sex couples. Generally, the more successful the company, the greater is the chance that it offers domestic partner benefits. Fifty-one percent of *Fortune* 500 companies offer domestic partner health benefits, as do 80 percent of the *Fortune* 50. Clearly, although some companies are passively discouraging diversity with respect to sexual orientation, others encourage it, much to their own—and their employees'—advantages.

PREJUDICE BASED ON RACE AND NATIONAL ORIGIN. The history of the United States is marked by struggles over acceptance for people of various racial and ethnic groups. Although the American workplace is now more racially diverse than ever, it is clear that prejudice lingers.

Not only do members of various minority groups believe they are the victims of prejudice and discrimination, but they also are taking action. For example, the number of complaints of discrimination based on national origin filed at the Equal Employment Opportunity Commission (EEOC) has been increasing steadily in recent years—and discrimination victims have been winning such cases. For example, the Supreme Court of the state of Washington upheld a $389,000 judgment against a Seattle bank brought by a Cambodian American employee who was fired because of his accent. Outside the courtroom, companies that discriminate pay in other ways as well—notably, in lost talent and productivity. According to former EEOC Commissioner Joy Cherian, employees who feel victimized "may not take the initiative to introduce inventions and other innovations," adding, "every day, American employers are losing millions of dollars because these talents are frozen."[24]

PREJUDICE BASED ON RELIGION. Although freedom of religion is the law of the land in the United States (primarily because of the Civil Rights Act of 1964), it's sad but true that many people in the workplace have been made to feel uneasy, or even unwelcome, because of their religious beliefs. In extreme cases, people have suffered through acts of **religious intolerance,** defined as actions taken against persons or groups based on their faith.[25] Such acts might take many forms, ranging from subtle, yet painful ridicule, to physical attacks on people and vandalism in places of worship.

religious intolerance
Actions (e.g., personal ridicule, vandalism) taken against persons or groups based on their faith.

A survey of a broad cross-section of Americans has shown that religious bias is a reality in the U.S. workplace.[26] This poses a serious concern for management, given that almost half of the people who report religious discrimination indicate that their job performance also is affected adversely as a result. Equally disturbing, 45 percent of employees have considered quitting because of religious discrimination. Not all religious groups are affected equally. Long having a presence in the United States, Christians and Jews are least likely to be victims of discrimination. However, groups such as Buddhists and Hindus, whose members have entered the U.S. workforce in growing numbers in recent years, have experienced more religious bias. In addition, as waves of Islamic immigrants from the Middle East have come aboard, many Muslims also have found themselves targets of intolerance.[27]

This problem is fueled by the fact that less than a quarter of the people who experience religious discrimination report it to their bosses. Generally, this is because they either don't know where to go in the company to express their concerns or because they feel that nothing would happen if they did. In fact, most companies fail to address matters of religious tolerance in their policy manuals and, not surprisingly, few managers are versed in how to handle religious discrimination. In general, then, it appears that issues of religious prejudice remain largely ignored in many companies.

Strategies for Overcoming Workplace Prejudice: Managing a Diverse Workforce

It's one thing to identify prejudicial attitudes and quite another to eliminate them. Two major approaches have been taken toward doing precisely this—*affirmative action* and *diversity management*. As you'll see, their overall goals and orientations are quite different.

Affirmative Action

In the United States, **affirmative action** is a policy that has been used to promote the nondiscriminatory treatment of women and members of minority groups in the workplace. Derived from civil rights initiatives of the 1960s, affirmative action involves efforts to give employment opportunities

affirmative action laws
Legislation designed to give employment opportunities to groups that historically have been underrepresented in the workforce, such as women and members of minority groups.

to qualified individuals belonging to groups that traditionally have been disadvantaged. The rationale is straightforward. By encouraging the hiring of qualified women and minority group members into positions in which they traditionally have been underrepresented two things occur. First, such individuals will be given opportunities that they historically have been denied in the past (an immediate benefit). Second, more people will come to see that women and members of minority groups are able to succeed in the workplace, leading them to perceive that their negative stereotypes were misguided. Then, eventually, as these stereotypes begin to crumble, discrimination will be reduced, along with the prejudicial attitudes on which it is based (a potential long-term benefit).

nonpreferential affirmative action
Efforts to get companies to conduct ongoing, conscious appraisals of their rules and procedures and to eliminate those that exclude women and members of minority groups without sufficient justification.

Over the years, some confusion has arisen with respect to the objectives of affirmative action, so let's clarify.[28] What the U.S. government had in mind may be referred to as **nonpreferential affirmative action**—efforts to get companies to conduct ongoing, conscious appraisal of their rules and procedures and to eliminate those that exclude women and members of minority groups without sufficient justification. Typically, this involves the following:

1. Taking steps to ensure that there is a diverse pool of applicants.
2. Based on the racial composition of this pool, predicting what the workforce would look like if the selection of employees were nondiscriminatory (this is the so-called *affirmative-action goal*).
3. Comparing results with goals and revising procedures and policies to alleviate the discrepancy.

Over the years, controversies emerged with respect to the ideal of affirmative action goals because the language of the law was misleading. Although a goal is something you aim at, this is not what the government intended. What they had in mind was not so much a finite number that had to be met (despite the language used) so much as an image of what things *should* be like. Despite this, courts interpreted the law literally and held companies to specific numeric goals. So if, say, 20 percent of a company's broad labor pool consisted of African Americans, then courts required it to hire this percentage of African Americans. This form of affirmative action, known as **preferential affirmative action**, is generally what the public has in mind when they think of affirmative action. Today, although some people are enlightened, many remain unaware of the spirit of the law.

preferential affirmative action
The practice of hiring women and members of minority groups in proportion to their representation in the population near organizations.

After approximately 40 years of experience with affirmative action programs, major gains have been made in the opportunities available for women and members of minority groups. Indeed, most problems with affirmative action have occurred in its preferential form.[29] However, nonpreferential affirmative action policies have been effective in increasing the attraction, selection, inclusion, and retention of underrepresented group members.

Diversity Management: Orientation and Rationale

Over the past few decades, organizations have become increasingly proactive in their attempts to eliminate prejudice and have taken it upon themselves to go beyond affirmative action requirements. Their approach has involved not merely hiring a broader group of people than usual but creating an atmosphere in which diverse groups can flourish.[30] This is the idea behind **diversity management**.

diversity management programs
Programs in which employees are taught to celebrate the differences between people and in which organizations create supportive work environments for women and minorities.

inclusion
Making people feel valued as worthwhile members of the organization.

ORIENTATION. Specifically, efforts to manage diversity are aimed at promoting supportive, not just neutral, work environments for women and minorities.[31] Diversity management calls not for simply treating everyone alike and ignoring their differences, but recognizing and celebrating the differences between people with respect to the lifestyles and practices associated with their racial and ethnic heritages, their religions, their appearance, and so on. The notion of **inclusion** is key—that is, making people feel valued as worthwhile members of the organization. And when people feel that they are welcomed, accepted and valued instead of just tolerated, everyone benefits.[32] Diversity management may be distinguished from affirmative action in four key ways, as summarized in Table 6.2.[33]

THE BUSINESS CASE FOR DIVERSITY. One cannot deny that companies are interested in managing diversity so that they can avoid becoming defendants in lawsuits claiming illegal discrimination. However, this generally is not the main reason. Instead, the primary motive is a

TABLE 6.2 Affirmative Action Versus Diversity Management

Both *affirmative action* and *diversity management* are designed to promote positive attitudes and to reduce discrimination toward women and members of minority groups. As outlined here, however, their rationales and approaches differ with respect to several key dimensions.

Dimension	Affirmative Action	Diversity Management
Objective	Adherence to legal regulations and bureaucratic procedures	Systemic transformation of an organization's culture (see Chapter 14)
Focus	Avoiding penalties associated with discrimination	Positive images of people and celebration of what they can contribute to an organization
Motivation	Legal compliance	Belief that there's a good "business case" associated with promoting diversity
Groups targeted	Gender and race	Any and all differences between people (e.g., religion, sexual preference, etc.)

Source: Based on suggestions by Greene & Kirton 2009; see Note 33.

traditional one—to improve business. With this in mind, we ask an important question: Can a "business case" be made for having a diverse workforce? In other words, do organizations with diverse workforces have advantages over those that don't?

Several studies reveal that the answer is yes.[34] One investigation, for example, examined the financial success of banks that actively pursued a growth strategy (i.e., deliberate efforts to grow larger in size). Among these institutions, the more highly diverse their workforces, the better they performed financially.[35] This, in turn, added value to these banks, giving them advantages over their competitors.

Researchers conducting another study reasoned that when companies use their human resources effectively they can lower their costs and thereby perform better than their competitors.[36] To test this notion, they compared two groups of companies from 1986 through 1992. One group was composed of organizations that received awards from the U.S. Department of Labor for their exemplary efforts at managing diversity. The other group was composed of companies that had settled large claims against them for employment discrimination. To compare the performance of these organizations, the researchers relied on a key index of economic success—stock returns. Their findings were striking: Companies that made special efforts to use their diverse human resources were considerably more profitable than those that discriminated against their employees.

The researchers explained that organizations that capitalized on the diversity of their workforces were better able to attract and retain the talented people needed for them to thrive. Indeed, this seems to be a major key to diversity. Organizations that effectively manage diversity are successful because they are especially adept at attracting and retaining pools of talented people from diverse backgrounds.[37] And, of course, it comes as no surprise that having the best people is essential to the success of any business.

Clearly, managing diversity makes sense not only because it is the right way to treat people, but also because it is good business! With this in mind, it is not surprising that one consultant claimed that, "A corporation's success will increasingly be determined by its managers' ability to naturally tap the full potential of a diverse workforce."[38] And, as a recruiter for an executive search firm emphasized, "There is a strong business case [for diversity]. A diverse workplace isn't a luxury, it's a necessity."[39]

Diversity Management: What Are Companies Doing?

Considering the practical value of diversity management, you probably won't be surprised that efforts to manage diversity are popular in today's organizations. This is evidenced in a survey revealing that the number of companies with diversity management policies in place has been growing rapidly, with 75 percent already having them and 14 percent planning to add them soon.[40] What exactly are these companies doing to promote diversity? We now identify four such tactics.

CONDUCT DIVERSITY TRAINING. Many companies conduct regular programs designed to develop people's skills with respect to managing diversity.[41] The best such programs do more than simply raise employees' awareness about the nature and importance of diversity, but train them in ways to interact effectively with people who are different from themselves. The main techniques used for this purpose are as follows.[42]

- *Cross-cultural understanding.* Understanding the cultural differences responsible for why different coworkers behave differently on the job.
- *Intercultural communication.* Learning to ensure that verbal and nonverbal barriers to communication across cultures are overcome.
- *Facilitation skills.* Training in how to help others alleviate misunderstandings that may result from cultural differences.
- *Flexibility and adaptability.* Cultivating the patience to take new and different approaches when dealing with others who are different.

As you might imagine, the nature and extent to which companies are involved in diversity management training vary widely. At some companies, training efforts are minimal and informal. However, others take diversity training very seriously and are highly methodical about assessing its impact. One such organization is Sodexo, the leading provider of food and facilities management services in North America (see Figure 6.5). For example, after the training has been conducted (which focuses on virtually all employees), the company administers a follow-up survey to assess the extent to which behavioral change is occurring (e.g., are members of minority groups being treated more respectfully?). The company also uses an extensive questionnaire known as the "Sodexo Diversity Index" to determine the extent to which its executives are demonstrating the company's diversity values. This measure assesses quantitatively and qualitatively both efforts and results (which, in turn, are used to determine compensation).

affinity groups
Informal collections of individuals who share a common identity with respect to such factors as race, ethnicity, or sexual preference.

USE LEADERS TO SEND STRONG MESSAGES ABOUT DIVERSITY. In many of the most diversity-minded companies, top leaders are involved actively in diversity management initiatives. For example, at the pharmaceutical giant Merck & Co., there are many different **affinity groups**—that is, informal collections of individuals who share a common identity with respect to such factors as race, ethnicity, or sexual preference (e.g., Asian American, African American, Hispanic, Native Indigenous, lesbian/gay/bisexual/transgendered people, and

FIGURE 6.5

Diversity Is Valued Highly at Sodexo

Sodexo's commitment to providing a workplace where everyone feels accepted and valued is reflected in the extensive diversity training programs it has for employees. And the company's successes in doing so has been recognized for many years by dozens of groups.

Newscom.

others). Acknowledging that understanding what people from different groups have to say is important. Chairman, President, and CEO Richard T. Clark personally meets with members of these groups.

At Capitol One Financial Corporation, Founder, Chairman, and CEO Richard D. Fairbank has been involved actively in the company's efforts to become a national leader in diversity. Among other things, he spearheaded the development of a set of company values in which diversity figures prominently (e.g., the company's "Best People" program requires employees to "value diversity of people") and takes the lead in promoting them. Not only are the actions of these leaders likely to be effective directly but indirectly too because of the strong messages they send about the importance of diversity in their companies.

REQUIRE SUPPLIERS TO PROMOTE DIVERSITY. Several companies are not only content to promote diversity within their walls, but also use their influence to get their suppliers to promote diversity. For example, FedEx awards contracts to suppliers that promote diversity. As a corporate member of the National Minority Supplier Development Council (NMSDC), FedEx requires all minority, woman, and small business suppliers to obtain certification from a recognized third party such as the Small Business Administration (SBA), a supplier development council, or a state or local body.

Starwood Hotels and Resorts expresses a commitment to diverse suppliers in its "Starwood Supplier Diverse Policy Statement." It defines diverse vendors as those certified to be 51 percent or more owned, managed, or controlled by one or more members of the following groups: African Americans, Asian Indian Americans, Asian/Pacific-Islander Americans, Hispanic Americans, persons with disabilities, Native Americans, U.S. veterans, disabled U.S. veterans, and women.

MAKE DIVERSITY A TOP PRIORITY. Being truly effective at managing diversity means far more than conducting some training programs and having executives talk to various people. To make everyone feel included and welcome in an organization, diversity must be made a top priority. This may be done in the following ways.

■ *Use ongoing diversity teams.* Devoting permanent teams to diversity helps ensure that any gaps between diversity initiatives (e.g., multicultural skills learning, affinity groups, etc.) are filled. This enables a company's diversity principles to be satisfied (i.e., attracting, developing, supporting a diverse workforce). Consider, for example, Convergys Corporation, a firm that provides customer service solutions to large corporate clients. This organization has permanent "Diversity Action Teams" that strive to identify and recommend solutions to diversity-related issues that arise anywhere in the company.

■ *Create reporting relationships that emphasize diversity.* At Johnson & Johnson, for example, the company's chief diversity officer reports directly to its chairman and CEO, William C. Weldon, assuring that it cannot get overlooked. At the pharmaceutical firm Abbott, each of the 13 people who report to the CEO is responsible for attaining diversity goals. By putting diversity at the top levels of these organizations, its high priority is assured.

■ *Establish accountability.* If an organization is going to be serious about promoting diversity, then its key people need to be held accountable for it. An effective way of doing this is by using pay policies that reward accomplishments with respect to diversity. At IBM, for example, for a manager to receive the top performance evaluation, he or she must provide evidence of having fostered a spirit of inclusion among employees and of having promoted the company's diversity values. If you want to be promoted at IBM, then you obviously need to go out of your way to do something that promotes diversity.

As you might suspect, the companies that are involved most actively in promoting diversity do all these things plus a lot more. For a look at what's done at a one company whose commitment to promoting diversity has been well established, see the OB in Practice section on page 190.

OB in Practice

How the "Good Hands People" Use Diversity as a Competitive Weapon

Promoting diversity in an organization is a challenging and important objective that takes a considerable commitment from everyone. It doesn't just happen by itself. For some guidelines as to how to go about doing this, it's useful to benchmark the best practices from a successful firm, such as the Allstate Insurance Company, the "good hands people."[43]

Allstate is so committed to diversity that it uses the opportunity to promote diversity as a strategic weapon. The idea is straightforward: By reflecting the racial and ethnic diversity of its customers in its own workforce, Allstate can be sensitive to needs that otherwise may go unrecognized and, therefore, unfulfilled by a more homogeneous group of employees. In the words of one former Allstate CEO, "Our competitive advantage is our people and our people are diverse. Nothing less than an integrated diversity strategy will allow the company to excel."[44]

Allstate's diversity management program takes a broad perspective. Not limited only to gender and ethnicity, it also pays attention to diversity with respect to age, religion, and sexual orientation. Specifically, it promotes diversity along three major fronts.

- Allstate recruiters visit Historically Black Colleges and Universities to attract members of the African American community. It also recruits from schools in Puerto Rico in an effort to expand its Hispanic customer base. From the many awards it has received for its efforts in these areas (e.g., named one of the "Best Companies for Hispanics to Work"), such initiatives appear to be working. And the more such recognition the company receives, the easier it is for it to attract more individuals from these groups.

- Attracting recruits is half the battle, but retaining them is far trickier. With this in mind, Allstate carefully trains all its employees to know that they are expected to show no bias toward others. It also goes out of its way to encourage development of minority candidates by showing them the routes to promotion within the company. In fact, minority candidates are considered seriously when it comes time to plan for succession up the ranks.

- Within his or her first six months on the job, each new Allstate employee receives diversity training (about three-quarters of a million person-hours have been invested thus far). This consists of classroom training that encourages people to recognize the way they see themselves and others as well as ways of sustaining a trusting environment among people who are different. Refresher courses also are given to managers from time to time.

Allstate keeps careful statistical records of its diversity efforts and the company's financial success. Twice a year, the company's employees complete a questionnaire known as the "Diversity Index" asking them to indicate, among other things, the extent to which they witness insensitive or inappropriate behavior at work, the amount of dignity and respect they are shown, and their beliefs about the company's commitment to delivering services to customers regardless of their ethnic background.

Interestingly, the higher the overall score on the Diversity Index, the more managers are successful in promoting a diverse work environment, and the more satisfied they are. And the company's statistics show that when this happens, Allstate does a better job of satisfying and retaining its customers. Indeed, Allstate is the top insurer of lives and automobiles among African Americans and also ranks as the top insurer of homes and lives among Hispanic Americans. Clearly, at Allstate, "good hands" come in many different colors, and making this happen is a highly successful business strategy.

Job Satisfaction: Its Nature and Major Theories

job satisfaction
Positive or negative attitudes held by individuals toward their jobs.

Some of the most widely studied of all workplace attitudes are those assessing people's feelings toward their jobs, referred to as **job satisfaction.** In this section of the chapter, we will address some fundamental issues about job satisfaction and describe some of the major theories that have been used to explain it.

The Nature of Job Satisfaction: Fundamental Issues

Would you say you are satisfied with your job? When tens of thousands of American workers were asked much the same question in a multiyear survey conducted in 2009, fewer than half reported that they were, in fact, satisfied. This number has dropped steadily since 1987 and is now at its lowest level (see Figure 6.6).[45]

How can this trend be explained? Although several factors may be responsible, two key ones appear to be involved. First, people's expectations have risen over the years, leading them to look for more and more from their jobs. And as the bar rises, it becomes increasingly difficult for companies to give employees what they want, resulting in dissatisfaction. Second, it's also likely that people find work less gratifying because the nature of jobs is changing.[46] In particular, many people find that their jobs have become so highly specialized and narrow that they are not

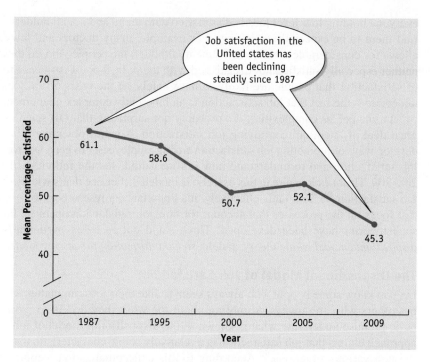

FIGURE 6.6

U.S. Job Satisfaction: Lowest Level in Over Two Decades

Systematic surveys of a broad spectrum of American workers have revealed that their job satisfaction has been declining regularly in recent decades. In fact, the current percentage who report feeling satisfied with their jobs is the lowest ever recorded in this survey.

Source: Based on data reported by Smith, 2009; see Note 45.

especially gratifying. Regardless of the underlying reason for this trend, it may be considered alarming in view of the adverse effects that result when people's job satisfaction levels are low.[47] We will discuss these consequences in the next section of this chapter.

As you might expect, the degree to which people are satisfied with their jobs also depends on exactly what those jobs are. For example, as you'll see in Figure 6.7, the percentages of people who consider their jobs to be very satisfying vary considerably.[48] Jobs that are the least satisfying tend to be ones that are low level and require the most rudimentary skills, whereas the ones that people find most satisfying tend to be more creatively fulfilling and allow workers to have a greater sense of accomplishment. This is only part of the story, however. Not

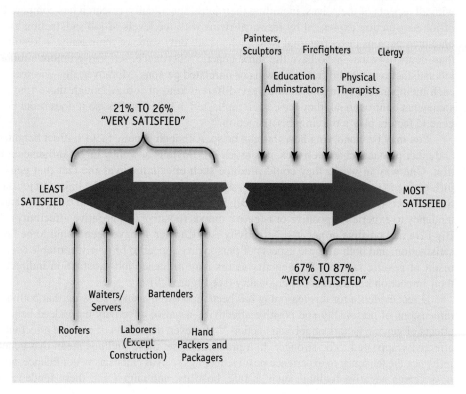

FIGURE 6.7

Who's Most and Least Satisfied with Their Jobs?

Systematic differences exist in the levels of job satisfaction expressed among people in different occupational groups. Those ranking highest and lowest in job satisfaction are shown here.

Source: Based on data reported by Smith, 2009; see Note 45.

everyone holding low-level jobs is dissatisfied with them, and not all holders of high-level jobs find them to be especially satisfying. For example, many doctors and lawyers do work that allows for considerable creative fulfillment, although the people who do these jobs tend to be neither especially satisfied nor dissatisfied with them. In short, it isn't easy to predict the level of satisfaction that people are likely to have solely on the basis of the jobs they hold. This underscores the fact that job satisfaction is an inherently complex phenomenon.

In view of its complexities, it's probably not surprising that OB scientists have devoted a great deal of attention to studying job satisfaction. A major objective of such research is to develop ways of promoting job satisfaction among employees. (To get a feel for your own level of job satisfaction and to understand how it's measured, see the Individual Exercise on pages 208–209. The questionnaire in this exercise is modeled after one that's widely used in research on job satisfaction.[49]) To do this effectively, it's important for researchers to be guided by theories that focus on the processes that account for how job satisfaction operates. Fortunately, several such theories have been developed. Three stand out as being particularly insightful—the *dispositional model, value theory,* and the *social information processing model.*

The Dispositional Model of Job Satisfaction

Do you know some people who always seem to like their jobs, no matter what they are doing, but others who are always grumbling about the work they do? If so, you are aware of the basic premise underlying what is known as the **dispositional model of job satisfaction.** This approach claims that job satisfaction is a relatively stable characteristic that stays with people through various situations.[50] According to this conceptualization, people who like the jobs they are doing at one time also tend to like the jobs they may be doing at another time, even if the jobs are different.

dispositional model of job satisfaction
The conceptualization proposing that job satisfaction is a relatively stable disposition of an individual—that is, a characteristic that stays with people through situations.

Supporting this approach, researchers have found that people are consistent in liking or disliking their jobs over as long as a 10-year period, although they may have had several different positions during that time. Such evidence is in keeping with the idea that job satisfaction operates much like the stable dispositions toward positive and negative affect described in Chapter 4. Indeed, research has shown that people who tend to be positive and cheerful most of the time do indeed tend to express higher job satisfaction than ones who tend to be "down" and gloomy.[51]

In keeping with this, research has shown that *genetic factors* play a role in job satisfaction. In other words, some people possess inherited tendencies to be either satisfied or dissatisfied with all aspects of their lives, including their jobs. Specifically, research has compared the levels of job satisfaction expressed by identical twins with the levels of job satisfaction expressed by unrelated persons or by fraternal twins, who share only some of their genes.[52] Results indicated that identical twins—who have the same genetic inheritance—expressed more similar levels of job satisfaction than did fraternal twins or unrelated persons. Moreover, this was true even when each member of a twin pair held a very different kind of job. Although these findings remain somewhat controversial, they have been replicated in other studies, so it does seem possible that genetic factors play a role in job satisfaction.[53]

You may be wondering how this can be so. Although genetic factors affect height, eye color, and other physical characteristics, it is much less obvious how they might influence job satisfaction. One way in which they could produce such effects involves the fact that genetic factors influence certain aspects of personality—aspects that might, in turn, be linked to job satisfaction. Such aspects of personality include the Big Five dimensions discussed in Chapter 4 and a general tendency to experience positive or negative moods (positive and negative affectivity).[54] Both the Big Five and positive or negative affectivity (see Chapter 4) have been found to be linked to job satisfaction, and both of these aspects of personality appear to be partly heritable (i.e., partly the result of genetic factors). So, genetic factors may influence job satisfaction indirectly through their impact on key aspects of personality (see Figure 6.8).

Direct evidence for this reasoning has been reported in a study showing that both the Big Five dimensions of personality and positive affectivity–negative affectivity did indeed help explain the effects of genetic factors on job satisfaction.[55] However, the effects of positive affectivity–negative affectivity appeared to be stronger. In a practical sense, these findings mean that genetic factors influence the tendency to experience positive feelings such as enthusiasm, confidence, and cheerfulness versus negative feelings such as fear, hostility, and anger, and these tendencies, in turn,

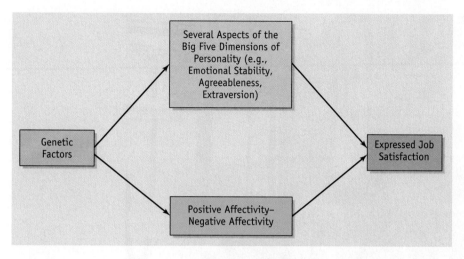

FIGURE 6.8

Genetic Factors and Job Satisfaction: The Effects Are Indirect

Genetic factors appear to influence job satisfaction, but these effects are indirect. Research suggests that genetic factors influence certain aspects of personality (e.g., positive affectivity–negative affectivity, emotional stability, extraversion) and these, in turn, play a role in job satisfaction.

Source: Based on findings reported by Ilies & Judge, 2003; see Note 55.

influence job satisfaction. If you've ever known someone who seemed happy and cheerful in most situations or someone who was just the opposite, you get the picture. Of course, people are satisfied or dissatisfied with their jobs for lots of reasons. But some individuals, it appears, experience relatively high or low levels of job satisfaction because they possess personality traits that are linked to genetic factors.

Value Theory of Job Satisfaction

Another approach to job satisfaction, known as **value theory of job satisfaction,** takes a broader look at the question of what makes people satisfied. This theory argues that almost any factor can be a source of job satisfaction so long as it is something that people value. The less people have of some aspect of the job (e.g., pay, learning opportunities) relative to the amount they desire, the more dissatisfied they will be—especially for those facets of the job that are highly valued. Thus, value theory focuses on discrepancies between what people have and what they want: The greater those discrepancies, the more dissatisfied they will be.

    This approach to job satisfaction implies that an effective way to satisfy workers is to find out what they want and, to the extent possible, give it to them. However, because it often is unknown what employees want, this is easier said than done. In fact, organizations sometimes go through great pains to find out how to satisfy their employees. With this in mind, a growing number of companies, particularly big ones, survey their employees systematically. For example, FedEx is so interested in tracking the attitudes of its employees that it has started using a fully automated online survey. The company relies on information gained from surveys of its 212,000 U.S.-based employees as the key to identifying sources of dissatisfaction and testing possible remedies.

value theory of job satisfaction
A theory suggesting that job satisfaction depends primarily on the match between the outcomes individuals value in their jobs and their perceptions about the availability of such outcomes.

Social Information Processing Model

It's your first day on a new job. You arrive at the office excited about what you will be doing, but you soon discover that your coworkers are far less enthusiastic. "This job stinks," they all say, and you hear all the details when you hang out with them during lunch. Soon, your own satisfaction with the job begins to fade. What once seemed exciting now seems boring, and your boss, who once seemed so pleasant, now looks more like an ogre. Your attitudes changed not because of any objective changes in the job or your boss, but because you changed your outlook based on the messages you received from your coworkers.

Chris Cooper-Smith/Alamy Images.

FIGURE 6.9

Social Information Contributes to Job Satisfaction

According to the *social information processing model* of job satisfaction, the way people feel about their jobs is based on the attitudes expressed by others with whom they come into contact. By virtue of sharing their feelings about their jobs with one another, these workers are likely to be shaping one anothers' attitudes.

social information processing model
A conceptualization specifying that people adopt attitudes and behaviors in keeping with the cues provided by others with whom they come into contact.

The idea that people's attitudes toward their jobs are based on information they get from other people is inherent in the **social information processing model.** This approach specifies that people adopt attitudes and behaviors in keeping with the cues provided by others with whom they come into contact.[56] The social information processing model is important insofar as it suggests that job satisfaction can be affected by such subtle things as the offhand comments others make (see Figure 6.9). With this in mind, it makes sense for managers to be very careful about what they say. A few well-chosen remarks may go a long way toward raising employees' job satisfaction. By the same token, a few offhand slips of the tongue may contribute to lowering morale.

Consequences of Job Dissatisfaction—and Ways to Reduce Them

Thus far, we alluded to the negative effects of job dissatisfaction, but without specifying exactly what these are. Now, we ask: What consequences may be expected among workers who are dissatisfied with their jobs? Several effects have been well documented. We now examine these.

Employee Withdrawal: Voluntary Turnover and Absenteeism

A few years ago, employees at a Safeway bakery in a small Oregon town were not particularly satisfied with their jobs. The bakery's 130 employees were so upset that they frequently were absent and quit their jobs. And these were no minor problems. In one year alone, accidents resulted in 1,740 lost workdays—a very expensive situation. At unpopular working times, such as Saturday nights, it was not unusual for as many as 8 percent of the workers to call in sick. Conditions were so bad that almost no one stayed on their jobs for more than a year.

As this situation reveals, all too extremely, people who are dissatisfied with their jobs want little to do with them—that is, they go out of their way to minimize the extent to which they are involved with them. This process is known as **employee withdrawal.** The two major forms of employee withdrawal are *voluntary turnover* and *absenteeism*, which as we see are linked to job dissatisfaction.

VOLUNTARY TURNOVER. The most extreme form of employee withdrawal is quitting, formally ending the employee–employer relationship for good, what is referred to as **voluntary turnover.** When employees quit their jobs, the costs to their organizations can be substantial. Most prominent among these are costs due to lost productivity as well as the recruiting and training of replacements. These costs vary considerably for different jobs, as you might imagine. For example, these have been estimated as ranging from 30 to 50 percent of the annual base salary for unskilled, entry-level workers to 200 to 400 percent of the annual base salary for specialists in information technology (IT).[57] Beyond dollars and cents, companies also are concerned about the quality of their workforces when people leave. As Bill Gates, cofounder of Microsoft, once said, "Take my 20 best people, and virtually overnight, Microsoft becomes a mediocre company."[58]

This raises a very practical question—namely, why do employees quit their jobs? Knowing the answers certainly promises to provide valuable insights into ways of reducing the problem of turnover (and, of course, its associated expenses). Scientists addressed this question a few years ago by interviewing a sample of employees who resigned from a variety of positions. Their findings, summarized in Table 6.3, reveal that employees left for eight key reasons.[59] As you review these reasons for quitting, you'll notice that although some may have little to do with job satisfaction (e.g., learning about alternatives—although, a dissatisfied employee is more likely to be proactive in seeking such alternatives than one who is highly satisfied), others (e.g., affective, constituent, calculative, and normative) may be considered direct expressions of job dissatisfaction.

In general, low levels of job satisfaction are associated with high levels of turnover, but this relationship is complex. As suggested in Table 6.3, there are many factors at play, and only some of them appear to have any connection to job satisfaction. For example, if conditions are such that alternative positions are available, people may be expected to resign when feeling dissatisfied. However, when such options are limited—such as when the economy is weak and companies are not hiring—voluntary turnover is a less viable option. In other words, knowing that one is dissatisfied with his or her job does not automatically suggest that he or she will be inclined to quit. Indeed, many people stay on jobs that they dislike.

THE HONEYMOON-HANGOVER EFFECT FOR VOLUNTARY TURNOVER. Thus far, we've shown that some people who are dissatisfied with their jobs are inclined to resign. This isn't surprising. At that

employee withdrawal
Actions, such as chronic absenteeism and voluntary turnover (i.e., quitting one's job), that enable employees to escape from adverse organizational conditions.

voluntary turnover
A form of employee withdrawal in which an individual resigns freely from his or her job.

TABLE 6.3 Why Do Employees Leave Their Organizations?

In a series of interviews with people who voluntarily quit their jobs, scientists found that their underlying reasons fit into the eight distinct categories shown here.

Reason	Explanation (the person . . .)
1. Affective	Does not enjoy the job or experiences in the organization.
2. Contractual	Desire to get even with someone in the company who hasn't done something that was expected.
3. Constituent	Desire to end relationships with one or more of the people in the workplace.
4. Alternative	Has more attractive job opportunities outside the organization.
5. Calculative	Believes that the future with the organization will be unpleasant in one or more ways.
6. Normative	Faces pressure from within the company to leave.
7. Behavioral	Believes that leaving the organization is easy because remaining there isn't highly valued by others.
8. Moral	Believes that quitting is ethically appropriate because it avoids stagnation.

Source: Based on suggestions by Maertz & Campion, 2004; see Note 59.

point, of course, they seek new positions. And, to their delight, they tend to be happier in those positions. This is welcome, because these individuals move to new jobs in search of higher levels of job satisfaction. That they find it, however, is not particularly surprising for several reasons. First, people in new positions need to justify their decision to leave their old jobs, which they can do by rationalizing about how wonderful their new positions are. In addition to this psychological reason, satisfaction on new jobs is likely to be high because the people associated with them are inclined to "put their best feet forward" by going out of their way to help their new colleagues feel welcome. So, for these reasons, people are likely to enjoy high levels of satisfaction on new jobs that they have taken in response to dissatisfaction with their old jobs. This is known as the **honeymoon effect.**

On the job, as in life, honeymoons only last so long. Eventually, reality sets in and that honeymoon glow soon fades. If one's initial satisfaction with a new job is based on limited, and often unrealistic, information, then it follows that as time goes on, people will have more realistic information about their jobs. Reality, although not necessarily harsh, is likely to make things more negative than they appear in the honeymoon glow. In other words, people's levels of satisfaction are inclined to drop over time from when a position is brand new to when one gains more experience with it. In keeping with the idea that today's reality is harsher than yesterday's good times, this is dubbed the **hangover effect.**

Given that the honeymoon effect describes a rise in satisfaction in response to a new job and that the hangover effect describes a decline in satisfaction as that new job becomes less new, what you get when you put these together is referred to the **honeymoon-hangover effect.** That the honeymoon effect is followed by the hangover effect was demonstrated in a study in which scientists assessed the job satisfaction levels of several thousand high-level managers over a five-year period.[60] The changes in their satisfaction levels over this period were precisely in keeping with the honeymoon-hangover effect. We see this in Figure 6.10, which shows levels of job satisfaction among employees who took new jobs in the third year of the study. As satisfaction dropped over the first two years, participants in the study found new jobs, as you might expect. Then, reflecting the honeymoon effect, their satisfaction was particularly high during this third year, when they were new to their jobs. However, as they became more used to those jobs (i.e., when the honeymoon was over), their levels of job satisfaction dropped to about where they were when the study began. Interestingly, this pattern describes shifts in job satisfaction in lots of

honeymoon effect
The tendency for people to enjoy high levels of satisfaction on new jobs that they have taken in response to dissatisfaction with their old jobs.

hangover effect
The tendency for people's levels of satisfaction to drop over time from when a position is brand new to when one gains more experience with it.

honeymoon-hangover effect
The tendency for the *honeymoon effect* to occur (i.e., for job satisfaction to increase as a dissatisfied person takes a new job) followed by the *hangover effect* (i.e., for the high levels of satisfaction associated with a new job to decline over time).

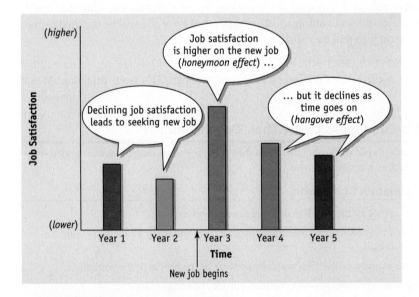

FIGURE 6.10

The Honeymoon-Hangover Effect

Recent research has shown that people's levels of job satisfaction tend to shift somewhat over time. As people become dissatisfied with their jobs, they take new ones. Immediately thereafter, satisfaction increases dramatically (the *honeymoon effect*), but soon thereafter, it declines (the *hangover effect*).

Source: Based on data reported by Boswell, Boudreau, & Tichy, 2005; see Note 60.

people, suggesting that how satisfied they are with the work they do depends on where in their job tenure a researcher happens to assess their attitudes.

THE UNFOLDING MODEL OF VOLUNTARY TURNOVER.   As you might imagine, the decision to quit one's job is not taken lightly; people consider a variety of different factors before making such an important decision. These have been described in a conceptualization known as the **unfolding model of voluntary turnover,** which is summarized in Figure 6.11.[61] According to this model, whether or not someone quits a job is said to depend on the way two key factors unfold. These are as follows:

unfolding model of voluntary turnover
A conceptualization that explains the cognitive processes through which people make decisions about quitting or staying on their jobs.

- *Shock to the system.* An attention-getting event that gets employees to think about their jobs (e.g., merger with another company)
- *Decision frames.* A set of internalized rules and images regarding how to interpret something that has occurred (e.g., "based on what I know from the past, is there an obvious response?")

As shown in Figure 6.11, the unfolding model of voluntary turnover recognizes that four possible *decision paths* can result. Trace these paths through the diagram as you read about each.

1. In *Decision Path 1,* a shock to the system occurs that matches an existing decision frame. So, for example, suppose your company loses a large account. This unusual occurrence constitutes a shock to your system, leading you to think about what occurred and to assess what it means. If it has been your experience that when accounts are lost, jobs are lost too, you may decide to quit (before the company decides it for you). This doesn't take much consideration. Likewise, it's an easy decision for you if you reach the conclusion that lost accounts don't really mean anything, so you decide to stay.

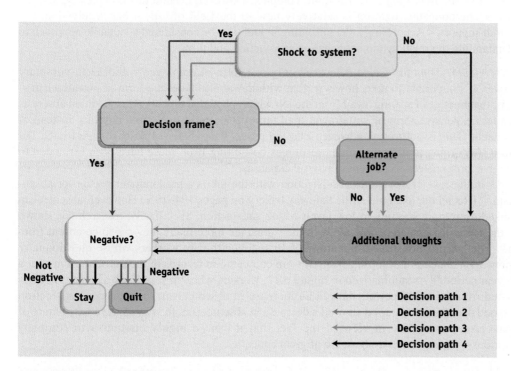

FIGURE 6.11

The Unfolding Model of Voluntary Turnover

According to the unfolding model of voluntary turnover, people make decisions about staying or leaving their current jobs based on a complex set of cognitive processes. The major considerations are whether or not there is a shock to the system (i.e., if something occurs that makes you consider leaving) and your decision frame (i.e., the things you believe). The various decision paths are summarized here.

Source: Based on suggestions by Mitchell & Lee, 2001; see Note 61.

2. In *Decision Path 2,* a shock to the system occurs, but in this case it fails to match a decision frame, and there is no specific job alternative. For example, suppose a leveraged buyout occurs (i.e., your company was taken over by another). This comes as a shock, but it's not exactly clear to you what it means. In such a case, you might assess how you feel about your organization. If, upon further reflection, you decide you like it, you probably will stay, especially since there is no alternative. If, however, this gets you to think about how awful the job is, you might decide to leave anyway, even without another job to fall back on. In either case, it's not immediately obvious to you what to do because you lack a decision frame, so you are forced to give the matter a lot of thought.

3. In *Decision Path 3,* a shock to the system occurs and it fails to match a decision frame, but here, there is a specific job alternative available. Again, suppose there's a leveraged buyout, which comes as a shock, and you find it difficult to interpret because it does not match any existing decision frames. However, in this case, because there's an alternate job available, you compare your current job to this possible new one. If you think the future will be better by staying, you will be likely to do so. However, if you are so dissatisfied with your current job that you think the new one will be better, you will be inclined to leave. This, too, will be a difficult decision, although it's made easier by the presence of an alternative.

4. Finally, in *Decision Path 4,* there is no shock to the system (e.g., no lost account and no leveraged buyout). As a result, no decision frame is considered, leaving you unlikely to consider leaving in the first place. Under such circumstances, if you're feeling dissatisfied, you may be inclined to quit if other conditions suggest that it's a good idea. Otherwise, however, you probably would be unwilling to bother leaving, leading you to stay. In either case, it may take a while for you to make the decision since no shock to the system has occurred to stimulate you into thinking about things.

Clearly, the unfolding model is quite complex. However, despite this complexity, and the fact that the conceptualization is relatively new to the field of OB, it has received strong research support.[62] Accordingly, the unfolding model may be considered a valuable approach to understanding the relationship between job satisfaction and turnover.

absenteeism
The practice of staying away from the job when scheduled to work.

ABSENTEEISM. Thus far, we've discussed only one form of employee withdrawal, voluntary turnover. It's important to note, however, that withdrawal also takes the form of **absenteeism**—that is, the practice of staying away from the job when scheduled to work. Unscheduled absences are a less expensive form of withdrawal than turnover because they are temporary instead of permanent. This is not to say, however, that the costs of unscheduled absences are trivial. Far from it. According to a major human resources consulting firm, these have been estimated to average approximately 15 percent of payroll expenses.[63]

As in the case of turnover, dissatisfaction with the job is a predominant reason for absenteeism.[64] (Recall our example of the Safeway bakery on pages 194–195.) However, absenteeism is linked even more strongly to low levels of job satisfaction. Specifically, research has shown that the more dissatisfied people are with their jobs, the more likely they are to be absent from work. This was demonstrated in a study of British health-care workers whose questionnaire responses on a measure of job satisfaction were compared to records of their absenteeism over a two-year period.[65] As summarized in Figure 6.12, workers whose levels of job satisfaction deteriorated over the study period showed an increase in absenteeism; those whose satisfaction increased over the study period showed a decrease in absenteeism. In view of the costly nature of absenteeism—especially in view of the fact that it can be highly disruptive to company operations—findings such as these are of great concern.

Job Performance: Are Dissatisfied Employees Poor Performers?

Although some dissatisfied employees leave their jobs, of course, not all do. What can be expected of those who remain? Does job performance suffer among dissatisfied employees? As in the case of turnover, the correlation between job performance and satisfaction also is positive but relatively modest.[66] However, research shows that happier workers are, in fact, more productive.[67]

For some insight into why this relationship exists, let's consider a study that goes beyond individual performance to something that matters greatly to organizations—their financial success. The possibility of a connection between individual job satisfaction and the financial

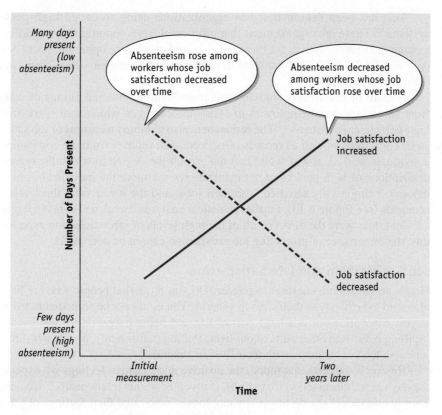

FIGURE 6.12

Relationship Between Job Satisfaction and Absence

A study tracing the levels of job satisfaction and absenteeism of health-care workers over a two-year period found the relationship depicted here. Absenteeism declined among those whose satisfaction rose whereas absenteeism rose among those whose job satisfaction declined.

Source: Based on data reported by Hardy, Woods, & Wall, 2003; see Note 65.

performance of companies was examined by a team of researchers who assessed the satisfaction of thousands of employees working over an eight-year period in some of the largest companies in the United States.[68] The scientists also computed the financial performance levels of the organizations in which these individuals worked using two key indexes that are widely used by financial analysts, return on assets and earnings per share. Because the data were collected during a period in which the economy showed a variety of ups and downs (1987–1995), there was reason to believe that the study's findings were not the results of any fluke conditions that might have occurred.

By conducting sophisticated statistical analyses, the scientists arrived at two fascinating conclusions. First, job satisfaction and financial performance were, in fact, associated with each other to a considerable degree. Second, and perhaps more interestingly, this was *not* the result of the tendency for highly satisfied workers to perform at higher levels (i.e., job satisfaction enhances financial performance), as you might expect. Instead, it was the other way around: The good financial performance of the companies promoted high levels of job satisfaction (i.e., financial performance promotes job satisfaction).

Let's consider how this appears to work. Imagine that because the company adopts policies that have been found to enhance employees' performance (e.g., involving them in key decisions, paying them for acquiring new skills), employees show high levels of performance. In turn, this good performance enhances the company's financial success. And, since it is successful, it can offer good benefits and increased pay, and enjoy a very positive reputation. The result? Employees feel well treated and are proud to work for their companies, and this leads them to experience high levels of job satisfaction. This is not just conjecture; the research found that this is precisely what occurred.

Job Satisfaction and Injuries: Are Happy Workers Safe Workers?

Injuries at work are a serious matter—both for the employees who are hurt and their organizations. So anything that can reduce the risk of serious workplace accidents is, potentially, very valuable. Efforts to reduce workplace injuries often have focused on the design of equipment and jobs, and on restricting the number of hours employees can work so as to protect them from fatigue—all major factors in accidents. Although these practices are indeed effective there is more involved. Evidence suggests that enhancing job satisfaction also has beneficial effects on job safety.

high-performance work systems
Organizations that offer employees opportunities to participate in decision making, provide incentives for them to do so, and emphasize opportunities to develop skills.

This has been demonstrated in organizations using so-called **high-performance work systems.**[69] These are organizations that offer employees opportunities to participate in decision making, provide incentives for them to do so, and emphasize opportunities to develop skills. Not only are employees highly satisfied in such organizations, but within them, they also perform their jobs very safely.[70]

A team of researchers studying this phenomenon obtained ratings of work environments from several thousand employees to assess the extent to which their work environments were high-performance systems.[71] The researchers also obtained measures of job satisfaction from the same employees as well as records of occupational injuries from the companies in which these individuals worked. It was found that the greater the degree to which the organizations met the descriptions of high-performance organizations, the more the individuals who worked in them reported being highly satisfied with their jobs, and the lower were the levels of work-related accidents (see Figure 6.13). Further statistical analyses revealed also that to some extent the low accident rates were the direct result of the high levels of job satisfaction experienced. In view of this, the importance of promoting job satisfaction cannot be overstated.

Job Satisfaction and Life Satisfaction

Here's an interesting question to ponder: Do you think that people who are happy on their jobs also tend to be happy in their lives in general? You might not be surprised to learn that the answer is yes. After all, work is a large part of life and being happy on the job has a good chance of "spilling over" into other parts of our lives. Putting it differently, people who are happy with their jobs also tend to be happy with their lives in general.[72]

Research suggests that mood, the positive and negative feelings we experience throughout the day (as we discussed in Chapter 5), is involved in this relationship.[73] Consider, for example, a study conducted among university employees who rated their feelings of job satisfaction and their mood states several times each day.[74] Participants did this both on workdays and nonworkdays, so they rated their moods and job satisfaction both at work and at home. Results indicated that job satisfaction and mood were closely linked at work; in fact, each influenced the other. High job satisfaction led to positive moods, and positive moods, in turn, triggered high job satisfaction.

Perhaps even more interesting, job satisfaction at work also influenced the moods these employees experienced at home. High job satisfaction at work generated positive moods away from work, whereas low job satisfaction at work generated negative moods. In other words, job satisfaction spilled over into employees' moods at home.

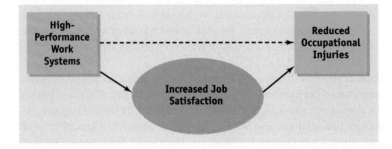

FIGURE 6.13

Job Satisfaction and Injuries at Work

Research indicates that high-performance work systems (i.e., ones that provide employees with opportunities to participate in decision making, incentives that encourage them to do so, and human resource practices designed to ensure skill development) can increase performance and job satisfaction and offer the added benefit of reducing accidents. This effect appears to stem, at least in part, from enhanced job satisfaction among employees. Apparently, positive attitudes toward their work make employees more careful, thus helping them to avoid accidents.

Source: Barling, et al., 2003; see Note 71.

The Ethics Angle

Promoting Job Satisfaction by Treating People Ethically

In view of the negative consequences of dissatisfaction, it makes sense to consider ways of raising people's levels of satisfaction on the job. But avoiding the organizational costs of dissatisfaction is not the only consideration. Many managers also are motivated by a more humanistic consideration—namely, they feel an ethical obligation to keep their employees happy not because of any benefits that stem from it (e.g., productivity) but for its own sake. With this in mind, what can managers do to raise people's levels of job satisfaction? We offer two recommendations.

Allow Employees to Select Their Own Benefits

Growing numbers of companies, including the data-management giant Oracle, are instituting so-called *cafeteria-style benefit plans,* which give employees opportunities to select the particular fringe benefits they desire from a menu of available options. We will discuss this more in Chapter 7, but for now, consider two key benefits that result from such programs. First, as we discussed in Chapter 2, people believe they've been treated in a procedurally fair manner when they are given a say in decisions affecting them. Not surprisingly then, employees who have such plans available to them are likely to be pleased because they believe that their companies are treating them fairly.

Second, according to the value theory of job satisfaction described earlier in this chapter, people who are given opportunities to select benefits they desire will be likely to feel satisfied with their jobs. After all, the programs provide opportunities for employees to minimize discrepancies between what they have and what they want, at least with respect to fringe benefits.

With these considerations in mind, there's good reason for companies to allow employees to select their own benefits whenever possible.

Improve the Quality of Supervision

It probably comes as no surprise that job satisfaction is high among employees who believe that their supervisors are competent, treat them with respect, and have their best interests in mind. To illustrate this, let's return to the case of the dissatisfied bakery employees that plagued the Safeway store described earlier (see pages 194–195). In response to the serious turnover problems, company officials transformed their management style. Instead of being highly intimidating, leaving employees feeling powerless and discouraged, they loosened their controlling ways and began treating people with the dignity and respect they deserved. The results were dramatic: Absenteeism fell from 8 percent to 0.2 percent, and voluntary turnover plummeted from almost 100 percent annually to less than 10 percent.

There can be no doubt that improving the quality of supervision at this store helped reduce the vexing organizational problem of employee withdrawal. But looking at it from an ethical perspective highlights a major point. Why was absenteeism reduced? It's because employees were treated so much better that they no longer felt the need to escape from being mistreated by staying home. Maybe instead of framing the absenteeism as a business problem, it should have been viewed as an indication of a managerial breech of ethics—that is, not treating employees in a way to which they are entitled as human beings. Managers who treat people as they deserve can be quite effective simply because they've done the right thing.

In summary, there is no doubt that job satisfaction is very important in organizations. Under some conditions, satisfied employees are more productive than dissatisfied ones; they also are less likely to quit their jobs or to experience serious accidents, and are more likely to experience positive feelings and moods at home. These reflect many practical reasons to promote job satisfaction. However, there's also an ethical consideration—making employees satisfied happens to be the right thing to do. For a discussion of this point, see The Ethics Angle section above.

Organizational Commitment: Attitudes Toward Companies

Thus far, our discussion has centered on people's attitudes toward one another and toward their jobs. However, to fully understand work-related attitudes we also must focus on people's attitudes toward the organizations in which they work—that is, their **organizational commitment.** The concept of organizational commitment is concerned with the degree to which people are involved with their organizations and are interested in remaining within them.[75]

It is important to note that organizational commitment generally is independent of job satisfaction. Consider, for example, that a nurse may really like the kind of work she does, but dislike the hospital in which she works. This may lead her to seek a similar job elsewhere. By the

organizational commitment
The extent to which an individual identifies and is involved with his or her organization and/or is unwilling to leave it (see *affective commitment, continuance commitment,* and *normative commitment*).

same token, a waiter may have positive feelings about the restaurant in which he works, but may dislike waiting on tables. This may lead him to consider taking another position in the restaurant, such as host or bartender. These complexities illustrate the importance of studying organizational commitment. Our presentation of this topic will begin by examining the different dimensions of organizational commitment. We then will review the impact of organizational commitment on organizational functioning and conclude by presenting ways of enhancing commitment.

Varieties of Organizational Commitment

Being committed to an organization is not only a matter of "yes or no" or even "how much?" Distinctions also can be made with respect to "what kind?" of commitment. Specifically, scientists have distinguished among three distinct forms of commitment, which we review here (see the overview in Figure 6.14).[76]

continuance commitment
The strength of a person's desire to continue working for an organization because he or she needs to do so and cannot afford to do otherwise.

CONTINUANCE COMMITMENT. Have you ever stayed on a job because you just didn't want to bother to find a new one? If so, you are already familiar with the concept of **continuance commitment.** This refers to the strength of a person's desire to remain working for an organization due to the belief that it will be costly to leave. The longer people remain in their organizations, the more they stand to lose what they have invested in them over the years (e.g., retirement plans, close friendships). Many people are committed to staying on their jobs simply because they are unwilling to risk losing these things. They also may be unwilling to forego any job security they might have based on their seniority in their current organizations. This is a particular concern in an era in which companies are cutting jobs regularly and new ones are hard to find. Individuals who have such beliefs may be said to have high degrees of continuance commitment.

normative commitment
The strength of a person's desire to continue working for an organization because he or she feels obligations from others to remain there.

NORMATIVE COMMITMENT. A second type of organizational commitment is **normative commitment.** This refers to employees' feelings of obligation to stay with their organizations because of pressures from others. People who have high degrees of normative commitment are concerned greatly about what others would think of them for leaving. They would be reluctant to disappoint their employers and concerned that their fellow employees might think poorly of them for resigning. If you were a tax accountant who was thinking of taking a position in a new firm, for example, your colleagues may encourage you strongly not to leave until the busy season preceding the April 15 personal income tax filing deadline has passed. And if you have a high degree of continuance commitment, you would be likely to satisfy their requests by not leaving your colleagues until they could find and train a suitable replacement.

AFFECTIVE COMMITMENT. The two types of commitment we've discussed thus far are not especially positive in that they do not suggest anything about an individual's connections to

FIGURE 6.14

Three Types of Organizational Commitment

Scientists have distinguished among the three different types of organizational commitment summarized here.

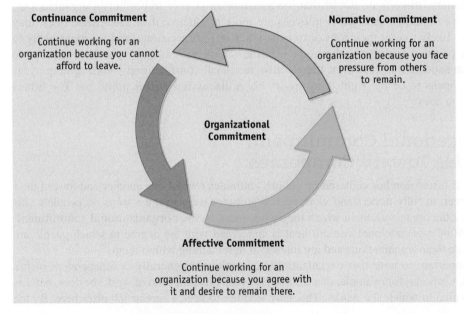

Continuance Commitment
Continue working for an organization because you cannot afford to leave.

Normative Commitment
Continue working for an organization because you face pressure from others to remain.

Organizational Commitment

Affective Commitment
Continue working for an organization because you agree with it and desire to remain there.

an organization based on their liking and attraction to it. However, the third type of organizational commitment, *affective commitment*, takes this into account. Specifically, **affective commitment** refers to the strength of people's desires to continue working for an organization because they regard it positively and agree with its underlying goals and values. People feeling high degrees of affective commitment desire to remain in their organizations because they endorse what these companies stand for and are interested in supporting their missions.

Sometimes, particularly when an organization is undergoing change, employees may wonder whether their personal values continue to be in line with those of the organizations in which they continue to work. When this happens, they may question whether they still belong, and if they believe they do not, they resign. A few years ago, Ryder Truck Company successfully avoided losing employees on this basis by publicly reaffirming its corporate values. Ryder was facing a situation in which it was not only expanding beyond its core truck leasing business, but also facing changes due to deregulation (e.g., routes, tariffs, taxes). To help guide employees through the tumultuous time, chief executive Tony Burns went out of his way to reinforce the company's core values—support, trust, respect, and striving. He spread the message far and wide throughout the company, using videotaped interviews, articles in the company magazine, plaques, posters, and even laminated wallet-size cards carrying the message of the company's core values. Along with other Ryder officials, Burns is convinced that reiterating the company's values was responsible for the high level of affective commitment that the company enjoyed during this turbulent period.

Why Strive for an Affectively Committed Workforce?

As you might imagine, people who feel high degrees of affective commitment toward their organizations behave differently from those who do not. Specifically, several key aspects of work behavior have been linked to affective commitment.[77]

AFFECTIVELY COMMITTED EMPLOYEES CONTRIBUTE TO SUCCESSFUL ORGANIZATIONAL PERFORMANCE. Naturally, officials are concerned greatly with how well their companies perform financially (e.g., with respect to such key factors as profit, sales growth, market share, etc.). Interestingly, a study conducted recently in the People's Republic of China found that these important indexes are linked to organizational commitment.[78] Surveying managers from 463 companies, the researchers distinguished between organizations in terms of the practices used to manage human resources. Some were oriented toward maximizing performance (such as by training employees in the latest developments in their fields) whereas others were geared more toward maintaining performance and stability (such as by retaining managers as long as they wish to remain in the company). The managers also completed scales assessing their degrees of affective commitment and continuance commitment to their companies.

The connections between these variables, as summarized in Figure 6.15, were quite interesting. As you might expect, the researchers found that companies using performance-oriented management practices were more successful financially than those focusing on merely maintaining the status quo. Organizational commitment played important roles in these relationships. Specifically, the reason why performance-oriented practices boosted performance was that these practices enhanced managers' feelings of affective commitment and these, in turn, led people to behave in ways that enhanced their companies' financial success.

However, companies using maintenance-oriented practices did not fare as well. Not feeling particularly inspired, managers in these companies did *not* experience high levels of affective commitment. Instead, maintenance-oriented practices raised feelings of continuance commitment, and of course, people who stay on their jobs while simply "going through the motions" and believing they have no better options are not especially productive. In fact, research has found that continuance commitment is *not* associated with high levels of job performance (sometimes, it even interferes with it, in fact).[79] Accordingly, companies in the Chinese study that used maintenance-oriented practices, and whose managers experienced high levels of affective commitment as a result, were found *not* to be high performers financially. Based on this study, it's clear that managers will want to be keenly interested in promoting affective commitment. Later in this chapter, we will offer some suggestions about how to do so.

affective commitment
The strength of a person's desire to work for an organization because he or she regards it positively and agrees with its goals and values.

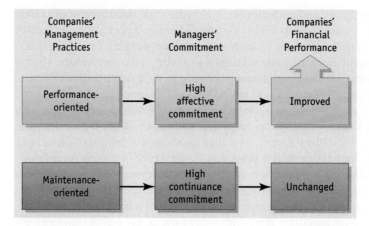

FIGURE 6.15

The Financial Benefits of Affective Commitment

Research has shown that when companies use performance-oriented management practices, it enhances affective commitment among managers. This, in turn, helps boost those companies' financial performance. In contrast, when companies use maintenance-oriented management practices, it enhances continuance commitment among managers. This, in turn, has no effect on the financial performance of those companies.

Source: Based on findings by Gong et al. (2009); see Note 78.

AFFECTIVELY COMMITTED EMPLOYEES ARE UNLIKELY TO WITHDRAW. The higher degrees of affective commitment employees have for their organizations, the less likely they are to resign from them or to be absent from them (what we referred to as *withdrawal behavior* in the context of job satisfaction). Affective commitment leads people to stay on their jobs and to show up ready to work when they are expected to do so.[80]

This phenomenon has been demonstrated in a large-scale study in which dropout rates among U.S. Air Force cadets were traced over the four years required to get a degree. The higher the affective commitment cadets had toward the Air Force upon entering the program, the less likely they were to drop out.[81] The fact that affective commitment levels at one time could predict turnover several years later provides a strong indication of the importance of organizational commitment as a work-related attitude. (Is affective commitment related to absenteeism and turnover all around the world, or do cultural factors affect this relationship? For a discussion of this issue, see the Today's Diverse and Global Organizations section on page 205.)

AFFECTIVELY COMMITTED EMPLOYEES ARE WILLING TO MAKE SACRIFICES FOR THEIR ORGANIZATIONS. Beyond remaining in their organizations, those who are highly committed to them demonstrate a willingness to make sacrifices required for their organizations to thrive. We see this, for example, among the many employees in recent years who have remained with their companies despite reluctantly facing pay cuts. Airline employees are a good example, as many have endured several rounds of pay cuts but have remained on their jobs (see Figure 6.16).

Some of the most extreme examples may be seen among CEOS who, in recent years, have passed up huge financial rewards for the sake of helping their companies.[82] In recent years, CEOs of companies such as Google, Capital One Financial, Pixar, and Apple Computer have given up their usual multimillion-dollar salaries to take only $1. Of course, they're not always being totally noble, and they won't be going hungry anytime soon because they still receive stock options worth many millions of dollars. Although cynics may claim that these $1 salaries are merely publicity stunts, there's at least one way that those who take them are helping their companies. By showing that they are willing to take only company stock, these individuals are sending a strong message about their confidence in their companies. And as economists tell us, this can help a company greatly.

Today's Diverse and Global Organizations

Does Absenteeism Mean the Same Thing in Canada and China?

It is easy to understand why people who have low commitment to their jobs may want to stay away from them. However, the degree to which people actually express their low commitment through absence may well be influenced by cultural factors. This idea was tested in an interesting study in which large groups of employees from Canada and the People's Republic of China were surveyed about their attitudes toward being absent from work.[83]

In general, Chinese managers pay far greater attention to absenteeism than their Canadian counterparts. For the most part, absence is very strongly discouraged—so much so, that even an uncommitted Chinese employee is unlikely to stay home from work. In keeping with this, the Chinese frown on absence based on illness, whereas the Canadians generally accept illness as a valid excuse for being out of work. This is consistent with the idea that in Chinese culture, a person of good character is expected to maintain self-control, and taking time off work due to illness would be an indication of lack of control.[84]

But there was an interesting exception to this general tendency for the Chinese to frown on absenteeism. Specifically, compared to the Canadians, the Chinese are more likely to take time off from work to deal with personal or family issues. What's more, they believe that doing this is much more appropriate than do Canadians. There are two reasons for this. First, unlike their Canadian counterparts, the Chinese are not paid when they do not go to work. As such, they are not receiving pay for work they didn't do, avoiding the potential guilt of overpayment inequity (feeling that they were getting larger rewards than they deserved; see Chapter 7). Furthermore, during the time of the study, it first became possible in China for citizens to own private homes. Recognizing this, employers generally considered it acceptable for employees to take time off work to attend to household maintenance.

These findings underscore a key point: Whereas lack of commitment may encourage absenteeism, low affective commitment may not, in and of itself, lead specific employees to be absent. At least one other factor, values inherent in employees' national cultures, also plays a role.

FIGURE 6.16

Committed Employees Make Tough Sacrifices

Weeks after US Airways pilot Captain Chesley "Sully" Sullenberger safely ditched his stalled Airbus A320 in the Hudson River in January 2009, saving 155 lives, he explained to the aviation subcommittee of the U.S. House of Representatives that safety was being compromised as pay cuts by airlines were leading experienced pilots to leave their jobs. His own pay had been cut 40 percent in recent years, and his once secure pension was terminated and replaced with a promise worth pennies on the dollar. Some, such as Captain Sullenberger, expressed their commitment to their airlines by remaining with them and "sharing their pain" during a recessionary period. Others, however, couldn't afford to remain committed and reluctantly were forced to seek new careers.

This example should not be taken as an indication that only highly magnanimous gestures result from commitment. In fact, small acts of good organizational citizenship (see Chapter 11), such as voluntarily pitching in to help others are also likely to occur among people who are highly committed to their organizations.[85] This makes sense if you consider that it would take people who are highly committed to their organizations to be willing to make the investments needed to give of themselves for the good of their companies.

In view of these benefits of affective commitment, organizations often take the steps necessary to enhance commitment among employees. We now describe various ways of doing this.

How to Promote Affective Commitment

Some determinants of organizational commitment fall outside of managers' spheres of control, giving them few opportunities to enhance these feelings. For example, commitment tends to be lower when the economy is such that employment opportunities are plentiful. An abundance of job options surely will lower continuance commitment, and there's not too much a company can do about it. However, although managers cannot control the economy, they can do several things to make employees want to stay working for the company—that is, to enhance affective commitment.

ENRICH JOBS. People tend to be highly committed to their organizations to the extent that they have a good chance to take control over the way they do their jobs and are recognized for making important contributions. When people get to perform jobs they believe are interesting and that provide opportunities to do work that challenges them mentally, they demonstrate their commitment to the organizations by working hard. In view of this, the practice of *enriching jobs* is an effective way of enhancing motivation. As such, we will discuss it more thoroughly in Chapter 7. For now, however, we simply wish to make it clear that enriching jobs also is an effective way to build commitment.

ALIGN THE INTERESTS OF THE COMPANY WITH THOSE OF THE EMPLOYEES. Whenever making something good for the company also benefits employees, those employees are likely to be highly committed to those organizations. Many companies establish this directly by introducing **gain-sharing plans**—that is, incentive plans in which employees receive bonuses in proportion to their companies' profitability. Such plans are often quite effective in enhancing organizational commitment, especially when they are administered fairly.

gain-sharing plans
Incentive plans in which employees receive bonuses in proportion to their companies' profitability.

An example of a gain-sharing plan may be found at Sheridan Memorial Hospital, located in the small town of Sheridan, Wyoming.[86] In 2009, this 88-bed hospital introduced a gain-sharing plan to give its 400 employees a direct stake in the hospital's success. Employees are rewarded for doing things that contribute to improvements in patient satisfaction scores and profitability. By tying the hospital's success to their own, the plan is expected to have a beneficial effect on building commitment.

RECRUIT AND SELECT NEW EMPLOYEES WHOSE VALUES CLOSELY MATCH THOSE OF THE ORGANIZATION. Recruiting new employees is important not only insofar as it provides opportunities to find people whose values match those of the organization, but also because of the dynamics of the recruitment process itself. Specifically, the more an organization invests in someone by working hard to lure him or her to the company, the more that individual is likely to return the same investment of energy by expressing commitment to the organization. In other words, companies that show their employees they care enough to work hard to attract them are likely to find those individuals, in turn, strongly committed to them.

In conclusion, it is useful to think of organizational commitment as an attitude that may be influenced by managerial actions. Not only might people be selected who are predisposed to be committed to the organization, but also various measures can be taken to enhance commitment in the face of indications that it is suffering.

Summary and Review of Learning Objectives

1. **Define attitudes and work-related attitudes, and describe the basic components of attitudes.**

   Attitudes are the stable clusters of feelings, beliefs, and behavioral tendencies directed toward some aspect of the external world. *Work-related attitudes* involve such reactions toward various aspects of work settings or the people in them. All attitudes consist of a *cognitive component* (what you believe), an *evaluative component* (how you feel), and a *behavioral component* (the tendency to behave a certain way).

2. **Distinguish between prejudice and discrimination, and identify various victims of prejudice in organizations.**

   Prejudice refers to negative attitudes toward members of specific groups, and *discrimination* refers to treating people differently because of these prejudices. Today's workforce is characterized by high levels of diversity, with many groups finding themselves victims of prejudicial attitudes and discriminatory behaviors (based on many different factors, including age, sexual orientation, physical condition, racial or ethnic group membership, gender, and people from different religions than our own). Although people are becoming more tolerant of individuals from diverse groups, prejudicial attitudes persist.

3. **Describe some of the things being done by today's organizations to manage diversity in their workforces and the effectiveness of these practices.**

   To help tap the rich pool of resources available in today's highly diverse workforce, many companies are using *diversity management programs*—techniques for systematically teaching employees to celebrate the differences among people. Typically, these programs go beyond efforts to recruit and hire women and members of minority groups, to creating supportive work environments for them. To promote diversity, organizations are conducting diversity training, using leaders to send strong messages about diversity, requiring suppliers to promote diversity, and making diversity a top priority. Although implementing diversity management programs is potentially difficult, experts acknowledge that the benefits, both organizational and personal, are considerable. For example, research has shown that companies whose employees systematically embrace diversity tend to be more profitable than those that allow discrimination to occur.

4. **Explain the concept of job satisfaction, and summarize three major theories of job satisfaction.**

   Job satisfaction involves positive or negative attitudes toward one's work. The *dispositional model of job satisfaction* suggests that job satisfaction is a relatively stable characteristic that stays with people over various situations. *Value theory* suggests that job satisfaction reflects the apparent match between the outcomes individuals desire from their jobs (what they value) and what they believe they are actually receiving. Finally, the *social information processing model* specifies that people adopt attitudes and behaviors in keeping with the cues provided by others with whom they come into contact.

5. **Describe the consequences of job dissatisfaction and ways to promote job satisfaction.**

   When people are dissatisfied with their jobs, they tend to withdraw. That is, they are frequently absent and are likely to quit their jobs. However, evidence suggests that job performance is only very weakly associated with dissatisfaction. Levels of job satisfaction can be raised by paying people fairly, improving the quality of supervision, decentralizing control of organizational power, and assigning people to jobs that match their interests.

6. **Describe the concept of organizational commitment, its major forms, the consequences of low levels of organizational commitment, and how to overcome them.**

   Organizational commitment focuses on people's attitudes toward their organizations. There are three major types of organizational commitment. One is *continuance commitment*—the strength of a person's tendency to continue working for an organization because he or she has to and cannot afford to do otherwise. Another is *affective commitment*—the strength of a person's tendency to continue working for an organization because he or she agrees with its goals and values, and desires to stay with it. A third is *normative commitment*—commitment to remain in an organization stemming from social obligations to do so. Low levels of organizational commitment have been linked to high levels of absenteeism and voluntary turnover, the unwillingness to share and make sacrifices for the company, and negative personal consequences for employees. However, organizational commitment may be enhanced by enriching jobs, aligning the interests of employees with those of the company, and recruiting and selecting newcomers whose values closely match those of the organization.

Points to Ponder

Questions for Review

1. What are the three main components of attitudes?
2. What is job satisfaction; what are its major causes and the consequences of dissatisfaction?
3. What is organizational commitment; what are its major causes and the consequences of low levels of organizational commitment?
4. What steps can be taken to promote job satisfaction and organizational commitment?
5. What is the difference between prejudice and discrimination?
6. What steps are today's organizations taking to promote diversity, and are these efforts effective?

Experiential Questions

1. Think of a particular job you have enjoyed most. What did you like about it so much? Now, think of a particular job that you enjoyed least. What made you dislike it so much? Did the factors you liked fall into the "motivator" category of two-factor theory? Did the factors you disliked fall into the "hygiene" category of the two-factor theory?
2. Think about the particular organization at which you have worked the longest. What were the main reasons you stayed there? How do these compare to the three forms of organizational commitment described in this chapter?
3. If you have ever participated in a diversity management training program, what effects did it have on you? In what ways, if any, did your attitudes or behavior change? If you have never participated in a diversity

management training program, how do you think you would react to being in one? Do you think you would find it enjoyable? Useful? What challenges to effectiveness, if any, do you suspect you might encounter?

Questions to Analyze

1. One of the strategies that has been recommended for enhancing job satisfaction is to make jobs more fun. We all like having fun, of course, but do you really think this matters when it comes to job satisfaction? In other words, is job satisfaction promoted by just having a pleasant, joking atmosphere in the workplace? Or, is what really matters making the work itself more interesting and enjoyable to perform? Explain your answer.
2. In today's economy, where replacing employees can be an expensive proposition, it pays to be able to maintain a highly committed workforce. Of the various things that can be done to promote commitment to an organization, which tactics do you believe may be most effective? Explain the basis for your answer.
3. Racial prejudice has been a serious problem in American society for a long time. How do you reconcile this with the fact that diversity management training generally seems to be successful? In other words, do you think diversity training actually changes people's prejudicial attitudes? Or, do you think that such programs get people to change their behavior—at least long enough to allow different kinds of people to be accepted? Explain.

Experiencing OB

Individual Exercise

How Satisfied Are You with Your Job?

Questionnaires similar to this one are used to assess job satisfaction. Completing this questionnaire will help you appreciate the level of satisfaction you feel toward your own job. It also illustrates one of the most popular tools for measuring this important work-related attitude.

Directions

Each of the following statements refers to a particular aspect of your job. In the space to the left of each, write the one number that reflects the extent to which you are satisfied or dissatisfied with this particular aspect of your present job. Express your answers using the following scale:

1 = very dissatisfied

2 = dissatisfied

3 = neither satisfied nor dissatisfied

4 = satisfied

5 = very satisfied

    ———— 1. The opportunity to do things I find enjoyable.
    ———— 2. Being able to count on a steady paycheck.
    ———— 3. The feeling that I've accomplished something important.
    ———— 4. The environment or surroundings in which I work.
    ———— 5. The people with whom I work most of the time.
    ———— 6. Opportunities to advance to higher positions.
    ———— 7. A chance to be responsible for my accomplishments.
    ———— 8. The opportunity to do things that I find challenging.
    ———— 9. A chance to learn interesting new skills.
    ———— 10. Having a chance to socialize and have fun with people.

Scoring and Interpretation

1. Add your scores for the 10 items. This will yield a number between 10 and 50.
2. Higher scores reflect higher degrees of job satisfaction.

Questions for Discussion

1. What did this questionnaire reveal about your level of job satisfaction? Were you surprised at what it suggested, or did it tell you something you already knew?
2. Although this questionnaire includes only 10 items, statements about other aspects of the job might have been added to the list. Thinking about other aspects of the job that may be particularly important to you, what might some of these items be? If such items were included, how might your score have been affected?
3. To what extent do you believe that your score on this questionnaire is likely to change as you move into new positions over the years? Do you expect it to become higher or lower in the future? Why?

Group Exercise

Stereotyping and Being Stereotyped: Comparing Experiences

You've probably been a victim of stereotyping by others, undoubtedly more often than you'd like. At the same time, you may have engaged in stereotyping others, even if you're not especially proud of it. This exercise is designed to make you sensitive to these processes so that hopefully you'll think twice before stereotyping anyone in the future.

Directions

1. Divide the class into pairs of students.
2. One student in each pair should recall a time in which he or she was stereotyped by someone else. To keep the facts straight, describe what occurred in a few lines. Also describe how this made you feel. Spend about 5 to 10 minutes on this.
3. At the same time, the other student in each pair should recall a time in which he or she engaged in stereotyping someone else. To keep the facts straight, describe what you did in a few lines. Also describe what led you to do this.
4. The members of each pair should take turns describing their experiences as "stereotypers" or victims of stereotyping. Be sure to explain your reactions (if you were a stereotype victim) or the things that led you to engage in stereotyping (if you were a stereotyper). Take about 5 to 10 minutes on this process.

Questions for Discussion

1. How did the other person's experiences as a victim or stereotyper compare to your own experiences in these roles?
2. Thinking about the experiences shared in this exercise, what factors associated with an organization may have led to the willingness to stereotype or to the reactions experienced as a victim of stereotyping? Did something about the company or its people make things better or worse? What are these factors?
3. Did this exercise make you any more sensitive to the costs of stereotyping? Do you think it will make a difference, at least for a little while?

Practicing OB

"I Quit!"

The president of a small manufacturing firm comes to you with a problem: The company is spending a lot of money training new employees, but 75 percent of them quit after working less than a year. Worse, they take jobs at the company's biggest competitor. Answer the following questions relevant to this situation based on the material in this chapter.

1. Drawing on research and theory on job satisfaction, what would you suspect is the cause of the turnover?

What advice can you offer about how to eliminate the problem?

2. Drawing on research and theory on organizational commitment, what would you suspect is the cause of the turnover? What advice can you offer about how to eliminate the problem?
3. Suppose you find out that the greatest levels of dissatisfaction exist among employees belonging to minority groups. What would you recommend doing to eliminate the prejudice that may be responsible for the turnover?

Case in Point

■ Domino's Pizza Takes a Bite Out of Turnover

Nine million miles—that's how far you'd travel if you went to the moon 37 times. Coincidentally, that's also how far Domino's Pizza delivery drivers travel each week in more than 60 countries. The 170,000 employees who work in the 8,800 stores in these nations get 1.3 million pizzas out the door each day. And they've been doing this every day since 1960, when the brothers, Tom and James Monaghan, bought their first small pizzeria in Ypsilanti, Michigan. The recipe for keeping these employees working happily at their jobs is something the company takes as seriously as its pizza recipe. And just as Domino's totally redesigned its pizzas "from the crust up" in 2010 to keep customers coming back for more, it also has been rethinking its approach to employees to keep them coming back to work.

This is no minor concern for Domino's Pizza, considering that annual turnover within stores has been more than 150 percent, resulting in an entirely new crew about every nine months. Although these figures are lower than the industry average for fast food, the fact that it costs upward of $2,500 to replace an entry-level worker (and 10 times more for a manager) was enough to make boosting employee retention a priority for the Domino's corporate management team in Ann Arbor. In 2005, under the leadership of David Brandon, Domino's

launched several initiatives to tackle the turnover problem, which continued when Patrick Doyle assumed the CEO post in 2010.

Brandon's approach was straightforward. Because employees tended to leave when managers resigned, he focused primarily on managers. Unlike some other CEOs facing the same problem in their companies, he opted *not* to buy his managers' loyalty by raising their pay. He believed that would have only a small and temporary effect on retention. Instead, he initiated a three-prong approach, beginning by hiring better managers. With this in mind, Domino's officials worked with researchers to develop an online test to select managers who had adequate levels of financial know-how and whose management styles were appropriate for the company. Once managers were selected, they were trained thoroughly in ways of effectively recruiting employees and interviewing them so as to ensure their success.

The second focus of the retention effort involved giving store managers tools to assess how well their employees are performing. This consisted of computerized tracking systems that enable them to learn precisely how long the pizza production process is taking and to identify star performers as well as those who need additional help.

Third, although Brandon is not a fan of across-the-board pay increases, he believes firmly in creating

(Continued)

incentives for managers that reward them for outstanding performance. This led to a system of bonuses based on store profits in addition to stock options for managers whose store sales grew while also creating highly satisfied customers. The effect was to align the financial interests of the managers with those of the company.

Since these efforts were put in place, turnover at Domino's Pizza has been cut in half—a vast improvement whose impact has been felt on the bottom line. And in an era of crust-thin margins, such developments are welcomed for sure.

Questions for Discussion

1. Of the three initiatives put into place to boost retention, which one do you believe will prove to be most effective? Why?

2. Based on the material in this chapter, what else could Domino's Pizza do to reduce its turnover problem?

3. How might making an effort to promote job satisfaction contribute to reducing turnover? As a manager of a Domino's store, what exactly could you do to help in this way?

7 Motivation in Organizations

Learning Objectives

After reading this chapter, you should be able to:

1. Define motivation and explain its importance in the field of organizational behavior.
2. Describe the motivational-fit approach and what it suggests about how to improve motivation in organizations.
3. Identify and explain the conditions through which goal setting can be used to improve job performance.
4. Describe equity theory and explain how it may be applied to motivating people in organizations.
5. Describe expectancy theory and how it may be applied in organizations.
6. Distinguish among job enlargement, job enrichment and the job characteristics model as techniques for motivating employees.

Chapter Outline

- Motivation in Organizations: Its Basic Nature
- Motivating by Enhancing Fit with an Organization
- Motivating by Setting Goals
- Motivating by Being Equitable
- Motivating by Altering Expectations
- Motivating by Structuring Jobs to Make Them Interesting

Preview Case

■ Costco: Doing Something Right

What company refused to sell Coca-Cola products for one month in the fall of 2009 until the soft drink giant eventually agreed to lower its wholesale prices? The answer is Costco, the third largest retailer in the United States. Considering its willingness to go to bat for customers with Coca-Cola, it's not surprising that shoppers love Costco—so much, in fact, that it has earned the coveted number one spot in the American Customer Satisfaction Index. They like the broad product mix (from candy bars to automobiles, even burial caskets), the generous return policy (almost anything can be returned at any time), and most of all, the low prices (no more than 15 percent over wholesale). It's no surprise, then, that Costco enjoys a larger share of the wholesale "club" market—some 54 percent—than its competitors Sam's Club and BJ's Wholesale Club. And, although membership costs $50 annually, about 86 percent of its 55 million members renew each year, making the cash registers sing to the tune of $71.42 billion, even in the recession year of 2009.

It's not only customers who like Costco but employees, too. As evidence, consider the fierce loyalty of its workforce. In the retail sector, it's generally considered good to keep about half your employees annually, but Costco retains about 94 percent. What exactly is Costco doing that spurs its employees to keep coming to work? According to a former schoolteacher who now works at a Costco lunch counter, opportunities for promotion are key. Recognizing that the company prefers to develop new managers from within its workforce, she says, "I know that sooner or later, I'll be given a bigger job—perhaps one with management responsibility, and that excites me." Although it may be a huge leap from selling hotdogs to managing a department, advancements abound at Costco, making it not unrealistic for employees to aspire to bigger things.

This is only part of the story when it comes to motivating Costco employees. Better-than-average wages and benefits also are key. Because large retailers struggle to keep expenses low, the wages they pay tend to be low, and whatever benefits they offer are not especially generous. This isn't so at Costco. Although less than half of Wal-Mart and Target employees receive health insurance, 85 percent of Costco's employees enjoy this important benefit. And because of the money saved by keeping turnover low, employees are paid relatively highly, up to $20 per hour for some nonsupervisory positions. This isn't quite as costly to Costco as it may seem because many employees, well aware of the stores' bargains, spend some of their paychecks at the very places they earn them. In fact, Costco's employees are among its most loyal shoppers.

Another key to Costco's success is its good customer service. Compared to many discount retail establishments where surly clerks might bark one-word answers to your questions, if you even can find a clerk in the first place, most Costco employees are interested in helping. Company officials are convinced that this is an extension of the company's friendly relations with its employees. They show respect and concern for them, creating an atmosphere in which people are motivated to treat one another like family. Although none of this may be at the top of your mind when you visit your local Costco to stock up on a year's supply of paper towels or shaving cream, it just may give you a new appreciation for what's going on behind the scenes.

There can be no doubt that Costco's success can be attributed to a great extent to its low prices and good service. As this case suggests, however, another important consideration is the high motivation of its employees. This factor, which leads people to work hard and remain loyal, is an invaluable asset for Costco—or any other business, for that matter. Companies strive to build their assets, and Costco has been actively committed to developing the motivation of its employees. With this in mind, it pays its employees well, it rewards them with promotions, and it treats them in a friendly and welcoming manner.

It's obvious that we certainly like these things, but do they really stimulate people into action? And if so, why? In other words, what psychological mechanisms explain what gets people to work hard? We will focus on the answer to these important questions in this chapter. And in keeping with the simultaneously theoretical and applied orientation of the field of OB, we also will consider how managers can put this information to practical use in attempting to motivate their employees.

Over the years, the question of what it takes to motivate workers has received a great deal of attention by organizational scientists and practicing managers.[1] In addressing this matter, we examine five different approaches that have been popular in the field of OB. Specifically, these focus on motivating by (1) fitting people's traits and skills with the nature of their work, (2) setting goals, (3) treating people equitably, (4) enhancing people's beliefs that desired rewards can be attained, and (5) designing jobs so as to make them more desirable. We will describe each of these approaches to motivation in this chapter, highlighting the research bearing on it and its practical implications.

Our discussion of these approaches to motivation will give you a sound understanding of how to answer a key question that's on the mind of a lot of managers these days: How can I motivate my employees? As you will see, the answer isn't exactly straightforward. Of course, if motivating people were easy, everyone would be doing it. At the same time, however, it is far from impossible. Costco and a good number of other organizations have leaders that demonstrate a firm understanding of the principles described within this chapter. Before getting to all this, however, it's important to touch briefly on a fundamental matter—namely, what exactly is meant by *motivation*.

Motivation in Organizations: Its Basic Nature

motivation
The set of processes that arouse, direct, and maintain human behavior toward attaining some goal.

Although motivation is a broad and complex concept, organizational scientists have agreed on its basic characteristics.[2] We define **motivation** as the set of processes that arouse, direct, and maintain human behavior toward attaining some goal. The diagram in Figure 7.1 will guide our explanation as we elaborate on this definition.

Components of Motivation

The first part of our definition deals with *arousal*. This has to do with the drive or energy behind our actions. For example, people may be guided by their interest in making a good impression on others, doing interesting work, being successful at what they do, and so on. This motivates people to do what it takes to accomplish these objectives.

But how will people go about satisfying their motives? Motivation is also concerned with the choices people make, the *direction* their behavior takes. For example, employees interested in cultivating a favorable impression on their supervisors may do many different things: compliment them on their good work, do them special favors, work extra hard on an important project, and the like. Each of these options may be recognized as a path toward meeting the person's goal.

The final part of our definition deals with *maintaining* behavior. How long will people persist at attempting to meet their goals? To give up in advance of goal attainment means not satisfying the need that stimulated behavior in the first place. Obviously, people who do not persist at meeting their goals (e.g., salespeople who give up before reaching their quotas) cannot be said to be highly motivated.

To summarize, motivation requires all three components: the arousal, direction, and maintenance of goal-directed behavior. An analogy may help tie these components together. Imagine that you are driving down a road on your way home. The arousal part of motivation is like the

FIGURE 7.1

Basic Components of Motivation

Motivation involves the arousal, direction, and maintenance of behavior toward a goal.

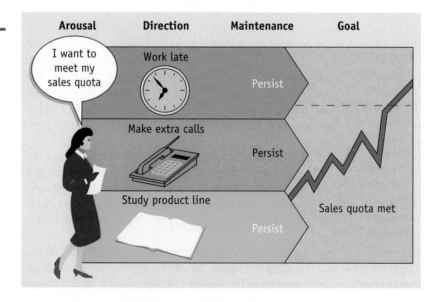

energy created by the car's engine. The direction component is like the steering wheel, taking you along your chosen path. Finally, the maintenance aspect of the definition is the persistence that keeps you going until you arrive home, reaching your goal. In both cases, any one missing part will keep you from getting where you want to go.

Three Key Points About Motivation

Now that we have defined motivation, we should note three important points you should keep in mind as you think about motivation on the job.

MOTIVATION AND JOB PERFORMANCE ARE NOT SYNONYMOUS. Just because someone performs a task well does not mean that he or she is highly motivated. Motivation is just one of several possible determinants of job performance. The person who performs well may be very skillful but not put forth much effort at all. If you're a mathematical genius, for example, you may breeze through your calculus class without trying. By contrast, someone who performs poorly may put forth a great deal of effort but fall short of a desired goal because he or she lacks the skills needed to succeed. If you've ever tried to learn a new sport but found that you couldn't get the hang of it no matter how hard you tried, you know what we mean.

MOTIVATION IS MULTIFACETED. People are likely to have several different motives operating at once. Sometimes, these conflict with one another. For example, a word processing operator might be motivated to please her boss by being as productive as possible. However, being too productive may antagonize her coworkers, who fear that they're being made to look bad. The result is that the two motives may pull the individual in different directions, and the one that wins is the one that's stronger in that situation.

PEOPLE ARE MOTIVATED BY MORE THAN JUST MONEY. Suppose you struck it big in the lottery. Would you keep your current job? Interestingly, although some make it clear that they would pack up and move to a tropical island where they would relax in the sun for the rest of their lives, most insist that they would continue to work. They might take a different job, but they'd continue to work even if they didn't need the money. Why? The answer is simple: Money isn't people's only motive for working.

This raises two interesting questions: (1) What is, in fact, the top motivator, and (2) Where is money on the list? Different research teams have sought answers in recent years. One group of researchers surveyed lower- and mid-level employees.[3] Another research team examined junior and senior executives.[4] Both surveys asked respondents from a variety of companies in different industries to consider the importance of a large number of possible motives. The rankings of the top factors for each group are shown in Table 7.1.

Despite some minor differences in orderings, the top four responses of both groups were remarkably similar. The top two factors for both groups were "doing challenging work" and

TABLE 7.1 What Motivates People to Work?

Pay, although important, is not at the very top of the list of the most important sources of work motivation in people's lives. This applies to both lower- to mid-level employees and to junior and senior executives.

Factor	Lower- to Mid-Level Employees	Junior and Senior Executives
Challenging work	1	2
Supportive, team-oriented environment	2	1
Adequate compensation	3	4
Opportunities for promotion, achievement	4	6
Fit between life on and off the job	—	3
Incentives to succeed	5	—
Working at a company that has high values	—	5
Peer group respect	6	—

Sources: Robson, 2004; see Note 3; Gallinsky et al., 2009; see Note 4.

"having a supportive, team-oriented atmosphere." Money came in consistently below these factors, ranking third among mid-lower-level employees and fourth among executives. As you will see in the rest of this chapter, the field of OB examines a variety of factors that motivate people—those indicated here as well as many others.

Having established these basic qualities of motivation, we now turn to the first of five different orientations to motivation discussed in this chapter. This particular approach, which focuses on motivating by enhancing fit with an organization, casts an interesting light on some issues we already have considered in this book.

Motivating by Enhancing Fit with an Organization

Imagine yourself in the following situation. You started a new job as a salesperson at an auto dealership. After a little while, however, you find that it's not really your thing. You're not the type of person to push someone into a sale, and as customers walk away, your self-confidence erodes. Realizing this about yourself makes you feel anxious as you approach a prospect on the floor or as you try to close a sale. And this, of course, interferes with your capacity to succeed. In turn, this lowers your motivation to work ("why even bother?"), further interfering with your performance, lowering your motivation, and so on. The downward cycle is spiraling you right out of the showroom and into a new job. Because your particular qualities are a poor match with the requirements of the job, your motivation and performance suffer.

In Chapter 4, we noted that many different personality traits and abilities influence job performance. In the context of motivation, however, scientists have found that a few particular traits and skills have especially profound effects. This is the basic idea behind a relatively new way of looking at motivation known as the **motivational fit approach.**[5] Specifically, this framework stipulates that motivation is based on the connection between qualities of individuals and requirements of the jobs they perform in their organizations. The better people's traits and skills fit the requirements of the work environment, the more highly motivated they will be (for an overview, see Figure 7.2). We now will explain the motivational fit approach in more detail and describe its implications for motivating people on the job.

motivational fit approach
The framework stipulating that motivation is enhanced by a good fit between the traits and skills of individuals and the requirements of the jobs they perform in their organizations.

FIGURE 7.2

The Motivational Fit Approach: An Overview

According to the motivational fit approach, people are most highly motivated to perform when there is a good fit between various traits and skills they possess and certain important characteristics of the work they perform. These are summarized here.

Source: Based on suggestions by Kanfer & Heggestad, 1997; see Note 5.

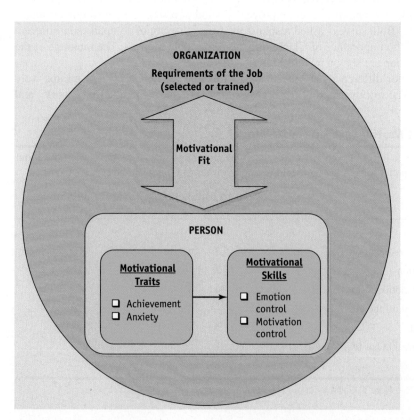

Motivational Traits and Skills

The motivational fit approach specifies that two particular individual characteristics, referred to as *motivational traits,* are important. These are as follows:

- *Achievement:* a person's interests in excelling at what he or she does and in accomplishing desired objectives
- *Anxiety:* a person's tendency to be excessively apprehensive or nervous about things in everyday life

Because achievement and anxiety are considered traits, they are assumed to be relatively stable differences between people (see Chapter 4), making some individuals more successful than others. As it works out, the most highly motivated employees tend to be those characterized by high levels of achievement and low levels of anxiety. Such individuals not only are inclined to strive for excellence, but they also lack the emotional problems associated with being excessively worried.

In addition to the traits they possess, an individual's motivation also is determined by what are known as *motivational skills*—the particular strategies used when attempting to meet objectives. Unlike traits, which are relatively stable within individuals over time, people can be trained in skills, and these also develop naturally over time as people gain experience over their careers (see Appendix 2). Two particular motivational skills are important:

- *Emotion control:* a person's capacity to control his or her own emotions and to stay focused on the task at hand without allowing emotions to interfere
- *Motivation control:* a person's capacity to push himself or herself by directing attention to the job and to continue exerting effort even when his or her interest begins to wane

As you might expect, employees with highly developed motivational skills are not only more strongly motivated to succeed but ultimately also more successful on their jobs than those with less developed motivational skills. Specifically, individuals with high levels of emotional control are more successful than those with low levels of emotional control. Also, those with high levels of motivation control are more successful than those with low levels of motivation control. This is probably not surprising, given that individuals with high levels of these skills are adept at overcoming key problems such as boredom and the frustration that inevitably occurs at work. Importantly, because these are skills rather than traits, anyone is capable of developing them.

People's motivational traits and skills do not operate independently. Rather, traits influence skills. Consider, for example, someone with high amounts of the achievement trait. Such an individual is particularly likely to seek out challenging situations. And, because such situations present considerable opportunities for failure, the person has to learn to overcome the negative emotional reactions that are likely to result (emotion control) and is likely to be driven to continue even in the face of obstacles (motivation control). By contrast, because individuals who are low in the achievement trait are inclined to avoid challenging situations, they are unlikely to face situations that allow them to develop motivational skills.

Organizational Factors: Enhancing Motivational Fit

Recognizing that people do not operate in a vacuum, the motivational fit approach specifies that it is important for people's motivational traits and skills to match the requirements of their work environments. Although this idea is admittedly abstract, we already provided a good illustration. Recall your unsuccessful attempt to make it as an auto salesperson? Given the nature of the work, it's understandable that you would be a bad fit with the organization.

Fortunately, however, there's hope for you yet. Fit can be enhanced in two ways. First, the dealership can prescreen job applicants in a manner that keeps individuals with your particular profile out of such positions. This would save you, the company, and some unsuspecting customers a lot of grief. Indeed, research has shown that motivational fit is enhanced when people's characteristics match the unique requirements of the positions they seek.[6] Second, the company can improve motivational fit by training people in ways of building their motivational skills. Although this might not come to you naturally at this time, becoming more of the way you have to be to perform the job is not out of the question. It involves learning a new skill (which we discussed in Chapter 3), and you surely are capable of doing so. This may take the form, for example, of training you in building self-confidence so you can avoid the self-doubts that interfere with your motivation to perform this job.

Dr. David Saltzberg.

FIGURE 7.3

High Motivational Fit: A Chilly Example

UCLA research scientist David Saltzberg has been working on a project designed to detect high-energy neutrinos produced by collisions between cosmic rays and photons in the universe. This led Dr. Saltzberg to Cape Evans, Antarctica, where he placed sensors in holes in the ice, a job that requires him to be highly innovative, often in the face of frustrating setbacks (not to mention frigid conditions). He is likely to be highly motivated to perform well because he is very interested in achieving success and has the capacity to push himself hard to attain it.

Another organizational factor with which people's motivational traits and skills must fit has to do with the inherent nature of the job. On some jobs, such as research scientist, success requires the capacity to work independently, to innovate, and to persist when attempting to solve difficult problems. The individuals most highly motivated to pursue positions of this type are those with high amounts of achievement and strong motivational skills (see Figure 7.3). By contrast, among people performing more routine jobs, such as factory worker or call center operator, such characteristics are not as likely to contribute to motivation. After all, the highly structured nature of these jobs is likely to make these traits and skills less important. Please note that "less important" does not mean "unimportant." Indeed, even among call center operators, motivational fit has been identified as a key to productivity.[7]

Because the motivational fit approach is new, it has not received as much research attention as the other frameworks described in this chapter. However, existing research has been highly supportive.[8] As a result, it already has been acknowledged as an important and especially promising way of understanding motivation on the job.[9]

Motivating by Setting Goals

Just as people are motivated to satisfy their needs on the job and to fit with their organizations, they also are motivated by another very basic interest—to strive for, and to attain, goals—a process known as **goal setting.** The process of setting goals is one of the most important motivational forces operating on people in organizations.[10] With this in mind, we will describe the underlying psychological processes that make goal setting effective and identify some practical suggestions for setting goals on the job.

goal setting
The process of determining specific levels of performance for workers to attain and then striving to attain them.

Goal-Setting Theory

Suppose that you are doing a task, such as word processing, when a performance goal is assigned. You are now expected to type 70 words per minute instead of the 60 words per minute you've been keyboarding all along. Would you work hard to meet this goal, or would you simply give up?

Some insight into the question of how people respond to assigned goals is provided by a popular theory known as **goal-setting theory**.[11] This approach claims that an assigned goal influences people's beliefs about being able to perform the task in question (i.e., a personality variable known as **self-efficacy**) and their personal goals. Both of these factors, in turn, influence performance.

The basic idea behind goal-setting theory is that a goal serves as a motivator for three key reasons. First, when goals are set, people direct their attention to them and gauge how well they are doing. In other words, they compare their current capacity to perform with that required to succeed at the goal. To the extent that people believe they will fall short of a goal, they will feel dissatisfied and will work harder to attain it so long as they believe it is possible for them to do so. When they succeed at meeting a goal, they feel competent and successful.[12] Having a goal enhances performance in large part because the goal makes clear exactly what type and level of performance is expected (see Figure 7.4).

Second, goal-setting theory also claims that assigned goals will lead to the acceptance of those goals as personal goals.[13] In other words, they will be accepted as one's own. This is the idea of **goal commitment**—the extent to which people invest themselves in meeting a goal. Indeed, people become more committed to a goal to the extent that they desire to attain it and believe they have a reasonable chance of doing so. Likewise, the more strongly people believe they are capable of meeting a goal, the more strongly they will accept it as their own. By contrast, workers who perceive themselves as incapable of meeting goals will not be committed to meeting them, and as a result, will not strive to do so.

Finally, goal-setting theory claims that beliefs about both self-efficacy and goal commitment influence task performance. After all, people are willing to exert greater effort when they believe they will succeed than when they believe their efforts will be in vain.[14] Moreover, goals that are not personally accepted will have little capacity to guide behavior. In fact, the more strongly people are committed to meeting goals, the better they perform.[15]

Although this sounds fairly abstract, the ideas are really quite straightforward and they will come to life with an illustration. Let's use an example of a situation with which college students easily can relate. Suppose you don't care about getting good grades in school (i.e., you are not committed to achieving academic success). In this case, you would not work very hard regardless of how easy or difficult a course may be. By contrast, if you are highly committed to achieving success, then a difficult (but not impossible) goal (e.g., getting a good grade in a very challenging

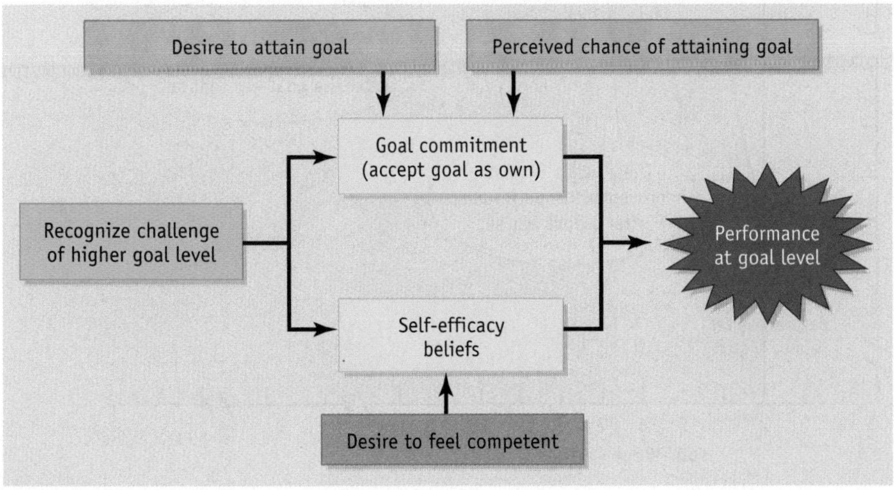

goal-setting theory
A popular theory specifying that people are motivated to attain goals because doing so makes them feel successful.

self-efficacy
One's belief about having the capacity to perform a task.

goal commitment
The degree to which people accept and strive to attain goals.

FIGURE 7.4

The Goal-Setting Process
When people are challenged to meet higher goals, several things happen. First, they assess their desire to attain the goal as well as their chances of attaining the goal. Together, these judgments affect their goal commitment. Second, they assess the extent to which meeting the goal will enhance their beliefs in their own self-efficacy. When levels of goal commitment and self-efficacy are high, people are motivated to perform at the goal level.

course) will have more meaning to you than an easy goal (e.g., getting a good grade in an easy course) because it enhances your self-efficacy. As a result, you will work harder to achieve it.

Goal-setting theory has been supported by research conducted over 40 years, suggesting that it is a valuable source of insight into how the goal-setting process works.[16] In fact, goal-setting theory is so highly regarded that it has been ranked as the most influential of all OB theories by management scholars.[17] One team of scientists even referred to goal-setting theory as being "quite easily the single most dominant theory in the field [of organizational behavior]."[18] Let's now examine what this theory suggests about the most effective way to set goals.

Guidelines for Setting Effective Performance Goals

Because researchers have been involved actively in studying the goal-setting process for many years, it is possible to summarize their findings in the form of principles. These may be taken as practical suggestions for managers to consider when attempting to enhance motivation.

ASSIGN SPECIFIC GOALS. Probably the best-established finding of research on goal setting is that people perform at higher levels when asked to meet a specific high-performance goal than when simply asked to "do your best," or when no goal at all is assigned. Generally, people find specific goals quite challenging and are motivated to meet them—not only to fulfill others' expectations but also to convince themselves that they have performed well.

A classic study conducted at an Oklahoma lumber camp provides a particularly dramatic demonstration of this principle.[19] The participants in this research were lumber camp crews who hauled logs from forests to their company's nearby sawmill. Over a three-month period before the study began, it was found that the crew loaded trucks to only about 60 percent of their legal capacities, wasting trips that cost the company money. Then a specific goal was set, challenging the loggers to load the trucks to 94 percent of their capacity before returning to the mill. How effective was this goal in raising performance? The results, summarized in Figure 7.5, show that the goal was

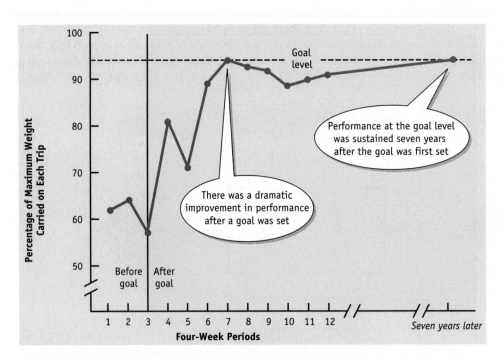

FIGURE 7.5

Goal Setting: Some Impressive Effects

The performance of loggers loading timber onto trucks markedly improved after a specific, difficult goal was set. The percentage of the maximum possible weight loaded onto the trucks rose from approximately 60 percent before any goal was set to approximately 94 percent—the goal level—after the goal was set. Performance remained at this level as long as seven years.

Source: Adapted from Latham & Baldes, 1975; see Note 19.

extremely effective. Not only was the specific goal effective in raising performance to the goal level after just a few weeks, but these effects were also long-lasting: Loggers sustained this level of performance throughout the next seven years. The resulting savings for the company were considerable.

This is just one of many studies that clearly demonstrate the effectiveness of setting specific performance goals. Research also has found that specific goals help bring about other desirable organizational objectives, such as reducing absenteeism and industrial accidents.[20] To reap such benefits, however, goals must be not only highly specific, but also challenging.

ASSIGN DIFFICULT, BUT ACCEPTABLE, PERFORMANCE GOALS. The goal set at the logging camp was successful not only because it was specific, but also because it pushed crew members to a higher standard. Obviously, a goal that is too easily attained will *not* bring about the desired increments in performance. For example, if you already type at 70 words per minute, the goal of 60 words per minute—although specific—would likely *lower* your performance because it is too easy (for some additional examples, albeit highly unlikely ones, see Figure 7.6). The key point is that a goal must be difficult as well as specific for it to raise performance.

It is interesting to consider *why* this occurs. The loggers were not paid any more for meeting the goal than for missing it. Still, they worked hard to meet it. Why? The answer is that the goal instilled purpose and meaning to the otherwise monotonous task of loading trucks. Loggers who met the goal took pride in doing so and found the task more interesting as a result. In fact, the challenge of meeting the goal made the job so much more fascinating that within a week after it was set, the loggers showed great improvements in attendance.[21]

Importantly, there is a limit to this effect. Although people will work hard to reach challenging goals, they only will do so when the goals fall within the limits of their capability. As goals become *too* difficult, performance suffers because people reject the goals as unrealistic and unattainable.[22] Let's consider an example to which you can relate as a student. You may work much harder in a class that challenges your ability than one that is very easy. At the same time, however, you probably

FIGURE 7.6

Some Goals Are Just Too Easy

Goals that can be attained very easily are not especially challenging and won't motivate people to work very hard. You probably wouldn't feel that you've accomplished much by reaching the goals shown here.

would give up trying if you had to get a perfect score on all exams to pass the course—a standard you would reject as unacceptable. The underlying principle applies in most situations. Specific goals are most effective if they are set high enough to challenge people, but not so high as to be rejected.

This principle is applied in many organizations, where goals are set with respect to many important criteria. Consider these varied examples:

- The Web site for the blogging community, YouSayToo.com, set the goal of raising $30,000 to aid the relief effort for victims of 2010's massive earthquake in Haiti.[23]
- Bell Canada's telephone operators are required to handle calls within 23 seconds, and FedEx's customer service agents are expected to answer customers' questions within 140 seconds.[24]
- The Dietetic Internship Program of the U.S. Department of Veterans Affairs in Bay Pines, Virginia, set the following goals: 90 percent of the people starting the program will finish it, and 90 percent of those completing the program will "agree" or "strongly agree" on the Program Evaluation form that the program prepared them for dietetic practice.[25]
- In 2009, Idaho's Coeur d'Alene Mines, set the "aggressive" goal of boosting production levels by 66 percent in its two newest silver mines.[26]

Despite the differences in these goals and the nature of the companies in which they were established, they have something in common. In all cases, the goals were considered difficult when first imposed, but the people involved eventually met—or even exceeded—them over time. They were likely to enjoy the satisfaction of knowing they succeeded at doing so.

Sometimes, the difficult goals set by companies are so far beyond levels currently being achieved that employees lack a clear idea how to go about reaching them. Such goals are known as **stretch goals.** By their very nature, stretch goals are so difficult that they challenge people to rethink the way they work, thereby establishing unprecedented levels of performance.

General Electric's former CEO, Jack Welch, regularly used stretch goals at his company to help it achieve vast improvements in quality and efficiency.[27] In describing them to his colleagues, Welch likened stretch goals to the bullet trains in Japan, which run at about 200 mph. Had engineers sought only modest speed improvements, they would have limited their thinking in ways leading to minor alterations in design. However, by specifying previously unheard of speeds, engineers were challenged to think completely differently—and therefore to achieve amazing results. Stretch goals of this type, in which higher levels of current activities are aggressively pursued (e.g., more speed, more profit, etc.), are known as **vertical stretch goals.**

Some companies also use stretch goals for other purposes. At the investment firm Goldman Sachs, for example, stretch goals are used to aid professional development, such as by challenging managers to perform tasks that they never have done before. According to the firm's head of Global Investment Reach, Steve Strongin, "Our people thrive on change, stretch goals and tough circumstances."[28] Efforts of this type are known as **horizontal stretch goals.** Such initiatives help develop the company's most talented employees so they can be as successful as possible in many different ways. Not only do horizontal stretch goals make employees' jobs more interesting, but they also make them more valuable assets to the company. For a summary comparison of vertical and horizontal stretch goals, see Table 7.2.

stretch goals
Goals that are so difficult that they challenge people to rethink the way they work.

vertical stretch goals
Stretch goals that challenge people to achieve higher levels of success in current activities.

horizontal stretch goals
Stretch goals that challenge people to perform tasks that they have never done.

TABLE 7.2 Two Types of Stretch Goals

Goals that extend performance far beyond present levels, known as *stretch goals,* take two distinct forms—*vertical stretch goals* and *horizontal stretch goals.* The major differences between them are summarized here.

	Vertical Stretch Goals	Horizontal Stretch Goals
Description	Aggressive goals aligned with current activities	Goals that require significant new responsibilities
Purpose	To improve individual and/or organizational effectiveness	To improve the development of professional skills among individuals
Example	Instead of working to boost annual sales by 10% as usual, strive to raise sales by 50%	An engineer is asked to lead a sales team in an effort to attain unheard of levels of sales performance

Source: Based on information in Kerr & Landauer, 2004; see Note 27.

As you read this, you may be wondering how goals should be set in a manner that strengthens employees' commitment to them. One obvious way of enhancing goal acceptance is to involve employees in the goal-setting process. Research on workers' participation in goal setting has demonstrated that people better accept goals that they have been involved in setting than goals that have been assigned by their supervisors—and they work harder as a result.[29] In other words, participation in the goal-setting process tends to enhance goal commitment. Not only does participation help people better understand and appreciate goals they had a hand in setting, but it also helps ensure that the goals set are not unreasonable.

PROVIDE FEEDBACK ON GOAL ATTAINMENT. The final principle of goal setting appears to be glaringly obvious, although in practice it is often not followed: Feedback helps people attain their performance goals. Just as golfers interested in improving their swings need feedback about where their balls are going, so do workers need feedback about how closely they are approaching their performance goals. In both instances, the feedback helps in two important ways. First, it helps people determine how well they are doing, which potentially enhances their feelings of self-efficacy. Second, feedback also helps people determine the nature of the adjustments to their performance that are required to improve (e.g., adjusting the grip on a golf club to avoid "hooking" or "slicing" the ball down the fairway).

The importance of using feedback in conjunction with goal setting has been demonstrated in a study of pizza delivery drivers.[30] These individuals have a critical mission: to deliver their customers' pizzas quickly. But, of course, they must do so safely and in compliance with all traffic laws. All too often, however, in the interest of keeping their pizzas hot, some delivery people's driving styles are even hotter (and saucier). To speed up delivery, for example, some have been known to fail to come to complete stops at intersections.

To curb this behavior, officials of pizza shops in two different towns participated in a study in which their deliverers' driving behavior was observed systematically over a nine-month period. Trained observers who were hidden from view of the drivers recorded various aspects of the deliverers' driving behavior during prime-time hours—in particular, the percentage of time they came to complete stops at intersections. Over a six-week period, drivers from both locations were found to come to complete stops, on average, just under half the time. Because this was unacceptable, the drivers in one location, the experimental group, were asked to come to a complete stop 75 percent of the time. And, over a four-week period, they were given regular feedback on how successfully they met this goal. Drivers in the control group were not asked to meet any goals and were not given any feedback on their driving. Following this feedback period, drivers in the experimental group were asked to maintain the 75 percent goal, but stopped getting feedback. Observations of their driving behavior, and that of control group drivers, continued during this six-month period.

How did the drivers do? The results of the study, summarized in Figure 7.7, show that goal setting in conjunction with feedback was highly successful. Specifically, it led drivers to come very close to the assigned goal of coming to a complete stop at intersections three-quarters of the time. However, once that feedback was withdrawn, drivers returned to stopping only half the time—as often as they did before the study began (and as often as drivers in the control group, who received neither goals nor feedback). These findings clearly demonstrate the importance of accompanying specific, difficult goals with clear feedback about the extent to which those goals are being met. Not giving feedback on performance relative to goals forces workers to do their jobs blindly. Providing feedback, however, shines a spotlight on task performance that is essential to success.

When it comes to pizza delivery drivers, the ways of measuring performance are relatively straightforward. However, this is not usually the case among individuals who have more complex jobs with responsibilities over others, such as managers. Although it is more challenging to set, assess, and give feedback on goals for managerial performance, the same basic rules that we have been describing apply as well.

To illustrate this, let's consider how the goal-setting process is used among managers at Microsoft.[31] Although the company refers to goals as "commitments" (which makes sense, since one must commit to meeting a goal) and goal setting as "commitment setting," the process is the same. First, managers and their supervisors meet to determine specific goals to meet—ones in keeping with the company's objectives. Second, a specific plan is put in place for each of those

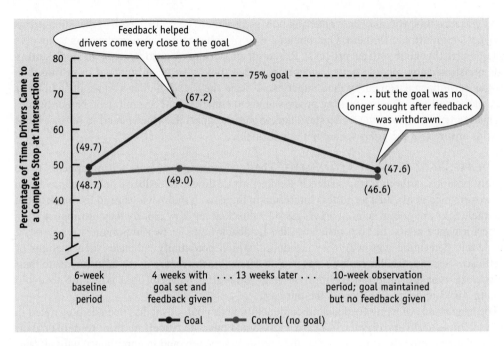

FIGURE 7.7

Feedback: An Essential Element of Goal Setting

Pizza delivery drivers came very close to reaching a goal—coming to a complete stop at intersections 75 percent of the time—during the period in which they were given regular feedback on goal performance. Several months later, however, after such feedback was no longer given, their performance returned to previous levels.

Source: Based on data reported by Ludwig & Geller, 1997; see Note 30.

commitments, making it clear precisely how it can be attained. Third, managers and their supervisors determine "accountabilities"—that is, specific ways of measuring each of the commitments, so that progress can be gauged.

As we have shown, goal setting is a very effective tool managers can use to motivate people. Setting a specific, acceptably difficult goal and providing feedback about progress toward that goal greatly enhance job performance. Companies, both large and small, rely on the technique of goal setting, and its effectiveness has been established widely.

Motivating by Being Equitable

Earlier in this chapter, we explained that although money isn't the top motivator for workers, it's still extremely important to them. It would be overly simplistic and misleading to suggest that people only want to earn as much money as possible. Even the highest-paid executives, sports figures, and celebrities sometimes complain about their pay despite receiving multimillion-dollar salaries.[32] Are they being greedy? Not necessarily. Often, the issue is not the actual amount of pay received, but rather, pay *equity*—that is, how one's pay compares to that of others doing similar work or to themselves at earlier times.

As we noted in Chapter 2, organizational scientists are keenly interested in understanding fairness on the job and how people respond when they believe they have been treated unfairly. One particular approach to distributive justice, known as *equity theory,* focuses on the motivational aspects of fairness. We examine it closely here.

Equity Theory: Balancing Outcomes and Inputs

Equity theory proposes that people are motivated to maintain equitable (i.e., fair) relationships between themselves and others and to avoid those relationships that are inequitable.[33] In judging equity, people compare themselves to others by focusing on two variables: **outcomes**—what we

equity theory
The theory stating that people strive to maintain ratios of their own outcomes (rewards) to their own inputs (contributions) that are equal to the outcome/input ratios of others with whom they compare themselves.

outcomes
The rewards employees receive from their jobs, such as salary and recognition.

get out of our jobs (e.g., pay, fringe benefits, and prestige)—and **inputs**—the contributions made (e.g., time worked, effort exerted, units produced). It helps to think of these judgments in the form of ratios—that is, the outcomes received relative to the inputs contributed (e.g., $1,000 per week in exchange for working 40 hours). It is important to note that equity theory deals with outcomes and inputs as they are *perceived* by people, not necessarily objective standards. As you might imagine, well-intentioned people sometimes disagree about what constitutes equitable treatment.

According to equity theory, people make equity judgments by comparing their own outcome/input ratios to the corresponding outcome/input ratios of others. This so-called "other" may be someone else in one's work group, another employee in the organization, an individual working in the same field, or even oneself at an earlier point in time—in short, almost anyone against whom we compare ourselves. As shown in Figure 7.8, these comparisons can result in any of three different states: *overpayment inequity, underpayment inequity,* or *equitable payment.*

Let's consider a simple example. Suppose Alice and Beth work together as paralegals in a law firm. Both women have equal amounts of experience, training, and education, and work equally long and hard at their jobs. In other words, their inputs are equivalent. But suppose Alice is paid an annual salary of $45,000 while Beth is paid only $35,000. In this case, Alice's ratio of outcomes/inputs is higher than Beth's, creating a state of **overpayment inequity** for Alice (since the ratio of her outcomes/inputs is higher than Beth's), but **underpayment inequity** for Beth (since the ratio of her outcomes/inputs is lower than Alice's). According to equity theory, Alice, realizing that she is paid more than an equally qualified person doing the same work, will feel *guilty* in response to her *overpayment.* By contrast, Beth, realizing that she is paid less than an equally qualified person for doing the same work, will feel *angry* in response to her *underpayment.* Guilt and anger are negative emotional states that people are motivated to

inputs
People's contributions to their jobs, such as their experience, qualifications, or the amount of time worked.

overpayment inequity
The condition, resulting in feelings of guilt, in which the ratio of one's outcomes to inputs is more than the corresponding ratio of another person with whom that person compares himself or herself.

underpayment inequity
The condition, resulting in feelings of anger, in which the ratio of one's outcomes to inputs is less than the corresponding ratio of another person with whom one compares himself or herself.

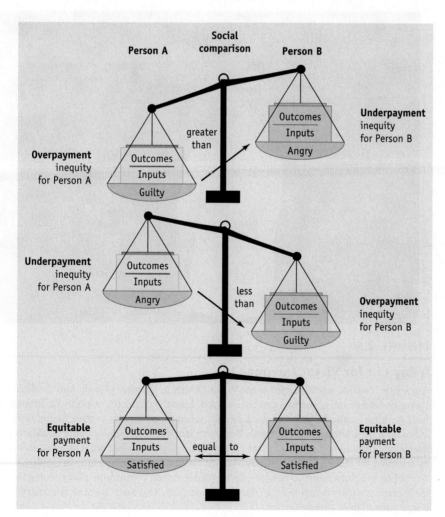

FIGURE 7.8

Equity Theory: An Overview

To judge equity or inequity, people compare the ratios of their own outcomes to inputs with the corresponding ratios of others (or of themselves at earlier points in time). The resulting states— overpayment inequity, underpayment inequity, and equitable payment— are summarized here, along with their associated emotional responses.

equitable payment
The state in which one person's outcome to input ratios is equivalent to that of another person with whom this individual compares himself or herself.

change. As a result, they will seek to create a state of **equitable payment** in which their outcome/input ratios are equal, leading them to feel *satisfied*.

Sometimes, people's emotional reactions to underpayment inequity can be quite intense, even if they are making millions of dollars. In recent years, people in many industries have been forced to take pay cuts as a serious economic recession hit businesses very hard. This has been the case in television broadcasting, where advertising revenues have plummeted. One person who has been affected by this is actor Eric Braeden, who, for 30 years, played the part of Victor Newman in CBS TV's top daytime drama, *The Young and the Restless*. Despite making a seven-figure salary, Braeden was so angry in the fall of 2009 when the production company told him that he'd have to take "a substantial salary cut" that he stormed off the set (see Figure 7.9).[34] Ultimately, he returned to the show, where he did, in fact, take a lower salary. Although few of us make anywhere near the amount of money that he makes, Braeden's feelings are understandable from the perspective of equity theory. If one day you make less money than you did the day before, even if it's still millions of dollars, you are likely to feel underpaid.

CREATING EQUITY. How can inequitable states be turned into equitable ones? The answer lies in adjusting the balance of outcomes and/or inputs. Among people who are underpaid, equity can be created by raising one's outcomes and/or lowering one's inputs. Likewise, those who are overpaid either may lower their outcomes or raise their inputs. Either action effectively would make the two outcome/input ratios equivalent. For example, the underpaid person, Beth, might lower her inputs, such as by slacking off, arriving at work late, leaving early, taking longer breaks, doing less work or lower quality work—or, in an extreme case, quitting her job. She also may

Photos 12/Alamy Images.

FIGURE 7.9

A Pay Cut for Victor Newman?

Actor Eric Braeden (shown right) is not Victor Newman, but after playing him for three decades on *The Young and the Restless*, the two can be confused. Like the character he portrays, Braeden is well paid for what he does. Similarly, both are quick to react when things are not to their liking. Although Newman's antics have been known to be extreme, Braeden's reactions are far more understandable. When declining television revenues required him to take a pay cut, Braeden was not reticent about sharing his discontent by storming off the set, leaving co-star Melody Thomas Scott (shown left) in a difficult position.
According to *equity theory*, when people are paid less than comparable others doing the same work, or themselves at earlier points in time, they feel underpaid. This leads them to feel angry—even if their pay is still quite high in absolute terms.

attempt to raise her outcomes, such as by asking for a raise, or even taking home company property, such as office supplies. By contrast, the overpaid person, Alice, may do the opposite—raise her inputs or lower her outcomes. For example, she might put forth much more effort, work longer hours, and try to make a greater contribution to the company. She also might lower her outcomes, such as by working while on a paid vacation, or not taking advantage of fringe benefits the company offers.

These are all specific *behavioral* reactions to inequitable conditions—that is, things people can *do* to turn inequitable states into equitable ones. However, people may be unwilling to do some of the things necessary to respond behaviorally to inequities. In particular, they may be reluctant to steal from their employers, or unwilling to restrict their productivity, for fear of getting caught "goofing off." In such cases, people may attempt to resolve inequity *cognitively,* by changing the way they think about the situation. As noted earlier, because equity theory deals with perceptions, inequitable states may be redressed by altering one's thinking about one's own—and others'—outcomes and inputs. For example, underpaid people may rationalize that others' inputs really are higher than their own (e.g., "I suppose she really *is* more qualified than me"), thereby convincing themselves that their higher outcomes are justified. Similarly, overpaid people may convince themselves that they really *are* better and deserve their relatively higher pay. Thus, by changing the way they see things, people can come to perceive inequitable situations as equitable, effectively relieving their feelings of guilt and anger, and transforming them into feelings of satisfaction. For a summary of behavioral and psychological reactions to inequity, see Table 7.3.

RESPONDING TO INEQUITIES ON THE JOB. From personal experience, how do you feel when you believe you have been unfairly paid? Equity theory suggests that you will find this highly distressing. Indeed, research has shown that the more people believe they are unfairly paid, the more negative symptoms of stress they display, such as coronary heart disease, depression, and insomnia.[35] Obviously unwilling to allow such conditions to develop, people are motivated to redress inequities at work, and they respond much as equity theory suggests. Consider two examples from the world of sports. Research has shown that professional basketball players who are underpaid (i.e., ones who are paid less than others who perform as well or better) score fewer points than those who are equitably paid.[36] Similarly, among baseball players, those paid less than others who play comparably well tend to change teams or even leave the sport when they are unsuccessful at negotiating higher pay.

We also know that underpaid workers attempt to raise their outcomes. For example, in an organization studied by the author, workers at two manufacturing plants suffered an underpayment created by the introduction of a temporary pay cut of 15 percent.[37] During the 10-week period

TABLE 7.3 Possible Reactions to Inequity: A Summary

People can respond to overpayment and underpayment inequities in behavioral and/or psychological ways. A few of these are summarized here. These reactions help change the perceived inequities into a state of perceived equity.

Type of Inequity	Form of Reaction	
	Behavioral: What You Can Do Is . . .	Psychological: What You Can Think Is . . .
Overpayment inequity	Raise your inputs (e.g., work harder) or lower your outcomes (e.g., work through a paid vacation).	Convince yourself that your outcomes are deserved based on your inputs (e.g., rationalize that you work harder than others and so you deserve higher pay).
Underpayment inequity	Lower your inputs (e.g., reduce effort) or raise your outcomes (e.g., get a raise in pay).	Convince yourself that others' inputs are really higher than your own (e.g., rationalize that the comparison worker is really more qualified and so deserves higher outcomes).

under which workers received lower pay, company officials noticed that theft of company property increased dramatically, approximately 250 percent. However, in another factory in which comparable work was done by workers paid at their normal rates, the theft rate remained low. This pattern suggests that employees may have stolen property from their company to compensate for their reduced pay. Consistent with this possibility, it was found that when the normal rate of pay was reinstated in the two factories, the theft rate returned to its normal, low level. These findings suggest that companies that seek to save money by lowering pay may be merely encouraging their employees to find other ways of making up for what they believe is rightfully theirs.

In extreme cases, people respond to inequity by quitting their jobs.[38] This, of course, is a very costly thing to do. However, many who take this drastic step do so because they feel that their current situations are intolerable and hope that more equitable conditions can be found elsewhere. (Interestingly, people also perceive inequities in one of the most common jobs they do—housework. Here too, they quit, so to speak, by getting divorced. As chronicled in the Today's Diverse and Global Organizations section below, married men and women perceive workplace inequities differently.)

Managerial Implications of Equity Theory

Equity theory has important implications for ways of motivating people.[39] We highlight three key ones here.

AVOID UNDERPAYMENT. Companies that attempt to save money by reducing employees' salaries may find that employees respond in many different ways so as to even the score. For example, they may steal, or they may shave a few minutes off their workdays, or otherwise withhold production.

Today's Diverse and Global Organizations

Inequity in Housework: Comparing Married Women and Men

Suppose you're working with a partner on an important job on which there's a recurring inequity with respect to the division of labor: The other individual does far less than his or her fair share of the work but reaps the same benefits as you. From the perspective of equity theory, this is clearly inequitable. You are underpaid and that other person is overpaid. Interestingly, this exact situation occurs regularly with respect to one of the most important jobs people perform—housework—and among the most important partners we have—our spouses. In this case, although the outcome is not money, but rather, living in a healthy and well-organized environment, the possibility that our partner's contributions to this end may be inequitable is a considerable source of conflict.

Despite the trend toward equality of the sexes, it remains the case in most households that wives do more of the housework than their husbands, even in dual-wage-earner households. Not surprisingly, this is a source of dissatisfaction in many marriages.[40] Importantly, research has found that the long-term effects of this particular source of inequity pose a serious threat to people's marriages.[41] In this investigation, a large sample of married men and women from dual-wage-earner families across the United States were polled at two times eight years apart. Participants were asked to indicate the proportion of routine household tasks (e.g., house cleaning, laundry) they did and the extent to which they believed this constituted a fair division of labor as opposed to being too much or too little. The findings were dramatic. Women who perceived that they did more than their fair share of the housework were more than twice as likely to be divorced from their spouses eight years later than those who perceived the division of labor to be fair. Among men, however, no such differences were found.

That women divorce husbands with whom they have an inequitable division of labor follows from equity theory and research showing that people often resign from jobs on which they feel underpaid.[42] The fact that men did not respond this way, however, reveals that husbands and wives have different thresholds as to what constitutes an equitable share of housework. Compared to men, women did a far greater proportion of the housework before believing it was too much. This is in keeping with traditional sex roles, according to which women do more housework than men. In the case of dual-earner households, however, such arrangements are impractical and generally give way to more egalitarian ones. When such expectations are violated, as often occurs because many men resent doing traditional "women's work," women experience considerable stress because they are completing most of the housework while also working outside the home. Because this puts such women in a highly stressful situation (see Chapter 5), it therefore is not surprising that they were likely to seek relief by ending their marriages.

This research is noteworthy because of the message it sends about gender equality (or lack thereof) in what is surely among the most universal of all jobs, housework. These findings provide some insight into why, even in today's allegedly enlightened era, many married women still face difficult choices between working inside and outside the home.

In extreme cases, employees express their feelings of extreme underpayment inequity by going on **strike,** that is, by engaging in a systematic stoppage of work designed as a protest against one or more organizations believed to have treated them unfavorably. This practice has been used numerous times over the years. In fact, the first known strike in recorded history (recorded on papyrus, in this case) occurred well over 3,000 years ago when artisan tomb makers in ancient Egypt struck to protest low wages and poor working conditions.[43] (For a more recent and broadly focused example—occurring, ironically, just across the Mediterranean Sea from this site—see Figure 7.10.)

Over the years and across the world, groups such as builders of railroad sleeping cars, miners, garment workers, teachers, autoworkers, airline pilots, and professional athletes (e.g., football, hockey, and baseball players), among many others, have relied on strikes to send their messages of discontent to management.[44] Although the exact natures of these workers' grievances differ from case to case, feelings of underpayment inequity are the overwhelming common theme.

AVOID OVERPAYMENT. You may think that because overpaid employees work hard to deserve their pay, it would be a useful motivational technique to pay people more than they merit. However, there are two key reasons why this would be problematic.[45]

- Any increases in performance in response to overpayment inequity are only temporary. As time goes on, people begin to believe that they actually deserve the higher pay they're getting and drop their work level down to normal.
- When you overpay one employee, you are underpaying all the others. When the majority of the employees feel underpaid, they will lower their performance, resulting in a net *decrease* in productivity—and widespread dissatisfaction.

With these concerns in mind, the conclusion is clear: *Managers should strive to pay all employees equitably.*

strike
The practice in which workers engage in a systematic stoppage of work designed as protest against one or more organizations believed to have treated them unfavorably.

Aris Messinis/Newscom.

FIGURE 7.10

Sorry, Greece Is Closed Today

Ordinarily bustling, Athens International Airport was nearly empty on February 10, 2010, as customs agents participated in a one-day strike by Greek civil service employees. Also staying home were thousands of teachers, taxi drivers, bankers, and hospital workers, bringing this usually thriving metropolis to a halt. Strikers were protesting Prime Minister George Papandreou's plan to freeze wages and pensions, which the government claimed was necessary to avert its impending bankruptcy. Protesters countered that the plan would help the rich at the expense of the working class.

transparency
The practice of making information about pay available openly instead of keeping it secret.

expectancy theory
The theory that asserts that motivation is based on people's beliefs about the probability that effort will lead to performance (*expectancy*), multiplied by the probability that performance will lead to reward (*instrumentality*), multiplied by the perceived value of the reward (*valence*).

expectancy
The belief that one's efforts will positively influence one's performance.

instrumentality
An individual's beliefs regarding the likelihood of being rewarded in accord with his or her own level of performance.

valence
The value a person places on the rewards he or she expects to receive from an organization.

BE TRANSPARENT. One of the major challenges with attempting to treat people equitably is that people perceive things differently. To some extent, of course (as suggested in Chapter 3), the process of perception is bound to be imperfect because people are biased. However, companies can do something to help everyone perceive things accurately: They can share information about pay openly. This is the notion of **transparency,** which refers to the practice of making information about pay available openly instead of keeping it secret.

Most companies are rather secretive about pay information, probably fearing backlash when employees learn what others are making. However, research has shown that it tends to work pretty much the opposite. People tend to overestimate how much their superiors are paid and as a result they feel that their own pay is not as high as it should be.[46] However, when information about pay is shared, inequitable feelings are less likely to materialize. With this in mind, transparency can be useful because it helps employees understand the basis for their pay (recall our discussion of procedural justice in Chapter 2). This, in turn, leads people to trust their companies, motivating them to put forth the effort required to excel.[47]

Motivating by Altering Expectations

Instead of focusing on individual traits and skills, goals, or social comparisons, another well-established approach to motivation, **expectancy theory,** takes a broader approach. It looks at the role of motivation in the overall work environment. The basic idea behind expectancy theory is that people are motivated to work when they expect that they will be able to achieve the things they want from their jobs. Expectancy theory is a cognitively oriented approach because it characterizes people as rational beings who think about what they have to do to be rewarded and how much the reward means to them. But, as we will see, the theory doesn't focus only on what people think. It also recognizes that these thoughts combine with other aspects of the organizational environment to influence job performance.

Basic Elements of Expectancy Theory

Although several different versions of expectancy theory have been proposed, all conceive of motivation as the result of three different types of beliefs that people have.[48] These are **expectancy**—the belief that one's effort will result in performance; **instrumentality**—the belief that one's performance will be rewarded; and **valence**—the perceived value of the rewards to the recipient (see Figure 7.11). We now describe each of these basic components of expectancy theory.

EXPECTANCY. Sometimes people believe that putting forth a great deal of effort means that they will get a lot accomplished. However, in other cases, people do not expect that their efforts will have much effect on how well they do. For example, an employee operating a faulty piece of

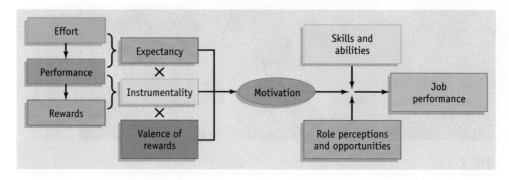

FIGURE 7.11

Expectancy Theory: An Overview

According to *expectancy theory,* motivation is the result of three types of beliefs. These are *expectancy* (the belief that one's effort will influence performance), *instrumentality* (the belief that one will be rewarded for his or her performance), and *valence* (the perceived value of the rewards expected). The theory also recognizes that motivation is only one of several factors responsible for job performance.

equipment may have a very low *expectancy* that his or her efforts will lead to high levels of performance. Naturally, someone working under such conditions probably would not continue to exert much effort.

INSTRUMENTALITY. Even if an employee works hard and performs at a high level, motivation may falter if that performance is not suitably rewarded—that is, if the performance is not perceived as *instrumental* in bringing about rewards. So, for example, a worker who is extremely productive may be poorly motivated to perform if the pay system doesn't recognize his or her success. Often, this occurs among people who already have reached the top pay grades in their companies. Even if they have become more successful, because they cannot be paid at higher levels in recognition of this, their motivation suffers.

VALENCE. Finally, even if employees believe that hard work will lead to good performance *and* that they will be rewarded commensurate with their performance, they still may be poorly motivated if those so-called rewards don't mean that much to them—that is, if they have low *valence.* In other words, someone who doesn't care about the rewards offered by the organization is not motivated to attain them. For example, a reward of $100 would be unlikely to motivate a multibillionaire like Bill Gates, although it may be a very desirable reward for someone of more modest means. Only those rewards that have a high positive valence to their recipients will motivate behavior.

One important factor that enhances the valence of rewards is the extent to which they satisfy people's fundamental *needs.* Psychologists have studied the nature of needs for many years and offer complex descriptions of their nature.[49] Most would agree, however, that **needs** are forces that motivate people to satisfy states that they inherently require for biological and/or social reasons. For example, we have a need to be satisfied physiologically, such as by having food and water, and socially, such as being admired and accepted by others. As suggested by the various needs identified and summarized in Table 7.4, there are quite a few needs that motivate people in the workplace.[50]

needs
Forces that motivate people to satisfy states that they inherently require for biological and/or social reasons.

As you review this list, please keep three things in mind. First, this list is not exhaustive; various theorists focus on different needs, so you may think of others that are not on this list. Second, some of these needs overlap with others. Like anything else having to do with human beings, clear lines between needs cannot always be drawn. Third, scientists disagree on whether or not people's needs are universal in nature. Some believe that everyone has the same needs and they are relatively equal in importance all the time. Others believe that some needs are more important at some times as opposed to others. Still other scholars suggest that people's needs differ based on the cultures in which they live and a variety of other factors.[51] What's important for our purposes in the field of OB, however, is much simpler. You should recognize the widespread nature and importance of these various needs, and that rewards that help satisfy human needs generally have high valence (i.e., they are considered most important and valuable to people).

With this in mind, many of today's companies are going out of their way to motivate employees by giving them the kinds of job perks they most desire. One particularly interesting example may be seen at Toyota. As a benefit to its U.S. employees, among whom the cost of medicine is a major concern, the company pays for the entire cost of the generic equivalent of prescription medicines, allowing employees to get them for free. Both online and on-site "Toyota Family Pharmacies" are available to employees, contributing greatly to their motivation.[52]

COMBINING ALL THREE TYPES OF BELIEFS. Expectancy theory claims that motivation is a multiplicative function of all three components. This means that higher levels of motivation will result when expectancy, instrumentality, and valence are all high than when they are all low. The multiplicative assumption of the theory also implies that if any one of these three components is zero, the overall level of motivation will be zero. So, for example, even if an employee believes that her effort will result in performance, which will result in reward, motivation will be zero if the valance of the reward she expects to receive is zero (i.e., if she believes that what she stands to receive in exchange for her effort has no value to her).

OTHER DETERMINANTS OF JOB PERFORMANCE. Figure 7.11 also highlights a point we made in our opening remarks about motivation—that motivation is not equivalent to job performance. Specifically, expectancy theory recognizes that motivation is one of several important determinants of job performance.

TABLE 7.4 Human Needs in the Workplace

Our *needs* as human beings influence behavior in all life activities. On the job, these needs are often satisfied in a variety of ways, as summarized here. Expectancy theory recognizes that rewards with the most positive valence often are ones that satisfy needs.

Need	Description/Example	How Satisfied on the Job
Biological and physiological needs	Need for basic things such as air, food, water	Companies have cafeterias for employees.
Psychological and physiological safety needs	Need to feel protected from harsh environments or dangerous people	Safety (e.g., goggles) and security procedures (e.g. guards) are used.
Affiliation, relatedness, and intimacy needs	Need to feel that one has friends with whom they enjoy being and who appreciate and accept them	Companies sponsor social events (e.g., picnics).
Esteem needs	Need to feel recognized for accomplishing things	Companies conduct ceremonies in which employees receive awards (e.g., certificates, cash).
Cognitive needs	Need to feel that one has learned something new	Company training programs help employees acquire new knowledge.
Aesthetic needs	Need to experience and appreciate beautiful things	Companies put interesting pieces of art throughout their facilities.
Self-actualization needs	The need to realize one's personal potential	Companies offer ongoing opportunities for growth and development (e.g., exposure to new people and places).
Transcendence needs	The need to help others grow and develop	Companies provide opportunities to coach and mentor other employees.
Autonomy needs	The need to have the freedom to decide how to do things without interference	Some jobs are designed in an effort to give people this ultimate freedom (see page 238).
Competence and success needs	The need to believe that one has mastered some skill and is capable of succeeding when performing it	Companies provide ongoing training and give feedback to help people to recognize when they have succeeded (see Chapter 3).
Power needs	The need to have an impact on other people	Leading and managing others satisfies this need (see Chapters 12 and 13).

Sources: Maslow, 1998; Deci et al., 2001; see Note 50.

For example, the theory assumes that *skills and abilities* also contribute to a person's job performance. It's no secret that some people are better suited to performing their jobs than others by virtue of their unique characteristics and special skills and abilities. For example, a tall, strong, well-coordinated person is likely to make a better professional basketball player than a very short, weak, uncoordinated one—even if the shorter person is highly motivated to succeed. Being highly motivated can help, of course, but it's not always enough to compensate for lack of physical or mental prowess. This is important for managers to keep in mind when diagnosing performance problems. If an employee is performing poorly, it might be a motivation problem (in which case, it's worth following the suggestions in the next section of this chapter) but it also may be due to a lack of skills (in which case the guidelines for training discussed in Chapter 3 should be followed).

Expectancy theory also recognizes that job performance will be influenced by people's *role perceptions*—in other words, what they believe is expected of them on the job. To the extent that there are disagreements about what one's job duties are, performance may suffer. For example, an assistant manager who believes her primary job duty is to train new employees may find that her performance is downgraded by a supervisor who believes she should be spending more time doing routine paperwork instead. In this case, the person's performance wouldn't suffer as a result of any deficit in motivation, but simply because of misunderstandings regarding what the job entails. As fundamental as this seems, many instances of poor job performance are, with surprising regularity, simply misunderstandings about role perceptions.

Finally, expectancy theory also recognizes the role of *opportunities to perform* one's job. Even the best employees may perform at low levels if their opportunities are limited. For example, a highly motivated salesperson may perform poorly if opportunities are restricted (such as if the territory is suffering from a financial downturn, or if the available inventory is limited). Here, once again, even a highly motivated person may perform poorly under certain (not too unusual) circumstances.

These examples underscore our point that motivation is just one of several determinants of job performance. The key thing to keep in mind is that motivation—combined with a person's skills and abilities, role perceptions, and opportunities—influences job performance.

Expectancy theory has generated a great deal of research and has been successfully applied to understanding behavior in many different organizational settings.[53] A key reason for expectancy theory's popularity is the many useful suggestions it makes for practicing managers. We now describe some of the most essential applications of expectancy theory, giving examples from organizations in which they have been implemented.

Putting Expectancy Theory to Work: Key Managerial Implications

Expectancy theory is a very practical approach to motivation. It identifies several important things that can be done to motivate employees.

MAKE IT CLEAR THAT EFFORT WILL LEAD TO PERFORMANCE. Motivation may be enhanced by training employees to do their jobs more efficiently, thereby achieving higher levels of performance. It also may be possible to enhance effort-performance expectancies by following employees' suggestions about ways to change their jobs. To the extent that employees are aware of problems in their jobs that interfere with their performance, attempting to alleviate these problems may help them perform more effectively. In essence, what we are saying is: *Make the desired performance attainable.* Good supervisors don't only make it clear to people what is expected of them, but they also help them attain that level of performance. When this occurs, workers will have a good understanding that working hard to perform the job correctly will lead to good performance.

ADMINISTER REWARDS THAT PROVIDE POSITIVE VALENCE TO EMPLOYEES. The carrot at the end of the stick must be tasty for it to have potential as a motivator. These days, with a demographically diverse workforce, it would be misleading to assume that all employees care about having the same rewards. Some might recognize the incentive value of a pay raise, whereas others might prefer additional vacation days, improved insurance benefits, day care, or elder-care facilities (see Chapter 1).

With this in mind, many companies have introduced **cafeteria-style benefit plans**—incentive systems allowing employees to select their fringe benefits from a menu of available alternatives. Given that fringe benefits constitute about 40 percent of payroll costs, more and more companies are recognizing the value of administering them flexibly. In fact, cafeteria-style benefit plans are in place in half of all larger companies (those employing more than 5,000) and about a quarter of smaller companies (those with less than 1,000 employees). For an example of one company that has had considerable success with its cafeteria-style benefits plan, see Figure 7.12.[54]

cafeteria-style benefit plans
Incentive systems in which employees have an opportunity to select the fringe benefits they want from a menu of available alternatives.

CLEARLY LINK VALUED REWARDS AND PERFORMANCE. There are several ways companies can link reward to performance (supporting a principle of operant conditioning described in Chapter 3). Whatever the particulars may be, the key is to make it absolutely clear what has to be done in order to be rewarded.

As an example, consider the pay plan IBM uses for its sales representatives. Previously, most of the pay these reps received was based on flat salary; their compensation was not linked to how well they did. Today, however, their pay is tied carefully to two factors that are essential to the company's success—profitability and customer satisfaction. So, instead of receiving commissions on the amount of the sale, as so many salespeople do, 60 percent of the commissions received by IBM sales reps are tied to the company's profit on the sales they make. As a result, the more money the company makes, the more the reps make. And, to make sure that the reps don't push only high-profit items that customers might not need, the remaining 40 percent of their commissions are based on customer satisfaction (assessed in regular surveys). Since introducing this plan, IBM has been effective in reversing its unprofitable trend. Although there are certainly many

Aerial Archives/Alamy Images.

FIGURE 7.12

Flexible Benefits at Oracle

Oracle, the large business software company, occupies this sprawling campus in Redwood Shores, California. Because the company hires people at many different career stages, a one-size-fits-all benefits plan is unlikely to make all of its 100,000 worldwide employees happy. To avoid this problem, the cafeteria-style benefits plan called "ORACLEflex" offers employees far more choices and greater flexibility than traditional health and insurance benefits plans. Staff members can design a custom benefits package for their unique situations. They are awarded flex credits that can be exchanged for whatever benefits they need, allocating any unused credits to a 401(k) savings plan or even regular taxable income. It's all up to them.

factors responsible for this turnaround, experts are confident that this practice of clearly linking desired performance to individual rewards is a key factor.

Compensation systems that reward people directly based on how well they perform their jobs are known as **pay-for-performance plans.** These may take such forms as the *commission plans* used for salespeople or the *piece-rate systems* used to pay some factory workers and field hands. Although the details vary from job to job, along with the names used to identify them, the underlying principle behind these programs is the same: Reward people in proportion to what they do and so long as the rewards have value to them, they will work hard to attain them. About three-quarters of all companies base the pay of at least some of their employees on measures of their performance, and report that this practice is generally quite effective.

As you might imagine, it is far easier to apply this principle to some jobs than others. In all cases, the trick is to identify exactly what behaviors are desired and to reward them without also unintentionally rewarding undesirable behaviors.[55] IBM was aware of this when it incorporated customer service into its compensation plan to ensure that short-term sales weren't promoted at the expense of long-term problems in the form of dissatisfied customers. Not all compensation programs are attuned equally to the important behaviors that really need to be rewarded, leading them to be misused. We see this, for example, when executives are rewarded with huge bonuses for making their companies profitable in the short run although their actions also may lead to long-term losses. Such executives did what they were rewarded for doing, and as rational beings, this is not unexpected. The problem in such cases lies not in the principle, but in the way it's implemented. If you reward people for short-term results, that's what they will focus on. (In recent years, pay-for-performance plans have been used to determine the compensation of a particular group of individuals who traditionally have not been associated with them, physicians.

pay-for-performance
A payment system in which employees are paid differentially, based on the quantity and quality of their performance. Pay-for-performance plans strengthen *instrumentality* beliefs.

The Ethics Angle

Should Doctors Be Paid for Their Performance?

Traditionally, physicians have been paid on a fee-for-service basis. They complete the service, such as examining a patient or performing a medical procedure, and they are paid for this by patients and their insurance companies. Now, however, a movement has been emerging in the United States and Great Britain that promises to change this. Some health insurance providers currently are rewarding doctors not for *what* they do, but *how well* they do it—that is, for meeting preestablished standards of quality and efficiency for the services they deliver. Although sometimes referred to as "value-based purchasing," by any other name, these are still pay-for-performance plans.

For the most part, professional groups, such as the American Medical Association, are supportive of this practice so long as several important considerations are satisfied. Most importantly, the indicators of quality have to be completely appropriate for all services provided. Otherwise, doctors may do what they have to do to satisfy these standards at the expense of their patients. Although this principle may be relatively easy to implement for salespeople, the unforeseen complexities of some medical cases may make it extremely challenging to apply to physicians.

The key is to have valid indicators of quality. For treating straightforward problems, metrics such as improvements in values revealed in laboratory tests are reasonable indicators that the doctor's course of treatment was effective. However, when it comes to diagnosing and managing complex diseases, where patients see multiple doctors, exactly what constitutes a "quality target" is likely to be very difficult to specify.[56] In such cases,

quality targets are essentially moving targets. This concern was expressed clearly by the Endocrine Society, which cautioned, "it is difficult to develop standardized measure across medical specialties . . . variations must be allowed to meet the unique needs of the individual patient."[57]

Another concern, and a potentially serious one for some patients, is that doctors whose performance is being assessed in terms of certain criteria might be inclined to refuse to accept new patients who they believe will be unable to help with respect to those criteria.[58] These may be individuals whose diseases are too advanced or whose symptoms make diagnosis challenging. Also likely to be refused service under pay-for-performance plans may be groups who require special attention because doctors might not be able to treat them as quickly or as effectively as others. This includes people who are poor, who cannot afford certain medical treatments, and who aren't responsive to their doctors' orders.[59]

Believing that such individuals—all patients, regardless of their conditions—deserve treatment and should have a right to medical care, some find it difficult to support a system that threatens to compromise these rights.[60] Medical ethics requires that physicians "do no harm," but questions are being raised about the appropriateness of a pay-for-performance system that encourages doctors to harm patients by providing disincentives to treat those who are in greatest need of attention. Of course, the system is new and it may need to be revised. Perhaps it may be used only selectively as a basis for compensating some physicians on certain occasions. It's too soon to tell. Although it's unclear how all these details will play out in the future, one thing's for certain: The debate about pay-for-performance among health-care professionals will continue for years to come.

For a discussion of this relatively new, and controversial, way of paying medical doctors, see The Ethics Angle section above.)

When rewards are linked to performance, it's not necessary for them to be monetary in nature. Even symbolic and verbal forms of recognition for a job well done can be very effective. For example, companies that verbally acknowledged their employees' good attendance records acknowledged dramatic improvements in attendance.[61] With this in mind, many organizations help recognize their employees' contributions by acknowledging them in their corporate newsletters.

As a case in point, consider CalPERS, the Sacramento-based firm that manages the pension and health benefits of 1.6 million Californians. In recent years, this company has been involved so actively in acknowledging the hard work of its employees that it has won a Best Practice Award from the National Association for Employee Recognition. The employee recognition—through printed and online newsletters, among other methods—has been so extensive and has generated so much goodwill that the company has been able to take on more work without having to hire additional employees.[62] Obviously, recognizing employees need not be lavish or expensive. It can involve nothing more than a heartfelt thank-you.

Some companies are so serious about paying employees for their performance that they are giving them pieces of the company in exchange for their contributions—a practice that is sure to link performance with rewards in their minds.[63] One form this has taken, particularly in many high-tech start-ups, is known as **incentive stock option (ISO) plans.** In such programs, a company grants an employee the opportunity to purchase its stock in the future at a specified price. So, over time, if the value of the company's stock increases, the employee can "exercise the option" by selling the stock at a profit, and with certain income tax advantages.[64]

incentive stock option (ISO) plans
Corporate programs in which a company grants an employee the opportunity to purchase its stock at some future time at a specified price.

Although the exact rules for ISOs are complex, the underlying rationale is straightforward: They give employees a stake in the success of the company. So, what's good for the company also is good for the employee. In expectancy theory terms, ISOs may be beneficial insofar as they enhance instrumentality beliefs by rewarding employees when their company does well. And this motivates them to put forth the effort to succeed. For example, at Merck & Co., the large pharmaceutical firm, the availability of ISOs has proven to be a very successful motivational device.[65] They encourage employees to help make the company perform at higher financial levels, and as this occurs, the more its stock value rises, making employees wealthier.

Motivating by Structuring Jobs to Make Them Interesting

job design
An approach to motivation suggesting that jobs can be created so as to enhance people's interest in doing them. See *job enlargement, job enrichment,* and the *job characteristics model.*

The final approach to motivation we consider, *job design,* is the broadest in scope because it is directed at improving the essential nature of the work performed. The idea behind **job design** is that motivation can be enhanced by making jobs more appealing to people. As you may recall from Chapter 1, Frederick W. Taylor's principle of *scientific management* attempted to stimulate performance by designing jobs in the most efficient fashion. However, treating people like machines often meant having them engage in repetitive movements, which they found highly routine and monotonous. Not surprisingly, people became bored with such jobs and frequently quit.[66] Fortunately, today's organizational scientists have found several ways of designing jobs that can not only be performed very efficiently, but are also highly pleasant and enjoyable.

Job Enlargement and Job Enrichment

job enlargement
The practice of expanding the content of a job to include more variety and a greater number of tasks at the same level.

Imagine that you have a highly routine job, such as tightening the lugs on the left rear wheel of a car as it rolls down the assembly line. Naturally, such a highly repetitive task would be monotonous and not very pleasant. One of the first modern approaches to redesigning jobs suggested that such consequences could be minimized by having people perform an increased number of different tasks all at the same level. This approach is known as **job enlargement.** To enlarge the jobs in our example, workers could be required to tighten the lugs on all four wheels. As a result, employees would have no more responsibility nor use any greater skills, but they would perform a wider variety of different tasks at the same level. Adding tasks in this fashion is said to increase the *horizontal job loading* of the position.

A few years ago, the 100-year-old American Greetings Corporation, in Cleveland, Ohio, enlarged some 400 jobs in its creative division, where employees design greeting cards.[67] Now, rather than always working exclusively on Christmas cards, for example, employees are able to move back and forth between different teams, such as those working on birthday ribbons, humorous mugs, and Valentine's Day gift bags. Employees at American Greetings reportedly enjoy the variety, as do those at RJR Nabisco, Corning, and Eastman Kodak, other companies that have allowed employees to make such lateral moves.

Although most reports of the effectiveness of job enlargement have been anecdotal, a few carefully conducted empirical studies also have examined their impact. For example, one group of researchers studied the effects of a job enlargement program instituted at a large financial services company.[68] The unenlarged jobs had different employees perform separate paperwork tasks such as preparing, sorting, coding, and keypunching various forms. By contrast, in the enlarged jobs these various functions were combined into larger jobs performed by single individuals. Although it was more difficult and expensive to train people to perform enlarged jobs than separate, unenlarged jobs, employees performing enlarged jobs expressed higher levels of job satisfaction and lower levels of boredom. And, because one person performing an enlarged job followed it all the way through from beginning to end, greater opportunities to correct errors existed. Not surprisingly, customers were satisfied with the result.

Unfortunately, in a follow-up investigation of the same company conducted two years later, it was found that not all the beneficial effects continued.[69] Notably, employee satisfaction leveled off and the rate of errors rose, suggesting that as employees get used to enlarged jobs they find them less interesting, and pay less attention to details. Hence, although job enlargement may help improve job performance, its effects may be short-lived.[70]

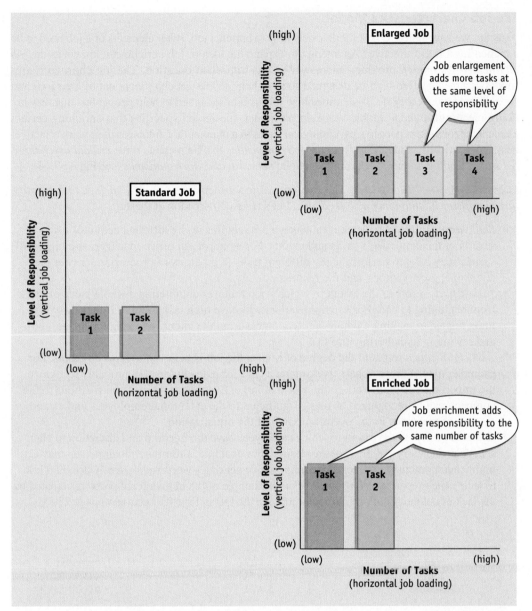

FIGURE 7.13

Job Enlargement and Job Enrichment: A Comparison
Redesigning jobs by increasing the number of tasks performed at the same level (horizontal job loading) is referred to as *job enlargement.* Redesigning jobs by increasing employees' levels of responsibility and control (vertical job loading) is referred to as *job enrichment.*

A more effective approach, **job enrichment,** gives employees not only more tasks to perform, but also ones requiring higher levels of skill and responsibility (see Figure 7.13). Specifically, job enrichment gives employees the opportunity to take greater control over how to do their jobs. Because people performing enriched jobs have increased opportunities to work at higher levels, the job enrichment process is said to increase a job's *vertical job loading.* The idea underlying job enrichment is that by making the jobs more interesting to people, they will be more highly motivated to perform them. Generally speaking, this is the case. In fact, an interesting by-product of enriching jobs has been found—people performing enriched jobs tend to procrastinate (i.e., put off things they are supposed to do) less than those who perform more standard jobs.[71]

Although evidence suggests that job enrichment programs generally have been successful, several factors limit their popularity.[72] Most obvious is the *difficulty of implementation.* To redesign existing facilities so that jobs can be enriched is often prohibitively expensive. Besides, the technology needed to perform certain jobs makes it impractical for them to be redesigned. Another impediment is the *lack of employee acceptance.* Although many people desire the additional responsibility associated with performing enriched jobs, others prefer to avoid it. In particular, individuals low in achievement motivation (see Chapter 4) are especially frustrated with enriched jobs.[73] Clearly, enriched jobs are not for everyone.

job enrichment
The practice of giving employees a high degree of control over their work, from planning and organization, through implementing the jobs and evaluating the results.

The Job Characteristics Model

Thus far, we have failed to specify precisely *how* to enrich a job. *What* elements of a job need to be enriched for it to be effective? An attempt to expand the idea of job enrichment, known as the *job characteristics model,* provides an answer to this important question. The **job characteristics model** assumes that jobs can be designed so as to help people get enjoyment out of their jobs and care about the work they do. It identifies how jobs can be designed to help people feel that they are doing meaningful and valuable work. In particular, the model specifies that enriching certain elements of jobs alters people's psychological states in a manner that enhances their work effectiveness.[74] Specifically, it identifies five *core job dimensions* that help create three *critical psychological states,* leading, in turn, to several beneficial *personal and work outcomes* (see Figure 7.14).

job characteristics model

An approach to job enrichment specifying that five core job dimensions (skill variety, task identity, task significance, autonomy, and job feedback) produce critical psychological states that lead to beneficial outcomes for individuals (e.g., high job satisfaction) and the organization (e.g., reduced turnover).

COMPONENTS OF THE MODEL. The five critical job dimensions are *skill variety, task identity, task significance, autonomy,* and *feedback.* Let's take a closer look at these.

- *Skill variety* refers to the extent to which a job requires doing different activities using several of the employee's skills and talents. For example, an office manager with high skill variety may have to perform many different tasks (e.g., do word processing, answer the telephone, greet visitors, and file records).
- *Task identity* refers to the extent to which a job requires completing a whole piece of work from beginning to end. For example, tailors will have high task identity if they do everything related to making a whole suit (e.g., measuring the client, selecting the fabric, cutting and sewing it, and altering it to fit).
- *Task significance* refers to the degree of impact the job is believed to have on others. For example, medical researchers working on a cure for a deadly disease probably recognize the importance of their work to the world at large. Even more modest contributions to the company can be recognized as being significant to the extent that employees understand the role of their jobs in the overall mission of the organization.
- *Autonomy* refers to the extent to which employees have the freedom and discretion to plan, schedule, and carry out their jobs as desired. For example, a furniture repair person may act highly autonomously by freely scheduling his or her day's work and by freely deciding how to tackle each repair job confronted. (For an example of the motivational problems created by the lack of autonomy in one particular job, see the OB in Practice section on page 239.)

FIGURE 7.14

The Job Characteristic Model: Basic Components

The *job characteristics model* stipulates that certain core job dimensions lead to certain critical psychological states, which, in turn, lead to several beneficial personal and work outcomes. The model also recognizes that these relationships are strongest among individuals with high levels of growth need strength.

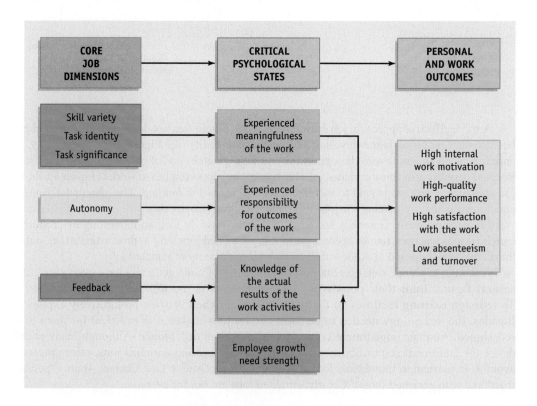

OB in Practice

Autonomy Is Not Music to the Maestro's Ears

When you think of people with limited autonomy on the job, the image probably comes to mind of assembly-line workers in factories who are required to work in a routinized fashion. It's easy to imagine how the highly mechanical nature of such jobs can limit their potential to motivate. You probably don't realize that a similar situation also exists among one of the most highly prestigious and sought-after jobs—musicians in professional orchestras. Indeed, research has shown that orchestra musicians tend to be less satisfied with their jobs (a key variable predicted by the job characteristics model) than their counterparts in small chamber groups, such as string quartets.[75]

Despite the apparent glamour, orchestra musicians generally have little freedom to perform their jobs as they wish. In fact, for centuries, tradition has held that orchestra musicians be subservient to the sometimes dictatorial whims of the maestros who conduct them. The musicians play their instruments, but following the explicit hierarchy of the symphony orchestra, the conductor very carefully regulates precisely *how* they play them, demanding perfection down to the slightest inflection of the final note. There is no doubt who's in charge and who makes all the decisions. Believe it or not, it was only in the past few years that orchestra unions won the right for musicians to take regularly scheduled bathroom breaks during rehearsal sessions. Until then, it was not unusual for orchestra musicians to face the wrath of angry conductors if they felt the need to heed nature's call.

By contrast, members of small musical ensembles enjoy considerable autonomy to interpret musical pieces, thereby allowing them to be highly involved in their performances, tapping more of their own talents. This is especially so in the case of jazz musicians, among whom the freedom to improvise is not only permitted, but encouraged. In keeping with the job characteristics model, it therefore is not surprising that such individuals are generally more satisfied with their jobs than members of orchestras, whose work is designed in a far less enriching fashion (assuming that they have high amounts of growth need strength).

Although it is not our intention to rob you of the glory of the musical experience by explaining this to you, it is fascinating to know that the field of OB has much to say about the personal experiences of these individuals who are entertaining you. After all, as unique as their positions may be, musicians—if they are fortunate enough to be working—still hold jobs, and as such, their behavior stands to be informed by the field of OB. Your takeaway is clear: To promote autonomy, taking a page from maestros will only lead to sour notes.

- *Feedback* refers to the extent to which the job allows people to have information about the effectiveness of their performance. For example, telemarketing representatives regularly receive information about how many calls they make per day and the number and values of the sales made.

The model specifies that these job dimensions have important effects on various critical psychological states. For example, skill variety, task identity, and task significance jointly contribute to a task's *experienced meaningfulness*. A task is considered to be meaningful to the extent that it is experienced as being highly important, valuable, and worthwhile. Jobs that provide a great deal of autonomy are said to make people feel *personally responsible and accountable for their work*. When they are free to decide what to do and how to do it, they feel more responsible for the results, whether good or bad. Finally, effective feedback is said to give employees *knowledge of the results of their work*. When a job is designed to provide people with information about the effects of their actions, they are better able to develop an understanding of how effectively they have performed—and such knowledge improves their effectiveness.

The job characteristics model indicates that the three critical psychological states affect various personal and work outcomes—namely, people's feelings of motivation, the quality of work performed, satisfaction with work, absenteeism, and turnover. The higher the experienced meaningfulness of work, responsibility for the work performed, and knowledge of results, the more positive the personal and work benefits will be. When they perform jobs that incorporate high levels of the five core job dimensions, people should feel highly motivated, perform high-quality work, be highly satisfied with their jobs, be absent infrequently, and be unlikely to resign from their jobs.

DOES THE JOB CHARACTERISTICS MODEL APPLY TO EVERYONE? At the end of the section on job enrichment, we indicated that there are individual differences in its effectiveness. Considering that the job characteristics model is a formal and expanded way to enrich jobs, it shouldn't be surprising that individual differences in effectiveness occur here, too. In particular, the

growth need strength
The personality variable describing the extent to which people have a high need for personal growth and development on the job. People who have high levels of growth need strength are most inclined to behave in accordance with the *job characteristics model.*

motivating potential score (MPS)
A mathematical index describing the degree to which a job is designed so as to motivate people, as suggested by the *job characteristics model.* It is computed on the basis of a questionnaire known as the Job Diagnostic Survey (JDS). The lower the MPS, the more the job may stand to benefit from redesign.

model is theorized to be especially effective in describing the behavior of a certain group of individuals—those who have high amounts of **growth need strength.** These are individuals who have a high need for personal growth and development. People not particularly interested in improving themselves on the job are not expected to experience the theorized psychological reactions to the core job dimensions, nor consequently, to enjoy the beneficial personal and work outcomes predicted by the model.[76]

PUTTING IT ALL TOGETHER. Based on the proposed relationship between the core job dimensions and their associated psychological reactions, the model claims that job motivation will be highest when the jobs performed rate high on the various dimensions. To assess this, a questionnaire known as the Job Diagnostic Survey (JDS) has been developed to measure the degree to which various job characteristics are present in a particular job.[77] Based on responses to the JDS, we can make predictions about the degree to which a job motivates people who perform it. The JDS yields an index known as the **motivating potential score (MPS),** which is a summary index of a job's potential for motivating people. The higher the score for a given job, the greater the likelihood of experiencing the personal and work outcomes specified by the model. Knowing a job's MPS helps one identify jobs that might benefit by being redesigned.

EVIDENCE FOR THE MODEL. The job characteristics model has been the focus of many empirical tests, most of which are supportive of many of its aspects.[78] One study conducted among a group of South African clerical workers found particularly strong support.[79] The jobs of employees in some of the offices in this company were enriched in accordance with techniques specified by the job characteristics model. Specifically, employees performing the enriched jobs were given opportunities to choose the kinds of tasks they perform (high skill variety), do the entire job (high task identity), receive instructions regarding how their job fit into the organization as a whole (high task significance), freely set their own schedules and inspect their own work (high autonomy), and keep records of their daily productivity (high feedback). Another group of employees, equivalent in all respects except that their jobs were not enriched, served as a control group.

After employees performed the newly designed jobs for six months, comparisons were made between them and their counterparts in the control group. With respect to most of the outcomes specified by the model, individuals performing redesigned jobs showed superior results. Specifically, they reported feeling more internally motivated and more satisfied with their jobs. There were also lower rates of absenteeism and turnover among employees performing the enriched jobs.

The only outcome predicted by the model that was not affected was actual job performance; people performed equally well in enriched and unenriched jobs. This isn't particularly surprising in this study because the complexity of the work allowed many factors to affect job performance, not all of which were likely to be affected by job design. However, recent research has shown that for more simple types of jobs, one particular job characteristic, task significance, does indeed have a beneficial effect on job performance.

Participants in this study were telephone solicitors for a university who called alumni requesting donations to fund a scholarship at their alma mater.[80] Before work one day, a randomly selected group of callers was asked to read brief stories explaining the beneficial impact of these scholarships on the lives of former students. Through this procedure, the significance of their jobs was enhanced in their minds. Another group of callers assigned to the control group received no information of any kind. As shown in Figure 7.15, explaining the significance of their jobs dramatically improved callers' performance on those jobs. Compared to the control group, workers who were led to understand the significance of their jobs performed them at much higher levels. In fact, these callers raised more than twice as much money from the alumni they phoned, suggesting that appreciating the significance of their jobs encourages people to put more effort into performing them.

Designing Jobs That Motivate: Managerial Guidelines

The job characteristics model specifies several ways in which jobs can be designed to enhance their motivating potential.[81] In Table 7.5 we present these in the form of general principles.

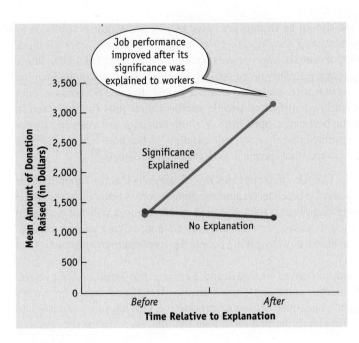

FIGURE 7.15

The Significance of Task Significance: An Experimental Demonstration

An experiment compared the job performance levels of groups of telephone solicitors seeking donations for a university alumni fund. One group, whose members were selected at random, received explanations of the importance of their jobs; the other group received no information of any kind. As shown here, the callers who were led to understand the significance of the donations they were seeking solicited more than twice as much money.

Source: Grant, A. M. (2008). The significance of task significance: Job performance effects, relational mechanisms, and boundary conditions. *Journal of Applied Psychology, 93*, 108–124.

COMBINE TASKS. Instead of having several workers each perform a separate part of a whole job, it would be better to have each person perform the entire job. Doing so helps provide greater skill variety and task identity. For example, Corning Glass Works redesigned jobs so that people who assembled laboratory hot plates put together entire units instead of contributing a single part to the assembly process.[82]

TABLE 7.5 Principles for Enriching Jobs Following the Job Characteristics Model

The job characteristics model suggests four important principles that can be followed to enrich jobs. These incorporate various core job dimensions responsible for enhancing motivation and performance.

Principle	Core Job Dimensions Incorporated
1. Combine tasks, enabling workers to perform the entire job.	Skill variety Task identity
2. Open feedback channels, giving workers knowledge of the results of their work	Feedback
3. Establish client relationships, allowing providers of a service to meet the recipients.	Skill variety Autonomy Feedback
4. Load jobs vertically, allowing greater responsibility and control over work	Autonomy

Source: Based on information in Hackman, 1976; see Note 81.

OPEN FEEDBACK CHANNELS. Jobs should be designed to give employees as much feedback as possible. The more people know how well they're doing (be it from customers, supervisors, or coworkers), the better equipped they are to take appropriate corrective action and plan for the future (see Figure 7.16). (You may recall that we already noted the importance of feedback in the learning process in Chapter 3, and in conjunction with goal setting earlier in this chapter.) Sometimes, cues about job performance can be clearly identified as people perform their jobs (as we noted in conjunction with goal setting). In the best cases, open lines of communication between employees and managers are so strongly incorporated into the corporate culture—as has been reported to exist at Boise Cascade's paper products group—that feedback flows without hesitation.[83]

ESTABLISH CLIENT RELATIONSHIPS. The job characteristics model suggests that jobs should be set up so that the person performing a service (such as an auto mechanic) comes into contact with the recipient of the service (such as the car owner). Jobs designed in this manner will not only help the employee by providing feedback, but also provide skill variety (e.g., talking to customers in addition to fixing cars) and enhance autonomy (by giving people the freedom to manage their own relationships with clients).

This suggestion has been implemented at Sea-Land Service, the large containerized ocean-shipping company.[84] Once this company's mechanics, clerks, and crane operators started meeting with customers, they became much more productive. Having faces to associate with the once-abstract jobs they did clearly helped them take the jobs more seriously.

LOAD JOBS VERTICALLY. As we described earlier, loading a job vertically involves giving people greater responsibility for their jobs. Taking responsibility and control over performance away from managers and giving it to their subordinates increases the level of autonomy the jobs offer these lower-level employees. And, according to a recent poll, autonomy is among the most important things people look for in their jobs—even more important than high pay.[85] In view of this, a growing number of companies are yielding control and giving employees increasing freedom to do their jobs as they wish (within limits, at least).

AFP Photo/Valery Hache/Files/Newscom.

FIGURE 7.16

What Is the Future of the Olympics? Your Feedback Is Invited

It's not unusual for organizations to ask their customers what they think of them so they can use the feedback to improve their products and services. Most rely on questionnaires, but the International Olympic Committee (IOC) used a more creative method. With assistance from triple gold medal winner Usain Bolt, the general public was invited to submit answers to the question, "What is the future of the Olympics?" in the form of videos posted on YouTube. In exchange for their efforts, people submitting the two best entries won trips to Copenhagen, Denmark, where they were invited to share their ideas in person at a meeting of the Olympic Congress, where discussions are held about how to improve the Olympic Games.

Summary and Review of Learning Objectives

1. **Define motivation and explain its importance in the field of organizational behavior.**
   Motivation is concerned with the set of processes that arouse, direct, and maintain behavior toward a goal. It is not equivalent to job performance, but is one of several determinants of job performance. Today's work ethic motivates people to seek interesting and challenging jobs, instead of just money.

2. **Describe the motivational-fit approach and what it suggests about how to improve motivation in organizations.**
   The *motivational-fit approach* highlights the importance of motivational traits (achievement and anxiety) and motivational skills (emotion control and motivation control) in work motivation. This framework specifies that people will be most highly motivated when these traits and skills best fit the requirements of the job and the organization in which someone works.

3. **Identify and explain the conditions through which goal setting can be used to improve job performance.**
   Goal-setting theory claims that an assigned goal influences a person's beliefs about being able to perform a task (referred to as *self-efficacy*) and his or her personal goals. Both of these factors, in turn, influence performance. Research has shown that people will improve their performance when specific, acceptably difficult goals are set and feedback about task performance is provided. The task of selecting goals that are acceptable to employees is facilitated by allowing employees to participate in the goal-setting process.

4. **Describe equity theory and explain how it may be applied to motivating people in organizations.**
   Equity theory claims that people desire to attain an equitable balance between the ratios of their work rewards (outcomes) and their job contributions (inputs) and the corresponding ratios of comparison to others. Inequitable states of *overpayment inequity* and *underpayment inequity* are undesirable, motivating people to try to attain equitable conditions. Responses to inequity may be either behavioral (e.g., raising or lowering one's performance) or psychological (e.g., thinking differently about work contributions). To avoid negative reactions (e.g., strikes, reduced work, resignations), overpayment inequity and underpayment inequity should be avoided. It also is useful to explain how outcomes and inputs were determined in an open and honest fashion.

5. **Describe expectancy theory and how it may be applied in organizations.**
   Expectancy theory recognizes that motivation is the product of a person's beliefs about *expectancy* (effort will lead to performance), *instrumentality* (performance will result in reward), and *valence* (the perceived value of the rewards). In conjunction with skills, abilities, role perceptions, and opportunities, motivation contributes to job performance. Expectancy theory suggests that motivation may be enhanced by linking rewards to performance (as in *pay-for-performance plans*) and by administering rewards that are highly valued (as may be done using *cafeteria-style benefit plans*).

6. **Distinguish among job enlargement, job enrichment and the job characteristics model as techniques for motivating employees.**
   Motivation may be enhanced at the organizational level by designing or redesigning jobs in certain ways. Popular approaches include *job enlargement* (performing more tasks at the same level) and *job enrichment* (giving people greater responsibility and control over their jobs). A more sophisticated approach, the *job characteristics model,* identifies the specific job dimensions that should be enriched (skill variety, task identity, task significance, autonomy, and feedback), and relates these to the critical psychological states influenced by including these dimensions on a job. These psychological states will, in turn, lead to certain beneficial outcomes for both individual employees (e.g., job satisfaction) and the organization (e.g., reduced absenteeism and turnover). Jobs may be designed to enhance motivation by combining tasks, opening feedback channels, establishing client relationships, and loading jobs vertically (i.e., enhancing responsibility for one's work).

Points to Ponder

Questions for Review

1. What are Maslow's five categories of needs and how might each be satisfied on the job?
2. What particular traits and skills are most important when it comes to enhancing motivation by promoting fit with one's job and organization?
3. What rules should be followed when setting goals to motivate workers?
4. What does equity theory say about the role of money as a motivator?
5. What are the basic components of expectancy theory, and how are they combined to predict performance?
6. How, specifically, can jobs be designed in an effort to enhance motivation?

Experiential Questions

1. What experiences have you had in setting personal goals (e.g., for saving money, for losing weight, for getting a certain job)? Which rules of goal setting did you follow? Which rules might you have followed to be even more successful?

2. Think of a time in which you felt inequitably underpaid by your employer or manager. How did it make you feel, and how did you respond as a result?
3. Think of the job you currently do, or one that you have done recently. Describe two specific things that could be done to redesign that job so that employees will be more motivated to perform it.

Questions to Analyze

1. An employee claims to be trying very hard but is not attaining acceptable levels of job performance. According to expectancy theory, what factors would contribute to such effort? What additional factors, besides motivation, contribute to task performance?
2. Money is not the only source of work motivation, but it plays a key role. Explain the specific role of money as a motivator in each of the theories of motivation presented in this chapter.
3. Imagine that you are devising an incentive plan for your company. What particular guidelines will you follow to ensure that it is effective? What problems do you anticipate as the plan takes effect?

Experiencing OB

Individual Exercise

Are You Equitably Paid?

The desire to be paid equitably is very strong among people in the workplace. Too often, however, employees believe that they are inequitably paid—either overpaid or underpaid. The following questionnaire will help you assess how you stand in this regard.

Directions

Respond to each of the following questions by selecting the one response that most accurately describes your situation as you believe it to be.

_____ 1. Compared to equally experienced others doing the same job as me in my company, I am:
   a. paid less
   b. paid about the same
   c. paid more

_____ 2. Given my training and experience, I would say that my pay is:
   a. too low
   b. about right
   c. too high

_____ 3. Considering how much effort I put into my job, I would say that my pay is:
   a. too low
   b. about right
   c. too high

_____ 4. Over the years, my level of pay has:
   a. not kept up with my accomplishments
   b. kept up with my accomplishments
   c. exceeded my accomplishments

_____ 5. So far as I know, people doing the same job as me at other companies are paid:
   a. more than me
   b. about the same as me
   c. less than me

Scoring

1. Give yourself 1 point each time you answer with response "a." These responses reflect underpayment. The more points you have in this category, the more underpaid you feel.
2. Give yourself 1 point each time you answer with response "b." These responses reflect equitable payment. The more points you have in this category, the more equitably paid you feel.
3. Give yourself 1 point each time you answer with response "c." These responses reflect overpayment. The more points you have in this category, the more overpaid you feel.

Questions for Discussion

1. What do your responses to this questionnaire reveal about the perceived equitableness of your pay? Are you overpaid or underpaid? Does your score confirm what you believe about the fairness of your pay?
2. If you are equitably paid, do you feel satisfied on the job? If you are inequitably paid (either overpaid or underpaid), do you feel dissatisfied on the job?
3. On occasions in which you felt inequitably underpaid, how did you respond? Did you lower your inputs? If so, how? Did you attempt to raise your outcomes? If so, how?

Group Exercise

Does Goal Setting Really Work? Demonstrate It for Yourself

Specific, difficult goals tend to enhance task performance. The following exercise is designed to help you demonstrate this effect for yourself. All you need is a class of students willing to participate and a few simple supplies.

Directions

1. Select a page of text from a book and make several photocopies. Carefully count the words and number each word on one of the copies. This will be your score sheet.
2. Find another class of 30 or more students who do not know anything about goal setting. (We do not want their knowledge of the phenomenon to bias the results.) On a random basis, divide the students into three equal-size groups.
3. Ask the students in the first group—the "baseline" group—to copy as much of the text as they can onto another piece of paper, and give them exactly one minute to do so. Direct them to work quickly. Using the score sheet created in step 1, identify the highest number of words copied by any one of the students and then multiply this number by 2. This will be the specific, difficult goal level.
4. Ask the students in the second group—the "specific goal" group—to copy the number of words on the same printed page for exactly one minute. Tell them to try to reach the specific goal number identified in step 3.
5. Repeat this process with the third group—the "do your best" group—but instead of giving them a specific goal, direct them to "try to do your best at this task."
6. Compute the average number of words copied in the "difficult goal" group and the "do your best" group. Have your instructor compute the appropriate statistical test (a _t_-test, in this case) to determine the statistical significance of this difference in performance levels.

Questions for Discussion

1. Was there a statistically significant difference between the performance levels of the two groups? If so, did students in the "specific goal" group outperform those in the "do your best" group, as expected? What does this reveal about the effectiveness of goal setting?
2. If the predicted findings were not supported, why do you suppose this happened? What was it about the procedure that may have led to this failure? Was the specific goal

(i.e., twice the fastest speed in the "baseline" group) too high, thus making the goal unreachable? Alternatively, was it too low, thus making the specific goal too easy?

3. What do you think would happen if the goal was lowered, thus making it easier, or raised, thus making it more difficult?

4. Do you think that providing feedback about goal attainment (e.g., someone counting the number of words copied and calling this out to the performers as they worked) would have helped?

5. For what other kinds of tasks do you believe goal setting may be effective? Specifically, do you believe that goal setting can improve your own performance on something? Explain this possibility.

Practicing OB

Motivating Nurses at a Hospital

You have been hired by the director of a large suburban hospital to help resolve problems of poor morale that have been plaguing the nursing staff. Unfortunately, the nurses don't find their jobs particularly interesting. As a result, turnover and absenteeism have been high, and patient care is at an all-time low. The problem is apparent to everyone; both doctors and patients have been complaining. Answer the following questions relevant to this situation based on the material in this chapter.

1. After interviewing the nurses, you found that they believed that no one cared how well they were doing. What theories could help explain this problem?

Applying these approaches, what would you recommend the hospital should do to resolve this problem?

2. Hospital officials tell you that the nurses are well paid, adding to your surprise about the low morale. However, your interviews reveal that the nurses themselves feel otherwise. Why might this occur and why is this a problem? What could be done to help?

3. "I'm bored with my job," one highly experienced nurse tells you, and you believe she speaks for many within the hospital. What could be done to make their jobs more interesting to those who perform them? What are the limitations of your plan? Would it work equally well for other members of the hospital staff (e.g., clerical and janitorial employees)?

Case in Point

■ *Google: Searching for a Better Way to Work*

Google, the immensely popular Web search engine, has been touted as "the closest thing the Web has to an ultimate answer machine." Although this is debatable, of course, it is far more difficult to deny that the company is, in fact, the closest thing we have to an ultimate example of business success. Founded by two computer science graduate students at Stanford University in the late 1990s, Larry Page and Sergy Brin, Google has grown astronomically. In late 1998, the search engine had 10,000 queries per day, a figure that grew to 300 million by 2009. More than just a search engine, Google now has 12 product lines, including its highly regarded Android cell phone. On the heels of these accomplishments, financial success likewise has been impressive. Only four months after the initial public offering of Google stock in August 2004, its price more than doubled and has risen much higher ever since.

Although Google is in the technology business, its founders acknowledge that the company's greatest challenges lie more with people than computers. At first, Page and Brin worked with just a handful of employees out of a converted garage, but today the company has some 10,000 employees in its sprawling headquarters, known as the "Googleplex," in Mountain View, California. With such rapid growth, how can Page and Brin ensure that their many new employees share their passion for innovation and work hard to achieve it? Brin explains his strategy quite simply: "To have a good lifestyle, we have to have a good lifestyle at work."

Just about all the people who work at Google, from the most advanced computer engineers to the lowest level employees, are hand selected (or, at least, approved) by Page and Brin. They look for people who are inspired not by money, but by love of the work they do. After all,

(Continued)

they are expected to work long hours and to achieve unparalleled levels of excellence, to come up with "the next big thing." To make this happen, they go out of their way to make Google a great place to work. As Brin put it, "Work should be challenging, and the challenge should be fun."

With this in mind, Page and Brin have taken strides to ensure that there's a comfortable and friendly atmosphere at Google. For example, there is no dress code; you dress however you wish to be comfortable (as stated in the company's philosophy, "You can be serious without a suit"). People even can bring their dogs to work, keeping them company throughout the day. To help everyone stay fit and to build a spirit of teamwork, there's also a very strong spirit of play at Google; at noon each day there's a volleyball game outside.

Google puts users first when it comes to online service, and it puts employees first when it comes to daily working life. Employees are treated very well. A fantastic on-site cafeteria serves gourmet meals of every kind, catering to a variety of dietary needs and preferences—all absolutely free of charge. According to CEO Eric E. Schmidt, this is just good business because it keeps people at their desks instead of leaving the building to eat. The company also invests in its employees in another interesting way. Every year, the company takes all its employees on an all-expenses-paid ski trip. Again, this is seen as good for the business because it promotes the spirit of càmàràderie that's necessary in their work environment, in which the sharing of ideas is critical.

This is not to say that Google is lavish or wasteful. Although Page and Brin each made $6 billion when the company went public, and 1,000 employees also became millionaires, it is not money that keeps people going at Google. Page and Brin still share a small office and live modestly, as do most of their employees. Although they have the means to be living extremely well (and surely will do so someday), right now, the thing that keeps everyone going at Google is their zeal to use computer technology to change the world. It's all about innovation, and not getting rich quick.

Questions for Discussion

1. What does Google do to motivate its employees?
2. Based on the material in this chapter, what recommendations would you make to Google about additional things it could do to enhance motivation?
3. What particular problems or limitations do you envision in the recommendations you offered in answering the previous question? For example, under what conditions are they likely to be effective? Would they work for everyone?

■ *Diversity at KPMG*

According to Kathy Hannan, diversity is essential to the culture at KPMG. Hannan heads both the company's Women's Advisory Board and the Diversity Advisory Board. In fact, KPMG has established a number of other advisory boards, including one for African Americans, one for Latinos, and one for gay, lesbian, bisexual, and transgender employees.

KPMG's commitment to a more diverse workforce is also evident in its efforts to recruit and hire minorities. The company has implemented several programs designed to attract students to the firm with the expectation that they could become future hires. These programs include internships and other kinds of educational opportunities. Furthermore, KPMG believes that a diverse workforce attracts more minority workers. Nigel Franklin of KPMG's African American Network agrees. He notes that prospective hires want to see other people like themselves in an organization so that they know that there is someone to relate to—someone who has traveled their path already.

Kathy Hannan says that the Women's Advisory Board is actively focusing on retaining young women; to that end, she has established goals of how the firm should look from a gender perspective and created a network that acts as a forum for women to reach out to each other. Kristen Johnston of KPMG's Gay, Lesbian, Bisexual and Transgender Network believes that education is the key to a more diverse organization. Johnston says that is important to help people understand differences and accept them. She feels that there is a long road ahead, but is optimistic that, at some point in time, stereotypes and prejudices will be a thing of the past. Hannan agrees, and believes that one day there no longer will be a need for the different networks to support the various groups. Until then, though, they perform a valuable role.

Discussion Questions

1. Which of the major training approaches to diversity management as discussed in Chapter 6 is KPMG following?
2. How does Kristen Johnston of KPMG's Gay, Lesbian, Bisexual and Transgender Network hope the group will help her avoid the prejudice and discrimination described in Chapter 6 that is found commonly in many organizations?
3. Which of the guidelines presented in Chapter 6 for making diversity programs successful is KPMG following?

(Continued)

Part 3 Video Cases

■ *Motivating Employees at KPMG*

KPMG believes that it is important for employees to feel valued and motivated to work. Just a few years ago, however, this was not the case. Workers at the company were not engaged in their jobs, turnover was high, and overall performance was suffering as a result. KPMG recognized that a fundamental shift was needed if it were to maintain its track record of success.

KPMG identified four things that were important to motivating employees and improving job performance. First, employees wanted to work for a winning organization of which they could be proud. Second, workers wanted to have the resources and information necessary to allow them to achieve their objectives in a timely fashion. Third, they wanted to be treated well, and fourth, they wanted to enjoy their work. This knowledge, together with the commitment of the CEO and senior management, allowed the company to make changes in several areas.

Today, KPMG workers enjoy better compensation packages, improved work/family arrangements, and more career development opportunities. The changes appear to have been successful. Employee turnover at KPMG has dropped, and individuals at all levels are more committed to their jobs and to the company as a whole.

Discussion Questions

1. What would equity theory (as presented in Chapter 7) imply about employee satisfaction and performance at KPMG?
2. What does expectancy theory (as presented in Chapter 7) suggest about the habits of workers at KPMG?
3. How does KPMG go about meeting the varied needs of its employees?

CHAPTER

8 Group Dynamics and Work Teams

Preview Case

■ Making a "Better Place" One Electric Vehicle at a Time

Can a tiny company change the world? Although it's unlikely, it's possible that if its members work together in a carefully coordinated and focused fashion they just might make a difference. And this is precisely what Shai Agassi intends to do. As founder and CEO of Better Place, he works with governments and auto manufacturers to develop personal transportation systems that eliminate our dependence on oil and the environmental and economic damage that comes with it. His vehicle of choice to make the earth a "better place" is the electric vehicle (EV).

In 2010, Agassi opened the company's first EV demonstration center. It's housed in a giant refurbished oil tank, an ironic symbol that incorporates the company's belief in transitioning to electric transportation. Only three years earlier, he launched the company with $200 million in venture capital funds. Better Place's business plan is straightforward: Pay for the transportation you need as a sustainable service. First, automakers have to replace their gasoline-guzzling engines with powerful, but quiet and smooth-running electric motors powered by batteries. Then, drivers pay a fee to access a network of charging spots and places where they can replace their batteries. Better Place operates the electric recharge grid that makes this possible.

According to Chairman of the Board Idan Ofer, this strategy benefits everyone. Drivers benefit by getting to enjoy their cars in cleaner environments. The auto industry benefits by getting to service a brand new market segment. Energy companies benefit by getting to introduce new technologies. The world's nations benefit by aligning economic and environmental interests. And, finally, of course, our planet benefits by being spared the pollution caused by the internal combustion engine.

Getting all this to work, as you might imagine, requires great teamwork, and Better Place has this covered. Aliza Peleg, vice president of planning and operations, works carefully with Karen Alter, vice president of marketing, to bring the company's ideas to international auto companies. They then hand off the plans to Agassi, who comes in to finalize the deal. It's like a relay race—and one they seem to be winning: Within the company's first six months, deals poured in.

Soon after the launch, Renault-Nissan signed on with Better Place to develop a line of battery-powered electric cars. Then, in January 2008, with the help of Moshe Kaplinsky, CEO of Better Place Israel, that nation became the first in the world to declare a plan for oil independence by 2020, using solar-powered electric recharge grids to power EVs. Only two months later, in March 2008, Denmark came onboard, working with Better Place to develop a recharge grid powered by energy from wind turbines. Since then, the United States, Canada, Australia, and Japan have gotten involved. And with an infusion of $350 million in financing in 2010, additional growth is in the cards.

If there's been any one problem with EVs thus far, it's that they're actually too quiet. This makes the driving less than gratifying and takes away the auditory cues that blind pedestrians rely on when crossing the street. Better Place has a solution. Agassi is planning on "drivetones," which are similar to ringtones for your phone, that can be downloaded and controlled through a dashboard switch. So, even if you don't have a Ferrari, with a little digital wizardry, your electric car can at least sound like one.

To return to our opening question, it's hard to say whether Better Place will ever change the world, but it's clear that Agassi and his team would be delighted to save it from pollution, thereby making it truly a better place. And this, after all, is something special.

What's going on at Better Place is, no doubt, quite amazing. Few entrepreneurs can pull off the kind of successes that Agassi has enjoyed, creating an entirely new product that promises to revolutionize the world in such a short time. But he clearly isn't doing it alone. Instead, he is part of a hard-working team of talented individuals who share his vision and are willing to work with one another to make things happen. Indeed, *work teams* are extremely popular today in all kinds of organizations—and, in view of Better Place's experiences, there's little wonder why. In the second half of the chapter, we will take a look at the nature of teams in the modern workplace. Acknowledging that they don't always operate as successfully as the team led by Agassi, we will describe the general effectiveness of teams and outline steps that can be taken to make them as productive as possible.

To help you understand the underlying factors that contribute to team success and failure, we first must examine the basic nature of *groups* in general. As you know, a great deal of the work performed in organizations is done by people working together in groups. In view of this, it makes sense to understand the types of groups that exist and the variables governing the interrelationships between them and individuals—commonly referred to as *group dynamics*. The topic of **group dynamics** focuses on the nature of groups—the variables governing their formation and development, their structure, and their interrelationships with individuals, other groups, and the organizations within which they exist.[1] Because groups exist in all types of social settings, the study of group dynamics has a long history in the social sciences—including OB.[2]

In the first half of this chapter, we will draw on this work. Specifically, we will describe the nature of groups by defining what groups are, identifying various types of groups and why they form, explaining the various stages through which groups develop, and describing the dynamics of the way groups are structured. Following this, we shift our attention to how effectively groups operate. Specifically, we will describe how people are affected by the presence of others, and the tendency for people to withhold their individual performance under certain conditions. Finally, in the second half of this chapter, we focus on *teams*, special types of groups that are in widespread use in today's organizations. After differentiating between groups and teams, we describe the factors that make teams effective along with ways to promote team success in the workplace.

Groups at Work: Their Basic Nature

To understand the dynamics of groups and their influence on individual and organizational functioning, we begin by addressing three fundamental issues—namely, what groups are, the types of groups that exist, and why people join groups.

What Is a Group?

Imagine three people waiting in a checkout line at a supermarket. Now, compare them to the board of directors of a large corporation. Which collection of individuals would you consider to be a "group"? Although in our everyday language we may refer to the people waiting in line as a group, they clearly are not a group in the same sense as the members of the board. Obviously, a group is more than simply a collection of people. But what exactly is it that makes a group a group?

Formally, social scientists define a **group** as a collection of two or more interacting individuals with a stable pattern of relationships between them who share common goals and who perceive themselves as being a group.[3] Examining this definition more closely, we summarize the four key characteristics of groups in Figure 8.1. To be considered a group, the collection of people in question must satisfy all four of these criteria.

group dynamics
Factors governing a group's formation and development, structure, and interrelationships with individuals, other groups, and the organizations within which it exists.

group
A collection of two or more interacting individuals who maintain stable patterns of relationships, share common goals, and perceive themselves as being a group.

- ☑ Two or more people in social interaction
- ☑ Stable structure
- ☑ Members share common goals
- ☑ Members perceive themselves as being a group

Nonmembers

Members

GROUP

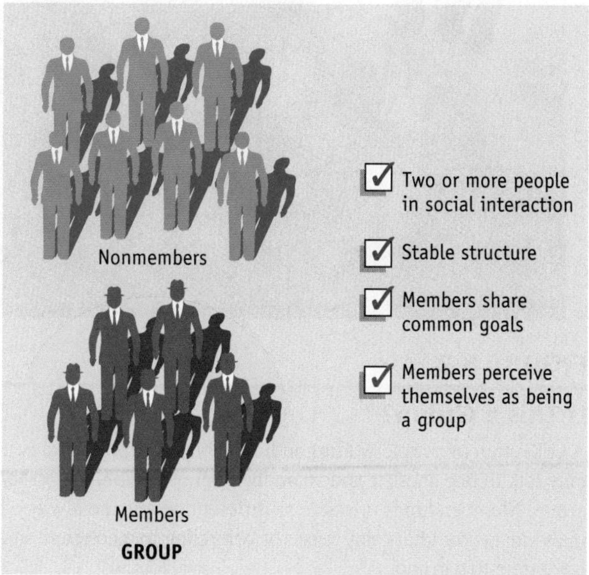

FIGURE 8.1

A Group: Its Defining Characteristics

To be a group, the four criteria specified here must be met.

SOCIAL INTERACTION.   One of the most obvious characteristics of groups is that they are composed of *two or more people in social interaction.* In other words, the members of a group must have some influence on one another. The interaction between the parties may be either verbal (such as sharing strategies for a corporate takeover) or nonverbal (such as exchanging smiles in the hallway), but the parties must have some impact on one another to be considered a group.

STABILITY.   Groups also must possess a relatively *stable structure.* Although groups can change, and often do, they must have some stable relationships that keep members together and functioning as a unit. A collection of individuals that constantly changes (e.g., the people inside an office waiting room at any given time) may not be considered a group, for example, because the set of people involved is unstable, changing all the time.

COMMON INTERESTS OR GOALS.   A third characteristic of groups is that *members share common interests or goals.* For example, members of a chess club constitute a group that is sustained by the mutual interest of members. Some groups form because members with common interests help each other achieve a mutual goal. For example, the owners and employees of a sewing co-op constitute a group formed around a common interest in sewing and the common goal of making money.

RECOGNITION AS BEING A GROUP.   Finally, to be a group, the individuals involved must *perceive themselves as a group.* Groups are composed of people who recognize one another as members of their group and can distinguish these individuals from nonmembers. The members of a corporate finance committee or a camera club, for example, know who is in their group and who is not. In contrast, shoppers in a checkout line probably don't think of each other as being members of a group. Although they stand physically close to one another and may have passing conversations, they have little in common (except, perhaps, a shared interest in reaching the end of the line) and fail to identify with the others in the line.

By defining groups in terms of these four characteristics, we have identified a group as a very special collection of individuals (see Figure 8.2). As we shall see, these characteristics are

FIGURE 8.2

Is This a Group?

A collection of people waiting in line to buy an Apple iPad is not considered a group. Although the people may talk to one another and share the goal of wanting to get the latest hot product, they are not considered a group. Membership is unstable as different people are always entering and leaving the line. In addition, the individuals don't have any sense of belonging to a coherent unit and, as a result, don't think of themselves as belonging to a group.

responsible for the important effects groups have on organizational behavior. To better understand these effects, we now review the wide variety of groups that operate within organizations.

What Types of Groups Exist?

What do the following have in common: a military combat unit, three couples getting together for dinner, the board of directors of a large corporation, and the three-person cockpit crew of a commercial airliner? As you probably guessed, the answer is that they are all groups. But, of course, they are very different kinds of groups, ones people join for different reasons.

FORMAL GROUPS. The most basic way of identifying types of groups is to distinguish between *formal groups* and *informal groups* (see Figure 8.3). **Formal groups** are created by an organization and are designed intentionally to direct members toward some important organizational goal. One type of formal group is referred to as a **command group**—a group created by connections between individuals who are a formal part of the organization (i.e., those who legitimately can give orders to others). For example, a command group may be formed by the vice president of marketing who gathers together the regional marketing directors from around the country to share ideas about a new national advertising campaign. The point is that command groups are determined by the organization's rules regarding who reports to whom, and usually consist of a supervisor and his or her subordinates.

A formal organizational group also may be formed around some specific task. Such a group is referred to as a **task group.** Unlike command groups, a task group is composed of individuals with some special interest or expertise in a specific area regardless of their positions in the organizational hierarchy. For example, a company may have a committee on equal employment opportunities whose members monitor the fair hiring practices of the organization. It may be composed of personnel specialists, corporate vice presidents, and workers from the shop floor. Whether they are permanent committees, known as **standing committees** or temporary ones formed for special purposes (such as a committee formed to recommend solutions to a parking problem), known as **ad hoc committees** or **task forces,** task groups are common in organizations.

INFORMAL GROUPS. As you know, not all groups found in organizations are as formal as those we've identified. Many groups are informal in nature. **Informal groups** develop naturally among an organization's personnel without any direction from the management of the organization within which they operate. One key factor in the formation of informal groups is a common interest shared by members. For example, a group of similar employees (e.g., members of a particular racial or ethnic group) who get together to share ideas about how to advance within the company may be called an **interest group.** The common goal sought by members of an interest group may unite workers at different organizational levels. The central idea is that membership in an interest group is voluntary—it is not created by the organization, but develops naturally based on common interests.

Of course, sometimes the interests that bind individuals together are diffuse in nature. For example, groups may develop out of a common interest in participating in sports, or going to the movies, or just getting together to talk. These kinds of informal groups are known as **friendship groups.** A group of coworkers who hang out together during lunch may also bowl or play cards

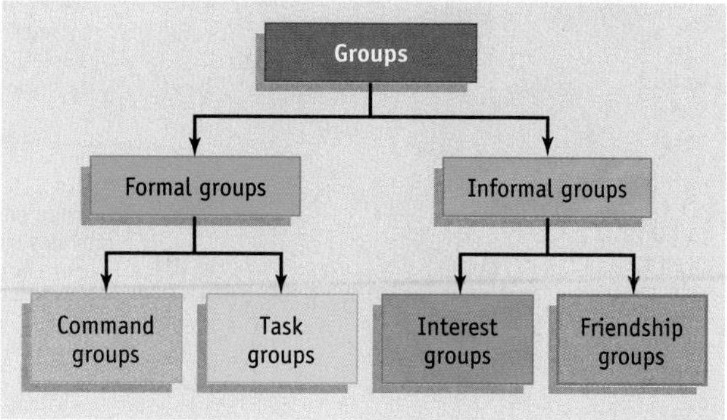

formal groups
Groups that are created by the organization, intentionally designed to direct its members toward some organizational goal.

command group
A group created by connections between individuals who are a formal part of the organization (i.e., those who legitimately can give orders to others).

task group
A formal organizational group formed around some specific task.

standing committees
Committees that are permanent, existing over time.

ad hoc committee
A temporary committee formed for a special purpose.

task force
See *ad hoc committee.*

informal groups
Groups that develop naturally among people, without any direction from the organization within which they operate.

interest group
A group of employees who come together to satisfy a common interest.

friendship groups
Informal groups that develop because their members are friends, often seeing each other outside of the organization.

FIGURE 8.3

Varieties of Groups in Organizations

Within organizations one may find *formal* groups (such as *command groups* and *task groups*) and *informal groups* (such as *interest groups* and *friendship groups*).

together after work. Friendship groups extend beyond the workplace because they provide opportunities for satisfying the social needs of workers, which are key to their well-being.

Informal work groups are an important part of life in organizations. Although they develop without intervention from management, friendships often originate out of formal organizational contact. For example, three employees working alongside each other on an assembly line may get to talking and discover their mutual interest in basketball, and decide to get together to shoot hoops after work. As we will see in Chapter 11, friendships can bind people together, helping them cooperate with one another, having beneficial effects on organizational functioning.

Why Do People Join Groups?

We already have noted that people often join groups to satisfy their mutual interests and goals. To the extent that getting together with others allows us to achieve ends that would not be possible alone, forming groups makes a great deal of sense. In fact, organizations can be thought of as collections of groups that are focused toward attaining the mutual goal of achieving success for the company. But this is not peoples' only motivation for joining groups. There are also several additional reasons (see the summary in Figure 8.4).

Not only do groups form for purposes of mutually achieving goals, they also frequently form for purposes of seeking protection from other groups. If you've ever heard the phrase "there's safety in numbers," you know what we mean. People sometimes join groups because they seek the security of group membership. Historically, for example, trade unions such as the AFL/CIO, the UAW, and the Teamsters have been created by labor to seek protection against abuses by management. Similarly, professional associations such as the American Medical Association and the American Bar Association were created, in large part, for purposes of protecting their members against undesirable governmental legislation.

This is not to say that groups always are designed to promote some instrumental good; they also exist because they appeal to a basic psychological need to be social (recall our discussion of needs in Chapter 7). People are social animals; they have a basic need to affiliate with others. Groups provide good opportunities for friendships to develop—hence, for social needs to be fulfilled.

FIGURE 8.4

Why Do People Join Groups?

People join groups for many different reasons. Four of the most important reasons are identified and explained here.

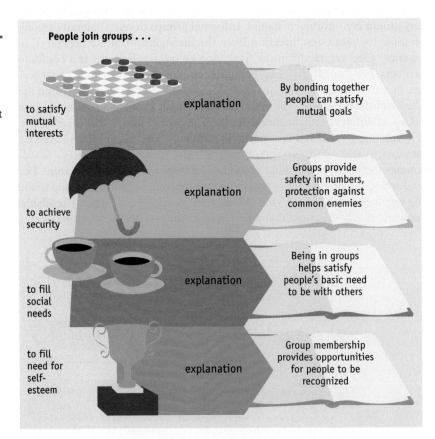

People join groups . . .

to satisfy mutual interests	explanation	By bonding together people can satisfy mutual goals
to achieve security	explanation	Groups provide safety in numbers, protection against common enemies
to fill social needs	explanation	Being in groups helps satisfy people's basic need to be with others
to fill need for self-esteem	explanation	Group membership provides opportunities for people to be recognized

People have a basic desire for self-esteem, to feel good about themselves. Group memberships can be a very effective way of nurturing self-esteem. For example, if a group to which one belongs is successful (such as a sales group that meets its quota), the self-esteem of all members (and supporters) is likely to be boosted. Similarly, election to membership in an exclusive group (e.g., a national honor society) will surely raise one's self-esteem.

As we have indicated, people are attracted to groups for a variety of different reasons. Although people may have different motivations for joining groups, once they are formed, groups develop in remarkably similar ways. We now examine this issue.

The Formation of Groups

As you might imagine, groups don't simply emerge out of thin air. Scientists have observed that groups form in systematic fashion. Specifically, they have proposed two particular conceptualizations of how groups are formed to which we now turn our attention.

The Five-Stage Model of Group Formation

One popular way of explaining how people form groups involves examining the various stages through which groups develop. Just as infants develop in certain ways during their first months of life, groups also show relatively stable signs of maturation and development.[4] One popular approach, the **five-stage model of group formation,** identifies five distinct stages through which groups develop.[5] As we describe these stages, please refer to the summary in Figure 8.5.

STAGE 1: FORMING. The first stage of group development is known as *forming.* During this stage, members get acquainted with each other. They establish the ground rules by trying to find out what behaviors are acceptable with respect to both the job (how productive they are expected to be) and interpersonal relations (who's really in charge). During the forming stage, people are a bit confused and uncertain about how to act in the group and how beneficial it will be to become a member of the group. Once the individuals come to think of themselves as members of a group, the forming stage is complete.

STAGE 2: STORMING. The second stage of group development is referred to as *storming.* As the name implies, this stage is characterized by a high degree of conflict within the group. Members often resist the control of the group's leaders and show hostility toward each other. If these conflicts are not resolved and group members withdraw, the group may disband. However, as conflicts are resolved and the group's leadership is accepted, the storming stage is complete.

STAGE 3: NORMING. The third stage of group development is known as *norming.* During this stage, the group becomes more cohesive, and members begin to identify more strongly with it.

five-stage model of group formation
The conceptualization claiming that groups develop in five stages— forming, storming, norming, performing, and adjourning.

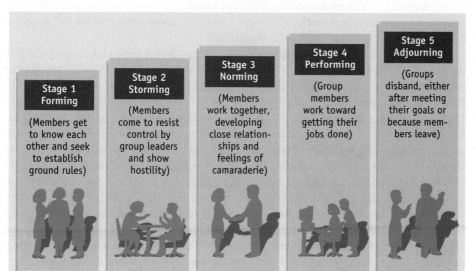

FIGURE 8.5

The Five Stage-Model of Group Development

In general, groups develop according to the five stages summarized here.

Source: Based on information in Tuckman & Jensen, 1977; see Note 5.

Close relationships develop, shared feelings become common, and a keen interest in finding mutually agreeable solutions develops. Feelings of camaraderie and shared responsibility for the group's activities are heightened. The norming stage is complete when the members of the group accept a common set of expectations about how to do things.

STAGE 4: PERFORMING. The fourth stage of group development is known as *performing*. During this stage, questions about group relationships and leadership have been resolved and the group is ready to work. Having fully developed, the group now devotes energy to getting the job done. The group's good relations and acceptance of the leadership help it perform well.

STAGE 5: ADJOURNING. Recognizing that not all groups last forever, the final stage is known as *adjourning*. Groups may cease to exist because they have met their goals and are no longer needed (such as an ad hoc group created to raise money for a charity project), in which case the end is abrupt. Other groups may adjourn gradually as the group disintegrates, either because members leave or because the norms that have developed are no longer effective for the group.

EXAMPLE. To illustrate these various stages, imagine that you just joined several of your colleagues on your company's newly created budget committee. At first, you and your associates feel each other out: You watch to see who comes up with the best ideas, whose suggestions are most widely accepted, who seems to take charge, and the like (the forming stage). Then, as members struggle to gain influence over others, you see a battle over control of the committee (the storming stage). Soon, this is resolved, and an accepted leader emerges. At this stage, group members become highly cooperative, work together in harmony and do things together, such as go out to lunch as a group (the norming stage). Now, it becomes possible for committee members to work together at doing their best, giving it their all (the performing stage). Then, once the budget is created and approved, the group's task is over, and it disbands (the adjourning stage).

It is important to keep in mind that groups may be in any one stage of development at a given time. Moreover, the amount of time a group may spend in a particular stage is highly variable. In fact, some groups may fail long before they have had a chance to work together. Research has revealed that the boundaries between the various stages may not be clearly distinct, and that several stages may be combined, especially as deadline pressures force groups to take action.[6] It is best, then, to think of this five-stage model as a general framework rather than a specific set of requirements. Although many of the stages may be followed, the dynamic nature of groups makes it unlikely that they will progress through all of the stages in a completely predictable order.

The Punctuated-Equilibrium Model

Not all scientists agree that groups develop in the order identified in the five-stage model. In fact, it has been argued that although there may not be a universal sequence of stages, there are some remarkable consistencies in the ways groups form and change. These patterns are described in what's known as the **punctuated-equilibrium model.** This approach to group formation recognizes that group members working to meet a deadline approach their task differently in the first half of their time together than in the second half.[7]

During the first half of the time, *phase 1,* groups define their task, setting a mission that is unlikely to change until the second half of the group's life. Even if group members have new ideas, these are generally not acted on. Interestingly, as soon as groups reach the midpoints of their lives (whether this is just a few hours or several months), something curious happens: Groups experience a sort of "midlife crisis"—a time when they recognize that they are going to have to change the way they operate if they are going to meet their goals. This begins *phase 2* of their existence—a time when groups drop old ways of thinking and adopt new perspectives. Groups then carry out these missions until they reach the end of phase 2, when they show bursts of activity needed to complete their work. For a summary of these processes, see Figure 8.6.

The idea is straightforward: Groups develop inertia, which keeps them going (i.e., an "equilibrium") until the halfway point, when they realize that deadlines loom large. This stimulates them to confront important issues and to initiate changes, beginning (i.e., "punctuating") a new equilibrium phase. This phase lasts until the group kicks into a final push just before the deadline. Although the punctuated-equilibrium model is relatively new, studies suggest that it does a good job of describing how groups develop.[8]

punctuated-equilibrium model
The conceptualization of group development claiming that groups generally plan their activities during the first half of their time together, and then revise and implement their plans in the second half.

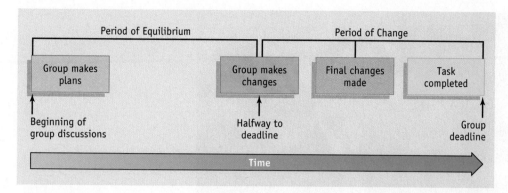

FIGURE 8.6

The Punctuated-Equilibrium Model

According to the punctuated-equilibrium model, groups go through two stages marked by the midpoint of the group's time together. The first half is a period of equilibrium, in which the group makes plans, but accomplishes little. During the second half, group members make changes that lead them to accomplish the group's task as the deadline approaches.

Source: Based on suggestions by Gersick, 1989; see Note 7.

To illustrate the punctuated-equilibrium model, consider what might occur in a group of people working to elect a political candidate. When the group first meets, one January, the members get to know each other and plan their campaign strategy. They figure out what they have to do in the 10 months that follow to get their candidate into office, and they spring into action. Then, by May or June, it becomes clear that there are problems, and the original plan needs to be changed. People working on the campaign begin taking critical looks at what they've been doing and take active steps to change things. This continues through October. Then, in the weeks or days right before the November election, the group will meet for a long time and make its final push. You might find it interesting to compare this scenario to your own experiences working with others in groups (e.g., on class projects).

The Structural Dynamics of Work Groups

As noted earlier, one of the key characteristics of a group is its stable structure. When social scientists use the term **group structure,** they are referring to the interrelationships between the individuals constituting a group, the characteristics that make group functioning orderly and predictable. In this section, we will describe four different aspects of group structure: the various parts played by group members (*roles*), the informal rules and expectations that develop within groups (*norms*), the prestige of group membership (*status*), and members' senses of belonging to their groups (*cohesiveness*).

Roles: The Hats We Wear

Social scientists use the term *role* in much the same way as a director of a play would refer to the character who plays a part. Indeed, the specific part one plays in the overall group structure is what we mean by a role. More formally, we may define a **role** as the typical behaviors that characterize a person in a social context.[9] An individual in a group may play one or more specific roles.

In organizations, many roles are assigned by virtue of an individual's formal position within an organization. For example, a boss may be expected to give orders, and a teacher may be expected to lecture and to give exams. These are behaviors expected of the individual in a particular position (i.e., the person in that role). The person holding the role is known as a **role incumbent,** and the behaviors expected of that person are known as **role expectations.** The person holding the office of the president of the United States (the role incumbent) has certain role expectations simply because he or she currently holds that post. When a new president takes office, that individual assumes the same role and has the same formal powers as the previous president. This is the case although the new president may have very different ideas about key issues facing the nation. (As you might

group structure
The pattern of interrelationships between the individuals constituting a group; the guidelines of group behavior that make group functioning orderly and predictable.

role
The typical behavior that characterizes a person in a specific social context.

role incumbent
A person holding a particular role.

role expectations
The behaviors expected of someone in a particular role.

Ron Sachs/CNP/Newscom.

FIGURE 8.7

Cultural Differences in Roles

In Japan, the role of company president is largely symbolic. Unlike their American counterparts, presidents of Japanese companies are not usually the ones making key decisions. Like royalty, their roles are largely symbolic and they are highly revered. This is especially so for Toyota President Akio Toyoda, grandson of the company's founder, who has been groomed as a morale booster and consensus builder. Toyoda learned the hard way that Americans are largely unaware of his role in February 2010 when he testified before the U.S. House Committee on Oversight and Government Reform about faulty gas pedals on 8.5 million of his company's vehicles. Toyoda knew the lawmakers wouldn't be pleased, but he was unprepared for the confrontational barrage of questions he faced. He deferred to other executives who were better equipped to address the details of the defects and politely assumed his symbolic role by appologizing for the problem and providing his assurance that the esteemed "Toyota Way" would not fail again.

expect, the roles played by people in organizations are inclined to differ in various countries throughout the world; see Figure 8.7.)

The role incumbent's recognition of the expectations of his or her role helps avoid the disorganization that surely would result if no clear role expectations existed. Sometimes, however, workers are confused about what is expected of them on a job, such as their level of authority or their particular responsibilities. **Role ambiguity,** as this is called, typically is experienced by new members of organizations who have had only limited opportunities to "learn the ropes." High levels of role ambiguity often result in job dissatisfaction, a lack of commitment to the organization, and an interest in leaving the job (recall our discussion of these important outcomes in Chapter 6).[10]

As groups develop, their various members come to play different roles in the social structure—a process referred to as **role differentiation.** By definition, the division of people into various jobs constitutes role differentiation—different people perform different functions in an organization. In other words, role differentiation can occur on a formal basis in a work group.[11] This is not the only basis for role differentiation, however. Roles also may emerge as part of a naturally occurring process. For example, think of committees on which you may have served. Was there someone who joked and made people feel better, and perhaps another member who always worked hard to get the group to focus on the issue at hand? These examples of different roles are typical of role behaviors that emerge in groups. Organizations, for example, often have their "office comedian" who makes everyone laugh, or the "grand old man" who tells newcomers the stories about the company's "good old days."

In keeping with this, scientists have noted that many organizational roles are, in fact, differentiated in some pre-specified ways. For example, in any group there tends to be one person who, more than anyone else, helps the group reach its goal.[12] Such a person is said to play the **task-oriented role.** In addition, another group member may emerge who is quite supportive and nurturing, someone who makes everyone else feel good. Such a person (like Mr. Toyoda, described

role ambiguity
Confusion arising from not knowing what one is expected to do as the holder of a role.

role differentiation
The tendency for various specialized roles to emerge as groups develop.

task-oriented role
The activities of an individual in a group who, more than anyone else, helps the group reach its goal.

TABLE 8.1 Roles Commonly Played by Group Members

Organizational roles may be differentiated into *task-oriented roles, relations-oriented roles* (or *socioemotional roles*), and *self-oriented roles*—each of which has several subroles. Several of these are shown here.

Task-Oriented Roles	Relations-Oriented Roles	Self-Oriented Roles
Initiator-contributors	*Harmonizers*	*Blockers*
Recommend new solutions to group problems	Mediate group conflicts	Act stubborn and resistant to the group
Information seekers	*Compromisers*	*Recognition seekers*
Attempt to obtain the necessary facts	Shift own opinions to create group harmony	Call attention to their own achievements
Opinion givers	*Encouragers*	*Dominators*
Share own opinions with others	Praise and encourage others	Assert authority by manipulating the group
Energizers	*Expediters*	*Avoiders*
Stimulate the group into action whenever interest drops	Suggest ways the group can operate more smoothly	Maintain distance, isolate themselves from fellow group members

Source: Based on Benne & Sheats, 1948; see Note 12.

in the caption for Figure 8.7) is said to play a **relations-oriented role (socioemotional role)** Still others may be recognized for the things they do for themselves, often at the expense of their groups—individuals recognized for playing a **self-oriented role.** Many specific role behaviors fall into one or more of these categories. For a listing of some of the most common forms that these three types of roles long have been known to take, see Table 8.1.

Norms: A Group's Unspoken Rules

One feature of groups that enhances their orderly functioning is the existence of group *norms.* **Norms** may be defined as generally agreed-upon informal rules that guide group members' behavior.[13] They represent shared ways of viewing the world. Norms differ from organizational rules in that they are informal and unwritten. In fact, group members may not even be aware of the subtle group norms that exist and regulate their behavior. Yet norms have profound effects on what they do. Norms regulate the behavior of groups in important ways, such as by fostering workers' honesty and loyalty to the company, by establishing appropriate ways to dress, and by dictating when it is acceptable to be late or absent.

If you recall the pressures placed on you by your peers as you grew up to dress or wear your hair in certain styles, then you are well aware of the profound normative pressures exerted by groups. Some norms, known as **prescriptive norms,** dictate the behaviors that *should be performed.* Other norms, known as **proscriptive norms,** dictate specific behaviors that *should be avoided* (see Figure 8.8). For example, groups may develop prescriptive norms to follow their leaders or to help group members who need assistance. In addition, they may develop proscriptive norms to avoid absences or to refrain from telling each other's secrets to the boss.

Sometimes the pressure to conform to norms is subtle, as in the dirty looks given a manager by his peers for going to lunch with one of the assembly-line workers. This would be the case if norms prohibit fraternizing with people at lower organizational levels. Other times, normative pressures may be quite severe, such as when one production worker sabotages another's work because he is performing at too high a level, making his coworkers look bad. This would be the case if norms require working within certain ranges deemed acceptable. (Scientists first observed this particular norm in the Hawthorne studies described in Chapter 1.)

Although our examples emphasize the underlying social dynamics responsible for how groups develop norms, they illustrate only one reason. There are, in fact, several factors responsible for the formation of norms.[14] For a summary of these, see Table 8.2.

relations-oriented role (socioemotional role)
The activities of an individual in a group who is supportive and nurturing of other group members and who helps them feel good.

self-oriented role
The activities of an individual in a group who focuses on his or her own good, often at the expense of others.

norms
Generally agreed-upon informal rules that guide group members' behavior.

prescriptive norms
Expectations within groups regarding what is supposed to be done.

proscriptive norms
Expectations within groups regarding behaviors in which members are not supposed to engage.

FIGURE 8.8

Norms Dictate What to Do and Not to Do

Norms are informal rules about behaviors that are considered acceptable and unacceptable in groups. As illustrated here, it is not unusual for norms to be communicated explicitly in an effort to get others to conform to them.

PC Vey/Cartoonbank.

"Everybody's getting together after work to do some more work-- you in?"

Status: The Prestige of Group Membership

Have you ever been attracted to a group because of the prestige accorded its members? You may have wanted to join a particular fraternity or sorority because it is held in high esteem by other students. No doubt, members of championship-winning N.F.L. teams proudly sport their Super Bowl rings to identify themselves as members of that highly regarded team. Clearly, one potential reward of group membership is the status associated with being in that group. Even within groups, various members are accorded different levels of prestige. Fraternity and sorority officers and committee chairpersons, for example, are likely to be recognized as being among the most important members of their respective groups. This is the idea behind **status**—the relative social position or rank given to a social unit (e.g., an individual, group, or organization) by others.[15]

Within most organizations, status may be recognized as both formal and informal in nature. **Formal status** refers to attempts to differentiate between the degrees of formal authority given employees by their organizations. Typically, this is accomplished through the use of **status symbols**—objects reflecting the position of an individual within an organization's hierarchy. Some common examples of status symbols include job titles (e.g., director); perquisites, or perks (e.g., a reserved parking space); the opportunity to do desirable and highly regarded work (e.g., serving on important committees); and luxurious working conditions (e.g., a large, private office that is lavishly decorated).[16]

Status symbols help groups in many ways.[17] For one, status symbols remind organizational members of their relative positions in their companies' hierarchies, thereby reducing uncertainty and

status
The relative prestige, social position, or rank given to groups or individuals by others.

formal status
The prestige one has by virtue of his or her official position in an organization.

status symbols
Objects reflecting the position of any individual within an organization's hierarchy of power.

TABLE 8.2 Norms: How Do They Develop?

Group norms are likely to form for several different reasons. The major ones are summarized here.

Basis of Norm Development	Example
Precedents set over time	Seating location of each group member around a table
Carryovers from other situations	Professional standards of conduct
Explicit statements from others	Working a certain way because you are told "that's how we do it around here"
Critical events in group history	After the organization suffers a loss due to one person's divulging company secrets, a norm develops to maintain secrecy

Source: Based on Feldman, 1984; see Note 14.

providing stability to the social order (e.g., your small desk reminds you of your lower organizational rank). In addition, they provide assurance of the various rewards available to those who perform at a superior level (e.g., "maybe one day I'll have a reserved parking spot"). They also provide a sense of identification by reminding members of the group's values (e.g., a soldier's uniform may remind its wearer of his or her commitment to the nation). It is, therefore, not surprising that organizations do much to reinforce formal status through the use of status symbols.

Symbols of **informal status** within organizations are also widespread. These refer to the prestige accorded individuals with certain characteristics that are not formally recognized by the organization. For example, employees who are older and more experienced may be perceived as being higher in status by their coworkers. Those who have certain special skills (such as the home-run hitters on baseball teams) also may be regarded as having higher status than others. In some organizations, the lower value placed on the work of women and members of minority groups by some unenlightened individuals also can be considered an example of informal status in operation—albeit a highly dysfunctional and insulting one.[18]

informal status
The prestige accorded individuals with certain characteristics that are not formally recognized by the organization.

One of the best-established findings in the study of group dynamics is that higher-status people tend to be more influential than lower-status people. This phenomenon may be seen in a classic study of decision making in three-man bomber crews in old military aircraft.[19] After the crews had difficulty solving a problem, the experimenter planted clues to the solution with either a low-status group member (the tail gunner) or a high-status group member (the pilot). It was found that the solutions offered by the pilots were far more likely to be adopted than the same solutions presented by the tail gunners. Apparently, the greater status accorded the pilots (because they tended to be more experienced and held higher military ranks) was responsible for the greater influence they wielded.

Cohesiveness: Getting the Team Spirit

One obvious determinant of any group's structure is its **cohesiveness**—the strength of its members' desires to remain part of their groups. Highly cohesive work groups are ones in which members are attracted to each other, accept their groups' goals, and help work toward meeting them. In very incohesive groups, the members dislike each other and may even work at cross-purposes.[20] In essence, cohesiveness refers to a *we feeling,* an *esprit de corps,* a sense of belonging to a group.

cohesiveness
The strength of group members' desires to remain a part of their groups.

Several important factors influence the extent to which group members tend to "stick together." One such factor involves the severity of initiation into the group. Research has shown that the greater the difficulty people overcome to become a member of a group, the more cohesive the group will be.[21] To understand this, consider how highly cohesive certain groups may be that you have worked hard to join. Was it particularly difficult to "make the cut" on a sports team, fraternity, or sorority to which you belong? If so, the levels of cohesiveness in those groups are likely to be very high, making the members "tight" with one another, agreeing with each other and being highly loyal to the group. The rigorous requirements for gaining entry into elite groups, such as the most prestigious medical schools and military training schools, may well be responsible for the high degree of camaraderie found in such groups. Having "passed the test" tends to keep individuals together and separates them from those who are unwilling or unable to "pay the price of admission."

Group cohesion also tends to be strengthened under conditions of high external threat or competition. When groups face a "common enemy" they tend to draw together (see Figure 8.9). Such cohesion not only makes workers feel safer and better protected, but also aids them by encouraging them to work closely together and to coordinate their efforts toward the common enemy. Under such conditions, petty disagreements that may have caused dissension within groups tend to be put aside so that a coordinated attack on the enemy can be mobilized.

Research also has shown that the cohesiveness of groups is established by several additional factors.[22] For one, cohesiveness generally tends to be greater the more time group members spend together. Obviously, limited interaction cannot help but interfere with opportunities to develop bonds between group members. Similarly, cohesiveness tends to be greater in smaller groups. Generally speaking, groups that are too large make it difficult for members to interact and, therefore, for cohesiveness to reach a high level. Finally, because "nothing succeeds like success," groups with a history of success tend to be highly cohesive. It is often said that "everyone loves a winner," and the success of a group tends to help unite its members as they rally around their success. For this reason, employees tend to be loyal to successful companies.

Thus far, our discussion has implied that cohesiveness is a positive thing. Indeed, it can be. For example, people are known to enjoy belonging to highly cohesive groups. Members of

David Guttenfelder/AP Wide World.

FIGURE 8.9

Confronting Common Enemies Breeds Group Cohesiveness

Spc. Zachary Boyd (far left), was so eager to join his fellow platoon members in battling the Taliban in Afghanistan that he rushed to join them before getting a chance to cover his pink "I Love NY" boxer shorts with standard uniform pants. The tendency for groups to become highly cohesive as they work together to ward off common enemies is an established principle of group dynamics. This applies not only to military groups, such as these American soldiers, but also to groups in business organizations whose members face less physical (but no less hostile) battles against their own enemies.

closely knit work groups participate more fully in their group's activities, more readily accept their group's goals, and are absent from their jobs less often than members of less cohesive groups.[23] Not surprisingly, cohesive groups tend to work together quite well, are sometimes exceptionally productive, and have low levels of voluntary turnover.[24]

However, highly cohesive groups also can be problematic. For example, if a highly cohesive group's goals are contrary to the organization's goals, that group is in a position to inflict a great deal of harm by working against an organization's interests.[25] Highly cohesive group members who conspire to sabotage their employers are a good example. That same high level of focus that can help organizations when cohesion is high can be used against it when a group's interests run counter to those of the organizations within which they operate. With this in mind, it's important to recognize that when it comes to organizational performance, group cohesiveness is a double-edged sword: Its effects can be both helpful (if the group supports the organization) and harmful (if the group is against organization).

Individual Performance in Groups

Now that we have reviewed the basic nature of groups, we turn to an aspect of group dynamics that's especially relevant to the field of organizational behavior—the effects of groups on individual performance. Specifically, we will examine two different issues: how people's work performance is affected by the presence of others, and how it is affected by group size.

Social Facilitation: Working in the Presence of Others

Imagine that you have been studying drama for five years and you are now ready for your first acting audition in front of some Hollywood producers. You have been rehearsing diligently for several months, preparing for the part. Now you are no longer alone at home with your script in front of you. Your name is announced, and silence fills the auditorium as you take the stage. The spotlight hits you. How will you perform now that you are in front of an audience? Will you freeze, forgetting the lines you studied so diligently when you practiced alone? Or will the audience spur you on to your best performance yet? In other words, what impact will the presence of the audience have on your behavior?

After studying this question for a century using a variety of tasks and situations, social scientists found that the answer to this question is not straightforward.[26] Sometimes people perform better in the presence of others than when alone but at other times they perform better alone than in the presence of others. This tendency for the presence of others to enhance an individual's performance at times and to impair it at other times is known as **social facilitation.** (Although the word *facilitation* implies improvements in task performance, scientists use the term *social facilitation* to refer to both performance improvements and decrements stemming from the presence of others.) What accounts for these seemingly contradictory findings?

EXPLAINING SOCIAL FACILITATION. Many scientists believe the phenomenon boils down to several basic psychological processes.[27] First, social facilitation is the result of the heightened emotional arousal (e.g., feelings of tension and excitement) people experience when in the presence of others. (Wouldn't you feel more tension playing the piano in front of an audience than alone?) Second, when people are aroused, they tend to perform their most dominant response— that is, what they have learned most strongly to do in that setting. (Returning the smile of a smiling coworker may be considered an example of a dominant act; it is a very well learned act to smile at another who smiles at you.) If someone is performing a very well learned act, the dominant response would be a correct one (such as speaking the right lines during your 50th performance). However, if the behavior in question is relatively novel, newly learned, the dominant response would likely be incorrect (such as speaking incorrect lines during an audition).

Together, these ideas describe the **drive theory of social facilitation.**[28] According to this theory, the presence of others increases arousal, which increases the tendency to perform the most dominant responses. If these responses are correct, the resulting performance will be enhanced; if they are incorrect, the performance will be impaired. Based on these processes, performance may be either helped (if the task is well learned) or hindered (if the task is not well learned). (For a summary of this process see Figure 8.10.)

Research has shown considerable support for this theory: People perform better on tasks in the presence of others if that task is very well learned, but poorer if it is not well learned. Although there are several good explanations for this effect, a key one is based on the idea of **evaluation apprehension**—the fear of being evaluated or judged by another person.[29] Indeed, people may be aroused by performing a task in the presence of others because of their concern over what those

social facilitation
The tendency for the presence of others sometimes to enhance an individual's performance and at other times to impair it.

drive theory of social facilitation
The theory according to which the presence of others increases arousal, which increases people's tendencies to perform the dominant response. If that response is well learned, performance will improve. But if it is novel, performance will be impaired.

evaluation apprehension
The fear of being evaluated or judged by another person.

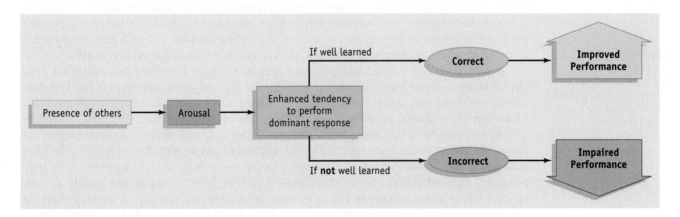

FIGURE 8.10

The Drive Theory of Social Facilitation

According to the drive theory of social facilitation, the presence of others is arousing. This, in turn, enhances the tendency to perform the most dominant (i.e., strongest) responses. If these are correct (such as if the task is well learned), then performance will be improved. However, if these are incorrect (such as if the task is novel), then performance will suffer.

others might think of them. For example, lower-level employees may suffer evaluation apprehension when they are worried about what their supervisors think of their work.

Similarly, in the example that opened this section of the chapter, you may face evaluation apprehension in your big acting audition. After all, what the producers think of you will go a long way in determining the success of your career. Applying the drive theory of social facilitation to this situation, if you know the part well, you will perform better at the audition than when rehearsing alone. You will be driven "to shine" for this important audience and rise to the occasion. However, if the part is new to you and you can't quite get the hang of it, fear of what these important others will think of you will interfere with your performance. Unfortunately, this will lead you to blow this big opportunity.

computerized performance monitoring
The process of using computers to monitor job performance.

SOCIAL LOAFING IN COMPUTER-MONITORED GROUPS. Given the widespread use of computers in today's workplaces, it's not unusual for the presence of others to be "virtual" rather than physical in nature. That is, instead of having an individual who is physically present to observe one's work, **computerized performance monitoring** makes it possible to watch over others indirectly, by computer—an "electronic presence." Imagine, for example, that you are entering data into a computer terminal. You may be monitored in a direct physical way by an individual looking over your shoulder, or indirectly by someone checking a computerized record of the speed and accuracy of your every keystroke. According to the drive theory of social facilitation, if the task being performed is complex, errors are likely, leading the physical presence of an observer to lower performance. But what if the others' presence is virtual in nature? Does the same thing occur? Research has shown that the answer is yes: Social facilitation occurs even when the "other person" is present only electronically.[30] If the job allows you to be monitored via computer then knowing that a supervisor is observing you appears to trigger evaluation apprehension just as if his or her presence were physical in nature.

From a practical perspective, this is important because it suggests that the practice of monitoring job performance to keep performance levels high may backfire.[31] That is, instead of causing people to improve their performance, monitoring actually might interfere with performance. Accordingly, if "Big Brother" is watching over workers to ensure that they are performing well, he just might be defeating his own purpose. This is not to say that performance monitoring always is harmful (indeed, see our discussion in Chapter 9). However, it's important to note that the "virtual presence" of others sometimes may have unintended negative effects when it comes to performance on tasks that are not well learned.

Social Loafing: "Free Riding" When Working with Others

Have you ever worked with several others helping a friend move into a new apartment, each carrying part of the load from the old place to the new one? Or, have you ever sat around a table with others stuffing political campaign letters into envelopes and addressing them to potential donors? Although these tasks are surely quite different in many ways, they share an important common characteristic: Each requires only a single individual to perform it, but several people's work can be pooled to yield greater outcomes. Reflecting the idea that each person's contributions can be added together with another's, such activities are known as **additive tasks.**[32]

additive tasks
Types of group tasks in which the coordinated efforts of several people are added together to form the group's product.

If you've ever performed additive tasks such as the ones described here, there's a good chance that you found yourself working not quite as hard as you would have if you had done them alone. Does this sound familiar to you? Indeed, a considerable amount of research has found that when several people combine their efforts on additive tasks, each individual contributes less than he or she would when performing the same task alone.[33] As suggested by the old saying "Many hands make light the work," a group of people would be expected to be more productive than any one individual. However, when several people combine their efforts on additive tasks, each individual's contribution tends to be less. In other words, five people working together raking leaves will *not* be five times more productive than one person working alone. As you probably know from personal experience, there are likely to be some individuals who go along for a "free ride." In fact, the more individuals who are contributing to an additive task, the less each individual's contribution tends to be—a phenomenon known as **social loafing.**[34]

social loafing
The tendency for group members to exert less individual effort on an additive task as the size of the group increases.

This effect was first noted 100 years ago by the engineer Maximilien Ringelmann, who compared the amount of force exerted by different-sized groups of people pulling on a rope.[35] Specifically, he found that one person pulling on a rope alone exerted an average of 63 kilograms of force. However, in groups of three, the per-person force dropped to 53 kilograms, and in groups of eight it was reduced to only 31 kilograms per person—less than half the effort exerted by

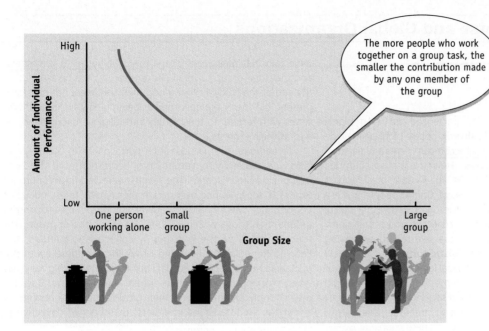

FIGURE 8.11

Social Loafing: Its General Form

According to the social loafing effect, when individuals work together on an additive task, the more people contributing to the group's task, the less effort each individual exerts.

people working alone! As more people pulled the rope, the total force exerted by the group as a whole rose but the average force exerted per person dropped. Social loafing effects of this type have been observed in many different studies conducted not only a century ago, but in recent years as well.[36] The general form of the social loafing effect is shown in Figure 8.11.

The phenomenon of social loafing has been explained by **social impact theory.**[37] According to this theory, the impact of any social force acting on a group is divided among its members. The larger the size of the group, the lower the impact of its force on any one member. As a result, the more people who might contribute to a group's product, the less pressure each person faces to perform well—that is, the responsibility for doing the job is diffused over more people. As a result, each group member feels less responsible for behaving appropriately, and social loafing occurs. Another way to understand this is by recognizing that social loafing occurs because people are more interested in themselves (getting the most for themselves while doing the least) than their fellow group members (who are forced to do their work for them). (As you might imagine, however, people in all countries throughout the world are not equally predisposed to think this way. For a look at research investigating this possibility, see the Today's Diverse and Global Organizations section on page 266.)

social impact theory
The theory that explains social loafing in terms of the diffused responsibility for doing what is expected of each member of a group (see *social loafing*). The larger the size of a group, the less each member is influenced by the social forces acting on the group.

OVERCOMING SOCIAL LOAFING. Obviously, the tendency for people to reduce their effort when working with others could be a serious problem in organizations. Fortunately, research has shown that there are several ways in which social loafing may be overcome.

1. *Make each performer identifiable.* Social loafing occurs when people feel they can get away with "taking it easy"—namely, under conditions in which each individual's contributions cannot be determined. However, it is unlikely to occur when individual performers are identified. A variety of studies on the practice of *public posting* support this idea.[38] This research has found that when each individual's contribution to a task is displayed where it can be seen by others (e.g., weekly sales figures posted on a chart), people are less likely to slack off than when only overall group (or company-wide) performance is made available. In other words, the more one's individual contribution to a group effort is highlighted, the more pressure each person feels to make a group contribution. Thus, social loafing can be overcome if one's contributions to an additive task are identified: Potential loafers are unlikely to loaf if they fear getting caught.

2. *Emphasize the importance of the work.* Research has revealed that people also are unlikely to go along for free rides when the tasks they are performing are believed to be vital to their organizations.[39] For example, research has found that the less meaningful salespeople believe their jobs are, the more they engage in social loafing—especially when they think their supervisors know little about how well they are working.[40] To help in this

Today's Diverse and Global Organizations

Is Social Loafing a Universal Phenomenon?

American culture has been characterized as being highly *individualistic*. In **individualistic cultures,** people highly value individual accomplishments and personal success. However, in other countries, such as Israel and the People's Republic of China, people place a high value on shared responsibility and the collective good of all. Such nations are referred to as having **collectivistic cultures.** If you think about social loafing in these terms, it makes sense that Americans would engage in social loafing because they are looking out for themselves.

individualistic cultures
National groups whose members place a high value on individual accomplishments and personal success.

collectivistic cultures
Cultures in which people place high value on shared responsibility and the collective good of all.

However, you wouldn't expect Israelis or Chinese people to do the same because in these cultures, social loafing would represent a failure of people's responsibilities to their groups. In fact, to the extent that people in collectivistic cultures are strongly motivated to help their fellow group members, they might even be expected to be *more* productive in groups than alone. That is, not only wouldn't they loaf, but they would work especially hard!

These ideas were tested in an interesting experiment involving managers from the United States, Israel, and the People's Republic of China.[41] Each group completed an exercise simulating the daily activities of managers in all three countries, such as writing memos, filling out forms, and rating job applicants. They were asked to perform this task as well as they could for a period of one hour under one of two randomly assigned conditions: either *alone,* or as part of a *group* of 10. Participants who worked alone were asked to write their names on each item they completed and to turn it in. In the group condition, participants were told that their work would be combined with the others' and that their group's overall performance would be assessed at the end of the study. Fellow group members were not physically present, but they were described as being highly similar to themselves with respect to their family and religious backgrounds as well as their interests.

To compare the groups, each participant's in-basket exercises were scored by converting his or her responses to standardized performance scores. The results were very interesting. As expected, social loafing occurred in the United States: Individual performance was significantly lower among people working in groups than those working alone. However, the opposite was found in each of the two highly collectivistic cultures, the People's Republic of China and Israel. In both these countries, managers not only failed to loaf, but performed at *higher* levels when working in groups than when working alone. Because they strongly identified with their groups and were concerned about the welfare of its members, members of collectivistic cultures placed their group's interests ahead of their own.

This research suggests that culture plays an important role in determining people's tendencies to engage in social loafing. Although it is tempting to think of social loafing as an inevitable aspect of human nature, that's not the case. Instead of being universal, social loafing occurs only in certain cultures. Among cultural groups in which individualism is stressed (e.g., Americans), individual interests guide performance, but among groups in which collectivism is stressed (e.g., Chinese and Israelis), group interests prevail and guide performance. This has interesting implications that are worth considering if you ever conduct business abroad.

If nothing else, these findings reinforce a key point we made in Chapter 1—namely, because culture influences behavior, it would be misleading to assume that people in other nations would respond to the same situations as you would. This doesn't make either one right or wrong, but as products of our respective cultures, just different.

---

regard, it would be useful for company officials to go out of their way to explain to employees the nature of the contributions they are making to their organizations (recall our discussion of task significance as a motivator, which we discussed in Chapter 7).

3. *Reward individuals for contributing to their group's performance.* Envision a situation in which each of the salespeople working in a territory are given a bonus if they jointly exceed a sales goal. In this situation, each person would benefit from the group's success, encouraging individual salespeople to contribute to their group's performance.[42] Individuals who are rewarded for their groups' successes are inclined to focus more on collective concerns and less on individualistic ones, enhancing their obligations to their fellow group members. This is important, of course, in that the success of an organization is more likely to be influenced by the collective efforts of groups than by the contributions of any one individual.

4. *Use punishment threats.* Social loafing is reduced when people believe they will be punished for slacking off. This was demonstrated in an experiment involving members of high school swim teams who swam either alone or in relay races during practice sessions.[43] In some conditions, the coach threatened the team by telling them that everyone would have to swim "penalty laps" if anyone on the team failed to meet a specified difficult time for swimming 100 meters freestyle. In a control group, no punishment threats were issued. The researchers found that people swam faster alone than as part of relay teams when no punishment was threatened, thereby confirming the social loafing effect. However, when punishment threats were made, group performance increased, thereby eliminating the social loafing effect.

Together, these findings suggest that social loafing is a potent force—and one that can pose a serious threat to organizational performance. Importantly, however, social loafing can be reduced in several ways that counteract the desire to loaf, such as by making loafing socially embarrassing or harmful to other individual interests.

Teams: Special Kinds of Groups

In recent years, as organizations have been striving to hone their competitive advantages, many have organized work around specific kinds of groups known as *teams*. Because the team movement frequently takes different forms and because the term "team" often is misused, some confusion has arisen regarding exactly what teams are. We address this here by clarifying the basic nature of teams. To do this we identify the various types of teams that exist and describe how teams form and develop. First, however, we begin by describing the key characteristics of teams, focusing on what distinguishes them from ordinary groups.

Defining Teams and Distinguishing Them from Groups

At the Miller Brewing Company in Trenton, Ohio, groups ranging from six to nineteen employees work together to perform all operations, including brewing, packaging, and distributing Miller Genuine Draft beer. They schedule their own work assignments and vacations, conduct assessments of their peers' performance, maintain the equipment, and perform other key functions. Each group is responsible for meeting prespecified targets for production, quality, and safety—and to help, data regarding costs and performance are made available to members.

Clearly, these groups differ in key respects from the ones we have been describing thus far. The particular ways in which they differ are in keeping with special kinds of groups known as *teams*. Formally, we define a **team** as a group whose members have complementary skills and are committed to a common purpose or set of performance goals for which they hold themselves mutually accountable. Given the unique nature of teams, we will highlight some of their key characteristics and distinguish teams from the traditional ways in which work is structured.[44] As you read these descriptions, you may find it useful to refer to the summary in Table 8.3.[45]

> **team**
> A group whose members have complementary skills and are committed to a common purpose or set of performance goals for which they hold themselves mutually accountable.

TEAMS ARE ORGANIZED AROUND WORK PROCESSES RATHER THAN FUNCTIONS. Instead of having traditional departments focusing on a specialized function (such as engineering, planning, quality control, and so on), it is likely that team members have many different skills and come together to perform key processes, such as designing and launching new products, manufacturing, and distribution. As an example, 3M used to have many separate departments working on various aspects of the manufacturing process. Today, all facets of production (e.g., ordering supplies, blending chemical formulations, scheduling work, etc.) are carried out by members of teams who work together on the production process.

TEAMS "OWN" THE PRODUCT, SERVICE, OR PROCESSES ON WHICH THEY WORK. By this, we mean that people feel part of something meaningful and understand how their work fits into the big picture (recall our discussion of the motivating properties of these kinds of beliefs described

TABLE 8.3 Groups Versus Teams

Teams differ from groups with respect to the six key distinctions identified here.

Groups	Teams
Design around functions.	Design around work processes.
No sense of ownership over the work products.	Ownership of products, services, or processes.
Workers have single skills.	Team members have many skills.
Outside leaders govern workers.	Team members govern themselves.
Support staff and skills are found outside the group.	Support staff and skills are built into teams.
Organizational decisions are made by managers.	Teams are involved in making organizational decisions for themselves.

Source: Adapted from Wellins R.S., Byham, W.C., & Dixon, G.R., (1994). *Inside Teams*. San Francisco: Jossey-Bass.

in Chapter 7). For example, employees at Florida's Cape Coral Hospital work in teams within four "minihospitals" (surgical, general, specialty medical, and outpatient)—not only to boost efficiency but also to help staff feel more responsible for their patients. By working in small units, team members have greater contact with patients and are more aware of the effects of their work on patient care. This is in contrast to the traditionally more distant ways of organizing hospital work, in which employees tend to feel less connected to the results of their actions.

MEMBERS OF TEAMS ARE TRAINED IN SEVERAL DIFFERENT AREAS AND HAVE A VARIETY OF DIFFERENT SKILLS. For example, at State Farm Insurance, business insurance policies are now processed by team members who rate applications, underwrite policies, and enter them into the computer system. Before the switch to teams, these three tasks were performed by specialists in three separate departments. In fact, this type of separation of tasks is typical within traditional work groups. Before the advent of work teams, it was usual for people to learn only single jobs and perform them over and over again unless there was some specific need for retraining (or interest in doing so on the part of the employee). In work teams, however, this practice of learning to perform a variety of different tasks, known as **cross-training,** occurs regularly.

Cross-training is an important aspect of what makes teams effective, and research suggests that this is based on the development of what are called **shared mental models.** These are areas of common understanding among team members regarding how their team operates, including how people are expected to work together and what each particular person is expected to do at any given time. Shared mental models help people understand how to coordinate their efforts with others and, of course, how to assist others who may need help (i.e., how to back them up). And, as you might expect, these particular skills contribute to team success. By contrast, people who are not cross-trained fail to develop any shared mental models with their teammates, thereby lowering the degree of coordination and capacity to help one another that is responsible for team success.

TEAMS GOVERN THEMSELVES—AT LEAST TO SOME EXTENT. Because team members tend to be so highly trained and involved in a variety of organizational activities, it often is unnecessary for them to be governed closely in the traditional top-down manner in which bosses supervise their subordinates. Instead, many team leaders serve as *coaches* who help team members achieve their goals rather than as traditional, more authoritarian leaders (see Chapter 13). In other words, teams are *empowered* to make decisions on their own behalf.

Here's a case in point. At the century-old company Mine Safety Appliances (based in Pittsburgh, Pennsylvania), members of global engineering teams located around the world join forces as they deem necessary to develop new devices (e.g., respirators and hard hats). Team members take turns as "captains," handling all the paperwork for a few weeks until the job is rotated to someone else. It is important to note that not all teams enjoy such total self-regulatory freedom. As you might imagine, because many company officials are reluctant to give up power (see Chapter 12), complete self-governance by teams is not always possible. Still, at least some degree of self-governance tends to occur in today's work teams.

IN TEAMS, SUPPORT STAFF AND RESPONSIBILITIES ARE BUILT IN. Traditionally, such functions as maintenance and human resources operate as separate departments that provide support to other groups requiring their services. Insofar as this often causes delays, teams often include members who have expertise in these crucial support areas. For example, at Clarks, the 175-year-old British footwear manufacturing firm, there are no longer any quality inspectors. Instead, all team members are trained in matters of inspection and quality control techniques. Sometimes, organizations hire people with highly advanced or specialized skills who are assigned to work as members of several teams at once. For example, this is done at Texas Instruments to give teams access to specialized engineering services. Regardless of how it's done, the point is that teams do not always rely on outside support services to get their jobs done; they are relatively self-contained and self-sufficient.

TEAMS ARE INVOLVED IN MAKING COMPANY-WIDE DECISIONS. Traditionally, it's only high-level managers who make important organizational decisions. In work teams, however, members often take on this responsibility themselves. For example, team members at Tennessee Eastman, a manufacturer of chemicals, fibers, and plastics, participate actively on company-level committees

cross-training
The practice of training team members in several different areas of expertise so that they are qualified to help their teammates by members performing a variety of tasks required for team success.

shared mental models
The common understanding that develops between team members regarding how their team operates, including how people are expected to work together and what each particular person is expected to do at any given time.

that develop policies and procedures affecting everyone. The underlying idea is that the people who are closest to the work performed are the ones most involved in making the decisions. As we noted earlier, the reluctance of some corporate leaders to completely empower teams may temper this process somewhat. In other words, although some companies may be reluctant to give teams total decision-making power, the granting of at least some decision-making authority is a hallmark of modern teams.

Teams are getting so much attention in the workplace these days that you'd almost think they are the latest management fad. But they are not. In fact, teams have been around for more than a century. For example, when Thomas Edison invented the electric lightbulb in 1879, he was part of a team of five scientists with different areas of expertise who joined forces. Apple's Macintosh computer was developed by a team headed by Steven Jobs, who along with other engineers worked together on the project for four years in the early 1980s. And, it also was a team at the advertising agency McCann Erickson that is credited with MasterCard's successful and popular "priceless" ad campaign.[46] With examples such as these as inspiration, it looks like teams are here to stay.

Types of Teams

In view of their popularity, it should not be surprising to learn that there are many different kinds of teams. To help make sense out of these, scientists have categorized teams into several different commonly found types, which vary along five major dimensions (see Figure 8.12).[47]

PURPOSE OR MISSION. The first dimension has to do with teams' major *purpose or mission*. In this regard, some teams—known as **work teams**—are primarily concerned with the work done by the organization, such as developing and manufacturing new products, providing services for customers, and so on. Their principal focus is on using the organization's resources to effectively create its results (be they goods or services). Other teams—known as

work teams
Teams whose members are concerned primarily with using the organization's resources to effectively create its results.

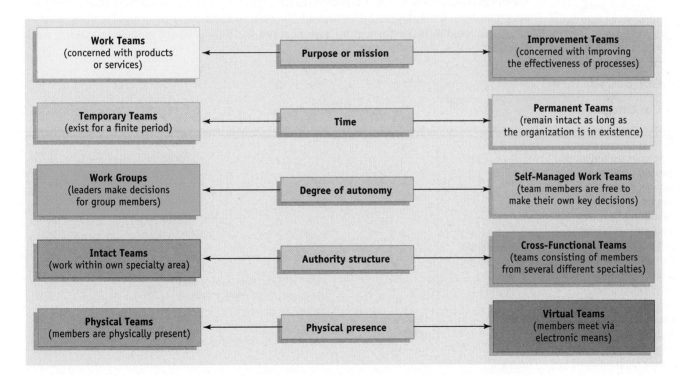

FIGURE 8.12

Types of Teams

The teams found in organizations may be distinguished from each other with respect to the five major dimensions identified here.

Source: Based on suggestions by Mohrman, 1993; see Note 47.

improvement teams
Teams whose members are oriented primarily toward the mission of increasing the effectiveness of the processes used by the organization.

semi-autonomous work groups
Work groups in which employees get to share in the responsibility for decisions with their bosses and are jointly accountable for their work outcomes.

self-managed work teams (self-directed teams)
Teams whose members are permitted to make key decisions about how their work is done.

improvement teams—are primarily oriented toward the mission of increasing the effectiveness of the processes that are used by the organization. For example, Texas Instruments has relied on teams to help improve the quality of operations at its plant in Malaysia.[48]

TIME. A second dimension has to do with *time*. Specifically, some teams are only *temporary* and are established for a specific project with a finite life. For example, a team set up to develop a new product would be considered temporary. As soon as its job is done, it disbands. However, other kinds of teams are *permanent* and stay intact as long as the organization is operating. For example, teams focusing on providing effective customer service tend to be permanent parts of many organizations.

DEGREE OF AUTONOMY. A third dimension has to do with the degree to which teams operate autonomously.[49] This reflects the extent to which employees are responsible for making their own decisions (as opposed to having their bosses make them) and the degree to which they (as opposed to their bosses) are accountable for their own work outcomes. As shown in Figure 8.13, various points along the resulting continuum of autonomy can be conceptualized as different types of groups or teams.

At the extreme low end of the scale (where bosses are responsible for decisions and accountable for work outcomes), we find standard *work groups*. Within these units, leaders make decisions on behalf of group members, who in turn, are responsible for following their leaders' orders. In recent years this traditional kind of group has waned in popularity as more organizations have granted employees higher degrees of responsibility for decisions and have made them more accountable for their outcomes. These are known as **semi-autonomous work groups**—collections of employees who get to share in the responsibility for decisions with their bosses and who are held jointly accountable for their work outcomes.

At the opposite end of the scale we find employees who are free to make their own key decisions and who are accountable for them. Such groups are commonly referred to as **self-managed work teams** (also known as **self-directed teams**). Typically, self-managed work teams consist of small numbers of employees, often around 10, who, in addition to their regular work, take on duties that used to be performed by their supervisors. This is likely to include making work

FIGURE 8.13

A Continuum of Autonomy

In *work groups*, bosses have responsibility over decisions and are accountable for work outcomes. The workers themselves have very little autonomy. By contrast, in *self-managed work teams*, the workers themselves have responsibility for decisions and are accountable for work outcomes. They are highly autonomous. *Semi-autonomous work groups* are positioned between these two extremes.

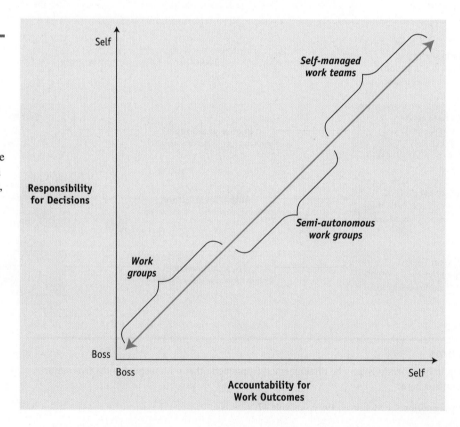

assignments, deciding on the pace of work, determining how quality is to be assessed, and even specifying who gets to join their teams.[50]

Self-managed work teams are growing in popularity. In fact, it has been estimated that close to 50 percent of companies have at least one team in place that is self-directed to at least some extent.[51] The list of companies using self-managed work teams includes many large corporations such as Xerox, Hewlett-Packard, Honeywell, PepsiCo, Procter & Gamble, Cummins Engine, and General Electric, which have used self-managed work teams for around 50 years.[52] All self-managed work teams are not alike. In fact, they differ considerably with respect to the specific aspects of the jobs they get to manage (for a summary, see Figure 8.14).[53] When you consider that different self-managed teams get to manage themselves to different degrees, it becomes clear why we depict the degree of autonomy in Figure 8.13 as a continuum.

AUTHORITY STRUCTURE. The fourth dimension reflects the team's connection to the organization's overall *authority structure*—that is, the connection between various formal job responsibilities. In some organizations, teams remain *intact* with respect to their organizational functions. For example, at Ralston-Purina projects are structured such that people work together on certain products all the time and do not apply their specialties to a wide range of products. Within such organizations, teams can operate without the ambiguities created when members stray from their areas of expertise.

With growing frequency, however, we are seeing teams that cross over various functional units (e.g., marketing, finance, human resources, and so on). Such teams are commonly referred to

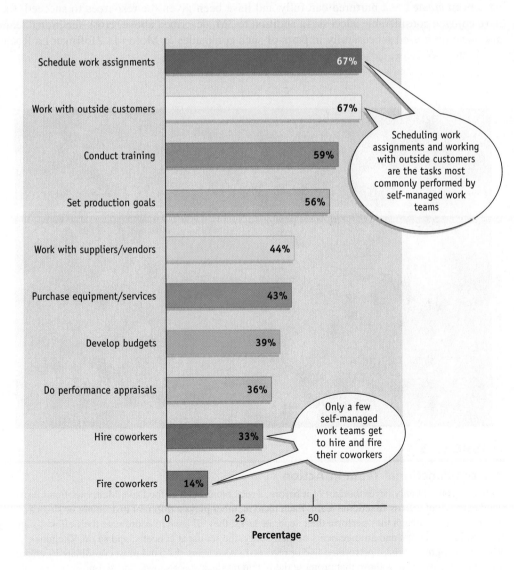

FIGURE 8.14

Self-Managed Work Teams: What Do They Manage?

As shown here, all self-managed work teams are not alike. Whereas the vast majority are able to schedule their own work assignments and to work with outside customers, far fewer are able to do other things, such as hire and fire coworkers.

Source: What Self-Managing Teams Manage. (1996, October). *Training*, p. 69.

**cross-functional
teams**
Teams represented by people from different specialty areas within organizations.

as **cross-functional teams.** These are teams composed of employees from different specialty areas who work together on tasks. Cross-functional teams represent an effective way of bringing people together from throughout an organization to cooperate with each other on the diverse tasks needed to complete large projects. A particularly good example of cross-functional teams may be found at 3M's Industrial Specialties Division.[54] Here, all product families (e.g., adhesives, fasteners, urethane films) are managed entirely by cross-functional teams that incorporate employees from the laboratory, manufacturing, and sales. Together, they are responsible for both the daily operation of the business and the development of new products.

In organizations using cross-functional teams, the boundaries between all teams must be considered permeable. Indeed, people frequently are members of more than one team—a situation often required for organizations to function effectively. For example, members of an organization's manufacturing team must carefully coordinate their activities with members of its marketing team. To the extent that people are involved in several different kinds of teams, they may gain broader perspectives and make more important contributions to their various teams (for another very different example, see Figure 8.15).

As you might imagine, cross-functional teams are difficult to manage. You can't simply throw together people from different units and expect them to be successful. It takes time for specialists in different areas to learn to communicate with each other and to coordinate their efforts. (In the case of Figure 8.15, for example, just any combination of musicians will not make a successful band.) It also takes time to develop the mutual trust and acceptance that is required for people to work closely with one another. However, where cross-functional teams have been created and nurtured carefully and have been given the resources to succeed, they have enjoyed considerable success. In addition to 3M, described above, cross-functional teams also have been used successfully in parts of such companies as Motorola, Hoffman La Roche, and Pratt & Whitney.[55]

Dana Edelson/NBCU Photo Bank/AP Wide World.

FIGURE 8.15

A Cross-Functional Team in Action

Although you probably never thought of it before, a rock band, such as the Dave Matthews Band, is a good example of a cross-functional team. Each band member plays a different instrument or sings a different part. Although they perform their separate tasks, they all have to coordinate their efforts, such as by deciding the tempo and arrangements of their songs, the set list at concerts, and so on. The music they make is their product (be it performed live or recorded). As a team, the band must coordinate its efforts with other teams, such as those that promote them, that produce stage shows, and so on.

PHYSICAL PRESENCE. The teams we have been describing thus far may be considered *physical teams* insofar as they involve people who physically meet to work together. Although teams have operated this way for many years, and surely will continue to do so, today's technology has made it possible for teams to exist without ever having their members physically meet. Teams of this sort are known as **virtual teams**—teams that operate across space, time, and organizational boundaries, communicating with each other predominantly through electronic technology.[56]

Sometimes, virtual teams form quite unintentionally, such as when valued team members begin telecommuting (the practice of working from home, but communicating via e-mail, which we described in Chapter 1). They also may be formed very deliberately, such as when it is important to bring together the most talented people in the world on a project.[57] Sun Microsystems did this, for example, when it developed a new electronic customer order system. The virtual team was composed of 15 engineers from three different companies in three different countries.[58] They worked together over a seven-month period without ever being together in the same room. Instead, intranets, teleconferencing, conference calls, and e-mails were used to enable team members to communicate with one another.

virtual teams
Teams that operate across space, time, and organizational boundaries, communicating with each other only through electronic technology.

Creating and Developing Teams: A Four-Stage Process

As you might imagine, assembling a team and keeping it going is no easy task. Doing so requires not only having the right combination of skilled people, but also individuals who are willing to work together with others as a team. When done properly, designing a work team involves the four distinct stages summarized in Figure 8.16.[59] Note that these processes occur before, during, and after teams are formed.

STAGE 1: PREWORK. Before teams are created, a decision has to be made about whether or not a team should be formed—a stage known as *prework*. One of the most important objectives of this phase is to determine whether a team should be created at all. A manager may decide to have several individuals working alone answer to him, or a team may be created if it is believed that it may develop the most creative and insightful ways to get things done. In considering this, it is important to note exactly what work needs to be created. The team's objectives must be established, and an inventory of the skills needed to do the job should be made. In addition, decisions should be made in advance about what authority the team should have. They may just be advisory to the manager, or they may be given full responsibility and authority for executing their task (i.e., self-regulating).

STAGE 2: CREATE PERFORMANCE CONDITIONS. Building on the prework, organizational officials must ensure that the team has the proper resources needed to carry out its work. This involves

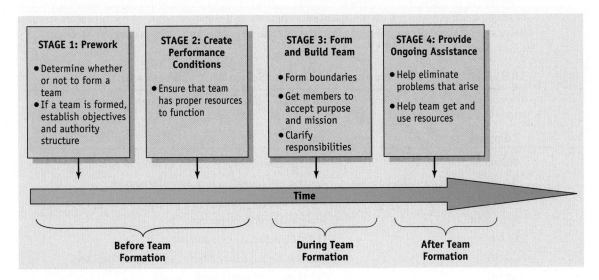

FIGURE 8.16

The Four Stages of Team Creation and Development

Successful teams are created and nurtured following the four steps summarized here.

Source: Based on suggestions by Hackman, 2002; see Note 57.

material resources (e.g., tools, equipment, and money), human resources (e.g., the appropriate blend of skilled professionals), and support from the organization (e.g., willingness to let the team do its own work as it sees fit). Unless managers help create the proper conditions for team success, like it or not, they are contributing to its failure.

STAGE 3: FORM AND BUILD THE TEAM. Three things may be done to help a team get off to a good start. First, managers should form boundaries—clearly establish who is and who is not a member of the team. Some teams fail simply because membership in it is left unclear. Reducing such ambiguity can help avoid confusion and frustration. Second, members must accept the team's overall mission and purpose. Unless they do, failure is inevitable. Third, organizational officials should clarify the team's mission and responsibilities—make perfectly clear exactly what it is expected to do (but not necessarily *how* to do it). Will team members be responsible for monitoring and planning their own work? If so, such expectations should be spelled out explicitly.

STAGE 4: PROVIDE ONGOING ASSISTANCE. Finally, once a team is functioning, supervisors may be needed to help the team eliminate problems and perform even better. For example, disruptive team members either may be counseled or replaced. Similarly, material resources may have to be replenished or upgraded. Although it may be unwise for a manager to intervene in the successful affairs of a team that has taken on its own life, it also may be unwise to neglect opportunities to help a team do even better.

As you ponder these suggestions, you doubtlessly will recognize the considerable managerial skill and hard work it takes to create and manage teams effectively. However, as managers learn these skills, and as individuals gain successful experiences as members of effective work teams, the four steps we outlined here are likely to become second nature. In the words of one expert, "When that stage is reached, the considerable investment required to learn how to use work teams well can pay substantial dividends—in work effectiveness and in the quality of the experience of both managers and [team] members."[60]

Effective Team Performance

In recent years, the popular press has been filled with impressive claims about the success of teams in improving quality, customer service, productivity, and the bottom line.[61] For a sampling of some findings cited, see Table 8.4.[62]

Clearly, we are led to believe that teams in general can produce very impressive results. However, it is important to consider whether or not such claims are valid. In this section, we will examine evidence bearing on this question. Then we will focus on some of the obstacles to team success, and some of the things that can be done to help promote highly successful teams.

TABLE 8.4 The Effectiveness of Teams: Some Impressive Results

Teams have helped many organizations enjoy dramatic gains in productivity. Here is a sampling of these impressive results.

Company	Result
Wilson Sporting Goods	Average annual cost savings of $5 million
Kodak Customer Assistance Center	Accuracy of responses increased 100 percent
Corning	Defects dropped from 1,800 parts-per-million (ppm) to 3 ppm
Sealed Air	Waste reduced by 50 percent
Exxon	$10 million saved in six months
Carrier	Unit turnaround reduced from two weeks to two days
Xerox	Productivity increased by 30 percent
Westinghouse	Product costs down 60 percent
Texas Instruments	Costs reduced by more than 50 percent

Sources: Based on information in Redding, 2000; and Blanchard & Bowles, 2001; see Note 61.

How Successful Are Teams?

The most straightforward way to learn about companies' experiences with work teams is to survey the officials of organizations that use them. One large-scale study did precisely this.[63] The sample consisted of several hundred of the 1,000 largest companies in the United States. About 47 percent used some work teams, although these were typically in place in only a few selected sites as opposed to the entire organization. Where they were used, however, they were generally successful, and in some instances the successes were dramatic. For example, using teams, FedEx was able to reduce incorrect billing errors by 13 percent in one year, Procter & Gamble was able to trim manufacturing costs by 30 to 50 percent, and companies such as General Electric, Best Foods, and Weyerhaeuser were able to boost production by more than 200 percent in some cases.

These impressive reports are further supported by in-depth case studies of numerous teams in many different organizations.[64] General Motors, for example, has used teams for many years. In 2010, as part of its financial reorganization plan, the company opened a new plant in Michigan, where they assemble battery packs for its electric car, the Chevy Volt. As in the conventional battery plants GM used to have, employees at the new facility operate in various teams. This includes managers working together in *support teams,* middle-level employees (e.g., technicians) working in *coordination teams,* and natural work units of various sizes performing specific tasks as members of *employee teams.* Although the teams work closely together, coordinating their activities, they function almost as separate businesses. By many measures, the traditional battery plant was very effective. Production was high, as was employee satisfaction. GE is hoping to match this level of success at its new facility.

Although case studies report successful experiences with teams, they are not entirely objective. After all, companies may be unwilling to broadcast their failures to the world. This suggests that more objective empirical research is needed. Overall, the results of such studies have been mixed. Some studies have shown that autonomous teams have significantly fewer accidents as well as lower rates of absenteeism and turnover than traditional work groups,[65] Other studies, however, have found that although many team members are satisfied with their arrangements, they are not any more productive than they were when working individually.[66]

So, what's the conclusion? Are teams effective? Taken together, research suggests that teams are well received. Most people enjoy working in teams, at least after they have adjusted to them (which can take some time and effort). Certainly, teams help enhance commitment among employees, and as we described in Chapter 6, there are benefits to be derived from this (e.g., reduced absenteeism and turnover). From an organizational perspective, teams appear to be an effective way of eliminating layers of management, thereby allowing more work to be done by fewer people, which also can be a valuable money-saving contribution. All of these benefits are tangible. However, it is important to keep in mind that teams do not always make individuals and organizations any more productive. Cases of companies becoming wildly successful after adopting teams, although compelling, cannot be generalized to all teams in all situations.

Potential Obstacles to Success: Why Some Teams Fail

Although we have reported many success stories about teams, we also have hinted at several possible problems and difficulties in implementing them. After all, working in a team demands a great deal, and not everyone is ready for them. Fortunately, we can learn from these experiences.[67] Analyses of failed attempts at introducing teams into the workplace suggest several obstacles to team success, pitfalls that can be avoided if you know them. We now discuss these.

UNWILLINGNESS TO COOPERATE. To begin, some teams fail because their members are unwilling to cooperate with one another. This is what happened once at Dow Chemical Company's plastics group in Midland, Michigan, where a team was put into place to create a new plastic resin.[68] Some members (those in the research field) wanted to spend several months developing and testing new options, while others (those on the manufacturing end) wanted to alter existing products slightly and start up production right away. Neither side budged, and the project eventually stalled. By contrast, when team members share a common vision and are committed to attaining it, they are generally very cooperative with each other, leading to success.

LACK OF MANAGEMENT SUPPORT. A second reason why some teams are not effective is that they fail to receive support from management. Consider, for example, the experience at the Lenexa, Kansas, plant of the Puritan-Bennett Corporation, a manufacturer of respiratory equipment for medical patients.[69] After seven years of working to develop improved software for its respirators, product development teams failed to get the job done despite the fact that it should have taken only three years. According to Puritan-Bennett's director of research and development, the problem was that company officials never made the project a priority and refused to free up another key person needed to do the job. As he put it, "If top management doesn't buy into the idea . . . teams can go nowhere."[70]

MANAGERS' RELUCTANCE TO RELINQUISH CONTROL. A third obstacle to group success, and a relatively common one, is that some managers are unwilling to relinquish control. Good supervisors work their way up from the plant floor by giving orders and having them followed. However, team leaders have to build consensus and must allow team members to make decisions together. As you might expect, yielding control isn't always easy for some to do. This was the problem some years back at Bausch & Lomb's sunglasses plant in Rochester, New York.[71] About 1,400 employees were put into 38 teams. After a few years, approximately half the supervisors failed to adjust to the change, despite receiving thorough training in how to work as part of a team. They argued bitterly with team members whenever their ideas were not accepted by the team, and eventually they were reassigned.

FAILURE TO COOPERATE BETWEEN TEAMS. Fourth, teams might fail not only because members do not cooperate with each other, but also because they fail to cooperate with other teams. This problem occurred in General Electric's medical systems division when it assigned two teams of engineers, one in Waukesha, Wisconsin, and another in Hino, Japan, the task of creating software for two new ultrasound devices.[72] Teams pushed features that made their products popular only in their own countries and duplicated each other's efforts. When teams met, language and cultural barriers separated them, further distancing the teams from one another. Without close cooperation between teams (as well as within them!), organizations are unlikely to reap the benefits they hoped for when creating teams in the first place.[73]

Developing Successful Teams

Making teams work effectively is no easy task. Success is not automatic. Rather, teams need to be carefully nurtured and maintained for them to accomplish their missions.[74] As one expert expressed it, "Teams are the Ferraris of work design. They're high performance but high maintenance and expensive."[75] What, then, could be done to help make teams as effective as possible? Based on analyses of successful teams, several keys to success may be identified, which we now describe.[76]

Compensate Team Performance

In general, people in the United States and Canada tend to be highly individualistic, making them most comfortable with compensation systems that recognize individual performance. However, when it comes to teams, it also is very important to recognize overall team performance. Teams are no places for hotshots who want to make their individual marks at the expense of the team; for them to be successful they need "team players." And the more organizations reward employees for their teams' successes, the more strongly team spirit will be reinforced. Several companies in which teams are widely used—including the Hannaford Brothers retail food distribution company in New York and Westinghouse's defense and commercial electronics plant in Texas—rely on **gain-sharing plans** to reward teams. These are plans that reward team members for reaching company-wide performance goals, allowing them to share in the company's profits.

gain-sharing plans
Compensation plans that reward team members for reaching company-wide performance goals, allowing them to share in their company's profits.

This is not to say that individual performance should be ignored. Indeed, research suggests that teams perform best when members are paid based both on how well they perform individually and how well their teams perform overall. This was determined in a recently conducted experiment in which college students performed a computer-based simulation game requiring them to coordinate their efforts carefully with others in their four-person teams.[77] The task required teams to gain access to enemy territories while also defending their own territories from invasions by enemy troops. Each team member was assigned to a particular job in his or her team, and they were told that many different teams would be playing the same game over the course of a semester. How they were paid was determined in one of three ways.

- In the "team pay" condition, each of the four top-performing teams would receive $160, with $40 paid to each member regardless of his or her individual contribution.
- In the "individual pay" condition, each of the four top-performing individuals in each of the four jobs would receive $40 regardless of how well their teams as a whole performed.
- In the "hybrid" condition, pay would be based on how well individuals performed their particular jobs compared to others in addition to how their teams performed as a whole.

Performance was assessed on the basis of how effective teams were at entering enemy territories while keeping enemies out of their own territories. Teams' scores were standardized so that they could be compared with one another, with higher scores representing superior overall performance. Figure 8.17 reveals performance across the three conditions. Specifically, teams given hybrid pay outperformed the other two. In fact, teams paid on an individual basis did least well since the system discouraged members from cooperating with one another, which was required for success at the task. It was found that people in the team pay condition engaged in social loafing (described earlier in this chapter). This makes sense considering that a lack of attention to individual contributions encouraged team members to "go along for the ride" by not doing their share of the work.

As a study conducted in the laboratory, this experiment reveals how things work, which is insightful, but it doesn't reveal anything about what organizations actually do. Fortunately, many companies recognize the potential pitfalls of pay systems oriented entirely toward individual performance or team performance and are using hybrid pay systems as a result. British Telecom is one such organization. Members of this company's network service team are paid bonuses that combine both their individual performance levels and the overall effectiveness of their teams on such key measures as their efficiency and the satisfaction of their customers.[78] (Our discussion of the most effective way to compensate teams raises a pair of related questions: What do members

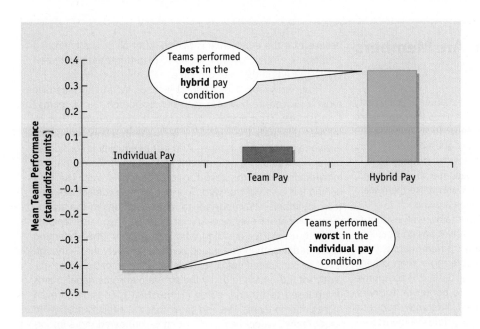

FIGURE 8.17

The Benefits of Hybrid Pay: An Experimental Demonstration

Should members of teams be paid based on their individual performance or on the overall success of their teams? Recent research has revealed that the answer is *both*. Teams in this study, whose members were paid using a hybrid system (i.e., taking into account both individual performance and overall team performance) performed significantly better than those whose members were paid based on individual performance or team performance alone.

Source: Based on data reported by Pearsall et al., 2010; see Note 76.

of teams believe constitutes a fair way to distribute reward within them? Also, what kinds of procedures do they believe constitute a fair way to determine those rewards? For a look at these issues, see The Ethics Angle section below.)

Finally, we note that because it's important for team members to have a variety of different skills, many companies are paying employees not only on the basis of how well they perform but on the breadth of their skills as well. Such a system is known as **skill-based pay.** A highly innovative skill-based pay system has been in use at Tennessee Eastman, for example. This company's "pay-for-applied-skills-and knowledge" plan (*PASK,* as it is known) requires employees to demonstrate their skills in several key areas, including technical skills and interpersonal skills. The pay scale is linked carefully to the number of skills acquired and the level of proficiency attained. By encouraging the development of vital skills in this manner, the company is ensuring that it has the resources for its teams to function effectively.

skill-based pay
Paying employees not only on the basis of how well they perform but on the breadth of their skills as well.

Recognize the Role of Team Leaders

When a sports team has a poor season, the coach is likely to be ousted, often to the delight of disappointed fans hoping for a turnaround. Similarly, executives of underperforming companies serving in periods of economic downturn also are likely to be removed from office, pleasing stockholders looking for greater returns on their investments. It would seem fair for the person at the top to pay for failure by leaving his or her post, and it would seem reasonable to expect that the ouster of the ineffective leader would bring an improvement as well. This follows from the idea that poor leaders may undermine the performance of even the most talented team members (be they athletes or employees in other industries), whereas exceptional leaders can bring out the best in team members and get them to perform at extremely high levels (see Chapter 13).

Despite their actual contributions, and the importance we accord them in society, it's important to acknowledge that leaders are only one determinant of a team's success. In fact, it's possible that

---

The Ethics Angle

Fairness in Teams: What Are Members Looking For?

Our references to justice and fairness (Chapter 2) and equity (Chapter 7) have focused on individuals. But given the importance of teams illustrated in this chapter, we must focus on justice in teams as well. In this connection, two key questions arise. First, what do team members believe constitutes distributive justice in teams (i.e., how rewards are divided between members)? Second, what procedures for determining those rewards make them seem fair? Research provides good insight into the answers.[79]

When it comes to paying individuals fairly, we've emphasized that an *equity* rule prevails. This involves paying people in proportion to their relative contributions, differentiating them from one another by giving some people more than others. When people are working on an individual basis, it is acceptable to pay more to better performers than to poorer performers. However, when people in teams are paid differently from one another, it encourages members to focus more on themselves than on one another. And this, as we have shown, can interfere with team success.

What's the alternative? The answer is to pay people following an *equality* rule—that is, giving each member the same amount of reward, overlooking any differences in their relative contributions. Do people believe this to be fair? Yes, it has been shown that people consider it more fair to use the equality rule in teams than for individuals. Overall, however, people still

believe that the equity rule is fairest. After all, it is a cherished tradition in individualistic societies to differentiate between people based on their performance.

Now, how about procedural justice? What characteristic must a procedure have for it to be considered fair in teams? Consistency is particularly important in this regard. That is, fairness demands that decisions be made in a way that treats everyone in the same manner. And just as equality is considered more important as a determinant of fairness in teams than for individuals, this is the case for consistency as well. The idea behind this is straightforward: To avoid possible conflict between team members, it's important to make decisions in exactly the same manner for everyone. So, for example, if you use seniority as the criterion for deciding who gets priority when selecting vacation dates, then this should be done for everyone. Although it will be considered unfair to implement the procedure inconsistently for individuals (e.g., by the standard in some departments as opposed to others), being inconsistent is considered even *more* unfair in teams. We also know that this effect is stronger in larger teams, where being consistent is considered more important, than in smaller teams, where being somewhat inconsistent, although still unfair, is better accepted.

We conclude by noting that being ethical requires being fair, and as shown here, what's considered fair differs somewhat in teams than among individuals. Given the popularity of teams and the possibility for them to be very successful if run properly, managers are advised to take these considerations into account.

some teams may succeed or fail regardless of—or even despite—their leaders' influence. This raises an interesting and important question: Under what conditions do team leaders matter most?

Scientists have identified two sets of external factors that constrain team performance in ways that limit the extent to which even the best leaders can make a difference.[80] These are (1) team-level constraints (i.e., aspects of the technological and organizational context within which the team operates), and (2) contextual constraints (i.e., factors associated with the broad institutional context within which the team operates).

TEAM-LEVEL CONSTRAINTS. Consider the nature of work on a mechanized assembly line. Machines are paced at fixed speeds, the assembly procedures are predetermined, and the operations involved always are performed in the same highly routinized ways. In this case, the performance of the team is unlikely to be influenced by the leader. Rather, the design of the job itself largely dictates how well the team performs (recall our discussion of job design in Chapter 7).

Now, consider the opposite situation, such as a product development team at a company like 3M. Scientists work at rates they determine themselves, performing highly complex work in which they have a great deal of discretion. Under such conditions, it makes sense that team leaders can make a big difference. By intervening, team leaders can contribute to their team's effectiveness by helping members gather and use resources most effectively. By contrast, of course, a leader also may disrupt task performance by interfering with what the team needs to succeed.

CONTEXTUAL CONSTRAINTS. Just as aspects of a team's work may affect the extent to which leaders matter, so too may aspects of the organizational environments in which they operate. Consider, for example, the work done by members of an emergency rescue squad. Given the highly noble and important cause for which they labor—saving lives—it's unlikely that their leaders may have much impact on members' capacity to work any harder than they already do.

Similarly, in many jobs constraints also are imposed by laws that dictate what must (or must not) be done. For example, members of a human resources team have to refrain from making hiring decisions on the basis of applicants' race regardless of what their leader may say or do. Finally, the labor market also constrains a team leader's impact. Consider our example of an athletic coach. Even the most talented coach can only have so much impact on a team of weak, clumsy, unmotivated players. Although the coach may help make them as good as they can be, the players' own limitations surely will make a big difference. After all, as they say, "you can't make a silk purse out of a sow's ear." In fact, it is with this in mind that leaders endeavor to select the best members for their teams.

In conclusion, we have to be careful when it comes to blaming team leaders for their team's failure or crediting them for their team's success. Leaders make a difference, to be sure, but the degree to which they deserve the credit or blame requires taking into account a variety of conditions under which their teams operate.

Communicate the Urgency of the Team's Mission

Team members are prone to rally around challenges that compel them to meet high performance standards. As a result, the urgency of meeting those standards should be expressed. For example, a few years ago, employees at Ampex Corporation (a manufacturer of recording equipment for the broadcasting industry) worked hard to make their teams successful when they recognized the changes necessitated by the shift from analog technology (recording on tape) to digital technology (recording on hard drives and solid state drives). Unless the company met these challenges, the plug surely would be pulled. Realizing that the company's very existence was at stake, work teams fast-forwarded Ampex into a position of prominence in its industry by ramping up development of digital recording technology.

Train Members in Team Skills

To be effective, team members must have the right blend of skills needed to satisfy their teams' objectives. Rather than simply putting together teams and hoping they will work, many companies are taking proactive steps to ensure that team members will get along and perform as they should. Formal efforts directed toward making teams effective are referred to as **team building.** Team building usually is used when established teams are showing signs of trouble, such as when members lose sight of their objectives and when turnover is high. Workers who have high

team building
Formal efforts directed toward making teams more effective.

degrees of autonomy on their jobs require a depth of skills and knowledge that surpasses that of others performing narrower, traditional jobs. For this reason, successful teams are those in which investments are made in developing the skills of team members and leaders. In the words of one expert, "Good team members are trained, not born."[81]

Illustrating this maxim is Development Dimensions International, a printing and distribution facility for a human resource company, located in Pittsburgh, Pennsylvania. This small company trains each of its 70 employees for approximately 200 hours (in such areas as interaction skills, customer service skills, and various technical areas) during their first year—even more for new leaders. Then, after this initial period, all employees receive a variety of training on an ongoing basis. (Recall our detailed discussion of training in Chapter 3.)

KEY AREAS OF TEAM TRAINING. Two areas of emphasis are essential to the success of any team training effort—training in being a team member, and training in self-management.

- *Being a team member.* Linda Godwin, a mission specialist at NASA's Johnson Space Center in Houston, likens team success to the kind of interpersonal harmony that must exist within space shuttle crews. "We have to be willing to compromise and to make decisions that benefit everyone as a whole," says Godwin, a veteran of two successful shuttle missions.[82] In this regard, there are several key interpersonal skills in which training is most useful, and these are summarized in Table 8.5.
- *Self-management.* Most employees are used to being told what to do and don't know how to manage their own behavior. However, for teams to operate effectively, members must be able to manage themselves. To accomplish this, managers have to learn a variety of skills— most notably, the ones summarized in Figure 8.18.[83]

TEAM TRAINING EXERCISES. Typically, team building involves having team members participate in several different exercises designed to help employees learn how to function effectively as a team member. Among the most widely used are the following.[84]

- *Role definition exercises.* Are team members doing what others expect them to be doing? Teams whose members answer no are destined for trouble. To avoid such problems, some team-building exercises ask members to describe their own roles and the roles of others on their teams. Members then systematically discuss these perceptions and highlight areas of disagreement so these can be addressed.
- *Goal-setting exercises.* As we described in Chapter 7, successful performance is enhanced by the setting of goals. As a team-building strategy, team members meet to clarify the various goals toward which they are working and to identify ways they can help achieve them.

TABLE 8.5 Interpersonal Skills Required by Team Members

Experts have recommended that team members be trained in the various interpersonal skills summarized here. Many of these skills are described in more detail elsewhere in this book (their locations are indicated in parentheses).

Skill	Description
Advocating	Ways of persuading others to accept one's point of view (see Chapter 12)
Inquiring	Listening effectively to others and drawing information out of them (see Chapter 9)
Tension management	Managing the tension that stems from conflict with others (see Chapter 11)
Sharing responsibility	Learning to align personal and team objectives
Leadership	Understanding one's role in guiding the team to success (see Chapter 13)
Valuing diversity	Acceptance—and taking advantage—of differences between members (see Chapter 6)
Self-awareness	Willingness to criticize others constructively and to accept constructive criticism from others (see Chapters 9 and 11)

Source: Based on information Caudron, 1994; see Note 83.

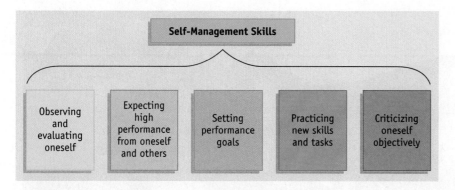

FIGURE 8.18

Self-Management Skills: A Key to Team Success

For teams to function successfully, it is essential for members to know how to manage themselves. Training in self-management focuses on the five skills summarized here.

- *Problem-solving exercises.* Building successful teams requires ensuring that members are able to work together at solving important problems. To help in this regard, some team-building sessions require members to get together to identify and discuss systematically ways of solving problems more effectively.
- *Interpersonal process exercises.* Some of the most popular team-building exercises involve activities that attempt to build trust and to open communication among members. After all, those members who harbor hostility toward each other or who have hidden agendas are unlikely to work together well. Often, there is a fun aspect to interpersonal process training. Black & Decker, for example, had members of its design team participate in a "spider web" activity requiring members to crawl through a large web of woven rope suspended between two trees without touching the rope. The underlying idea is that by helping one another through these exercises, team members can develop more positive relationships with their colleagues and come to learn how they can influence each other's potential back on the job (in Chapter 16 we will discuss similar exercises used to promote organizational development). In doing this, companies have used such diverse activities as trekking in the wilderness, going through obstacle courses, and having paintball wars. For a particularly important example, see Figure 8.19.[85]

As you might imagine, this list of training topics reflects only the most fundamental areas in which training in teamwork is useful. Depending on the exact nature of the work being performed and the specific working conditions involved, additional training may be required. This often is the case when team members are located in different countries throughout the world. (For a discussion of how to promote special skills required in such circumstances, see the OB in Practice section on page 283.)

IS TEAM TRAINING EFFECTIVE? Although these various meetings and physical exercises may be fun, we must ask: Do they have any value? In other words, are they worth the time and money invested in them? The answer is *yes, but only when the training is conducted properly.* Too often, exercises are used without first thoroughly analyzing precisely what the team needs. When it comes to team building, one size does not fit all!

Another problem is that team-building exercises often are used as a one-time panacea. For them to be most effective, however, team-building exercises should be repeated regularly (or, at least, at the very first sign of problems) to keep the team in tip-top shape. And then, when on the job, everyone should be reminded of the lessons learned off-site.

Research has revealed just how effective training in teamwork skills can be.[86] One particular study involved more than 1,000 officers in the U.S. Air Force who were trained in a variety of teamwork skills. After the training, officers took tests to see how effectively they picked up the relevant skills. Subsequently, various military teams that contained these officers were compared with respect to three key measures: (1) performance in the field when

FIGURE 8.19

Teamwork Training at NASA

Although hiking in the Bridger-Teton National Forest in the Rocky Mountains near Lander, Wyoming) is a far cry from working on a space mission, NASA officials recognize that the experience can provide a valuable learning opportunity for astronauts by simulating the interpersonal tensions crew members are likely to face while in flight. With this in mind, astronauts go on such expeditions as part of their ongoing training to work well together as a team. According to astronaut Ron Garan, "You could be the best pilot, scientist, or astronaut in the world, but if you can't work as part of a team or live with people for six months, you're no good to NASA."

conducting military operations, (2) success in solving problems, and (3) performance on physical tasks. Independently of these measures, observers also rated the effectiveness of the teams overall. As summarized in Figure 8.20 (on page 284), teams consisting of members who, as a whole, scored highly on the tests of team-relevant skills outperformed the teams whose officers performed less well. These findings highlight the potential value of administering training in teamwork skills.

Promote Cooperation Within and Between Teams

Team success requires not only cooperation within teams, but between them as well. As one expert put it, "Time and time again, teams fall short of their promise because companies don't know how to make them work together with other teams. If you don't get your teams into the right constellations, the whole organization can stall."[87]

Boeing successfully avoided such problems in the course of developing its 777 passenger jet—a project involving some 200 teams. As you might imagine, on such a large project coordination of effort between teams is essential. To help, regular meetings were held between various team leaders who disseminated information to members. And team members could go wherever needed within the organization to get the information required to succeed. As one Boeing employee, a team leader, put it, "I can go to the chief engineer. Before, it was unusual just to see the chief engineer."[88] Just as importantly, if after getting the information they need, team members find problems, they are empowered to take action without getting management's approval. According to Boeing engineer Henry Shomber, "We have the no-messenger rule. Team members must make decisions on the spot. They can't run back to their functions [department heads] for permission."[89]

OB in Practice

Making Cross-National Teams Successful

There can be no mistaking the growth of cross-national teams in today's organizations. The majority of large companies already use teams in different nations, and most others plan to do so. This creates opportunities to tap a variety of viewpoints and talent, creating conditions that enhance team effectiveness. At the same time, however, cultural differences between people in the same team may cause problems.

Specifically, we are referring to the natural tendency for teams consisting of culturally diverse combinations of people to break into subgroups sharing common characteristics. The extent to which this occurs, however, depends on the way characteristics are distributed across people in those subgroups. Consider, for example, a team composed of engineers and designers, some of whom are men and some of whom are women. If all the engineers happen to be of one gender while all the designers are of the opposite gender, then a so-called **faultline** will be created. This refers to a condition in which the key attributes of group members are correlated across group membership instead of cutting across team membership.[90] This precisely describes our example. Just as geologists are concerned about faultlines in the earth

faultline
A condition in which the key attributes of group members are correlated across group membership instead of cutting across team membership.

because of the unstable geological conditions they create, managers also need to be concerned about faultlines in teams because they weaken overall cohesion by promoting disruptive conflict (see Chapter 11).

When team members are geographically distributed, particularly across national boundaries, people become keenly aware of the particular subgroups in each location. This encourages **ethnocentrism**— a bias toward one's own subgroup and against other subgroups. Thus, team members who are distributed across national borders, as often

ethnocentrism
A bias toward one's own subgroup and against other subgroups.

occurs, are inclined to favor their own groups at the expense of others. The resulting faultline makes cooperation between subgroups unlikely. And this, as you might imagine, interferes with the success of teams.

If naturally occurring conditions (i.e., the use of cross-national teams) are inclined to promote ethnocentrism and the inevitable conflict it creates, then managers face a challenge. How can they capitalize on the diverse viewpoints of people in different nations in a harmonious manner? An important part of the answer involves promoting **ethnorelativistic thinking,** taking the perspective of another group and understanding how they see the world, including one's own group.[91] Essentially, the idea is to expand people's perspectives and to show greater empathy for other groups.

ethnorelativistic thinking
Taking the perspective of another group and understanding how they see the world, including one's own group.

Promoting ethnorelativistic learning requires getting group members to understand and to respect the differences between them and to help them relate to one another despite those differences. In all cases, this involves three key foci:

- *Perspective-taking:* Considering the way others see things
- *Empathy:* Being aware of others' feelings
- *Adaptability:* Willingness to change one's own views and behaviors

Practically, this can be accomplished using diversity training of the types described in Chapter 6.

Another way of avoiding faultlines involves using technology in ways that promote inclusive communication—that is, taking everyone's views into account. Often, this requires using teleconferences in which subgroup members share information freely about things that help team members interpret their behavior correctly. This may include topics such as local customs, including holidays, work hours, use of breaks, and so on. Absent such information, misunderstandings are likely to develop.

It's also worthwhile to use such sessions to emphasize each subgroup's relative strengths and weaknesses so people in one subgroup can understand what to expect of those in another. This information, of course, is quite valuable to groups attempting to perform their tasks—and far more useful than focusing on difficulties associated with getting along with others.

In conclusion, because cross-national teams are growing in popularity, everyone should be prepared for the interpersonal challenges they create. Hopefully, this discussion will help prepare you to meet these challenges.

Select Team Members Based on Their Skills or Potential Skills

Because the success of teams demands that members work together closely on a variety of tasks, it is essential for them to have a complementary set of skills. This includes not only job skills but also interpersonal skills (especially since getting along with one's teammates is very important). With this in mind, at Ampex, three-person subsets of teams are used to select their own new members because as they have the best idea about what skills are needed and who would best fit into the teams. Frequently, it also is important for teams to project future skills that may be

FIGURE 8.20

Training in Teamwork Skills Promotes Successful Team Performance

After being trained in various teamwork skills, U.S. Air Force officers were tested on how well they learned the material. The higher the scores of officers in various military teams, the better those units performed on several important performance measures.

Source: Based on findings reported by Hirschfeld, et al., 2006; see Note 86.

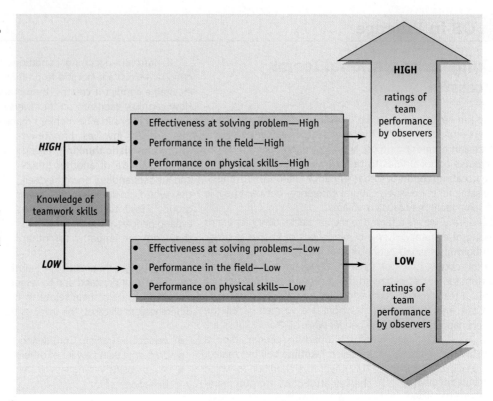

needed and to train team members in these skills. With this in mind, work teams at Colgate-Palmolive Company's liquid detergents plant in Cambridge, Ohio, initially received 120 hours of training in such skills as quality management, problem solving, and team interaction, and subsequently received advanced training in all these areas.

In an effort to keep team members' skills current, it is important to confront members with new facts on a regular basis. Fresh approaches are likely to be prompted by fresh information, and introducing new facts may present the kind of challenges that teams need to stay innovative. For example, when information about pending cutbacks in defense spending was introduced to teams at Florida's Harris Corporation (an electronics manufacturer), new technologies were developed that positioned the company to land large contracts in nonmilitary government organizations—including a $1.7 billion contract to upgrade the FAA's air traffic control system.

A Cautionary Note: Developing Successful Teams Requires Patience

It is important to caution that although these suggestions are important, they alone do not ensure the success of work teams. Many other factors, such as the economy, the existence of competitors, and the company's financial picture also are important determinants of organizational success. Still, the fact that the practices described here are followed in many highly successful teams certainly makes them worthy of consideration.

However, developing effective teams is difficult, and the path to success is riddled with obstacles. It is also time-consuming. According to management expert, the late Peter Drucker, "You can't rush teams. It takes five years just to learn to build a team and decide what kind you want."[92] And it may take most organizations over a decade to make a complete transition to teams. Clearly, teams are not an overnight route to success. But, with patience and careful attention to the suggestions outlined in this chapter, teams have ushered many companies into extraordinary gains in productivity. For this reason, they must be considered a viable option for organizing groups of work groups.[93]

Summary and Review of Learning Objectives

1. **Define what is meant by a group and identify different types of groups operating within organizations.**

   A *group* is a collection of two or more interacting individuals with a stable pattern of relationships between them who share common goals and who perceive themselves as being a group. Within organizations, there are two major classes of groups—*formal groups* (which include *command groups* and *task groups*), and *informal groups* (which include *interest groups* and *friendship groups*).

2. **Describe the importance of roles, norms, status, and cohesiveness within organizations.**

   Roles are the typical pattern of behavior in a social context. Norms are generally agreed-upon informal rules. *Status* refers to the prestige accorded group members. *Cohesiveness* is the pressures faced by group members to remain in their groups. Together, these factors determine the dynamics of people working in groups.

3. **Explain how individual performance in groups is affected by the presence of others (social facilitation), and the number of others with whom one is working (social loafing).**

   Individual productivity is influenced by the presence of other group members. Sometimes, a person's performance improves in the presence of others (when the job he or she is doing is well learned), and sometimes performance declines in the presence of others (when the job is novel). This phenomenon is known as *social facilitation*. On *additive tasks* (i.e., ones in which each member's individual contributions are combined), *social loafing* occurs. According to this phenomenon, the more people who work on a task, the less each group member contributes to it.

4. **Define what teams are and describe the various types of teams that exist in organizations.**

   Teams are special kinds of groups—ones whose members focus on collective, rather than individual, work products; are mutually accountable to each other; share a common commitment to purpose; and are usually self-managing. Teams differ with respect to several dimensions: their purpose or mission (*work teams* versus *improvement teams*), time (*temporary teams* or *permanent teams*), degree of autonomy (*work groups, semi-autonomous work groups, self-managed teams*), authority structure (*intact teams* versus *cross-functional teams*), and physical presence (*physical teams* versus *virtual teams*).

5. **Describe the effectiveness of teams in organizations.**

   In general, teams are well received. Most people enjoy working in teams, at least after they have adjusted to them (which can take some time and effort). Teams help enhance commitment among employees and are effective in promoting organizational efficiency by eliminating layers of management. However, teams are not always responsible for making individuals and organizations any more productive. Cases of companies becoming wildly successful after adopting teams, although compelling, cannot always be generalized to all teams in all situations.

6. **Explain the factors responsible for the failure of some teams to operate as effectively as possible and steps that can be taken to build successful teams.**

   Despite some evidence of team successes, some teams fail. This is often because team members are unwilling to cooperate with each other, they fail to receive support from management, some managers are unwilling to relinquish control, and some teams fail to coordinate their efforts effectively with other teams. With some effort, teams can yield exceptionally high levels of performance. To build successful teams, it helps to do the following: provide training in team skills, compensate team performance, provide managerial support, promote employee support, promote cooperation within and between teams, and select team members based on their skills or potential skills.

Points to Ponder

Questions for Review

1. What is a group and how do groups form?
2. How do norms, roles, status, and cohesiveness influence the operation of groups?
3. How do the phenomena of social facilitation and social loafing influence the performance of individuals in group settings?
4. What are teams and how do they differ from groups?
5. What does the evidence reveal about the effectiveness of work teams?
6. What are the major obstacles to team success and how can they be overcome?

Experiential Questions

1. Think of a group in which you have been working. How do the *five-stage model* and the *punctuated-equilibrium model* apply to this experience?
2. Describe an incident of *social loafing* in which you may have been involved (e.g., a class project). What might be done to overcome this effect?

3. How have your own experiences in work teams compared to those described in this chapter? Based on what you read, what could be done to make your own team experiences more successful?

Questions to Analyze

1. Imagine that you are about to go on stage to give a solo piano recital. How would the phenomenon of social facilitation account for your performance?
2. Based on the evidence regarding the effectiveness of teams, would you say that the popularity of teams today is well-founded?
3. Think of any professional sports team, such as a professional baseball, football, or basketball team. In what ways do they fit the description of teams used in this chapter? In what ways do they *not* fit the description of teams used in this chapter?

Experiencing OB

Individual Exercise

Are You a Team Player?

Let's face it, some people find it easier to work in teams than others. Are you already a "team player," or have you not yet developed the skills needed to work effectively with others in teams? Knowing where you stand along this dimension may come in handy when it comes to considering a new job or planning your next work assignment. The following questionnaire will give you insight into this question.

Directions

1. Read each of the following statements and carefully consider whether or not it accurately describes you on the job most of the time.
2. Then, on the line next to each statement, write "Yes" if the statement describes you most of the time, or "No" if it does not describe you most of the time. If you are uncertain, write a question mark ("?").
3. Do your best to respond to all items as honestly as possible.

Most of the time, on the job, I . . .

1. —— demonstrate high ethical standards.
2. —— deliver on promises I make.
3. —— take initiative, doing what's needed without being told.
4. —— follow the norms and standards of the groups in which I work.
5. —— put team goals ahead of my own.
6. —— accurately describe my team to others in the organization.
7. —— pitch in to help others learn new skills.
8. —— do at least my share of the work.
9. —— coordinate the work I do with others.
10. —— try to attend all meetings and arrive on time for them.
11. —— come to meetings prepared to participate.
12. —— stay focused on the agenda during team meetings.

13. ——— share with others new knowledge I may have about the job.
14. ——— encourage others to raise questions about the way things are.
15. ——— affirm positive things about others' ideas before noting concerns.
16. ——— listen to others without interrupting them.
17. ——— ask others questions to make certain I understand them.
18. ——— make sure I attend to a speaker's nonverbal messages.
19. ——— praise others who have performed well.
20. ——— give constructive, nonjudgmental feedback to others.
21. ——— receive constructive feedback without acting defensively.
22. ——— communicate ideas without threats or ridicule.
23. ——— explain the reasoning behind my opinions.
24. ——— demonstrate my willingness to change my opinions.
25. ——— speak up when I disagree with others.
26. ——— show disagreement in a tactful, polite manner.
27. ——— discuss possible areas of agreement with others with whom I am in conflict.

Source: Based on material appearing in McDermott et al., 1998; see Note 93.

Scoring

1. Count the number of times you responded with yes.
2. Then, count the number of times you responded with no.
3. Add these two numbers together.
4. To compute your *team player score,* divide the number of times you responded yes (step 1) by the total (step 3). Then, multiply by 100. Your score will be between 0 and 100. Higher scores reflect greater readiness for working in teams.

Questions for Discussion

1. What was your score, and how did it compare to those of others in your class?
2. What underlying criteria of team success are assessed by this questionnaire?
3. What does this questionnaire reveal about the ways in which you are best equipped to work in teams?
4. What does this questionnaire reveal about the ways in which you are most deficient when it comes to working in teams? What do you think you could do to improve your readiness for working in teams?

Group Exercise

Demonstrating the Social Loafing Effect

The social loafing effect is quite strong and is likely to occur in many different situations in which people make individual contributions to an additive group task. This exercise is designed to demonstrate the effect firsthand in your own class.

Directions

1. Divide the class into groups of different sizes. Between 5 and 10 people should work alone. In addition, there should be a group of two, a group of three, a group of four, and so on, until all members of the class have been assigned to a group. (If the class is small, assign students to groups of vastly different sizes, such as 2, 7, and 15.) Form the groups by putting people from the same group together at tables.
2. Each person should be given a page or two from a telephone directory and a stack of index cards. Then, have the individuals and the members of each group perform the same additive task—copying entries from the telephone directory onto index cards. Allow exactly 10 minutes for the task to be performed, and encourage everyone to work as hard as they can.
3. After the time is up, count the number of entries copied.
4. For each group, and for all the individuals, compute the average per-person performance by dividing the total number of entries copied by the number of people in the group.

5. At the board, the instructor should graph the results. Along the vertical axis show the average number of entries copied per person. Along the horizontal axis show the size of the work groups—one, two, three, four, and so on. The graph should look like the one in Figure 8.11 (see page 265).

Questions for Discussion

1. Was the social loafing effect demonstrated? What is the basis for this conclusion?
2. If the social loafing effect was not found, why do you think this occurred? Do you think it might have been due to the possibility that your familiarity with the effect led you to avoid it? Test this possibility by replicating the exercise using people who do not know about the phenomenon (e.g., another class), and then compare the results.
3. Did members of smaller groups feel more responsible for their group's performance than members of larger groups?
4. What could have been done to counteract any "free riding" that may have occurred in this demonstration?

Practicing OB

Gearing Up for Self-Managed Teams

Officials of a large manufacturing company are concerned about the stagnant productivity they've seen in the past year. Although sales have been good, employees in the company's manufacturing plant are having a hard time keeping up with demand. Right now, they are working on an assembly line, requiring each individual to perform only one or two highly specific tasks. To remedy the situation, they are considering moving to self-managed teams. You have been asked to give your advice on this matter.

1. Do you think teams would be effective in this situation? Why or why not?
2. What potential problems do you think would be associated with the move to teams, and how might these be overcome?
3. What advice would you give to help the teams work as effectively as possible?

■ *Inside the Peloton: Social Dynamics of the Tour de France*

Case in Point

Each July, bicyclists race across the French countryside in the Tour de France. The race, first run in 1903, now consists of about 180 of the world's best cyclists, who meander through tiny villages, up and down steep mountain grades, and after a grueling 3,407 kilometers (slightly over 2,117 miles), complete their 23-day-long journey along Paris's famed Champs-Elysées. To the winner goes €400,000 (currently about US$517,840). For seven consecutive years (until 2009, when Alberto Contador became the official winner), American Lance Armstrong crossed the finish line first, but despite how it may look from the outside, the Tour, as it is called for short, is very much a team sport.

To appreciate the team dynamics, it's necessary to understand what goes on inside the *peloton,* a cycling term for "pack"—a picturesque mob of competing teams seen gliding along the route. The complex social arrangements that occur within them belie the bucolic surroundings in which they peddle. As one observer put it, "What appears to be a random mass of bicycles is really an ordered, complex web of shifting alliances, crossed with brutal competition, designed to keep or acquire the market's most valued currency: energy."

Pelotons consist of about 20 teams of nine riders, each of whom has a specialty. For example, there are *roulers,* two or three particularly fast riders who help create drafts for their team's leader in flat terrain; *hill specialists,* who have the strength and stamina to support the leader in gaining ground by creating a slipstream (a field of low wind resistance) as they go up mountains; and *domestiques,* usually new riders who wear shoulder bags to help carry supplies between the team car and various team members. Together, these individuals have a common objective: to position leaders for a win.

It's not only members of one's own teams who work together; sometimes, tiny groupings of enemies from different teams form momentary alliances when race decisions dictate—sometimes hundreds per day. For example, members of two opposing teams riding knuckle-to-knuckle at 60 mph may help one another by cutting temporary

(Continued)

deals, each taking turns blocking others through upcoming twists and turns. As longtime Tour commentator Phil Liggett observed, "You have to make friends of enemies. And just as quickly, enemies of friends."

Within the peloton, unspoken rules develop. For example, riders may be given a chance to lead the pack, such as when they enter their hometowns (allowing them to enjoy the glory and admiration) and when they go to areas with lots of television coverage (allowing them to please their sponsors). Cooperation between teams also is important when nature calls. Usually, bathroom breaks (more actually, trips to the woods) occur when everyone agrees they will.

During one race, however, French rider Dante Coccolo took it upon himself to defy the rules. When everyone stopped for a break, he charged ahead. Later, when he took his own bathroom break, some other cyclists grabbed his bike and threw it into a ditch. Slowed down and ostracized, Coccolo's team had to get him another bike. He finished in next-to-last place that year and never again rode in the Tour. Lesson learned.

Questions for Discussion

1. What examples of role differentiation are found in this case? To what extent do they help achieve the desired goals?

2. What social norms are illustrated? How do they help each team's mission, and how are they enforced?

3. Teams of nine are used in this case. Do you think they would be more effective if they were smaller in size, or does the situation dictate the team size used? To what extent would larger teams help or hinder effectiveness?

9 Communication in Organizations

Learning Objectives

After reading this chapter, you should be able to:

1. Describe the process of communication and its purposes in organizations.
2. Identify various forms of verbal media used in organization, and explain which ones are most appropriate for communicating messages of different types.
3. Describe how technology has influenced organizational communication.
4. Describe how people's communication patterns differ based on their sex and culture.
5. Distinguish between the various forms of formal and informal communication that occur in organizations and how they operate.
6. Explain how you can improve your effectiveness as a communicator in organizations.

Chapter Outline

- Communication: Its Basic Nature
- Verbal and Nonverbal Communication: Messages With and Without Words
- The Role of Technology: Computer-Mediated Communication
- Formal Communication in Organizations
- Informal Communication Networks: Behind the Organization Chart
- Individual Differences in Communication
- Improving Your Communication Skills

Preview Case

■ *Reducing Interruptions High-Tech Style at Microsoft and IBM*

Human beings are readily distracted, psychologists tell us, because distractions signal changes in the environment of which we must be aware. The doorbell rings and we answer it. Someone calls our name and we look up. This fact of nature wasn't a problem before we were busily multitasking and faced with e-mails, phone calls, instant messages, and people stopping by to chat. Today, however, the sheer number of distractions takes its toll on productivity. In fact, most people "switch gears" every few minutes, and when this occurs, it takes about a half hour to recover. Overall, people lose an average of 28 percent of their daily work hours due to disruptions, costing the U.S. economy some $650 billion each year.

As you might imagine, such an expensive problem has prompted a search for a solution. One fascinating fix comes from the company responsible for developing the technology that made possible many distractions in the first place—Microsoft. For more than 10 years, Microsoft scientist Eric Horvitz has been working on an artificial-intelligence system that emulates the behavior of people at work. His computer program, Priorities, tracks everything that people do at their computers and handheld devices and then uses sophisticated statistical techniques to determine the costs and benefits of being interrupted by various e-mail messages. If the program determines that it's too costly to interrupt you with a particular message, it will keep it from you until such time as the interruption is less expensive. So, for example, word of a corporate shake-up is more likely to be presented to you

than, say, a message about the day's cafeteria offerings. For better or worse, Microsoft is considering including some version of this technology in a forthcoming version of its Windows operating system.

Not to be outdone, IBM is taking a different approach to the problem of disruption. Their program, IMSavvy, is like an answering machine for instant messages. Based on the nature and extent of keyboard activity, the program senses when you're busy or away from your desk and tells people who are demanding your attention that you are unavailable. There's still something important that the program hasn't yet worked out—namely, what if you're quiet because you are reading or thinking about something? Somehow, the silence or keyboard inactivity needs to be able to interpret this, but that's something for Version 2.0.

Probably the most fascinating feature of IMSavvy is the way it gives people the opportunity to determine whether their message is sufficiently important to let the recipient decide if it warrants an interruption. The so-called "whisper" option is designed to emulate what might happen if someone knocks on your door while you're on the phone. You may wave the visitor away but listen to an important message whispered to you (e.g., "Hey, we closed the deal"). This way, people, rather than software, can determine the importance of any potential interruption. Of course, if this is abused, then we're back to the beginning by creating yet another (albeit softer) form of interruption.

Surely, few among us are unable to relate to the problem of interruptions. After all, they threaten to affect our productivity adversely at work and at home, too. Then again, what you consider an interruption may simply be a message that you don't want to hear at that particular moment. The information, in reality, may be quite important to you or to someone else, although it might better be attended to at some later time. Matters of this nature are involved in the fundamental—and vital—process of *communication*. We refer to it as vital because there can be no organizations without people communicating with one another. Waiters must take their customers' orders and pass them along to the chef. Store managers must describe special promotions to their sales staffs. And the football coach must tell his team what plays to run. Clearly, communication is the key to these attempts at coordination. Without it, people would not know what to do, and groups and organizations would not be able to operate effectively—if at all!

With this in mind, communication has been referred to as "the social glue . . . that continues to keep organizations tied together,"[1] and "the essence of organizations."[2] Given its importance in organizations, you may not be surprised to learn that managers spend as much as 80 percent of their time engaged in one form of communication or another (e.g., writing reports, sending e-mails, talking to others in person, etc.). Communication involves everyone in an organization (and outside it, too), from the lowest-level employee to the head of a large corporation. Not only is this function essential, but it also has been observed that it is more important in today's business environment than ever before.[3] There are several key reasons for this.

- **Technology has sped up the pace of work.** As work gets done faster than ever, communication must be more effective because there is less time to correct errors or misunderstandings.
- **Teams enhance the need for coordination.** Because of the popularity of teams (as described in Chapter 8), people interact with lots of others who perform wide varieties of jobs. This requires coordinating information very carefully.
- **Employees are likely to be distributed geographically.** It's not unusual for people to work from home (see Chapter 1) and to keep in close contact with their offices while traveling on business. And, when people are out of sight, the normal opportunities to communicate when seeing someone in person are eliminated.
- **Knowledge and information are keys to success.** For today's organizations to be successful, they not only must be productive, but they also must stay abreast of rapidly changing markets. This requires information to be accessed and shared in a coordinated fashion.
- **Technology has transformed the way people do their jobs.** In today's electronically sophisticated world, we count on a variety of communication media that have transformed the way people do their jobs (see Figure 9.1).

Given the central role of communication in organizations, we will examine this process closely in this chapter. We begin by defining the process of communication and characterizing its role in organizations. Following this, we will describe two basic forms of communication: verbal and nonverbal. Because much of today's communication is high tech in nature, we will highlight

FIGURE 9.1

Technology Has Transformed Communication, Opening up Work Options

Advances in communication technology have made it possible for countless men and women to work full-time from their homes. Using the Internet and telephone, they are able to transmit work and maintain regular contact with their colleagues. The practice of *telecommuting*, popular today, not only allows people to spend time with their children, but also to save time and money by not having to travel to a distant office.

Mylife photo/Alamy.

computer-mediated communication techniques. Next, we will distinguish between two major types of communication in which we all engage—formal communication and informal communication. Then, recognizing that people don't always communicate in the same fashion, we will examine two key individual differences with respect to communication—sex differences and cross-cultural differences. Finally, we conclude this chapter by offering practical suggestions about how to become a better communicator.

Communication: Its Basic Nature

To appreciate fully the process of organizational communication, we must address some fundamental issues. We begin by defining formally the concept of communication and then elaborating on the process by which it occurs. Following this, we will describe the various purposes and levels of communication in organizations.

Defining Communication and Describing the Process

Although you probably already have a good idea of what communication entails, we can better understand communication in organizations by defining it precisely and describing the nature of the communication process. With this in mind, we define **communication** as the process by which a person, group, or organization (the *sender*) transmits some type of information (the *message*) to another person, group, or organization (the *receiver*). To clarify this definition and to further elaborate on how the process works, we have summarized it in Figure 9.2. You may find it helpful to follow along with this diagram as we review the various steps.

ENCODING. The communication process begins when one party has an idea that it wishes to transmit to another (either party may be an individual, a group, or an entire organization). It is the sender's mission to transform the idea into a form that can be sent to and understood by the receiver. This is what happens in the process of **encoding**—translating an idea into a form, such as written or spoken language, that can be recognized by a receiver. We encode information when we select the words we use to write a letter or speak to someone in person. This process is critical if we are to communicate our ideas clearly. If you've ever had difficulty finding the right words to express your ideas (and who hasn't!), then you know that people are far from perfect when it comes to encoding their ideas. Fortunately, as we will note later, this skill can be improved.

CHANNELS OF COMMUNICATION. After a message is encoded, it is ready to be transmitted over one or more **channels of communication**—that is, the pathways along which information travels—to reach the desired receiver. Telephone lines, radio and television signals,

communication
The process by which a person, group, or organization (the sender) transmits some type of information (the message) to another person, group, or organization (the receiver).

encoding
The process by which an idea is transformed so that it can be transmitted to, and recognized by, a receiver (e.g., a written or spoken message).

channels of communication
The pathways over which messages are transmitted (e.g., telephone lines, mail, etc.).

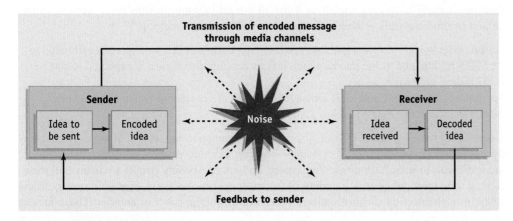

FIGURE 9.2

The Communication Process

Communication generally follows the steps outlined here. Senders *encode* messages and transmit them via one or more communication channels to receivers, who then *decode* them. The process continues as the original receiver sends feedback to the original sender. Factors distorting or limiting the flow of information, known as *noise,* may enter into the process at any point.

fiber-optic cables, cell phone signals, mail routes, satellite transmissions to GPS devices, and even the air waves that carry the vibrations of our voices are all potential channels of communication. Of course, the form of encoding largely determines the way information may be transmitted. Visual information—such as pictures and written words—may be mailed, delivered in person by a courier, shipped by an express delivery service, or sent electronically, such as via e-mail, uploaded onto a Web site, or faxed. Oral information may be transmitted over the telephone, via radio and television signals, using online sound files—and, of course, the old-fashioned way, in person. Whatever channel is used, the goal is the same: to send the encoded message accurately to the desired receiver.

decoding
The process by which a receiver of messages transforms them back into the sender's ideas.

DECODING. Once a message is received, the recipient must begin the process of decoding—converting the message back into the sender's original ideas. This involves many different subprocesses, such as comprehending spoken and written words, interpreting facial expressions, and the like. To the extent that the sender's message is decoded accurately by the receiver, the ideas understood will be the ones intended. Of course, our ability to comprehend and interpret information received from others may be imperfect. For example, this may be restricted by unclear messages, by our own language skills, or by one's existing knowledge. Thus, as in the case of encoding, limitations in our ability to decode information represent another potential weakness in the communication process—but, as we will describe later in this chapter, one that can be developed.

feedback
Knowledge about the impact of messages on receivers.

FEEDBACK. Finally, once a message has been decoded, the process can continue, with the receiver transmitting a new message back to the original sender. This part of the process is known as feedback—knowledge about the impact of messages on receivers. Receiving feedback allows senders to determine whether their messages have been understood properly. At the same time, giving feedback can help convince receivers that the sender really cares about what he or she has to say. Once received, feedback can trigger another idea from the sender, and another cycle of transferring information may begin. For this reason, we have characterized the process of communication summarized in Figure 9.2 as continuous.

noise
Factors capable of distorting the clarity of messages at any point during the communication process.

NOISE. Despite the apparent simplicity of the communication process, it rarely operates as flawlessly as we have described it here. As we will see, there are many potential barriers to effective communication. The name given to factors that distort the clarity of a message is noise. As we have suggested in Figure 9.2, noise can occur at any point along the communication process. For example, messages that are poorly encoded (e.g., written in an unclear way) or poorly decoded (e.g., not comprehended), or channels of communication that are too full of static (e.g., receivers' attentions are diverted from the message) may reduce communication's effectiveness.

spam
Unsolicited commercial e-mail messages.

One particularly annoying source of noise in e-mail communication these days is spam, unsolicited commercial bulk e-mail messages. The statistics are shocking:[4]

■ Based on technical expenses and lost productivity, the annual cost of spam is estimated to be $20.5 billion, and at the rate at which it is increasing, that figure is expected to rise to $257 billion very soon.

■ As much as 75 percent of e-mail messages received are considered spam, and despite efforts to stop it, the figure is rising rapidly.

Considering these statistics, it's not surprising that spam, a modern form of noise, contributes greatly to the inefficiency of e-mail systems—bogging them down with unwanted information, making it difficult to search for desired messages, and often exposing people to distasteful material. It's not only spam, of course; a variety of factors (e.g., time pressure, organizational politics) contribute to the distortion of information transmitted from one party to another. These factors and many others, as we will see in this chapter, make the process of organizational communication so very complex.

Purposes and Levels of Organizational Communication

In a sense, discussing the purpose of communication in organizations seems unnecessary since it's so obvious: You have to communicate with others to share information with them, which is necessary to get things done. This is true, of course, but communication actually serves a much broader range of purposes. In fact, communication serves at least eight critical functions in organizations.[5] These are as follows:

- **Directing action.** Communication between people is necessary to get others to behave in a desired fashion. Managers must communicate with subordinates to tell them what to do, to give them feedback on their performance, to discuss problems with them, to encourage them, and so on.

- **Linking and coordination.** For organizations to function effectively, individuals and groups must carefully coordinate their efforts and activities, and communication makes this possible. In a restaurant, for example, a waiter must take customers' orders and pass them along to the chef.

- **Building relationships.** Communication is essential to the development of interpersonal relationships. Building friendships and promoting trust (see Chapter 11) requires careful communication. Doing so can help create a pleasant atmosphere in the workplace. However opportunities to use technology for social networking can interfere with performing one's job, and so it's frequently prohibited (see Figure 9.3).[6]

- **Explaining organizational culture.** By communicating with others, employees come to understand how their companies operate, what is valued, and what matters most to people. In other words, they learn about the *culture* of their organizations (we will discuss organizational culture in detail in Chapter 14).

- **Interorganizational linking.** People communicate not only with others in their own organizations but also with representatives of other organizations. This makes it possible for companies to coordinate their efforts toward achieving mutual goals, such as occurs in *joint ventures* (see Chapter 15).

- **Presenting an organization's image.** Organizations send messages about themselves to broad groups of others. For example, companies publish information about goods and

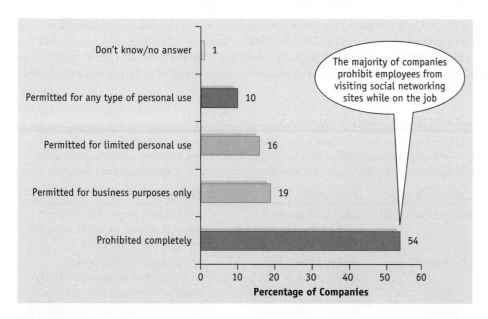

FIGURE 9.3

Social Networking on the Job Is Banned for Most: No Tweeting While Working

Recently, 1,400 chief information officers (CIOs) were polled about their companies' policies concerning employees' visiting social networking sites (e.g., Facebook, MySpace, and Twitter) while on the job. Recognizing that these sites may be used for effective business purposes for some jobs, CIOs permitted their use in approximately one in five companies. The majority, however, considered them to be diversions from productive work and prohibited visits during working hours. As these sites have gained popularity, so too have "No Tweeting while working" policies been springing up among employers.

Source: Robert Half Technology, 2009; see Note 6.

services to attract prospective customers. These forms of communication are designed to present certain images of the organization to the world.

■ *Generating ideas.* Communication is used to generate ideas and to share them as necessary. When people brainstorm with one another, for example, the communication process helps create new ideas (see Chapter 10 for a discussion of the brainstorming process).

■ *Promoting ideals and values.* Many organizations "stand for something" and have purposes that must be communicated clearly. For example, a stated purpose of the National Organization for Women (NOW) is to help women participate fully in society. Communication is required for word of this mission to reach people, for it to be understood—and, of course, for it to be accomplished.

As these descriptions suggest, communication plays a vital role at all organizational levels. Specifically, organizational communication occurs at the five distinct levels summarized in Table 9.1. These range from *interpersonal communication* at one end, involving people on an individual basis, all the way to *mass communication*, in which information is shared with large numbers of people. This broad range of approaches lends itself to study by a variety of professional groups. Besides specialists in the field of OB, as this table suggests, communication also is of great interest to psychologists and sociologists, as well as scientists and practitioners in the fields of marketing, journalism, and political science. Among OB specialists, the focus primarily is on the three lowest levels, interpersonal communication, group-level communication, and organizational-level communication. You will see these various emphases in this chapter.

Now that we have established the nature of communication in organizations, we will continue by examining the two major forms it takes—*verbal communication* (communicating by using words) and *nonverbal communication* (communicating without words).

Verbal and Nonverbal Communication: Messages With and Without Words

verbal communication
The transmission of messages using words, either written or spoken.

Because you are reading this book, we know you are familiar with **verbal communication**—the process of using words to transmit and receive ideas. Whether it's a face-to-face chat with a coworker, a phone call from a supplier, an e-mail message from the boss, or a faxed memo from company headquarters, people in today's organizations use a variety of different communications

TABLE 9.1 Levels of Organizational Communication

As summarized here, communication occurs at many different levels. These range from the "micro-level" communication between individuals through broader, "macro-level" forms, involving communication within and between organizations, to societal-level communication, such as occurs in the case of mass communication.

Level of Communication	Description	Example
Interpersonal communication	Individuals sharing information, formally or informally	A supervisor meets with her direct report to discuss ways of improving this person's work.
Group-level communication	Sharing of information within groups or teams	The members of a sales team coordinate their efforts at developing a new sales campaign.
Organizational-level communication	Sharing of information between subunits of the same organization	Representatives of various company departments assemble to create a strategic plan.
Interorganizational communication	Sharing of information between organizations	Firms working together on a joint venture make plans for sharing resources required to create a new product.
Mass communication	A company sending messages to large numbers of people	An automobile manufacturer notifies its dealers and owners of a safety recall.

media. When we speak of verbal media, we are referring to communication involving the use of words. Whether the words are transmitted orally or in written form, both play an important role in organizations.

As you know, much of what people communicate also occurs without using words, which is known as **nonverbal communication.** Whether we're talking about people's facial expressions or body language, the distances they maintain from others, or other subtle cues that we will describe here, nonverbal communication carries a great deal of weight when it comes to sending messages in organizations. In this section of the chapter, we discuss both verbal and nonverbal communication.

nonverbal communication
The transmission of messages without the use of words (e.g., by gestures, the use of space).

Verbal Media

When most of us think about communication, we focus on **verbal media**—forms of communication involving the use of words. Face-to-face conversations, letters, and telephone conversations are clear examples. The various forms of verbal media can be distinguished with respect to their capacity to convey information.[7]

verbal media
Forms of communication involving the use of words (e.g., telephone messages, faxes, books, etc.).

Some verbal media, such as *face-to-face conversations,* are considered especially *rich* because they provide vast amounts of information. They also are highly personal in nature and provide opportunities for immediate feedback. A bit less rich are non-face-to-face interactive media, such as the *telephone.* However, not all business communication requires a two-way flow of information. For example, further toward the *lean* end of the continuum are personal, but static media, such as *memos* (written messages used for communication within an organization) and *letters* (written messages used for external communication).[8] This includes one-way communications sent either physically (e.g., letter) or electronically (e.g., fax or e-mail). (Given their prevalence in today's organizations, we will describe high-tech forms of communication in more detail in the next major section of this chapter, beginning on page 302.) Finally, at the leanest end of the continuum are highly impersonal, static media, such as *flyers* and *bulletins*—written information that is targeted broadly and not aimed at any one specific individual. For an overview of this continuum of verbal media, see Figure 9.4.

FORMS OF WRITTEN COMMUNICATION. Although organizations rely on a variety of written media, three particular forms—*newsletters, employee handbooks,* and *recruitment ads*—deserve

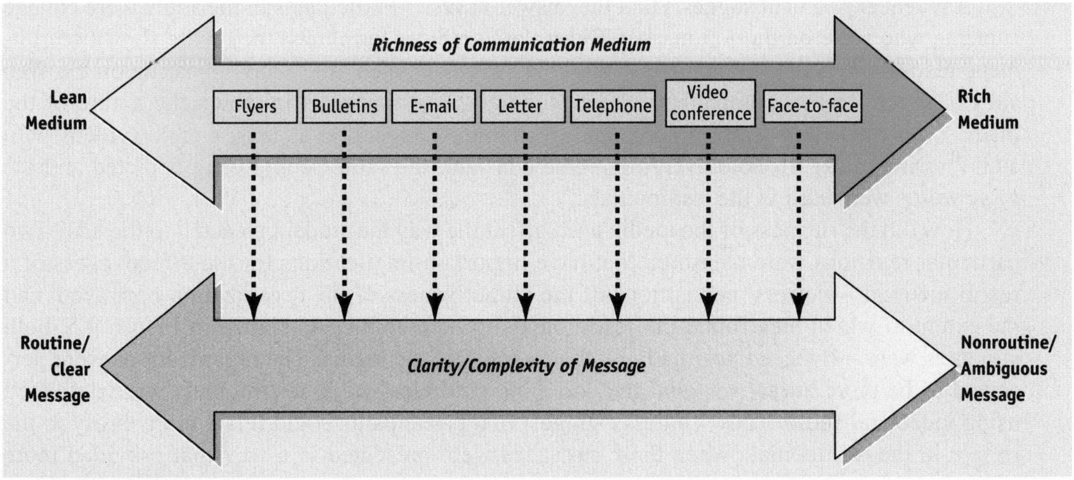

FIGURE 9.4

Matching the Medium to the Message: Media Richness Theory

Verbal communication media may be characterized along a continuum ranging from highly rich, interactive media, such as face-to-face discussions, to lean, static media, such as bulletins. According to *media richness theory,* lean media are most effectively used to communicate routine/clear messages, whereas rich media are most effectively used to communicate nonroutine/ambiguous messages.

Source: Based on material in Lengel & Daft, 1988; see Note 7.

newsletters
Regularly published internal documents, either hard copy or electronic in nature, describing information of interest to employees regarding an array of business and nonbusiness issues affecting them.

intranet
A private Web site that can be accessed only by a company's employees.

employee handbook
A document describing to employees basic information about a company; a general reference regarding a company's background, the nature of its business, and its rules.

recruitment ads
Written documents prepared for the purpose of sharing information about the organization for purposes of soliciting new employees.

special mention because of the important roles they play. **Newsletters** are regularly published internal documents describing information of interest to employees regarding an array of business and nonbusiness issues. Traditionally, these have been printed on paper, but today a great many newsletters are published online, using a company's **intranet**—a private Web site that can be accessed only by its employees. Many companies have found newsletters to be useful devices for explaining official policies and reminding everyone of important decisions made at group meetings. At the public relations firm Widmeyer Communications, with offices in New York and Washington, DC, for example, employees use the company's intranet to access an online newsletter that provides key information about what's going on in the firm.[9] Particularly popular is a column called "The Buzz," which serves as a sort of electronic watercooler around which people gather to share information about others in the company.

Employee handbooks also are important vehicles of internal organizational communication. These are formal documents describing basic information about the organization—its formal policies, mission, and underlying philosophy. Handbooks are widely used today. Not only do they do an effective job of helping new employees learn all about the company, including its code of ethics (see Chapter 2), but the explicit statements they provide also may help avoid serious misunderstandings and conflict between employees and their company's top management (see Chapter 11).

Newsletters and employee handbooks are focused on communication within organizations, but another important variety of written communication is aimed externally (although intended ultimately to bring people inside). We're speaking here of **recruitment ads.** These are written documents that share information about the organization for purposes of soliciting new employees. These ads often appear on companies' Web sites, allowing them to impart information to prospective employees about why they might want to work for them. Many of these ads include testimonials by current employees about how they like working for the company. Testimonials are particularly useful features because they make it possible to present information in ways to which prospective employees may be able to relate. Sometimes these are photos of employees accompanied by testimonials appearing in the form of text. At other times, however, companies leverage the power of technology to use richer media, such as videos in which employees appear and talk to viewers about their jobs. This raises a question: Does the richness of the media used in testimonials influence how job seekers feel about the organizations being portrayed?

A recent experiment suggests that the answer is yes.[10] Participants in the study were college students who were on the job market. Sitting at computer terminals, they were shown recruitment ads for a hypothetical company; these ads were modeled after ones appearing on the Web sites of several actual companies. The ads contained testimonials in which the nature of the media used was either lean (pictures and testimonials appearing as text) or rich (videos with audio testimonials). To hold everything else constant, the same people were depicted and the same words were used in the testimonials.

How did the richness of the media used affect the way the students reacted to the ads? Two particular reactions were measured that have important implications for the effectiveness of a recruitment ad—viewers' perceptions of the attractiveness of the organization portrayed, and the extent to which they found the testimonials to be credible. As shown in Figure 9.5, both variables were influenced positively by the richness of the media. The organizations were perceived to be more attractive—and the ads more credible—when testimonials were delivered using video and audio. These findings suggest that participants could relate more easily to the people in the testimonials when their messages were presented in a way that provided more complete information about them. This, in turn, reflected positively on the organizations they represented.

Matching the Medium to the Message

What types of communication are most effective under various circumstances? In general, communication is most effective when it uses multiple channels, such as both oral and written messages.[11] Apparently, oral messages are useful in getting people's immediate attention, and the follow-up written portion helps make the message more permanent, something that can be referred to in the future. Oral messages also have the benefit of allowing for immediate two-way

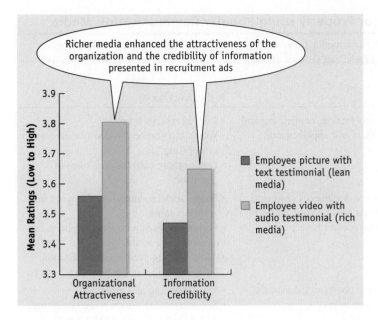

FIGURE 9.5

Rich Media Enhances the Impact of Recruitment Ads

A recent experiment found that the richness of media used in recruitment ads appearing on a company Web site affects how job seekers respond. Participants rated organizations as more attractive and the ads as being more credible when employee testimonials were presented via video with audio, as opposed to being presented via picture with text.

Source: Based on data reported by Walker et al., 2009; see Note 10.

communication between parties, whereas written communiqués frequently are only one-way, or require too long for a response.

Not surprisingly, two-way communications (e.g., face-to-face discussions, telephone conversations) are used more commonly in organizations than one-way communications (e.g., memos). For example, in a study of civilian employees of a U.S. Navy agency, approximately 83 percent of the communications taking place used two-way media.[12] In fact, 55 percent of all communications were individual face-to-face interactions. One-way, written communications tended to be reserved for more formal, official messages that needed to be referred to in the future at the receiver's convenience (e.g., official announcements about position openings). Clearly, both written and spoken communications have their places in organizational communication. The trick to any communication medium is not only *when* to use it but how to use it properly.[13] For some valuable suggestions in this regard, see Table 9.2.

MEDIA RICHNESS THEORY. In essence, a medium's effectiveness depends on how appropriate it is for the kinds of message being sent. Specifically, according to a conceptualization known as **media richness theory,** the effectiveness of any verbal medium depends on the extent to which it is appropriate when taking into account the ambiguity of the message being sent. In particular, oral media (e.g., telephone conversations, face-to-face meetings) are more effective than written media (e.g., notes, memos) when messages are nonroutine or ambiguous.[14] This is because the information contained in such messages is likely to be unclear to recipients, requiring the additional assistance in interpretation that oral media provide. If you've ever found yourself giving up on e-mail and calling someone to discuss something that is too complex, then you know what we mean.

By contrast, written media are more effective when messages are clear. For example, using e-mail to send someone a billing address or a phone number or directions to a company location—all very clear and highly specific information—is effective because it avoids errors. Problems of mishearing a number, for example, are eliminated, and people easily can refer to

media richness theory
A conceptualization specifying that the effectiveness of any verbal medium depends on the extent to which it is appropriate for ambiguity of the message being sent.

TABLE 9.2 Guidelines for Properly using Popular Communication Media

The most widely used communication media are e-mail, fax, postal mail, telephone, and, of course, face-to-face discussions. Each of these can be very useful if a few simple rules are followed, such as those summarized here.

Medium	Best Use	Rules for Use
E-mail	Sending key information, confirming and documenting facts and appointments	• Keep messages brief. • Words last forever, so don't be sarcastic or insulting. • Don't ignore conventional rules of grammar.
Fax	Sending complete documents requiring a signature, drafts for approval, or notes to someone who doesn't have e-mail	• Phone ahead to announce that your fax is forthcoming. • Follow up faxes with a quick phone call or e-mail to confirm receipt. • Avoid sending personal or confidential information that might be seen by others.
Postal mail	Sending long and complicated material or short thank-you notes	• Verify spelling and grammar. • Summarize key points at the beginning. • Avoid long sections; break up with bullet points.
Telephone	Communicating information in which emotion must be conveyed (if face-to-face discussions are not possible)	• Stay focused; avoid multitasking while on the phone. • Make appointments to have important phone calls ("phone dates"). • Let the other person finish speaking before you respond.
Face-to-face	Communicating highly sensitive and delicate information	• Keep discussions brief and focused on the issues. • Make sure personal discussions cannot be overheard. • Plan for meetings and arrive prepared to discuss the topic.

Source: Based on information in Gantenbein, 2002; see Note 13.

the written message when the information it contains is called for. In view of this, the quest for effective communication should be seen not simply as a question of what communication medium is best, but rather, what medium is best suited to the particular message being sent (recall the summary in Figure 9.4).

Importantly, managers who follow these practices by matching the type of communications media they use to the kind of message they are sending, considered *media-sensitive,* generally perform their jobs more effectively than those who fail to do so, considered *media-insensitive.*[15] Fortunately, many of us are likely to have a good intuitive sense for selecting the appropriate medium for the messages we wish to send. If you've ever found yourself thinking that it's best to discuss some "sensitive" or "delicate" matters in person instead of via e-mail or phone, then you know what we mean. Matters that are "difficult" because they are emotionally charged—those pertaining to serious illness or job termination, for example—are best handled in person instead of in writing because of the added opportunities they offer to demonstrate sensitivity and concern. (Considering that layoffs have been prevalent in organizations these days, questions arise about the appropriateness of the media used to announce them. For a discussion of this, see the OB in Practice section on page 301.)

Nonverbal Communication

It has been claimed that people communicate at least as much *nonverbally* (i.e., without words) as they do verbally.[16] Indeed, there can be no doubt that many of the messages we send

OB In Practice

The Downside of Communicating Layoffs Via E-Mail

There can be no mistaking the widespread nature of layoffs in today's organizations. The U.S. Bureau of Labor Statics reported that in 2009 alone, more than 11,000 mass layoffs occurred in the United States, resulting in more than 2 million lost jobs.[17] This means that a lot of company officials had the unpleasant task of having to announce these layoffs to their unsuspecting employees. Although we'll never know how all these companies went about communicating the bad news to their employees, business experts have debated the merits of making these announcements in person or more impersonally, such as via e-mail. We present both sides here, but as you'll see, OB research and theory point to the merits of the more personal approach.

From time to time, news accounts tell of layoffs being announced to employees in shockingly insensitive ways. The story in these cases is not that the layoffs occurred. With just about all companies cutting their staffs in recent years, layoffs are not particularly newsworthy anymore. Rather, the focus of these accounts is on *how* the companies went about sending their messages. As an extreme example, administrators in one California school district not only informed teachers that they were being laid off by giving them curt written notices, but they also delivered these while the teachers were standing in front of their classes![18] Their reactions are almost too frightening to envision.

Even in (slightly) less extreme cases, where the layoffs are announced to employees via e-mail (and there have been quite a few), many people are still aghast. It's as if the companies involved have violated a norm suggesting that important messages should be communicated in person. The lack of personal contact, denial of the opportunity to ask questions on the spot, and of course, not being there to console the victim—these appear to be the missing elements at the root of people's indignation. By its willingness to violate this norm, a company is sending the message that it doesn't care about the employees it's letting go.

This was precisely the crux of the backlash against the large pharmaceuticals firm Pfizer, which sent e-mail messages to 2,000 sales reps announcing their layoffs (this comprised 20 percent of its sales force of 10,000). From the company's perspective, this was undoubtedly an incredibly efficient way to reach such a large number of people. What's more, it precluded requiring any officials from having to drop the axe in person, which would have been distasteful for them. How about the victims, you ask? Shouldn't the message be sent in a way that minimizes the damage—that is, without adding insult (using e-mail) to injury (the layoff itself)?

One business analyst has suggested that using e-mail was actually the better approach because it made the overall level of pain less than it would have been if the messages were announced individually to sales reps 2,000 times. To him, the issue boils down to either "a lot of pain for a few people in a short period of time, or a little bit of pain for a larger group of people over a longer period of time."[19] He argues that it's best to get it over and done with as quickly as possible, even if that means being impersonal. Although others aren't saying much about this in public, the fact that Pfizer is not alone in using e-mail to announce layoffs suggests that other company leaders share the belief that the costs of not making the announcement in person are outweighed by the benefits of doing the job by e-mail.

From the perspective of media richness theory, the counterargument is straightforward. It suggests that the sensitive nature of the message's content demands using a richer medium. More information can be communicated in face-to-face contact than in e-mail, making it better suited as a medium for presenting messages that are likely to make people upset. The additional cues from richer media may help mitigate those negative reactions. Company officials should have been more media-sensitive, but the fact that they weren't suggests that they might not be sufficiently concerned about the welfare of these individuals, as if to imply, "they're out the door, anyway."

No matter how badly victims feel because of the layoffs themselves, companies also need to be mindful of the survivors of those layoffs. And in the case of Pfizer's sales reps, there are 8,000 of them. Research has shown that survivors are highly sensitive to the manner in which their colleagues are laid off.[20] This sends a strong message to them about what their companies value. And when 2,000 of their colleagues got the axe in what may be believed to be an insensitive fashion, that message is not likely to be very flattering. As a result, the 8,000 survivors may be feeling that their company treats its employees in an interactionally unfair manner (see Chapter 2). This, in turn, may lead some of these survivors to consider leaving the company themselves, voluntarily in these cases. And given that the employees who remain behind following layoffs are presumably the better performing ones, companies are unlikely to be pleased by their departures. This may be viewed as an unintended, and potentially costly, consequence of communicating mass layoffs via e-mail.

Companies also should be concerned about consequences to layoff victims themselves. Not only are they out of a job, but they also were sent a parting message that their soon-to-be former employer didn't even care enough about them to talk to them in person. Putting aside thoughts of "doing the right thing," there's a very practical reason for companies to be concerned about laying people off in ways they consider to be unfair. Employees who believe they have been treated unfairly in the course of being laid off are inclined to strike back at their former employers by suing them for wrongful termination.[21] And no matter how the case turns out, this is a costly ordeal for the companies involved, in terms of both direct legal expenses and damage to their corporate reputations.

Taking all this into account, it would be wise for company officials to think twice before communicating layoffs via e-mail. The costs of doing so may be greater than envisioned.

others are transmitted without words. Here are just a few examples of how we communicate nonverbally in organizations.

- ■ *Mode of dress.* Much of what we say about ourselves to others comes from the way we dress. For example, despite the general trend toward casual clothing in the workplace, higher-status people tend to dress more formally than lower-ranking employees.[22]
- ■ *Waiting time.* Higher-status people, such as managers and executives at all ranks, tend to communicate their organizational positions nonverbally by keeping lower-ranking people waiting to see them—a gesture that sends the message that one's time is more important.[23]
- ■ *Seating position.* Higher-ranking people also assert their higher status by sitting at the heads of rectangular tables. Over the years, this position has come to symbolize the high status of the individuals who occupy these seats. The benefits are not merely symbolic; individuals seated at the heads of tables are in excellent positions to maintain eye contact with others.[24] This, in turn, facilitates opportunities to influence those individuals (see Chapter 12).
- ■ *Body language.* When communicating in other countries, it's useful to learn not only the verbal language spoken, but also the nonverbal, body language used. People from various cultures interpret certain nonverbal signs very differently than people do in the United States.[25] Avoiding serious miscommunications requires familiarizing oneself with such information. For some useful recommendations in this regard, see Table 9.3.

The Role of Technology: Computer-Mediated Communication

computer-mediated communication
Forms of communication that are aided by the use of computer technology (e.g., e-mail, instant messaging).

As we have indicated, a great deal of communication that takes place in organizations these days occurs online, such as through e-mail, and video conferences. These are considered forms of **computer-mediated communication** because the messages are transmitted using computers.[26] Because of its widespread use, we focus on computer-mediated communication in this section of the chapter.

In today's uncertain period for General Motors, the company has been making a concerted effort to use computer-mediated communication to get messages out to key employees—and,

---

TABLE 9.3 To Avoid Embarrassment Abroad, Watch that Gesture!

In today's global business environment, Americans are likely to be communicating with people from other nations. Although you can learn a few words of another language, it's easy to overlook the messages you may be sending unintentionally with your gestures. As shown here, many gestures that are completely proper among Americans may mean very different—and extremely negative—things in other parts of the world. Once you get off that plane, be mindful of your hands. Ignore this advice and you may be in for an unpleasant surprise.

Where	What	What it Means
Muslim and most Asian cultures	Taking or giving something with your left hand	This is considered very rude.
Asia	Placing your hand on another's head	This is offensive because the head is considered the residence of the soul.
Middle East	Firm handshake	This is considered highly aggressive.
Australia	"V" for victory with palm facing out	This is considered to be an obscene gesture.
East Asian countries	Putting hands on hips	This is considered to be an aggressive gesture.
Asia	Holding up hand so as to signal "stop"	You are seeking permission to speak.
Singapore	Curled finger as if to say "come here"	This signifies death.
Asian and Islamic countries	Thumbs up, as if to indicate your approval	This is a rude gesture.
Brazil and Germany	"OK" sign with your fingers	This is a rude gesture.
Middle East and Near East	Showing the soles of your shoes while sitting	This is a sign of disrespect.
Bulgaria and Greece	Nodding head up and down to say "yes"	This means "no."

importantly, to hear back from them. For example, the company has been using bi-weekly *podcasts* (titled "For Immediate Release") and *RSS feeds* on various topics (e.g., high-tech advances) to get the latest developments to engineers. A **podcast** (an iPod broadcast) is a message distributed for playback on an MP3 player, such as Apple's iPod; an **RSS feed** is information, usually news, delivered to Web sites as events occur. And, as a means of hearing back from these engineers, the company has been relying on **blogs** (short for **Web logs**)—Web pages in which an individual expresses personal feelings and experiences, an Internet-based diary.

A useful way of distinguishing among various forms of computer-mediated communication is by noting differences between those in which communication occurs in *synchronous* fashion and those in which it occurs in *asynchronous* fashion. **Synchronous communication techniques** are ones in which the parties can send and receive messages at once. Telephone conversations fall into this category, for example. However, some other communication technologies—push-to-talk cell phone service and radio transmissions between airline pilots and air traffic controllers being two popular examples—are considered **asynchronous communication techniques** because people must take turns sending and receiving messages (in other words, the sender's message and the receiver's messages are not synchronized). Some widely used forms of computer-mediation communication may be found in each category.

Synchronous Communication: Video-Mediated Communication

These days, it's not unusual for people to work together although they are physically in different locations. This is because technology can be used to bring them together, allowing people to communicate by sharing information in real time whether they are across the street or across the planet. Just as the telephone revolutionized business communications a century ago, today, advances in technology have driven down the costs of more advanced techniques, such as *videoconferences* or *Webcasts* (short for Web broadcasts), making them extremely popular communication tools. These are known more generally as forms of **video-mediated communication (VMC).** Simply put, these are ways of simultaneously transmitting audio and video between two or more computers. The inexpensive "Webcams" used with personal computers are, in fact, rudimentary forms of this technology. Given the widespread availability of wifi service, people can participate in VMC from almost anywhere (see Figure 9.6).

Companies use VMC as inexpensive ways of linking employees in distant locations—allowing them to have *cybermeetings*. Not only are these considerably less expensive than air travel—with respect to both money and time—but because they require limited preparation, they also allow for meetings to be scheduled at the last minute. Boeing, for example, regularly uses VMC to connect the employees in the company's Chicago headquarters with others in satellite locations.[27]

podcast
A prerecorded message distributed for playback on an MP3 player, such as Apple's iPod (i.e., an iPod broadcast).

RSS feed
Information, usually news, delivered to Web sites on a real-time basis, as events occur.

blogs (Web logs)
Web pages in which people express their personal experiences and feelings; an Internet-based diary.

synchronous communication techniques
Forms of communication in which the parties can send and receive messages at the same time.

asynchronous communication techniques
Forms of communication in which senders and receivers must take turns sending and receiving messages.

video-mediated communication (VMC)
Conferences in which people can hear and see each other using computers.

FIGURE 9.6

Cybermeetings at 30,000 Feet?

Some airlines, such as Virgin America Airlines offers wifi service to passengers. This has made it possible for many businesspeople (including rapper MC Hammer, shown here) not only to stay in touch using e-mail but even to conduct video conferences when necessary.

Casey Rodgers/AP World Wide.

Asynchronous Communication: E-Mail and Instant Messaging

Some of the most widely used forms of communication technology fall into the asynchronous category. Because they rely on less sophisticated technologies, asynchronous forms of communication—such as fax machines and voice mail—are older (around since the 1980s and 1990s), making them very well established. In these techniques, one party must complete a message before the other can respond to it. Also in this category are two especially popular forms of communication—*e-mail* and *instant messaging.*

e-mail (electronic mail)
A system whereby people use personal computer terminals to send and receive messages between one another using the Internet.

E-MAIL. Short for electronic mail, **e-mail** refers to messages sent via the Internet, usually in text form (although graphics, videos, and audio files also are sent all the time). Based on your own experiences, it probably comes as no surprise to you that e-mail is the most widely used communication tools in organizations (see Figure 9.7).[28] The statistics are staggering.[29] About 247 billion e-mails are sent each day. In fact, in the time it took you to read that sentence, some 20 million new e-mails entered cyberspace. Every second of every day, the messages sent by the world's e-mail users equal the size of 16,000 copies of the *Complete Works of William Shakespeare.* The main reason for e-mail's popularity is the freedom it provides people to send and receive messages quickly and efficiently to people located anyplace at any time of day or night, and to organize and store messages as well.

E-mail is the preferred means of communicating facts, such as information needed to coordinate effort between individuals and work groups. Brief, factual messages (e.g., about schedule changes) and announcements (e.g., about forthcoming events) are popular uses of e-mail. E-mail also has made it easier to break down status barriers between people that often make it difficult to share ideas. For example, whereas one may find it difficult to get an in-person appointment with the head of a company, it's just as simple to send an e-mail message to that individual as it is to reach anyone else, effectively altering the flow of information within an organization.[30] Not surprisingly, many top executives rely on e-mail as an effective means of reaching out to everyone in their companies.

information overload
The feeling of being overwhelmed by more information than one can process.

As popular as e-mail is today, it is far from perfect. One major problem is that e-mail contributes to **information overload**—that is, the feeling of being overwhelmed by more information than one can process. Frequently, people receive so much information that it's tiring,

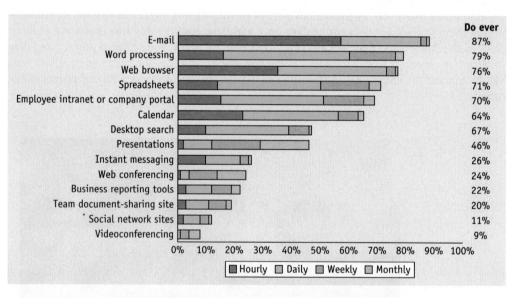

FIGURE 9.7

Popularity of Various Computer-Based Products and Services

In a recent survey, 2,001 information workers in the United States indicated the frequency with which they use various computer-based products and services. Not surprisingly, e-mail topped the list.

Source: The State of Workforce Technology Adoption: *US BenchMark 2009.* Forrester Research, Inc., October 2009. Used with permission of Forrester Research, Inc.

frustrating, and challenging to have to sift through it all to find what's most important. Given the statistics we just cited, this is not too surprising.

Another key problem with e-mail is that people usually find it a highly limiting medium for expressing their emotions. After all, traditional e-mail is restricted to alphanumeric characters and lacks the nonverbal information that makes face-to-face communication so rich. So, although you can change the tone of your voice or make a face to express how you feel about something in person, it's harder to do this using only the tools of the keyboard.

One way of getting around this is by using **emoticons** (short for emotional icons). These are simple graphic representations of facial expressions used to express feelings. They are created by typing characters such as commas, hyphens, and parentheses, which when tilting one's head to the side, resemble facial expressions. The smiley face—typed as :-) or :) —is the most commonly used emoticon. People generally use emoticons to qualify their emotions in important ways. Most simply, the presence of the smiley face in a message can be used to emphasize the point being made, as in "you make me happy :)" or it can be used sarcastically, as in the message, "he's really smart :-)" to connote that the person in question is really not so smart at all.

Research has revealed two particularly interesting things about emoticons. First, emoticons do *not* always qualify the meanings of written messages.[31] For example, a negative message accompanied by a wink or a frown is generally not seen as being any more sarcastic or negative in tone than the words by themselves. One possible reason for this is that emoticons tend to be overused, and as a result, their impact has diminished over time. Second, there are gender differences with respect to using emoticons.[32] In general, women use emoticons more frequently than men. However, when men are communicating with women, they use emoticons more frequently than when communicating with other men. This is in keeping with research showing that in general men feel more comfortable expressing their emotions to women than to other men. Interestingly, men and women use emoticons for different purposes. Whereas women usually use emoticons to be humorous, men use them to be teasing and sarcastic. Yeah, right ;-).

emoticons (emotional icons)
Symbols typed using characters such as commas, hyphens, and parentheses for purposes of expressing emotions in online communication.

INSTANT MESSAGING. Another form of asynchronous communication that has become very popular in recent years is known as **instant messaging.** Services of this type (such as those offered by AOL and MSN) allow people who are online to share messages with one another instantaneously, without having to go through an e-mail program. Sending an instant message (IM) opens up a small onscreen window into which each party can type messages for the other to read. This makes it possible to exchange written notes in real time, as well as to share Web links and files of all types. Although e-mail is quite fast, sometimes even the rapid response of e-mail is not fast enough given that it requires checking for incoming messages and then having to click through a few steps to read, reply, and send the e-mail. This accounts for the popularity of instant messaging. In fact, on a typical day, Facebook users alone send 1 billion instant messages.[33]

instant messaging
The practice of communicating with another online by typing messages into boxes that pop up on the screen as needed.

Although intended originally for home users, instant messaging is becoming increasingly popular as a communications medium for business as well. Currently, only about one in four people use IM to communicate with others at work. Some people like it, but for many others it's a mixed blessing.[34] Those in favor of it feel that IMs save time, provide relief from the daily grind, and improve teamwork. Others, though, believe IMs encourage gossip, are too distracting, and promotes stress. (Another concern regarding IM, and all forms of electronic communication, for that matter, involves possible violations of employee privacy—the focus of this chapter's The Ethics Angle section on page 306.) Despite mixed reactions to instant messaging as a tool for organizational communication, IM has been seeing slow and steady growth as a communication medium in organizations.

Does High-Tech Communication Dehumanize the Workplace?

When computers first entered the workplace, experts became concerned about the tendency for people's social needs to go unfulfilled because they come into contact with fewer others in the course of their days.[35] To a large extent, this is a valid concern.

The Ethics Angle

Should Employers Be Monitoring Employees' Computer Activities?

Before advances in technology, when the major forms of organizational communication were speaking face-to-face, writing letters, and talking on the telephone, concerns about violating privacy were not especially great. After all, social norms discouraged people from listening in on others' conversations and peeking at their mail. Although dramatically useful, technology changed all this. Messages being communicated today, because they are heavily mediated by computers, can be—and frequently are—monitored by others. Indeed, today's companies spend an estimated $655 million monitoring their employees' actions on the Internet.[36]

Although most employees generally dislike this practice because it violates their privacy, employers counter that they have to monitor their employees because today's communication technology makes it easier than ever for employees to "goof off." Just consider these statistics:[37]

- 86.5 percent of employees use their company's e-mail systems to send personal messages.
- 30 percent of American workers watch sports online and 24 percent admit to shopping online while at work.
- 70 percent of the visits to Internet pornography sites occur during regular 9:00 A.M. to 5:00 P.M. working hours.

Given these figures, it's not surprising that nonwork-related use of the Internet has been estimated to result in a 40 percent loss in productivity for American businesses.

Beyond concerns about lost productivity, companies are monitoring their employees' communications for two additional reasons. Both involve security. First, in recent years, terrorist attacks (e.g., in New York, Madrid, and London) have put the world on notice that being vigilant for terrorism in the workplace is wise. Second, many companies are losing untold millions of dollars through industrial espionage and other breaches of information security.[38] These are vitally important considerations, of course. At the same time, they raise questions about where to draw the line between personal liberties and the need for security, both national and industrial.[39]

The trick, then, is to find ways to balance people's rights to privacy in the workplace with the rights of organizations to confirm that their employees are doing what they are paid to do and to protect their property, as well as the obligation of government to protect its citizens. Although this surely isn't a simple matter, several suggestions for balancing these considerations may be noted.

- *Establish a clear monitoring policy and follow it carefully.* All employees should be made aware of the conditions under which certain messages will be monitored. This gives them the opportunity to decide whether or not to engage in inappropriate behavior while at work, knowing all along that they might get caught.
- *Apply the privacy policy equally.* Too often, policies applied to lower-level employees are ignored at the top. However, if it is wrong for low-level employees to use company e-mail for personal purposes, so too is it wrong for top executives to do the same.
- *Maintain complete privacy of all company records.* Organizations never should use company records for purposes other than those to which employees have agreed when providing the information. For example, performance information may be used to make training decisions, but health records should not be used in making decisions about suitability for promotion. Clearly, information never should be shared with third parties without employees' full consent—unless, of course, a company is required to do so by court order.

Research has revealed a particularly interesting side to this issue. Specifically, the inherently solitary nature of communication via the Internet makes it a particularly appealing communication channel for individuals lacking in interpersonal skills—those who find traditional, face-to-face communication awkward and difficult. Frequently, such individuals rely on the Internet (e.g., through e-mail, chat rooms, or instant messaging) to satisfy their basic needs for affiliation (i.e., to be connected to others) in ways that compensate for their uneasiness with in-person social interaction. However, this appears to be a double-edged sword.[40]

On the positive side, it's clear that the Internet opens up avenues of communication to individuals who otherwise might be inclined to be left out of the loop. The downside, however, is that many such individuals tend to overcompensate by being highly compulsive in their use of the Internet, finding it difficult to limit the considerable hours spent in front of the computer. The problem is so serious for some that, as a result, the time spent online causes them to miss work or social engagements (for a summary, see Figure 9.8). As such, we note that computer-mediated communication is a valuable organizational tool, but one that is not without limits or problems.

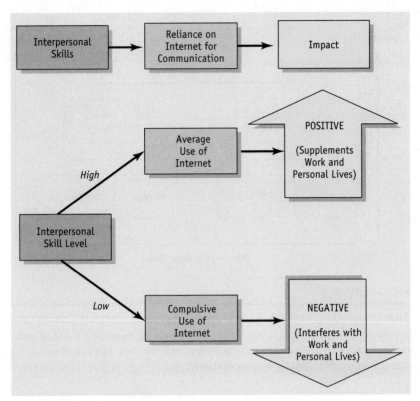

FIGURE 9.8

The Positive and Negative Sides of Computer-Mediated Communication

Research has shown that among individuals who are lacking in interpersonal skills, computer-mediated communication might be problematic. In contrast, people with good interpersonal skills reap benefits from computer-mediated communication. The specific connections responsible for these patterns are summarized here.

Source: Based on findings reported by Caplan, 2005; see Note 40.

Formal Communication in Organizations

Think of the broad range of messages that are communicated to you in the course of a workday. For example, your boss may ask you to complete an important sales report, another manager from across the hall may hand you a memo regarding the status of a new project, you may read an e-mail message from a coworker regarding who won the office football pool, and the custodian may tell you a joke. From just these few examples, it's easy to distinguish between two basic types of communication that occur in organizations: **formal communication**—the sharing of messages regarding the official work of the organization, and **informal communication**—the sharing of messages that are unrelated to the organization's official activities. Because both formal and informal communication are so widespread in organizations, we describe both in this chapter. First, in this section we will focus on formal communication; then, in the next section we will turn to informal communication.

Organizational Structure Influences Communication

Although the basic process of communication described thus far is similar in many different contexts, a unique feature of organizations has a profound impact on the communication process—namely, their *structure*. Organizations often are set up in ways that dictate who may and may not communicate with whom. Given this, we may ask: How is the communication process affected by the structure of an organization?

The term **organizational structure** refers to the formally prescribed pattern of interrelationships existing between the various units of an organization (a topic we will examine in detail in Chapter 15). An organization's structure may be described using a diagram like the one shown in Figure 9.9, known as an **organization chart.** Such diagrams provide graphic representations of the formal pattern of communication in an organization (this one is fictitious). An organization chart may be likened to an X-ray showing the organization's skeleton, an outline of the planned, formal connections between individuals in various departments.[41]

Note the various boxes in the diagram and the lines connecting them. Each box represents a person performing a specific job. The diagram shows the titles of the individuals performing

formal communication
The sharing of messages regarding the official work of the organization.

informal communication
The sharing of messages that are unrelated to the organization's official activities.

organizational structure
The formally prescribed pattern of interrelationships existing between the various units of an organization.

organization chart
A diagram showing the formal structure of an organization, indicating who is to communicate with whom.

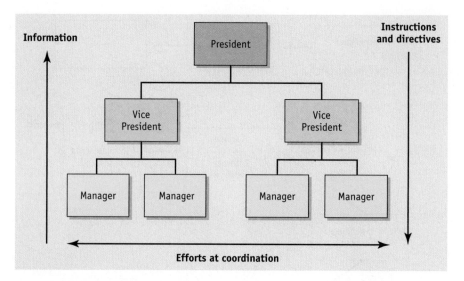

FIGURE 9.9

The Organization Chart: An Organization's Formal Communication Network

An organization chart, such as this simple one, shows the formally prescribed patterns of communication in an organization. Different types of messages typically flow upward, downward, and horizontally throughout organizations, as summarized here.

the various jobs and the formally prescribed pattern of communication between them. These are relatively fixed and defined. Each individual is responsible for performing a specified job. Should the people working in the organization leave their jobs, they must be replaced if their jobs are to be performed. The formal structure of an organization—hence, the prescribed pattern of communication between individuals—does not change just because the personnel change. As you will see in the next section of this chapter, however, the pattern of informal communication may change dramatically under such circumstances.

The lines connecting the boxes in the organization chart are lines of *authority* showing who must answer to whom—that is, **reporting relationships.** Each person is responsible to (or answers to) the person at the next higher level to which he or she is connected. At the same time, people also are responsible for (or give orders to) those who are immediately below them—individuals known as **direct reports.** The boxes and lines form a sort of blueprint of an organization, showing not only what people have to do, but with whom they have to communicate for the organization to operate properly.

As you might imagine, the nature and form of communication vary greatly according to people's relative positions within an organization. Even a quick look at an organization chart reveals that information may flow up (from lower to higher levels within the same functional area), down (from higher to lower levels within the same functional area), or horizontally (between people at the same level in different functional areas). However, as summarized in Figure 9.9, and as we now describe, different types of information typically travel in different directions within a hierarchy.

Downward Communication: From Supervisor to Subordinate

Communication from supervisors to their subordinates is known as **downward communication** because it flows from one level to the next lowest one, slowly trickling down to the bottom of the organization chart. What types of messages do supervisors typically send their direct reports? Although many things may be communicated, official messages flowing downward generally consist of instructions, directions, and orders—messages telling subordinates what they should be doing.[42] We also would expect to find feedback on past performance flowing in a downward direction (such as when managers tell subordinates how well they have been working). A sales manager, for example, might direct members of her sales force to promote a certain product and then congratulate them for being successful.

reporting relationships
Formal connections between people indicating who must answer to whom in an organization.

direct report
Someone in an organization, a subordinate, who must answer directly to a higher-level individual in that organization.

downward communication
Communication from people at higher organizational levels to those at lower organizational levels.

WHAT DO SUBORDINATES WANT TO HEAR? Generally, employees are satisfied only moderately with the nature of the communication they receive from their superiors. A large-scale survey found that 71 percent of employees believe their superiors keep them well informed, 65 percent believe that they are given sufficient information to do their jobs, and 51 percent believe that the downward messages they receive are candid and accurate.[43] Although the problem does not appear dire, these statistics suggest that there's clearly something missing from the information people are receiving from their superiors. This raises an interesting question: When listening to their superiors, what topics interest employees most? To what questions are they searching for answers? There appear to be six key areas of interest to employees.[44] These are as follows:

- What, exactly, does my job entail?
- How well am I doing?
- Does anyone care about me?
- How is my work unit doing?
- Where is the organization headed?
- How can I help the company meet its objectives?

Armed with this information, it's obvious that managers should have a clear agenda when communicating downward with their subordinates. Answering these questions, whether directly in the form of one-on-one discussions, or in broader media, such as company newsletters, is a sure way of improving communication. Not only does addressing these issues stand to make workers more satisfied with the messages received from their superiors, but also with those superiors themselves. In fact, addressing these issues in messages to one's subordinates is an excellent way of managing their job performance.[45]

THE MUM EFFECT. An interesting phenomenon that often occurs in the course of downward communication is known as the **MUM effect.** This refers to people's reluctance to transmit bad news to others (as in "Mum's the word," being silent about something).[46] For example, a manager may feel reluctant to explain to a subordinate that he or she has performed a job poorly. As a result, the manager may be inclined to respond in several different ways, each of which is problematic.

MUM effect
The reluctance to transmit bad news, shown either by not transmitting the message at all, or by delegating the task to someone else.

- The manager may downplay the seriousness of a problem, making things seem better than they really are. As a result, an employee is unlikely to come away with good sense of the magnitude of the problem—or even that there is a problem at all.
- The manager may "pass the buck" by having someone else, such as an assistant, give the bad news to the employee. Because the assistant is unlikely to be equally familiar with the problems and because this person's word doesn't carry the same weight as the manager's, the employee has a good chance of not understanding or appreciating fully the problem at hand.
- Possibly worst of all, the manager may be so reluctant to address the bad news that he or she simply avoids saying anything whatsoever.[47] Employees who receive no information about the need to change something that they're doing are inclined to keep doing it. And, of course, a problem that goes unaddressed has a good chance of becoming more serious in the future.

Any way you look at it, failing to overcome the MUM effect can be very problematic. Keeping employees from the corrective feedback they need will prevent them from taking steps to improve their work (see Chapter 3). Although it's difficult to counteract the MUM effect, the task of transmitting bad news can be made less difficult by becoming more supportive as a communicator. Later in this chapter we offer some guidelines for developing this important skill (see pages 325–326).

Upward Communication: From Subordinate to Superior

Information flowing from lower levels to higher levels within an organization, from subordinates to supervisors, is referred to as **upward communication.** Messages flowing in this direction tend to contain the information managers need to do their jobs, such as data required for decision making and the status of various projects. In short, upward communication is designed to keep managers aware of what is going on. Among the most typical types of information flowing upward are suggestions for improvement, status reports, reactions to work-related issues, and new ideas.

upward communication
Communication from people at lower organizational levels to those at higher organizational levels.

Upward communication is not simply the reverse of downward communication. The difference in status between the communicating parties makes for some important distinctions. For one, upward communication occurs much less frequently than downward communication. A classic study found that 70 percent of assembly-line workers initiated communication with their supervisors less than once a month.[48] In addition, managers direct less than 15 percent of their total communication to their superiors.[49] And, when people do communicate upward, their conversations tend to be shorter than discussions with their peers.[50] Although the flattening of organizational structures (see Chapter 15) and the advent of teams in organizations (see Chapter 8) are likely to have made these figures less extreme over the years, it's safe to say that upward communication still remains relatively restricted.[51]

Importantly, upward communication is often inaccurate. For example, subordinates frequently feel they must highlight their accomplishments and downplay their mistakes if they are to be looked on favorably.[52] Similarly, some individuals fear that they will be rebuked by their supervisors if they anticipate that their remarks will be perceived as threatening.[53] As a result, many people frequently avoid communicating bad news to their supervisors, or simply "pass the buck" for doing so to someone else.[54] This, of course, represents another instance of the MUM effect discussed earlier in conjunction with downward communication. Clearly, this same phenomenon occurs here as well. As you might imagine, because superiors rely on information when making decisions, keeping silent about important news, even if it's bad, may be one of the worst things a subordinate can do. As one executive put it, "All of us have our share of bonehead ideas. Having someone tell you it's a bonehead idea before you do something about it is really a great blessing."[55]

It's an intriguing possibility that managers may be to blame for their subordinates' reluctance to communicate with them. Time pressure seems to be the key. Specifically, many subordinates complain that they would communicate with their superiors more frequently if they believed their superiors welcomed them, but too often they are led to believe that their superiors are unwilling to make the time for them.[56] Given the importance of accurate upward messages, managers should make time to listen to their subordinates—and importantly, to let them know that they are doing so. Also to avoid the problem of limited upward communication, many companies have incorporated large-scale programs through which employees can send messages to top company officials by completing *employee surveys*. Because of their general value in improving communication (including upward and downward communication), later in this chapter (see pages 324–325) we will describe in detail this and other valuable tools for sending and receiving feedback.

Lateral Communication: Coordinating Messages Among Peers

lateral communication
Communication between individuals at the same organizational level.

Finally, we note the nature of **lateral communication** within organizations. This refers to messages that flow between different people at the same organizational level.[57] Typically, lateral communication is characterized by efforts at coordination (attempts to work together). Consider, for example, how a vice president of marketing would coordinate her efforts to initiate an advertising campaign for a new product with information from the vice president of production about when the first products will be rolling off the assembly line. Such communication is essential for organizations to operate effectively. These days, as organizations are eliminating layers of hierarchy (see Chapter 15) and are having people work together in teams in which individuals are relatively equal (see Chapter 8), lateral communication is becoming increasingly common (for an example, see Figure 9.10).

Because lateral communication involves people at the same organizational level, it is often friendlier in nature and less awkward than either upward or downward communication, in which the parties are at different levels. Communication between peers also tends to be more casual and occurs more quickly because fewer social barriers exist between them. Not surprisingly, people generally are satisfied with the nature of the lateral communication they experience—85 percent, according to one survey.[58] This is not to say, however, that lateral communication is free of challenges. One common problem that occurs is that people in different departments have rivalries that make them feel that they are competing against one another for valued organizational resources. As a result, they may show resentment toward one another, substituting an antagonistic, competitive orientation for the friendlier, cooperative one needed to get things done.[59] Fortunately, the

The Star-Ledger/Gerry McCrea/The Image Works.

FIGURE 9.10

Lateral Communication in Progress

Staff meetings are venues in which lateral communication is inclined to occur. Such sessions provide opportunities for individuals at the same organizational level to work together so they can plan and coordinate their efforts.

various suggestions for improving communication that appear later in this chapter can be used to minimize this problem and to improve the quality of lateral communication.

Communicating Inside Versus Outside the Organization: Strategic Communication

All corporate communication can be distinguished with respect to whether it is aimed at other people within the organization (e.g., fellow employees) or outside the organization (e.g., the general public).[60] This prompts an interesting question: Do executives say different kinds of things when aiming their remarks inside versus outside the company?

Research suggests that they do.[61] Illustrating this, consider a study in which scientists analyzed the comments made by CEOs of 10 forest products companies appearing in their letters to shareholders (external communications) over a 10-year period. They also examined various planning documents (internal communications) for these same companies during this period. These messages were categorized with respect to how they were framed—that is, whether the statements focused on threats the company faced (e.g., the rising cost of materials) or on opportunities (e.g., growth in demand for the product).

The results were quite interesting. In general, because the industry improved during the period studied, the proportion of documents framed in terms of threat dropped. However, mentions of threat were not equally likely to occur in both internal and external statements. For each year studied, a greater proportion of internal documents than external documents referred to threats. Likewise, with only few exceptions, a greater proportion of external documents than internal documents focused on opportunities.

These findings suggest that executives were attempting to present their companies in a positive light to the public (by focusing on opportunities), but were more willing to address threats internally. They may have been thinking that it is important not to frighten the investing public, while at the same time keeping employees appraised of threats the company faces so that their help can be enlisted in defending against these threats.

This is the idea behind what is called **strategic communication**—the practice of presenting information about the company to broad, external audiences, such as the press. The more effectively companies manage this process, the better they will be received by the general public, yielding considerable benefits, such as enhanced customer loyalty and increased sales. Given the importance of clearly and appropriately managing a corporate image through strategic communication, public relations firms are often hired to do the work.

strategic communication
The practice of presenting information about the company to broad, external audiences, such as the press.

Informal Communication Networks: Behind the Organization Chart

Think about the people with whom you communicate during the course of an average day. Friends, family members, classmates, and colleagues at work are among those with whom you may have *informal communication,* information shared without any formally imposed obligations or restrictions. It's easy to recognize how widespread our informal connections can be. You know someone who knows someone else, who knows your best friend—and before long, your informal reach is very extensive. (Film buffs may recall that this was the premise behind the 1993 movie, *Six Degrees of Separation.*) The pattern of informal connections between people is known as an **informal communication network.**

As you might imagine, informal communication networks, because they are so widespread, constitute an important avenue by which information flows in organizations.[62] In fact, middle managers ranked informal networks as better sources of organizational information than formal networks.[63] It may be said, therefore, that if an organization's formal communication network represents its skeleton, then its informal communication network constitutes its central nervous system.[64]

Organizations' Hidden Pathways

It is easy to imagine how important the flow of informal information may be within organizations. In general, we transmit information to others with whom we come into contact, thereby providing conduits through which messages can travel.

THE OLD BOYS' NETWORK. People are inclined to communicate most with individuals who are similar to themselves on key dimensions (e.g., age, seniority).[65] Because we are more comfortable with similar people than with dissimilar ones, we tend to spend more time with them and, of course, communicate with them more frequently. As a result, many informal gender-segregated networks tend to form in organizations—what, among men, has been referred to as the **old boys' network.** Over the years, this term has come to be used in a derogatory fashion because of the tendency to exclude women from the communication network, thereby interfering with their career advancement (see Chapter 6 and Appendix 2).

To the extent that such restricted associations isolate people from others in power who may be different from themselves, this practice is seriously limiting.[66] At the same time, however, exposure to similar others with whom people feel comfortable provides valuable sources of information. For example, many business leaders from various racial and ethnic minority groups have formed informal networks with others of their same group so as to help them share ways of succeeding in a business world in which they constitute an ethnic minority—alliances that have proven helpful to the careers of many.[67] This informal observation is in keeping with scientific evidence showing that the more involved people are in their organizations' communication networks, the more powerful and influential they become.[68]

THE SNOWBALL EFFECT. The idea that people are connected informally also has been used to explain a very important organizational phenomenon—turnover. Do people resign from their jobs in ways that are random and unrelated to each other? Research suggests that they do not, but rather, that turnover is related to the informal communication patterns between people.[69] In fact, voluntary turnover (employees freely electing to resign from their jobs) occurs in a kind of **snowball effect.** A snowball does not accumulate snowflakes randomly, but collects those that are in its path. Analogously, patterns of voluntary turnover are not independently distributed within a work group, but are the result of people's influences on each other. Thus, predicting which people will resign from their jobs may be based, in large part, on knowledge of the informal communication patterns within work groups. A person who leaves his or her job for a better one in another organization is likely to be an individual who knows someone who already has done so. The individual in the new organization can provide information about positions there, potentially opening the door to new opportunities. For a suggestion regarding how this may operate, see Figure 9.11.

An important quality of informal communication networks is that the people in them can communicate anything to anyone else, even if they are at different organizational levels that one dare not cross in formal communications. For example, informal messages such as jokes and funny stories tend to cross levels and departments in an organizational hierarchy and are freely shared by people in both the managerial and nonmanagerial ranks of organizations.[70] This is

FIGURE 9.11

Informal Communication Networks: A Predictor of Turnover Patterns

The informal networks of communication between people (shown in dotted lines) provide channels through which messages about better job opportunities may be communicated. Patterns of voluntary turnover have been linked to the existence of such informal networks.

Source: Based on suggestions by Krackhardt & Porter, 1986; see Note 69.

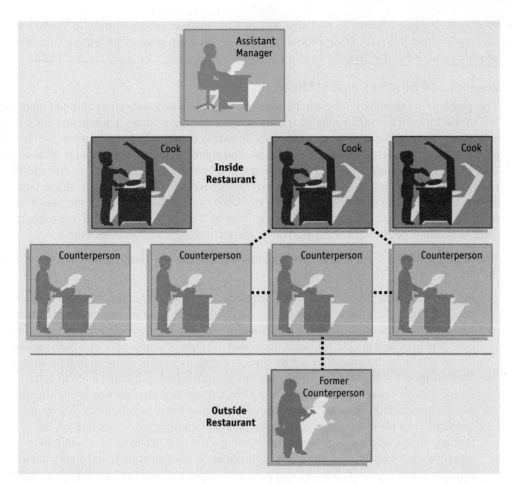

information that's unrelated to the job. On the other hand, in many organizations it would be quite unlikely—indeed, seriously "out of line"—for a lower-level employee to communicate something to an upper-level employee about how to do the job.

The Nature of the Grapevine

When anyone can tell something informal to anyone else, it results in a very rapid flow of information along what is commonly referred to as the **grapevine**—the pathways along which unofficial, informal information travels. In contrast to a formal organizational message, which might take several days to reach its desired audience, information traveling along the organizational grapevine tends to flow very rapidly, often within hours. One reason for this is that informal communication can cross formal organizational boundaries. For example, you can tell a good joke to almost anyone, not just your boss or subordinates with whom you are required to communicate. Another reason for the rapid flow of informal information is that it tends to be communicated orally. Spoken messages, of course, easily can reach several people at the same time whereas people don't always attend to written messages immediately upon receiving them.

grapevine
An organization's unofficial channels of communication, through which informal information travels.

The downside to informal oral communication is that it tends to become increasingly inaccurate as messages flow from person to person. It is important to note, however, that *some* of the information communicated along the grapevine is accurate. In fact, one study found that 82 percent of the information communicated along a particular company's organizational grapevine on a single occasion was accurate.[71] The problem with interpreting this figure is that the inaccurate portions of some messages may alter their overall meaning. If, for example, a story is going around that someone got passed by for promotion in favor of a lower-ranking employee, it may cause quite a bit of dissension in the workplace. However, suppose everything is true except that the person turned down the promotion because it involved relocating. This important fact completely alters the situation. Only one fact needs to be inaccurate for the accuracy of the entire message to suffer.

Although this can be problematic, of course, it would be misleading to suggest that the grapevine is necessarily bad. Informally socializing with coworkers can help make work groups more cohesive (see Chapter 8), and also may provide excellent opportunities for desired human contact, keeping the work environment stimulating. Whether good or bad, grapevines must be considered an inevitable fact of life in organizations.[72]

Rumors and How to Combat Them

rumors
Information with little basis in fact, often transmitted through informal channels. (See *grapevine*.)

This problem of inaccuracy is clearly responsible for giving the grapevine such a bad reputation. In extreme cases, information may be transmitted that is almost totally without any basis in fact and usually is unverifiable. Such messages are known as **rumors.** Typically, rumors are based on speculation, an overactive imagination, and wishful thinking, rather than on facts. Rumors race like wildfire through organizations because the information they present is so interesting and ambiguous. The ambiguity leaves it open to embellishment as it passes orally from one person to the next. Before you know it, almost everyone in the organization has heard the rumor, and its inaccurate message becomes taken as fact ("It must be true, everyone knows it"). Hence, even if there was, at one point, some truth to a rumor, the message quickly becomes untrue.

TYPES OF RUMORS. Scientists have noted that rumors can be classified as falling into four distinct categories.[73] These are as follows.

pipe dreams
Types of rumor that express people's wishes.

- *Pipe dreams.* Imagine a rumor going around your company that this year's bonuses will be much larger than usual. Although this may reflect the positive wishes of those who are spreading the word, if it is untrue it eventually will lead to disappointment. Rumors of this type, which reflect people's wishes, are known as **pipe dreams.** Although they may be positive, to the extent that they are untrue, pipe dreams have no place in organizations.

bogie rumors
Rumors that are based on people's fears and anxieties.

- *Bogie rumors.* A few years ago, information was posted on an Internet bulletin board stating that the Washington, DC, law firm Dow, Lohnes & Albertson was laying off vast numbers of its staff attorneys. This so enraged many of the firm's staffers that they threatened to walk out. Although, in fact, a handful of attorneys were dismissed, the postings were completely overblown. According to managing partner B. Dwight Perry, the reports were "not only inaccurate" but "scurrilous . . . not to mention, potentially libelous."[74] Rumors of this type, which are based on people's fears and anxieties, are known as **bogie rumors.** As the example suggests, such rumors are likely to arise under conditions in which people are uneasy about things, such as when budgets are exceptionally tight.

wedge drivers
Rumors in which people intentionally say malicious things about someone with the intent of damaging that individual's reputation.

- *Wedge drivers.* Sometimes, people go out of their way to spread malicious rumors about someone with the intent of damaging that individual's reputation. Rumors of this type, known as **wedge drivers,** are the most damaging type because they are used in an intentionally aggressive fashion. Suppose, for example, someone were to come up to you and say, "Did you see that Ms. X was seen leaving the building late last night with Mr. Y, and they were holding hands?" Intending to harm Ms. X and/or Mr. Y, the person using such a wedge driver is using the rumor as a form of attack.

home-stretchers
Rumors designed to reduce the degree of ambiguity in a situation by telling a story about something before it happens.

- *Home-stretchers.* Suppose talks have been going on in your company about an impending merger with another firm. You've been waiting for the announcement, but it hasn't come yet. Under such conditions, rumors may spread about the specifics of the merger in anticipation of something happening. Such rumors, known as **home-stretchers,** are designed to reduce the degree of ambiguity in a situation by "completing the puzzle," telling a story about something before it happens (and that may be inaccurate as a result). As people become anxious about impending decisions, rumors of this type are likely to emerge.

The important thing to keep in mind about rumors, regardless of the type they may be, is that they do everyone a disservice and should not be spread. Although part of the story may be true, the fact that they are misleading makes them dangerous forms of communication that should be avoided at all costs.

TODAY'S HIGH-TECH GRAPEVINE. These days, technology has made it possible for rumors to spread at lightning speed. Not only might rumors be passed along via e-mail, but also Internet bulletin boards. Today, blogs are especially popular since anyone can create a site at which he or she opens up about whatever is on the person's mind. And because it can be accessed by anyone, the blog is an opportunity to broadcast one's messages to the world on an ongoing basis. It's been estimated that more than 133 million blogs were created from 2002–2009 and that these are read by about three-quarters of all Internet users.[75] It's no wonder that anyone interested in using a blog to spread a rumor will have a large audience waiting to take it in. Although the Internet is one of the most important communication tools of all time, the fact that it's both easy and inexpensive to use magnifies its potential for misuse, especially when it comes to spreading rumors.

Sometimes the rumors spread online come from disgruntled employees. More often, however, they are meant as jokes. A few years ago, for example, a seemingly innocuous hoax, targeting clothing retailer J. Crew, reached thousands of people after a Massachusetts teenager sent an e-mail to just 27 other people. Sometimes, however, hoaxes and unproven assertions originate with corporate rivals. For example, a rumor going around the Internet alleged that a certain popular cooking product was unsafe. A competitor had deliberately spread obsolete medical data to imply that this brand was dangerous to consumers. Not surprisingly, one Internet security firm found that Internet-based rumors have been responsible for millions of dollars in lost sales and have tarnished the reputations of victims. The problem has been so extensive that a new industry has developed—companies specializing in finding and eliminating Internet rumors.[76]

HOW TO COMBAT RUMORS. If you've ever been the victim of a personal rumor, then you know how difficult they can be to crush, and how profound their effects can be. This is especially so when organizations are the victims of rumors. For example, rumors about the possibility of corporate takeovers may not only influence the value of a company's stock, but also are likely to threaten its employees' feelings of job security. Sometimes, rumors about company products can be very costly. To illustrate that rumors thrived long before the Internet, here are two classic examples:

- A rumor about the use of worms in McDonald's hamburgers circulated in the Chicago area in the late 1970s. Although the rumor was completely untrue, sales dropped as much as 30 percent in some restaurants.[77]
- The consumer products giant Procter & Gamble has been subject to consistent, nagging rumors linking it to Satanism.[78] Since 1980, rumors have swirled that the company's moon-and-stars trademark was linked to witchcraft. Although the company denied the rumor emphatically and has won court judgments against various individuals spreading such rumors, it has persisted. In an effort to quash the rumor once and for all, the company changed its logo.

What can be done to counter the effects of rumors? One's immediate temptation is to refute the rumor, noting its implausibility and presenting information to the contrary. For example, Coca-Cola has been the victim of so many rumors that the company has a page on its Web site at which it identifies rumors targeted against it (see Table 9.4).[79]

Unfortunately, however, directly refuting a rumor is not always completely effective. As the P&G rumor illustrates, some rumors are difficult to disprove and do not die quickly. In such cases, directly refuting the rumors only fuels the fire. When you directly refute a rumor (e.g., "I didn't do it"), you actually may help spread it among those who have not already heard about it ("Oh, I didn't know people thought that") and strengthen it among those who have already heard it ("If it weren't true, they wouldn't be protesting so much"). In the case of P&G, the problem is

TABLE 9.4 Coca-Cola's Battle Against the Rumor Mill

Rumors involving Coca-Cola have been so extensive at times and have concerned such a variety of issues that the company has devoted space on its Web site to setting the record straight. Here is just a small sampling of these rumors. The company has denied each one. So, remember as you review this list, *these statements are false!*

Topic	Rumor
The Middle East	• People have been warned not to buy Coca-Cola because of possible contamination by terrorists. • The Coca-Cola trademark, when read backwards, reveals an anti-Muslim slogan.
Ingredients	• The acidity of cola drinks is strong enough to dissolve teeth and bones. • Phosphoric acid in Coca Cola leads to osteoporosis.
Product and packaging	• Soft drinks can be used by farmers as pesticides for their crops. • Aluminum from soft drink cans leads to Alzheimer's disease.

Source: Coca-Cola Web site, 2010; see Note 79.

compounded by the allegation that some parties may be making a concerted effort to keep the rumor alive. In such cases, directing the public's attention away from the rumor may help minimize its adverse impact. For example, the company can focus its advertising on other positive things the public knows about it. In research studying the McDonald's rumor, for example, it was found that reminding people of other things they thought about McDonald's (e.g., that it is a clean, family-oriented place) helped counter the negative effects of the rumor.[80]

So, what's the takeaway for you as an individual? If you should ever become the victim of a rumor, try immediately to refute it with indisputable facts if you can. But, if the rumor lingers, try directing people's attention to other positive things they already believe about you (a long list, no doubt). Although rumors may be difficult to stop, with some effort their effects can be managed effectively.

Individual Differences in Communication

As you know from experience, people tend to communicate in different ways. Two individuals saying the same thing might do so very differently and communicate their messages in ways that may have different effects on you. Scientists have verified that such individual differences in how people communicate are indeed real. We now examine such differences with respect to two major factors—gender and nationality.

Sex Differences in Communication: Do Women and Men Communicate Differently?

Infuriated and frustrated, Kimberly stormed out of Jason's office. "I explained the problem I was having with the freelancers," she grumbled, "but he just doesn't listen!" If this situation sounds at all familiar to you, chances are good that you are already aware of the communication barriers that often exist between women and men. Sociolinguists have explained that men and women frequently miscommunicate with one another because they have learned different ways of using language.[81] In general, what appears "natural" to women doesn't come easily to men, and vice versa (see Figure 9.12).

With respect to communication, the basic difference between women and men, experts have observed, is that men emphasize and reinforce their status when they speak, whereas women downplay their status. Instead, women focus on creating positive social connections between themselves

FIGURE 9.12

Men and Women Have Different Communication Styles

Whereas men generally seek to reinforce their status when they communicate (e.g., by saying "I"), women are more interested in creating positive social connections between themselves and others (e.g., by saying "we"). Too often, this leads to miscommunication between the sexes.

and others. Thus, whereas men tend to use the word "I," women tend to say "we." Similarly, whereas men try to exude confidence and boast, thinking of questions as signs of weakness, women usually downplay their confidence (even when they are sure they are correct) and are not afraid to ask questions. (What comes to mind here is the stereotypical image of the couple that gets hopelessly lost because the man overrules the woman's pleas to ask for directions.)

This difference in style between women and men explains why they respond differently to problems. Whereas women tend to listen and lend social support, men tend to take control by offering advice. When men do this, they are asserting their power, contributing to a communication barrier between the sexes. Not surprisingly, whereas men may complain that women are "too emotional," women may complain that men "do not listen." Similarly, men tend to be much more direct and confrontative than women. Although a man might come right out and say "I think your sales figures are inaccurate," a woman might ask, "Have you verified your sales figures by comparing them to this morning's daily report?" A man may consider this approach to be sneaky, whereas a woman may believe it to be kinder and gentler than a more direct statement. Likewise, women may interpret a man's directness as being unsympathetic.

The implications of this set of differences come to the surface once we point out another key finding: People in powerful positions tend to reward individuals whose linguistic styles match their own.[82] As a result, in most organizations, where men tend to be in charge, the contributions of women are often downplayed because the things they say tend to be misinterpreted. The woman who politely defers to a dominant male speaker at a meeting may come across to men as being passive. As a result, her contributions may never be heard. However, the woman who breaks from this pattern and interjects her ideas may be perceived by men as being pushy and aggressive. And here too, her contributions may be discounted. In both cases, the communication barrier has caused a situation in which organizations are not only breeding conflict, but they also are not taking advantage of the skills and abilities of their female employees.

The solution, although not easy, lies in appreciating and accepting the different styles that people have. As one expert put it, "Talk is the lifeblood of managerial work, and understanding that different people have different ways of saying what they mean will make it possible to take advantage of the talents of people with a broad range of linguistic styles."[83]

Cross-Cultural Differences in Communication

In Chapter 1 we noted that the phenomenon of globalization presents many challenges. Clearly, one of the most immediate challenges has to do with communication. When people speak different languages, it follows that communication between them may be imperfect.

Part of the problem is that different words may mean different things to different people.[84] For example, as hard as it might be for people from countries with long-standing capitalist economies to realize, Russians have difficulty understanding words such as "efficiency" and "free market," which have no direct translation in their own language. People who have never known a free-market economy while they were growing up under Communist rule certainly may find it difficult to grasp the concept. It is therefore not surprising to find that communication barriers have been found to exist among American executives who are attempting to conduct business in Russia.[85] (Interestingly, however, because this book has been published in Russia, we take it as a sign that things are improving.)

Another factor that makes cross-cultural communication difficult is that different cultures sometimes have very different cultural norms about using certain words. Take the simple word "no," for example. Although the term exists in the Japanese language, the Japanese people are reluctant to say no directly to someone because doing so is considered insulting. For this reason, they often rely on other ways of saying no that can be quite difficult for foreigners to understand (see Table 9.5).[86] As such, it frequently is considered wise for foreign visitors to other countries to learn not only the language of that country, but the customs about using language as well.

In addition to different vocabularies, cross-cultural communication is made difficult by the fact that in different languages even the same word can mean different things. Just imagine, for example, how confused an American executive might become when she speaks to her counterpart in Israel, where the same Hebrew word *shalom* means both "hello" and "good-bye" (as well as "peace"). Confusion is bound to arise. The same may be said for cultural differences in the tone of speech used in different settings. Whereas Americans might feel free to say the word "you" in both formal and informal situations, Spanish people have different words in each (*tu* for informal

TABLE 9.5 How to Say "No" in Japan

Although most Americans are not reluctant to come out directly and say "no" when necessary, doing so is frowned upon in Japanese culture. Instead, the Japanese rely on the following more indirect ways of communicating "no."

Saying "no" in a highly vague and roundabout manner

Saying "yes or no" in an ambiguous fashion

Being silent and not saying anything at all

Asking questions that change the topic

Responding in a highly tangential manner

Leaving the room

Making a polite excuse

Saying, "yes, but . . . "

Delaying the answer, such as by promising a future letter

Source: Based on information in Hodgson, Sango, & Graham, 2000; see Note 86.

speech and *usted* for formal speech). To confuse these may be tantamount to misinterpreting the nature of the social setting, a potentially costly blunder—and all because of a failure to recognize the subtleties of cross-cultural communication. (What can be done to eliminate blunders likely to be caused by the barriers inherent in cross-cultural communication? In the Today's Diverse and Global Organizations section below, we outline several key suggestions.)

Today's Diverse and Global Organizations

Promoting Cross-Cultural Communication

As we have noted, the potential for miscommunication between people from different cultures is considerable. However, short of becoming expert in foreign languages and cultures, there are several steps that can be taken to promote cross-cultural communication.[87]

1. *Observe, but do not evaluate.* Suppose while touring a factory in a foreign country you observe several assembly-line workers sitting down and talking instead of working. Based on your own country's culture, this would be inappropriate, a sure sign of laziness. Fearing what this means about the plant's productivity, you develop second thoughts about doing business with that company. However, as you learn more about these workers' national culture, you discover that they were engaging in a traditional work break ritual: resting while remaining on the work site. The people in question were merely doing what was expected of them culturally, and they may not be lazy after all. The point is that you evaluated the situation by applying your own cultural values and were misled by them. To avoid such problems, it is advisable in cross-cultural communications to describe what you observe (i.e., the workers are resting) rather than to use these observations as the basis for making evaluations (i.e., the workers are lazy). Doing so can help you avoid serious misinterpretation. (This relates to our discussion of the attribution process in Chapter 3.)

2. *Do not jump to conclusions.* When we perceive various situations, we tend to assume that our judgments are correct. However, when it comes to cross-national settings, we should consider our judgments more as educated guesses than as certain conclusions. If you think that something is correct (such as your interpretation of the lazy workers in the previous example), it is best to compare these to the judgments of experts in the local culture than to assume you are correct. By confirming the accuracy of your judgments misinterpretation is less likely.

3. *Assume that people are different from yourself.* Most of us assume that others are similar to ourselves until we learn otherwise. However, in cross-cultural communication, such an assumption may lead us down the wrong path. Seasoned international managers know this. They take the opposite stance, assuming that others are different until proven otherwise. Because they "know that they don't know," they are less likely to be surprised by differences they don't expect—but which are inevitable.

4. *Take the other person's perspective.* Try to see situations through the eyes of your foreign colleague. Consider this individual's values and experiences, asking yourself how he or she might view things. To the extent that you can switch roles, you will be able to avoid the narrow-mindedness—referred to as *cultural myopia*—with which we tend to perceive things.

Although these measures may be easier said than done, they can be mastered with practice. Given that such steps are key to the success of international managers, the effort involved in doing so would appear to be well worthwhile.

Improving Your Communication Skills

Throughout this chapter we have noted the central role of communication in organizational functioning. Given this, it is easy to understand how any efforts at improving the communication process in organizations may have highly desirable payoffs for organizations as well as for the individuals and groups working in them. Several steps can be taken to obtain the benefits of effective communication.[88] In this final section of the chapter, we describe some of these techniques, including measures that can be taken by individuals, as well as tactics for improving communication that involve entire organizations.

Use Jargon Sparingly

All organizations, social groups, and professions have their own **jargon**—specialized language limited to use by people in certain fields. No doubt, you've encountered a great many words and phrases in this book that may at first sound strange to you. Our point is that the use of jargon is inevitable when people within the same field or groups communicate with one another. Some degree of highly specialized language may help communication by providing an easy way for people in the same fields to share complex ideas. This is the case among football players, for example, who understand the seeming gibberish uttered by quarterbacks calling plays in the huddle.

Jargon also plays another important function. It allows professionals to identify unknown others as people in their field because they "speak the same language." For example, management professors would describe this book as dealing with the field of OB, a term that would have a very different meaning to medical doctors (for whom the acronym refers to the field of obstetrics). Obviously, within professions jargon helps communication, but it can lead to confusion when used outside the groups within which it has meaning. Although jargon may be useful to those who are in the know, it only confuses messages sent to the uninitiated.

In many cases, jargon takes the form of *acronyms*, a series of letters serving as an abbreviation for a particular entity of some type, usually pronounced as if it were a word. As such, they serve as useful shortcuts—if, of course, you know what they mean (see Figure 9.13).

The military services in the United States, for example, use hundreds of different acronyms.[89] Among these are the following: BETA (battlefield exploitation and target acquisition), CAEX (computer-aided exploration), JATT (joint air attack team), and WAGE (weapons aerospace ground equipment). Even within the military, various acronyms can have multiple meanings. For example, to some, "DAB" may refer to the Defense Acquisition Board, while to others it may mean Directory of the Army Budget—two very different things. Likewise, the acronym "MAC" may be taken to mean any of 17 different things, including maintenance action code and military agency check. Here too, unless you know the acronym and the context in which it is used, communication may not be facilitated by using them. In fact, it even may suffer serious confusion. This underscores our point: Be mindful when and how you use acronyms, or any form of jargon.

jargon
The specialized language used by a particular group (e.g., people within a profession).

© Randy Glasbergen
glasbergen.com

—GLASBERGEN

Randy Glasbergen.

"I knew it was time to simplify our organization when we started creating acronyms for our acronyms."

FIGURE 9.13

Time for AAPE (Acromm Abatement Policy Enforcement)

Acronyms can be useful shortcuts that facilitate communication. However, because they may not be known to everyone, it's important to use them selectively.

Be Consistent in What You Say and Do

Managers communicating with their subordinates often send inconsistent messages by saying one thing but doing another. We're not necessarily even talking about major things such as speaking out against fraud but committing it oneself. Inconsistencies in even small things can lead to problems. Consider, for example, the case of Kristen J., the operations manager of a large consumer products company. For years, she has been telling her direct reports to complete expense reports in a certain way that helps the accounting department—specifically, by itemizing the various expenses in a hotel bill, such as the nightly room rate, various taxes, phone charges, and so on. However, when submitting her own expense reports, Kristen hasn't been following her own directives. Rather, she simply lumps together all the expenses when submitting them for reimbursement. Although this doesn't sound like a big deal—and on its own, it surely is not—repeated instances of saying one thing but doing another have led Kristen's subordinates not to take her seriously when she issues a directive. When questioned about it one day, Kristen wasn't embarrassed, admonishing the subordinate to "Do as I say, not as I do." As you might imagine, this didn't go over very well.

say-do matrix
A way of differentiating systematically with respect to consistencies and inconsistencies in what people say and what they do.

To help understand such situations, one organizational analyst has developed what is known as the **say-do matrix,** a way of differentiating systematically between the consistencies and inconsistencies in communication with respect to one's actions (do) and one's words (say).[90] This conceptualization distinguishes between sending a specific message by way of one's actions (high do) or by failing to do so (low do). It also distinguishes between telling someone to do something specific (high say) or by not doing so (low say). Combining these results in a say-do matrix like the one depicted in Figure 9.14.

The various combinations of "say" and "do" create different communication situations. These are as follows.

- In the upper right corner is the *high say–high do* combination. This is the ideal—the case in which a person's words and deeds with respect to a certain message match perfectly. Making it clear that one is expected to drive safely and then following safe driving practices oneself is an example of this. There is a high degree of consistency between messages communicated verbally and behaviorally.

- In the upper left corner is the *high say–low do* case. This occurs when a manager's words and deeds do not match, such as in our example of Kristen, who fails to follow her own directives about filling out expense reports. As you might imagine, in this case communication tends to be confusing and less effective than in the high say–high do case.

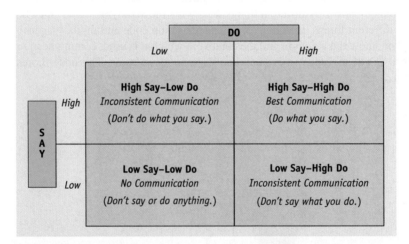

FIGURE 9.14

The Say-Do Matrix

The say-do matrix systematically distinguishes between saying things (high say) and not saying things (low say) and doing things (high do) and not doing things (low do). The most effective communication for managers occurs when there is a high consistency between what they say and do (the high say–high do combination).

Source: Based on information in D'Aprix, 1996; see Note 44.

- In the lower right corner is the *low say–high do* case. Here, a manager fails to articulate what to do verbally although he or she expresses it clearly by his or her actions. In such cases, the fact that the individual did not express the message verbally is likely to lead to confusion insofar as it sends the message that the manager's actions are not worthy of noting. For example, our safe-driving manager is unlikely to communicate his or her concerns about road safety by not saying anything about it. This provides a missed opportunity to articulate the right thing to do.

- In the lower left corner, finally, we have the *low say–low do* case. In this situation, no communication with respect to a given issue is occurring whatsoever. As odd as this may sound, such "communication voids" are not at all unusual, especially when conditions are so hectic that insufficient time is made to communicate clear expectations. In one company, for example, an office manager was hired but told almost nothing about what was expected of her.[91] The supervisor assumed that the manager would know what to do and how to do it. He handed her three file folders and told her to "work on these projects," and then was out of touch. A month later, the supervisor realized that the new employee had taken on responsibilities for which she was neither prepared nor able to complete. As a result, she made serious mistakes. All of this could have been avoided, of course, by simply making expectations clear in advance.

The practical advice is clear: Be a high say–high do manager. Communicate your intentions clearly and consistently by way of your words and your deeds. As suggested by our examples, failing to do so can have serious consequences.

Become an Active, Attentive Listener

Just as it is important to make your ideas understandable to others (i.e., sending messages), it is equally important to be a good listener (i.e., receiving messages). After all, communication cannot be effective unless a sender's messages are received and understood accurately—and this involves listening.

Unfortunately, however, many people ignore this part of the communication process, focusing more on the messages they send than on those they receive. To some extent, this occurs because based on outward appearances, people who are talking may appear to be "taking charge," or at least being "involved," whereas those who are listening may come across as doing nothing at all. Of course, to equate listening with doing nothing could not be farther from the truth. Although we cannot see it occurring, listening is an extremely active process.[92]

What Do Good Listeners Do? In the words of former U.S. President, Calvin Cooledge, "No man ever listened himself out of a job." To this, we would add that quite a few probably have found themselves out of jobs because they have *failed* to listen. Given its importance, it makes sense to examine what can be done to improve our effectiveness as listeners. With this in mind, some recommendations can be identified by examining exactly what it is that good listeners do.

1. Good listeners ask questions if they don't understand something, and they nod or otherwise signal when they understand. Such cues provide critical feedback to communicators about the extent to which they are coming across to you. As a listener, you can help the communication process by letting the sender know if and how his or her messages are coming across to you. *Asking questions* and *putting the speaker's ideas into your own words* are helpful ways of ensuring you are taking in all the information presented.

2. Good listeners avoid distractions in the environment and concentrate on what the other person is saying. When listening to others, avoid jumping to conclusions or evaluating their remarks. It is important to completely take in what is being said before you respond. Simply dismissing someone because you don't like what is being said is much too easy. Doing so, of course, poses a formidable barrier to effective communication.

3. Good listeners make sure they are aware of others' main points. What is the speaker trying to say? *Make sure you understand another's ideas before you formulate your reply.* Too many of us interrupt speakers with our own ideas before we have fully heard theirs. If this sounds like something you do, rest assured that it is not only quite common, but also correctable if you work on it.

Although it requires some effort, incorporating these three suggestions into your own listening habits cannot help but make you a better listener. Indeed, many organizations have sought to help their employees in this way. For example, the corporate giant Unisys has for some time systematically trained thousands of its employees in effective listening skills (using seminars and self-training cassettes). Clearly, Unisys is among those companies acknowledging the importance of good listening skills in promoting effective organizational communication. Executives are so interested in training their employees in listening skills that specialized training companies have sprung up to accommodate them.

Listening Skills: The HURIER Model. The development of listening skills requires identifying the individual elements of listening, the separate skills that contribute to listening effectiveness. These may be clustered into six groups known as the **HURIER model.**[93] The term HURIER is an acronym composed of the initials of the words reflecting the component skills of effective listening: *h*earing, *u*nderstanding, *r*emembering, *i*nterpreting, *e*valuating, and *r*esponding. For a summary of these individual skills, see Figure 9.15. Although it might seem easy to do the six things needed to be a good listener, we are not all as good as we think we are in this capacity, suggesting that listening might not be as easy as it seems.

Management consultant Nancy K. Austin would agree, and she explains that when you invite people to talk to you about their problems on the job, you're implicitly making a promise to listen to them.[94] Of course, when you do, you may feel hostile and defensive toward the speaker, and become more interested in speaking up and setting the record straight if you don't like what you hear. This is the challenge of listening. Good listeners should resist this temptation and pay careful attention to the speaker. When they cannot do so, they should admit the problem and reschedule another opportunity to get together.

Austin also advises people to "be an equal opportunity listener," that is, to pay attention not only to those whose high status commands our attention, but also to anyone at any level, and to make time to hear them all in a democratic fashion. The idea is not only that people at any job level might have something to say, but also that they may feel good about you as a manager for having shown consideration to them. Austin notes that by listening to an employee, you are saying, "You are smart and have important things to say; you are worth my time."[95] Such a message is critical to establishing the kind of open, two-way communication essential for top management.

Research has confirmed the importance of listening as a management skill. In fact, it has shown that the better a person is as a listener, the more likely he or she is to rapidly rise up the organizational hierarchy and to perform well as a manager.[96] Good listening skills are an important aspect of one's ability to succeed as a manager. However, people tend to think they are much better listeners than others think they are.[97] This is unfortunate because overconfidence in one's own listening ability can be a barrier to seeking training in listening skills. After all, people who believe they are already good listeners may have little motivation to seek training in this important skill. Managers who complete formal training programs to enhance their listening skills generally benefit considerably.[98] (To get some practice in this important management skill, complete the Group Exercise on page 330.)

HURIER model

The conceptualization that describes effective listening as made up of the following six components: *h*earing, *u*nderstanding, *r*emembering, *i*nterpreting, *e*valuating, and *r*esponding.

FIGURE 9.15

The HURIER Model: Components of Effective Listening

Research has shown that the six skills identified here—hearing, understanding, remembering, interpreting, evaluating, and responding— contribute greatly to the effectiveness of listening.

Source: Based on suggestions by Brownell, 1985; see Note 94.

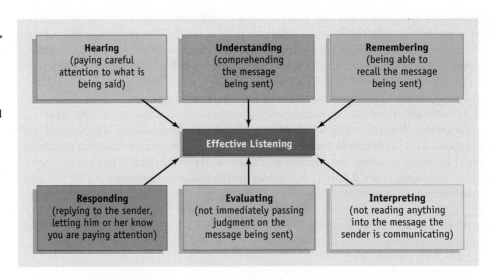

Gauge the Flow of Information: Avoiding Overload

Imagine a busy manager surrounded by a tall stack of papers, with a telephone receiver at each ear and a crowd of people gathered around, waiting to talk to her. Obviously, the many demands put on this person can slow down the system and make its operation less effective. When any part of a communication network becomes bogged down with more information than it can handle effectively, a condition of **overload** is said to exist. Consider, for example, the bottleneck in the flow of routine financial information that might result when the members of the accounting department of an organization are tied up preparing corporate tax returns. Naturally, such a state poses a serious threat to effective organizational communication. Because today's managers face more information overload than ever before, they tend to ignore a great deal of the information they need to do their jobs. Fortunately, however, several concrete steps can be taken to manage information more effectively.

For one, organizations may employ **gatekeepers,** people whose jobs require them to control the flow of information to potentially overloaded units. For example, administrative assistants are responsible for making sure that busy executives are not overloaded by the demands of other people or groups. Newspaper editors and television news directors also may be thought of as gatekeepers, since such individuals decide what news will and will not be shared with the public. It is an essential part of these individuals' jobs to avoid overloading others by gauging the flow of information to them.

Overload also can be avoided through **queuing.** This term refers to lining up incoming information so that it can be managed in an orderly fashion. A simple and mundane example is the practice of taking a number at a busy supermarket deli counter. By attending to customers on a first-come-first-served basis, confusion can be avoided, along with some dirty glances from other shoppers. Another example, and a more serious one, is the practice of "stacking" jets as they approach a busy airport (i.e., defining their position in the line). Establishing a queue for the incoming planes, determining the order in which they land, will avoid the chaos, and resulting tragedy, that otherwise would result when no such clearcut basis exists for establishing a service queue exists.

Overload also can be avoided by *establishing priorities for incoming information*—that is, determining the order in which you're going to do things because, after all, you can't do everything at once. As an example, consider hospital emergency rooms. Because they are usually understaffed, *triage* nurses are used to determine the order in which incoming patients are treated. As the name implies, these nurses make one of three decisions.

- The lowest priority goes to those whose conditions appear to be minor and will not worsen if they wait (e.g., patients who have superficial cuts).
- The highest priority goes to patients whose lives can be saved if they receive immediate medical attention (e.g., victims of gunshot wounds who are quickly losing blood).
- Finally, some individuals' conditions may be so serious that their lives are unlikely to be saved even if they receive treatment. And, although it sounds cruel, until staff members have finished working on patients in the highest priority group, patients in this gravely serious group will go untreated.

By assigning priorities in this manner, hospitals can do the most good for the greatest number of people.

When systems are overloaded, *distortion* and *omission* are likely to result. That is, messages may be either changed or left out when they are passed from one organizational unit to the next. If you've ever played the parlor game "Telephone" (in which one person whispers a message to another, who passes it on to another, and so on until it reaches the last person), you have likely experienced—or contributed to—the ways messages get distorted and omitted. When you consider the important messages that are often communicated in organizations, these problems can be very serious. They also tend to be quite extreme.

A dramatic demonstration of this was reported in a study tracing the flow of downward communication in more than 100 organizations. The researchers found that messages communicated downward over five levels lost approximately 80 percent of their original information by the time they reached their destination at the lowest level of the organizational hierarchy.[99] Obviously, something needs to be done.

overload
The condition in which an individual or unit of an organization becomes over-burdened with too much incoming information.

gatekeepers
People responsible for controlling the flow of information to others to keep them from becoming overloaded.

queuing
Lining up incoming information so it can be managed in an orderly fashion.

One strategy that has proven effective in avoiding the problems of distortion and omission is *redundancy*. Making messages redundant involves transmitting them again, often in another form or via another channel. For example, in attempting to communicate an important message to her subordinates, a manager may tell them the message and then follow it up with a written memo. In fact, managers frequently encourage this practice.[100]

Another practice that can help avoid distortion and omission is *verification*. This refers to making sure messages have been received accurately. Pilots use verification when they repeat the messages given them by air traffic controllers. Doing so assures both parties that the messages the pilots heard were the actual messages the controllers sent. Given how busy pilots may be during takeoffs and landings and the interference inherent in radio transmissions, coupled with the vital importance of the messages themselves, the practice of verifying messages is a wise safety measure. The practice not only is used in airline communication systems, but may be used by individual communicators as well. Active listeners may wish to verify that they correctly understood a speaker. They do so by paraphrasing the speaker's remarks within a question, asking "If I understood, you were saying. . . . "

Give and Receive Feedback: Opening Channels of Communication

To operate effectively, organizations must be able to communicate accurately with those who keep them running—their employees. Unfortunately, the vast majority of employees believe that the feedback between themselves and their organizations is not as good as it should be.[101] For various reasons, people are often unwilling or unable to communicate their ideas to top management. Part of the problem is the lack of available channels for upward communication and people's reluctance to use whatever ones exist. How, then, can organizations obtain information from their employees, improving the upward flow of communication? Several approaches have been used widely.

360-degree feedback
The process of systematically giving and receiving feedback between individuals at various organizational levels.

360-DEGREE FEEDBACK. A popular technique for promoting the sharing of information and ideas is known as **360-degree feedback.** As we described in Chapter 8, this technique calls for having people at various organizational levels complete questionnaires in which they give feedback to and share ideas with others with whom they work in their organization. Essentially, everyone gives feedback to everyone else. At a restaurant, for example, waiters may be evaluated by restaurant managers, chefs, the other waiters with whom they work, service personnel, and customers. Although the process tends to be complex in operation, the basic idea is simple: By gathering information from multiple sources, information is communicated about areas of performance that need to be improved. The technique is useful because it allows such information to be collected systematically and from people who are likely to have diverse perspectives on one's work.

suggestion systems
Formal mechanisms through which employees can present ideas to their companies.

SUGGESTION SYSTEMS. Too often, employees' good ideas about how to improve organizational functioning fail to work their way up the organization chart because the people with the ideas do not know how to reach the people who can implement them. Even worse, they may feel they will not be listened to even if they can reach the right person. **Suggestion systems** are procedures designed to help avoid these problems by providing a formal mechanism through which employees can present their ideas to the company. Research has found that about 15 percent of employees use their companies' suggestion boxes, and that about 25 percent of the suggestions made are implemented.[102] Employees are usually rewarded for their successful suggestions, either with a flat monetary award or some percentage of the money saved by implementing the suggestion. Employee suggestion systems make good sense because the people who perform jobs every day are in good positions to conceive of ways to improve them. And the many successful ideas that have come from suggestion systems (see Table 9.6) indicate that such programs may be well worthwhile.[103]

corporate hotlines
Telephone lines staffed by corporate personnel ready to answer employees' questions, listen to their comments, and the like.

CORPORATE HOTLINES. Growing numbers of companies are using **corporate hotlines**—telephone lines staffed by corporate personnel ready to answer employees' questions, listen to their comments, and the like.[104] A good example of this is the hotline that Atlanta's Flag Bank set up in 2005 when it merged with First Capital Bank. As thousands of customers and employees sought information about what the merger would mean for them, the hotline proved to be a useful means of sharing needed information. In general, by providing personnel with easy access to information,

TABLE 9.6 It's the Little Things That Count: Big Results from Small Suggestions

Over the years, companies using suggestion systems have found them to be valuable sources of ideas for improvement. As these examples suggest, it's sometimes employees' seemingly minor suggestions that bring some of the biggest savings.

Placement of elevator	When the El Cortez Hotel in San Diego was planning to construct a new elevator for guests, a janitor who worked at the hotel suggested that by placing the elevator outside the building instead of inside, the hotel wouldn't have to close some floors during construction, thereby preventing the hotel from losing revenue.
Boxed lunches at airports	An employee at Marriott Hotels noticed that people in airports were buying food at shops and stuffing it into their luggage. This led him to suggest selling prepackaged boxes lunches.
Move site of medical tests	An employee at a California juvenile detention center saved the county almost $12,000 per year by suggesting that medical tests for the youngsters be conducted at the facility instead of transporting them to a doctor's office.
Changing the paper	At a boat manufacturing company, the floor of the lamination department was lined with paper before each shift to prevent a buildup of fiberglass on the floor. One employee recommended changing the paper supplier to one who used recycled paper, saving the company a half-million dollars annually.

Source: Based on information reported by Turner, 2010; see Note 103.

companies benefit in several ways. Doing so not only showed employees that the company cares about them, but it also encouraged them to address their concerns before the issues became more serious. In addition, by keeping track of the kinds of questions and concerns voiced, top management is given invaluable insight into ways of improving organizational conditions.[105]

INFORMAL MEETINGS. Many companies have found it useful to hold informal meetings between employees at a variety of corporate levels as a means of facilitating communication. Sometimes called *brown bag meetings* or *skip-level meetings,* such sessions are designed to facilitate communication between people who don't usually get together because they work at different organizational levels.[106] **Brown bag meetings** are informal get-togethers over breakfast or lunch (brought in from home, hence the term "brown bag") at which people discuss what's going on in the company. The informal nature of the meetings is designed to encourage the open sharing of ideas (eating a sandwich out of a bag is an equalizer!). **Skip-level meetings** do essentially the same thing. These are gatherings of employees with corporate superiors who are more than one level higher than themselves in the organizational hierarchy. The idea is that new lines of communication can be established by bringing together people who are two or more levels apart, individuals who usually don't come into contact with one another.

EMPLOYEE SURVEYS. Many companies attempt to gather feedback from employees systematically by giving them questionnaires referred to as **employee surveys.** Often, these are used to collect information about employees' attitudes and opinions about key areas of organizational operations. Surveys administered at regular intervals may be useful for spotting changes in attitudes as they occur. Such surveys tend to be quite effective when their results are shared with employees, especially when the feedback is used as the basis for changing the way things are done. Some managers even go so far as to ask their employees to rate them on a "report card."[107]

brown bag meetings
Informal get-togethers over meals in which people discuss what's going on in their companies.

skip-level meetings
Gatherings of employees with corporate superiors who are more than one level higher than themselves in an organizational hierarchy.

employee surveys
Questionnaires designed to assess how employees feel about their organizations.

Be a Supportive Communicator: Enhancing Relationships

To be an effective communicator, you must be supportive of others. By **supportive communication** we are referring to any communication that is accurate and honest, and that builds and enhances relationships instead of jeopardizing them.

Simply put, how you act toward another influences the nature of your relationship with that person, which in turn affects the quality of communication, which may influence various work-related attitudes (see Chapter 6) and job performance. Suppose, for example, you send someone a very abrasive, insensitive message. That person is likely to become distant and distrustful, believing that you are uncaring. This, in turn, will lead the attacked person to become defensive, spending more time and energy constructing a good defense rather than listening carefully to your message. And, of course, a message that is not carefully attended to will not be comprehended, leading to problematic job performance.

supportive communication
Any communication that is accurate and honest, and that builds and enhances relationships instead of jeopardizing them.

This discussion prompts an important question: What can you do to become a supportive communicator? Several tried-and-true tactics can be identified.[108]

■ *Focus on the problem, not the person.* Referring to an individual's characteristics (e.g., saying, "You are lazy") is likely to make that person defensive (e.g., thinking, "No, I'm not"). However, focusing on the problem itself (e.g., saying, "We lost the account") is likely to move the conversation toward a solution (e.g., asking, "What can we do about it?"). Communication tends to be far more supportive when it focuses on the problem and possible solutions than one person's beliefs about the characteristics of another who caused it. (This is in keeping with the difficulties of making accurate attributions of others noted in Chapter 3.)

■ *Honestly say what you mean.* Too often, people avoid difficult matters by disguising their true feelings. Instead of saying that everything's fine when it clearly isn't, for example, it helps to make clear how you feel. Don't be afraid of saying, "I'm upset by what you did," if that's how you really feel.

■ *Own up to your decisions.* Don't hesitate to make it clear exactly what you did and how you feel. It's far more supportive, for example, to explain to someone precisely why you voted to deny his or her request than to hide behind a general statement, such as "The committee saw problems in your proposal." If you were on the committee, speak for yourself. This may be awkward and socially difficult, but by explaining your decision the other person may learn a great deal.

■ *Use validating language.* Of course, when you do speak your mind, always avoid language that arouses negative feelings about one's self-worth, such as "What can you expect from a lawyer?" Statements of this type use what is referred to as **invalidating language.**[109] It's far more effective to state your point in a way that makes people feel recognized and accepted for who they are—that is, to use **validating language.** For example, you might say, "I'm not sure I agree, but I'm interested in hearing your side." Although you might disagree with the speaker, this is a far more supportive approach.

■ *Strive to keep the conversation going.* You can keep people talking about what's on their mind by probing them for additional information (e.g., by saying, "Tell me about it") or by reflecting back what you think the speaker said (e.g., "If I heard you correctly, you feel . . ."). Another trick for helping conversations move along is to use **conjunctive statements**—comments that connect what you will be saying to the speaker's remarks, instead of **disjunctive statements**—comments that are disconnected from the speaker's remarks. So, for example, it's better to say something like, "On that same topic, I think . . . ," as opposed to saying something on a completely different subject. Doing so is sure to end the conversation. (To see how supportive you are as a communicator, you may enjoy completing the Individual Exercise on pages 328–329.)

invalidating language
Language that arouses negative feelings about one's self-worth.

validating language
Language that makes people feel recognized and accepted for who they are.

conjunctive statements
Statements that keep conversations going by connecting one speaker's remarks to another's.

disjunctive statements
Statements that are disconnected from a previous statement, tending to bring conversations to a close.

Summary and Review of Learning Objectives

1. **Describe the process of communication and its purposes in organizations.**
   The process of *communication* occurs when a sender of information *encodes* a message and transmits it over communication channels to a receiver, who *decodes* it and then sends *feedback*. Factors interfering with these processes are known as *noise*. Communication serves many functions in organizations. These include directing action, linking and coordinating, building relationships, explaining organizational culture, linking people with other organizations, presenting an organization's image, generating ideas, and promoting ideals and values.

2. **Identify various forms of verbal media used in organizations and explain which ones are most appropriate for communicating messages of different types.**
   Communication in both oral and written forms is commonly used in organizations. Verbal media range from those that are *rich* (highly personal and provide opportunities for immediate feedback), such as face-to-face discussions, to those that are *lean* (impersonal and

one-way), such as flyers. According to *media richness theory,* rich forms of communication are best for communicating ambiguous and nonroutine matters, whereas leaner forms of communication are adequate for more routine matters.

3. **Describe how technology has influenced organizational communication.**
Technology has been a major force in facilitating organizational communication. Indeed, computer-mediated communication has been responsible for making communication faster and by making the distances between people irrelevant as a barrier to sending and receiving information. Such techniques as video-mediated communication (video conferences), e-mail, and instant messaging have revolutionized people's access to information. These media are not without problems, however. For example, people receive so many e-mails that they suffer information overload. They also find it a very limiting medium for expressing emotions. Although also very useful, many people find instant messaging too intrusive. Finally, the rapid speed of electronic communication poses another problem—it allows rumors to flow extremely rapidly, making them difficult to control, often causing damage in the process.

4. **Describe how people's communication patterns differ based on their sex and culture.**
Despite similarities, women and men communicate in several different ways that may be problematic unless understood. Whereas men tend to communicate with the intent of emphasizing their status, women tend to focus on making positive social connections. Such differences frequently lead to miscommunication between men and women. Cross-cultural communication is hampered by the fact that people from different cultures frequently misunderstand each other's intentions. This may stem from different vocabularies and subtle differences in the meanings of words that may not be understood outside the culture.

5. **Distinguish between the various forms of formal and informal communication that occur in organizations and how they operate.**
Formal communication is governed by *organizational structure,* the formally prescribed pattern of interrelationships between people in organizations. Structure dictates who must communicate with whom (as reflected in an *organization chart,* a diagram outlining these reporting relationships) and the form that communication takes. Orders flow down an organizational hierarchy, and information flows upward. However, the downward and upward flow of information is often distorted insofar as people are reluctant to share bad news with their superiors (known as the *MUM effect*). Attempts at coordination characterize *horizontal (or lateral) communication,* messages between organizational members at the same level. Information flows rapidly along *informal communication networks.* These informal connections between people are responsible for spreading information very rapidly because they transcend formal organizational boundaries. Informal pathways known as the *grapevine* are often responsible for the rapid transmission of partially inaccurate information known as *rumors.* Rumors may be costly to organizations as well as individuals. Fortunately, there are several ways they can be combated.

6. **Explain how you can improve your effectiveness as a communicator in organizations.**
There are several things you can do to become a better communicator. First, keep your messages clear by avoiding *jargon* while communicating with those who may not be familiar with specialized terms. Second, you can become a better communicator by demonstrating consistency between what you say and do. Third, you can improve your *listening* skills, learning to listen actively (thinking about and questioning the speaker) and attentively (without distraction). Fourth, you can minimize the problem of *overload* by using *gatekeepers* (individuals who control the flow of information to others) or by *queuing* (the orderly lining-up of incoming information). And you can minimize the problems of *distortion* and *omission* of messages by making messages *redundant* and by encouraging their *verification.* Fifth, you can improve communication at the organizational level by using techniques that open upward channels of communication to employee feedback (e.g., *suggestion systems, corporate hotlines,* and *employee surveys*). Finally, you should attempt to be a *supportive communicator*—someone who makes an effort to enhance his or her relationships with others, such as by focusing attention on the problem instead of the person, using *validating language.*

Points to Ponder

Questions for Review

1. What are the various steps in the communication process?
2. What types of verbal media are best suited to various situations?
3. How does technology facilitate communication in organization?
4. What can be done to improve the quality of formal and informal communication in organizations?
5. How do women and men differ in their styles of communication?
6. What steps can be taken to improve the quality of communication in organizations?

Experiential Questions

1. Think of an instance in which you had to transmit bad news to another person (e.g., firing, unwanted transfer). Were you reluctant to share this information (as per the MUM effect)? How did you respond in this situation?
2. Think of an instance in which you used a particular communication medium (e.g., e-mail) in a manner that proved to be ineffective. What occurred? In retrospect, what could you have done to avoid the problems you encountered?
3. Do you regard yourself to be a good listener? What might you do to improve your skills as a listener?

Questions to Analyze

1. What particular communication problem do you believe occurs most frequently in organizations? Why is this so? What would you recommend to combat this particular problem?
2. There's no doubt that technology has facilitated organizational communication. However, it also has brought problems. What are these limitations and how might they be overcome? Has technology been more of a help or hindrance to the communication process? Why?
3. In what ways has rapidly advancing technology helped communication in organizations and in what ways has it been a hindrance? Explain your answer.

Experiencing OB

Individual Exercise

Are You a Supportive Communicator?

As noted on pages 325–326, one key to being effective as a communicator is to be supportive of people. Supportive communication involves being accurate and honest with people in a manner that builds, rather than jeopardizes, relationships with them. This exercise will give you a good feel for how supportive you are as a communicator.

Directions

Answer each of the following questions by indicating which of the options indicated, A or B, you would be most likely to follow when interacting with someone else in the situation indicated.

1. _____ You are discussing the performance of a subordinate whose work has not been up to standards. Which of the following statements comes closest to what you might say?
   A: Your sales have been lagging in the last few weeks. What do you think is wrong, and how might I be able to help?
   B: You haven't been meeting your sales quota lately. Unless you improve, you might find yourself looking for a new job pretty soon.
2. _____ One of your employees has arrived at the office late many times this past week, making it difficult for his customers to reach him. Which of the following statements comes closest to what you might say?
   A: You would say nothing.
   B: I've noticed that you've been late this week, and I'm concerned about how this will affect your job performance.
3. _____ Because of changes in your organization, it has become necessary to lay off a member of your work group. When discussing this with the individual to

be laid off, which of the following statements comes closest to what you might say?

A: Because of some changes we've been making here at the company, it has become necessary to lay off some employees. I have decided that you will be released.

B: Because of some changes we've been making here at the company, it has become necessary to lay off some employees. It has been decided that you will be released.

4. _____ In a meeting with the members of your work team, someone expresses an idea that seems totally ridiculous to you and, you suspect, to everyone else as well. Which of the following statements comes closest to what you might say?

A: I don't think that's a very useful idea. Please stop wasting our time so we can continue our meeting.

B: I don't quite understand that idea, but please explain it to us so we can consider it more fully.

5. _____ One of your employees has been having problems with a project lately, and she has been coming up to you to complain about it. You don't understand the nature of the problem and believe she should be able to do the job. Which of the following statements comes closest to what you might say?

A: Tell me more about this so I can try to help.

B: I can't figure out why you're having this problem. You'll have to work it out yourself because I have my own work to do.

Scoring and Interpretation

1. Count the number of times you responded as follows: 1 = A; 2 = B; 3 = A; 4 = B; 5 = A.
2. The more times you responded as indicated here, the more supportive you are being as a communicator.

Let's examine each response.

Question 1: Response A is more supportive because it focuses on the problem without making negative judgments about the person. This is likely to help, whereas Response B is too threatening and may discourage the employee from trying.

Question 2: Response B is more supportive because it involves honestly saying what you mean. Merely ignoring the problem by saying nothing will not help and may make things worse because it suggests that you don't think anything is wrong.

Question 3: Response A is more supportive because you own up to your decision. This invites the person to discuss the situation with you so you can explain how the difficult decision was made. Response B is less supportive because it depersonalizes the decision, leaving the impression that nobody cares enough to stand behind it.

Question 4: Response B is more supportive because it uses validating language. It encourages the person to fully explain the idea and makes him or her feel worthwhile. Although you may not like what the person is saying, shutting the individual up, as in Response A, will discourage him or her from speaking in the future. Assuming that everyone may make a useful contribution, this is to be avoided.

Question 5: Response A is the more supportive option because it is more likely to keep the person talking to you, coming up with ways of making things better. Response B, however, makes the person feel marginalized—unimportant and not worthwhile. It gets the person off your back for now, but it also risks keeping that person from contributing anything in the future.

Questions for Discussion

1. Based on this questionnaire, how supportive are you? Did you score high, such as 4 or 5, or low, such as 1 or 2? Does this score surprise you? Did you expect to score higher or lower than you did?
2. Of the five aspects of supportive communication described in the text and assessed here, which ones are most challenging for you? How do you think you can overcome these limitations and become even more supportive in the future?
3. Based on your own past experiences, how supportive are the various people with whom you have communicated? Who are the most supportive individuals and how do they make you feel when communicating with you?

Group Exercise

Sharpening Your Listening Skills

Are you a good listener, a *really* good listener—one who understands exactly what someone else is saying to you? Most of us tend to think that we are much better than we really are when it comes to this important skill. After all, we've been listening to others our whole lives. And, with that much practice, we must certainly be okay. To gain some insight into your own listening skills, try the following group exercise.

Directions

1. Divide the class into pairs of people who do not already know each other. Arrange the chairs so that the people within each pair are facing each other, but separated from the other pairs.
2. Within each pair, select one person as the speaker and the other as the listener. The speaker should tell the listener about a specific incident on the job in which he or she was somehow harmed (e.g., disappointed by not getting a raise, being embarrassed by another, losing a battle with a coworker, getting fired, etc.), and how he or she felt about it. The total discussion should last about 10–15 minutes.
3. Listeners should carefully attempt to follow the suggestions for good listening described on pages 321–322. To help, the instructor should discuss these with the class.
4. After the conversations are over, review the suggestions with your partner. Discuss which ones the listener followed and which ones were ignored. Try to be as open and honest as possible about assessing your own and the other's strengths and weaknesses. Speakers should consider the extent to which they felt the listeners were really paying attention to them.
5. Repeat steps 2 through 4, but change roles. Speakers now are listeners, and listeners now are speakers.
6. As a class, share your experiences as speakers and listeners.

Questions for Discussion

1. What did this exercise teach you about your own skills as a listener? Are you as good as you thought? Do you think you can improve?
2. Was there general agreement or disagreement about each listener's strengths and weaknesses? Explain.
3. After the discussion about the first listener's effectiveness, you might expect the second listener to do a better job. Was this the case in your own group or throughout the class?
4. Which particular listening skills were easiest and most difficult to put into practice? Are there certain conditions under which good listening skills may be difficult to implement?
5. Do you think you will learn something from this exercise that will help you to improve your listening skills in other situations? If so, what? If not, why not?

Practicing OB

Phone Center Chaos

The employees in a company's phone center are not paying any attention to new procedures for taking orders from clients. They are following the old procedures, which they prefer, and avoiding the changes that they dislike. What's more, they are spending so much time bickering with one another that overall productivity has been suffering. You are called in to handle this situation.

1. How might sex differences or cross-cultural differences in communication styles lie at the heart of this situation? What can be done about this?
2. How might technology be used to improve this situation?
3. What can be done to make the employees better listeners and more supportive of one another? How do you think these measures would help address the problem?

■ *The Home Depot's Extreme Communication Makeover*

With some 2,200 "orange box" stores throughout North America and more than 322,000 employees, The Home Depot has become the world's largest home improvement retailer. Although it's a landmark today, the company is relatively new—founded in 1978. To say that its growth has been staggering is an understatement: The Home Depot is the fastest growing retailer in history and the youngest retailer in the *Fortune* 50. Its sales volume is so enormous that in 2005 alone, it sold enough carpet to pave a two-lane road from company headquarters in Atlanta to Los Angeles, then up to New York and back again to Atlanta. The company enjoys annual sales of more than $71.28 billion.

As impressive as these figures are, The Home Depot's vast size, rapid growth, and geographic diversity have created a number of challenges—not the least important of which are the complexities of communication. After all, employees speak not only English, but Spanish (in parts of the United States and in Mexico) as well as French (in Québec)—not to mention the various mother tongues spoken by suppliers and immigrant employees. And of course, the company faces the Herculean task of getting the word out to store employees about such vital issues as price changes, promotional campaigns, and product recalls. To make all this happen, The Home Depot has developed a two-pronged plan that capitalizes on technology.

The challenge of communicating in multiple languages is so extensive that The Home Depot employs a full-time translation supervisor who oversees the translation of everything from the labeling of boxes and the creation of training manuals to in-store promotional campaigns. To receive perfect translations very quickly, the company has partnered with a firm specializing in international translation services, Bowne Global Solutions (BGS). They installed a Web-based system through which Home Depot managers can submit translation projects, ranging from simple in-store notices to lengthy operational manuals, for rapid translations that sound completely natural to native speakers. To date, BGS has completed thousands of translation projects not only for Home Depot departments in the United States, Canada, and Mexico, but also its numerous suppliers throughout the world. The quick turnaround and high-quality translations The Home Depot gets from BGS have been instrumental to its success.

Another communication challenge at The Home Depot is the need to coordinate all the information sent to sales associates and managers in a way that ensures that nothing is missed—but without overwhelming them. Over the years, these have been problems for the giant retailer, as messages in various forms would pour into stores daily, creating a deluge of phone calls, faxes, snail mails, and e-mails. According to the director of store operations, there was a need to coordinate this ongoing stream of information. To streamline and prioritize the information, The Home Depot again sought the expertise of an outside firm, Reflexis Systems, which developed a Web-based system in which all messages are organized in a single place. Now, not only can managers access all the information required to plan and track their assignments, but they also can track their progress and report their results on a real-time basis.

The biggest challenge in implementing the system involved training thousands of employees in every store, but it has been working well. Now, they've got a single pipeline that all managers can use for all action-required communication, completely eliminating duplication in communication. Before this system was put into place, it was not unusual for store managers to receive the same e-mail several times because it was sent to them by various people. Now, the clarity and greater visibility of important messages has made it possible for stores to be in perfect compliance with requirements for handling product recalls and safety alerts, which benefits customers. And this, of course, contributes to The Home Depot's efforts to provide outstanding customer service.

Questions for Discussion

1. What major communication problems did The Home Depot have and manage to solve?
2. In what ways did The Home Depot leverage the power of technology to facilitate communication? How else might it do so?
3. Based on the material in this chapter, what else could be done at The Home Depot to improve communication within the company?

10 Decision Making in Organizations

Learning Objectives

After reading this chapter, you should be able to:

1. Identify the steps in the analytical model of decision making and distinguish between the various types of decisions that people make.

2. Describe different individual decision styles and the various organizational factors that influence the decision-making process.

3. Distinguish among three approaches to how decisions are made: the rational-economic model, the administrative model, and image theory.

4. Identify the various factors that lead people to make imperfect decisions.

5. Compare the conditions under which groups make superior decisions than individuals and when individuals make superior decisions than groups.

6. Describe various techniques that can be used to enhance the quality of individual decisions and group decisions.

Chapter Outline

- A General, Analytical Model of the Decision-Making Process
- The Broad Spectrum of Organizational Decisions
- Factors Affecting Decisions in Organizations
- How Are Individual Decisions Made?
- The Imperfect Nature of Individual Decisions
- Group Decisions: Do Too Many Cooks Spoil the Broth?
- Techniques for Improving the Effectiveness of Decisions

Preview Case

■ *How Should We Handle the Tiger Affair?*

Few athletes have dominated their sports like Tiger Woods has dominated golf. Since turning pro in 1996, he has won 95 tournaments, including 71 on the PGA (Professional Golfers' Association) Tour. He has held each of the four major championships (e.g., the Masters Tournament) at least three times, winning one by a record-setting 15 strokes. He also was the youngest person ever to win all four championships in the same season. Eight times from 2000–2009 he was awarded the PGA's coveted Golfer of the Year award, and in this same 520-week period, he held the top position in the Official World Golf Ranking for all but 32 of those weeks. It's little wonder that as 2009 drew to a close, the Associated Press named Tiger Woods its Athlete of the Decade.

This accolade was eclipsed, however, by headlines of a more tawdry nature that captured the world's attention only a few days before the AP's big announcement. It came to light that Tiger had had extra-marital affairs with several women over the years, sullying his squeaky clean image. Immediately, he admitted that the allegations were true, and, acknowledging personal issues to work on, sought inpatient counseling for 45 days to help address them. In a public statement made in February 2010, a contrite Tiger apologized to his family, his fans, the golfing community, his business partners, and his sponsors. All now faced decisions, some tougher than others.

Foremost, of course, was Tiger's wife, Elin Nordegren, who, with the couple's two children, returned to her homeland of Sweden, seeking distance from her estranged spouse and hoping to escape prying journalists. She had a difficult decision to make about the fate of her marriage and the future of her family. Also having to decide whether to forgive Tiger were legions of golf fans, whose hero had fallen from grace. Would they once again be willing to make Tiger the focus of their unwavering support and admiration?

Companies endorsing Tiger Woods faced very different kinds of issues—business decisions that left them in a sand trap without a wedge. Should they stick with him in the wake of the lurid allegations? If they remain loyal, they risk alienating consumers put off by the scandals in Tiger's private life. Cutting ties with the golf icon was immediate for Accenture, which sells business services on the basis of trust. With their spokesperson's trustworthiness now destroyed, their decision was easy. Cautious about possible backlash, AT&T also ended its relationship with Woods. Until then, AT&T had been the title sponsor of a PGA event that Tiger hosted, and its logo once proudly adorned his golf bag.

Several companies (e.g., Upper Deck, Nike) took the opposite approach, continuing to back Woods. Even before the hoopla could settle, Tag Heuer boldly featured Tiger's image in their ads, prominently proclaiming that the luxury watchmaker "stands with Tiger Woods." Exactly why they've decided to back the embattled star we may never know, but at least one public relations analyst has suggested that such a move has a considerable upside. By sticking with Tiger, they stand to ride the crest of a legendary sports comeback story if he emerges from his self-imposed hiatus forgiven by his wife and playing better than ever. If redeemed by the court of public opinion, Tiger's new value would be greater than ever, and Tag Heuer would cash in.

That's a big "if," of course, since no one knows for sure exactly how Tiger's tale will play out. Bearing this uncertainty in mind, several of Tiger's sponsors, most notably, Gillette, have been laying low, not using him in campaigns until they can better assess the situation. The final decision came from Tiger, himself. The beleaguered champion returned to the links 5 months later at the 2010 Master's Tournament.

Despite the uncertainties associated with Tiger's situation, several things are quite clear. As Tiger might tell us directly, the decisions we make can have profound effects on others and ourselves. And as his sponsors might indicate, other people's decisions may influence the decisions we have to make ourselves. Such decisions, of course, can be very difficult when what the future holds is uncertain (as it usually is). If Tiger only knew the consequences of his infidelities, if his sponsors only knew how the public will react to their decisions about accepting or rejecting him, if his publicity team only knew if Tiger will reemerge as a sympathetic and beloved athlete who will regain the public's trust—these are questions that only the future will answer. Not being fortune-tellers, of course, predicting these "ifs" isn't always clear. In fact, it rarely is.

Even if we're not a world-class athlete or a top business executive (yet, a least), we all have our own "ifs" to confront us, and the consequences of our own decisions can be just as monumental for us as the ones described here are for the individuals and companies involved Your personal decisions about what college to attend, what classes to take once you're there, and what job to accept after you graduate will have a major impact on the direction your life takes. If

decision making
The process of making choices from among several alternatives.

you think about the difficulties involved in making decisions in your own life, you surely can appreciate how complicated—and important—the process of *decision making* can be in organizations, where the stakes are often considerable and the impact is widespread. In both cases, however, the essential nature of **decision making** is identical. It may be defined as the process of making choices from among several alternatives.

It's safe to say that decision making is one of the most important—if not *the* most important—of all managerial activities.[1] Management theorists and researchers agree that decision making is one of the most common and most crucial work roles of executives. However true this may be, it's important to note that it's not only executives who make decisions in organizations; in one way or another, everyone participates in decision making. As the late management consultant Peter F. Drucker put it,

> Most discussions of decision making assume that only senior executives make decisions or that only senior executives' decisions matter. This is a dangerous mistake . . . Making good decisions is a crucial skill at every level.[2]

Every day, people in organizations make decisions about a variety of topics ranging from the mundane to the monumental.[3] Understanding how these decisions are made, and how they can be improved, is an important goal of the field of organizational behavior.

In this chapter we will examine theories, research, and practical managerial techniques concerned with decision making in organizations, both by individuals and groups. Beginning with individuals, we will review various perspectives on how people go about making decisions. We then will identify factors that may adversely affect the quality of individual decisions and ways of combating them—that is, techniques for improving the quality of individual decisions. Then we will shift our focus to group decisions, examining the conditions under which individuals and groups are each better suited to making decisions. Finally, we will describe some of the factors that make group decisions imperfect, and various techniques that can be used to improve the quality of group decisions. But first, we begin by outlining the general nature of the decision-making process and the wide varieties of decisions made in organizations.

A General, Analytical Model of the Decision-Making Process

analytical model of the decision-making process
A conceptualization of the eight steps through which individuals and groups make decisions: identify the problem, define objectives, make a predecision, generate alternatives, evaluate alternatives, make a choice, implement the choice, and follow up to determine whether the problem still exists.

Scientists have found it useful to conceptualize the process of decision making as a series of steps that groups or individuals take to solve problems.[4] This is accomplished by the **analytical model of the decision-making process,** which can help us understand the complex nature of organizational decision making (see Figure 10.1).[5] This approach highlights three important phases of the general decision-making process:[6]

- *Formulation:* The process of coming to understand the nature of the problem that is being confronted
- *Consideration:* The process of determining and selecting a possible decision to solve that problem
- *Implementation:* The process of carrying out the decision that has been made so as to solve the problem

As we present this model, it's important to keep in mind that all decisions might not fully conform to the neat, eight-step pattern described (e.g., steps may be skipped and/or combined).[7] However, for the purpose of pointing out the *general* way the decision-making process operates, the model is quite useful. To show how it works, we'll use a simple running example: The owner of a small business finds that her cash reserves are insufficient to meet her company's payroll obligations.

Decision Formulation

The first three steps in the decision-making process involve *formulation*. It is through these steps that people think about and come to grips with the problem at hand.

1. *Identifying the problem.* The first step in the decision-making involves *identifying the problem*. To decide how to solve a problem, one first must acknowledge its existence. This might sound obvious, but it's not always the case that people are aware of the problems

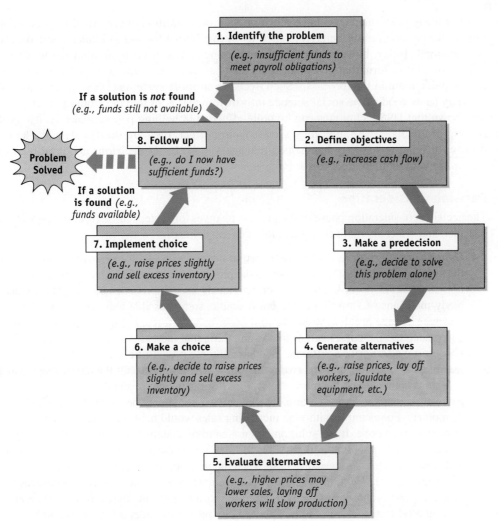

FIGURE 10.1

Overview of the Decision-Making Process

The *analytical model of the decision-making process* describes most decisions as following the eight general steps shown here. Note how each step may be applied to a hypothetical organizational problem (in this example, not having sufficient funds to meet payroll obligations).

Source: Based on information in Wedley & Field, 1984; see Note 5.

they face. Substance abuse counselors, for example, tell us that a major step in the recovery process involves getting patients to admit that they have problems in the first place. Even among people who don't suffer from this disease, as you may recall from our discussion of the social perception process (see Chapter 3), people in general don't always perceive social situations accurately. It's easy to distort, omit, ignore, and/or discount information that might have provided important cues about the existence of problems.[8] In the case of our cash-short business owner, realizing the existence of a problem may be as easy as checking the bank balance, or having a bookkeeper or accountant point this out.

2. *Defining objectives.* After a problem is identified, the next step is to *define the objectives to be met in solving the problem.* It is important to conceive of problems in such a way that possible solutions can be identified. Since the problem in our example is inadequate cash reserves, the objective may be to improve cash flow. Any possible solution to the problem should be evaluated relative to this objective. A good solution is one that meets it.

3. *Making a predecision.* The third step in the decision-making process calls for *making a predecision.* A **predecision** is a decision about how to make a decision. This may sound like doubletalk, but it isn't. To illustrate what we mean by this, consider how our business owner must determine how to go about deciding what to do about her company's cash flow problem. After assessing the nature of the situation, she may opt to put together an ad hoc group to study the problem and make recommendations (see Chapter 8); she may hire an outside consultant to help her decide (an expensive option under the circumstances); she might delegate the task of figuring out what to do to the company's accountant; or she may decide to take on the problem herself. Regardless of the particular course of action she ultimately takes, she is making a decision about how to go about making that decision (i.e., a predecision). In our example, let's say that the owner decides to make the decision herself.

predecision
A decision about what process to follow in making a decision.

For many years, managers have relied on their own intuition or empirically-based information about organizational behavior (such as in this book) for the guidance needed to make predecisions. Today, however, computer programs can be used to summarize much of this information into a form that gives managers ready access to a wealth of social science information to guide them in this process.[9] Such **decision support systems (DSS),** as they are called, can only be as good as the social science information that goes into developing them. Research has shown that DSS techniques can be quite effective in helping people make decisions about solving problems.[10] Although they are far from perfect, they are used widely.[11] The use of decision-making technology has helped managers make better decisions about problems than they make without these decision aids.[12]

**decision support
systems (DSS)**
Computer programs in
which information about
organizational behavior is
presented to decision
makers in a manner that
helps them structure their
responses to decisions.

Decision Consideration

The decision consideration phase of the process involves three steps through which people create, consider, and select alternatives to solve the problem at hand.

4. *Generating alternatives.* The fourth step in the process calls for *generating alternatives,* the stage in which possible solutions to the problem are identified. In attempting to come up with solutions, people often rely on previously used approaches that might provide ready-made answers for them.[13] In our example, some possible ways of solving the revenue shortage problem would be to reduce the workforce, to liquidate unnecessary equipment, to take out a loan, or to do something that increases sales immediately.

5. *Evaluating alternative solutions.* Because all these possibilities may not be equally feasible, the fifth step calls for *evaluating alternative solutions.* Of the alternatives, which is best? What would be the most effective way of raising the revenue needed to meet the payroll? Among the various alternatives identified, some may be more effective and feasible than others. For example, although increasing sales would help solve the problem, it's much easier said than done. It is a solution, but not an immediately practical one. Borrowing money might help, but all it might do is forestall the problem until the next payroll period—and create even greater needs for cash when the time comes to repay the loan.

6. *Making a choice.* Next, in the sixth step, *a choice is made.* After several alternatives are evaluated, one is chosen. As we will describe shortly, different approaches to decision making offer different views of how thoroughly people consider alternatives and how optimal their chosen alternatives are. Choosing which course of action to take is the step that most often comes to mind when we think about the decision-making process. In this case, after carefully considering the alternatives, our business owner may decide to liquidate a lot of unused equipment (generating immediate cash), using some of it for payroll and the remainder to develop new products that are inclined to boost sales.

Decision Implementation

Once a problem has been identified and a decision has been made, the time has come to carry out the decision and to assess its impact.

7. *Implementing the decision.* The seventh step calls for *implementing the chosen alternative—* that is, carrying out the decision that was made in step 6. So now, the business owner would actually go about liquidating the equipment and developing the new products as decided upon in step 6.

8. *Following up.* The eighth and final step involves *following up.* Did liquidating the equipment and developing the new products solve the problem as required? Monitoring the effectiveness of the decisions that were put into action is important to the success of the organization. Does the problem still exist? Have any new problems been created by implementing the solution? In other words, it is important to seek feedback about the effectiveness of any attempted solution. For this reason, the decision-making process in Figure 10.1 is depicted as circular. If the solution works, then the problem is solved. If not, a new solution will have to be attempted.

Having outlined the basic steps through which people go in making decisions, you may assume that everyone makes decisions the same way. This would be misleading because although there are strong similarities in the basic steps, there are some fascinating differences in

Today's Diverse and Global Organizations

How Does National Culture Affect the Decision-Making Process?

Because we take for granted our own ways of making decisions, different methods used by people in other cultures may seem strange to us. However, one should be mindful of such differences when doing business with people from around the world. Accordingly, it makes sense to familiarize yourself with these interesting ways in which people from various nations differ in the way they make decisions.

Identifying Problems

The first step in the analytical model of decision making specifies that the process begins by observing a problem. As obvious as this may seem, people from different countries do not always agree on what constitutes a problem. Suppose, for example, you are managing a large construction project and discover that your most important supplier will be delivering some important materials several months late. If you are from the United States, Canada, or Western Europe, you may decide to get another supplier. However, if you are from Thailand, Indonesia, or Malaysia, you would be likely to accept the situation as fate and allow the project to be delayed.

Making Predecisions

In the United States, where people tend to have a highly *individualistic orientation* (i.e., their primary focus is on themselves as individuals), they are inclined to make decisions alone. However, in Asian countries, people have a more *collectivistic orientation* (i.e., their primary focus is on the groups to which

they belong). As such, it would be inconceivable for a Japanese businessperson to make a decision without first checking with his or her colleagues. Individuals from such cultures are inclined to make group decisions rather than individual ones. As such, they are unlikely to include the option of making decisions individually among the predecisions they consider.

Generating and Evaluating Alternatives

In Sweden, employees at all levels expect to be involved in making whatever decisions involve them. In fact, employees of the Swedish auto manufacturers Saab and Volvo routinely make decisions about how to do their jobs. In India, by contrast, the hierarchy of an organization matters a great deal. People there expect decisions to be made by others of higher rank. Empowered decision making (which we will describe more fully later in this chapter) is not well accepted.

Making Choices

In the United States, we generally respect people who make decisions quickly, referring to them as "decisive," a quality that is valued. In other cultures, however, time urgency is downplayed. For example, in the Middle East, selecting a course of action quickly would be taken as a sign of being overly hasty. In Egypt in particular, the more important the matter at hand, the more time one is expected to take when making a decision about it.

As these examples illustrate, there are some interesting and important differences in how people from various countries consider and formulate decisions. Understanding such differences is an important first step toward developing appropriate strategies for conducting business at a global level.[14]

---

the way people from various nations go about making decisions.[15] (For a discussion of this point, see the Today's Diverse and Global Organizations section above.)

The Broad Spectrum of Organizational Decisions

As you might imagine, because decision making is so fundamental to organizations, decisions themselves tend to be of many different kinds. Understanding the variety of decisions that are made in organizations is an important first step toward understanding the nature of the decision-making process. With this in mind, we will distinguish among decisions in three important ways: how routine they are, how much risk is involved, and who in the organization gets to make them.

Programmed Versus Nonprogrammed Decisions

Think of a decision that is made repeatedly, according to a preestablished set of alternatives. For example, a word processing operator may decide to make a backup copy of the day's work on a network server, or an assistant manager of a fast-food restaurant may decide to order hamburger buns as the supply starts to dwindle. Decisions such as these are known as **programmed decisions**—routine decisions, made by lower-level personnel, that rely on predetermined courses of action.

By contrast, we may identify **nonprogrammed decisions**—ones for which there are no ready-made solutions. The decision maker confronts a unique situation in which the solutions are novel. A research scientist attempting to find a cure for a rare disease faces a problem that is

programmed decisions
Highly routine decisions made according to preestablished organizational routines and procedures.

nonprogrammed decisions
Decisions made about a highly novel problem for which there is no prespecified course of action.

FIGURE 10.2

Comparing Programmed and Nonprogrammed Decisions

Two major types of organizational decisions—programmed decisions and nonprogrammed decisions—differ with respect to the three dimensions summarized here.

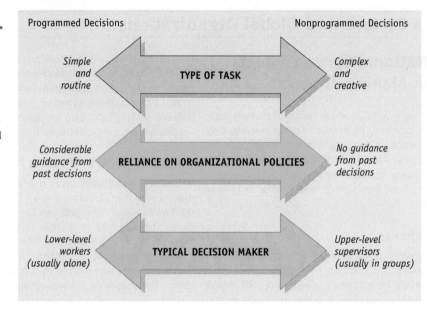

strategic decisions
Nonprogrammed decisions typically made by high-level executives regarding the direction their organization should take to achieve its mission.

poorly structured. Unlike the order clerk, whose course of action is clear when the supply of paper clips runs low, the scientist in this example must rely on creativity rather than preexisting answers to solve the problem at hand.

The differences between programmed and nonprogrammed decisions can be described with respect to three important questions (see Figure 10.2). First, *what types of tasks are involved?* Programmed decisions are made on tasks that are common and routine, whereas nonprogrammed decisions are made on unique and novel tasks. Second, *how much reliance is there on organizational policies?* In making programmed decisions, the decision maker can count on guidance from statements of organizational policy and procedure. However, nonprogrammed decisions require the use of creative solutions that are implemented for the first time; past solutions may provide little guidance. Finally, *who makes the decisions?* Not surprisingly, nonprogrammed decisions typically are made by upper-level organizational personnel, whereas the more routine, well-structured, programmed decisions are usually relegated to lower-level personnel.[16]

Certain types of nonprogrammed decisions are known as **strategic decisions.**[17] Such decisions typically are made by groups of high-level executives and have important long-term implications for the organization. Strategic decisions reflect a consistent pattern for directing the organization in some specified fashion—that is, according to an underlying organizational philosophy or mission. For example, an organization may make a strategic decision to grow at a specified yearly rate, or to be guided by a certain code of corporate ethics. Both decisions may be considered "strategic" because they guide the future direction of the organization. Some good examples of both highly successful and unsuccessful strategic decisions made in business settings may be found in Table 10.1.[18]

Certain Versus Uncertain Decisions

Just think of how easy it would be to make decisions if we knew what the future had in store. Making the best investments in the stock market simply would be a matter of looking up the prices in tomorrow's newspaper. Of course, we never know exactly what the future holds, but we can be more certain at some times than others. Certainty about the factors on which decisions are made is highly desired in organizational decision making.

UNDERSTANDING RISK: OBJECTIVE AND SUBJECTIVE PROBABILITIES. Degrees of certainty and uncertainty are expressed as statements of *risk*. All organizational decisions involve some degree of risk—ranging from complete certainty (no risk) to complete uncertainty, "a stab in the dark" (high risk). To make the best possible decisions in organizations, people seek to "manage" the risks they take—that is, minimizing the riskiness of a decision by gaining access to information relevant to the decision.[19]

What makes an outcome risky or not is the *probability* of obtaining the desired outcome. Decision makers attempt to obtain information about the probabilities, or odds, of certain events

TABLE 10.1 Successful and Unsuccessful Strategic Decisions: Some Examples

The history of business is full of examples of major successes and equally serious failures in strategic decision making. Here are a few of the most visible examples.

Unsuccessful Strategic Decisions	Successful Strategic Decisions
• 1927: Warner Brothers rejected the idea of producing motion pictures with soundtracks.	• 1905: Sears widened its audience by presenting its products in the form of a catalog.
• 1938: IBM, GM, and DuPont turned down photocopying technology.	• 1914: Ford created a market for its cars by paying autoworkers enough money ($5/day) to buy one.
• 1962: Decca records refused to sign the Beatles to a recording contract.	• 1944: Coca-Cola developed brand loyalty by selling soft drinks to soldiers for 5 cents per bottle.
• 1975: Sony decided not to license its Betamax technology, allowing Matsushita to dominate the home videotape market with VHS.	• 1981: Microsoft decided to license its computer operating system (DOS) to IBM.
• 1984: Coca-Cola changed its long-successful formula (at least until public outcry forced the company to change it back).	• 1994: Amazon.com launched the Web commerce market by selling books over the Internet.
• 2006: Toshiba released the first HD DVD player, but despite a three-month head start on the market, it was forced to cease production only two years later, after the competing Blu-ray disc format gained dominance.	• 2007: Sony designed its PS3 game units to play Blu-ray discs, defeating HD DVD in the format wars and creating a large market for its movies on Blu-ray discs.
• 2009: NBC made Conan O'Brien host of its long-running *The Tonight Show* and gave former host, Jay Leno, a new nightly comedy show during prime time. Leno's new show fared poorly, and two months later NBC returned him to *The Tonight Show*, ousting O'Brien from his new spot.	• 2008: At little or no cost to his campaign for U.S. president, Senator Barack Obama leveraged the power of the Internet to organize his supporters in a way that previously would have required an army of volunteers and paid organizers, leading to his victory.
• 2010: BP minimized the seriousness of its oil leak in the Gulf of Mexico, adding a public relations disaster to its environmental nightmare.	

occurring given that other events have occurred. For example, a financial analyst may report that a certain stock has risen 80 percent of the time that the prime interest rate has dropped, or a meteorologist may report that the precipitation probability is 50 percent (i.e., in the past it rained or snowed half the time certain atmospheric conditions existed). These may be considered reports of *objective probabilities* because they are based on concrete, verifiable data (for another example, see Figure 10.3).

Risk does not occur only in organizations, of course: A certain degree of risk is associated with every decision we make in life.[20] Given that roughly half of all marriages end in divorce, having a successful marriage is a fairly risky proposition (especially under some circumstances).[21] However, the odds of becoming president of the United States are far less, only 1 in 10 million, which gives you about the same chance of getting killed by parts falling off an airplane.[22] Of course, knowing such odds helps people make decisions about certain precautions to take (e.g., getting counseling to improve the odds of having a successful marriage), or even whether they want to engage in certain behavior at all (e.g., running for president is desirable to many, but the low chances of success keep even more from trying).

In addition to making decisions using objective probabilities, people also make decisions based on *subjective probabilities*—personal beliefs or hunches about what will happen. For example, a gambler who bets on a horse because it has a name similar to one of his children's, or a person who suspects it's going to rain because he just washed his car, is basing these judgments on subjective probabilities. Despite the considerable effort that's put into making rational, objective decisions, we cannot deny the fact that people, on at least some occasions, base their decisions on subjective probabilities, or "gut feelings."

REDUCING UNCERTAINTY IN DECISION MAKING. Obviously, uncertainty is an undesirable characteristic in decision-making situations. We may view much of what decision makers do in organizations as attempting to reduce uncertainty (i.e., putting the odds in their favor) so they can make better decisions. How do organizations respond when faced with highly uncertain

FIGURE 10.3

Relying on Objective Probabilities: Important in Restaurants

This manager of a Jamba Juice store in Los Angeles is presenting an upcoming work schedule to some members of his staff. It's relatively common in retail businesses for employees' schedules to be based on *objective probabilities* of business levels expected on various days and times. An effective way of doing this is by consulting records of customer-counts at such times in the past and adjusting them based on other factors (e.g., overall rises or declines in business levels, publication of a good or bad review in the newspaper, sales, and so on). Decisions made in this manner make it possible to minimize waste (by not ordering more fresh food than is likely to be used) and labor costs (by not scheduling more employees than needed to staff shifts).

conditions, when they don't know what the future holds for them? Studies have shown that decision uncertainty can be reduced by *establishing linkages with other organizations*. The more an organization knows about what another organization will do, the greater certainty it will have in making decisions.[23] This is part of a general tendency for organizational decision makers to respond to uncertainty by reducing the unpredictability of other organizations in their business environments. Those outside organizations with which managers have the greatest contact are most likely to be the ones whose actions are easiest to predict.[24]

In general, what reduces uncertainty in decision-making situations? The answer is *information*. Knowledge about the past and the present can be used to help make projections about the future. A modern executive's access to data needed to make important decisions may be as close as the nearest computer. Indeed, technology has aided greatly managers' abilities to make decisions quickly, using the most accurate and thorough information available.[25] A variety of online information services (e.g., government reports and statistics, stock market filings) are designed to provide organizational decision makers with the latest information relevant to the decisions they are making.

Of course, not all information needed to make decisions comes from computers. Many managerial decisions are based as well on decision makers' past experiences and intuitions.[26] This is not to say that managers rely solely on subjective information in making decisions (although they might), but that their history of past decisions—both successes and failures—is often given great weight in the decision-making process. In other words, when it comes to making decisions, people often rely on what has worked for them in the past. Part of the reason this strategy is often successful is because experienced decision makers tend to make better use of information relevant to the decisions they are making.[27] Individuals who have expertise in certain subjects know what information is best to use and how to interpret it once collected, when making decisions. It is therefore not surprising that people seek assistance from experienced professionals, such as doctors and lawyers who are seasoned veterans in their fields, when it comes to making important decisions. With high levels of expertise comes information relevant to assessing the riskiness of decision alternatives and knowledge about how to reduce it.

Top-Down Versus Empowered Decisions

Traditionally, in organizations the job of making all but the most menial decisions belonged to managers. (In fact, organizational scientist Herbert Simon, who won a Nobel prize for his work on the economics of decision making, has gone so far as to describe decision making as synonymous with managing.[28]) Subordinates collected information and gave it to superiors, who used it to make decisions. This approach, known as **top-down decision making,** puts decision-making power in the hands of managers and leaves lower-level workers little or no opportunities to make decisions. If this sounds familiar to you, it's probably because this is how most organizations have operated over the years.

Today, however, a new approach has come into vogue, which is in many ways exactly the opposite. The idea of **empowered decision making** allows employees to make the decisions required to do their jobs without first seeking supervisory approval. As the name implies, it gives them the power to decide what they need to do so as to perform their jobs effectively. (For a comparison between top-down decision making and empowered decision making, see Figure 10.4.) The rationale for this philosophy of decision making is that the people who do the jobs know what's best, so having someone else make the decision may not make the most sense. In addition, when people are empowered to make their own decisions, they are more likely to accept the consequences of those decisions. If the decision was a good one, they can feel good about it. If not, then they have learned a valuable lesson for the next time. In either case, people are more committed to courses of action based on decisions they have made themselves than ones based on decisions that others have made (particularly if those decisions affect them). And such commitment can be important to keeping the organization functioning effectively.

It is important to note that managers who empower their subordinates to make their own decisions are not abdicating their responsibility. Rather, they are delegating some of their power

top-down decision making
The practice of vesting decision-making power in the hands of superiors as opposed to lower-level employees.

empowered decision making
The practice of vesting power for making decisions in the hands of employees themselves.

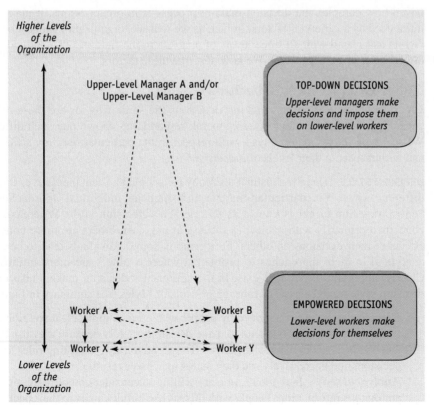

FIGURE 10.4

Top-Down Versus Empowered Decisions: A Comparison

Traditionally, decision making in organizations was a top-down practice. Upper-level workers made decisions, which they then imposed on lower-level workers, who carried them out. Although this still goes on, of course, many decisions today are made by lower-level workers who are empowered to make certain decisions for themselves.

(see Chapter 12) to others who are capable of making decisions. When empowering workers, managers provide general guidance about how to make decisions, but they do not set up specific rules to be followed in each possible circumstance. This gives workers discretion about what to do. For example, a manager at a car rental agency may empower agents at rental counters to offer free upgrades or discounts as appeasement to customers who have reasonable complaints. In this case, the worker is making the decision as deemed necessary but within guidelines set by the manager (who, of course, ultimately is responsible). Not only does empowerment motivate many workers (as noted in Chapter 7) and serve as a source of job satisfaction (as noted in Chapter 6), but it also frees up the time of higher-level personnel. Instead of "micro-managing" by making small decisions, empowering lower-level workers enables higher-level managers to concentrate on making the higher-level decisions that only they, themselves, can make.

We find illustrations of empowerment in many different organizations. Consider these examples.

- Individual employees at the Ritz-Carlton Hotel chain are empowered to spend up to $2,000 of the company's money per day to resolve any customer problem they find.[29] Instead of getting approval, they can make arrangements directly with the appropriate individuals in the company to fix the problem.
- Teams at the Chesapeake Packaging Company's box plant in Baltimore, Maryland, are organized into eight separate internal companies.[30] Each such unit is empowered to make its own decisions about key issues, such as ordering, purchasing new equipment, and measuring its performance (see the discussion of self-management in Chapter 8).
- At Disney World, empowering employees to deal with customers is the rule rather than the exception.[31] "Cast members," as they are called, are given the authority to do whatever it takes (within reason, of course) to make customers happy on the spot. Management interference is discouraged.

These examples illustrate not only some of the great lengths to which companies are going to empower their employees to make decisions, but they also highlight a key trend. Empowering workers is not a fad, but a practice that is here to stay.[32]

Factors Affecting Decisions in Organizations

Given how complex the decision-making process is in organizations, it makes sense that it is influenced by a variety of factors. In fact, as we will see, organizational decisions are affected by factors associated with all three levels of analysis in the field of OB—individuals, groups, and organizations (see Chapter 1). We now describe these factors.

Individual Differences in Decision Making

Do all individuals go about making decisions the same way, or are there differences in the general approaches people take? In general, research has shown that such differences do exist. We see these in two major ways—with respect to the particular *decision style* that people have and with respect to their levels of *indecisiveness*.

decision style
Differences between people with respect to their orientations toward decisions.

DECISION STYLE. There is a distinct tendency for people to orient themselves toward decisions in different ways. The particular manner in which an individual approaches the decisions confronting him or her is known as this person's **decision style.** Whereas some people are concerned primarily with achieving success at any cost, others are more concerned about the effects of their decisions on others. Furthermore, some individuals tend to be more logical and analytical in their approaches to problems, whereas others are more intuitive and creative. Clearly, important differences exist in the approaches decision makers take to problems. The **decision style model** classifies four major decision styles (see summary in Figure 10.5).[33]

decision style model
The conceptualization according to which people use one of four predominant decision styles: *directive, analytical, conceptual,* or *behavioral.*

- *Directive style*—Characterized by people who prefer simple, clear solutions to problems. Individuals with this style tend to make decisions rapidly because they use little information and do not consider many alternatives. They tend to rely on existing rules to make their decisions and aggressively use their status to achieve results.
- *Analytical style*—Individuals who are willing to consider complex solutions based on ambiguous information. People with this style carefully analyze their decisions using as

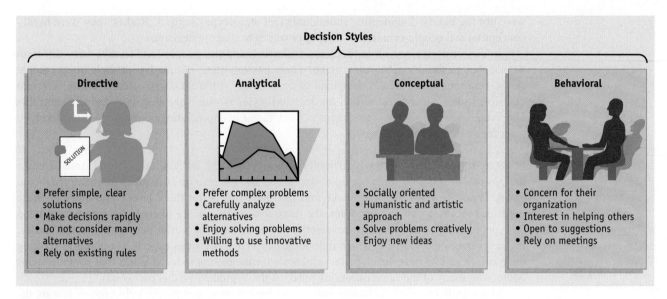

Decision Styles

Directive	Analytical	Conceptual	Behavioral
• Prefer simple, clear solutions • Make decisions rapidly • Do not consider many alternatives • Rely on existing rules	• Prefer complex problems • Carefully analyze alternatives • Enjoy solving problems • Willing to use innovative methods	• Socially oriented • Humanistic and artistic approach • Solve problems creatively • Enjoy new ideas	• Concern for their organization • Interest in helping others • Open to suggestions • Rely on meetings

FIGURE 10.5

Decision Style Model: A Summary

According to the *decision style model,* people may be characterized as adhering to one of the four decision styles summarized here.

Source: Based on information in Rowe et al., 1984; see Note 33.

much data as possible. Such individuals tend to enjoy solving problems. They want the best possible answers and are willing to use innovative methods to achieve them.

■ *Conceptual style*—People who are socially oriented in their approach to problems. Their approach is humanistic and artistic. Such individuals tend to consider many broad alternatives when dealing with problems and to solve them creatively. They have a strong future orientation and enjoy initiating new ideas.

■ *Behavioral style*—People who are concerned deeply about the organizations in which they work and about the personal development of their coworkers. They are highly supportive of others and very concerned about others' achievements, frequently helping them meet their goals. Such individuals tend to be open to suggestions from others, and therefore tend to rely on meetings for making decisions.

It is important to point out that although most managers may have one dominant style, they use many different styles. In fact, those who can shift between styles—that is, those who are most flexible in their approaches to decision making—have highly complex, individualistic styles of their own. Despite this, people's dominant styles reveal a great deal about the way they tend to make decisions. Not surprisingly, conflicts often occur between individuals with different styles. For example, a manager with a highly directive style may have a hard time accepting the slow, deliberate actions of a subordinate with an analytical style.

Researchers have noted that being aware of people's decision styles is a potentially useful way of understanding social interactions in organizations. With this in mind, scientists have developed an instrument known as the *decision style inventory,* a questionnaire designed to reveal the relative strength of people's decision styles.[34] The higher an individual scores with respect to a given decision style, the more likely that style is to predominate in his or her decision making. (To give you a feel for how the various decision styles are measured, and for your own decision style, see the Individual Exercise on pages 370–371.)

Research using the decision style inventory has revealed some interesting findings. For example, when it was given to a sample of corporate presidents, their scores on each of the four categories were found to be approximately equal. Apparently, they had no one dominant style, but were able to switch back and forth between categories with ease. Further research has shown that different groups tend to have, on average, different styles that dominate their decision making. For example, military leaders were found to have high conceptual style scores. They were not the highly domineering individuals that stereotypes suggest. Rather, they were highly conceptual and people-oriented in their approaches to making decisions.

In conclusion, research on decision styles reveals that people tend to take very different approaches to the decisions they make. Their personalities, coupled with their interpersonal skills, lead them to approach decisions in consistently different ways—that is, using different decision styles. Although research on decision styles is relatively new, it already is clear that understanding such stylistic differences is a key factor in appreciating potential conflicts likely to arise between decision makers.

INDECISIVENESS. Do you have difficulty making choices? Do you take a long time to make decisions? Do you delay the making of decisions? Do you change your mind frequently? Do you worry about the decisions you make and find that you regret them later? The more of these questions to which you answered yes, the more *indecisive* you are likely to be. Beyond studying *how* people approach decisions, researchers also are interested in a personality characteristic **indecisiveness**, the degree to which individuals approach decisions eagerly as opposed to putting them off. Scientists have developed a valid scale for measuring indecisiveness that contains items addressing many of the same questions posed at the beginning of this paragraph.[35]

indecisiveness
An individual difference variable reflecting the degree to which people approach decisions eagerly as opposed to wanting to put them off.

In a simple experiment, female college students who scored particularly high or low on the indecisiveness scale were brought into a room where they were seated at a desk in front of a monitor. On the screen they were presented with photos of pairs of items and were asked to make a decision about each pair. In one part of the study, what was shown on the screen were pairs of photos of items of clothing taken from a catalogue. For each of the pairs, they were asked to indicate which one of the items they would prefer to buy. They also were presented with pairs of items in other categories (e.g., pairs of course descriptions from class catalogues, pairs of activities from lists, and pairs of items on restaurant menus). The researcher measured the amount of time the participants took to make each of these decisions. In addition, participants were asked to indicate the degree to which they found it difficult to make these choices and the degree to which they had difficulties making similar decisions in real life.

The differences were in line with what you'd expect for decisive and indecisive people. Specifically, compared to women whose scores on the scale revealed that they were highly decisive, those who were found to be highly indecisive took significantly more time making the decisions in all four categories. They also reported having more problems with the decision-making task and greater difficulty with similar problems in real life. Obviously, indecisiveness is more than just a term we use to describe people in everyday life and a legitimate and potentially important personality characteristic.

Research on indecisiveness has provided some interesting insight into precisely why indecisive people take longer to make decisions. For one, people who are highly indecisive tend to be perfectionists—but not in a good way.[36] They tend to be overly concerned about making mistakes and to have doubts about the quality of their decisions. In contrast, people who set high goals for themselves and who do not obsess over minor details tend to be highly decisive.

Additional research has found that decisive and indecisive people also differ with respect to the way they process information when making decisions. Specifically, a study was conducted in which people were given a decision task presented on a computer monitor. As they watched the screen, a device was used that allowed researchers to record participants' eye movements.[37] This research allowed scientists to determine differences in how people scanned the information in front of them. Decisive people, it was found, narrow down their decisions based on a particular attribute that they find most important. However, indecisive people focus on all the information, even if it's not especially important. In fact, they also spent time looking at nothing, just blank spaces on the screen. Taking these findings into account, it becomes clear why it takes indecisive people longer to make decisions—namely, they approach the task in a less efficient manner.

It's interesting to consider how people who differ in levels of indecisiveness may behave when making decisions on the job. As in the case of most personality variables (as we noted in Chapter 4), their impact is likely to depend on the nature of the situations they're facing. It's easy to envision jobs in which being indecisive can be problematic, such as when quick action is required. This would be the case, for example, among airline pilots, astronauts, or soldiers in combat, where indecisiveness could be deadly. However, in some other positions, such as executives making decisions about important business matters, making decisions too quickly may be a sign of hastiness and lack of care. In this case, not taking in all that extra information can be a serious liability because it may interfere with making effective decisions. Of course, one also can take too much time to make a decision, slowing things down so that problems may result by causing other important decisions to be delayed (for an example, see Figure 10.6).

Group Influences: A Matter of Trade-Offs

As you might imagine, groups influence organizational decisions in a vast array of ways, potentially positive and negative. We say "potentially" because the variety of factors influencing organizational decisions make it difficult to predict whether anticipated benefits or problems actually will occur. Still, it is useful to understand some of the major forces that have the potential to affect the way groups make decisions in organizations.

POTENTIAL BENEFITS OF DECISION-MAKING GROUPS. Much can be gained by using decision-making groups. For example, bringing people together may increase the amount of knowledge and information available for making good decisions. In other words, there may be a *pooling of resources* in which everyone involved contributes something to the joint effort. A related benefit is that in decision-making groups there can be a *specialization of labor*. In other words, with enough people around to share the workload, individuals can perform only those tasks at which they are best, thereby potentially improving the quality of the group's efforts.

AP Photo/Gene J. Puskar.

FIGURE 10.6

Indecisiveness Can Be Hazardous to Your Coach

There can be no questioning Brett Favre's extraordinary skills as a quarterback. However, Favre has questioned his own future as either a retiree or a player over such long periods that it has made life challenging for his coaches, who are attempting to plan their offensive strategies and their rosters for the season. You may even remember humorous pokes that Favre took at himself on television commercials in which he parodied his own indecisiveness in making a decision about which TV set to purchase.

Another benefit is that group decisions are likely to enjoy *greater acceptance* than individual decisions. People involved in making decisions generally understand those decisions better and are more committed to carrying them out than decisions made for them by someone else.[38]

POTENTIAL PROBLEMS OF DECISION-MAKING GROUPS. Despite these potential benefits, there also are some possible problems associated with using decision-making groups. One drawback of which you already might be aware is that groups are inclined to *waste time*. The time spent socializing before getting down to business, for example, may distract groups from the tasks at hand and be very costly to organizations as a result.

Another possible problem is that potential disagreement over important matters may breed ill will and *group conflict*. Although constructive disagreement may lead to better group outcomes, highly disruptive conflict may interfere with group decisions. Indeed, with corporate power and personal pride at stake, it is not at all surprising to find that lack of agreement can cause bad feelings to develop between group members (see Chapter 11).

Finally, we may expect groups to be ineffective sometimes because of members' *intimidation by group leaders*. A group composed of several "yes men" or women trying to please a dominant leader tends to discourage open and honest discussion of solutions. In view of these problems, it is easy to understand the old adage, "A camel is a horse put together by a committee."

GROUPTHINK: TOO MUCH COHESIVENESS CAN BE A DANGEROUS THING. As we described in Chapter 8, sometimes members of groups become so concerned about not "rocking the boat" that they are reluctant to challenge the group's decisions. When this happens, group members tend to isolate themselves from outside information, and the process of critical thinking deteriorates. This phenomenon is referred to as **groupthink**.[39]

groupthink
The tendency for members of highly cohesive groups to so strongly conform to group pressures regarding a certain decision that they fail to think critically, rejecting the potentially correcting influences of outsiders.

To illustrate the phenomenon of groupthink, consider the tragic decision to launch the space shuttle *Challenger* in January 1986. Analyses of conversations between key personnel suggested that NASA officials made the decision to launch the shuttle under freezing conditions while ignoring admonitions from engineers.[40] Given that NASA had such a successful history, the decision makers operated with a sense of invulnerability. They also worked so closely together and were under such intense pressure to launch the shuttle without further delay that they all collectively went along with the launch decision, creating the illusion of unanimous agreement. For a more precise description of groupthink and a practical guide to recognizing its symptoms, see Figure 10.7.

Groupthink doesn't occur only in governmental decision making, as you might imagine, but in the private sector as well (although in such cases, the failures may be less well publicized). For example, analyses of the business policies of large corporations such as British Airways, Lockheed, and Chrysler have suggested that it was the failure of top management teams to respond to changing market conditions that at one time led these firms to the brink of disaster (in the case of Chrysler, multiple times).[41] The problem is that members of very cohesive groups may have considerable

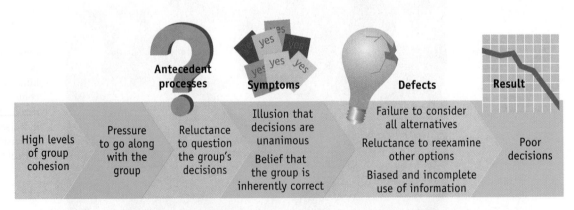

FIGURE 10.7

Groupthink: An Overview
Groupthink occurs when highly cohesive conditions in groups discourage members from challenging their group's overall decision. Poor-quality decisions result.

confidence in their groups' decisions, making them unlikely to raise doubts about these actions (i.e., "the group seems to know what it's doing"). As a result, they may suspend their own critical thinking in favor of conforming to the group. When group members become fiercely loyal to each other, they may ignore potentially useful information from other sources that challenges their groups' decisions. The result of this process is that a group's decisions may suffer, such as by being uninformed, irrational, or immoral.[42] (Fortunately, several steps can be taken to avoid groupthink. For some suggestions in this regard, see the OB in Practice section below.)

Organizational Influences on Decision Making

In addition to individual and group forces that affect decision making, we also have to be aware of forces stemming from within organizations themselves. Two key ones in this regard are political pressures and time pressures.

POLITICAL PRESSURES. Sometimes, the quality of decisions people make in organizations is limited by the pressures they face to look good to others (i.e., to "save face") even though the resulting decisions might not be in the best interest of their organizations. Imagine, for example, how an employee might distort the available information needed to make a decision if the correct information would jeopardize his job. This would be the case if a sales rep inflated his quarterly sales figures to make himself look good although this might lead to an overly optimistic picture of a product's popularity. Unfortunately, such misuses of information to support desired decisions are all too common.

A study on the topic of political face-saving found that businesspeople working on a group decision-making problem opted for an adequate—although less than optimal—decision rather than risk generating serious conflicts with their fellow group members.[43] In an actual case, a proponent of medical inoculation for the flu was so interested in advancing his pro-inoculation position that he proceeded with the inoculation program although there was only a 2 percent

---

OB in Practice

Strategies for Avoiding Groupthink

Because scientists have such a good feel for why groupthink occurs, it is possible to identify tactics aimed at weakening the dynamics that trigger it in the first place. With this in mind, here are several tried-and-true recommendations.

1. *Promote open inquiry.* Remember, groupthink arises in response to group members' reluctance to "rock the boat." Thus, group leaders should encourage members to be skeptical of all solutions to problems and to avoid reaching premature agreements about them. Toward this end, it sometimes helps to play the role of *devil's advocate* by intentionally finding fault with a proposed solution and challenging others to improve upon it.[44] Research has shown that when this is done, groups make higher-quality decisions.[45] In fact, some corporate executives use exercises in which conflict is intentionally generated just so the negative aspects of a decision can be identified before it's too late.[46] This is not to say that leaders should be argumentative. Rather, raising a nonthreatening question to force both sides of an issue can be very helpful in improving the quality of decisions.

2. *Use subgroups.* Because the decisions made by any one group may be the result of groupthink, basing decisions on the recommendations of two groups is a useful check. If the two groups disagree, a discussion of their differences is likely to raise important issues. However, if the

two groups agree, you can be relatively confident that their conclusions are not *both* the result of groupthink.

3. *Admit shortcomings.* When groupthink occurs, group members feel very confident that they are doing the right thing. Such feelings of perfection discourage people from considering opposing information. However, if group members acknowledge some of the flaws and limitations of their decisions, they may open themselves to corrective influences. No decision is perfect, of course, so asking others to point out misgivings about a group's decisions may help avoid the illusion of perfection that contributes to groupthink.

4. *Hold second-chance meetings.* Before implementing a decision, it is a good idea to hold a *second-chance meeting* during which group members are asked to express any doubts and propose any new ideas they may have. Alfred P. Sloan, longtime head of General Motors in its heyday, is known to have postponed acting on important matters until any group disagreement was resolved.[47] As people get tired of working on problems, it's not unusual for them to reach agreement on a solution in a hasty fashion. Second-chance meetings can be useful for seeing if a solution still seems good even after "sleeping on it."

Given the adverse effects groupthink can have on organizations, managers would be wise to put these suggestions into practice. The alternative—facing the consequences of groupthink—clearly suggests that they should be taken seriously.

chance of an epidemic.[48] Apparently, people often make the decisions they need to make to cultivate favorable impressions, although these may not be the best ones for their organizations.

TIME PRESSURE: MAKING DECISIONS IN EMERGENCIES. An unavoidable fact of life in contemporary organizations is that people often have only limited amounts of time to make important decisions. The rapid pace with which businesses operate these days results in severe pressures to make decisions almost immediately. Among firefighters, emergency room doctors, and fighter pilots, it's clear that time is of the essence. But, even those of us who toil in less dramatic settings also face the need to make good decisions quickly. The practice of thoroughly collecting information, carefully analyzing it, and then leisurely reviewing the alternatives is a luxury few modern decision makers can afford. In one survey, 77 percent of a broad cross-section of managers polled felt that the number of decisions they were required to make each day has increased, and 43 percent reported that the time they can devote to making decisions has decreased.[49] Often, the result is that bad—and inevitably, costly—decisions are made.

Highly experienced experts, psychologists tell us, are able to make good decisions quickly because they draw on a wealth of experiences collected over the years.[50] Whereas novices are very deliberate in their decision making, considering one option at a time, experts are able to make decisions quickly because they are able to assess the situations they face and compare them to experiences they have had earlier in their careers. They know what matters, what to look for, and what pitfalls to avoid. What is so often considered "gut instinct" is really nothing more than the wealth of accumulated experiences. The more experiences a person has from which to draw, the more effectively he or she can "size up" a situation and take appropriate action (see Figure 10.8).

FIGURE 10.8

Feeding That Gut Instinct

This man is not the only person who relies on his gut to make decisions. To some extent, we all do. Making "gut decisions" involves drawing on the repository of our past experiences, which can be considerable in many cases. As any experienced medical doctor can tell you, when combined with more systematic, analytical tools, gut instinct can be quite valuable when making decisions.

Paul Steiner/Cartoonbank.com.

"I make decisions as much with my gut as I do with my brain. Let's eat."

How Are Individual Decisions Made?

Now that we have identified the types of decisions people make in organizations and the factors that influence them, we are prepared to consider the matter of *how* people go about making them. Perhaps you are thinking, "What do you mean? You just think things over and do what you think is best!" It's not that simple, however; there's a lot more to decision making than meets the eye. In fact, scientists have considered several different approaches to how individuals make decisions. Here, we review three of the most important ones.

The Rational-Economic Model: In Search of the Ideal Decision

We all like to think that we are "rational" people who make the best possible decisions. But what exactly does it mean to make a *rational* decision? Organizational scientists view **rational decisions** as ones that maximize the attainment of goals, whether they are the goals of a person, a group, or an entire organization.[51] What is the most rational way for an individual to go about making a decision? Economists interested in predicting market conditions and prices have relied on a **rational-economic model** of decision making, which assumes that decisions are optimal in every way. An economically rational decision maker will attempt to maximize his or her profits by searching systematically for the *optimum* solution to a problem. For this to occur, the decision maker must have complete and perfect information and be able to process all this information in an accurate and unbiased fashion.[52]

In many respects, rational-economic decisions follow the same steps outlined in our analytical model of decision making (recall Figure 10.1, page 335). However, what makes the rational-economic approach special is that it calls for the decision maker to recognize *all* alternative courses of action (step 4), and to evaluate each one accurately and completely (step 5). In other words, it views decision makers as attempting to make *optimal* decisions.

Of course, the rational-economic approach to decision making does not take into account the fallibility of the human decision maker. Based on the assumption that people have access to complete and perfect information and use it to make perfect decisions, the model can be considered a *normative* (also called *prescriptive*) approach—one that describes how decision makers ideally ought to behave so as to make the best possible decisions. (Many conceptualizations of decision making used by economists are of this type.) It does not describe how decision makers actually behave in most circumstances. This task is undertaken by the next major approach to individual decision making, the *administrative model*.

The Administrative Model: Acknowledging the Limits of Human Rationality

As personal experience undoubtedly tells you, people do not act in a completely rational-economic manner. In fact, we cannot; we're just not built for it. To illustrate this point, consider how a company's human resources manager might go about selecting a new receptionist. After several applicants are interviewed, the manager might choose the best candidate seen so far and stop interviewing. Had the manager been following a rational-economic model, he or she would have had to interview *all* possible candidates before deciding on the best one. This is impractical, however, making it impossible ever to fill the position. However, by ending the search after finding someone considered reasonably good enough to do the job, the manager is using a much simpler approach.

The process used in this example characterizes an approach to decision making known as the **administrative model**.[53] This conceptualization recognizes that decision makers may have a limited and imperfect view of the problems confronting them. The number of solutions that can be recognized or implemented is limited by the innate capabilities of decision makers and the resources available to the organization. For example, decision makers rarely have enough time to consider all the information available to them before having to make a decision. Even if they did, the information available is often too limited or too imperfect to predict the consequences of many decisions, making it difficult or impossible to determine which is best.

How, then, are decisions made according to the administrative model? The answer is that instead of considering all possible solutions, decision makers consider solutions as they become available. Then they decide on the first alternative that meets their criteria for acceptability. Thus, the decision maker selects a solution that may be just good enough, although not

rational decisions
Decisions that maximize the chance of attaining an individual's, group's, or organization's goals.

rational-economic model
The model of decision making according to which decision makers consider all possible alternatives to problems before selecting the optimal solution.

administrative model
A model of decision making that recognizes that people have imperfect views of problems, which limits the making of optimally rational-economic decisions.

satisfacing decisions
Decisions made by selecting the first minimally acceptable alternative as it becomes available.

optimal. Such decisions are referred to as **satisficing decisions.** Of course, a satisficing decision is much easier to make than an optimal decision. In most decision-making situations, people consider satisficing decisions to be acceptable and strive to make them instead of trying to make the optimal decision.[54] The following analogy highlights the difference between the two types of decisions: Making an optimal decision is like searching a haystack for the sharpest needle, but making a satisficing decision is like searching a haystack for a needle just sharp enough with which to sew.

One major factor that contributes to less than optimal decisions has to do with limitations in people's innate cognitive capacities. In other words, the administrative model recognizes the **bounded rationality** under which most organizational decision makers must operate. The idea is that people lack the cognitive skills required to formulate and solve highly complex business problems in a completely objective, rational way.[55] Although computers help a great deal when it comes to organizing information, of course, it's ultimately we human beings who attempt to make sense out of what all the information means and what courses of action to take. And let's face it, we're just not perfect.

bounded rationality
The major assumption of the administrative model—that organizational, social, and human limitations lead to the making of *satisficing*, rather than optimal decisions.

For example, although marketing experts regularly assess consumers' reactions to prospective new products—sometimes quite thoroughly and systematically—some new products still fail. A classic case from the annals of marketing research illustrates this point. In response to rising market share by chief competitor Pepsi, in 1985 Coca-Cola decided to tweak the flavor of its flagship beverage. Despite extensive market testing revealing that people loved the new drink, "new Coke," as it became known, proved to be an epic flop.[56] The public clamored for the return of their favorite beverage, and a few months later, they got it. This tale of fizzled decision making illustrates the flawed nature of decisions that can result because of the inherently imperfect nature of human decision making. Bounded rationality led Coca-Cola's decision makers straight down what proved to be a blind alley.

It may sound strange, but another factor that keeps people from making decisions that maximize some important criteria, such as profitability, is their tendency to conform to moral and ethical standards. Using the terminology of the administrative model, people use **bounded discretion.**[57] In other words, people limit their consideration of decision options to ones that fall within ethical and legal boundaries. For example, although a grocery store might take in more money if it doctored scales at the deli counter to display higher than actual weights, most proprietors, wanting to treat their customers ethically, would be unwilling to do so—even if they had no chance of getting caught. If people were motivated solely by interest in maximizing outcomes, they wouldn't let these ethical considerations interfere with their decision making. But this isn't the case. Instead, people generally are inclined to restrict their decision options to ones that are ethical even if they lead to less than the maximum possible results. As the regular proliferation of ethical scandals appearing in headlines suggests, however, many people do, in fact, decide to behave unethically.[58] For a discussion of the major factors responsible for unethical decisions, see The Ethics Angle section on page 351.

bounded discretion
The tendency to restrict decision alternatives to those that fall within prevailing ethical standards.

It should not be surprising that the administrative model does a better job than the rational-economic model of describing what decision makers really do. The administrative approach is said to be *descriptive* (also called *proscriptive*) in nature because it describes what actually occurs. This interest in examining the real, imperfect behavior of decision makers, rather than specifying the ideal, economically rational behaviors that decision makers ought to engage in, lies at the heart of the distinction between the administrative and rational-economic models. Our point is not that decision makers do not want to behave rationally, but that restrictions posed by their innate capabilities and by the environments in which they work preclude "perfect" decisions.

Image Theory: An Intuitive Approach to Decision Making

If you think about it, you'll probably realize that some, but certainly not all, decisions are made following the logical steps of our general model of decision making. Consider Elizabeth Barrett Browning's poetic question "How do I love thee? Let me count the ways."[59] It's unlikely that anyone would ultimately answer the question by carefully counting what one loves about another (even if many such characteristics could be enumerated). Instead, a more intuitive-based decision making is likely, not only for matters of the heart, but for a variety of important organizational decisions as well.[60]

The Ethics Angle

Why Do People Make Unethical Decisions? Bad Apples, Bad Cases, and Bad Barrels

Noting a multitude of reasons why people make unethical decisions, scientists have found it useful to organize these into three different categories.

- *Bad apples* are qualities of individuals that lead to unethical decisions made by a few unsavory individuals. The focus in this category is on various personality variables (e.g., Machiavellianism; see Chapter 4) that predispose people to behave unethically.
- *Bad cases* are circumstances surrounding particular ethical dilemmas that provoke unethical choices. These are features of moral dilemmas within organizations that influence how people experience them (e.g., limited or no consequences expected when behaving unethically).
- *Bad barrels* are characteristics of the organizational environment that may influence ethical behavior (e.g., absence of a code of ethics; see Chapter 2).

Recently, a team of OB scientists thoroughly reviewed 30 years of research on these three factors, providing a good sense of what we know about them.[61] Among the individual factors, so-called bad apples, associated with unethical behavior were several we already have discussed in other connections. Particularly important, for example, were Machiavellianism (Chapter 4; the more Machiavellian people are, the more unethically they behave) and cognitive moral development (Chapter 2; the higher degree of moral development people have attained, the less unethically they behave). The picture painted here is that individuals who behave unethically are ones who are highly focused on doing what's best for themselves, even at the expense of others—that is, people who are "looking out for number one."

With respect to characteristics of the ethical dilemma being faced—that is, bad cases—several factors were involved. Specifically, unethical behavior was found to be greater when the *probability of effect* (i.e., the likelihood that an action will bring harm) was lower, and also when the *magnitude of consequences* (i.e., the total harm resulting from unethical choices) was lower. Interestingly, when these factors and others related to them were considered all together—that is, when the *general moral intensity* as a whole was lowest—unethical behavior was at its highest.

Finally, bad barrels were important as well. In fact, two particular characteristics of the organizational environment were related strongly to unethical behavior. First, unethical behavior was found to be lower in organizations that had higher *ethical cultures*—that is, ones in which behaving ethically was emphasized and practiced—than in ones with lower ethical cultures (we will discuss the general nature of *organizational culture* in Chapter 14). Second, codes of ethics (see Chapter 2) also were important. However, although the mere presence of a code of ethics was unrelated to unethical behavior, the extent to which that code was enforced made a huge difference. The more strictly companies' code of ethics were enforced, the less unethically their employees behaved. In other words, codes were effective not merely by having them, but by enforcing them as well. As obvious as this may seem, companies do not always do good jobs of enforcing their codes of ethics.

Managers certainly will want to keep these various factors in mind. Although it's inappropriate for managers to consider changing people's personalities (nor is this easy even for psychologists to do), it may be wise for them to assign people with certain characteristics to positions in which they cannot do much harm. Also, managers are in a good position to regulate various environmental factors (e.g., enforcing ethical codes) so as to influence the way people behave—in this context, keeping them from behaving unethically. In fact, this is precisely what they're supposed to do.

The point is that selecting the best alternative by weighing all the options is not always a major concern when making a decision. People also consider how various decision alternatives fit with their personal standards as well as their personal goals and plans. The best decision for someone might not be the best for someone else. In other words, people may make decisions in a more automatic, *intuitive* fashion than traditionally is recognized. Representative of this approach is **image theory**.[62] This conceptualization is summarized in Figure 10.9.

Image theory deals primarily with decisions about adopting a certain course of action (e.g., should the company develop a new product line?) or changing a current course of action (e.g., should the company drop a current product line?). According to the theory, people make decisions on the basis of a simple two-step process. The first step is the *compatibility test*, a comparison of the degree to which a particular course of action is consistent with various images—particularly individual principles, current goals, and plans for the future. If any lack of compatibility exists with respect to these considerations, a rejection decision is made.

If the compatibility test is passed, then the *profitability test* is carried out. That is, people consider the extent to which using various alternatives best fits their values, goals, and plans. The decision is then made to accept the best available candidate. These tests are used within a certain *decision frame*—that is, with consideration of meaningful information about the

image theory
A theory of decision making that recognizes that decisions are made in an automatic, intuitive fashion. According to the theory, people will adopt a course of action that best fits their individual principles, current goals, and plans for the future.

FIGURE 10.9

Image Theory: An Overview and Example

According to *image theory*, decisions are made in a relatively automatic, intuitive fashion following the two steps outlined here.

Source: Adapted from Beach & Mitchell, 1990; see Note 62.

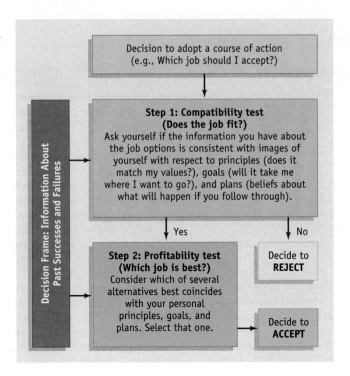

decision context (such as past experiences). The basic idea is that we learn from the past and are guided by it when making decisions. The example shown in Figure 10.9 highlights this contemporary approach to decision making.

According to image theory, the decision-making process is very rapid and simple. The theory suggests that people do not ponder and reflect over decisions, but make them using a smooth, intuitive process with minimal cognitive processing. If you've ever found yourself saying that something "seemed like the right thing to do," or "something doesn't feel right," you're probably well aware of the kind of intuitive thinking that goes on in a great deal of decision making. Recent research suggests that when it comes to making relatively simple decisions, people do, in fact, tend to behave as suggested by image theory.[63] For example, it has been found that people decide against various options when past evidence suggests that these decisions may be incompatible with their images of the future.[64]

To summarize, we have described three major approaches to decision making. The rational-economic approach represents the ideal way optimal decisions may be made. However, the administrative model and image theory represent ways that people actually go about making decisions. Both have received support, and neither should be seen as a replacement for the other. Instead, several different processes are likely to be involved in decision making. Not all decision making is carried out the same way: Sometimes decision making might be analytical, and sometimes it might be more intuitive. Modern organizational behavior scholars recognize the value of both approaches, each of which recognizes the fallibility of the human decision maker. With this in mind, we now turn attention to the imperfect nature of individual decisions.

The Imperfect Nature of Individual Decisions

Let's face it: As a whole, people are less than perfect when it comes to making decisions. Mistakes are made all the time. Obviously, people have limited capacities to process information accurately and thoroughly, like a computer. For example, we often focus on irrelevant information in making decisions.[65] We also fail to use all the information that's available to us, in part because we may forget some of it.[66] Beyond these general limitations in human information-processing capacity, we may note several systematic determinants of imperfect decisions, factors that contribute to the imperfect nature of people's decisions. These variables reside not only within individuals themselves (e.g., biases in the way people make decisions) but also the organizations within which we operate. We now examine three major factors contributing to the imperfect nature of individual decisions: *framing*, *heuristics*, and *biases*.

Framing Effects

Have you ever found yourself changing your mind about something because of *how* someone explained it to you? If so, you might have said something like, "Now that you put it that way, I agree." This may sound familiar to you because it describes a well-established decision-making characteristic known as **framing**—the tendency for people to make different decisions based on how a problem is presented to them. Scientists have identified three major forms of framing effects that occur when people make decisions.[67] As we describe these, you might find it helpful to follow along with the summary in Figure 10.10.[68]

RISKY CHOICE FRAMING. For many years, scientists have noted that when problems are framed in a manner that emphasizes the positive gains to be received, people tend to shy away from taking risks and go for the sure thing (i.e., decision makers are said to be *risk-averse*). However, when problems are framed in a manner that emphasizes the potential losses to be suffered, people are more willing to take risks so as to avoid those losses (i.e., decision makers are said to make *risk-seeking* decisions).[69] This is known as the **risky choice framing effect.** To illustrate this phenomenon consider the following example:

> The government is preparing to combat a rare disease expected to take 600 lives. Two alternative programs to combat the disease have been proposed, each of which, scientists believe, will have certain consequences. *Program A* will save 200 people, if adopted. *Program B* has a one-third chance of saving all 600 people, but a two-thirds chance of saving no one. Which program do you prefer?

When such a problem was presented to people, 72 percent expressed a preference for Program A, and 28 percent for Program B. In other words, they preferred the "sure thing" of saving 200 people over the one-third possibility of saving them all. However, this did not occur when the description of the programs was framed in negative terms such as the following:

> *Program C* was described as allowing 400 people to die, if adopted. *Program D* was described as allowing a one-third probability that no one would die, and a two-thirds probability that all 600 would die. Now which program would you prefer?

Compare these four programs. Program C is just another way of stating the outcomes of Program A, and Program D is just another way of stating the outcomes of Program B. However,

framing
The tendency for people to make different decisions based on how the problem is presented to them.

risky choice framing effect
The tendency for people to avoid risks when situations are presented in a way that emphasizes positive gains, and to take risks when situations are presented in a way that emphasizes potential losses that may be suffered.

Type of Framing	Negative Frame		Positive Frame
Risky choice framing	Avoid losses (lives lost)	Likelihood of taking risks	Experience gains (lives saved)
	more likely ⟵	⟶	less likely
Attribute framing	Negative qualities (25% fat)		Positive qualities (75% lean)
	negative ⟵	Evaluation ⟶	positive
Goal framing	Suffer loss (no breast exam leads to decreased chance of finding early tumor)		Experience gain (breast exam leads to increased chance of finding early tumor)
	more likely ⟵	Likelihood of performing exam ⟶	less likely

FIGURE 10.10

Framing Effects: A Summary of Three Types

Information presented (i.e., framed) negatively is perceived differently than the same information presented positively. This takes the three different forms summarized here— *risky choice framing, attribute framing,* and *goal framing.*

Source: Based on suggestions by Levin et al., 1998; see Note 67.

Programs C and D are framed in negative terms, which led to opposite preferences: 22 percent favored Program C and 78 percent favored Program D. In other words, people tended to avoid risk when the problem was framed in terms of "lives saved" (i.e., in positive terms), but to seek risk when the problem was framed in terms of "lives lost" (i.e., in negative terms). This classic effect has been replicated in several studies.[70]

ATTRIBUTE FRAMING. Risky choice frames involve making decisions about which course of action is preferred. However, the same basic idea applies to situations not involving risk, but involving evaluations. Suppose, for example, you're walking down the meat aisle of your local supermarket when you spot a package of ground beef labeled "75% lean." Of course, if the same package were to say "25% fat," you would know exactly the same thing. However, you probably wouldn't perceive these situations identically. In fact, consumer marketing research has shown that people rated the same sample of ground beef as being better tasting and less greasy when it was framed with respect to a positive attribute (i.e., 75% lean) than when it was framed with respect to a negative attribute (i.e., 25% fat).[71]

attribute framing effect
The tendency for people to evaluate a characteristic more positively when it is presented in positive terms than when it is presented in negative terms.

Although this example is easy to relate to, its generalizability goes way beyond product evaluation situations. In fact, the **attribute framing effect,** as it is known, occurs in a variety of organizational settings. In other words, people evaluate the same characteristic more positively when it is described in positive terms than when it is described in negative terms. Take performance evaluation, for example. In this context, people whose performance is framed in positive terms (e.g., percentage of shots made by a basketball player) tend to be evaluated more positively than those whose identical performance is framed in negative terms (e.g., percentage of shots missed by that same player).[72]

GOAL FRAMING. A third type of framing, *goal framing,* focuses on an important question: When attempting to persuade someone to do something, is it more effective to focus on the positive consequences of doing it or the negative consequences of not doing it? For example, suppose you are attempting to get women to engage in self-examination of their breasts to check for signs of cancer. You may frame the desired behavior in positive terms:

> "Research shows that women who *do* breast self-examinations have an *increased* chance of finding a tumor in the early, more treatable stages of the disease."

Or you may frame it in negative terms:

> "Research shows that women who *do not* do breast self-examinations have a *decreased* chance of finding a tumor in the early, more treatable stages of the disease."

goal framing effect
The tendency for people to be more strongly persuaded by information that is framed in negative terms than information that is framed in positive terms.

Which approach is more effective? Research has shown that women were significantly more likely to engage in breast self-examination when they were presented with the consequences of not doing it rather than the benefits of doing it.[73] This is an example of the **goal framing effect** in action. According to this phenomenon, people are more strongly persuaded by the negatively framed information than by the positively framed information.

A GENERAL NOTE ABOUT FRAMING. The three kinds of framing we have described here, although similar in several key ways, are also quite different. Specifically, they focus on different types of behavior: preferences for risk in the case of *risky choice framing*; evaluations of characteristics in the case of *attribute framing*; and taking behavioral action in the case of *goal framing*. (Now that we're reviewed all three types of framing, you may find it helpful to compare and contrast them as presented in Figure 10.10.)

Scientists believe that framing effects are due to the tendency for people to perceive equivalent situations framed differently as not really equivalent.[74] In other words, focusing on the glass as "half full" leads people to think about it differently than when it is presented as being "half empty," although they might recognize intellectually that the two are really the same. Such findings illustrate our point that people are not completely rational decision makers, but are systematically biased by the cognitive distortions created by simple differences in the way situations are framed.

Reliance on Heuristics

Framing effects are not the only cognitive biases to which decision makers are subjected. It also has been established that people often attempt to simplify the complex decisions they face by using **heuristics**—simple rules of thumb that guide them through a complex array of decision alternatives.[75] Although heuristics are potentially useful to decision makers, they also represent potential impediments to decision making. Two very common types of heuristics may be identified—the *availability heuristic* and the *representativeness heuristic* (see Figure 10.11).

THE AVAILABILITY HEURISTIC. The **availability heuristic** refers to the tendency for people to base their judgments on information that is readily available to them—even though it might not be accurate. Suppose, for example, that a real estate executive needs to know the percentage of available houses in a particular neighborhood. There is not enough time to gather the appropriate statistics, so she bases her judgments on her knowledge of available property nationwide. If the neighborhood in question is atypical, her estimate will be off accordingly (see the top portion of Figure 10.11). In other words, basing judgments solely on information that just happens to be available increases the possibility of making inaccurate decisions. Yet, people use the availability heuristic on a regular basis when making decisions.[76]

THE REPRESENTATIVENESS HEURISTIC. The **representativeness heuristic** refers to the tendency to perceive others in stereotypical ways if they appear to be typical representatives of the category to which they belong.

As an example, suppose you believe that accountants are bright, mild-mannered individuals, whereas salespeople are less intelligent, but much more extroverted. Further, imagine that you

heuristics
Simple decision rules (rules of thumb) used to make quick decisions about complex problems. (See *availability heuristic* and *representativeness heuristic*.)

availability heuristic
The tendency for people to base their judgments on information that is readily available to them although it may be potentially inaccurate, thereby adversely affecting decision quality.

representativeness heuristic
The tendency to perceive others in stereotypical ways if they appear to be typical representatives of the category to which they belong.

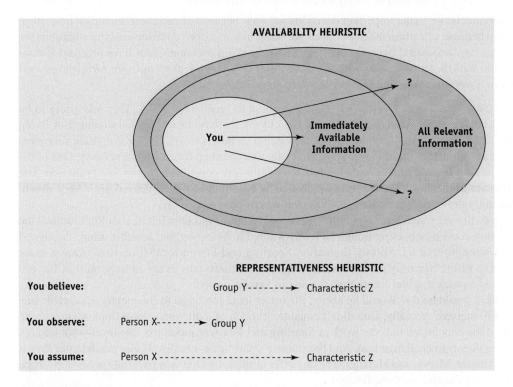

FIGURE 10.11

The Availability Heuristic and the Representativeness Heuristic

People making decisions often rely on simple rules of thumb, known as *heuristics*, to help them. Sometimes, however, these actually hinder decision-making quality. This occurs in the case of the *availability heuristic,* in which people are inclined to consider immediately available information (e.g., what they already know) instead of all relevant information. The *representativeness heuristic* is another example. Here, decision makers are likely to assume that people possess the characteristics they associate with others in those individuals' groups—that is, that people we meet are representative of the groups to which they belong.

are at a party at which there are twice as many salespeople as accountants. You meet someone at the party who is bright and mild-mannered. Although mathematically the odds are two-to-one that this person is a salesperson rather than an accountant, chances are you will guess that the individual is an accountant because she possesses the traits you associate with accountants (see the bottom portion of Figure 10.11). In other words, you believe this person to be representative of accountants in general—so much so that you would knowingly go against the mathematical odds in making your judgment. Research has found that people tend to make this type of error in judgment, thereby providing good support for the existence of the representativeness heuristic.[77]

THE HELPFUL SIDE OF HEURISTICS. It is important to note that heuristics do not *always* deteriorate the quality of decisions made. In fact, they can be quite helpful. People often use rules of thumb to help simplify the complex decisions they face. For example, management scientists employ heuristics to aid decisions regarding where to locate warehouses and stock brokers use heuristics when deciding how to assemble an investment portfolio.[78] We also use heuristics in our everyday lives, such as when we play chess ("control the center of the board") or blackjack ("hit on 16, stick on 17").

Despite this, the representativeness heuristic and the availability heuristic may be recognized as impediments to superior decisions because they discourage people from collecting and processing as much information as they should. Making judgments on the basis of only readily available information, or on stereotypical beliefs, although making things simple for the decision maker, does so at a potentially high cost—poor decisions. Thus, these systematic biases represent potentially serious impediments to individual decision making.

The Inherently Biased Nature of Individual Decisions

As individuals, we make imperfect decisions not only because of our overreliance on heuristics, but also because of certain inherent biases we bring to the various decision-making situations we face. Among the several biases people have when making decisions, four have received special attention by OB scientists—the bias toward *implicit favorites,* the *hindsight bias,* the *person sensitivity decision bias,* and the *escalation of commitment* bias.

BIAS TOWARD IMPLICIT FAVORITES. Don was about to receive his MBA. This was going to be his big chance to move to San Francisco, the city by the bay. Don long had dreamed of living there, and his first "real" job, he hoped, was going to be his ticket. As the corporate recruiters made their annual migration to campus, Don eagerly signed up for several interviews. One of his first was with Baxter, Marsh, and Hidalgo, a medium-size consulting firm in San Francisco. The salary was right and the people seemed nice, a combination that pleased Don very much. Apparently the interest was mutual; soon Don was offered a position.

Does the story end here? Not quite. It was only March, and Don felt he shouldn't jump at the first job to come along, even though he really wanted it. So, to do "the sensible thing," he signed up for more interviews. Shortly thereafter, Sparling and Fox, a local firm, made Don a more attractive offer. Not only was the salary higher, but there was every indication that the job promised a much brighter future than the one in San Francisco.

What would he do? Would he accept the better local job or go to the merely acceptable one in San Francisco? Actually, Don didn't consider it much of a dilemma. After thinking it over, he reached the conclusion that the work at Sparling and Fox was much too low-level—not enough exciting clients to challenge him. And the starting salary wasn't really all *that* much better than it was at Baxter, Marsh, and Hidalgo. The day after graduation Don was packing for his new office overlooking the Golden Gate Bridge.

implicit favorite
One's preferred decision alternative, selected even before all options have been considered.

confirmation candidate
A decision alternative considered for purposes of convincing oneself of the wisdom of selecting the *implicit favorite.*

Do you think the way Don made his decision was atypical? He seemed to have his mind made up in advance about the job in San Francisco, and didn't really give the other one a chance (even though it was better in several ways). Research suggests that people make decisions in this way all the time. That is, people tend to pick an **implicit favorite** option (i.e., a preferred alternative) very early in the decision-making process.[79] Then, the other options they consider subsequently are not given serious consideration. Rather, they are merely used to convince oneself that the implicit favorite is indeed the best choice. An alternative considered for this purpose is known as a **confirmation candidate.** It is not unusual to find that people psychologically distort their beliefs about confirmation candidates so as to justify selecting their implicit favorites. Don did this when

TABLE 10.2 Bias Toward Implicit Favorites: Some Likely Steps

Although the bias toward implicit favorites may take many forms, it usually follows a pattern of steps similar to those outlined here.

Step	I think this . . .	And, so I do this . . .	Job referred to as . . .
1	I need a job and I heard that Job A is great, so I . . .		
2		Look at Job A	Implicit favorite
3	I like Job A, as I thought I would, but I shouldn't take the first job, so I . . .		
4		Look at Job B	Confirmation candidate 1
5	I don't like Job B, but I'll keep looking just to make sure that Job A is the best one for me, so, I . . .		
6		Look at Job C	Confirmation candidate 2
7	I don't like Job C either. Now, I have looked at enough alternatives (confirmation candidates) to convince myself that Job A really is the best, and so I am now ready to . . .		
8		Accept Job A (finally)	My job

he convinced himself that the job offered by the local firm really wasn't as good as it seemed. (For an outline of some steps likely to be occurring in this process, see Table 10.2.)

Research shows that people make decisions very early in the decision process. For example, in one study of the job recruitment process, investigators found that they could predict 87 percent of the jobs that students would take as early as two months before the students acknowledged that they actually had made a decision.[80] Apparently, people's decisions are biased by the tendency for them to not consider all the relevant information available to them. In fact, they tend to bias their judgments of the strengths and weaknesses of various alternatives so as to make them fit their already-made decision—that is, to select their implicit favorite.[81] This phenomenon clearly suggests that people not only fail to consider all possible alternatives when making decisions, but that they even fail to consider all readily available alternatives. Instead, they tend to make up their minds very early and convince themselves that they are right about this decision. As you might imagine, this bias toward implicit favorites is likely to limit severely the quality of decisions that are made.

HINDSIGHT BIAS. "Hindsight is 20-20" is a phrase commonly heard. It means that when we look back on decisions that already have been made, we know better what we should have done. Indeed, research has revealed that this phenomenon is quite pervasive. For example, studies have shown that people tend to distort the way they see things so as to conform to what they already know about the past. This effect, known as the **hindsight bias,** refers to the tendency for people to perceive outcomes as more inevitable after they have occurred (i.e., in hindsight) than before they occurred (i.e., in foresight). A sign that hindsight bias has occurred is when people believe that they could have predicted past events better than they actually did—that is, when they say, "I knew it all along."

hindsight bias
The tendency for people to perceive outcomes as more inevitable after they have occurred (i.e., in hindsight) than before they occurred (i.e., in foresight).

The hindsight bias occurs because people feel good about being able to judge things accurately. As such, we may expect that people will be more willing to say that they expected events from the past to have occurred whenever these are positive about themselves or their work team, but not when these events are negative. After all, we look good when we can take credit for predicting successes, but we look bad when we anticipated negative outcomes without doing anything to stop them. Indeed, recent research has shown precisely this.[82] This qualification of the hindsight bias may have important effects on the way people make decisions (for example, see Figure 10.12).

Let's consider a classic example. During the 1970s, a group of public utilities known as the Washington Public Power Supply System (WPPSS) made plans to build seven nuclear power plants in an effort to meet the need for energy, estimated as growing by 7 percent each year. Through the early 1980s, 27,000 investors bought bonds to support this project. As things worked out, however, consumers found ways to conserve energy as energy prices rose, resulting

Mark Richards/PhotoEdit.

FIGURE 10.12

Hindsight Bias: An Example

These doctors from the Family Medical Center in Bakersfield, California, are meeting to make important decisions about medical procedures to be followed at their facility. In keeping with the *hindsight bias,* when reviewing cases that had positive outcomes, they are likely to claim that they "knew it all along." However, they are unlikely to acknowledge that they were able to predict the outcomes of cases having negative results.

in far smaller increases in energy demands than anticipated. As a result, only one of the seven planned power plants was ever completed, and in 1983, the WPPSS defaulted on bonds valued at $2.25 billion. When investors sued, they claimed that the WPPSS "should have known" that the demand for energy was going to change, thereby precluding the need for the power plants. In other words, they were biased such that they saw the decision to invest in ways that made themselves look good and the WPPSS look bad. In response, officials from the WPPSS claimed that they had no way of anticipating the changes the future was going to bring, therefore justifying their decision to raise money and build power plants as a wise one.

PERSON SENSITIVITY BIAS. President George W. Bush first took office in January 2001, following a highly controversial election that many didn't believe he won fairly. As time went on, many people disapproved of his foreign policy, claiming that he was ill-suited to the position. Then, only eight months later, following the September 11 terrorist attacks, President Bush unified the country with impassioned speeches that sent his approval ratings into the stratosphere. His stance with respect to foreign policy was now widely praised. Then, years later when the war in Iraq faltered, his approval rating plummeted. This mini history lesson nicely illustrates an interesting aspect of human nature (beyond the fickle nature of politics, that is): When things are going poorly, nobody likes you, but when things are going well, everyone's your friend. Scientists refer to this as **person sensitivity bias.** Formally, this refers to the tendency for people to blame others too much when things are going poorly and to give them too much credit when things are going well.

Evidence for the person sensitivity bias has been reported in an interesting experiment.[83] Participants in the study were asked to judge the performance of either individuals who staffed an assembly line or machines that performed the same assembly task. The people or the machines also were described either as exceeding the company standards or not meeting them. When people were said to be responsible for exceeding the standards, they were perceived more positively than machines that also exceeded the standard. However, when the standards were not

person sensitivity bias
The tendency for people to give too little credit to others when things are going poorly and too much credit when things are going well.

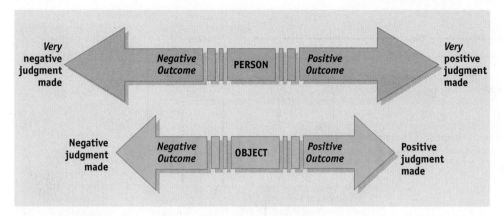

FIGURE 10.13

Person Sensitivity Bias: An Overview

According to the *person sensitivity bias,* we are likely to blame people too much when things are going poorly and to give them too much credit when things are going well. The same positive decision outcomes are perceived as being more positive when caused by people than by inanimate objects, such as computers. Likewise, equally negative decision outcomes are perceived as being more negative when caused by people than by objects.

Source: Based on suggestions by Moon & Conlon, 2002; see Note 83.

met, participants judged other people more harshly than the machines (see Figure 10.13). These findings are in keeping with both the positive and negative aspects of the person sensitivity bias.

The person sensitivity bias is important insofar as it suggests that the decisions we make about others are not likely to be completely objective. As people, we need to understand others (as we emphasized in Chapter 3), and it makes things easier for us if we keep our perceptions consistent: what's good is very good; what's bad is very bad. With such a bias underlying our judgments of others, it's little wonder that the decisions we make about them may be highly imperfect. After all, to the extent that effective decisions rely on accurate information, biases such as the person sensitivity bias predispose us to perceive others in less than objective ways.

ESCALATION OF COMMITMENT BIAS. Because decisions are made all the time in organizations, some of these inevitably will be unsuccessful. What would you say is the rational thing to do when a poor decision has been made? Obviously, the ineffective action should be stopped or reversed. In other words, it would make sense to "cut your losses and run." However, people don't always respond in this manner. In fact, it is not unusual to find that ineffective decisions are sometimes followed up with still further ineffective decisions.

Imagine, for example, that you have invested money in a company that now appears to be failing. Rather than lose your initial investment, you may invest still more money in the hope of salvaging your first investment. The more you invest, the more you may be tempted to save those earlier investments by making later investments. That is to say, people sometimes may be found "throwing good money after bad" because they have "too much invested to quit." This is known as the **escalation of commitment phenomenon**—the tendency for people to continue to support previously unsuccessful courses of action because they have sunk costs invested in them.[84]

Why do people do this? If you think about it, you may realize that the failure to back your own previous courses of action in an organization would be taken as an admission of failure— a politically difficult act to face in an organization. In other words, people may be very concerned about "saving face"—looking good in the eyes of others and oneself.[85] Researchers have recognized that this tendency for *self-justification* is primarily responsible for people's inclination to protect their beliefs about themselves as rational, competent decision makers by convincing themselves and others that they made the right decision all along and are willing to back it up.[86] Although there are other possible reasons for the escalation of commitment phenomenon, research supports the self-justification explanation.[87] For a summary of the escalation of commitment phenomenon, see Figure 10.14.

escalation of commitment phenomenon
The tendency for individuals to continue to support previously unsuccessful courses of action.

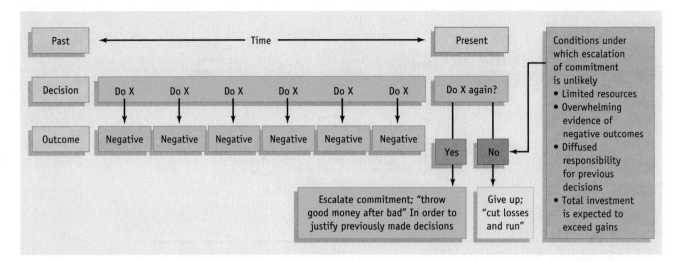

FIGURE 10.14

Escalation of Commitment: An Overview

According to the escalation of commitment phenomenon, people who have repeatedly made poor decisions continue to support those failing courses of action to justify their earlier decisions. Under some conditions, however, as summarized here, this effect will not occur.

Researchers have noted several conditions under which people will refrain from escalating their commitment to a failing course of action.[88] Notably, it has been found that people will stop making failing investments under conditions in which the available funds for making further investments are limited and the threat of failure is overwhelmingly obvious.[89] For example, when the Long Island Lighting Company decided to abandon plans to operate a nuclear power plant in Shoreham, New York, it was in the face of 23 years' worth of intense political pressure (a strong antinuclear movement) and financial pressure (billions of dollars in cost overruns).[90]

It also has been found that people will refrain from escalating commitment when they can diffuse their responsibility for the earlier failing actions. That is, the more people feel they are just one of several individuals responsible for a failing course of action, the less likely they are to commit to further failing actions.[91] In other words, the less one is responsible for an earlier failure, the less one may be motivated to justify those earlier failures by making further investments in them.

Third, escalation of commitment toward a losing course of action will be low in organizations in which the people who have made ineffective decisions have left and are replaced by others who are not linked to those decisions. In other words, turnover lessens an organization's commitment to a losing course of action. Illustrating this, research has shown that although some banks continue to make bad (i.e., uncollectable) loans to customers to whom they have loaned money in the past, this is less likely to occur in banks whose top executives (individuals who are considered responsible for those loans) have vacated their posts.[92]

Finally, it has been found that people are unwilling to escalate commitment to a course of action when it is made clear that the total amount invested exceeds the amount expected to be gained.[93] Although people may wish to invest in projects that enable them to recoup their initial investments, there is little reason for them to do so when it is obvious that doing so will be a losing proposition. Under such conditions, it is difficult to justify doing so, even if one "hopes against hope" that it will work out. Indeed, research has shown that decision makers do indeed refrain from escalating commitment to decisions when it is made clear that the overall benefits to be gained are less than the overall costs to be borne.[94] This finding was more apparent among students with accounting backgrounds than those without such backgrounds, presumably because their training predisposed them to be more sensitive to these issues.

To conclude, the escalation of commitment phenomenon represents a type of irrational decision making that has the potential to occur. However, whether or not it does occur will depend on the various circumstances that decision makers confront.

Group Decisions: Do Too Many Cooks Spoil the Broth?

Decision-making groups are well-established facts of modern organizational life. Groups such as committees, study teams, task forces, or review panels are often charged with the responsibility for making important business decisions.[95] They are so common, in fact, that it has been said that some administrators spend as much as 80 percent of their time in committee meetings.[96]

In view of this, it is important to ask how well groups do at making decisions compared to individuals. Given the several advantages and disadvantages of having groups make decisions we described earlier, this question is particularly important. Specifically, we may ask: Under what conditions might individuals or groups be expected to make superior decisions? Fortunately, research provides some good answers.[97]

When Are Groups Superior to Individuals?

Whether groups will do better than individuals or worse than individuals depends on the nature of the task. Specifically, any advantages that groups may have over individuals will depend on how complex or simple the task is. We now will explain how this works, but as you read this, you might find it useful to follow along with the summary in Figure 10.15.

COMPLEX DECISION TASKS. Imagine a situation in which an important decision has to be made about a complex problem—such as whether one company should merge with another. This is not the kind of problem about which any one individual working alone would be able to make a good decision. After all, its highly complex nature may overwhelm even an expert, thereby setting the stage for a group to do a better job.

However, this doesn't happen automatically. In fact, for groups to outperform individuals, several conditions must exist. First, we must consider who is in the group. Successful groups tend to be composed of *heterogeneous group members with complementary skills*. So, for example, a group composed of lawyers, accountants, real estate agents, and other experts may make much better decisions on the merger problem than would a group composed of specialists in only one field. Indeed, research has shown that the diversity of opinions offered by group members is one of the major advantages of using groups to make decisions.[98]

As you might imagine, it is not enough simply to have skills. For a group to be successful, its members must also be able to freely communicate their ideas to each other in an open, nonhostile

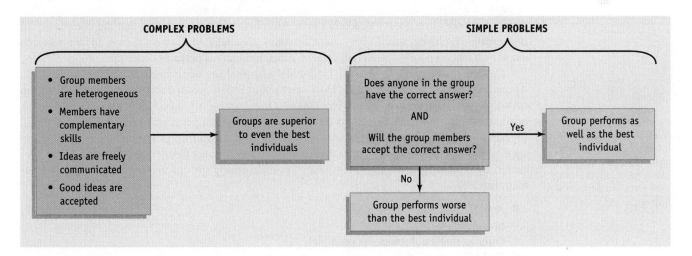

FIGURE 10.15

When Are Group Decisions Superior to Individual Decisions?

When performing complex problems, groups are superior to individuals if certain conditions prevail (e.g., when members have heterogeneous and complementary skills, when they can freely share ideas, and when their good ideas are accepted by others). However, when dealing with simple problems, groups perform only as well as the best individual group member—and then, only if that person has the correct answer and if that answer is accepted by others in the group.

manner. Conditions under which one individual (or group) intimidates another from contributing his or her expertise can easily negate any potential gain associated with composing groups of heterogeneous experts. After all, *having* expertise and being able to make a contribution by *using* that expertise are two different things. Indeed, research has shown that only when the contributions of the most qualified group members are given the greatest weight does the group derive any benefit from that member's presence.[99] Thus, for groups to be superior to individuals, they must be composed of a heterogeneous collection of experts with complementary skills who can freely and openly contribute to their group's product.

SIMPLE DECISION TASKS. In contrast to complex decision tasks, imagine a situation in which a judgment is required on a simple problem with a readily verifiable answer. For example, make believe that you are asked to translate a phrase from a relatively obscure language into English.

Groups might do better than individuals on such a task, but primarily because the odds are increased that someone in the group knows the language and can perform the translation on behalf of the group. However, there is no reason to expect that even a large group will be able to perform such a task better than a single individual who has the required expertise even if someone in the group can perform the task. In fact, an expert working alone may do even better than a group. This is because an expert individual performing a simple task may be distracted by others and suffer from having to convince them of the correctness of his or her solution. For this reason, exceptional individuals tend to outperform entire committees on simple tasks.[100] In such cases, for groups to benefit from a pooling of resources, there must be some resources to pool. The pooling of ignorance does not help.

In sum, the question "Are two heads better than one?" can be answered this way: On simple tasks, two heads may be better than one if at least one of those heads contains what it takes to succeed and if others allow that head to prevail. Thus, whether groups perform better than individuals depends on the nature of the task performed and the expertise of the people involved. Recall our graphic summary of these considerations in Figure 10.15.

When Are Individuals Superior to Groups?

As we have described thus far, groups may be expected to perform better than the average or even the exceptional individual under certain conditions. However, there are also conditions under which individuals are superior to groups.

Most of the problems faced by organizations require a great deal of creative thinking. For example, a company deciding how to use a newly developed adhesive in its consumer products is facing decisions on a poorly structured task. Although you would expect that the complexity of such creative problems would give groups a natural advantage, this is not the case. In fact, research has shown that on poorly structured, creative tasks, individuals perform better than groups.[101]

Despite this, groups tend to be used widely for making decisions on these kinds of tasks. Accordingly, it is important to ask: How can the quality of group decisions be improved when making poorly structured, creative tasks? One commonly used approach is known as **brainstorming.** This technique was developed by advertising executive Alex Osborn as a tool for coming up with creative, new ideas.[102] When brainstorming, group members are encouraged to present their ideas in an uncritical way and to discuss freely and openly all ideas presented by others. Specifically, members of brainstorming groups are required to follow four main rules:

brainstorming
A technique designed to foster group productivity by encouraging interacting group members to express their ideas in a noncritical fashion.

- ■ Avoid criticizing others' ideas.
- ■ Share even far-out suggestions.
- ■ Offer as many comments as possible.
- ■ Build on others' ideas to create your own.

Does brainstorming improve the quality of creative decisions? To answer this question, researchers compared the effectiveness of individuals and brainstorming groups working on creative problems.[103] Specifically, participants were given 35 minutes to consider the consequences of situations such as "What would happen if everybody went blind?" or "What would the world be like if everybody grew an extra thumb on each hand?" Clearly, the novel nature of such problems requires a great deal of creativity. The researchers compared the number of solutions generated by groups of

TABLE 10.3 Tips for Using Brainstorming Successfully

The rules of brainstorming are simple enough, but doing it effectively requires some guidance. Many brainstorming sessions fail because people don't fully appreciate the finer points of how to conduct them. Following these guidelines stands to make your own brainstorming sessions more effective.

Suggestion	Explanation
Brainstorm frequently, at least once per month.	Practice makes perfect. The more frequently people engage in brainstorming, the more comfortable they are with it—hence, the more effective it becomes.
Keep brainstorming sessions brief, less than an hour in length.	Brainstorming effectively can be very exhausting, so limit the time dedicated to it. After about an hour, people become too inefficient to make it worthwhile to continue.
Focus on the problem at hand.	The best brainstorming sessions begin with a clear statement of the problem at hand. These shouldn't be too broad or too narrow.
Don't forget to "build" and "jump."	The best ideas to result from brainstorming sessions are those that build on other ideas. Everyone should be encouraged to jump from one idea to another as they build on the earlier one.
Prepare for the session.	Brainstorming is much more effective when people prepare in advance by reading up on the topic than when they come in "cold."
Don't limit yourself to words—use props.	Some of the most effective brainstorming sessions result when people introduce objects to help model their ideas.

Source: Based on suggestions by Kelley, 2001; see Note 104.

four or seven people and a like number of individuals who worked on the same problems alone. The results were clear: Individuals were significantly more productive than groups.

In summary, groups perform worse than individuals when working on creative tasks. A great part of the problem is that some individuals feel inhibited by the presence of others even though one rule of brainstorming is that even far-out ideas may be shared. To the extent that people wish to avoid feeling foolish as a result of saying silly things, their creativity may be inhibited when in groups. Similarly, groups may inhibit creativity by slowing down the process of bringing ideas to fruition. Yet, many creative professionals strongly believe in the power of brainstorming.[104] What, then, could be done to make brainstorming more effective? For some specific suggestions on how to reap the benefits of brainstorming, see Table 10.3.

Techniques for Improving the Effectiveness of Decisions

As we have suggested in this chapter, certain advantages can be gained from sometimes using individuals and sometimes using groups to make decisions. A decision-making technique that combines the best features of groups and individuals, while minimizing their disadvantages, would be ideal. Several techniques designed to realize the "best of both worlds" have been used widely in organizations. These include techniques that involve the structuring of group discussions in special ways. An even more basic approach to improving the effectiveness of group decisions involves training decision makers in ways of avoiding some of the pitfalls of group decision making. We will begin this section of the chapter with a discussion of this training approach to improving group decisions and then go on to consider various ways of creating specially structured groups.

Training Individuals to Improve Group Performance

Earlier in this chapter we noted that how well groups solve problems depends in part on the composition of those groups. If at least one group member is capable of coming up with a solution, groups may benefit by that individual's expertise. Based on this reasoning, it follows that the more qualified individual group members are to solve problems, the better their groups as a whole will perform. What, then, might individuals do to improve the nature of the decisions they make?

Researchers looking into this question have found that people tend to make four types of mistakes when attempting to make creative decisions, and that they make better decisions when trained to avoid these errors.[105] Specifically, these are as follows.

hypervigilance

The state in which an individual frantically searches for quick solutions to problems, and goes from one idea to another out of a sense of desperation that one idea isn't working and that another needs to be considered before time runs out.

unconflicted adherence

The tendency for decision makers to stick to the first idea that comes to their minds without more deeply evaluating the consequences.

unconflicted change

The tendency for people to quickly change their minds and to adopt the first new idea to come along.

defensive avoidance

The tendency for decision makers to fail to solve problems because they go out of their way to avoid working on the problem at hand.

- *Hypervigilance.* The state of **hypervigilance** involves frantically searching for quick solutions to problems, going from one idea to another out of a sense of desperation that one idea isn't working and that another needs to be considered before time runs out. A poor, "last chance" solution may be adopted to relieve anxiety. This problem may be avoided by keeping in mind that it is best to stick with one suggestion and work it out thoroughly, and reassuring the person solving the problem that his or her level of skill and education is adequate to perform the task at hand. In other words, a little reassurance may go a long way toward keeping individuals on the right track and avoiding the problem of hypervigilance.

- *Unconflicted adherence.* Many decision makers make the mistake of sticking to the first idea that comes into their heads without more deeply evaluating the consequences, a mistake known as **unconflicted adherence.** As a result, such people are unlikely to become aware of any problems associated with their ideas or to consider other possibilities. To avoid unconflicted adherence, decision makers are urged (1) to think about the difficulties associated with their ideas, (2) to force themselves to consider different ideas, and (3) to consider the special and unique characteristics of the problem they are facing and avoid carrying over assumptions from previous problems.

- *Unconflicted change.* Sometimes people are very quick to change their minds and adopt the first new idea to come along—a problem known as **unconflicted change.** To avoid unconflicted change, decision makers are encouraged to ask themselves about (1) the risks and problems of adopting that solution, (2) the good points of the first idea, and (3) the relative strengths and weaknesses of both ideas.

- *Defensive avoidance.* Too often, decision makers fail to solve problems effectively because they go out of their way to avoid working on the task at hand. This is known as **defensive avoidance.** People can do three things to minimize this problem. First, they should attempt to *avoid procrastination.* Don't put off the problem indefinitely just because you cannot come up with a solution right away. Continue to budget some of your time on even the most frustrating problems. Second, *avoid disowning responsibility.* It is easy to minimize the importance of a problem by saying "It doesn't matter, so who cares?" Avoid giving up so soon. Finally, *don't ignore potentially corrective information.* It is tempting to put your nagging doubts about the quality of a solution to rest in order to be finished with it. Good decision makers would not do so. Rather, they use their doubts to test and potentially improve the quality of their ideas.

Techniques for Enhancing Group Decisions

Just as there are various things individuals can do to improve decision making, so too are there steps that groups can take to enhance the quality of their decisions. The basic idea underlying these techniques is identical: Structure the group experience so as to enable the many benefits of groups to occur without also experiencing the weaknesses.

Delphi technique

A method of improving group decisions using the opinions of experts, which are solicited by mail and then compiled. The expert consensus of opinions is used to make a decision.

THE DELPHI TECHNIQUE: DECISIONS BY EXPERT CONSENSUS. According to Greek mythology, people interested in seeing what fate the future held for them could seek the counsel of the Delphic oracle. Today's organizational decision makers sometimes consult experts to help them make the best decisions as well. A technique developed by the RAND Corporation, known as the **Delphi technique,** represents a systematic way of collecting and organizing the opinions of several experts into a single decision.[106] For a summary of the steps in this process, see Figure 10.16.

The Delphi process starts by enlisting the cooperation of experts and presenting the problem to them, usually in a letter or an e-mail message. Each expert then proposes what he or she believes is the most appropriate solution. The group leader compiles all of these individual responses and reproduces them so they can be shared with all the other experts in a second mailing. At this point, each expert comments on the others' ideas and proposes another solution.

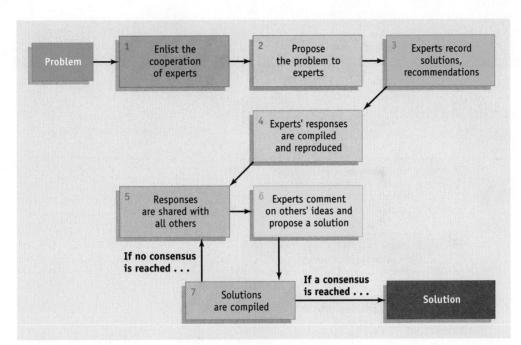

FIGURE 10.16

The Delphi Technique

The Delphi technique allows decisions to be made by several experts while avoiding many of the pitfalls of face-to-face group interaction. Its general steps are outlined here.

These individual solutions are returned to the leader, who compiles them and looks for a consensus of opinions. If a consensus is reached, the decision is made. If not, the process of sharing reactions with others is repeated until a consensus eventually is obtained.

The obvious advantage of using the Delphi technique to make decisions is that it allows expert judgments to be collected without the great costs and logistical difficulties of bringing experts together for a face-to-face meeting. However, the technique is not without limitations. As you might imagine, the Delphi process can be very time-consuming. Sending out letters or e-mail messages, waiting for everyone to respond, transcribing and disseminating the responses, and repeating the process until a consensus is reached can take quite a long time. Experts have estimated that the minimum time required to use the Delphi technique would be more than 44 days. In one case (using regular postal mail), the process took five months to complete.[107] With the widespread use of e-mail, the Delphi approach can be sped up considerably, but it is still slow. Obviously, the Delphi approach is not appropriate for making decisions in crisis situations, or whenever else time is of the essence. However, the approach has been successfully employed to make decisions such as what items to put on a conference agenda and what the potential impact of implementing new land-use policies would be.[108]

THE NOMINAL GROUP TECHNIQUE: A STRUCTURED GROUP MEETING. When there are only a few hours available to make a decision, group discussion sessions can be held in which members interact with each other in an orderly, focused fashion aimed at solving problems. The **nominal group technique (NGT)** brings together a small number of individuals (usually about 7 to 10) who systematically offer their individual solutions to a problem and share their personal reactions to others' solutions.[109] The technique is referred to as *nominal* because the individuals involved form a group in name only. The participants do not attempt to agree as a group on any solution, but rather vote on all the solutions proposed. For a summary of this process, see Figure 10.17.

As shown in Figure 10.17, the nominal group process begins by gathering the group members together around a table and identifying the problem at hand. Then each member writes down his or her solutions. Next, one at a time, each member presents his or her solutions to the group as the leader writes these down on a chart. This process continues until all the ideas have been expressed. Following this, each solution is discussed, clarified, and evaluated by the group members. Each member is given a chance to voice his or her reactions to each idea. After all the ideas have been evaluated, the group members privately rank-order their preferred solutions. Finally, the idea that receives the highest rank is taken as the group's decision. (To experience the NGT firsthand, complete the Group Exercise on pages 371–372.)

nominal group technique (NGT)
A technique for improving group decisions in which small groups of individuals systematically present and discuss their ideas before privately voting on their preferred solution. The most preferred solution is accepted as the group's decision.

FIGURE 10.17

The Nominal Group Technique

The nominal group technique structures face-to-face group meetings in such a way that the open expression and evaluation of ideas are encouraged. It follows the six steps summarized here.

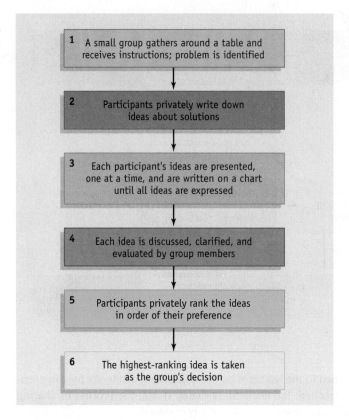

1. A small group gathers around a table and receives instructions; problem is identified

2. Participants privately write down ideas about solutions

3. Each participant's ideas are presented, one at a time, and are written on a chart until all ideas are expressed

4. Each idea is discussed, clarified, and evaluated by group members

5. Participants privately rank the ideas in order of their preference

6. The highest-ranking idea is taken as the group's decision

The NGT has several advantages and disadvantages.[110] We have already noted that it can be used to arrive at group decisions in only a few hours. This can be useful for many types of decisions—but, of course, not for urgent decisions that have to be made on the spot. The benefit of the technique is that it discourages any pressure to conform to the wishes of a high-status group member because all ideas are evaluated openly and the preferences are expressed in private balloting. The technique must be considered limited, however, in that it requires the use of a trained group leader. In addition, using NGT successfully requires that only one narrowly defined problem be considered at a time. So, for very complex problems, many NGT sessions would have to be run—and only *if* the problem under consideration could be broken down into smaller parts.

It is important to consider the relative effectiveness of nominal groups and Delphi groups over face-to-face interacting groups. In general, research has shown the superiority of these special approaches to decision making in many ways on a variety of decision problems.[111] Overall, members of nominal groups tended to be the most satisfied with their work and made the best-quality judgments. In addition, both nominal groups and Delphi groups are much more productive than interacting groups.

As we noted earlier, however, there is a potential benefit to be derived from face-to-face interaction that cannot be realized in nominal and Delphi groups—that is, acceptance of the decision. Groups are likely to accept their decisions and be committed to them if members have been actively involved in making them in traditional face-to-face discussions. Thus, the more detached and impersonal atmosphere of nominal and Delphi groups sometimes makes their members less likely to accept their groups' decisions. We may conclude, then, that there is no one best type of group used to make decisions. Which type is most appropriate depends on the trade-offs decision makers are willing to make in terms of speed, quality, and commitment.[112]

THE STEPLADDER TECHNIQUE: SYSTEMATICALLY INCORPORATING NEW MEMBERS. Another way of structuring group interaction is known as the **stepladder technique.**[113] This approach minimizes the tendency for group members to be unwilling to present their ideas by adding new members to a group one at a time and requiring each to present his or her ideas independently to a group that already has discussed the problem at hand. To begin, each of two people works on a

stepladder technique
A technique for improving the quality of group decisions that minimizes the tendency for group members to be unwilling to present their ideas by adding new members to a group one at a time and requiring each to present his or her ideas independently to a group that already has discussed the problem at hand.

problem independently, and then come together to present their ideas and discuss solutions jointly. While the two-person group is working, a third person working alone also considers the problem. Then, this individual presents his or her ideas to the group and joins in a three-person discussion of a possible solution. During this period a fourth person works on the problem alone, and then presents his or her ideas to the group and joins into a four-person group discussion. After each new person has been added to the group, the entire group works together at finding a solution. (For a summary of the steps in this technique, see Figure 10.18.)

In following this procedure, it is important for each individual to be given sufficient time to work on the problem before he or she joins the group. Then, each person must be given enough time to present his or her ideas to the group in thorough fashion. Groups then must have sufficient time to discuss the problem at hand and reach a preliminary decision before the next person is added. Next, the final decision is made only after all individuals have been added to the group.

The rationale underlying this procedure is that by forcing each person to present independent ideas without knowing how the group has decided, the new person will not be influenced by the group, and the group is required to consider a constant infusion of new ideas. If this is so, then groups solving problems using the stepladder technique would be expected to make better decisions than conventional groups meeting all at once to discuss the same problem. Research has found that this is exactly what happens. Moreover, members of stepladder groups report feeling more positive about their group experiences than their counterparts in conventional groups. Although the stepladder technique is new, this evidence suggests that it holds a great deal of promise as a way of enhancing the decision-making capacity of groups.

Group Decision Support Systems

Suppose you need to collaborate with people who are located in different places who all cannot meet at the same time. Today, this is not such an unusual situation. One solution that has been growing in popularity involves leveraging the power of the Internet to allow people to meet virtually, using what are known as **group decision support systems (GDSS).** These are interactive computer-based systems that combine communication, computer, and decision technologies to improve the effectiveness of group problem-solving meetings. Typically, they involve having people type their ideas into a networked program so that they can be "discussed" with others online. This may be done in real time among individuals who happen to be available. When this isn't possible, that's okay because a record of all discussions is left for others to examine as needed when they join in.

Some software vendors have been claiming that using their products promotes the efficiency of group decision meetings, and although scientific research on this is limited, this is reasonable given the nature of the process. Additionally, users of GDSS expect that it will improve the quality of group decisions by removing some of the impediments to decision making we identified earlier. Specifically, it may accomplish this in three key ways.

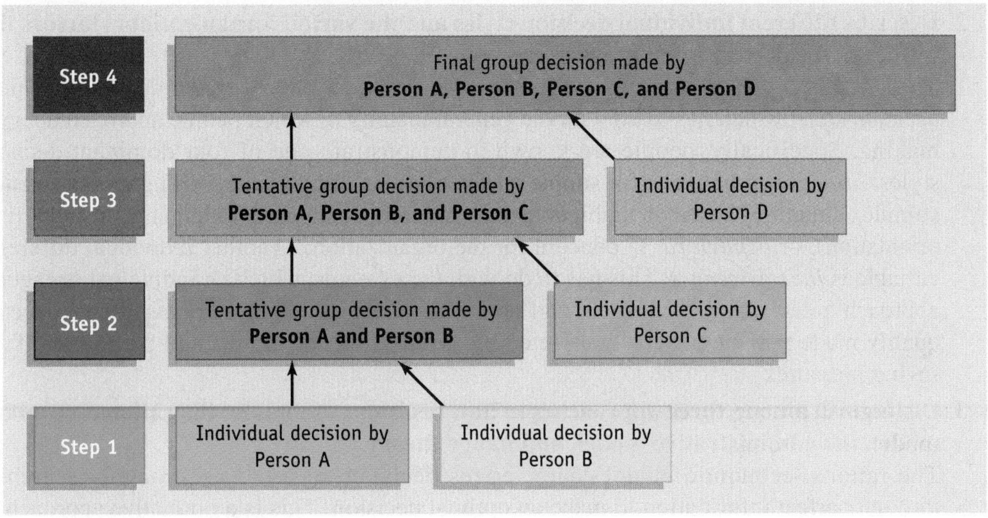

group decision support systems (GDSS)
Interactive computer-based systems that combine communication, computer, and decision technologies to improve the effectiveness of group problem-solving meetings.

FIGURE 10.18

The Stepladder Technique

By systematically adding new individuals into decision-making groups, the stepladder technique helps to increase the quality of the decisions made.

Source: Adapted from Rogelberg & O'Connor, 1998; see Note 113.

- GDSS helps meetings stay focused, and participants avoid overload because the software directs the flow of information.
- GDSS sessions allow the appropriate experts to contribute to meetings at their convenience—even though they may be far away—instead of receiving input only from those who physically can attend the meeting.
- Because GDSS sessions can be configured so as to keep contributors anonymous, no participants have to worry about getting "put down" for sharing certain points. Intimidation by powerful leaders is all but eliminated as a result. Also, because even unpopular ideas can be shared with impunity, the problem of groupthink is reduced.

Research has found that GDSS has, in fact, improved group decisions. An experiment was conducted comparing the effectiveness of groups of managers asked to solve simulated management problems in face-to-face groups and using GDSS.[114] As expected, the results showed that compared to face-to-face groups, groups using GDSS not only shared considerably more information, but they also made far better decisions as a result.

For now, it seems that group decision support systems appear to be quite effective. However, because they are very new, we don't yet know all the conditions under which they will continue to be successful. As OB researchers conduct further research on this topic, we surely will learn more about this promising technique in the future.

Summary and Review of Learning Objectives

1. **Identify the steps in the analytical model of decision making and distinguish between the various types of decisions that people make.**

   According to the analytical model of decision making, the making of decisions is a multistep process through which (1) a problem is identified, (2) solution objectives are defined, (3) a predecision is made (i.e., a decision about how to make a decision), (4) alternatives are generated, (5) these alternatives are evaluated, (6) an alternative is chosen, (7) that alternative is implemented, and then (8) a follow-up occurs to determine if the problem still exists. Decisions made in organizations can be characterized as being either programmed, routine decisions made according to preexisting guidelines, or nonprogrammed decisions requiring novel and creative solutions. Decisions also differ with respect to the amount of risk involved, ranging from those in which the decision outcomes are relatively certain to those in which the outcomes are highly uncertain. Uncertain situations are expressed as statements of probability based on either objective or subjective information. Decisions also differ with respect to whether they are made by high-level organizational officials (top-down decisions) or by employees themselves (empowered decisions).

2. **Describe different individual decision styles and the various organizational factors that influence the decision-making process.**

   There are two major individual differences in the way people make decisions. One is *decision style*, which has to do with the general manner in which people approach decision making. Specifically, people are known to demonstrate one of four dominant decision styles: *directive* (preference for simple, clear solutions), *analytical* (willingness to consider complex situations based on ambiguous information), *conceptual* (a humanistic and artistic orientation), or *behavioral* (a concern for the organization). Another individual difference variable is *indecisiveness*. This has to do with the extent to which an individual is eager to approach a decision or is hesitant and prefers to put it off. Within organizations, decision quality made may be adversely affected by severe time constraints and by political face-saving pressures.

3. **Distinguish among three approaches to how decisions are made: the rational-economic model, the administrative model, and image theory.**

   The rational-economic model characterizes decision makers as thoroughly searching through perfect information to make an optimal decision. This is a normative approach, in that it describes how decision makers ideally ought to behave to make the best possible decisions. In contrast, the administrative model is a descriptive approach, which describes how decision makers actually behave. It recognizes that limitations imposed by people's ability to process the information needed to make complex decisions (bounded rationality and bounded discretion) restrict decision makers to making satisficing decisions—solutions that are not optimal, but good enough. An alternative approach, image theory, recognizes that decisions are made in an automatic, intuitive fashion. It claims that people will adopt a course of action that best fits their individual principles, current goals, and plans for the future.

4. **Identify the various factors that lead people to make imperfect decisions.**

   People make imperfect decisions due to cognitive biases. One such bias, framing, refers to the tendency for people to make different decisions based on how a problem is presented. For example, when a problem is presented in a way that emphasizes positive gains to be received, people tend to make conservative, risk-averse decisions, whereas when the same problem is presented in a way that emphasizes potential losses to be suffered, people tend to make riskier decisions. Simple rules of thumb, known as heuristics, also may bias decisions. For example, according to the availability heuristic, people base their judgments on information readily available to them, and according to the representativeness heuristic, people are perceived in stereotypical ways if they appear to be representatives of the categories to which they belong. People also are biased toward implicit favorites, alternatives they prefer in advance of considering all the options. Other alternatives, confirmation candidates, are considered for purposes of convincing oneself that one's implicit favorite is the best alternative. Decisions also are biased because of the tendency to believe that we were far better at judging past events than we actually were (known as the hindsight bias) and the tendency for people to give too little credit to others when things are going poorly and too much credit when things are going well (known as the person sensitivity bias). Finally, decisions are biased insofar as people tend to escalate commitment to unsuccessful courses of action because they have sunk costs invested in them. This occurs in large part because people need to justify their previous actions and wish to avoid having to admit that their initial decision was a mistake.

5. **Compare the conditions under which groups make superior decisions than individuals and when individuals make superior decisions than groups.**

   Groups make superior decisions than individuals when these are composed of a heterogeneous mix of experts who possess complementary skills. However, groups may not be any better than the best member of the group when performing a task that has a simple, verifiable answer. Individuals make superior decisions than face-to-face brainstorming groups on creative problems. However, when brainstorming is done electronically—that is, by using computer terminals to send messages—the quality of decisions tends to improve.

6. **Describe various techniques that can be used to enhance the quality of individual decisions and group decisions.**

   Decision quality may be enhanced in several different ways. First, the quality of individual decisions has been shown to improve following individual training in problem-solving skills. Training in ethics also can help people make more ethical decisions. Group decisions may be improved in four ways. First, in the Delphi technique, the judgments of experts are systematically gathered and used to form a single joint decision. Second, in the nominal group technique, group meetings are structured so as to elicit and evaluate systematically the opinions of all members. Third, in the stepladder technique, new individuals are added to decision-making groups one at a time, requiring the presentation and discussion of new ideas. Contemporary techniques also employ the use of computers as aids in decision making. Finally, group decision support systems may be used. These are interactive computer-based systems that combine communication, computer, and decision technologies to improve the effectiveness of group problem-solving meetings.

Points to Ponder

Questions for Review

1. What are the general steps in the decision-making process, and how can the different types of organizational decisions be characterized?
2. How do individual decision style, group influences, and organizational influences affect decision making in organizations?
3. What are the major differences between the rational-economic model, the administrative model, and the image theory approach to individual decision making?
4. How does each of the following factors contribute to the imperfect nature of decisions: framing effects, reliance on heuristics, decision biases, and the tendency to escalate commitment to a losing course of action?
5. When it comes to making decisions, under what conditions are individuals superior to groups and under what conditions are groups superior to individuals?
6. What traditional techniques and computer-based techniques can be used to improve the quality of decisions made by groups or individuals?

Experiential Questions

1. Think of any decision you recently made. Would you characterize it as programmed or nonprogrammed?

Highly certain or highly uncertain? Top-down or empowered? Explain your answers.
2. Identify ways in which various decisions you have made were biased by framing, heuristics, the use of implicit favorites, and the escalation of commitment.
3. Think of various decision-making groups in which you may have participated over the years. Do you think that groupthink was involved in these situations? What signs were evident?

Questions to Analyze

1. Imagine that you are a manager facing the problem of not attracting enough high-quality personnel to your organization. Would you attempt to solve this problem alone or by committee? Explain your reasoning.
2. Suppose you were on a committee charged with making an important decision, and that committee was composed of people from various nations. How do you think this might make a difference in the way the group operates?
3. Argue pro or con: "All people make decisions in the same manner."

Experiencing OB

Individual Exercise

What Is Your Personal Decision Style?

As you read about the various personal decision styles, did you put yourself into any one of the categories? To get a feel for what the *decision style inventory* reveals about your personal decision style, complete this exercise. It is based on questions similar to those appearing in the actual instrument (Rowe et al., 1984; see Note 33).

Directions

For each of the following questions, select the one alternative that best describes how you see yourself in your typical work situation.

1. When performing my job, I usually look for:
   a. practical results
   b. the best solutions to problems
   c. new ideas or approaches
   d. pleasant working conditions
2. When faced with a problem, I usually:
   a. use approaches that have worked in the past
   b. analyze it carefully
   c. try to find a creative approach
   d. rely on my feelings
3. When making plans, I usually emphasize:
   a. the problems I currently face
   b. attaining objectives

    c. future goals

    d. developing my career

  4. The kind of information I usually prefer to use is:

    a. specific facts

    b. complete and accurate data

    c. broad information covering many options

    d. data that is limited and simple to understand

  5. Whenever I am uncertain about what to do, I:

    a. rely on my intuition

    b. look for facts

    c. try to find a compromise

    d. wait, and decide later

  6. The people with whom I work best are usually:

    a. ambitious and full of energy

    b. self-confident

    c. open-minded

    d. trusting and polite

  7. The decisions I make are usually:

    a. direct and realistic

    b. abstract or systematic

    c. broad and flexible

    d. sensitive to others' needs

Scoring

1. For each "a" you select, give yourself a point in the *directive* category.
2. For each "b" you select, give yourself a point in the *analytical* category.
3. For each "c" you select, give yourself a point in the *conceptual* category.
4. For each "d" you select, give yourself a point in the *behavioral* category.
5. The points reflect the relative strength of your preferences for each decision style.

Questions for Discussion

1. What style did the test reveal that you have? How did this compare to the style you thought you had before you took the test?
2. Based on the descriptions of the personal decision styles in the text, were you able to guess in advance which test items were indicative of which styles?
3. What additional items may be added to the test to assess each style?

Group Exercise

Running a Nominal Group: Try It Yourself

A great deal can be learned about nominal groups by running one—or, at least, participating in one—yourself. Doing so will not only help illustrate the procedure, but demonstrate how effectively it works as well.

Directions

1. Select a topic suitable for discussion in a nominal group composed of students in your class. It should be a topic that is narrowly defined and on which people have many different opinions (these work best in nominal groups). Some possible examples include the following:
   - What should your school's student leaders be doing for you?
   - What can be done to improve the quality of instruction in your institution?
   - What can be done to improve the quality of jobs your school's students receive when graduating?
2. Divide the class into groups of approximately 10 students. Arrange each group in a circle, or around a table, if possible. In each group, select one person to serve as the group facilitator.

3. Following the steps outlined in Figure 10.17 (page 366), facilitators should guide their groups in discussions regarding the focal question identified in step 1. Allow approximately 45 minutes to 1 hour to complete this process.

4. If time allows, select a different focal question and a different group leader, and repeat the procedure.

Questions for Discussion

1. Collectively, how did the group answer the question? Do you believe that this answer accurately reflected the feelings of the group?

2. How did the various groups' answers compare? Were they similar or different? Why?

3. What were the major problems, if any, associated with the nominal group experience? For example, were there any group members who were reluctant to wait their turns before speaking up?

4. How do you think your group experiences would have differed had you used a totally unstructured, traditional face-to-face group instead of a nominal group?

Practicing OB

The Intrusive Manager

A large product-distribution company is having a problem during its group meetings: One department manager is constantly disrupting the meetings while trying to get his ideas across. He has so consistently intimidated his coworkers that they are reluctant to speak up. As a result of his intrusiveness, people's good ideas are not coming across.

1. Explain what steps might be taken to avoid this problem.

2. What is your rationale for this advice?

3. What are the advantages and disadvantages of the tactic you identified?

■ Coca-Cola: Deciding on the Look

Case in Point

What do Yao Ming, LeBron James, and Earl R. Dean have in common? The first two are professional basketball stars, of course, but who's Earl R. Dean? He happens to be the person who designed Coca-Cola's familiar "contour bottle," the shapely container with a middle diameter that's larger than its base. That was back in 1915. How do Yao and LeBron fit in, you ask? They too designed Coca-Cola bottles, but more recently, in 2008 to be exact. Now, before you start thinking that only celebrities such as Yao, LeBron, and the now-departed Earl get to do such cool things, you too could have designed your own bottle. In fact, in conjunction with the Olympic Games in Beijing and Vancouver, tens of thousands of people from around the world visited Coca-Cola's Web site, where, with the aid of a drawing application, they put stunningly beautiful finishing touches on classic Coke bottles.

Why did Coke bother with this? The answer is simple: Coca-Cola has been in the process of deciding on a new bottle design and they stand to get great ideas from the submissions. And because visitors to the site are asked to vote on the various designs submitted, company officials can get a good sense of what consumers like.

But designs by consumers were only one source of inspiration. The head of Coca-Cola's design team was charged with creating a consistent new look for the company's products and needed as much input as possible. That was the same situation a century ago, when Coca-Cola officials turned to its bottle suppliers for suggestions. They wanted a bottle that people enjoyed using and that was so easily recognizable that it could be identified if felt in the dark, or even if it were broken into pieces. That's when our hero, Earl R. Dean, bottle designer at the Root Glass Company, came up with the winning deign, earning him a prize of a lifetime job with the company.

Today, with 450 different brands, more than 300 different models of vending machines, and different design standards being used throughout the world, the design task is a bit larger in scope. But like a century ago, clear criteria are being used to specify exactly what the company is trying to achieve. Today's design team identified three considerations. The design had to identify the brand clearly; it should create a good experience for the user; and the container

(Continued)

should be made from environmentally friendly materials. Interestingly, the first two criteria remained unchanged from 100 years ago.

With these considerations in mind, and with the Root Glass Company long gone, the job was turned over to design staff at the branding and packaging firm Turner Duckworth. Their new design was an aluminum contour bottle in traditional Coke red with the white script logo wrapped prominently around the middle. It was a sexier, updated version of Mr. Dean's Coke bottle—immediately recognizable but up-to-date. And being made of aluminum instead of glass, the container feels colder when held, is lighter to ship, is much less expensive to produce, and is eco-friendly. In fact, the bottle is made of recycled aluminum that, itself, can be recycled. So highly regarded was the design that it won the prestigious Grand Prix at the Cannes Lions advertising festival.

Although this bottle is in only limited use, such as in a few upscale clubs, its success has inspired Coca-Cola to redesign the remaining products in the company's vast portfolio. As overwhelming as this may seem, with a consistent look and design strategy to guide them, these decisions promise to be a little less challenging. Too bad Earl R. Dean isn't here to help this time around.

Questions for Discussion

1. How do you think the analytical model of decision making (see Figure 10.1, page 335) might have been applied by Coca-Cola when designing new bottles? What specific tasks might have been done at each step in the process?

2. What errors or biases might have contributed to less-than-perfect decisions in this case? How might they have been overcome?

3. What recommendations for improving the decision-making process identified in this chapter might be applied in this case? How do you think they would help?

11

Interpersonal Behavior at Work: Conflict, Cooperation, Trust, and Deviance

Learning Objectives

After reading this chapter, you should be able to:

1. Describe three types of psychological contracts and the two basic kinds of trust that play a role in work relationships.
2. Describe organizational citizenship behavior and ways in which it may be encouraged.
3. Identify ways in which cooperation can be promoted in the workplace.
4. Describe the causes and effects of conflict in organizations along with techniques that can be used to manage conflict in organizations.
5. Explain why deviant organizational behavior can produce positive as well as negative effects.
6. Describe the major forms of workplace deviance.

Chapter Outline

- Psychological Contracts and Trust: Building Blocks of Working Relationships
- Organizational Citizenship Behavior: Going Above and Beyond Formal Job Requirements
- Cooperation: Providing Mutual Assistance
- Conflict: The Inevitable Result of Incompatible Interests
- Deviant Organizational Behavior

Preview Case

■ *NASCAR: The Etiquette of Drafting*

To the uninitiated, there's really not much to it. A commentator once described a NASCAR race as simply a matter of "go straight, turn left, go straight, turn left," round and round again. Do this faster than anyone else 200 times and you've won NASCAR's biggest, richest, and most prestigious race, the Daytona 500, pocketing about $1.5 million for your troubles. Ask any of NASCAR's 75 million fans who are in the know, however, and they'll tell you that there's far more to the sport of racing high performance stock cars than meets the untrained eye.

A great car, a talented crew, and drivers with nerves of steel can be taken for granted as keys to success, but to win races, drivers also must know "how to compete by cooperating." And this, in a word, requires "drafting," the practice of following closely behind the car ahead of you so as to get sucked into its vacuum. Due to aerodynamics, this boosts the speed of both cars—not much, but enough to make all the difference in a long race, such as the annual 500-mile events at Daytona and Talladega. The more cars in a drafting line—at any given time, these typically range from a pair of cars to about 10—the more each benefits.

Knowing that if they don't draft, they lose, the best NASCAR drivers are adept at working multi-car draft lines and out-competing the others by out-cooperating them. Suppose a driver wants to pull ahead by swinging out of the pack, for example. He or she can do so, but unless another car pulls up behind, the absence of a draft will cause it to lose momentum and fall back several places. In the new draft line, both drivers benefit, but because each wants to win, these partnerships are fleeting. One moment, a driver may seek a nearby drafting partner to help move ahead but inevitably, and just as quickly, he or she will defect in search of another. These ephemeral partnerships between rivals at 190 mph may last a few seconds or a few laps, but they are essential.

Winning drivers know when to join draft lines (or to invite others to join theirs) and when to defect. This interplay between cooperating and competing requires trusting other drivers to know and abide by the unspoken rules of the game. For this reason, veteran racers are wary of having rookies as draft partners until they have earned the confidence of the other drivers on the track. Trust also is an issue for allies, members of the same racing team. Confident that cooperation will be forthcoming, other cars from the driver's racing team are inclined to be multi-lap draft partners. Still, because drivers seek individual glory, even members of their own teams become rivals when the end of the race is near and the driver of the second-place car wants to "slingshot" ahead of the lead car to cross the finish line at the last second.

As you might imagine, having drafting partners enter a line requires close communication. Drivers sometimes have pre-race arrangements to cooperate with one another, but most drafting partnerships emerge on the fly. To broker these deals, drivers may use hand gestures, but these might be difficult to see and, of course, removing one's hands from the steering wheel for even a second can spell disaster. Instead, most deals are made by drivers communicating by radio with spotters, diplomatic envoys in the stands who negotiate drafting deals with the spotters of other drivers. These partnerships may last only the 10 seconds required to pull ahead of another rival, but of course, the helping driver is expected to return the favor later in the race if needed. After all, on the racetrack, as in other things in life, "one hand washes the other."

Although you might be unaware of these dynamics as you watch a NASCAR race, they are potent illustrations that it involves far more than just driving around in circles. Being a winning NASCAR driver also requires good interpersonal relationships with other drivers. As one expert put it, "A driver's reputation as a trustworthy person may affect the outcome as much as his reputation as a driver."[1] Of course, the same could be said of people in many other lines of work, including ones that are less glamorous and far safer. Indeed, the themes highlighted here—trust, negotiation, cooperation and competition—play prominent roles in just about any line of work. These processes of working with others and against them, broadly referred to as **interpersonal behavior,** are the focus of this chapter. Specifically, we will summarize an array of interpersonal behaviors that occur in the workplace, describing how they influence the way people work and their feelings about their jobs and organizations.

Figure 11.1 identifies the major forms of interpersonal behavior in the workplace that we'll be discussing in this chapter. This diagram organizes interpersonal behaviors along a continuum, ranging from those that involve working with others (shown on the left) to those that involve working against others (shown on the right). This forms a useful road map for how we will proceed. Beginning on the left, we first will examine **prosocial behavior**—the tendency for people to help others on the job, sometimes even when there doesn't appear to be anything in it for them. Following this, we will

interpersonal behavior
A variety of behaviors involving the ways in which people work with and against one another.

prosocial behavior
The tendency for people to help others on the job, even when they will not personally benefit from assisting.

FIGURE 11.1

Varieties of Interpersonal Behavior

The five types of interpersonal behavior observed in organizations and presented in this chapter can be summarized as falling along a continuum ranging from those involving working with other people to those involving working against them.

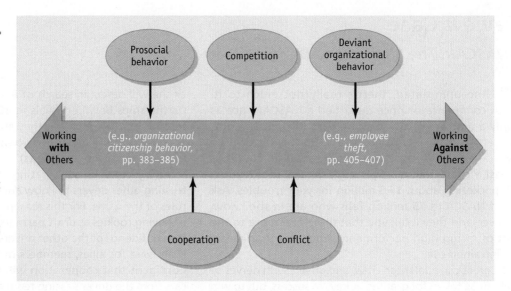

discuss situations in which people help each other and receive help from them—that is, the tendency to *cooperate*. In NASCAR races and elsewhere in the world of business, as you know, people and entire companies don't always work with each other; they also *compete* against each other—that is, as one tries to win, it forces the other to lose. Under such circumstances, it is not unusual for *conflict* to emerge, breeding ill-will. And, when taken to the extreme, this results in *deviant* behavior—acts intended to bring harm, such as stealing from the company or even harming another person.

Before examining these various forms of behavior, though, we consider two processes that play a role in all interpersonal relationships: developing *psychological contracts* and building *trust*. These processes are important because they often affect the extent to which people choose either to work with or against one another.

Psychological Contracts and Trust: Building Blocks of Working Relationships

Interpersonal relationships are complex, to say the least. They range in nature from ones that are relatively short-term and have little or no emotional ties between the persons involved (e.g., interactions between temporary employees and regular employees; customers and salespersons at a used car lot) to ones that are long-term and involve powerful emotional bonds (e.g., cofounders of a new venture; employees who have worked closely together for many years). In a sense, then, all interpersonal relationships are unique. Yet, despite this fact, there are basic themes or building blocks that play a role in most, if not all, of them. Among these, two that are especially important are *psychological contracts* and *trust*.

Psychological Contracts: Our Expectations of Others

When people enter into relationships with each other, they quickly develop expectations about what these relationships will be like—what each side is expected to do. For instance, if you leave a phone message for a friend, you expect her to return your call. If you report for work on a regular basis and do your job, you expect to be compensated at the end of the pay period. These examples illustrate what is known as the **psychological contract**—a person's perceptions and expectations about the mutual obligations in an employment relationship (or, for that matter, any other relationship).[2]

Although psychological contracts generally are not recorded formally on paper, they guide what we expect of others much as if they were. However, unlike legal contracts, in which the terms are made explicit, psychological contracts exist primarily in the beliefs and perceptions of the persons involved. Not surprisingly, there may well be differences of opinion regarding psychological contracts: What one person expects may not be exactly what another expects. As you know from experience, such disagreements often can lead to interpersonal friction (see Figure 11.2).

psychological contract
A person's beliefs about what is expected of another in a relationship.

Blend Images/SuperStock.

FIGURE 11.2

Psychological Contracts: Open to Interpretation

Because psychological contracts are not written and formal in nature, they are open to interpretation. If two parties to such a contract have contrasting perceptions of their mutual obligations, the result may be interpersonal friction between them—or worse!

TYPES OF PSYCHOLOGICAL CONTRACTS. Although psychological contracts can vary in many ways and are, in a sense, unique to each working relationship, most can be described in terms of two basic dimensions.[3] First, psychological contracts vary with respect to *time frame*—how long they are expected to last. In keeping with the nature of their employment arrangements, temporary employees anticipate having only short-term relationships with their employers. At the other extreme, employees of most large Japanese companies—at least until the economic crises of the 2000s—expected *lifetime employment* with their organizations, resulting in long-term, family-like relationships with their employers.

Second, psychological contracts vary in terms of *performance requirements*—how close the relationship is between performance demands (i.e., what employees are expected to do) and the rewards they receive.[4] For some jobs, pay is related directly to output, while for others, this relationship is less clear-cut, and much more than pay is involved: The relationship is *not* defined purely in economic terms (e.g., employees expect emotional and social support from their companies as well as pay). Together, these two dimensions point to the existence of three basic kinds of psychological contracts: *transactional, relational,* and *balanced.*[5] We summarize these in Figure 11.3.

Transactional contracts are informal expectations between individuals whose relationships are exclusively economic in nature and of relatively brief duration. Suppose, for example,

transactional contract
A variety of psychological contract in which the parties have a brief and narrowly defined relationship that is primarily economic in focus.

Three Kinds of Psychological Contracts: A Summary

Psychological contracts may be considered transactional, relational, or balanced. The key characteristics of transactional and relational contracts are shown at opposite ends of each continuum. Balanced contracts, however, combine various aspects of each, typically at the point indicated by "X" along each dimension.

Source: Based on suggestions by Dabos & Rousseau, 2004; see Note 2.

Transactional Contracts	Balanced Contracts	Relational Contracts
Concerned about economic factors	**Primary focus** ⟵X⟶	*Concerned about people*
Closed-ended and short-term	**Time frame** ⟵ X⟶	*Open-ended and indefinite*
Static, rarely changing	**Stability of relationship** ⟵X⟶	*Dynamic, frequently changing*
Narrow	**Scope of relationship** ⟵ X⟶	*Broad and pervasive*
Well defined	**Tangibility of terms** ⟵X⟶	*Highly subjective*

that you are a student working at a summer job. You have been hired to take over for regular employees while they are on vacation. You know that your relationship with your employer is short-term and that it is based on a clearly defined set of economic terms. You go to work each day as scheduled, you do your job, you get your paycheck, and at the end of the season, it's over—and you go back to school.[6]

By contrast, **relational contracts** are informal expectations between individuals whose relationships are close and personal in nature. They are not tied to specific pay or other rewards and generally are longer-term in nature. For example, if you have worked in the same company for the same boss for more than 20 years, chances are good that your relationship is based not simply on an exchange of specific benefits and contributions that are largely economic in nature; rather, other factors, such as friendship, loyalty, and years of shared experiences matter, too. You expect that relationship to last well into the future, and you feel a sense of commitment to your boss, your job, and your company that no temporary employees, working under transactional psychological contracts, can share. It is precisely because of these feelings that employees tend to feel betrayed when their long-term employers find it necessary to lay off such, often highly paid, individuals.

A third type of psychological contract combines the open-ended, long-term features of relational psychological contracts with the well-specified reward-performance contingencies of transactional contracts. Such **balanced contracts,** as they are known, are informal expectations between people that result in each side receiving some benefit from the other.[7] As an example, consider an individual who wants to start her own company. She may spend several years working in a large organization because this helps her develop the skills and contacts needed for founding a new venture. She is committed to staying in this company until she acquires these skills and contacts (perhaps for several years), and forms close relationships with the people who are helping her toward her goal. Clearly, then, she is exchanging her time, effort, and talent for pay and these other, less tangible benefits. The term "balanced contracts" reflects the fact that each side receives benefits from the arrangement between them. It is with this in mind that balanced relationships are depicted as falling between the two extremes shown in Figure 11.3.

EFFECTS OF PSYCHOLOGICAL CONTRACTS. As you might expect, the three different kinds of psychological contracts have contrasting effects both for individuals and organizations. For instance, relational and balanced contracts encourage individuals to go beyond the basic requirements of their jobs, helping others or their companies on a voluntary basis (we will

relational contract
A variety of psychological contract in which the parties have a long-term and widely defined relationship with a vast focus.

balanced contracts
Psychological contracts that combine the open-ended, long-term features of relational psychological contracts with the well-specified reward-performance contingencies of transactional contracts.

describe this kind of behavior, known as *organizational citizenship behavior,* in the next major section of this chapter).[8]

Similarly, individuals with certain personal characteristics are more likely to form relational contracts, while others are more likely to form transactional ones. Specifically, people who are low in emotional stability (see Chapters 4 and 5) and who also are highly sensitive to being treated fairly (see Chapter 2) are inclined to form transactional contracts, whereas those who are high in conscientiousness and self-esteem (see Chapter 4) are inclined to form longer-term relational contracts.[9] Can you see why? People who are low in emotional stability do not like long-term commitments, ones that demand high levels of social skills and trust.[10] On the other hand, individuals who are high in conscientiousness and self-esteem are more inclined to be concerned with doing a good job and with opportunities for growth and achievement than with purely economic benefits, especially short-term ones. As a result, they tend to prefer—and to develop—relational contracts.

In sum, although psychological contracts aren't written on paper, they play important roles in many aspects of organizational behavior, including the extent to which individuals work with or against each other—the main theme of this chapter. (Do these three kinds of psychological contracts exist around the world? For a discussion of this issue, see the Today's Diverse and Global Organizations section below.)

Trust in Working Relationships

One thing that makes relationships based on transactional contracts so different from those based on relational contracts is the degree to which the parties *trust* one another. By **trust,** we are referring to the degree to which one person (a trustor) is willing to make himself of herself vulnerable to another (a trustee) based on the trustor's positive expectations about the trustee. In other words, trust reflects one person's degree of confidence in the words and actions of another.[11] Suppose, for example, that your supervisor, the local sales manager of a retail store, will be talking to his boss, the district sales manager, about getting you transferred to a new location you find more desirable. You are counting on your boss to come through for you because he says he will. To the extent you believe that he will do what he promises—that is, make a strong case on your behalf—you trust him. However, if you believe that his recommendation will not be too

trust
A person's degree of confidence in the words and actions of another.

Today's Diverse and Global Organizations

Psychological Contracts in China and the United States: Are They the Same?

Because cultures differ in many respects, it's an interesting possibility that the types of psychological contracts that people use in various nations reflect these differences. Interestingly, though, research indicates that psychological contracts are actually very much the same across various cultures.[12]

This has been shown in a study of psychological contracts in China.[13] The researchers asked Chinese employees to complete a scale designed to measure the types of psychological contracts they use. In the United States, it has been clear that people use transactional, relational, and balanced psychological contracts, but was this also the case in China? The study's results suggested that in China, just as in the United States, all three types of contracts are used. Just like their American counterparts, Chinese employees are aware of the nature of their relationships with their employers and understand that these can vary in terms of time frame (length of duration) and performance requirements (strictly pay-for-specific performance or a much broader array of mutual obligations).

In the same research project, the researchers also examined the extent to which people were interested in helping others in their organizations and the types of relationships they had with them. Employees in relational or balanced relationships with their employers were inclined to help their colleagues and the organization itself in an effort to strengthen their relationships with their supervisors. However, employees whose relationships with their employers were transactional in nature also helped, but for different reasons—as a means of demonstrating respect. Again, these findings matched those found among employees in the United States.

Overall, this research suggests that the basic nature of psychological contracts is identical in the United States and China, despite their very different cultures. However, it was clear from the research that the specific nature of these contracts and the forms they took were influenced by cultural factors to some degree. As is often the case, then, basic processes of organizational behavior are much the same around the world, but they should be viewed through the lens of specific cultures to obtain an accurate understanding of the forms they take in different countries.

enthusiastic or that he will not recommend you at all, you will trust him much less. As you might expect, the concept of trust is more complex than suggested by our simple example. In fact, there are three distinct kinds of trust (for an overview, see Figure 11.4).

calculus-based trust
A form of trust based on deterrence; whenever people believe that another will behave as promised out of fear of getting punished for doing otherwise.

CALCULUS-BASED TRUST. One kind of trust, known as **calculus-based trust,** is based on the use of threats and deterrents.[14] Calculus-based trust exists whenever people believe that another person will behave as promised out of fear of getting punished for doing otherwise. We trust our employers to contribute their shares to our Social Security accounts because they risk fines and penalties if they fail to do so. Similarly, if your company hires a catering firm to provide the food for an important social function, you trust this business to show up with the items you have ordered; if they fail to do so, you won't pay them and you're likely to warn others not to hire them.

Calculus-based trust is characteristic of many business relationships—ones based on transactional contracts, in which each side knows what it is expected to deliver. Although calculus-based trust may not sound like the kind you would like others to have in you, it is essential for most businesses: It is the basis for a good reputation, and that, as everyone knows, often is the foundation for success. Various deterrents for the trustor help ensure the trustee that he or she is safe from exploitation. If you find yourself saying about a person, Y, "If Y messes with me, X will give it to him," then X provides your insurance policy, of sorts, that Y will not harm you. Such relationships are ones in which calculus-based trust is involved.

identification-based trust
A form of trust based on accepting the wants and desires of another person.

IDENTIFICATION-BASED TRUST. A very different kind of trust, and one that is grounded less in deterrents and more in the power of personal relations, is known as **identification-based trust.** This kind of trust is based on accepting and understanding another person's wants and desires. Identification-based trust occurs when people know and understand one another so well that they are willing to allow that individual to act on their behalf. The example we described earlier in which you allow your boss to discuss your transfer with a higher-ranking official illustrates identification-based trust.

What is the foundation on which identification-based trust is based? In other words, what elements of a relationship between trustor and trustee must be established for the trustor to trust the trustee? Research has established that several important factors are involved.[15] The major ones are as follows.

- *Familiarity.* The trustor knows something about the trustee based on having had a relationship in the past.
- *Shared experience.* Having spent time together, the trustor and the trustee have experienced many of the same things (i.e., they have a history with one another).
- *Reciprocal disclosure.* The trustor and the trustee have shared information about one another, which breeds closer interpersonal relationships between them.

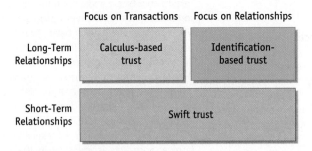

FIGURE 11.4

Three Major Forms of Trust: A Comparison

Different types of trust can be categorized with respect to whether their focus is on transactional or interpersonal factors and whether they exist in long-term or short-term relationships. Specifically, *calculus-based trust* exists in long-term relationships that focus on transactional considerations, whereas *identification-based trust* exists in long-term relationships that focus on interpersonal considerations. A third type of trust, *swift trust,* incorporates both transactional and interpersonal considerations but occurs only in short-term relationships (e.g., virtual teams).

- *Fulfilled promises.* The trustee has already shown the trustor that he or she will do what was promised; there is a history of coming through for the trustee in the past.
- *Demonstrations of nonexploitation and vulnerability.* In the past, the trustor has had opportunities to exploit the trustee but has not taken advantage of them; despite having made himself or herself vulnerable to the trustor, the trustee was not harmed.

SWIFT TRUST. The types of trust we've discussed thus far are ones that exist in ongoing, long-term relationships. This makes sense given that some degree of history between the parties would appear to be necessary for trust to develop. Interestingly, however, it has been found that trust develops even within relationships that are short-term and temporary in nature—that is, ones that have a finite lifespan, whose members have a shared purpose, and in which activities are carefully coordinated. This would describe, for example, a crew of technicians from throughout the country who gather at a remote location to record a television commercial. The unit assembles for a day or two and then disbands, never to see one another again unless a job happens to bring them together sometime in the future. As we described in Chapter 8, teams (e.g., virtual teams) and work groups of this type are not uncommon.

Although it would appear that conditions don't exist for trust to exist in such temporary systems, it does, in fact, occur in them. It's not just a scaled-down version of what we've described earlier but something different, known as **swift trust.**[16] This refers to trust that occurs as a set of collective perceptions develops among members of temporary groups. In fact, various features of the temporary arrangement are responsible for this trust to develop. These are as follows:

> **swift trust**
> Trust that occurs as a set of collective perceptions develops among members of temporary groups.

- *Outcomes are interdependent.* In the type of temporary groups we're describing, people's successes or failures depend on one another. To meet your objectives, you have to help others meet theirs. People who are put "in the same boat" eventually "sink or swim" together, so they work together. Recognizing this leads people to develop trust in one another.
- *Time constraints exist.* Because time is limited and the pace of work is exaggerated in temporary groups, trust cannot develop in its usual, more leisurely manner. With little or no slack time, people are unlikely to engage in selfish activities that would make them untrustworthy. Believing this also encourages people to trust others.
- *Group members focus on task and professional roles.* Learning what someone is like (including his or her trustworthiness) usually takes time, making the development of such attributions (see Chapter 3) unlikely in temporary groups (unless, of course, someone does something out of the ordinary right away). Because individual information isn't available, people are inclined to judge their teammates in keeping with their professional roles. By focusing on individuals as professionals who contribute to the success of the joint task, people are unlikely to have any reasons to doubt their trustworthiness. To the contrary, their high professional regard for these individuals is likely to promote a willingness to trust them.
- *A trust broker is in place.* In temporary work units, the individual who hires and fires the team members is available to ensure that everyone involved will behave appropriately and not let others down. This central person is the "designer of the system," so to speak—likely, a producer in the case of our television commercial—to whom anyone can turn should concerns arise. The existence of such an individual provides a sort of "safety net" that provides a reason to trust strangers who there otherwise would be no reason to feel comfortable enough to trust.

As suggested in Figure 11.4, swift trust incorporates both the transactional aspects of calculus-based trust and the interpersonal aspects of identification-based trust. What's different, of course, is the focus on short-term relationships instead of long-term ones. Given that so many teams and groups are being formed virtually, for temporary purposes, it's not surprising that there have been many opportunities to conduct research on swift trust. Indeed, several studies have supported the notion that swift trust operates in a variety of temporary groups, including ones whose members come from all around the world.[17]

DEVELOPING TRUSTWORTHINESS. What factors influence the development of trust? Although many play a role, research has established that three are especially important in promoting followers' trust in their leaders.[18] Each contributes somewhat, but trustworthiness develops most strongly when all three factors are combined. These are as follows.

- *Ability.* As we described in Chapter 4, ability refers to one's knowledge and capacity to perform various tasks. In the case of trust, it's not only important to have knowledge about how to perform a particular job, but also general managerial ability—that is, knowing how to work effectively with people (such as described throughout this book). The role of ability in trustworthiness is straightforward: People are inclined to trust leaders whose abilities they recognize. This isn't all, of course, but subordinates can hardly trust leaders who they believe cannot perform their jobs well and who are ineffective in helping them do their own work.

- *Benevolence.* Some people are more inclined than others to be considerate and to demonstrate concern and support as necessary. Individuals who are especially sensitive in this manner are said to display high degrees of **benevolence.** Not surprisingly, the more benevolent leaders have been to their followers, the more likely those followers are to trust them. After all, we certainly wouldn't be willing to trust someone who is inconsiderate, unconcerned, and unsupportive of us.

- *Integrity* As we suggested in Chapter 2, people demonstrate high degrees of integrity when they adhere to moral and ethical principles (e.g., not stealing company property) and when they behave fairly. People are disinclined to put their trust in others who have revealed themselves to be not of high moral character. Why, for example, would you even think of trusting someone who has lied consistently?

benevolence
Disposition of people to be considerate and to demonstrate concern and support for others.

Research has shown that when people perceive their leaders as being high in ability, benevolence, and integrity, they perceive them to be especially trustworthy.[19] And when this occurs, they behave in a variety of beneficial ways. Among other things, they are willing to go beyond their job descriptions and take risks required to succeed because they believe that their leaders will be supportive. They also perform their jobs particularly well because they are not worried about having to "watch their backs." For this same reason, people remain highly committed to organizations when they trust their leaders, which, as we discussed in Chapter 6, brings about several benefits, such as reducing turnover. Taking all these factors into account, precisely what can you do to promote trust in your own working relationships? For some useful suggestions in this regard, see Table 11.1.

TABLE 11.1 Guidelines for Promoting Trust in Working Relationships

Our discussion has identified several general factors that promote trustworthiness. However, what exactly can you do to put these ideas into practice? Several particular recommendations may be offered.

Suggestion	Explanation
Always meet deadlines.	If you promise to get something done on time, it is essential to meet that deadline. People who are chronically late in meeting deadlines rapidly gain a reputation for being untrustworthy. And, when others believe that you will not meet vital deadlines, they are unlikely to trust you with important assignments.
Follow through as promised.	It's not only important to do things on time, but also to perform those tasks in the manner in which others expect them to be done. If you do not (e.g., if you provide only part of what others expect you to do), you may acquire a reputation for being untrustworthy.
Share your personal values and goals with others.	Trusting someone requires a keen understanding and appreciation of that person. Gaining this understanding requires spending time together discussing common interests, common objectives, and so on.
"Walk the talk" (i.e., do what you say).	We certainly wouldn't trust someone who says one thing (e.g., "don't cheat") but does another (e.g., claims personal expenses on his business travel reimbursement form), so be sure to "walk the talk." We also don't trust people who fail to follow fair procedures or who treat us in ways that are interpersonally unfair (e.g., not demonstrating the dignity and respect we deserve).
Give people a chance to express themselves.	When someone tells you something and you respond by having a warm and accepting conversation, you have revealed that you are benevolent, contributing to being considered as a confidant. Also, by inviting someone to express his or her ideas, you are likely to be seen as being procedurally fair (and, as a result, more trustworthy).
Make sure that people know about you.	We're unlikely to trust people with whom we've worked for some time but still don't know (you may wonder what they have to hide). Making an effort to ensure that people know who you are and what particular skills and abilities you bring to the table will make them feel comfortable with you.

Organizational Citizenship Behavior: Going Above and Beyond Formal Job Requirements

Imagine the following scene: It's coming up on 5:00 P.M. and you're wrapping up your work for the day. You're eagerly looking forward to getting home and relaxing. While this is going on, the scene is quite different at the next cubicle. One of your colleagues has been working feverishly to complete an important report, but appears to have hit a snag. She now has little hope of getting the report on the boss's desk before he leaves for the day—that is, without your help. Pitching in to help your colleague is something you don't have to do. After all, there's nothing in your formal job description that makes it necessary for you to do so. What's more, you're quite weary after your own long day's work. However, when you see the bind your colleague is in, you put aside your own feelings and offer to stay and help her out.

In this case, although you're probably not going to win any medals for your generosity, you are being helpful, and you have gone "above and beyond the call of duty." Actions such as these, which exceed the formal requirements of one's job, are known as **organizational citizenship behavior** (**OCB,** for short).[20] It is easy to imagine how such behaviors, although informal and sometimes minor in nature, may play an important role when it comes to the smooth functioning of organizations.

Forms of OCB

The example we just gave of volunteering to help one of your coworkers is just one of five different forms that OCB can take. For a summary of all five, including examples of each, see Table 11.2.

If you look at the examples in Table 11.2, it becomes apparent that organizational citizenship behavior can be directed both at an *individual* (in which case it is referred to as **OCB-I**) and at the *organization* itself (in which case it is referred to as **OCB-O**).[21] Some examples of OCB-I include the following:

- Doing a favor for someone
- Assisting a coworker with a personal problem
- Bringing in food to share with others
- Collecting money for flowers for sick coworkers or for funerals
- Sending birthday greetings to others in the office

organizational citizenship behavior (OCB)
An informal form of behavior in which people go beyond what is formally expected of them to contribute to the well-being of their organization and those in it.

OCB-I
Acts of organizational citizenship directed at other individuals in the workplace (i.e., helping coworkers in ways that go beyond what is expected).

OCB-O
Acts of organizational citizenship directed at the organization itself (i.e., helping the company in ways that go beyond what is expected).

TABLE 11.2 Organizational Citizenship Behavior: Specific Forms and Examples

Organizational citizenship behavior (OCB) can take many different forms, most of which fall into the five major categories shown here.

Form of OCB	Examples
Altruism	■ Helping a coworker with a project
	■ Switching vacation dates with another at his or her request
	■ Volunteering
Conscientiousness	■ Never missing a day of work
	■ Coming to work early if needed
	■ Not spending time on personal calls
Civic virtue	■ Attending voluntary meetings and functions
	■ Reading memos; keeping up with new information
Sportsmanship	■ Making do without complaint ("Grin and bear it!")
	■ Not finding fault with the organization
Courtesy	■ "Turning the other cheek" to avoid problems
	■ Not "blowing up" when provoked

Some examples of OCB-O include the following:

■ Speaking favorably about the organization to outsiders
■ Being receptive to new ideas
■ Being tolerant to temporary inconveniences without complaining
■ Offering ideas to improve the functioning of the organization
■ Expressing loyalty toward the organization

Why Does OCB Occur?

As you know, people sometimes are selfish and do not engage in OCB. What, then, lies behind the tendency to be a good organizational citizen? Although there are several factors involved, evidence strongly suggests that people's beliefs that they are being treated fairly by their organizations (especially their immediate supervisors) is a critical factor. Specifically, the more people believe they are treated fairly by their organizations, the more they trust its management, and the more willing they are to go the extra mile to help out when needed.[22] By contrast, people who feel that their organizations are taking advantage of them are untrusting and highly unlikely to engage in OCB.

OCB also occurs for other reasons. For example, OCB tends to occur when employees hold positive attitudes toward their organizations[23] and when they have good relationships with their supervisors.[24] It's interesting to note that not everyone is equally predisposed to engage in OCB. Personality characteristics also are linked to OCB. Specifically, individuals who are highly conscientious (see Chapter 4) and who are highly empathic (i.e., those who are inclined to take others' perspectives and to share their feelings and reactions) are inclined to engage in OCB.[25] This isn't too surprising, of course, since such individuals probably would be interested in "going the extra mile" to make others feel good.

Does OCB Really Matter?

OCB has several important effects on organizational functioning. Specifically, people's willingness to engage in various types of OCB is related to such work-related measures as job satisfaction and organizational commitment, which, as we described in Chapter 6, are related to organizational functioning in a number of complex ways.[26] In addition, being a good organizational citizen can have important effects on recruiting efforts. After all, the more positive statements current employees make about the companies where they are employed, the more favorably those organizations will be regarded, thereby enhancing their capacities to attract the best new employees.[27]

As we indicated, OCB is an unofficial aspect of people's jobs. It's considered *extra-role behavior* because it refers to things that people do that go beyond their formal job descriptions. However, because OCB can make such a big difference in job satisfaction and organizational commitment—not to mention just making life more pleasant for everyone— several companies do, in fact, take it into account as part of employees' formal performance appraisals.[28] This seems reasonable since even when OCB is *not* taken into account in a formal way, it still has great impact. For example, research has shown that OCB has a greater impact on employees' performance appraisal ratings than such "official" factors as the knowledge, skills, and abilities people need to do their jobs.[29] As such, it's not surprising that many managers go out of their way to gather information about OCB so that they can take it into account in their performance ratings (even though they may have to make written comments about it since there's no official place for OCB on the evaluation form).[30]

core task behavior (CTB)
Formal behaviors that traditionally are recognized as part of a particular job.

This raises an interesting question: If OCB *were* to be incorporated into employees' formal performance appraisals, how heavily weighted should it be relative to **core task behavior (CTB)**—that is, the formal behaviors that traditionally are recognized as part of a particular job? If it's considered important by managers, then they would want to weight it highly since these ratings would send an official message to employees about how well they are performing as organizational citizens.

Recently, researchers have shed light on this issue.[31] Participants in their study were employees from a wide range of industries who were asked to read several brief scenarios depicting situations in which employees were described as performing at various levels of CTB and OCB. For each of these they were shown a list of 11 possible ways in which OCB was rated relative to CTB. These ranged from 100 percent for CTB and 0 percent for OCB (the usual, official way, totally disregarding OCB) to 0 percent for CTB and 100 percent for OCB (the opposite, counting only OCB and disregarding CTB), with steps in between that varied in 10 percent intervals. For each of these divisions between CTB and OCB participants were asked to rate their perception of its fairness (the set of questions focused primarily on distributive justice; see Chapter 2).

Several interesting findings emerged. Overall, ratings that incorporated OCB were believed to be significantly more fair than ones that did not take OCB into account. Digging deeper into the results, the researchers found that participants considered some weightings of OCB to be fairer than others. Figure 11.5 shows the perceived fairness of each of these as they were judged separately by men and women in the study. Interestingly, men perceived the 30 percent weighting for OCB as being most fair whereas women preferred the 50 percent weighting. It is noteworthy that such high percentages were considered fair since, officially, OCB isn't taken into account at all.

Also interesting were differences in the ratings made by women and men. Women believed that it would be fair to give OCB more weight than did men. This is in keeping with the general tendency for women to be more interested than men in being kind and helpful and to believe that behaving this way (such as occurs in many forms of OCB) is appropriate.[32] (It is important to note that this is not simply a guess based on stereotypes, but a description based on thorough research by social scientists.) Reflecting this general tendency, women's ratings showed that being fair required giving OCB greater weight than did men.

Considering the actual importance of OCB, and that people believe it would be fair to make it a sizable portion of formal performance evaluations, it would appear to be worthwhile for managers to consider ways of encouraging people to engage in OCB. For some recommendations, see the OB in Practice section on page 386.

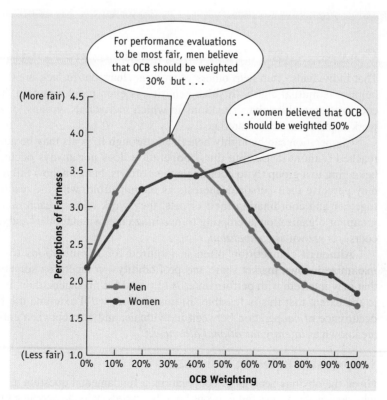

FIGURE 11.5

How Much Should OCB Contribute Toward Performance Evaluations?

Although OCB doesn't usually count toward employees' official performance evaluations, recent research suggests that people believe it should. In fact, men believe it would be fair for OCB to contribute 30 percent toward overall performance overall ratings; women believe it should be even higher, 50 percent.

Source: Adapted from Johnson et al., 2009; see Note 29.

OB in Practice

How to Promote OCB

Although many people view OCB as something that comes from within individuals—either they want to help or they do not—in fact, such behavior can be encouraged or discouraged by conditions existing within organizations. Here are some steps managers can take to increase OCB in their work groups.

1. *Be a model of helpful behavior.* Helping, it appears, is contagious. Once it begins, it tends to increase. Managers can get the ball rolling by being helpful to their subordinates and to their peers. In this way, they become models of helpful behavior and may encourage its occurrence.

2. *Demonstrate courtesy.* Courtesy, too, is contagious, so managers always should be sure to demonstrate it in their own behavior. Show respect for employees, treat them politely—and the result will be that these aspects of OCB also will become the norm.

3. *Make voluntary functions worth attending.* Why should employees attend voluntary meetings if these are dull and boring? Making meetings interesting and fun, on the other hand, may encourage employees to attend and to show the civic virtue aspect of OCB. For instance, if you are having a voluntary meeting in the morning, be sure to provide coffee and something to eat. There's nothing like food to draw a crowd!

4. *Don't complain!* If managers complain a lot, this sets the tone for similar behavior by employees—and OCB will go

right out the window. So even if conditions are not ideal, be a "good sport" and refrain from complaining. This, too, will increase OCB in your work group.

5. *Demonstrate conscientiousness.* If *you,* as manager, aren't willing to come in early, stay late, and go beyond the formal requirements of your position, you cannot expect your subordinates to do so. Thus, you should be sure to demonstrate these aspects of OCB clearly and openly yourself. Doing so will encourage your subordinates to do the same.

6. *Treat employees fairly.* Perhaps the single factor that exerts the strongest effects on OCB is perceived fairness: When employees perceive that they are being treated fairly, their willingness to engage in OCB increases. So it is *essential* to ensure that all actions and procedures in an organization lead to this conclusion (see Chapter 2). This may require considerable effort (e.g., to ensure that performance appraisals are conducted fairly), but it is well worthwhile in terms of the significant increases in OCB it will generate.

Although these suggestions may all seem like common sense, they certainly are *not* common practice. Often, managers do not set very good examples for their subordinates where OCB is concerned. They complain frequently, "pull rank" on subordinates, are discourteous, and take advantage of their positions such as by disappearing for two-hour lunches. Needless to say, such actions will discourage helpfulness by employees: Why should they go beyond the requirements of their jobs if their boss doesn't? The bottom line is clear: Promoting OCB begins by demonstrating OCB.

Cooperation: Providing Mutual Assistance

That individuals often help others at work is clear; but in fact, another pattern—one in which helping is mutual and both sides benefit—is even more common. This pattern is known as **cooperation** and involves situations in which individuals, groups, or even entire organizations work together to attain shared goals.

cooperation
A pattern of behavior in which assistance is mutual and two or more individuals, groups, or organizations work together toward shared goals for their mutual benefit.

Cooperation can be highly beneficial; through it, goals may be attained that never could be reached without it. Despite this, cooperation does *not* always occur. Frequently, individuals belonging to a group try to coordinate their efforts, but somehow fail to do so. Even worse, they may perceive their personal interests as incompatible, with the result that instead of working together and coordinating their efforts, they work *against* each other, with each individual, group, or organization attempting to maximize its own outcomes and defeat the others. This, of course, is known as *competition*.

Although competition often is required for organizations to succeed—each seeks to maximize its own market share and profitability—competition sometimes also occurs in ways that may interfere with performance. A key goal for managers, then, is to maximize cooperation to the extent that this is feasible. In this section, we'll examine the factors that influence the occurrence of cooperation between individuals, and also between entire organizations in what are known as *interorganizational alliances.*[33]

Cooperation Between Individuals

Given the obvious benefits of cooperation, a fundamental question arises: If it is so useful, then why does it sometimes fail to occur? In other words, why do people with similar goals sometimes keep from joining forces? Although there are many possibilities, the answer in some situations is that cooperation cannot occur because the goals sought by the individuals or groups involved are incompatible—that is, they cannot be shared. For example, two people going after the same job cannot both get it. Likewise, when two companies court the same merger candidate, only one can be victorious. This describes a type of behavior known as **competition**—the pattern of behavior in which each person, group, or organization seeks to maximize its own gains at the expense of others. (For a comparison between cooperation and competition, see Figure 11.6.) With this background, we now consider some of the factors associated with people's tendencies to cooperate with one another.

SOCIAL DILEMMAS: SITUATIONS IN WHICH COOPERATION COULD OCCUR, BUT OFTEN DOESN'T. Another way to think about situations in which cooperation potentially could develop but does not is to view them as ones involving what are known as **social dilemmas**—situations in which each person can increase his or her individual gains by acting in a purely selfish manner, but if others also act selfishly, the outcomes experienced by all are reduced.[34] As a result, the persons in such situations must deal with **mixed motives:** There are reasons to cooperate (avoid negative outcomes for all), but also reasons to *compete*—to do what is best for oneself, since if only one or a few persons engage in such behavior, they will benefit while the others will not.

A good example of such a situation may be seen in a professional basketball team. Each player has much to gain by cooperating with his team members because coordinating efforts with one another (in the form of "assists") increases the chances of defeating opponents. At the same time, each player also has much to gain from "grandstanding"—that is, improving their individual point totals by shooting instead of passing the ball to teammates. This may help them get higher salaries and bonuses. So again, there is a strong basis for cooperating and at the same time, a strong temptation for each player to maximize his individual points. It is with this in mind that we refer to basketball, or other team sports, as mixed motive situations.

THE RECIPROCITY PRINCIPLE. For a moment, think about the following well-known popular expressions.

> *An eye for an eye and a tooth for a tooth*
> *One hand washes the other*
> *You scratch my back and I'll scratch yours*

competition
A pattern of behavior in which each person, group, or organization seeks to maximize its own gains at the expense of others.

social dilemmas
Situations in which each person can increase his or her individual gains by acting in a purely selfish manner, but if others also act selfishly, the outcomes experienced by all are reduced.

mixed motives
Contexts in which people have reasons both to cooperate and to compete.

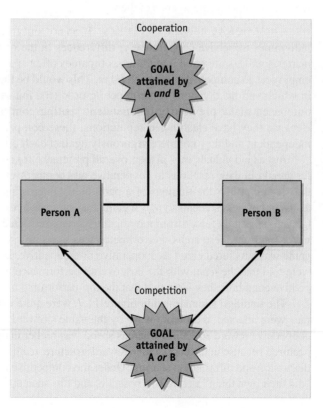

FIGURE 11.6

Cooperation Versus Competition: A Comparison

When cooperating with each other, people work together to attain the same goal, which they share. However, when competing against one another, each person works to attain the same goal to the exclusion of the other.

Besides the fact that they all refer to body parts, what else do they have in common? In one way or another, they all describe the fundamental human tendency to treat others as they have treated us. Social scientists refer to this as the principle of **reciprocity.** For example, if someone gives you a generous gift on your birthday, then you would feel obligated to reciprocate by giving that person an equally generous gift on his or her birthday.

reciprocity
The tendency to treat others as they have treated us.

To a great extent, the principle of reciprocity describes the way people behave when cooperating with others.[35] Because this is so, the key task in establishing cooperation in organizations is straightforward: getting it started. Once individuals or teams have begun to cooperate, the process may be largely self-sustaining. That is, one unit's cooperation encourages cooperation among the others. To encourage cooperation, therefore, managers should get the process under way by cooperating with other units and making it clear that they expect them to reciprocate.

PERSONAL ORIENTATION. As you know from experience, by nature, some people tend to be more cooperative than others. In contrast, others tend to be far more competitive—interested in doing better than others in one way or another. Not surprisingly, scientists have found that people can be classified reliably into four different categories in terms of their natural predispositions toward working with or against others.[36] These are as follows:

competitors
People whose primary motive is doing better than others, beating them in open competition.

individualists
People who care almost exclusively about maximizing their own gain and don't care whether others do better or worse than themselves.

cooperators
People who are concerned with maximizing joint outcomes, getting as much as possible for their team.

equalizers
People who are primarily interested in minimizing the differences between themselves and others.

- **Competitors:** People whose primary motive is doing better than others, beating them in open competition
- **Individualists:** People who care almost exclusively about maximizing their own gain, and don't care whether others do better or worse than they do
- **Cooperators:** People who are concerned with maximizing joint outcomes, getting as much as possible for their team
- **Equalizers:** People who are interested primarily in minimizing the differences between themselves and others

Because these differences exist and are the result of a lifetime's experience, they tend to be difficult to change. In view of this fact, it often is useful for managers to take the time to get to know their subordinates' personal orientations (e.g., by observing them carefully in past situations) so that they can match these to the kinds of tasks they ask them to perform. For example, competitors may be effective in negotiation situations whereas cooperators may be most effective in teamwork situations. In other words, managers should attempt to put these existing individual preferences to work rather than trying to change them.

ORGANIZATIONAL REWARD SYSTEMS. It is not only differences between people that lead individuals to behave cooperatively; differences in the nature of organizational reward systems matter, too. Despite good intentions, companies often create reward systems that encourage their employees to compete against each other. This would be the case, for example, in an organization in which various divisions sell competing products. For instance, Lennox International Inc. has purchased many previously independent heating contractors throughout the United States. Because they have established reputations, these companies continue to operate as if they are independent and they compete vigorously against each other for business.

Just as individuals vary in their overall preference for competition or cooperation, they also differ greatly in their reactions to cooperative and competitive reward structures. As an illustration of this, let's consider the findings of a particularly interesting study.[37] The researchers arranged for teams of business students to play a game that simulated complex military situations. Their task was to keep unfriendly forces from moving into certain restricted areas while allowing friendly forces to move freely in these areas. Performance was measured with respect to speed and accuracy. The game was structured either as cooperative or competitive. In the cooperative condition, participants were told that the *team* with the best overall performance would receive a cash award. In the competitive condition, they were told that the top-performing *individuals* would receive cash awards.

The findings, summarized in Figure 11.7, were quite interesting. In particular, speed and accuracy were affected in different ways by the game's reward structures. Accuracy was higher under a cooperative reward structure, whereas speed was higher under a competitive reward structure. This occurred because in the cooperative reward structure, teams worked together closely, taking time for discussion and information sharing. Under the competitive reward structure, in contrast, individuals "did their own thing" as much as possible, and this sped up the performance of the entire team.

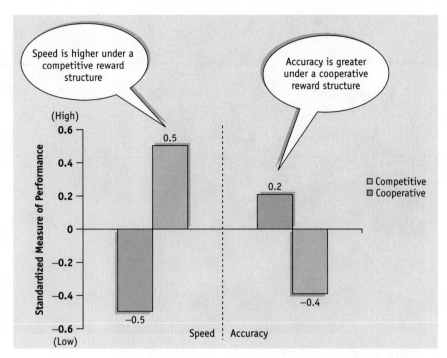

FIGURE 11.7

Effects of Competitive and Cooperative Reward Structures on Performance

Research has found that, speed is increased by a competitive reward structure, whereas accuracy is enhanced by a cooperative reward structure. This suggests that the choice between these two possible reward structures should take into account whether speed or accuracy is of primary importance.

Source: Based on data from Beersma et al., 2003; see Note 37.

Whatever the precise basis for these findings, they suggest that the task of choosing between these two different ways of structuring tasks is trickier than most people would guess. Managers wanting to do a good job in this respect should take into account whether speed or accuracy is more important. Although such decisions will be complex, given the strong effects of these factors on performance they are well worth considering carefully.

Cooperation Between Organizations: Interorganizational Alliances

In business, competition is the natural order of things; company competing against company is the standard state of affairs. This does not mean, however, that it must always be the case. Sometimes, in fact, companies find it beneficial to work together to maximize their joint profits—that is, to cooperate. This occurs in several different ways that we now discuss.

PARTNERING WITH SUPPLIERS. Years ago, companies used to think of suppliers (other companies from whom they purchase goods and services) as more or less interchangeable. They'd select the best one and ignore the others, and if the situation changed, they switched suppliers quickly. Today, however, companies are far more likely to work closely with their suppliers to ensure that they can provide high-quality products.

Consider Kontron, a German company that provides data to Microsoft about the effectiveness of its new operating systems. Rather than being forced to guess what Microsoft wants, Kontron officials work closely with Microsoft engineers to provide the kind of information that is most useful to them. Many auto companies also have developed close, cooperative relationships with their suppliers (e.g., various manufacturing companies) to ensure a constant flow of high-quality components required to stay competitive.

RESEARCH AND DEVELOPMENT (R&D) PARTNERSHIPS. In certain industries, the costs of research and development can present a staggering burden to individual companies, especially ones that are relatively small in size. Under these conditions, it often makes sense for two or more organizations to pool their resources and share in the potential rewards.[38]

This occurs in many different industries, but the biotech industry is the best single example. In this industry, hundreds of small start-up firms struggle to advance the drugs they are developing through the rigorous testing procedures required by the U.S. government. Because modern science is expensive, these small companies often form research and development partnerships. In these arrangements, each company often brings something unique to the table—special facilities, specific kinds of knowledge, useful ties with larger companies. The hope, of course, is that by

AP Photo/Mike Derer.

FIGURE 11.8

Wanted: R&D Partners for Developing Biopharmaceutical Medicine

Each year, the Johnson & Johnson (J&J) pharmaceuticals group enters into R&D partnerships with more than 50 companies. Despite its own state-of-the-art facilities and extensive experience in bringing products to market, the company considers these partnerships essential to harnessing the latest biotech knowledge required to develop new medical compounds. With this in mind, J&J actively seeks partnerships as part of its strategy for conducting research and developing new business.

cooperating in this manner, all participants in the partnership ultimately will benefit, accomplishing something together—bringing a drug to market—that they otherwise could not accomplish on their own. (For an example of one company that actively invites such relationships, see Figure 11.8.)

INTERORGANIZATIONAL ALLIANCES AND SOCIAL DILEMMAS. Recall our discussion of social dilemmas—situations in which there are strong reasons to cooperate with others *and* strong reasons to defect (to compete while one's opponent is still acting cooperatively). If you think about it for a moment, you will see that this basic model fits many instances of interorganizational cooperation. Yes, the participating companies have much to gain by working together; but at the same time the temptation to take advantage of the situation and seek selfish, individual gain can be strong.

Research has called attention to this possibility.[39] Specifically, it was noted that in a multiparty alliance (i.e., one in which many companies participate), noncooperative behavior by one is relatively easy to conceal—much easier than in a situation involving just two companies. Similarly, any harm produced by selfish actions on the part of one company is diffused across the many partners, leading to the belief that one's own gain will not bring much harm to any individual partner. Finally, since there are many partners in the alliance, it is difficult for each to influence the decisions of the others through its own actions, and therefore, more difficult to insist on cooperation by the threat of withdrawal. The result is that multiparty alliances between organizations are especially subject to the risks inherent in all social dilemma situations: One or more participants will stop cooperating while the others continue to cooperate, potentially reaping large individual gains (at least in the short term) at the expense of others.

How can these risks be reduced? Several procedures may be effective, including (a) taking steps to ensure that the payoffs for universal cooperation are greater than those for universal defection, (b) increasing the level of communication between members (c) focusing the alliance on long-term rather than short-term goals, and (d) establishing a high level of identification with the alliance. Through these and other steps—which are all designed to strengthen incentives for cooperation and weaken temptations to compete (i.e., defect from the alliance)—the likelihood that interorganizational alliances will succeed is increased. And as we noted earlier in this discussion, this is the essential nature of cooperation. When it works, it provides larger rewards for the persons or groups who participate in it than they could obtain alone.

Conflict: The Inevitable Result of Incompatible Interests

You may recall from Figure 11.1 that we conceived of cooperation as being at one end of a continuum and *conflict* as approaching the opposite end. In the context of organizations, **conflict** may be defined as a process in which one party perceives that another party has taken or will take actions that are incompatible with one's own interests. As you might imagine, conflict occurs quite commonly in organizations. In fact, it has been estimated that about 20 percent of managers' time is spent dealing with conflict and its effects.[40] Considering this, it makes sense to examine the types of conflict that exist, the causes and consequences of conflict, and ways to manage conflict that occurs in the workplace.

conflict
A process in which one party perceives that another party has taken or will take actions that are incompatible with one's own interests.

Types of Conflict

As you might imagine, all conflict is not alike. In fact, scientists have distinguished among three major types of conflict that commonly occur.[41] These are as follows:

- *Substantive conflict.* It is not unusual for people to have different viewpoints and opinions with respect to a decision they are making with others. This variety of conflict is known as **substantive conflict.** In most cases, substantive conflict can be very beneficial to helping groups make effective decisions because it forces the various sides to articulate their ideas clearly. (You may recall that we discussed group decision making in Chapter 10.)
- *Affective conflict.* When people experience clashes of personalities or interpersonal tension of some sort, the frustration and anger that result are signs of **affective conflict.** It is not unusual for affective conflict to result whenever people from different backgrounds are put together to perform tasks. Until they learn to accept one another, affective conflict is likely, resulting in disruption to group performance. After all, people who do not see the world in the same manner are likely to clash, and when they do, their joint performance tends to suffer.
- *Process conflict.* In many work groups, controversies arise about how they are going to operate—that is, how various duties and resources will be allocated and with whom various responsibilities will reside. This is known as **process conflict.** Generally, the more process conflict exists, the more group performance will suffer.[42]

substantive conflict
A form of conflict that occurs when people have different viewpoints and opinions with respect to a decision they are making with others.

affective conflict
A form of conflict resulting when people experience clashes of personality or interpersonal tension, resulting in frustration and anger.

process conflict
A form of conflict resulting from differences of opinion regarding how work groups are going to operate, such as how various duties and resources will be allocated and with whom various responsibilities will reside.

As this discussion suggests, conflict takes several different forms and it can have effects that are both positive and negative in nature. With this in mind, let's now turn to a discussion of the underlying causes of conflict.

Causes of Conflict

The conflicts we face in organizations may be viewed as stemming from a variety of causes, including both our interactions with other people and the organization itself. Here are just a few of the most important sources of organizational conflict.

GRUDGES. All too often, conflict is caused when people who have lost face in dealing with someone attempt to "get even" with that person by planning some form of revenge. Employees involved in this kind of activity are not only going out of their way to harm one of their coworkers, but by holding a grudge, they also are wasting energy that could be devoted to more productive organizational endeavors. (And as suggested by Figure 11.9, the same applies to families as well.)

MALEVOLENT ATTRIBUTIONS. Why did someone do something that hurt us? To the extent that we believe that the harm we suffer is due to an individual's malevolent motives (e.g., the desire to hurt us), conflict is inevitable. However, whenever we believe that we suffered harm because of factors outside someone's control (e.g., an accident), conflict is less likely to occur. (This is an example of the attribution process addressed in Chapter 3.) This causes problems in cases in

FIGURE 11.9

Holding Grudges: An All-Too-Common Source of Conflict

Hopefully, you cannot relate at all to the tale being told here. Despite their disruptive effect on both families and organizations, grudges are quite common, and the conflicts resulting from them are inevitable.

"*My family likes to set up our grudges at Thanksgiving, stew over them through December, then take our revenge at Christmas.*"

which we falsely attribute the harm we suffer to another's negative intent when, in reality, the cause was externally based.

DESTRUCTIVE CRITICISM. Communicating negative feedback in organizations is inevitable. All too often, however, this process arouses unnecessary conflict. The problem is that some people make the mistake of using **destructive criticism**—that is, negative feedback that angers the recipient rather than helps this person do a better job. The most effective managers attempt to avoid conflict by using constructive criticism instead. For some important comparisons between these two forms of criticism, see Table 11.3.

DISTRUST. The more strongly people suspect that some other individual or group is out to get them, the more likely they are to have a relationship with that person or group that is riddled with

destructive criticism
Negative feedback that angers the recipient instead of helping him or her do a better job.

TABLE 11.3 Constructive Versus Destructive Criticism: A Comparison

The factors listed here distinguish *constructive criticism* (negative feedback that may be accepted by the recipient because it improves his or her performance) from *destructive criticism* (negative feedback likely to be rejected by the recipient because it is not helpful and triggers anger and defensiveness).

Constructive Criticism	Destructive Criticism
Considerate—protects the recipient's self-esteem	Inconsiderate—harsh, sarcastic, biting
Does not contain threats	Contains threats
Timely—occurs as soon as possible after the substandard performance	Not timely—occurs after an inappropriate delay
Does not attribute poor performance to internal causes	Attributes poor performance to internal causes (e.g., lack of effort, motivation, ability)
Specific—focuses on aspects of performance that are inadequate	General—a sweeping condemnation of performance
Focuses on performance, not on the recipient	Focuses on the recipient—his or her personal characteristics—instead of performance
Motivated by desire to help the recipient improve	Motivated by anger, desire to assert dominance over the recipient, desire for revenge
Offers specific useful suggestions for improvement	Offers no useful suggestions for improvement

conflict. In general, companies that are considered great places in which to work are characterized by high levels of trust between people at all levels.

COMPETITION OVER SCARCE RESOURCES. Because organizations never have unlimited resources (such as space, money, equipment, or personnel), it is inevitable that conflicts will arise over the distribution of those resources. This occurs in large part because of a self-serving tendency in people's perceptions (see Chapter 3)—that is, people tend to overestimate their own contributions to their organizations. Believing that we made greater contributions leads us to feel more deserving of resources than others. Inevitably, conflict results when others do not see it this way.

Consequences of Conflict

As you know from experience, conflict can be a major source of stress (see Chapter 5). However, stress marks only the beginning of a chain of reactions that can have harmful effects.

The negative reactions, besides being quite stressful, also are problematic in that they trigger negative emotions that divert people's attention from the task at hand (see Chapter 5). For example, people who are focused on getting even with a coworker and making that person look bad in front of others are unlikely to be attending to the most important aspects of their jobs. In particular, communication between individuals or teams may be affected so adversely that any coordination of effort between them is compromised (see Chapter 9). Not surprisingly, such lowered coordination tends to lead to decrements in organizational functioning that can have costly effects on organizational performance. Unfortunately, this is all too common. For some helpful suggestions on how to manage organizational conflict in an effective manner, see Table 11.4.[43]

As we have been suggesting, organizational conflict—especially when it gets out of hand—is stressful, unpleasant, distracting, interferes with communication, and can damage long-term relationships and organizational performance.[44] That's quite a list—and it suggests that conflict is a serious issue, one that every manager and every organization should take seriously. However, it is very important to note that, despite what often is said about conflict, it also can have positive effects on behavior in organizations. For a discussion of this key point, see The Ethics Angle section on page 394.

Managing Conflict Through Negotiation

When conflicts arise between individuals, groups, or even entire organizations, the most common way to resolve them is to work together to find a solution that is acceptable to all parties involved. This process is known as **bargaining (negotiation)**. Formally, we may define

bargaining (negotiation)
The process by which two or more parties in dispute with one another exchange offers, counteroffers, and concessions in an attempt to find a mutually acceptable agreement.

TABLE 11.4 How to Manage Conflict Effectively

Although conflict is inevitable in the workplace, there are steps that managers can take to avoid the negative consequences that result.

■ Agree on a process for addressing conflict *before* conflict arises. This way, when a conflict needs to be addressed, everyone knows how it is going to be handled.

■ Make sure everyone knows his or her specific areas of responsibility, authority, and accountability. Clarifying these matters avoids potential conflicts when people either ignore their responsibilities or overstep their authority.

■ Recognize conflicts stemming from faulty organizational systems, such as a pay system that rewards one department at the expense of another. In such cases, work to change the system rather than training employees.

■ Acknowledge the emotional reactions to conflict. Conflicts will not go away until people's hurt feelings are addressed.

■ Consider how to avoid problems rather than assign blame for them. Questions such as "Why did you do that?" only make things worse. It is more helpful to ask, "How can we make things better?"

■ Conflicts will not go away by making believe they don't exist; doing so will only make them worse. Avoid the temptation not to speak to the other party but instead, discuss your misunderstandings thoroughly.

Source: Based on suggestions by Bragg, 1999; see Note 43.

The Ethics Angle

The Benefits of Promoting Conflict

Have you ever worked on a team project and found that you disagreed with someone on a key matter? If so, how did you react? Chances are good that you fell short of sabotaging that person's work or acting aggressively. In fact, the conflict may have even brought the two of you to the table to have a productive discussion about the matter at hand. As a result of this discussion, you may have even improved relations between the two of you and the quality of the decisions that resulted from your joint efforts. If you can relate to this scenario, then you already recognize an important fact about organizational conflict—that sometimes its effects can be positive. With this in mind, it may, in fact, be highly ethical to promote conflict—so long, of course, as you do it correctly.

When asked about his management philosophy, Starbucks CEO and founder Howard Schultz touted the importance of conflict and debate, saying, "If there's no tension, I don't think you get the best result."[45] As this successful business leader suggests, organizational conflict can be the source of several benefits. Among these are the following:

- Conflict may improve the quality of organizational decisions.
- Conflict may bring out into the open problems that have been previously ignored.
- Conflict may motivate people to appreciate each other's positions more fully.
- Conflict may encourage people to consider new ideas, thereby facilitating change.

In view of these positive effects of conflict, the key is to make sure that it's only these benefits that occur and none of the costs. It is with this in mind that managers work so diligently to manage organizational conflict, trying to promote a productive result while keeping away from destructive effects (e.g., sabotage). We consider several ways of doing this in this chapter. For now, though, our point is that you shouldn't have a knee-jerk reaction, grimacing when you hear the word "conflict," because it's not necessarily a bad thing. As you continue reading, make it a point to identify ways of promoting conflict so as to bring about positive results.

bargaining as the process in which two or more parties in dispute with each other exchange offers, counteroffers, and concessions in an attempt to find a mutually acceptable agreement.

Obviously, bargaining does not work when the parties rigidly adhere to their positions without budging—that is, when they "stick to their guns." For bargaining to be effective, the parties involved must be willing to adjust their stances on the issues at hand. And for the people involved to be willing to make such adjustments, they must believe that they have found an acceptable outcome—one that allows them to claim victory in the negotiation process. For bargaining to be most effective in reducing conflict, this must be the case for all sides. That is, outcomes must be found for all sides that allow them to believe that they have "won" the negotiation process—results known as **win-win solutions.** In win-win solutions, everybody benefits, precisely as the name implies.

win-win solutions
Resolutions to conflicts in which both parties get what they want.

TIPS FOR NEGOTIATING WIN-WIN SOLUTIONS. Several effective ways of finding such win-win solutions may be identified. (For practice in putting these techniques to use, see the Group Exercise on page 409.)

1. *Avoid making unreasonable offers.* Imagine that a friend of yours is selling a used car with an asking price of $10,000—the car's established "book value." If you were to attempt to "lowball" the seller by offering only $1,000, your bad-faith offer might end the negotiations right there. A serious buyer would offer a more reasonable price, say $9,000—one that would allow both the buyer and the seller to come out ahead in the deal. In short, extreme offers tend to anger one's opponents, sometimes ending the negotiation process on a sour note, allowing none of the parties to get what they want.
2. *Seek the common ground.* All too often people in conflict with others assume that their interests and those of the other party are completely incompatible. When this occurs, they tend to overlook the fact that they actually might have several areas of interest in common. When parties focus on the areas of agreement between them, it helps bring them together on the areas of disagreement. So, for example, in negotiating the deal for purchasing the used car, you might establish the fact that you agree to the selling price of $9,000. This verifies that the interests of the buyer and the seller are not completely incompatible, thereby encouraging them to find a solution to the area in which they disagree, such as a payment schedule. By contrast, if either party believed that they were completely far apart on all aspects of the deal, they would be less likely to negotiate a win-win solution.

3. *Broaden the scope of issues considered.* Sometimes, parties bargaining with one another have several issues on the table. When this occurs, it is often useful to consider the various issues together as a total package. Labor unions often do this in negotiating contracts with company management whenever they give in on one issue in exchange for getting what they want on another. So, for example, in return for not freezing wages, a company may agree to concede to the union's other desires, such as gaining representation on key corporate committees. In other words, compared to bargaining over single issues (e.g., the price of the used car), when the parties get to bargaining across a wide array of issues, it often is easier to find solutions that are acceptable to all sides.

4. *Uncover "the real" issues.* Frequently, people focus on the conflicts between them in only a single area although they may have multiple sources of conflict—some of which are hidden. Suppose, for example, that your friend is being extremely stubborn when it comes to negotiating the price of the used car. He's sticking firmly to his asking price, refusing to budge despite your reasonable offer, possibly adding to the conflict between you. However, it may be the case that there are other issues involved. For example, he may be trying to "get even" with you for harming him several years ago. In other words, what may appear to be a simple conflict between two people may actually have multiple sources, only some of which are apparent. Finding long-lasting solutions requires identifying *all* the important issues—even the hidden ones—and bringing them to the table.

As you might imagine, it is almost always far easier to say these things than to do them. Indeed, when people cannot come to agreement about something, they sometimes become irrational, not seeking common ground, and not taking the other's perspective needed to find a win-win solution, but thinking only of themselves. In such circumstances, third parties can be useful to break the deadlock. One widely used way of helping out in such situations is by turning to *alternative dispute resolution* techniques, a topic to which we now turn.

Alternative Dispute Resolution

When a customer canceled a $60,000 wedding reception, Anthony Capetola, a caterer from Long Island, New York, was able to fill that time slot with an event bringing in only half as much.[46] Although Capetola was harmed by the customer's actions, as you might imagine, that customer was unwilling to cough up the $30,000 lost revenue (after all, it was bad enough that the wedding was called off). Many business owners in Capetola's situation would seek restitution by taking the customer to court, resulting in a long delay and a huge bill for litigation, not to mention adverse publicity. Fortunately, in their contract, Capetola and the customer agreed to settle any future disagreements using what is known as **alternative dispute resolution (ADR).** This refers to a set of procedures in which disputing parties work together with a neutral party who helps them settle their disagreements out of court. There are two popular forms of ADR—*mediation* and *arbitration* (see Figure 11.10).

MEDIATION. The process of **mediation** involves having a neutral party (the *mediator*) work together with both sides to reach a settlement. Typically, mediators meet with each side together and separately, attempting to find a common ground that will satisfy everyone. Mediators do not consider who's wrong and who's right, but set the stage for finding a resolution. They have no formal power and cannot impose any agreements. Instead, they seek to clarify the issues involved and to promote communication between the parties.

Sometimes, mediators offer specific recommendations for compromise or **integrative agreements.** These are solutions that involve taking many different factors into account. In other cases, they merely guide the parties toward developing such solutions themselves. Their role is primarily that of a facilitator—that is, someone who helps the two sides toward agreements that each will find acceptable. Because it requires voluntary compliance by the disputing parties, mediation is sometimes ineffective. Indeed, when the mediation process fails, it simply underscores the depth of the differences between the two sides.

ARBITRATION. As you might imagine, for mediation to work the two sides must be willing to communicate with each other. When this doesn't happen, ADR may take the form of **arbitration.** This is a process in which a third party (the *arbitrator*) has the power to impose, or at least to

alternative dispute resolution (ADR)
A set of procedures, such as *mediation* and *arbitration*, in which disputing parties work together with a neutral party who helps them settle their disagreements out of court.

mediation
The process in which a neutral party (known as a *mediator*) works together with two or more parties sides to reach a settlement to their conflict.

integrative agreement
A type of solution to a conflict situation in which the parties consider joint benefits that go beyond a simple compromise.

arbitration
A process in which a third party (known as an *arbitrator*) has the power to impose, or at least to recommend, the terms of an agreement between two or more conflicting parties.

FIGURE 11.10

Mediation Versus Arbitration: A Summary

Mediation and *arbitration* are both popular techniques for resolving conflicts. Third parties known as *arbitrators* can impose terms of agreement between the disputants, whereas *mediators* can only recommend such terms.

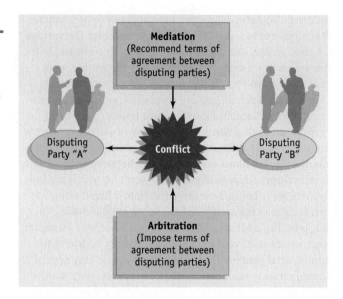

recommend, the terms of an agreement between two parties.[47] Four types of arbitration are most common. These are as follows:

binding arbitration
A form of arbitration in which the two sides agree in advance to accept the terms set by the arbitrator, whatever he or she may be.

voluntary arbitration
A form of arbitration in which the two sides retain the freedom to reject the agreement recommended by an arbitrator.

conventional arbitration
A form of arbitration in which an arbitrator can offer any package or terms he or she wishes.

final-offer arbitration
A form of arbitration in which the arbitrator chooses between final offers made by the disputing parties themselves.

- **Binding arbitration.** The two sides agree in advance to accept the terms set by the arbitrator, whatever they may be.
- **Voluntary arbitration.** The two sides retain the freedom to reject the recommended agreement.
- **Conventional arbitration.** The arbitrator can offer any package of terms he or she wishes.
- **Final-offer arbitration.** The arbitrator chooses between final offers made by the disputing parties themselves.

ADR TODAY. ADR is very popular these days because it helps disputants reach agreements rapidly (often in a matter of a day or two, compared to months or years for court trials) and inexpensively (usually for just a few thousand dollars split between the parties, compared to astronomical sums for attorney fees). Moreover, it keeps people who otherwise might end up in court out of the public eye, which could be damaging to their reputations—even the party in whose favor the judgment goes.

Because it is low key and nonconfrontational, mediation is particularly valuable in cases in which the parties have an ongoing relationship (business or personal) that they do not want to go sour.[48] After all, the mediation process brings the parties together, helping them see each other's side—something that is usually lost in the heat of a courtroom battle. Not surprisingly, the popularity of ADR has led to the development of several companies specializing in rendering mediation and arbitration services. The largest of these is the American Arbitration Association, a public-service, not-for-profit organization that has been providing ADR services to the public since 1926.

Although conflict can be both distressing and costly, we now turn to behaviors that are often even more damaging and sometimes downright frightening—various forms of *deviant organizational behavior.*

Deviant Organizational Behavior

deviant organizational behavior
Actions on the part of employees that intentionally violate the norms of organizations and/or the formal rules of society, resulting in negative consequences.

Tragically, you hear about it all too frequently these days: An angry, terminated employee enters his former place of business and with gun in hand exacts revenge on those who fired him. Assaults of this type were reported so often in the 1990s among disgruntled employees of the U.S. Postal Service that the phrase "going postal" became part of the vernacular. Clearly, acts of this type may be positioned at the far negative end of the continuum of positive to negative behaviors we have been discussing.

Although acts of physical violence have been the subject of news stories, they represent just one very extreme form of what is often described as **deviant organizational behavior**—actions on the part of employees that intentionally violate the norms of organizations and/or the formal rules of society.[49] At first glance, you might assume that all forms of deviant organizational behavior produce negative effects. In fact, though, the issue is more complex. As we'll now see, deviant organizational behaviors—ones that violate the norms of a particular company—can produce beneficial effects if, at the same time, they are consistent with other norms, those of the broader society or culture.

Constructive and Destructive Workplace Deviance

To illustrate the fact that departures from existing organizational norms can produce a variety of effects, consider the following example. Imagine that an employee of a large company is ordered to find a way to dump toxic waste into a nearby river without being observed. Further, assume that the river is one used by many people for fishing, boating, and swimming. The employee follows these orders and comes up with an effective means of dumping the chemicals. How would you describe this person's behavior? From the point of view of the organization, it is *constructive:* The employee has performed an assigned task well. From the point of view of society, though, it is highly *destructive:* Many innocent people, wildlife, and the ecosystem will be harmed by the toxic chemical waste.

Now, imagine that when ordered to dump the waste, the employee refuses and, in fact, reports the company's intentions to the Environmental Protection Agency and a local newspaper. In this case, the employee's behavior is destructive from the point of view of the organization (its reputation may be harmed and it may receive a large fine), but constructive from society's perspective.

Here's another example. Suppose that the norms in an organization support sexual discrimination: Women do not receive the raises or promotions they deserve simply because they are women. Under these conditions, managers who discriminate against women are behaving in a way consistent with organizational norms, but they also are violating societal norms against such discrimination—not to mention federal laws prohibiting such practices. If you think this sounds far-fetched, then consider the fact that Morgan Stanley, one of the largest brokerage companies in the United States, agreed in 2004 to pay $54 million to settle lawsuits by former employees who claimed they had been the victims of sexual discrimination and sexual harassment. In this case and many others that have been filed, the employees involved allegedly went along with their company's unstated norms of discrimination, thus violating fundamental societal norms and laws.

Basically, the framework we have been discussing suggests that it is useful to think about workplace deviance in terms of both constructive and destructive forms (see Figure 11.11). **Destructive organizational deviance** is a form of behavior that violates both organizational and societal norms (e.g., workplace aggression and violence). However, **constructive organizational deviance** refers to actions that deviate from organizational norms but are consistent with societal

destructive organizational deviance
A form of behavior that violates both organizational and societal norms.

constructive organizational deviance
Actions that deviate from organizational norms but are consistent with societal norms.

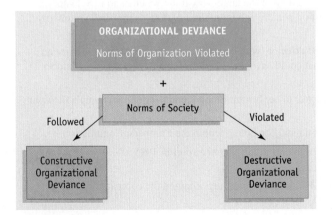

FIGURE 11.11

Constructive Versus Destructive Organizational Deviance

Behavior directed toward an organization is considered deviant if it violates its norms or rules, thereby bringing harm. If that behavior is consistent with the norms of society, it is considered *constructive organizational deviance.* However, if it is inconsistent with the norms of society and those of the organization, it is considered *destructive organizational deviance.*

norms (e.g., the act of going public with an organizational wrongdoing, or what is called *whistle-blowing*). We now take a closer look at each.

Whistle-Blowing: Constructive Workplace Deviance

whistle-blowing
The disclosure by employees of illegal, immoral, or illegitimate practices by employers to people or organizations able to take action.

Sometimes employees face situations in which they recognize that their organization is behaving improperly. To right the wrong, they reveal the improper or illegal practice to someone who may be able to correct it—an action known as **whistle-blowing.**[50] Formally, whistle-blowing is the disclosure by employees of illegal, immoral, or illegitimate practices by employers to people or organizations able to take action; these may be either internal to the organization, or when that doesn't work, external (e.g., to the press).

Is whistle-blowing a constructive action? Although some people in the organization might not think so, from the point of view of society, it usually is. In many instances, the actions of whistle-blowers can protect the health, safety, or security of the general public. For example, an employee of a large bank who reports risky or illegal practices to an appropriate regulatory agency may be protecting thousands of depositors from considerable delay in recovering their savings. Similarly, an individual who blows the whistle on illegal dumping of toxic chemicals by his or her company may save many people from serious illness. For a summary of some actual cases of whistle-blowing, see Table 11.5.[51]

Key questions about whistle-blowing include "Why do people do it?" and "What happens as a result—what are the effects on both employees and their organizations?" Unfortunately, there is no clear-cut answer to the first question. Individual employees appear to engage in whistle-blowing for a variety of reasons, ranging from a desire to "get even" with a company they feel has treated them unfairly, through a genuine desire to stop illegal and harmful actions. A survey of Australian employees, though, suggests that uneasiness about being party to unlawful and dangerous or unsafe action is often a key motivator.[52]

TABLE 11.5 Whistle-Blowing: Some Examples

As these examples illustrate, employees blow the whistle on many different types of organizations accused of committing a wide range of questionable activities.

Whistle-Blower	Incident
Harry Markopolos	In 2009, after investigating the financial affairs of Bernard Madoff for almost 8 years, he testified to authorities, providing details of Mr. Madoff's Ponzi scheme, and the Security and Exchange Commission's unresponsiveness to his many earlier efforts to convince them of the problem.
Bradley Birkenfeld	In 2007, this banker went to authorities about one of the largest tax fraud schemes in U.S. history, resulting in UBS bank paying a $780 million penalty and more than 14,000 "taxpayers" voluntarily disclosing their illegal offshore accounts.
Coleen Rowley	This special agent wrote a letter to the FBI director (with copies to two key members of Congress) about the bureau's failure to take action that could have prevented the terrorist attacks of September 11, 2001.
Sherron Watkins	In 2001, she notified the press about her letter to her boss at Enron identifying the company's fictitious accounting practices.
Paul van Buitenen	In 1999, he went public with claims of fraud and corruption within the European Commission.
An unnamed U.S. Customs inspector	This person alerted Congress of security problems at the Miami airport in 1995 after management took no action.
Tonya Atchinson	This former internal auditor at Columbia-HCA Healthcare Corp. charged the company with illegal Medicare billing.
Daniel Shannon	An in-house attorney for Intelligent Electronics protested the company's alleged misuse of marketing funds from computer manufacturers.
Robert Young	This agent for Prudential Insurance Co. in New Jersey accused company agents of encouraging customers to needlessly sell some policies and buy more expensive ones, boosting their commissions.
Bill Bush	This manager at the National Aeronautics and Space Administration (NASA) went public with the administration's policy of discouraging the promotion of employees older than 54 years of age.

Sources: See Note 51.

As you might imagine, blowing the whistle on one's employer is likely to be a very costly act for employees, as they often find themselves facing a long, uphill battle attempting to prove the wrongdoing. They also frequently face ostracism and job loss in response to their disloyalty. For example, five agents from State Farm Insurance were fired after they accused the company of various consumer abuses.[53] Jennifer P. Day was fired from her job as a Boston schoolteacher after she reported that the principal of her school gave answers to fourth-grade students taking a standardized statewide exam.[54] (For an example of an even more serious penalty, see Figure 11.12.[55])

It's not unusual for whistle-blowers to become targets of retaliation by the organizations whose wrongdoings they have reported. Several whistle-blowers have reported fearing for their lives, and a good many get fired for their actions. This, of course, is a major reason why many people are highly reluctant to engage in this action.[56] Although various laws, such as the Whistleblower Protection Act in the United States, prevent employers from firing people directly because they blew the whistle, organizations frequently find alternative official grounds for dismissing "troublemakers."[57] It is not surprising, therefore, that six senior employees of the company that runs the 900-mile Trans-Alaskan pipeline chose to remain anonymous when voicing their complaints about safety violations to BP Amoco.[58]

Despite the risks involved, of course, many individuals do decide to blow the whistle on their companies, and although they often are discarded by their organizations, they sometimes

rcapphotos/Newscom.

Charles Trainer Jr./Miami Herald/MCT/Newscom.

FIGURE 11.12

Is This Whistle-Blower Doing Time for His Good Deed?

Bradley Birkenfeld, former UBS banker, single-handedly helped the U.S. Justice Department bring an end to the practice of using Swiss banks as tax shelters for wealthy Americans. The information he provided triggered a massive investigation that led to a $780 million fine for UBS. Shortly thereafter, Mr. Birkenfeld, who admits he's "no angel," was sentenced to 40 months in a federal penitentiary for his own tax evasion activities. Many have suggested that the assistance he gave federal authorities in the UBS case should have earned him immunity for his misdeeds, which were considerably more minor by comparison.

become true heroes and heroines to their societies. Illustrating this, Bradley Birkenfeld, who blew the whistle on UBS (see Figure 11.12) was named by the publication, *Tax Notes* as its inaugural "Person of the Year" and the *NY Daily News* has suggested that he be given a "statue on Wall Street."

Cyberloafing: Deviant Behavior Goes High-Tech

The advent of Internet technology has brought with it increased efficiency in accessing information and communicating with others—both of which are vital benefits. However, it also has created new ways for employees to loaf, or "goof off." Although workers have devised ways to slack off ever since people have been employed, access to the Internet and e-mail has provided tempting and more insidious opportunities than ever before. Employees who use their company's computers, such as its e-mail and/or Internet facilities, for personal use are considered to be engaged in **cyberloafing.**[59] (See Figure 11.13.)

In the United States, approximately 40 million people have Internet and/or e-mail access at work, use it regularly, and are referred to as *online workers*. However, further statistics reveal that much of what online workers are doing while online is not work-related. For example:

- According to an MSNBC survey, one-fifth of all people who have visited pornographic Web sites have done so while on the job.
- One-third of workers surveyed by the Society of Financial Service Professionals reported playing computer games while at work.
- Eighty-three percent of companies surveyed by the Privacy Foundation indicated that their employees were using e-mail for personal purposes.

cyberloafing
The practice of using a company's e-mail and/or Internet facilities for personal use.

FIGURE 11.13

Cyberloafing: Inaction in Action

Does this scene—playing games on a computer while at work—look familiar to you? If so, we're not surprised. Far too many people engage in *cyberloafing*, the practice of using the company's computer system for personal purposes. This form of workplace deviance is both widespread and extremely costly to organizations.

Rod Morata/Photonica/Getty.

These and other forms of cyberloafing are costing U.S. organizations, both private and public, untold millions of dollars a year. In fact, just one $40,000/year employee can cost his or her employer as much as $5,000 annually by playing around on the Internet for one hour a day.

Executives are implicitly aware of this problem, and more than three-quarters believe that some types of online monitoring and filtering efforts are needed. Recent polls found, however, that only about a third of online workers are monitored, and most of this monitoring is highly sporadic. In fact, only 38 percent of companies acknowledge monitoring the online work of employees who already have been suspected of cyberloafing. Bottom line: Cyberloafing is a costly problem about which little is being done.

Although various software products make it possible to monitor employees and such products are growing in popularity, this technology is not a panacea. Some problems are technical in nature, but the most notable ones are social-psychological. Specifically, employees believe that being monitored constitutes an invasion of their privacy and reject the practice as being unfair.

Decisions in federal courts are in agreement. A few years ago, for example, the 27-judge Judicial Conference of the United States repealed a proposed monitoring policy for their own employees, which they feared would violate their constitutional rights to privacy. Speaking for the group, federal appeals court judge Alex Kozinski objected to the policy's assertion that "court employees should have no expectation of privacy at any time while at work." The resulting policy permitted virtually no monitoring of employees' e-mail and only highly limited monitoring of their Internet use.

Where we stand now is quite interesting: Although cyberloafing is admittedly a widespread and costly problem, efforts aimed at addressing it that involve employee monitoring are not well accepted (or even legally permissible, in some cases). Clearly, the key is to find additional ways of discouraging people from cyberloafing. Admittedly, given the ancient problem of "goofing off" coupled with the vast opportunities to goof off provided by Internet access, cyberloafing looks like it's going to be a problem that stays around for years to come. Fortunately, organizational behavior specialists are now beginning to study this phenomenon, which hopefully will provide useful suggestions in the years to come.[60]

Workplace Aggression and Violence

Approximately 1.5 million Americans annually become victims of violence while on the job, resulting in direct and indirect costs to their companies of more than $4.2 billion.[61] Despite all the publicity given to such incidents, though, violence is actually a rare occurrence in workplaces. Only about 800 people are murdered at work each year in the United States, and most of these crimes are committed by outsiders, such as customers or criminals during robberies, not by fellow employees.[62]

Although violence is relatively rare, other forms of **workplace aggression**—any efforts by individuals to harm others with whom they work or have worked in the past, or their organizations—are much more common.[63] What forms does workplace aggression take? Why does it occur? And who are the persons most likely to engage in it? These are the questions to which we now turn.

workplace aggression
Acts of verbal and physical abuse toward others in organizations, ranging from mild to severe.

WORKPLACE AGGRESSION: ITS MANY FORMS. When it comes to aggression, most people would like to maximize the harm they do their intended victims while simultaneously minimizing the likelihood of retaliation. In view of this, it's not surprising that many instances of workplace aggression are largely covert (hidden, disguised) in nature. This type of aggression is especially likely in workplaces because aggressors in such settings expect to interact with their intended victims frequently in the future. Using covert forms of aggression reduces the likelihood that the victims will retaliate against them.

Of course, not all forms of workplace aggression are covert. People do indeed sometimes assault others directly, either with words or in physical assaults. Overall, it appears that most aggression occurring in workplaces can be described as falling into three major categories.

■ **Incivility:** Behaviors demonstrating a lack of regard for others, denying them the respect they are due. Often such acts are verbal or symbolic in nature (e.g., belittling others' opinions, talking behind their backs, spreading malicious rumors about them).

incivility
Demonstrating a lack of regard for others, denying them the respect they are due.

obstructionism
Attempts to impede
another's job performance.

overt aggression
Acts that are outwardly
intended to harm other
people or organizations.

■ **Obstructionism:** Behaviors designed to obstruct or impede the target's performance (e.g., failure to return phone calls or respond to memos, failure to transmit needed information, interfering with activities important to the target).

■ **Overt aggression:** Behaviors that have typically been included under the heading "workplace violence" (e.g., physical assault, destruction of property, threats of physical violence, direct verbal abuse).

How common are these forms of behavior? More common than you might guess. In fact, a large proportion of employees report that they either have been on the receiving end of workplace aggression or that they have behaved aggressively toward others at some time during their careers. So, although overt violence involving physical assaults is relatively rare, other forms of workplace aggression are quite common. In fact, in some workplaces, they are everyday occurrences.

WORKPLACE AGGRESSION: ITS CAUSES. What are the causes of workplace aggression? As is true of aggression in any context, many factors play a role. However, one that has emerged repeatedly in research on this topic is *perceived unfairness*.[64] When individuals feel that they have been treated unfairly by others in their organization—or by their organization itself—they experience intense feelings of anger and resentment, and often seek to "even the score" by harming the people they hold responsible in some manner (see Chapter 2).

In addition, the likelihood that a specific person will engage in workplace aggression is influenced by the overall level of aggression in his or her work group or organization.[65] In other words, to the extent that individuals work in environments in which aggression is common, they, too, are likely to engage in such behavior. Moreover, this seems to be true for aggression outside as well as inside organizations. For instance, one study found that the greater the incidence of violence in communities surrounding U.S. Post Offices, the higher were the rates of aggression within these branch offices.[66] It was as if acceptance of violence in the surrounding communities paved the way for similar behavior inside this large organization.

Additional factors that play a role in workplace aggression involve changes that have occurred recently in many workplaces: downsizing, layoffs, and increased use of part-time employees, to name a few. In fact, the greater the extent to which such changes have occurred, the greater is the level of stress and uncertainty experienced by employees. This, in turn, promotes workplace aggression. Since such changes have been widespread in recent years, it is quite likely that the incidence of workplace aggression is increasing as well. In sum, workplace aggression, like aggression in other contexts, derives from many different factors rather than a single dominant cause.

WHO ENGAGES IN WORKPLACE AGGRESSION? What kind of person is most likely to engage in workplace aggression? Existing evidence concerning this issue paints a fairly clear picture of the characteristics that seem to equip individuals with "short fuses":[67]

■ *High trait anger:* The tendency to respond to situations in a predominantly angry manner
■ *Positive attitude toward revenge:* The belief that it is justifiable to get back at others who have caused one harm
■ *Past experience with aggression:* A history that involves exposure to aggressive behavior
■ *Overt expressions of anger:* The tendency to express anger rather than to suppress it

Can we use these findings to create a "profile" of individuals who are likely to harm others in their organization? Findings of a *USA Today* study indicate that at least in the case of the most violent offenders, perhaps we can.[68] This study examined a total of 224 fatal incidents spanning 28 years (1975–2003) to gain insight into the motives and traits of employees who kill. Results suggested that the desire for revenge was important for many of these persons, but that others—persons high in trait anger—were started down the path toward violence by an initially minor on-the-job argument or disagreement.

WHAT JOB CHARACTERISTICS PUT PEOPLE AT RISK FOR VIOLENCE OR AGGRESSION? In addition to identifying individuals whose personal characteristics predispose them to behave aggressively, scientists also have considered the possibility that aggressive behavior is triggered by the nature of the work people perform. The possibility that people doing certain kinds of jobs are more likely to become victims of aggression than those doing other kinds of jobs is important to know in advance so that appropriate precautions can be taken. With this in mind, scientists conducted a study in which they assessed the relationship between two variables in a broad sample of workers—characteristics of the work they performed (i.e., the extent to which their jobs put them in a position to do certain things, such as caring for other people, handling valuable goods, etc.) and the extent to which they experienced various forms of violence or aggression at work.[69] Their findings were quite interesting. Specifically, it was found that people are most likely to experience violence on the job to the extent that their jobs require them (a) to exercise control over others (e.g., high-level managers), (b) to handle weapons (e.g., police officers), or (c) to take care of individuals who are on medication (e.g., nurses). Figure 11.14 identifies the seven job characteristics that are most strongly associated with experiencing violence on the job.

MANAGING WORKPLACE AGGRESSION. Although it often is very difficult for individual employees to deal with aggression, organizations can take steps to reduce it. Here are a few that may prove helpful.

- *Establish clear norms against abusive treatment of employees—and clear procedures for assuring that they are followed.* If it is made clear in an organization from the top down that abusiveness toward employees will not be tolerated, and employees are provided with procedures for reporting such treatment, even highly aggressive managers will be likely to get the message. After all, assuming they want to protect their own careers, they will be inclined to reduce their abusiveness, if only to avoid the negative consequences it may bring.
- *Train managers in interpersonal skills.* Some abusive supervisors simply don't know how else to communicate with their subordinates. For them, destructive criticism

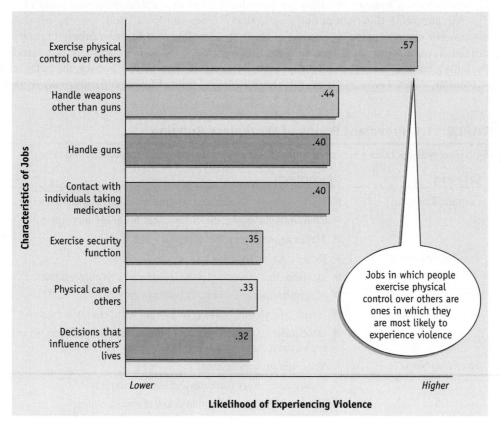

FIGURE 11.14

Job Characteristics That Put People at Risk for Violence

The seven job characteristics listed here were found to be related most strongly to experiencing violence on the job. Insofar as these are characteristic of the work performed by police officers and nurses, it is not surprising that individuals performing these jobs experience the highest occurrences of violence.

Source: Based on data reported by LeBlanc & Kelloway, 2002; see Note 69.

is the only style they know. Training programs designed to equip such managers with better communication skills and greater sensitivity to others can help reduce such problems.

- *Conduct periodic assessments of employee satisfaction and commitment.* If such assessments are conducted in a confidential manner that protects the identities of individual employees, managers who are acting in a hostile, abusive manner may be identified before their behavior becomes worse. Then, these individuals can be provided with appropriate training or counseling, and if that does not succeed, disciplinary procedures designed to change their behavior can be initiated (see Chapter 3).

Although none of these procedures is perfect, together, they can help get the message to abusive managers that their behavior is inappropriate and will not be tolerated. And this, in turn, will this create a more positive work environment. As such, it is well worth following these suggestions.

Abusive Supervision: Workplace Bullying

abusive supervision
A pattern of supervision in which a boss engages in sustained displays of hostile verbal and nonverbal behaviors.

workplace bullying
The repeated mistreatment of an individual at work in a manner that endangers his or her physical or mental health.

In recent years, OB scientists and practitioners have become interested in studying **abusive supervision**—a pattern of supervision characterized by sustained displays of hostile verbal and physical behaviors. A particularly widespread form of abusive supervision is known as **workplace bullying.**[70] This refers to the repeated mistreatment of individuals at work in a manner that endangers their physical or mental well-being.[71] Workplace bullying occurs by virtue of things people do intentionally to bring harm (e.g., chastising another) as well as things they don't do (e.g., withholding valuable information). Unlike harassment based on race or gender, bullying is not strictly illegal (unless, of course, it results in harm), and it is quite widespread.

According to a recent survey, 1 in 6 workers in the United States has been the victim of bullying in the past year.[72] Typically, bullies tend to be bosses (81 percent) who are abusing their power. Interestingly, bullies are equally likely to be women or men, but the vast majority of the targets of bullying tend to be women (especially when the bullies are themselves women).[73] For a summary of some of the most prevalent forms of workplace bullying, see Table 11.6.

An interesting thing about bullying is that it tends to repeat itself, thereby escalating its effects. For example, a bully's target is likely to complain to a higher-ranking organizational official. Typically, most higher-level managers will take some form of action (e.g., admonishing the bully), but will leave the bully in place to strike again. This time, however, the bully is likely to retaliate with vengeance. Often, this results in high levels of fear that paralyze the workplace,

TABLE 11.6 Prevalent Forms of Workplace Bullying

Workplace bullying takes a variety of forms. Some of the most prevalent are summarized here.

Category	Description
Constant Critic	■ Uses insulting and belittling comments, engages in name-calling ■ Constantly harangues the victim about his or her incompetence ■ Makes aggressive eye contact
Two-Headed Snake	■ Denies victims the resources needed to work ■ Demands that coworkers provide damning evidence against the victim ■ Assigns meaningless work as punishment
Vindictive Gatekeeper	■ Isolates the victim, ignoring him or her with "the silent treatment" ■ Deliberately cuts the target out of the communication loop but expects the victim to have the missing information
Screaming Mimi	■ Yells, screams, and curses ■ Makes loud, angry outbursts and throws tantrums ■ Intimidates by slamming things and throwing objects

Source: Based on information in Namie & Namie, 2000; see Note 73.

causing people to seek new jobs and exposing employers to litigation. Part of the difficulty in dealing with this problem is that bullies often are so highly effective that they bring other employees into their webs, getting them either to join in on the abuse or to agree to keep silent about it. Soon, the inappropriate behavior of a lone individual becomes a serious problem for the entire organization.

Today's workplace bully is not simply a grown-up version of the schoolyard bully who threatened to beat you up in second grade. Rather, workplace bullies are best understood from the same perspective as those who perpetrate domestic violence—they are individuals whose desires to control others are so extreme that they are in need of psychological counseling. As you might imagine, the workplace bully, once rooted out, should be dealt with in a swift and effective manner. This might result in a leave of absence during which professional help is provided—or, in many cases, termination. As you might imagine, of course, this is far easier said than done. After all, few among us would be willing to admit that we have a bully working in our midst, causing us to take only mild action, which, as we noted, can only make things worse. In many cases, the best offense is likely to be "a good defense"—that is, to be on the lookout for bullies and to step in before they can get a foothold into the organization.

Although bullies are not commonplace in organizations, almost anyone can engage in bullying if prompted by adverse situations. For example, frequent mergers and acquisitions make working conditions insecure for lots of people, causing almost anyone to behave aggressively from time to time. This makes it more important than ever for managers to identify and respond to bullies (as they would respond to any employees who engage in aggressive behavior).

Employee Theft

Retail stores are very concerned with problems of shoplifting, as you know. What you might not know, however, is that companies lose more money and goods from their own employees than from customers. In 2009, in fact, they lost almost seven times more (about $969.14 per employee compared to $135.81 per shoplifter).[74] Although estimates of costs of employee theft are quite varied, it is clear that the figures are staggering, amounting to many billions of dollars per year.[75] Worse yet, theft by employees has been rising steadily in recent years in response to the weak economy (see Figure 11.15). As one expert it, "People not getting raises are starting to take them."[76]

To understand these statistics fully, it is important to recognize an important fact: Almost everyone takes home some company property—a pencil, a note pad, some paper—for personal

Michael Newman/PhotoEdits, Inc.

FIGURE 11.15

Employee Theft: Widespread and on the Rise

One of the largest sources of economic loss for businesses, particularly retail stores, is employee theft. During weak economic conditions, many employees find illegal ways to supplement their incomes at the expense of their employers. This often takes the form of pilfering office supplies, as this employee is doing.

use, but in general, they don't consider this to be theft. Many consider this to be an accepted benefit of their jobs. Whether or not this is justified, taking company property for nonbusiness uses does indeed constitute **employee theft** in the legal sense of the term. Although taking home a few pens or pencils may seem innocent enough, *petty theft* or *pilferage,* as it is known, is widespread. It becomes a problem since so many people do it, and because they don't think it's wrong, they're disinclined to stop. However, the facts are clear: It costs companies more money when a lot of people steal small things than when just a few people steal large things (e.g., the embezzlers who capture headlines with their clever and bold antics).[77] To understand these dynamics, let's turn to a critical question: Why do employees steal?

WHY DO EMPLOYEES STEAL? Some employees steal because they are troubled in some way (e.g., they are in serious debt or have a narcotics or gambling habit). But this appears to be the minority. Instead, many people engage in employee theft for a more innocuous reason—*they see their coworkers doing it.*

To the extent that everyone around you is taking home tools, office supplies, and even petty cash, it quickly seems appropriate for you to do it, too. (This is a good example of the influence of *norms,* which we discussed in Chapter 8.) Although this doesn't make it right, of course, and it clearly costs the company money, people are quick to rationalize that petty theft is "no big deal" and not worth worrying about. After all, we convince ourselves, "If everyone's doing it, it must be okay." Similarly, many employees engage in theft because in some companies, *not* stealing goes against the informal norms of the work group.[78] Unspoken rules go a long way toward determining how people behave on the job, and in some companies, an employee has to steal to feel accepted and to belong. In some retail stores, for example, so many clerks steal goods that those who don't go along are socially ostracized by their workmates.

Finally, employees frequently engage in theft because they want to "even the score" with employers who they believe have mistreated them. In fact, people who feel underpaid frequently steal from their employers because in so doing they are righting a wrong by taking what they believe they should have had all along. (This is in keeping with equity theory, described in Chapter 7.)

REDUCING EMPLOYEE THEFT. Although we now see security cameras just about everywhere, employees continue to steal from their employers, suggesting that surveillance is not an entirely effective deterrent.[79] Fortunately, there are several people-based practices that can be followed to help lessen the problem. Although they won't be able to stop theft by employees completely, they can make a difference.

- *Involve employees in the creation of a theft policy.* It is not always clear what constitutes theft. Does your company prohibit personal phone calls or using the copy machine for personal purposes? If so, violating these policies constitutes theft of company resources, although chances are good that few will think of them as such. The trick is to develop very clear policies about employee theft and to involve employees in the process of doing so. The more involved they are, the more they will "buy into" the policies and follow them.

- *Communicate the costs of stealing.* Many employees would be truly shocked to learn how much their companies are losing each year through theft; they don't realize how quickly pencils, pads, papers, and other items add up—especially when everyone takes them. To the extent that this information is shared with other employees, along with a clear indication of how it costs them (e.g. through smaller raises and bonuses), many will think twice before they take company property for personal use.

- *Treat people fairly.* Many employees who steal from their employers do so because they are trying to strike back at their companies, which they believe have treated them unfairly. So, treating people fairly—and making sure they feel that they are being treated this way—can go a long way toward reducing such resentment and employee theft. (For suggestions as to how to behave fairly, see Chapter 2.)

- *Be a good role model.* One of the most effective things managers can do to discourage theft is to not engage in theft themselves. After all, to the extent that employees see their managers making personal phone calls, padding their expense accounts, or taking home office supplies, they are left with the message that doing these kinds of things is perfectly acceptable. When it comes to discouraging employee theft, "walking the talk" is very important.

Again, none of these steps by themselves will be completely effective, but together they can make a considerable difference,. And because even slight reductions in the rate of employee theft can go right to the bottom line and significantly increase an organization's profitability, these suggestions deserve to be taken seriously.

Summary and Review of Learning Objectives

1. **Describe three types of psychological contracts and the two basic kinds of trust that play a role in work relationships.**
   One type of psychological contract is the *transactional contract*. It is characteristic of relationships that have an exclusively economic focus, last for a brief period of time, are unchanging in nature, and have a narrow, well-defined scope. Another kind is the *relational contract*. It applies to relationships that are longer-term in scope and go beyond basic economic issues such as pay for performance. A third type is the *balanced contract;* this involves elements of both transactional and relational contracts. With respect to trust, one type is known as *calculus-based trust*. It is a form of trust based on deterrence, whenever people believe that another will behave as promised out of fear of getting punished for doing otherwise. A second type is *identification-based trust*. It is based on understanding another person plus the acceptance of this person's wants and desires.

2. **Describe organizational citizenship behavior and ways in which it may be encouraged.**
   Organizational citizenship behavior consists of acts that go above and beyond one's formal job requirements in helping one's organization or fellow employees. It is influenced by many factors, including employees' beliefs about whether they are being treated fairly, their relationships with their supervisors, their attitudes toward their company, and several personal characteristics (e.g., conscientiousness).

3. **Identify ways in which cooperation can be promoted in the workplace.**
   Although by nature some people are more cooperative than others, interpersonal cooperation may be promoted by following the reciprocity principle and by adopting reward systems that encourage cooperation with others.

4. **Describe the causes and effects of conflict in organizations along with techniques that can be used to manage conflict in organizations.**
   Conflict is caused by a variety of factors, including grudges, malevolent attributions, destructive criticism, distrust, and competition over scarce resources. Conflict can be not only a source of negative emotions, but it also can lead to a lack of coordination, which can make performance suffer in organizations. But conflict also can have beneficial effects. These include bringing out into the open problems that have been previously ignored, motivating people to appreciate one another's positions more fully, and encouraging people to consider new ideas. Bargaining is the single most effective technique for resolving conflicts. Many factors influence the course and outcomes of bargaining, including specific tactics used by bargainers (e.g., the "big lie" technique), their overall approach to the situation (win-win versus win-lose), cognitive factors such as faulty beliefs and perceptions on the part of negotiators (e.g., the belief that keeping deadlines secret is best), and the motives and emotions of the negotiators. *Alternative dispute resolution* is another approach to resolving conflicts. It involves *mediation* (in which a neutral third party works with the conflicting parties to find a mutually satisfying solution to the conflict) and *arbitration* (in which a neutral third party proposes solutions for conflicting parties).

5. **Explain why deviant organizational behavior can produce positive as well as negative effects.**
   Deviant organizational behavior (sometimes termed *workplace deviance*) involves actions on the part of employees that intentionally violate the norms of organizations and/or the rules of society. Depending on whether such actions violate one or both of these sets of norms, they can result in beneficial or harmful effects both for the organization and society. For instance, if an employee's behavior is consistent with organizational norms but violates societal ones (e.g., dumping toxic chemical wastes into a nearby river), it produces positive effects for the organization but negative ones for society. If it violates organizational norms but is consistent with societal norms, then the opposite occurs (as occurs in the case of *whistle-blowing*).

6. **Describe the major forms of workplace deviance.**

Workplace aggression is usually covert (i.e., hidden) in nature. Direct physical or verbal assaults by one employee against another are much rarer than indirect attacks, such as spreading malicious rumors about another person or withholding important information from them. Workplace aggression stems from many different factors including employees' beliefs that they have been treated unfairly, their personal characteristics, and the general level of aggression in a work group or organization. Abusive supervision is a style of supervision involving sustained displays of hostile verbal and nonverbal behaviors by a supervisor. *Cyberloafing* is a form of deviance in which employees "goof off" by using their computers for nonwork activities. *Employee theft,* another form of deviant organizational behavior, occurs when employees take company property for personal use. It can be reduced by involving employees in the creation of a theft policy, communicating the costs of stealing, and having managers be a good role model by not stealing themselves.

Points to Ponder

Questions for Review

1. What are psychological contracts and why do different kinds develop in various working relationships?
2. What is the difference between calculus-based trust and identification-based trust?
3. What forms does organizational behavior take? Why do people engage in it?
4. What are the major determinants of cooperation between individuals and between organizations?
5. What are the major causes and consequences of organizational conflict?
6. In what ways can organizational conflict be managed effectively?
7. Why can deviant organizational behavior result in negative consequences for an organization but positive consequences for society?

Experiential Questions

1. Think of individuals whom you trust and those you don't trust. In what key ways do your relationships with these people differ?

2. What are the major sources of conflict at work within the company at which you are employed? How do you think these conflicts may be resolved?
3. Have you ever been the target of some form of workplace aggression? Why do you think this happened? What did you do to deal with it?

Questions to Analyze

1. Do you agree or disagree with the following statement: People are inherently good, but are forced into behaving in negative ways by virtue of compelling forces they encounter within their organizations.
2. What would you say are the major barriers to interpersonal cooperation within the workplace?
3. What do you think *you* would do if faced with a situation in which obeying the norms of your organization would lead you to perform actions you considered illegal or unethical? Would you resist? What would be the consequences of resisting or "going along"?

Experiencing OB

Individual Exercise

Assessing Your Personal Orientation Toward Others

On page 388, you read descriptions of four different personal orientations toward others—*competitors, individualists, cooperators,* and *equalizers.* As you read these, you probably developed some ideas as to which orientation best described you. This exercise is designed to help you find out.

Directions

Use the following scale to indicate how well each of the following statements describes you.

1 = Does not describe me at all/never

2 = Describes me somewhat/some of the time

3 = Describes me moderately/half of the time

4 = Describes me greatly/much of the time

5 = Describes me perfectly/all of the time

1._____ I don't care how much money one of my coworkers earns, so long as I make as much as I can.

2._____ When playing a game with a close friend, I always try to keep the score close.

3._____ So long as I do better than the next guy, I'm happy.

4._____ I will gladly give up something for myself if it can help my team get ahead.

5._____ It's important to me to be the best in the class, even if I'm not doing my personal best.

6._____ I feel badly if I do too much better than my friends on a class assignment.

7._____ I want to get an "A" in this class regardless of what grade you might get.

8._____ I enjoy it when the people in my work team all pitch in together to beat other teams.

Scoring

Insert the numbers corresponding to your answers to each of the questions in the spaces corresponding to those questions. Then, add the numbers in each column (these can range from 2 to 10). The higher your score, the more accurately the personal orientation heading that column describes you.

Competitor	Individualist	Cooperator	Equalizer
3. _____	1. _____	4. _____	2. _____
5. _____	7. _____	8. _____	6. _____
Total = _____	Total = _____	Total = _____	Total = _____

Questions for Discussion

1. What did this exercise reveal about yourself?
2. Were you surprised at what you learned, or was it something you already knew?
3. Do you tend to maintain the same orientation most of the time, or are there occasions on which you change from one orientation to another? What do you think this means?

Group Exercise

Negotiating the Price of a Used Car

This exercise is designed to help you put into practice some of the skills associated with being a good negotiator. In completing this exercise, follow the steps for negotiating a win-win solution found on pages 394–395.

Directions

1. Find a thorough description of a recent-model used car in a newspaper or online.
2. Divide the class into groups of six. Within each group, assign three students to the role of buyer and three to the role of seller.
3. Each group of buyers and sellers should meet in advance to plan their strategies. Buyers should plan on getting the lowest possible price; sellers should seek the highest possible price.
4. Buyers and sellers should meet to negotiate the price of the car within the period of time specified by the instructor. Feel free to meet within your groups at any time to evaluate your strategy.
5. Write down the final agreed-upon price and any conditions that may be attached to it.

Questions for Discussion

1. Did you reach an agreement? If so, how easy or difficult was this process?
2. Which side do you think "won" the negotiation? What might have changed the outcome?
3. How might the negotiation process or the outcome have been different had this been a real situation?

Practicing OB

Your Worst Nightmare Boss

You work for a moderate-size office-supply company. Most of the people in your work group are pleasant and easy to get along with. But your boss—that is something else entirely. She always seems to be in a bad mood, and shows it. Almost every day one or more of your coworkers (including you!) becomes the target of her harsh verbal abuse. She frequently storms out of her office, shouting at any subordinate unlucky enough to be in her path. And she seems to take great pleasure out of raking people over the coals publicly—humiliating them in front of others. Her management style is so obnoxious that everyone hates her, and several good people have already quit to find other jobs. Answer the following questions based on the material in this chapter.

1. Why do you think she acts this way? Is it her job? Something about her personality? Or has she merely learned that intimidation works—at least for her?
2. What effects do you think her behavior is having on the performance of your work group? Morale, clearly, has been wrecked, but what about efficiency and the quality of the work done?
3. What can members of your work group do to change her obnoxious behavior? Or are you stuck with her as long as she is the supervisor and you stay with the company?

Case in Point

■ Southwest Airlines: Profits from People

"**W**e are extremely proud to report our 2009 earnings, which represents our 37th consecutive year of profitability." That's a statement that almost no airline executives were making as 2009 slipped into 2010. However, Gary C. Kelly, CEO of Southwest Airlines spoke these words with considerable pride as he addressed company stockholders. Indeed, he had every reason to be proud of the company's capacity to turn a profit at a time when just about all of its competitors were either at, or beyond, the brink of bankruptcy. The secret, as he boasts, is "our people."

For many years, Southwest Airlines was famous for having good relations between employees and management. The company and its employees saw eye-to-eye and agreements about working conditions and pay were met readily. Although that appears to be the case today as well, conditions soured a decade ago. In 2002 and 2003, negotiations focusing around labor practices ground to a painful halt. Even worse, the tone of the negotiations became so angry and bitter that for the first time in the company's history union leaders issued strong verbal attacks against top management, including Southwest's then-CEO, James F. Parker.

Employees accused Parker of being inflexible and unreasonable, and expressed strong concerns about the quality of his leadership. Ultimately, the situation became so tense that Parker removed himself from the negotiations and asked Southwest's former CEO, Herbert D. Kelleher, to come out of retirement just to resolve the bitter dispute. Fortunately, he succeeded quickly, resolving in less than eight weeks a dispute that had lasted over two years.

For Parker, this failure on his part was the last straw, leading him to resign in mid-2004. In his resignation speech, he stated that he had never found the job to be fun and that the company deserved a leader who could take it to the next level.

Today, Kelleher remains sensitive to his company's relations with its employees. Addressing an audience at Stanford Business School, Kelleher said, "We've never treated them [employees] as adversaries. We've always treated them as partners, because if that canoe goes down, we're all going down with it." He said Southwest makes a point of including union leaders in company functions, and "if they have an issue, we take care of it as quickly as we possibly can." During labor negotiations, "We have fights, but not vendettas. We yell, we throw things, we get a contract and then it's behind us. It's not like the Hatfields and McCoys, feuding and still killing each other after generations for reasons they don't remember." And, in today's highly competitive airline business, this surely gives Southwest an edge up on the other carriers. If the figures Mr. Kelly reports are any indication, this surely is the case.

Questions for Discussion

1. What forms of trust are involved in this case and how were they violated?
2. How are issues of cooperation and competition involved in this case?
3. To what extent might the excellent state of labor relations at Southwest have contributed to the company's record of financial success—especially in a challenging business environment?

■ *Effective Versus Ineffective Communication*

Effective communication in business is essential to success. Top managers spend approximately 85 percent of their time communicating with others. However, at the advertising agency The Factory, Mike, the new art director, is finding out just how difficult this can be, and why he needs to improve his skills.

In a conversation with Natalie, an account director at the firm, Mike finds out that his efforts at connecting with people so far have been lacking. Mike points out that he is finding it is more difficult to speak with clients than with other employees. Benny, the creative director, notes that Mike needs to learn how to communicate internally with upper management and externally with clients. Benny points out that having external communication skills is particularly important because, when he is dealing with clients, Mike is the face of the company. A Messenger tells Mike that this requires him to be practical, factual, concise, clear, and persuasive.

After Mike takes the advice of the Messenger, his communications skills improve, and he receives positive feedback for his efforts. Mike's clients are happier because they believe that he really understands their needs and goals. Mike knows that he still has much to learn, but recognizes that he already has come a long way.

Discussion Questions

1. In which phases of the communication process discussed in Chapter 9 is Mike having the most trouble when he communicates with clients?
2. How does the Messenger in the video clip suggest that Mike improve the process of encoding?
3. Mike is having trouble with both internal and external communication. Using the techniques to improve communication presented in Chapter 9, what would you recommend Mike do?

■ *Groups and Teams at Kluster*

The concept of teamwork is essential to the success of Kluster. The company's Illuminator project, a community-driven product development platform, requires the involvement of many different people. Tom Pasley, the project manager, notes that each individual on the Illuminator team brings a different set of skills to the table. Members meet daily, either electronically or physically, to discuss the project and generate new ideas.

According to Pasley, self-management is important to the project's success. Each person must stay on task and provide feedback to the other members. The graphic designer on the project says that each individual plays a different role. One person provides the voice of reason; a second gives a perspective of how ideas will affect the internal situation. A third member of the team thinks outside the box; a fourth considers the project from a future point of view, and so on. The founder of Kluster, Ben Kaufman,

generates many of the ideas for the project, and is the leader of the team.

However, engineer Peter Wadsworth, claims that Kaufman also values the perspectives and inputs of the other team members. Wadsworth notes that self-discipline is important, and that it quickly becomes apparent when someone fails to pull his or her weight. Strong communication skills contribute to the success of the project.

Discussion Questions

1. Using the definitions presented in Chapter 8, how would you characterize the Illuminator project at Kluster? Is it a group or a team?
2. Use the five dimensions of teams outlined in Chapter 8 to describe the Illuminator team at Kluster.
3. Considering the keys to successful teams presented in Chapter 8, what would you recommend that Kluster do to ensure that its Illuminator team is successful?

■ *Technology and the Tools of Communication*

Effective communication is essential for organizations. Communicators face two main challenges. The first is to ensure that information is easy to comprehend. The second is to get a message noticed. This is particularly important because people are bombarded continually with new information. This involves choosing the right media and delivery vehicle for a particular audience. When choosing the right tools, it is essential to consider the audience's expectations, the development time and cost of the message, how long it will take to distribute it,

how many people it will reach, and whether the audience will read it.

Tools available to communicators include traditional methods, such as interoffice memos, bulletin boards, and brochures, and technology-enhanced methods, such as on-demand custom-printed booklets, e-mail, and Web sites. Making messages more interesting has become an important component in an organization's overall communication strategy.

Not only does technology allow firms to develop highly personalized messages, but it also facilitates measuring

(Continued)

return on investment. Communicators can develop a decision matrix to identify which tool will be most effective in a given situation. In some cases, they may choose to combine options.

Discussion Questions

1. The video explores the importance of choosing the right media and delivery vehicle when communicating. Using the model presented in Chapter 9, explain which stage of the communication process this involves.

2. Technology has had a significant effect on communication within and between companies. Using the discussion of technology in Chapter 9 as a basis, explain how technology has increased the speed of communication in the workplace.

3. Using media richness theory presented in Chapter 9, explain which medium would be most effective for communicating: (a) highly sensitive material, (b) messages of an emotional nature, and (c) a short thank-you note.

CHAPTER

12 Power: Its Uses and Abuses in Organizations

Learning Objectives

After reading this chapter, you should be able to:

1. Describe the nature of influence in organizations and its major forms.
2. Distinguish between various forms of individual power in organizations.
3. Define empowerment and indicate how it operates among individuals and in teams.
4. Describe how the resource-dependency model and the strategic contingencies model explain the nature of power between organizational units.
5. Describe how sexual harassment constitutes an abuse of organizational power and ways of reducing its occurrence.
6. Explain when and where organizational politics occur and the forms such behavior takes.

Chapter Outline

- Influence: A Basic Organizational Process
- Individual Power: Sources and Uses
- Empowerment: Sharing Power with Employees
- The Power of Organizational Groups
- Sexual Harassment: A Serious Abuse of Power
- Organizational Politics: Selfish Uses of Power

Preview Case

■ *Abuse of Power or "An Indiscriminate Jerk"?*

Company policy at Holland & Knight—one of the largest and most respected law firms in the world—makes it perfectly clear: "The firm is committed to fostering a collegial work environment in which all individuals are treated with dignity and respect." To nine of the firm's female attorneys in its Tampa, Florida, office, however, this sentiment is a far cry from the treatment they allegedly received from Douglas Wright, one of the firm's partners. One by one, they reported incidents in which Wright touched them in ways they believed were inappropriate and/or spoke to them in sexually explicit ways.

One of the accusations was that Wright told the women to "feel my guns," referring to his muscular arms. In the context of other things he did and said that were suggestive in nature and tone, the female associates felt highly uneasy, went out of their way to avoid Wright at the office, and even stayed away from social functions he was attending. They filed internal charges of sexual harassment against Wright, citing incidents going back five years.

Two investigations followed, one by an outside law firm and another by an internal body, Holland & Knight's Fair Employment Practices Committee (FEPC). Wright denied the charges against him. However, he admitted to using the phrase "feel my guns" regularly, albeit in a friendly fashion, as "an icebreaker," and not in a sexual manner. Most of the investigators didn't buy it, countering that the charges against Wright were credible. With this, the FEPC recommended reprimanding him personally and privately (although these reprimands, and the accounts themselves, subsequently were made public).

Among the recommendations were that Wright be told to refrain from asking others in the firm to "feel his muscles, guns, and/or pipes"; to no longer ask people about their sex lives; to stop monitoring adherence to the firm's dress code; and to be given professional counseling about sexual harassment. In July 2004, Howell Melton, Jr., the firm's managing partner, agreed to adhere to these guidelines for reprimanding Wright, but refused to go along with specific recommendations to bar Wright from participating in the hiring of summer interns and regular firm associates.

Furious and dissatisfied by his unwillingness to accept all the recommendations, four female accusers responded to Melton in a sharply worded memo: "The message that you have sent us . . . is that cruel behavior is tolerated so long as the perpetrator is in a position of power." This sentiment was in keeping with the FEPC's recommendation that Wright's behavior be monitored because he "has been entrusted with leadership positions" and "has made questionable use of the power inherent in those positions."

In an interview, the burly attorney with the frat-boy personality told the *St. Petersburg* (Florida) *Press* that he denied targeting women. "I joke and tease with everyone," he stated—adding, "I suppose some might think that makes me an indiscriminate jerk."

As you might suspect, people hold varied ideas about this incident.[1] Regardless of where you might stand, however, it's noteworthy that claims about Mr. Wright's misuse of power feature prominently in this account of sexual harassment. Being far more senior than his accusers, Wright was able to influence their careers by the things he did and said. He could play a key role in determining their fates. Moreover, this capacity to affect the young female attorneys was based on the formal power he held over them by virtue of his high-ranking position in the law firm. The accusers cried foul in response to the managing partner's actions, suggesting that he might have been succumbing to organizational politics by giving Wright "a slap on the wrist"—going too easy on a colleague, who was "one of the guys." Again, although these perspectives all are matters of opinion, to be sure, it cannot be denied that uses and abuses of power play vital roles in this episode. Indeed, they are central themes in all organizations in general, warranting their attention as the focus of this chapter.

To begin, we examine the nature of the *influence* process in general by describing a range of tactics used by individuals and groups in work settings to change others' behavior. Then, building on this, we turn to the nature of *power*. In this connection, we examine separately power as it is acquired and used by individuals and as it is used by groups or units in an organization. For both discussions, the key issues will be how power is gained and used, and—in the case of individuals—how it sometimes is shared with others. Then, we will focus on various ways in which people abuse power in organizations. At this point, we will be more explicit about what we've been discussing here: *sexual harassment* in the workplace, including information about the extent of the problem and how to address it. Finally, in closing, we will cover a fascinating form of behavior known as *organizational politics*, examining the tactics individuals use to attain their personal (and selfish) goals, as well as the ethical issues raised by these actions.

Influence: A Basic Organizational Process

Imagine that you are a supervisor heading a small group of staff members who are working on an important project for your company. Tomorrow, you're scheduled to make a big presentation to company officials, but the report isn't quite ready. If only several staff members would work late this evening, the job could be done on time. There's a problem, however. This happens to be a night when several major events are occurring—a key basketball game, a special concert featuring a famous entertainer, and a big fund-raising benefit for a local museum. Most of the people on your team have tickets to one of these events, so if anything, they'd prefer to leave early rather than stay late. What can you do to get them to change their plans and work late to complete the project? In other words, how can you *influence* them to do what you want?

Every day, managers confront situations like this in which they attempt to influence others. **Influence** refers to attempts to affect another in a desired fashion. In one way or another, supervisors seek to change others' behavior in a manner consistent with organizational objectives. Yet, it isn't always apparent how they can, or should, go about doing so. What specific tactics do they use, and which are most effective? These are the issues to which we now turn.

influence
Attempts to affect another in a desired fashion, whether or not these are successful.

Tactics for Exerting Influence

It is acknowledged widely that successful managers are adept at influencing others.[2] But precisely how do they do so? And how do *you* attempt to influence others—that is, get them to do what you want them to do? Table 12.1 identifies and describes the influence techniques that are used most often.

As you might imagine, the 10 tactics in Table 12.1 are not likely to be used by all people on every occasion. What is it exactly that determines their usage? One key factor is differences in the formal organizational levels of the people involved—that is, whether one is attempting to influence another who is at a higher, lower, or equivalent level as oneself.[3] For example, leaders often use inspirational appeals, or even pressure, when necessary, to influence their subordinates. In contrast, subordinates are unlikely to use these techniques when attempting to influence their bosses. Instead, they generally rely on consultation or rational persuasion.

Adding to this, people believe overall that procedures that involve dealing with others directly (e.g., consultation) are more appropriate than pressuring someone or "cutting the ground from under them" (e.g., pressure).[4] Accordingly, the most popular techniques used to influence people at all levels of an organization are consultation, inspirational appeals, and rational persuasion.[5] Generally, these methods are viewed as appropriate for attempting to influence others regardless of their organizational levels. In contrast, more coercive forms of influence, such as

TABLE 12.1 Influence Techniques

To exert *influence* over others (target persons)—that is, to get them to behave in some desired fashion—people use one or more of the following techniques.

Technique	Description
Rational persuasion	Using logical arguments and facts to persuade one or more others that a desired result will occur
Inspirational appeals	Arousing enthusiasm by appealing to a target person's values and ideals
Collaboration	Making it easier for someone to agree to a request
Consultation	Asking an individual to participate in decision making or planning a change
Ingratiation	Getting somebody to do what you want by putting him or her in a good mood or otherwise getting him or her to like you
Exchange	Promising some benefits to a person upon complying with a request
Personal appeal	Appealing to feelings of loyalty or friendship before making a request
Coalition-building	Persuading by seeking the assistance of others in a coalition, or by telling them about the support you already enjoy from elsewhere
Legitimating	Calling attention to one's formal authority to make a request, or verifying that it is consistent with prevailing organizational policies and practices
Pressuring	Seeking compliance by making demands or threats, or otherwise intimidating someone

pressure and legitimating, are viewed as less appropriate and are used more infrequently. In fact, pressure, when it is used, is more likely to be relied upon as a follow-up technique than as a tool for an initial influence attempt—and then, only for subordinates. Also, it is interesting that some techniques—such as ingratiation, coalition, personal appeal, and exchange—are more likely to be used in combination with other methods than by themselves.

A very dramatic illustration of the range of these tactics involves the many ways in which Las Vegas casinos try to lure the business of the world's biggest gamblers.[6] The casinos even categorize these customers into such groups as "high rollers" (who risk no less than $10,000 over 4 days) and "whales" (who risk more than $1 million during a 4-day period). Casinos welcome such customers because they contribute significantly to corporate earnings. As Glenn Schaeffer, president and CEO of Mandalay Resort Group, put it, "It's very difficult, when you've got a $1 billion building, to make a living on slot machines." So the large casinos do many things to lure the biggest whales to their facilities when they come to town. Free lavish suites and sumptuous meals are just the beginning. Some casinos have built private entrances for these valuable customers, and it is not unknown for management do whatever it takes to bring these top gamblers through their (private) doors.[7] As tempting as it may be to dream about receiving such royal treatment, we return to the point at hand: If you have something that people want (money, in this case), you can influence them—and in this extreme example, even to the point of having them do whatever you may ask.

Can Managers Learn to Use Influence More Effectively?

As we noted earlier, managers' successes are determined greatly by their ability to influence others effectively. For instance, a supervisor who can't induce his subordinates to put forth extra effort on important projects probably will not advance very far. Similarly, an employee who can't persuade her boss to consider her views on various topics carefully probably won't be seen as a good candidate for promotion. And managers who can't get their peers to assist them in various ways will have considerable difficulty in getting ahead. So influence is certainly an important skill, and one all managers should develop. But can they learn it? Or is it something with which people simply are born and that they cannot modify?

Fortunately, the news is encouraging. We all have a chance at being influential because influence is a skill, and, like other skills (see Chapter 3), it can be improved. This was revealed in research involving employees of a regional bank who were asked to rate the extent to which their managers employed the various methods of influence described earlier.[8] The participants also rated themselves on their use of these tactics, so that the two ratings—those by subordinates and the self-ratings—could be compared. On the basis of these ratings, the researchers then prepared feedback reports summarizing the use of the four tactics described earlier—*rational persuasion, inspirational appeals, consultation,* and *collaboration.* These reports were given to the managers, who then participated in a seven-hour workshop on using these skills. The workshop involved showing videotapes illustrating how these tactics could be used in various situations that typically arise at banks. Examples of upward, downward, and lateral influence were included. Then, groups met to discuss effective ways of using these tactics.

After the workshops were completed, subordinates of the participants again rated the managers' usage of various influence tactics. By comparing the pre-workshop and post-workshop ratings, training effectiveness could be assessed. In other words, the researchers were able to determine the extent to which the exercises helped supervisors learn to use influence tactics more effectively. A control group from the same bank received feedback, but did not participate in the workshop. (Later, after the study was completed, they, too, participated in the same workshop.)

As shown in Figure 12.1, participation in the workshop did indeed increase managers' use of these highly effective tactics of influence. Those who participated showed a significant increase in the frequency with which they used these methods (as rated by their subordinates). In contrast, managers in the control group, who did not participate in the workshop before the ratings were completed, showed no increase in their skill at using these tactics of influence.

In sum, effective use of influence tactics can be learned. Given the benefits of being able to influence others effectively, it seems clear that this is one skill managers should work hard to acquire. This raises an important question: How can you increase your own use of core influence tactics? For some suggestions in this regard, see the OB in Practice section on page 417.

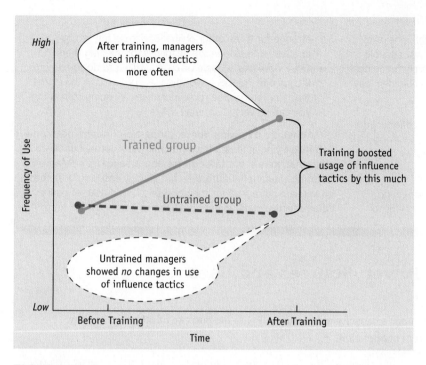

FIGURE 12.1

Learning to Be More Influential

Managers who participated in a workshop designed to give them feedback on how they were currently using various influence tactics, plus information on how they could use these techniques more successfully, benefited greatly from this experience. They used these effective tactics of influence more frequently after the workshop than before it. In contrast, managers who did not receive such training did not show a similar increase in use of influence tactics.

Source: Based on data reported by Seifert et al., 2003; see Note 8.

OB in Practice

Cultivating Your Own Influence Skills

Although formal training may be required to help people become comfortable using various influence techniques, there are several things that anyone can do to become more influential in the workplace.

For example, to improve your use of *rational persuasion*, it's important to base your arguments on valid data and to present that information in a clear and unemotional manner. Specifically, to do this, you should consider the following suggestions.

- *Gather the facts.* Base your arguments on clear and comprehensive information from objective and verifiable sources. Be prepared to share and explain all the evidence upon which your opinion is drawn.
- *Present balanced information.* There are two sides to every story, as they say, so to enhance credibility, be sure to explain not only why you think you are right but also why you believe the other side is wrong. Showing that you are aware of both sides will make you more credible, and influential as a result.

It's also important to use *inspirational appeals* in the most appropriate fashion. This requires focusing on the other side's values and feelings. To accomplish this, it helps to do the following.

- *Focus on what's best for the company.* Explaining how your position on a matter benefits yourself is likely to be of little interest. Instead, remove the personal angle by basing your argument on something that the other cannot argue against—what's best for the company.
- *Point to a higher ideal.* If you present an ethical perspective (what's right) or a legal perspective (it's against the law), it's hard for someone to take the opposing side.

It's also important for managers to use *consultation skills*, such as encouraging others to get involved in the making of a decision. Some specific ways of doing this are as follows:

- *Invite everyone to participate.* People like to feel that their ideas matter, making it important to ensure that everyone is invited to get involved. Someone who is not saying anything, for example, might be called upon to share his or her ideas at a meeting.

(Continued)

■ *Encourage dissenting views.* To be influential, it helps to demonstrate one's concern for making the best possible decisions. And doing this effectively requires encouraging people to share thoughts about how a particular idea may be flawed.

Managers should develop skills regarding *collaboration.* This refers to making it easier for someone to go along with your requests. Doing this can be accomplished by doing the following.

■ *Eliminate obstacles.* If someone cannot do something because he or she has other responsibilities, it helps to arrange for those other obligations to be fulfilled by another or to extend the deadlines for meeting them.

■ *Offer incentives.* People often are willing to do something if someone "makes it worthwhile" to do so. To the extent that you can provide some incentives for doing something, you can be very influential.

Although following these suggestions might not come naturally, trying at least a few of them is well worthwhile. Keep in mind that we are not talking here about being manipulative by misusing managerial authority, but rather, ensuring that those powers are harnessed for the good of all. And that, of course, is what effective management is all about.

Individual Power: Sources and Uses

Power consists in one's capacity to link his will with the purpose of others, to lead by reason and a gift of cooperation.

Woodrow Wilson, 28th President of the United States (1856–1924),
letter to Mary A. Hulbert, September 21, 1913

power
The capacity to exert influence over others.

In this insightful comment, President Wilson made a key point about the nature of power. Putting it less articulately, **power** refers to the capacity to exert influence over others. This raises a key question: From where do people derive this capacity? In other words, what are the bases of individual power in organizations? As we now describe, there are several key answers to this important question.

Position Power: Influence That Comes with the Office

position power
Power based on one's formal position in an organization.

A great deal of the power people have in organizations comes from the specific jobs or titles they hold. In other words, they are able to influence others because of the formal power associated with their jobs. This is known as **position power.** For example, there are certain powers that the president of the United States has simply because of the office (e.g., signing bills into law, making treaties, etc.). These remain vested in the position and are available to anyone who holds it. When the president's term is up, they transfer to the new office-holder. There are four bases of position power: *legitimate power, reward power, coercive power,* and *information power.*

legitimate power
The individual power base derived from one's position in an organizational hierarchy; the accepted authority of one's position.

LEGITIMATE POWER. The power that people have because others recognize and accept their authority is known as **legitimate power.** As an example, students recognize that their instructors can formulate class policies and assign grades, giving them legitimate power over the class.

It is important to note that legitimate power covers a relatively narrow range of influence, and that it may be inappropriate to overstep these bounds. For example, although a boss may require her secretary to type and fax a company document, it would be an abuse of power to ask that secretary to type her son's homework. This is not to say that the secretary might not take on the task as a favor, but doing so would *not* be the direct result of the boss's formal authority. Legitimate power applies only to the range of behaviors that are recognized and accepted as appropriate by the parties involved.

reward power
The individual power base derived from an individual's capacity to administer valued rewards to others.

REWARD POWER. Along with certain jobs comes the power to control the rewards others want to receive—that is, **reward power.** For example, professors have a degree of reward power over students, since they can give them high grades and write glowing letters of recommendation. In the case of managers, the rewards available may be tangible ones such as raises and promotions, or intangible ones such as praise and recognition. In both cases, access to these desired outcomes gives power to the individuals who control them.

COERCIVE POWER. In contrast, power also results from the capacity to dole out punishments— that is, **coercive power.** Although most managers do not like using threats, it is a fact of organizational life that many people rely them. If any boss has ever directly told you, "Do what I say, or else," or even implied it, you are probably all too familiar with coercive power. Often, people have power simply because others know that they have the opportunity to punish them, even if the threat of doing so is not made explicit. For example, in the military, when your commanding officer "asks" you to do something, you almost certainly will comply since that apparent request is really an order in disguise, and there are severe consequences for failing to obey. In organizations, implied threats of suspensions without pay and reassignments to undesirable duties may enhance the coercive power of many managers.

INFORMATION POWER. The fourth source of power available to people by virtue of their positions is based on the data and other knowledge they have at their disposal—known as **information power.** Traditionally, people in top positions have access to unique sources of information that are unavailable to others (e.g., knowledge of company performance, market trends, and so on), which makes them powerful. Often, it is said that "Knowledge is power," and to a large extent, this is true.

Today, as technology has made it possible for more information to be available than ever before (which is why the field is known as *information technology*), it is an intriguing possibility that information power may be losing ground as a potent source of influence in many organizations. We note, however, that although much information no longer is the unique property of a few people holding special positions, it remains the case that managers, by virtue of their positions, still have access to proprietary data—that is, closely guarded information about people and processes. For example, only the owners may know for sure how profitable a privately held company truly is. Similarly, managers are expected to maintain confidentiality concerning their employees. Thus, although far more information is available to people today than ever before, it seems safe to say that even today information remains an important source of power.

Personal Power: Influence That Comes from the Individual

So far, the sources of influence we've discussed have been based on an individual's position in an organization. However, this is not the only way people gain power. Frequently, it also derives from an individual's own unique qualities or characteristics. This is known as **personal power,** and there are four basic types: *rational persuasion, expert power, referent power,* and *charisma.*

RATIONAL PERSUASION. In Table 12.1 (page 415) we noted that rational persuasion is a key tactic for exerting influence—perhaps the most frequently used approach in organizations. When it is used effectively and repeatedly, however, it also can serve as a means for acquiring personal power. In other words, individuals who are truly expert at influencing others through the strength of their logic and by means of an effective style for delivering their arguments often acquire power over others. Not only can they influence them in specific situations or about special issues, but they also gain power within their organizations by virtue of their effectiveness in doing so.

EXPERT POWER. Another basis of personal power lies in *expertise.* People who possess expert knowledge of a business or some facet of it often gain what is known as **expert power,** power based on others' beliefs that one has superior knowledge, skills or abilities in a certain area. Consider, for example, the conductor of an orchestra or band. The musicians follow this person's directions and lead not only because he or she is in charge formally (i.e., because of legitimate power), but also because this individual is a recognized expert in the field of music. When people believe that you know what you are doing, you have power over them because they are inclined to do what you say.

REFERENT POWER. Imagine that you are friends with your supervisor. One day, she asks you to take on a special project that you really don't like. To anyone else, you might be inclined to say no, but because of your closeness to this individual, you may be likely to do it as a favor. In this case, it could be said that the supervisor has power over you by virtue of your positive relationship. This illustrates another source of personal power, one not based on expertise, but rather, the fact that one is admired or respected by others. This type of power is known as **referent power.** For example, senior managers who possess desirable qualities and good reputations may

---

coercive power
The individual power base derived from the capacity to administer punishment to others.

information power
The extent to which a supervisor has power by virtue of the information available to him or her.

personal power
The power that one derives because of one's individual qualities or characteristics.

expert power
The individual power base derived from an individual's recognized superior knowledge, skills or abilities in a certain area.

referent power
The individual power base derived from the degree to which one is liked and admired by others.

find that they have referent power over younger managers who identify with them and wish to emulate them. These younger individuals might go along with their senior colleague not only because they feel they have to do so (i.e., legitimate power) or because they believe that he knows what he's doing (i.e., expert power), but also because they like him. That represents referent power.

CHARISMA. As you know, some people seem to possess an almost magical quality: Their personalities are so powerful and magnetic that they seem to put others in a kind of trance. Such individuals are described as possessing **charisma,** and one benefit they gain from this quality is a big boost in personal power. (We will have more to say about charisma in Chapter 13, in our discussion of leadership.)

What makes charismatic people so influential, so capable of getting others to do what they want? The answer is that such individuals have "that special something" that gets others to go along with them. Although their power seems to be magical, the "spell" cast by highly charismatic individuals, in reality, is based on several key elements. People possessing this quality have the following characteristics in common. Specifically, they

- Express clear visions of the future and how to get there
- Excite crowds by using colorful metaphors and exciting language
- Inspire trust because their integrity is beyond reproach
- Make people feel good about themselves

In your opinion, who can be described in this manner, either currently or from the past? The Rev. Dr. Martin Luther King, President John F. Kennedy, or Steve Jobs, cofounder of Apple Computer? Indeed, all these individuals have been noted for their charisma. Of course, there also are countless other individuals who are not famous but who may be considered highly charismatic in their own worlds—and who, by virtue of this, also have power over others.

In summary, people may influence others because of the jobs or positions they hold (position power), their individual characteristics (personal power), or both. When you consider these factors, it's not difficult to understand why in most organizations large differences exist with respect to individual power: Some people have it and some do not. (For a review of the sources of position and personal power discussed in this section, see Figure 12.2.)

How Is Individual Power Used?

What bases of power do you use? Chances are good that you don't rely on just one, but several, including different types on different occasions. Not surprisingly, the various power bases are closely related to each other with respect to how they are used.[9]

For example, the more someone uses coercive power, the less that person is liked, and the lower his or her referent power tends to be. Similarly, managers with expert power also are likely to have legitimate power because people accept their expertise as a basis for having authority

---

charisma
An attitude of enthusiasm and optimism that is contagious; an aura of leadership.

FIGURE 12.2

Sources of Individual Power: An Overview

As shown here, *individual power* can derive either from formal positions within an organization *(position power)* or from various personal characteristics *(personal power).*

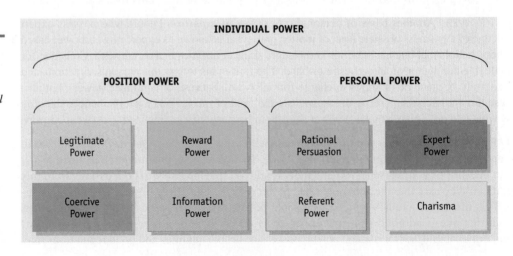

over them. In addition, the higher someone's rank is in the organizational hierarchy, the more legitimate power that person has. And this, in turn, tends to be accompanied by greater opportunities to use reward and coercion.[10] Clearly, then, the various bases of power should not be thought of as completely separate and distinct from each other. Often, they are used together in varying combinations.

What bases of power do people prefer to use? Although the answer depends on many considerations, overall people prefer to use expert power most and coercive power least.[11] Although this is the case with respect to the specific power bases we've identified so far, an interesting picture emerges when you ask people to report exactly what sources of power they have on their jobs. Figure 12.3 presents the results of a survey in which 216 CEOs of American corporations were asked to rank-order the importance of a series of specific sources of power.[12] The numbers reflect the percentage of executives who included each source of power among their top three choices. These findings indicate not only that top executives derive their power from multiple sources, but also that their power rests mainly on their personal characteristics (personal power) and on support from people located throughout their organizations.

Although executives use a variety of powers to influence their subordinates, they rely most on expert power when attempting to influence peers and superiors.[13] After all, it is almost always appropriate to try to get others to go along with you if you base your efforts on your expertise. In contrast, coercive tactics tend to be rejected in general, and are especially inappropriate when attempting to influence a higher-ranking person.[14]

Influencing superiors is tricky because of the **counterpower** they have—that is, the capacity to neutralize another's attempts at control. When trying to sway the opinion of someone who is believed to have no power at his or her disposal, one doesn't have to worry about possible retaliation. When dealing with an individual with considerably greater power, however, this is a real possibility and can lead to greater compliance with the wishes of the powerful party. Flexing one's muscles in a power struggle, then, is a sure way to get the other party to flex theirs, too. After all, in organizations wielding power is vitally important.

The situation is complicated still further, however, by the fact that one party may have higher power on one dimension, and another may have more power on a different dimension. Consider, for example, the case of administrative assistants who have acquired power because they have been with their companies for many years. They know the ropes and they know where important documents are filed, so they can get things done for you if they want, or they can get you hopelessly bogged down in red tape. Their expert knowledge gives them a great sense of power over others. Although

counterpower
The capacity to neutralize another's influence attempts.

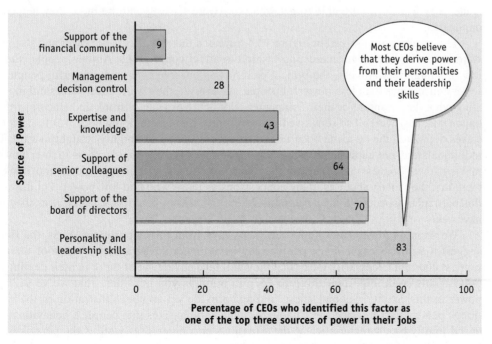

FIGURE 12.3

American CEOs: What Are Their Power Bases?

A survey of American CEOs revealed that they obtained their power primarily by cultivating the support of others at different levels throughout the organization and by virtue of their personality and leadership skills.

Source: Based on data appearing in Stewart, 1999; see Note 12.

they may lack the legitimate power of their executive bosses, the expertise of many administrative assistants can be a valuable source of counterpower over those with more formal power.

When Can Being Powerful Be a Liability?

In Chapter 11 we described negotiation as a means of reducing conflict with others. One of our key points was that for this process to be successful, it's often necessary for one of the sides to make concessions to the other. And, that party is likely to be the one with lower level of power. Suppose, for example that an employee is negotiating with her employer about a salary increase. Really wanting the raise, she may say, "If you pay me the salary I'm requesting, I'll take those awful assignments that nobody wants." She's thinking that this will be a win-win situation because it gives each side the desired outcome (i.e., she gets the salary she seeks and the company gets someone to staff the undesirable assignments). This is where power comes in. It only works this way if the parties are relatively equal in power.

If one party has more power than the other, however, the sides will not be equally inclined to make concessions. Instead, the parties with the greater power can more easily get what they want, enabling them to concede less to the other side. In this case, for example, if the company has workers who are willing to take those undesirable assignments, it has the greater power and need not concede to the employee. However, if the employee has attractive job offers from other companies, then she has the greater power—leaving the company "over a barrel," or having "the upper hand," as they say. In this case, she's unlikely to back down and the company will have to concede to her if it wants to keep her onboard.

As plausible as this is—and research has established that this is indeed how power is involved in negotiations—it is only part of the story. Another factor that makes a difference is a personality variable known as **straightforwardness.** This refers to the tendency for people to behave in ways that are frank, sincere, and candid in their dealings with others. In addition to being concerned about his or her own welfare, someone who is highly straightforward also is greatly concerned about the other party in a negotiation. When it comes to negotiating, is being highly straightforward an asset or a liability?

A recent experiment has examined this question.[15] Participants in the study were students who worked in pairs on a simulation exercise requiring them to assume the role of one of two companies involved in negotiating a series of human resource management decisions. One of the companies, it was explained, had more power because it was about to acquire the other. As an incentive to ensure that the students took the exercises seriously, they were promised monetary prizes for performing well. The researchers examined the number and amount of concessions made by the participants. As in real-life negotiations, the more concessions the sides made, they less they were able to get what they were seeking and the more they helped their opponents.

The results, summarized in Figure 12.4, revealed that the effects of power and straightforwardness combined in an interesting fashion to affect concessions. Among people who were low in straightforwardness, the typical pattern was observed. That is, powerful people made fewer concessions than less powerful people. As a result, they were more successful in negotiating what they wanted for their companies. Not being especially frank and sincere with their opponents, they weren't so sensitive that it prevented them from doing what was best for themselves. However, the opposite occurred among people who were highly straightforward. These individuals did *not* capitalize on the advantage that they had due to their greater power by making fewer concessions. Instead, they were so attuned to their opponents and frank with them that they made about as many concessions as those who had low power. Put differently, this particular aspect of their personalities kept them from being as successful as they might have been.

We should point to two important takeaways from this experiment. First, the findings suggest that just because some people may have power advantages by virtue of their positions, it does not necessarily mean that they will take advantage of these in their dealings with others. This is an important thing to keep in mind as you consider what we've said about power in this chapter. Second, these findings provide yet another illustration of the interactionist perspective described in Chapter 4, which emphasizes that people's behavior is influenced jointly by characteristics of the situations encountered as well as the personalities of the individuals in those situations.

straightforwardness
The tendency for people to behave in ways that are frank, sincere, and candid in their dealings with others.

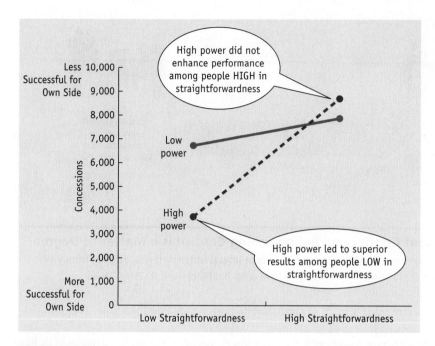

FIGURE 12.4

Power as a Liability: An Experimental Demonstration

Pairs of participants in a recent experiment negotiated for outcomes in a simulation exercise. One person in each pair had more power than the other. When they had higher power, people who had a high amount of *straightforwardness* did not use that power to negotiate favorable outcomes for themselves. However, high power individuals who had low amounts of straightforwardness successfully negotiated favorable outcomes for their sides.

Source: Adapted from DeRue et al., 2009; see Note 15.

Empowerment: Sharing Power with Employees

Former U.S. President Theodore Roosevelt was quoted as saying, "The best executive is the one who has sense enough to pick good men to do what he wants done, and self-restraint enough to keep from meddling with them while they do it."[16] Although this remark was made about 100 years ago, it's as true today as ever. In fact, an important trend has been occurring in organizations these days: Power is shifting downward. Top managers are granting more power to lower-level managers, and supervisors are putting power into the hands of employees themselves.

In other words, many of today's employees are not being "managed" in the traditional, top-down styles that were used by managers of generations past. Instead, power often is shifted down the ladder to teams that are allowed to make decisions themselves (see Chapter 8). Survey findings tell the story clearly: When asked about how much power they currently had compared to 10 years ago, only 19 percent of CEOs surveyed reported that they now had more power. Thirty-six percent indicated that they had the same amount of power. However, the largest group, 42 percent, indicated that they had less power.[17]

These figures are in keeping with the idea of **empowerment**—the process of delegating authority to individuals at the lowest levels in organizations at which competent decisions can be made.[18] Although empowerment involves many specific steps and policies, three are particularly important. These are:

- *Information sharing:* Providing potentially sensitive information on costs, productivity, quality, and financial performance to employees throughout the organization
- *Autonomy through boundaries:* Using organizational designs (see Chapter 15) and practices that encourage autonomous action by employees, including work procedures, areas of responsibilities, and goals
- *Team accountability:* Ensuring that both decision-making authority and performance accountability reside in teams (see Chapter 8)

empowerment
The passing of responsibility and authority from managers to lower-level employees.

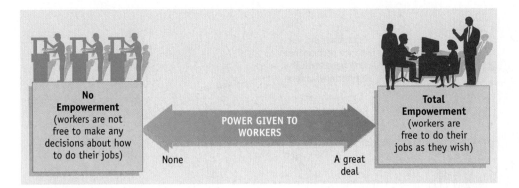

FIGURE 12.5

The Empowerment Continuum: Relinquishing Control Is a Matter of Degree

As shown here, empowering subordinate workers may take several different forms, ranging from giving employees complete power to determine how to do their jobs, to giving them no power at all.

Overall, then, empowerment is a trend toward sharing power with employees in several important ways.[19]

As you might imagine, empowerment is not just a simple yes-or-no option, but a matter of degree (see Figure 12.5).[20] At one end of the scale are companies (such as ones using traditional assembly lines) in which workers have virtually no power to determine how to do their jobs. At the opposite end are jobs in which employees have complete control over what they do and how they do it.

We see this at companies using self-managed work teams (as described in Chapter 8). For example, at Chaparral Steel managers are free to hire, train, and use new employees however they think best.[21] At W. L. Gore & Associates, manufacturers of specialty fabrics, the empowerment philosophy is so strongly entrenched that employees work without any fixed, assigned sets of responsibilities.[22] Government bureaus and departments, too, have jumped on the empowerment bandwagon. For instance, in Canada, government downsizing and restructuring, undertaken to increase efficiency, has been linked with empowerment of employees. According to an account of these new policies:

> In accordance with the 'New Public Management,' narrow jobs have become enriched, enlarged (see Chapter 7) and more fluid. More information and decisions are delegated to self-directed teams. Work arrangements are more flexible, with increased overtime, and more choice for employees.[23]

When employees are empowered, their supervisors cannot be thought of as "bosses" who use coercive power to "push people around." Rather, they are more likely to serve as teachers or "facilitators" who guide their work groups by using their knowledge and experience (i.e., their expert power). Traditional managers may tell people what to do and how and when to do it, but supervisors of empowered workers are more inclined to provide assistance. They ask questions that help others solve problems and that allow them to make decisions on their own (see Figure 12.6).

Do Employees Like Being Empowered?

Empowerment is indeed a trend in today's organizations; it's important to consider how employees react to it. In general, most respond quite favorably.[24] As an illustration, consider Xerox. Years ago, corporate reorganization led to having the employees take greater responsibility for their work, especially at its distribution center outside Atlanta. The head of that facility considers its 24 hourly-paid union workers as managers, and treats them as such. They are free to take responsibility for their own jobs and to solve problems as they see fit. And that's just what they've done. For example, employees have found ways to save the company money on trash removal (by recycling) and in shipping costs (by using lighter-weight pallets). They even have reorganized warehousing procedures; 99.9 percent of orders now ship on time. Absenteeism is almost nonexistent and productivity is up dramatically.[25]

Another example of the benefits of empowerment is provided by Omni Hotels. The company implemented a program called "Power of One" to help combat exceptionally high employee turnover and low levels of satisfaction among guests. This involves training all employees to make

FIGURE 12.6

Empowered "Hog"-Makers

Employees at Harley-Davidson's 358,000-square-foot vehicle and powertrain operations plant in Kansas City, Missouri, such as Jim Parker, shown here, are empowered to make decisions regarding how to perform their jobs. From fabrication and finishing through final assembly, they produce the company's Sportster®, Dyna® and VRSC™ families of bikes. (Originally, "H.O.G." stood for "Harley Owners' Group." Although the group is still so designated, the term "hog" has come to refer to any large motorcycle.)

independent decisions that benefit guests—even if it means bending the rules. Frontline employees also are empowered to listen to angry customers and to give them whatever they want (within reason, of course).[26] Within the program's first month, customer satisfaction surged 16 percent, and after the first year, turnover was reduced to 42 percent—still high, but much lower than the 65 percent that existed before the plan was introduced.

These and many similar success stories suggest that empowerment often yields important benefits for both employees and their organizations.[27] But we don't want to paint too rosy a picture. It would be misleading to suggest that workers always react positively to empowerment. Although many like some aspects of it, they may find it challenging and stressful to take on new responsibilities. This point is in keeping with ones we made earlier, suggesting that not all employees are motivated to perform enriched jobs (Chapter 7) or to work in teams where they have freedom to make decisions (see Chapter 10). There seem to be clear individual differences in the degree to which people are attracted to jobs that empower them. To many of us, this seems like a wonderful opportunity; to others, it's merely an obligation they would rather not undertake. (In view of this, we pose an interesting question: Do employees all over the world react in the same way to empowerment? Is it perceived differently in different countries? For a look at this matter, see the Today's Diverse and Global Organizations section on page 426.)

Empowerment Climate

So far, we have focused on the effects of empowerment on individual employees. However, empowerment also may influence teams and work units of various types, and research reveals precisely how this may occur.[28] Researchers conducting the study reasoned that organizations adopting various empowerment-giving practices will create what they called an **empowerment climate**—a relatively enduring atmosphere in the workplace that is supportive of empowerment. Specifically, the scientists hypothesized that the more strongly organizations encourage information sharing, autonomy, and holding teams accountable for their work (key aspects of

empowerment climate
A relatively enduring atmosphere in the workplace that is supportive of empowerment.

Today's Diverse and Global Organizations

Comparing Reactions to Empowerment in Four Different Nations

Cultures differ greatly, and one of the ways in which they vary involves the extent to which inequalities among people in status or power are seen as appropriate. In *high-power-distance* cultures (so-called "vertical" societies, such as India and Japan), such differences are viewed as natural and acceptable and people are comfortable with hierarchical distinctions.[29] In *low-power-distance* cultures (so-called "horizontal" societies, such as the United States and Mexico), in contrast, differences in power are viewed as less acceptable and people feel uncomfortable with distinctions based on position or rank.

How do people in these two kinds of cultures react to empowerment? Presumably, people in low-power-distance cultures will react more favorably. After all, empowerment reduces distinctions based on hierarchies so that managers and their subordinates are on a more equal footing, and this would be consistent with the basic values of a low-power-distance culture. In contrast, people in high-power-distance cultures might find it somewhat disturbing: They are comfortable with differences based on hierarchies and might be somewhat uncomfortable with the blurring of such differences.

Research has shown that this, in fact, is the case. In one intriguing project, a team of researchers asked employees of a multinational corporation to rate the extent to which empowerment was occurring in their company and their satisfaction with their work, supervisors, and coworkers.[30] These measures were collected in four different countries: the United States, Poland, and Mexico (which are low in power distance) and India (which is relatively high in power distance). As you might expect, the researchers found a positive relationship between empowerment and job satisfaction in the United States, Poland, and Mexico. That is, when empowerment was high, job satisfaction was high as well. However, there was a negative relationship between these factors in India: When empowerment was high, job satisfaction was low.

These findings indicate that although empowerment is often a positive development in many organizations, its benefits may not be universal in scope. In fact, in cultures where people are used to distinctions based on hierarchies, employees may find empowerment a strange concept and—more importantly—inconsistent with traditional cultural values. Clearly, then, for management practices to succeed, they must take into account the cultures in which they are applied. Failing to do so runs the real risk of accepting a "one-practice-fits-all" mentality, and that, in turn, can undermine the very benefits that inspired their use in the first place.

empowerment), the more those organizations would have an empowerment climate. And this, in turn, would enhance the performance of teams—and also, by generating feelings of empowerment among individuals, enhance both individual performance and job satisfaction (see Figure 12.7).

To test these predictions, employees of a high-tech manufacturing company were asked to complete a questionnaire assessing their organizations' empowerment climate (e.g., one item was, "We create structures and procedures that encourage people to take initiative in improving organizational performance"). Team performance was assessed via ratings by higher-level

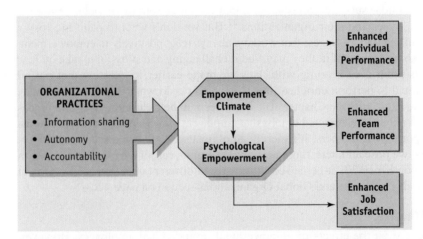

FIGURE 12.7

The Importance of an Empowerment Climate

Creating an empowerment climate in an organization facilitates team performance. It also promotes feelings of psychological empowerment, which in turn, enhance individual performance and job satisfaction.

Source: Based on findings reported by Seibert et al., 2004; see Note 30.

managers who were responsibility for these work units. Individual performance was measured by ratings from team leaders, and job satisfaction was assessed by questionnaire responses from team members (see Chapter 6).

The study's results were in keeping with Figure 12.7. Not only did empowerment climates enhance team performance, but they also contributed to feelings of psychological empowerment among employees. This, in turn, enhanced both individual performance and job satisfaction. In short, an empowerment climate enhanced the job performance of both individuals and teams.

Additional research has shown that team empowerment also leads to beneficial effects for teams whose members do not work together physically—that is, *virtual teams* (see Chapter 8).[31] One study examined empowerment in teams of employees who worked in a high-tech service organization in the travel industry, whose members met one another in person only rarely. Interestingly, the more these teams were empowered to do their work, the higher was the level of satisfaction among the customers they served. All things considered, it's clear that empowering employees can be a very effective organizational practice.

The Power of Organizational Groups

To this point, we have examined the uses of power by individuals and teams. However, in organizations, it is not only people acting alone or in small teams who wield power, but also large groups and subunits, such as departments.[32] For instance, just as some individuals are considered more powerful than others, so too are some bodies of people, including branch offices, trade unions, and so on.

This is based on the tendency for power within organizations to be distributed unequally across different departments. These subunits have responsibility for different functions, such as finance, human resource management, marketing, and research and development (we will describe these arrangements more fully in Chapter 15), and some clearly have more power than others. Why? What are the sources of such power? By what means do some groups come to control the activities of other groups? Answers to these questions are offered by two theoretical models—the *resource-dependency model* and the *strategic contingencies model*. We now consider each of these, noting what they reveal about power at the group or subunit level.

The Resource-Dependency Model: Controlling Critical Resources

It is not difficult to think of an organization as a complex set of subunits that are constantly exchanging resources with each other. By this, we mean that formal organizational departments may both give to and receive from other departments such valued commodities as money, personnel, equipment, supplies, and information. These critical resources are necessary for the successful operation of organizations.

Various subunits often depend on others for such resources. To illustrate this point, imagine a large organization that develops, produces, and sells its products in retail outlets. The sales department generates financial resources that enable the research and development division to create new products. Naturally, it cannot do so effectively without information from the marketing staff about what consumers are interested in buying and how much they might be willing to pay. The production unit has to do its part, of course, by manufacturing the goods on time, but only if the purchasing group can supply the needed raw materials—and at a price the finance department accepts.

It is easy to see how the various organizational subunits are involved in a complex set of interrelationships. To the extent that one controls the resources upon which another depends, it may be said to have power over it. After all, controlling valued resources allows the group that has such control to successfully influence the actions of other groups. Subunits that control more resources than others are considered more powerful. Indeed, such imbalances, or *asymmetries,* in the pattern of resource dependencies occur normally in organizations. The more one group depends on another for needed resources, the less power it has (see Figure 12.8).

The **resource-dependency model** proposes that a subunit's power is based on the degree to which it controls the resources required by other subunits.[33] Thus, although all subunits may contribute something to an organization, the most powerful ones are those that contribute the most important resources. Controlling the resources other departments need puts a subunit in a better position to bargain for the resources it, in turn, requires.

resource-dependency model
The view that power resides within subunits that are able to control the greatest share of valued organizational resources.

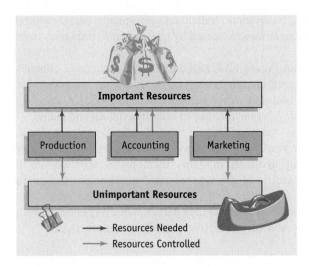

FIGURE 12.8

The Resource-Dependency Model: An Example

The resource-dependency model of organizational power explains that subunits acquire power when they control critical resources needed by other subunits. In this example, the accounting department would be considered more powerful than either the production department or the marketing department.

To illustrate this point, let's consider a classic study of differences in power wielded by departments in a large university.[34] Within a university, the various academic departments may be very unequal with respect to the power they possess. For example, relative to others, some may have more students, be more prestigious in their national reputations, receive greater grant support, and have more representatives on important university committees. As such, they would be expected to have greater control over valued resources. This was found to be the case within the large state university examined in this study. Specifically, the more powerful departments proved to be ones that were most successful in gaining scarce and valued resources from the university (e.g., funds for graduate student fellowships, faculty research grants, summer faculty fellowships). As a result, they became even more powerful, suggesting that within organizations, the rich subunits tend to get richer.

A question that follows from this conclusion is: How do various organizational subunits gain such power to begin with? That is, why do certain departments come to control the most resources when an organization is newly formed? Insight into this question is provided by a study of the semiconductor industry in California.[35] Using personal interviews, market research data, and archival records, it was found that two main factors account for how much power an organizational subunit has: (1) the period within which the company was founded, and (2) the background of the entrepreneur starting the company. For example, because research and development functions were critical for the earliest semiconductor firms (founded 1958–1966), this department had the most power among the oldest firms—the ones founded in the semiconductor industry's early years. Because research and development became somewhat less important, while sales became more important in later years as the industry matured, these departments were found to be relatively more powerful in younger companies—ones founded in the 1970s and 1980s. In short, the importance of each area of corporate activity at the time the company started operations determined the relative power of that area years later (here, in 1985, when the study was conducted).

It also was found that the most powerful organizational subunits tended to be those that represented the founder's area of expertise. Thus, for example, the marketing and sales departments of companies founded by experts in these fields tended to have the greatest amounts of power. This research provides an important missing link in our understanding of the attainment of subunit power within organizations. This tendency for the greatest corporate power to reside in areas of the founder's expertise can be seen in companies all over the world (for a significant example, see Figure 12.9).

In short, the resource-dependency model suggests that a key determinant of subunit power is the control of valued resources: The greater this control, the greater the power the subunit or department can wield. However, as we now will see, control over resources is not

AFP Photo/JIJI Press/Newscom.

FIGURE 12.9

Masaru Ibuka: Cofounder of Sony

In 1950, a young engineer from Tokyo named Masaru Ibuka was traveling the United States in search of new ideas when he came across an invention called the transistor. Although it had been developed initially for military purposes, Mr. Ibuka immediately envisioned its commercial value and convinced officials at AT&T's Bell Labs to license it to him. Shortly thereafter, he developed what became the world's first commercially viable transistor radio and sold it in his new company, Sony. On the heels of its success, Mr. Ibuka led the company in an unprecedented direction: Instead of creating new products by incorporating modified Western technology, Sony would develop its own entirely new technology to be used in consumer electronics. The rest, as they say, is history. For 60 years, Sony has been a world leader in developing new electronic products—and in the company itself, those units that are most closely involved with this function wield the most power. This illustrates a point emphasized by the *resource-dependency model*: The most powerful units in a company are those reflecting the founder's expertise.

the only factor that determines organizational power; control over the *activities* of other sub-units is important, as well.

The Strategic Contingencies Model: Power Through Dependence

In many businesses, the accounting department has the responsibility for approving or disapproving funds requested by other areas of the company. To the extent that it has this power, its actions greatly affect the activities of other units, which depend on its decisions. Specifically, other operations are *contingent* on what the accounting department does. To the extent that a department is able to control the relative power of various organizational subunits by virtue of its actions, it is said to have control over *strategic contingencies*. For example, if the accounting department consistently approved the budget requests of the production department but rejected those of the marketing department, it would be making the production department more powerful.

Where do the strategic contingencies lie within organizations? In a classic study, researchers found that power was distributed differently (i.e., across various departments) in various industries.[36] Specifically, they found that within successful firms, strategic contingencies are controlled by the departments that are most important for organizational success. For example, within the food-processing industry, where it is critical for new products to be developed and sold, successful firms have strategic contingencies controlled by the sales and research departments. In the container manufacturing field, where the timely delivery of high-quality goods is a critical determinant of organizational success, successful firms place most of the decision-making power in the sales and production departments. Thus, successful companies focus the control over strategic contingencies within the subunits most responsible for their success.

What factors give subunits control over strategic contingencies? The **strategic contingencies model** suggests that several are crucial. First, power may be enhanced by subunits that have the capacity to reduce the levels of **uncertainty** faced by others—that is, the degree to which it can provide information about the likelihood of certain events occurring in the future. For example, departments that can shed light on projections of future markets, changes in government regulations, and the availability of needed supplies, for example, can be expected to wield the most power. Accordingly, the balance of power within organizations may be expected to change as organizational conditions shift.

Consider, for example, changes that have taken place over the years in public utility companies. When public utilities first began, the engineers tended to wield the most power. But now that these companies have matured and face problems of litigation and governmental regulation (particularly over nuclear power), power has shifted to attorneys.[37] A similar shift toward greater power to the legal department has occurred in recent years in the area of human resource management, where a complex set of laws and governmental regulations has created a great deal of uncertainty for organizations. Powerful subunits are ones that can help reduce such uncertainty.

Second, subunits control power to the extent that they possess a high degree of *centrality* in the organization. **Centrality** refers to the degree to which an organizational unit has a key impact on others because it has to be consulted and because its activities have immediate effects on an organization. Some organizational subunits perform functions that are more central, whereas others perform ones that are more peripheral. For example, a firm's accounting department may have to be consulted before expenditures can be approved. As a result, it occupies a very central position in its organization. A unit's centrality also is considered high to the extent that its actions have immediate effects. So, for example, in an auto company, the effects would be far more dramatic and immediate if production lines stopped than if the research and development activities ceased. Thus, the units in charge of manufacturing or production would have greater centrality— hence, wield more power—than those responsible for research and development. In other words, the central connection of some departments to immediate organizational success provides them with considerable power.

Third, a subunit controls power when its activities are **nonsubstitutable**—that is, the degree to which it is the only unit that can perform its particular duties. So, if *any* group can perform a certain function, then the particular subunits responsible for controlling that function are not especially powerful. In a hospital, for example, personnel on surgical teams are certainly more nonsubstitutable than maintenance workers because fewer individuals have the skills needed to perform surgery than to mop a floor. Because an organization easily can replace some employees with others either from within or outside, subunits composed of individuals who are most easily replaced tend to wield very little organizational power. A summary of the three major factors included in the strategic contingencies model is provided by Figure 12.10.[38]

Taken together, the resource-dependency and strategic contingencies models offer important insights into the question, "Why, in a given organization, are some subunits or departments more powerful than others?" This question focuses on the power of organizational units as a whole instead of individuals. Interestingly, the power that individuals and groups have in organizations generally is used for good—that is, to promote the objectives of the organization and the well-being of the individuals within them. Sometimes, however, as you know probably only too well, we see abuses of power, situations in which people use their power in ways that are harmful or destructive. In each of the remaining parts of this chapter, we address particularly important forms of abuses of power—*sexual harassment* and *organizational politics*. Both constitute what may be considered "the dark side" of organizational power.

---

strategic contingencies model
A view explaining power in terms of a subunit's capacity to control the activities of other subunits. A subunit's power is enhanced when (1) it can reduce the level of uncertainty experienced by other subunits, (2) it occupies a central position in the organization, and (3) its activities are nonsubstitutable.

uncertainty
Lack of knowledge about the likelihood of certain events occurring in the future.

centrality
The degree to which an organizational unit has a key impact on others because it has to be consulted and because its activities have immediate effects on an organization.

nonsubstitutable
The degree to which an organizational unit is the only one that can perform its particular duties.

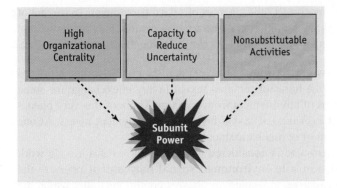

FIGURE 12.10

Strategic Contingencies Model: Identifying Sources of Subunit Power

The strategic contingencies model explains intraorganizational power in terms of the capacity of some subunits to control the actions of others. Subunit power may be enhanced by the factors shown here.

Sexual Harassment: A Serious Abuse of Power

Recall this chapter's Preview Case about a prominent male attorney who was alleged to have sexually harassed as many as nine of his female colleagues over a five-year period. His inappropriate behavior—or even claims about this behavior—harmed not only the victims, but also sullied his own reputation and tarnished the image of his otherwise distinguished firm. Unfortunately, this represents only one episode of a form of behavior that is all too common in many workplaces. And because it represents an abuse of power, *sexual harassment* is a theme we address in this section of the chapter.

Before moving forward, let's underscore this point: Almost always, sexual harassment is about power. In the majority of instances, it is an abuse of power: A more powerful person (usually, but not always, a male) gives unwanted sexual attention to a less powerful person (usually, but not always, a female). And because there's a power difference between the parties, the less powerful individual is put in a difficult situation.

Nature and Scope of Sexual Harassment

To understand why there is such concern about sexual harassment, we begin by defining this concept and presenting some statistics about its prevalence and forms. This information will make it clear that sexual harassment is an issue about which we all must be concerned.

DEFINITION. Although the working definitions used in various organizations may differ, the definition of **sexual harassment** from the U.S. Equal Employment Opportunity Commission is as follows:

> Unwelcome sexual advances, requests for sexual favors, and other verbal or physical conduct of a sexual nature constitute sexual harassment when this conduct explicitly or implicitly affects an individual's employment, unreasonably interferes with an individual's work performance, or creates an intimidating, hostile, or offensive work environment.[39]

To understand this definition fully, it helps to keep in mind the following facts:

- The victim, as well as the harasser, may be a woman or a man; the victim does not have to be of the opposite sex.
- The harasser can be the victim's supervisor, an agent of the employer, a supervisor in another area, a coworker, or a nonemployee.
- The victim may not be only the person harassed but anyone affected by the offensive conduct.
- Unlawful sexual harassment may occur without economic injury to or discharge of the victim.
- The harasser's conduct must be unwelcome.

Because sexual harassment is covered under Title VII of the Civil Rights Act of 1964, the U.S. Equal Employment Opportunity Commission (EEOC) keeps statistics on charges filed at the federal

sexual harassment
Unwelcome sexual advances, requests for sexual favors, and other verbal or physical conduct of a sexual nature constitute sexual harassment when this conduct explicitly or implicitly affects an individual's employment, unreasonably interferes with an individual's work performance, or creates an intimidating, hostile, or offensive work environment.

level. In 2009, for example, the EEOC received 12,696 charges of sexual harassment, 16 percent of which were filed by males. It recovered $51.5 million in monetary benefits for charging parties and other aggrieved individuals (not including monetary benefits obtained through litigation).[40]

quid pro quo sexual harassment
A form of sexual harassment in which the harasser requires sexual favors in exchange for some tangible conditions, privileges, or terms of employment from a victim.

hostile environment sexual harassment
A form of sexual harassment in which individuals are subjected to negative, unwanted, or abusive conditions under which their ability to work effectively and comfortably is compromised.

MAJOR FORMS. The law recognizes two major forms of sexual harassment. So-called **quid pro quo sexual harassment** occurs when the harasser requires sexual favors in exchange for some tangible conditions, privileges, or terms of employment from a victim. Think of this very blatant form of sexual harassment as a direct exchange of sexual favors for employment favors. At one time, this was the only recognized form of sexual harassment.

Today, however, sexual harassment also is considered to have occurred if a hostile work environment is created. This so-called **hostile environment sexual harassment** refers to the practice of subjecting individuals to negative, unwanted, or abusive conditions under which the ability to work effectively and comfortably is compromised. Hostile environments may exist not only because of the words or actions of particular individuals, but also by virtue of management's failure to prevent such actions among employees. This describes the form of sexual harassment depicted in this chapter's Preview Case (page 414). Although it was not claimed that Mr. Wright engaged in quid pro quo harassment, he was alleged to have created a hostile work environment for his accusers. This particular form of harassment is most prevalent. And, as you might imagine, by virtue of its inherent ambiguity, it also is most challenging to establish. Over the years, some cases of sexual harassment have become quite famous. For an overview of several of these, see Table 12.2.[41]

OCCURRENCE. As you might imagine, only a small proportion of cases of sexual harassment are brought to federal court; the vast majority are addressed as internal matters by the human resources departments within organizations. Exact figures about the prevalence of sexual harassment are difficult to come by because about 95 percent of all such incidents go unreported. However, it has been estimated that about 42 percent of women and 15 percent of men report being victims of sexual harassment.[42]

Interestingly, these figures have remained relatively unchanged in recent years. This appears to be the result of two countervailing forces. On the one hand, as people have become increasingly aware of sexual harassment because of accounts in the popular press, they have grown more sensitive to its inappropriate nature and the fact that they can (and should) do something about it. This leads them to report the behavior to appropriate authorities in their organizations, thereby contributing to a rising trend. However, the apparent rate of sexual harassment hasn't risen overall because, at the same time, awareness of the problem has inhibited some prospective perpetrators from engaging in such behavior. Thus, there also may be less of it occurring. Overall, then, fewer incidents coupled with more widespread reporting of those incidents makes it easy to see why occurrences of sexual harassment appear not to be on the rise. Still, there can be no doubt that it remains a serious problem.

Because sexual harassment has received so much attention in the popular press, it's not surprising that some people have become confused about it. This is worrisome because misunderstandings may lead to trivialization of the problem and its subsequent dismissal in some people's minds. And this, of course, can only make things worse by promoting further unethical and illegal behavior. With this in mind, it's important to dispel some key myths about sexual harassment, which is the task we undertake in The Ethics Angle section on page 434.

Managing Sexual Harassment in the Workplace: What to Do

Earlier, we noted that organizations are held legally responsible for the hostile work environments created by their employees. Unless they step in to remedy the problem, they will be seen as having contributed to it by virtue of their inaction. As such, it's important to consider what managers' responsibilities are with respect to sexual harassment in the workplace. How can management help discourage sexual harassment? The success of several practices has been established.[43]

HAVE—AND COMMUNICATE—A CLEAR POLICY. In the employee handbook or in some other established regulations, it's necessary for all companies to have clearly articulated statements

TABLE 12.2 Famous Sexual Harassment Cases

In recent years, some famous people have been involved in sexual harassment cases. These, along with other cases involving individuals who initially were less well known, have gained notoriety. Although the guilt or innocence of the accused parties has not always been established—nor should it be inferred by these accounts—high-profile cases such as these have heightened the public's awareness of the seriousness of sexual harassment.

Parties Involved or Case Names	Description
Bill Clinton and Monica Lewinsky	Investigations targeting President Clinton's relationship with a former White House intern led to his impeachment.
Bill Clinton and Paula Jones	While Governor of Arkansas, Bill Clinton allegedly propositioned Paula Jones, but he has steadfastly denied this accusation. A special prosecutor for the Lewinsky case, however, indicated that while president, Mr. Clinton perjured himself when giving a deposition about his relationship with Ms. Jones.
Maxine Henderson and Gwen	Impressionistic artist Maxine Henderson painted a portrait of a nude woman named Gwen that hung on the wall of the City Hall building in Murfreesboro, Tennessee. Claiming that she was offended by it, a female city official filed a sexual harassment claim with the city, which subsequently took the painting down. In response to this, the artist sued the city on the grounds that this violated her rights under the First Amendment. A U.S. District Court decided in favor of the artist, claiming that the city's sexual harassment policy was insufficiently detailed regarding what constituted offensive material.
Burlington Industries versus Kimberly Ellerth	Kimberly Ellerth sued her employer, Burlington Industries, alleging that she was harassed by her supervisor, leading her to suffer considerable humiliation and embarrassment. The company's defense was that she never reported any of these incidents internally and that she did not suffer any professional setbacks. Subsequently, the U.S. Supreme Court ruled that claims of sexual harassment do not require victims to report the harassment to company officials or to provide evidence of harm to their careers.
Anita Hill versus Clarence Thomas	While Clarence Thomas was being investigated as nominee for Supreme Court Justice, it was brought to light that one of his former employees at the Equal Employment Opportunity Commission, Anita Hill, had accused him of sexual harassment. Some speculated that Ms. Hill's claims were inaccurate and that this was made public in an effort to discredit this conservative nominee.
Joseph Onacle versus Sundowner Offshore Services	Mr. Onacle worked on an oil rig on a platform in the Gulf of Mexico. He claimed that he was repeatedly sodomized, threatened, and humiliated by crew members. After reporting these events to company officials, no action was taken against the alleged offenders, and Mr. Onacle subsequently resigned. He filed sexual harassment charges in the District Court of Eastern Louisiana, which dismissed the case on the grounds that, as a male, he was not protected by Title VII of the Civil Rights Act of 1964. Subsequently, the U.S. Supreme Court reversed this ruling, specifying that sexual harassment in the workplace applies as well to members of the same sex.
Lois Jenson versus Eveleth Taconite Co.	This is the story on which the 2005 film *North Country* was based. Lois Jenson reported being harassed regularly by male workers. After filing sexual harassment charges, her tires were slashed. Eventually, other women in the company came forward to indicate that they too were being sexually harassed. Eventually, Ms. Jenson and other plaintiffs settled with the company for $3.5 million.

Source: HR World Editors, 2010; see Note 41.

about sexual harassment. These generally indicate the company's intolerance of it and the actions taken against violators. Specifically, such statements make it clear that:

- The employer will not tolerate harassment based on race, sex, religion, national origin, age, or disability.
- Retaliation against anyone who complains of harassment or who participates in an investigation will not be tolerated.

It is imperative for all employees to familiarize themselves with these policies (some of which are likely to be quite extensive) and for managers to ensure that their subordinates are well versed in them. After all, having a policy that is neither communicated clearly nor followed consistently is worthless. This is important because the absence of a clear policy sends the message

The Ethics Angle

Dispelling Myths about Sexual Harassment

Sexual harassment may be considered an ethical issue because it violates the rights of its victims. If we are to end such abuses, it's important not to give anyone a chance to dismiss it as silly, as some people do. Such individuals simply don't understand what sexual harassment is all about and harbor misconceptions about it. With an eye toward turning this around, we now identify and explode some of the more common myths about sexual harassment and exchange them with underlying truths.[44]

Myth 1. If women would only would say "no," harassment would stop.

Fact. This is problematic on two counts. First, it often is difficult and very embarrassing for women of lower organizational ranks to confront higher-ranking harassers by telling them to stop what they are doing. It is up to the higher-ranking men to refrain from putting women in this position by not harassing them in the first place.

Second, even if a woman says "no," some men rationalize that "no really means yes," leading them to continue harassing their victims. The fact could not be any simpler. As you've undoubtedly heard before, no means no. Bottom line: It's preferable to not put anyone in a situation in which they have to say "no," but if and when it is said, the offender should take it seriously and stop immediately.

Myth 2. Harassment will stop if the victim simply ignores it.

Fact. The opposite is true: When harassment is ignored, it either continues or gets worse. This occurs because the harasser interprets the victim's silence as a sign of approval or encouragement. Remember, victims, quite understandably, may be too embarrassed to speak up, so they never should be put in a position where they have to do so. If necessary, however, any victim of sexual abuse, or witnesses to such abuse on the part of others, should report it to the proper authorities.

Myth 3. If women dressed less provocatively, there would be no sexual harassment.

Fact. Anyone can be a victim of sexual harassment, no matter how that individual dresses. Often, harassment is about demonstrating power, rather than sexual interest sparked by attractiveness. Besides, dressing in any particular way does not grant permission to touch or otherwise harass.

Myth 4. Most behavior considered sexual harassment is merely natural flirting and teasing between people.

Fact. This is an all-too-common rationalization. There's nothing friendly or playful about unwanted sexual innuendos, inappropriate touching, and making lewd comments. Instead of considering these innocuous expressions of friendship, recognize them for what they are—abuses of power and a need to control. If the behavior were friendly, it would not be so hurtful.

Myth 5. What some may mistake for harassment is really just a harmless compliment.

Fact. There's nothing harmless about being humiliated, or even frightened, by something that someone else says or does. Nobody should be required to endure such treatment, even if it's well intended and seemingly innocuous. If the target isn't taking it this way, then it's not so harmless after all.

Myth 6. "Nice" people, such as professionals, cannot be harassers.

Fact. Sexual harassers may not be perverts; they do not match any particular profile. Almost anyone—even a popular, highly admired professional—might be a sexual harasser. In fact, highly regarded and trusted individuals might be especially capable of engaging in harassment precisely *because* potential victims are not suspicious of them.

Sexual harassment is a very serious and all too widespread form of behavior in organizations. It occurs in large part because of common misconceptions that allow people to get away with it. Hopefully, by substituting truths for myths, we have taken at least a small step toward reducing its occurrence.

---

that sexual harassment is condoned (even if that is untrue). As you might imagine, because they are more formal in nature and have sophisticated human resources experts to help, larger companies are more likely to have formal sexual harassment policies in place than smaller ones.[45]

TRAIN EMPLOYEES ABOUT WHAT CONSTITUTES INAPPROPRIATE BEHAVIOR. Just as employees need to be trained in how to perform their jobs, they also need to be trained regarding what constitutes appropriate and inappropriate behavior toward others in the workplace. Because the lines sometimes are gray, it's important to establish the kinds of things that can and cannot be done and said. For example, although many may consider it innocuous, others may find it offensive to tell sexually oriented jokes, to say sexual things about people, to refer to people's body parts, or to refer to people in sexually related or demeaning ways. Although some individuals already may be sensitive to these things, others may not, making such training appropriate for individuals at all levels. In fact, the higher a person's rank is in an organization, the greater is that person's potential to abuse power—and hence, the more important it is for him or her to be well trained (see Figure 12.11).

MAKE SURE THERE'S A CLEAR AND EFFECTIVE COMPLAINT PROCEDURE. Any policy prohibiting sexual harassment isn't going to be particularly effective if there's no mechanism in place to report

Kathleen Lange/AP Wide World Photos.

FIGURE 12.11

Sexual Harassment Training: A Widely Used Approach for Reducing an All-Too-Common Abuse of Power

To help curtail sexual harassment most organizations provide training aimed at getting employees to learn precisely what constitutes inappropriate behavior. These programs are a fundamental part of training at the various military service academies, including the United States Naval Academy, whose cadets are shown here receiving such training.

any violations that might occur. As a result, most companies, as well as colleges and universities, have offices to which incidents of sexual harassment may be reported. The professionals in this office, usually staffed by experts in human resources management, are well equipped not only to take complaints, but also to investigate them and to make recommendations. (As you may recall, such a unit, the FEPC, existed in the law firm described in this chapter's Preview Case.)

TAKE IMMEDIATE STEPS TO STOP HARASSMENT. If an employer determines that harassment has occurred, it should take immediate measures to stop it and to ensure that it does not recur. Perpetrators found guilty should be disciplined using measures proportional to the seriousness of the offense (for general guidelines on using discipline, see Chapter 3). In addition, the employer should correct any effects of the harassment. For example, any negative performance evaluations resulting from the situation should be corrected.

CONTRIBUTE TO A NONHOSTILE ENVIRONMENT YOURSELF. One of the most effective things any manager can do to reduce the likelihood of sexual harassment occurring is to contribute to a positive and supportive culture himself or herself. Not only should you, as a manager, show support for the company policy (e.g., by expressing its importance, distributing information about it, encouraging discussions about it, etc.), but it's also important to conform with it yourself. Any violations on a manager's part may be modeled by subordinates, thereby suggesting the manager's own lack of regard for it. In other words, supervisors must be good role models.

Organizational Politics: Selfish Uses of Power

When individuals working in many industries and companies are asked to list the key problems they face at work, they mention many different issues. Near the top of most lists, though, is **organizational politics.** This refers to actions by individuals that are directed toward the goal of furthering their own self-interest without regard for the well-being of others or their organizations.[46] If this sounds selfish and unprincipled—an abuse of power—you are correct. Organizational politics

organizational politics
Unauthorized uses of power that enhance or protect one's own or one's group's personal interests.

does involve placing one's self-interests above the interests of the company. Indeed, this use of power to foster one's own interests distinguishes organizational politics from uses of power that are approved and accepted by organizations.[47]

Not surprisingly, many people condemn organizational politics and those who engage in such behavior. For example, as the outspoken billionaire and former presidential candidate H. Ross Perot once put it, "I don't want any corporate politicians . . . some guy that wants to move ahead at the expense of others."[48] Similarly, in describing why they have chosen to leave secure jobs with good companies to start their own businesses, many people note that they simply got tired of life in a big company—and especially, of having to deal with organizational politics![49]

To provide a broad overview of what we currently know about organizational politics, we'll first consider the roots of such behavior—why it occurs. Then we'll describe some of the important forms it takes and its impact on individuals and organizations.

Forms of Political Behavior

To understand precisely what organizational politics involves, it's helpful to examine the various forms it takes. We do this here by focusing on a key question: What do people do to promote their own selfish ends? There are many answers to this question but we describe several of the most prominent ones here.[50]

GAINING CONTROL OVER—AND SELECTIVELY USING—INFORMATION. Information is considered the lifeblood of organizations. Therefore, controlling it and determining who knows what is one of the most important ways to gain and exercise power in organizations. Although outright lying and falsifying information are relatively rare (in part because of the consequences of getting caught), there are other ways of controlling information to gain political advantage. For example, you might (1) withhold information that makes you look bad (e.g., negative sales information), (2) avoid contact with those who may ask you something you would prefer not to disclose, (3) be very selective about what you say, or (4) overwhelm others with information that may not be completely relevant. These are all ways of controlling the nature and degree of data that people have at their disposal. Such control often plays a key role in organizational politics.

CULTIVATING A FAVORABLE IMPRESSION. People interested in enhancing their power in an organization often engage in some type of image building—attempts to enhance the favorableness of the impressions they make on others. Such efforts take many forms, such as (1) "dressing for success," (2) associating oneself with the successful accomplishments of others (or, in extreme cases, taking credit for others' successes), or (3) simply calling attention to one's own successes and positive characteristics.[51] Of course, not everyone who does these things (or engages in other efforts to look good to others) is doing so for political reasons. However, it's quite likely that a person who engages in extreme levels of these behaviors may well have political motives in mind.

BUILDING POWERFUL COALITIONS. To exert influence successfully, it often is useful to gain the support of others within the organization. Managers, for example, may lobby for their ideas before they officially present them at meetings, ensuring that others are committed to them in advance and thereby avoiding the embarrassment of public rejection. Sometimes, of course, it's difficult even to assemble an audience of high-ranking company officials to whom to make your argument. This is where the "elevator pitch" often comes in: Politically active people have been known to hang around specific elevators at particular times of day, hoping to ride next to a top executive—to whom they can "pitch" their projects or ideas along the way.

BLAMING AND ATTACKING OTHERS. One of the most popular political tactics involves blaming and attacking others when bad things happen. A commonly used political tactic is finding a **scapegoat,** a person who is made to take the blame for someone else's failure or wrongdoing. A supervisor, for example, may explain that the failure of a sales plan she designed was based on the serious mistakes of one of her subordinates—even if this is not entirely true. Explaining that "it's *her* fault" sometimes can get the real culprit "off the hook" for it.

Finding a scapegoat can allow the politically astute individual to avoid (or at least minimize) association with the negative situation (see Figure 12.12). For example, when corporate performance drops, powerful chief executives often resort to placing the blame on lower-ranking individuals, protecting themselves from getting fired while their subordinate gets the axe.[52]

scapegoat
Someone who is made to take the blame for someone else's failure or wrongdoing.

"The new scapegoats are in."

FIGURE 12.12

Finding a Scapegoat Is Never Quite This Easy

Although scapegoats are never so conveniently identified, politically astute individuals still manage to find people on whom they can affix blame for their own wrongdoings.

ASSOCIATING WITH POWERFUL OTHERS. One of the most direct ways to gain power is by connecting oneself with more powerful others. There are several means of accomplishing this goal. For example, a lower-power person may become more powerful if she has as a mentor a higher ranking and better-established person, who can look out for and protect her interests (for a thorough discussion of careers, see Appendix 2).

People also may align themselves with more powerful others by giving them "positive strokes" in the hope of getting these persons to like them and help them—a process known as **ingratiation**.[53] Agreeing with someone more powerful may be an effective way of getting that person to consider you an ally. Such an alliance, of course, may prove valuable when you are looking for support within an organization. To summarize, having a powerful mentor, forming coalitions, and using ingratiation are all potentially effective ways of gaining power by aligning oneself with others.

ingratiation
The practice of cultivating someone's favor by agreeing with that individual.

CREATING OBLIGATIONS AND USING RECIPROCITY. Still another way to gain power is to gather a lot of obligations—IOUs from others that will be paid back with interest. People who are adept at using this tactic do favors for others in their organization—favors that cost them relatively little. Later, they attempt to wring major benefits from such obligations. "I helped you," they suggest, "now it's your turn." They do relatively little for others, but expect a lot in return.

Why Does Political Behavior Occur?

If you have worked in several different organizations, you probably realize that although organizational politics occur almost everywhere, the amount of such activity varies greatly. In some settings people spend large amounts of time engaging in organizational politics, although in others, such actions are far less frequent. This raises an important question: What factors encourage—or discourage—such behavior? Both personal and organizational variables play a role.

PERSONAL DETERMINANTS OF ORGANIZATIONAL POLITICS. Turning first to personal factors, it appears that people high in Machiavellianism, an aspect of personality we discussed in Chapter 4, are especially likely to engage in such behavior.[54] Given that high Machiavellians believe that it is acceptable to use others for their personal needs, this is hardly surprising.

We also know that some individuals, ones who are particularly adept at monitoring the effects of their behavior on others, are inclined to engage in organizational politics. After all, such "**social chameleons**" do whatever it takes to get others to like them.[55]

Finally, people who engage in organizational politics have a particular set of skills and traits that equip them to engage in this behavior. In particular, they are very socially adept, highly popular, extroverted, self-confident, aggressive, ambitious, devious, intelligent, and articulate. Given this particular set of variables, it's little wonder that such individuals often succeed in their efforts to get ahead, no matter what.[56]

social chameleons
Individuals who do whatever it takes to get others to like them.

ORGANIZATIONAL DETERMINANTS OF ORGANIZATIONAL POLITICS. Turning next to organizational factors, it appears that to the extent certain conditions exist, political behavior is likely to occur. Specifically, political behavior occurs when goals and roles are ambiguous, the organization has a history or climate of political activity, and resources are scarce.[57] This raises an interesting question: If ambiguous conditions promote political activity, then how does having political skills affect actual job performance?

This question was addressed in a recent study conducted in a division of a state government.[58] Participants in the research were employees (who completed various questionnaires) and these individuals' supervisors (who rated their employees' performance levels). The researchers conducting this study examined ambiguity from the perspective of procedural justice (as noted in Chapter 2); this refers to the extent to which people believe that fair procedures are used in their organization. When procedural justice is low, people don't know what to expect because there's a degree of uncertainty about what decisions will be made. Under these circumstances, employees may turn to their political skills to help them navigate the ambiguity. So, for example, people who have connections to help them may find such individuals especially useful. Thus, when procedural justice is low, people with high levels of political skill are likely to outperform those who have low levels of political skill. If you look at the red line on Figure 12.13, you'll see that this is precisely what the researchers found.

What about when employees perceive that procedural justice levels are high? Under these circumstances things are clear to employees; they can count on fair procedures being used, making it apparent what they have to do to perform appropriately. Under such conditions, having political skill actually may interfere with job performance because it keeps employees from going about their jobs the right way. Those with low levels of political skill may perform better because they are disinclined to engage in any political behavior that might lead them in the wrong direction. Thus, when procedural justice is high, people with low levels of political skill are likely to outperform those who have high levels of political skill. The green line in Figure 12.13 reveals that this is indeed what occurred.

FIGURE 12.13

Political Skill Can Help or Hinder Job Performance

A recent study found that when procedural justice was low (i.e., when people can't count on fair procedures being used, making conditions ambiguous), people with high levels of political skill outperformed those who have low levels of political skill. However, when procedural justice was high (i.e., people can count on fair procedures being used, making conditions clear), people with low levels of political skill outperformed those who have high levels of political skill.

Source: Adapted from Andrews et al., 2009; see Note 58.

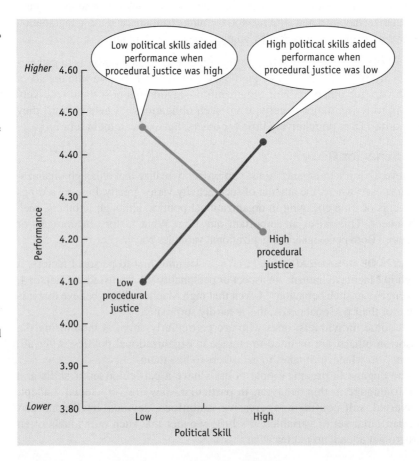

This study is interesting because it reveals the complex ways in which OB variables come together to tell a rich story about the way people behave on the job.

POLITICS IN HUMAN RESOURCE MANAGEMENT. Another important finding concerning organizational politics is that they often occur in connection with key human resource management activities such as performance appraisal, personnel selection, and compensation decisions.[59] Given that there is often a certain amount of ambiguity associated with evaluating another's performance, this leaves lots of room for individuals to cultivate certain images as they perform this task. As a result, performance ratings are sometimes more a reflection of the rater's interest in promoting a particular image of himself or herself (e.g., being tough, or easy to please) than in accurately evaluating another's behavior.[60] Similarly, when making personnel decisions, people are concerned at least as much about the implications of their hires for their own careers (e.g., will this person support me or make me look bad?) as they are concerned about doing what's best for the organization.[61]

Finally, pay raise decisions have been shown to be politically motivated, at least in some instances. For example, researchers conducting a management simulation exercise found that managers gave the highest raises to individuals who threatened to complain if they didn't get a substantial raise, particularly if it was known that these people had political connections within the organization.[62] Taken together, these findings suggest that the very nature of human resource management activities in organizations makes them prime candidates for various forms of organizational politics.

POLITICS IN LARGE MULTINATIONAL ORGANIZATIONS. Although organizational politics often involves actions by individuals designed to boost their own power and status, it also occurs at the corporate level between units of large multinational companies. For instance, consider Vodafone Group, the huge European mobile phone company. It has subsidiaries around the world, from Australia to Europe, and works hard to attain a high level of equipment and software compatibility in all its units.

Yet, because its subsidiaries retain considerable independence (often under the laws of their respective countries), Vodafone lacks the power to order them to adopt a uniform array of products. How does it attempt to deal with this situation? Through the political tactic of *creating accomplished fact*: It strives to create the perception that the systems and products it recommends are the established standard. And to some extent, this works. In some instances, however, subsidiaries carefully guard their independence and make their own choices. The result is that Vodafone, like many other companies facing the same situation, must continue to use political tactics and maneuvering to strengthen its power; under current circumstances there is, literally, no other option.

The Impact of Organizational Politics

By definition, political behavior is selfish in nature. So when people engage in such actions, and do so effectively, they benefit personally: They get the promotions, raises, or power that they are seeking. The effects on other persons and the organization itself, however, can be far more negative.

We know, for example, that the more frequently political behavior occurs in an organization, the less satisfied its employees are with their jobs and the less committed they are to working in those companies.[63] Similarly, the greater the incidence of political behavior, the stronger is the intention of employees to leave (voluntary turnover).[64] As we saw in Chapter 6, job satisfaction, commitment, and turnover are all important factors in an organization's performance, so to the extent these are affected by politics, important consequences may result. Finally, the greater the incidence of politics, the less employees believe that they are supported by their organizations.[65] And since such feelings play a key role in work motivation (see Chapter 7), the impact of organizational politics can take its toll in a very important way.

In general, although organizational politics may benefit those who are skilled at carrying it out, at least over the short term, its occurrence tends to undermine employees' satisfaction with, and commitment to, their organizations. And in extreme cases, many persons—often the best—may choose to leave rather than put up with an environment they view as unfair, corrupt, and deceptive.

Interestingly, however, not everyone reacts to organizational politics in the same way. Some people are bothered by it more than others. In particular, people low in *conscientiousness*—one of the Big Five dimensions of personality we examined in Chapter 4—are more strongly affected. The less conscientious they are, the more adversely their job performance is affected by political behavior.[66] It's interesting to consider why this occurs. The answer lies in the fact that people who are highly conscientious are reliable, responsible, and persistent, giving them the tenacity and diligence to get things done even in a politically charged work environment. In contrast, individuals who are low in conscientiousness lack these adaptive characteristics, allowing them to become more easily distracted or discouraged by politics. In a sense, therefore, politics are most harmful to the "weakest links" in an organization's chain—those employees who are not top performers anyway.

Summary and Review of Learning Objectives

1. **Describe the nature of influence in organizations and its major forms.**

   When someone attempts to change the behavior or views of one or more others, they are engaging in attempts at exerting *influence*. Influence can take many different forms, including rational persuasion, inspirational appeal, consultation, ingratiation, exchange, personal appeal, coalition-building, legitimating, and pressure.

2. **Distinguish between various forms of individual power in organizations.**

   Overall, power refers to the capacity to influence others. One major type of power, *position power*, resides within one's formal organizational position. It includes (1) *reward power* and (2) *coercive power*, the capacity to control valued rewards and punishments, respectively, (3) *legitimate power*, the recognized authority that an individual has by virtue of his or her organizational position, and (4) *information power*, power that stems from having special data and knowledge. A second major type of power, *personal power*, resides within an individual's own unique qualities or characteristics. It includes (1) *rational persuasion*, using logical arguments and factual evidence to convince others that an idea is acceptable, (2) *expert power*, the power an individual has because he or she is recognized as having some superior knowledge, skill, or expertise, (3) *referent power*, influence based on the fact that an individual is admired by others, and (4) *charisma*, having an engaging and magnetic personality.

3. **Define empowerment and indicate how it operates among individuals and in teams.**

   Empowerment is a process in which authority is delegated to the lowest level in an organization at which competent decisions regarding various issues can be made. At the individual level, it has been found to enhance both performance and job satisfaction, although these beneficial effects are greater in some cultures (low-power-distance cultures) than others (high-power-distance cultures). To the extent organizations create an *empowerment climate*, they can empower teams as well as individuals. This can enhance the performance of both teams and individuals.

4. **Describe how the resource-dependency model and the strategic contingencies model explain the nature of power between organizational units.**

   The *resource-dependency model* asserts that power resides within the subunits that control the greatest share of valued organizational resources. The *strategic contingencies model* explains power in terms of a subunit's capacity to control the activities of other subunits. Such power may be enhanced by the capacity to reduce the level of uncertainty experienced by another unit, having a central position within the organization, or performing functions that other units cannot perform.

5. **Describe how sexual harassment constitutes an abuse of organizational power and ways of reducing its occurrence.**

   Almost always, sexual harassment constitutes an abuse of power in which a more powerful person (usually, but not always, a male) gives unwanted sexual attention to a less powerful person (usually, but not always, a female). Because there's a power difference between the parties, the less powerful individual is put in a difficult situation. Unfortunately, this form of behavior is not uncommon, although most instances go unreported. Not only is sexual harassment patently illegal, but it also is highly costly to all involved parties, both financially and psychologically. To help reduce the occurrence of sexual harassment, it is useful for management to do the following: (1) have—and communicate—a clear policy prohibiting sexual harassment, (2) train employees about what constitutes inappropriate behavior, (3) make sure there's a clear and effective complaint procedure in place, (4) take immediate steps to stop harassment before it gets worse, and (5) as a manager, contribute to a nonhostile work environment yourself.

6. **Explain when and where organizational politics occur and the forms such behavior takes.**

   Political behavior is likely to occur in situations where goals and roles are ambiguous, the organization has a history or climate of political activity, and resources are scarce. In addition, politics is also encouraged by a high level of centralization and when different individuals or units in the organization have conflicting interests or goals. Politics often occurs in connection with human resources issues and tends to increase as organizations mature and increase in size. Political tactics vary greatly and include such things as blaming and attacking others, controlling access to information, and cultivating a favorable impression.

Points to Ponder

Questions for Review

1. What is influence and how does it differ from power? From organizational politics?
2. What are the tactics of influence used most frequently in organizations?
3. What is position power? How does it differ from personal power?
4. What is empowerment? Can it work on the team as well as individual level?
5. According to the resource-dependency model of subunit power, what are the most important foundations of subunit power in an organization?
6. According to the strategic contingencies model, what is the basis of subunit power in an organization?
7. What, exactly, is sexual harassment, and what can be done to minimize its occurrence in organizations?
8. What are some of the most important causes of organizational politics?
9. What are the effects of organizational politics?

Experiential Questions

1. How do you attempt to influence the people with whom you work?
2. If you hold power in an organization, what is its basis? How do you prefer to exert power over others?
3. Have you ever felt empowered in an organization? If so, why? And what effects, if any, did such feelings of being empowered have on your performance?

4. Answer the following questions only if you don't mind talking about this personal issue: Have you ever engaged in sexual harassment? What, precisely, did you do that was wrong and what might have been done to prevent you from doing it?
5. Answer the following questions only if you don't mind talking about this personal issue: Have you ever been a victim of sexual harassment? How did it make you feel?
6. Have you ever engaged in organizational politics? If so, what tactics did you use?

Questions to Analyze

1. Do you think that highly influential people gain power? In other words, are influence and power related?
2. Aside from rational persuasion, what techniques of influence do you believe are used most often in organizations? Why are these particular techniques used more frequently than others?
3. Why do you think most executives prefer personal bases of power to positional bases of power?
4. Do you think that sexual harassment ever can be eliminated entirely or that some degree of harassment is inevitable in the workplace?
5. Politics often produces negative effects for organizations as a whole. What steps can an organization wishing to reduce politics take to reach this goal?

Experiencing OB

Individual Exercise

What Kinds of Influence Does Your Supervisor Use?

One of the main ways of learning about social influence in organizations is to use questionnaires in which people are asked to describe the behaviors of their supervisors. If a consistent pattern emerges with respect to the way subordinates describe supervisors, some very strong clues are provided as to the nature of that person's influence style. Questionnaires similar to this one are used for this purpose. Completing this exercise will give you an idea of the types of social influence favored by your supervisor.

Directions

Indicate how strongly you agree or disagree with each of the following statements as it describes your immediate supervisor. Answer by using the following scale:

1 = strongly disagree

2 = disagree

3 = neither agree nor disagree

4 = agree

5 = strongly agree

For each statement select the number corresponding to the most appropriate response; then, score your responses.

My supervisor can:

1. _____ Recommend that I receive a raise.
2. _____ Assign me to jobs I dislike.
3. _____ See that I get the promotion I desire.
4. _____ Make my life at work completely unbearable.
5. _____ Make decisions about how things are done.
6. _____ Provide useful advice on how to do my job better.
7. _____ Comprehend the importance of doing things a certain way.
8. _____ Make me want to look up to him or her.
9. _____ Share with me the benefit of his or her vast job knowledge.
10. _____ Get me to admire what he or she stands for.
11. _____ Find out things that nobody else knows.
12. _____ Explain things so logically that I want to do them.
13. _____ Have access to vital data about the company.
14. _____ Share a clear vision of what the future holds for the company.
15. _____ Come up with the facts needed to make a convincing case about something.
16. _____ Put me in a trance when he or she communicates to me.

Scoring

1. Add the numbers assigned to statements 1 and 3. This is the *reward power* score.
2. Add the numbers assigned to statements 2 and 4. This is the *coercive power* score.
3. Add the numbers assigned to statements 5 and 7. This is the *legitimate power* score.
4. Add the numbers assigned to statements 6 and 9. This is the *expert power* score.
5. Add the numbers assigned to statements 8 and 10. This is the *referent power* score.
6. Add the numbers assigned to statements 11 and 13. This is the *information power* score.
7. Add the numbers assigned to statements 12 and 15. This is the *rational persuasion* score.
8. Add the numbers assigned to statements 14 and 16. This is the *charisma* score.

Questions for Discussion

1. With respect to which dimensions did your supervisor score highest and lowest? Are these consistent with what you would have predicted in advance?
2. Does your supervisor behave in ways consistent with the dimension along which you gave him or her the highest score? In other words, does he or she fit the description given in the text?
3. How do you think your own subordinates would answer the various questions with respect to yourself?
4. Which of the eight forms of social influence do you think are most common and least common, and why?

Group Exercise

Recognizing Organizational Politics When You See It

A good way to make sure you understand organizational politics is to practice enacting different political tactics, and to attempt to recognize these tactics portrayed by others. This exercise is designed with these objectives in mind. The more practiced you are at recognizing political activity when you see it, the better equipped you may be to defend yourself against political adversaries.

Directions

1. Divide the class into groups of approximately four students each.
2. Each group should select at random one of the six major political tactics described on pages 436–437.
3. Meeting together for about 30 minutes, each group should prepare a brief role-play in which the four members enact the particular political tactic selected. These should be as realistic as possible, and not written simply to broadcast the answer. That is, the tactic should be presented much as you would expect to see it used in a real organization.
4. Each group should take a turn presenting its role-play to the class. Feel free to announce the setting or context in which your portrayal is supposed to occur. Don't worry about giving an award-winning performance; it's okay to keep a script or set of notes in your hand. The important thing is that you attempt to depict the political tactic in a realistic manner.
5. After each group presents its skit, members of the class should attempt to identify the specific political tactic depicted. This should lead to a discussion of the clues that suggested that answer and additional things that could have been done to depict the particular tactic portrayed.

Questions for Discussion

1. How successful was the class in identifying the various political tactics portrayed? Were some tactics more difficult to portray than others?
2. Based on these portrayals, which tactics do you believe are most likely to be used in organizations, and under what circumstances?
3. Which political tactics do you believe are most negative? Why

Practicing OB

Politics Is Powering the Exit Door

A rapidly growing high-tech company has recently experienced resignations by several of its best people. These individuals have left, expressing strong annoyance over the high level of politics within the company. This is a serious situation because these former employees are also spreading the word that "politics is king" in the company.

1. What steps can the top management of this company take to turn this situation around—to reduce the role of politics within the company?

2. How can the company counter the negative image it is acquiring as a result of disparaging comments by former employees concerning politics within the company?

3. Why do you think politics has become such an important issue in this company? Is it a matter of personalities—the specific persons who work there—or something about the nature of the business—how it is structured, the industry within which it works?

■ *The Smith Brothers' Low-Key Approach to Organizational Power*

Case in Point

Two brothers who have both run major companies? That's certainly a rarity in the modern world of business. But it is exactly the situation for the Smith brothers, John F. and Michael. John is vice president of Corporate Planning and Alliances at General Motors, while his brother Mike is retired CEO of Hughes Electronics Corp. and serves on the boards of directors of several large electronics companies. So both have held powerful positions, indeed. But how, you may be wondering, did they both acquire so much power—and such a

high level of success? Was it because they lusted after power and focused their lives on attaining it? People who know them well would disagree. They attribute the Smiths' rise to power more to their interests than to any powerful desire for power.

Long-time friends and acquaintances note that even as children, the Smith brothers showed tremendous interest in business. Sally Mahoney, who knew the Smith brothers and their parents, recalls that as children, they loved to play board games, especially Monopoly. "I can just remember them stacking up those hotels and houses. Money was

(Continued)

always very interesting to them," she notes. And the Smiths themselves were aware of this interest from childhood on. "We like business. We grew up in a business-oriented family," Mike says.

Although they attended different schools, the Smith brothers were both described by people who knew them as bright, hard-working, and unassuming. "Ego doesn't show," says M. Hoglund, a retired GM executive who worked with both brothers. "They are great guys to work around and as a result, generate a lot of loyalty." "Jack will wander down the halls, his head down, trying to be obscure, where the king would be looking around for recognition," says Dr. David E. Cole, director of the University of Michigan's Center for Automotive Research. So, it does not appear that the Smiths gained their power through organizational politics. Instead, they seemed to acquire it naturally because other people liked, trusted, and respected them.

In addition, the fact that they were "organization-oriented" rather than "my own career–oriented" seems to have played an important role in their rise to power. Both Smith brothers are true team players, with genuine concern for the people with whom they work as well as their companies. More top executives prefer to gather power from their personal characteristics—their charisma, expertise, personalities—than from their positions. The Smith brothers seem to appreciate this fact and have used it to build their successful careers—along with huge helpings of power. Individually and together, they suggest that the road to power in today's organizations does *not* have to follow a route dictated by selfish self-interest. On the contrary, individuals who gain power often seem to do so because their skills and talents suit them to this role rather than because they set out, early in life, to seek it.

Questions for Discussion

1. What bases of personal power contribute to the Smith brothers' success?
2. Is their low-key, unassuming approach the best for obtaining—and keeping—power?
3. How might organizational politics have played a role in the Smith brothers' rise to the top?

13 Leadership in Organizations

Learning Objectives

After reading this chapter, you should be able to:

1. Differentiate between leadership and management, contrasting the things people in these roles typically do.

2. Identify the major characteristics that make leaders effective and that help transformational leaders inspire followers to make major changes in their organizations.

3. Distinguish between the two basic forms of leader behavior: person-oriented behavior and production-oriented behavior, explaining how grid training helps develop them.

4. Explain what the leader-member exchange (LMX) model says about the relationships between leaders and followers.

5. Summarize what LPC contingency theory and situational leadership theory say about the connection between leadership style and situational variables.

6. Describe various techniques used to develop successful leaders in organizations.

Chapter Outline

- The Nature of Leadership
- The Trait Approach to Leadership: Having the Right Stuff
- Leadership Behavior: What Do Leaders Do?
- Leaders and Followers
- Contingency Theories of Leader Effectiveness
- Leadership Development: Bringing Out the Leader Within You

Preview Case

■ *The Woman Who Saved the Chicken Fajitas*

With only 97 restaurants in 20 states, Houlihan's doesn't have the presence of its larger competitors in the $83.5 billion casual-dining business, Applebee's, Chili's, and T.G.I. Friday's. Neither does it have their multi-million dollar advertising budgets to lure customers. What Houlihan's does have, though, is a particularly valuable human asset—Jen Gulvik, a leader who listens.

As vice president of marketing, Gulvik recognized that the time had come for a total makeover of Houlihan's. Even most of the people who lived near one of the restaurants had never visited. Individuals who were most familiar with the chain were employees, of course, and previous customers, most of whom were repeat guests who really loved the restaurants. Often, they'd come in with friends who also enjoyed dining there. But word-of-mouth advertising, although satisfactory, wasn't good enough.

Gulvik realized that it was necessary to bring new customers through Houlihans' doors, which required delivering precisely what diners were looking for. And this, in turn, meant listening to prospective customers. Comment cards on the tables reached only current diners. What she really needed was to reach out to the broader community, especially younger "Millennials," among whom the restaurant had the most appeal. So, moving people from recognizing Houlihan's appeal to becoming its customers became her mission.

As her major weapon in this battle, Gulvik relied on one of the favorite communication tools of her target market: the social networking site. Harnessing this power, in the summer of 2009 she sent e-mails to 100,000 people who had expressed interest in Houlihan's (such as by visiting its Web site) and invited them to join its private, by-invitation-only social networking site, HQ. This was to be a brand community that could serve as a

"virtual comment card." It became wildly popular, and today HQ consists of some 10,500 "Houlifans," as the community's members have chosen to call themselves.

The unrestricted feedback from Houlifans has proven invaluable in transforming the previously stodgy, pub-style restaurants into hipper, suburban-chic spots, complete with popular music in the background and even new forks on the tables. Their input has enabled Houlihan's to change menu items on-the-fly, such as when Houlifans made it clear that several of the restaurant's new tapas-style (small plate) items needed work. The white bean hummus and pita, for example, was described as "thick and spongy." Because Gulvik schedules at least an hour a day in the online community, her ears perked up as she discovered this problem. Immediately, she got word to Chef Dan that some tweaking was required. Today, the tapas menu—containing all high-profit margin items—comprises about a quarter of total sales.

In the eyes (and tastebuds) of many, the single most important benefit from HQ has been its capacity to share concerns directly with Jen Gulvik. Apparently, one revision of the menu led to the removal of chicken fajitas, a low-profit item. Customers, however, loved them so much that they purchased the sauce from the restaurants to take home, and many guests visited only to have them, never venturing anyplace else on the menu.

Acknowledging the importance of giving customers what they want—and reinforcing contributions to HQ as well—Gulvik returned the chicken fajitas to the menu. The HQ community was abuzz, and excited customers tweeted photos of the dish to their friends as proof if its return. One customer who came to the restaurant in search of them spotted Jen Gulvik and introduced her to her dining companion as "The Woman Who Saved the Chicken Fajitas." And so she forever will be known.

Jen Gulvik is not your ordinary leader. Instead of envisioning a bold new menu and inspiring eagerly waiting staffers to bring it to fruition, as many leaders would have done, she took another approach. Ms. Gulvik envisioned listening to customers and she has inspired Houlihan's many servers, chefs, and bartenders to do the same, joining online chats and spreading the word about their restaurants. Her objective, and now theirs too, is classic: Give customers what they want. Although this is hardly a novel orientation, Ms. Gulvik's vision incorporated a way to make it happen that was quite new indeed. It was really quite ingenious, too. Besides using HQ as a portal for getting valuable feedback from thousands of people, she recognized that it would help the company in another way. By participating in the discussions, so-called Houlifans have come to identify with the restaurant, considering it their own. Not surprisingly, they visit regularly and often bring friends to join them in experiencing "my restaurant."

Although Jen Gulvik might not be famous (yet, at least), her story is likely quite similar to those of untold thousands of other leaders who toil in relative anonymity every day. They are known within their organizations, of course, and maybe in their industries, but theirs are not household names. This does not make them any less vital as leaders. Their organizations count on these individuals for bringing them huge successes. In fact, if you were to ask a group of top executives to name the single most important determinant of organizational success, most would likely point to "effective leadership." Indeed, it is widely believed in the world of business that *leadership* is the key ingredient in the recipe for corporate achievement. And this view is by no means restricted to business organizations. As you know from experience, leadership also is important when it comes to politics, sports, and many other activities.[1]

Is this view justified? Do leaders really play crucial roles in shaping the fates and fortunes of businesses? A century of research on this topic suggests that they do. Effective leadership is indeed a key determinant of organizational success.[2] Given its importance, it makes sense that leadership has been one of the most widely studied phenomena in the social sciences.[3] In view of this, we will devote this chapter to describing various approaches to the study of leadership as well as their implications for managerial practice.

To make manageable the task of summarizing this wealth of information, we will proceed as follows. First, we will consider some basic points about leadership—what it is and how leadership differs from management. Then, we will examine views of leadership focusing on the traits of leaders, followed by a discussion of leader behaviors. Next, we will examine several major theories of leadership that look at the relationship between leaders and their followers. Following this, we will review several contrasting theories dealing with the conditions under which leaders are effective or ineffective in their important role. Finally, we conclude by describing various techniques used to enhance and develop leaders, making them highly effective.

The Nature of Leadership

In a sense, leadership resembles love: It is something most people believe they can recognize, but often find difficult to define. What, precisely, is it? And, how does being a leader differ from being a manager? We now focus on these questions.

Defining Leadership

Imagine that you have accepted a new job and entered a new work group. How would you recognize its leader? One possibility, of course, is through the formal titles and assigned roles each person in the group holds. In short, the individual designated as department head or project manager would be the one you would identify as the group's leader.

Imagine, however, that during several staff meetings, you noticed that this person was really not the most influential. Although she or he held the formal authority, these meetings were dominated by another individual who, ostensibly, was the top person's subordinate. What would you conclude about leadership then? Probably, you would say that the real leader was the person who actually ran things—not the one with the formal title and the apparent authority.

In many cases, of course, the disparity we have just described does not exist. The individual possessing the greatest amount of formal authority is also the most influential. In some situations, however, this is not so. And in such cases, we typically identify the person who actually exercises the most influence over the group as its **leader.** These facts point to the following definition of leadership—one accepted by many experts on this topic: **Leadership** is the process whereby one individual influences other group members toward the attainment of defined group or organizational goals.[4]

Important Characteristics of Leadership

Now that we've formally defined leadership, let's examine more closely three key points appearing within this definition. Appreciating these ideas will help you better understand the general nature of the leadership process. We outline this general process here (see Figure 13.1) and expand upon it fully throughout this chapter.

LEADERSHIP INVOLVES NONCOERCIVE INFLUENCE. According to our definition, leadership is a process involving influence—one in which a leader changes the actions or attitudes of several group members or subordinates. As we saw in Chapter 12, many techniques for exerting such influence exist, ranging from relatively coercive ones—the recipient has little choice but to do what is requested—to relatively noncoercive ones—the recipient can choose to accept or reject the influence attempted. Of note, leadership refers to the use of noncoercive influence techniques.

leader
An individual within a group or an organization who wields the most influence over others.

leadership
The process whereby one individual influences others toward the attainment of defined group or organizational goals.

FIGURE 13.1

The Leadership Process: A Summary

Leadership is a process in which one person, a *leader*, influences a follower in a noncoercive manner to attain a goal. Note, of course, that leaders also may be influenced by their followers.

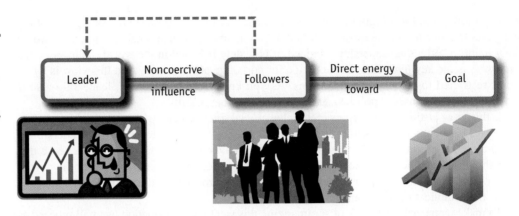

Former U.S. President Dwight D. Eisenhower emphasized this point by saying, "You do not lead by hitting people over the head; that's assault, not leadership."

People who rely on coercive forms of influence are considered *dictators* instead of leaders. Thus, whereas dictators get others to do what they want by using physical coercion or threats of physical force but leaders do not. Contrast President Eisenhower's remarks with those of Mao Zedong,[5] founder of the People's Republic of China: "Power grows out of the barrel of a gun." This may be true with respect to the power of dictators, but *not* the power of leaders. In most cases, leadership rests, at least in part, on positive feelings between leaders and their subordinates. Subordinates are inclined to follow leaders because they respect, like, or admire them—not simply because they hold positions of formal authority. (This point is in keeping with our discussion of referent power and coercion in Chapter 12.)[6]

LEADERSHIP INFLUENCE IS GOAL-DIRECTED. Our definition of leadership also suggests that it involves the exercise of influence for a purpose—that is, to attain some clearly specified group or organizational goal. In other words, leaders focus on altering those actions or attitudes of their subordinates that are related to specific outcomes; they are far less concerned with altering actions or attitudes that are irrelevant to such goals.

LEADERSHIP REQUIRES FOLLOWERS. Finally, note that our definition, by emphasizing the central role of influence, implies that leadership is somewhat reciprocal. Although leaders do indeed influence subordinates in various ways, leaders are also influenced by their subordinates. In fact, it may be said that leadership exists only in relation to followers. After all, one cannot lead without followers! As former British statesman Benjamin Disraeli once put it, "I must follow the people. Am I not their leader?"

We cannot help but conclude this section by noting how often we pointed out what famous world leaders have said about leadership. Although they sometimes disagree with one another about the content of their messages[7] (as world leaders are inclined to do), the fact that they have had so much to say about leadership provides a clear indication of their appreciation for its importance.

Leaders Versus Managers: A Key Distinction—At Least in Theory

In everyday speech, the terms *leader* and *manager* tend to be used interchangeably. Although we understand the temptation to do so, the two roles are not identical and need to be clearly distinguished. In essence, the primary function of a *leader* is to envision and articulate the essential purpose or mission of an organization and the strategy for attaining it. By contrast, the job of the *manager* is to implement that vision.

Essentially, the manager's job is to put into practice a means for achieving the vision created by the leader. Thus, whereas management is about dealing with complexity, leadership is about coping with change. Specifically, managers create plans and monitor results relative to those plans. However, leaders establish direction by creating a vision of the future. Effective leaders then get people to buy into their visions and to go along with them.[8]

Although these differences are simple to articulate, the distinction between establishing a mission and implementing it is often blurred in practice (see Figure 13.2). This happens because many leaders, such as top corporate executives, frequently take it upon themselves not

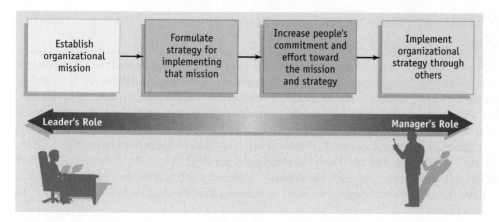

FIGURE 13.2

Leaders and Managers: Distinguishing Their Roles

Leaders are primarily responsible for establishing an organizational mission, whereas *managers* are primarily responsible for implementing that mission through others. The intermediate steps—formulating a strategy and increasing people's commitment toward the goal—tend to be performed by either leaders or managers. These overlapping functions often make the distinction between leaders and managers blurred in actual practice.

only to create a vision, but also to formulate a strategy for implementing it—and play a role in increasing people's commitment toward that vision and plan. By contrast, managers are charged with responsibility for implementing organizational strategy through others. At the same time, they also are frequently involved in helping to formulate strategy and increasing people's commitment and effort toward implementing that plan.

In other words, leaders and managers play several overlapping roles in actual practice—a fact that blurs the distinction between them. Some managers are considered leaders, whereas others are not. Similarly, some leaders assume more of a management role than others. Thus, although the differences are not always obvious, they are real. For this reason, we will distinguish carefully between leaders and managers throughout this chapter (for an overview, see Table 13.1).

TABLE 13.1 Leaders Versus Managers: A Summary Comparison

According to a well-known management theorist, the distinction between managers and leaders is reflected by the 12 points of difference summarized here. Although some of these are a bit general, they provide a good comparison. Also, because some managers do the things in the "leaders" column and some leaders do the things in the "managers" column, the practical distinctions between them are not always clear.

Managers . . .	Leaders . . .
• Administer	• Innovate
• Ask how	• Ask what and why
• Focus on systems	• Focus on people
• Do things right	• Do the right things
• Maintain	• Develop
• Rely on control	• Inspire trust
• Take a short-term perspective	• Take a longer-term perspective
• Accept the status quo	• Challenge the status quo
• Keep an eye on the bottom line	• Keep an eye on the horizon
• Imitate	• Originate
• Emulate the classic good soldier	• Are their own person
• Copy	• Show originality

Source: Bennis, 2009; see Note 3.

The Trait Approach to Leadership: Having the Right Stuff

At one time or another, many of us dream about being leaders. We fantasize about taking charge of large groups and being viewed with great awe and respect. Despite the prevalence of such daydreams, however, relatively few individuals convert them into reality by becoming leaders. Further, among those who do make it into leadership positions, only some are considered particularly effective in this role.

This raises an intriguing question: What sets effective leaders apart from most others? Why, in short, do some people, but not others, become good leaders? One of the most widely studied approaches to this question suggests that effective leadership is based on the characteristics that people have. In other words, people become leaders because they are different from others in some special ways.[9]

The Great Person Theory

Are some people born to lead? Common sense suggests that this is so. Great leaders of the past, such as Alexander the Great, Queen Elizabeth I, and Abraham Lincoln do seem to differ from ordinary people in several respects. The same applies to some contemporary leaders as well, such as a president of the United States (e.g., Barack Obama), a military general (e.g., Stanley McChrystal), or a business tycoon (e.g., Bill Gates). No matter what you may feel about these individuals, you'd have to agree that they all possess high levels of ambition coupled with clear visions of precisely where they want to go. To a lesser degree, even leaders lacking in such history-shaping fame seem different from their followers. This applies not only to top executives, but also to some politicians, and even sports heroes or heroines. One scientist expressed this idea as follows.

> [I]t is unequivocally clear that *leaders are not like other people.* Leaders do not have to be great men or women by being intellectual geniuses or omniscient prophets to succeed, but they do need to have the "right stuff" and this stuff is not equally present in all people. Leadership is a demanding, unrelenting job with enormous pressures and grave responsibilities. It would be a profound disservice to leaders to suggest that they are ordinary people who happened to be in the right place at the right time . . . In the realm of leadership (and in every other realm), the individual does matter.[10]

great person theory
The view that leaders possess special traits that set them apart from others, and that these traits are responsible for their assuming positions of power and authority.

This orientation expresses an approach to the study of leadership known as the **great person theory.** According to this approach, great leaders possess key traits that set them apart from most other human beings. Further, these traits remain stable over time and across different groups.[11] Thus, it suggests that all great leaders share these characteristics regardless of when and where they lived, or the precise role in history they fulfilled.

What are these traits? In other words, in precisely what measurable ways do successful leaders differ from people in general? Researchers have identified several such characteristics, and these are listed in Table 13.2.[12] As you review these, you will readily recognize and understand most of

TABLE 13.2 Characteristics of Successful Leaders

Research indicates that successful leaders possess high degrees of the traits listed here.

Trait or Characteristic	Description
Drive	Desire for achievement; ambition; high energy; tenacity; initiative
Honesty and integrity	Trustworthy; reliable; open
Leadership motivation	Desire to exercise influence over others to reach shared goals
Self-confidence	Trust in own abilities
Cognitive ability	Intelligence; ability to integrate and interpret large amounts of information
Knowledge of the business	Knowledge of industry and relevant technical matters
Creativity	Originality
Flexibility	Ability to adapt to needs of followers and requirements of situation

them (e.g., drive, honesty and integrity, self-confidence), which require no elaboration. However, we now explain several that are not quite as obvious.[13]

LEADERSHIP MOTIVATION: THE DESIRE TO LEAD. First, consider what has been termed **leadership motivation.** This refers to leaders' desires to influence others and, in essence, to lead.[14] Such motivation can take two distinct forms. On the one hand, it may cause leaders to seek power as an end in itself. People who demonstrate such **personalized power motivation,** as it is called, wish to dominate others, and their desire to do so often is reflected in an excessive concern with status.

In contrast, leadership motivation also can cause people to seek power as a means to achieve desired, shared goals. Leaders who evidence such **socialized power motivation** cooperate with others, develop networks and coalitions, and generally work with subordinates instead of trying to dominate or control them. Needless to say, this type of power motivation is usually far more adaptive for organizations than personalized power motivation.

FLEXIBILITY. Another special characteristic of effective leaders is *flexibility*. This refers to the ability to recognize what actions are required in a given situation and then to act accordingly. Evidence suggests that the most effective leaders are not prone to behave in the same ways all the time, but to be adaptive, matching their styles to the needs of followers and the demands of the situations they face.[15]

FOCUS ON MORALITY. In view of all the attention that has been paid to the dishonest dealings of many top business leaders in recent years (for a reminder, see Chapter 2), it's important to note that successful leaders do, in fact, place considerable emphasis on ethics and morality. This is in keeping with what has been called *authentic leadership*. **Authentic leaders** are highly moral individuals who are confident, hopeful, optimistic, and resilient, and who are highly aware of the contexts in which they operate.[16, 17]

The underlying idea is that people who are characterized in these ways tend to have highly positive perspectives that are in keeping with moral values and ethical behavior. Accordingly, authentic leaders play key roles in promoting the growth and development of their subordinates and, as a result, the sustained performance of their organizations. (Toward the end of this chapter, in The Ethics Angle section on page 473, we will describe these processes in conjunction with our discussion of leadership development practices.)

MULTIPLE DOMAINS OF INTELLIGENCE. Scientists have acknowledged that leaders have to "be smart" in a variety of ways. In other words, they have to demonstrate what is known as **multiple domains of intelligence.**[18] In particular, leaders need to be intelligent in three special ways. One of these, cognitive intelligence, was discussed in Chapter 4; another, emotional intelligence, was covered in Chapter 5.

A third kind of intelligence that also is very important for leaders to have, especially today, is known as *cultural intelligence*. The idea is that because national culture is likely to influence the way people respond to the things leaders say and do, it is essential for leaders to be intimately familiar with the cultural rules of the countries where they work. Sensitivity to this fact is referred to as **cultural intelligence.**[19] In today's global economy, this is more important than ever. In the words of C. R. "Dick" Shoemate, former chairman and CEO of Best Foods, "It takes a special kind of leadership to deal with the differences of a multicountry, multicultural organization such as ours."[20] Not surprisingly, most of the organizations on *Fortune* magazine's list of the "Global Most Admired Companies" (such as General Electric, BASF, Berkshire Hathaway, and SBC Communications) are involved actively in training leaders in ways to enhance their cultural intelligence, thereby preparing them to deal with the realities of the global economy.[21]

Transformational Leaders: Special People Who Make Things Happen

For organizations to thrive—let alone survive—they must be led by individuals who have a strong commitment to change. As such, leaders must have clear visions about what the future holds. The world's top leaders tend to agree. In a large-scale survey of CEOs from 20 different countries, having "a strong sense of vision" was identified by 98 percent as the most important characteristic for a CEO to have. Not surprisingly, companies with the most visionary leaders tend to outperform those with less visionary leaders in all important financial respects.

leadership motivation
The desire to influence others, especially toward the attainment of shared goals.

personalized power motivation
The desire to dominate others.

socialized power motivation
Leaders' interest in cooperating with others, developing networks and coalitions, and generally working with subordinates rather than trying to control them.

authentic leaders
Highly moral individuals who are confident, hopeful, optimistic, and resilient, and who are highly aware of the contexts in which they operate.

multiple domains of intelligence
Intelligence as measured in several different ways, such as cognitive intelligence (traditional measures of the ability to integrate and interpret information), emotional intelligence (the ability to be sensitive to one's own and others' emotions), and cultural intelligence (awareness of cultural differences between people).

cultural intelligence
The degree to which one is sensitive to the cultural differences between people.

FIGURE 13.3

This Company Is *Not* Looking for a Transformational Leader

Transformational leaders are not afraid to dream big, hoping to change the world. Just the opposite appears to be going on here.

Drew Demavich/cartoonbank.com.

"We need a leader who is not afraid to dream incremental dreams."

Now think of some of the great leaders throughout history—people who have changed the world because of their visions. Among others, the names of Rev. Dr. Martin Luther King, Jr., and President John F. Kennedy are certain to come to mind. These individuals surely were effective at envisioning ways of changing society and then bringing these visions to reality. People who do **transformational** things to revitalize and transform society or organizations are known as **transformational leaders.**[22] Rev. King's famous "I have a dream" speech inspired people to adopt the civil rights movement, and President Kennedy's shared vision of "landing a man on the moon and returning him safely to earth" before 1970 inspired the "space race" of the 1960s. In short, transformational leaders dream about bringing great change to the future instead of merely incremental changes (see Figure 13.3). It is precisely because of these interests that such leaders are considered to be transformational.

Although these examples are useful, we must ask: Exactly what makes a leader transformational? Their key characteristics are as follows.

- ■ *Charisma.* Transformational leaders have a mission and inspire others to follow them, often in a highly emotional manner.
- ■ *Self-confidence.* They are highly confident in their ability and judgment, and others readily become aware of this.
- ■ *Vision.* Transformational leaders have ideas about how to improve the status quo and do what it takes to change things for the better, even if it means making personal sacrifices.
- ■ *Environmental sensitivity.* These leaders are highly realistic about the constraints imposed on them and the resources needed to change things. They know what they can and cannot do.
- ■ *Intellectual stimulation.* Transformational leaders help followers recognize problems and identify ways of solving them.
- ■ *Interpersonal consideration.* These leaders give followers the support, encouragement, and attention they need to perform their jobs well.
- ■ *Inspiration.* They clearly communicate the importance of the company's mission and rely on symbols (e.g., pins and slogans) to help focus their efforts.
- ■ *Morality.* Transformational leaders tend to make decisions in a manner showing advanced levels of moral reasoning (recall this concept from Chapter 2). For a summary of some research evidence bearing on this, see Figure 13.4.[23]

In the world of business, Jack Welch, the former CEO of General Electric (GE), is a classic example of a transformational leader.[24] Under Welch's leadership, GE underwent a series of major changes with respect to the way it does business.[25] At the individual level, GE abandoned its highly bureaucratic ways and now does a good job of listening to its employees. Not surprisingly, GE consistently has ranked among the most admired companies in its industry in *Fortune* magazine's annual survey of corporate reputations (including a number-one ranking for several

transformational leaders
People who do things to revitalize and transform organizations or society.

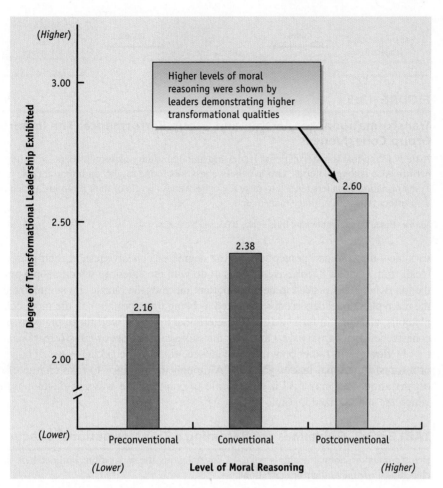

FIGURE 13.4

Transformational Leadership and Morality: Evidence of a Connection

Based on a sample of workers from Canada and the United Kingdom, scientists determined the degree to which leaders were judged by their subordinates as having the characteristics of transformational leaders. Using a paper-and-pencil test, these leaders also were assessed in terms of the moral reasoning they displayed. The findings, summarized here, were clear: The more the leaders were considered transformational, the higher were their levels of moral reasoning.

Source: Based on data reported by Turner et al., 2002; see Note 23.

years!).[26] In the 1980s, Welch bought and sold many businesses for GE, using as his guideline that GE would only keep a company if it placed either number one or number two in market share. If this meant closing plants, selling assets, and laying off personnel, he did it, earning him the nickname "Neutron Jack." Did Welch transform and revitalize GE? Having added well over $100 billion to the company's coffers, making it the most valuable company in the United States at the time, there can be no doubt about it.[27]

What we know about the effectiveness of transformational leadership goes beyond anecdotal examples and is based on sound scientific research.[28] Overall, transformational leadership is positively related to key aspects of job performance. For example, a study of secondary school teachers found that the more highly transactional their schools' principals were (as measured using a special questionnaire), the more they engaged in organizational citizenship behavior (see Chapter 11), and the higher were the levels of job satisfaction and organizational commitment among the teachers (Chapter 6).[29] Further research has shown that managers at FedEx who are rated by their subordinates as being highly transformational tend to be better performers and are recognized by their superiors as being highly promotable.[30] These studies and others suggest that the benefits of being a transformational leader are considerable.[31]

Although this is a useful conclusion as it stands, it raises an important question for OB scientists: Why? Specifically, what is it about being a transformational leader that tends to improve performance among followers? A study was done that sheds light on this issue. The researchers assessed the transformational leadership behavior of platoon leaders in the U.S. Army by administering a questionnaire to the soldiers who worked under them on military exercise missions.[32] They also used judgments by military experts to evaluate the performance of these leaders' platoons as a whole. The findings were clear: The more strongly the leaders demonstrated transformational characteristics, the more successfully their platoons performed. So far, this is consistent with other studies. However, in this research, the scientists went a step further by also assessing another key

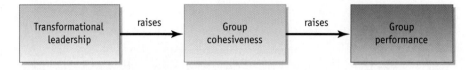

FIGURE 13.5

Transformational Leadership and Group Performance: The Important Role of Group Cohesiveness

A study found that transformational leadership among military platoon leaders led to improved performance among platoons. Group cohesiveness was found to play an important role in this process. Transformational leaders tended to raise the cohesiveness levels of their platoons, which in turn improved their effectiveness in military maneuvers.

Source: Based on suggestions by Bass et al., 2003; see Note 32.

variable—the soldiers' perceptions of the degree of cohesiveness in their platoons (as you may recall from Chapter 8, cohesiveness has to do with the extent to which people pull together to get the job done). This proved to be an important piece of the puzzle. As summarized in Figure 13.5, the more platoon leaders were recognized as being transformational, the more cohesive were their platoons, and this, in turn, was a key determinant of how well those platoons performed. Thus, cohesiveness is a partial explanation for the successful impact of transformational leaders.

In view of this rather convincing evidence, you may be asking yourself how to become more of a transformational leader yourself. Although it isn't easy to take charge of changing one's organization, you may find it worthwhile to consider the ways of developing these qualities, which are summarized in Table 13.3.

TABLE 13.3 Guidelines for Becoming a Transformational Leader

Being a transformational leader is not easy, but following the suggestions outlined here may help leaders change and revitalize their organizations.

Suggestion	Explanation
Develop a vision that is both clear and highly appealing to followers.	A clear vision will guide followers toward achieving organizational goals and make them feel good about doing so.
Articulate a strategy for bringing that vision to life.	Don't present an elaborate plan; rather, state the best path toward achieving the mission.
State your vision clearly and promote it to others.	Visions should not only be clear but also compelling, such as by using anecdotes.
Show confidence and optimism about your vision.	If a leader lacks confidence about success, followers will not try very hard to achieve that vision.
Express confidence in followers' capacities to carry out the strategy.	Followers must believe that they are capable of implementing a leader's vision and leaders should build subordinates' self-confidence.
Build confidence by recognizing small accomplishments toward the goal.	If a group experiences early success, it will be motivated to continue working hard.
Celebrate successes and accomplishments.	Formal or informal ceremonies are useful for celebrating success, thereby building optimism and commitment.
Take dramatic action to symbolize key organizational values.	Visions are reinforced by things leaders do to symbolize them. For example, one leader demonstrated concern for quality by destroying work that was not up to standards.
Set an example; actions speak louder than words.	Leaders serve as role models. If they want followers to make sacrifices, for example, they should do so themselves.

Sources: Based on suggestions by Yukl, 2009; see Note 1; Bass, 1998; see Note 22.

Leadership Behavior: What Do Leaders Do?

The approach to leadership we just reviewed dealt with the appealing idea that various traits distinguish effective leaders from others. In short, it focused on *who leaders are.* As plausible as this approach may be, it also makes sense to consider the idea that leaders may be distinctive with respect to the way they behave. In other words, we can supplement our emphasis on leadership traits with attention to leadership behavior—that is, by examining *what leaders do.*

The behavioral approach is appealing because it offers an optimistic view of the leadership process. After all, although we may not all be born with "the right stuff," we certainly can at least strive to do "the right things"—that is, to do what it takes to become a leader. The general question underlying the behavior approach is quite simple: What do leaders do that makes them effective as leaders? As we now describe, there are several good answers to this question.

Participative Versus Autocratic Leadership Behaviors

When it comes to describing the behavior of leaders, a key variable involves how much influence they allow subordinates to have over the decisions that are made. As we will see, there are two ways to do this.

THE AUTOCRATIC-DELEGATION CONTINUUM MODEL. Think about the different bosses you have had in your life. Can you remember one who wanted to control virtually everything—someone who made all the decisions, told people precisely what to do, and desired, quite literally, to run the entire show? Such a person is said to be **autocratic.** In contrast, can you recall a boss or supervisor who allowed employees to make their own decisions? This individual would be described as relying on **delegation**.

You probably also know supervisors who have acted in ways that fall between these extremes—that is, bosses who invited your input before making decisions, were open to suggestions, and who allowed you to carry out various tasks in your own way. These individuals may be said to be using a so-called **participative leadership style.**[33] More precisely, they may be *consulting* with you or involving you in a *joint decision* of some sort. In either case, you were more involved than you would have been in the case of an autocratic leader but less involved than with a leader who delegated all responsibility to you. (For a summary of the **autocratic-delegation continuum model,** see Figure 13.6.)

Although the autocratic-delegation continuum model does a reasonable job of describing the role of the leader in organizational decision making, it is regarded as being overly simplistic. In fact, upon more carefully studying the way leaders make decisions, researchers have observed that describing a leader's participation in decision making involves two separate dimensions.[34]

THE TWO-DIMENSIONAL MODEL OF SUBORDINATE PARTICIPATION. Acknowledging the need for a more sophisticated approach, scientists have proposed the **two-dimensional model of subordinate participation.** As the name implies, this conceptualization describes subordinates' participation in decisions in terms of two dimensions.

autocratic (leadership style)
A style of leadership in which a leader makes all decisions unilaterally.

delegation (leadership style)
A style of leadership in which a leader allows employees to make their own decisions.

participative leadership style
A style of leadership in which a leader solicits opinions from subordinates before making decisions.

autocratic-delegation continuum model
An approach to leadership recognizing that leaders allow followers to have different degrees of decision-making power, ranging from autocratic, through participative, to delegating.

two-dimensional model of subordinate participation
An approach to leadership that distinguishes between leaders who are *directive* or *permissive* toward subordinates, and the extent to which they are *participative* or *autocratic* in their decision making.

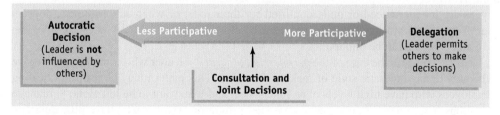

FIGURE 13.6

The Autocratic-Delegation Continuum Model

Traditionally, the amount of influence leaders give followers has been summarized as a continuum ranging from autocratic behavior (no influence) to delegation behavior (high influence). Consultation and joint decisions are intermediate forms of participation in decision making.

Source: Based on suggestions by Yukl, 2009; see Note 1.

TABLE 13.4 The Two-Dimensional Model of Subordinate Participation

Leaders can be described as having different styles based on how they involve subordinates in making decisions about how to do their jobs. Four distinct styles are summarized here.

Are Subordinates Told Exactly How to Do Their Jobs?	Are Subordinates Permitted to Participate in Making Decisions?	
	Yes (*Democratic*)	No (*Autocratic*)
Yes (*directive*)	**Directive democrat** (*makes decisions participatively; closely supervises subordinates*)	**Directive autocrat** (*makes decisions unilaterally; closely supervises subordinates*)
No (*permissive*)	**Permissive democrat** (*makes decisions participatively; gives subordinates latitude in carrying out their work*)	**Permissive autocrat** (*makes decisions unilaterally; gives subordinates latitude in carrying out their work*)

Source: Based on suggestions by Muczyk & Reimann, 1987; see Note 34.

The first characterizes the extent to which leaders permit subordinates to take part in decisions; this is the *autocratic-democratic* dimension. The autocratic extreme is marked by no participation, whereas the democratic extreme is marked by high participation. The second dimension involves the extent to which leaders direct the activities of subordinates and tell them how to carry out their jobs; this is the *permissive-directive* dimension. The permissive extreme is marked by not telling subordinates how to do their jobs, whereas the directive extreme is marked by telling subordinates precisely how to do their jobs. Combining these two variables yields the four possible patterns described in Table 13.4. These are:

- The *directive autocrat*
- The *permissive autocrat*
- The *directive democrat*
- The *permissive democrat*

Although any attempt to divide human beings into discrete categories can't be perfect, these patterns do seem to make good sense. Indeed, many managers adopt a leadership style that fits, at least roughly, within one.

Given that leaders differ along these two dimensions and can, as a result, be classified as falling into one of the four patterns shown in Table 13.4, do any of them have a clear-cut edge? In short, is one pattern superior to the others in many, if not most, situations? Existing evidence suggests that this is doubtful. All four styles involve a mixed pattern of advantages and disadvantages. Moreover—and this is the crucial point—the relative success of each depends heavily on conditions existing within a given organization and its specific stage of development.

To illustrate this point, consider a manager who is a *directive autocrat*. Such a person makes decisions without consulting subordinates and supervises their work activities very closely. It is tempting to view such a pattern as undesirable insofar as it runs counter to the value of personal freedom. However, this approach may be highly successful in some settings—such as when employees are inexperienced or underqualified for their jobs, or when subordinates adopt an adversarial stance toward management and must be closely supervised. As you might imagine, directive autocrats tend to be unpopular.

In contrast, consider the case of the *permissive autocrat*—a leader who combines permissive supervision with an autocratic style of making decisions. This pattern may be useful in dealing with employees who have high levels of technical skill and who want to be left alone to manage their own jobs (e.g., scientists, engineers, computer programmers), but who have little desire to participate in routine decision making.

The remaining two patterns (*directive democrat* and *permissive democrat*) are also well suited to specific organizational conditions. The key task for leaders, then, is to match their own style to the needs of their organization, and to change as these needs shift and evolve. What happens when leaders in organizations lack such flexibility? Actual events in one now-defunct, and short-lived company—People Express Airlines—are instructive.[35] (The fact that it wasn't around very long is a good indication that something was wrong, and we'll identify a key factor.)

Don Burr, the founder and CEO, had a very clear managerial style: He was a highly permissive democrat. He involved employees in many aspects of decision making, and emphasized autonomy in work activities. Indeed, he felt that everyone at People Express should be viewed as a "manager." This style worked well while the company was young, but as it grew and increased in complexity, such practices created mounting difficulties. New employees were not necessarily as committed as older ones, so permissive supervision was ineffective with them. And, as decisions increased in both complexity and number, a participative approach became less appropriate. Unfortunately, top management was reluctant to alter its style; after all, it seemed to have been instrumental in the company's early success. This poor match between the style of top leaders and changing external conditions seems to have contributed (along with many other factors, of course) to People Express's ultimate demise.

To conclude, no single leadership style is best under all conditions or in every situation. However, recognizing the importance of differences in this respect can be a constructive first step toward assuring that the style most suited to a given set of circumstances is, in fact, adopted. (Specific ideas regarding the most appropriate style for a given situation are described in our discussion of so-called *contingency theories of leader effectiveness* beginning on page 462.)

Person-Oriented Versus Production-Oriented Leaders

Think about all the bosses you have had in your career. Now, divide these into two categories—those who were relatively effective and those who were ineffective. How do the two groups differ? If you think about this carefully, your answers are likely to take one of two forms. First, you might reply, "My most effective bosses helped me to get the job done. They gave me advice, answered my questions, and let me know exactly what was expected of me. My most ineffective bosses didn't do this." Second, you might answer, "My most effective bosses seemed to care about me as a person. They were friendly, listened to me when I had problems or questions, and seemed to help me toward my personal goals. My ineffective bosses didn't do this."

A large body of research suggests that leaders do, in fact, differ greatly along these two dimensions.[36] Those at the high end of the first dimension, known as **initiating structure (production-centered)**, are concerned mainly with production and focus primarily on getting the job done. They engage in actions such as organizing work, inducing subordinates to follow rules, setting goals, and making leader and subordinate roles explicit. In contrast, other leaders are lower on this dimension and show less of a tendency to engage in these actions.

Leaders at the high end of the second dimension, known as **consideration (person-centered)**, are concerned primarily with establishing good relations with their subordinates and being liked by them. They engage in actions such as doing favors for subordinates, explaining things to them, and ensuring their welfare. Others, in contrast, are low on this dimension and don't care much about how they get along with subordinates.

At first glance, you might assume that initiating structure and consideration are linked so that people high on one of these dimensions are automatically low on the other. In fact, this is not the case. The two dimensions are largely independent.[37] Thus, a leader may be high on both concern with production and for people, high on one of these dimensions and low on the other, moderate on one and high on the other, and so on (see Figure 13.7).

Is any one of these possible patterns best? Careful study over a half-century indicates that this is a complex issue; production-oriented and people-oriented leadership behaviors both offer a mixed pattern of strengths and limitations.[38] With respect to showing consideration (high concern with people and human relations), the major benefits are improved group atmosphere and morale.[39] However, since leaders high on this dimension are reluctant to act in a directive manner toward subordinates and often shy away from presenting them with negative feedback, productivity sometimes suffers. Regarding initiating structure (high concern with production), efficiency and performance are indeed sometimes enhanced by this leadership style. If leaders focus entirely on production, however, employees may soon conclude that no one cares about them or their welfare. Then work-related attitudes such as job satisfaction and organizational commitment may suffer (and, as we describe in Chapter 6, this is problematic).

Having said all this and pointed out the complexities, we add that one specific pattern appears to have an edge in many settings. This is a pattern in which leaders demonstrate high

initiating structure (production-centered)
Activities by a leader designed to enhance productivity, having a task-oriented style.

consideration (person-centered)
Actions by a leader that demonstrate concern with the welfare of subordinates, having a person-oriented style.

FIGURE 13.7

Two Basic Dimensions of Leader Behavior

Leaders' behavior can vary from low to high with respect to *consideration* (person orientation) and *initiating structure* (task orientation). Patterns of leader behavior produced by variations along these two dimensions are illustrated here.

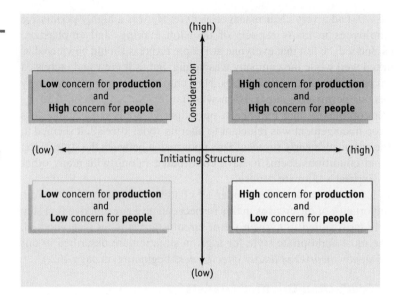

degrees of concern with both people *and* production.[40] Indeed, research has shown that high amounts of concern with people (showing consideration) and concern with productivity (initiating structure) are not incompatible. Rather, skillful leaders can combine both of these orientations into their overall styles to produce favorable results. Thus, although no one leadership style is best, leaders who combine these two concerns may often have an important edge over leaders who show only one or the other. In the words of U.S. Army Lieutenant General William G. Pagonis:

> To lead successfully, a person must demonstrate . . . expertise and empathy. In my experience, both of these traits can be deliberately and systematically cultivated; this personal development is the first important building block of leadership.[41]

Developing Successful Leader Behavior: Grid Training

grid training
A multistep process designed to cultivate within leaders a concern for people and a concern for production.

How can one go about developing these two forms of leadership behavior—demonstrating concern for production and concern for people? A technique known as **grid training** proposes a multistep process designed to cultivate these two important skills.[42]

The initial step consists of a *grid seminar*—a session in which an organization's managers (who have been previously trained in the appropriate theory and skills) help organization members analyze their own management styles. This is done using a specially designed questionnaire that allows managers to determine how they stand with respect to their *concern for production* and their *concern for people*. Each participant's approach on each dimension is scored using a number ranging from 1 (low) to 9 (high).

Managers who score low on both concern for production and concern for people are scored 1,1—evidence of what is called *impoverished management*. A manager who is highly concerned about production but shows little interest in people, the *task management* style, scores 9,1. In contrast, ones who show the opposite pattern—high concern with people but little concern for production—are described as having a *country club* style of management; they are scored 1,9. Those scoring moderately on both dimensions, the 5,5 pattern, are said to follow a *middle-of-the-road* management style. Finally, there are individuals who are highly concerned with both production and people, those scoring 9,9. This is the most desirable pattern, representing what is known as *team management*. These various patterns are represented in a diagram like that shown in Figure 13.8, known as the *managerial grid.*®

After a manager's position along the grid has been determined, training is implemented to develop concern for production (planning skills) and concern for people (communication skills) to reach the ideal 9,9 state. This consists of organization-wide sessions aimed at helping individuals interact more effectively with each other. Then, these concepts are expanded to reducing conflict between groups that work with each other. Additional training includes efforts to identify the extent

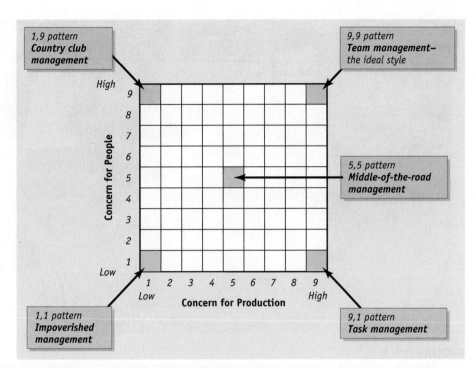

FIGURE 13.8

The Managerial Grid

A manager's standing allowing two basic dimensions, concern for production and for people, can be illustrated by means of a diagram such as this, known as the *managerial grid.* In *grid training,* people learn to be effective leaders by demonstrating high amounts of both dimensions.

Source: Based on suggestions by Blake & Mouton, 1969; see Note 42.

to which the organization is meeting its strategic goals and then comparing this performance to an ideal. Next, plans created to meet these goals are implemented in the organization. Finally, progress toward the goals is assessed continuously, and problem areas are identified.

Grid training is widely considered an effective way to improve the leadership behaviors of people in organizations. Indeed, the grid approach has been used to train hundreds of thousands of people in developing the two key forms of leadership behavior.

Leaders and Followers

Thus far throughout this chapter, we have focused on leaders—their traits and their behaviors. Followers, by and large, have been ignored. But, in a crucial sense, followers are the essence of leadership. Without them, there really is no such thing as leadership (see Figure 13.9). As someone once put it, "Without followers leaders cannot lead . . . Without followers, even John Wayne becomes a solitary hero, or, given the right script, a comic figure, posturing on an empty stage."[43]

The importance of followers, and the complex, reciprocal relationship between leaders and followers, is widely recognized by organizational researchers. Indeed, major theories of leadership, such as those we consider in this section, note—either explicitly or implicitly—that leadership is really a two-way street. We will now consider two such approaches: the *leader-member exchange model,* and the practice of *team leadership.*

The Leader-Member Exchange (LMX) Model: The Importance of Being in the "In-Group"

Do leaders treat all their subordinates in the same manner? Informal observation suggests that, clearly, they do not. Yet many theories of leadership ignore this fact. They discuss leadership behavior in terms that suggest similar actions toward all subordinates. The importance of potential differences in this respect is brought into sharp focus by the **leader-member exchange (LMX) model.**[44]

This conceptualization suggests that for various reasons leaders form different kinds of relationships with various groups of subordinates. One group, referred to as the *in-group,* is favored by the leader. Members of in-groups receive considerably more attention from the leader and larger shares of the resources they have to offer (such as time and recognition). By contrast, other

leader-member exchange (LMX) model
A theory suggesting that leaders form different relations with various subordinates and that the nature of such dyadic exchanges can exert strong effects on subordinates' performance and satisfaction.

Getty Images, Inc.

FIGURE 13.9

Leaders and Followers: An Essential Connection

You might not know Reed Hastings, but you surely know the company he founded in 1997—Netflix. With more than 2 billion DVDs shipped so far, there's a good chance that you're also familiar with having its red envelopes hit your mailbox on a regular basis. As a successful CEO, Mr. Hastings' leadership effectiveness is based on his capacity to gain the support of a vast array of followers, including approximately 2,000 employees and, as a publicly traded organization, legions of stockholders. Given the company's ongoing financial success and with cause for optimism about the future (based largely on growth in video streaming), these followers have good reason to be loyal to their leader.

subordinates fall into the *out-group*. These individuals are disfavored by leaders. As such, they receive fewer valued resources from their leaders.

Leaders distinguish between in-group and out-group members very early in their relationships with them—and on the basis of surprisingly little information. Sometimes, perceived similarity with respect to personal characteristics such as age, gender, or personality is sufficient to categorize followers into a leader's in-group.[45] Similarly, a particular follower may be granted in-group status if the leader believes that person to be especially competent at performing his or her job.[46]

Research has supported the idea that leaders favor members of their in-groups. For example, one study found that supervisors inflated the ratings they gave poorly performing employees when these individuals were members of the in-group, but not when they were members of the out-group.[47] Given the favoritism shown toward in-group members, it follows that such individuals would perform their jobs better and would hold more positive attitudes toward their jobs than members of out-groups.

In general, research has supported this prediction. For example, it has been found that in-group members are more satisfied with their jobs and more effective in performing them than out-group members.[48] In-group members are also less likely to resign from their jobs than out-group members.[49] And, as you might imagine, members of in-groups tend to receive more mentoring from their superiors than do members of out-groups, helping them become more successful in their careers (for a summary, see Figure 13.10).[50]

Together, these studies provide good support for the LMX model. Such findings suggest that paying attention to the relations between leaders and their followers can be very useful. The nature of such relationships can strongly affect the morale, commitment, and performance of employees. Helping leaders to improve such relations, such as through training, therefore, can be extremely valuable in these key respects.

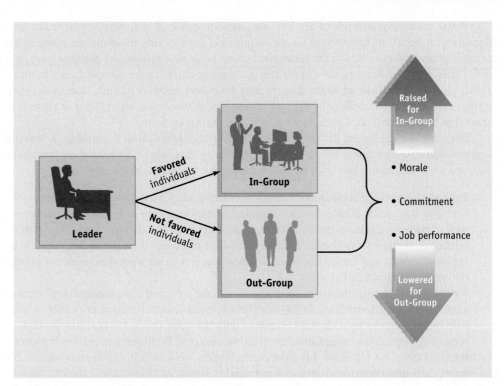

FIGURE 13.10

**The LMX Model:
A Summary**
According to the *leader-member exchange (LMX) model,* leaders distinguish between groups they favor (in-groups) and those they do not (out-groups). Members of in-groups generally enjoy higher levels of morale, commitment, and job performance than members of out-groups.

The Challenge of Leading Work Teams

Traditionally, leaders make strategic decisions on behalf of followers, who are responsible for carrying them out. In many of today's organizations, however, where *teams* are used (see Chapter 8), leaders play a somewhat different role. For the most part, they are called upon to provide special resources to team members, who are empowered to implement their own missions in their own ways. Instead of "calling the shots," team leaders help subordinates take responsibility for their own work. As such, they are quite different from the traditional "command and control" leadership role we have been discussing.[51] Table 13.5 summarizes the key differences.

TABLE 13.5 Leading Groups Versus Leading Teams

The popularity of teams in today's organizations has important implications for how leaders go about fulfilling their roles. Some of the key differences between leading traditional work groups and leading teams are summarized here.

In Traditional Work Groups, Leaders . . .	But, in Teams, Leaders . . .
Tell people what to do.	Ask people what they think and share responsibility for organizing and doing the work.
Take all the credit.	Share the limelight with all their teammates.
Focus on training employees.	Concentrate on expanding their team's capabilities by functioning primarily as coaches who build confidence in team members, cultivating their untapped potential.
Relate to others individually.	Create a team identity by helping the team set goals, helping members meet them, and celebrating when they have been met.
Work at reducing conflict between individuals.	Make the most of team differences by building respect for diverse points of view and ensuring that all team members' views are expressed.
React to change.	Recognize that change is inevitable and foresee it, better preparing the organization to make appropriate adaptations.

When most people think of leaders, they tend to think of individuals who make strategic decisions on behalf of followers who are responsible for carrying them out. In many of today's organizations, however, where the movement toward *self-managed teams* predominates, it is less likely than ever that leaders are responsible for getting others to implement their orders to help fulfill their visions. Instead, team leaders may be called upon to provide special resources to groups empowered to implement their own missions in their own ways. They don't call all the shots, but help subordinates take responsibility for their own work.

Because leading teams differs from the traditional approach to leadership in hierarchical organizations, many leaders are ill-prepared to assume this role.[52] To help meet this challenge, here are a few guidelines that may be followed to achieve success as a team leader.

- Instead of directing people, *team leaders work at building trust and inspiring teamwork.* One way this can be done is by encouraging interaction among all members of the team as well as between the team and its customers and suppliers. Another key ingredient is to take initiatives to make things better. Instead of taking a reactive, "if it ain't broke, don't fix it" approach, teams may be led to success by individuals who set a good example for improving the quality of their team's efforts.
- Rather than focusing simply on training individuals, effective *team leaders concentrate on expanding team capabilities.* In this connection, team leaders function primarily as coaches, helping the team by providing all members with the skills needed to perform the task, removing barriers that might interfere with success, and finding the necessary resources required to get the job done. Likewise, team leaders work at building the confidence of the team, cultivating members' untapped potential.
- Instead of managing one-on-one, *team leaders attempt to create a team identity.* In other words, leaders must help teams understand their missions and recognize what they're doing to help fulfill them. In this connection, team leaders may help the group set goals—pointing out ways they may adjust their performance when they do not meet them, and planning celebrations when team goals are attained.
- Although traditional leaders work at preventing conflict between individuals, *team leaders are encouraged to make the most of differences between members.* Without doubt, it is a considerable challenge to meld a diverse group of individuals into a highly committed and productive team, but doing so is important. This can be done by: (a) building respect for diverse points of view, (b) making sure that all team members are encouraged to present their views, and (c) respecting these ideas once they are expressed.
- Unlike traditional leaders who simply react to change, team leaders try to *foresee and influence change.* To the extent that leaders recognize that change is inevitable (a point we will emphasize in Chapter 16), they may be better prepared to make the various adaptations required. Effective team leaders continuously scan the business environment for clues as to changes that appear to be forthcoming and help teams decide how to be responsive to them.

In conclusion, leading teams is a far cry from leading individuals in the traditional directive (or even participative) manner. The special nature of teams makes the leader's job very different. Although appreciating these differences is easy, making the appropriate adjustments may be extremely challenging—especially for individuals who are well practiced in the ways of traditional leadership. However, given the prevalence of teams in today's work environment, the importance of making the adjustments cannot be overstated. Leading new teams using old methods is a surefire formula for failure.

Contingency Theories of Leader Effectiveness

contingency theories of leader effectiveness
Any of several theories that recognize that certain styles of leadership are more effective in some situations than others.

That leadership is a complex process should be obvious by now. It involves intricate social relationships and is affected by a wide range of factors. Given all these complications, you may wonder why so many researchers focus so much time and energy on attempting to understand all of its intricacies. The answer, of course, is that effective leadership is an essential ingredient in organizational success. With it, organizations can grow, prosper, and compete effectively. Without it, many simply cannot survive. Recognition of this basic point lies behind several modern theories of leadership collectively referred to as **contingency theories of leader effectiveness.**

As soon will be clear, these theories differ sharply in their content, terminology, and scope. Yet all are linked by two common themes. First, all adopt a *contingency approach*—they recognize that there is no one best style of leadership, and that the key task of organizational behavior researchers is determining which leadership styles will prove most effective under which specific circumstances. Second, all are concerned with the issue of *leader effectiveness*. They seek to identify the conditions and factors that determine whether, and to what degree, leaders will enhance the performance and satisfaction of their subordinates. Several theories fall into this category.[53] Among these are three that we will describe here: *LPC contingency theory, situational leadership theory, and path-goal theory.*

LPC Contingency Theory: Matching Leaders and Tasks

Earlier, we explained that the behaviors associated with effective leadership fall into two major categories—concern for people and concern for production. Both types of behavior contribute to a leader's success. However, a more refined look at this issue leads us to ask exactly *when* each type of behavior works best. That is, under what conditions are leaders more successful when they demonstrate a concern for people compared to a concern for production?

THE BASICS OF THE THEORY. This question is addressed by a widely studied approach to leadership known as **LPC contingency theory.** The contingency aspect is reflected by the assumption that a leader's contribution to successful performance by his or her group is determined both by the leader's own traits and by various features of the situation. Different levels of leader effectiveness occur under different combinations of conditions. To fully understand leader effectiveness, both types of factors must be considered.

According to the theory, *esteem (liking) for least preferred coworker* (**LPC** for short) is the most important personal characteristic. This refers to a leader's tendency to evaluate in a favorable or unfavorable manner the person with whom she or he has found it most difficult to work. Leaders who perceive this person in negative terms (low LPC leaders) are concerned primarily with attaining successful task performance. In contrast, those who perceive their least preferred coworker in a positive light (high LPC leaders) mainly are concerned with establishing good relations with subordinates. A questionnaire is used to measure one's LPC score. It is important to note that the theory views LPC as being fixed—that is, an aspect of an individual's leadership style that cannot be changed. As we will explain, this has important implications for applying the theory so as to improve leader effectiveness.

Which type of leader—one low in LPC or one high in LPC—is more effective? As suggested by the word *contingency*, the answer is: "It depends." And, what it depends upon is the degree to which the situation is favorable to the leader—that is, how much it allows the leaders to have control over their subordinates. This, in turn, is determined largely by three factors:

- The nature of the *leader's relations with group members* (the extent to which he or she enjoys their support and loyalty)
- The *degree of structure* in the task being performed (the extent to which task goals and subordinates' roles are clearly defined)
- The leader's *position power* (as described in Chapter 11, his or her formal capacity to enforce compliance by subordinates)

Combining these three factors, the leader's situational control can range from very high (positive relations with group members, a highly structured task, and high position power) to very low (negative relations, an unstructured task, and low position power).

What types of leaders are most effective under these various conditions? According to the theory, low LPC leaders (ones who are task-oriented) are superior to high LPC leaders (ones who are relations-oriented) when situational control is either very low or very high. In contrast, high LPC leaders have an edge when situational control falls within the moderate range (refer to Figure 13.11).

The rationale for these predictions is as follows. Under conditions of low situational control, groups need considerable guidance to accomplish their tasks. Without such direction, nothing would get done. For example, imagine a military combat group led by an unpopular platoon leader under battle conditions in which things are falling apart and the troops are thinking of mutinying. Any chance of effectiveness this person has would result from paying careful attention to the task at hand, rather than hoping to establish better relations with the group. Since low LPC leaders are more likely to provide structure than high LPC leaders, they usually will be superior in such cases.

LPC contingency theory
A theory suggesting that leader effectiveness is determined both by characteristics of leaders (their *LPC* scores) and by the level of situational control they are able to exert over subordinates.

LPC
Short for "esteem for least preferred coworker"—a personality variable distinguishing between individuals with respect to their concern for people (high LPC) and their concern for production (low LPC).

FIGURE 13.11

LPC Contingency Theory: An Overview

LPC contingency theory predicts that low LPC leaders (ones who are primarily task-oriented) will be more effective than high LPC leaders (ones who are primarily people-oriented) when situational control is either very low or very high. However, the opposite is true when situational control is moderate.

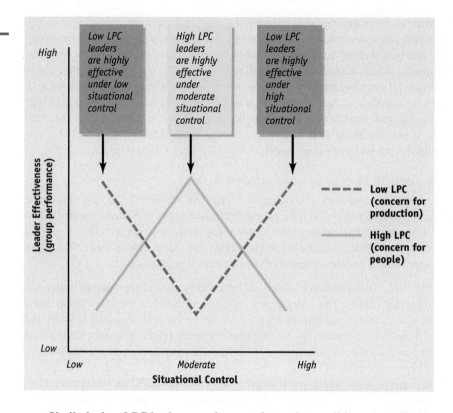

Similarly, low LPC leaders are also superior under conditions that offer them a high degree of situational control. Indeed, when leaders are liked, their power is not challenged. When the demands of the task make it clear what leaders should be doing, it is perfectly acceptable for them to focus on the job at hand. Subordinates expect their leaders to exercise control under such conditions and accept it when they do so. And this leads to task success. For example, an airline pilot leading a cockpit crew is expected to take charge and not to seek the consensus of others as she guides the plane onto the runway for a landing. Surely, she would be less effective if she didn't take charge but instead asked the co-pilot what he thought she should do. In other words, this is not the proper occasion to consult with others and take their opinions into account but instead to tell them what to do.

Things are different, however, when circumstances offer leaders moderate situational control. Consider, for example, a condition in which a leader's relations with subordinates are good, but the task is unstructured, and the leader's power is somewhat restricted. This describes what might be found within a research and development team attempting to find creative new uses for a company's products. Here, it clearly would be inappropriate for a low LPC leader to tell people what to do. Rather, a highly nurturant leader who is considerate of the feelings of others would likely be most effective—that is, a high LPC leader. (Figure 13.12 shows some examples of how leadership style can be matched to a situation).

APPLYING LPC CONTINGENCY THEORY. Practitioners have found LPC contingency theory to be quite useful when it comes to suggesting ways of enhancing leader effectiveness. Because the theory assumes that certain kinds of leaders perform best under certain kinds of situations, and that leadership style is fixed, the best way to enhance effectiveness is to fit the right kind of leaders to the situations they face.

Doing this involves completing questionnaires that can be used to assess both the LPC score of the leader and the amount of control he or she faces in the situation. Then, using these indexes, a match can be made such that leaders are put into situations that best suit their leadership styles—a technique known as **leader match.** This approach also focuses on ways of changing the situational control variables—leader-member relations, task structure, and leader position power—when it is impractical to change leaders. For example, a high LPC leader may be moved to a job in which situational control is either extremely high or extremely low. Alternatively, we may attempt to change the situation (such as by altering relations between leaders and group members, or raising or lowering the leader's position power) so as to increase or decrease the amount of situational control encountered.

leader match
The practice of matching leaders (based on their LPC scores) to the groups whose situations best match those in which they are expected to be most effective (according to LPC contingency theory).

FIGURE 13.12

Matching Leadership Style to the Situation

LPC contingency theory recognizes that the most appropriate leadership style depends on circumstances. The aircraft cockpit crew (pictured top left) may be most effective when its leader, the pilot, uses a highly directive (low LPC) style. So, too, would a military troop in a difficult battle situation (pictured bottom left) perform best when its commanding officer adopts a low LPC style. However, a research and development team would perform poorly if its leader (pictured top right) behaved this same way. In that setting, a less directive (high LPC) style would be more effective.

Source: (top left) Newscom, (bottom left) Mitchell Prothero/Newscom, (top right) A.P. World Wide Photos.

Several companies—most notably, Sears—have used the leader match approach with some success. In fact, several studies have found it to be effective in improving group performance on at least some occasions.

Situational Leadership Theory: Adjusting Leadership Style to the Situation

Another theory of leadership, **situational leadership theory,** also is considered a contingency theory because it focuses on the best leadership style for a given situation. Specifically, the scientists who developed this theory argue that leaders are effective when they select the right leadership style for the conditions they face.[54] Specifically, this depends on the *maturity* of followers—that is, their readiness to take responsibility for their own behavior. This, in turn, is based on two variables with which we already are familiar (although they are referred to using different terminology here): (1) *task behavior* (the degree to which followers have the appropriate job knowledge and skills—that is, their need for guidance and direction), and (2) *relationship behavior* (the degree to which followers are willing to work without taking direction from others—that is, their need for emotional support.)

As shown in Figure 13.13, by combining high and low levels of these independent dimensions, four different types of situations are identified (denoted by "S" in the diagram), each of which is associated with a particular leadership style that is most effective.

situational leadership theory
A theory suggesting that the most effective style of leadership—either delegating, participating, selling, or telling—depends on the extent to which followers require guidance and direction, and emotional support.

- *Lower-right corner of Figure 13.13 (S1):* Situations in which followers need a great deal of direction from their leaders but don't need much emotional support from them. The practice of *telling* followers what to do is most useful in such circumstances. That is, giving followers specific instructions and closely supervising their work may be the best approach.
- *Upper-right corner of Figure 13.13 (S2):* Followers still lack the skill to be able to succeed, although in this case, they require more emotional support. Under these conditions, *selling* works best. Being very directive may make up for the follower's lack of ability, while being very supportive will help get them to go along with what the leader is asking of them.
- *Upper-left corner of Figure 13.13 (S3):* Conditions in which followers need very little guidance with respect to how to do their jobs, but considerable emotional hand-holding and support

FIGURE 13.13

Situational Leadership Theory: Its Basic Dimensions

Situational leadership theory specifies that the most appropriate leadership style depends on the amount of emotional support followers require in conjunction with the amount of guidance they require to do their jobs.

Source: Hersey & Blanchard, 1988; see Note 54.

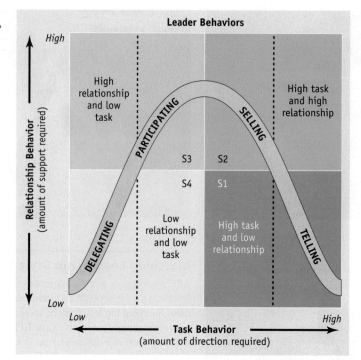

to motivate them. That is, low levels of task behavior, but high levels of relationship (supportive) behavior are required. A *participating* style of leadership works well in such situations because it allows followers to share their expertise while enhancing their desire to perform.

■ *Lower-left corner of Figure 13.13 (S4):* Followers are both willing and able to do what is asked of them. In other words, low levels of task behavior and low levels of relationship behavior are required. Under such conditions, *delegating* is the best way to treat followers—that is, turning over to them the responsibility for making and implementing their own decisions.

According to this situational leadership theory, leaders must be able to (1) diagnose the situations they face, (2) identify the appropriate behavioral style, and then (3) implement that response. Because the situations leaders face may change all the time, they must constantly reassess them, paying special attention to followers' needs for guidance and emotional support. To the extent that they do so, they are likely to be effective.

Specialized training in these skills has been found to be quite useful. In fact, the approach has been used to train leaders at such corporate giants as Xerox, Mobil Oil, and Caterpillar, as well as in the U.S. military services. (Which style of leadership are you most prone to follow in your own treatment of others? To give you some insight into this question, complete the Individual Exercise on pages 475–476.)

Path-Goal Theory: Leaders as Guides to Valued Goals

Suppose you conducted an informal survey in which you asked 100 people to indicate what they expect from their leaders. What kind of answers would you receive? Although they would vary greatly, one common theme you might uncover would be, "I expect my leader to *help*—to assist me in reaching goals I feel are important." This basic idea plays a central role in the **path-goal theory** of leadership.[55]

path-goal theory
A theory of leadership suggesting that subordinates will be motivated by a leader only to the extent they perceive this individual as helping them to attain valued goals.

In general terms, this theory contends that subordinates will react favorably to a leader only to the extent that they perceive that leader as helping them progress toward various goals by clarifying actual paths to such rewards. That is, effective leaders clarify for followers what they need to do to get from where they are to where they should be, and help them do so. More specifically, the theory contends that actions by a leader that clarify the nature of tasks and that reduce or eliminate obstacles will increase perceptions on the part of subordinates that working hard will lead to good performance, which in turn will be recognized and rewarded. Under such conditions, the theory suggests, job satisfaction, motivation, and job performance will all be enhanced.

How, precisely, can leaders best accomplish these tasks? The answer, as in other contingency theories of leadership, is: "It depends." And what it depends on is a complex interaction between key aspects of *leader behavior* and certain *contingency* factors. Specifically, with respect to leader behavior, path-goal theory suggests that leaders can adopt four basic styles:

- *Instrumental (directive):* An approach focused on providing specific guidance, and establishing work schedules and rules
- *Supportive:* A style focused on establishing good relations with subordinates and satisfying their needs
- *Participative:* A pattern in which the leader consults with subordinates, permitting them to participate in decisions
- *Achievement-oriented:* An approach in which the leader sets challenging goals and seeks improvements in performance

According to the theory, these styles are not mutually exclusive; in fact, the same leader can adopt them at different times and in different situations. Indeed, as described on page 451, showing such flexibility is one important aspect of an effective leader. (Recognizing that it is important to embrace these styles, many of today's leaders use an approach to leadership known as *coaching*. For a look at this orientation to leadership, see the OB in Practice section below.)

OB in Practice

Coaching Tips from Some of the Best

If you have ever played on a sports team, you have experienced firsthand the important leadership function of a coach. What did your coach do? Chances are that he or she was actively involved in helping you in the following manner:

- Analyzing ways of improving your performance and extending your capabilities
- Creating a supportive climate, one in which barriers to development are eliminated
- Encouraging you to improve your performance, no matter how good you already may be

In athletics, coaching has been used for a long time. However, only recently has it emerged as a philosophy of leadership in organizations.[56] To a large extent this appears to have been stimulated by books in which football coaches (such as the famed former college coach Lou Holtz and NFL coach Bill Belichick) and executives (such as the Green Bay Packers' executive VP and general manager, Ron Wolf) have shared insight into the coaching process.[57]

These insiders to big-time sports tell us that what makes coaching a unique form of leadership is the special nature of the relationship between the coach and team members. The key to this relationship is trust (see Chapter 11). Team members acknowledge the coach's expertise and trust the coach to have his, and the team's, best interests in mind. At the same time, the coach believes in the team member's capacity to profit from his or her advice. In other words, coaching is a partnership in which both the coach and the team member play an important part in achieving success.

Additional dimensions of the coach's leadership power have been described by basketball hall of famer and former U.S. Senator Bill Bradley.[58] A key to coaching, Bradley emphasizes, is to get players to commit to something bigger than themselves.

In sports this may mean winning a championship; in other businesses, it may mean landing a huge contract or surpassing a long-standing sales record. Focusing on the goal itself, and identifying how each individual may contribute to it, is key.

Bradley also advises that the best coaches don't do all the talking when someone gets out of line. Rather, they harness the power of team members to put pressure on the problem person. As a case in point, consider an incident from basketball lore. In 1994, the Chicago Bulls' Scottie Pippin angrily took himself out of a semifinal championship game after coach Phil Jackson called for teammate Toni Kukoc to make the final, game-deciding shot. Naturally, Coach Jackson came down hard on Pippin in his postgame interview, but that was mostly for show. The real work in getting Pippin to see the error of his ways came not from the coach, but from his teammates. After the game, the coach left the locker room, announcing that the team had something to say to Pippin. Then, one by one, members of the Bulls expressed their disappointment in Pippin for letting down the team. Seeing the error of his ways, Pippin apologized on the spot and immediately went back to being the team player he had been all along. Had the coach not orchestrated this session, the effects surely would not have been as successful.

One way coaches can be supportive and earn the trust of their team members is to refrain from bad-mouthing them to others. Athletic coaches who use the media to send critical messages to their players live to regret it, Bradley tells us. However, behind the closed doors of the locker room, it's quite a different story. In that setting, there's no such thing as being too frank. The same applies in the office or shop as well. A manager who complains to other managers about what a poor job one of her employees has been doing is not only making herself look bad, but more importantly, also is betraying that employee's trust. And, as we said earlier, trust is the heart of the coaching game.

These suggestions from successful athletic coaches on the field or court also go a long way toward making leaders successful in the office or shop floor.

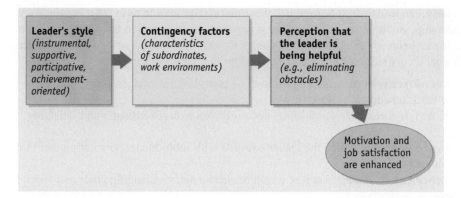

FIGURE 13.14

Path-Goal Theory: An Overview

According to *path-goal theory*, perceptions among employees that leaders are helping them reach valued goals enhance their motivation and job satisfaction. Such perceptions, in turn, are encouraged when a leader's style is consistent with the needs and characteristics of subordinates (e.g., their level of experience) and aspects of the work environment (e.g., the requirements of the tasks being performed).

Which of these styles is best for maximizing subordinates' satisfaction and motivation? The answer depends on two contingency factors. First, the choice is strongly affected by several *characteristics of subordinates.* For example, if followers are high in ability, an instrumental style of leadership may be unnecessary; instead, a less structured, more supportive approach may be preferable. On the other hand, if subordinates are low in ability, the opposite may be true; people with poor ability need considerable guidance to help them attain their goals. Similarly, people high in need for affiliation (that is, those desiring close, friendly ties with others) may strongly prefer a supportive or participative style of leadership. Those high in the need for achievement may strongly prefer an achievement-oriented leader.

Second, the most effective leadership style also depends on several *aspects of the work environment.* For example, path-goal theory predicts that when tasks are unstructured and nonroutine, an instrumental approach by the leader may be best; much clarification and guidance are needed. However, when tasks are structured and highly routine, an instrumental approach may interfere with good performance, and may be resented by subordinates who think the leader is engaging in unnecessary meddling. (See Figure 13.14 for an overview of all these aspects of path-goal theory.)

Path-goal theory has been subjected to empirical testing in several studies.[59] In general, results have been consistent with major predictions derived from the theory, although not uniformly so. Thus, at present, path-goal theory appears to be a reasonably useful framework offering valuable insights into leadership and the many factors that determine the degree to which individual leaders are successful in this role.

Leadership Development: Bringing Out the Leader Within You

In case it's not clear by now, being an effective leader isn't easy. If you happen to be fortunate enough to be born with "the right stuff," it helps. It also is beneficial to find yourself in the kind of situation in which an opportunity exists to demonstrate your capacity as a leader. However, anyone can improve his or her leadership skills, honing his or her capacity to inspire others in an organization. Although we all cannot become a Jack Welch (the highly successful former CEO of General Electric described earlier), it is possible for almost anyone to develop the skills needed to become more successful as a leader.

The systematic process of training people to expand their capacity to function effectively in leadership roles is known as **leadership development.** In recent years, many organizations have invested

leadership development
The practice of systematically training people to expand their capacity to function effectively in leadership roles.

heavily in these efforts, recognizing that effective leadership is a source of competitive advantage for an organization. Such efforts have focused on three major areas of emphasis. These are as follows:

- Developing networks of social interaction between people, close ties within and between organizations (see Chapter 9)
- Developing trusting relationships between oneself and others (see Chapter 11)
- Developing common values and shared visions with others

In essence, these skills emphasize the development of emotional intelligence—one of the key characteristics of effective leaders we described earlier (see Chapter 5).

All leadership development programs are based on two key assumptions: (1) that leadership makes a difference in an organization's performance, and (2) that it is possible for leaders to be developed (i.e., made, if not born).[60] However, the various leadership development tools go about the mission of promoting leaders' skills in different ways. We now identify some of the most widely used techniques.[61]

360-Degree Feedback

In Chapter 3 we described **360-degree feedback,** the process of using multiple sources from inside and outside an organization to evaluate the work of an individual. This practice has proven to be an effective way for leaders to learn what key others, such as peers, direct reports, and supervisors, think about them.[62] This is a useful means of identifying aspects of one's leadership style that are in need of change. Its basic assumption is that different people will have varying perspectives on someone's leadership.

The practice of collecting 360-degree feedback is extremely popular these days. In fact, nearly all of the *Fortune* 500 companies rely on this technique in one way or another.[63] However, collecting feedback and taking appropriate action based on it are two entirely different things. After all, many people are threatened by negative feedback and defend against it psychologically by dismissing it as invalid. Even those who agree with it might not be willing to change their behavior (a topic we will revisit in Chapter 16). Furthermore, even the most well-intentioned leaders may fail to take action on the feedback they receive if that information is too complex or inconsistent, which is not too unusual. To help in this regard, many companies have found that leaders who have face-to-face meetings with others in which they get to discuss the feedback they receive are particularly likely to follow up in an effective manner.

It's not at all unusual for 360-degree feedback to be given within exercises conducted in **assessment centers.**[64] These are sessions (lasting from only a few hours to several days) in which a variety of techniques are used to determine how people behave under various standardized conditions. For example, people in assessment centers often participate in *role-playing exercises*. Typically, the individual being assessed assumes the role of a person in a particular job who is asked to respond to various things being said by a trainer who is playing another role. The way the individual responds can provide insight into what he or she is like. Discussing this insight is part of the assessment.[65] This information can be extremely useful for leaders to gain insight into new ways of behaving.

Networking

Far too often, leaders find themselves isolated from things that are going on in other departments. As a result, when they need help, they don't know where to go to get it. As a leadership development tool, **networking** is designed to break down these barriers. Specifically, it is aimed at helping leaders learn to whom they should turn for information, finding what problem-solving resources are available to them (for an example, see Figure 13.15).

Networking is beneficial to leadership development because it promotes peer relationships in work settings. These are valuable insofar as they involve mutual obligations, thereby promoting cooperation. What's more, they tend to be long-lasting. In fact, it is not unusual for some peer relationships to span an entire 30-year career. Importantly, personal networks tend to be effective because they transcend organizational boundaries, thereby bringing together people from different parts of an organization who otherwise would not normally come into contact with one another. (Although networking is beneficial to businesses in all countries, it is especially important in China, where, as we describe in the Today's Diverse and Global Organizations section on page 470, it is an essential aspect of doing business.)

360-degree feedback
The process of using multiple sources from around an organization, and outside it, to evaluate the work of an individual—often used for leaders to learn what people think about them.

assessment centers
Sessions in which a variety of techniques are used to determine how people behave under various standardized conditons.

networking
A leadership development tool designed to help people make connections to others to whom they can turn for information and problem solving.

Peter Wynn Thompson/Redux Pictures.

FIGURE 13.15

Networking: Not Leaving It to Chance

Networking is so important to Accenture, the worldwide consulting firm, that it holds an annual five-day seminar designed to give its global partners a chance to meet one another and to exchange views. The goal is to allow partners to strengthen their personal networks, making it possible to address problems and take on projects that otherwise would have been overlooked, thereby developing participants' leadership skills.

Today's Diverse and Global Organizations

Guanxi: Social Networking in China

If making connections with other people is a useful skill for American leaders, it is an absolutely essential one for Chinese leaders, or anyone doing business in China, for that matter. In **guanxi** Chinese, the term **guanxi** refers to interpersonal relationships—specifically, one's network of personal and business connections.[66] For several centuries, guanxi has been a pervasive part of the Chinese business world, binding literally millions of Chinese companies into a vast social and business web. Business cannot be conducted in China without guanxi; one must have the proper network of connections to get things done. One party supports another, exchanging favors. It's not considered bribery, and it's perfectly legal. In fact, it's the glue that holds together the Chinese business enterprise. In today's fast-paced world, this is truer than ever.[67]

guanxi
In China, a person's network of personal and business connections.

Behind the penchant for networking in China is the tendency for the Chinese to prefer working with people they know and trust. They are unlikely to make deals with strangers, so becoming a trusted associate is essential (and time consuming, too). Leaders who cultivate strong interpersonal relationships become powerful because they are given opportunities that are denied to others. Doors open up for them. Suppose, for example, you want to obtain a license to market your product in a new region of China. With the right guanxi, the process can be accelerated and much less expensive. Without it, you might be hopelessly tied up in a mountain of red tape.

Guanxi is developed by cultivating a network of reciprocal obligations over time.[68] One person does a favor for another, and that original favor subsequently is returned by another, and so on. Often, "money talks," as they say, when it comes to cultivating favors, but guanxi is more about good will and personal support. For example, in China, one wouldn't think of doing business with a supplier, a bank, or even a government official without bringing a small gift, such as wine or cigarettes. Although to some Westerners the process might seem intrusive to the point of being blatantly pushy, it is considered completely proper in China. In fact, the giving of small gifts is absolutely necessary to cultivate, develop, and nurture the vast network of relationships needed to succeed.

Management consultant Tom Peters once noted that a sure sign of a successful leader is one who has a Rolodex (a card file of business contacts) that grows larger each year. Former President Bill Clinton was considered a master of developing a vast network of business relationships. Whenever he needed a favor from someone, he would just find the Rolodex card of someone he met who might be able to help. Peters and Clinton worked their network contacts to their strategic advantages. In China, however, leaders must do the same thing just to stay in the game.

Executive Coaching

A highly effective method of developing leaders involves custom-tailored, one-on-one learning aimed at improving an individual leader's performance. This approach, known as **executive coaching,** is an extension of the practice of career counseling described in Appendix 2. Coaching can be either a one-time process aimed at addressing some specific issues, or it can be an ongoing, continuous process. In either case, executive coaching typically includes an integrative assessment of a leader's strengths and weaknesses along with a comprehensive plan for improvement. Specifically, these programs tend to follow the specific steps outlined in Figure 13.16.

In some organizations, being assigned a coach is seen as a remedial measure, a sign of weakness. In such cases, any benefits of coaching may be minimized as leaders fail to get involved in the process out of embarrassment. For this reason, organizations that use coaches are advised to provide these services to an entire executive group, thereby removing any stigma and putting all leaders on an equal footing. Research has found that this approach is particularly effective when it is used following a formal training program. In fact, the customized, one-on-one coaching provided after a standardized training program was found to increase leaders' productivity by 88 percent.[69]

Mentoring

In Chapter 6 we discussed how minority group members stand to benefit by having relationships with *mentors,* more senior associates who help show them the ropes. Again, in Appendix 2, we describe the formal process of *mentoring*, in which employees receive help, either formally or informally, from more experienced colleagues in the organization as a means of helping them develop their careers. (Mentors also may come from outside the organization, but such relationships are more likely to take the form of coaching.) Although this approach is unlikely to include a formal assessment of a leader's strengths and limitations, it tends to focus on personal and professional support. Recent research shows that officials from a wide array of organizations consider mentoring one of the most effective forms of leadership development they have in place.[70]

A potential problem with mentoring (as we note in Appendix 2) is that protégés (i.e., the individuals helped by mentors) may become so highly connected to their mentors that they fail to think independently. Soon, what a mentored employee does is just what the mentor would have done. Although this is beneficial, it also can be potentially limiting, leading to a narrowness of thought. This problem is especially likely to occur in the case of executive coaching because

executive coaching
A technique of leadership development that involves custom-tailored, one-on-one learning aimed at improving an individual leader's performance.

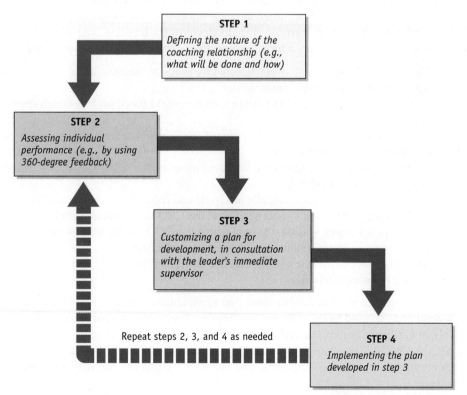

FIGURE 13.16

Steps in the Executive Coaching Process

The process of executive coaching generally follows the four steps outlined here.

STEP 1
Defining the nature of the coaching relationship (e.g., what will be done and how)

STEP 2
Assessing individual performance (e.g., by using 360-degree feedback)

STEP 3
Customizing a plan for development, in consultation with the leader's immediate supervisor

STEP 4
Implementing the plan developed in step 3

Repeat steps 2, 3, and 4 as needed

individuals making important decisions may fear straying from the tried-and-true solutions of their mentors. And whenever this occurs, the organization is denied any fresh new perspective that the less seasoned executive might be able to provide.

Job Assignments

When it comes to leadership, the phrase "experience is the best teacher" holds true. Indeed, one of the most effective ways of training leaders is by assigning them to positions that allow them to gain "on the job" experience.

With this in mind, many companies intentionally assign personnel to relatively unfamiliar positions in other countries so they can broaden their experiences by developing new areas of familiarity. For example, the Coca-Cola Company recently transferred more than 300 professional and managerial employees from the United States to facilities abroad for one year in an effort to develop leadership skills before returning them home to assume new leadership positions. Procter & Gamble does the same thing on a regular basis, assigning prospective leaders to positions at foreign affiliates for periods of one to three years. In many ways, this is akin to the practice used in Major League Baseball of developing players by sending them to a team's minor league "farm teams."

For job assignments to serve their developmental function, it is necessary for the newly assigned positions to provide the kind of opportunities that make learning possible. Ideally, these jobs give newly developing leaders opportunities to try out different approaches to leadership so they can determine what works for them. In other words, they should be given the latitude to try different approaches, even if they fail. It is important to keep in mind that the purpose of the job assignment is to facilitate learning, in which case some degree of failure is inevitable (as is the case for all students). However, should an emphasis be placed on job performance instead, it's unlikely that the new assignment will have the intended benefits, and it is destined to be looked upon unfavorably.

Action Learning

action learning
A leadership development technique involving a continuous process of learning and reflection that is supported by colleagues and that emphasizes getting things done.

Traditionally, much of the learning that takes place when people are taught to lead occurs in the classroom. The problem with this approach, however, is that shortly after the formal training sessions are over, people revert to their old ways when back at their jobs, resulting in little if any developmental progress. To combat this problem, many organizations have been turning to **action learning,** which is a continuous process of learning and reflection that is supported by colleagues and that emphasizes getting things done.[71] The underlying assumption of action learning is that leaders develop most effectively when they are working on real organizational problems.[72]

Citibank used action learning to help develop its leaders, who were having difficulty thinking about problems from a broad perspective.[73] Specifically, they took the following steps.

1. The issues to be worked on were selected by heads of business units. These had to be ones that affected total Citibank performance.
2. Participants were selected from throughout the world based on a thorough review of their talents.
3. A three-day orientation session was held off-site in which team-building skills were practiced (these are discussed in Chapter 8).
4. For two to three weeks, data were collected about effective banking practices from both inside and outside Citibank.
5. These findings were systematically analyzed and recommendations were developed.
6. Findings were presented to area heads and the CEO in 90-minute meetings.
7. A one-day debriefing session was held with a coach. These focused on the recommendations, team processes, and individual development opportunities.
8. One to two weeks later, senior managers followed up and made decisions regarding the various recommendations.

Although the business imperatives that drive action learning differ from case to case, the general process used tends to follow the steps outlined here. Action learning has been used not only at Citibank, but also at such organizations as General Electric (to develop new markets), ARAMARK (to promote cross-cultural opportunities), Shell Oil (to alter perceptions of the company's financial strength), and the U.S. Army (to share lessons from battlefield experiences).[74] Because action learning is a general idea that takes different forms in various organizations, its effectiveness has been difficult to assess. However, research generally confirms the effectiveness of training leaders by using the kind of active approaches described here instead of more passive, classroom training (see also our discussion of the factors that make training effective in Chapter 3).

The various leadership development techniques we have described in this section of the chapter are useful for developing a variety of characteristics and skills in leaders or potential leaders. These focus on many of the topics considered elsewhere in this book (e.g., communication, motivation, etc.) as well as ones addressed in this chapter (e.g., when it's best to delegate, how to be people-centered and production-centered, etc.). In addition to using these techniques for these purposes, they also have been used to promote what we earlier referred to *as authentic leadership* (see page 451)—that is, leadership associated with being ethical. In this chapter's The Ethics Angle section below, we describe specific qualities of authentic leaders and indicate how the leadership development techniques described here may be used to enhance them.

The Ethics Angle

Using Leadership Development Techniques to Promote Authentic Leaders

Individuals considered *authentic leaders* may be effective because of their emphasis on morality and ethics in their relationships with others. Specifically, scientists have observed that they possess four particular qualities that contribute to their effectiveness in this regard.[75] These are as follows:

- *Self-awareness:* The extent to which people are aware of their own strengths and weaknesses and also understand their own emotions and personalities
- *Unbiased processing:* The degree to which individuals are capable of judging and accepting their positive and negative qualities in an objective fashion
- *Authentic behavioral acting:* The ability to act in ways that are consistent with personal values and preferences instead of ones designed merely to get others to respond positively (e.g., by offering rewards)
- *Relational authenticity:* The ability to share information about oneself, developing close and trusting relations with others who recognize both good and bad in them

The various leadership development techniques described in this chapter, in addition to being used to enhance a variety of other abilities, have been used to help develop these four skills. Here's how.

Self-awareness may be developed by using 360-degree feedback

The idea is that by gaining insight into how we are viewed by others (e.g., followers, peers, supervisors), it becomes possible to discover inconsistencies between the ways we see ourselves and how others see us. Focusing on this can help people derive insight into their own values and beliefs. And, of course, it is useful as a means of identifying strengths and weaknesses.

Unbiased processing may be developed by using assessment centers

As we suggested in conjunction with our discussion of the attribution process (Chapter 3), we are highly biased and unlikely to be objective when it comes to perceiving ourselves (and others, too). With this in mind, it has been recommended that people being trained participate in assessment centers, where they can take part in experiential exercises that allow them to gain insight into themselves. In these, participants are asked to adopt various roles (e.g., supervisor, employee) in the course of discussing various topics others (e.g., giving performance feedback). Analyzing these dialogues with the help of others in attendance allows people to learn unbiased information about themselves.

Authentic behavior/acting may be developed by using coaching or mentoring

Inherent in the experience of being coached or mentored is the potential to observe role models who are especially good at behaving in ways that are consistent with their own values. So, for example, a highly authentic leader (coach or mentor) may be paired with an aspiring leader (trainee or protégé), allowing the trainee to observe what the authentic leader is doing and the beneficial reactions that result. The underlying process that makes this effective is observational learning, which we described in Chapter 3.

Relational authenticity can be developed by using 360-degree feedback

Authentic relations are ones characterized by openness and truthfulness. As a first step toward developing these qualities, it's quite useful to receive information from others who know you well (e.g., because you've worked together over the years). If the setting is structured appropriately, feedback may emerge that may prove invaluable when it comes to developing relational authenticity.

In conclusion, we note that becoming an authentic leader requires certain knowledge (about oneself) and skills. Several of the standard leadership development skills promise to be very useful in this regard.

Summary and Review of Learning Objectives

1. **Differentiate between leadership and management, contrasting the things people in these roles typically do.**

   Leadership involves influencing others (followers) in ways that help attain goals and in a manner that is noncoercive and goal-directed. A leader's primary function is to envision and articulate the essential purpose or mission of an organization and the strategy for attaining it. The job of the manager is to implement the leader's vision, putting into practice ways of bringing that vision to fruition. In practice, this distinction is often difficult to make because many leaders and followers also do things that are in keeping with the other's role.

2. **Identify the major characteristics that make leaders effective and that help transformational leaders inspire followers to make major changes in their organizations.**

   The *trait approach to leadership,* referred to as *great person theory,* claims that successful leaders have characteristics that set them apart from other people. Such individuals tend to be higher in *leadership motivation* (i.e., the desire to be a leader), drive, honesty, self-confidence, and several other traits. Successful leaders also tend to have multiple sources of intelligence (e.g., cognitive intelligence, emotional intelligence, and cultural intelligence) and demonstrate high amounts of *flexibility*—that is, the ability to adapt their style to the followers' needs and to the requirements of specific situations. Transformational leaders also have several important characteristics that help them inspire people to make major changes in their organizations. Most notably, transformational leaders generally have many of the following traits: charisma, self-confidence, vision, environmental sensitivity, intellectual stimulation, interpersonal consideration, inspiration, and morality.

3. **Distinguish between the two basic forms of leader behavior: person-oriented behavior and production-oriented behavior, explaining how grid training helps develop them.**

   Leaders differ with respect to the extent to which they focus on efforts to attain successful task performance—known as *initiating structure* (or being *task-oriented*)—and their concern with maintaining favorable personal relations with subordinates—known as *consideration* (or being *person-oriented*). *Grid training* is a systematic way of training managers to raise their concern for people as well as their concern for production (by training them in communication skills and planning skills).

4. **Explain what the leader-member exchange (LMX) model says about the relationships between leaders and followers.**

   This conceptualization suggests that for various reasons leaders form different kinds of relationships with various groups of subordinates. One group, referred to as the *in-group,* is favored by the leader. Members of in-groups receive considerably more attention from the leader and larger shares of the resources they have to offer (such as time and recognition). By contrast, other subordinates fall into the *out-group.* These individuals are disfavored by leaders. As such, they receive fewer valued resources from their leaders. Leaders distinguish between in-group and out-group members very early in their relationships with them—and on the basis of surprisingly little information. Sometimes, perceived similarity with respect to personal characteristics such as age, gender, or personality is sufficient to categorize followers into a leader's in-group. Similarly, a particular follower may be granted in-group status if the leader believes that person to be especially competent at performing his or her job.

5. **Summarize what LPC contingency theory and situational leadership theory say about the connection between leadership style and situational variables.**

   LPC contingency theory suggests that a leader's characteristics in conjunction with various situational factors determine his or her group's effectiveness. Task-oriented leaders (termed *low-LPC leaders*) are more effective than people-oriented leaders (termed *high-LPC leaders*) under conditions in which the leader has either high or low control over the group in question. In contrast, people-oriented leaders are more effective under conditions where the leader has moderate control. The *situational leadership theory* suggests that the most effective style of leadership—either delegating, participating, selling, or telling—depends on the extent to which followers require guidance and direction, and emotional support. Effective leaders are required to diagnose the situations they face and implement the appropriate behavioral style for that situation.

6. **Describe various techniques used to develop successful leaders in organizations.**

One popular technique of leadership development, *360-degree feedback,* involves giving people multiple sources of feedback about their strengths and weaknesses. *Networking,* another technique, is aimed at helping leaders learn to whom they should turn for information, both inside and outside their organization. *Executive coaching* is a one-on-one experience in which a leader is given an integrative assessment of his or her strengths and weaknesses. Leadership development also involves giving people special *job assignments* that allow them to develop new skills. Finally, *action learning* is a leadership development technique in which people get to learn by experiencing real organizational problems.

Points to Ponder

Questions for Review

1. What is the difference between leadership and management? What are the characteristics that distinguish successful leaders from ordinary managers?
2. What is the difference between person-oriented leadership and production-oriented leadership?
3. How are the relationships between leaders and followers explained by the LMX model? What assumptions must be made about the relationships between leaders and followers when leading work teams?
4. What makes charismatic leaders and transformational leaders so special in organizations?
5. What are the basic assumptions of contingency theories of leadership? What particular theories fall into this category?
6. What is meant by "leadership development," and what techniques are used to bring it about?

Experiential Questions

1. Do you know anyone who you consider a charismatic leader or a transformational leader? If so, what is this person like? What has this individual done that suggests that he or she is so special?
2. Think about the leaders of teams in which you have worked and how they compare to the leaders of other groups that do not operate as teams. In what ways do these leaders behave similarly or differently?
3. Have you ever participated in a leadership development program? If so, what exactly was done? In what ways was the program effective or ineffective?

Questions to Analyze

1. As we noted, the lines between leading and managing sometimes are blurred in practice. What factors (e.g., technology, the economy, etc.) do you believe are responsible for making this distinction so vague?
2. As technology advances further in the years to come, how do you think the nature of leadership in work organizations is likely to change?
3. What techniques of leadership development do you believe would be most effective in the company in which you work? What do you see as the major impediments to the effectiveness of leadership development?

Experiencing OB

Individual Exercise

Determining Your Leadership Style

As noted on pages 465–466, *situational leadership theory* identifies four basic leadership styles. To be able to identify and enact the most appropriate style of leadership in any given situation, it is first useful to understand the style to which you are most strongly predisposed. This exercise will help you gain such insight into your own leadership style.

Directions

Following are eight hypothetical situations in which you have to make a decision affecting you and members of your work group. For each, indicate which of the following actions you are most likely to take by writing the letter corresponding to it in the space provided.

- Action A: Let the members of the group decide themselves what to do.
- Action B: Ask the members of the group what to do, but make the final decision yourself.
- Action C: Make the decision yourself, but explain your reasons.
- Action D: Make the decision yourself, telling the group exactly what to do.

———— 1. In the face of financial pressures, you are forced to make budget cuts for your unit. Where do you cut?

———— 2. To meet an impending deadline, someone in your secretarial pool will have to work late one evening to finish typing an important report. Who will it be?

———— 3. As coach of a company softball team, you are required to trim your squad to 25 players from 30 currently on the roster. Who goes?

———— 4. Employees in your department have to schedule their summer vacations to keep the office appropriately staffed. Who decides first?

———— 5. As chair of the social committee, you are responsible for determining the theme for the company ball. How do you do so?

———— 6. You have an opportunity to buy or rent an important piece of equipment for your company. After gathering all the facts, how do you make the choice?

———— 7. The office is being redecorated. How do you decide on the color scheme?

———— 8. Along with your associates you are taking a visiting dignitary to dinner. How do you decide what restaurant to go to?

Scoring

1. Count the number of situations to which you responded by marking "A." This is your *delegating* score.
2. Count the number of situations to which you responded by marking "B." This is your *participating* score.
3. Count the number of situations to which you responded by marking "C." This is your *selling* score.
4. Count the number of situations to which you responded by marking "D." This is your *telling* score.

Questions for Discussion

1. Based on this questionnaire, what was your most predominant leadership style? Is this consistent with what you would have predicted in advance?
2. According to situational leadership theory, in what kinds of situations would this style be most appropriate? Have you ever found yourself in such a situation, and if so, how well did you do?
3. Do you think that it would be possible for you to change this style if needed?

Group Exercise

Identifying Great Leaders in All Walks of Life

A useful way to understand the great person theory is to identify those individuals who may be considered great leaders and then to consider what it is that makes them so great. This exercise is designed to guide a class in this activity.

Directions

1. Divide the class into four equal-size groups, arranging each in a semicircle.
2. In the open part of the semicircle, one group member—the recorder—should stand at a flip chart, ready to write down the group's responses.
3. The members of each group should identify the 10 most effective leaders they can think of—living or dead, real or fictional—in one of the following fields: business, sports, politics/government, humanitarian endeavors. One group should cover each of these domains. If more than 10 names come up, the group should vote on the 10 best answers. The recorder should write down the names as they are identified.
4. Examining the list, group members should identify the traits and characteristics that the people on the list have in common, but that distinguish them from others who are not on the list. In other words, what is it that makes these people so special? The recorder should write down the answers.
5. One person from each group should be selected to present his or her group's responses to members of the class. This should include both the names of the leaders identified and their special characteristics.

Questions for Discussion

1. How did the traits identified in this exercise compare to the ones identified in this chapter (see pages 450–451 and Table 13.2) as important determinants of leadership? Were they similar or different? Why?

2. To what extent were the traits identified in the various groups different or similar? In other words, were different characteristics associated with leadership success in different walks of life? Or were the ingredients for leadership success more universal?

3. Were some of the traits identified surprising to you, or were they all what you would have expected?

Practicing OB

"I Don't Get No Respect"

The president and founder of a small tool and die casting firm tells you, "Nobody around here has any respect for me. The only reason they listen to me is because this is my company." Company employees report that he is a highly controlling individual who does not let anyone do anything for themselves.

1. What behaviors should the president attempt to emulate to improve his leadership style? How might he go about doing so?
2. Under what conditions would you expect the president's leadership style to be most effective?
3. Do you think that these conditions might exist in his company? If not, how might they be created?

■ *A New Era for Newark*

In the 1970s, *Harper's* magazine named Newark, New Jersey—still unrecovered from the 1967 riots that drove away middle-class citizens and thriving businesses— "America's worst city." Flash forward four decades and although high crime and substandard housing make Newark, just 10 miles from New York City, a textbook picture of urban blight, conditions have improved in recent years—and dramatically, at that. Since 2006, the city's homicide rate has fallen sharply, new townhomes with green spaces have replaced decrepit high-rises for low-income residents, and adding still more green space, new parks have been springing up throughout the city. And little by little, new businesses have been coming to town as well. Not coincidentally, 2006 is exactly when Cory Booker was elected mayor, only the city's third since 1970.

Mayor Booker would be the first to tell you that the turnaround has been the result of hard work more than anything else. Downplaying his Ivy League background as a graduate of Yale Law School and a former Rhodes scholar, he has gone out of his way to show that he's "willing to work as hard or harder than anybody in city hall." Over the objections of the city's police director, Booker sat beside Newark police officers in squad cars as they patrolled the city nightly until 4:00 A.M. His objective was not only to learn firsthand exactly what's going on but also to demonstrate his high level of commitment to the city's police officers, who he regards as soldiers on the front lines of his crusade against crime.

The mayor, in his early 40s, is unapologetic about his hands-on approach to leadership—and with good reason. Booker's personal efforts on behalf of the city have paid off big, resulting in $25 million raised from private donors (most from John Walton, son of Wal-Mart's founder) to develop Newark's charter schools. Despite this and other direct efforts on behalf of the city, it would be misleading to suggest that Mayor Booker views himself as a one-man show. Rather, he has adopted a lead-by-example philosophy—an ethos he credits to his mother, who taught him that, "who you are speaks so loudly that I can't hear what you say."

In the mayor's case, who he is comes across loudly, at least at the City of Newark's Web site. There, he proudly shares his dream that Newark "will set a national standard" by making "transformative change," resulting in "a renewed feeling of hope and optimism in our city." Proclaiming that Newark is "5 to 10 years away from a massive tipping point," Mayor Booker has demonstrated his commitment to leading this charge, even if it meant declining President Obama's invitation to run his administration's Urban Affairs Office. It's little wonder that in 2009 *U.S. News & World Report* named Cory Booker one of "America's Best Leaders."

Questions for Discussion

1. What particular characteristics does Cory Booker appear to have that make him well suited to his leadership position?
2. Would you consider Cory Booker to be a transformational leader, or a potential one, at least? Why or why not?
3. How might Cory Booker benefit from any of the leadership development techniques described in this chapter? What particular techniques would appear to be most helpful, and why?

■ Leadership at Kluster

Kluster, a company that produces a Web-based platform called the Illuminator, is the latest in a string of companies founded by 20-year-old Ben Kaufman, who launched his first business as a high school student. Despite founding the company, Kaufman is not Kluster's CEO. He demoted himself from that position when he realized that his youth and inexperience made investors uneasy. Although he lacks a formal title, Kaufman is very much a visionary leader and is committed to the success of the Illuminator.

Design coordinator Andres Arango claims that Kaufman inspires everyone at the firm. Peter Wadsworth, an engineer, agrees. He believes that Kaufman's key strength is his ideas and that Kaufman knows exactly where he wants to go. Wadsworth notes that although everyone is encouraged to voice their opinions, Kaufman will campaign for ideas he thinks are best, and tell people when he believes their suggestions lack merit.

At the same time, however, Kaufman knows his limitations and is willing to pass responsibility to those who are more skilled. He also possesses a high level of self-confidence and believes strongly in the value of his ideas and decisions. Wadsworth believes these characteristics are an asset when Kaufman meets with other companies and celebrities. Indeed, Arango notes that it was Kaufman's charisma and commitment to his vision that prompted him to join the Illuminator team.

Discussion Questions

1. Using the discussion of effective leaders in Chapter 13 as a starting point, identify the qualities of effective leadership that Ben Kaufman appears to have.
2. Has Ben's effectiveness as a leader been diminished by his decision to step down as CEO? Why or why not?
3. Based on the description in Chapter 13, do you believe that Ben Kaufman is a transformational leader?

■ Decision Making at Insomnia Cookies

Insomnia Cookies was founded by Seth Berkowitz when he was a college student. The company, a chain of late-night cookie stores located on college campuses, began with a delivery-only concept, but more recently has incorporated retail outlets.

When Insomnia Cookies was founded, Berkowitz did everything from baking cookies to delivering them. Today, however, the company has expanded to include COO Joe Essenfeld and Elise Piatkowski, the marketing director. Both Piatkowski and Essenfeld play important roles in decision making at Insomnia Cookies. In fact, Berkowitz says that he welcomes their input because it forces him to look at issues in different ways.

Essenfeld feels that the team works well because members continually critique one another by challenging decisions and ideas. Pitakowski, for example, believes she pays more attention to detail and has a better feel for the brand's aesthetics than either Berkowitz or Essenfeld. She feels that Essenfeld has a tendency to leap before he looks, which sometimes can be problematic. Piatkowski also notes

that the nature of the interaction between Essenfeld and Berkowitz has been beneficial for the company: Essenfeld encourages Berkowitz to explore areas he otherwise might have avoided, and Berkowitz helps Essenfeld moderate his more extreme thinking. According to Berkowitz, the team has been successful at separating members' personal feelings from their professional feelings, which has facilitated the decision-making process.

Discussion Questions

1. Applying the steps in the phases of the decision-making process presented in Chapter 10, explain how Insomnia Cookies likely made the decision to close its Binghampton store.
2. In your opinion, does Insomnia Cookies' decision to use a purple truck constitute a strategic decision? Explain your answer.
3. Using the decision style model making presented in Chapter 10, how would you characterize the decision-making styles of Seth Berkowitz, Joe Essenfeld, and Elise Piatkowski?

CHAPTER

14 Organizational Culture, Creativity, and Innovation

Learning Objectives

After reading this chapter, you should be able to:

1. Define organizational culture and identify its core characteristics and the various functions it serves in organizations.

2. Describe the four major forms of organizational culture specified by the competing values framework.

3. Explain the factors responsible for creating and transmitting organizational culture and for getting it to change.

4. Define creativity and describe the basic components of individual and team creativity.

5. Describe various approaches to promoting creativity in organizations.

6. Identify the basic forms and targets of innovation and the stages of the innovation process.

Chapter Outline

- Organizational Culture: Its Basic Nature
- Creating, Transmitting, and Changing Organizational Culture
- Creativity in Individuals and Teams
- Promoting Creativity in Organizations
- The Process of Innovation

Preview Case

■ *Zipcar: Wheels on Demand*

When you own a car, how much time do you actually spend driving it? For many people, their cars spend more time in the garage than on the road. But even when parked, they rack up bills for insurance and interest on an auto loan, not to mention depreciation of the vehicle's worth. Then, when you drive the car, of course, the costs of gasoline and parking are sky-high. You can always go to one of the traditional car rental companies, but these tend to be very expensive and inconvenient. Still, you need wheels, so what's the alternative?

Antje Danielson had an answer inspired by something she saw while on vacation in Germany—a car-sharing service. Why not have fleets of cars stationed throughout a city that you could rent on a short-term, on-demand basis by phoning in a last-minute, no-hassle reservation? Just walk up to the parked vehicle, swipe a card, and drive away. When you're done, drop the car off at one of the many conveniently located lots, leave the keys, and walk away. You're billed a reasonable daily or hourly fee for a rental that includes everything—all insurance, fuel, and parking.

One day in 1999, in Cambridge, Massachusetts, Danielson approached Robin Chase with her "wheels when you want them" idea, and the following year Zipcar was launched. Their plan was to introduce facilities into congested areas, such as downtowns of major cities and areas around the campuses of large universities, where people are inclined to need cars for short trips but where ownership is prohibitively expensive. It would work, they reasoned, if they could meet four requirements: (1) develop a phone and online reservation system that was blazingly fast and easy to use, (2) offer a variety of different kinds of vehicles for different occasions, (3) have pick-up and drop-off locations that are as easy to find as ATMs, and, of course (4) keep rental fees reasonable.

This required considerable start-up funds, so Danielson and Chase partnered with major investors, including a company backed by AOL cofounder Steve Case

and Staples founder Thomas G. Stemberg. With strong financial support, Zipcar now operates in 65 U.S. cities, plus two in Canada and one in the United Kingdom, and has some 270,000 members ("Zipsters," as the company calls them), making it the largest car-sharing company in the world. And with soaring fuel costs, this figure is rising fast. For an annual fee of $50, members can rent cars for $8 per hour (and up, depending on the vehicle—about 70 different varieties—and location), or $66 for a whole day, with 180 miles included.

Zipcar has been so popular with customers that more than 40 percent either put off buying a car or sell their vehicles within their first year of membership. This not only saves lots of money for members (reported to be about $600 per month) but also takes 15 to 20 personal cars off the road, doing a great deal to reduce both carbon emissions and traffic congestion. The key to its success is its simplicity and convenience. After joining, you get a Zipcard. Then, using your phone, an online site, or even an iPhone app, you reserve your car. At the time and place you select, your vehicle is waiting for you. When you hold either your Zipcard or iPhone to the window, the door unlocks and you can drive away.

In 2010 Zipcar expanded its horizons by partnering with Zimride to promote ridesharing. Now, even people who don't own cars get to participate in sharing rides to popular locations. In recognition of how it has changed America's relationship with driving, Zipcar was ranked second among the most innovative companies in the transportation industry in *Fast Company* magazine's list of most innovative companies for 2010. The previous year, *Time* magazine named the Zipcar App one of "The Best Travel Gadgets of 2009." And with revenues bounding over 674 percent between 2005 and 2008, *Inc.* magazine ranked Zipcar as number 375 on its list of the "Top 500 Fastest Growing Companies for 2009." It sure looks like Zipcar's simple, "join, reserve, unlock, drive" approach to car rental has changed the game.

Zipcar's founders didn't invent the car rental business, of course, but they surely came up with an entirely new way of operating. Its convenient new twist on picking up and returning short-term rental vehicles makes it the proverbial "better mousetrap" of this $50 billion industry. Behind it were founders who demonstrated considerable *creativity*. Of course, coming up with a creative idea that makes you say, "why didn't I think of that?" and bringing it to fruition are two different things. And just as some individuals are more creative than others, some companies—3M, General Electric, and Rubbermaid, for example—are particularly adept at routinely doing the nonroutine. They take creative ideas and turn them into cutting-edge solutions, making them highly *innovative*. Considering the importance of creativity and innovation in today's rapidly changing, technologically oriented business environment, we examine these topics in this chapter.

When thinking about why some organizations are more innovative than others, it's tempting to speculate that because people have different personalities, the companies in which they work are likely to vary as well. However, when you consider that entire organizations are often so consistently different from one another, it's apparent that there's more involved than simply the personalities of the employees. Even companies where employees are constantly changing do not reinvent themselves. If you've held jobs in different organizations, you probably recognize that they have unique styles and ways of operating and that employees have to adapt to them. For example, some are more formal while others are more casual; some are more high-pressured but others are more laid-back, and so on. In other words, organizations have stable existences of their own that make them unique, and these go beyond the composition of employees at any given time. This is the idea behind *organizational culture*—the shared beliefs, expectations, and core values of people in an organization.[1]

Because it provides much of the foundation for individual creativity and an organization's tendency toward innovation, we begin this chapter by examining organizational culture. Specifically, we describe the basic nature of organizational culture—its role in organizations, the processes through which it is formed and maintained, its effects on individual and organizational functioning, and finally, how culture is subject to change. With this foundation in place, we shift attention to creativity and innovation. This includes a discussion of not only their fundamental characteristics, but also specific tips and suggestions on how to bring out your own creativity and how to make your own organization more innovative.

Organizational Culture: Its Basic Nature

To appreciate organizational culture fully, we have to understand its basic nature. With this in mind, we now examine six fundamental aspects of culture: (1) its formal definition, (2) the key characteristics on which it is based, (3) the strength of organizational culture, (4) whether there is generally only one or more than one culture within an organization, (5) the role that culture plays in organizational functioning, and (6) the various forms that culture takes.

Organizational Culture: A Definition

Although we have been talking about organizational culture in general terms thus far, a formal definition is in order. Accordingly, we define **organizational culture** as a cognitive framework consisting of attitudes, values, behavioral norms, and expectations shared by organization members.[2] You may think of it as a set of basic assumptions about an organization that are accepted widely by its members. (Please note that organizational culture sometimes is referred to as *corporate culture,* and if you see that term someplace, its meaning is the same. However, because a company doesn't have to be designated legally as a corporation to have a culture, organizational culture is the more appropriate term.)

organizational culture
A cognitive framework consisting of attitudes, values, behavioral norms, and expectations shared by organization members; a set of basic assumptions shared by members of an organization.

Some management experts have likened organizational culture to the roots of trees. What roots do for the lives of trees, culture does for organizations. Roots provide stability and nourishment for trees; culture provides stability and nourishment for organizations. Culture supports and feeds everything that goes on inside an organization. As one expert put it, "The strength of a firm's 'root system' ultimately shapes and determines its ability to perform in the marketplace."[3] With this in mind, the importance of organizational culture cannot be emphasized too strongly (see Figure 14.1).[4]

Core Cultural Characteristics

Fundamental to any organization's culture is a set of six core characteristics that are valued collectively by its members. We now describe these.[5]

SENSITIVITY TO OTHERS. Years ago, the culture at UPS was relatively rigid and inflexible with respect to customer needs. With some arrogance, it operated however it thought best, and forced customers to adjust to its ways. No more. Today, UPS's culture places high value on service and satisfaction. UPS now strives to suit the needs of its customers; changes are driven by better opportunities to serve.[6]

Paul Ellis/Newscom.

FIGURE 14.1

Embarrassment for the "Toyota Way"

For decades, Toyota was well-served by its *Toyota way* culture, emphasizing excellence and quality in the "4Ps"—philosophy, processes, people, and problem solving. In 2010 the foundations of that culture were rocked as a half-million vehicles were recalled due to sticking gas pedals that led to some fatal accidents. Allegations that Toyota downplayed safety defects raised questions about the company's ultimate commitment to quality and customer safety. There can be no mistaking that the "Toyota way" was badly bruised as the company was publicly embarrassed. Time will tell, however, if industry analysts are correct in predicting that the "Toyota way" ultimately will prevail, leading the company to reemerge with an even stronger commitment to quality and satisfaction. Meanwhile, this technician and thousands of others are busily replacing gas pedals with safer ones.

INTEREST IN NEW IDEAS. Walt Disney Co. employees—or "cast members," as they are called—traditionally have had lengthy orientation programs to ensure that they know exactly what to say and how to behave toward guests.[7] For the most part, their behavior is scripted. By contrast, people working at Southwest Airlines are encouraged to be unique and to bring fresh ideas to their work. In fact, company founder Herb Kelleher is so adamant about this that managerial training is geared toward hiring people who bring to the job an orientation toward openness and fun.[8]

WILLINGNESS TO TAKE RISKS. At some companies, such as the Bank of America, the culture is very conservative, and employees make only the safest investments. By contrast, buyers at The Limited are discouraged from making too many "safe" choices. Taking risks in the purchasing of fashion merchandise is valued.[9]

toxic organizational cultures
Organizational cultures in which people feel that they are not valued (opposite of healthy organizational cultures).

THE VALUE PLACED ON PEOPLE. Some companies consider their employees as valuable only insofar as they contribute to production, much as they view machinery. Such organizations, where people do not feel valued, are considered to have **toxic organizational cultures**. A survey found that 48 percent of people believe they work in toxic cultures.[10] Organizations like these tend to lose good employees, and struggle to be profitable as a result.

healthy organizational cultures
Organizational cultures in which people feel that they are valued (opposite of toxic organizational cultures).

By contrast, organizations that treat people well and that inspire employees—said to have **healthy organizational cultures**—tend to have very low turnover, and generally thrive (for an example of a company with a healthy culture, see Figure 14.2).[11] What, exactly, makes for a healthy organizational culture? How do you know one when you see it? The following characteristics play huge roles.[12]

■ *Everyone in the organization is open and humble.* Arrogance is absent. This is good because it encourages people to learn from everyone else.

FIGURE 14.2

Healthy Organizational Culture at The Container Store

Kip Tindell, president and CEO of the The Container Store, is proud of his company's healthy organizational culture, which has consistently contributed to its ranking at or near the top of *Fortune* magazine's annual list of the "Best Companies to Work For." The company is so committed to valuing its employees that on Valentine's Day in 2010, officials surprised workers in the company's stores, offices, and distribution centers with its first "National We Love Our Employees Day." In most retail stores annual turnover averages more than 100 percent, but at The Container Store it's less than 10 percent. These are good indications of a healthy culture.

- *Individuals are held accountable and accept personal responsibility for their actions.* Denial, blame, and excuses are absent. By accepting responsibility, conflict is lowered and opportunities for success are raised.
- *Within appropriate limits, people are free to take risks.* Neither reckless risk-taking nor stiflingly high levels of control are found. Hence, freedom exists to follow new ideas.
- *The commitment to doing things well is very high.* Mediocrity is not tolerated. Everyone is expected to do things appropriately, not taking shortcuts to quality.
- *Mistakes are tolerated because they are considered learning opportunities.* Attempts at innovation assist the organization, but some failures are inevitable. These are accepted because they provide opportunities to learn how to improve things next time.
- *Integrity is unquestioned.* Dishonesty undermines trust, which is essential to success. As a result, efforts to promote integrity, such as being transparent about decisions and following up on promises, are key.
- *Collaboration and integration between units is ongoing.* Turf wars and narrow thinking are discouraged. Instead, people work together in open, friendly, collaborative environments.
- *Courage and persistence are encouraged.* Work often is challenging. In healthy cultures everyone is encouraged to persist even in the face of failure, so long as they remain realistic about what can be accomplished.

OPENNESS OF AVAILABLE COMMUNICATION OPTIONS. At some companies, such as Yahoo!, employees are expected to make decisions freely and to communicate with whoever is needed to get the job done—even if it means going right to the CEO.[13] At IBM, however, the culture has called for working within the proper communication channels and to vest power in the hands of only a few key individuals, although this has been changing in recent years.[14]

FRIENDLINESS AND CONGENIALITY. At some companies, such as Nokia Corp., the employees tend to get along well. Friendships often run deep, and employees see each other outside of work.[15] At the toymaker Mattel, however, the culture has been depicted as being far more cutthroat and competitive.[16]

Strength of Organizational Culture: Strong and Weak

As we have been suggesting, organizations differ in many key ways with respect to their cultures. They also vary in the degree to which their cultures impact employees. In some businesses, there is widespread agreement concerning the elements of organizational culture we just described (i.e. sensitivity to others, willingness to take risks, etc.), paving the way for culture to exert major influences on the way people behave. An organization of this type may be said to have a **strong culture**. By contrast, other organizations may be characterized as having weaker agreement with respect to the various elements of organizational culture, thereby giving its culture only limited impact on the way people behave. An organization described in this manner may be said to have a **weak culture**.

In an organization with a strong culture, the core values are held intensely and shared widely. The more members accept these values and the greater their commitment to those concepts, the stronger a culture may be said to be. Specifically, organizations with strong cultures are characterized in the following ways.

- A clear philosophy exists about how business is to be conducted.
- Considerable time is spent communicating values and beliefs.
- Explicit statements are made that describe the organization's values.
- A set of values and norms exists that is shared widely and rooted deeply.
- New employees are screened carefully to ensure fit with the culture.

Research has shown that organizations differ in some interesting ways as to culture.[17] For example, stronger organizational cultures are likely to be found in companies that are newer and that have fewer employees. This suggests that perhaps as organizations grow older and larger in size, the effects of culture become diffused. This would be the case, for example, as the influence of a company founder grows smaller because his or her impact is felt less in a maturing organization. Also, organizations are more successful financially when their leaders hold views that are in keeping with the organizational culture than when leaders' personal perspectives are at odds with the prevailing culture. This makes sense given that workers may find themselves responding to inconsistent and competing messages. Together, these findings suggest that strong cultures shape the preferences and actions of people in the organizations that have them.

Cultures Within Organizations: One or Many?

Our discussion thus far has implied that each organization has only a single, uniform culture—one set of shared values, beliefs, and expectations. In fact, this is rarely the case. Instead, organizations, particularly large ones, typically have *several* cultures operating within them.

People generally have attitudes and values that are more in common with others in their own fields or work units than they do with those in other parts of the organization. These various groups may be said to have several different **subcultures**—cultures existing within parts of organizations rather than entirely through them. These typically are distinguished with respect to either functional differences (i.e., the type of work done) or geographic distances (i.e., the physical separation between people). Indeed, research suggests that several subcultures based on occupational, professional, or functional divisions usually exist within any large organization.

This is not to say, however, that there also may not be a **dominant culture**, a distinctive, overarching "personality" of an organization—the kind of culture to which we have been referring. An organization's dominant culture reflects its core values, the prevailing perceptions that are generally shared throughout the organization. Typically, members of subcultures who share additional sets of values also usually accept the core values of their organizations as a whole. Thus, subcultures should not be thought of as a bunch of totally separate cultures but, rather, as "mini" cultures operating within a larger, dominant one.

The Role of Culture in Organizations

As you read about the various cultural values that make organizations special, it probably strikes you that culture is an intangible force—albeit one with far-reaching consequences. Indeed, culture plays several important roles in organizations (for a summary, see Figure 14.3).

---

strong culture
An organization in which there is widespread agreement with respect to the core elements of culture, making it possible for culture to exert major influences on the way people behave.

weak culture
An organization in which there is limited agreement with respect to the core elements of culture, giving culture little influence on the way people behave.

subcultures
Cultures existing within parts of organizations rather than entirely through them.

dominant culture
The distinctive, overarching "personality" of an organization.

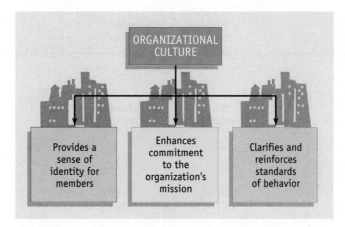

FIGURE 14.3

The Basic Functions of Organizational Culture

Organizational culture serves the three major functions summarized here.

CULTURE PROVIDES A SENSE OF IDENTITY. The more clearly an organization's shared perceptions and values are defined, the more strongly people can associate with its mission and feel a vital part of it. For example, employees at Southwest Airlines feel special because of their company's emphasis on having fun and joking around on the job, a widespread practice initiated by founder Herb Kelleher.[18] Southwest's employees feel strongly connected to the company, believing that they belong there. As a result, they only infrequently resign to take other positions in the airline industry.

CULTURE GENERATES COMMITMENT TO AN ORGANIZATION'S MISSION. Sometimes it's difficult for people to go beyond thinking of their own interests (i.e., how will this affect me?). When there is a strong, overarching culture, however, people feel that they are part of that larger, well-defined whole and involved in the entire organization's work. Bigger than any one individual's interests, culture reminds people of what their organization is all about.

CULTURE CLARIFIES AND REINFORCES STANDARDS OF BEHAVIOR. Culture guides employees' words and deeds, making it clear what they should do or say in a given situation, which is especially useful to newcomers. In this sense, culture provides stability to behavior, both with respect to what an individual might do at different times, but also with what various employees may do at the same time. For example, in a company with a culture that strongly supports customer satisfaction, workers will have clear guidance as to how they are expected to behave: doing whatever it takes to please the customer.

By serving these three important roles, it is clear that culture is an important force influencing behavior in organizations.

Forms of Organizational Culture: The Competing Values Framework

As you might imagine, just as there are many different organizations, there also are many different organizational cultures. Although each organization may be unique in several ways, key similarities may be noted. Fortunately, scientists have developed useful ways of organizing and identifying these cultures. One of the most popular approaches is known as the **competing values framework**.[19] According to this approach, the cultures of organizations differ with respect to two sets of opposite values (hence, the name). These are:

- Valuing *flexibility* and *discretion* as opposed to stability, order, and control.
- Valuing *internal affairs* as opposed to what's going on in the external environment.

By combining both dimensions, as shown in Figure 14.4, scientists have been able to identify the four unique types of organizational culture we now describe.

HIERARCHY CULTURE. Organizations described as having a **hierarchy culture** (shown in the lower-left corner of Figure 14.4) have an internal focus and emphasize stability and control. Here, the most effective leaders are good coordinators of projects and emphasize smooth-running procedures, often relying on formal rules and policies to do so.

Governmental agencies and large corporations tend to fall into this category. At McDonald's, for example, key values center on maintaining efficient and reliable production, and to ensure this, both the equipment used and the procedures followed—described in a 350-page manual—are

competing values framework
A conceptualization of organizational culture that specifies that cultures of organizations differ with respect to two sets of opposite values: (1) valuing flexibility and discretion as opposed to stability, order, and control, and (2) valuing internal affairs as opposed to what's going on in the external environment.

hierarchy culture
In the competing values framework, a form of organizational culture in which organizations have an internal focus and emphasize stability and control.

FIGURE 14.4

The Competing Values Framework

According to the *competing values framework,* the cultures of organizations can be distinguished in terms of the two opposite dimensions identified here. Combining these two sets of competing values results in the four types of organizational cultures shown.

Source: Adapted from Cameron & Quinn, 1999; see Note 19.

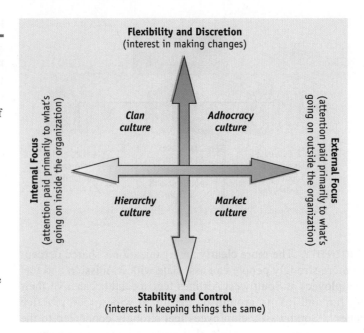

designed with this in mind. Sometimes, because organizations with hierarchy cultures are so attuned to internal concerns at the expense of external ones, and so focused on stability as opposed to making necessary changes (which often are necessary; see Chapter 16), serious problems result.

Not surprisingly, as a large government agency, the National Aeronautics and Space Administration (NASA) has a hierarchy culture.[20] Its sharp focus on stability created a culture that was blind to the threat posed by foam debris on its space shuttles. Furthermore, its attention to internal issues as opposed to external matters reinforced employees' convictions that the agency was far more attuned to making decisions based on safety than was the case in reality. Tragically, according to the Columbia Accident Investigation Board, flawed organizational culture was among the factors that led to the explosion of the space shuttle *Columbia* on February 1, 2003. Although not all hierarchy cultures are doomed to fail, this incident represents an extreme example of what may occur when they do.

market culture
In the competing values framework, a form of organizational culture in which organizations are concerned with stability and control, and are external in their orientation.

MARKET CULTURE. The term **market culture** describes organizations that are concerned with stability and control but that are external in their orientation (see the lower-right corner of Figure 14.4). In such organizations, the core values emphasize competitiveness and productivity, focusing on bottom-line results. They do this by carefully identifying the markets in which they are going to compete and then taking a very hard-driving, results-oriented approach to getting things done.

Perhaps the classic example of a market culture was General Electric (GE) during the two decades (1981–2001) that it was led by CEO Jack Welch. The culture called for making each of GE's business units either first or second in its respective market. Otherwise, the mandate from Welch was clear—fix, sell, or close the unsuccessful business.[21] He explained this as follows:

> When you're number four or five in a market, when number one sneezes, you get pneumonia. When you're number one, you control your destiny. The number fours keep merging; they have difficult times. That's not the same if you're number four, and that's your only business. Then you have to find strategic ways to get stronger. But, GE had a lot of number ones.[22]

clan culture
In the competing values framework, an organization characterized by a strong internal focus along with a high degree of flexibility and discretion.

His approach to market success involved not making small, incremental changes slowly, but rather, making major changes quickly. In this respect, GE operates more like a small company than the enormous one it is.

CLAN CULTURE. An organization is said to have a **clan culture** when it has a strong internal focus along with a high degree of flexibility and discretion (see the upper-left corner of Figure 14.4). With goals that are highly shared by members of the organization and high levels of cohesiveness (see Chapter 8), such organizations feel more like extended families than economic entities. Given their highly friendly nature, it's not surprising that most people prefer clan cultures to any of the other forms of organizational culture.[23]

In the clan culture, the predominant focus is on flexibility when it comes to external needs. This is attained by concentrating on the excellence of the employees, which reflects the internal focus. An example of a company that fits the clan culture is the Finnish conglomerate Nokia, best known for its cellular phones. At this company, the well-being of employees is a top priority. In contrast to the attention-grabbing element of most high-tech firms, Nokia's emphasis is on collegiality. As the firm's former CEO Jorna Ollila put it, "We don't snap our suspenders."[24]

Of importance, clan cultures often are characterized as enjoyable places to work, organizations in which a great deal of attention is paid to doing things to make work fun for employees. Although this makes life pleasant, of course, it's important to note that cultures in which having fun is stressed also must pay serious attention to meeting business objectives.

ADHOCRACY CULTURE. Organizations that have an **adhocracy culture** emphasize flexibility while also paying a great deal of attention to the external environment (see upper-right corner of Figure 14.4). As defined by management consultant Robert H. Waterman, Jr., an **adhocracy** is a form of organization that cuts across normal bureaucratic lines to capture opportunities, solve problems, and get results.[25] The term *adhocracy* is a reference to the absence of hierarchy, making it the opposite of *bureaucracy* (an organizational form we discuss in Chapters 1 and 15). Typical of contemporary companies, which often have to make rapid changes in the way they operate (see Chapter 16), the adhocracy culture is characterized by recognition that, to succeed, organizations need to be highly innovative (a concept we will describe later in this chapter) and constantly assess what the future requires for survival, let alone growth.

Typical of companies with adhocracy cultures are those in the software development and filmmaking businesses, where it is widely recognized that highly innovative products and services are essential to success (for an example, see Figure 14.5). Not surprisingly, these cultures also

adhocracy culture
In the competing values framework, organizations that emphasize flexibility while also paying a great deal of attention to the external environment.

adhocracy
A form of organization that cuts across normal bureaucratic lines to capture opportunities, solve problems, and get results.

FIGURE 14.5

Lights, Camera, Adhocracy Culture

Although you probably don't think of it when you're watching one of the *Harry Potter* movies (the highest grossing film series of all times), you're enjoying a product of Warner Brothers. Despite its enormous size (annual revenues exceed $11.7 billion), most of the company's operating units are considered to have *adhocracy cultures*, in which individual welfare is valued. This type of organizational culture is typical of that found in most motion picture studios.

exist in organizations in which research and development is essential. This is the case, for example, at 3M, the large American company that has been producing innovative products (currently, some 55,000 of them) for more than 100 years. To promote the innovative spirit at 3M, one of its earliest presidents, William McKnight, recognized the importance of a culture in which people were respected and felt free to take risks. Consider the three principles he articulated back in 1948, which describe an adhocracy culture (although he didn't refer to it as such):[26] (1) Delegate responsibility to encourage people to take initiative; (2) expect mistakes to be made, so be tolerant of them; and (3) criticize in a constructive, not destructive, manner (see Chapter 9).

Creating, Transmitting, and Changing Organizational Culture

Now that we have described the basic nature and forms of organizational culture, we turn attention to three additional issues of importance: how culture is created initially, how it is transmitted, and when and how it changes.

How Is Organizational Culture Created?

Why is it that many individuals within an organization share basic attitudes, values, and expectations? Two key factors contribute to this state of affairs and, hence, to the emergence of organizational culture—the influence of company founders and experiences with the external environment.

COMPANY FOUNDERS. Organizational culture may be traced, at least in part, to the founders of the company.[27] These individuals often possess dynamic personalities, strong values, and clear visions of how their businesses should operate. Since they are on the scene first and play a key role in hiring initial staff, their attitudes and values are readily transmitted to new employees. As a result, founders' views become the accepted ones in the organization and persist as long as they are on the scene—and often, long afterward. For a summary of the four major steps involved in this process, see Figure 14.6.

Several good illustrations of the important role of founders may be identified. For example, the culture at Microsoft calls for working exceptionally long hours, in large part because that's what cofounder Bill Gates has always done. Sometimes, founders' values can continue to drive an organization's culture long after that individual is no longer alive. For example, the late Ray Kroc founded the McDonald's restaurant chain on the values of tasty food at a good value served in clean, family-oriented surroundings—key cultural values that persist today. Likewise, Walt Disney's wholesome family values are still cherished at the company that bears his name—in large part because employees ask themselves, "What would Walt think?"[28] These individuals' principles continue to permeate their entire companies and are central parts of their dominant cultures.

EXPERIENCES WITH THE EXTERNAL ENVIRONMENT. As critical events occur in organizations based on their experiences with the external environment, it's not surprising that their effects contribute to the development of the culture. It's as if companies learn from these events and the memories are passed along from person to person, contributing to the development of the cultural framework. In this connection, the term **organizational memory** is used to describe information from an organization's history that its leaders draw upon later as needed.[29] That information is stored through the recollections of these events and their shared interpretations by key individuals in the organization who pass it along to others.

organizational memory
Information from an organization's history that is stored through the recollections of events and their shared interpretations by key individuals in the organization who pass it along to others.

As an example, consider Sony's experience with its Betamax format for home videocassette tapes. Introduced in 1975, Betamax competed with the VHS format introduced by JVC the following year. If you're thinking that you've heard of VHS, but not Betamax, that's indeed the story. Sony made two critical errors. First, unlike JVC, which permitted open sharing of its technology, Sony licensed its technology, which made it less popular among equipment manufacturers. Second, Sony failed to anticipate the demand for prerecorded movies, leading studios to release films on VHS instead. As a result, Sony's product never captured the market, and in 1988 it gave up, abandoning Betamax, and began making VHS-format video cassette recorders.

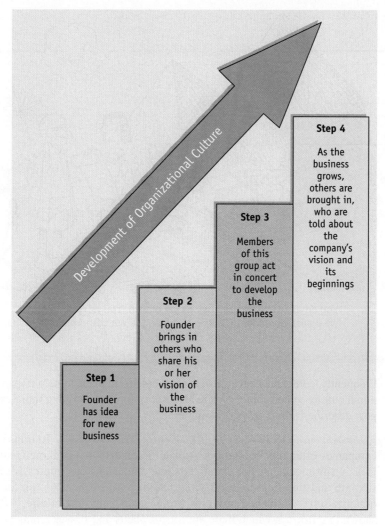

FIGURE 14.6

How Do Founders Influence Organizational Culture?

The cultures of organizations are affected by their founders. This tends to occur over time, generally according to the four steps summarized here.

In the aftermath of this incident, it appeared that Sony executives had learned an important lesson about what it takes to win a battle of formats. From 2006 to 2008 Sony once again found itself in a battle over format dominance. This time it was over high-definition DVDs and the competitor was Toshiba. Having lost the videotape battle, Sony was more aggressive this time in making strategic decisions (see Chapter 10). It signed up more movie studios (including its own, Sony Pictures Studio) to its Blu-ray disc (BD DVD) format than Toshiba did for its High Definition DVD (HD DVD) format, and it also promoted sales by making its popular PS3 game units compatible with Blu-ray. This time around, Sony won, and without a protracted battle. Toshiba threw in the towel after only two years.

The mechanism by which organizational memories help transmit culture is not surprising. It has to do with the natural tendency of individuals within organizations to come into contact with one another—and to share interpretations of events when doing so. Indeed, the dynamics of people in groups (as discussed in Chapter 8) and their tendencies to communicate with one another (as discussed in Chapter 9) make it possible for incidents to be explained and interpreted to others, thereby perpetuating organizational culture.[30]

Tools for Transmitting Culture

How are cultural values transmitted between people? In other words, how do employees come to learn about their organizations' cultures? Sometimes, one person will come right out and tell someone else, "This is how it's done here." This is especially likely when the other person is new to the organization. In such cases, the person explaining the cultural information may be a superior, but even a peer can tell a colleague about the prevailing expectations (see Figure 14.7).

FIGURE 14.7

You Probably Wouldn't Be Very Happy if Your Organization's Culture Were Like This

It's not entirely unusual for someone to describe aspects of their shared organizational culture with a coworker. We suspect, however, that it never goes quite like this.

www.Cartoonstock.com/Jim Sizemore.

"You do as you're told, we pay as we please. You work like a slave, we punish at random. That, in a nutshell, is our corporate culture."

Frequently, companies have various mechanisms in place to help impart facts about the organizational culture to newcomers while also to reinforcing it among more established employees. We now describe various ways of doing this.

SYMBOLS: OBJECTS THAT SAY MORE THAN MEETS THE EYE.   To transmit organizational culture, companies often rely on **symbols**—material objects that connote meanings that extend beyond their intrinsic content. For example, some companies use impressive buildings to convey their strength and significance, signifying that they are large, stable places. In addition, the way an organization is furnished provides useful insight into its culture.[31] Specifically, research has shown that firms in which there are lots of plants and flower arrangements are believed to have friendly, person-oriented cultures, whereas those in which waiting areas are adorned with awards and trophies are believed to be highly interested in achieving success. These findings suggest that material symbols are potent tools for sending messages about organizational culture. (To demonstrate this phenomenon for yourself, complete the Group Exercise on pages 513–514.)

SLOGANS: PHRASES THAT CAPTURE ORGANIZATIONAL CULTURE.   When you think of the catchy phrases that companies use to call attention to their products and services, you may dismiss them as being merely advertising gimmicks. It should be noted, however, that many slogans also communicate important aspects of an organization's culture, both to the public at large and to the company's own employees. For some examples of such slogans and what they communicate about organizational culture, see Table 14.1. As you peruse this list, you will see that these words help convey important information about an organization's culture, such as what the company stands for and what it values.

STORIES: "IN THE OLD DAYS, WE USED TO . . . ."   Organizations also transmit information about culture by virtue of the *stories* that are told, both formally and informally. Stories illustrate key aspects of an organization's culture, and telling them can effectively introduce or reaffirm underlying values to employees.[32] It is important to note that these anecdotes need not involve some great event, such as someone who saved the company with a single wise decision, but may be less dramatic tales that become legends because they communicate a message so effectively. An example may be found at Nike, where employees are told stories about how the company was founded in an effort to help athletes (for some examples, see Table 14.2).[33]

JARGON: THE SPECIAL LANGUAGE THAT DEFINES A CULTURE.   Even without telling stories, the everyday language used in companies helps sustain culture. For example, the slang or

symbols
Material objects that connote meanings that extend beyond their intrinsic content.

TABLE 14.1 Slogans That Reflect Organizational Culture

Corporate *slogans* often send messages about the cultures of the organizations that use them. The slogans they use allow customers, employees, and prospective employees to learn about the cultures of the companies listed here. Can you think of other slogans that reflect the culture of the businesses with which they are associated?

Company	Slogan	Message
Staples	*That was easy.*	The office products we sell make your life easy, and purchasing from us is a pleasurable experience.
Gillette	*The best a man can get.*	The company's products are superior and/or they give men confidence
Wal-Mart	*Save money. Live better.*	You can count on us to offer low prices on items that will improve your quality of life.
Home Box Office (HBO)	*It's more than you imagined. It's HBO.*	Our service is special; our programs will surpass your expectations.
Four Seasons Hotels & Resorts	*Fifty hotels. Twenty-two countries. One philosophy.*	We are very exclusive; no matter where you might travel in the world, you can count on us for excellence.
McDonald's	*I'm lovin' it.*	You will enjoy eating here.
Apple Store	*There's an app for just about anything.*	You can download a broad range of applications to your iPhone.
Microsoft Windows 7	*Your PC, simplified.*	This operating system is easy to use.
State Farm	*Like a good neighbor, State Farm is there.*	You can count on friendly and reliable service when you need it.

jargon that is used in a company or particular a field helps people define their identities as members of that group (see Chapter 9). Illustrating this, for many years employees at IBM referred to disk drives as "hard files" and circuit boards as "planar boards," terms that defined the insulated nature of their culture.[34] Today's jargon continues to predominate in the high-tech world. For example, within the information technology (IT) community, the term "geek keys" is used to refer to a loose deck of electronically encoded pass cards that are used to gain access to restricted areas, and "egosurfing" refers to the practice of entering one's own name in search engines and visiting the resulting hits.[35] Over time, as departments, organizations,

TABLE 14.2 The Nike Story: Just Tell It—And Keep It Alive

New employees at Nike are told stories that transmit the company's underlying cultural values. The themes of some of the most important ones are summarized here, along with several of the ways the company helps keep its heritage alive.

New Employees Are Told the Following Stories ...

• Founder Phil Knight was a middle-distance runner who started the business by selling shoes out of his car.

• Knight's running coach and company cofounder, Bill Bowerman, developed the famous "waffle sole" by pouring rubber into the family waffle iron.

• The late Steve Prefontaine, coached by Bowerman, battled to make running a professional sport and was committed to helping athletes.

To Ensure That These Tales of Nike's Heritage Are Kept Alive, the Company ...

• Takes new hires to the track where Bowerman coached and the site of Prefontaine's fatal car crash.

• Has created a "heritage wall" in its Eugene, Oregon, store.

• Requires salespeople to tell the Nike story to employees of the retail stores that sell its products.

Source: Based on information in Ransdell, 2000; see Note 33.

or professional groups develop unique language, their terms, although strange to newcomers, serve as a common factor that brings together individuals belonging to a corporate culture or subculture.

ceremonies
Celebrations of an organization's basic values and assumptions.

CEREMONIES: SPECIAL EVENTS THAT COMMEMORATE CORPORATE VALUES. Organizations also do a great deal to sustain their cultures by conducting various types of **ceremonies**. If you want to know what a company values, just attend their award ceremonies. Whatever it is that gets someone to the stage to receive a plaque is what's valued. Award ceremonies may be seen as celebrations of an organization's basic values and assumptions. Just as a wedding ceremony symbolizes a couple's mutual commitment and a presidential inauguration marks the beginning of a new presidential term, various organizational ceremonies also celebrate some important accomplishment. These events have importance that go beyond the individuals involved—in this example, the bride and groom, and the new president and vice president. They send clear messages about the institutions of marriage and the presidency to all who participate in or view the ceremony. In this manner, it's easy to see how they function as important transmitters of organizational culture.

For example, one accounting firm celebrated its move to much better facilities by throwing a party, an event signifying that it "has arrived," or "made it to the big time." Such ceremonies convey meaning to people inside and outside the organization. As one expert put it, "Ceremonies are to the culture what the movie is to the script ... values that are difficult to express in any other way."[36]

statements of principle
Explicitly written statements describing the beliefs that guide an organization, helping to reinforce its culture.

STATEMENTS OF PRINCIPLE: DEFINING CULTURE IN WRITING. Organizational culture also may be transmitted directly using written **statements of principle**. Some companies have explicitly written their principles for all to see. For example, Forrest Mars, the founder of the candy company M&M Mars, developed his "Five Principles of Mars," which still guide his company today.[37] These are as follows.

- *Quality.* Everyone is responsible for maintaining quality.
- *Responsibility.* All employees are responsible for their own actions and decisions.
- *Mutuality.* Creating situations in which everyone can win.
- *Efficiency.* Most of the company's factories operate continuously.
- *Freedom.* Employees are given opportunities to shape their futures.

Not only are these principles practiced, but employees also are given opportunities to share their feelings about them and their experiences with each one at the company's Web site. This technique helps reinforce the company's messages about what it stands for.

Some companies have chosen to make explicit the moral aspects of their cultures by publishing *codes of ethics,* which, as you will recall from Chapter 2, are statements of a company's ethical values and expectations. According to Hershey Foods' former CEO, Richard Zimmerman, this is an effective device: "[O]ften, an individual joins a firm without recognizing the type of environment in which he will place himself and his career. The loud and clear enunciation of a company's code of conduct ... [allows] that employee to determine whether or not he fits that particular culture."[38]

Why and How Does Organizational Culture Change?

Our comments about the relative stability of organizational culture may have left you wondering why and how culture ever changes. In other words, why isn't culture simply passed down from one generation of organizational members to the next in unchanging fashion? The answer lies in the fact that the worlds in which organizations operate are in a constant state of flux (see Chapter 16). Shifts in market conditions, new competitors, emerging technologies, altered government policies, and many other factors necessitate changing how companies operate, and with it, their cultures. We now consider several factors that promote changes in organizational culture.

COMPOSITION OF THE WORKFORCE. Over time, the people entering an organization may differ in important ways from those already in it, and these differences may impinge on the existing culture of the organization. For example, people from different ethnic or national backgrounds may have contrasting views about various aspects of behavior at work. They may hold dissimilar views about style of dress, the importance of being on time (or even what constitutes "on-time" behavior), the level of deference one should show to higher-status people, and even what foods should be served in the company cafeteria. When people have different views, existing cultural norms are likely to be challenged. And when this occurs, changes in organizational culture can be expected to follow suit.

It's important to note that any such effects may be slow in coming. For the most part, individuals adapt to the cultures of their organizations as forces lead them in this manner. What we're saying here is that people also may affect the culture somewhat, but such changes tend to be gradual (e.g., eventually changing the cafeteria menu) and are unlikely to influence the organization's core ideas. With some effort, top executives may be able to change the culture, but an influx of new people generally will have little or no immediate impact on the core values of an organization. This is in keeping with the idea that organizational culture is relatively stable.

MERGERS AND ACQUISITIONS. Another, and even more dramatic, source of cultural change is *mergers* (two companies join forces as relative equals) and *acquisitions* (one organization purchases or otherwise acquires another).[39] When these events occur, there is likely to be a careful analysis of the financial and material assets of the acquired company. However, it is unusual for any consideration also to be given to the acquired organization's culture. This is unfortunate, since several high-profile cases over the years have illustrated how the merger of two organizations with conflicting cultures leads to serious problems.[40] These are referred to as **culture clashes.**

culture clashes
Problems resulting from attempts to merge two or more organizational cultures that are incompatible.

Interestingly, just as some newlywed couples have problems due to their differing styles of spending money, so too have some newly merged companies. For example, Time Warner's 2001 merger with AOL was short-lived in large part because AOL's free-spending executives never saw eye-to-eye with their financially conservative counterparts from Time Warner. It was the same story in the 1998 merger between Chrysler and Daimler-Benz. After the new DaimlerChrysler was created, former Chrysler officials traveled to meetings in minivans and flew economy class while Daimler-Benz officials showed up in Mercedes sedans and flew first class. It took six months of attempting to iron out the differences in their corporate cultures before realizing they were at an impasse. Divorces resulted in both cases. (See Figure 14.8 for an example of a recent merger where concerns about incompatible corporate cultures were expressed even before the wedding.[41])

cultural due diligence analysis
Before a merger or acquisition is finalized, the process of analyzing the cultures of both organizations to ensure their compatibility.

As you might imagine, life in companies with incompatible cultures tends to be conflict-ridden and highly disruptive, often resulting in arguments and considerable uncertainty about what to do. In some cases, organizations have even been known to disband because of extreme culture clashes. With this in mind, some experts have called for conducting a **cultural due diligence analysis**

Zuma Wire West Photos/Newscom.

FIGURE 14.8

Kraft Swallows Cadbury in a Bittersweet Deal

In 2010 Cadbury approved a takeover bid from Kraft worth a sweet $19.5 billion. Even as the ink was drying on the deal, industry analysts expressed concern about how the culture of the 190-year-old British confectioner founded on Quaker principles would blend with that of the giant American firm. As shown here, some individual Britons also were opposed to the deal and were not reticent to share their disapproval.

TABLE 14.3 Conducting a Cultural Due Diligence Analysis

Just as company officials carefully analyze the financial and legal ramifications of mergers and acquisitions before finalizing the deals, it is advised that they also study the cultures of the individual companies to determine their cultural compatibility. This so-called *cultural due diligence* analysis involves the following activities.

Action	Description
Audit the prevailing cultures.	Compare such fundamental aspects of the culture as how compensation is determined, how leaders emerge, what business practices are valued, what the tolerance is for taking risks, and so on.
Assess *intellectual capital.*	Interview people in both organizations to determine who knows what. Determine who really knows what to do and how to do it. Knowing this will help the new company put people's talents and skills to best use.
Involve different people from both companies in designing the new enterprise.	By involving diverse groups (e.g., customers, the sales force, people from different departments) in a discussion of how the new company should operate, a better understanding of each group's culture is likely to emerge.
Communicate early and often.	Throughout the process, everyone should be completely open and honest about what's going on. This should involve not only top-down communication, but discussions within and between people at all levels of both organizations.

Source: Based on suggestions by Smith, 2005; see Note 42.

to ensure compatibility before a merger or acquisition is finalized.[42] This involves analyzing the cultures of both organizations in as much depth as typically is used in exploring the financials, the legal implications, and the intellectual property of the companies involved. For some useful guidelines to follow in conducting such an analysis, refer to the summary in Table 14.3. The idea is straightforward: By determining in advance the potential areas in which the companies might experience culture clashes, they may begin to focus on mutual understanding and working together on developing a totally new culture.

STRATEGIC CULTURAL CHANGE. Sometimes, company officials deliberately decide to change organizational culture as a means of adjusting to evolving conditions—even positive ones, such as fantastic growth. It's probably not too surprising that the culture of a small organization has to change as the company grows in size. What once worked for a small company may no longer be successful as it becomes a much larger organization.

This was the situation Robert Nardelli inherited when he took over as The Home Depot's CEO in 2000.[43] When The Home Depot first opened its doors in 1978, it was a small business, complete with a small-company culture that reflected the personality of one of its cofounders, Bernie Marcus. It had a high-spirited, entrepreneurial way of doing things. Employees were willing to take risks and showed a passionate commitment to customers, colleagues, and the company as a whole. Anything bureaucratic was rejected, but things had to change. As Nardelli put it, "What so effectively got [The] Home Depot from zero to $50 billion in sales wasn't going to get it to go to the next $50 billion."[44] As 1978 slipped into 2000, the small-company culture that had once worked still existed, but it now was strangling an enormous enterprise with 1,000 stores. Nardelli introduced more formal operations where the processes were centralized and data-driven instead of intuitive. The culture shift was abrupt and some key players left. However, the change was overdue and it came not a minute too soon. Only five years after Nardelli's orchestrated cultural changes were in place, The Home Depot's financial picture was much brighter. It now had a culture that was appropriate for its size.

Recently, companies that desire to make strategic changes in their own organizational cultures have had an interesting new opportunity available to them. Zappos.com (the successful online shoe store purchased by Amazon.com in 2009) has started running seminars in which staff members teach corporate leaders from a variety of organizations how to recreate the essence of its own customer service–driven culture.[45] For $4,000, attendees at the two-day seminar are shown what Zappos.com does, which is coddle customers. Although 95 percent of the company's customers place Web orders, the 5 percent who call are looking for special treatment—and they get it. Instead of reading from a script, Zappos.com's sales agents—members of the "customer loyalty team," as they are called—are empowered to "wing it" with customers. Sometimes they even chat with them for hours, write them notes, or recommend other Web sites for them to visit. It's all okay. In an industry in which employees at call centers are regularly measured in terms of their hourly call counts and sales figures, Zappos.com's "extreme customer service" culture is unique. Learning how it works may be worth the price of admission, but just as culture clashes sometimes result when companies merge, executives who leave the seminars hoping to incorporate what they learned into their own corporate cultures may find it challenging, if not risky.

One of the ways in which organizations are attempting to make strategic changes in their cultures is by making them more ethical. For some recommendations about how to do this, see The Ethics Angle section below.

The Ethics Angle

Building an Ethical Organizational Culture

As we discussed in Chapter 2, many organizations rely on some type of *ethics training* to promote desired behaviors. Among other things, this training focuses primarily on communicating to employees what is expected of them. Although such information is always valuable, by itself, ethics training has only limited impact on reducing undesirable workplace behavior. Research has shown that what's far more valuable, instead, is to take steps to build an *ethical organizational culture*.[49] This prompts two key questions. First, what is ethical organizational culture? Second, how can one be developed?

ethical organizational culture
Set of attitudes, behavioral norms, and expectations about what constitutes "doing the right thing" inside an organization.

The term **ethical organizational culture** is used to refer to a set of attitudes, behavioral norms, and expectations about what constitutes "doing the right thing" inside an organization. When a company's ethical culture is strong, it influences employees' decisions about how to make decisions, how to treat others, and generally how to behave in ways that are considered appropriate. It helps to think of an ethical culture as a set of invisible forces that guide employees in doing what society considers right as applied to the activities of an organization.

Research has identified several things that can be done to promote ethical cultures within organizations.[50] These suggestions should be taken seriously because to some extent, they each contribute to reducing organizational misconduct (see Chapter 11).

Demonstrate ethical leadership

Leaders are role models and this gives them opportunities to set their organizations' ethical tones. They do this by virtue of the things they say and do. As a result, it's critical for leaders to do the following.

- *Set an example.* As obvious as it seems, some fail to recognize that when it comes to ethical behavior, "actions speak louder than words." There can be no hope of having an ethical culture unless the "tone at the top" is highly ethical itself.

- *Keep promises.* Not following up on promises sends strong messages that one is untrustworthy, which contributes to the belief that "anything goes." By itself, keeping promises won't make an organizational culture ethical, but not doing so surely will keep that from happening.

- *Reinforce ethical behavior.* Employees look to their immediate supervisors for signs that ethical behavior is really taken seriously. Because of this, consistent messages should be sent concerning its importance. This may be done by acknowledging any particularly ethical things that subordinates may have done.

Showcase peer commitment

Employees pick up messages about ethical behavior not only from superiors but from peers as well. When ethical culture is strong, everyone receives messages about the importance of ethics from everyone else. Because of this, it's a good idea to showcase that commitment among one's peers. This may be done by holding regularly scheduled meetings in which employees share experiences about how they have addressed any ethical dilemmas they may have confronted. Such sessions provide good opportunities to communicate commitment to ethics among peers.

Incorporate ethical values into daily activities

Make it clear that ethical behavior is everyone's responsibility and that acting in this manner is not something to consider only on certain "red-flag" occasions (e.g., if one is offered a bribe). It would be useful to ask employees to identify any particular daily activities that present opportunities to behave ethically or unethically.

Doing the things outlined here will help promote ethical values and embed them into the fabric of an organization. When it becomes clear that behaving ethically is "how we do it around here," then it just may be that the roots of an ethical organizational culture have taken hold.

RESPONDING TO THE INTERNET. There can be no doubt that the Internet is a major influence on organizational culture these days. Compared to traditional brick-and-mortar businesses, where things move slowly and in which people look at change skeptically, the culture of Internet businesses is agile, fast-paced, and receptive to new solutions.[46] Information sharing is key, as such organizations not only accept, but also embrace, the expansion of communication networks and business relationships across organizational boundaries. When traditional, "brick-and-mortar" companies expand into e-commerce (in which case they sometimes are referred to as "click-and-mortar businesses"), changes in their organizational cultures follow suit. We see this, for example, at the investment firm Merrill Lynch, which launched a Web site for trading stock in an effort to compete with other brokerage firms, such as E*Trade, which do business only online. The organizational culture at this venerable, traditional firm has become far more fast-paced ever since adapting to today's Internet economy.

To conclude, it is clear that although organizational culture is generally stable, it is not immutable. In fact, culture often evolves in response to outside forces (e.g., changes in work-force composition and information technology) as well as deliberate attempts to change the design of organizations (e.g., through mergers and corporate restructuring). An important quality that an organization frequently strives to alter is the degree to which it approaches problems in creative and innovative ways. With this in mind, we now turn attention to the topics of *creativity* and *innovation* in organizations.

Creativity in Individuals and Teams

creativity
The process by which individuals or teams produce novel and useful ideas.

Although you probably have no difficulty recognizing creativity when you see it, defining it can be a bit more challenging. Scientists define **creativity** as the process by which individuals or teams produce novel and useful ideas.[47] With this definition to guide us, we will explain how this process operates. Specifically, we begin by describing the components of individual and team creativity and then outline several steps you can take to enhance your own creativity.

Components of Individual and Team Creativity

Creativity in individuals and teams is composed of three basic components—*domain-relevant skills, creativity-relevant skills,* and *intrinsic task motivation.*[48]

DOMAIN-RELEVANT SKILLS. Whether it's the manual dexterity required to play the piano or to use a computer keyboard, or the sense of rhythm and knowledge of music needed to conduct an orchestra, specific skills and abilities are necessary to perform these tasks. In fact, any task you might under-take requires certain talents, knowledge, or skills. These skills and abilities that we already have constitute the raw materials needed for creativity to occur. After all, without the capacity to perform a certain task at even a basic level, one has no hope of demonstrating creativity on that task. For example, before he or she can begin to create dramatic automotive stunts, a stunt driver must have the basic skills of dexterity and eye–hand coordination required to drive a car.

CREATIVITY-RELEVANT SKILLS. Beyond the basic skills, being creative also requires additional skills—special abilities that help people approach the things they do in novel ways. Specifically, when fostering creativity, it helps to do the following.

divergent thinking
The process of reframing familiar problems in unique ways.

- *Break mental sets and take new perspectives.* Creativity is enhanced when people do not limit themselves to old ways of doing things. Restricting oneself to the past can inhibit creativity. Take a fresh look at even the most familiar things. This involves what is known as **divergent thinking**—the process of reframing familiar problems in unique ways, producing multiple or alternative answers from available information. Divergent thinking requires creating unexpected combinations, recognizing associations between things, and transforming information into unexpected forms. Often, the result of divergent thinking is something novel and surprising, something that never before has existed.[51] For some examples of ways to promote divergent thinking, see Table 14.4, and to practice this yourself, see the Individual Exercise on pages 512–513.
- *Understand complexities.* Instead of making things overly simplistic, don't be afraid to consider complex ways in which ideas may be interrelated.

TABLE 14.4 Ways of Triggering Divergent Thinking

To encourage divergent thinking, exercises often are conducted in which people are asked open-ended questions to which there are no correct answers. Responses are free to fall outside normal ways of thinking about things. The following are typical examples.

- List various uses for a hat other than wearing it.

- Make as many sentences as possible that include the following words: *melon, consider, flower, paper.*

- How could you turn a cardboard box into a temporary tent for use on a camping trip in the woods?

- Think carefully about a stone. Then indicate what you believe to be its hidden meanings.

- If you were going to host a party for a group of elves (other than those cookies they make), what would you serve?

- Your car is stuck in a ditch along a deserted road. Using only the things likely to be found in and around the car, how could you summon help?

■ *Keep options open and avoid premature judgments.* Creative people are willing to consider all options. To do so, they consider all the angles and avoid reaching conclusions prematurely. People are particularly good at this when they are new to an organization and, therefore, don't know enough to accept everything the way it is. With this in mind, some companies actually prefer hiring executives from outside their industries.

■ *Follow creativity heuristics.* People sometimes follow certain strategies, known as **creativity heuristics**, to help them come up with creative new ideas. These are rules that people follow to help them approach tasks in novel ways. They may involve such techniques as considering the counterintuitive, and using analogies.

■ *Use productive forgetting.* Sometimes, our creativity is inhibited by becoming fixated on certain ideas that we just can't get out of our heads. With this in mind, it helps to practice **productive forgetting**—abandoning unproductive ideas and temporarily putting aside stubborn problems until new approaches can be considered.

creativity heuristics
Rules that people follow to help them approach tasks in novel ways.

productive forgetting
The ability to abandon unproductive ideas and temporarily put aside stubborn problems until new approaches can be considered.

To help individuals and teams become more creative, many organizations are inviting employees to participate in training exercises designed to promote some of these skills. Although the results are not assessed scientifically, several companies have reported anecdotal success using these techniques to boost creativity in the workplace.[52]

INTRINSIC TASK MOTIVATION. The first two components of creativity, domain-relevant skills and creativity-relevant skills, focus on what people are *capable* of doing. However, the third component, *intrinsic task motivation*, refers to what people are *willing* to do. The idea is simple: For someone to be creative, he or she must be interested in performing the task in question. In other words, there must be a high degree of **intrinsic task motivation**—the motivation to do work because it is interesting, engaging, or challenging in a positive way. Someone who has the capacity to be creative, but who isn't motivated to do what it takes to produce novel outcomes, certainly wouldn't become creative. People are most likely to be creative when they are passionate about their work.[53]

intrinsic task motivation
The motivation to do work because it is interesting, engaging, or challenging in a positive way.

Intrinsic task motivation tends to be high under several conditions. For example, when an individual has a *personal interest* in the task at hand, he or she will be motivated to perform it—and may go on to do so creatively. However, anyone who doesn't find a task interesting surely isn't going to perform it long enough to demonstrate any signs of creativity. Likewise, intrinsic task motivation will be high whenever an individual perceives that he or she has internal reasons to be performing that task (e.g., because it is fun to do). People who come to believe that they are performing a task for some external reason—such as high pay or pressure from a boss—are unlikely to find the work inherently interesting, in and of itself, and are unlikely to show much creativity.

PUTTING IT ALL TOGETHER. As you might imagine, the components of creativity are important insofar as they paint a picture of when creativity will occur. Specifically, people will be at their most creative when they have high amounts of all three of the components shown in Figure 14.9.

FIGURE 14.9

Components of Creativity

Scientists claim that people will be at their most creative when they exhibit high levels of the three factors shown here.

Source: Adapted from Amabile & Fisher, 2009; see Note 47.

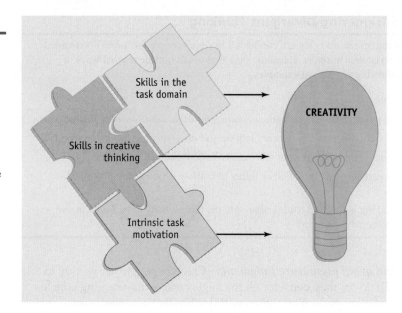

It has been claimed that there is a multiplicative relationship among these three components. Thus, people will not be creative at all if any one of these elements is at zero (i.e., if it is missing completely). After all, you would be unlikely to be creative at a job if you didn't have the skills needed to do it, regardless of how motivated you were to be creative and how well-practiced you were at coming up with new ideas. Likewise, creativity would be nonexistent if either creativity-relevant skills or intrinsic task motivation were zero. The practical implications are clear: To be as creative as possible, people must strive toward attaining high levels of all three components of creativity.

A Model of the Creative Process

Although it isn't always obvious how people come up with creative ideas, scientists have developed a model that outlines the general steps in this process.[54] Specifically, the model summarized in Figure 14.10 specifies that the process of creativity adheres to the following four stages.

1. *Prepare to be creative.* Although we often believe that our most creative ideas come "out of thin air," people are at their most creative when they have made suitable preparations. This involves gathering the appropriate information and concentrating on the problem.
2. *Allow ideas to incubate.* Because ideas take time to develop, creativity can be enhanced by putting the problem out of our conscious minds and allowing it to incubate. If you've ever been successful at coming up with a fresh approach to a problem by putting it aside and working on something else, you know what we are describing. The phrase "sleep on it" captures this stage of the process.
3. *Document insight.* At some point during the first two stages, you are likely to come up with a unique idea. However, that idea may be lost if it is not documented. With this in mind, many people carry small notebooks that allow them to capture their ideas before they become lost in a maze of other thoughts. Likewise, writers keep diaries, artists keep sketch pads, and songwriters keep digital recorders handy to capture ideas whenever inspiration strikes.
4. *Verify ideas.* Coming up with an idea is one thing but ensuring that it's any good is quite another. Assessing the usefulness of an idea requires consciously thinking about it and verifying its quality, such as by seeing what others have to say about it. In other words, you want to see if those ideas that came to you in a moment of inspiration in the middle of the night still are any good in the morning light.

Knowing about the creative process is particularly useful insofar as it can be applied to promoting individual and team productivity. We now examine this process.

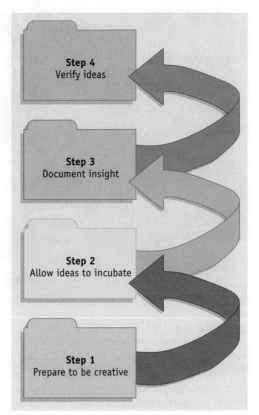

FIGURE 14.10

Steps in the Creative Process

Scientists have proposed that the creative process follows the four steps outlined here.

Source: Kabanoff & Rossiter, 1994; see Note 54.

Promoting Creativity in Organizations

Highly creative people are an asset to any organization. But what exactly do companies do to promote creativity within their ranks? In general terms, the answer lies in things that we can do as individuals and that organizations can do as a whole. Specifically, two major approaches may be identified: training people to be creative, and developing creative work environments.

Training People to be Creative

It is true that some people, by nature, are more creative than others. Such individuals are inclined to approach various situations in new ways and tend not to be bogged down by previous ways of doing things.[55] However, there are skills that anyone can develop to become more creative, and firms have sprung up that assist organizations in promoting creativity among employees. Generally, training people to become more creative involves two key practices.[56]

ENCOURAGE OPENNESS TO NEW EXPERIENCES. Many good ideas go undeveloped because they are not in keeping with current ways of doing things. Becoming more creative requires allowing oneself to be open to new ideas, or as it is often described, *thinking outside the box.* Some people are, by nature, more highly open to new experiences than others. In fact, **openness to experience** is a personality variable that reflects the degree to which people are interested in things that are new and different and get excited by new ideas.

At the same time, it's possible to make anyone more open to new experiences. In fact, some companies do this by sending their employees on *thinking expeditions*—trips specifically designed to put people in challenging situations in an effort to help them think differently and become more creative. According to the CEO of a company that specializes in running such expeditions for clients, these trips "push people out of their 'stupid zone'—a place of mental and physical normalcy—so that they can start to think differently," adding "it's an accelerated unlearning experience."[57] For an example of how this has been accomplished at one large company, see Figure 14.11.[58]

TAKE THE TIME TO UNDERSTAND THE PROBLEM—MAYBE. Meaningful ideas rarely come to those who don't fully understand the problem at hand, and this is likely to take time. In many

openness to experience
Personality variable that reflects the degree to which people are interested in things that are new and different and get excited by new ideas.

ASP/Cal Sport Media/Newscom.

FIGURE 14.11

How Does This Make Betty Crocker More Efficient?

To develop new ideas about how to improve efficiency in their Betty Crocker factories, General Mills officials went to an unlikely place—the pit of a NASCAR racetrack, where they carefully studied how pit crews changed tires on cars in the midst of a race. What they learned led them to creative ways of making the changes necessary to swap factory configurations from one product to another, ultimately reducing the process from 4.5 hours to only 12 minutes. Clearly, General Mills' openness to new ideas led to some creative ways to solve a problem.

support for creativity
The degree to which people believe that others in their workplaces are supportive of their efforts to come up with novel ideas.

organizations, however, it's not unusual for people to report that they are "under pressure" to create. Suppose you have to come up with some creative idea but you have a deadline that restricts your time? How would you do? In other words, are you more creative when you experience time pressure or less creative? As in so many cases in the field of OB, the answer is "it depends." In this case, what it depends on is two factors.

The first factor is one we just identified, openness to experience. The second one is not a personality trait, but a characteristic of the work environment—namely, **support for creativity.** This refers to the degree to which people believe that others in their workplaces (e.g., superiors, peers) are supportive of their efforts to come up with novel ideas. Some people, of course, perceive their workplaces as being more supportive than others. If you take into account an individual's openness to experience and the degree to which that person perceives support for creativity, it's clear that high levels of both make for the best conditions to nurture creativity. In other words, it puts the right person in the right situation.

As it works out, research has shown the answer to our question about the relationship between pressure to be creative and actually being creative depends on the combination of these variables.[59] The particular study involved employees who were expected to be creative in their jobs at a large cereal company. The participants completed rating scales measuring support for new ideas and openness to experience. They also completed a third questionnaire assessing the degree to which they experienced time pressure to come up with creative ideas. While the employees were completing these questionnaires, their supervisors were completing a different questionnaire—one to determine the degree to which each of the employees demonstrated actual creativity on their jobs.

Figure 14.12 reveals the relationship between the degree of creative time pressure the workers experienced and the extent to which their supervisors considered them to be creative. Remember the question we asked earlier: Are you more creative or less creative when experiencing time pressure? Now you can see the "it depends" part of the answer. The study found that the answer depends on a particular combination of openness to experience and support for creativity. For most people, the more time pressure they experienced, the less creative they were considered to be. Put the other way, the most creative people were the ones who experienced the least time

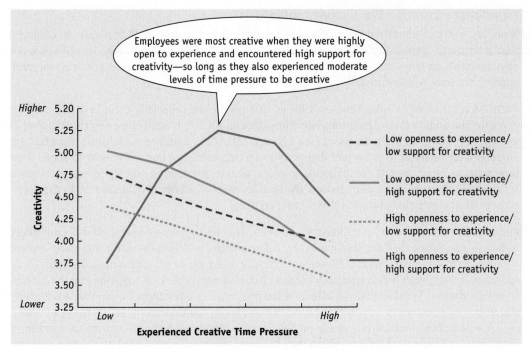

FIGURE 14.12

Are People More Creative or Less Creative Under Time Pressure?

As summarized here, the answer to this question depends on two factors—the degree to which someone is *open to experience* and who also believes that there is *support for creativity* in the organization.

Source: Adapted from Baer & Oldham, 2006; see Note 59.

pressure, but this did not apply to everyone. Instead, this relationship characterized three groups of people: (1) those who scored low in openness to experience and who encountered low support for creativity, (2) those who also scored low in openness to experience and who faced high levels of support for creativity, and finally (3) those who scored high in openness to experience but encountered low support for creativity. These results are reflected in the three almost-straight lines running from the upper-left part of the graph down to the lower-right corner.

However, there's a fourth line in Figure 14.12, one that's hard to miss—the inverted *U*-shaped line in blue. As the key indicates, this represents those individuals who are both extremely open to experience and who work in environments in which they believe their creativity is supported. These are the people to whom we referred earlier as "the right people in the right situation." You would expect that this combination of conditions would lead to high levels of creativity. Indeed, as shown by the very top of the inverted *U*, this is precisely when the highest levels of creativity were observed. However, as you also can see, this was found only when these individuals experienced a moderate level of time pressure.

Why do you think this occurred? The answer is not difficult to understand. When time pressure was very low, these individuals were insufficiently stimulated to be creative. They could always put off their creative work since, after all, they were capable of doing it at other times. However, as time pressure mounted, these individuals felt "under the gun" to be more creative and this stimulated them to "rise to the occasion" by demonstrating that creativity. But, after the time pressure began to mount, they didn't have adequate time to fulfill their creative potential and, as a result, their creativity began to fall. Tracing this line, we can see the *curvilinear relationship* between time pressure for creativity and actual creativity among people in this group.

The reason why this relationship didn't occur in the three other conditions is easy to explain: Because of their low openness to experience and/or the low support for creativity they encountered, such individuals were not especially well-suited to being creative in the first place. So, the only opportunity for them to be at all creative occurred when they had plenty of time to devote to it. As that time shrunk, however, the fact that they were not well-suited to this process became a handicap and their creativity began to fall.

This poses a bit of a dilemma for managers. Should they give people plenty of time to be creative or should they create a more leisurely environment in the hope of promoting creativity? As this study suggests, they should aim for some intermediate level of time pressure—so long as they also have either selected people who are, by nature, highly open to experience or have trained their employees to become open to experience on the job.

Developing Creative Work Environments

Thus far, we have identified ways of making people more creative as individuals. In conjunction with these approaches, it also is useful for organizations to take steps to change work environments in ways that bring out people's creativity.[60] Based on research, several such approaches may be identified.[61]

PROVIDE AUTONOMY. It has been established that people are especially creative when they are given the freedom to control their own behavior—that is, when they have *autonomy* (see Chapter 7) and are *empowered* to make decisions (see Chapter 12). At the Japanese video game manufacturer Nintendo, creativity is so important that people are empowered to determine how to spend their time so as to bring out that creativity. As a result, no one considers it odd when designers leave work to go see a movie or a play. Indeed, the high levels of creativity at Nintendo led to the development of its enormously successful Wii game console.

PROVIDE EXPOSURE TO OTHER CREATIVE PEOPLE. It is widely assumed that workers are likely to be creative when they are surrounded by other creative individuals. After all, being around creative people is inspirational. Moreover, one can learn creativity-relevant skills from these individuals. Although this is true under some circumstances, research suggests that the picture is not so simple. Specifically, the effect of having creative coworkers on another's creativity depends on the extent to which that individual is closely monitored by his or her supervisor.

A researcher conducting a study on this topic administered questionnaires to a group of employees to assess the extent to which they believed they were surrounded by creative coworkers as well as their beliefs about how closely they were monitored by their supervisors.[62] In addition, supervisors who were familiar with the work of each of these workers were asked to rate the degree of creativity they demonstrated in their work. The results showed that the presence of creative coworkers promoted creativity when supervisory monitoring was low, but that it actually discouraged creativity when supervisory monitoring was high.

These findings may be explained as follows. Workers who feel that they are constantly being watched, evaluated, and controlled by their bosses are reluctant to take the chances required to behave in a creative fashion for fear of doing something that is considered inappropriate. As a result, they tend to "play it safe" by simply imitating what others are doing, thereby demonstrating less creativity than they are capable of showing. By contrast, employees who are not closely monitored by their supervisors are likely to be more willing to experiment with new ideas, thereby allowing them to reap the benefits of having creative coworkers around them.

ALLOW IDEAS TO CROSS-POLLINATE. People who work on just one project run the risk of getting stale, whereas those who work on several are likely to come into contact with different people and have a chance of applying to one project an idea they picked up on another one. This is done all the time at the design firm IDEO. For example, in coming up with an idea about how to make a more comfortable handle for a scooter, designers might use ideas they developed while working on a project involving the design of a more comfortable computer mouse. Because of the upheaval that is bound to result when companies are downsizing, ideas are unlikely to cross-pollinate. It is, therefore, not surprising that creativity tends to be considerably lower at such times.[63]

MAKE JOBS INTRINSICALLY INTERESTING. Research has shown that people are inclined to be creative when they are intrinsically interested in the work they do. After all, nobody will want to invest the effort it takes to be creative at a task that is boring. With this in mind, creativity can be promoted by enhancing the degree to which tasks are made intrinsically interesting to people. The essence of the idea is to turn work into play.

This approach is used routinely at a marketing agency in Richmond, Virginia, appropriately named "Play." Instead of coming up with ideas by sitting in boring meetings, staff members are encouraged to play. For example, to aid the process of coming up with a new marketing campaign for the Weather Channel play employees spent time developing costumes for superheroes. According to Play's cofounder Andy Stefanovich, the idea is simple: "When you work in a place that encourages people to be themselves, have fun, and take risks, you fuel and unleash their creativity. The best ideas come from playful minds. And the way to tap into that playfulness is to play—together."[64] (To view Play in action for one of its clients, see Figure 14.13.)

Courtesy of www.prophet.com.

FIGURE 14.13

Play Turns Work into Play

Many well-known companies have hired Play (now part of the consulting firm, Prophet) to help them promote creativity by encouraging them to play. This is intended to get their clients' employees to view things from a fresh perspective and to uncover new insights.

SET YOUR OWN CREATIVE GOALS. Being free to do as you wish does not necessarily imply goofing off. In fact, the freedom to make your own decisions pays off most handsomely when people set their own creative goals. For example, the famous inventor Thomas A. Edison set the goal of having a minor invention every 10 days and a major invention every six months. This kept Edison focused on being creative—and, with more than 1,000 patents in his name, he clearly did an outstanding job of meeting his goals. We are not talking about strict external pressure to be creative, which rarely results in anything positive. However, creativity is aided when people strive to meet their own difficult goals for achieving creativity.[65] Aim to be creative instead of merely hoping that creativity comes about.

SUPPORT CREATIVITY AT HIGH ORGANIZATIONAL LEVELS. Nobody in an organization is going to go out of his or her way to be creative if it is not welcomed by the bosses. Supervisors, team leaders, and top executives must encourage employees to take risks if they are to have any chance of being creative. At the same time, this involves accepting any failures that result. This idea was embraced by Livio D. DeSimone, a former CEO of 3M, who helped make it one of the most creative companies in the world. "Failure is not fatal," he has said, noting that success requires taking chances, "and when you take a chance, there is always the possibility of a failure."[66]

PROMOTE DIVERSITY. When companies are staffed by people from diverse ethnic and cultural groups, they are bound to think differently about the situations they face. And, as we noted earlier, divergent thinking is a key element of creativity. Therefore, companies with ethnically diverse workforces are inclined to have cultures that allow creativity to flourish. In fact, some high-tech experts attribute the highly creative ideas emanating from California's Silicon Valley to the fact that more than one-third of its resident engineers and scientists come from countries throughout the world.[67]

Many of today's most successful multinational corporations attribute their successes to the fact that the adjustments they have made in the course of getting different kinds of people to work together in harmony have had a beneficial, if sometimes unintended by-product—namely, boosting creativity. Although having a diverse population does not ensure creativity, to be sure, it is safe to say that *not* having one can limit creativity. Today's multinational corporations are unwilling to be denied this benefit. One hotel executive expressed this well when referring to his "principle of the United Nations" when it comes to recruiting—hiring the best people in the world, regardless of their nationality.[68] (This discussion raises an interesting question as to whether people in some countries are more creative than those in other countries. For some insight into this matter, see the Today's Diverse and Global Organizations section on page 504.)

Today's Diverse and Global Organizations

Where in the World Is Entrepreneurial Creativity Promoted?

To be a successful entrepreneur, it helps to live someplace where the culture supports creative thinking and innovation. Not only is entrepreneurship likely to thrive under such conditions, but the reverse is especially true: The entrepreneurial spirit is likely to be snuffed out whenever creativity and innovation are frowned upon. This applies not only to differences in organizational cultures, but to national cultures as well. With this in mind, it is interesting to consider the possibility that various countries differ with respect to how strongly their cultures support creativity and innovation.[69]

In an interesting study, scientists administered a questionnaire to people from Spain, Norway, Sweden, Germany, Italy, and the United States to assess citizens' perceptions of (1) their society's admiration for people who start their own businesses, (2) the extent to which they believe that innovative and creative thinking are good, and (3) the belief that starting one's own business is a valued career option.[70]

The results were striking: People from the United States scored considerably higher than their counterparts in the European countries. That is, Americans, as a whole, believed their country was more supportive of entrepreneurial activity and the creativity and innovativeness required to make that activity successful than did people from Sweden, Norway, Spain, Italy, or Germany. Furthermore, the Europeans all scored remarkably similar to one another.

Although these findings are interesting on their own, three important points should be taken into account when interpreting them. First, considerations in addition to the value placed on creativity also are likely to make a difference. In fact, the same study found that knowledge of how to finance, structure, and manage new businesses, and the extent to which the government provides helpful support along the way, also were important. Along these dimensions, people from the two Scandinavian countries ranked highly along with the Americans.

Second, these findings do *not* mean that American entrepreneurs are destined to be more successful than their European counterparts. Clearly, many different factors are involved in determining the ultimate success of any entrepreneurial venture. Still, the findings reveal that when it comes to nurturing the creative activities that promote entrepreneurial activity, Americans appear to have the edge.

Finally, it is important to recognize that the study considered only a small number of countries. To the extent that entrepreneurs come from all over the world, it would be interesting to extend these findings to people from places such as Asia, Latin America, Africa, and the Middle East.

The Process of Innovation

Having examined individual and group creativity, we now extend our analysis to situations in which people implement their creative skills for the sake of improving their organizations. This is the process of *innovation* to which we referred earlier. Specifically, **innovation** may be defined as the process of making changes to something already established by introducing something new. Put differently, innovation is the successful implementation of creative ideas within an organization. Thus, whereas creativity involves coming up with new ideas, innovation involves putting them into action. To understand the nature of innovation, it helps to identify the companies considered most innovative and to examine some of the special things they do. For such an overview, see Table 14.5.[71]

To understand this process, we identify the major forms of innovation, the various targets of innovation, and its key components. Then, we review the various stages through which innovation progresses. Before doing this, however, for the record, let's make it clear why companies are so interested in innovation. A very strong business case can be made for innovation: It pays off on the bottom line.

Take the top 50 most innovative companies (the first five of which are identified in Table 14.5), for example. These organizations have enjoyed increases in annual profit margin that were considerably higher than those of the average Standard & Poor's Global 1200 companies. In observing the financial successes of highly innovative companies over the years, one consultant noted that, "Innovation is allowing companies to grow faster [and to] have a richer product mix."[72] As you read about some of the innovative things companies are doing in the remainder of this chapter, you probably will find it easy to understand the positive financial impact of innovative practices.

Major Forms of Innovation

Our definition leaves open the possibility that innovation may take several different forms. In fact, it's possible to differentiate among these with respect to three key factors: its impact on existing business, the degree of uncertainty involved, and its sources (for a summary comparison, see Figure 14.14).

innovation
The process of making changes to something already established by introducing something new; the successful implementation of creative ideas within an organization.

TABLE 14.5 The Five Most Innovative Companies in the World

Highly innovative companies do not get that way by accident. As summarized here, the world's most innovative companies, as identified by *Fast Company* magazine in 2010, engage in a variety of practices to help promote innovation—and they've enjoyed considerable successes as a result. We've included the top five companies on this list—all of which happen to be in the high-tech industry. This reflects the fact that rapid advances in technology have driven innovation in high-tech firms.

Rank	Company	Innovative Practices and Results
1	Facebook	New features are added to the site regularly. Engineers are encouraged to champion entirely new ideas. If they fail, their jobs remain safe. In 2009 Facebook more than doubled its number of active users, which now include more than 350 million people from every country in the world.
2	Amazon	After adding video streaming to its product line, Amazon introduced the first major successful reading device, the "Kindle," into which over a half million books can be downloaded wirelessly from any-place in the world.
3	Apple	The iPhone has revolutionized the "smartphone" business. Users have downloaded apps 3 billion times, selecting from more than 200,000 different choices. The phone is so popular that it sold 8.7 million units during the 2009 Christmas season alone. The iPad sold over 2 million units in its first 2 months after launch in April 2010.
4	Google	Google has introduced several new services, such as camera-based and voice-powered searches. It also introduced a highly regarded Android smartphone. Google is used for 86 percent of the searches conducted on mobile units.
5	Huawei Technologies	This Chinese company has developed a line of telecom equipment that is so advanced, yet so inexpen-sive, that it is has made major inroads into markets long dominated by Ericsson and Nokia Siemens. In 2009 its share of the global market doubled to 20 percent.

Source: Fast Company, 2010; see Note 71.

IMPACT ON EXISTING BUSINESS. Over the years, wireless networking standards have changed to allow increasingly faster transmissions of data through the air. First there was 802.11a, then the faster 802.11b, followed by 802.11g, and still faster networking standards such as today's 802.11n. An improvement of this type is referred to as a **sustaining innovation** because it allows companies to approach their markets in the same manner.[73] It gives existing customers better performance. A sustaining innovation is, quite simply, the proverbial "better mousetrap."

Sustaining innovations may be contrasted with others that bring significant changes to the market. For example, before it introduced its personal computer (PC), IBM was in the market of

sustaining innovation
A form of innovation that is incremental in nature; inno-vation that allows companies to approach their markets in the same manner as they have done in the past.

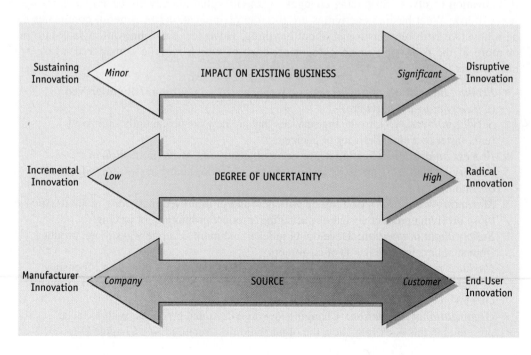

FIGURE 14.14

Forms of Innovation

Various forms of innovation may be distinguished with respect to the three dimensions summarized here.

selling minicomputers, and before that, mainframe computers. The mini disrupted the market for the mainframe and the PC disrupted the market for the mini. As this description suggests, an innovation of this type, which completely changes the market, is known as a **disruptive innovation**. Despite what the name suggests, a disruptive innovation is desirable for the company that produces it—although, of course, it is meant to be highly disruptive to competitors.

DEGREE OF UNCERTAINTY. Another way to categorize innovation is with respect to the degree of uncertainty involved. On some occasions, organizations face conditions in which things have evolved slowly, making it clear what may be done. Moving ahead with innovation isn't particularly risky because the future is relatively certain. This slow-and-steady approach to innovation is known as **incremental innovation**. Companies engaging in incremental innovation exploit existing technology and operate under conditions in which uncertainty about the future is low. In other words, you can pretty much figure out what the future will be.

GE's former CEO Jack Welch didn't favor the incremental approach to innovation. Instead, he was inclined to do the opposite, shocking his competitors by making quantum leaps in innovation. This approach is known as **radical innovation**. In contrast to companies making incremental innovations, those making radical innovations explore new technology and operate under highly uncertain conditions.[74] Instead of making continuous, linear changes that are slow and steady, radical innovation involves a trajectory that is sporadic and discontinuous. And when it works, the payoffs of radical innovation tend to be huge. For example, radical innovations resulted in the Colgate-Palmolive Company's development of Colgate Total, a new kind of toothpaste that unseated Crest as the world's leading toothpaste brand.

SOURCE OF INNOVATION. Traditionally, the source of innovation is the company itself. This process, known as **manufacturer innovation**, occurs when an individual or organization develops an innovation for the purpose of selling it. Intel, for example, develops faster computer chips, which it sells to customers demanding more powerful computers.

Although manufacturer innovation has been going on for some time, many of today's organizations are finding inspiration from the individuals who use their goods or services. This process, known as **end-user innovation**, is very popular today because users of products provide useful guidance with respect to what is needed.[75] Companies seeking feedback from the users of its products about what features they desire in the future are likely to be focusing on end-user innovation. Microsoft's Windows 7 operating system is said to be the result of this process.

Targets of Innovation

If innovation involves introducing changes to activities that already are established, it makes sense to ask: What business activities are the foci of innovation? In general, companies can be innovative with respect to just about anything. However, most innovation falls into one or more of the following seven categories, each of which may be considered a target of innovation.[76]

- *Product innovation:* Introducing goods that are new or substantially improved (e.g., easier-to-use software)
- *Service innovation:* Introducing services that are new or substantially improved (e.g., faster overnight delivery of packages)
- *Process innovation:* Creating a new or significantly improved production or delivery method (e.g., an easier and more accurate order-taking system for call center operators)
- *Marketing innovation:* Coming up with new and/or improved marketing methods, such as those involving product design or packaging, product promotion, or pricing[77]
- *Supply chain innovation:* Developing quicker and more accurate ways to get products from suppliers into the hands of customers
- *Business model innovation:* Revising the basic way business is done (e.g., focusing on high volume and low prices or on offering extremely high-quality goods to exclusive clients)
- *Organizational innovation:* Changing key organizational practices, such as those presented in this book (e.g., how the organization is structured; see Chapter 15)

As you might imagine, companies attempting to be innovative tend to follow more than one of these practices at a time. For example, consider a financial investment firm that is trying to be more innovative. This may involve developing new financial products (e.g., new money market funds) and services (e.g., new interest-bearing checking accounts) for clients, combining basic financial attributes (e.g., risk-sharing, liquidity, credit) in innovative ways, and finding legal ways to minimize clients' income tax liabilities. Not only does this require creating new products and services, but also new business models, improved business processes, and so on. In other words, innovation often involves multiple activities that are followed in concert.

Conditions Required for Innovation to Occur

Creativity is necessary for innovation to occur, but it is not sufficient. What other factors, then, are required for innovation to occur? As it works out, the answer lies in the same basic components that are essential for creativity to occur, albeit in different ways. These are *motivation, resources,* and *skills.*

MOTIVATION TO INNOVATE. Just as individual creativity requires that people be motivated to do what it takes to be creative, organizational innovation requires that companies have the kinds of cultures that encourage innovation. When top executives fail to promote a vision of innovation and accept the status quo, change is unlikely. However, at organizations such as Microsoft, where leaders envision innovation as being part of the natural order of things, it is not surprising that innovative efforts are constantly underway.

RESOURCES TO INNOVATE. Again, a parallel to individual creativity is in order. Just as people must have certain basic skills to be creative, so too must organizations possess certain basic resources that make innovation possible. For example, to be innovative, at the very least, organizations must have what it takes in terms of human and financial resources. After all, unless the necessarily skilled people and deep pockets are available to do what it takes to innovate, stagnation is likely to result.

SKILLS TO MANAGE INNOVATION. Finally, just as individuals must hone special skills needed to be creative, so too must organizations develop special ways of managing people so as to encourage innovation—that is, *skills in innovation management.* Most notable in this regard is the matter of *balance.* Specifically, managers help promote innovation when they show balance with respect to three key matters: goals, reward systems, and time pressure.

- Organizational innovation is promoted when *goals* are linked carefully to the corporate mission. However, they should not be so specific as to tie the hands of those who put them into practice. Innovation is unlikely when such restrictions are imposed.
- *Reward systems* should recognize one's contributions generously and fairly, but they should not be so specific as to connect literally every move to a bonus or some type of monetary reward. To do so discourages people from taking the kinds of risks that make innovation possible.
- Innovation management requires carefully balancing the *time pressures* under which employees are placed. If pressures are too great, people may be unimaginative and offer routine solutions. By the same token, if pressure is too weak, employees may have no sense of time urgency and believe that the project is too unimportant to warrant any creative attention on their part.

Stages of the Organizational Innovation Process

Any CEO who snaps her fingers one day and expects her troops to be innovative on command surely will be in for disappointment. Innovation does not happen all at once. Rather, innovation occurs gradually, through a series of stages. Specifically, scientists have identified five specific

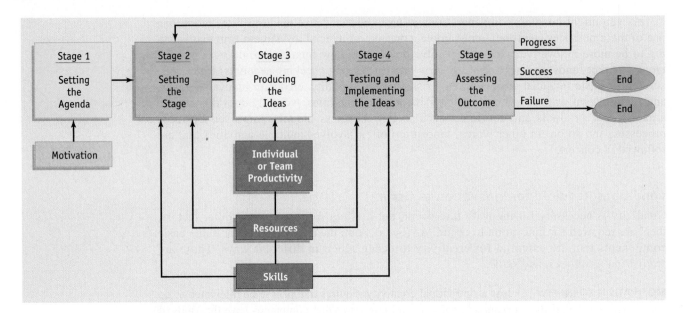

FIGURE 14.15

The Process of Innovation

The innovation process consists of the various components, and follows the steps, shown here.

Source: Adapted from Amabile, 2000; see Note 48.

stages through which the process of organizational innovation progresses.[78] We now describe each of these (see the summary in Figure 14.15).

STAGE 1: SETTING THE AGENDA. The first stage of the process of innovation begins by setting the agenda for innovation. This involves creating a **mission statement**—a document describing an organization's overall direction and general goals. The component of innovation that is most involved here is *motivation* (see Chapter 7). After all, the highest-ranking officials of the organization must be highly committed to innovation before they will initiate a push toward it.

STAGE 2: SETTING THE STAGE. Once an organization's mission has been established, it is prepared to set the stage for innovation. This may involve narrowing down certain broad goals into more specific tasks and gathering the resources to meet them. It also may involve assessing the environment, both outside and inside the organization, searching for anything that either may support or inhibit later efforts to "break the rules" by being creative. To set the stage for innovation most effectively requires using the skills necessary for innovation management as well as full use of the organization's human and financial resources.

STAGE 3: PRODUCING THE IDEAS. This stage of the process involves coming up with new ideas and testing them. It is in this third stage that individual and small group creativity enters the picture. As a result, all of the components of individual creativity mentioned earlier are involved. What's more, these may combine in important ways with various organizational factors. For example, an individual who has the skills and motivation to be highly creative might find his motivation waning as he attempts to introduce novel ideas in an organization that is not committed to innovation and that fails to make the necessary resources available. By contrast, the highly innovative nature of a company may bring out the more creative side of an individual who may not have been especially creative.

In recent years, growing numbers of organizations have turned to using **innovation labs** to help them through this stage of the innovation process. These are physical facilities that are built specifically as venues for employees to use when attempting to develop creative solutions. Although it may be difficult to imagine that any special place is required for this, there are benefits

mission statement
A document describing an organization's overall direction and general goals.

innovation labs
Physical facilities that are built specifically as venues for employees to use when attempting to develop innovative solutions.

associated with using neutral locations (so as to minimize turf wars) that also are free of distractions (e.g., ringing phones, interruptions by colleagues).[79] Companies have been using innovation labs of different scales for varied purposes. As just one example, Bell Canada relied on very large innovation labs over several years in their effort to develop new communications facilities for use at the 2010 Winter Olympics in Vancouver.[80]

STAGE 4: TESTING AND IMPLEMENTING THE IDEAS. This is the stage where implementation occurs. Now, after an initial group of individuals has developed an idea, other parts of the organization get involved. For example, a prototype product may be developed and tested, and market research may be conducted. In short, input from the many functional areas of the organization is provided. As you might imagine, resources in the task domain are important at this stage. After all, unless adequate amounts of money, personnel, material systems, and information are provided, the idea will be unlikely to survive.

Interestingly, even a good idea and resources are not enough to bring innovation to life. Skills in innovation management are critical, because for good ideas to survive it is necessary for them to be "nourished" and supported throughout the organization. Even the best ideas may be "killed off" if people in some parts of the company are not supportive. For some remarkable examples of this, see Table 14.6.[81] When you see all the great ideas that didn't quite make it at first, you come to realize that you are in excellent company if your own ideas are rejected.

STAGE 5: ASSESSING THE OUTCOME. The final stage of the process involves evaluating the new idea that arises. What happens to that concept depends on the results of the assessment. Three outcomes are possible. If the resulting idea (e.g., a certain product or service) has been a total success, it will be accepted and carried out in the future. This ends the process. Likewise, the process is over if the idea has been a complete failure. In this case, there is no good reason to continue. However, if the new idea shows promise and makes some progress toward the organization's objectives, but still has problems, the process starts all over again at stage 2.

Although this five-stage process does not account for all innovations you may find in organizations, this general model does a good job of identifying the major steps through which most go as they travel along their path from a specific organizational need to a product or service that meets that need. (For some further suggestions on how to promote innovation in an organization, see the OB in Practice section on page 510.)

TABLE 14.6   Is Your Innovative Idea Rejected? If So, You're in Good Company

Some of the best, most innovative ideas were rejected at first because one or more powerful people failed to see their merit. When you look at these examples, you can imagine how bad these individuals must have felt about "the one that got away."

Product	Rejection Story
Star Wars	This movie was turned down by 12 Hollywood studios before finally being accepted.
Photocopying process	Photocopying was rejected as a viable technology by IBM, GM, and DuPont.
Velcro	Victor Kiam (of Remington Razor fame) turned down the patent for $25,000.
Transistor radio	In the 1950s, Sony's founder, Akio Morita, was unsuccessful in marketing this idea.
The Beatles	The Beatles were turned down by Decca Records in 1962 because it was believed that "groups with guitars were on the way out."
Movies with soundtracks	In 1927, Harry Warner, president of Warner Brothers, said "nobody wanted to hear actors talk."

Source: Based on information reported by Davila et al., 2005; Ricchiuto, 1997; see Note 81.

OB in Practice

How to Inspire Innovation

The noted organizational consultant Gary Hamel believes that top management plays an important role when it comes to inspiring innovation in their companies. Radical innovation, he argues, "is no longer an option for big companies—it's the imperative," adding that top management's job is "to build an organization that can continually spawn cool new business concepts."[82] Hamel identifies several ways in which managers can go about doing this.[83] These are as follows.

Set very high expectations

In Chapter 7 we emphasized that people strive to meet performance goals. When employees are confronted with goals they find to be especially challenging—but still not impossible, of course—they are forced to consider highly novel ways of accomplishing them. At GE Capital, for example, executives are expected to grow annual earnings by at least 20 percent. This leads them to consider more novel approaches and to develop more innovative products than they would if they were required to meet a more modest goal, such as the more typical 5 percent.

Listen to new voices

If you ask questions of the same old people, you get the same old answers. But, if you seek the opinions of outsiders free from industry prejudices, they are less likely to say "you can't do it." Indeed, Jeff Bezos was not a retailing mogul when he started Amazon.com (see the Case in Point on pages 514–515), and neither was Ted Turner a seasoned broadcast journalist when he founded CNN. With this in mind, many of today's most innovative companies are doing things like seeking out the revolutionaries in the company, those whose voices are getting muffled by the hierarchy. They also are paying special attention to newcomers, especially the youngest people. Again, GE Capital provides a good example: Intentionally seeking a youthful perspective, many members of the management team at this well-established financial services firm are hired when under 30 years of age.

Create opportunities for talented employees

It is widely believed that the better people are always interested in the best opportunities within a company. The most effective organizations capitalize on this by allowing employees to move to other jobs within the company that they find more exciting. Sometimes, this involves making the best use of human resources by training employees for new positions that enable their organizations to be innovative. For example, IBM has committed to spending $200 million to train 100,000 employees in high-skill jobs, such as those involving Linux systems and middleware (i.e., software that connects two otherwise separate applications, such as linking a database system and a Web server).[84]

Recognize innovation

Many experts believe that to get people to innovate, it helps to reward them for doing so. This is practiced at South Africa's First National Bank (FNB), which in 2005 initiated the FNB Innovators competition.[85] This program identifies and rewards employees who think creatively and come up with innovations to ensure efficient and effective systems and procedures. According to Michael Jordaan, CEO of FNB, innovation can either be a new approach to an old process or a totally novel idea. In its first year, 3,000 ideas were entered. The bank's Cellphone Banking Division won first prize in 2005 for creating an entirely new way to do online banking, netting team members a whopping ZAR 1 million (approximately US$166,668).

It is important to note that the recognition for innovative activity need not always be monetary in nature. Many companies find that simply acknowledging employees for their innovations contributes to efforts to keep them going. At 3M, for example, which we have mentioned several times in this chapter, a "Hall of Inventors" showcases the work of the firm's most innovative engineers. The company even has published its own book to celebrate the contributions of its innovators.[86]

Identify a cause

Most think of Charles Schwab as a well-established, rather traditional investment firm. Although in many ways it is, that's not how president and co-CEO David Pottruck prefers to think of it. Rather, Pottruck envisions Charles Schwab's mission in far loftier terms—as guardians of its customers' financial dreams. By sharing this vision, Pottruck has gotten his employees to recognize that they are doing something important, contributing to a cause that will make a difference in people's lives. It was such thinking that inspired Schwab employees to take innovative steps, such as offering its services online, and at a sizable discount.

If you are thinking that implementing these guidelines is akin to being innovative about innovation, we are inclined to agree. Indeed, although these suggestions may be challenging to adopt, their considerable impact makes it unwise to ignore them.

Summary and Review of Learning Objectives

1. **Define organizational culture and identify its core characteristics and the various functions it serves in organizations.**
   Organizational culture is a cognitive framework consisting of attitudes, values, behavioral norms, and expectations shared by organization members. Scientists often think of organizational culture as a set of basic assumptions shared by members of a company. Organizational

culture consists of six core characteristics by which organizations may be differentiated. These are (1) sensitivity to others, (2) interest in new ideas, (3) willingness to take risks, (4) value placed on people, (5) openness of available communication options, and (6) friendliness and congeniality. Culture plays three major roles in organizations. It provides a sense of identity for its members, it generates commitment to the organization's mission, and it also serves to clarify and reinforce standards of behavior.

2. **Describe the four major forms of organizational culture specified by the competing values framework.**

   According to the competing values framework, organizations have one of four different forms of organizational culture. Organizations that have an internal focus and that emphasize stability and control are said to have a *hierarchy culture*. In this case, effective leaders are good coordinators of projects and emphasize smooth-running procedures, often relying on formal rules and policies to do so. Organizations that are concerned with stability and control, but that are external in their orientation, are said to have a *market culture*. In such organizations, the core values emphasize competitiveness and productivity, focusing on bottom-line results. They do this by carefully identifying the markets in which they are going to compete and then taking a very hard-driving, results-oriented approach to getting things done. Organizations that have a strong internal focus along with a high degree of flexibility and discretion are said to have a *clan culture*. With goals that are highly shared by members of the organization and high levels of cohesiveness, such companies feel more like extended families than economic entities. Organizations that emphasize flexibility while also paying attention to external environments are said to have *adhocracy cultures*. Such cultures are characterized by the recognition that, to succeed, organizations need to be highly innovative and constantly assess what the future requires for survival.

3. **Explain the factors responsible for creating and transmitting organizational culture and for getting it to change.**

   Organizational culture is created by two key factors—the influence of company founders and experiences with the external environment. Organizational culture is transmitted in several ways, including symbols, slogans, stories, jargon, ceremonies, and statements of principle. Although organizational culture tends to be stable, it is subject to change. Among the factors most responsible for changing organizational culture are the composition of the workforce, mergers and acquisitions, strategic (i.e., planned) organizational changes, and changes necessitated by the Internet.

4. **Define creativity and describe the basic components of individual and team creativity.**

   Creativity is the process by which individuals or small groups produce novel and useful ideas. Creativity in organizations is based on three fundamental components: domain-relevant skills (basic knowledge needed to perform the task at hand), creativity-relevant skills (special abilities needed to generate creative new ideas), and intrinsic task motivation (people's willingness to perform creative acts).

5. **Describe various approaches to promoting creativity in organizations.**

   Creativity in organizations may be promoted by training people to be creative, by encouraging openness to new ideas (e.g., "thinking outside the box"), by taking the time to understand the problem at hand, and by developing divergent thinking. It also may be accomplished by developing creative work environments. These are ones in which autonomy is provided, people are exposed to creative individuals, ideas are permitted to cross-pollinate, jobs are made intrinsically interesting, creative goals are set, creativity is supported within the organization, people have fun, and diversity is promoted.

6. **Identify the basic forms and targets of innovation and the stages of the innovation process.**

   Innovation refers to the implementation of creative ideas within organizations. It takes different forms depending on three factors: impact on existing business (*sustaining innovation* if impact is minor, and *disruptive innovation* if impact is major), the degree of uncertainty involved (*incremental innovation* if uncertainty is low, and *radical innovation* if uncertainty is high), and its sources (*manufacturer innovation* if ideas come from within, and *end-user innovation* if ideas come from customers). The innovation process generally proceeds in the following five stages: setting the agenda, setting the stage, producing the ideas, testing and implementing the ideas, and assessing the outcome.

Points to Ponder

Questions for Review

1. What is organizational culture, what role does it play in organizations, and how is it created?
2. How does organizational culture influence individuals and organizations, and what makes organizational culture change?
3. What are the three components of individual and team creativity, and what can be done to promote creativity in individuals, work teams, and the whole work environment?
4. What are the basic components of innovation and the stages through which the process of innovation progresses?

Experiential Questions

1. Think of an organization in which you have worked. In what ways was its culture transmitted to the people who worked in it and those who remained outside, such as the public?
2. Have you ever worked for an organization whose culture is in need of change? If so, what was the problem? What could have been done to change the culture? What obstacles would have had to be overcome for the changes to be effective?

3. Do you think of yourself as a creative person? What could you do to become more creative when it comes to the work you do?
4. Have you ever worked for a highly innovative company? If so, what was done that made it so innovative? If not, what could have been done to make it more innovative?

Questions to Analyze

1. Organizational culture is a "mushy" concept. You can't see it, yet you know it's there. What indications are there that organizational culture really does exist?
2. Think of an organization in which you have worked. Was its culture predominantly hierarchy, market, clan, or adhocracy? Was this an effective culture given the nature of the people employed there and the type of work done?
3. Think of an instance in which you were especially creative. Did it involve a task at which you were particularly skillful and that you found interesting (e.g., composing music)? Also, did you use any of the creativity-relevant skills identified here (e.g., divergent thinking, productive forgetting)? In retrospect, what additional skills might you have used to be even more creative in that situation?

Experiencing OB

Individual Exercise

Who's Most Like a Giraffe?

A highly effective way of "getting your creative juices flowing" is by thinking of things in unusual ways. (This is the concept of *divergent thinking* that we described on page 496.) Doing this opens you up to considering new approaches to things, unusual ways of looking at them. And this, in turn, is key to promoting creative thinking. This exercise is designed to get this process going.

Directions

1. On the left in the following table is a list of animals. For each one, think of a famous person (a celebrity from any walk of life, such as a well-known performer, politician, athlete, etc.), alive or dead, who you believe is most similar to it in one way or another. The match can be based on a physical similarity, personality, whatever, so long you think there's some strong similarity. Write that person's name on the corresponding line in the "Celebrity" column.
2. For each of the celebrities, think of one particular food that you associate with that person for one reason or another. Write the name of that food on the corresponding line in the "Food" column.

Animal	Celebrity	Food
Giraffe		
Snake		
Tiger		
Rat		
Panda		
Moose		
Monkey		
Flamingo		
Crab		
Grasshopper		
Cougar		
Parrot		

Questions for Discussion

1. Do you think that completing this exercise was helpful in getting you to think about things in usual ways? Why or why not?
2. Do you believe that thinking about things from unusual perspectives will help you think more creatively in other ways, such as on your job? If so, for how long do you think this will last?
3. In what ways do you think that being more creative will help you on your current job? How about in a job you hope to have someday? Might there be any ways in which being especially creative will be a hindrance?
4. So, who's most like a giraffe, anyway?

Group Exercise

What Does Your Workspace Suggest About Organizational Culture?

Newcomers' impressions of an organization's culture depend greatly on visual images. Even without knowing anything about a company, just seeing the workplace sends a message, intentional or unintentional, regarding what that organization is like. The following exercise is designed to demonstrate this phenomenon.

Directions

1. Each member of the class should take several photographs of his or her workplace and select the three that best capture, in his or her own mind, the essence of what that organization is like.
2. One member of the class should identify the company depicted in the photos, describe the type of work it does, and present the photos to the rest of the class.
3. Members of the class should then rate the organization shown in the photos using the following dimensions. Circle the number that comes closest to your feelings about the company shown.

```
      unfamiliar:__1__:__2__:__3__:__4__:__5__:__6__:__7__:familiar
    unsuccessful:__1__:__2__:__3__:__4__:__5__:__6__:__7__:successful
      unfriendly:__1__:__2__:__3__:__4__:__5__:__6__:__7__:friendly
    unproductive:__1__:__2__:__3__:__4__:__5__:__6__:__7__:productive
   not innovative:__1__:__2__:__3__:__4__:__5__:__6__:__7__:innovative
        uncaring:__1__:__2__:__3__:__4__:__5__:__6__:__7__:caring
    conservative:__1__:__2__:__3__:__4__:__5__:__6__:__7__:risky
          closed:__1__:__2__:__3__:__4__:__5__:__6__:__7__:open
```

5. Take turns sharing your individual reactions to each set of photos. Compare the responses of the student whose company pictures were examined with those of the students who were seeing the photos for the first time.
6. Repeat this process using the photos of other students' organizations.

Questions for Discussion

1. For each set of photos examined, how close did the descriptions of members of the class come to the photographers' assessments of their own companies? In other words, how well did the photos capture the culture of the organization as perceived by an "insider"?
2. As a whole, were people more accurate in assessing the culture of companies with which they were already familiar than those they didn't already know? If so, why do you think this occurred?
3. Was there more agreement regarding the cultures of organizations in some types of industries (e.g., manufacturing) than in others (e.g., service)? If so, why do you think this occurred?

Practicing OB

Stimulating a Creative Culture

The president of your organization, a small manufacturing company, has been complaining that sales are stagnant. A key problem, you discover, is that the market for the products your firm makes is fully developed—and frankly, the products themselves are not very exciting. No one seems to care about doing anything innovative. Instead, the employees seem more interested in doing things the way they have always done them.

1. What factors do you suspect are responsible for the way the culture in this organization has been over the years?
2. What do you recommend should be done to enhance the creativity of this company's employees?
3. What could be done to help make the company's products more innovative?

Case in Point

■ *Amazon.com: Innovation via the "Two-Pizza Team"*

Amazon.com widely is considered the world's best online retail site, the undisputed leader of Internet commerce. Although many e-tailers pulled their plugs during the dot-com bust of the late 1990s, Amazon has become a profitable multibillion-dollar business. The man behind the company's success is its founder and CEO, Jeff Bezos. And his secret to success, he proudly proclaims, is his willingness to innovate.

His secret is simple (to explain, at least)—being willing to take risks. As Bezos put it, "Innovation is part and parcel with going down blind alleys. You can't have one without the other." And at Amazon, being innovative is possible because it's engrained into the culture of the organization. Indeed, the very idea of starting an Internet-based bookstore in 1993 was then as unusual as it is unremarkable today.

To keep innovation going at Amazon, Bezos does several things. First, company officials go out of their way to select people who are interested in being innovative.

Those who are unwilling to take risks or who demand stable working environments "flee Amazon.com in hordes," says Bezos. However, because Amazon is known for its pioneering focus, it also tends to attract individuals who buy into the company's highly innovative orientation.

Second, to keep ideas percolating, managers form teams that introduce and test ideas constantly. And, because the company's only presence is Web-based, it's easy to test ideas without making large investments. For example, it's possible to expose some customers, but not others, to some features or descriptions or prices. Then, comparisons can be made to provide instant feedback on how people behave.

Within the company's Seattle headquarters, these teams that test innovations are called "two-pizza teams." All projects involve only small numbers of people—"small enough that they can be fed on two pizzas," Bezos explains, explaining that six-person teams constitute a good size for getting things done.

(Continued)

At Amazon, "getting things done" is all about making the best possible experience for customers. Recently, this has taken such popular forms as "inside the book" (which allows guests to the Web site to examine and search through books before purchasing) and various deals that allow customers to have their items shipped free of charge. Both have been wildly successful.

When asked if he considers himself to be an innovator, Bezos readily acknowledges that this description fits him perfectly. "I absolutely think of myself as an innovator," he says, adding that too often "we learn that we can't improve things." However, being innovative means learning that anything can be improved upon. And if Amazon's success is any indication, this clearly is so.

Questions for Discussion

1. As Amazon.com has grown in size over the years, do you think it has become easier or more difficult for innovation to occur? Or do you think that the company's size makes no difference in this regard?
2. What role do you think Jeff Bezos has played in instilling the innovative culture at Amazon.com? How, if at all, do you think he is involved in maintaining an innovative culture?
3. Personally, would you like to work at a highly innovative company like Amazon.com, or would you be among those who leave because you prefer a more stable environment?

15 Organizational Structure and Design

Learning Objectives

After reading this chapter, you should be able to:

1. Describe what is meant by organizational structure and the basic characteristics of organizational structure revealed in an organization chart.

2. Describe different approaches to departmentalization—functional organizations, product organizations, and matrix organizations.

3. Distinguish between classical and neoclassical approaches to organizational design and between mechanistic organizations and organic organizations, as described by the contingency approach to organizational design.

4. Describe the five organizational forms identified by Mintzberg: simple structure, machine bureaucracy, professional bureaucracy, divisional structure, and adhocracy.

5. Explain how organizations can be designed with strategy in mind.

6. Characterize three forms of intraorganizational design—boundaryless organizations, conglomerates, and strategic alliances.

Chapter Outline

- Organizational Structure: The Basic Dimensions of Organizations
- Departmentalization: Ways of Structuring Organizations
- Organizational Design: Coordinating the Structural Elements of Organizations
- A Strategic Approach to Designing Organizations
- Interorganizational Designs: Joining Multiple Organizations

Preview Case

■ *Verizon and McAfee Head for "the Cloud" Together*

For three decades companies purchased computers to run software that enabled them to be productive, and they connected them in networks to facilitate communication. This model served them well although the investments in hardware, software and networking infrastructure were enormous, and keeping everything up and going was an ongoing battle. Today, this is changing. Many organizations are finding it far easier, less expensive, and more efficient to give up all this and simply plug into "the cloud," an array of computer services accessed via the Internet. It's akin to utilities. We don't own sources of electricity, but we can get all we want by plugging into outlets fed by our local electric companies. They provide the service, maintain it, and upgrade it to meet demands. Cloud computing operates the same way. As organizations grow, shrink, move in new directions, open facilities abroad, and join forces with others, their computing needs change accordingly.

By using cloud computing, companies can focus their resources on their core businesses instead of investing in the technology and enormous IT (information technology) staffs that support it. For cloud computing to succeed, two ingredients are essential: there must be an incredibly sophisticated and powerful hardware and software infrastructure in place that readily meets the needs of clients, and it must be perfectly secure. If the system breaks down or is compromised by hackers, that cloud will burst, triggering a massive storm of angry users.

As you might expect, organizations will reach for the cloud only when they feel assured that they can count on it to meet their needs effectively and securely. Making this a reality often requires the expert resources of more than one company. It was with this in mind that in October 2009, Verizon Business, a major provider of communication and IT solutions for businesses throughout the world, joined forces with McAfee, the world's largest dedicated security technology company. In announcing their strategic alliance, company officials explained that their objective was "to provide integrated security solutions to businesses and government agencies worldwide."

Beyond using this arrangement as a springboard for tomorrow's cloud computing business, it also enhances each company's capacity to serve today's customers. For example, Verizon now is able to offer McAfee's full range of enterprise security solutions to clients. It also will tap McAfee's secure technology that makes it economically feasible to process credit card payments for companies with fewer than 1 million annual transactions, about a third of all business. At McAfee's end, the alliance gives it access to the vast distribution capabilities of Verizon and its army of 1,200 security specialists who provide on-site, "feet on the street" service to business customers.

These current benefits are only just the beginning of a more ambitious plan. Both companies hope that, soon, their deal will serve as a springboard to dominance in the nascent cloud computing business.

Although the complete story has not yet been written, McAfee and Verizon Business are counting on it having a happy ending, and they're investing considerable resources to see that it does. In today's complex and rapidly changing business environment, it's not unusual for companies to join forces. Sometimes it's intended to gain a strategic advantage over competitors, but at other times, it's necessary to gain new capacities that enable them simply to remain in business. At the core of the matter is the issue of how companies can best organize themselves to accomplish their objectives. This example focuses on external forms of organization but this is a relatively new phenomenon. Traditionally, companies have examined ways of coordinating their efforts internally, organizing themselves into separate units that make them most effective. The question of how to do this is a venerable one for organizations—and, as we explain in this chapter, one whose answers have far-reaching implications.

OB researchers and theorists have provided considerable insight into the matter by studying what is called *organizational structure*—the way individuals and groups are arranged with respect to the tasks they perform—and *organizational design*—the process of coordinating these structural elements in the most effective manner.[1] As you may suspect, finding the best way to structure and design organizations is no simple matter. However, because understanding the structure and design of organizations is key to appreciating their functioning fully—and, ultimately, their success—organizational scientists have devoted considerable attention to this topic.

We describe these efforts in this chapter. Specifically, we examine how these structural elements can be most effectively combined into productive organizational designs. In so doing, we cover some of the traditional ways of designing organizations as well as some of the rapidly developing organizational forms emerging today. We also will examine an approach to designing organizations that takes into account the organization's strategic plans. Finally, we conclude by presenting designs that bring together multiple organizations. Before getting to this, we begin by examining the basic structural dimensions of organizations—the various qualities that characterize what they're like.

Organizational Structure: The Basic Dimensions of Organizations

Think about how a simple house is constructed. Typically, it is composed of a wooden frame positioned atop a concrete slab covered by a roof and siding materials. Within this basic structure are separate systems operating to provide electricity, water, and telephone services. Similarly, the structure of the human body is composed of a skeleton surrounded by various systems of organs, muscle, and tissue serving bodily functions such as respiration, digestion, and the like. Although you may not have thought about it much, we also can identify the structure of an organization in a similar fashion.

Consider, for example, the college or university you attend. It probably is composed of various groupings of people and departments working together to serve special functions. Individuals and groups are dedicated to tasks such as teaching, providing financial aid, maintaining the physical facilities, and so on. Of course, within each group, even more distinctions can be found between the jobs people perform. For example, it's unlikely that the instructor for your organizational behavior course also is teaching seventeenth-century French literature. Similarly, you also can distinguish between the various tasks and functions people perform in other organizations. In other words, an organization is not a haphazard collection of people, but a meaningful combination of groups and individuals working together purposefully to meet the goals of the organization.[2] The term **organizational structure** refers to the formal configuration between individuals and groups with respect to the allocation of tasks, responsibilities, and authority within organizations.[3]

Strictly speaking, one cannot see the structure of an organization; it is an abstract concept. However, the connections between various clusters of functions of which an organization is composed can be represented in the form of a diagram known as an *organization chart* (which we also described in conjunction with communication in Chapter 9). In other words, an organization chart can be considered a representation of a company's internal structure. As you might imagine, organization charts are useful tools for avoiding confusion regarding how various tasks or functions are interrelated.

Organization charts provide information about the various tasks performed within a company and the formal lines of authority between them. For example, look at the chart depicting part of a hypothetical manufacturing organization shown in Figure 15.1. Each box represents a specific job, and the lines connecting them reflect the formally prescribed *reporting relationships* between the individuals performing those jobs. (In other words, it reveals "who answers to whom.") To specialists in organizational structure, however, such diagrams reveal a great deal more. Specifically, they reveal five basic dimensions of organizational structure that we now will describe: *hierarchy of authority, span of control, division of labor, line versus staff positions*, and *decentralization*.

Hierarchy of Authority: Up and Down the Organizational Ladder

Among the first things you see when examining an organization chart is the distinction between higher-level individuals (toward the top) and lower-level individuals (toward the bottom)—what is referred to as **hierarchy of authority.** The diagram reveals which particular lower-level employees are required to report to which particular individuals immediately above them in the organizational hierarchy. In our hypothetical example in Figure 15.1, the various regional salespeople (at the bottom of the hierarchy and the bottom of the diagram) report to their respective

organizational structure
The formal configuration between individuals and groups with respect to the allocation of tasks, responsibilities, and authorities within organizations.

hierarchy of authority
The distinction between members of organizations with respect to the degree of authority they have; higher positions in an organization chart reflect higher degrees of formal authority.

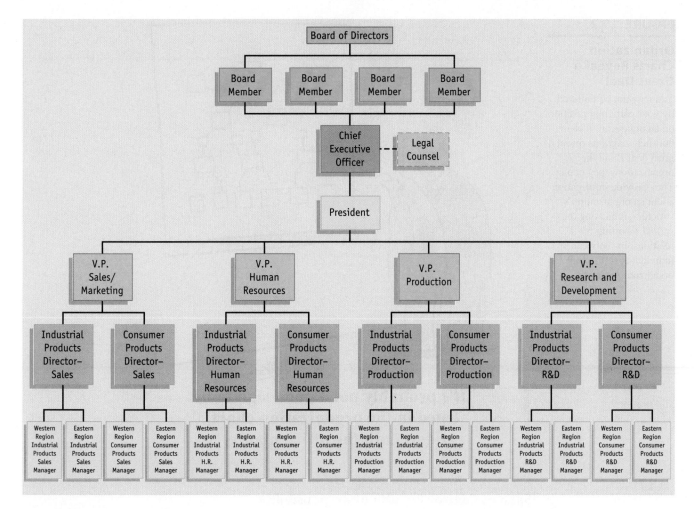

FIGURE 15.1

Organization Chart of a Hypothetical Manufacturing Firm

An organization chart, such as this one, identifies pictorially the various functions performed within
an organization and the lines of authority between the individuals performing those functions.

regional sales directors, who report to the vice president of sales, who reports to the president,
who reports to the chief executive officer, who reports to the board of directors. (For an indication of life at the very bottom of an organizational hierarchy, see Figure 15.2.)

As we trace these reporting relationships, we work our way up the organization's hierarchy.
In this case, the organization has six levels. Some may have many levels, in which case their
structure is considered *tall* (as in the top of Figure 15.3 on page 521), or only a few, in which case
the structure is considered *flat* (as in the bottom of Figure 15.3).

Even before today's practice of eliminating jobs as a cost-saving measure, organizations have,
since the mid-1980s, been restructuring their workforces, seeking to eliminate waste by flattening
them out.[4] This is the practice of **downsizing** that has received so much attention in the press.
Sometimes, it's referred to as "rightsizing," "delayering," or "retrenching," but whatever it may be
called, it essentially refers to the same thing—that is, eliminating entire layers of organizational
structure (we will return to this topic again in Chapter 16).[5] Typically, when jobs are lost through
restructuring, they are positions found in the middle layers of organizational hierarchies. To a great
extent, this follows from the trend toward getting work done through teams (see Chapter 8). As this
occurs, tall organizational hierarchies become unnecessary. The underlying assumption is that
fewer layers reduce waste and enable people to make better decisions (by moving decision-making
authority into the hands of the individuals who are closer to the problems at hand), thereby leading
to greater profitability. "Doing more with less" is the mantra of proponents of delayering.

downsizing
Practice of eliminating jobs,
typically at the middle layers
of organization charts.

FIGURE 15.2

Organization Charts Reveal a Great Deal

You may not be flattered by your particular position on an organization chart, but such diagrams reveal a great deal about the organizations they depict. They provide information about an organization's structure, indicating the formal reporting relationships between individuals at different organizational levels.

www.cartoonstock.com/Jonny Hawkins.

"It's probably not a good sign to be listed in the organization chart underneath the office plants."

span of control
The number of subordinates in an organization who are supervised by managers.

Span of Control: Breadth of Responsibility

Over how many individuals should a manager have responsibility? The earliest management theorists and practitioners alike (even the Roman legions) addressed this question.[6] When you look at an organization chart, the number of people formally required to report to each individual manager is immediately clear. This number constitutes what is known as a manager's **span of control.** Supervisors responsible for many individuals are said to have a *wide* span of control, whereas those responsible for fewer are said to have a *narrow* span of control. In our organization chart in Figure 15.3, note how the managers in the top portion of this figure have relatively narrow spans of control (only two workers), whereas the ones in the bottom have relatively broader spans of control (twice as many people). In real companies, some managers have spans of control so broad that they may be responsible for dozens of subordinates.

Figure 15.3 shows something important about the relationship between the tallness of a hierarchy and the span of control of its supervisory personnel. Generally speaking, when a manager's span of control is wide, the organization itself tends to have a flat hierarchy. In contrast, when a manager's span is narrow, the organization tends to have a tall hierarchy. Specifically, notice that in the "Tall Organization" (at the top of the diagram), there are many levels in the hierarchy and that the span of control is relatively narrow (i.e., the number of people supervised is low). By contrast, in the "Flat Organization" (at the bottom of the diagram), there are only a few levels in the hierarchy, and the span of control is relatively wide. Both organizations depicted here have 31 positions, but these are arranged differently, as you can see.

It is important to note that the organization chart may not reflect a manager's actual span of control perfectly. Other factors not immediately forthcoming from the chart itself may be involved. For example, supervisors may have additional responsibilities that do not appear on the chart—notably, assignments on various committees. Moreover, some subordinates (e.g., people new to the job) might require more attention than others. Also, the degree of supervisory control needed may increase (e.g., when jobs change) or decrease (e.g., when subordinates become more proficient).

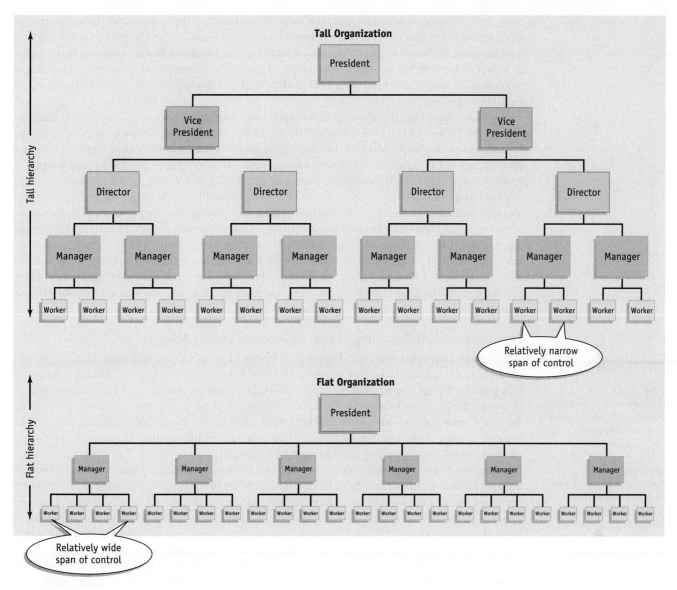

FIGURE 15.3

Tall Versus Flat Organizations: A Comparison

In tall organizations, the hierarchy has many layers, and managers have a narrow span of control (i.e., they are responsible for few subordinates). However, in flat organizations, the hierarchy has few layers and managers have a wide span of control (i.e., they are responsible for many workers). Both of the organizations depicted here have 31 members, although each one is structured differently.

It is not readily possible to specify the "ideal" span of control that should be sought. Instead, it makes better sense to consider what form of organization is best suited to various purposes. For example, because supervisors in a military unit must have tight control over subordinates and get them to respond quickly and precisely, a narrow span of control is likely to be effective. As a result, military organizations tend to have extremely tall hierarchies (in the Army, for example, ranging in rank from Private to Four-Star General). In contrast, people working in a research and development lab must have an open exchange of ideas and typically require little managerial guidance to be successful. Units of this type tend to have very flat structures.

Division of Labor: Carving Up the Work to Be Done

The standard organization chart makes clear that the many tasks to be performed within a company are divided into specialized jobs, a process known as the **division of labor**. The more that

division of labor
The process of dividing the many tasks performed within an organization into particular jobs.

tasks are divided into separate jobs, the more those jobs are *specialized* and the narrower the range of activities that job incumbents are required to perform. In theory, the fewer tasks a person performs, the better he or she may be expected to execute them, freeing others to do the tasks at which they excel. Taken together, an entire organization is composed of people performing a collection of specialized jobs. This is probably the most obvious feature that can be observed from the organization chart.

As you might imagine, the degree to which employees perform specialized jobs is likely to depend on the size of the organization. The larger the organization, the more opportunities for specialization are likely to exist. For example, an individual working in a large advertising agency may get to specialize in a very narrow field, such as writing jingles for radio and TV spots for automobiles. By contrast, someone employed at a much smaller agency may be required to do all writing of print and broadcast ads in addition to helping out with the artwork meeting with clients, and even making coffee. Obviously, the larger company might be expected to reap the benefits of using the talents of employees efficiently (a natural result of an extensive division of labor). As companies downsize, however, many jobs become less specialized. For example, at General Electric, quite a few middle-management positions have been eliminated in recent years. As a consequence, the remaining managers must perform a wider variety of jobs, making their own jobs less specialized.[7] You can see this relationship in our summary in Table 15.1.

Line Versus Staff Positions: Decision Makers Versus Advisers

The organization chart shown in Figure 15.1 (page 519) reveals an additional distinction that deserves to be highlighted—that between *line positions* and *staff positions*. People occupying **line positions** (e.g., the various vice presidents and managers) have decision-making power. However, the individual shown in the dotted box set off to the right—the legal counsel—cannot make decisions, but provides advice and recommendations to be used by the line managers. For example, such an individual may help corporate officials decide whether a certain product name can be used without infringing on copyright restrictions.

In many of today's organizations, human resource managers occupy **staff positions,** providing specialized services regarding testing and interviewing procedures as well as information about the latest laws on personnel discrimination. However, the ultimate decisions on personnel selection, such as who to hire for key positions, are likely to be made by more senior managers in specialized areas—that is, staff managers. Various assistants also fall into this category, holding staff positions. For an example from a large government agency, see Figure 15.4.

Sociologists have noted that staff managers tend to be younger, better educated, and more committed to their fields than to the organizations employing them.[8] Line managers might feel more committed not only because of the greater opportunities they have to exercise decisions, but also because they are more likely to perceive themselves as being part of a company rather than an independent specialist (whose identity lies primarily within his or her specialty area).

Decentralization: Delegating Power Downward

During the first half of the twentieth century, as companies grew larger and larger, they shifted power and authority into the hands of a few upper-echelon administrators—executives whose decisions influenced the many people below them in the organizational hierarchy. In fact, it was during

line positions

Positions in an organization in which people can make decisions related to doing its basic work.

staff positions

Positions in organizations in which people make recommendations to others, but are not themselves involved in making decisions concerning the organization's day-to-day operations.

TABLE 15.1 Division of Labor: A Summary

Low and high levels of division of labor can be characterized with respect to the three dimensions shown here.

Dimension	Division of Labor	
	Low	High
Degree of specialization	General tasks	Highly specialized tasks
Typical organizational size	Small	Large
Economic efficiency	Inefficient	Highly efficient

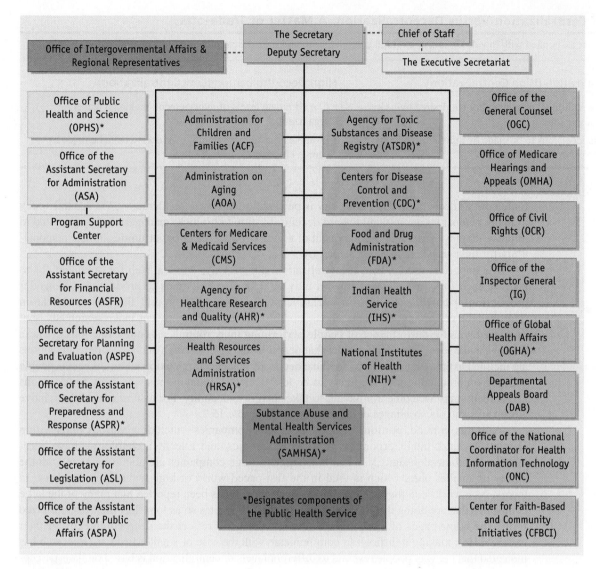

FIGURE 15.4

Line Versus Staff Positions in the U.S. Department of Health and Human Services

The upper echelons of the U.S. Department of Health and Human Services are organized as shown here. Note how the Chief of Staff, the Executive Secretariat, and the Office of Intergovernmental Affairs and Regional Representatives are staff positions (designated by broken lines) whereas all others on this organization chart are line positions (designated by solid lines).

Source: U.S. Department of Health and Human Services, 2010.

the 1920s that Alfred P. Sloan, Jr., president of General Motors at the time, introduced the notion of a "central office"—the place where a few individuals made policy decisions for the entire company.[9] As part of Sloan's plan, decisions regarding the day-to-day operation of the company were pushed further down the organizational hierarchy, allowing those individuals who were most affected to make the decisions. This process of delegating power from higher to lower levels within organizations is known as **decentralization.** It is the opposite, of course, of **centralization,** the tendency for just a few powerful individuals or groups to hold most of the decision-making power.

Earlier, we mentioned that flattening hierarchies has made it possible to streamline organizations by eliminating many middle-management jobs. This is in keeping with the tendency toward decentralization. After all, as people are empowered to make their own decisions, it's unnecessary for them to report to as many supervisors. As a result, organization charts will

decentralization
The extent to which authority and decision making are spread throughout all levels of an organization rather than being reserved for top management (centralization).

centralization
The tendency for just a few powerful individuals or groups to hold most of the decision-making power.

TABLE 15.2 Centralization Versus Decentralization: A Matter of Trade-offs

Various benefits are associated with low decentralization (high centralization) and high decentralization (low centralization) within organizations.

Low Decentralization (High Centralization)	High Decentralization (Low Centralization)
• Eliminates the additional responsibility not desired by people performing routine jobs	• Can eliminate levels of management, making a leaner organization
• Permits crucial decisions to be made by individuals who have the "big picture"	• Promotes greater opportunities for decisions to be made by people closest to problems

flatten out as decision-making authority is pushed farther down the hierarchy. We see this today as many companies are moving toward decentralization to promote managerial efficiency and to improve employee satisfaction (the result of giving people greater opportunities to take responsibility for their own actions; see Chapter 6).[10]

It is important to note that decentralization is *not* always an ideal step for organizations to take. In fact, for some types of jobs, it may be a serious hindrance to productivity. Consider production-oriented positions: In a classic study, researchers found that decentralization improved the performance on some jobs—notably, the work of employees in a research lab—but interfered with the performance of people performing more routine, assembly-line jobs.[11] These findings make sense once you consider that people working in research and development positions are inclined to enjoy the autonomy to make decisions that decentralization allows, whereas people working on production jobs are likely to be less interested in taking responsibility for decisions and actually may welcome *not* having to take such responsibility. For a summary of the relative advantages and disadvantages of centralization, see Table 15.2.

With this in mind, portions of many high-tech companies—including various units within Hewlett-Packard, Intel Corporation, Philips Electronics, and Lucent Technology—have introduced decentralized designs.[12] When this happens, large companies are able to operate with the agility of smaller ones, which is vital in the fast-paced world of high technology—at least, in theory. As it works out, they are not doing so perfectly. It has been reported that many of the large companies that are doing this are not setting up their Web sites so as to reflect their decentralized form. The home pages of many high-tech companies still reflect the deep complexity of their massive sizes, making it difficult to communicate with the ease of smaller firms.[13] (Research has indicated that the way people respond to different levels of centralization is based on their perceptions of fairness. For a look at this phenomenon, see The Ethics Angle section on page 525).

Departmentalization: Ways of Structuring Organizations

Thus far, we have been talking about "the" organization chart of company. Typically, such charts, like the one shown in Figure 15.1 (page 519), divide the organization into different units based on the particular functions they perform. However, as we will explain in this section, this is only one option. Organizations can be divided not only by function, but also by product or market, and by a special blend of function, product, or market known as the *matrix form*. We now will take a closer look at these various ways of organizing companies into coherent units—that is, the process of **departmentalization**.

departmentalization
The process of breaking up organizations into coherent units.

functional organization
The type of departmentalization based on the activities or functions performed (e.g., sales, finance).

Functional Organizations: Departmentalization by Task

Because it is the form organizations usually take when they are first created, and because it is how we usually think of businesses, the **functional organization** can be considered the most basic approach to departmentalization. Essentially, functional organizations departmentalize individuals according to the nature of the tasks they perform, with people who perform similar jobs assigned to the same department. For example, a manufacturing company might consist of separate departments devoted to basic functions such as production, sales, research and development, and accounting (see Figure 15.5).

The Ethics Angle

How Fair Is Centralization? It Depends Who You Ask

It's easy to envision that the experience of working in a highly centralized organization may be very different for various individuals. People who hold high-level positions in centralized organizations are the ones with the most power, whereas those in lower-level positions are in less powerful, more peripheral positions. However, this isn't the case in decentralized organizations. In these organizations, one's position in a status hierarchy reveals less about power because decentralization tends to equalize the levels of power people have.

These considerations raise two interesting questions: Does centralization influence the degree to which people believe that they are treated in an interactionally fair manner in their organizations? (As we discussed in Chapter 2, this refers to the extent to which people believe that things are explained to them in a manner that shows them dignity and respect.) And, do these relationships differ for people who occupy high-level and low-level positions in their organizations?

Some interesting studies have addressed these questions.[14] Researchers conducting one investigation examined the degree to which employees from a variety of organizations perceived that their work unit was centralized.[15] This was measured in terms of their frequency of participation in organizational decisions (the more people believed to have participated, the less centralized their unit was labeled as being). They also measured these workers' perceptions of interactional justice. Interestingly, the researchers found that the relationship between these variables depended on the employees' organizational level. Specifically, the found the following:

■ High-level employees perceived that they were treated fairly regardless of the degree to which organizational decisions were centralized. This reflects the general tendency for higher-level workers (who tend to enjoy greater levels of participation as a whole) to feel positively about their work.

■ Among low-level employees, level of centralization made a very big difference. Specifically, the more low-level workers were allowed to participate in the making of decisions (i.e., the less decision making was considered centralized), the more fairly they believe they were treated. This reflects the tendency for lower-level employees to place a high value on participation because as a whole they are not inclined to have many opportunities to get involved in making organizational decisions.

These findings are interesting because they reveal something important that typically never gets taken into account when deciding to make an organization more centralized or more decentralized—that is, the nature of people's reactions. Because people who believe they are unfairly treated are inclined to respond in a variety of negative ways (as we discussed in Chapter 2), it would seem important for such factors to be given serious consideration when planning ways to design organizations. Although certain organizational designs may be well-suited to performing some kinds of tasks, we need to take into account the possibility that such benefits might be counteracted by the negative reactions of some individuals.

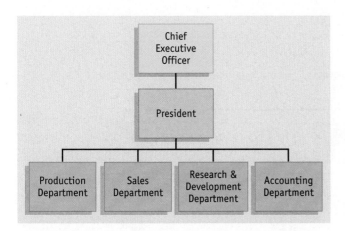

FIGURE 15.5

Functional Organization of a Typical Manufacturing Firm

Functional organizations are ones in which departments are formed on the basis of common foci, directions, or tasks performed. In the hypothetical manufacturing firm shown in this simplified organization chart, four typical departments are identified. In specific organizations, the actual functions may differ.

Naturally, as organizations grow and become more complex, additional departments are added or deleted as the need arises. As certain functions become centralized, resources can be saved by avoiding duplication of effort, resulting in a higher level of efficiency. Not only does this type of structure take advantage of *economies of scale* (by allowing employees performing the same jobs to share facilities and not duplicating functions), but it also allows individuals to specialize, thereby performing only those tasks at which they are most expert. The result is a highly skilled workforce, a direct benefit to the organization.

Partly offsetting these advantages, however, are several potential limitations. The most important of these stems from the fact that functional organizational structures encourage separate units to develop their own narrow perspectives and to lose sight of overall organizational goals. For example, in a manufacturing business, an engineer might see the company's problems in terms of the reliability of its products and lose sight of other key considerations, such as market trends, overseas competition, and so on. Such narrow-mindedness is the inevitable result of functional specialization—the downside of people seeing the company's operations through a narrow lens.

A related problem is that functional structures discourage innovation (see Chapter 14) because they channel individual efforts toward narrow, functional areas instead of encouraging coordination and cross-fertilization of ideas between areas. As a result, such organizations are slow to respond to the challenges and opportunities they face from the environment (such as the need for new products and services). In summary, although functional organizations certainly are logical in nature and have proven useful in many contexts, they are by no means the perfect way to departmentalize people.

Product Organizations: Departmentalization by Type of Output

Organizations—at least successful ones—do not stand still; they change constantly in size and scope. As they develop new products and seek new customers, they might find that a functional structure doesn't work as well as it once did. Manufacturing a wide range of products using a variety of different methods, for example, might put a strain on the manufacturing division of a functional organization. Similarly, keeping track of the varied tax requirements for different types of business (e.g., restaurants, farms, real estate, manufacturing) might pose quite a challenge for a single financial division of a company. In response to such strains, a **product organization** might be created. This type of departmentalization creates self-contained divisions, each of which is responsible for everything to do with a certain product or group of products. (For a look at the structure of a product organization, see Figure 15.6.)

product organization
The type of departmentalization based on the products (or product lines) produced.

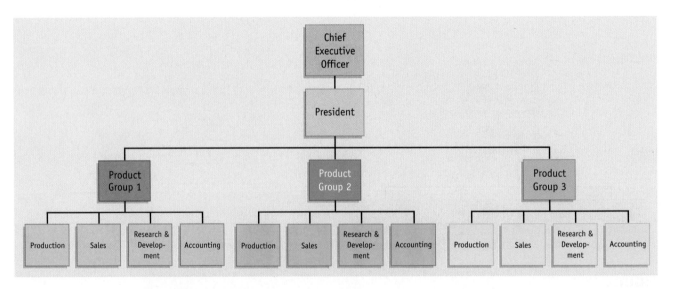

FIGURE 15.6

A Product Organization

In a *product organization,* separate units are established to handle different products or product lines. Each of these divisions contains all of the departments necessary for operating as an independent unit.

When organizations are departmentalized by products, separate divisions are established, each of which is devoted to a certain product or group of products. Each unit contains all the resources needed to develop, manufacture, and sell its particular goods. The organization is composed of separate divisions operating independently, the heads of which report to top management. Although some functions might be centralized within the parent company (e.g., human resources management or legal staff), on a day-to-day basis each division operates autonomously as a separate company or, as accountants call them, *cost centers* of their own.

Such arrangements allow companies to benefit from a marketing perspective, as many auto companies are aware. Take Toyota, for example. In 1989 it introduced its Lexus line of luxury cars. By creating a separate division, manufactured in separate plants and sold by a separate network of dealers, the company made its higher-priced cars look special and avoided making its less expensive cars look less appealing by putting them together with superior products on the same showroom floors. Applying the same reasoning to a completely different market, Toyota launched its Scion line in 2003 to appeal to younger car buyers.

Product organizations also have several drawbacks. The most obvious of these is the loss of economies of scale stemming from the duplication of various departments within operating units. For example, if each unit carries out its own research and development functions, the need for costly equipment, facilities, and personnel is multiplied. Another problem associated with product designs involves the organization's ability to attract and retain talented employees. Since each department within operating units is necessarily smaller than a single, combined one would be, opportunities for advancement and career development are limited. This, in turn, may pose a serious problem with respect to the long-term retention of talented employees. Finally, problems of coordination across product lines may arise. In fact, in extreme cases, actions taken by one operating division may have adverse effects on the outcomes of one or more others.

Hewlett-Packard provides a clear example of such problems.[16] For most of its history, Hewlett-Packard adopted a product design. It consisted of scores of small, largely autonomous divisions, each concerned with producing and selling certain products. As it grew—merging with Compaq in 2002—the company found itself in an increasingly untenable situation in which sales representatives from different divisions sometimes attempted to sell different lines of equipment, often to be used for the same basic purposes, to the same customers. To address this problem, top management reorganized the company into four sectors—what they call "business groups"—based on the markets they serve: the Enterprise Systems Group (which provides information technology hardware for businesses), the Imaging and Printing Group (which focuses on printers for businesses and consumers), the Personal Systems Group (which focuses on personal computers for home and office use), and HP Services (which offers information technology services).[17] In short, driven by market considerations, Hewlett-Packard switched from a traditional product organization to an internal structure driven by market considerations.

Matrix Organizations: Departmentalization by Both Function and Product

When the aerospace industry was first developing, the U.S. government demanded that a single manager in each company be assigned to each of its projects so that it was immediately clear who was responsible for the progress of each project. In response to this requirement, the large aerospace company at the time, TRW, established a "project leader" for each project, someone who shared authority with the leaders of the existing functional departments.[18] This temporary arrangement later evolved into what is called a **matrix organization,** the type of organization in which an employee is required to report to both a functional (or division) manager and the manager of a specific project (or product). In essence, they developed a complex type of structure that combines both the function and product forms of departmentalization.[19] To better understand matrix organizations, examine the partial organization chart shown in Figure 15.7.

Employees in matrix organizations have two bosses (or, more technically, they are under *dual authority*). One line of authority, shown by each vertical axis on Figure 15.7, is *functional*, managed by vice presidents in charge of various functional areas. The other, shown by each horizontal axis, is *product* (or it may be a specific project or temporary business), managed by specific individuals in charge of certain products (or projects).

In matrix designs, there are three major roles. First, there is the *top leader*—the individual who has authority over both lines (the one based on function and the one based on product or

matrix organization
The type of organization in which a product or project form is superimposed on a functional form.

FIGURE 15.7

A Typical Matrix Organization

In a *matrix organization,* a portion of which is depicted here, a product structure is superimposed on a basic functional structure. This results in a dual system of authority in which some managers report to two bosses— a project (or product) manager and a functional (departmental) manager.

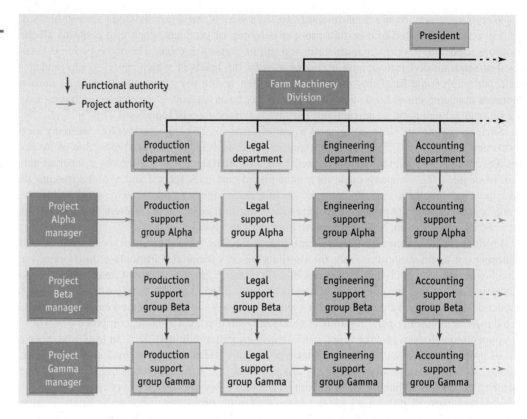

project). It is this individual's task to enhance coordination between functional and product managers and to maintain an appropriate balance of power between them. Second, there are the *matrix bosses*—people who head functional departments or specific projects. Since neither functional managers nor project managers have complete authority over subordinates, they must work together to ensure that their efforts mesh rather than conflict. In addition, they must agree on issues such as promotions and raises for specific people working under their joint authority. Finally, there are *two-boss managers*—people who must report to both product and functional managers and attempt to balance the demands of each.

Organizations are most likely to adopt matrix designs when they confront certain conditions. These include a complex and uncertain environment (one with frequent changes) and the need for economies of scale in the use of internal resources. Specifically, a matrix approach is often adopted by medium-size organizations with several product lines that do not possess sufficient resources to establish fully self-contained operating units. Under such conditions, a matrix design provides a useful compromise. Some companies that have adopted this structure, at least on a limited basis, are Liberty Mutual Insurance and Citibank (for another example, see Figure 15.8).[20]

DEGREE OF PERMANENCE. Not all organizations using the matrix structure do so on a permanent basis. Several partial, or temporary, types of matrix design have been identified.[21] First, the *temporary overlay* is a form of matrix structure in which projects are crossed with functions on a special, short-term basis. This is in contrast to a *permanent overlay,* in which project teams are kept going after each project is completed. Finally, there are *mature matrix organizations,* those in which both the functional lines and the product lines are permanent and equally strong within the organization.

With a matrix design that has been in effect for more than three decades, Dow Corning is an example of a mature matrix organization.[22] At this company, each functional representative reports to the leaders of his or her own department, while also contributing to the design and operation of the particular product line for which he or she is responsible. Because people working in this fashion have two bosses, they must have sufficient freedom to attain their objectives. As you might imagine, a fair amount of coordination, flexibility, openness, and trust is essential for such a program to work, suggesting that not everyone adapts well to such a system.

FIGURE 15.8

A Venti-Sized Matrix Organization

Starbucks uses a matrix organizational design in several places within the company. Separate managers are responsible for various functions (e.g., sales) and geographic divisions (e.g., Western region), requiring store managers to report to two different bosses.

ADVANTAGES AND DISADVANTAGES. Several key advantages offered by matrix designs may be identified.[23] First, they permit flexible use of an organization's human resources. Individuals within functional departments can be assigned to specific products or projects as the need arises and then return to their regular duties when this task is completed. Such arrangements allow project costs to be shared because it reduces the number of full-time employees required. Second, matrix designs offer organizations an efficient means of responding quickly to a changing, unstable environment. Third, such designs often enhance communication among managers; indeed, they literally force matrix bosses to discuss and agree on many matters.

Disadvantages of such designs include the frustration and stress faced by two-boss managers. By reporting to two different supervisors, there's a danger that one of the two authority systems (functional or project) will overwhelm the other, along with the consistently high levels of cooperation required from the people involved for the organization to succeed.[24] In situations where organizations must stretch their financial and human resources to meet challenges from the external environment or take advantage of new opportunities, however, matrix designs often can play a useful role.

Organizational Design: Coordinating the Structural Elements of Organizations

Earlier in this chapter we likened the structure of an organization to the structure of a house. Now we are prepared to extend that analogy for purposes of introducing the concept of *organizational design.* Just as a house is designed in a particular fashion by combining its structural elements in various ways, so too can an organization be designed by combining its basic elements in different ways. Accordingly, **organizational design** refers to the process of coordinating the structural elements of organizations in the most appropriate manner.

As you might imagine, this is no easy task. Although we might describe some options that sound neat and rational on the next few pages, in reality this is hardly ever the case. Even the most precisely designed organizations will face the need to change at one time or another, adjusting to the realities of technological changes, political pressures, accidents, and so on. Organizational designs also might be changed intentionally, as may occur when companies enter new businesses, when they merge with others, or simply just because they seek a higher level of operating efficiency. In recent decades, concerns about waste and inefficiency have driven many efforts at redesigning organizations, especially among U.S. government agencies, where the need to streamline has been considerable.

organizational design
The process of coordinating the structural elements of organizations in the most appropriate manner.

Our point is simple: Because organizations operate within a changing world, their own designs must be flexible as well. Those organizations that are either poorly designed or inflexible cannot survive. If you consider the large number of banks and airlines that have gone out of business in the last few years because of their inability to deal with rapid changes brought about by deregulation and a shifting economy, you'll get a good idea of the ultimate consequences of ineffective organizational design.

Classical and Neoclassical Approaches: The Quest for the One Best Design

The earliest theorists interested in organizational design did not operate out of awareness of the point we just made regarding the need for organizations to be flexible. Instead, they approached the task of designing organizations as a search for "the one best way." Although today we are more attuned to the need to adapt organizational designs to various economic and social conditions, theorists in the early and middle part of the twentieth century sought to establish the ideal form for all organizations under all conditions—that is, the universal design.

In Chapter 1, we described the efforts of the earliest organizational scholars such as Max Weber, Frederick Taylor, and Henri Fayol. These theorists believed that effective organizations were ones that had a formal hierarchy, a clear set of rules, specialization of labor, highly routine tasks, and a highly impersonal working environment. You may recall that Weber referred to this form as a *bureaucracy.* Such **classical organizational theory,** as it is known, has fallen into disfavor because it is insensitive to human needs and is not suited to a changing environment. Unfortunately, the "ideal" form of an organization, according to Weber, did not take into account the realities of the world within which it operates. Apparently, what is ideal is not necessarily what is realistic.

In response to these conditions, and with inspiration from the Hawthorne studies, the classical approach of the bureaucratic model gave way to more of a human relations orientation. Organizational scholars such as McGregor, Argyris, and Likert attempted to improve upon the classical model—which is why their approach is labeled **neoclassical organizational theory**. These theorists argued that economic effectiveness is not the only goal of an industrial organization, but also employee satisfaction.

Specifically, Douglas McGregor was an organizational theorist who objected to the rigid hierarchy imposed by Weber's bureaucratic form because it was based on negative assumptions about people—primarily that they lacked ambition and wouldn't work unless coerced (the *Theory X* approach described in Chapter 1).[25] In contrast, McGregor argued that people desire to achieve success by working and that they seek satisfaction by behaving responsibly (the *Theory Y* approach also described in Chapter 1). Another neoclassical theorist, Chris Argyris, expressed similar ideas.[26] Specifically, he argued that managerial domination of organizations blocks basic human needs to express oneself and to accomplish tasks successfully. This results in feelings of dissatisfaction, he argues, that encourage turnover and lead to poor performance.

An additional neoclassical theorist, Rensis Likert, shared these perspectives, arguing that organizational performance is enhanced not by rigidly controlling people's actions, but by actively promoting their feelings of self-worth and their importance to the organization.[27] An effective organization, Likert proposed, is one in which individuals would have a great opportunity to participate in making organizational decisions—what he called a *System 4* organization. Doing this, he claimed, would enhance employees' personal sense of worth, motivating them to succeed. Likert called the opposite type of organization *System 1*, the traditional form in which power is distributed in the hands of a few top managers who tell lower-ranking people what to do. (*System 2* and *System 3* are intermediate forms between the System 1 and System 4 extremes.)

The organizational design implications of these neoclassical approaches are clear. In contrast to the classical approach, calling for organizations to be designed with a rigid, tall hierarchy with a narrow span of control (allowing managers to maintain close supervision over their subordinates), the neoclassical approach argues for designing organizations with flat, hierarchical structures (minimizing managerial control over workers) and a high degree of decentralization (encouraging employees to make their own decisions). (For a summary of these differences, see Figure 15.9.) Indeed, such design features may well serve the underlying neoclassical philosophy.

Like the classical approach, the neoclassical approach also may be faulted on the grounds that it has been promoted as "the one best approach" to organizational design. Although the benefits of flat, decentralized designs may be many, to claim that this represents the universal,

classical organizational theory
Approaches assuming that there is a single best way to design organizations.

neoclassical organizational theory
An attempt to improve upon classical organizational theory, claiming that economic effectiveness is not the only goal of organizational structure, but also employee satisfaction.

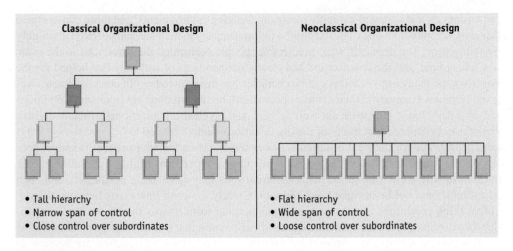

FIGURE 15.9

Classical Versus Neoclassical Designs: A Summary

The *classical approach* to designing organizations assumed that managers needed to have close control over their subordinates. As such, it called for designing organizations with tall hierarchies and narrow spans of control. In contrast, the *neoclassical approach* to designing organizations assumed that managers did not have to carefully monitor their workers. As such, it called for designing organizations with flat hierarchies and wide spans of control.

ideal form for all organizations would be naive. In response to this criticism, more contemporary approaches to organizational design have given up on finding the one best way in favor of finding designs that are most appropriate to various circumstances and contexts within which companies operate. We now turn to such approaches.

The Contingency Approach: Design According to Environmental Conditions

The idea that the best design for an organization depends on the nature of the environment in which it is operating lies at the heart of the modern **contingency approach to organizational design.** We use the term *contingency* here in a manner similar to the way we used it in our discussion of leadership (see Chapter 13). But rather than considering the best approach to leadership for a given situation, we now discuss the best way to design an organization given the environment within which it functions.

THE EXTERNAL ENVIRONMENT: ITS CONNECTION TO ORGANIZATIONAL DESIGN. It is widely accepted that the most appropriate type of organizational design depends on its *external environment*. In general, the external environment is the sum of all the forces impinging on an organization with which it must deal effectively if it is to survive.[28] These forces include general work conditions, such as the economy, geography, and national resources, as well as the specific task environment within which the company operates—notably, its competitors, customers, workforce, and suppliers.

Banks represent a good example. Financial institutions operate within an environment that is highly influenced by the economy (e.g., interest rates and government regulations) as well as by competition that makes customers sensitive to other banks' products (e.g., types of accounts), fees (e.g., charges for ATM transactions and overdrafts), and services (e.g., drive-through hours, sophistication of online banking services). Banking also is affected by the availability of trained personnel (e.g., individuals suitable for entry-level positions) in addition to the nature of suppliers providing goods and services (e.g., automated teller equipment, surveillance equipment, computer workstations). These have been the standard environmental factors affecting banks for many years, but since 2008, additional ones have emerged as the subprime mortgage crisis has made banks more sensitive than ever to the creditworthiness of the customers to whom they issue loans.

Although many features of the environment may be taken into account when considering how an organization should be designed, a classic investigation provides some useful guidance.[29] Scientists interviewed people in 20 industrial organizations in the United Kingdom to determine the relationship between managerial activities and the external environment. In so doing, they distinguished

contingency approach to organizational design
The contemporary approach that recognizes that no one approach to organizational design is best, but that the best design is the one that best fits with the existing environmental conditions.

between businesses that operated in highly *stable*, unchanging environments, and those that operated in highly *unstable*, turbulent ones. For example, a rayon company in their sample operated in a highly stable environment: The demands were predictable, people performed the same jobs in the same ways for a long time, and the organization had clearly defined lines of authority that helped get the job done. (Not too many organizations can be characterized this way today.) In contrast, a new electronics development company in their sample operated in a highly turbulent environment: Conditions changed on a daily basis, jobs were not well defined, and no clear organizational structure existed.

The researchers noted that many of the organizations studied tended to be described in ways that were appropriate for their environments. For example, when the environment is stable, people can do the same tasks repeatedly, allowing them to perform highly specialized jobs. However, in turbulent environments, many different jobs may have to be performed, and such specialization should not be designed into the jobs. Clearly, a strong link exists between the stability of working conditions and the proper organizational form. It was the researchers' conclusion that two different approaches to management existed and that these are largely based on the degree of stability within the external environment. These two approaches are known as *mechanistic organizations* and *organic organizations.* A **mechanistic organization** is one that is stable in nature, where people perform jobs that do not change much over the years. In contrast, an **organic organization** is one that changes frequently, making it likely that people will have to alter the nature of the jobs they perform over the years.

MECHANISTIC VERSUS ORGANIC ORGANIZATIONS: DESIGNS FOR STABLE VERSUS TURBULENT CONDITIONS. If you've ever worked at a McDonald's restaurant, you probably know how highly standardized each step of the most basic operations must be.[30] Boxes of fries are to be stored two inches from the wall in stacks one inch apart. Making those fries is another matter—one that requires 19 distinct steps, each clearly laid out in a training film shown to new employees. The process is the same, whether it's done in Melbourne, Florida, or Melbourne, Australia. This is an example of a highly mechanistic task. Organizations can be highly mechanistic when conditions don't change. Although the fast-food industry has changed a great deal in recent years (with the introduction of healthier choices, $1 menu items, gourmet coffee drinks, and the like), the making of fries at McDonald's has changed very little. The key to mechanization is the lack of change. If the environment doesn't change, a highly mechanistic organizational form can be very efficient.

An environment is considered stable whenever there is little or no unexpected change in product, market demands, or technology. Examples are hard to come by these days, but if you've ever seen bottles of Dickinson's witch hazel (used to cleanse the skin surrounding a wound) in drugstores, you've found one. Despite changing ownership on several occasions and relocating facilities (although remaining in eastern Connecticut), the company has been making the product following the same distillation process since 1866, suggesting that it certainly is operating in a relatively stable manufacturing environment.[31] As we described earlier, stability affords the luxury of high employee specialization. Without change, people easily can specialize. When change is inevitable, however, this is impractical.

Mechanistic organizations can be characterized in several additional ways (for a summary, see Table 15.3). Not only do mechanistic organizations allow for a high degree of specialization,

TABLE 15.3 Mechanistic Versus Organic Designs: A Summary

Mechanistic designs and *organic designs* differ along several key dimensions identified here. These represent extremes; organizations can be relatively organic, relatively mechanistic, or somewhere in between.

Dimension	Structure	
	Mechanistic	Organic
Stability	Change unlikely	Change likely
Specialization	Many specialists	Many generalists
Formal rules	Rigid rules	Considerable flexibility
Authority	Centralized, vested in a few top people	Decentralized, diffused throughout the organization

mechanistic organization
An internal organizational structure that is stable in nature, where people perform jobs that do not change much over the years.

organic organization
An internal organizational structure that changes frequently, making it likely that people will have to alter the nature of the jobs they perform over the years.

but they also impose many rules. Authority is vested in a few people located at the top of a hierarchy who give direct orders to their subordinates. Mechanistic organizational designs tend to be most effective under conditions in which the external environment is stable and unchanging.

Now, let's consider the other extreme by thinking about high-technology industries, such as those dedicated to telecommunications, aerospace, and biotechnology. Their environmental conditions are changing all the time. These industries are so prone to change that as soon as a new way of operating is introduced, it sometimes has to be altered. It isn't only technology, however, that makes an environment turbulent. Turbulence also can be high in industries in which adherence to rapidly changing regulations is essential. For example, times were turbulent in the nuclear power industry when governmental regulations dictated the introduction of many new standards that had to be followed; times also were turbulent in the hospital industry when new Medicaid legislation was passed. Today's renewed interest in further developing nuclear power capabilities and in completely rebuilding the health-care system in the United States already is beginning to make these industries more turbulent once again.

The pure organic form of organization may be characterized in several different ways (see Table 15.3). The degree of job specialization possible is very low; instead, a broad knowledge of many different jobs is required. Very little authority is exercised from the top. Rather, self-control is expected, and an emphasis is placed on coordination between peers. As a result, decisions tend to be made in a highly democratic, participative manner. Be aware that the mechanistic and organic types of organizational structure described here are ideal forms. The mechanistic–organic distinction should be thought of as opposite poles along a continuum rather than as completely distinct options for organization. Certainly, organizations can be relatively organic or relatively mechanistic compared with others, but may not be located at either extreme.

Finally, organizational effectiveness is related to the degree to which an organization's structure (mechanistic or organic) is matched to its environment (stable or turbulent). In a classic study, researchers evaluated four departments in a large company—two of which manufactured containers (a relatively stable environment at the time) and two of which dealt with communications research (a highly unstable one).[32] One department in each pair was evaluated as being more effective than the other. It was found that for the container manufacturing departments, the more effective unit was the one structured in a highly mechanistic form (roles and duties were clearly defined). In contrast, the more effective communications research department was structured in a highly organic fashion (roles and duties were vague). Additionally, the other, less effective departments were structured in the opposite manner (i.e., the less effective manufacturing department was organically structured, and the less effective research department was mechanistically structured; see Figure 15.10 on page 534).

Taken together, the results made it clear that departments were most effective when their organizational structures fit their environments. This question of "Which design is best under which conditions?" lies at the heart of the modern orientation—the contingency approach—to organizational structure. Rather than specifying *which* structure is best, the contingency approach specifies *when* each type of organizational design is most effective.

Mintzberg's Framework: Five Organizational Forms

Although the distinction between mechanistic and organic designs is important, it is not terribly specific with respect to exactly how organizations should be designed. Filling this void, however, is the work of contemporary organizational theorist Henry Mintzberg.[33] Specifically, Mintzberg claims that organizations are composed of five basic elements, or groups of individuals, any of which may predominate in an organization. The one that does will determine the most effective design in that situation. The five basic elements are as follows:

- *The* **operating core**: Employees who perform the basic work related to the organization's product or service. Examples include teachers (in schools) and chefs and waiters (in restaurants).
- *The* **strategic apex**: Top-level executives responsible for running the entire organization. Examples include the entrepreneur who runs her own small business, and the general manager of an automobile dealership.
- *The* **middle line**: Managers who transfer information between the strategic apex and the operating core. Examples include middle managers, such as regional sales managers (who

operating core
In Mintzberg's framework, employees who perform the basic work related to an organization's product or service.

strategic apex
In Mintzberg's framework, top-level executives responsible for running an entire organization.

middle line
In Mintzberg's framework, managers who transfer information between the strategic apex and the operating core. (See *strategic apex* and *operating core*.)

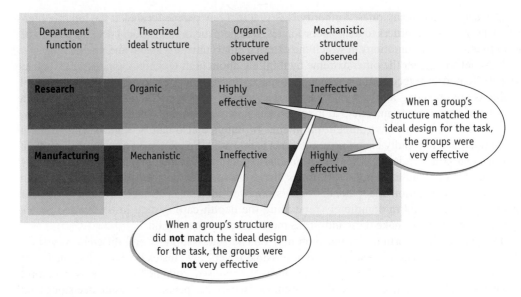

FIGURE 15.10

Matching Organizational Design and Industry: The Key to Effectiveness

In a classic study, researchers evaluated the performance of four departments in a large company. The most effective units were ones in which the way the group was structured (mechanistic or organic) matched the most appropriate form for the type of task performed (i.e., organic for research work and mechanistic for manufacturing work).

Source: Based on suggestions by Morse & Lorsch, 1970; see Note 32.

technostructure
In Mintzberg's framework, organizational specialists responsible for standardizing various aspects of an organization's activities.

support staff
In Mintzberg's framework, individuals who provide indirect support services to an organization.

connect top executives with the sales force) and the chair of an academic department in a college or university (an intermediary between the dean and the faculty).

■ *The* **technostructure:** Those specialists responsible for standardizing various aspects of the organization's activities. Examples include accountants, auditors, and computer systems analysts.

■ *The* **support staff:** Individuals who provide indirect support services to the organization. Examples include consultants on technical matters and corporate attorneys.

What organizational designs best fit under conditions in which each of these five groups dominate? Mintzberg has identified five specific designs: *simple structure, machine bureaucracy, professional bureaucracy,* the *divisionalized structure,* and the *adhocracy* (see summary in Table 15.4).

TABLE 15.4 Mintzberg's Five Organizational Forms: A Summary

Mintzberg has identified five distinct organizational designs, each of which is likely to occur in organizations in which certain groups are in power.

Design	Description	Dominant Group	Example
Simple structure	Simple, informal, authority centralized in a single person	Strategic apex	Small, entrepreneurial business
Machine bureaucracy	Highly complex, formal environment with clear lines of authority	Technostructure	Government office
Professional bureaucracy	Complex, decision-making authority is vested in professionals	Operating core	University
Divisional structure	Large, formal organizations with several separate divisions	Middle line	Multidivisional business, such as General Motors
Adhocracy	Simple, informal, with decentralized authority	Support staff	Software development firm

Source: Based on suggestions by Mintzberg, 1983, 2009; see Note 33.

SIMPLE STRUCTURE. Imagine that you open an antique shop and hire a few people to help you out in the store. You have a small, informal organization in which there is a single individual with ultimate power. There is little in the way of specialization or formalization, and the overall structure is organic in nature. The hierarchy is quite flat, and all decision-making power is vested in a single individual—you. An organization so described, simple in nature, with the power residing at the strategic apex, is referred to by Mintzberg as having a **simple structure.**

As you might imagine, organizations with simple structure can respond quickly to the environment and be very flexible. For example, the chef-owner of a small, independent restaurant can change the menu to suit the various tastes of customers whenever needed, without first consulting anyone else. The downside to this, however, is that the success or failure of the entire enterprise is dependent on the wisdom and health of the individual in charge. Not surprisingly, organizations with simple structure are risky ventures.

MACHINE BUREAUCRACY. If you've ever worked for your state's department of motor vehicles, you probably found it to be a very large place, with numerous rules and procedures for employees to follow. The work is highly specialized (e.g., one person gives the vision tests, and another completes the registration forms), and decision making is concentrated at the top (e.g., you need to get permission from your supervisor to do anything other than exactly what's expected). This type of work environment is highly stable and does not have to change. An organization so characterized, where power resides with the technostructure, is referred to as a **machine bureaucracy.** Although machine bureaucracies can be highly efficient at performing standardized tasks, they tend to be dehumanizing and very boring for the employees.

PROFESSIONAL BUREAUCRACY. Suppose you are a doctor working at a large city hospital. You are a highly trained specialist with considerable expertise in your field. You don't need to check with anyone else before authorizing a certain medical test or treatment for your patient; you make the decisions as they are needed, when they are needed. At the same time, the environment is highly formal (e.g., there are lots of rules and regulations for you to follow). Of course, you do not work alone; you also require the services of other highly qualified professionals such as nurses and laboratory technicians. Organizations of this type—and these include universities, libraries, and consulting firms as well as hospitals—maintain power with the operating core, and are called **professional bureaucracies.** Such organizations can be highly effective because they allow employees to practice those skills for which they are best qualified. However, sometimes specialists become so overly narrow that they fail to see the "big picture," leading to errors and potential conflict between employees.

DIVISIONAL STRUCTURE. When you think of large organizations, such as General Motors, DuPont, Xerox, and IBM, the image that comes to mind is probably closest to what Mintzberg describes as **divisional structure.** Such organizations consist of a set of autonomous units coordinated by a central headquarters (i.e., they rely on departmental structure based on products, as described on pages 526–527). In such organizations, because the divisions are autonomous (e.g., a General Motors employee at Cadillac does not have to consult with another at Chevrolet to do his or her job), division managers (the *middle line* part of Mintzberg's basic elements) have considerable control. Such designs preclude the need for top-level executives to think about the day-to-day operations of their companies and free them to concentrate on larger scale, strategic decisions. At the same time, companies organized into separate divisions frequently tend to have high duplication of effort (e.g., separate order processing units for each division). Having operated as separate divisions for about a century, General Motors is considered the classic example of divisional structure.[34] Although the company has undergone significant periods of growth and decline, it has maintained much of its divisional structure (see Table 15.5).

ADHOCRACY. After graduating from college, where you spent years learning how to program computers, you take a job at a small software company. Compared to your friends who found positions at large accounting firms, your professional life is much less formal. You work as a member of a team developing a new time-management software product. There are no rules, and schedules are made to be broken. You all work together, and although there is someone who is "officially" in charge, you'd never know it. Using Mintzberg's framework, you work for an **adhocracy**—an organization in which power resides with the support staff. Essentially, this is the epitome of the

simple structure
An organization characterized as being small and informal, with a single powerful individual, often the founding entrepreneur, who is in charge of everything.

machine bureaucracy
An organizational form in which work is highly specialized, decision making is concentrated at the top, and the work environment is not prone to change (e.g., a government office).

professional bureaucracy
Organizations (e.g., hospitals and universities) in which there are lots of rules to follow, but employees are highly skilled and free to make decisions on their own.

divisional structure
The form used by many large organizations, in which separate autonomous units are created to deal with entire product lines, freeing top management to focus on larger scale, strategic decisions.

adhocracy
A highly informal, organic organization in which specialists work in teams, coordinating with each other on various projects (e.g., many software development companies).

TABLE 15.5 GM Reorganization: 2007–Present

General Motors (GM) has maintained a divisional structure for more than a century. In response to mounting financial losses in 2008, however, GM dropped some product lines and organized others into four "sales channels." The following year, as part of its bankruptcy reorganization plan, some brands were sold or dismantled, leaving only four divisions. Although GM has maintained its potentially inefficient, decentralized divisional structure, it is hopeful that by devoting its more limited resources into divisions representing fewer, more successful brands, it will be able to regain its dominance in the auto business. (Note that this information is limited to automotive operations for brands sold in the United States. The overall organizational design of GM is far more complex.)

"Old GM"	"Streamlined GM"	"New GM"
Through 2007	2008	2009–present (post-bankruptcy)
• 9 divisions	• 7 divisions in 4 channels	• 4 divisions
• Chevrolet	*Chevrolet Channel*	• Chevrolet
	• Chevrolet	
• Pontiac	*Buick-Pontiac Channel*	
	• Pontiac	• Buick
• Buick	• Buick	
• Cadillac	*Premium Channel*	• Cadillac
	• Cadillac	
• Hummer	• Hummer	
• Saab	• Saab	
• Oldsmobile		
• Saturn	*Saturn Channel*	
	• Saturn	
• GMC		• GMC

organic structure identified earlier. Specialists coordinate with each other not because of their shared functions (e.g., accounting, manufacturing), but as members of teams working on specific projects.

The primary benefit of the adhocracy is that it fosters innovation. Some large companies, such as Johnson & Johnson (J&J), nest within their formal divisional structures units that operate as adhocracies. In the case of J&J, it's the New Products Division, a unit that has been churning out an average of 40 products per year.[35] As in the case of all other designs, there are disadvantages. In this case, the most serious limitations are their high levels of inefficiency (they are the opposite of machine bureaucracies in this regard) and their considerable potential for disruptive conflict (see Chapter 11).

The Vertically Integrated Organization

For many years, Ford has owned its own steel mills and its own financing company. The steel mills have pre-supplied customers as Ford purchases the steel to manufacture cars. The financing company also has built-in business as Ford dealers rely on it to finance purchases for their customers. Organizations that own their own suppliers and/or their own customers who purchase their products are said to be relying on **vertical integration.** By contrast, other companies only assemble products that they buy from outside suppliers and sell to customers. Companies of this type are not vertically integrated. Dell presents a good example because it purchases computer components from other companies and assembles them into finished computers for customers who have ordered them configured in certain ways. For a comparison between vertically integrated companies and non–vertically integrated companies, see Figure 15.11.

The fact that companies don't have to worry about attracting customers would appear to be a big advantage for vertical integration. Although this is true, there also are challenges associated with vertical integration.[36] For one, they tend to find it difficult to balance their resources in the most effective manner, providing exactly enough resources to be used in manufacturing and the right number of finished products to be sold. A second drawback of vertical integration comes from the fact that because the company's suppliers are internal, they don't face competition to

vertical integration
The practice in which companies own their own suppliers and/or their own customers who purchase their products from them.

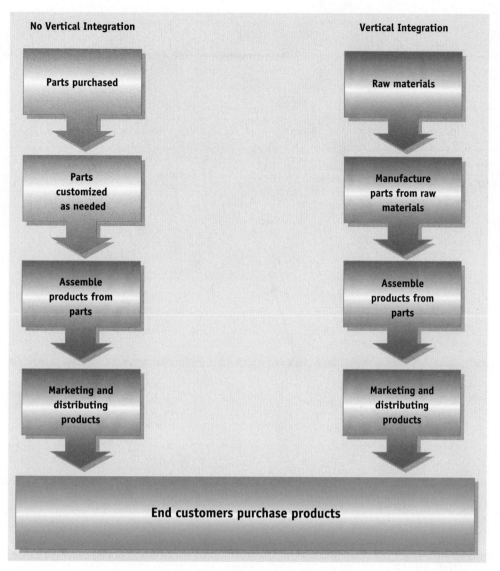

No Vertical Integration

Parts purchased

Parts customized as needed

Assemble products from parts

Marketing and distributing products

Vertical Integration

Raw materials

Manufacture parts from raw materials

Assemble products from parts

Marketing and distributing products

End customers purchase products

FIGURE 15.11

The Vertically Integrated Organization

A vertically integrated organization, like the one summarized on the right, owns the suppliers and/or the customers with whom it does business (the blue boxes in this diagram). It even may own the sources of the raw materials it requires. Because it is involved only in the assembly and selling products, the organization summarized on the left is not considered vertically integrated.

keep their prices down, potentially resulting in higher costs for the company. Third, because the various parts of the organization are so tightly interconnected, it is very difficult for the company to respond to changes, such as developing new products. Because this would involve changes in supplies, manufacturing, and sales, the vertically integrated company faces more challenges than its non–vertically integrated counterpart when it comes to making such changes.

Team-Based Organizations

The organizational designs we have described thus far have been around for a long time, and because they are so well known and often so effective, they are not likely to fade away anytime soon. However, based on the growing popularity of work teams (see Chapter 8), it's not surprising that many of today's organizations rely on teams as their basic organizing structure. These are referred to *team-based organizations*. Specifically, **team-based organizations** are organizations in which autonomous work teams are organized in parallel fashion such that each performs many different steps in the work process.

The underlying idea is simple. Instead of organizing jobs in the traditional, hierarchical fashion by having a long chain of groups or individuals perform parts of a task (e.g., one group that sells the advertising job, another that plans the ad campaign, and yet another that produces the ads), team-based organizations have flattened hierarchies. Essentially, this approach calls for designing organizations around *processes* instead of tasks (see Figure 15.12).[37] For example, members of an advertising team may combine their different skills and expertise and become responsible for all aspects of advertising.

team-based organizations
Organizations in which autonomous work teams are organized in parallel fashion such that each performs many different steps in the work process.

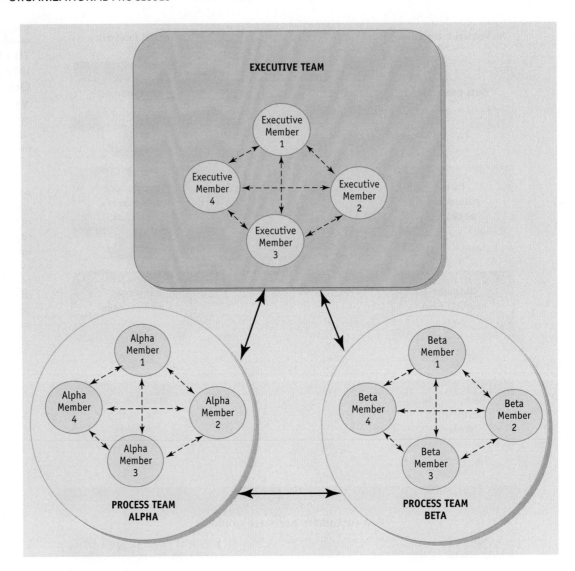

FIGURE 15.12

Team-Based Organizations

Instead of arranging individuals and tasks in hierarchical fashion, *team-based organizations* are designed with respect to the processes performed by various teams and the interconnections between them.

Source: Adapted from Mohrman et al., 1997; see Note 37.

A Strategic Approach to Designing Organizations

A major reason why organizational structure and design are so important is that they contribute to a company's success. Specifically, it has been suggested that for an organization to be able to satisfy its long-term plans and objectives (i.e., to implement its *strategy* successfully), various factors have to be taken into account. In other words, structure is what makes it possible to implement strategy successfully—or, as one scientist succinctly put it, "structure follows strategy."[38]

The conditions that must be met are referred to as *contingency factors* because the organization's ultimate success in implementing its strategies is contingent upon meeting these conditions. These factors, in turn, influence the nature of the *qualities of the tasks* that people are required to perform. And this requires using particular *coordination mechanisms*. Finally, this is made possible by certain features of organizational structure and design. Figure 15.13 summarizes the processes through which strategy dictates organizational structure.[39] Please refer to this as we highlight these processes in this section of the chapter. At this point, the chain of events must appear quite abstract, but as we begin explaining it, things will become clear.

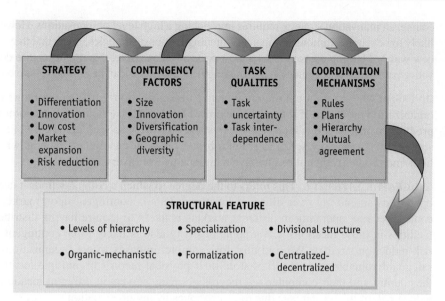

FIGURE 15.13

Structure Follows Strategy: An Overview

An organization's strategy is facilitated by various features of organizational structure and design, as summarized here.

Source: Based on suggestions by Donaldson, 2009; see Note 39.

Strategy

An organization's **strategy** refers to the particular objectives it has for the future and how it plans to focus its business activities so as to create and sustain value for the organization. Businesses can have a variety of different strategies, of course, but some of the major ones are as follows.

strategy
Particular objectives a company has for the future and how it plans to focus its business activities so as to create and sustain value.

- *Differentiation strategy.* The company decides to market different products to different groups of customers. For example, General Motors sells a wide range of cars—from inexpensive subcompacts to expensive luxury cars.
- *Innovation strategy.* An organization selects its particular approach to introducing innovations. For example, it can resolve to be the first to introduce major new developments to the market (a first-mover strategy), such as has been Sony's and Toshiba's approaches to LCD televisions. At the other extreme, a company might prefer to be less innovative by manufacturing a product that already is known to be successful, make some incremental changes in it, and sell it more cheaply (which it can do because it has spent less on research and development). This is known as a late-mover strategy, and has been used in the consumer television business by Westinghouse.
- *Low-cost strategy.* As the name implies, this is a plan in which a business attempts to gain a large share of a market by undercutting the prices of its competitors. Vizio has done just this with its LCD television, becoming the top-selling brand since 2007.
- *Market expansion strategy.* The organization seeks new opportunities to increase sales by expanding into new markets, such as ones in other geographic areas. For many years, companies such as Ford and Coca-Cola have been aggressive in their efforts to open up large new markets, such as China.
- *Risk reduction strategy.* A strategy in which organizations focus on ways of minimizing losses. For example, many companies have been implementing risk reduction strategies by using plans to keep their data and company records safe in the event of natural disasters or terrorist attacks.

Contingency Factors

When an organization adopts a particular strategy, it affects them in various ways. These are called *contingency factors* because they depend upon the particular strategy adopted.

SIZE. This refers to the volume of work performed by an organization. In the case of a manufacturing business (e.g., a cosmetics company), it might be the number of items produced; in the case of a service business (e.g., a house-cleaning service), it might be the number of customers served. As related to strategy, size would have to increase among companies adopting market expansion strategies.

INNOVATION. When we refer to innovation as a contingency factor, we are referencing the introduction of new processes in an organization within a particular period of time. By definition, of course, an innovation strategy requires introducing a high level of innovations. However, this is also likely to be required among companies pursuing low-cost strategies, given that they have to develop new ways of cutting costs to reduce their prices. For example, this might require developing innovative packaging that reduces space or weight so that items can be shipped less expensively.

DIVERSIFICATION. As a contingency factor, diversification refers to the range of products an organization produces. If they produce only a few products, then diversification is low, but if it produces many, then it is high. The clearest example may be seen in the case of a differentiation strategy. If a company seeks to reach a broad range of customers, such as with low-end and high-end products, then it has to have a high degree of diversification.

GEOGRAPHIC DIVERSITY. This refers to the degree to which a company finds it necessary to have operations spread out over different locations. This is contingent upon market expansion, of course, because operating in different markets is likely to require having distribution and sales facilities in those locations. Geographic diversity also is likely to be contingent upon having a risk reduction strategy. We find this, for example, in cases where organizations attempting to safeguard valuable company files store their physical records in multiple locations throughout the country and their computerized records on many servers in different locations. Such efforts reduce risk of loss or damage due to catastrophes in any one location.

Task Qualities and Coordination Mechanisms

Next, we focus on the characteristics of tasks that are affected by the contingencies to which we just referred. Two particular task qualities are of interest here—*task uncertainty* and *task interdependence*.

TASK UNCERTAINTY. This refers to the degree of predictability that performing a task a particular way will result in completing it successfully. The higher the uncertainty, the less predictable are the results. The degree of uncertainty encountered in any situation suggests that particular **coordination mechanisms** be used. These are different ways of governing how things get done in an organization. Four different coordination mechanisms may be identified. We now identify each of these and specify how they should be used under different levels of uncertainty. For a summary, see Figure 15.14.[40]

coordination mechanisms
Different ways of governing how things get done in an organization.

- *Govern by rules.* These are specifications regarding what is supposed to occur under certain conditions. For example, a rule might be in place stipulating that an employee who scores below a certain level on a proficiency test be retrained. Rules should be used whenever the tasks being performed are low in uncertainty. Under these conditions, it's so clear what needs to be done to succeed that it can be specified in advance in the form of rules.
- *Govern by plans.* This refers to schedules specifying who will do what, and when. Plans are particularly useful when uncertainty is moderately low. Under these conditions, you

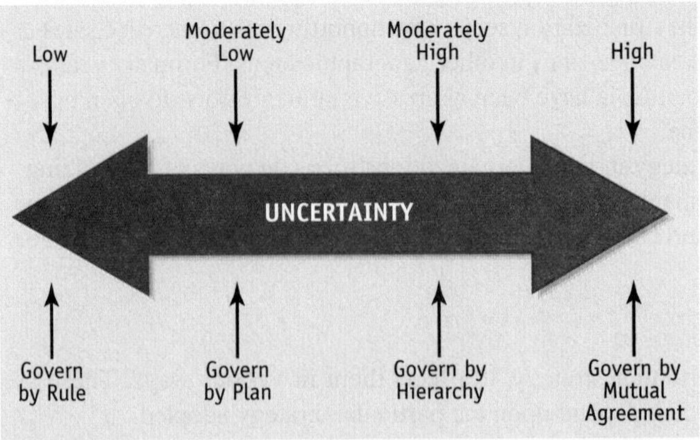

FIGURE 15.14

Uncertainty and Coordination Mechanisms

As summarized here, different coordination mechanisms are most effective for use under different conditions of uncertainty.

Source: Based on suggestions by Donaldson, 2009; see Note 39.

have a fairly good sense of how things will be. They're not so clear that actions can be specified in advance in the form of rules, but they are sufficiently certain to make it possible for benefits to result from establishing plans and following them.

- *Govern by hierarchy.* Hierarchies are used in organizations to specify in advance exactly who is responsible for directing the activities of specific others. Hierarchies are useful when uncertainty is moderately high because they allow for decisions to be overseen by persons who have more formal authority and, presumably, higher expertise.
- *Govern by mutual agreement.* This refers to having individuals decide among themselves exactly what each will do. Mutual agreement is especially useful when uncertainty is very high. The main reason for this is that it allows multiple people to contribute perspectives to the task at hand, enhancing expertise that can be brought to the situation. And the more light that is shed on the problem by information from various sources, the greater is the opportunity to reduce the effective level of uncertainty.

TASK INTERDEPENDENCE. This refers to the degree to which two or more tasks are connected to one another. The greater the degree of connection, the more closely they have to be coordinated. Say, for example, that an electronics company has adopted an innovation strategy. In keeping with this, its engineers have developed a revolutionary new product, the "Thought Writer," a device that sends someone's thoughts directly to a PC. Small sensors inside a hat (the "thinking cap") make contact with the skull, through which brain waves are picked up and sent wirelessly to a PC, where they are transformed into language recognized by a word processing program. You now have a computer file that reveals your thoughts. You can dictate in silence or, better yet (maybe), literally "gather your thoughts" so you can review them later. It also may have scores of other uses that are too scary to imagine. Prototypes exist, and now the engineers who developed it have to coordinate their efforts with experts in manufacturing to ensure that it can be mass produced and with people from the marketing department who have to determine how the device can be used, who would want it, and how to sell it to them. The stakes are high because, if these organizational units can carefully coordinate their efforts, they have a good chance of bringing a revolutionary new product to market, bringing fame and fortune to the company. In this case, a high degree of interdependence exists.

Structural or Design Feature

We've now reached the part of the process where specific structural features or organizational designs are indicated. Let's illustrate this by continuing our example. Having established that a high degree of task interdependence required, how should the organization be structured so as to facilitate this coordination? In this case, coordination through a hierarchy is best. Rules and plans are not at all possible given the highly novel nature of the product. And, mutual agreements are unlikely to work here because there are so many aspects of the task that some parts can be overlooked. So, a hierarchy would be most effective in this case because it ensures that individuals from specific areas of the company will be able to attend to their specialized parts of the challenge.

However, to ensure success in this situation the organization should not only be hierarchical in nature, but the particular units involved (manufacturing, marketing, and research and development, in this case) should be close to one another in the hierarchy, as well. As a general rule, if one unit is much higher or lower than another, then coordination is made difficult. In addition, coordination is easier for units within the same division. In a typical functional organization, this isn't the case because people from R&D, marketing, and manufacturing are unlikely to be in touch with one another. So, in the case we've been describing, what particular divisional design would be most effective? It'd be a product organization, such as shown in Figure 15.6 (page 526). In this case, the individuals involved in coordinating their efforts would be close to one another both vertically (being at the same level) and laterally (being within the same product group). In this case, coordination would be facilitated and the chances of success would be enhanced. (For some additional considerations regarding the use of organizational design for strategic purposes in today's organizations, see the OB in Practice section on page 542.)

Although space does not allow us to examine all the remaining possibilities, we can identify some of the key connections in the form of principles linking contingency factors to the various characteristics of organizational structure and design that we identified earlier in this chapter. For a summary of these, see Table 15.6.[41]

TABLE 15.6 Connections Between Contingency Factors and Organizational Structure

The effectiveness of organizational strategies requires meeting certain conditions known as *contingency factors*. These are facilitated when various structural characteristics are incorporated into organizational designs. Some of the best-established connections between contingency factors and structural features are identified here.

Contingency Factor	Strategies Are Most Effective When . . .
Size is large.	• Specialization of labor is high.
	• Hierarchy is tall.
	• Decision making is decentralized.
Innovation rate is great.	• Organic structure is used.
Diversification is high.	• Many divisions are used.
	• Decision making is decentralized.
Geographic diversity is high.	• Divisions are based on geographic locations.

Source: Based on suggestions by Donaldson, 2009; see Note 39.

OB in Practice

Organizational Design Strategies for the Information Age

Most of what we know about organizational design has been based on conditions that existed in the middle of the twentieth century. That was an era in which the essential nature of work was mechanical and physical. Designing organizations effectively required a sharp focus on hierarchy and coordination. In today's digital era, however, work is based primarily on the flow of information. This also requires attention to hierarchy and coordination, of course, but not in the same way. Today, it's not just possible, but necessary, to use hierarchies and coordination more efficiently than ever before.[42] This can be accomplished in several ways.

Promote collaboration by measuring "assists"

On the court, basketball players are measured not only by the number of baskets they score but also by the number of "assists" they make—that is, getting the ball to someone else on the team who takes a shot at the basket. It has been suggested that employees in all organizations be measured in this way as well. The idea is that collaboration can be promoted by creating a sense of mutual self-interest, making people accountable not only for their own performance but also for that of others. Enhancing collaboration in this fashion is an effective way of building coordination into the system. And given the team-oriented nature of today's workplaces, this is more important than ever (recall our discussion of team-based pay in Chapter 8).

Streamline the vertical hierarchy

The legacy of the twentieth century is such that many organizations have inherited hierarchies that are too tall and overly complex, resulting in inefficiencies. Many talented employees are still relying on their superiors to make decisions for them even though they may be capable of making them themselves.

Employees also may be better positioned to do so because they are closer to the work itself. Of course, pushing decision making down the hierarchy requires that the decision makers be held accountable for the outcomes of their decisions. After all, one thing that hasn't changed over the years is that people still do the things for which they are rewarded and refrain from doing the things for which they are punished (this is a basic principle of learning we discussed in Chapter 3).

Encourage informal networks for sharing ideas

Instead of relying on work getting done only by individuals who are assigned formally to projects, it's been found useful in contemporary organizations to allow employees to venture outside their formal hierarchies and allow them to create **communities of practice**—that is, informal networks of professionals and managers who share common interests, such as those based on similar skills (recall our discussion of informal networks in Chapter 9). Such arrangements encourage people to collaborate with others who have a mutual interest in the project. This involves creating within an organization a *talent marketplace* of sorts in which people are able to attract one another on the basis of their capacities to contribute to the success of interesting projects.

communities of practice
Informal networks of professionals and managers who share common interests, such as those based on similar skills.

Together, these suggestions represent ways of lifting barriers that all too often keep talented people from doing everything possible to contribute their best to their organizations. Although these recommendations might not have been advisable when most work was routine and performed in factories, this is much less prevalent today. The organizational structures required for doing today's information-based work require some adjustment. The good news is that this takes into account principles of OB already identified in this book.

Interorganizational Designs: Joining Multiple Organizations

All the organizational designs we have examined thus far have concentrated on the arrangement of units within one organization—what may be termed **intraorganizational designs.** However, sometimes parts of different organizations come together to operate jointly, coordinating efforts on projects. When this is the case, businesses must create **interorganizational designs,** plans by which two or more organizations come together. (For a tragic example of what occurs when such coordination fails to occur, see Figure 15.15.[43]) We now examine several such designs.

Boundaryless Organizations: Eliminating Walls

Often, when today's organizations join forces, it's done in ways that give them considerable flexibility, allowing them to respond to rapidly changing conditions in the business environment. Keenly aware of the need for successful organizations to turn on a dime, Jack Welch, the former CEO of General Electric, introduced the **boundaryless organization.** This refers to a type of organization in which chains of command are eliminated, spans of control are unlimited, and rigid departments give way to empowered teams. The idea is that replacing rigid distinctions between people with roles that are fluid, intentionally ambiguous, and ill-defined, makes it much easier to be flexible. Welch's vision was that GE would operate like a family grocery store (albeit a $60 billion one)—one in which barriers that separate employees from one another would be eliminated.[44]

This part of Welch's idea focuses on breaking down boundaries within organizations. However, he also advocated eliminating external boundaries so that organizations could join forces quickly and as needed to take advantage of opportunities. With this in mind, two popular forms of externally oriented boundaryless organizations have emerged.[45] These are the following:

- **Modular (networked) organizations.** These are businesses that outsource noncore functions to other companies while focusing on their own core business. In other words,

intraorganizational designs
Designs that concentrate on the arrangement of units within one organization.

interorganizational designs
Plans by which two or more organizations come together.

boundaryless organization
An organization in which chains of command are eliminated, spans of control are unlimited, and rigid departments give way to empowered teams.

modular (networked) organizations
Businesses that outsource noncore functions to other companies while focusing on their own core business.

UPI/A. J. Sisco/Newscom.

FIGURE 15.15

Poor Interorganizational Coordination Makes a Bad Situation Worse

On April 20, 2010, BP's oil rig Deepwater Horizon exploded in the Gulf of Mexico, killing 11 workers. Adding to this tragedy, the resulting oil leak created the worst environmental disaster in U.S. History, causing untold loss of wildlife, habitat damage, and severe setbacks to the livelihoods of the region's fisherman. Making matters worse, although various governmental and private agencies arrived on the shores of Louisiana to help in the cleanup, a lack of communication between them hampered their efforts.

they have a central hub and are surrounded by networks of outside specialists that can be added or subtracted as needed.[46] Reebok is a good example. It focuses on designing and marketing athletic shoes and apparel but outsources all production to companies in Taiwan and South Korea that specialize in manufacturing. This allows the company to concentrate on what it does best—tapping the changing tastes of its customers.[47]

■ **Virtual organizations.** These are organizations composed of a continually evolving network of companies linked together to share skills, costs, and access to markets. They form a partnership to capitalize on their existing talents, pursuing common objectives. In most cases, after these objectives have been met, the organizations disband.[48] This arrangement allows each participating company to contribute only its core competencies (i.e., its areas of greatest strength), resulting in products that no one company could have created on its own. Corning, the giant glass and ceramics manufacturer, is a good example of a company that builds upon itself by developing partnerships with other companies (including Siemens, the German electronics firm, and Vitro, the largest glass manufacturer from Mexico). In fact, Corning officials see their company not as a single entity, but as "a network of organizations."[49]

virtual organizations
Organizations composed of a continually evolving network of companies linked together to share skills, costs, and access to markets. They form a partnership to capitalize on their existing talents, pursuing common objectives.

Conglomerates: Diversified "Megacorporations"

When an organization diversifies by adding an entirely unrelated business or product to its organizational design, it may be said to have formed a **conglomerate.** Some of the world's largest conglomerates may be found in Asia. For example, in Korea, companies such as Samsung and Hyundai produce home electronics, automobiles, textiles, and chemicals in large, unified conglomerates known as *chaebols*.[50] These are all separate companies overseen by leaders in the same parent company. In Japan, the same type of arrangement is known as a *keiretsu*.[51] A good example of a keiretsu is the Matsushita Group.[52] This enormous conglomerate consists of a bank (Asahi Bank), a consumer electronics company (Panasonic), and several insurance companies (e.g., Sumitomo Life, Nippon Life). These examples are not meant to suggest that conglomerates are unique to Asia. Indeed, many large U.S.-based corporations, such as IBM and Tenneco, also are conglomerates.

conglomerate
A form of organizational diversification in which an organization (usually a very large, multinational one) adds an entirely unrelated business or product to its organizational design.

Companies form conglomerates for several reasons. First, as an independent business, the parent company can enjoy the benefits of diversification. Thus, as one industry languishes, another may excel, allowing for a stable economic outlook for the parent company. In addition, conglomerates may provide built-in markets and access to supplies, since companies typically support other organizations within the conglomerate. For example, General Motors' cars and trucks are fitted with Delco radios, and Ford cars and trucks have engines with Autolite spark plugs, separate companies that are owned by their respective parent companies. In this manner conglomerates can benefit by providing a network of companies that are dependent on each other for products and services, thereby creating considerable advantages.

Strategic Alliances: Joining Forces for Mutual Benefit

A **strategic alliance** is a type of organizational design in which two or more separate firms join their competitive capabilities to operate a specific business. The goal of a strategic alliance is to provide benefits to each individual organization that could not be attained if they operated separately. They are low-risk ways of diversifying (adding new business operations) and entering new markets. Some companies, such as GE and Ford, have strategic alliances with many others. Although some alliances last only a short time, others have remained in existence for well over 30 years and are still going strong.[53]

strategic alliance
A type of organizational design in which two or more separate companies combine forces to develop and operate a specific business. (See *mutual service consortia, joint ventures,* and *value-chain partnerships.*)

THE CONTINUUM OF ALLIANCES. A study of 37 strategic alliances from throughout the world identified three types of cooperative arrangements between organizations.[54] These may be arranged along a continuum from those alliances that are weak and distant, at one end, to those that are strong and close, at the other end (see Figure 15.16).

At the weak end of the continuum are strategic alliances known as **mutual service consortia.** These are arrangements between two similar companies from the same or similar industries to pool their resources to receive a benefit that would be too difficult or expensive for either to obtain alone. Often, the focus is some high-tech capacity, such as an expensive piece of diagnostic equipment that might be shared by two or more small, rural hospitals (e.g., a magnetic resonance imaging, or MRI unit).

mutual service consortia
A type of strategic alliance in which two similar companies from the same or similar industries pool their resources to receive a benefit that would be too difficult or expensive for either to obtain alone.

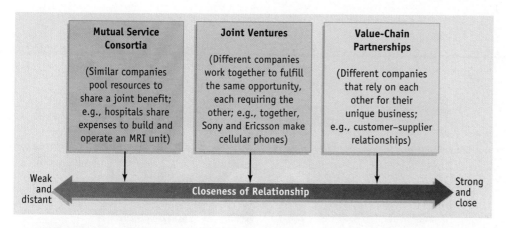

FIGURE 15.16

Strategic Alliances: A Continuum of Interorganizational Relationships

The three types of strategic alliances identified here may be distinguished with respect to their location along a continuum ranging from weak and distant to strong and close.

Source: Based on suggestions by Kanter, 1994; see Note 53.

At the opposite end of the scale are the strongest and closest type of collaborations, referred to as **value-chain partnerships.** These are alliances between companies in different industries that have complementary capabilities. Customer–supplier relationships are a prime example. In such arrangements one company buys necessary goods and services from another so that it can do business. Because each company greatly depends on the other, each party's commitment to their mutual relationship is high. As noted earlier, Toyota has a vast network of hundreds of suppliers with whom it regularly does business. The relationship between Toyota and these various companies represent value-chain partnerships.

Between these two extremes are **joint ventures.** These are arrangements, either temporary or permanent, in which companies work together to fulfill opportunities that require the capabilities of the other. For example, two companies might enter into a joint venture if one has a valuable technology and the other has the marketing knowledge to help transform that technology into a viable commercial product.

Joint ventures have been especially popular between organizations from different nations. One such joint venture with which you are probably familiar is Sony Ericsson, a joint venture created in 2001 to make cellular phones. This company combined the consumer electronics expertise of the Japanese company, Sony, with telecommunications expertise of the Swedish company, Ericsson. Joint ventures between international partners have been particularly popular in the oil and gas industry. For example, over the years Royal Dutch Shell has been involved in quite a few joint ventures with foreign partners. In most cases, companies from different nations form joint ventures voluntarily. However, in some cases, companies that wish to enter markets in another country—China, in particular—discover that they are required to do so by way of finding joint venture partners in those countries (for an example, see Figure 15.17). (For an overview of the challenges associated with forming joint ventures with Chinese firms, see the Today's Diverse and Global Organizations section on page 547.)

STRATEGIC ALLIANCES IN THE GLOBAL ECONOMY. It is not just joint ventures but strategic alliances in general that have become popular between companies from different nations. In particular, strategic alliances have been popular between companies in established nations and those with transforming economies (such as China, India, and eastern Europe). This allows companies from richer nations to gain entry into the markets of other countries.[55] Such arrangements also may allow for an exchange of technology and manufacturing services. For example, over the years, Korea's Daewoo has received technical information and has been paid to manufacture automobiles for companies with which it has entered into strategic alliances, such as General Motors, as well as Germany's Opel and Japan's Isuzu and Nissan.[56]

value-chain partnerships
Strategic alliances between companies in different industries that have complementary capabilities.

joint ventures
Strategic alliances in which several companies work together to fulfill opportunities that require one another's capabilities.

FIGURE 15.17

McDonald's (Joint) Ventures into China

When attempting to enter the enormous Chinese market, McDonald's officials learned that the Chinese government required the company to have a local partner. It formed joint ventures with Chinese companies as a first step toward establishing franchises in that nation.

Greg Baker/AP Wide World Photos.

In addition to the financial incentives (circumventing trade and tariff restrictions) and marketing benefits (access to internal markets) associated with strategic alliances, direct managerial benefits also are associated with extending one company's organization chart into another's. These benefits come primarily from improved technology and greater economies of scale (e.g., sharing functional operations across organizations). For these benefits to be derived, a high degree of coordination and fit must exist between the parties, each delivering on its promise to the other. Finally, it is noteworthy that strategic alliances with companies in nations with transforming economies provide good opportunities for those nations' economies to develop.[57] Given the rapid move toward globalization of the economy, we may expect to see many companies seeking strategic alliances in the future as a means for gaining or maintaining a competitive advantage.[58]

AN ALTERNATIVE TO THE JOINT VENTURE. Although forming joint ventures with other organizations is a popular way for companies to grow in new directions, it is not the only way. An alternative that has been popular in many companies has been to create a **spinoff**—that is, an entirely new company that is separate from the original parent organization, one with its own identity, a new board of directors, and a different management team. The idea is that instead of looking around for a suitable partner, a rich and powerful company can create its own partner.

spinoff
An entirely new company that is separate from the original parent organization, one with its own identity, a new board of directors, and a different management team.

Consider, for example, the development of Expedia, Microsoft's online travel service. In 1996, Expedia was launched as just another Microsoft product.[59] As it became more successful, Expedia was set up as a separate operating unit. Then, in November 1999, Expedia was "spun off" into a separate publicly traded company (i.e., it can be purchased by anyone on the stock market). This raised $84 million for Microsoft, and because the company retains 85 percent of Expedia's stock, it promises to make even more money in the future. Despite the highly competitive market within which it operates, Expedia has been flourishing, enjoying record profits in recent years. This is in large part because it was the offspring of a wealthy and successful parent (which gave Expedia a head start), but also because it was allowed to develop on its own as needed, without too much "parental supervision," so to speak. Further extending the parent-child metaphor, the spinoff company is forever associated with the parent company, provides services to it, and gets help from it. However, it also is free to develop other business relationships that stand to strengthen it further.

Today's Diverse and Global Organizations

Challenges of Launching Joint Ventures in China

With an enormous market that is opening its doors to Western capitalism, it's not surprising that the idea of forming joint ventures with Chinese companies is very appealing to organizations in other parts of the world. Some companies, such as Johnson & Johnson, have enjoyed considerable success in joint ventures with Chinese firms. Most others, however, are finding it difficult to make these relationships work.[60]

Consider, for example, the experiences of a U.S.-based household-products company that formed a joint venture with Shanghai Jahwa Corporation, China's largest cosmetics manufacturer. The U.S. company was looking for help introducing its products into the large Chinese market by tapping into Jahwa's distribution system. It also was hoping to find what the Chinese call *guanxi*, the social and political connections required to become successful in China (see Chapter 13). Jahwa officials were looking for help in upgrading its technology and boosting its capacity to compete in the international marketplace. Unfortunately, the two companies became paralyzed by serious disagreements over directions and resources, resulting in a failed deal. Making matters worse, joint ventures are difficult to dissolve in Chinese culture because the relationship between the two companies is based on trust. Walking away from such relationships comes at a considerable loss of face (i.e., esteem in the eyes of others).

Several factors make the prospects of forming joint ventures with Chinese firms difficult, at best. To begin, there is the obvious matter of cultural differences. Compared to Western countries, Chinese culture and traditions are profoundly different. In particular, its social, governmental, and economic systems are far more complex. Compared to Western companies, for example, Chinese companies are more likely to become lax after achieving success, and they are less likely to consider strategies that take a long-term approach. If this were the only challenge, however, it most likely would be overcome. After all, executives interested in conducting business in various countries have been successful in learning all about the cultural ways of their hosts.[61] In China, however, there are several more unique problems.

First is the fact that the Chinese market is becoming extremely competitive as many Western companies are attempting to be the first to introduce their products to the vast Chinese population. Competition has become so fierce in some industries (e.g., construction, pharmaceuticals, and electronics), in fact, that companies have been aggressively pursuing market share, even if it meant lowering prices so much that they were selling at a loss. This is a game that very few companies can afford to play for long.

Another challenge associated with forming joint ventures with Chinese companies is that very few have presence throughout the country. Most operate either regionally or locally. This is a vestige of the country's planned economic system, in effect until 1979, which required companies to operate in very narrow market niches. Because only the earliest companies to form joint ventures with Chinese companies (e.g., Coca-Cola Co.) managed to make contact with the few that operate nationally, it is very difficult for today's foreign companies to find suitable partners.

A consideration problem has to do with government intervention. Although governments are involved in one way or another in businesses in all countries, their connection to Chinese businesses runs deep—so much so, in fact, that many companies are actually owned, in part, by government agencies. What makes this particularly frustrating is that different governmental rules operate in different territories. As a case in point, consider the difficulties that companies such as AT&T and Siemens have been having in establishing telephone service through their various Chinese partners. The problem resides in the fact that Shanghai Bell has a Chinese partner, which just happens to be the Ministry of Post and Telecommunication—the government agency that controls communications. To say that Shanghai Bell has a distinct advantage, as a result, probably comes as no surprise.

In view of these considerations, experts advise companies seeking joint ventures with Chinese firms to consider all their options carefully. The benefits that stand to be gained from an enormous market may be challenging to realize because several formidable obstacles stand in the way.

Summary and Review of Learning Objectives

1. **Describe what is meant by organizational structure and the basic characteristics of organizational structure revealed in an organization chart.**
   The formal configuration between individuals and groups with respect to the allocation of tasks, responsibilities, and authority within organizations is known as *organizational structure*. It is an abstract concept that can be represented by an *organization chart*, a diagram revealing the relationships between the various units (individuals or departments) in an organization. Organization charts depict five different elemental building blocks of organizational structure. These are *hierarchy of authority* (a summary of reporting relationships), *span of control* (the number of individuals over which a manager has responsibility), *division of labor* (the degree to which jobs are specialized), *line* versus *staff positions* (jobs permitting direct decision-making power versus jobs in which advice is given), and

decentralization (the degree to which decisions can be made by lower-ranking employees as opposed to a few higher-ranking individuals).

2. **Describe different approaches to departmentalization—functional organizations, product organizations, and matrix organizations.**

Within organizations, groups of people can be combined into departments in various ways. The most popular approach is the *functional organization,* an organization created by combining people in terms of the common functions they perform (e.g., sales, manufacturing). An alternative approach is to departmentalize people by virtue of the specific products for which they are responsible, known as the *product organization.* Another form of departmentalization combines both of these approaches into a single form known as the *matrix organization.* In such organizations, people have at least two bosses; they are responsible to a superior in charge of the various functions and a superior in charge of the specific product. Employees also may have to answer to high-ranking people responsible for the entire organization, the top leader.

3. **Distinguish between classical and neoclassical approaches to organizational design and between mechanistic organizations and organic organizations, as described by the contingency approach to organizational design.**

Organizational design is the process of coordinating the structural elements of organizations in the most appropriate way. *Classical organizational theories* (such as Weber's notion of bureaucracy) claim that a universally best way to design organizations exists, an approach based on high efficiency. *Neoclassical organizational theories* (such as those advanced by McGregor, Argyris, and Likert) also believe that there is one best way to design organizations. Their approach, however, emphasizes the need to pay attention to basic human needs to succeed and express oneself. The *contingency approach* to organizational design is predicated on the belief that the most appropriate way to design organizations depends on the external environments within which they operate. Specifically, a key factor has to do with the degree to which the organization is subject to change: A stable environment is one in which business conditions do not change, whereas a turbulent environment is one in which conditions change rapidly. When conditions are stable, a *mechanistic organization* is effective. This is one in which people perform specialized jobs, many rigid rules are imposed, and authority is vested in a few top-ranking officials. However, when conditions are turbulent, an *organic organization* is effective. This is one in which jobs tend to be very general, there are few rules, and decisions can be made by low-level employees.

4. **Describe the five organizational forms identified by Mintzberg: simple structure, machine bureaucracy, professional bureaucracy, divisional structure, and adhocracy.**

Mintzberg identified five specific organizational forms. Organizations with *simple structure* are small and informal and have a single powerful individual, often the founding entrepreneur, who is in charge of everything (e.g., a small retail store owned by a sole proprietor). In a *machine bureaucracy* work is highly specialized, decision making is concentrated at the top, and the work environment is not prone to change (e.g., a government office). In *professional bureaucracies,* such as hospitals and universities, there are lots of rules to follow, but employees are highly skilled and free to make decisions on their own. *Divisional structure* characterizes many large organizations (such as General Motors) in which separate autonomous units are created to deal with entire product lines, freeing top management to focus on larger scale, strategic decisions. Finally, the *adhocracy* is a highly informal, organic organization in which specialists work in teams, coordinating with each other on various projects (e.g., many software development companies).

5. **Explain how organizations can be designed with strategy in mind.**

An organization's strategy is its long-term plans and objectives. Five major types include differentiation, innovation, low cost, market expansion, and risk reduction. To implement its strategy successfully, various contingency factors have to be taken into account. These are size, innovation, diversification, and geographic diversity. These factors, in turn, influence the nature of the *qualities of the tasks* that people are required to perform (i.e., task uncertainty and task interdependence). And this requires using particular *coordination mechanisms* to govern the organization, such as rules, plans, hierarchy, and mutual agreement. This is made possible by certain dimensions of organizational structure and design—most notably, levels of hierarchy, organic-mechanistic, specialization, formalization, divisional structure, and centralized-decentralized.

6. **Characterize three forms of intraorganizational design—boundaryless organizations, conglomerates, and strategic alliances.**
   Some organizational designs, known as interorganizational designs, combine more than one organization. One of these is the *boundaryless organization*. This involves not only eliminating all internal boundaries (such as those between employees) but also external boundaries (such as those between the company and its suppliers). Popular forms of boundaryless organizations include *modular (or networked) organizations* and *virtual organizations*. Another type of interorganizational design is the *conglomerate*, a large corporation that diversifies by getting involved in unrelated businesses. A third type of interorganizational design is the *strategic alliance*, one or more organizations that combine forces to operate a specific business. There are three major types of strategic alliances: *mutual service consortia, joint ventures,* and *value-chain partnerships.*

Points to Ponder

Questions for Review

1. What are the fundamental dimensions of organizations that are described by organizational structure?
2. What are the major ways that traditionally have been used to organize departments in organizations?
3. What are the major differences between classical, neoclassical, and contingency approaches to organizational design?
4. What are the five organizational forms identified by Mintzberg?
5. What is meant by "the boundaryless organization" and what forms does it take?
6. What are the major types of interorganizational design, in which two or more organizations can coordinate their efforts?

Experiential Questions

1. Think of the organization in which you currently work—specifically, the work group or department with which you are most closely affiliated. How would you characterize this unit with respect to division of labor, span of control, and centralization?
2. Based on your own experiences, do you think that traditional, hierarchical organizations are giving way to less well-structured, boundaryless forms of organization? In other words, do you see this trend in your own organizational life?
3. Have you ever worked for a company that was involved in a strategic alliance of some kind? How about a virtual organization? If so, how was the experience different from working for a traditional company?

Questions to Analyze

1. How have advances in information technology changed the way organizations are structured and designed today?
2. For what types of business endeavors do you think virtual organizations are particularly well suited, and for what type do you believe they should be avoided?
3. What particular organizations would appear to benefit from the use of boundaryless designs? Explain why.

Experiencing OB

Individual Exercise

How Centralized Is Your Organization?

Organizations differ in terms how highly centralized they are. This questionnaire is designed to help you identify the degree to which your organization is centralized.

Directions

Read each of the following statements and think about the extent to which it describes the organization in which you currently work. In the space to the left of each statement, mark "T" if you believe it is mostly true in your organization or "F" if you believe it is mostly false.

1. _____ Decisions are made mostly by top executives.
2. _____ Many employees at lower levels are empowered to make decisions.

3. ———Power generally resides in the hands of only a few individuals.
4. ———For my boss to get an answer to a question, he or she has to ask someone who pushes the question up the organization.
5. ———The company would operate more effectively if some of the people separating me from top management were eliminated.

Scoring and Interpretation

1. Give yourself 1 point for answering each of the following questions as indicated:
   1 = T, 2 = F, 3 = T, 4 = T, 5 = T
2. Your score could range from 0 to 5. The higher your score, the more centralized your organization appears to be.

Questions for Discussion

1. Based on your score, how centralized does your organization appear to be? How does this fit with your own informal assessment of its degree of centralization?
2. Complete the same questionnaire, but this time, answer with respect to another job you've held at some time. Is your current organization more centralized or less centralized than this other one?
3. What particular advantages or disadvantages does your organization have because of its current degree of centralization? What additional advantages or disadvantages would result if it were more centralized?
4. What particular changes would have to be made for the organization to become more centralized? Less centralized?

Group Exercise

Comparing Span of Control in Organization Charts

One of the easiest things to determine about a company by looking at its organization chart is its span of control. This exercise will allow you to learn about and compare span of control within companies in your area.

Directions

1. Divide the class into four equal-size groups.
2. Assign one of the following industry types to each group: (a) manufacturing companies, (b) financial institutions, (c) public utilities, and (d) charities.
3. Within the industry assigned to each group, identify one company per student. Also, consider larger organizations inasmuch as these are more likely to have formal organization charts. For example, if there are five students in the "financial institutions" group, name five different banks or savings and loan institutions.
4. Each student should search the Internet for a copy of the organization chart for the company assigned to him or her in step 3.
5. Meet as a group to discuss the spans of control of the organizations in your sample.
6. Gather as a class to compare the findings of the various groups.

Questions for Discussion

1. How easy or difficult was it to find organization charts on the Internet?
2. Did you find that there were differences with respect to span of control?
3. Were spans of control different at different organizational levels? If so, how? And, were these differences the same for all industry groups?
4. In what ways did spans of control differ for the various industry groups? Were the spans broader for some industries and narrower in others? How do you explain these differences? Do these differences make sense to you?

Practicing OB

Reconsidering an Organizational Design

Fabricate-It, Inc., is a medium-size manufacturing company that uses standard assembly lines to produce its products. Its employees tend to be poorly educated and perform monotonous work. Think-It, Inc., is a software design firm that writes customized programs to solve its customers' problems. Its employees tend to be highly educated and perform highly creative work. Both are reconsidering their current organizational designs.

1. What type of organizational design would you imagine would best suit the needs of Fabricate-It? Explain your decision.
2. What type of organizational design would you imagine would best suit the needs of Think-It? Explain your decision.
3. How might each of these organizations benefit by entering into strategic alliances with other organizations?

■ Commercial Metals Company "Steels" the Show

Although you've probably never heard of the Commercial Metals Company (CMC), chances are good that you've driven across a bridge or spent time in a building made of its steel products. And when builders repaired the Pentagon after the September 11 terrorist attack, they turned to CMC for ultra-strong structural steel girders. To industry insiders, the choice seemed obvious. Since 1915, companies building bridges, skyscrapers, vehicles, and industrial equipment have relied on CMC to provide steel and metal products of every conceivable type. The company's high-quality products coupled with its reputation for outstanding service has paid off on the bottom line. Even in an economically rocky period, the company has consistently been performing well. In fact, the fourth quarter of 2009 was the 180th consecutive quarter that CMC paid dividends to its shareholders.

The company's president and CEO, Murray R. McClean, has emphasized that the key to its success is CMC's high level of efficiency. Indeed, CMC operates a network of companies that carefully feed one another in a manner that minimizes waste. Specifically, the firm is organized into five segments: Domestic Mills; the Polish company, CMC Zawiercie (CMCZ); Domestic Fabrication; Recycling; and Marketing and Distribution. The Domestic Mills segment consists of four steel "minimills" and the Howell Metals Company, which manufactures copper tubes in Virginia. Servicing the European market, CMCZ mills 1.1 million tons of steel a year. CMC's Recycling Segment ensures a constant supply of raw materials for these units. Operating 34 metals-processing plants across the Sunbelt, CMC is one of the largest processors of scrap metals in the United States, providing metal products of all types to steel mills (including the company's own facilities) and manufacturing plants.

Supporting these divisions is CMC's Marketing and Distribution segment. This portion of the business, which itself is composed of four different divisions, focuses on marketing steel, nonferrous metals, and other commodities and products through a network of offices located around the world. One of these divisions is the International Division, which knits together CMC's operations in 130 countries and coordinates business ventures with companies in other nations (e.g., Australia and Germany). To help promote the manufacturing business, the Marketing and Distribution segment also performs vital service functions for its customers, such as providing technical information, financing, transportation and shipping, and even insurance. In short, if it's something that a metals customer may need, this segment of CMC is there to provide it. And the more seamlessly customers have their needs met, the more metal products they buy from the organization.

To say that nothing goes to waste at CMC is an understatement. Take scrap, for instance. For a quarter century, CMC has been holding an annual "Scrap Can Be Beautiful" contest for art students at a high school in the Dallas area (where the company is headquartered). The company donates scrap metal to students in a metal sculpture class and awards cash prizes for the best entries. Some of the projects are displayed in the corporate office for a year, others are displayed in local galleries and museums, and still others are auctioned off to benefit Dallas-area arts organizations.

Questions for Discussion

1. What type of organizational design does CMC appear to use? On what do you base your answer?
2. How might CMC be redesigned to make it even more efficient than it is already? How would this fit what you would regard to be its strategy?
3. How might CMC benefit from entering into some form of strategic alliance with other companies? What particular form of strategic alliance should be used and why?

Case in Point

16 Managing Organizational Change: Strategic Planning and Organizational Development

Learning Objectives

After reading this chapter, you should be able to:

1. Characterize the prevalence of the change process in organizations.
2. Explain what, exactly, happens when organizational change occurs, and the forces responsible for unplanned organizational change.
3. Describe what is meant by strategic planning and the types of strategic changes that organizations make.
4. Identify the 10 steps in the strategic planning process.
5. Explain why people are resistant to organizational change and how this resistance may be overcome.
6. Identify and describe the major organizational development techniques that are used today.

Chapter Outline

- The Prevalence of Change in Organizations
- The Nature of the Change Process
- Strategic Planning: Deliberate Change
- Resistance to Change: Maintaining the Status Quo
- Organizational Development Interventions: Implementing Planned Change

Preview Case

■ *Saving Campbell's from the Soup*

With its iconic red and white cans a staple on grocers' shelves for about 145 years, no one would have suspected that the Campbell Soup Company was struggling. But that was exactly the case a decade ago when the venerable organization, which sells a range of packaged foods in 120 different countries, admittedly suffered what was called "a precipitous decline in market value and employee engagement."

Engineering a turnaround was the challenge Douglas R. Conant faced in January 2001, when he assumed the reins as the company's eleventh president and CEO. A decade later, all accounts suggest that he did precisely this, revitalizing the company by winning back customers, retaining employees, and developing new products. Even when the 2008 recession hit the consumer packaged goods industry hard, slashing investors' earnings by 25 percent, Campbell Soup Company investors' earnings rose 7 percent.

Conant's recipe for success focused on promoting changes from the inside out: "You can't win in the marketplace unless you win first in the workplace." And in an industry where "you evolve and grow or you die," as he says, this approach has served the company well. At the heart of Conant's approach to driving change has been an emphasis on building trust, which, he empathizes, has made it possible for people to work together to do amazing things. As he explains it, the more management delivers on its commitments, the more people are inspired to execute with excellence, creating what he refers to as a "flywheel of performance."

Conant went about this in several ways. To begin, during his first 30 months on the job, he replaced 300 of the company's top 350 executives, individuals who he believed were underperforming. Not only were these high-ranking leaders unproductive, but many contributed to what appeared to be a toxic work environment that was poisoning 20,000 others in the workplace who looked up to them. Half were replaced from outside the company. and the rest were insiders with exciting new ideas who were hungry to put them into place.

To ensure that these problems weren't going to reoccur—and to encourage just the opposite—Conant vowed to keep his finger on the pulse of the company's culture. He has been doing this by annually assessing "employee engagement" with a questionnaire developed by the Gallup Organization. These metrics have allowed him to track how emotionally committed Campell's 580 managers are feeling, and to compare this with the levels of engagement found in managers from other organizations. The first time Campbell's administered the questionnaire, the results were off the chart—in the negative direction. A harsh picture was painted of an organization in which managers simply didn't care—far worse than conditions found in other *Fortune* 500 companies.

Sensing urgency, Conant developed a process in which managers became more actively involved in everything. Their voices were heard, they were held accountable for results, and they developed action plans aimed at turning things around. The very next year, a marked improvement was found, along with rises in performance at all levels. Conant believes that this is so important that each year he presents employees' engagement scores in Campbell's annual report.

To the delight of shareholders and employees alike, Mr. Conant has led dramatic turnarounds at the Campbell Soup Company. He introduced changes that have sparked a chain reaction of improvements. Building a healthier organizational culture (see Chapter 14) characterized by trust (see Chapter 11) and tracking it systematically, he improved the quality of life at the company, making the Campbell Soup Company a place with renewed excitement, where people enjoy and care about what they're doing. This environment made it possible for the company to be more productive and more innovative (Chapter 14), contributing to improved financial success.

This case depicts a talented leader who stepped in heroically to rescue his company. Although not all efforts are equally successful, you can be sure that officials in most organizations are, in one way or another, striving to bring about changes and to make them work. Mr. Conant's approach focused on people, which, of course, we believe is critical. Other leaders have sought to usher in changes in different ways. As we described in Chapter 15, organizations frequently are redesigned in an effort to alter them for the better. And, of course, the continuous introduction of new technology has had dramatic effects on the nature of the work we do. Add to this such factors as a volatile economic environment, new government regulations, and competition from companies around the world, and one thing becomes perfectly clear: For organizations, *change is not the exception, but the rule.* With this in mind, it would be an

organizational change
Planned or unplanned transformations in an organization's structure, technology, and/or people.

understatement to say that the impact of organizational change can be found everywhere. **Organizational change** may be defined as planned or unplanned transformations in an organization's structure, technology, and/or people.

To understand this important process, we examine it from several key perspectives in this chapter. To begin, we describe the nature of the process of change, describing the forces that require it. Then we shift our focus to changes that are more deliberate, describing what is known as *strategic planning*. This involves deliberately making radical changes in the way an organization operates. As you might imagine, most people have difficulty accepting that they may have to redefine the group of people they work with and the basic nature of the jobs they do. After all, if you're used to working a certain way, a sudden change can be very unsettling. In other words, as we will describe, for various reasons, people are resistant to this process. Fortunately, such resistance can be overcome. With this in mind, social scientists have developed various methods, known collectively as *organizational development* techniques, which are designed to implement needed organizational change in a manner that is acceptable to employees and that enhances the effectiveness of the organizations involved.

The Prevalence of Change in Organizations

A century ago, advances in machine technology made farming so highly efficient that fewer hands were needed to plant and reap the harvest. Displaced laborers fled to nearby cities, seeking jobs in newly opened factories, opportunities created by some of the same technologies that sent them from the farm. The economy shifted from agrarian to manufacturing, and the *industrial revolution* was underway. With it came drastic shifts in where people lived, how they worked, how they spent their leisure time, how much money they made, and how they spent it.

In recent years, another industrial revolution has been occurring—one driven by a new wave of global economic forces and rapid technological transformation. As one observer put it, "This workplace revolution . . . may be remembered as a historic event, the Western equivalent of the collapse of communism."[1] And, like the revolution that occurred 100 years ago, this one is bringing with it broad transformations in the workplace to which we all must adapt.

Today's business leaders readily acknowledge that the pace of change in organizations is more rapid than ever. And when asked why this is so, they identify a variety of reasons. As shown in Figure 16.1, most prominent among these are innovations in products, services, or business models, and greater ease of obtaining information.[2] Indeed, we already have highlighted the importance of these factors elsewhere in this book (see Chapters 9 and 14).

The Message Is Clear: Change or Disappear!

Remember Mr. Conant's admonition (in the Preview Case on page 553) that "you evolve and grow or you die"? As harsh as it may seem, this Darwinian (survival of the fittest) notion is reality for more than just the packaged foods industry. Take the auto industry, for example. As recently as the 1980s, it was pretty much the case that the nameplate on a vehicle identified the owner of the company that manufactured it. With sales and purchases of companies (or portions of them) over the years, the owners of nameplates have been moving targets. For example, after struggling financially, the British luxury car company Jaguar was sold to Ford in 1989. Then as Ford began to struggle itself, it sold Jaguar to the large Indian company Tata Motors. In addition, some companies have swallowed-up several others over the years. At the moment, for example, Audi, Bentley, Lamborghini, and Porsche are subsidiaries of Volkswagen. Our point is that ownership of auto companies has been changing. In great part, this is the result of some businesses being more successful than others in adapting to changing conditions. And when this occurs, the more successful companies have been able to build their assets by acquiring less successful ones at attractive prices.

There can be no mistaking the fact that the world is changing in many different ways, and those companies that fail to adapt when required find themselves either acquired or simply out of existence as a result.[3] For example, in 2010 General Motors was unsuccessful in finding a buyer for its Hummer brand and simply liquidated its assets. That same year, Ford also discontinued its venerable Mercury brand. With all this in mind, it shouldn't be surprising that support

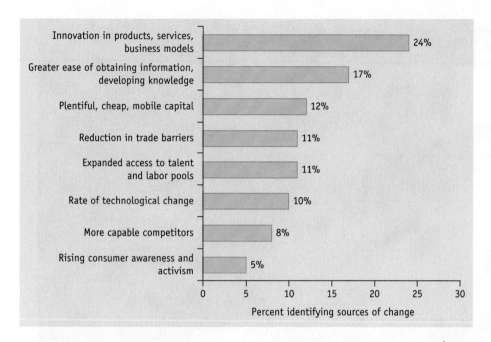

FIGURE 16.1

Why Are Things Changing So Rapidly?

In 2006, a large group of executives was asked to identify one factor that contributes most to the accelerating pace of change in today's global business environment. The percentage of respondents who named various factors is summarized here.

Source: McKinsey & Company. (2006, April). An executive take on the top business trends: A McKinsey Global Survey. *McKinsey Quarterly*. From https://www.mckinseyquarterly.com/An_executive_take_on_the_top_business_trends_A_McKinsey_Global_Survey_1754.

for organizational change among senior managers is a characteristic that distinguishes the most successful organizations from their less successful counterparts. Specifically, research has revealed that leaders of successful organizations support change 94 percent of the time, whereas all others support change only 76 percent of the time.[4] Although this alone does not mean that support for change directly causes success, of course, the sizable difference surely suggests that it may be a factor.

This is important because business failure is the rule rather than the exception: Fully 62 percent of new ventures fail to last as long as five years, and only 2 percent make it as long as 50 years.[5] In view of this, it is particularly impressive that some companies have beaten the odds—so soundly, in fact, that they have remained in existence for hundreds if years. At least one has been around for nearly 400 years, and as you'd expect, has made quite a few changes along the way (see Figure 16.2).[6]

Change Is a Global Phenomenon

Interestingly, the forces for organizational change are not isolated to the United States; they appear to be global in nature. This point is illustrated clearly in a study in which more than 12,000 managers from 25 different countries were asked to identify the major changes their organizations had encountered in the past two years.[7] The most-cited factors turned out to be large restructurings, mergers, divestitures and acquisitions, reductions in employment, and international expansion.

As you might suspect, it was reported that a few forms of change occurred more often in some countries than in others. What was particularly striking, however, was that organizations in all 25 countries were involved actively in each of these change efforts. This evidence suggests that organizational change is occurring throughout the world. Although many forces may be

FIGURE 16.2

A "Cymbal" of Change

Founded in 1623, the Avedis Zildjian Company is the oldest continually family-owned business in America. The alloy used in its cymbals has been passed down between Zildjian heirs for 14 generations. Although this formula has remained constant, the company has changed designs and manufacturing processes to be responsive to the shifting tastes of percussionists over the centuries.

Michael Fein/Bloomberg/Getty Images.

shaping change at different rates in various places, it is safe to conclude that change is a universal fact of life in today's organizations.

The Nature of the Change Process

Given that change is so frequent, it is important to understand the basic nature of the process. With this in mind, we turn attention to two key questions: (1) What, exactly, happens when organizational change occurs? and (2) What forces are responsible for unplanned organizational change?

Targets: What, Exactly, Is Changed?

Imagine that you are a facilities manager responsible for overseeing a large office building. The property owner has noted a dramatic increase in the use of heat in the building, leading operating costs to skyrocket. As such, a need for change exists—specifically, doing something that results in reducing heating bills. You cannot get the power company to lower its rates, of course, so it's up to you to take action, but what can you do?

As in many cases of organizational change, the options focus on three prospective targets— changes in *organizational structure, technology,* and/or *people* (see Figure 16.3). In describing each one, let's consider how it might be applied to our heat usage example.

CHANGES IN ORGANIZATIONAL STRUCTURE. In Chapter 15 we described the key characteristics of organizational structure. Here, we note that altering the structure of an organization can be an effective way of responding to a need for change. In our example, the structural solution to the heat-regulation problem would be to rearrange job responsibilities so that only maintenance personnel can adjust thermostats. Essentially, this involves moving from a decentralized system (in which anyone can make adjustments) to a centralized one (in which only maintenance personnel are permitted to reset the temperature). Where this is done in office buildings, you tend to find lockboxes covering thermostats with only authorized personnel holding keys. Putting it differently, the people with the keys are the ones who control the power.

In other situations, structural shifts may take different forms. For example, changes may be made in an organization's span of control, altering the number of employees for which supervisors are responsible. Structural changes also may take the form of revising the basis for creating departments—such as from product-based departments to functional ones. Other structural changes may be much simpler, such as clarifying someone's job description or the written policies and procedures followed.

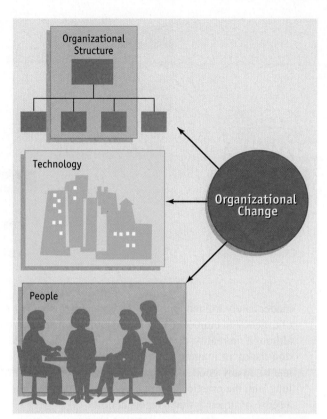

FIGURE 16.3

Organizational Change Targets: Structure, Technology, People
To create change in organizations, one can rely on altering organizational structure, technology, and/or people. Changing in any one of these areas may impact the others.

CHANGES IN TECHNOLOGY. In many organizational settings, the most straightforward way to make changes is by introducing new technology. Essentially, technology dictates the way jobs must be done, thereby ensuring change. When computers were introduced into offices in the mid-1980s, they revolutionized how people went about creating, storing, and transmitting documents. Typewriters became relics as the jobs of administrative staff members changed and entirely new ways of working were introduced.

How could technology be used to drive change in our thermostat example? One solution would be to install programmable thermostats that adjust temperatures (lowering them in cool winter months and raising them during the summer) so as to save energy when the building is not in use. Combining this with the structural solution we just described, a centralized, multiple-zone system could be used in which sensors appear in several different locations but the mechanisms for making adjustments appear only in one centralized locked office.

CHANGES IN PEOPLE. You've probably seen stickers next to light switches in hotels asking guests to turn off the lights when not in use. Something of this nature could be done in our example. Very inexpensive, printed labels requesting that occupants not adjust the thermostats could be affixed to them. Indeed, asking people to change their behavior can be a very straightforward way of introducing organizational change. The only problem is that it doesn't always work. Of course, individuals don't always do what's requested of them. If you said to yourself, "If I'm cold—I'm going to turn up the heat no matter what the sign says," then you know exactly what we mean.

The point at which we're hinting probably comes as no surprise: Changing people isn't easy. Indeed, it lies at the core of most of the topics discussed in this book. Despite unique differences found in various situations, in one way or another, the process of changing people involves the following three steps (see Figure 16.4).

■ *Unfreezing.* This is the process of recognizing that the current state of affairs is undesirable. Realizing that change is needed may be the result of some serious organizational crisis or threat (e.g., a serious financial loss, a strike, an accident, or a major lawsuit) or simply becoming aware that current conditions are unacceptable (e.g., antiquated equipment,

FIGURE 16.4

Changes Involving People: A Three-Step Process

Many organizational changes require people to do things differently. For this to occur it's necessary to follow the three general steps outlined here. As you will see later in this chapter, there are several specific ways in which this may be carried out.

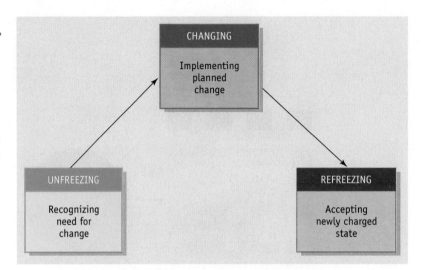

doomsday management
The practice of introducing change by suggesting that an impending crisis is likely.

inadequately trained employees). To bring this about, managers sometimes create a sense of urgency in employees by introducing the idea that there is an impending crisis although, in reality, conditions are currently acceptable. This approach, referred to as **doomsday management,** effectively unfreezes people, stimulating change before it's too late to do any good. Although lying is inappropriate and is bound to be ineffective in the long run, the practice of emphasizing the troublesome aspects of a situation may help create a sense of urgency that triggers action.

■ *Changing.* Following unfreezing changes are made to create more desirable states for organizations and their members. Change attempts may be quite ambitious (e.g., an organization-wide restructuring) or only minor (e.g., a revision to a training program). (We will discuss such planned change techniques in the next major part of this chapter.)

■ *Refreezing.* This happens when the changes made are incorporated into employees' new ways of thinking and the organizations' ways of operating. Hence, the new attitudes and behaviors become a new part of life in the organization. Inevitably, these new threads in the organizational fabric are likely to become targets of subsequent organizational change efforts at some time in the future.

Magnitude: How Much Is Changed?

The changes that organizations make differ in magnitude. Whereas some are limited in scope and complexity (e.g., the addition of a new sales rep to an already large sales force), others are more extensive in nature (e.g., the acquisition of a new firm).

Change that is continuous in nature and involves no major shifts in the way an organization operates is known as **first-order change**. This is apparent in the very deliberate, incremental changes that Lexus has been making in continuously improving the environmentally friendly nature of its production process.[8] Similarly, a restaurant may be seen as making first-order changes as it gradually adds new items to its menu and gauges their success before completely revamping its concept.

As you might imagine, however, other types of change are far more complex and dramatic. **Second-order change** is the term used to refer to more radical change, major shifts involving many different levels of the organization and many different aspects of business.[9] (For a comparison between these two forms of change, see Figure 16.5.) Citing only some of the most publicized examples of second-order change from recent years, General Electric and Tenneco have radically altered the ways they operate, their cultures, the technologies they use, their structures, and the nature of their relations with employees.[10]

first-order change
Change that is continuous in nature and involves no major shifts in the way an organization operates.

second-order change
Radical change; major shifts involving many different levels of the organization and many different aspects of business.

unplanned changes
Shifts in organizational activities due to forces that are external in nature, those beyond the organization's control.

Forces: Why Does Unplanned Change Occur?

As organizations encounter forces in the environments in which they operate, they face formidable challenges to adapt. Indeed, as we noted earlier, businesses must be responsive to **unplanned changes**. We now examine several forces that lead to unplanned change.

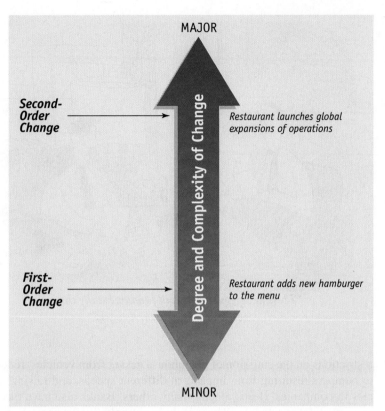

FIGURE 16.5

Comparing First-Order and Second-Order Change

Changes occurring in organizations differ with respect to scope and complexity. A change that is relatively minor is referred to as *first-order change,* whereas one that is more major is referred to as a *second-order change.* One example of each is shown here.

SHIFTING EMPLOYEE DEMOGRAPHICS. It is easy to see how, even within your own lifetime, the composition of the workforce has changed. As noted in Chapters 1 and 6, the American workforce is now more highly diverse than ever. To people concerned with the long-term operation of organizations, these are not simply curious sociological trends, but shifting conditions that require organizations to adjust.

Human resources experts need to know how the workforce is changing so they can compensate. For example, in recent years the growth of minority groups in the United States has been considerable. Among other things, this has made it possible to hire people from different ethnic groups in many companies and to serve members of these groups who seek service providers with whom they share common language and cultural backgrounds.[11] Besides facility in language, growing ethnic diversity has made it necessary in some businesses to offer diversity management programs designed to help people from different backgrounds get along with one another. Sometimes, the changes are small. For example, additions to the menu in the company cafeteria to accommodate the varied tastes of people from different ethnic groups can make a big difference to employees, who come to feel at home as a result.

PERFORMANCE GAPS. If you've ever heard the phrase "If it's not broken, don't fix it," you already have a good feel for one of the most potent sources of unplanned internal changes in organizations—*performance gaps.* A product line that isn't moving, a vanishing profit margin, a level of sales that isn't up to corporate expectations—these are examples of gaps between real and expected levels of organizational performance.

Few things force change more than sudden and unexpected information about poor performance. Organizations usually stay with a winning course of action and change in response to failure. Indeed, a performance gap is one of the key factors providing an impetus for organizational innovation (for an example, see the Case in Point on pages 585–586). Those organizations that are best prepared to mobilize in response to unexpected downturns are expected to be the ones that succeed.

GOVERNMENT REGULATION. Some of the most commonly witnessed unplanned organizational changes are those stemming from government regulations (see Figure 16.6). Consider, for example, rulings imposed on the auto industry. The U.S. federal government has imposed

FIGURE 16.6

Governmental Regulation Is a Source of Organizational Change

When government agencies introduce new regulations or eliminate old ones, organizations are required to change accordingly. These may or may not take the form indicated here.

P. C. Vey/Cartoonbank.com.

"These new regulations will fundamentally change the way we get around them."

restrictions on the emission of greenhouse gasses from vehicles, reducing the levels of damage to bumpers resulting from impacts at different speeds, and raising the fuel economy of vehicles in companies' fleets, among many others. Banks also have faced changes in response to governmental regulations. These include not only 2010's changes regarding the imposition of over-limit fees for credit cards but also older requirements, such as those limiting the amount of time checks can be held before clearing.

In addition to the imposition of regulations, industries also have experienced changes due to their removal. Again, in the banking business, today's financial institutions are free to compete against one another in determining the interest they pay depositors, although this used to be regulated. Likewise, deregulation also has occurred over the years with respect to the pricing of airline tickets and long-distance telephone services.

GLOBAL COMPETITION. It happens every day—someone builds a better mousetrap, or at least a less expensive one. As a result, companies often must fight to maintain their shares of the market, such as by advertising more effectively and lowering their costs. This kind of economic competition not only forces organizations to change, but also demands that they do so effectively if they are to survive.

Although competition always has been crucial to organizational success, today it comes from all over the world. As it has become increasingly less expensive to transport materials around the world, the industrialized countries have found themselves competing with one another for shares of the marketplace in many nations. This extensive globalization of the economy presents a strong need to change and to be innovative (see Chapter 14). For example, for many years the large American automobile manufacturers have suffered from being unprepared to meet the world's growing demand for small, high-quality cars—products their Japanese competitors were only too glad to supply to an eager marketplace. With this rapidly changing growth in globalization, one thing is certain: Only the most adaptive organizations can survive.

FLUCTUATING ECONOMIC CONDITIONS. The constantly changing economy has been very challenging for organizations in recent years. A prolonged recession beginning in 2008 hit many companies hard, forcing them to reduce their workforces—sometimes, dramatically. In fact, the unemployment rate in the United States more than doubled between December 2007 and October 2009.[12] And, of course, as people lose their jobs, they have less money to spend, leading to more economic problems. The cycle, as economists tell us, is devastating to individuals and organizations alike. Clearly, this is a major source of unplanned organizational change.

It hasn't been only lost jobs that have resulted from economic downturns. There also have been adjustments to work schedules (resulting in people working fewer hours in exchange for lower pay), reductions in pay and benefits, and hiring freezes. Taken together, all this suggests that employees who have managed to keep their jobs are required to do more work but get paid less at the same time. Not surprisingly, feelings of inequity (Chapter 7) and the stress associated with it (Chapter 5) have taken their toll on people.

By way of countering all this doom-and-gloom, we should note that there has been one particularly interesting positive effect associated with economic fluctuation. Namely, employee misbehavior has dropped. In fact, between 2007 (when economic conditions were stronger) and 2009 (when those conditions were weaker), there was a decline in the amount of employee misconduct observed.[13] In fact, it's most interesting to note that there was a sharp parallel between the percentage of the U.S. workforce observing bad behavior and the average monthly S&P 500 Index (an indication of financial performance based on the prices of major stocks) (see Figure 16.7).

These findings appear to run counter to ones reported in Chapter 11, revealing that as the economy suffers, people are likely to suffer adverse experiences (e.g., pay cuts) to which they respond by stealing company property. Because most employee theft is covert in nature, people are unlikely to observe its occurrence, making it unlikely to be involved in this study. However, when it comes to forms of misbehavior that are observed (e.g., being rude and inconsiderate to others), as measured in this research, just the opposite occurred: Misbehavior was lowest when the economy was weakest.

Although there are likely several good reasons for this, two seem especially appealing. First, it is an intriguing possibility that during weak economic conditions, employees were least willing to do anything (such as misbehaving in any way) that might jeopardize their jobs. A second possibility is that external events affected both variables in parallel fashion. Specifically, when events such as the Enron scandal and the Madoff scandal (see Chapter 2) occurred, two things happened at the same time. First, investors became concerned, leading financial markets to decline. Second, the talk about stepped-up legal enforcement and prosecution of wrongdoing that was going on at those same times appears to have led people to think twice about engaging in any ethical misbehavior. With these two dynamics occurring simultaneously, it's not surprising to find the parallel trends shown in Figure 16.7.

ADVANCES IN TECHNOLOGY. As you know, advances in technology have produced changes in the way organizations operate. Senior scientists and engineers, for example, can probably tell you how their work was drastically altered in the mid-1970s, when their ubiquitous plastic slide rules gave way to pocket calculators. Things changed again only a decade later, when calculators

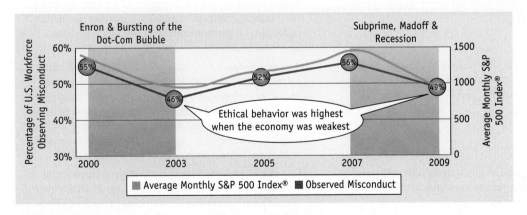

FIGURE 16.7

Ethical Behavior Parallels Financial Performance

The S&P 500 Index® fluctuated between 2000 and 2009. So too did the percentages of people in the U.S. workforce who engaged in various forms of ethical misconduct. Interestingly, these trends paralleled one another in striking fashion. When the economy was weakest, percentages of individuals engaging in misconduct were lowest.

Source: Ethics Resource Center, 2009; "2009 National Business Ethics Survey: Ethics in the Recession" Arlington, VA. used with permission of the Ethics Resource Center.

were supplanted by powerful desktop microcomputers, which have revolutionized the way documents are prepared, transmitted, and filed in an office. Today, powerful handheld devices make portable, wireless communication a reality, further changing the way work is done.

Companies that in the late 1980s and early 1990s may have considered jumping on the technology bandwagon to gain an advantage over their competitors quickly found out that doing so wasn't an option needed to get ahead—but rather, a requirement just to stay in the game. In the late 1990s, technology made it possible for people to develop new, Web-based businesses with only limited start-up capital. Businesses started by *Internet entrepreneurs* became commonplace, although vast numbers of these went bust by 2000. Today, although the Internet no longer is seen as a path to instant riches, it is clear that Internet technology has transformed the way many people work. (For a summary of ways in which computer technology has changed the way we work, see Table 16.1.)

Strategic Planning: Deliberate Change

Thus far, we have been describing unplanned organizational change. However, not all changes that companies make fall into this category. Organizations also make changes that are very carefully planned and deliberate. This is the idea behind **strategic planning**, which we define as the process of formulating, implementing, and evaluating decisions that enable an organization to achieve its objectives.[14]

strategic planning
The process of formulating, implementing, and evaluating decisions that enable an organization to achieve its objectives.

Basic Assumptions About Strategic Planning

To clearly understand the nature of strategic plans used in organizations today, it is important to highlight three fundamental assumptions about them.[15]

TABLE 16.1   How Has Computer Technology Changed the Way We Work?

Advances in computer technology have revolutionized many of the ways we work. Some key ways in which this has been occurring are summarized here.

Area of Change	Old Way	New Technology Examples
Use of machines	Materials were moved by hand, with the aid of mechanical devices (e.g., pulleys and chains).	*Automation* is prevalent—the process of using machines to perform tasks that otherwise might be done by people. For example, computer-controlled machines manipulate materials and perform complex functions, a process known as *industrial robotics* (*IR*).
Work by employees with disabilities	People with various physical or mental disabilities either were relegated to the most simple jobs, or they didn't work at all.	*Assistive technology* is widespread—devices and other solutions that help individuals with physical or mental problems perform the various actions needed to do their jobs. For example, *telephone handset amplifiers* make it possible for people with hearing impediments to use the telephone and *voice recognition systems* read to people with visual impairments.
Monitoring employees	Supervisors used to enter the offices of employees at work and observe them from afar.	*Computerized performance monitoring* systems are in widespread use, which allow supervisors to access their subordinates' computers for purposes of assessing how well they are performing their jobs.
Customer service	Individual service providers did things to help employees, customizing goods and services as time and skill allowed.	*Personalized service* is likely to take the form of greeting visitors to one's Web page with information customized to match the goods and services in which they expressed interest in their last visit (e.g., Amazon.com does this).
Environmental friendliness	Products at the end of their lives were buried in landfills, often polluting the earth.	*Design for disassembly* (*DFD*) is the process of designing and building products so that their parts can be reused several times and then disposed of at the end of the product's life without harming the environment.

STRATEGIC PLANNING IS DELIBERATE. When organizations make strategic plans, they make conscious decisions to alter fundamental aspects of themselves. These changes tend to be radical in nature (e.g., changing the nature of the business), as opposed to minor (e.g., changing the color of the office walls).[16] Changes in this category may be inspired by any of several factors, such as the presence of new competitors, the introduction of new technologies, and the like.

STRATEGIC PLANNING OCCURS WHEN CURRENT OBJECTIVES CAN NO LONGER BE MET. For the most part, when a company's current strategy already is bringing about the desired results, change is unlikely to occur. In other words, "don't mess with success" seems to be the rule that's followed. However, when it becomes clear that current objectives can no longer be met, new strategies are formulated to turn things around.

NEW ORGANIZATIONAL OBJECTIVES REQUIRE NEW STRATEGIC PLANS. Whenever a company takes steps to move in a completely different direction, it establishes new objectives—and a strategic plan is designed to meet them. Acknowledging that the various parts of an organization are all interdependent, the new plan is likely to involve all functions and levels of the organization. Moreover, the plan will require adequate resources from throughout the organization to bring it to fruition.

To illustrate how these assumptions come to life, we now will describe some examples of the kinds of issues about which companies tend to make strategic plans.

About What Do Companies Make Strategic Plans?

As you might imagine, organizations can make strategic plans to change just about anything. However, most of the ones we see these days involve changing either (a) a company's products and services, or (b) its organizational structure.

PRODUCTS AND SERVICES. Imagine that you and a friend have a small janitorial business. The two of you divide the duties, each doing some cleaning, buying supplies, and performing some administrative work. Before long, the business grows, leading you to add additional employees to be able to accommodate the new business. At this point, you're merely doing more of the same thing. Then, suppose that in response to inquiries about window cleaning from many of your commercial clients, you and your partner think it over and decide to expand into that business as well. This decision to take a different direction with the business, to add a new, specialized service, will require a bit of organizational change. Not only will new equipment and supplies be needed, but new personnel also will have to be hired and trained, additional insurance will need to be purchased, and new accounts will have to be secured. In short, you made a strategic decision to add to the company's line of services, and this necessitates organizational change.

Organizations are required to make these kinds of changes all the time. History reveals that some have done it more successfully than others, however. For example, Canon, Minolta, and Nikon, dominant players in the market for film cameras, responded to the digital revolution of the 1990s by adding digital cameras to their product mix. By contrast, Polaroid, the longtime leader in instant film-based photography, was slow to jump on the digital photography bandwagon.[17] Because Polaroid executives stuck to their beliefs about the relative benefits of their instant film products, which proved to be unfounded, the company ultimately was forced to declare bankruptcy. (As an interesting aside, the company's assets, including the Polaroid name, were purchased, and in 2010 the new owner of the Polaroid brand named pop star Lady Gaga as its creative director for a specialty line of imaging products.[18])

ORGANIZATIONAL STRUCTURE. It is not only changes in products and services that prompt companies to make strategic changes. As we noted in Chapter 15, organizations also make strategic plans to change their structures. For example, consider IBM's 2004 decision to reorganize by selling its personal computer division to the China-based Lenovo Group.[19] Although IBM was the world's third largest PC maker (behind market leaders Dell and HP), company officials made a strategic decision to strengthen its focus on the company's core business—developing information technology for corporate customers. This, of course, represents a significant departure for IBM because it was the original leader of the personal computer revolution with the release of the first IBM PC on August 12, 1981—four months before *Time* magazine named the personal computer its "man of the year."[20]

outsourcing
The practice of eliminating parts of organizations that focus on noncore sectors of the business and hiring outside firms to perform these functions instead.

offshoring
Short for *offshore outsourcing*, the practice of using outsourcing services of overseas companies.

Another way organizations are restructuring is by completely eliminating parts of themselves that focus on noncore sectors of the business and hiring outside firms to perform these functions instead—a practice known as **outsourcing**. For example, companies like ServiceMaster, which provides janitorial services, and ADP, which provides payroll processing services, make it possible for other organizations to concentrate on the business functions most central to their missions, thereby freeing them from having to attend to these peripheral support functions.

Outsourcing is particularly popular in various high-tech businesses, as when firms contract with other, specialized companies to provide such services as data storage or disaster recovery. Another widely outsourced function in computer-related businesses is customer service (see Figure 16.8). The vast majority of these services are provided by companies located in other countries, in which specialized facilities have developed to house them. The practice of using outsourcing services of overseas companies is known as **offshoring** (short for *offshore outsourcing*).[21] Typically, this practice allows companies to take advantage of lower labor costs and to leverage the expertise of talented workers in other parts of the world.[22] Three major types of offshoring are popular.

- *Product offshoring.* This involves relocating the manufacturing of existing products to new locations. Electronic components are often made in Costa Rica, for example, and clothing and toys frequently are made in Chinese factories.
- *Services offshoring.* Telecommunications technology is used to provide services for clients. As we noted earlier, most of the work of this type occurs in call centers staffed by workers who provide support services for customers of high-tech companies. This is not the only use of services offshoring. Although it's a bit unorthodox, DuPont has been using a staff of 30 lawyers based in the Philippines to do routine legal work.[23] The work has been of high quality and savings to the company has been considerable.
- *Innovation offshoring.* This is the process of using companies in other nations to make its products more innovative (see Chapter 14). Many high-tech firms have relied on innovation offshoring to reduce the time required to bring new products to market.

Indranil Mukherjee/Newscom.

FIGURE 16.8

Offshoring Technical Support Is Big Business

The ready availability of well-educated, English-speaking experts in information technology (IT), like these in the southern Indian city of Bangalore, have made their nation a haven for companies seeking the services of technical support representatives. Many businesses here, and in the Philippines as well, provide these services to American firms in 24/7 call centers, located in gigantic "IT Cyberparks."

Some critics have expressed concerns that outsourcing represents a "hollowing out" of companies—a reduction of functions that weakens organizations by making them more dependent on others. Others counter that outsourcing makes sense when the work that is outsourced is not highly critical to competitive success (e.g., janitorial services) or when it is so highly critical that the only way to succeed requires outside assistance. If you think that outsourcing is an unusual occurrence, guess again. One industry analyst has estimated that 30 percent of the largest American industrial firms outsource over half their manufacturing—and this practice is growing rapidly.[24]

The Strategic Planning Process: Making Change Happen

The process of strategic planning typically follows 10 ordered steps, which we now describe.[25] Although these steps are not immutable and are not always followed in the exact order specified, they do a reasonably good job of describing the way companies go about planning change strategically. As we discuss these, you may find it useful to follow along with the summary of steps appearing in Figure 16.9.

1. *Define goals.* A strategic plan must begin with a stated goal. Typically, goals involve a company's market (e.g., to gain a certain position in the product market) and/or its financial standing (e.g., to achieve a certain return on equity). Organizational goals also involve society (e.g., to benefit certain groups, or the environment) or organizational culture (e.g., to make the workplace more pleasant).

   It is important to note that a company's overall goals must be translated into corresponding ones to be achieved by various organizational units. For example, suppose a company wants to change its position in the market from a manufacturer of wholesale machinery to a maker of consumer products. It identifies as its goal achieving 10 percent market share within the first two years. This must then be translated into goals for the various departments. For example, the marketing department must have objectives with respect to reaching certain consumers in its advertising. Likewise, the production department must be able to manufacture certain numbers of products within a specific period of time.

2. *Define the scope of products or services.* For a strategic plan to be effective, company officials must clearly define their organization's *scope*—that is, the businesses in which it

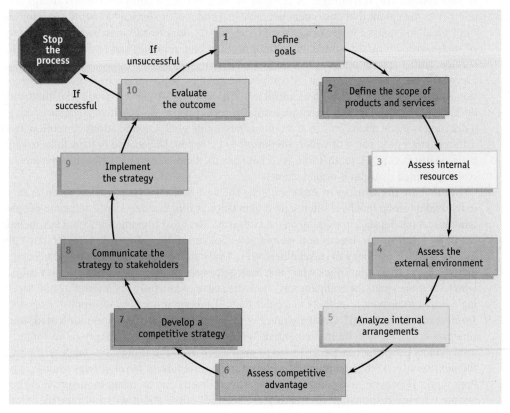

FIGURE 16.9

Strategic Planning: A 10-Step Process

Strategic planning—the process of formulating, implementing, and evaluating decisions that enable an organization to achieve its objectives—generally follows the 10 steps summarized here.

Source: Based on suggestions by Christensen, 1994; see Note 25.

already operates and the new ones in which it aims to participate. If scope is defined too narrowly, the company will overlook opportunities; if it is defined too broadly, the effectiveness of its plan will be diluted.

The matter of defining scope involves answering questions about what business a company is in, and what it could be in. For example, Beech-Nut, long known for its infant food, faced a challenge created by lowered birthrates, thereby lowering the size of its market. That's when company officials recognized that its scope could be broadened to include the elderly—another group that has difficulty digesting hard food. Broadening its scope in this manner has been a key part of the company's strategic plan for success.[26]

3. *Assess internal resources.* The question with respect to internal resources is: What resources does the company have available to plan and implement its strategy? The ones in question involve funds (e.g., money to make purchases), physical assets (e.g., required space), and human assets (e.g., knowledge and skills of the workforce).

4. *Assess the external environment.* As we have said throughout this book, organizations do not operate in a vacuum. Rather, they function within environments that influence their capacity to operate and to grow as desired. The extent to which the environment either helps or hinders a company's growth (or even its existence) depends on several key factors. Specifically, a company has a competitive advantage over others when its resources (a) cannot be easily imitated by others, (b) will not depreciate anytime soon, and (c) are better than those its competitors might have.[27]

5. *Analyze internal arrangements.* By "internal arrangements," we are referring to the nature of the organization itself as identified by the characteristics described in this book. For example, are the employees paid in a way that motivates them to strive for corporate goals (Chapter 7)? Also, does the culture of the organization encourage people to be innovative and to make changes, or does it encourage them to be stagnant (see Chapter 14)? Furthermore, do people communicate with each other clearly (Chapter 9) and do they cooperate with one another sufficiently well (Chapter 11) to accomplish their goals? These and other basic questions must be answered to formulate an effective plan for change. After all, unless the organization is operating properly in these key respects, even the best strategic plans may not pan out.

6. *Assess competitive advantage.* A company is said to have a **competitive advantage** over another to the extent that customers perceive its products or services as being superior and offered at an equal or lower price (see Figure 16.10). Superiority may be assessed in terms of such factors as quality, price, breadth of product line, reliability of performance, styling, service, and company image.

7. *Develop a competitive strategy.* A competitive strategy is the means by which an organization achieves its goal. Based on a careful assessment of a company's standing on the factors described earlier (e.g., the company's available resources, its competitive advantage, etc.), a decision is made about how to go about achieving its goal. Organizations can follow many different strategies, some of which we outlined in Chapter 15 because of their links to organizational structure. Here, in Table 16.2, we identify some additional strategies that are widely adopted by today's organizations.

8. *Communicate the strategy to stakeholders.* The term **stakeholder** is used to describe an individual or group in whose interest an organization is run. In other words, these are people who have a special stake, or claim, on the company. The most important stakeholders include employees at all levels, boards of directors, stockholders and customers. It is essential to communicate a firm's strategy to stakeholders very clearly so they can contribute to its success, either actively (e.g., employees who pitch in to help meet goals) or passively (e.g., investors who pour money into the company). Without the stakeholders fully understanding and accepting a firm's strategy, it is unlikely to receive the full support it needs to accomplish its goals.

9. *Implement the strategy.* Once a strategy has been formulated and communicated, the time has come for it to be implemented. When this occurs, there is likely to be some upheaval as people scramble to adjust to new ways of doing things. As we describe in the next section of this chapter, people tend to be reluctant to make changes in the way they work. However, as we also will note, several steps can be taken to ensure that the people who are responsible for making the changes come about will embrace them rather than reject them.

competitive advantage
The benefits enjoyed by an organization to the extent that customers perceive its products or services as being superior to those of another organization.

stakeholder
Any individual or group in whose interest an organization is run.

Frances Roberts/Alamy Images.

FIGURE 16.10

Local Television News: What Is Its Competitive Advantage?

A key part of developing a company's strategic plan involves assessing its competitive advantage. Local television news producers have had to do this a great deal in recent years as online sources, such as bloggers and small, independent news organizations, have become formidable competitors. Almost always, the Internet services are quicker, making it increasingly difficult for TV newscasters to be "first on the scene." This has led them to reassess their competitive advantages. What can they do that the less experienced and generally more poorly staffed online sources cannot? For many TV news units, the answer is no longer speed or exclusivity, but rather, depth of coverage. As a result, many news programs are now covering key stories from more different angles. They've also been stepping up coverage from local perspectives, on which Internet news agencies are unlikely to focus.

10. *Evaluate the outcome.* Finally, after a strategy has been implemented, it is crucial to determine whether the goals have been met. If so, then new goals may be sought. If not, then different goals may be defined, or different strategies may be followed, so as to achieve success next time. (The process of strategic planning we have been describing here may strike you as perfectly rational—so much so, in fact, that you may expect it to be universal. However, as we explain in the Today's Diverse and Global Organizations section on page 568, this is not the case.)

TABLE 16.2 Varieties of Competitive Strategies

Some of the most popular competitive strategies used by today's organizations are summarized here.

Strategy	Description
Market-share increasing strategies	Developing a broader share of an existing market, such as by widening the range of products, or by forming a joint venture (see Chapter 15) with another company that already has a presence in the market of interest
Profit strategies	Attempting to derive more profit from existing businesses, such as by training employees to work more efficiently or salespeople to sell more effectively
Market concentration strategies	Withdrawing from markets where the company is less effective and, instead, concentrating resources in markets where the company is likely to be more effective
Turnaround strategies	Attempting to reverse a decline in business by moving to a new product line or by radically restructuring operations
Exit strategies	Withdrawing from a market, such as by liquidating assets

Today's Diverse and Global Organizations

Strategic Values: More American Than Universal

Although you may not have realized it, the process of strategic planning we have been describing has several underlying values associated with it. Specifically, the process (a) is highly deliberate, (b) is based on competition, (c) assumes that radical change is possible and desirable, and (d) assumes shareholder ownership of the company. As we will outline here, these values are not universally held, thereby casting doubt on the generalizability of this process outside American culture.

One of the most obvious features we have been describing is its *deliberate nature*. In the United States, companies that are most successful are ones that carefully analyze, plan, and implement key decisions.[28] Despite this, such a deliberate process is not always used in other countries. In Southeast Asian countries, for example, intuition (gut feeling) and informal knowledge are used instead of deliberate analyses. In the words of one expert in the field, companies in these countries "don't have strategies. They do deals. They respond to opportunities."[29]

It's clear that our analysis of strategic planning is strongly based on one's position relative to the competition. However, outside the United States open expressions of *competitiveness* are not as common. Japan provides a fascinating example. In that nation, almost nothing is ever said about being competitive. Rather, the good work of the company is likely to be stressed in formal company publications. Ironically, however, Japanese companies tend to be fierce competitors in the international market. Thus, although competitive values may not be expressed in Japan (where, as a result, they are not likely to appear in any strategic plans), they certainly exist.

Our discussion of strategic planning is based on the idea that radical change is not only possible, but also desirable. Again, we use Southeast Asian culture as a counterexample. In Vietnam and Thailand, for example, experts warn that radical change is doomed to fail. Instead, minor incremental adjustments to ways of operating are advised.[30]

Finally, in the United States, strategic decisions tend to be made primarily in the interest of stockholders. In fact, it often is said that the mission of a company is to raise stockholder value. Outside the United States, the interests of other stakeholders are given more weight. For example, in Germany and France, the interests of the employees tend to be accorded far greater importance in the planning process. And, in Japan, companies are considered to belong to all the stakeholders, with employees being given precedence over others.[31]

In conclusion, it is clear that the values underlying the strategic planning process tend to prevail in the United States, but are not equally widespread elsewhere throughout the world. As a result, it appears questionable whether the strategic planning process we've described here would work—or that it is even worth attempting—outside the United States.

Resistance to Change: Maintaining the Status Quo

Even if people are unhappy with the state of affairs confronting them in organizations, they may be afraid that any changes will be potentially disruptive and only make things worse. Indeed, fear of new conditions is quite real, and it creates unwillingness to accept change. For this reason people may react to organizational change quite negatively. Then again, if the process is managed effectively, people may respond in a very enthusiastic manner. Scientists have summarized the nature of people's reactions to organizational change as falling along a continuum ranging from acceptance, through indifference and passive resistance, to active resistance.[32] For a summary of the various forms these reactions may take, see Figure 16.11.

As you might imagine, for organizations to make the changes needed to remain competitive—let alone to survive—they must tackle the problem of **resistance to change** head on. With this in mind, we discuss the issue of readiness for change and examine both its individual and organizational barriers. Then we conclude this section of the chapter by identifying specific steps that can be taken to overcome resistance to change.

resistance to change
The tendency for employees to be unwilling to go along with organizational changes based on some combination of individual and organizational barriers.

Individual Barriers to Change

People resist changes in organizations for a variety of reasons stemming from their own individual concerns, qualities, and interests.[33] Key ones are as follows.

- *Economic insecurity.* Because any changes on the job have the potential to threaten one's livelihood—by either loss of job or reduced pay—some resistance to change is inevitable.
- *Fear of the unknown.* Employees derive a sense of security from doing things the same way, knowing who their coworkers will be, and whom they're supposed to answer to from day to day. Disrupting these well-established, comfortable patterns creates unfamiliar

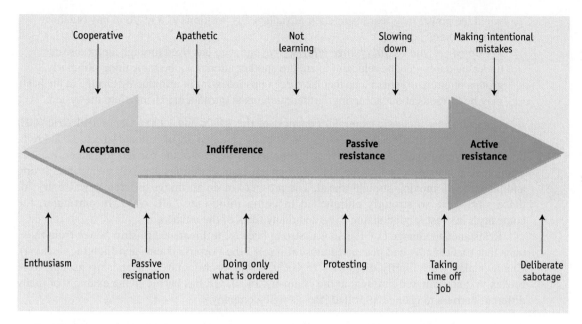

FIGURE 16.11

A Continuum of Reactions to Organizational Change

People's reactions to organizational change can range from acceptance (left) to active resistance (right). Some of the specific forms these reactions might take are indicated here.

Sources: Based on suggestions by Goldstein, 2001; Judson, 1991; see Note 32.

conditions, a state of affairs that is often rejected. It is not unusual for such fears to be based on adjustments required to adapt to the use of new technology.

- *Threats to social relationships.* As people continue to work within organizations, they form strong bonds with their coworkers. Many changes (e.g., the reassignment of job responsibilities) threaten the integrity of friendship groups that provide valuable social rewards.
- *Habit.* Jobs that are well learned and become habitual are easy to perform. The prospect of changing the way jobs are done challenges people to develop new job skills. Doing this is clearly more difficult than continuing to perform the job as it was originally learned.
- *Failure to recognize need for change.* Unless employees can recognize and fully appreciate the need for changes in organizations, any vested interests they may have in keeping things the same may overpower their willingness to accept change. Using the terminology of Figure 16.4 (page 558), unfreezing is necessary before change can occur.

Organizational Barriers to Change

In addition to the effects of individual factors, resistance to change stems also from conditions associated with organizations themselves.[34] Several such factors are as follows.

- *Structural inertia.* Organizations are designed to promote stability. To the extent that employees are carefully selected and trained to perform certain jobs, and rewarded for doing them well, the forces acting on individuals to work in certain ways are very powerfully determined—that is, jobs have **structural inertia.** Thus, because jobs are designed to have stability, it is often difficult to overcome the resistance created by the forces that create stability.
- *Work group inertia.* Inertia to continue performing work in a specified way comes not only from the jobs themselves but also from the social groups within which people work— **work group inertia.** Because of the development of strong social norms within groups (see Chapter 8), potent pressures exist to perform jobs in certain ways. Introducing change disrupts these established normative expectations, leading to formidable resistance.
- *Threats to existing balance of power.* If changes are made with respect to who's in charge, a shift in the balance of power between individuals and organizational subunits is likely to occur (see Chapter 12). Those units that now control the resources, have the expertise, and

structural inertia
The organizational forces acting on employees, encouraging them to continue performing their jobs in certain ways, thereby making them resistant to change.

work group inertia
Forces within a work group that encourage employees to perform their jobs in certain ways, thereby making them resistant to change.

wield the power may fear losing their advantageous positions as a result of any organizational change.

■ *Previously unsuccessful change efforts.* Anyone who has lived through a past disaster understandably may be reluctant to endure another attempt at the same thing. Similarly, groups or entire organizations that have been unsuccessful in introducing change in the past may be cautious about accepting further attempts at introducing change into the system.

Let's consider a classic example. For most of the 1980s and 1990s, General Electric (GE) underwent a series of widespread changes in its basic strategy, organizational structure, and relationship with employees. In this process, it experienced several of the barriers just identified. For example, GE managers had mastered a set of bureaucratic traditions that kept their habits strong and their inertia moving straight ahead. The prospect of doing things differently was scary for those who were so strongly entrenched in doing things the "GE way." In particular, the company's interest in globalizing triggered many fears of the unknown.

Resistance to change at GE also was strong because it threatened to strip power from those units that traditionally had possessed most of it (e.g., the Power Systems and Lighting division). Changes also were highly disruptive to GE's "social architecture"; friendship groups were broken up and scattered throughout the company. In all, GE has been a living example of many different barriers to change all rolled into a single company.

Readiness for Change: When Will Organizational Change Occur?

As you might imagine, there are times when organizations are likely to change and others during which change is less likely. In general, change is inclined to occur when the people involved believe that the benefits associated with making a change outweigh the costs.[35] The factors contributing to the benefits of making a change are:

■ The amount of dissatisfaction people have with current conditions. Change is most likely when dissatisfaction with the status quo is high.

■ The availability of a desirable alternative. Change is most likely when clearly desirable alternatives are recognized.

■ The existence of a plan for achieving that alternative. Change is most likely when it is clear how an alternative may be made to come about.

Theorists consider that these three factors combine multiplicatively to determine the benefits of making a change (see Figure 16.12). Thus, if any one of these factors is zero, the benefits of

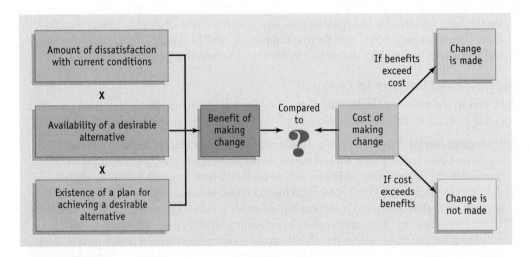

FIGURE 16.12

Organizational Change: When Will It Occur?

Whether or not an organizational change will be made depends on people's beliefs regarding its relative benefits and costs. The benefits are reflected by three considerations reviewed here.

Source: Based on suggestions by Beer, 1980; see Note 35.

making a change, and its likelihood, will be zero. If you think about it, this makes sense. After all, people are unlikely to initiate change if they are not dissatisfied, if they don't have any desirable alternative in mind, or if they fail to recognize any way of attaining that alternative if they do have one in mind. Of course, for change to occur, the expected benefits must outweigh the likely costs involved (e.g., disruption, uncertainties).

Factors Affecting Resistance to Change

To overcome resistance to change, it helps to discover the individual variables (e.g., personality) and aspects of the work setting to which such opposition is most closely linked. Doing this makes it possible to identify specific ways of changing people and/or changing situations so as to promote acceptance of organizational change.

This approach was taken in a study of officials who worked for a large governmental agency.[36] Using questionnaires that assessed a variety of individual differences and situational factors, the researchers sought to identify the factors that were linked most closely to an important concept—openness to change (i.e., the extent to which someone is willing to accept changes in his or her organization). The researchers found that three variables in particular were linked most strongly to openness to change. These were as follows:

- **Resilience:** The extent to which people are capable of bouncing back from adversity (recall our discussion of this variable in Chapter 5 as it pertains to stress)
- **Information about change:** Specific facts about how things will be different
- **Change self-efficacy:** Beliefs in one's ability to function effectively despite the demands of change

As summarized at the top of Figure 16.13, the relationship between each of these variables and openness to change was positive—in other words, greater amounts of these variables were associated with greater openness to change.

Of course, it's not only what people report on a questionnaire that matters, but also how such openness is related to key aspects of people's work attitudes and behavior. To learn about this, the researchers also assessed a number of variables. What they found was interesting. Three particular variables were associated strongly with openness to change (see bottom portion of Figure 16.13). The first was job satisfaction (see Chapter 6). The more open to change employees were, the more satisfied they were with their jobs. Furthermore, the more open the workers were to change, the less work-related irritation they showed (i.e., the less they tended to get

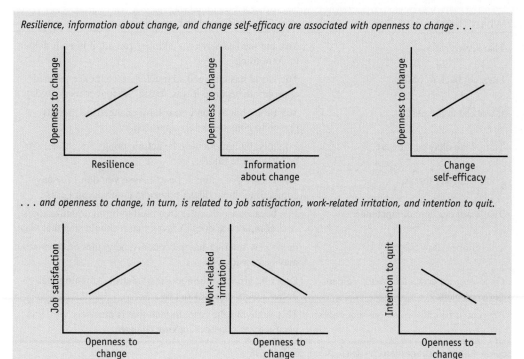

Resilience, information about change, and change self-efficacy are associated with openness to change . . .

. . . and openness to change, in turn, is related to job satisfaction, work-related irritation, and intention to quit.

FIGURE 16.13

Variables Linked to Openness to Change: Research Findings

As summarized at the top of this diagram, three factors—resilience, information about change, and change self-efficacy—are associated positively with openness to change. And, as shown at the bottom, openness to change is in turn related to job satisfaction, work-related irritation, and intention to quit.

Source: Based on findings reported by Wanberg & Banas, 2000; see Note 36.

angry or aggravated at work), and the less likely they were to quit their jobs. Thus, openness to change can make a big difference when it comes to these important aspects of the job.

In view of this, it makes sense to try to make people more resilient to change, to increase the amount of information they have available about how their organizations will change, and to show them how they will benefit from new work situations. As you will see in the next section, several of these suggestions are incorporated into specific approaches to overcoming resistance to organizational change.

How Can Resistance to Organizational Change Be Overcome?

Because organizational change is inevitable, managers should be sensitive to its barriers so that resistance can be overcome. This, of course, is easier said than done. However, several useful approaches have been suggested, including the key ones summarized here.[37]

GAIN LEADERSHIP SUPPORT. For change to be accepted, it often is useful (if not absolutely necessary) to win the support of the most powerful and influential individuals in the company. Doing so builds a critical internal mass of support for change. Demonstrating clearly that key organizational leaders endorse the change is an effective way to get others to go along with it—either because they share the leader's vision or because they fear his or her retaliation. Either way, their support will facilitate acceptance of change.

IDENTIFY AND NEUTRALIZE CHANGE RESISTERS. An important way of supporting change initiatives involves neutralizing those who resist change. Often, resistance occurs because people say things publicly that express their fears, but organizational officials fail to respond. An offhand remark that expresses concerns and fears about impending change can be contagious, sending fear into the workplace. Not saying anything to counter such statements is to support that concern tacitly. As such, it is important for individuals promoting organizational change to identify and neutralize those who resist it. Several statements reflecting a fear of change and ways of responding to them are identified in Table 16.3.[38]

TABLE 16.3 Recognizing and Responding to People Who Resist Change

It generally is not difficult to identify employees who are most resistant to change. The things they say give them away. Unless such statements are immediately countered, they run the risk of spreading resistance further throughout the company. Here are some statements that reflect an underlying resistance to change and some guidelines for responding to them.

When They Say . . .	You Should Counter by Saying . . .
That seems risky.	Yes, but the risk is worth taking. After all, it is even riskier to do nothing.
Let's get back to basics.	The world has changed so much that what once seemed appropriate because it was "basic" no longer works today.
It worked in the past.	Maybe so, but as conditions have changed, so there is reason to consider a new approach.
Things are okay as they are.	Possibly, but unless we take action, things are unlikely to be okay in the future.
I don't see any threat.	There's always a threat. Just because you don't see any compelling threat doesn't mean that one doesn't exist.
That's not our core competence.	Just because a particular area used to be an organization's core competence doesn't mean that it should stay that way.
The numbers don't work.	In the new Internet-based economy, new rules of accounting may be considered.
Once we start down that road, we can never go back.	Don't be afraid of relinquishing control. Anything that doesn't work can be stopped.
There will be unforeseen consequences.	This is always the case. In fact, that is precisely why it is necessary to consider making changes.

Source: Based on suggestions by Reich, 2000; see Note 38.

EDUCATE THE WORKFORCE. Often, people are reluctant to change because they fear what the future has in store for them. Fears about economic security, for example, may be put to rest by a few reassuring words from powerholders. As part of educating employees about what organizational changes may mean for them, top management must show a considerable amount of emotional sensitivity. Doing so makes it possible for the people affected by change to help make it work. Some companies have found that simply answering the question, "what's in it for me?" can help allay a lot of fears.

"SELL" THE NEED FOR CHANGE. For organizational change to occur, top management must accept the idea that change is required. And quite often, it's lower-level supervisors, those who toil daily in the trenches, who offer the best ideas. For these ideas to be accepted and implemented, however, it's necessary for leaders to be convinced that the ideas are worthwhile. How, then, do supervisors "sell" their bosses on the need for change?

An interesting study has examined this question.[39] Scientists interviewed supervisors from various departments in a large hospital, inquiring as to how they went about presenting their ideas for change to top management. Carefully analyzing the responses led them to identify three major approaches, known as "issue selling" techniques (for a summary, see Figure 16.14). These are as follows:

- *Packaging moves.* This involves combining several ideas into a coherent whole. It includes such approaches as presenting one's ideas in the form of a clear business plan and "bundling" the idea together with other key organizational concerns, such as profitability.
- *Involvement moves.* This has to do with involving other people in the selling of the idea, such as other top-level personnel, others at the same level, or even others outside the organization.
- *Process moves.* This concerns paying attention to matters of form and style, such as giving a thorough presentation with all the issues carefully thought out, and presenting ideas at the most opportune time and in a persistent fashion.

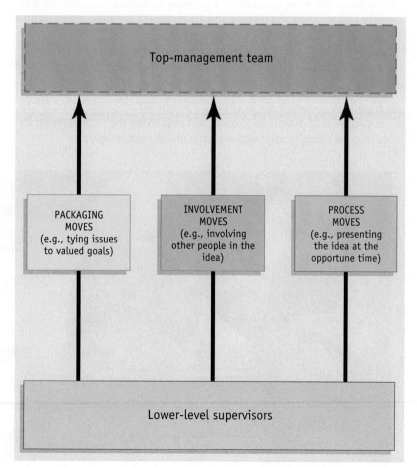

FIGURE 16.14

How Do Managers "Sell" Ideas About Change to Their Superiors?

Interviews with supervisors have revealed that to "sell" their superiors on ideas about organizational change, they rely on the three kinds of "moves" identified here.

Source: Based on suggestions by Dutton et al., 2001; see Note 39.

Although one cannot guarantee that top leaders always will follow the advice of lower-level supervisors, for these supervisors to have any chance of doing so, top officials must be convinced of the merit of their ideas. And, to increase the chances that good ideas will come across, it helps to follow these moves.

INVOLVE EMPLOYEES IN THE CHANGE EFFORTS. People who participate in making a decision tend to be more committed to its outcomes than are those who are not involved. Accordingly, employees who participate in responding to unplanned change, or who are made part of the team charged with planning a needed organizational change, may be expected to have very little resistance to change. Organizational changes that are "sprung" on the workforce with little or no warning, however, might be expected to encounter resistance simply as a knee-jerk reaction until employees have a chance to assess how the change will affect them. In contrast, employees who are involved in the change process are better able to understand the need for change, and are therefore less likely to resist it. As a manager at Hewlett-Packard once put it, "I don't think people really enjoy change, but if they can participate in it and understand it, it can become a positive [experience] for them."[40]

REWARD CONSTRUCTIVE BEHAVIORS. One rather obvious, and quite successful, mechanism for facilitating organizational change, as we noted in Chapter 3, is to reward people for behaving in the desired fashion. Changing operations may necessitate altering the kinds of behaviors that need to be rewarded by an organization. This is especially critical when a company is in the transition period of introducing the change. For example, employees who are required to learn to use new equipment should be praised for their successful efforts along the way. Feedback on how well they are doing not only provides a great deal of useful assurance to uncertain workers, but also helps shape the desired behavior.

CREATE A "LEARNING ORGANIZATION." Although all organizations change, whether they want to or not, some do so more effectively than others. Those that have developed the capacity to

adapt and change continuously are known as **learning organizations**.[41] In learning organizations, people set aside old ways of thinking, freely share ideas with others, form a vision of the organization, and work together on a plan for achieving that goal. As a result, learning organizations are said to transform themselves. Examples of learning organizations include Ford, General Electric, Wal-Mart, Xerox, and Motorola (see Figure 16.15).

As you might imagine, becoming a learning organization is no simple feat. In fact, it involves implementing many of the principles of organizational behavior described throughout this book. Specifically, for a firm to become a continuous learner, management must take the following steps.

■ *Establish commitment to change.* Unless all employees clearly see that top management is committed strongly to altering and improving the organization, they will be unlikely to make the changes necessary to bring about improvements.

FIGURE 16.15

Motorola: A Learning Organization

This woman works at a Motorola factory in Penang, Malaysia, which makes two-way radios, walkie talkies, and cellular phones. Her company has been actively engaged in becoming a *learning organization*—that is, one in which people set aside old ways of thinking in an effort to make continuous changes that help the business.

TABLE 16.4 Situation-Based Strategies for Overcoming Resistance to Change

An effective way to approach overcoming resistance to change is to consider the nature of the situation in which change is required and to respond accordingly. Some important ways of doing so are summarized here.

In Situations in Which . . .	Resistance to Change Should Be Overcome by . . .	This Is Effective Because . . .
Information is lacking or is inaccurate.	Educating employees and communicating with them	Employees can help make the changes once they appreciate their importance.
Management doesn't know what type of change is best.	Involving employees in the process of making the change	Employees' may provide valuable insight and their commitment to change will be enhanced.
Employees are concerned about losses resulting from change.	Negotiating an agreement about other aspects of work	It finds a way for employees to win, thereby offsetting any possible losses.
Changes are vital and must be made immediately.	Imposing the required changes	Time is of the essence; explanations can follow.

Sources: Based on suggestions by Kotter, 1995; Kotter & Schlesinger, 1979; see Note 42.

- **Adopt an informal organizational structure.** Change is more readily accepted when organizational structures (described in Chapter 15) are flat, cross-functional teams are created (see Chapter 8), and the formal boundaries between people are eliminated.
- **Develop an open organizational culture.** As we described in Chapter 14, managers play a key role in forming *organizational culture*. To adapt effectively to changes in their environments, organizations should have cultures that embrace risk-taking, openness, and growth. Companies whose leaders are reluctant to confront the chance of failure are ones that will be unlikely to grow and develop.

TAKE THE SITUATION INTO ACCOUNT. Although the suggestions we have identified thus far may be very useful, they fail to take into account the nature of the situation in which change efforts are to be undertaken. Should changes be imposed on employees or should they be involved in the process of designing the change efforts? Organizational scientists have determined that precisely how one should approach the change process depends on the nature of the situation being faced.[42] Some strategies for ways to overcome resistance to change in various situations are summarized in Table 16.4.

Although these suggestions may be easier to state than to implement, efforts at following them will be well rewarded. Given the many forces that make employees resistant to change, managers should keep these guidelines in mind. (For some suggestions as to how some effective organizations promote change, see the OB in Practice section on page 576.)

Organizational Development Interventions: Implementing Planned Change

Now that we've shed some light on the basic issues surrounding organizational change, we are prepared to examine planned ways of implementing it—collectively known as techniques of **organizational development (OD)**. Formally, we may define organizational development as a set of social science techniques designed to plan and implement change in work settings for purposes of enhancing the personal development of individuals and improving the effectiveness of organizational functioning. By planning organization-wide changes involving people, OD seeks to benefit organizations and the people who work in them.

Over the years, many different strategies for implementing planned organizational change (referred to as *OD interventions*) have been used by specialists known to as *OD practitioners*.[43] All the major methods of organizational development attempt to produce some kind of change in individual employees, work groups, and/or entire organizations. This is the goal of the five OD interventions we review here.

organizational development (OD)
A set of social science techniques designed to plan change in work settings for purposes of enhancing the personal development of individuals and improving the effectiveness of organizational functioning.

Management by Objectives: Clarifying Organizational Goals

In Chapter 7 we discussed the motivational benefits of setting specific goals. As you might imagine, not only individuals, but also entire organizations stand to benefit from this. For example, an executive

OB in Practice

Making Changes Stick: Tips from Three Established Organizations

If you want to understand change, it makes sense to look at successful organizations that have been around for a while. After all, to have made it for more than 100 years, a company must be managing change quite effectively. This clearly applies to three of the world's largest organizations—Royal Dutch Shell, Sears, and the U.S. Army. By analyzing what they have done to manage change effectively, it's possible to identify several practices that are worth emulating.[44]

1. *Fully incorporate employees into challenges faced by the organization.* This means more than simply involving employees in an organization's operations, but engaging them actively about the problems it faces. Officials from Shell Malaysia had long been unsuccessful in getting employees to work together to beat the competition. They were far too complacent, and the competition was rapidly gaining market share. In response to this, Shell officials called together all 260 managers for a session in which the problem of the rapidly encroaching competition was put before them. They emerged with a firm plan that was put into place. Back on the job, regular follow-up meetings were held to make sure the plan was implemented. Finally, because the employees bought into the problem and met the challenge themselves, Shell was successful in changing the way it operated.

2. *Lead in a way that stresses the urgency of change.* It's not unusual for company officials to get in a rut, becoming lazy and complacent about the way they operate—even if it's necessary to take decisive action. This is *almost* what

happened to Sears a few years ago. The retailing giant was losing customers rapidly as officers sat by, merely lowering sales goals. That's when CEO Arthur Martinez lit a fire under everyone by stressing the importance of turning things around—or else! He generated a sense of urgency by setting very challenging goals (e.g., quadrupling market share and increasing customer satisfaction by 15 percent). Although Martinez didn't have all the answers to Sears' problems, he provided something even more important—straightforward, honest talk about the company's problems, creating a sense of urgency that got everyone moving in the right direction.

3. *Create relentless discomfort with the status quo.* Following military maneuvers, the U.S. Army thoroughly debriefs all participants in what is called an "After Action Review." In these sessions, careful feedback is given about what soldiers did well and where they stand to improve. By focusing in a relentless, detailed manner on work that needs to be done, officers eventually get soldiers to internalize the need for excellence. Soldiers return to their home bases asking themselves how they can do something better (faster, cheaper, or more accurately), or if there is a new and more effective approach that could be taken. In short, the status quo is the enemy; current performance levels are never accepted. Things always can be better. Army brass liken this commitment to continuous improvement to painting a bridge: The job is never over.

Although these measures are rather extreme measures—and may not always be easy to implement—they certainly warrant careful consideration. After all, they have worked well for some of the most successful organizations in the world.

---

may express interest in "raising productivity" and "improving the quality" of her company's goods or services. These objectives, well-intentioned though they may be, are not as useful as more specific ones, such as, "increase production of widgets by 15 percent" or "lower the failure rate of widgets by 25 percent." After all, as the old saying goes, "It's usually easier to get somewhere if you know where you're going." The late management expert Peter Drucker was well aware of this idea while consulting for General Electric during the early 1950s and is credited with promoting the benefits of specifying clear organizational goals—a technique known as **management by objectives (MBO)**.

As summarized in Figure 16.16, the MBO process consists of four basic steps. First, goals are selected that employees will try to attain to best serve the needs of the organization. These should be selected by managers and their subordinates working together and not simply imposed on subordinates by managers. Further, these goals should be directly measurable and have some time frame attached to them. Goals that cannot be measured (e.g., "make the company better"), or that have no time limits, are useless.

In step two, managers and their subordinates work together to plan ways of attaining the goals they have selected—developing what is known as an *action plan*. Specifically, an **action plan** is a carefully specified set of guidelines indicating exactly what needs to be done to attain desired results.

Once goals are set and action plans have been developed to accomplish them, the third step calls for *implementation*—carrying out the plan and regularly assessing its progress. Is the plan working? Are the goals being approximated? Are there any problems being encountered in attempting to meet the goals? Such questions need to be considered while implementing an action plan. If the plan is failing, a midcourse correction may be in order—changing the plan, the way it's carried out, or even the goal itself.

management by objectives (MBO)
The technique by which managers and their subordinates work together to set, and then strive to attain organizational goals.

action plan
A carefully specified set of guidelines indicating exactly what needs to be done to attain desired results.

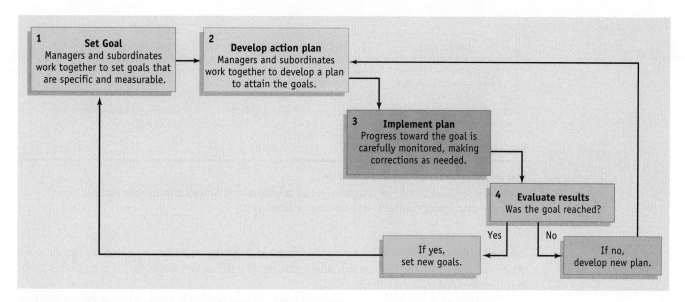

FIGURE 16.16

Management by Objectives: Developing Organizations Through Goal Setting

The organizational development technique of *management by objectives* requires managers and their subordinates to work together on setting and trying to achieve important organizational goals. The basic steps of the process are outlined here.

Finally, after monitoring progress toward the goal, the fourth step may be instituted: *evaluation*—assessing goal attainment. Were the organization's goals reached? If so, what new ones should be set to improve things still further? If not, what new plans can be initiated to help meet the goals? Because the ultimate assessment of the extent to which goals are met helps determine the selection of new goals, MBO is a continuous process.

MBO represents a potentially effective source of planning and implementing strategic change for organizations. Systematic efforts to meet organizational goals get individual employees and their organizations working together toward common ends. When this happens, system-wide change results. Of course, for MBO to work, everyone involved has to buy into it. Because MBO programs typically require a great deal of participation by lower-level employees, top managers must be willing to accept and support the cooperation and involvement of all.

Making MBO work also requires a great deal of time—anywhere from three to five years. Hence, MBO may be inappropriate in organizations that do not have the appropriate time to commit to the process. Despite these considerations, MBO has become one of the most widely used techniques for affecting organizational change in recent years. Not only is it used on an ad hoc basis by many organizations, but it also constitutes an ingrained element of the organizational culture in some companies, such as Hewlett-Packard and Intel.

Survey Feedback: Inducing Change by Sharing Information

For effective organizational change to occur, employees must understand the company's current strengths and weaknesses. That's the underlying rationale behind the **survey feedback** method. This technique follows the three steps summarized in Figure 16.17.

First, data are collected that provide information about matters of general concern to employees, such as organizational culture (see Chapter 14), leadership style (see Chapter 13), and job satisfaction (see Chapter 6). This may take the form of intensive interviews or structured questionnaires, or both. Because it is important that this information be as unbiased as possible, employees providing feedback should be assured that their responses will be kept confidential. For this reason, this process is usually conducted by outside consultants who keep the responses of individual employees from management.

The second step calls for reporting the information obtained back to the employees during small group meetings. Typically, this consists of summarizing the average scores on the information

survey feedback
An OD technique in which questionnaires and interviews are used to collect information about issues of concern to an organization. This information is used as the basis for planning organizational change.

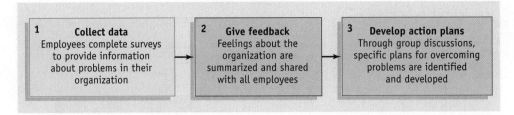

FIGURE 16.17

Survey Feedback: An Overview

The *survey feedback* technique of organizational development follows the three steps outlined here: collecting data, giving feedback, and developing action plans.

assessed in the survey. Profiles are created of feelings about the organization, its leadership, the work done, and related topics. Discussions also focus on why the scores are as they are, and what problems are revealed by the feedback.

The final step involves analyzing problems dealing with communication, decision making, and other organizational processes to make plans for dealing with them. Such discussions are usually most effective when they are documented carefully and a specific plan of implementation is made, with someone put in charge of carrying it out.

Survey feedback is used widely as an organizational development technique. This is not surprising in view of the advantages it offers. It is efficient, allowing a great deal of information to be collected relatively quickly. Also, it is very flexible and can be tailored to the needs of different organizations facing a variety of problems. However, the technique can be no better than the quality of the questionnaire used—it must measure the things that really matter to employees. Of course, to derive the maximum benefit from survey feedback, it must have the support of top management. The plans developed by the small discussion groups must be capable of being implemented with the full approval of the organization. When these conditions are met, survey feedback has proven to be a very effective OD technique.

Appreciative Inquiry

Although survey feedback and MBO are highly regarded OD techniques, they focus only on deficiencies, such as negative feedback and unmet goals. By contrast, a relatively new approach to organizational development known as *appreciative inquiry* helps organizations focus on the positive and the possible.[45] Specifically, **appreciative inquiry (AI)** is an OD intervention that focuses attention away from an organization's shortcomings and toward its capabilities and its potential. It is based on the assumption that members of organizations already know the problems they face and that they stand to benefit more by focusing on what is possible.

As currently practiced, the process of appreciative inquiry involves assembling small groups of people from an organization and guiding them through four straightforward steps. These are as follows.[46]

1. *Discovery.* The discovery step involves identifying the positive aspects of the organization, the best of "what is." This frequently is accomplished by documenting the positive reactions of customers or people from other organizations.
2. *Dreaming.* Through the process of discovering the organization's strengths, it is possible to begin dreaming by envisioning "what might be." By discussing dreams for a theoretically ideal organization, employees are free to reveal their ideal hopes.
3. *Designing.* The designing stage involves having a dialogue in which participants discuss their ideas about "what should be." The underlying idea is that by listening to others in a highly receptive manner, it is possible to understand others' ideas and to come to a common understanding of what the future should look like.
4. *Delivering.* After having jointly discussed the ideal state of affairs, members of the organization are ready to begin instituting a plan for delivering their ideas. Specifically, this involves establishing specific objectives and directions regarding "what will be."

appreciative inquiry (AI)
An OD intervention that focuses attention away from an organization's shortcoming, and toward its capabilities and its potential; based on the assumption that members of organizations already know the problems they face and that they stand to benefit more by focusing on what is possible.

Although appreciative inquiry is a newer approach to OD than the others we've discussed, it has been used a great deal and with considerable success.[47]

Action Labs

Usually, bringing about change is a very slow process. At a typical large company, it involves painstakingly analyzing and planning ideas and then rolling out only small changes in a deliberate sequence. However, in today's rapidly moving world, this pace is likely to be far too slow. To accelerate the change process, a technique known as the *action lab* has been introduced in recent years. The action lab is meant to be a "greenhouse" in which change can be created by insulating a group of decision makers from daily operations and getting them to focus on a business problem. Specifically, an **action lab** is an OD intervention in which teams of participants work off-site to develop and implement new ways of solving organizational problems by focusing on the ineffectiveness of current methods.[48]

One of the unique features of action labs is that the participants are in contact with one another for such extended periods of time (e.g., every day for four weeks) that they eventually find it impossible to cling to their established ways. For example, in one particular action lab, participants faced a frustrating few days in which bold proposals constantly were being shot down. Inevitably, an executive would find some flaw and the idea was dropped in an attempt to avoid conflict. Soon, however, team members realized that despite the aim of treating everyone as equals, they inevitably retreated to the safety of the company's established practice of pleasing the bosses. Eventually, the lab participants figured out that the very forces that were blocking changes in the company were also present within the lab. They were more concerned with avoiding conflict than with getting new ideas out into the open. Only once this insight occurred was the way paved for the team to develop innovative new ideas.

AN EXAMPLE. Let's consider an example of how an action lab helped facilitate change in one large but faltering organization. The Cummins Engine Company used an action lab to develop a strategy consisting of several teams that focused on ways in which the company could regain its former leadership in the diesel engine manufacturing business. An action lab was formed consisting of several teams, one of which included union stewards, manufacturing supervisors, and plant managers.[49] Carefully analyzing the situation, they discovered that customers were turning to competitors because they offered less expensive products. Cummins' long-time strategy was to attract customers by emphasizing "lifetime customer value," that is, by getting them to realize that the high quality of their engines made them less expensive over the products' lifetimes. This image served the company well, but it didn't compensate for the competitors' lower initial prices, causing sales to slip.

Analyzing the problem, the team figured out that, to remain competitive, Cummins had to reduce prices by 20 percent. The barrier was the long-standing practice of manufacturing all components in-house to ensure the highest quality standards. The lab team realized that this cherished practice had to be abandoned. Within one month's time, the team established strategic alliances (see Chapter 15) with various suppliers who could manufacture the parts less expensively. Cummins would assemble the final products and serve as the "quality watchdog" for the overall manufacturing process. Although this process has been in place for only a few years, it seems to be very successful thus far. Quality has been high and Cummins is well on its way to regaining its dominance in the diesel engine business.

Quality of Work Life Programs: Humanizing the Workplace

When you think of work, do you think of drudgery? Although many people believe these two terms go together naturally, it has grown increasingly popular to improve systematically the quality of life experienced on the job. As more people demand satisfying and personally fulfilling places to work, OD practitioners have attempted to create work situations that enhance employees' motivation, satisfaction, and commitment—factors that may contribute to high levels of organizational performance. Such efforts are known collectively as **quality of work life (QWL) programs**. These programs are ways of increasing organizational output and improving quality by involving employees in the decisions that affect them on their jobs. Typically, QWL programs support highly democratic treatment of employees at all levels and encourage their participation in decision making. Although many approaches to improving the quality of work life exist, they all share a common goal: humanizing the workplace.

---

action lab
An OD intervention in which teams of participants work off-site to develop and implement new ways of solving organizational problems by focusing on the ineffectiveness of current methods.

quality of work life (QWL) programs
OD techniques designed to improve organizational functioning by humanizing the workplace, making it more democratic, and involving employees in decision making.

work restructuring
The process of changing the way jobs are done to make them more interesting to workers.

quality circles (QCs)
An approach to improving the quality of work life, in which small groups of volunteers meet regularly to identify and solve problems related to the work they perform and the conditions under which they work.

SPECIFIC PROGRAMS.   One popular approach to improving the quality of work life involves **work restructuring**—the process of changing the way jobs are done to make them more interesting to workers. We already discussed several such approaches to redesigning jobs—including *job enlargement, job enrichment,* and the *job characteristics model*—in our discussion of motivation in Chapter 7. If you recall many employee's positive responses to these programs, it should not be surprising that these techniques also are considered effective ways of improving the quality of work life for employees.

Another approach to improving the quality of work life involves using **quality circles (QCs)**. These are small groups of volunteers (usually around 10) who meet regularly (usually weekly) to identify and solve problems related to the quality of the work they perform and the conditions under which people do their jobs. An organization may have several QCs operating at once, each of which deals with a particular work area about which it has the most expertise. To help them work effectively, the members of the circle usually receive some form of training in problem solving. Although QCs originated in Japan and have been used extensively there, many large American companies also have included QCs as part of their QWL efforts. Groups have dealt with issues such as how to reduce vandalism, how to create safer and more comfortable working environments, and how to improve product quality. Research has shown that although quality circles are very effective at bringing about short-term improvements in quality of work life (i.e., those lasting up to 18 months), they are less effective at creating more permanent changes.

POTENTIAL BENEFITS.   Three major benefits—even if short-term ones—may result from QWL programs. The most direct benefits usually are increased job satisfaction, organizational commitment, and reduced turnover within the workforce (see Chapter 6). A second benefit—and a major one—is increased productivity. A final benefit related to these first two is increased organizational effectiveness (e.g., profitability, goal attainment).

As you might imagine, achieving these benefits is not automatic. For success to be possible, it's crucial to incorporate the following two key provisions into any QWL program.

- *Both management and labor must cooperate in designing the program.* Should either believe that the program is really just a method of gaining an advantage over the other, it is doomed to fail.
- *The plans agreed to by all concerned parties must be implemented fully.* It is too easy for action plans developed in QWL groups to be forgotten. To keep this from occurring amidst the hectic pace of daily activities, it should be considered the responsibility of employees at all levels—from the highest-ranking executive to the lowest-level laborer—to follow through on their parts of the plan.

Over the years, some of the largest and best known companies, such as Ford and General Electric, have had active—and very successful—QWL programs. Their successes, in part, have been based on their careful attention to these two vitally important considerations.

Now that we've described a variety of OD techniques, you may find yourself wondering whether engaging in these practices is ethical. They may, after all, encourage people to change in ways that they might find undesirable. For a close-up look at this important issue, see The Ethics Angle section on page 581.

Critical Questions About Organizational Development

No discussion of organizational development would be complete without addressing two fundamental questions—do the techniques work (i.e., do they bring about the desired results), and if so, are they effective throughout the world (i.e., are they culture-bound)? We now consider these two important questions.

THE EFFECTIVENESS OF ORGANIZATIONAL DEVELOPMENT: DOES IT REALLY WORK?   Thus far, we have described some of the major techniques used by OD practitioners to improve organizational functioning. As is probably clear, carrying these out requires a considerable amount of time, money, and effort. Accordingly, it is appropriate to ask if this investment is worthwhile. In other words, does OD really work? Given the popularity of OD in organizations, this

The Ethics Angle

Is Organizational Development Inherently Unethical?

By its very nature, OD represents an attempt to change attitudes and behavior. Because of this, some people have claimed over the years that its practice is inherently unethical. They argued that changing people in ways they might not want is manipulative and inappropriate.[50]

For example, it has been suggested that OD techniques impose the values of the organization on the individual without taking the person's own attitudes into account. OD is a very one-sided approach, reflecting the imposition of the more powerful organization on the less powerful employee. A related claim is that OD fails to provide free choice on the part of workers. As a result, it may be seen as *coercive.* When faced with a "do it, or else" situation, employees tend to have little free choice and are forced to allow themselves to be manipulated, a potentially degrading prospect.

Another argument is that the unequal power relationship between the organization and its workers makes it possible for the true intent of OD techniques to be misrepresented. As an example, imagine that an MBO technique is presented to employees as a means of allowing greater organizational participation, whereas in reality it is used as a means for holding individuals responsible for their poor performance and punishing them as a result. Although such an event might not happen, the potential for abuse of this type does exist, and the temptation to misuse the technique—even if not originally intended—might later prove to be too great.

Despite these considerations, many professionals (the author, included) do not agree that OD is inherently unethical. Such a claim, it has been countered, is to say that the practice of management is itself unethical. After all, the very act of going to work for an organization requires one to submit to both the company's and society's values. One cannot help but face life situations in which others' ideals are imposed. This is not to say that organizations have opportunities to impose unethical values on people for the purpose of making a profit (e.g., stealing from customers). Indeed, because they have the potential to abuse their power organizations have a special obligation to refrain from doing so.

Although abuses of organizational power are all too common, OD itself is not necessarily the culprit. Indeed, like any other tool (even a gun!), OD is not inherently good or evil. Instead, many proponents argue that how the tool is used will depend upon the individual wielding it. With this in mind, the ethical use of OD interventions will require that they be supervised by professionals in an organization that places a high value on ethics. In fact, today's OD practitioners subscribe to a code of ethics that holds them to clear standards with respect to ensuring the benefits to organizations and the well-being of all employees.[51]

To the extent that top-management officials embrace ethical values and behave that way themselves, norms for good behavior are likely to develop in organizations. When an organization has a strong ethical culture, it is unlikely that OD practitioners would even think of misusing their power to harm individuals. The need to develop such a culture has been recognized as a way for organizations to take not only moral leadership in their communities, but financial leadership as well.

---

question is very important. Most of the studies bearing on the answer show the effects of the various OD interventions to be beneficial—particularly when it comes to improving organizational functioning.[52]

We hasten to add that any conclusions about the effectiveness of OD should be qualified in several important ways.

- *OD interventions tend to be more effective among blue-collar employees than among white-collar employees.* This likely occurs for a simple reason—namely, that most OD techniques are focused on changing the behavior of front-line people in operative roles rather than higher-level decision makers.
- *The beneficial effects of OD are enhanced by using a combination of several techniques (e.g., two or more together) instead of any single technique.* Given that the various techniques have strengths and weaknesses, it is not surprising that using one approach to offset the limitations of another is quite helpful.
- *The effectiveness of OD techniques depends on the degree of support they receive from top management.* The more programs are supported from the top, the more successful they tend to be. We already made this point in conjunction with QWL programs, but it is applicable to all OD interventions. If management is not fully supportive of such efforts, they are doomed to fail.

Despite the obvious importance of evaluating the effectiveness of OD interventions, a great many of them go unevaluated. There are two key reasons for this. First, we must note the difficulty of assessing change. Because many factors can cause people to behave differently in organizations, and because such behaviors may be difficult to measure, many OD practitioners avoid the problem of measuring change altogether. Second, political pressures to justify OD programs may discourage some professionals from honestly and accurately assessing their effectiveness. After all, in doing so, one runs the risk of revealing time and money were wasted. Although these considerations are understandable, they certainly are not advisable. Assessing the effectiveness of any OD program is wise insofar as it provides valuable feedback about precisely how things can be improved in the future. Just as a medical doctor must know the effectiveness of his or her efforts to cure illness to take an appropriate course of action, so too must organizational practitioners assess the impact of their own actions.

Overall, our conclusion is positive. Despite some limitations, organizational development techniques have considerable capacity to benefit both organizations and the individuals working within them. And, as you may recall from Chapter 1, these are among the fundamental purposes of the field of OB.

IS ORGANIZATIONAL DEVELOPMENT DEPENDENT ON NATIONAL CULTURE? For organizational development to be effective, people must be willing to share their ideas candidly with others, accept uncertainty, and show concern for others, especially members of their own teams. However, not all people are comfortable doing these things; this pattern better characterizes the people from some countries than others. For example, this profile closely describes people from Scandinavian countries, suggesting that OD may be most effective in such nations. However, people from Latin American nations are much the opposite, suggesting that OD interventions will be less successful when conducted there.[53] For a summary of the extent to which the basic assumptions of OD fit with the cultural styles of people from various nations, see Figure 16.18.

Although the predominant cultural values of people from the United States place it in the middle region of the diagram in Figure 16.18, this is not to say that OD is doomed to be ineffective in American companies. Not all OD techniques are alike with respect to their underlying cultural values.[54] For example, MBO has become a very popular OD technique in the United States in large part because it promotes the American values of willingness to take risks and working aggressively at attaining high performance. However, because MBO also encourages superiors and subordinates to negotiate freely with each other, the technique has been generally unsuccessful in France, where others' higher levels of authority are well accepted.[55] Reasoning similarly, one may expect survey feedback to be unsuccessful in the Southeast Asian nation of Brunei, where the prevailing cultural value is such that problems are unlikely to be confronted openly.

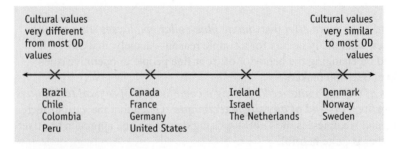

FIGURE 16.18

Organizational Development: Its Fit with National Values

Organizational development (OD) techniques tend to be successful when the underlying values of the technique match the cultural values of the nations in which it is used. General OD values tend to conform more to the cultural norms of some nations, shown on the right (where OD is more likely to be accepted), than others, shown on the left (where OD is less likely to be accepted).

Source: Based on suggestions by Jaeger, 1986; see Note 52.

These examples illustrate a key point: The effectiveness of OD techniques will depend, in part, on the extent to which the values of the technique match the underlying values of the national culture in which it is employed. As such, OD practitioners must appreciate fully the cultural norms of the nations in which they are operating. Failure to do so not only may make OD interventions unsuccessful, but they may even yield unintended negative consequences.

Summary and Review of Learning Objectives

1. **Characterize the prevalence of the change process in organizations.**

   Organizational change is very prevalent and is occurring at a rapid pace. Almost all organizations are changing in one way or another in order to survive. Inevitably, those that don't adapt, fail. Research has shown that the tendency for organizational change to occur is not limited to organizations in North America. Change is occurring rapidly in organizations of all nations throughout the world.

2. **Explain what, exactly, happens when organizational change occurs, and the forces responsible for unplanned organizational change.**

   The process of organizational change involves some combination of changing organizational structure, technology, and people. Unplanned change occurs in organizations due to shifting employee demographics, performance gaps, governmental regulation, economic competition in the global arena, and advances in technology.

3. **Describe what is meant by strategic planning and the types of strategic changes that organizations make.**

   Strategic planning is the process of formulating, implementing, and evaluating decisions that enable an organization to achieve its objectives. Typically, strategic plans are made about changing either a company's products and services, or its organizational structure.

4. **Identify the 10 steps in the strategic planning process.**

   The strategic planning process follows 10 steps: (1) define goals, (2) define the scope of products or services, (3) assess internal resources, (4) assess the external environment, (5) analyze internal arrangements, (6) assess competitive advantage, (7) develop a competitive strategy, (8) communicate the strategy to stakeholders, (9) implement the strategy, and (10) evaluate the outcome.

5. **Explain why people are resistant to organizational change and how this resistance may be overcome.**

   In general, people are resistant to change because of individual factors (e.g., economic insecurity, fear of the unknown) and organizational factors (e.g., the stability of work groups, threats to the existing balance of power). However, resistance to change can be overcome in several ways, including shaping political dynamics, educating the workforce about the effects of the changes and involving employees in the change process, involving employees in change efforts, rewarding constructive behaviors, and creating a learning organization.

6. **Identify and describe the major organizational development techniques that are used today.**

   Management by objectives (*MBO*) focuses on attempts by managers and their subordinates to work together at setting important organizational goals and developing a plan to help meet them. *Survey feedback* uses questionnaires and/or interviews as the basis for identifying organizational problems, which then are addressed in planning sessions. *Appreciative inquiry* (*AI*) is an OD intervention that focuses attention away from an organization's shortcomings and toward its capabilities and potential. It involves having small groups of workers discover, dream, design, and deliver changes to their organizations. An *action lab* is an OD intervention in which teams of participants work off-site to develop and implement new ways of solving organizational problems by focusing on the ineffectiveness of current methods. *Quality of work life* (*QWL*) programs seek to humanize the workplace by involving employees in the decisions affecting them (e.g., through quality circle meetings) and by restructuring the jobs themselves. The rationale underlying all of these techniques is that they may enhance organizational functioning by involving employees in identifying and solving organizational problems. Overall, research suggests that they generally are effective in this regard.

Points to Ponder

Questions for Review

1. When people talk about organizational change, what precisely is being changed and what forces lead to such change?
2. Under what conditions will people be most willing to make changes in organizations? Explain your answer and give an example.
3. What is meant by strategic planning, and what are the steps in the strategic planning process?
4. What are the major techniques of organizational development?
5. Overall, how effective is organizational development in improving organizational functioning? With respect to what factors does it work or not work?
6. Argue for or against the following statement: "Organizational development doesn't work." Explain your answer.

Experiential Questions

1. Think about the one job in a company with which you are most familiar (a job you have or one that a close friend or family member has). Based on what you know about this position, how has the nature of this job changed over the years? What is done differently, and why? In what ways has technology been involved? To what extent do you believe that the company benefited from these changes?

2. Think back to one particular change that was made in the organization in which you either work or have worked. What concerns did you have about it? Were you resistant to this change? If so, what, if anything, did management do to allay your fears? What might they have done?
3. Have you ever participated in some type of organizational development effort? If so, what was done? How did you feel about the program? Do you believe the effort was effective?

Questions to Analyze

1. Suppose you are having difficulty managing a small group of subordinates who work in an office 1,000 miles away from your home base. What kinds of changes in structure, technology, and people can be implemented to more closely supervise these distant employees?
2. Suppose that you are a top executive of a large organization about to undertake an ambitious restructuring plan that involves massive changes in job responsibilities for most employees. Explain why people might be resistant to such changes and what steps could be taken to overcome this resistance.
3. Imagine that you are a manager whose unit is suffering problems due to a lack of coordination between employees. How can OD techniques be used to address this problem? Which particular technique would you use and why? What do you need to do to help ensure its success?

Experiencing OB

Individual Exercise

Developing a Strategic Plan

Developing a strategic plan is not an easy matter. In fact, doing it right requires a great deal of information and lots of practice. This exercise will give you a feel for some of the challenges involved in developing such a plan.

Directions

1. Suppose that you are the president of a small software development firm that has for years sold a utility that has added functionality to the operating system used in most computers. Now, you suddenly face a serious problem: Microsoft has changed its operating system such that your product no longer serves any purpose.
2. Using the 10 steps outlined in Figure 16.9 (page 565), develop a strategic plan to keep your company alive. Make any assumptions you need to develop your plan, but state these in the process of describing it.

Questions for Discussion

1. How easy or difficult was it for you to develop this strategic plan? What would have made the process easier or more effective?
2. Which of the 10 steps would you imagine is easiest to implement? Which do you think would be most challenging?
3. Would you use competitive intelligence in the course of implementing your plan? If so, how?
4. What special challenges, if any, would the employees of your company face as they attempted to implement this plan? How would you attempt to overcome these challenges?

Group Exercise

Recognizing Impediments to Change—and How to Overcome Them

To confront the reality of organizational change, one of the most fundamental steps involves recognizing the barriers to change. Then, once these impediments have been identified, consideration can be given to ways of overcoming them. This exercise is designed to help you practice thinking along these lines while working in groups.

Directions

1. Divide the class into groups of approximately six and gather each group around in a circle.
2. All groups should consider each of the following situations.
   - *Situation A.* A highly sophisticated e-mail system is being introduced at a large university. It will replace the practice of transmitting memos on paper.
   - *Situation B.* A very popular employee who's been with the company for many years is retiring. He will be replaced by a completely new employee from the outside.
3. For each situation, discuss three major impediments to change.
4. Identify a way of overcoming each of these impediments.
5. Have someone from the group record the answers and present them to the class for a discussion session.

Questions for Discussion

1. For each of the situations, were the impediments to change similar or different?
2. Were the ways of overcoming the impediments similar or different?
3. How might the nature of the situation confronted dictate the types of change barriers confronted and the ease with which these may be overcome?

Practicing OB

Concerns About Downsizing

You are the manager of a poorly performing research and development department. In view of the performance problems, there has been talk in the company about the possibility of downsizing your unit. This has aroused a great deal of concern in the workplace as people begin to fear for the security of their jobs. This, in turn, has been disrupting the flow of work. Productivity is slowing down as some of your top engineers have been taking new jobs.

1. Does it make sense to expect your employees to have these fears? Why or why not?
2. Describe the steps you can take to help allay these fears and to return work to normal. How effective do you think these steps may be?
3. If large-scale downsizing were to occur, how might you use an organizational development technique to help smooth the transition?

■ Can P&G Turn the Tide?

It's a typical day. You wake up and brush your teeth with Crest toothpaste, bathe with Zest soap, wash your hair with Head & Shoulders shampoo, and apply your Cover Girl makeup. You then begin your household chores, washing clothes with Tide, putting fresh Luvs diapers on the baby, and cleaning the kitchen floor with your Swiffer dust mop. Taking a break, you sip your SunnyD as you pour yourself some Folgers coffee and munch on a few Pringles. If this sounds like you, then consider yourself a living advertisement for Procter & Gamble (P&G), the 170-year-old company whose products you've been using.

As you might imagine, a company that's been around this long has made more than a few changes in its day. Some have been in response to fundamental changes in society, such as in the 1920s, when the advent of electric light bulbs pushed P&G out of the candle business. Others have been aimed at proactively improving business operations, such as

Case in Point

(Continued)

in 1919, when the company sought to stabilize uneven sales cycles by eliminating wholesalers and selling directly to retail stores, a move that would revolutionize the grocery business. Perhaps more than anything, P&G has always been responsive to the ever-changing demands of consumers. Parents seeking modern conveniences in the 1960s, for example, found P&G on the scene with Pampers, the first disposable diaper.

Times may be different today, but P&G faces the same kinds of challenges to keep it at the top of the consumer products business. For example, although new products are the lifeblood of the company, P&G hasn't developed many successful new brands of its own recently (the Swiffer dust mop was the only one in the last 15 years!). Meeting the problem head on, former CEO Alan G. "A. G." Lafley was buying brands—Clairol in 2001 and Wella in 2003, among them. In 2002, P&G also entered into an agreement with Clorox to produce Glad food wraps and plastic food-storage containers. In a move to save money while also allowing the company to do what it does best—market products—Lafley has decided to outsource some business functions, including the manufacturing of bar soap (including Ivory, the company's oldest surviving brand). Another change has come in the form of marketing P&G brands more creatively. No longer just a toothpaste, for example, the Crest name now also appears on the company's SpinBrush electric toothbrush, and its line of tooth-whitening products.

Acknowledging that the culture at P&G has been resistant to adopting new ideas—"insular," some have complained—Lafley went out of his way to ensure that these fundamental changes will keep P&G vital for at least another 170 years. The key to his approach rests on building "understanding and commitment" among his personnel. With this in mind, he regularly spends Monday mornings in the office with a dozen other top corporate officers working on the week's game plan. To ensure that everyone gets the message, communication barriers—literally, walls on the eleventh floor of corporate headquarters—have been broken down and offices have been moved so that people now sit directly alongside those with whom they most often have to work.

One of his colleagues referred to Lafley as "an excellent listener . . . a sponge." From what he hears, Lafley patiently reshapes everything the company does. And with profits rising even in today's turbulent economy, it's clear that P&G has become "new and improved" from his efforts.

Questions for Discussion

1. What adjustments were required at P&G as changes were made?
2. What sources of resistance to change do you suspect were encountered at P&G and how do you think they were overcome?
3. What OD techniques might have been helpful for P&G to use? Explain your reasoning.

■ *Change, Creativity, and Innovation at Terra Cycle*

Part 6 Video Cases

Change, creativity and innovation are essential to the success of Terra Cycle, a company that makes consumer products from garbage. Tom Szaky, founder and CEO, hopes to reinvent consumer products and how they are made by capitalizing on the growing trend toward environmentally friendly lifestyles.

The notion of change, flexibility, and the ability to identify new ways to respond to consumer demand permeates every part of the culture at Terra Cycle. A core team is dedicated to innovation, but novel ideas are welcome from anyone, and employees are encouraged to try new things. Getting products to market quickly is an important component in Terra Cycle's competitive strategy, so the company looks for ways to circumvent traditional processes that can be time-consuming. In fact, although time to market at a traditional company is about three years, at Terra Cycle it's just nine months.

The company also prides itself on its ability to find quick fixes to problems in the production process. At one point, for example, the company used swimming pools and horse troughs to mix fertilizer in an effort to get around the time constraints involved in waiting for customized equipment. Milton Oppenheimer, assistant production manager, clams that being open-minded and willing to try new things is a characteristic of all employees at Terra Cycle. Change and thinking outside the box are part of the job, and everyone is expected to contribute ideas and find new solutions to problems. Tom Szaky also encourages employees to be innovative. His philosophy is that it is acceptable to fail because failing is better than not trying at all.

Discussion Questions

1. How does Terra Cycle promote a culture of creativity and divergent thinking as described in Chapter 14?
2. How are the basic components of creativity in teams and individuals as presented in Chapter 14 displayed at Terra Cycle?
3. In your opinion, is innovation at Terra Cycle radical or incremental in nature?

(Continued)

■ Organizational Culture at Terra Cycle

The commitment to making the world a better place drives just about everything at Terra Cycle, an eco-friendly company that makes consumer products entirely out of garbage. The company is staffed primarily by young people who share a vision of growing a better world. Founder and CEO Tom Szaky is devoted to the notion of eco-capitalism, which, he argues, involves a business model that differs from those of other companies that claim to be "green."

According to Szaky, other businesses simply take existing practices, look for ways to make them more environmentally friendly, and then pass the additional costs on to consumers. In contrast, eco-capitalism involves completely rethinking the entire process—and doing what is best for the environment—but without charging premium prices. Following this new model requires an organizational culture that demands flexibility from employees along with a willingness to change direction quickly and to occupy multiple roles.

According to Albe Zakes, director of public relations, employees at Terra Cycle are given many responsibilities and are empowered to handle them in their own way. He notes that although there is a set of checks and balances in place, it is not unusual for him to hand off a project with only very loose guidelines instructing a subordinate as to what to do. The sense of empowerment is evident in many areas at Terra Cycle, from R&D to production to marketing. Even interns at the company note that they receive far more freedom and responsibility than they would be given at most companies.

Inside the graffiti-covered walls of Terra Cycle's New Jersey headquarters is a scene of organized chaos, and the prevailing feeling is to get done what needs to be done and then move on. There are no rules as to how something is to be completed. Employees figure things out as they go. Zakes believes that the close relationships among employees at Terra Cycle and the shared belief that they are making the world a better place are significant factors in the company's success.

Discussion Questions

1. How are the core characteristics of organizational culture presented in Chapter 14 displayed at Terra Cycle?
2. Using the discussion of strong versus weak organizational culture presented in Chapter 14 as a starting point, how would you describe the organizational culture at Terra Cycle?
3. In which category of the competing values framework discussed in Chapter 14 would you place Terra Cycle?

■ Inside Student Advantage

Student Advantage is a company whose focus is capitalizing on the economic influence of college students. Recognizing that they usually do not have much money, but that most of what they do have is usually disposable, Ray Sozzi, president and CEO of Student Advantage, founded the company in 1992 with the idea that he could draw students across the country into an association that would give them more clout in the marketplace.

To some extent, the idea is modeled after the American Association of Retired Persons. Members receive a card that gives them discounts of 15 to 20 percent at a variety of Big Box stores and restaurants, as well as at many smaller "mom and pop" outlets. The company now employs approximately 450 people. Expansion has occurred primarily through mergers and acquisitions. Sozzi typically looks for companies that fit with his vision, and then acquires them. According to Todd Eichler, vice president, the new businesses are usually integrated and absorbed directly into the organization's existing operations.

Today, the company is expanding into a new product line called "Student Advantage Cash," which involves students, colleges, and merchants. With the new card, students will be able to do everything from using the laundry facilities in their dorms to buying pizzas at local retail outlets. Parents can add cash to the cards as needed. This new product complements many of the others that Student Advantage has launched since its inception, including Web sites that provide travel advice and academic assistance. Todd Eichler feels that because of its breadth and depth, Student Advantage has a strategic advantage in offering clients the opportunity to have a customized marketing package.

Discussion Questions

1. Which of the different organizational structures described in Chapter 15 does Student Advantage appear to have?
2. How do you think the division of labor within Student Advantage may have changed as the company has grown?
3. Using the discussions of strategy in Chapters 15 and 16, how would you characterize the strategic approach to change adopted by Student Advantage?

Appendix 1

Learning About Behavior in Organizations: Theory and Research

As noted in Chapter 1, organizational behavior (OB) is a science, and as such, it relies upon the scientific method to draw conclusions about behavior in organizations. As in other scientific fields, OB uses the tools of science to achieve its objectives. In this case, those goals are learning about organizations and the behavior of people working in them. With this in mind, it is useful to understand the basic methods that OB scientists use. In this appendix we will briefly describe some of these techniques. Our goal here is not to make you an expert in scientific methodology, but rather to give you an understanding of the techniques encountered in this book.

Isn't It All Just Common Sense?

Although you may not be a top executive of a large business firm with decades of experience in the work world, you doubtlessly know *something* about the behavior of people on the job. After all, you probably learned quite a bit from whatever jobs you have had or from talking to other people about their experiences. This isn't surprising, given that we all can observe a great deal about the behavior of people in organizational settings just by paying casual attention. So, whether you're the CEO of a *Fortune* 500 firm or a part-time pizza delivery driver, chances are good that you already have a few ideas about how people behave on the job.

Importantly, however, as indicated in Chapter 1, we cannot always trust our common sense about matters of organizational behavior. Several of the things we might assume to be true might not be the case. Many are likely to be far more complex than we ever envisioned. So, if we can't trust our common sense, on what can we rely? The answer is *research*. This is where the *scientific method* enters the picture. The **scientific method** is the systematic process of gathering and assessing information that identifies and helps explain the relationships between variables.

scientific method
The systematic process of gathering and assessing information that identifies and helps explain the relationships between variables.

Although social science research is far from perfect, the techniques used to study behavior in organizations can tell us a great deal. Naturally, not everything this research reveals contradicts common sense. In fact, a considerable amount confirms things we already believe to be true. If this occurs, is the research useless? The answer is emphatically *no!* After all, scientific evidence often provides a great deal of insight into the subtle conditions under which various events occur. Such complexities would not have been apparent from only casual, unsystematic observation and common sense. In other words, the field of OB is based solidly on carefully conducted and logically analyzed research. Although common sense may provide a useful starting point for getting us to think about behavior in organizations, there's no substitute for scientific research when it comes to understanding what really happens and why.

Now that you understand the important role of the scientific method in the field of OB, you are prepared to appreciate the specific approaches used to conduct scientific research in this field. We will begin our presentation of these techniques with a discussion of one of the best-accepted sources of ideas for OB research—*theory*.

Theory: An Indispensable Guide to Organizational Research

What image comes to mind when you think of a scientist at work? Someone wearing a white lab coat surrounded by microscopes and test tubes busily at work testing theories? Although OB scientists typically don't wear lab coats or use microscopes and test tubes, it *is* true that they make use of theories. This is the case despite the fact that OB is, in part, an applied science. Simply because a field focuses on theory does not imply that it is impractical or out of touch with reality. To the contrary, a theory is simply a way of describing the relationship between concepts. Thus, theories help, not hinder, our understanding of practical situations.

What Is a Theory and Why Are Theories Important?

Formally, a **theory** can be defined as a set of statements about the interrelationships between concepts that allows us to predict and explain various processes and events. As you might imagine, such statements may be of interest to both practitioners and scientists alike. We're certain that as you read this book you will come to appreciate the valuable role that theories play when it comes to understanding behavior in organizations—and putting that knowledge to practical use.

theory
A set of statements about the interrelationships between concepts that allows us to predict and explain various processes and events.

To demonstrate the value of theory in OB, let's consider an example based on a phenomenon described in more detail in Chapter 7—the effects of task goals on performance. Imagine observing that word-processing operators type faster when they are given a specific goal (e.g., 75 words per minute) than when they are told to try to do their best. You note as well that salespeople tend to make more sales when they are given quotas than when not given them. By themselves, these are useful observations insofar as they allow us to predict what will happen when goals are introduced. In addition, they suggest a way to change conditions so as to improve performance among people in these groups. These two accomplishments—*prediction* and *control*—are major goals of science.

Yet, there's something missing—namely, knowing that having specific goals improves performance fails to tell us anything about *why* this is so. What is going on here? After all, this was observed in two different settings and with distinct groups of people. Why is it that workers are so productive in response to specific goals? This is where theory enters the picture. In contrast to some fields, such as physics and chemistry, where theories often take the form of mathematical equations, those in OB generally involve verbal descriptions. For example, in the current cases, it might be theorized as follows:

- When workers are given specific goals they know exactly what's expected of them;
- When individuals know what's expected of them, they are motivated to work hard to find ways to succeed; and
- When people work hard to succeed, they perform at high levels.

This simple theory, like all others, consists of two basic elements: *concepts* (in this case goals and motives) and *assertions about how they are related.*

The Functions of Theories

In science, the formation of a theory is only the beginning of a sequence of events followed to understand behavior. It probably comes as no surprise to you to learn that the process of theory development and testing described here is very laborious. In view of this, why do scientists bother to fine-tune their assumptions? The answer lies in the very useful purposes of theories. Specifically, theories serve three important functions—organizing, summarizing, and guiding.

- Theories provide a way of *organizing* large amounts of data into meaningful propositions. In other words, they help us combine information so diverse that it might be difficult to grasp otherwise.
- Theories help us in *summarizing* this knowledge by making it possible to make sense out of bits and pieces of information that might be difficult—if not impossible—to understand.
- Theories provide an important *guiding* function. That is, they help scientists identify important areas of needed research that would not have been apparent without having a guide for their thinking.

As you read this text, you will come across many different theories attempting to explain various aspects of behavior in organizations. When you do, we think you will appreciate the useful organizing, summarizing, and guiding roles they play—in short, how theories help provide meaningful explanations of behavior.

The Theory-Testing Process

hypotheses
Logically derived, testable statements about the relationships between variables that follow from a theory.

Once a theory is proposed, it is used to introduce **hypotheses**—logically derived statements that follow from a theory. In our example, it may be hypothesized that specific goals will only improve performance when they are not so difficult that they cannot be attained. Next, this prediction needs to be tested in actual research to see if it can be confirmed. If our hypothesis is confirmed, we can be more confident about the accuracy of the theory. However, if it is not confirmed after several well-conducted studies are done, our confidence in the theory will be weakened. When this happens, it's time to revise the theory and generate new, testable hypotheses from it. As you might imagine, given the complexities of human behavior in organizations, theories are rarely—if ever—fully confirmed. In fact, many of the field's most popular and useful theories are constantly being refined and tested. We have summarized the cyclical nature of the scientific endeavor in Figure A1.1.

In all cases, the usefulness of any theory is based on the extent to which it can be confirmed or disconfirmed. In other words, theories must be *testable*.[1] A theory that cannot be tested serves no real purpose to scientists. Once it's tested, a theory—or, at least part of it—must be confirmed if it is to be considered an accurate account of human behavior. And, of course, that's what the field of OB is all about.

How are theories tested? The answer is: by conducting *research*. Unless we do research, we cannot test theories, and unless we test them, we are greatly limited in what we can learn about behavior in organizations.[2] This is why research is such a major concern of specialists in OB. So, for you to appreciate fully the field of organizational behavior, it's critical for you to understand something about the research techniques it on which is based—that is, how we come to know about the behavior of people at work. As a result, throughout this book, we not only explain *what* is known about organizational behavior, but also *how* that knowledge was derived. We are confident that the better you understand OB's "tools of the trade," the more you will come to appreciate its value as a field. With this in mind, we now will describe some of its major research techniques.

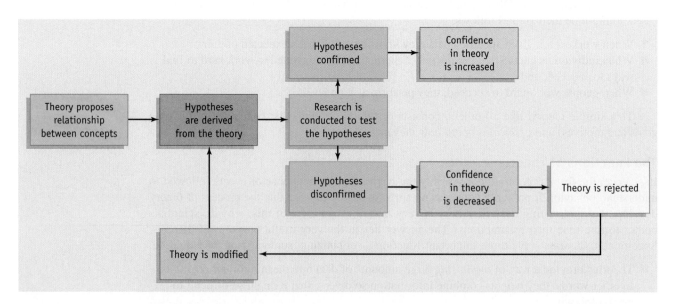

FIGURE A1.1

Theory Testing: The Research Process

Once a theory is formulated, research is conducted to test hypotheses derived from it. If these hypotheses are confirmed, confidence in the theory is increased. If these hypotheses are disconfirmed, confidence in the theory is diminished. At this point, the theory either is modified and retested, or it is rejected completely.

Survey Research: The Correlational Method

The most popular approach to conducting research in OB involves giving people written questions that ask them to report how they feel about various aspects of themselves, their jobs, and their organizations. Such questionnaires, also known as **surveys,** make it possible for organizational scientists to delve into a broad range of issues. This research technique is so very popular because it is applicable to studying a variety of topics. After all, you can learn a great deal about how people feel by asking them a systematic series of carefully worded questions. Moreover, questionnaires are relatively easy to administer (be it by mail, phone, or in person), and—as we will note shortly—they are readily quantifiable and lend themselves to powerful statistical analyses. These features make survey research a very appealing option to OB scientists. Not surprisingly, we will be describing quite a few survey studies throughout this text.

surveys
Questionnaires in which people are asked to report how they feel about various aspects of themselves, their jobs, and organizations.

Conducting Surveys

The survey approach consists of three major steps. First, the researcher must identify the variables in which he or she is interested. These may be various aspects of people (e.g., their attitudes toward work), organizations (e.g., the pay plans they use), or the environment in general (e.g., how competitive the industry is). They may be suggested from many different sources, such as a theory, previous research, or observations about conditions in the workplace.

Second, these variables are measured as precisely as possible. As you might imagine, it isn't always easy to tap precisely people's feelings about things (especially if they are uncertain about those feelings or reluctant to share them). As a result, researchers must pay a great deal of attention to the way they word the questions they use. For some examples of questions designed to measure various work-related attitudes, see Table A1.1.

Finally, after the variables of interest have been identified and measured, scientists must determine how—if at all—they are related to each other. With this in mind, they analyze their survey findings using a variety of different statistical procedures.

Scientists conducting survey research typically are interested in determining how variables are interrelated—or, put differently, how changes in one variable are associated with changes in another. For example, let's say that a researcher is interested in learning the relationship between how fairly people believe they are paid and various work-related attitudes, such as their willingness to help their coworkers and their interest in quitting. Based on various theories and previous research, a researcher may suspect that the more people believe they are unfairly paid, the less likely they will be to help their coworkers and the more likely they will be to desire new jobs. These predictions constitute the researcher's *hypothesis*—as we explained earlier, the as-yet-untested prediction based on the theory that the researcher wishes to investigate. After devising an appropriate questionnaire measuring these variables, the researcher would have to administer it to a large number of people so that the hypothesis can be tested.

Traditionally, people completing questionnaires have done so by marking responses with pen or pencil on a sheet of paper. Today, the practice of conducting surveys online has become very popular. **Online surveys** present questions to people either via e-mail or on a Web site; respondents

online surveys
Questionnaires presented to people either via e-mail or on a Web site that are completed and returned to administrators by using the same electronic means.

TABLE A1.1 Survey Questions Designed to Measure Work Attitude

Items such as these might be used to measure attitudes toward various aspects of work. People completing the survey are asked to circle the number that corresponds to the point along the scale that best reflects their feelings about the attitude in question.

1. Overall, how fairly are you paid?

    Not at all fairly: 1 2 3 4 5 6 7: Extremely fairly

2. Imagine that one of your colleagues needs to stay late to complete an important project. How likely or unlikely would you be to volunteer to help that person, even if you would not receive any special recognition for your efforts?

    Not at all likely: 1 2 3 4 5 6 7: Extremely likely

3. How interested are you in quitting your present job?

    Not at all interested: 1 2 3 4 5 6 7: Extremely interested

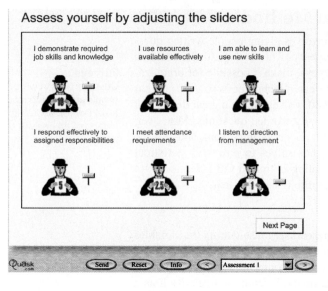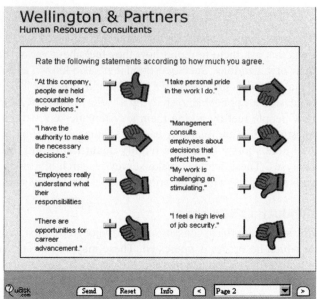

FIGURE A1.2

Online Surveys: Two Examples

Employee satisfaction questionnaires (left) and self-assessment questionnaires (right) are among the many different kinds of surveys that can be presented via e-mail or on Web pages using the "Form Caster" program by Quask. Companies such as GE Medical Systems, Lockheed Martin, and Procter & Gamble have benefited from using this technique.

then complete and return them to administrators by using the same electronic means. Many employees enjoy taking surveys online because modern software programs have made them highly user-friendly and, in some cases, fun to complete (see the samples in Figure A1.2). Many employers and researchers also prefer them to paper-and-pencil questionnaires because they are easier to administer and because they also can provide an instant summary and analysis of responses that would have taken many hours to enter by hand into a statistical analysis program.

This is not to say that online surveys are perfect, by any means. The greatest problem with them is that they cannot always be used because access to online networks is not universal. Thus, any survey results coming from people who complete questionnaires online may not be generalizable to those who either do not have access to computers or who avoid completing online questionnaires because they are uncomfortable working at computers. In short, online surveys should be considered a useful addition to the choices available to researchers interested in administering questionnaires, but not yet a replacement for more traditional, low-tech options. Until this turns around, you might want to keep that #2 pencil handy.

Analyzing Survey Results: Using Correlations

Once the survey data are collected, the investigator must statistically analyze them so as to compare the results to the hypothesis. Generally speaking, researchers are interested in seeing how the variables of interest are related to each other. That is, if they are "co-related"—or, that there exists a meaningful **correlation** between them. Variables are correlated to the extent that the level of one variable is associated with the level of another.

correlation
The extent to which two variables are related to each other.

POSITIVE AND NEGATIVE CORRELATIONS.   Suppose a researcher obtains results like those shown on the left side of Figure A1.3. In this case, the more fairly employees believe they are paid, the more willing they are to help their coworkers. In other words, the variables are related to each other such that the more that one increases, the more the other also increases. Any variables described in this way are said to have a **positive correlation.**

positive correlation
A relationship between two variables such that more of one variable is associated with more of the other.

Now, imagine what will be found when the researcher compares the sample's perceptions of pay fairness with their interest in quitting their jobs. If the experimenter's hypothesis is correct,

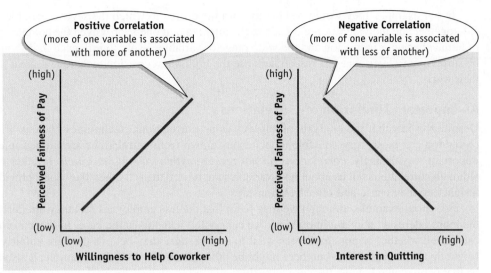

FIGURE A1.3

Positive and Negative Correlations: What They Mean

Positive correlations (left) exist when more of one variable is associated with more of another. Negative correlations (right) exist when more of one variable is associated with less of another.

the results will look like those shown on the right side of Figure A1.3. In other words, the more people believe their pay is fair, the less interested they are in looking for a new job. Any such case—in which the more one variable increases, the more another decreases—is said to have a **negative correlation.**

INTERPRETING CORRELATION COEFFICIENTS.   OB scientists are interested not only in the direction of the relationship between variables—that is, whether the association is positive or negative—but also in how strong that relationship is. To gauge this, researchers rely on a statistic known as the **correlation coefficient.** This is a number between -1.00 and $+1.00$ used to express the strength of the relationship between the variables studied. The closer this number is to 1.00 (either -1.00 or $+1.00$), the stronger the relationship is—that is, the more closely the variables are related to each other. However, the closer the correlation coefficient is to 0, the weaker the relationship between the variables—that is, the less strongly they are associated.

So, when interpreting a correlation coefficient, there are two things to keep in mind: its *sign* (in keeping with algebraic traditions, positive correlations are usually expressed without any sign) and its *absolute value* (that is, the size of the number without respect to its sign). For example, a correlation coefficient of $-.92$ reflects a much stronger relationship between variables than one of .22. The minus sign simply reveals that the relationship being described is negative (more of one variable is associated with less of another). The fact that the absolute value of this correlation coefficient is greater tells us that the relationship between the variables is stronger.

When variables are strongly correlated, scientists can make more accurate predictions about how they are related to each other. So, using our example, a negative correlation between perceptions of pay fairness and intent to quit, we may expect that in general, those who believe they are unfairly paid will be more likely to quit their jobs than those who believe they are fairly paid. If the correlation coefficient were high, say over $-.80$, we would be more confident that this would occur than if the correlation were low, say under $-.20$. In fact, as correlation coefficients approach 0, it's impossible to make any accurate predictions whatsoever. In such cases, knowing one variable would not allow us to predict anything about the other. As you might imagine, organizational scientists are extremely interested in discovering the relationships between variables and rely on correlation coefficients to tell them a great deal.

MORE THAN TWO VARIABLES.   Although the examples we've been using involve the relationship between only two variables at a time, organizational researchers frequently are interested in the interrelationships between many different variables at once.

For example, an employee's intent to quit may be related to several variables besides the perceived fairness of one's pay—such as satisfaction with the job itself, or liking for one's immediate supervisor. Researchers may make predictions using several different variables at once by using a technique known as **multiple regression.** Using this approach, researchers may be able to tell the extent to which each of several different variables contributes to predicting the behavior in question.

negative correlation
A relationship between two variables such that more of one variable is associated with less of the other.

correlation coefficient
A statistical index indicating the nature and extent to which two variables are related to each other.

multiple regression
A statistical technique through which it is possible to determine the extent to which each of several different variables contributes to predicting another variable (typically, where the variable being predicted is the behavior in question).

In our example, they would be able to learn the degree to which the several variables studied, together and individually, are related to the intent to quit one's job. Given the complex nature of human behavior on the job and the wide range of variables likely to influence it, it should not be surprising to learn that OB researchers use the multiple regression technique a great deal in their work.

An Important Limitation of Correlations

Despite the fact that the analysis of surveys using correlational techniques such as multiple regression can be so very valuable, conclusions drawn from correlations are limited in a very important way. Namely, *correlations do not reveal anything about causation.* In other words, although correlations tell us about how variables are related to each other, they don't provide any insight into their cause-and-effect relationships.

So, in our example, although we may learn that the less employees feel they are fairly paid the more interested they are in quitting, we cannot tell *why* this is the case. In other words, we cannot tell whether or not employees want to quit *because* they believe they are unfairly paid. Might this be the case? Yes, but there might be other reasons as well. For example, it also might be that people who believe they are unfairly paid tend to dislike the work they do and it is this that encourages them to find a new job. Another possibility is that people believe they are unfairly paid because their supervisors are too demanding—and this that raises their interest in quitting (see Figure A1.4). Our point is simple: Although all these possibilities are reasonable, knowing only that variables are correlated does *not* permit us to determine what causes what. Because it is important for researchers to establish the causal relationships between the variables they study, OB scientists frequently turn to another technique that *does* permit such conclusions to be drawn—the *experiment.*

Experimental Research: The Logic of Cause and Effect

experimental method
A research technique through which it is possible to determine cause–effect relationships between the variables of interest—that is, the extent to which one variable causes another.

Because both scientists and practitioners not only want to know the degree to which variables are related, but also how much one causes another, the **experimental method** is popularly used in OB. The more we know about the causal connections between variables, the better we can explain the underlying causes of behavior—and this, after all, is one of the major goals of OB.

FIGURE A1.4

Correlations: What They Don't Reveal About Causation

Even if a strong negative correlation exists between pay fairness and the desire to leave one's job, we cannot tell why this relationship exists. This correlation does not show that unfairness causes people to leave. As shown here, there are many possible underlying causes that are not identified by the knowledge of the correlation alone.

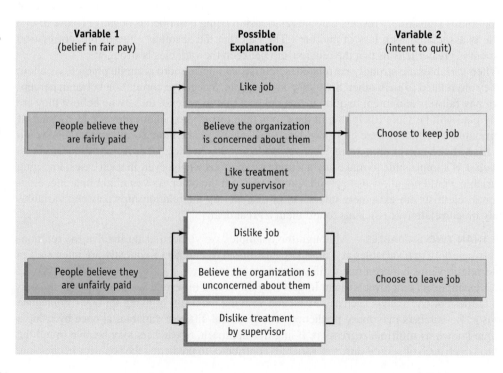

A Hypothetical Experiment

To illustrate how experiments work, let's consider an example. Suppose we're interested in determining the effects of social density (the number of people per unit of space) on the job performance of clerical employees—that is, the degree to which the crowdedness of working conditions in an office influences how accurately word-processing operators do their jobs.

Although this topic might be studied in many different ways, imagine that we do the following. First, we select at random a large group of word-processing operators working in a variety of organizations—the participants in our study. Then, we prepare a specially designed office, the setting for the experiment. Throughout the study, we would keep the design of the office and all the working conditions (e.g., temperature, light, and noise levels) alike with one exception—we would systematically vary the number of people working in the office at any given time.

For example, we could have one condition—the "high density" condition—in which 50 people are put into a 500-square-foot room at once (allowing 10 square feet per person). In another condition—the "low density" condition—we could put 5 people into a 500-square-foot room at once (allowing 100 square feet per person). Finally, we can have a "moderate density" condition in which we put 25 people into a 500-square-foot room (allowing 20 square feet per person).

Say we have several hundred people participating in the study and we assign them at random to each of these three conditions. Each word-processing operator is then given the same passage of text to type over two hours. After this period, the typists are dismissed, and the researcher counts the number of words accurately typed by each person, noting any possible differences between performance in the various conditions. Suppose we obtain the results summarized in Figure A1.5.

The Logic of Experimentation

Let's analyze what was done in this simple, hypothetical experiment to help explain the basic elements of the experimental method and its underlying logic. First, recall that we selected participants from the population of interest and assigned them to conditions on a *random* basis. This means that each person had an equal chance of being assigned to any one of the three conditions. This is critical because it is possible that differences between conditions could result from having many very good operators in one condition and many unproductive ones in another. So, to safeguard against this possibility, it is important to assign people to conditions at random. When this is done, we can assume that the effects of any possible differences among them would equalize over conditions.

Thus, by assigning people to conditions at random, we can be assured that there will be just as many fast as slow operators in each. As a result, there is no reason to believe that any differences in productivity that may be noted can be attributed to systematic discrepancies in the skills of the

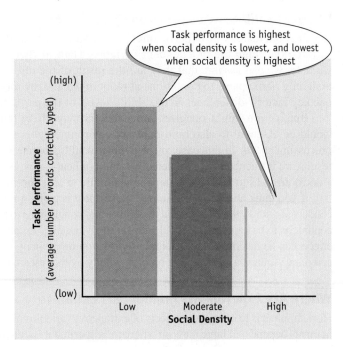

FIGURE A1.5

Example of Simple Experimental Results

Word-processing operators are put into rooms that differ with respect to only one variable—social density (i.e., the number of people per unit of space). The hypothetical results summarized here show that people perform best under conditions of lowest density and worst under conditions of highest density.

participants. Given "the luck of the draw," such differences can be discounted, thereby enhancing our confidence that they are solely the result of the social density of the rooms. This is the logic behind random assignment. Although it is not always feasible to use random assignment when conducting experiments in organizations, it is highly desirable whenever possible.

Recall that word-processing operators were assigned to conditions that differed with respect to only the variable of interest—in this case, social density. We can say that the experimenter *manipulated* this aspect of the work environment, systematically changing it from one condition to another. A variable altered in this way is called an **independent variable.** An independent variable is one that is systematically manipulated by the experimenter so as to determine its effects on the behavior of interest. In our example, the independent variable is social density. Specifically, it may be said to have three different *levels*—that is, degrees of the independent variable: high, moderate, and low.

The variable that is measured, the one influenced by the independent variable, is known as the **dependent variable.** A dependent variable is the behavior of interest that is being measured—the behavior that is dependent upon the independent variable. In this case, the dependent variable was word-processing performance, the quantity of words accurately typed. Besides studying this, we could have studied other dependent variables, such as satisfaction with the work or the perceived level of stress encountered. In fact, it would be quite likely for OB researchers to study several dependent variables in one experiment.

By the same token, scientists also frequently consider the effects of several different independent variables in a given experiment. The matter of which particular independent and dependent variables are being studied is one of the most important questions researchers make. Often, they base these decisions on suggestions from previous research (other experiments suggesting that certain variables are important) and existing theory (conceptualizations suggesting that certain variables may be important).

Generally speaking, the basic logic behind the experimental method is quite simple. In fact, it involves only two major steps. First, some variable of interest (the independent variable) must be systematically altered. Second, the effects, if any, of such changes must be measured. The underlying idea is that if the independent variable does indeed influence behavior, then people exposed to different amounts of it should behave differently. In our example, we can be certain that social density caused differences in processing performance because when all other factors were held constant, different amounts of density led to different levels of performance. Although our experiment is fabricated, it follows the same logic of all experiments—namely, it is designed to reveal the effects of the independent on the dependent variables.

Drawing Valid Conclusions from Experiments

For the conclusions of experimenters to be valid, it is critical for them to hold constant all factors other than the independent variable. Then, if there are differences in the dependent variable, we can assume that they are the result of the effects of the independent variable. By assigning participants to conditions at random we already took an important step to ensure that one key factor—differences in the ability levels of the participants—would be equalized.

But, as you might imagine, other factors may affect the results as well. For example, it would be essential to also hold constant environmental conditions that might influence word-processing speed. In this case, more people would generate more heat, so to make sure that the results are influenced only by density—and not heat—it would be necessary to air-condition the workroom so as to keep it the same temperature in all conditions at all times.

If you think about it, our "simple" experiment is really not that simple at all—especially if it is conducted with all the care needed to permit valid conclusions to be drawn. Thus, experiments require conditions to be kept identical with respect to all variables except the independent variable so that its effects can be determined unambiguously. As you might imagine, this is often easier said than done and often requires a considerable bit of ingenuity by the researcher.

Where Are Experiments Conducted? Laboratory and Field Settings

How simple it is to control the effects of extraneous variables (i.e., factors not of interest to the experimenter) depends, in large part, on where the experiment is conducted. In OB, researchers generally have two options available: Experiments can be conducted in either naturalistic organizational

independent variable
A variable that is systematically manipulated by the experimenter so as to determine its effects on the behavior of interest (i.e., the *dependent variable*).

dependent variable
A variable that is measured by the researcher, the one influenced by the *independent variable.*

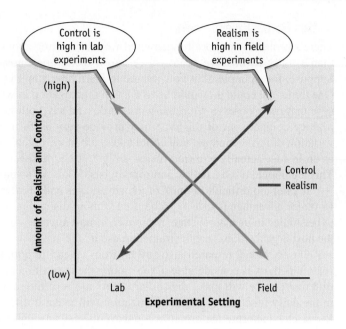

FIGURE A1.6

Trade-Offs Between Lab and Field Experiments

Researchers in OB may conduct experiments in laboratory or field settings, each of which has advantages and disadvantages. Generally, the lab offers more control but less realism, whereas the field offers less control but more realism.

settings (referred to as the *field*) or in settings specially created for the study itself, (referred to as the *laboratory,* or *lab* for short). As summarized in Figure A1.6, there are trade-offs involved with conducting research in each setting.

The study in our example is a lab experiment. It was conducted in carefully controlled conditions specially made for the research. The great amount of control possible in such settings improves the chances of creating the conditions needed to allow valid conclusions to be drawn from experiments. At the same time, however, lab studies suffer from a lack of realism. Although the working conditions can be carefully controlled, they may be relatively unrealistic, not carefully simulating the conditions found in actual organizations. As a result, it may be difficult to generalize the findings of lab studies to settings outside the lab, such as the workplace.

However, if we conducted our study in actual organizations, there would be many unknowns, many uncontrollable factors at work. To conduct such a study, we would have to distinguish between those who worked in offices differing with respect to social density and later compare people's performance. If we did this, we would be sure that the conditions studied were realistic. However, there would be so little control over the setting that many different factors could be operating. For example, because people would not be assigned to conditions at random, it might be the case that individuals would work in those settings they most desire. Furthermore, there would be no control over such factors as distractions and differences in environmental conditions (e.g., noise and temperature).

In short, field experiments, although strong in realism, are weak with respect to the level of control they provide. By contrast, lab experiments permit a great deal of control, but tend to be unrealistic. In view of these complementary strengths and weaknesses, it should be clear that experiments should be conducted in *both* types of sites. As researchers do so, our confidence can be increased that valid conclusions will be drawn about behavior in organizations.

Qualitative Research Methods

In contrast to the highly empirical approaches to research we have been describing thus far, we also should note that OB scientists sometimes use a less empirical method. After all, probably the most obvious way of learning about behavior in organizations is to observe it firsthand and to describe it after it occurs. Researchers have a long tradition of studying behavior using these nonempirical, descriptive techniques, relying on what is known as **qualitative research.**[3] The qualitative approach relies on preserving the natural qualities of the situation being studied, attempting to capture the richness of the context while disturbing naturalistic conditions only minimally, if at all. The two major qualitative methods used by OB scientists are *naturalistic observation* and the *case method.*

qualitative research
A nonempirical type of research that relies on preserving the natural qualities of the situation being studied.

Naturalistic Observation

naturalistic observation
A research technique in which people are systematically observed in situations of interest to the researcher.

There's probably no more fundamental way of learning about how people act in organizations than simply to observe them—a research technique known as **naturalistic observation.** Suppose, for example, that you wanted to learn how employees behave in response to layoffs. One thing you could do would be to visit an organization in which layoffs will be occurring and systematically observe what the workers do and say both before and after the layoffs occur. Making comparisons of this type may provide very useful insights into what's going on. As a variation of this technique, you could take a job in the organization and make your observations as an insider actually working there—giving you a perspective you might not otherwise gain. This technique, often used by anthropologists, is known as **participant observation.**

participant observation
A qualitative research technique in which people systematically make observations of what goes on in a setting by becoming an insider, part of that setting itself.

It's not too difficult to think of the advantages and disadvantages of observational research. Its major advantage is that it can be used without disrupting normal routines, allowing behavior to be studied in its natural state. Moreover, almost anyone—including people already working in the host organization—can be trained to use it.

Observational research also suffers from several important limitations. First, the potential for subjectivity is considerable. Even among the most diligent of researchers, it's inevitable that different people will make dissimilar observations of the same events. Second, being involved in the daily functioning of an organization will make it difficult for observers to be impartial. Researchers interpreting organizational events may be subject to bias due to their feelings about the people involved. Finally, because most of what goes on in an organization is fairly dull and routine, it's very easy to place a great deal of emphasis on unusual or unexpected events, possibly leading to inaccurate conclusions. Given these limitations, most OB scientists consider observational research to be more useful as a starting point for providing basic insight into behavior than as a tool for acquiring definitive knowledge about behavior.

The Case Method

Suppose that we conducted our hypothetical study of reactions to layoffs differently. Instead of observing behavior directly, we might fully describe the company's history leading up to the event and some statistics summarizing its aftermath (e.g., how long people were unemployed, how the company was restructured after downsizing, and the like). We might even include some interviews with people affected by the layoff, and quote them directly. The approach we are describing here is known as the **case method.** More often than not, the rationale behind the case method is *not* to teach us about a specific organization per se, but to learn what happened in that company as a means of providing cues as to what may be going on in others.

case method
A research technique in which a particular organization is thoroughly described and analyzed for purposes of understanding what went on in that setting.

The case method is similar to naturalistic observation in that it relies on descriptive accounts of events. However, it is different in that it often involves using post hoc accounts of occurrences from those involved as opposed to firsthand observations by scientists.

As you might imagine, a great deal can be learned by detailed accounts of events in organizations summarized in the form of written cases. Especially when these cases are supplemented by careful interviews (in which case the method would be considered quantitative rather than qualitative in nature), cases can paint a particularly detailed picture of events as they unfolded in a particular organization.

Of course, to the extent that the company studied is unique, it may be not be possible to generalize what is learned to others. To get around this limitation, some researchers have recommended that multiple, as opposed to single, cases should be used to test theories.[4] Another problem with the case method—a limitation it shares with naturalistic observation— is that the potential for bias is relatively high. As a result, many scientists believe that although the case method may serve as a valuable source of hypotheses about behavior on the job, testing those theories requires more rigorous research methods.[5]

Appendix 2

Understanding and Managing Your Career

Throughout this book we have spoken about the work people do at any given point in time. Here, however, we turn our attention to individuals' employment during their lives. Indeed, over the years we are likely to find ourselves holding a variety of jobs in several organizations. In fact, the average American holds eight different jobs in his or her lifetime.

In most cases, these positions are interconnected in some systematic way, weaving a path, however twisted and indirect, representing a career. This appendix discusses the basic nature of careers, along with some of the key issues associated with choosing a career and the challenges encountered as it develops. To fully understand these ideas, of course, let's begin with some basic definitions.

The Nature of Careers

We've all heard of, and use, the word *career,* but it begs to be defined more precisely. As you'll see, although we use the term rather loosely in everyday language, social scientists use it in far more precise fashion. With this in mind, we will define what we mean by *career,* along with various terms to which it is related; in addition, various types of careers will be identified and described.

Basic Definitions

Formally, a **career** can be defined as the evolving sequence of work experiences over time. In everyday language, however, people often use the terms *job, occupation,* and *career* interchangeably, so it makes sense to distinguish among these before going any further. Simply put, a **job** is a predetermined set of activities one is expected to perform. An **occupation**, by contrast, is a coherent set of jobs.[1] So, for example, a person working as a carpenter would be said to have an occupation in the field of construction. Eventually, he or she may shift to occupations in the field of sales, such as home sales manager. Overall, this succession of jobs represents the individual's career. For a summary, see Figure A2.1.

Careers mean a great deal to individuals—both financially and psychologically. After all, the career path you take has a major impact upon how much money you will make throughout your life. Historically, some careers are more lucrative than others. For example, in 2010 the average annual salary of an insurance claims adjustor was $57,550; for an aerospace engineer it was $92,980; the average attorney made $124,750 and the average surgeon made $206,770, but the average cook in a fast food restaurant made only $17,620.[2] Although money isn't everything, of course, these very large differences underscore the point that how much money you are likely to make depends greatly on your choice of career.

Careers also are important to us as individuals because they give us a sense of accomplishment and pride, and they also can give meaning to our lives (e.g., such as doctors who feel good about themselves because they save people's lives). Like it or not, your job defines your identity in the eyes of others. After all, when you meet someone at a party, the question often is asked, "What do you do?" Indeed, we define ourselves and others define us by the work we do.

Types of Careers

Although everyone's career is unique, scientists who have studied careers have observed that there are some general patterns or categories into which the vast majority fall.[3]

career
The evolving sequence of work experiences over time.

job
A predetermined set of activities one is expected to perform.

occupation
A coherent set of jobs.

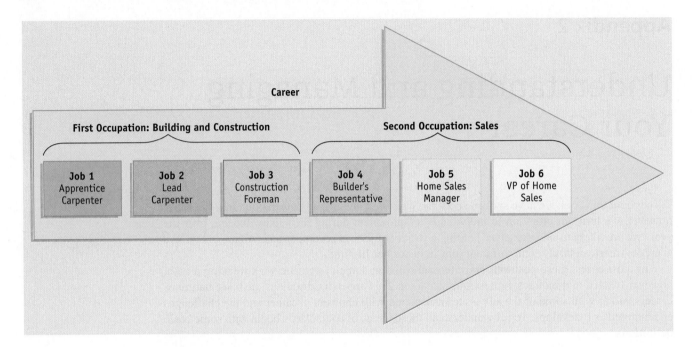

FIGURE A2.1

Distinguishing Among Career, Occupation, and Job

The typical career consists of several occupations (coherent sets of jobs), each of which is composed of a succession of individual jobs (predetermined sets of activities). A hypothetical example is presented here.

Specifically, four different types of careers have been identified (for a summary, see Figure A2.2).

STEADY-STATE CAREERS.   Bob's family owns a small bakery, Main Street Bakery. When Bob was a young boy, he used to hang out there after school, and he became interested in that line of work. After getting a degree in hospitality management from the local community college, Bob took over the family business. For all his working life, some 40 years, he ran Main Street Bakery, where he baked fine breads, cakes, and pies. Over the years, Bob had several opportunities to sell the business and do something else, but he didn't. When it came time for him to retire, he simply handed over the family business to his own son.

Bob made a career choice that led him to a lifetime commitment to a single job, what is called a **steady-state career**. People who have steady-state careers are generally very satisfied with what they are doing. Also, because they work at their jobs for so long, they tend to become highly skilled experts at what they do. After all, for Bob to have stuck it out in the bakery as long as he did, he must like what he does, and be pretty good at it, as well.

LINEAR CAREERS.   Claire always loved tinkering with computers, even as a young girl. Nobody was surprised, therefore, when she did an internship at a software development firm before getting a bachelor's degree in computer science. After graduating, she took an entry-level position at a Silicon Valley start-up, where she did lots of different jobs and got great experience. After about four years, it became clear that the company wasn't going anywhere (except out of business, perhaps), so she moved on to a much larger firm, where she took a position in which she helped develop and test new wireless products. Her assignments were small at first, but after a few years, Claire found herself taking on larger and larger projects, until eventually she became a vice president of technology for the company. It was a dream job for Claire, but she wanted more. At about the same time, the company decided to invest more of its resources in manufacturing and marketing and to outsource research and product development. So Claire sold her stock and started her own firm—not a competitor, but a lab that specialized in developing new wireless technology for her old employer, and lots of other companies as well.

steady-state career
The type of career in which there is a lifetime of employment in a single occupation.

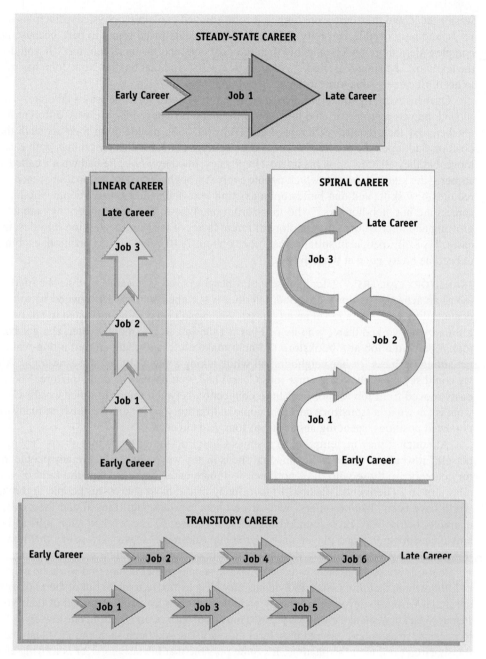

FIGURE A2.2

Four Major Types of Careers

Scientists have found it useful to distinguish among four different types of careers—steady-state, linear, spiral, and transitory—each of which is depicted here.

Claire had what's known as a **linear career**. That is, she stuck with a certain field and worked her way up the occupational ladder. Sometimes, she stayed at a single company, but at other times, she changed jobs. In all cases, however, she took on greater challenges. Linear careers are rather traditional paths. For many years, working one's way "up the corporate ladder" until "you made it" was considered the true sign of career success. Indeed, although achieving increasingly higher levels of success in a single line of work is a considerable accomplishment, it is no longer regarded as the only acceptable option for people today.

SPIRAL CAREERS. John always loved science, especially physics, so he kept going to school and getting higher degrees. Before he knew it, he had a PhD and found that he enjoyed studying thermal dynamics. Fortunately, a local aeronautics lab was looking for someone in that area to conduct research, and they were impressed with John's accomplishments. Working there was satisfying for him for a few years, but research wasn't his passion. Then, one day, he was asked to give a talk about his work to a group of students at a small college nearby. John became hooked on teaching and soon took a job as a physics instructor at that same school. The pay

linear career
The type of career in which someone stays in a certain field and works his or her way up the occupational ladder, from low-level jobs to high-level jobs.

wasn't great, and the hours were long, but John enjoyed explaining physical principles in simple ways, and he proved to be pretty good at it. The students loved him—in part, because he made complex ideas more understandable than the textbook, and far more fun, too. "If you don't like the textbook," he soon reasoned, "write one yourself." And that he did. Now, John has moved on to his third career—this time, as an author of textbooks.

Over his working life, John moved between three jobs. First, he was a laboratory scientist; second, he was a professor; and third, he was an author. These jobs are very different from one another, and each requires different skills. However, John pieced them together such that each position built upon the previous one. He did exciting, new, and different things with each career move, but they all drew upon his interest in physics. In other words, he had what's called a **spiral career**—the kind of career in which people evolve through a series of occupations, each of which requires new skills and that builds upon existing knowledge and skills. People who have spiral careers are not "job-hoppers," who move from one post to another. Rather, they are constantly growing and improving as they explore different facets of the same profession (physics, in John's case). Typically, people in spiral careers spend about 7–10 years in each position, enabling them to become pretty good at what they do.

spiral career
The kind of career in which people evolve through a series of occupations, each of which requires new skills and that builds upon existing knowledge and skills.

TRANSITORY CAREERS. After high school, Cheryl worked as a waitress while she tried to find a job as an actress. The tips were good, but after it became clear that Hollywood wasn't going to come calling, she took a job at an art gallery. She wasn't especially interested in art, but she had a friend who worked there, who helped her get the job. A few months later, she got bored and took a part-time job at a bookstore. To help make ends meet, she started a dog-walking and pet-sitting business for her neighbors, all while taking a few college classes at night. Although we could say more about the other jobs Cheryl had, you probably get the picture: She continuously moved from job to job, with little connection between them. In other words, Cheryl has what is known as a **transitory career**. People in transitory careers move between many different unrelated positions, spending about one to four years in each.

transitory career
The type of career in which someone moves between many different unrelated positions, spending about one to four years in each.

Although it may be tempting to dismiss Cheryl on the grounds that she is "trying to find herself," it would be unfair to assume that she is in any way inept. In fact, many people in transitory careers are those who have not been fortunate enough to discover the kind of work that allows them to derive satisfaction. In fact, many of the most successful people in the business world have been "late bloomers" who drifted between jobs until they found their calling. For example, before Ray Croc founded McDonald's at age 52, he worked such jobs as being an ambulance driver, a piano player, and a paper cup salesman.[4] Obviously, to say that he was anything other than a huge success, despite his transitory career, would be very misleading.

It also is important to acknowledge that some people simply do not find work the major source of fulfillment in their lives. Such individuals may elect to "make a career out of their hobbies," so to speak, preferring to devote their energy and talent to their avocations instead of their vocations. Perhaps you know someone who's a talented musician, but who moves from one low-level "day job" to the next, so as to have time to play local gigs at night. Although such an individual may have a transitory career during the daytime, it's quite possible that his or her career is moving along in a very linear fashion after the sun goes down. Even if the hobby brings personal satisfaction instead of occupational recognition, it clearly would be unfair to think any less of such an individual.

Getting Started: Making Career Choices

"What do you want to be when you grow up?" This is a question you probably heard many times in your youth (if not later in life, too!). As children, we learn about different careers, based mostly on the people with whom we come into contact in real life (e.g., teachers and doctors) and on television (e.g., athletes). This continues into our adult years as well, although as adults we come into contact with a broader range of professions, and we have had experiences at some. With this in mind, we will turn our attention to three major factors that determine people's career choices.

Person-Job Fit: Holland's Theory of Occupational Choice

Why is it that you may decide to become a lawyer whereas your sister is interested in being a doctor, a police officer, a musician, or a chef—anything other than a lawyer? To a great extent, the answer lies in the notion of **person-job fit**. That is the degree to which a particular job matches an individual's skills, abilities, and interests. This was the basic idea of John Holland, a scientist who has specialized in studying occupational choice. Specifically, he believed that a person's decision is based primarily on his or her personality (see Chapter 4).[5] His research has established two important findings:

- People from various occupations tend to have many similar personality characteristics.
- Individuals whose characteristics match those of people in a given field are predisposed to succeed in that field.

So, for example, assume for argument's sake that successful lawyers tend to have certain characteristics in common: They are very inquisitive, detail-oriented, and analytical—all characteristics that help them do their jobs well. According to *Holland's theory of vocational choice,* you would be attracted to the field of law to the extent that you share many of the same characteristics. In other words, because being a lawyer "suits you," and you "have what it takes" to succeed at that field, you are likely to select that occupation. In essence, **Holland's theory of vocational choice** says that people will perform best at occupations that match their traits and personalities.

Holland's theory is quite specific with respect to the various personality types and occupational types involved. Specifically, Holland identifies six different characteristics of work environments and the personality traits and interests of the people who are most successful in those environments. These are summarized in Figure A2.3. As you look at this diagram, you probably cannot help but consider what particular type best describes you. It is important to be very cognizant of this because the more closely your personality type matches the work you do, the more successful you will be and the less stress you are likely to encounter.[6]

It's clear from Figure A2.3 that people in each type should work in certain environments, but what happens when these don't occur? Holland has noted that for people of each type there are second-best matches, third-best matches, and some jobs that constitute the worst possible match of all. These are summarized in Figure A2.4, known as **Holland's hexagon**. Interpreting this diagram is straightforward. The position of each Holland type around the hexagon indicates those occupations for which people are best suited and worst suited, based on their types. The closer a job environment comes to the associated personality type on this diagram, the more effective the person will be.

For example, someone with an enterprising personality type is expected to be most successful when working in an occupation that permits those qualities to come out (e.g., a sales job). However, neither people nor jobs fit perfectly into only a single category. As such, fairly good matches may occur in cases in which individuals in a certain category perform work in environments that favor adjacent types. So, for example, an enterprising person may perform reasonably well at jobs in social or conventional environments, each of which is adjacent to the enterprising type in the hexagon. By the same token, poorer matches, such as with environments favoring artistic or realistic people, which are two steps away, are likely to be quite problematic for enterprising individuals. And finally, there's the point along the hexagon that lies directly opposite— in the case of the enterprising type, it's the investigative environment. These represent the poorest matches. So, for example, we would expect people who do well in enterprising occupations (such as salesperson) to do poorly in occupations (such as scientist) that require the more analytical talents of the investigative type.

Holland's theory has been used widely by vocational counselors, professionals specializing in helping people find the kind of work that best suits them. The rationale is straightforward. Individuals taking various vocational tests can determine how closely their traits and personality characteristics match those of people in various occupational groups. Then, using Holland's hexagon, they are encouraged to seek work in fields whose job incumbents tend to have those various qualities, and to avoid work in areas where workers have qualities that lie opposite their own along the hexagon. The happiest and most successful employees tend to be those for whom there is a close fit between their personality and their work environment. According to Holland, and supported by research, this is the key to successful career development.[7]

person-job fit
The degree to which a particular job matches an individual's skills, abilities, and interests.

Holland's theory of vocational choice
A theory that claims that people will perform best at occupations that match their traits and personalities.

Holland's hexagon
A conceptualization specifying the occupations for which people are best suited based on which of six personality types most closely describe them.

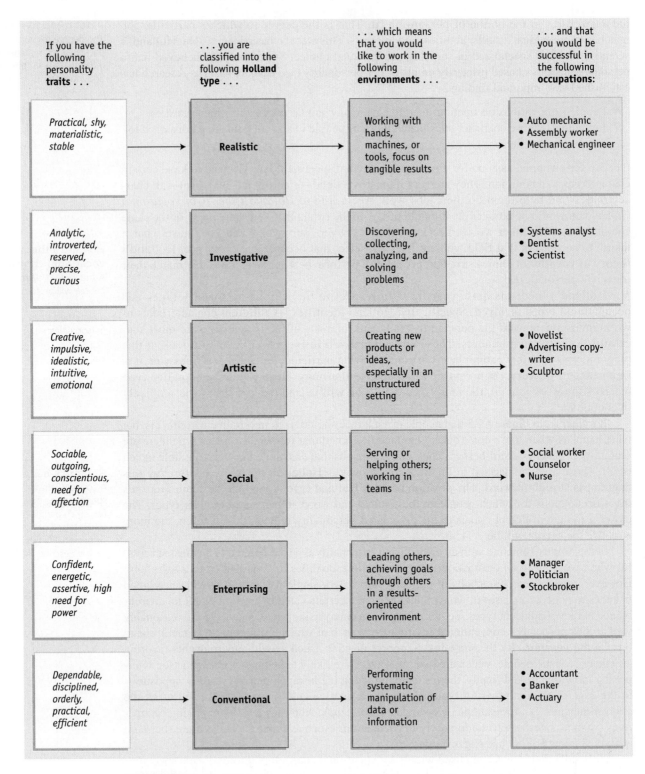

FIGURE A2.3

Holland's Theory of Vocational Choice: An Overview

Holland's theory of vocational choice specifies that people are most satisfied with occupations that match their personalities. People are classified into any of six distinct personality types, each of which is associated with a particular work environment that best suits them. These pairings and the occupations that most closely match them are summarized here.

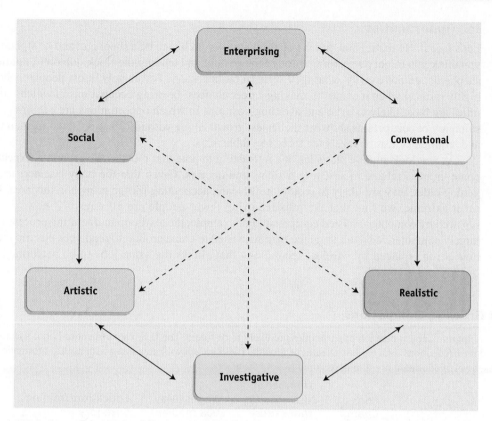

FIGURE A2.4

Holland's Hexagon

The diagram known as Holland's hexagon summarizes the relationship between each of the six personality and work environment types. According to Holland's theory of vocational choice, the closer these are, the more satisfied one will be with one's occupational choice. Occupations with demands opposite each personality type (shown here with dashed lines) identify those for which people are most poorly suited.

Career Anchors

Thus far, we've considered the extent to which a person's occupation matches his or her personality. However, another very important consideration when it comes to selecting careers has to do with the extent to which various jobs are in keeping with our self-image. For example, suppose you think of yourself as a creative kind of person, someone who likes to build or produce new things on your own. Because of this, based on your experiences and knowledge, you may find yourself moving into directions that bring out your creative side. So, instead of managing a restaurant, for example, you might come to think of yourself as a chef and be motivated to develop a new set of skills. In other words, these beliefs about yourself "anchor" your choice of careers—and, as such, they are known as *career anchors.*

Formally defined, a **career anchor** is a person's occupational self-concept based on his or her self-perceived talents, abilities, values, needs, and motives.[8] As people spend time working, they gradually develop career anchors. Scientists studying careers have identified five major career anchors.[9] These are as follows:

- *Technical or functional.* Concentration on jobs focusing on specific content areas (e.g., auto mechanics, graphic arts)
- *Managerial competence.* Focus on jobs that allow for analyzing business problems and dealing with people
- *Security and stability.* Attraction to jobs that are likely to continue into the future (e.g., the military)
- *Creativity or entrepreneurship.* Primary interest in starting new companies from visions of unique products or services, but not necessarily running them
- *Autonomy and independence.* Attraction to jobs that allow for freedom from constraints and working at one's own pace (e.g., novelists and creative artists)

Despite the fact that people have many interests and abilities, not all of these guide them toward careers. Instead, people are regularly attracted to careers that are in keeping with their particular career anchor. Scientists have used various questionnaires to assess people's career anchors. One of these, known as the "Career Orientation Inventory," is used by vocational counselors for the purpose of helping people decide the kind of occupations to which they are best suited.

career anchor
A person's occupational self-concept based on his or her self-perceived talents, abilities, needs, and motives.

Job Opportunities

Let's face it: No matter how much you think you would like to be a shepherd, and how good a job you think you might do roaming through the pasture and tending the flock, job opportunities for shepherds are not exactly what they were in biblical days. Fortunately, most people tend to be highly rational when it comes to making career choices, favoring occupations in which opportunities are most likely to exist and avoiding positions in which opportunities are declining. For a summary of occupations showing the fastest growth along with information about median wages and required education levels for each, see Table A2.1.

As you look at these statistics, it's interesting to note that most of the growth is expected to come in areas related to assisting patients and doctors. Given that the baby boomers are now getting older, they are likely to require health care, accounting for the growth in this area. At the other extreme, we find that the jobs requiring fewer people are all ones that now are being replaced by computer-assisted equipment. For example, the textile-manufacturing process is now largely computerized. And that nice man who used to come around to read your electric meter is now being replaced by wireless technology that allows the same jobs to be performed more quickly and accurately.

TABLE A2.1 Fastest Growing Occupations

When planning a career, it is helpful to know where job opportunities are likely to be found. The U.S. Department of Labor's Bureau of Labor Statistics has identified the occupations with the fastest rates of growth. These are shown here, along with useful information about median salaries and the level of education or training required to hold these jobs.

Occupations	Percent Change	Number of New Jobs (*in thousands*)	Wages (May 2008 median)	Education/Training Category
Biomedical engineers	72	11.6	$77,400	Bachelor's degree
Network systems data and communications analysts	53	155.8	71,100	Bachelor's degree
Home health aides	50	460.9	20,460	Short-term on-the-job training
Personal and home care aides	46	375.8	19,180	Short-term on-the-job training
Financial examiners	41	11.1	70,930	Bachelor's degree
Medical scientists, except epidemiologists	40	442.0	72,590	Doctoral degree
Physician assistants	39	29.2	81,230	Master's degree
Skin care specialists	38	147.0	28,730	Postsecondary vocational award
Biochemists and biophysicists	37	8.7	82,840	Doctoral degree
Athletic trainers	37	6.0	39,640	Bachelor's degree
Physical therapist aides	36	16.7	23,760	Short-term on-the-job training
Dental hygienists	36	62.9	66,570	Associate degree
Veterinary technologists and technicians	36	28.5	28,900	Associate degree
Dental assistants	36	105.6	32,380	Moderate-term on-the-job training
Computer software engineers, applications	34	175.1	85,430	Bachelor's degree
Medical assistants	34	163.9	28,300	Moderate-term on-the-job training
Physical therapist assistants	33	21.2	46,140	Associate degree
Veterinarians	33	19.7	79,050	First professional degree
Self-enrichment education teachers	32	81.3	35,720	Work experience in a related occupation
Compliance officers, except agriculture, construction, health and safety, and transportation	31	80.8	48,890	Long-term on-the-job training

Source: Bureau of Labor Statistics, 2010.

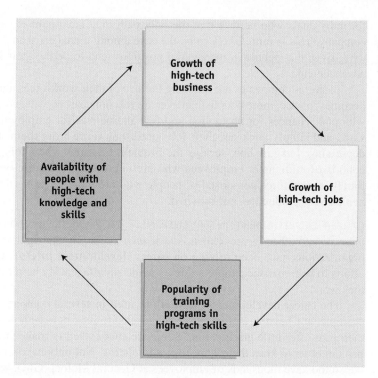

FIGURE A2.5

The Cyclical Nature of Job Growth, Training Opportunities, and Skilled Labor
As summarized here, the growth of high-tech companies leads to high-tech jobs, which leads to high-tech training, which leads to more people with high-tech skills, which further supports the growth of more high-tech jobs.

Because openings in many high-tech jobs and medical jobs are expected to grow in the years ahead, these positions tend to capture people's attention when considering occupations they might want to enter. Not surprisingly, they also capture the attention of those administering vocational programs in high schools, technical schools, and colleges. To be popular with prospective students, these programs offer training in areas where the jobs are likely to be. The availability of such training opportunities also attracts people to the kind of jobs that require this training, creating the cycle shown in Figure A2.5.

Managing Established Careers

Although getting started in one's career can be very difficult, so too do people face considerable challenges once they've been working for a while. Three such challenges are described in the following sections.

Confronting the Career Plateau

While people in their 20s and 30s are figuring out what they want to be, the 40-something crowd faces different challenges. This is sometimes a difficult period in which people look down the road and realize that they never may fulfill their career aspirations. As you might imagine, this can be problematic for both employees and their organizations. Fortunately, however, something can be done to help.

THE NATURE OF THE CAREER PLATEAU.   The point at which one's career has peaked and is unlikely to develop further is known as a **career plateau**. One way to identify this is by noting how long someone has been in his or her current position. Employees who have been in a particular post for five or more years would be considered immobile and to have reached a plateau. Another popular approach is subjective in nature: People may be considered to have plateaued whenever they no longer expect to move on to higher-status positions. Using either definition, about one employee in four is considered to have reached a career plateau.[10]

Although it is tempting to assume that employees whose careers have plateaued are no longer motivated or effective at their current jobs, this isn't always so. In fact, some people are quite satisfied to remain at their present jobs for a long time, finding it more relaxing and a source of contentment to be a "solid citizen" of the company instead of being one of its "fast trackers" or "high fliers." Of course, career plateauing can be a serious source of dissatisfaction

career plateau
The point at which one's career has peaked and is unlikely to develop further.

for individuals who believe that the only path to contentment is via upward movement in the company. This is more likely to be the case among managers than for employees holding other jobs, given that people in managerial positions tend to define their success in terms of upward advancement.

Today, as companies are reducing the size of their workforces and competition for good jobs becomes intense, more people than ever are reaching career plateaus earlier than expected. Faced with poor chances for promotion and few alternatives for employment, they may feel unmotivated and simply stick out their jobs until they retire from them. If you think this picture is depressing, imagine how serious the problem becomes when companies are faced with large cohorts of mid-career employees who are unmotivated because their careers have plateaued. Surely, a workforce composed of people who are merely "going through the motions" will be neither very productive, nor satisfied.

CAREER DEVELOPMENT INTERVENTIONS.   To avoid the problems associated with career plateaus and other career-related issues, such as finding the right job or adjusting to new ones, organizations have been relying on **career development interventions**. These are systematic efforts to help manage people's careers while simultaneously helping the organizations in which they work.

career development interventions
Systematic efforts to help manage people's careers while simultaneously helping the organizations in which they work.

The career development interventions used in several companies are quite interesting. For example, at Chevron, employees are counseled to seek outside hobbies during periods in which their jobs offer little gratification. Some are encouraged to make lateral moves within the company in order to keep their work lives stimulating. Not only have Chevron employees done this, but so too have thousands of employees at General Motors (GM), where the white-collar workforce has been reduced dramatically over the last few years. In fact, it has been reported that GM has spent some $10 million per year helping employees whose careers have reached plateaus find appropriate new positions within the company.

Much of what goes on in career development interventions involves helping employees assess the skills and interests they have so that they may be placed into positions for which they are well suited. Some companies, such as Hewlett-Packard and Lawrence Livermore Laboratories, provide self-assessment exercises for this purpose. Others, such as Coca-Cola and Disneyland, rely on individualized counseling sessions in which employees meet with trained professionals. Still others, including AT&T, IBM, Ford, Shell Oil, and Kodak, take it a step further, offering organizational assessment programs through which employees are systematically tested to discover their profiles of skills and interests.

At the very least, companies such as CBS, Merck, Aetna, and General Electric all provide services such as job posting systems and career resource centers through which employees can learn about new career options within their companies. And, when businesses find that they must reduce the size of their workforces, terminated employees at Exxon, Mutual of New York, General Electric, and other companies receive the services of **outplacement programs**. These generally include assistance in developing the skills needed to find new jobs (such as networking, interviewing skills, resume writing, and the like). Despite these various differences, it is safe to characterize the vast majority of career development interventions as following the six steps listed in Figure A2.6.

outplacement programs
Systematic efforts to find new jobs for employees who are laid off.

Making Career Changes

Changing jobs, or even entire occupations, is quite common today. In fact, most new graduates with MBA degrees expect to stay at their first jobs for no more than four years.[11] About two-thirds of all U.S. workers say that they would make major career changes if they could.[12] Each year, approximately 10 million workers do make these changes. And, of those who did this in recent years, 53 percent did so voluntarily, with the majority reporting that their incomes went up as a result.[13] People who make significant career changes do so for a variety of reasons. The major ones are that they recognize that:

- They either don't like, or can't succeed, at their chosen profession.
- Prospects are poor for future employment in their current occupation.
- Their needs or interests have shifted, requiring a life change.

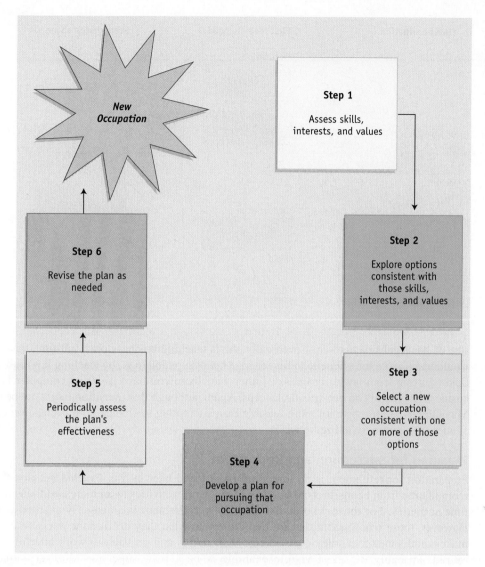

FIGURE A2.6

Career Development Interventions: Step-by-Step

Although each specific career development intervention may be unique in various ways, most involve the six steps summarized here.

The traditional way of making a major career change is by starting completely anew. You may, for example, quit your current job, return to school for new training, and then start over in your new career. People do this all the time. If you've done it, or if you know anyone who has, you probably know how very difficult it can be, both emotionally (because you're making a lot of changes at once) and financially (because you're likely to be without an income for awhile, and then have a lower income).

For example, suppose that Michelle is a lawyer who specializes in computers, but she is unhappy and looking to make a brand-new start by becoming, say, a business teacher. The hard way of doing this would be for Michelle to give up her job and go back to college, where she studies both education and business. Then, after graduating and receiving her teaching credentials, she can look for a new job. Although this would take Michelle to that new place she desires, this way of making the change would be very disruptive. So, how can Michelle go about making a major career change in a way that minimizes the disruption in her life?

Career experts advise making the changes in two steps: first changing either your occupation or your field of expertise, and then changing the other.[14] In our example Michelle has a current occupation, lawyer, and desires a new one, teacher. She also has a field, computers, and desires a new one, business. Using the two-step method, she first may change her field, such as by expanding her practice into business law. Then, after getting established, Michelle should consider changing occupations, such as by teaching a class or two during the evenings at a local community college. After awhile, she might want to take on more teaching responsibilities and limit the

FIGURE A2.7

Making Career Changes: A Two-Step Process

Career experts advise that the most effective way to make a major career shift is by changing your occupation and your field in two separate steps, as illustrated here.

Source: Based on suggestions by Bolles, 2006; see Note 13.

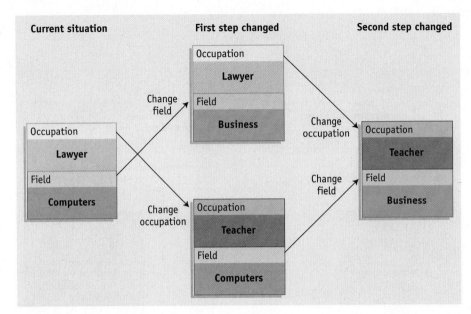

size of her legal practice, until eventually she is teaching business on a full-time basis. It also would be possible for Michelle to first change her occupation (e.g., by teaching law) and then her field (shifting from law to business). Either way, there you have it—from computer lawyer to business teacher in two not-so-simple steps. Again, although this transition might not be easy for Michelle, it certainly is a lot more feasible than attempting to change both occupation and field at once (see summary in Figure A2.7).

Planning for Succession and Retirement

Preparation for retirement is an important issue faced later in life. Psychologically, there is a reorientation from being directed in one's life by work activities to an increased focus on leisure time activities. For those who dislike their jobs, retirement is an eagerly awaited condition. However, those whose identities are tied closely to what they do find the decision difficult to make—and sometimes, they even change their minds and go back to work after once having retired. Probably the most visible example is basketball superstar Michael Jordan, who announced his retirement from the game in 1993 only to return in 1995. He then retired once more in 1999 before returning as a player for the 2002–2003 season and then retiring again at the end of the 2003 season (at age 40). Few of us have the option of changing our minds this often, but then again, we're not Michael Jordan.

retirement
The phase of people's lives in which they reach the end of their careers and stop working for their primary income.

RETIREMENT.   The phase of people's lives in which they reach the end of their careers and stop working for their primary income is known as **retirement**. It's important to recognize that retirement does not necessarily imply inactivity, but rather, a different kind of activity.[15] Many retired people lead very active lives, such as by working part-time, engaging in volunteer work, spending time in leisure pursuits, or some combination of these activities. Generous pension plans coupled with more sophisticated investors and a generally good economy have made it possible for many people to retire earlier than ever. This, coupled with the fact that advances in health care enable people to live longer, makes it not unusual for people to spend 20 years or more in retirement.

People retire for either voluntary or involuntary reasons (see Figure A2.8). Sometimes, people retire earlier than they originally planned—that is, involuntarily—because they fear that their jobs may be eliminated or because they are in ill health. In other words, like turnover and absenteeism, sometimes retirement is a form of withdrawal.[16] Fortunately, in most cases, this occurs voluntarily, with employees leaving their companies on good terms and happily moving on to the next stage of their lives. Research has shown that the underlying reasons why people leave make a difference in how their retirement goes.[17] Those who retire for work-related or health-related reasons tend to be less satisfied than those who retire as planned, by personal choice.

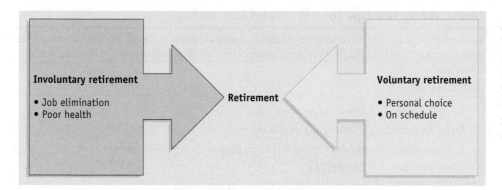

Voluntary Versus Involuntary Retirement

Retirement can occur for voluntary or involuntary reasons, some of which are identified here.

Today, rather than retiring from work completely, many people in their 60s are opting for brand-new careers. In fact, only about 37 percent of recent retirees expect to never return to work. The rest plan on staying active by working at least part-time.[18] Apparently, the image of retirees spending their golden years leisurely golfing and playing with their grandkids is fading fast. Speaking of golf, many professional golfers who find that aging makes it hard for them to compete against today's pros (e.g., Ernie Els, Phil Mickelson) no longer have to retire from the game. Instead, older golfers are discovering second careers by competing in the Senior PGA tour, where at age 50, they once again can rise to the top of their game.[19] Although precious few of us have the luxury of making a living by playing golf, many companies are finding it beneficial to hire semiretired executives as consultants. Instead of putting these talented, experienced people out to pasture, so to speak, they are taking full advantage of the expertise they can bring to the job—especially as *mentors* to young employees.[20]

SUCCESSION PLANNING AND MENTORING.   Before people retire—whether to a world of leisure or to an entirely new career—high-level executives typically assist their companies to prepare for the void created by their departure. This process is known as **succession planning**—a person's systematic attempt to identify possible holders of particular positions ahead of time as preparation for his or her departure.[21] After an individual spends years building a successful business, it is unlikely that he or she would feel comfortable retiring without taking steps to preserve what has been done and to ensure that the company is left in good hands. People generally also want to pass the baton to another whose goals and values match their own. And, of course, careful planning of this nature is in the best interest of the company as well.

Formal succession-planning efforts are more likely to occur in large organizations than small ones. Large firms generally have formal plans on record, specifying exactly who will move into certain positions once they are vacated. These typically include frequently updated information on the specific skills and qualifications of the individuals involved. Many succession plans identify **short-term successors**, individuals who are suitable candidates, at least temporarily, to fill a post vacated unexpectedly (e.g., through termination, resignation, or death).[22] This is not to say that leaders of small companies are unconcerned about succession. Indeed, their businesses' small size makes it crucial to consider how jobs will be filled in the event of an emergency. However, leaders of small companies are more likely to discuss these things among themselves than to have a formal plan specifying succession in any systematic fashion.

One way of identifying successors, particularly for top executives, is by having the retiring individual identify and develop a successor (over a course of years, if possible).[23] This may be accomplished through the process of **mentoring**. This involves having an experienced employee, known as a **mentor**, advise and counsel the professional development of a new employee, known as a **protégé**. If you've ever had an older, more experienced worker take you under his or her wing and guide you, then you probably already know how valuable mentoring can be. Indeed, it is strongly associated with career success: The more mentoring people receive, the more promotions and pay raises they subsequently receive during their careers.[24]

Mentors do many important things for their protégés.[25] For example, they provide much-needed emotional support and confidence. For those who are just starting out and are likely to be insecure about their abilities, this can be a big help. Mentors also help pave the way for their protégés' job success, such as by nominating them for promotions and by providing opportunities

succession planning
A person's systematic attempt to identify possible holders of particular positions ahead of time as preparation for his or her departure.

short-term successors
Individuals who are considered suitable candidates, at least temporarily, to fill the position of someone who leaves his or her job unexpectedly.

mentoring
The process by which a more experienced employee (see *mentor*) advises, counsels, and otherwise enhances the professional development of a new employee (see *protégé*).

mentor
A more experienced employee who guides a newer employee (see *protégé*) in learning about the job and organization.

protégé
An inexperienced employee who receives assistance from a more experienced employee (see *mentor*).

TABLE A2.2 Ten Tips for Successful Mentoring

The long-term success of mentoring can be enhanced by adhering to the suggestions identified here. Both mentors and protégés should familiarize themselves with these guidelines before entering into a relationship.

Mentors Should . . .

1. Be responsible *to* protégés, not *for* them.

2. Make the mentoring relationship fun and enjoyable.

3. Recognize that their involvement with their protégé extends beyond the workday.

4. Listen carefully to their protégés.

5. Openly acknowledge their failures as well as their successes.

6. Protect their protégés and expect their protégés to protect them.

7. Give their protégés not only directions but also options.

8. Recognize and encourage their protégés' small successes and accomplishments.

9. Encourage independent thinking among their protégés.

10. Focus not only on job skills but also on ethical values.

Source: Based on suggestions by Wickman & Sjodin, 1997; see Note 27.

for them to demonstrate their competence. They also suggest useful strategies for achieving work objectives—especially ones that protégés might not generate for themselves. In doing all these things, they help bring the protégé to the attention of top management—a necessary first step for advancement. Finally, mentors often protect their protégés from the repercussions of errors and help them avoid situations that may be risky for their careers.[26]

As you might suspect, it is not only mentors and protégés who come out ahead from mentoring programs, but also organizations themselves. At Scotiabank, for example, mentoring was used to reduce the time required for newly minted MBAs to become loan officers. This was necessary because these recent grads maintained traditional, not particularly service-oriented, beliefs about banking, which were holding them back. Through Scotiabank's Competency-Based Mentoring Program, however, branch managers reinforced what these new employees learned about service in their training programs. As a result, training time was reduced from a full year to nine months, allowing the bank to get these new employees fully functioning that much sooner. Clearly, mentoring can be very beneficial if it is handled properly. For a summary of some guidelines for effective mentoring, see Table A2.2.[27]

Endnotes

Chapter 1

Preview Case Sources

Taleo Closes Acquisition of Worldwide Compensation. (2010, January 4). *CNNMoney.com*. From http://money.cnn.com/news/newsfeeds/articles/marketwire/0582687.htm. Barret, V. (2010, January 28). Taleo: Managing during uncertainty. *Forbes.com*. From http://www.forbes.com/2010/01/28/taleo-oracle-sap-intelligent-technology-gregoire.html?feed=rss_home. Taleo Web Site. (2010). About Taleo. From http://new.taleo.com/company. Taleo 10 Talent Management Software Generally Available. (2010, February 2). *CNNMoney.com*. From http://money.cnn.com/news/newsfeeds/articles/marketwire/0582687.htm.

Chapter Notes

1. Barling, J., & Cooper, C. L. (2009). *The Sage handbook of organizational behavior (Vol. 1)*. Thousand Oaks, CA: Sage. Locke, E. A. (2009). *Handbook of principles of organizational behavior* (2nd ed.). London: Wiley.
2. Davenport, T. H. (2005). *Thinking for a living: How to get better performance and results from knowledge workers*. Boston, MA: Harvard Business School Press.
3. Risher, H. (1999). *Aligning pay and results*. New York: AMACOM.
4. Judge, T. A., & Church, A. H. (2000). Job satisfaction: Research and practice. In C. A. Cooper & E. A. Locke (Eds.), *Industrial and organizational psychology: Linking theory to practice* (pp. 166–198). Malden, MA: Blackwell.
5. Hackman, J. R., Wageman, R., Ruddy, T. M., & Ray, C. L. (2000). Team effectiveness in theory and in practice. In C. A. Cooper & E. A. Locke (Eds.), *Industrial and organizational psychology: Linking theory to practice* (pp. 109–129). Malden, MA: Blackwell.
6. Greenberg, J. (2010). Organizational justice: The dynamics of fairness in the workplace. In S. Zedeck (Ed.), *APA handbook of industrial and organizational psychology* (Vol. 3). Washington, DC: American Psychological Association.
7. Benavides, F. G., Benach, J., Diez-Roux, A. V., & Roman, C. (2000). How do types of employment relate to health indicators? Findings from the Second European Survey on working conditions. *Journal of Epidemiology & Community Health, 54*, 494–501. Roberts, S. (2000, June 26). Integrating EAPs, work/life programs holds advantages. *Business Insurance, 34*(36), pp. 3, 18–19. Vahtera, J., Kivimaki, M., Pentti, J., & Theorell, T. (2000). Effect of change on the psychosocial work environment on sickness absence: A seven year follow up of initially healthy employees. *Journal of Epidemiology and Community Health, 54*, 484–493.

8. The Corporate Research Foundation UK. (2000). *Britain's best employers: A guide to the 100 most attractive companies to work for*. New York: McGraw-Hill.
9. Bollinger, D. (1996). *Aiming higher: 25 stories of how companies prosper by combining sound management and social vision*. New York: AMACOM.
10. Katz, D., & Kahn, R. (1978). *The social psychology of organizations*. New York: Wiley.
11. Warner, M. (1994). Organizational behavior revisited. *Human Relations, 47*, 1151–1166.
12. Kennedy, C. (1991). *Instant management*. New York: William Morrow.
13. Drucker, P. F. (1974). *Management: Tasks, responsibilities, practices*. New York: Harper & Row.
14. Mayo, E. (1933). *The human problems of an industrial civilization*. London: Macmillan.
15. Crainer, S. (2000). *The management century*. San Francisco, CA: Jossey-Bass.
16. Roethlisberger, F. J., & Dickson, W. J. (1939). *Management and the worker*. Cambridge, MA: Harvard University Press.
17. Weber, M. (1921). *Theory of social and economic organization* (A. M. Henderson & T. Parsons, Trans.). London: Oxford University Press.
18. Colvin, G. (2000, March 6). Managing in the info era. *Fortune*, pp. F6–F9 (quote, p. F9).
19. Gardner, B., & Moore, G. (1945). *Human relations in industry*. Homewood, IL: Irwin.
20. See Note 18.
21. Gordon, R. A., & Howell, J. E. (1959). *Higher education for business*. New York: Columbia University Press.
22. See Note 21.
23. Collins, J. (2000, August 28). Don't rewrite the rules of the road. *BusinessWeek*, pp. 206–208.
24. Deresky, H. (2007). *International management*, 6th ed. Upper Saddle River, NJ: Prentice Hall.
25. Morgan, S. (2010, January 13). The Haitian earthquake's economic aftershocks. *SmartMoney.com*. From http://www.smartmoney.com/investing/economy/the-haitian-earthquakes-economic-aftershocks.
26. Lodge, G. C. (1995). *Managing globalization in the age of interdependence*. San Francisco, CA: Pfeifer.
27. *Fortune*. (2009, May). Global 500. From http://money.cnn.com/magazines/fortune/global500/2009/index.html.
28. Times Online. (2009, February 5). Driven down by debt, Dubai expats give new meaning to long-stay car park. *Times Online*. From http://business.timesonline.co.uk/tol/business/markets/the_gulf/article5663618.ece.
29. Ogbonna, E. (1993). Managing organizational culture: Fantasy or reality? *Human Resource Management Journal, 3*(2), 42–54.
30. DeCieri, H., & Dowling, P. J. (1995). Cross-cultural issues in organizational behavior. In C. L. Cooper & D. M. Rousseau (Eds.), *Trends in organizational behavior* (Vol. 2, pp. 127–145). New York: Wiley.

31. Hesketh, B., & Bochner, S. (1994). Technological change in a multicultural context: Implications for training and career planning. In H. C. Triandis, M. D. Dunnette, & L. Hough (Eds.), *Handbook of industrial and organizational psychology* (Vol. 4, pp. 190–240). Palo Alto, CA: Consulting Psychologists Press.

32. Janssens, M. (1995). Intercultural interaction: A burden on international managers? *Journal of Organizational Behavior, 16*, 155–167.

33. See Note 32.

34. *DM Review*. (2006, March 24). IBM to acquire Language Analysis Systems. From http://www.dmreview.com/article_sub.cfm?articleId=1051183.

35. IBM. (2006, March 16). IBM to acquire Language Analysis Systems. From http://www-306.ibm.com/software/data/globalname.

36. U.S. Department of Labor. (2009). *Women in the workplace*. Washington, DC: Author. Lerman, R. I., & Schmidt, S. R. (2002). *An overview of economic, social, and demographic trends affecting the labor market*. Report to the Urban Institute for U.S. Department of Labor (at www.dol.gov).

37. U.S. Department of Labor. (2009). *Women in the workplace*. Washington, DC: Author. Lerman, R. I., & Schmidt, S. R. (2002). *An overview of economic, social, and demographic trends affecting the labor market*. Report to the Urban Institute for U.S. Department of Labor (at www.dol.gov).

38. Hobbs, F, & Stoops, N. (2008). *Demographic trends in the 20th century: Census 2000 special reports*. Washington, DC: U.S. Census Bureau.

39. See Note 38.

40. Carnevale, A. P., & Stone, S. C. (1995). *The American mosaic: An in-depth report on the future of diversity at work*. New York: McGraw-Hill.

41. See Note 40.

42. Jayson, S. (2008, July 16). Is this the next baby boom? *USA Today*, pp. A1–A2.

43. It all depends where you sit. (2000, August 14). *BusinessWeek*, Frontier Section, p. F8.

44. Zuboff, S. (1988). *In the age of the smart machine*. New York: Basic Books.

45. Bridges, W. (1994). *Job shift: How to prosper in a workplace without jobs*. Reading, MA: Addison-Wesley.

46. Nirmala, M., & Akhliesh, K. B. (2009). *Organizational rightsizing*. Saarbrücken, Germany: Lambert Academic Publishing.

47. Hendricks, C. F. (1992). *The rightsizing remedy*. Homewood, IL: Business One Irwin.

48. Tomasko, R. M. (1993). *Rethinking the corporation*. New York: AMACOM.

49. Brown, D., & Wilson, S. (2005). *The black book of outsourcing*. New York: Wiley.

50. Haapaniemi, P. (1993, Winter). Taking care of business. *Solutions*, pp. 6–8, 10–13.

51. See Note 50.

52. Fong, M. W. L. (2005). *E-collaborations and virtual organizations*. Hershey, PA: IRM Press.

53. Byrne, J. A., Brandt, R., & Port, O. (1993, February 8). The virtual corporation: The company of the future will be the ultimate in adaptability. *BusinessWeek*, pp. 98–102.

54. Sadowski-Rasters, G., Duysters, G., & Sadowski, B. (2006). Communication and cooperation in the virtual workplace. Northampton, MA: Edward Elgar.

55. See Note 53 (quote, p. 99).

56. Victoria, E. (2009, August 11). *Telecommuting trends in the 2009 economy*. Bright Hub. From http://www.brighthub.com/office/home/articles/22829.aspx.

57. IATC. (2009, October 4). *Annual survey shows that Americans are working from many different locations outside their employer's office*. Silver Spring, MD: Author.

58. Telework Statistics for 2005. (2006). *The Information Society, London*. From http://www.noelhodson.com/index_files/2004_telework_statistics.htm.

59. Amigoni, M., & Gurvis, S. (2009). *Managing the telecommuting employee*. Cincinnati, OH: Adams Media.

60. See Note 59.

61. See Note 58.

62. See Note 59.

63. International Telework Advisory Council. (2006). *Can your organization survive a disaster? Exploring telework as a business continuity strategy*. Scottsdale, AZ: The Telework Advisory Group for World at Work. From http://www.workingfromanywhere.org/pdf/ITAC-ExecSummFINALweb.pdf.

64. Mariani, M. (2000, Fall). Telecommuters. *Occupational Outlook Quarterly*, pp. 10–17.

65. Bakker, A. B., & Leiter. M. P. (2010) *Work engagement: A handbook of essential theory and research*. New York: Psychology Press.

66. Krueger, J., & Killharn, E. (2006, March 9). Why Dilbert is right. *Gallup Management Journal*. From http://gmj.gallup.com/content/default.asp?ci=21802.

67. U.S. Office of Personnel Management. (2008). *Handbook of alternative work schedules*. Washington, DC: Author.

68. Armour, S. (2008, June 2). Souring fuel prices drive some to try four-day workweeks. *USA Today*, p. A3.

69. Padgett, M., Harland, L., & Moser, S. B. (2009). The bad news and the good news: The long-term consequences of having used an alternative work schedule. *Journal of Leadership & Organizational Studies, 16*, 73-84. Cohen, A. R., & Gadon, H. (1980). *Alternative work schedules*. Reading, MA: Addison-Wesley.

70. Bureau of Labor Statistics/ (2005, July 27). Contingent and alternative employment arrangement, February 2005. From http://www.bls.gov/news.release/conemp.nr0.htm. Galen, M., Palmer, A. T., Cuneo, A., & Maremont, M. (1993, June 28). Work and family. *BusinessWeek*, pp. 80–84, 86, 88.

71. Goldsmith, M. (2007, May 23). The contingent workforce. *BusinessWeek*. From http://www.businessweek.com/careers/content/may2007/ca20070523_580432.htm.

72. Coy, P., Conlin, M., & Herbst, M. (2010, January 18). The disposable worker. *BusinessWeek*, pp. 33–39.

73. Bureau of Labor Statistics (2009). Employed contingent and noncontingent workers by occupation and industry. From http://www.bls.gov/news.release/conemp.t04.htm.

74. See Note 71.

75. See Note 72.

76. See Note 73.

77. Rousseau, D. M., Ho, V. T., & Greenberg, J. (2006). I-deals: Idiosyncratic terms in employment relationships. *Academy of Management Review*. Rousseau, D. M. (2005). I-deals: Idiosyncratic deals employees bargain for themselves. New York: M. E. Sharpe.

78. Greenberg, J., Roberge, M. E., Ho, V. T., & Rousseau, D. (2004). Fairness as an "i-deal": Justice in under-the-table employment arrangements. In J. Martocchio (Ed.), *Research in personnel and human resources management* (Vol. 23, pp. 1–34). San Diego, CA: Elsevier.

79. O'Hanlon, M. & Morella, A. (2003). *Job sharing: Two heads are better than one*. Crow's Nest, Australia: Allen & Unwin.

80. See Note 79.

Case in Point Sources

Forgrieve, J. (2008, May 23). Five questions for Rob O'Brien. *Rocky Mountain News*. p. 19. O'Brien, K. (2008). The Floyd's story. *Floydsbarbershop.com*. Cho, C. H. (2006, August 16). Male-themed salons: Barbershops with style. *Los Angeles Times*, pp. C1, C7. Kretikos, E. (2005, July 8–14). Forget Mayberry, this new Floyd's cuts a hip profile. *Washington Business Journal*, p. 7.

Chapter 2

Preview Case Sources

Ng, S. (2010, February 3). Despite critics, AIG sets bonuses. *WallStreetJournal.com*. From http://online.wsj.com/article/SB10001424052748704402280457504 1300793298866.html. Gruenwald, M. (2010, January 15). Geithner gets a bad rap in the AIG scandal. *Time.com*. From http://www.time.com/time/business/article/0,8599,1953864,00.html. Gentry, P. (2009, March 19). Obama outraged with AIG. *BET.com*. From http://blogs.bet.com/news/pamela/2009/03/19/obama-outrage-with-aig. Board of Governors of the Federal Reserve System. (2009). Troubled asset relief program (TARP) information. From http://www.federalreserve.gov/bankinforeg/tarpinfo.htm.

Chapter Notes

1. Schminke, M. (2010). *Managerial ethics: Managing the psychology of morality*. New York: Psychology Press.

2. Ross, B. (2009). *The Madoff chronicles*. New York: Hyperion. McClean, B., & Elkind, P. (2004). *Smartest guys in the room: The amazing rise and scandalous fall of Enron*. New York: Penguin.

3. Bianco, A. (2010). *The big lie: Spying, scandal and ethical collapse at Hewlett Packard*. Jackson, TN: Public Affairs.

4. Sun, W. (2010). *How to govern corporations so they serve the public good: A theory of corporate governance emergence*. New York: Edwin Mellen.

5. Greenberg, J. (2010). Organizational justice: The dynamics of fairness in the workplace. In S. Zedeck (Ed.), *APA handbook of industrial-organizational psychology* (Vol.3). Washington, DC: American Psychological Association.

6. Fitness, J. (2000). Anger in the workplace: An emotion script approach to anger episodes between workers and their superiors, co-workers and subordinates. *Journal of Organizational Behavior, 21*, 147–162.

7. Cropanzano, R., Byrne, Z. S., Bobocel, D. R., & Rupp, D. E. (2001). Moral virtues, fairness heuristics, social entities, and other denizens of organizational justice. *Journal of Vocational Behavior, 58*, 164–209.

8. Colquitt, J. A. (2001). On the dimensionality of organizational justice: A construct validation of a measure. *Journal of Applied Psychology, 86*, 386–400. Greenberg, J. (1993). The social side of fairness: Interpersonal and informational classes of organizational justice. In R. Cropanzano (Ed.), *Justice in the workplace: Approaching fairness in human resource management* (pp. 79–103). Hillsdale, NJ: Erlbaum.

9. Richman, B. D., & Havinghurst, C. C. (2007). *Distributive injustice(s) in American health care*. Duke Law School Faculty Scholarship Series. From Nellco Legal Scholarship Repository at http://lsr.nellco.org/cgi/viewcontent.cgi?article=1079&context=duke_fs.

10. Greenberg, J. (2009). Promote procedural and interactional justice to enhance individual and organizational outcomes. In E. A. Locke (Ed.), *Blackwell handbook of principles of organizational behavior* (2nd ed., pp. 255–271). Malden, MA: Blackwell Publishers.

11. Allen, M. (1998, May 15). Giuliani threatens action if cabbies fail to cancel a protest. *New York Times*, p. C1.

12. See Note 10.

13. Halogen Software (2010). A sweet employee performance appraisal system for Jelly Belly. From http://www.halogensoftware.com/customers/case-studies/services-manufacturing/study_jbelly.php.

14. Greenberg, J., & Cropanzano, R. A. (2001). *Advances in organizational justice*. Stanford, CA: Stanford University Press.

15. Lind, E. A., Greenberg, J., Scott, K. S., & Welchans, T. D. (2000). The winding road from employee to complainant: Situational and psychological determinants of wrongful termination claims. *Administrative Science Quarterly, 45*, 557–590.

16. See Note 5.

17. Dulebohn, J. H., Conlon, D. E., Sarinopoulos, I., Davidson, R. B., & McNamara, G. (2009). The biological bases of unfairness: Neuroimaging evidence for the distinctiveness of procedural and distributive justice. *Organizational Behavior and Human Decision Processes, 110*, 140–151.

18. Colquitt, J. A., Greenberg, J., & Scott, B. (2005). Organizational justice: Where do we stand? In Greenberg, J., & Colquitt, J. A. (2005). *Handbook of organizational justice* (pp. 622–655). Mahwah, NJ: Erlbaum.

19. Greenberg, J. (2006). Positive organizational justice: Moving from fair to fairer—and beyond. In J. E. Dutton & B. R. Ragins (Eds.), *Exploring positive*

relationships at work: Building a theoretical and research foundation (pp. 159–178). Mahwah, NJ: Erlbaum.

20. Simons, T., & Roberson, Q. (2003). Why managers should care about fairness: The effects of aggregate justice perceptions on organizational outcomes. *Journal of Applied Psychology, 88,* 432–443.

21. Van den Bos, K. (2005). What is responsible for the fair process effect? In Greenberg, J., & Colquitt, J. A. (2004). *Handbook of organizational justice* (pp. 318–342). Mahwah, NJ: Erlbaum.

22. Kaufman, W. (2008, December 19). FedEx delivers salary cuts to managers. *NPR.org.* From http://www.npr.org/templates/story/story.php?storyId=98494929.

23. Schaubroeck, J., May, D. R., & Brown, F. W. (1994). Procedural justice explanations and employee reactions to economic hardship: A field experiment. *Journal of Applied Psychology, 79,* 455–460.

24. Skarlicki, D. P., & Latham, G. P. (2005). Can leaders be trained to be fair? In J. Greenberg & J. A. Colquitt (Eds.), *Handbook of organizational justice.* Mahwah, NJ: Erlbaum.

25. Greenberg, J. (2006). Losing sleep over organizational injustice: Attenuating insomniac reactions to under-payment inequity with supervisory training in interactional justice. *Journal of Applied Psychology, 81,* 58–69.

26. Goldgar, A. (2007). *Tulipmania: Money, honor, and knowledge in the Dutch golden age.* Chicago, IL: University of Chicago Press.

27. Mackay, C. (1852/2003). *Memoirs of extraordinary popular delusions and the madness of crowds.* Hampshire, UK: Harriman House.

28. McConahey, M. (2003, June 8). Ethics scandals reach epidemic level. *Press Democrat* (Santa Rosa, California), p. A8. (Also at http://www.jim-carroll.com/acrobat/publicity/pressdemocrat-1.pdf.)

29. New York Times uncovers dozens of faked stories by reporter. (2003, May 11). *Washington Post,* p. 1.

30. Sullivan, M. (2006, June 9). Two charged in VoIP hacking scandal. *Dark Reading.* From http://www.darkreading.com/document.asp?doc_id=96861.

31. Florida man arrested on Miss. Home repair fraud charges. (2008, February 21). *St. Cloud, FL Topix.* From http://www.topix.com/city/st-cloud-fl/2008/02/florida-man-arrested-on-miss-home-repair-fraud-charges.

32. Associated Press. (2007, October 28). Gap stores using child labor in Indian sweatshops, British newspaper reports. *Fox News.com.* From http://www.foxnews.com/story/0,2933,305703,00.html.

33. Weaver, J. (2003, June 4). Martha Stewart indicted on 9 counts. *MSNBC.* From http://stacks.msnbc.com/news/922014.asp.

34. Zellner, W., & Forest, S. A. (2001, December 17). The fall of Enron. *BusinessWeek,* pp. 30–34, 36.

35. Ferrell, O. C., Fraedrich, J., & Ferrell, L. (2002). *Business ethics: Ethical decision making and cases* (5th ed.). Boston, MA: Houghton Mifflin.

36. The Corporate Library. (2002, July). Spotlight topic: Adelphia scandal. From http://www.thecorporatelibrary.com/spotlight/scandals/adelq.html.

37. Henderson, V. E. (1992). *What's ethical in business?* New York: McGraw-Hill.

38. Ethics Resources Center. (2003). *2003 National business ethics survey.* Washington, DC: Author.

39. Ethics Resource Center. (2003). *What is ethics?* From http://www.ethics.org/faq.html#eth_what.

40. Salopek, J. J. (2001, July). Do the right thing. *American Society for Training and Development.* From http://www.astd.org/CMS/templates/index.html?template_id=1&articleid=26983.

41. Treviño, L. K., & Nelson, K. A. (1999). *Managing business ethics* (2nd ed.). New York: John Wiley & Sons (quote, p. 14).

42. MAALA Business for Social Responsibility. (2002). Corporate social responsibility. Tel Aviv, Israel: Author (also at http://www.maala.com). Verschoor, C. C. (1998). A study of the link between a corporation's financial performance and its commitment to ethics. *Journal of Business Ethics, 17,* 1509–1516. Embley, L. L. (1993). *Doing well while doing good.* Upper Saddle River, NJ: Prentice Hall.

43. See Note 42.

44. Delaware Sustainable Energy Utility. (2010). Helping Delaware businesses save money, create jobs and improve the environment. From http://www.energizedelaware.org/business/home/home.

45. Barton, L. (2007). *Crisis leadership now.* New York: McGraw-Hill.

46. See Note 45.

47. Johnson, D. C. (1997, November 9). United Way, faced with fewer donations, is giving away less. *New York Times,* p. A1.

48. See Note 45 (quote, pp. 30–31).

49. Ethics and Policy Integration Centre (2003). Toward an effective ethics and compliance program: The Federal Sentencing Guidelines for Organizations. Washington, DC: Author. From http://www.ethicaledge.com/appendix1.html.

50. Butler, H. N., & Ribstein, L. E. (2006). *The Sarbanes-Oxley debacle: What we've learned; how to fix it.* Washington, DC: AEI Press.

51. Public Company Accounting Oversight Board (2008, June 12). *Auditing standard number 5.* Washington, DC: Author.

52. Ramos, M. J. (2008) *How to comply with Sarbanes-Oxley Section 404: Assessing the effectiveness of internal control* (3rd ed.). New York: Wiley.

53. 18 U.S.C. Sec. 1519.

54. Treviño, L. K., & Youngblood, S. A. (1990). Bad apples in bad barrels: A causal analysis of ethical decision-making behavior. *Journal of Applied Psychology, 75,* 378–385.

55. Kohlberg, L. (1976). Moral stages and moralization: The cognitive-developmental approach. In T. Lickona (Ed.), *Moral development and behavior: Theory, research, and social issues* (pp. 2–52). New York: Holt, Rinehart, and Winston. Kohlberg, L. (1969). Stage and sequence: The cognitive-developmental approach to socialization. In D. A. Goslin (Ed.), *Handbook of socialization theory and research* (pp. 347–380). Chicago, IL: Rand McNally.

56. Greenberg, J. (2002). Who stole the money, and when? Individual and situational determinants of employee theft. *Organizational Behavior and Human Decision Processes, 89*, 895–1003. Blass, T. (1999). *Obedience to authority: Current perspectives on the Milgram paradigm.* Mahwah, NJ: Erlbaum. Grover, S. L. (1993). Why professionals lie: The impact of professional role conflict on reporting accuracy. *Organizational Behavior and Human Decision Processes, 55*, 251–272.

57. Treviño, L. K. (1992). Moral reasoning and business ethics. *Journal of Business Ethics, 11*, 445–459.

58. Brass, D. J., Butterfield, K. D., & Skaggs, B. C. (1998). Relationships and unethical behavior: A social-network perspective. *Academy of Management Review, 23*, 14–31.

59. Wolfe, D. M. (1988). Is there integrity in the bottom line: Managing obstacles to executive integrity. In S. Srivastava (Ed.), *Executive integrity: The search for high human values in organizational life* (pp. 140–171). San Francisco, CA: Jossey-Bass.

60. Jansen, E., & Von Glinow, M. A. (1985). Ethical ambivalence and organizational reward systems. *Academy of Management Review, 10*, 814–822.

61. See Note 60.

62. Cassell, C., Johnson, P., & Smith, K. (1997). Opening the black box: Corporate codes of ethics in their organizational context. *Journal of Business Ethics, 16*, 1077–1093.

63. Ethics Resource Center. (1994). *Ethics in American business: Policies, programs and perceptions.* Washington, DC: Author.

64. Ferrell, O. C., Fraedrich, J., & Ferrell, L. (2002). *Business ethics* (5th ed.). Boston, MA: Houghton Mifflin. Waddock, S., & Smith, N. (2000, Winter). Corporate responsibility audits: Doing well by doing good. *Sloan Management Review*, pp. 66–83.

65. Ferrell, O. C., Fraedrich, J., & Ferrell, L. (2005). *Business ethics* (6th ed.). Boston, MA: Houghton Mifflin. Waddock, S., & Smith, N. (2000, Winter). Corporate responsibility audits: Doing well by doing good. *Sloan Management Review*, pp. 66–83.

66. Singer, A. (2003, May/June). Excelon excels at reaching out. *Ethikos, 16*(6), 7–9, 13.

67. From http://www.exeloncorp.com/corporate/about/a_overview.shtml.

68. Donaldson, T. (1996, September/October). Values in tension: Ethics away from home. *Harvard Business Review*, pp. 48–62.

69. See Note 68.

70. Gap, Inc. (2004). *Social responsibility report, 2003.* New York: Author. (Also at http://ccbn.mobular.net/ccbn/7/645/696/index.html.)

71. See Note 68 (quote, p. 55).

72. From http://www.adviceonmanagement.com/advice_ethics.html.

73. Carroll, A. B. (1991). The pyramid of corporate social responsibility: Toward the moral management of organizational stakeholders. *Business Horizons, 34*(4), 39–48.

74. Business for Social Responsibility (2004). *Issue brief: Overview of corporate social responsibility.* From http://www.bsr.org/CSRResources.

75. McDonald's Corporation (2010). *2009 worldwide corporate responsibility report.* From http://www.aboutmcdonalds.com/mcd/csr/report/overview.printreport.html.

76. The CRO. (2009). *100 best corporate citizens, 2009.* From http://www.thecro.com/100best09.

77. Brady, D. (2002, February 19). The right mix of (yogurt) cultures? *BusinessWeek*, pp. 57–58. Key mining and oil companies pledge to keep hands off protected sites. (2003, September 7). *Business Respect Corporate Social Responsibility Dispatches No. 62.* From http://www.mallenbaker.net/csr/nl/62.html#anchor1058. U.S.: Boise Cascade announces zero old-growth wood policy. (2003, September 7). *Business Respect Corporate Social Responsibility Dispatches No. 62.* From http://www.mallenbaker.net/csr/nl/62.html#anchor1058. Waddock, S. A. (2001). *Leading corporate citizens.* Burr Ridge, IL: McGraw-Hill/Irwin.

78. UPS deploys 245 new "green" trucks. (2010, January 19). *Corporate Social Responsibility Newswire.* From http://www.csrwire.com/press/press_release/28619-S-Deploys-245-New-Green-Trucks.

79. Broder, J. (2010, January 28). S.E.C. adds climate risk to disclosure list. *New York Times*, p. B1.

80. See Note 79.

81. Orlitzky, M., Schmidt, F. L., & Rynes, S. L. (2003). Corporate social and financial performance: A meta-analysis. *Organization Studies, 24*, 403–441. Kelly, M. (2004, Winter). Holy grail found: Absolute, definitive proof CSR pays off. *Business Ethics*, pp. 4–5.

82. McIntosh, M. (2003). *Raising a ladder to the moon: The complexities of corporate social and environmental responsibility.* New York: Palgrave Macmillan. Rayner, J. (2002). *Corporate social responsibility monitor.* London: Gee. Kinder, P. D., Lydenberg, S. D., & Domini, A. L. (1994). *Investing for good: Making money while being socially responsible.* New York: HarperCollins. Domini, A. L., Lydenberg, S. D., & Kinder, P. D. (1992). *The social investment almanac: A comprehensive guide to socially responsible investing.* New York: Henry Holt.

83. Treviño, L., & Nelson, K. (2006). *Managing business ethics: Straight talk about how to do it right* (4th ed.). New York: Wiley.

84. ExxonMobil. (2009). 2008 giving report. From http://www.exxonmobil.com/Corporate/community_contributions_report.aspx.

85. Deane, B. (2005, January). Promoting accountability in the workplace: Starbucks and Dell first to adopt corporate code of conduct regarding women. From http://www.diversityhotwire.com/business/managers_update.html.

86. See Note 85.

87. See Note 85.

Case in Point Sources

AFX News Limited (2008, February 13). HP settles spying scandal claims. *Forbes.com*. From http://www. forbes.com/afxnewslimited/feeds/afx/2008/02/13/afx 4653525.html. Steffy, L. (2008, February 15). Privacy: Less and less is the trend. *Houston Chronicle*. From http://www.chron.com/disp/story.mpl/business/steffy/5546747.html. Fried, I. (2006, December 8). HP settles with California in spy scandal. *CNET News.com*. From http://www.zdnet.com.au/news/business/soa/-HP-settles-with-California-in-spy-scandal/0,139023166,339272604,00.htm?feed=pt_cnet. Ard, S., & Fried, I. (2006, September 12). Leak scandal costs HP's Dunn her chairman's job. *CNET News.com*. From http://news.cnet.com/Leak-scandal-costs-HPs-Dunn-her-chairmans-job/2100-1014_3-6114655.html. Sandoval, G. (2006, October 5). Dunn to surrender Thursday. *ZD Net*. From http://news.zdnet.com/2100-9584_22-6123054.html.

Chapter 3

Preview Case Sources

Who We Are (2010). *Enterprise*. From http://aboutus. enterprise.com/ who_we_are.html. Kazanjian, K. (2007). *Exceeding customer expectations: What Enterprise, America's #1 car rental company, can teach you about creating lifetime customers*. New York: Currency. Schelereth, J. (2003, July–August). Putting people first. *BizEd*, pp. 16–20.

Chapter Notes

1. Furnham, A. (2005). *The psychology of behavior of work: The individual in the organization*. New York: Psychology Press.
2. Ashforth, B. E., & Mael, F. (1989). Social identity theory and the organization. *Academy of Management Review, 14*, 20–29.
3. LaTendresse, D. (2000). Social identity and intergroup relations within the hospital. *Journal of Social Distress and the Homeless, 9*, 51–69.
4. Cialdini, R. B., Borden, R. J., Thorne, A., Walker, M. R., Freeman, S., & Sloan, L. R. (1999). Basking in reflected glory: Three (football) field studies. In R. F. Baumeister (Ed.), *The self in social psychology* (pp. 436–445). Philadelphia, PA: Psychology Press/Taylor & Francis.
5. Wann, D. L., Hamlet, M., Wilson, T., & Hodges, J. (1995). Basking in reflected glory, cutting off reflected failure, and cutting off future failure: The importance of group identification. *Social Behavior and Personality: An International Journal, 23*, 377–388.
6. Miller, C. B. (2009). Yes we did! Basking in reflected glory and cutting off reflected failure in the 2008 presidential election. *Analyses of Social Issues and Public Policy, 9*, 283–296.
7. Weiner, B. (1995). *Judgments of responsibility*. New York: Guilford.
8. Jones, E. E., & McGillis, D. (1976). Correspondent inferences and the attribution cube: A comparative reappraisal. In J. H. Harvey, W. J. Ickes, & R. F. Kidd (Eds.), *New directions in attribution research* (Vol. 1, pp. 389–420). Hillsdale, NJ: Erlbaum.
9. Kelley, H. H. (1972). Attribution in social interaction (pp. 1–26). In E. E. Jones, D. E. Kanous, H. H. Kelley, R. E. Nisbett, S. Valins, & B. Weiner (Eds.), *Attribution: Perceiving the causes of behavior*. Morristown, NJ: General Learning Press.
10. Burger, J. M. (1991). Changes in attribution errors over time: The ephemeral fundamental attribution error. *Social Cognition, 9*, 183–193.
11. Murphy, K. R., Jako, R. A., & Anhalt, R. L. (1993). Nature and consequences of halo error: A critical analysis. *Journal of Applied Psychology, 78*, 218–225.
12. Naquin, C. E., & Tynan, R. O. (2003). The team halo effect: Why teams are not blamed for their failures. *Journal of Applied Psychology, 88*, 332–340.
13. Pulakos, E. D., & Wexley, K. N. (1983). The relationship among perceptual similarity, sex, and performance ratings in manager–subordinate dyads. *Academy of Management Journal, 26*, 129–139.
14. Turban, D. B., & Jones, A. P. (1988). Supervisor–subordinate similarity: Types, effects, and mechanisms. *Journal of Applied Psychology, 73*, 228–234.
15. Dearborn, D. C., & Simon, H. A. (1958). Selective perception: A note on the departmental identification of executives. *Sociometry, 21*, 140–144.
16. Waller, M. J., Huber, G. P., & Glick, W. H. (1995). Functional background as a determinant of executives' selective perception. *Academy of Management Journal, 38*, 943–974.
17. Dougherty, T. W., Turban, D. B., & Callender, J. C. (1994). Confirming first impressions in the employment interview: A field study of interviewer behavior. *Journal of Applied Psychology, 79*, 659–665.
18. Eden, D., & Shani, A. B. (1982). Pygmalion goes to boot camp: Expectancy, leadership, and trainee performance. *Journal of Applied Psychology, 67*, 194–199.
19. Oz, S., & Eden, D. (1994). Restraining the Golem: Boosting performance by changing the interpretation of low scores. *Journal of Applied Psychology, 79*, 744–754.
20. Davidson, O. B., & Eden, D. (2000). Remedial self-fulfilling prophecy: Two field experiments to prevent Golem effects among disadvantaged women. *Journal of Applied Psychology, 85*, 386–398.
21. Eden, D. (1997). Leadership and expectations: Pygmalion effects and other self-fulfilling prophecies in organizations. In R. Vecchio (Ed.), *Leadership: Understanding the dynamics of power and influence in organizations* (pp. 177–193). Notre Dame, IN: University of Notre Dame Press.
22. Bethune, G. (1999). *From worst to first: Behind the scenes of Continental's remarkable comeback*. New York: Wiley.
23. Sherman, J. W. (2001). The dynamic relationship between stereotype efficiency and mental representation. In G. B. Moskowitz (Ed.), *Cognitive social psychology: The Princeton Symposium on the legacy and future of social cognition* (pp. 177–190). Mahwah, NJ: Erlbaum.

24. Steele, C. M., & Aronson, J. (1995). Stereotype threat and the intellectual performance of African Americans. *Journal of Personality and Social Psychology, 69,* 797–811.

25. Steele, C. M., Spencer, S. J., & Aronson, J. (2002). Contending with group image: The psychology of stereotype and social identity threat. In P. P. Zanna (Ed.), *Advances in experimental social psychology* (Vol. 34, pp. 379–440). San Diego, CA: Academic Press.

26. Martens, A., Johns, M., Greenberg, J., & Schimel, J. (2006). Combating stereotype threat: The effect of self-affirmation on women's intellectual performance. *Journal of Experimental Social Psychology, 42,* 236–243.

27. Aronson, J., Lustina, M. J., Good, C., & Keough, K. (1999). When white men can't do math: Necessary and sufficient factors in stereotype threat. *Journal of Experimental Social Psychology, 35,* 29–46.

28. Extra pounds, slimmer wages. (2001, January 15). *BusinessWeek,* p. 28.

29. Rosenfeld, P., Giacalone, R. A., & Riordan, C. A. (2002). *Impression management: Building and enhancing reputations at work.* London: Thomson Learning.

30. Blair, I. (2001). Implicit stereotypes and prejudice. In G. B. Moskowitz (Ed.), *Cognitive social psychology: The Princeton Symposium on the legacy and future of social cognition* (pp. 359–374). Mahwah, NJ: Erlbaum.

31. Sassenberg, K., & Moskowitz, G. B. (2005). Don't stereotype, think different! Overcoming automatic stereotype activation by mindset priming. *Journal of Experimental Social Psychology, 41,* 506–614.

32. Giacalone, R. A. & Rosenfeld, P. (1989). *Impression management in the organization.* Hillsdale, NJ: Erlbaum.

33. Stevens, C. K., & Kristof, A. L. (1995). Making the right impression: A field study of applicant impression management during job interviews. *Journal of Applied Psychology, 80,* 587–606.

34. Mohrman, A. M., Jr., Resnick-West, S. M., & Lawler, E. E., III. (1989). *Designing performance appraisal systems.* San Francisco, CA: Jossey-Bass.

35. Ilgen, D. R., Major, D. A., & Tower, S. L. (1994). The cognitive revolution in organizational behavior (pp. 1–22). In J. Greenberg (Ed.), *Organizational behavior: The state of the science.* Hillsdale, NJ: Erlbaum.

36. Hogan, E. A. (1987). Effects of prior expectations on performance ratings: A longitudinal study. *Academy of Management Journal, 30,* 354–368.

37. Wayne, S. J., & Liden, R. C. (1995). Effects of impression management on performance ratings: A longitudinal study. *Academy of Management Journal, 38,* 233–260.

38. Garbett, T. (1988). *How to build a corporation's identity and project its image.* Lexington, MA: Lexington Books.

39. America's most admired companies. (2006, February 19). *Fortune.* From http://money.cnn.com/magazines/fortune/mostadmired.

40. Davies, G. (2002). *Corporate reputation and competitiveness.* Oxfordshire, UK: Taylor & Francis.

41. Boehmer, J. (2010, February 9). Japan Airlines to stick with Oneworld, forge joint venture with AA. *BTNOnline.com.* From http://www.btnonline.com/businesstravelnews/headlines/article_display.jsp?vnu_content_id=1004066123.

42. Wick, C. W., & Leon, L. S. (1993). *The learning edge: How smart managers and smart companies stay ahead.* New York: McGraw-Hill.

43. Atkinson, R. C., Herrnstein, R. J., Lindzey, G., & Luce, R. D. (Eds.). (1988). *Stevens' handbook of experimental psychology* (2nd ed., Vol. 1, pp. 218–266). New York: Wiley.

44. Skinner, B. F. (1969). *Contingencies of reinforcement.* New York: Appleton-Century-Crofts.

45. Bandura, A. (1986). *Social foundations of thought and action.* Englewood Cliffs, NJ: Prentice Hall.

46. Harrison, J. K. (1992). Individual and combined effects of behavior modeling and the cultural assimilator in cross-cultural management training. *Journal of Applied Psychology, 77,* 963–963.

47. Goldstein, I. L. (1991). Training in work organizations. In M. D. Dunnette & L. M. Hough (Eds.), *Handbook of industrial and organizational psychology* (2nd ed., Vol. 2, pp. 507–620). Palo Alto, CA: Consulting Psychologists Press.

48. Schnake, M. E. (1986). Vicarious punishment in a work setting. *Journal of Applied Psychology, 71,* 343–345.

49. Bares, A. (2008, February 12). Companies spend an average of $1,200 per employee on training. *Workforce Management.* From http://compforce.typepad.com/compensation_force/2008/02/companies-spend.html.

50. Crane, M. (2006, December 4). To train or not to train? *Forbes.com.* From http://www.forbes.com/2006/12/04/hewlett-packard-general-electric-microsoft-ent-hr-cx_mc_1204training.html.

51. Del Valle, C. (1993, April 26). From high schools to high skills. *BusinessWeek,* pp. 110, 113.

52. Francesco, A. M., & Gold, B. A. (1998). *International organizational behavior.* Upper Saddle River, NJ: Prentice Hall.

53. Jarvis, P. (2000). *Universities, corporate universities, and the higher learning industries.* London: Kogan Page. Meister, J. C. (1998). *Corporate universities.* New York: McGraw-Hill.

54. Gist, M. E., Stevens, C. K., & Bavetta, A. G. (1991). Effects of self-efficacy and post-training intervention on the acquisition and maintenance of complex interpersonal skills. *Personnel Psychology, 44,* 837–861.

55. See Note 49.

56. O'Reilly, B. (1993, April 5). How execs learn now. *Fortune,* pp. 53–54, 58.

57. Rendon, J. (2000, October). Learning potential. *Grok,* pp. 58–60.

58. Liddle, A. J. (2003, March 10). Chains upgrade to online training, downgrade teaching expenses. *Nation's Restaurant News, 37*(10), pp. 62–63 (quote, p. 62).

59. Bell, B. S., & Kozlowski, S. W. J., (2008). Active leaning: Effects of core training design elements on self-regulatory processes, learning and adaptability. *Journal of Applied Psychology, 93,* 296–316.

60. See Note 59.

61. Argyris, C. (1991, May–June). Teaching smart people how to learn. *Harvard Business Review, 69*(3), 99–109.

62. Driskell, J. E., Cooper, C., & Moran, A. (1994). Does mental practice enhance performance? *Journal of Applied Psychology, 79,* 481–493.

63. See Note 59.

64. Tracey, B. J., Tannenbaum, S. I., & Kavanaugh, M. J. (1995). Applying trained skills on the job: The importance of the work environment. *Journal of Applied Psychology, 80,* 239–253.

65. Tannenbaum, S. I., & Yukl, G. A. (1992). Training and development in work organizations. *Annual Review of Psychology, 43,* 399–441.

66. Hoffman, R. (1995, April). Ten reasons you should be using 360-feedback. *HRMagazine,* pp. 83–85.

67. Edwards, M. R., & Ewen, A. J. (1996). *360° feedback: The powerful new model for employee assessment and performance improvement.* New York: AMACOM.

68. Pfau, B., & Kay, I. (2002, June). Does 360-degree feedback negatively affect company performance? *HR Magazine,* pp. 20–27.

69. Miller, L. (1978). *Behavior management.* New York: Wiley.

70. Beyer, J., & Trice, H. M. (1984). A field study of the use and perceived effects of discipline in controlling work performance. *Academy of Management Journal, 27,* 743–754.

71. Trahan, W. A., & Steiner, D. D. (1994). Factors affecting supervisors' use of disciplinary actions following poor performance. *Journal of Organizational Behavior, 15,* 129–139.

72. Oberle, R. J. (1978). Administering disciplinary actions. *Personnel Journal, 18*(3), 30–33.

73. Arvey, R. D., & Jones, A. P. (1985). The use of discipline in organizational settings: A framework for future research. In L. L. Cummings & B. M. Staw (Eds.), *Research in organizational behavior* (Vol. 7, pp. 367–408). Greenwich, CT: JAI Press.

74. Kiechell, W., III. (1990, May 7). How to discipline in the modern age. *Fortune,* pp. 179–180 (quote, p. 180).

75. Arvey, R. E., & Ivancevich, J. M. (1980). Punishment in organizations: A review, propositions, and research suggestions. *Academy of Management Review, 5,* 123–133.

Case in Point Sources

Our Company. (2006). *Safeway, the start-up.* From http://shop.safeway.com/superstore/default.asp?brandid=1&page=corphome. Safeway workers frowning upon service-with-a-smile policy (1998, September 3). *Columbus Dispatch,* p. C1. Kornheiser, T. (1998, September 13). Unsafe way? *Washington Post,* p. F1. McNichol, T. (1998, November 11). My supermarket, my friend. *SF Weekly.* From http://www.sfweekly.com/Issues/1998-11-11/news/feature.html.

Chapter 4

Preview Case Sources

Colvin, G. (2009, October 15). Crisis chief: AmEx's Chenault. *Fortune, CNNMoney.com.* From http://money.cnn.com/2009/10/14/news/companies/american_express_chenault.fortune/index.htm. Wilchins, D. (2008, July 25). MasterCard settles lawsuit with American Express. *Reuters.* From http://uk.reuters.com/article/bankingfinancial-SP/idUKN2542549620080625. Wilchins, D. (2008, July 22). American Express shares drop after gloomy earnings. *Reuters.* From http://uk.reuters.com/article/bankingfinancial-SP/idUKN2227942820080722. Farrell, G. (2005, April 24). A CEO and a gentleman. *USA Today,* p. C.1. Answers.Com (2007). Business biographies: Kennith I. Chenault. From http://www.answers.com/topic/kenneth-chenault. Colvin, G. (2007, September 19). Secrets of leadership from American Express. *Fortune,* pp. 15–16.

Chapter Notes

1. Tett, R. P., & Burnett, D. D. (2003). A personality trait–based interactionist model of job performance. *Journal of Applied Psychology, 88,* 500–517.

2. Steel, R. P., & Rentsch, J. R. (1997). The dispositional model of job attitudes revisited: Findings of a 10-year study. *Journal of Applied Psychology, 82,* 873–879.

3. Carver, C. S., & Scheier, M. F. (1992). *Perspectives on personality* (2nd ed.). Boston, MA: Allyn & Bacon.

4. George, J. M., & Zhou, J. (2001). When openness to experience and conscientiousness are related to creative behavior: An interactional approach. *Journal of Applied Psychology, 86,* 513–524.

5. Chatman, J. A., Caldwell, D. F., & O'Reilly, C.A. (1999). Managerial personality and performance: A semi-idiographic approach. *Journal of Research in Personality, 33,* 534–545.

6. See Note 1.

7. Osipow, S. H. (1990). Convergence in theories of career choice and development: Review and prospect. *Journal of Vocational Behavior, 36,* 122–131.

8. Caldwell, D. F., & O'Reilly, C. A., III (1990). Measuring person-job fit with a profile-comparison process. *Journal of Applied Psychology, 75,* 648–657.

9. Slaughter, J. E., Zickar, M. J., Highhouse, S., & Mohr, D. C. (2004). Personality trait inferences about organizations: Development of a measure and assessment of construct validity. *Journal of Applied Psychology, 89,* 85–103.

10. Allport, G. W., & Odbert, H. S. (1936). Trait names: A psycholexical study. *Psychological Monographs, 47,* 211–214.

11. Costa, P. T., & McCrae, R. R. (1992). *The NEO-PI personality inventory.* Odessa, FL: Psychological Assessment Resources.

12. Salgado, J. F. (1997). The five-factor model of personality and job performance in the European community. *Journal of Applied Psychology, 82,* 30–43.

13. Hurtz, G. M, & Donovan, J. J. (2000). Personality and job performance: The Big Five revisited. *Journal of Applied Psychology, 85,* 869–879.

14. Mount, M. K., & Barrick, M. R. (1995). The Big Five personality dimensions: Implications for research and practice in human resources management. In K. M. Rowland & G. Ferris (Eds.), *Research in personnel and human resources management* (Vol. 13, pp. 153–200). Greenwich, CT: JAI Press.

15. Barrick, M. R., Stewart, G. L., Neubert, M. J., & Mount, M. K. (1998). Relating member ability and personality to work-team processes and team effectiveness. *Journal of Applied Psychology, 83,* 377–391.

16. Raja, U., Johns, G. J., & Ntallanis, F. (2004). The impact of personality on psychological contracts. *Academy of Management Journal, 47,* 350–367.

17. Watson, D., & Clark, L. A. (1997). Extraversion and its positive emotional core. In R. Hogan, J. A. Johnson, & S. R. Briggs (Eds.), *Handbook of personality psychology* (pp. 767–793). San Diego, CA: Academic Press.

18. Judge, T. A., Bono, J. E., Ilies, R., & Gerhardt, M. W. (2002). Personality and leadership: A qualitative and quantitative review. *Journal of Applied Psychology, 87,* 765–780.

19. Zhao, H., & Seibert, S. E. (2006). The Big Five personality dimensions and entrepreneurial status: A meta-analytical review. *Journal of Applied Psychology, 91,* 259–271.

20. Zhao, H., Seibert, S. E., & Lumpkin, G. T. (2010). The relationship of personality in entrepreneurial intentions and performance: A meta-analytic review. *Journal of Management, 36,* 381–404. Ciaverall, M. A., Bucholtz, A. K., Riordan, C. M., Gatewood, R. D., & Stokes, G. (2004). The Big Five and venture survival: Is there a linkage? *Journal of Business Venturing, 19,* 465–583.

21. George, J. M., & Brief, A. P. (1992). Feeling good—doing good: A conceptual analysis of the mood at work—organizational spontaneity relationships. *Psychological Bulletin, 112,* 310–329.

22. Isen, A. M., & Baron, R. A. (1992). Positive affect as a factor in organizational behavior. In B. M. Staw & L. L. Cummings (Eds.), *Research in organizational behavior* (Vol. 13, pp. 1–54). Greenwich, CT: JAI Press.

23. Magruder, J. (2004, August 5). Negative employees costing companies money. *Arizona Republic,* p. B16.

24. Staw, B. M., & Barsade, S. G. (1993). Affect and managerial performance: A test of the sadder-but-wiser vs. happier-and-smarter hypotheses. *Administrative Science Quarterly, 38,* 304–331.

25. George, J. M. (1990). Personality, affect, and behavior in groups. *Journal of Applied Psychology, 75,* 107–116.

26. Aquino, K., Grover, S. L., Bradfield, M., & Allen, D. G. (1999). The effects of negative affectivity, hierarchical status, and self-determination on workplace victimization. *Academy of Management Journal, 42,* 260–272.

27. Judge, T. A., Locke, E. A., & Durham, C. C. (1997). The dispositional causes of job satisfaction: A core evaluations approach. *Research in Organizational Behavior, 19,* 151–188.

28. Grant, A. M., & Wrzesniewski, A. (2010). I won't let you down . . . or will I? Core self-evaluations, other orientation, anticipated guilt and gratitude, and job performance. *Journal of Applied Psychology, 95,* 108–121.

29. Judge, T. A., & Bono, J. E. (2001). Relationship of core self-evaluations traits—self-esteem, generalized self-efficacy, locus of control, and emotional stability—with job satisfaction and job performance: A meta-analysis. *Journal of Applied Psychology, 86,* 80–92.

30. See Note 27.

31. Grant, A. M., & Wrzesniewski, A. (2010). I won't let you down . . . or will I? Core self-evaluations, other orientation, anticipated guilt and gratitude, and job performance. *Journal of Applied Psychology, 95,* 108–121. Judge, T. A., Bono, J. E., Erez, A., & Locke, E. A. (2004). Core self-evaluations and job and life satisfaction: The role of self-concordance and goal attainment. *Journal of Applied Psychology, 90,* 257–268. Bono, J. E., & Judge, T. A. (2003). Core self-evaluations: A review of the trait and its role in job satisfaction and job performance. *European Journal of Personality, 17*(Suppl1), S5–S18.

32. Christie, R., & Geis, F. L. (1970). *Studies in Machiavellianism.* New York: Academic Press.

33. Paulhus, D. L. & Williams, K. M. (2002). The dark triad of personality: Narcissism, Machiavellianism, and psychopathy. *Journal of Research in Personality 36,* 556–563.

34. See Note 31.

35. Creswell, J., & Thomas, L., Jr. (2009, January 24). The talented Mr. Madoff. *New York Times.* From http://www.nytimes.com/2009/01/25/business/25bernie.html?pagewanted=1&_r=1.

36. Wilson, D. S., Near, D., & Miller, R. R. (1997). Machiavellianism: A synthesis of the evolutionary and psychological literatures. *Psychological Bulletin, 119,* 285–299.

37. Schultz, C. J., II. (1993). Situational and dispositional predictors of performance: A test of the hypothesized Machiavellianism × structure interaction among sales persons. *Journal of Applied Social Psychology, 23,* 478–498.

38. Moyer, L. (2009, January 5). Can new regulation stop another Madoff? *Forbes.com.* From http://www.forbes.com/2009/01/05/madoff-regulation-banking-biz-wall-cx_lm_0105madoff.html.

39. McClelland, D. C. (1985). *Human motivation.* Glenview, IL: Scott Foresman.

40. McClelland, D. C. (1977). Entrepreneurship and management in the years ahead. In C. A. Bramletter (Ed.), *The individual and the future of organizations* (pp. 12–29). Atlanta, GA: Georgia State University.

41. Miller, D., & Droge, C. (1986). Psychological and traditional determinants of structure. *Administrative Science Quarterly, 31,* 539–560.

42. Turban, D. B., & Keon, T. L. (1993). Organizational attractiveness: An interactionist perspective. *Journal of Applied Psychology, 78,* 184–193.

43. Dweck, C. S. (1999). *Self-theories: The role in motivation, personality, and development.* Philadelphia: Psychology Press.

44. VandeWalle, D. (1997). Development and validation of a work domain goal orientation instrument. *Educational and Psychological Measurement, 8,* 995–1015.

45. Chen, G., Gully, S. M., Whiteman, J. A., & Kilcullen, R. N. (2000). Examination of relationships among trait-like individual differences, state-like individual differences, and learning performance. *Journal of Applied Psychology, 85,* 835–847.

46. VandeWalle, D., Cron, W. K., & Slocum, J. W., Jr. (2001). The role of goal orientation following performance feedback. *Journal of Applied Psychology, 86,* 629–640.

47. National Institute for Occupational Safety and Health. (2010). Work schedules: Shift work and long work hours. *Centers for Disease Control.* From http://www.cdc.gov/niosh/topics/workschedules/. U.S. Department of Labor (2005, July 1). Workers on flexible and shift schedules in 2004 summary. From http://www.bls.gov/news.release/flex.nr0.htm.

48. Totterdell, P., Spelten, E., Smith, L., Barton, J., & Folkard, S. (1995). Recovery from work shifts: How long does it take? *Journal of Applied Psychology, 80,* 43–57.

49. McClelland, D. C. (1961). *The achieving society.* Princeton, NJ: Van Nostrand.

50. Lynn, R. (1991). *The secret of the miracle economy.* London: SAU.

51. Furnham, A., Kirkcaldy, B. D., & Lynn, R. (1994). National attitudes to competitiveness, money, and work among young people: First, second, and third world differences. *Human Relations, 47,* 119–132.

52. Chung, M.-H., Chang, F.-M., Yang, C. C. H., Kuo, T. B. J., & Hsu, N. (2009). Sleep quality and morningness-eveningness of shift nurses. *Journal of Clinical Nursing, 18,* 279–284.

53. Workplace Health and Safety Bulletin. (2004, June). *Fatigue, extended work hours, and safety in the workplace.* From http://employment.alberta.ca/documents/WHS/WHS-PUB_erg015.pdf.

54. Paine, S. J., Gander, P. H., & Travier, N. (2006). The epidemiology of morningness/eveningness: Influence of age, gender, ethnicity and socioeconomic factors in adults (30–49 years). *Journal of Biological Rhythms 21,* 68–76.

55. Guthrie, J. P., Ash, R. A., & Bendapudi, V. (1995). Additional validity evidence for a measure of morningness. *Journal of Applied Psychology, 80,* 186–190.

56. Wallace, B. (1993). Day persons, night persons, and variability in hypnotic susceptibility. *Journal of Personality and Social Psychology, 64,* 827–833.

57. Eysenk, M. W. (1994). *Individual differences.* Hillsdale, NJ: Erlbaum.

58. Salgado, J. F., Anderson, N., Moscoso, S., Bertua, C., de Fruyt, F., & Rolland, J. P. (2003). A meta-analytic study of general mental ability validity for different occupations in the European community. *Journal of Applied Psychology, 88,* 1068–1081.

59. Sternberg, R. J. (1986). *Intelligence applied.* New York: Harcourt Brace Jovanovich.

60. Neisser, U., Boodoo, G., Bouchard, T. J., Jr., Bykin, A. W., Brody, N., Ceci, S. J., et al. (1996). Intelligence: Knowns and unknowns. *American Psychologist, 51,* 77–101.

61. Sternberg, R. (2004). Successful intelligence. *Journal of Business Venturing, 19,* 189–202.

62. Sternberg, R. J., Wagner, R. K., Williams, W. M., & Horvath, J. A. (1995). Testing common sense. *American Psychologist, 50,* 912–927.

63. Binet. A., & Simon, T. (1916). *The development of intelligence in children.* Baltimore, MD: Williams & Wilkins. (Reprinted 1973, New York: Arno Press; 1983, Salem, NH: Ayer Company.)

64. Gray, J. R., & Thompson, P. M. (2004, June). Neurobiology of intelligence: Science and ethics. *Nature Reviews: Neuroscience, 5,* 471–482.

65. Loehlin, J. C. (2000). Group differences in intelligence. In R. J. Sternberg (Ed.), *Handbook of intelligence* (pp. 176–193). New York: Cambridge University Press.

66. Goleman, D. (1995). *Emotional intelligence.* New York: Bantam Books.

67. Mayer, J. D., Roberts, R. D., & Barsade, S. G. (2008). Human abilities: Emotional intelligence. *Annual Review of Psychology, 59,* 507–536.

68. See Note 58.

69. Davies, M., Stankow, L., & Roberts, R. D. (1998). Emotional intelligence: In search of an elusive construct. *Journal of Personality and Social Psychology 75,* 989–1015.

70. Joseph, D. L., & Newman, D. A. (2010). Emotional intelligence: An integrative meta-analysis and cascading model. *Journal of Applied Psychology, 95,* 54–78.

71. Roberts, B. W., Jackson, J. J., Fayard, J. V., Edmonds, G., & Meints, J. (2010). Conscientiousness. In M. Leary & R. Hoyle (Eds.), *Handbook of individual differences in social behavior.* New York: Guilford.

72. Côté, S., & Miners, C. T. H. (2006). Emotional intelligence, cognitive intelligence, and job performance. *Administrative Science Quarterly, 51,* 1–28.

73. Schneider, R. J. (2002). Exploring the structure and construct validity of a self-report social competence inventory. In L. M. Hough (Chair), *Compound traits: The next frontier of I/O personality research.* Symposium presented at the 17th annual meeting of the Society for Industrial and Organizational Psychology. Toronto, Ontario, Canada.

74. Riggio, R. E., & Throckmorton, B. (1988). The relative effects of verbal and nonverbal behavior, appearance, and social skills on valuations made in hiring interviews. *Journal of Applied Social Psychology, 18,* 331–348. Robbins, T. L., & DeNisi, A. S. (1994). A closer look at interpersonal affect as a distinct influence on cognitive processing in performance evaluations. *Journal of Applied Psychology, 79,* 341–353.

75. Wayne, S. J., Liden, R. C., Graf, I. K., & Ferris, G. R. (1997). The role of upward influence tactics in human resource decisions. *Personnel Psychology, 50,* 979–1006.

76. Witt, L. A., & Ferris, G. R. (2003). Social skill as moderator of the conscientiousness–performance

relationship: Convergent results across four studies. *Journal of Applied Psychology, 88,* 809–820.

Case in Point Sources

Behar, H. (2007). *It's not about the coffee: Lessons on putting people first from a life at Starbucks.* New York: Penguin. Michelli, J. (2006). *The Starbucks experience.* New York: McGraw Hill. Stories of Entrepreneurs: Howard Schultz. (2009). *ZeroMillion.com.* From http://www.zeromillion.com/entrepreneurship/stories/howard-schultz.html. Capon, N. (2007). *The marketing mavens.* New York: Crown. Schultz, H. (1999). *Pour your heart into it: How Starbucks built a company one cup at a time.* New York: Hyperion.

Chapter 5

Preview Case Sources

Dealing with stress on the job and elsewhere. (2006). *Schizophrenia.com Newsletter.* From http://www.schizophrenia.com.newsletter/697/697stress.htm. Kaiser Permanente. (2006). Life outside of work. From http://www .kaiserpermanentejobs.org/workinghere/lifeoutside.asp. Jacobs, L. (2003, Winter). Discovering a remedy for physician work stress. *The Permanente Journal.* From http://xnet.kp.org/permanentejournal/winter03/group.html.

Chapter Notes

1. American Institute of Stress. (2010). *Stress in the workplace.* From http://www.stress.org/topic-workplace.htm.
2. Lewis, M., Haviland-Jones, J. M., & Barrett, L. F. (2008). *Handbook of emotions* (3rd ed.). New York: Guilford.
3. Hatfield, E., Cacioppo, J. T., & Rhapson, R. L. (1994). *Emotional contagion.* New York: Cambridge University Press.
4. Barsade, S. G. (2002). The ripple effect: Emotional contagion and its influence on group behavior. *Administrative Science Quarterly, 47,* 644–675. Cherulnik, P. K., Donley, K. A., Wiewel, T. S. R., & Miller, S. R. (2001). Charisma is contagious: The effects of leaders' charisma on observers' affect. *Journal of Applied Social Psychology, 31,* 2149–2159.
5. Ekman, P., Friesen, W. V., & Ancoli, S. (2001). Facial signs of emotional experience. In W. G. Parrott (Ed.), *Emotions in social psychology* (pp. 255–264). Philadelphia, PA: Psychology Press.
6. Nakamura, N. (2000). Facial expression and communication of emotion: An analysis of display rules and a model of facial expression of emotion. *Japanese Psychological Review, 43,* 307–319.
7. Matsumoto, D., Yoo, S. H., & Fontaine, J. (2008). Mapping expressive differences around the world: The relationship between emotional display rules and individualism versus collectivism. *Journal of Cross-Cultural Psychology, 39,* 55–74.
8. Tangney, J. P., & Fischer, K. W. (Eds.). (1995). *Self-conscious emotions: The psychology of shame, guilt, embarrassment, and pride.* New York: Guilford Press. Tracy, J. L., & Robins, R. W. (2004). Putting the self into self-conscious emotions: A theoretical model. *Psychological Inquiry, 15,* 103–125.
9. Keltner, D., & Anderson, C. (2000). Saving face for Darwin: The functions and uses of embarrassment. *Current Directions in Psychological Science, 9,* 187–192.
10. Beer, J. S., Heery, E. A., Keltner, D., Scabini, D., & Knight, R. T. (2003). The regulatory function of self-conscious emotion: Insights from patients with orbitofrontal damage. *Journal of Personality and Social Psychology, 85,* 594–604.
11. Vecchio, R. P. (2005). Explorations of employee envy: Feeling envious and feeling envied. *Cognition and Emotion, 19,* 69–81. Poulson, C. F. II. (2000). Shame and work. In N. M. Ashkanasy, W. Zerbe, & C. E. J. Härtel (Eds.), *Emotions in the workplace: Research, theory, and practice* (pp. 490–541). Westport, CT: Quorum Books.
12. Huelsman, T. J., Furr, R. M., & Memanick, R. C., Jr. (2003). Measurement of dispositional affect: Construct validity and convergence with a circumplex model of affect. *Educational and Psychological Measurement, 63,* 655–673. Larsen, J., Diener, E., & Lucas, R. E. (2002). Emotion: Moods, measures, and differences. In R. G. Lord, R. J. Klimiski, & R. Kanfer (Eds.), *Emotions in the workplace* (pp. 64–113). San Francisco, CA: Jossey-Bass.
13. George, J. M., & Brief, A. P. (1996). Motivational agendas in the workplace: The effects of feelings on focus of attention and work motivation. In B. M. Staw & L. L. Cummings (Eds.), *Research in organizational behavior* (Vol. 18, pp. 75–109). Greenwich, CT: JAI Press.
14. 100 Best Companies to Work For. (2010). *Fortune.* From http://money.cnn.com/magazines/fortune/bestcompanies/2010.html.
15. Lyubomirsky, S., King, L., & Diener, E. (2005). The benefits of frequent positive affect: Does happiness lead to success? *Psychological Bulletin, 131,* 803–855.
16. Staw, B. M., Sutton, R. I., & Pelled, L. H. (1994). Employee positive emotion and favorable outcomes in the workplace. *Organization Science, 5,* 51–71.
17. Cropanzano, R., & Wright, T. A. (1999). A five-year study of change in the relationship between well-being and job performance. *Consulting Psychology Journal, 51,* 252–265. Wright, T. A., & Staw, B. M. (1999). Affect and favorable work outcomes: Two longitudinal tests of the happy-productive worker thesis. *Journal of Organizational Behavior, 20,* 1–23.
18. DeLuga, R. J., & Manson, S. (2000). Relationship of resident assistant conscientiousness, extraversion, and positive affect with rated performance. *Journal of Research in Personality, 34,* 225–235. Totterdell, P. (2000). Catching moods and hitting runs: Mood linkage and subjective performance in professional sports teams. *Journal of Applied Psychology, 83,* 848–859.
19. See Note 18.
20. Foster, J. B., Hebl, M. R., West, M., & Dawson, J. (2004, April). *Setting the tone for organizational success: The impact of CEO affect on organizational climate and firm-level outcomes.* Paper presented at the annual meeting of the Society for Industrial and Organizational Psychology,

Toronto, Ontario, Canada. Pritzker, M. A. (2002). The relationship among CEO dispositional attributes, transformational leadership behavior and performance effectiveness. *Dissertation Abstracts International, 62*(12-B), 6008. (UMI No. AA13035464.)

21. Lucas, R. E., Clark, A. E., Georgellis, Y., & Deiner, E. (2004). Unemployment alters the set points for live satisfaction. *Psychological Science, 15,* 8–13. Graham, C., Eggers, A., & Sukhtanar, S. (in press). Does happiness pay: An exploration based on panel data from Russia. *Journal of Economic Behaviour and Organization.*

22. Howell, C. J., Howell, R. T., & Schwabe, K. A. (in press). Does wealth enhance life satisfaction for people who are materially deprived? Exploring the association among the Orang Asli of Peninsular Malaysia. *Social Indicators Research.*

23. Vohs, K. D., Baumeister, R. F., & Loewenstein, G. (in press). *Do emotions help or hurt decision making?* New York: Russell Sage Foundation Press.

24. Weiss, H. M., Nicholas, J. P., & Daus, C. S. (1999). An examination of the joint effects of affective experiences and job beliefs on job satisfaction and variations in affective experiences over time. *Organizational Behavior and Human Decision Processes, 78,* 1–24.

25. Forgas, J., Goldenberg, L, & Unkelbach, C. (2009). Can bad weather improve your memory? An unobtrusive field study of natural mood effects on real-life memory. *Journal of Experimental Social Psychology, 45,* 254–257.

26. Clark, M. S., & Isen, A. M. (1982). Towards understanding the relationship between feeling states and social behavior. In A. H. Hastorf & A. M. Isen (Eds.), *Cognitive social psychology* (pp. 73–108). New York: Elsevier-North Holland.

27. Clore, G. L., Schwartz, N., & Conway, M. (1994). Affective causes and consequences of social information processing. In R. S. Wyer, Jr., & T. K. Srull (Eds.), *Handbook of social cognition* (Vol. 1, pp. 323–417). Hillsdale, NJ: Erlbaum.

28. Ashkanasy, N. M. (2004). Emotion and performance. *Human Performance, 17,* 137–144.

29. Weiss, H. M., & Cropanzano, R. (1996). An affective events approach to job satisfaction. In B. M. Staw & L. L. Cummings (Eds.), *Research in organizational behavior* (Vol. 18, pp. 1–74). Greenwich, CT: JAI Press.

30. Ashkanasy, N. M., & Daus, C. S. (2002). Emotion in the workplace: New challenges for managers. *Academy of Management Executive, 16,* 76–86.

31. See Note 12.

32. Miner, A. G., & Hulin, C. L. (2000). *Affective experience at work: A test of affective events theory.* Poster presented at the 15th annual conference of the Society for Industrial and Organizational Psychology; New Orleans, LA. Fisher, C. (1998, August). *Mood and emotions while working: Missing pieces of job satisfaction?* Paper presented at the annual meeting of the Academy of Management. San Diego, CA.

33. Ashkanasy, N. M., Hartel, C. E. J., & Daus, C. S. (2002). Diversity and emotion: The new frontiers in organizational behavior research. *Journal of Management, 28,* 307–338.

34. Goleman, D. (1998). *Working with emotional intelligence.* New York: Bantam.

35. Morris, J. A., & Feldman, D. C. (1997). Managing emotions in the workplace. *Journal of Managerial Issues, 9,* 257–274.

36. American Psychological Association. (2006). Topic: Anger. Controlling anger. From http://www.apa.org./topics/angersub1.html.

37. Bolles, R. N. (2010). *What color is your parachute?* (2010 edition). Berkeley, CA: Ten Speed Press.

38. American Institute of Stress (2009). Job stress. From http://www.stress.org/job.htm.

39. Goldin, R. (2004, September 23). Counting the costs of stress. *American Institute of Stress.* From http://stats.org/stories/2004/counting_costs_stress_sep23_04.htm.

40. Selye, H. (1976). *Stress in health and disease.* Boston, MA: Butterworths.

41. Bakker, A. B., Schaufeli, W. B., Sixma, H. J., Bosveld, W., & Van Dierendonck, D. (2000). Patient demands, lack of reciprocity, and burnout: A five-year longitudinal study among general practitioners. *Journal of Organizational Behavior, 21,* 425–441.

42. Nideffer, R. M., (1976). Test of attentional and interpersonal style. *Journal of Personality and Social Psychology, 34,* 394–404.

43. Stress at work (1997, April 15). *Wall Street Journal,* p. A12.

44. Heller, R., & Hindle, T. (1998). *Essential manager's manual.* New York: DK Publishing.

45. Major, V. S., Klein, K. J., & Erhart, M. G. (2002). Work time, work interference with family, and psychological distress. *Journal of Applied Psychology, 87,* 427–436.

46. Fisher, A. B. (1993, August 23). Sexual harassment: What to do. *Fortune,* pp. 84–86, 88.

47. Kolbert, E. (1991, October 10). Sexual harassment at work is pervasive. *New York Times,* pp. A1, A17.

48. U.S. Equal Employment Opportunity Commission. (2010). Sexual harassment charges, EEOC and FEPAs Combined FY 1997–FY 2009. From http://www.eeoc.gov/eeoc/statistics/enforcement/sexual_harassment.cfm.

49. Wright, B. E., & Millesen, J. L. (2008). Nonprofit board role ambiguity: Investigating its prevalence, antecedents, and consequences. *American Review of Public Administration, 38,* 322-338. McGrath, J. E. (1976). Stress and behavior in organizations. In M. D. Dunnette (Ed.), *Handbook of industrial and organizational psychology* (pp. 1351–1398). Chicago, IL: Rand McNally.

50. Niessen, B. (2000, November 15). Last straw survey—overworked, overwrought: "Desk rage" at work. *CNN.com.* From http://archives.cnn.com/2000/CAREER/trends/11/15/rage.

51. Stephens, C., & Long, N. (2000). Communication with police supervisors and peers as a buffer of work-related traumatic stress. *Journal of Organizational Behavior, 21,* 407–424.

52. Beehr, T. A., Jex, S. M., Stacy, B. A., & Murray, M. A. (2000). Work stressors and coworker support as predictors of individual strain and job performance. *Journal of Organizational Behavior, 21,* 391–405. Cohen, S., & Willis, T. A. (1985). Stress, social

support, and the buffering hypothesis. *Psychological Bulletin, 98,* 310–357.

53. Treharne, G. J., Lyons, A. C., & Tupling, R. E. (2001). The effects of optimism, pessimism, social support, and mood on the lagged relationship between stress and symptoms. *Current Research in Social Psychology, 7*(5), 60–81.

54. Sullivan, S. E., & Bhagat, R. S. (1992). Organizational stress, job satisfaction, and job performance: Where do we go from here? *Journal of Management, 18,* 353–374.

55. Cropanzano, R., Rupp, D. E., & Byrne, Z. S. (2003). The interrelationship of emotional exhaustion to work attitudes, job performance, and organizational citizenship behaviors. *Journal of Applied Psychology, 88,* 160–169. Motowidlo, S. J., Packard, J. S., & Manning, M. R. (1986). Occupational stress: Its causes and consequences for job performance. *Journal of Applied Psychology, 71,* 618–629.

56. Legree, P. J., Heffner, T. S., Psotka, J., Martin, D. E., & Medsker, G. J. (2003). Traffic crash involvement: Experiential driving knowledge and stressful contextual antecedents. *Journal of Applied Psychology, 88,* 5–26.

57. Daw, J. (2001, August). Road rage, air rage, and now desk rage. *Monitor on Psychology, 32*(7). 9–10. The list: Desk rage. *BusinessWeek* (2000, November 27), p. 12. Lorenz, I. (2004, December 20). 7 tips for combating desk rage. *CNN.com/CareerBuilder.com.* From http://www.cnn.com/2004/US/Careers/08/13/boss.spying/index.html.

58. Frese, M. (1985). Stress at work and psychosomatic complaints: A causal interpretation. *Journal of Applied Psychology, 70,* 314–328. Quick, J. C., & Quick, J. D. (1984). *Organizational stress and preventive management.* New York: McGraw-Hill.

59. Quick, J. C., Cooper, C, L., Gavin, J. H., & Quick, J. D. (2008). *Managing executive health.* New York: Cambridge University Press.

60. K. F., & Orioli, E. M. (1994). Gender differences in stress symptoms, stress-producing contexts, and coping strategies. In G. P. Keita & J. J. Hurrell, Jr. (Eds.), *Job stress in a changing workforce* (pp. 7–22). Washington, DC: American Psychological Association.

61. Iwanski, Y., MacKay, K., & Mactavysh, J. (2005, First Quarter). Gender-based analyses of coping with stress among professional managers: Leisure coping and non-leisure-coping. *Journal of Leisure Research.* From http://www.findarticles.com/p/articles/mi_qa3702/is_200501/ai_n9520740.

62. Latack, J. C., & Havlovic, S. J. (1992). Coping with job stress: A conceptual evaluation framework for coping measures. *Journal of Organizational Behavior, 13,* 479–508.

63. Society for Human Resource Management. (2006). *Annual benefits survey.* Alexandria, VA: SHRM.

64. Employee Assistance Professionals Association. (2006). Recent EAP cost/benefit statistics research: 2000–present. From http://www.eapassn.org/public/articles/EAPcostbenefitstats.pdf.

65. Flora, C. (2004, January/February). Keeping workers and companies fit. *Psychology Today,* pp. 36–40.

Also available from http://www.psychologytoday.com/articles/pto-3285.html.

66. See Note 67.

67. Robertson Cooper, Ltd. (2009, November). "Presenteeism" on the rise as an estimated quarter of UK employees admit to working when ill. From http://www.robertsoncooper.com/news/presenteeism.aspx.

68. See Note 67.

69. Singer, T. (2007, October 17). The balance of power. *Inc. 500,* pp. 105–108, 110.

70. Benson, H. (1993). The relaxation response. In D. Goleman & J. Gurin (Eds.), *Mind/body medicine* (pp. 233–257). New York: Consumer Reports Books. Domar, A. D., & Dreher, H. (1996). *Healing mind, healthy woman.* New York: Henry Holt.

71. Krajicinovic, I. (1997). *From company doctors to managed care: The United Mine Workers' noble experiment.* Ithaca, NY: Cornell University Press.

72. Business Ethics Memo. (2007, March 21). Mandating employee health? From http://businessethicsmemo.blogspot.com/2007/03/should-employers-mandate-healthy_21.html.

Case in Point Sources

Newsday.com. (2008, July 30). Tim Donaghy timeline. From http://www.newsday.com/sports/basketball/ny-sprefbox305782382jul30,0,6452591.story. Fortado, L., & Hurtado, P. (2008, July 29). Ex-NBA referee Donaghy gets 15-month term for betting. *Bloomberg.com.* From http://www.bloomberg.com/apps/news?pid=newsarchive&sid=arILgbEs3O_4. Hays, T. (2008, July 30). BBA scandal: Corrupt ref gets 15-month sentence. From http://www.bloomberg.com/apps/news?pid=newsarchive&sid=arILgbEs3O_4. Price, J., & Wolfers, J. (2007, June). *Racial discrimination among NBA referees* (NBER working paper no. 13206). Cambridge, MA: National Bureau of Economic Research.

Chapter 6

Preview Case Sources

Hyman, M. (2008, September 8). Paralympians break the ad barrier. *BusinessWeek,* p. 70. International Paralympic Committee. (2009). Paralympic games: Facts and figures. From http://www.parakympic.org/release. Prosthetics by Ossur. (2009). Marlon Shirley. From http://www.ossur.com/pages/3361. Cheri Blauwet. (2008). From http://www.cheriblauwet.com. Group Benefits from the Hartford. (2008). Cheri Blauwet. From http://groupbenefits.thehartford.com/usp/bios/blauwet.html.

Chapter Notes

1. McGuire, W. J. (1985). Attitudes and attitude change. In G. Lindzey & E. Aronson (Eds.), *Handbook of social psychology* (3rd ed., Vol. 2, pp. 233–346). New York: Random House.

2. U.S. Bureau of Labor Statistics (2010). *Labor participation rates.* Washington, DC: Author.

3. U.S. Bureau of Labor Statistics (2009, November). *Labor force characteristics by race and ethnicity* (Report 1020). Washington, DC: Author.

4. Joshi, A. (2006). The influence of organizational demography on the external networking behavior of teams. *Academy of Management Review, 31,* 583–595. Nicholson, N. (1995). Organizational demography. In N. Nicholson (Ed.), *Blackwell encyclopedic dictionary of organizational behavior* (pp. 833–834). Malden, MA: Blackwell. Pfeffer, J. (1985). Organizational demography: Implications for management. *California Management Review, 38,* 67–81.

5. Tsui, A. S., Egan, T. D., & O'Reilly, C. A., III. (1992). Being different: Relational demography and organizational attachment. *Administrative Science Quarterly, 37,* 549–579.

6. Wagner, W. G., Pfeffer, J., & O'Reilly, C. A. (1984). Work group demography and turnover in top management groups. *Administrative Science Quarterly, 29,* 74–92. Godthelp, M., & Glunk, U. (2003). Turnover at the top: Demographic diversity as a determinant of executive turnover in the Netherlands. *European Management Journal, 21,* 614–626.

7. Watson, W., Stewart, W. H., Jr., & BarNir, A. (2003). The effects of human capital, organizational demography, and interpersonal processes on venture partner perceptions of firm profit and growth. *Journal of Business Venturing, 18,* 145–164.

8. Webber, S. S., & Donahue, L. M. (2001). Impact of highly and less job-related diversity on work group cohesion and performance: A meta-analysis. *Journal of Management, 27,* 141–162.

9. Gregory, R. F. (2001). *Age discrimination in the American workplace: Old at a young age.* New Brunswick, NJ: Rutgers University Press.

10. Raines, C. (1997). *Beyond Generation X. A practical guide for managers.* Menlo Park, CA: Crisp.

11. Howe, N., & Strauss, W. (2000). *Millennials rising: The next great generation.* New York: Vintage.

12. Lieberman, S., Simons, G., & Berardo, K. (2009). *Putting diversity to work.* Mississauga, Ontario, Canada: Crisp.

13. Brault, M. (2008, February). *Disability status and the characteristics of people in group quarters.* U.S. Bureau of the Census. From http://www.census.gov/hhes/www/disability/GQdisability.pdf.

14. Magill, B. G. (1999). *Workplace accommodations under the ADA.* Washington, DC: Thomson Publishing Group.

15. U.S. Census Bureau. (2009, January 5). News release: Facts for features. From http://www.census.gov/Press-Release/www/releases/archives/facts_for_features_special_editions/013129.html.

16. U.S. Department of Labor. (2009, September). *Women in the labor force: A databook* (2009 edition). From http://www.bls.gov/cps/wlf-table10-2009.pdf.

17. CNNMoney.com (2009). Women CEOs. Fortune 500. From http://money.cnn.com/magazines/fortune/fortune500/2009/womenceos.

18. Foster, F. (1994). Managerial sex role stereotyping among academic staff within UK business schools. *Women in Management Review, 9,* 17–22.

19. Chynoweth, C. (2007, October 3). Clever ways to break through glass. *London Times Online.* From http://business.timesonline.co.uk/tol/business/career_and_jobs/top_50_women/article2568814.ece.

20. Barreto, M., Ryan, M. K., & Schmitt, M. (2008). *The glass ceiling in the 21st century: Understanding barriers to gender equity.* Washington, DC: American Psychological Association.

21. Hereck, G. M. (1998). *Stigma and sexual orientation: Understanding prejudice against lesbians, gay men, and bisexuals.* Newbury Park, CA: Sage.

22. Martinez, M. N. (1993, June). Recognizing sexual orientation is fair and not costly. *HRMagazine,* pp. 66–68, 70–72 (quote, p. 68).

23. Alternatives to Marriage Project. (2008). From http://www.unmarried.org/statistics.html.

24. Yang, C. (1993, June 21). In any language, it's unfair: More immigrants are bringing bias charges against employers. *BusinessWeek,* pp. 110–112 (quote, p. 111).

25. Niebuhr, G. (2008). *Beyond tolerance: Searching for interfaith understanding in America.* New York: Viking.

26. Tannenbaum Center for Religious Understanding. (2001). *Survey on religious bias in the workplace.* New York: Author.

27. Corrigan, J, & Neale, L. S. (2010). *Religious intolerance in America: A documentary history.* Charlotte, NC: University of North Carolina Press.

28. Philosophy and Public Policy. (2008). Civil rights and racial preferences: A legal history of affirmative action. From http://www.puaf.umd.edu/IPPP/2QQ.HTM.

29. Kravitz, D. A. (2008). The diversity-validity dilemma: Beyond selection—the role of affirmative action. *Personnel Psychology, 61,* 173–193.

30. Ragins, B. R., & Gonzales, J. A. (2003). Understanding diversity in organizations: Getting a grip on a slippery construct. In J. Greenberg (Ed.), *Organizational behavior: The state of the science,* 2nd ed., (pp. 125–163). Mahwah, NJ: Erlbaum.

31. Murray, K. (1993, August 1). The unfortunate side effects of "diversity training." *New York Times,* pp. E1, E3.

32. Gottfredson, L. S. (1992). Dilemmas in developing diversity programs. In S. E. Jackson (Ed.), *Diversity in the workplace* (pp. 279–305). New York: Guilford Press.

33. Greene, A., & Kirton, G. (2009). *Diversity management in the UK.* New York: Routledge.

34. Klein, K. J. & Harrison, D. A. (2007). On the diversity of diversity: Tidy logic, messier realities. *Academic of Management Perspectives, 21,* 26–33. Harrison, D. A. & Klein, K. J. (2007). What's the difference? Diversity constructs as separation, variety, or disparity in organizations. *Academy of Management Review, 32,* 1199–1228.

35. Richard, O. C. (2000). Racial diversity, business strategy, and firm performance: A resource-based view. *Academy of Management Journal, 43,* 164–177.

36. Wright, P., Ferris, S. P., Hiller, J. S., & Kroll, M. (1995). Competitiveness through management of diversity: Effects of stock price valuation. *Academy of Management Journal, 38,* 272–287.

37. Kandola, R., & Fullerton, J. (1998). *Managing the mosaic: Diversity in action* (2nd ed.). London: Chartered Institute of Personnel and Development.

38. Thomas, R. R., Jr. (1992). Managing diversity: A conceptual framework. In S. E. Jackson (Ed.),

Diversity in the workplace (pp. 306–317). New York: Guilford Press (quote, p. 309).

39. Kahn, J. (2001, July 9). Diversity trumps the downturn. *Fortune,* pp. 66–72 (quote, p. 70).

40. Fegley, S. (2006). *2006 workplace diversity and changes to the EEO-1 process: Survey report.* Alexandria, VA: Society for Human Resource Management.

41. Gardenswartz, L., & Rowe, A. (1994). *The managing diversity survival guide.* Burr Ridge, IL: Irwin.

42. Battaglia, B. (1992). Skills for managing multicultural teams. *Cultural Diversity at Work, 4,* 4–12.

43. Allstate Insurance Company. (2010). *Workforce diversity.* From http://www.allstate.com/diversity/workplace.aspx. Allstate Insurance Company. (2008). *One company for us all.* From http://www.allstate.com/Allstate/content/refresh-attachments/diversity_brochure.pdf.

44. What's it like to work at Allstate? Diversity. (2003). From http://www.allstate.com/Careers/PageRender.asp?Page=diversity.htm.

45. Smith, T. W. (2009, April 17). *Job satisfaction in the United States.* Chicago, IL: National Opinion Research Center at the University of Chicago.

46. Burke, R. J., & Ng, E. (2006). The changing nature of work and organizations: Implications for human resource management. *Human Resource Management Review, 16,* 86–94.

47. Judge, T. A., & Klinger, R. A. (2009). Promote job satisfaction through mental challenge. In E. A. Locke (Ed.), *Handbook of principles of organizational behavior* (pp. 107–121). Chichester, UK: Wiley.

48. See Note 47.

49. Weiss, F. J., Dawis, R. V., England, G. W., & Lofquist, L. J. (1967). *Manual for the Minnesota Satisfaction Questionnaire.* Minneapolis, MN: Industrial Relations Center, University of Minnesota.

50. Judge, T. A. (1992). Dispositional perspective in human resources research. In G. R. Ferris & K. M. Rowland (Eds.), *Research in personality and human resources management* (Vol. 10, pp. 31–72). Greenwich, CT: JAI Press.

51. Judge, T. A., & Ilies, R. (2004). Affect and job satisfaction: A study of their relationships at home and at work. *Journal of Applied Psychology, 89,* 661–673.

52. Arvey, R. D., Bouchard, T. J., Jr., Segal, N. L., & Abraham, L. M. (1989). Job satisfaction: Genetic and environmental components. *Journal of Applied Psychology, 74,* 187–192.

53. Cropanzano, R., & James, K. (1990). Some methodological considerations for the behavioral-genetic analysis of work attitudes. *Journal of Applied Psychology, 71,* 433–439.

54. Watson, D. (2000). *Mood and temperament.* New York: Guilford Press.

55. Ilies, R., & Judge, T. A. (2003). On the heritability of job satisfaction: The mediating role of personality. *Journal of Applied Psychology, 88,* 750–759.

56. Salancik, G. R., & Pfeffer, J. R. (1978). A social information processing approach to job attitudes. *Administrative Science Quarterly, 23,* 224–252. Zalesny, M. D., & Ford, J. K. (1990). Extending the social information processing perspective: New links to attitudes, behaviors, and perceptions. *Organizational Behavior and Human Decision Processes, 47,* 205–246.

57. Phillips, J. J., & O'Connell, A. (2003). *Managing employee retention: A strategic accountability approach.* San Diego, CA: Elsevier.

58. Quote cited in Staff Turnover Costs at PeoplePulse.com.au. From http://www.exitinterviews.com.au/staff-turnover.htm.

59. Maertz, C. P., & Campion, M. A., (2004). Profiles in quitting: Integrating process and content turnover theory. *Academy of Management Journal, 47,* 566–582.

60. Boswell, W. R., Boudreau, J. W., & Tichy, J. (2005). The relationship between employee job change and job satisfaction: The honeymoon-hangover effect. *Journal of Applied Psychology, 90,* 882–892.

61. Mitchell, T. R., & Lee. T. W. (2001). The unfolding model of voluntary turnover and job embeddedness: Foundations for a comprehensive theory of attachment. In B. M. Staw & R. I. Sutton (Eds.), *Research in organizational behavior* (Vol. 23, pp. 189–246). San Diego, CA: Elsevier.

62. Lee, T. W., Mitchell, T. R., Holtom, B. C., McDaniel, L., & Hill, J. W. (1999). Theoretical development and extension of the unfolding model of voluntary turnover. *Academy of Management Journal, 42,* 450–462.

63. Mercer Consulting. (2009). From http://www.mercer.com/absenteeism.

64. Harrison, D. A., & Martocchio, J. J. (1998). Time for absenteeism: A 20-year review of origins, offshoots, and outcomes. *Journal of Management, 24,* 305–350.

65. Hardy, G. E., Woods, D., & Wall, T. D. (2003). The impact of psychological distress on absence from work. *Journal of Applied Psychology, 88,* 306–314.

66. Iaffaldano, M. R., & Murchinsky, P. M. (1985). Job satisfaction and job performance: A meta-analysis. *Psychological Bulletin, 97,* 251–273.

67. Judge, T. A., Thorenson, C. J., Bono, J. E., & Patton, G. K. (2001). The job satisfaction–job performance relationship: A qualitative and quantitative review. *Psychological Bulletin, 127,* 376–407.

68. Schneider, B., Hanges, P. J., Smith, D. B., & Salvaggio, A. N. (2004). Which comes first: Employee attitudes or organizational financial and market performance? *Journal of Applied Psychology, 88,* 836–851.

69. Goddard, J. (2001). High performance and the transformation of work: The implications of alternative work practices for the experience and outcomes of work. *Industrial and Labor Relations Review, 54,* 776–806.

70. Gyeke, S. A., & Salminen, S. (2006). Making sense of industrial accidents: The role of job satisfaction. *Journal of Social Sciences, 2,* 127–134.

71. Barling, J., Kelloway, E. K., & Iverson, R. D. (2003). High-quality work, job satisfaction, and occupational injuries. *Journal of Applied Psychology, 88,* 276–283.

72. Tait, M., Padgett, M. Y., & Baldwin, T. T. (1989). Job and life satisfaction: A reevaluation of the strength of the relationship and gender effects as a function of the date of the study. *Journal of Applied Psychology, 74,* 502–507.

73. Ilies, R., & Judge, T. A. (2002). Understanding the dynamic relationships among personality, mood, and job satisfaction: A field experience sampling study. *Organizational Behavior and Human Decision Processes, 89,* 1119–1139. Weiss, H. M. (2002). Deconstructing job satisfaction: Separating evaluations, beliefs, and affective experiences. *Human Resource Management Review, 12,* 173–194.

74. Judge, T. A., & Ilies, R. (2004). Affect and job satisfaction: A study of their relationship at work and at home. *Journal of Applied Psychology, 89,* 661–673.

75. Klein, H. J., Becker, T. E., & Meyer, J. P. (2009). *Commitment in organizations: Accumulated wisdom and new directions.* New York: Routledge.

76. Snape, E., & Redman, T. (2003). An evaluation of a three-component model of occupational commitment: Dimensionality and consequences among United Kingdom human resource management specialists. *Journal of Applied Psychology, 88,* 152–159. Meyer, J. P., Allen, N. J., & Smith, C. A. (1993). Commitment to organizations and occupations: Extension and test of a three-component conceptualization. *Journal of Applied Psychology, 78,* 538–551.

77. Lee, K., Carswell, J. J., & Allen, N. J. (2000). A meta-analytic review of occupational commitment: Relations with person- and work-related variables. *Journal of Applied Psychology, 85,* 799–811.

78. Gong, Y., Law, K. S., Chang, S., & Xin, K. R. (2009). Human resources management and firm performance: The differential role of managerial affective and continuance commitment. *Journal of Applied Psychology, 94,* 263–275.

79. Meyer, J. P., Stanley, D. J., Herscovitch, L., & Topolnytsky, L. (2002). Affective, continuance, and normative commitment to the organization: A meta-analysis of antecedents, correlates, and consequences. *Journal of Vocational Behavior, 61,* 20–52.

80. Clugston, M. (2000). The mediating effects of multidimensional commitment on job satisfaction and intent to leave. *Journal of Organizational Behavior, 21,* 477–486.

81. Lee, T. W., Ashford, S. J., Walsh, J. P., & Mowday, R. T. (1992). Commitment propensity, organizational commitment, and voluntary turnover: A longitudinal study of organizational entry processes. *Journal of Management, 18,* 15–32.

82. Brush, M. (2006, February 1). CEOs for $1 a year—plus millions more. *MSN Money.* From http://moneycentral.msn.com/content/P143257.asp.

83. Bond, M. H. (1986). *The psychology of the Chinese people.* New York: Oxford University Press.

84. Hui, C., Lam, S. S. K., & Law, K. K. S. (2000). Instrumental values of organizational citizenship behavior for promotion: A field quasi-experiment. *Journal of Applied Psychology, 85,* 822–828.

85. Johns, G., & Xie, J. L. (1998). Perceptions of absence from work: People's Republic of China versus Canada. *Journal of Applied Psychology, 83,* 515–530.

86. Sheraton Memorial Hospital Employee Gainsharing Plan. (2009, June 30). From http://www.sheridanhospital.org/documents/GainsharingPlan2009.pdf.

Case in Point Sources

Domino's Pizza. (2010). Fun facts. From http://www.dominosbiz.com/Biz-Public-EN/Site+Content/Secondary/About+Dominos/Fun+Facts. White, E. (2005, February 15). To keep employees, Domino's decides it's all about pay. *Wall Street Journal*, p. 1. Boorstin, J. (2005, February 7). Delivering at Domino's Pizza. *CNNMoney.com, Fortune.* From http://money.cnn.com/magazines/fortune/fortune_archive/2005/02/07/8250433/index.htm. Coomes, S. (2005, May). Taming turnover. Pizza marketplace. From http://www.pizzamarketplace.com/article.php?id=4082. Domino's lowers corporate turnover with training program. Nation's Restaurant News. (2005, April 5). From http://findarticles.com/p/articles/mi_m3190/is_14_39/ai_n13596665.

Chapter 7

Preview Case Sources

Costco Wholesale. (2010). Member relations. From http://phx.corporate-ir.net/phoenix.zhtml?c=83830&p=irol-homeprofile. Costco Wholesale. (2008). Wikinvest. From http://www.wikinvest.com/stock/.Costco_Wholesale_(COST). Yukl, G., & Lepsinger, R. (2005). Why integrating the leading and managing roles is essential for organizational effectiveness. *Organizational Dynamics, 34*(4), 361–375. Holmes, S., & Zellner, W. (2004, April 12). The Costco way: Higher wages mean higher profits; but try telling Wall Street. *BusinessWeek*, pp. 76–77. Kiel, F. (2008, October 6). Flaws in the selfish-worker theory. *BusinessWeek*, p. 78. Greenhouse, S. (2005, July 17). How Costco became the anti Walmart. *New York Times.* From http://www.nytimes.com/2005/07/17/business/yourmoney/17costco.html.

Chapter Notes

1. Pinder, C. C. (2008). *Work motivation in organizational behavior* (2nd ed.). New York: Psychology Press.

2. Mitchell, T. R., & Daniels, D. (2003). Motivation. In W. C. Borman, D. R. Ilgen, & R. J. Klimoski (Eds.), *Handbook of psychology, Vol. 12: Industrial and organizational psychology* (pp. 215–254). New York: Wiley.

3. Robson, C. (2004). What motivates workers today? London: Hays Office Support. From http://www.hays.com/uk/index.jsp?Channel=office&Content=/uk/jobseekers/office/what-motivates-office-workers-today.htm.

4. Gallinsky, E., Carter, N., Bond, J. T., & Bloom, H. (2009). *Leaders in a global economy: Finding the fit for top talent.* New York: Families and Work Institute.

5. Kanfer, R., & Heggestad, E. D. (1997). Motivational traits and skills: A person-centered approach to work motivation. In L. L. Cummings & B. M. Staw (Eds.), *Research in organizational behavior* (Vol. 19, pp. 1–56). Greenwich, CT: JAI Press.

6. Kanfer, R., Wanberg, C. R., & Kantrowitz, T. M. (2001). Job search and employment: A personality-motivational analysis and meta-analytic review. *Journal of Applied Psychology, 86,* 837–855.

7. Cline, M. (2001, September). Cut agent turnover by hiring for motivational fit. *Call Center Management Review,* pp. 2–3.

8. Kanfer, R., & Ackerman, P. L. (2000). Individual differences in work motivation: Further explorations of a trait framework. *Applied Psychology: An International Review, 40,* 479–486.

9. See Note 8.

10. Latham, G. P. (2009). Motivate employee performance through goal setting. In E. A. Locke (Ed.), *Handbook of principles of organizational behavior* (pp. 161–178). Chichester, UK: Wiley. Locke, E. A. (2004). Goal-setting theory and its applications to the world of business. *Academy of Management Executive, 18,* 124–125

11. Locke, E. A., & Latham, G. P. (1990). *A theory of goal setting and task performance.* Englewood Cliffs, NJ: Prentice Hall.

12. Mento, A. J., Locke, E. A., & Klein, H. J. (1992). Relationship of goal level to valence and instrumentality. *Journal of Applied Psychology, 77,* 395–406.

13. Latham, G. P. (2004). The motivational benefits of goal-setting. *Academy of Management Executive, 18,* 126–129.

14. Gellatly, I. R., & Meyer, J. P. (1992). The effects of goal difficulty on physiological arousal, cognition, and task performance. *Journal of Applied Psychology, 77,* 696–704.

15. Latham, G. P., & Seijts, G. H. (1999). The effects of proximal and distal goals on performance on a moderately complex task. *Journal of Organizational Behavior, 20,* 421–429.

16. Locke, E. A., & Latham, G. P. (2002). Building a practically useful theory of goal setting and task motivation: A 35-year odyssey. *American Psychologist, 57,* 705–717.

17. Miner, J. B. (2003). The rated importance, scientific validity, and practical usefulness of organizational behavior theories. *Academy of Management Executive, 2,* 250–268.

18. Mitchell, T. R., & Daniels, D. (2003). Observations and commentary on recent research in work motivation. In L. W. Porter, G. A. Bigley, & R. M. Steers (Eds.), *Motivation and work behavior* (7th ed., pp. 26–44). Burr Ridge, IL: McGraw-Hill/Irwin (quote, p. 29).

19. Latham, G., & Baldes, J. (1975). The practical significance of Locke's theory of goal setting. *Journal of Applied Psychology, 60,* 122–124.

20. Locke, E. A., & Latham, G. P. (1984). *Goal setting: A motivational technique that works!* Englewood Cliffs, NJ: Prentice Hall.

21. See Note 20.

22. Wright, P. M., Hollenbeck, J. R., Wolf, S., & McMahan, G. C. (1995). The effects of varying goal difficulty operationalizations on goal setting outcomes and processes. *Organizational Behavior and Human Decision Processes, 61,* 28–43.

23. YouSayToo Sets a Donation Goal of US$30 Thousand to Hope for Haiti. (2010, January 27). *PR Hub.* From http://blog.taragana.com/pr/yousaytoo-sets-a-donation-goal-of-us30-thousand-to-hope-for-haiti-12315.

24. Bernstein, A. (1991, April 29). How to motivate workers: Don't watch 'em. *BusinessWeek,* p. 56.

25. United States Department of Veterans Affairs. (2010). *Bay Pines, Virginia Health Care System: Goals—dietetic internship program.* From http://www.baypines.va.gov/DieteticCareer/goals.asp.

26. Coeur d'Alene Mines Corporation Q1 2009 Earnings Call Transcript. (2009, May 11). *Seeking Alpha.* From http://seekingalpha.com/article/136985-coeur-dalene-mines-corporation-q1-2009-earnings-call-transcript?page=2.

27. Kerr, S., & Landauer, S. (2004). Using stretch goals to promote organizational effectiveness and personal growth: General Electric and Goldman Sachs. *Academy of Management Executive, 18,* 134–138.

28. Goldman Sachs Group. (2010). Global investment research: Who we look for. From http://www2.goldmansachs.com/careers/our-firm/divisions/gir/who-we-look-for/index.html.

29. Latham, G. P., Erez, M., & Locke, E. A. (1988). Resolving scientific disputes by the joint design of crucial experiments by the antagonists: Application to the Erez-Latham dispute regarding participation in goal setting. *Journal of Applied Psychology, 73,* 753–772.

30. Ludwig, T. D., & Geller, E. S. (1997). Assigned versus participative goal setting and response generalization: Managing injury control among professional pizza deliverers. *Journal of Applied Psychology, 82,* 253–261.

31. Shaw, K. N. (2004). Changing the goal-setting process at Microsoft. *Academy of Management Executive, 18,* 139–142.

32. Langley, M. (2003, June 9). Big companies get low marks for lavish executive pay. *Wall Street Journal,* p. C1.

33. Colquitt, J. A., & Greenberg, J. (2003). Organizational justice: A fair assessment of the state of the literature. In J. Greenberg (Ed.), *Organizational behavior: The state of the science* (2nd ed., pp. 165–210). Mahwah, NJ: Erlbaum. Adams, J. S. (1965). Inequity in social exchange. In L. Berkowitz (Ed.), *Advances in experimental social psychology* (Vol. 2, pp. 267–299). New York: Academic Press.

34. Star, M. (2009, October 9). "Restless" Braeden quits CNS soap. *New York Post.* From http://www.newyorkpost.com/p/entertainment/tv/item_FzcPxHGmhnurAvFP0m9UWL.

35. Greenberg, J. (2010). Organizational injustice as an occupational health risk. In J. P. Walsh & A. P. Brief (Eds.), *Academy of management annals* (Vol. 4 pp. 205–243). Oxford, England: Routledge.

36. Harder, J. W. (1992). Play for pay: Effects of inequity in a pay-for-performance context. *Administrative Science Quarterly, 37,* 321–335.

37. Greenberg, J. (1993). Stealing in the name of justice: Informational and interpersonal moderators of theft reactions to underpayment inequity. *Organizational Behavior and Human Decision Processes, 54,* 81–103.

38. Jones, D. A., & Skarlicki, D. P. (2003). The relationship between perceptions of fairness and voluntary turnover among retail employees. *Journal of Applied Social Psychology, 33,* 1226–1243.

39. Mowday, R. T., & Colwell, K. A. (2003). Employee reactions to unfair outcomes in the workplace: The contributions of Adams's equity theory to understanding work motivation. In L. W. Porter, G. A. Bigley, & R. M. Steers (Eds.), *Motivation and work behavior* (7th ed., pp. 65–82). Burr Ridge, IL: McGraw-Hill/Irwin.

40. Greenstein, T. N. (1995). Gender ideology and perception of the fairness of the division of household labor: Effects on marital quality. *Social Forces, 74,* 1029–1042.

41. Frisco, M. L., & Williams, K. (2003). Perceived housework equity, marital happiness, and divorce in dual-earner households. *Journal of Family Issues, 24,* 51–73.

42. Moon, M. A. (2008). Pay-for-performance boosts [HbA.sub.1c] testing, but not disease control. *OB GYN News, 43*(1), 24.

43. Romer, J. (1984). *Ancient lives: The story of the Pharaoh's tomb-makers.* London: Phoenix Press.

44. Dubofsky, M. (2000). *We shall be all: A history of the industrial workers of the world.* Champaign, IL: University of Illinois Press.

45. Colquitt, J. A., Greenberg, J., & Zapata-Phelan, C. P. (2005). What is organizational justice? A historical overview. In J. Greenberg & J. A. Colquitt (Eds.), *Handbook of organizational justice* (pp. 3–55). Mahwah, NJ: Erlbaum.

46. Hodge, W. A., (2003). *The role of performance pay systems in comprehensive school reform.* Lanham, MD: University Press of America. Lawler, E. E., III. (1967). Secrecy about management compensation: Are there hidden costs? *Organizational Behavior and Human Performance, 2,* 182–189.

47. Lewicki, R. J., Wiethoff, C., & Tomlinson, E. C. (2005). What is the role of trust in organizational justice? In J. Greenberg & J. A. Colquitt (Eds.), *Handbook of organizational justice* (pp. 222–257). Mahwah, NJ: Erlbaum.

48. Porter, L. W., & Lawler, E. E., III. (1968). *Managerial attitudes and performance.* Homewood, IL: Irwin.

49. Hall, C. S., & Lindzey, G. (1966). *Theories of personality.* New York: Wiley.

50. Deci, E. L., Ryan, R. M., Gagné, M., Leone, D. R., Usunov, J., & Kornazheva, B. P. (2001). Need satisfaction, motivation, and well-being in the work organizations of a former Eastern Bloc country. *Personality and Social Psychology Bulletin, 27,* 930–942. Maslow, A. (1998). *Maslow on management.* New York: Wiley.

51. Heine, S. J., Lehman, D. R., Markus, H. R., & Kitayama, S. (1999). Is there a universal need for positive self-regard? *Psychological Review, 106,* 766–794.

52. Serwer, A. (2005, January 25). Toyota rolls out a new economy-class drug plan. *Fortune,* p. 47.

53. Bilkovski, S. D. (2004). Work force motivation: A novel application of expectancy theory in emergency medicine. *Annals of Emergency Medicine, 44*(4), Supplement 1, S130. Lord, R. G., Hanges, P. J., & Godfrey, E. G. (2003). Integrating neural networks into decision-making and motivational theory: Rethinking VIE theory. *Canadian Psychology, 44,* 217.

54. Oracle. (2010). Benefits. From http://www.oracle.com/corporate/employment/college/ben.html.

55. Kerr, S. (1995). On the folly of rewarding A while hoping for B. *Academy of Management Executive, 9,* 7–14.

56. See Note 41.

57. The Endocrine Society. (2006, June). *Position statement: Pay-for-performance.* Chevy Chase, MD: Author.

58. Snyder, L., & Neubauer, R. L. (2007, December 4). Pay-for-performance principles that promote patient-centered care: An ethics manifesto. *Annals of Internal Medicine, 147,* 792–794.

59. Cannon, M. F. (2007). Pay-for-performance: Is Medicare a good candidate? *Yale Journal of Health Policy, Law, and Ethics, 7*(1), 1–38.

60. Schneider, M. E. (2007). Pay-for-performance ethical concerns explored. *Clinical Psychiatry News, 35*(6), 52.

61. Markham, S. E., Dow, S. K., & McKee, G. H. (2002). Recognizing good attendance: A longitudinal, quasi-experimental field study. *Personnel Psychology, 55,* 639–660.

62. National Association for Employee Recognition. (2002). From http://www.recognition.org/index.asp?cid=189&tid=694.

63. Ettore, B. (1998, May). The brave new world of executive compensation. *Management Review, 8.*

64. Rodric, S. (2001). *The stock options book.* Oakland, CA: National Center for Employee Ownership.

65. Merck & Co. (2004). *Annual report: 2004.* Whitehouse, NJ: Author.

66. Griffin, R. W., & McMahan, G. C. (1994). Motivation through job design. In J. Greenberg (Ed.), *Organizational behavior: The state of the science* (pp. 23–44). Hillsdale, NJ: Erlbaum.

67. Rigdon, J. E. (1992, May 26). Using lateral moves to spur employees. *Wall Street Journal,* pp. B1, B9.

68. Campion, M. A., & McClelland, C. L. (1991). Interdisciplinary examination of the costs and benefits of enlarged jobs: A job design quasi-experiment. *Journal of Applied Psychology, 76,* 186–198.

69. Campion, M. A., & McClelland, C. L. (1993). Follow-up and extension of the interdisciplinary costs and benefits of enlarged jobs. *Journal of Applied Psychology, 78,* 339–351.

70. Steers, R. M., & Spencer, D. G. (1977). The role of achievement motivation in job design. *Journal of Applied Psychology,* 472–479.

71. Lonergan, J. M., & Maher, K. J. (2000). The relationship between job characteristics and workplace procrastination as moderated by locus of control. *Journal of Social Behavior and Personality, 15,* 213–224.

72. Luthans, F., & Reif, W. E. (1974). Job enrichment: Long on theory, short on practice. *Organizational Dynamics, 2*(2), 30–43.

73. Hackman, J. R., & Oldham, G. R. (1980). *Work redesign.* Reading, MA: Addison-Wesley.

74. See Note 73.

75. Levine, R., & Levine, S. (1996). Why they are not smiling: Stress and discontent in the orchestral workplace. *Harmony, 2,* 15–25.

76. Graen, G. B., Scandura, T. A., & Graen, M. R. (1986). A field experimental test of the moderating effects of growth need strength on productivity. *Journal of Applied Psychology, 71,* 486–491.

77. Hackman, J. R., & Oldham, G. R. (1976). Motivation through the design of work: Test of a theory. *Organizational Behavior and Human Performance, 16,* 250–279.

78. Johns, G., Xie, J. L., & Fang, Y. (1992). Mediating and moderating effects in job design. *Journal of Management, 18,* 657–676. Fried, Y., & Ferris, G. R. (1987). The validity of the Job Characteristics Model: A review and meta-analysis. *Personnel Psychology, 40,* 287–322.

79. Orpen, C. (1979). The effects of job enrichment on employee satisfaction, motivation, involvement, and performance: A field experiment. *Human Relations, 32,* 189–217.

80. Grant, A. M. (2008). The significance of task significance: Job performance effects, relational mechanisms, and boundary conditions. *Journal of Applied Psychology, 93,* 108–124.

81. Hackman, J. R. (1976). Work design. In J. R. Hackman & J. L. Suttle (Eds.), *Improving life at work* (pp. 96–162). Santa Monica, CA: Goodyear.

82. Ropp, K. (1987, October). Candid conversations. *Personnel Administrator,* p. 49.

83. Callari, J. J. (1988, June). You can be a better motivator. *Traffic Management,* pp. 52–56.

84. Magnet, M. (1993, May 3). Good news for the service economy. *Fortune,* pp. 46–50, 52.

85. Finegan, J. (1993, July). People power. *Inc.,* pp. 62–63.

Case in Point Sources

Google. (2010). Google management. From http://www.google.com/corporate/execs.html. "Defining Google" (2005, January 2). *CBSNews.com, 60 Minutes.* From http://www.cbsnews.com/stories/2004/12/30/60minutes/main664063.shtml. Kennedy, S. D. (2004, April). A love/hate relationship. *Information Today, 27*(4), 15–16. Rubenking, N. J. (2004, December 28). MSN Search prepares to battle Google. *PC Magazine,* p. 41. Stone, B., & Levy, S. (2004, December 27). Google's two revolutions. *Newsweek,* p. 70.

Chapter 8

Preview Case Sources

Schwartz, A. (2010, March 23). Better Place, by the numbers. *Fast Company.* From http://www.fastcompany.com/1593916/better-place-by-the-numbers?partner=rss&utm_source=feedburner&utm_medium=feed&utm_campaign=Feed%3A+fastcompany%2Fheadlines+%28Fast+Company+Headlines%29&utm_content=Google+Feedfetcher. Thompson, C. S. (2009, April 16). Batteries not included. *New York Times,* p. M44. Roth, D. (2008, August 18). Driven: Shai Agassi's audacious plan to put electric cars on the road. *Wired Magazine,* p. 16. From http://www.wired.com/cars/futuretransport/magazine/16-09/ff_agassi. Ewing, J. (2008, September 1). My other car sounds like a Ferrari. *BusinessWeek,* p. 12. Better Place (2010). From http://www.betterplace.com. Better Place enters electric car network partnership with Ontario. (2009). *Green Car Congress.*

From http://www.greencarcongress.com/2009/01/better-place-en.html. Agassi, S. (2008, July 26). Tom Friedman's Column. *The Long Tailpipe.* From http://shaiagassi.typepad.com.

Chapter Notes

1. Turner, M. E. (2000). *Groups at work: Theory and research.* Mahwah, NJ: Erlbaum. Cartwright, D., & Zander, A. (1968). Origins of group dynamics. In D. Cartwright & A. Zander (Eds.), *Group dynamics: Research and theory* (pp. 3–21). New York: Harper & Row.

2. Toothman, J. (2000). *Conducting the experiential group: An introduction to group dynamics.* New York: John Wiley. Bettenhausen, K. L. (1991). Five years of groups research: What we have learned and what needs to be addressed. *Journal of Management, 17,* 345–381.

3. Forsyth, D. L. (1999). *Group dynamics* (3rd ed.). Belmont, CA: Wadsworth.

4. Long, S. (1984). Early integration in groups: "A group to join and a group to create." *Human Relations, 37,* 311–332.

5. Tuckman, B. W., & Jensen, M. A. (1977). Stages of small group development revisited. *Group and Organization Studies, 2,* 419–427.

6. Gersick, C. J. G. (1988). Time and transition in work teams: Toward a new model of group development. *Academy of Management Journal, 31,* 9–41.

7. Gersick, C. J. G. (1989). Marking time: Predictable transitions in task groups. *Academy of Management Journal, 32,* 274–309.

8. Romanelli, E., & Tushman, M. L. (1994). Organizational transformation as punctuated equilibrium: An empirical test. *Academy of Management Journal, 37,* 1141–1166.

9. Biddle, B. J. (1979). *Role theory: Expectations, identities, and behavior.* New York: Academic Press.

10. Jackson, S. E., & Schuler, R. S. (1985). A meta-analysis and conceptual critique of research on role ambiguity and role conflict in work settings. *Organizational Behavior and Human Decision Processes, 36,* 16–78.

11. O'Keefe, B. (2006, June 15). Hoop dreams. *Fortune,* p. 122.

12. Benne, K. D., & Sheats, P. (1948). Functional roles of group members. *Journal of Social Issues, 4,* 41–49.

13. Hackman, J. R. (1992). Group influences on individuals in organizations. In M. D. Dunnette & L. M. Hough (Eds.), *Handbook of industrial and organizational psychology* (2nd ed., Vol. 3, pp. 199–268). Palo Alto, CA: Consulting Psychologists Press.

14. Feldman, D. C. (1984). The development and enforcement of group norms. *Academy of Management Review, 9,* 48–53.

15. Wilson, S. (1978). *Informal groups: An introduction.* Englewood Cliffs, NJ: Prentice Hall.

16. Greenberg, J. (1988). Equity and workplace status: A field experiment. *Journal of Applied Psychology, 73,* 606–613.

17. Stryker, S., & Macke, A. S. (1978). Status inconsistency and role conflict. In R. H. Turner, J. Coleman, &

R. C. Fox (Eds.), *Annual review of sociology* (Vol. 4, pp. 58–90). Palo Alto, CA: Annual Reviews.

18. Jackson, L. A., & Grabski, S. V. (1988). Perceptions of fair pay and the gender wage gap. *Journal of Applied Social Psychology, 18,* 606–625.

19. Torrance, E. P. (1954). Some consequences of power differences on decision making in permanent and temporary three-man groups. *Research Studies: Washington State College, 22,* 130–140.

20. Hare, A. P. (1976). *Handbook of small group research* (2nd ed.). New York: Free Press.

21. Aronson, E., & Mills, J. (1959). The effects of severity of initiation on liking for a group. *Journal of Abnormal and Social Psychology, 59,* 178–181.

22. Long, S. (1984). Early integration in groups: "A group to join and a group to create." *Human Relations, 37,* 311–322.

23. Cartwright, D. (1968). The nature of group cohesiveness In D. Cartwright & A. Zander (Eds.), *Group dynamics: Research and theory* (3rd ed., pp. 91–109). New York: Harper & Row.

24. George, J. M., & Bettenhausen, K. (1990). Understanding prosocial behavior, sales performance, and turnover: A group-level analysis in a service context. *Journal of Applied Psychology, 75,* 698–709.

25. Douglas, T. (1983). *Groups: Understanding people gathered together.* New York: Tavistock.

26. Aiello, J. R., & Douthitt, E. A. (2001). Social facilitation from Triplett to electronic performance monitoring. *Group Dynamics: Theory, Research and Practice, 5,* 163–180.

27. Zajonc, R. B. (1965). Social facilitation. *Science, 149,* 269–274.

28. Zajonc, R. B. (1980). Compresence. In P. B. Paulus (Ed.), *Psychology of group influence* (pp. 35–60). Hillsdale, NJ: Erlbaum.

29. Geen, R. B., Thomas, S. L., & Gammill, P. (1988). Effects of evaluation and coaction on state anxiety and anagram performance. *Personality and Individual Differences, 6,* 293–298.

30. Aiello, J. R., & Svec, C. M. (1993). Computer monitoring of work performance: Extending the social facilitation framework to electronic presence. *Journal of Applied Social Psychology, 23,* 538–548.

31. Alge, B. J. (2001). Effects of computer surveillance on perceptions of privacy and procedural justice. *Journal of Applied Psychology, 86,* 797–804. Ambrose, M. L., Adler, G. S., & Noel, T. W. (1998). Electronic performance monitoring: A consideration of rights. In M. Schmeinke (Ed.), *Managerial ethics: Moral management of people and processes* (pp. 61–80). Mahwah, NJ: Erlbaum.

32. Steiner, I. D. (1972). *Group processes and productivity.* New York: Academic Press.

33. Shepperd, J. A. (1993). Productivity loss in performance groups: A motivation analysis. *Psychological Bulletin, 113,* 68–81.

34. Latané, B., Williams, K., & Harkins, S. (1979). Many hands make light the work: The causes and consequences of social loafing. *Journal of Personality and Social Psychology, 37,* 822–832.

35. Kravitz, D. A., & Martin, B. (1986). Ringelmann rediscovered: The original article. *Journal of Personality and Social Psychology, 50,* 936–941.

36. Jassawalla, A., Sashittal, H., & Malshe, A. (2009). Students' perceptions of social loafing: Its antecedents and consequences in undergraduate business classroom teams. *Academy of Management Learning and Education, 8,* 42–54. Karau, S. J., & Williams, K. D. (1993). Social loafing: A meta-analytic review and theoretical integration. *Journal of Personality and Social Psychology, 65,* 681–706.

37. Latané, B., & Nida, S. (1980). Social impact theory and group influence: A social engineering perspective. In P. B. Paulus (Ed.), *Psychology of group influence* (pp. 3–34). Hillsdale, NJ: Erlbaum.

38. Nordstrom, R., Lorenzi, P., & Hall, R. V. (1990). A review of public posting of performance feedback in work settings. *Journal of Organizational Behavior Management, 11,* 101–123.

39. Bricker, M. A., Harkins, S. G., & Ostrom, T. M. (1986). Effects of personal involvement: Thought-provoking implications for social loafing. *Journal of Personality and Social Psychology, 51,* 763–769.

40. George, J. M. (1992). Extrinsic and intrinsic origins of perceived social loafing in organizations. *Academy of Management Journal, 35,* 191–202.

41. Earley, P. C. (1993). East meets West meets Mideast: Further explorations of collectivistic and individualistic work groups. *Academy of Management Journal, 36,* 319–348.

42. Albanese, R., & Van Fleet, D. D. (1985). Rational behavior in groups: The free-riding tendency. *Academy of Management Review, 10,* 244–255.

43. Miles, J. A., & Greenberg, J. (1993). Using punishment threats to attenuate social loafing effects among swimmers. *Organizational Behavior and Human Decision Processes, 56,* 246–265.

44. Wellins, R. S., Byham, W. C., & Dixon, G. R. (1994). *Inside teams.* San Francisco, CA: Jossey-Bass.

45. See Note 44.

46. "Six Teams That Made Business History." (2006, June 12). *Fortune,* special section. Also available from http://money.cnn.com/2006/05/31/magazines/fortune/sixteams_greatteams_fortune_061206/index.htm.

47. Mohrman, S. A. (1993). Integrating roles and structure in the lateral organization. In J. R. Galbraith & E. E. Lawler, III (Eds.), *Organizing for the future* (pp. 109–141). San Francisco, CA: Jossey-Bass.

48. Tuckman, B. W., & Jensen, M. A. (1977). Stages of small group development revisited. *Group and Organization Studies, 2,* 419–427.

49. Ray, D., & Bronstein, H. (1995). *Teaming up.* New York: McGraw-Hill.

50. Wellins, R. S., Byham, W. C., & Wilson, J. M. (1991). *Empowered teams.* San Francisco, CA: Jossey-Bass.

51. Moravec, M., Johannessen, O. J., & Hjelmas, T. A. (1997, July/August). Thumbs up for self-managed teams. *Management Review,* 42–47. Manz, C. C., & Sims, H. P., Jr. (1993). *Business without bosses.* New York: Wiley.

52. Osburn, J. D., Moran, L., Musselwhite, E., & Zenger, J. H. (1990). *Self-directed work teams.* Burr Ridge, IL: Irwin.

53. 1996 Industry report: What self-managing teams manage. (1996, October). *Training,* p. 69.

54. Parker, G. M. (2003). *Cross-functional teams: Working with allies, enemies, and other strangers.* San Francisco, CA: John Wiley & Sons.

55. See Note 54.

56. Duarte, L. L., & Snyder, N. T. (2000). *Mastering virtual teams.* San Francisco, CA: Jossey-Bass.

57. Coovert, M. D., & Foster, L. L. (2001). *Computer supported cooperative work.* New York: Wiley.

58. Lipnak, J., & Stamps, J. (2000). *Virtual teams* (2nd ed.). New York: Wiley.

59. Hackman, J. R. (2002). *Leading teams: Setting the stage for great performance.* Boston, MA: Harvard Business School Press. Hackman, J. R. (1987). The design of work teams. In J. W. Lorsch (Ed.), *Handbook of organizational behavior* (pp. 315–342). Englewood Cliffs, NJ: Prentice Hall.

60. Robbins, H., & Finley, M. (1995). *Why teams don't work.* Princeton, NJ: Peterson's/Pacesetters Books (quote, p. 338).

61. Blanchard, K. H., & Bowles, S. M. (2001). *High five: The magic of working together.* New York: William Morrow. Redding, J. C. (2000). *The radical team handbook.* New York: Wiley.

62. Beyerlein, M. M., Kennedy, F., & Beyerlein, S. (2006). *Advances in interdisciplinary studies of work teams.* San Diego, CA: Elsevier. Fisher, K. (1993). *Leading self-directed work teams.* New York: McGraw-Hill.

63. Lawler, E. E., III., Mohrman, S. A., & Ledford, G. E., Jr. (1992). *Employee involvement and total quality management.* San Francisco, CA: Jossey-Bass.

64. Hackman, J. R. (Ed.) (1990). *Groups that work (and those that don't).* San Francisco, CA: Jossey-Bass.

65. Pearson, C. A. L. (1992). Autonomous workgroups: An evaluation at an industrial site. *Human Relations, 45,* 905–936.

66. Wall, T. D., Kemp, N. J., Jackson, P. R., & Clegg, C. W. (1986). Outcomes of autonomous workgroups: A long-term field experiment. *Academy of Management Journal, 29,* 280–304.

67. See Note 60.

68. Stern, A. (1993, July 18). Managing by team is not always as easy as it looks. *New York Times,* p. B14.

69. Maginn, M. D. (1994). *Effective teamwork.* Burr Ridge, IL: Business One Irwin.

70. See Note 68.

71. See Note 68.

72. See Note 68.

73. See Note 68.

74. Salas, E., Edens, E., & Nowers, C. A. (2000). *Improving teamwork in organizations.* Mahwah, NJ: Erlbaum.

75. Dumaine, B. (1994, September 5). The trouble with teams. *Fortune,* pp. 86–88, 90, 92 (quote, p. 86).

76. Barner, R. W. (2001). *Team troubleshooter.* Palo Alto, CA: Davies Black. Maruca, R. F. (2000, November). Unit of one. *Fast Company,* pp. 109–140.

77. Pearsall, M. J., Christian, M. S., & Ellis, A. P. J. (2010). Motivating interdependent teams: Individual rewards, shared rewards, or something in between? *Journal of Applied Psychology, 95,* 183–191.

78. Quader, S. Q., & Quader, R. Q. (2008). A critical analysis of high performing teams: A case study based on the British telecommunications (BT) PLC. *Journal of Services Research, 8,* 175–216.

79. Colquitt, J. A., & Jackson, C. L. (2006). Justice in teams: The context sensitivity of justice rules across individual and team contexts. *Journal of Applied Social Psychology, 36,* 868–899.

80. Hackman, J. R., & Wageman, R. (2005). When and how team leaders matter. In B. M. Staw & R. M. Kramer (Eds.), *Research in organizational behavior* (Vol. 26, pp. 37–74). San Diego, CA: Elsevier.

81. Redding, J. C. (2000). *The radical team handbook.* New York: Wiley. Caudron, S. (1994, February). Teamwork takes work. *Personnel Journal,* 41–46, 49 (quote, p. 43).

82. Caudron, 1994; see Note 81 (quote, p. 42).

83. Stewart, G. L., & Manz, C. C. (1997). Leadership for self-managing work teams: A typology and integrative model. In R. P. Vecchio (Ed.), *Leadership: Understanding the dynamics of power and influence in organizations* (pp. 396–410). Notre Dame, IN: University of Notre Dame Press.

84. Sundstrom, E., DeMeuse, K. P., & Futrell, D. (1990). Work teams: Applications and effectiveness. *American Psychologist, 45,* 128–137.

85. Levine, R. (2005, June 15). The new right stuff. *Fortune,* pp. 116, 118.

86. Hirschfeld, R. R., Jordan, M. H., Felid, H. S., Giles, W. F., & Armenakis, A. A. (2006). Becoming team players: Team members' mastery of teamwork knowledge as a predictor of team task proficiency and observed teamwork performance. *Journal of Applied Psychology, 91,* 467–474.

87. See Note 75 (quote, p. 88).

88. See Note 75 (quote, p. 90).

89. See Note 75 (quote, p. 88).

90. Lau, D. C., & Murnighan, J. K. (1998). Demographic diversity and faultlines: The compositional dynamics of organizational groups. *Academy of Management Review, 23,* 325–340.

91. Cramton, C. D., & Hinds, P. J. (2005). Subgroup dynamics in internationally distributed teams: Ethnocentrism or cross-national learning. In B. M. Staw & R. Kramer (Eds.), *Research in organizational behavior* (Vol. 26, pp. 231–263). San Diego, CA: Elsevier.

92. Anonymous. (1994, December). The facts of life for teambuilding. *Human Resources Forum,* p. 3.

93. McDermott, L. C., Brawley, N., & Waite, W. W. (1998). *World class teams.* New York: Wiley.

Case in Point Sources

Great Moments in the History of the Tour (2010). *Tour de France.* From http://www.letour.fr/2010/TDF/HISTO/us/index.html. Shields, D. (2006). *The tour.* Salt Lake City, UT: Three Story Press. Hochman, P. (2006, June 15). Pack mentality. *Fortune,* pp. 145, 147–150, 152. Wheatcroft, G. (2005). *Le Tour: A history of the Tour de France.* London: Simon & Schuster UK. Liggert, P., Raia, J., & Lewis, S. (2005). *Tour de France for dummies.* Hoboken, NJ: Wiley. Tour de France. (2006). From http://www.letour.fr/indexus.html.

Chapter 9

Preview Case Sources

Jackson, M. (2008). *Distraction.* New York: Prometheus Books. Jackson, M. (2008, June 23). May we have your attention, please? *BusinessWeek,* pp. 55–56. Marcus, G. (2008). *Kluge: The haphazard construction of the human mind.* New York: Houghton Mifflin. Eric Horvitz. (2008). From http://research.microsoft.com/~horvitz.

Chapter Notes

1. Roberts, K. H. (1984). *Communicating in organizations.* Chicago, IL: Science Research Associates (quote, p. 4).
2. Gillis, T. (2008). *The IABC handbook of organizational communication.* San Francisco, CA: Jossey-Bass. Weick, K. E. (1987). Theorizing about organizational communication. In F. M. Jablin, L. L. Putnam, K. H. Roberts, & L. W. Porter (Eds.), *Handbook of organizational communication* (pp. 97–122). Newbury Park, CA: Sage.
3. Von Krogy, G., Ichio, K., & Nonaka, I. (2000). *Enabling knowledge creation: How to unlock the mystery of tacit knowledge and release of the power of innovation.* New York: Oxford University Press. Witherspoon, P. D. (1997) *Communicating leadership: An organizational perspective.* Boston, MA: Allyn & Bacon.
4. Spam Statistics and Facts. (2010). *Spamlaws.com.* From http://www.spamlaws.com/spam-stats.html.
5. See Note 4.
6. Robert Half Technology. (2009, October 6). News release: *Whistle—but don't Tweet—while you work.* Menlo Park, CA: Author.
7. Lengel, R. H., & Daft, R. L. (1988). The selection of communication media as an executive skill. *Academy of Management Executive, 2,* 225–232.
8. Yates, J., & Orlikowski, W. J. (1992). Genres of organizational communication: A structurational approach to studying communication and media. *Academy of Management Review, 17,* 299–326.
9. Widmeyer Communications. (2008). Who we are. From http://www.widmeyer.com/contact. Esterson, E. (1998). Inner beauties. *Inc. Tech,* pp. 78–80, 84, 86, 88, 90.
10. Walker, H. J., Field, H. S., Giles, W. F., Armenakis, A. A., & Bernerth, J. B. (2009). Displaying employee testimonials on recruitment Web sites: Effects of communication media, employee race, and job seeker race on organizational attraction and information credibility. *Journal of Applied Psychology, 94,* 1354–1364.
11. Level, D. A. (1972). Communication effectiveness: Methods and situation. *Journal of Business Communication, 28,* 19–25.
12. Klauss, R., & Bass, B. M. (1982). *International communication in organizations.* New York: Academic Press.
13. Gantenbein, D. (2002, September). Communicate correctly. *Home Office Computing,* pp. 39–40.
14. Daft, R. L., & Lengel, R. H. (1984). Information richness: A new approach to managerial behavior and organizational design. In L. L. Cummings & B. M. Staw (Eds.), *Research in organizational behavior* (Vol. 6, pp. 191–233). Greenwich, CT: JAI. Daft, R. L., & Lengel, R. H. (1986). Organizational information requirements, media richness and structural design. *Management Science 32,* 554–571. Daft, R. L., Lengel, R. H., & Treviño, L. K. (1987). Message equivocality, media selection, and manager performance: Implications for information systems. *MIS Quarterly, 22,* 355–366.
15. Daft, R. L., Lengel, R. H., & Treviño, L. K. (1987). Message equivocality, media selection, and manager performance: Implications for information systems. *MIS Quarterly, 11,* 355–366.
16. Hickson, M. L., Stacks, D. W., & Moore, N-J. (2003). *Nonverbal communication: Studies and applications* (4th ed.). Los Angeles, CA: Roxbury.
17. Bureau of Labor Statistics. (2010, February 17). Economic news release: Mass layoffs summary. From http://www.bls.gov/news.release/mslo.nr0.htm.
18. East Side Teachers Association Update. (2003, March 20). San Jose, CA. From www.eastsideta.org/030321.htm.
19. Maister, D. (2006, December 5). How to layoff 2,000 people. From http://davidmaister.com/blog/273/How-to-Layoff-2-000-People.
20. Brockner, J., & Greenberg, J. (1990). The impact of layoffs on survivors: An organizational justice perspective. In J. Carroll (Ed.), *Advances in applied social psychology: Business settings* (pp. 45–75). Hillsdale, NJ: Erlbaum.
21. Lind, E. A., Greenberg, J., Scott, K. S., & Welchans, T. D. (2000). The winding road from employee to complainant: Situational and psychological determinants of wrongful termination claims. *Administrative Science Quarterly, 45,* 557–590.
22. Rafaeli, A., Dutton, J., Harquail, C., & Mackie-Lewis, S. (1997). Navigating by attire: The use of dress by female administrative employees. *Academy of Management Journal, 40,* 9–45.
23. Greenberg, J. (1989). The organizational waiting game: Time as a status-asserting or status-neutralizing tactic. *Basic and Applied Social Psychology, 10,* 13–26.
24. Zweigenhaft, R. L. (1976). Personal space in the faculty office: Desk placement and student-faculty interaction. *Journal of Applied Psychology, 61,* 628–632.

25. Barnum, C., & Wolnainsky, N. (1989, April). Taking cues from body language. *Management Review,* pp. 3–8.

26. DuBrin, A. J. (2001). *Leadership* (3rd ed.). Boston, MA: Houghton Mifflin.

27. Craiger, P., & Weiss, R. J. (1998, June). Traveling in cyberspace: Video-mediated communication. *The Industrial-Organizational Psychologist,* pp. 83–92. Boeing Company Web site: http://www.boeing.com.

28. Schadler T. (2009, October 7). The state of workforce technology adoption: US benchmark, 2009. *Forrester.* From http://www.forrester.com/rb/Research/state_of_ workforce_technology_adoption_us_benchmark/q/id/ 55367/t/2. Mackie, S. (2009, October 8). Only 1 in 4 uses IM at work, says study. *WebWorkerDaily.* From http://webworkerdaily.com/2009/10/08/only-1-in-4-uses-im-at-work-says-study.

29. Brownlow, M. (2010). Eight email statistics to use at parties. *Email Marketing Reports.* From http://www.email-marketing-reports.com/iland/ 2009/08/8-email-statistics-to-use-at-parties.html.

30. Saunders, C. C., Robey, D., & Vavarek, K. A. (1994). The persistence of status differentials in computer conferencing. *Human Communication Research, 20,* 443–472.

31. Walther, J. B., & Addario, K. P. (2001). The impacts of emoticons on message interpretation in computer-mediated communication. *Social Science Computer Review, 19,* 324–347.

32. Wolf, A. (2000). Emotional expression online: Gender differences in emoticon use. *CyberPsychology & Behavior, 3,* 827–833.

33. De Hoyos, B. (2010). Facebook engineer: 1 billion IMs sent daily. *About.com.* From http://im.about.com/od/ resources/a/facebook-chat-statistics.htm.

34. Zuboff, S. (1988). *In the age of the smart machine: The future of work and power.* New York: Basic Books.

35. See Note 34.

36. Employee Monitoring Guide. (2006). From http://www. computer-monitoring.com/employee-monitoring/ stats.htm.

37. Gartner Group. (2006). From http://www.gartner.com. Also see Note 34.

38. American Management Association. (2005). *Electronic monitoring and surveillance survey.* New York: Author.

39. Yang, C. (2005, August 8). The state of surveillance. *BusinessWeek,* pp. 55–56.

40. Caplan, S. E. (2005). A social skill account of problematic Internet use. *Journal of Communication, 55,* 721–736.

41. Argyris, C. (1974). *Behind the front page: Organizational self-renewal in a metropolitan newspaper.* San Francisco, CA: Jossey-Bass.

42. Hawkins, B. L., & Preston, P. (1981). *Managerial communication.* Santa Monica, CA: Goodyear.

43. Towers Perrin HR Services. (2005). From www.towersperrin.com/hrservices/global/default.htm.

44. D'Aprix, R. (1996). *Communicating for change: Connecting the workplace with the marketplace.* San Francisco, CA: Jossey-Bass.

45. Smith, M. (2005). *Performance measurement and management.* Newbury Park, CA: Sage.

46. Tesser, A., & Rosen, S. (1975). The reluctance to transmit bad news. In L. Berkowitz (Ed.), *Advances in experimental social psychology* (Vol. 8, pp. 192–232). New York: Academic Press.

47. Heath, C. (1996). Do people prefer to pass along good news or bad news? Valence and relevance of news as predictors of transmission propensity. *Organizational Behavior and Human Decision Processes, 68,* 79–94.

48. Walker, C. R., & Guest, R. H. (1952). *The man on the assembly line.* Cambridge, MA: Harvard University Press.

49. Luthans, F., & Larsen, J. K. (1986). How managers really communicate. *Human Relations, 39,* 161–178.

50. Kirmeyer, S. L., & Lin, T. (1987). Social support: Its relationship to observed communication with peers and superiors. *Academy of Management Journal, 30,* 137–151.

51. Hackman, J. R. (2002). *Leading teams.* Boston, MA: Harvard Business School Press.

52. Read, W. (1962). Upward communication in industrial hierarchies. *Human Relations, 15,* 3–16.

53. Glauser, M. J. (1984). Upward information flow in organizations: Review and conceptual analysis. *Human Relations, 37,* 613–643.

54. Lee, F. (1993). Being polite and keeping MUM: How bad news is communicated in organizational hierarchies. *Journal of Applied Social Psychology, 23,* 1124–1149.

55. Kiechel, W., III. (1990, June 18). How to escape the echo chamber. *Fortune,* pp. 129–130 (quote, p. 130).

56. Gibson, J. W. (1985, March). Satisfaction with upward and downward organizational communications: Another perspective. *Proceedings of the Southwest Academy of Management,* p. 150.

57. Spillan, J. E., Mino, M., & Rowles, S. M. (2002). Sharing organizational messages through effective lateral communication. *Qualitative Research Reports in Communication, 3,* 96–104.

58. Frank, A. D. (1984, December). Trends in communication: Who talks to whom? *Personnel,* pp. 41–47.

59. Rogers, E. M., & Rogers, A. (1976). *Communication in organizations.* New York: Free Press.

60. Kitchen, P. J., & Daly, F. (2002). Internal communication during change management. *Corporate Communications, 7*(1), 46–53.

61. Fiol, C. M. (1995). Corporate communications: Comparing executives' private and public statements. *Academy of Management Journal, 38,* 522–536.

62. Cheng, E. W., Li, H., Love, P. E. D., & Irani, Z. (2001). Network communication in the construction industry. *Corporate Communications, 6*(2), 61–70.

63. Harcourt, J., Richerson, V., & Waitterk, M. J. (1991). A national study of middle managers' assessment of organization communication quality. *Journal of Business Communication, 28,* 347–365.

64. Krackhardt, D., & Hanson, J. R. (1993, July–August). Informal networks: The company behind the chart. *Harvard Business Review,* pp. 104–111.

65. Zenger, T. R., & Lawrence, B. S. (1989). Organizational demography: The differential effects of age and tenure distributions on technical communication. *Academy of Management Journal, 32,* 353–376.

66. Ibarra, H. (1992). Homophily and differential returns: Sex differences in network structure and access in an advertising firm. *Administrative Science Quarterly, 37*, 422–447.

67. Lesley, E., & Mallory, M. (1993, November 29). Inside the Black business network. *BusinessWeek,* pp. 70–72, 77, 80–81.

68. Brass, D. J. (1985). Men's and women's networks: A study of interaction patterns and influence in an organization. *Academy of Management Journal, 28,* 327–343.

69. Krackhardt, D., & Porter, L. W. (1986). The snowball effect: Turnover embedded in communication networks. *Journal of Applied Psychology, 71,* 50–55.

70. Duncan, J. W. (1984). Perceived humor and social network patterns in a sample of task-oriented groups: A reexamination of prior research. *Human Relations, 37,* 895–907.

71. Walton, E. (1961). How efficient is the grapevine? *Personnel, 28,* 45–49.

72. Baskin, O. W., & Aronoff, C. E. (1989). *Interpersonal communication in organizations.* Santa Monica, CA: Goodyear.

73. Mishra, J. (1990, Summer). Managing the grapevine. *Public Personnel Management,* pp. 213–228.

74. Layoff rumors anger law firm. (2001, November 28). *New York Lawyer.* From www.nylawyer.com/pay/01/112801a.html.

75. State of the Blogosphere 2009. (2009, December). *Technorati.com.* From the Web at http://technorati.com/blogging/feature/state-of-the-blogosphere-2009/.

76. McCarthy, E. (2003, May 1). Jousting with rumor mills. *Washington Post,* p. E1.

77. Thibaut, A. M., Calder, B. J., & Sternthal, B. (1981). Using information processing theory to design marketing strategies. *Journal of Marketing Research, 18,* 73–79.

78. Schiller, Z. (1995, September 11). P&G is still having a devil of a time. *BusinessWeek,* p. 46.

79. The Coca-Cola Company. (2010). From http://www2.coca-cola.com/contactus/myths_rumors.

80. Adler, N. (1991). *International dimensions of organizational behavior* (2nd ed.). Boston, MA: PWS/Kent.

81. Tannen, D. (1995). *Talking 9 to 5.* New York: Avon.

82. Tannen, D. (1998, September–October). The power of talk: Who gets heard and why. *Harvard Business Review,* pp. 137–148.

83. See Note 45 (quote, p. 148).

84. Munter, M. (1993, May–June). Cross-cultural communication for managers. *Business Horizons,* pp. 75–76.

85. Mellow, C. (1995, August 17). Russia: Making cash from chaos. *Fortune,* pp. 145–146, 148, 150–151.

86. Hodgson, J. D., Sango, Y., & Graham, J. L. (2000). *Doing business with the new Japan.* Oxford, England: Rowman & Littlefield. Ueda, K. (1974). Sixteen ways to avoid saying no in Japan. In J. C. Condon & M. Saito (Eds.), *International encounters with Japan* (pp. 185–192). Tokyo: Simul Press.

87. See Note 80.

88. Alessandra, T., & Hunksaker, P. (1993). *Communicating at work.* New York: Fireside.

89. Federation of American Scientists. (2010). Military acronyms, initialisms, and abbreviations. From http://www.fas.org/news/reference/lexicon/acronym.htm.

90. See Note 45.

91. Ivy Sea Online. (2005). Think good communication's a "no-brainer"? Real-world results of unmindful communication. From www.ivysea.com/pages/ca0299_1.html.

92. Burley-Allen, M. (1982). *Listening: The forgotten skill.* New York: Wiley.

93. Brownell, J. (1985). A model for listening instructions: Management applications. *ABCA Bulletin, 48*(3), 39–44.

94. Austin, N. K. (1991, March). Why listening's not as easy as it sounds. *Working Woman,* pp. 46–48.

95. Vernyi, B. (1987, April 26). Institute aims to boost quality of company suggestion boxes. *Toledo Blade,* p. B2.

96. Penley, L. E., Alexander, E. R., Jernigan, I. E., & Henwood, C. I. (1991). Communication abilities of managers: The relationship to performance. *Journal of Management, 17,* 57–76. Seyper, B. D., Bostrom, R. N., & Seibert, J. H. (1989). Listening, communication abilities, and success at work. *Journal of Business Communication, 26,* 293–303.

97. Brownell, J. (1990). Perceptions of effective listeners: A management study. *Journal of Business Communication, 27,* 401–415.

98. High Gain. (2005). *The listening organization.* Sebastopol, CA: Author.

99. Nichols, R. G. (1962, Winter). Listening is good business. *Management of Personnel Quarterly,* p. 4.

100. See Note 96.

101. McCathrin, Z. (1990, Spring). The key to employee communication: Small group meetings. *The Professional Communicator,* pp. 6–7, 9.

102. See Note 96.

103. Turner, F. (2010). Employee suggestion programs save money. From http://www.chartcourse.com/articlesuggestion.html.

104. Taft, W. F. (1985). Bulletin boards, exhibits, hotlines. In C. Reuss & D. Silvis (Eds.), *Inside organizational communication* (2nd ed., pp. 183–189). New York: Longman.

105. Flag Bank. (2005, December). Merger information. From http://www.flagbank.com/merger_info.htm.

106. See Note 105.

107. Beck, S. M. (1997, September 7). How'm I really doing? No, really. *BusinessWeek,* pp. ENT10–ENT11.

108. Schnake, M. E., Dumler, M. P., Cochran, D. S., & Barnett, T. R. (1990). Effects of differences in superior and subordinate perception of superiors' communication practices. *Journal of Business Communication, 27,* 37–50.

109. Whetten, D. A., & Cameron, K. S. (1995). *Developing management skills* (3rd ed.). New York: Harper Collins.

Case in Point Sources

The Home Depot Web site (2010): www.homedepot.com/HDUS/EN_US/corporate/about/about.shtml. Brown, J. (2004, June). The Home Depot's communication makeover. Integrated Solutions for Retailers. From www.ismretail.com/articles/2005 _06/

040604.htm. Bowne Global Solutions (2005). Home Depot. From www.bowneglobal.com/english/exp_cs_homedepot.htm. Sharing success. (2005). *Hewitt Magazine Online,* Vol. 7, no. 3. From was4.Hewitt.com/Hewitt/resource/rptspubs/Hewitt_magazine/vol7_iss3.htm.

Chapter 10

Preview Case Sources

Associated Press. (2010, February 26). Nike: We'll continue to back Woods. *Philly.com/sports.* From http://www.philly.com/philly/sports/golf/85456572.html. Tse, A. (2010, February 26). Tiger Woods' sponsors jumping ship. *TheStreet.com.* From http://www.thestreet.com/story/10637017/1/tiger-woods-sponsors-jumping-ship.html. Associated Press. (2009, December 17). Woods named top athlete of decade. *ESPN.com.* From http://sports.espn.go.com/golf/news/story?id=4747530 . About Tiger Woods. (2010). *TigerWoods.com.* From http://web.tigerwoods.com/aboutTiger/bio. Gregory, S. (2009, December 16). Tiger Woods' sponsors: Will any stick by him? *Time.com.* From http://www.time.com/time/nation/article/0,8599,1948181,00.html. Tag Heuer, Tiger Woods sponsor, "Stands with" golfer. (2009, December 29). *The Huffington Post.* From http://www.huffingtonpost.com/2009/12/22/tag-heuer-tiger-woods-spo_n_400539.html.

Chapter Notes

1. Mintzberg, H. J. (1988). *Mintzberg on management: Inside our strange world of organizations.* New York: Free Press.
2. Drucker, P. F. (2006). Brainy quote. From http://www.brainyquote.com/quotes/authors/p/peter_f_drucker.html.
3. Allison, S. T., Jordan, A M. R., & Yeatts, C. E. (1992). A cluster-analytic approach toward identifying the structure and content of human decision making. *Human Relations, 45,* 410–472.
4. Harrison, E. F. (1987). *The managerial decision-making process* (3rd ed.). Boston, MA: Houghton Mifflin.
5. Wedley, W. C., & Field, R. H. G. (1984). A predecision support system. *Academy of Management Review, 9,* 696–703.
6. Nutt, P. C. (1993). The formulation process and tactics used in organizational decision making. *Organization Science, 4,* 226–251.
7. Nutt, P. (1984). Types of organizational decision processes. *Administrative Science Quarterly, 29,* 414–450.
8. Cowan, D. A. (1986). Developing a process model of problem recognition. *Academy of Management Review, 11,* 763–776.
9. Dennis, T. L., & Dennis, L. B. (1998). *Microcomputer models for management decision making.* St. Paul, MN: West.
10. Fulk, J., & Boyd, B. (1991). Emerging theories of communication in organizations. *Journal of Management, 17,* 407–446.
11. Power, D. J. (2000, September 24). Supporting business decision-making. From http://www.dssresources.com/dssbook/ch1sbdm.pdf.
12. Sainfort, F. C., Gustafson, D. H., Bosworth, K., & Hawkins, R. P. (1990). Decision support systems effectiveness: Conceptual framework and empirical evaluation. *Organizational Behavior and Human Decision Processes, 45,* 232–252.
13. Stevenson, M. K., Busemeyer, J. R., & Naylor, J. C. (1990). Judgment and decision-making theory. In M. D. Dunnette & L. M. Hough (Eds.), *Handbook of industrial and organizational psychology* (2nd ed., Vol. 1, pp. 283–374). Palo Alto, CA: Consulting Psychologists Press.
14. Roth, K. (1992). Implementing international strategy at the business unit level: The role of managerial decision-making characteristics. *Journal of Management, 18,* 769–789.
15. Brett, J. (2001). *Negotiating globally. How to negotiate deals, resolve disputes, and make decisions across cultural boundaries.* San Francisco, CA: Jossey-Bass. Adler, N. J. (1991). *International dimensions of organizational behavior.* Boston, MA: PWS Kent.
16. See Note 15.
17. Dutta, A. (2001). Business planning for network services: A systems thinking approach. *Information Systems Research, 12,* 260–283. Hill, C. W., & Jones, G. R. (1989). *Strategic management.* Boston, MA: Houghton Mifflin.
18. Crainer, S. (1998, November). The 75 greatest management decisions ever made. *Management Review,* pp. 16–23.
19. Amit, R., & Wernerfelt, B. (1990). Why do firms reduce business risk? *Academy of Management Journal, 33,* 520–533.
20. Roepik, D, & Gray, G. (2002). *Risk: A practical guide to deciding what's really safe and what's really dangerous in the world around you.* New York: Houghton Mifflin.
21. Bronson, P., & Merryman, A. (2006, June 30). Will this marriage last? *Time.com.* From http://www.time.com/time/nation/article/0,8599,1209784,00.html.
22. The Odds. (2006). *Funny2.com.* From http://funny2.com/odds.htm.
23. Provan, K. G. (1982). Interorganizational linkages and influence over decision making. *Academy of Management Journal, 25,* 443–451.
24. Galaskiewicz, J., & Wasserman, S. (1989). Mimetic processes within an interorganizational field: An empirical test. *Administrative Science Quarterly, 34,* 454–479.
25. Parsons, C. K. (1988). Computer technology: Implications for human resources management. In G. R. Ferris & K. M. Rowland (Eds.), *Research in personnel and human resources management* (Vol. 6, pp. 1–36). Greenwich, CT: JAI Press.
26. Simon, H. A. (1987). Making management decisions: The role of intuition and emotion. *Academy of Management Executive, 1,* 57–64.
27. Kirschenbaum, S. S. (1992). Influence of experience on information-gathering strategies. *Journal of Applied Psychology, 77,* 343–352.
28. Simon, H. (1977). *The new science of management decisions* (2nd ed.). Englewood Cliffs, NJ: Prentice Hall.

29. Lampton, B. (2003, December 1). "My pleasure"—
The Ritz-Carlton Hotel Part II. *Expert Magazine.* From
http://www.expertmagazine.com/artman/publish/article
_391.shtml.

30. Case, J. (1995). *Open-book management.* New York:
HarperBusiness.

31. Tschohl, J. (2006). Empowerment: The key to customer
service. *M&T Bank Business Resource Center.* From
http://www.mandtbank.com/smallbusiness/brc_humanr
esources_empowerment.cfm.

32. Sifonis, J. (2002, November–December). Empowering
employees. *IQ Magazine: Cisco Systems.* From http://
www.cisco.com/web/about/ac123/iqmagazine/archives/
2001_2002/empowering_employees.html.

33. Rowe, A. J., Boulgaides, J. D., & McGrath, M. R.
(1984). *Managerial decision making.* Chicago, IL:
Science Research Associates.

34. See Note 31.

35. Frost, R. O., & Shows, D. L. (1993). The nature and
measurement of compulsive indecisiveness.
Behavioral Research and Theory, 31, 683–692.

36. See Note 35.

37. Patalano, A. L., Juhasz, B. J., & Dicke, J. (2009).
The relationship between indecisiveness and eye
movement patterns in a decision making informational
search task. *Journal of Behavioral Decision Making,
22,* 560–560.

38. Murninghan, J. K. (1981). Group decision making:
What strategies should you use? *Management Review,
25,* 56–62.

39. Janis, I. L. (1982). *Groupthink: Psychological studies
of policy decisions and fiascoes* (2nd ed.). Boston,
MA: Houghton Mifflin.

40. Morehead, G., Ference, R., & Neck, C. P. (1991).
Group decision fiascoes continue: Space shuttle
Challenger and a revised groupthink framework.
Human Relations, 44, 531–550.

41. Eaton, J. (2001). Management communication: The
threat of groupthink. *Corporate Communication, 6,*
183–192. Janis, I. L. (1988). *Crucial decisions:
Leadership in policy making and crisis management.*
New York: Free Press.

42. Morehead, G., & Montanari, J. R. (1986). An empirical
investigation of the groupthink phenomenon. *Human
Relations, 39,* 391–410.

43. Johnson, R. J. (1984). Conflict avoidance through
acceptable decisions. *Human Relations, 27,* 71–82.

44. Schweiger, D. M., Sandberg, W. R., & Ragan, J. W.
(1986). Group approaches for improving strategic
decision making: A comparative analysis of dialectical
inquiry, devil's advocacy, and consensus. *Academy of
Management Journal, 29,* 51–71.

45. Schweiger, D. M., Sandberg, W. R., & Rechner, P. L.
(1989). Experiential effects of dialectical inquiry,
devil's advocacy, and consensus approaches to
strategic decision making. *Academy of Management
Journal, 32,* 745–772.

46. Cosier, R. A., & Schwenk, C. R. (1990). Agreement
and thinking alike: Ingredients for poor decisions.
Academy of Management Executive, 4, 610–74.

47. Sloan, A. P., Jr. (1964). *My years with General
Motors.* New York: Doubleday.

48. Neustadt, R. E., & Fineberg, H. (1978). *The swine flu
affair: Decision making on a slippery disease.*
Washington, DC: U.S. Department of Health,
Education and Welfare.

49. Hurry up and decide (2001, May 14). *BusinessWeek,*
p. 16.

50. Breen, B. (2000, September). What's your intuition?
Fast Company, pp. 290–294, 296, 298. 300. Klein, G.
(1999). *Sources of power.* Cambridge, MA: MIT Press.

51. Linstone, H. A. (1984). *Multiple perspectives for
decision making.* New York: North-Holland.

52. Simon, H. A. (1979). Rational decision making in
organizations. *American Economic Review, 69,*
493–513.

53. March, J. G., & Simon, H. A. (1958). *Organizations.*
New York: Wiley.

54. See Note 53.

55. Simon, H. A. (1957). *Models of man.* New York:
Wiley.

56. Prendergast, M. (1994). *For God, country and Coca-
Cola: The definitive history of the great American soft
drink and the company that makes it.* New York: Basic
Books.

57. Shull, F. A., Delbecq, A. L., & Cummings, L. L.
(1970). *Organizational decision making.* New York:
McGraw-Hill.

58. Tenbrunsel, A. E., & Smith-Crowe, K. (2008). Ethical
decision making: Where we've been and where we're
going. *Academy of Management Annals, 2,* 545–607.

59. Browning, E. B. (1850/1950). *Sonnets from the
Portuguese.* New York: Ratchford and Fulton.

60. Mitchell, T. R., & Beach, L. R. (1990). " . . . Do I love
thee? Let me count . . . " Toward an understanding of
intuitive and automatic decision making.
*Organizational Behavior and Human Decision
Processes, 47,* 1–20.

61. Kish-Gephart, J. J., Harrison, D. A., & Treviño, L. K.
(2010). Bad apples, bad cases, and bad barrels: Meta-
analytic evidence about sources of unethical decisions
at work. *Journal of Applied Psychology, 95,* 1–31.

62. Beach, L. R., & Mitchell, T. R. (1990). Image theory:
A behavioral theory of image making in organizations.
In B. Staw and L. L. Cummings (Eds.), *Research in
organizational behavior* (Vol. 12, pp. 1–41).
Greenwich, CT: JAI Press.

63. Dunegan, K. J. (1995). Image theory: Testing the role
of image compatibility in progress decisions.
*Organizational Behavior and Human Decision
Processes, 62,* 710–786.

64. Dunegan, K. J. (1993). Framing, cognitive modes, and
image theory: Toward an understanding of a glass half
full. *Journal of Applied Psychology, 78,* 491–503.

65. Gaeth, G. J., & Shanteau, J. (1984). Reducing the
influence of irrelevant information on experienced
decision makers. *Organizational Behavior and Human
Performance, 33,* 263–282.

66. Ginrich, G., & Soli, S. D. (1984). Subjective evaluation and allocation of resources in routine decision

making. *Organizational Behavior and Human Performance, 33,* 187–203.

67. Levin, I. P., Schneider, S. L., & Gaeth, G. J. (1998). All frames are not created equal: A typology and critical analysis of framing effects. *Organizational Behavior and Human Decision Processes, 76,* 141–188.

68. Levin, I. P. (1987). Associative effects of information framing. *Bulletin of the Psychonomic Society, 25,* 85–86.

69. Kahneman, D., & Tversky, A. (1984). Choices, values, and frames. *American Psychologist, 39,* 341–350.

70. Highhouse, S., & Yüce, P. (1996). Perspectives, perceptions, and risk-taking behavior. *Organizational Behavior and Human Decision Processes, 65,* 151–167.

71. Levin, I. P., & Gaeth, G. J. (1988). Framing of attribute information before and after consuming the product. *Journal of Consumer Research, 15,* 374–378.

72. See Note 71.

73. Meyerowitz, B. E., & Chaiken, S. (1987). The effects of message framing on breast self-examination attitudes, intentions, and behavior. *Journal of Personality and Social Psychology, 52,* 500–510.

74. Frisch, D. (1993). Reasons for framing effects. *Organizational Behavior and Human Decision Processes, 54,* 391–429.

75. Nisbett, R. E., & Ross, L. (1980). *Human inference: Strategies and shortcomings of social judgment.* Englewood Cliffs, NJ: Prentice Hall.

76. Maule, A. J., & Hodgkinson, G. (2002). Heuristics, biases and strategic decision making. *Psychologist, 15,* 68–71.

77. Kahneman, D., & Tversky, A. (1973). On the psychology of prediction. *Psychological Review, 80,* 251–273.

78. Gaeth, G. J., & Shanteau, J. (1984). Reducing the influence of irrelevant information on experienced decision makers. *Organizational Behavior and Human Performance, 33,* 187–203.

79. Power, D. J., & Aldag, R. J. (1985). Soelberg's job search and choice model: A clarification, review, and critique. *Academy of Management Review, 10,* 48–58.

80. Soelberg, P. O. (1967). Unprogrammed decision making. *Industrial Management Review, 8,* 110–129.

81. Langer, E., & Schank, R. C. (1994). *Belief, reasoning, and decision making.* Hillsdale, NJ: Erlbaum.

82. Loouie, T. A., Curren, M. T., & Harich, K. R. (2000). "I knew we would win": Hindsight bias for favorable and unfavorable team decision outcomes. *Journal of Applied Psychology, 85,* 264–272.

83. Moon, H., & Conlon, D. E. (2002). From acclaim to blame: Evidence of a person sensitivity decision bias. *Journal of Applied Psychology, 87,* 33–42.

84. Conlon, D. E., & Garland, H. (1993). The role of project completion information in resource allocation decisions. *Academy of Management Journal, 36,* 402–413.

85. Bobocel, D. R., & Meyer, J. P. (1994). Escalating commitment to a failing course of action: Separating the roles of choice and justification. *Journal of Applied Psychology, 79,* 360–363.

86. Staw, B. M. (1981). The escalation of commitment to a course of action. *Academy of Management Review, 6,* 577–587.

87. Whyte, G. (1993). Escalating commitment in individual and group decision making: A prospect theory approach. *Organizational Behavior and Human Decision Processes, 54,* 430–455.

88. Simonson, I., & Staw, B. M. (1992). Deescalation strategies: A comparison of techniques for reducing commitment to losing courses of action. *Journal of Applied Psychology, 77,* 411–426.

89. Garland, H., & Newport, S. (1991). Effects of absolute and relative sunk costs on the decision to persist with a course of action. *Organizational Behavior and Human Decision Processes, 48,* 55–69.

90. Ross, J., & Staw, B. M. (1993). Organizational escalation and exit: Lessons from the Shoreham nuclear power plant. *Academy of Management Journal, 36,* 701–732.

91. Whyte, G. (1991). Diffusion of responsibility: Effects on the escalation tendency. *Journal of Applied Psychology, 76,* 408–415.

92. Staw, B. M., Barsade, S. G., & Koput, K. W. (1997). Escalation at the credit window: A longitudinal study of bank executives' recognition and write-off of problem loans. *Journal of Applied Psychology, 82,* 130–142.

93. Heath, C. (1995). Escalation and de-escalation of commitment in response to sunk costs: The role of budgeting in mental accounting. *Organizational Behavior and Human Decision Processes, 62,* 38–54.

94. Tan, H., & Yates, J. F. (1995). Sunk cost effects: The influences of instruction and future return estimates. *Organizational Behavior and Human Decision Processes, 63,* 311–319.

95. Davis, J. H. (1992). Introduction to the special issue on group decision making. *Organizational Behavior and Human Decision Processes, 52,* 1–2.

96. Delbecq, A. L., Van de Ven, A. H., & Gustafson, D. H. (1975). *Group techniques for program planning.* Glenview, IL: Scott, Foresman.

97. Hill, G. W. (1982). Group versus individual performance: Are *N* + 1 heads better than one? *Psychological Bulletin, 91,* 517–539.

98. Wanous, J. P., & Youtz, M. A. (1986). Solution diversity and the quality of group decisions. *Academy of Management Journal, 29,* 141–159.

99. Yetton, P., & Bottger, P. (1983). The relationships among group size, member ability, social decision schemes, and performance. *Organizational Behavior and Human Performance, 32,* 145–149.

100. See Note 99.

101. See Note 99.

102. Osborn, A. F. (1957). *Applied imagination.* New York: Scribner's.

103. Bouchard, T. J., Jr., Barsaloux, J., & Drauden, G. (1974). Brainstorming procedure, group size, and sex as determinants of the problem-solving effectiveness of groups and individuals. *Journal of Applied Psychology, 59,* 135–138.

104. Kelley, T. (2001, June–July). Reaping the whirlwind. *Context,* pp. 56–58.

105. Bottger, P. C., & Yetton, P. W. (1987). Improving group performance by training in individual problem solving. *Journal of Applied Psychology, 72,* 651–657.

106. Dalkey, N. (1969). *The Delphi method: An experimental study of group decisions.* Santa Monica, CA: RAND Corporation.

107. Van de Ven, A. H., & Delbecq, A. L. (1971). Nominal versus interacting group processes for committee decision making effectiveness. *Academy of Management Journal, 14,* 203–212.

108. See Note 107.

109. Gustafson, D. H., Shulka, R. K., Delbecq, A., & Walster, W. G. (1973). A comparative study of differences in subjective likelihood estimates made by individuals, interacting groups, Delphi groups, and nominal groups. *Organizational Behavior and Human Performance, 9,* 280–291.

110. Ulshak, F. L., Nathanson, L., & Gillan, P. B. (1981). *Small group problem solving: An aid to organizational effectiveness.* Reading, MA: Addison-Wesley.

111. Willis, R. E. (1979). A simulation of multiple selection using nominal group procedures. *Management Science, 25,* 171–181.

112. Stumpf, S. A., Zand, D. E., & Freedman, R. D. (1979). Designing groups for judgmental decisions. *Academy of Management Review, 4,* 581–600.

113. Rogelberg, S. G., & O'Connor, M. S. (1998). Extending the stepladder technique: An examination of self-paced stepladder groups. *Group Dynamics, 2*(2), 82–91. Rogelberg, S. G., Barnes-Farrell, J. L., & Lowe, C. A. (1992). The stepladder technique: An alternative group structure facilitating effective group decision making. *Journal of Applied Psychology, 77,* 730–737.

114. Lam, S. S. K., & Shaubroeck, J. (2000). Improving group decisions by better pooling information: A comparative advantage of group decision support systems. *Journal of Applied Psychology, 85,* 564–573.

Case in Point Sources

Mooney, P. (2009, March 25). The contour bottle is born. *Coca-Cola Conversations.* From http://www.coca-colaconversations.com/my_weblog/2009/03/the-contour-bottle-is-born.html. Vigo County Public Library. (2010). Inventory: Earl R. Dean Collection. From http://www.vigo.lib.in.us/archives/inventories/business/dean.php. Scanlon, J. (2008, September 8). The shape of a new Coke. *BusinessWeek,* p. 72. *Coca-Cola.* From http://www.coke.com. Hays, C. (2004). *The real thing: Truth and power at the Coca-Cola Company.* New York: Random House. Prendergast, M. (1994). *For God, country and Coca-Cola: The definitive history of the great American soft drink and the company that makes it.* New York: Basic Books.

Chapter 11

Preview Case Sources

Leslie-Pelecky, D. (2008). *The physics of NASCAR: How to make steel + gas + rubber = speed.* New York: Dutton/Penguin. Clarke, L. (2008). *One helluva ride: How NASCAR swept the nation.* New York: Villard/Random House. History of NASCAR. (2008, July 17). *NASCAR.com.* From http://www.nascar.com/news/features/history. Ronfeldt, D. (2000, February). Social science at 190 mph on NASCAR's biggest speedways. First Monday, 5(2). From http://firstmonday.org/issues/ issue5_2/ronfeldt/index.html. Daytona International Speedway. (2008). Brief history of the 500. Daytona 500. From http://www.daytona500.com/content-display.cfm/cat/Brief-History-of-the-500.

Chapter Notes

1. Ronfeldt, D. (2000, February). Social science at 190 mph on NASCAR's biggest speedways. First Monday, 5(2). From http://firstmonday.org/issues/issue5_2/ronfeldt/index.html.

2. Dabos, G. E., & Rousseau, D. M. (2004). Mutuality and reciprocity in the psychological contracts of employees and employees. *Journal of Applied Psychology, 89,* 52–72.

3. Rousseau, D. M. (1995). *Psychological contracts in organizations: Understanding written and unwritten agreements.* Thousand Oaks, CA: Sage.

4. Rousseau, D. M. (2001). Schema, promise and mutuality: The building blocks of the psychological contract. *Journal of Occupational and Organizational Psychology, 74,* 511–541. Rousseau, D. M., & Schalk, R. (2000). *Psychological contracts in employment: Cross-national perspectives.* Thousand Oaks, CA: Sage.

5. See Note 2.

6. Rousseau, D. M., & Parks, J. M. (1993). The contracts of individuals and organizations. In L. L. Cummings & B. M. Staw (Eds.), *Research in organizational behavior* (Vol. 15, pp. 1–43). Greenwich, CT: JAI Press.

7. Hui, C., Lee, C., & Rousseau, D. M. (2004). Psychological contract and organizational citizenship behavior in China: Investigating generalizability and instrumentality. *Journal of Applied Psychology, 89,* 311–321.

8. See Note 4.

9. Raja, U., Johns, G., & Ntalianis, F. (2004). The impact of personality on psychological contracts. *Academy of Management Journal, 67,* 350–367.

10. Judge, T. A., Heller, D., & Mount, M. K. (2002). Five-factor model of personality and job satisfaction: A meta-analysis. *Journal of Applied Psychology, 87,* 530–541.

11. Schoorman, F. D., Mayer, R. C., & Davis, J. H. (2007). An integrative model of organizational trust: Past, present, and future. *Academy of Management Review, 32,* 344–354.

12. Lee, C., Tinsley, C. H., & Chen, Z. X. (2000). Psychological normative contracts of work group members in the U.S. and Hong Kong. In D. M. Rousseau & R. Schalk (Eds.), *Psychological contrasts in employment: Cross-cultural perspective* (pp. 87–103). Thousand Oaks, CA: Sage.

13. See Note 7.

14. Lewicki, R. J., & Wiethoff, C. (2000). Trust, trust development, and trust repair. In M. Deutsch &

P. T. Coleman (Eds.), *The handbook of conflict resolution* (pp. 86–107). San Francisco, CA: Jossey-Bass.

15. Bachman, R., & Zaheer, A. (2008). *Handbook of trust research.* Northampton, MA: Edgar Elgar.

16. Myerson, D., Weick, K. E., & Kramer, R. M. (1996). Swift trust in temporary groups. In R. M. Kramer & T. R. Tyler (Eds.), *Trust in organizations: Frontiers of theory and research* (pp. 166–195). Thousand Oaks, CA: Sage.

17. Peters, L., & Karren, R. J. (2009). An examination of the roles of trust and functional diversity performance ratings. *Group & Organization Management, 34*, 479–504. Henttonen, K., & Blomqvist, K. (2005). Managing distance in a global virtual team: The evolution of trust through technology-mediated relational communication. *Strategic Change, 14*, 107–119. Jarvenpaa, S. L., Knoll, K., & Leidner, D. E. (1998). Is anybody out there? Antecedents of trust in global virtual teams. *Journal of Management Information Systems, 14*, 29–64.

18. Colquitt, J. A., & Salam, S. C. (2009). Foster trust through ability, benevolence and integrity. In E. A. Locke (Ed.), *Handbook of principles of organizational behavior* (pp. 389–404). Chichester, UK: Wiley.

19. See Note 18.

20. Podsakoff, P. M., MacKenzie, S. B., Paine, J. B., & Bachrach, D. G. (2000). Organizational citizenship behaviors: A critical review of the theoretical and empirical literature and suggestions for future research. *Journal of Management, 26*, 513–563.

21. Settoon, R. P., & Mossholder, K. W. (2002). Relationship quality and relationship context as antecedents of person- and task-focused interpersonal citizenship behavior. *Journal of Applied Psychology, 87*, 255–267. McNeely, B. L., & Meglino, B. M. (1994). The role of dispositional and situational antecedents in prosocial organizational behavior: An examination of the intended beneficiaries of prosocial behavior. *Journal of Applied Psychology, 79*, 836–844.

22. Zellars, K. L., Tepper, B. J., & Duffy, M. K. (2002). Abusive supervision and subordinates' organizational citizenship behavior. *Journal of Applied Psychology, 87*, 1068–1076.

23. Podsakoff, P. M., MacKenzie, S. B., Paine, J. B., & Bachrach, D. G. (2000). Organizational citizenship behaviors: A crucial review of the theoretical and empirical literature and suggestions for future research. *Journal of Management, 26*, 513–563.

24. Tansky, J. W. (1993). Justice and organizational citizenship behavior: What is the relationship? *Employees' Responsibilities and Rights Journal, 6*, 195–207.

25. Ladd, D., & Henry, R. A. (2000). Helping coworkers and helping the organization: The role of support perceptions, exchange ideology, and conscientiousness. *Journal of Applied Social Psychology, 30*, 2028–2049.

26. See Note 1.

27. Fomburn, C. J. (1996). *Reputation.* Boston, MA: Harvard Business School Press.

28. Allen, T. D., & Rush, M. C. (1998). The effects of organizational citizenship behavior on performance judgments: A field study and laboratory experiment. *Journal of Applied Psychology, 83*, 247–260.

29. Johnson, J. (2001). The relative importance of task and contextual performance dimensions to supervisor judgments of overall performance. *Journal of Applied Psychology, 86*, 984–996.

30. Werner, J. M. (1994). Dimensions that make a difference: Examining the impact of in-role and extrarole behaviors on supervisory ratings. *Journal of Applied Psychology, 79*, 98–107.

31. Johnson, S. K., Holladay, C. L., & Quiñones, M. A. (2009). Organizational citizenship behavior in performance evaluations: Distributive justice or injustice? *Journal of Business and Psychology, 24*, 409–418.

32. Eagly, A. H. (1987). *Sex differences in social behavior: A social-role interpretation.* Hillsdale, NJ: Erlbaum.

33. Zeng, M., & Chen, X. P. (2003). Achieving cooperation in multiparty alliances: A social dilemma approach to partnership management. *Academy of Management Review, 38*, 587–605.

34. Komorita, M., & Parks, G. (1994). Interpersonal relations: Mixed-motive interactions. *Annual Review of Psychology, 46*, 183–207.

35. Falk, A., Gachter, S., & Kovacs, J. (1999). Intrinsic motivation and extrinsic incentives in a repeated game with incomplete contracts. *Journal of Economic Psychology, 20*, 251–284.

36. Knight, G. P., Dubro, A. F., & Chao, C. (1985). Information processing and the development of cooperative, competitive, and individualistic social values. *Developmental Psychology, 21*, 37–45.

37. Beersma, B., Hollenbecvk, U. R., Humphrey, S. E., Moon, E., Conlon, D. E., & Ilgen, D. R. (2003). Cooperation, competition, and team performance: Toward a contingency approach. *Academy of Management Journal, 46*, 572–590.

38. Koza, M., & Lewin, A. Y. (1998). The evo-evolution of strategic alliances. *Organizational Science, 9*, 255–264.

39. Zeng, M., & Chen, X. P. (2003). Achieving cooperation in multiparty alliances: A social dilemma approach to partnership management. *Academy of Management Review, 28*, 587–605.

40. Thomas, K. W., & Schmidt, W. H. (1976). A survey of managerial interests with respect to conflict. *Academy of Management Journal, 10*, 315–318.

41. Dirks, K. T., & McLean Parks, J. (2003). Conflicting stories: The state of the science of conflict. In J. Greenberg (Ed.), *Organizational behavior: The state of the science* (2nd ed., pp. 283–324). Mahwah, NJ: Erlbaum.

42. Jehn, K., & Mannix, E. (2001). The dynamic nature of conflict: A longitudinal study of intragroup conflict and performance. *Academy of Management Journal, 44*, 238–251.

43. Bragg, T. (1999, October). Ten ways to deal with conflict. *IIE Solutions,* pp. 36–37.

44. See Note 43.

45. Resume: Howard Schultz. (2002, September 9). *BusinessWeek Online.* From http://www.businessweek.com/magazine/content/02_36/b3798005.htm.

46. Lee, M. (1998, October 12). "See you in court—er, mediation." *BusinessWeek Enterprise,* pp. ENT22, ENT24.

47. Richey, B., Bernardin, J. J., Tyler, C. L., & McKinney, N. (2001). The effect of arbitration program characteristics on applicants' intentions toward potential employees. *Journal of Applied Psychology, 86,* 1006–1013.

48. Bordwin, M. (1999). Do-it-yourself justice. *Management Review,* pp. 56–58.

49. Bennett, R. J., & Robinson, S. L. (2003). The past, present, and future of workplace deviance research. In J. Greenberg (Ed.), *Organizational behavior: The state of the science* (pp. 52–70). Mahwah, NJ: Erlbaum.

50. Gundlach, M. J., Scott, D. S., & Martinko, M. J. (2003). The decision to blow the whistle: A social information processing framework. *Academy of Management Review, 28,* 107–123. Miceli, M., & Near, J. (1992). *Blowing the whistle.* Lexington, MA: New Lexington Press.

51. Edson, R. (2009, February 3). Madoff outrage: Whistleblower testimony rips SEC. *Foxbusiness.com.* From http://www.foxbusiness.com/story/markets/ industries/government/madoff-outrage-whistleblower-testimony-rips-sec. National Whistleblowers Center. (2010). Spotlight Bradley Birkenfeld. From http://www. whistleblowers.org/index.php?option=com_content& task=blogcategory&id=71&Itemid=108. Fricker, D. G. (2002, March 27). Enron whistle-blower honored in Dearborn. From www.freep.com/money/business/htm. Anonymous. (2000, April). Paul van Buitenen: Paying the price of accountability. *Accountancy, 125*(1), 280. Taylor, M. (1999, September 13). Another Columbia suit unsealed. *Modern Healthcare, 29*(37), 10. Ettore, B. (1994, May). Whistleblowers: Who's the real bad guy? *Management Review,* 18–23.

52. Australian Compliance Institute. (2004, July 16). Australians are reluctant whistleblowers. *The Age,* p. 112.

53. Gjersten, L. A. (1999). Five State Farm agents fired after accusing company of consumer abuse. *National Underwriter, 103*(51), 1, 23.

54. Rothstein, K. (2004, July 6). Class act for hire: Fired whistleblowing teacher looks for work. *Boston Herald,* p. B7.

55. Stier, K. (2009, October 6). Why is the UBS whistleblower headed to prison? *Time.com.* From http://www.time.com/time/business/article/ 0,8599,1928897,00.html.

56. See Note 55.

57. Martucci, W. C., & Smith, E. W. (2000). Recent state legislative development concerning employment discrimination and whistle-blower protections. *Employment Relations Today, 27*(2), 89–99.

58. Jones, M., & Rowell, A. (1999). Safety whistleblowers intimidated. *Safety and Health Practitioner, 17*(8), 3.

59. Bidoli, M., & Eedes, J. (2001, February 16). Big Brother is watching you. *Future Company.* From www.futurecompany.co.za/2001/02/16/covstory.htm.

60. Mastrangelo, P., Everton, W., & Jolton, J. (2001). *Computer misuse in the workplace.* Unpublished manuscript. University of Baltimore. Lim, V. K. G.,

Loo, G. L., & Teo, T. S. H. (2001, August). *Perceived injustice, neutralization and cyberloafing at the workplace.* Paper presented at the annual meeting of the Academy of Management, Washington, DC.

61. Douglas, S. C., & Martinko, M. J. (2001). Exploring the role of individual differences in the prediction of workplace aggression. *Journal of Applied Psychology, 86,* 547–559.

62. National Institute for Occupational Safety and Health, Centers for Disease Control and Prevention. (1993). *Homicide in the workplace.* [Document # 705003]. Atlanta, GA: Author.

63. Baron, R.A. (2004). Workplace aggression and violence: Insights from basic research. In R.W. Griffin & V. O'Leary-Kelly (Eds.), *The dark side of organizational behavior* (pp. 23–61). San Francisco, CA: Jossey-Bass.

64. Neuman, J. H. (2004). Injustice, stress, and aggression in organizations. In R.W. Griffin & V. O'Leary-Kelly (Eds.), *The dark side of organizational behavior* (pp. 62–102). San Francisco, CA: Jossey-Bass.

65. Glomb, T. M., & Liao, H. (2003). Interpersonal aggression in work groups: Social influence, reciprocal, and individual effects. *Academy of Management Journal, 46,* 386–396.

66. Dietz, J., Robinson, S. A., Folger, R., Baron, R. A., & Jones., T. (2003). The impact of societal violence and organizational justice climate on workplace aggression. *Academy of Management Journal, 46,* 317–326.

67. See Note 66.

68. Armour, S. (2004, July 15). Probe shows traits of violence-prone workers. *USA Today, p. A14.*

69. LeBlanc, M. M., & Kelloway, E. K. (2002). Predictors and outcomes of workplace violence and aggression. *Journal of Applied Psychology, 87,* 444–453.

70. Varita, M., & Jari, R. (2002). Gender differences in workplace bullying among prison officers. *European Journal of Work and Occupational Psychology, 11,* 113–126.

71. Cowie, H., Naylor, P., Rivers, I., Smith, P. K., & Pereira, B. (2002). Measuring workplace bullying. *Aggression and Violent Behavior, 7,* 33–51.

72. Namie, G. (2000). *U.S. hostile workplace survey, 2000.* Benicia, CA: Campaign Against Workplace Bullying.

73. Namie, G., & Namie, R. (2001). *The bully at work.* Naperville, IL: Sourcebooks.

74. Jack L. Hays International. (2009). Theft surveys. From http://www.hayesinternational.com/thft_srvys.html.

75. Kooker, N. R. (2000, May 22). Taking aim at crime— stealing the profits: Tighter controls, higher morale may safeguard bottom line. *Nation's Restaurant News, 34* (21), pp. 114–118.

76. Golden, A. (2009, November 6). As economy falters, employee theft on the rise. *Las Vegas Sun.* From http://www.lasvegassun.com/news/2009/nov/06/ managing-fraud-lesson-recession.

77. Jabbkerm, A. (2000, March 29). Agrium seeks $30 million in damages in embezzlement case. *Chemical Week, 162*(13), p. 22.

78. Greenberg, J. (1998). The cognitive geometry of employee theft: Negotiating "the line" between taking

and stealing. In. R. W. Griffin, A. O'Leary-Kelly, & J. M. Collins (Eds.), *Dysfunctional behavior in organizations: Nonviolent dysfunctional behavior* (pp. 147–194). Greenwich, CT: JAI Press.

79. Greenberg, J. & Tomlinson, E. (2004). The Methodological evolution of employee theft research: The DATA cycle. In R. Griffin & A. O'Leary-Kelley (Eds.), *The dark side of organizational behavior* (pp. 426–461). San Francisco, CA: Jossey-Bass. Tomlinson, E., & Greenberg, J. (2007). Employee theft and workplace justice. In J. Ranjan-Fox, C. L. Cooper, & R. J. Klimoski (Eds.), Research companion to the dysfunctional workplace: Management challenges and symptoms (pp. 121–142). Boston, MA: Edgar Elgar.

Case in Point Sources

Southwest Airlines News Release. (2010, January 21). Southwest Airlines reports fourth quarter profit and 37th consecutive year of profitability. *Southwest.com: Investor Relations.* From http://www.southwest.com/about_swa/financials/investor_relations_index.html?int=GFOOTER-ABOUT-INVESTOR. Harris, J. (2008, August 29). Labor relations at Southwest Airlines. From http://www.blogsouthwest.com/blog/labor-relations-southwest-airlines. Top Stories. (2006, April). View from the top: Southwest Airlines' Kelleher advises managing in good times for the bad. Stanford Graduate School of Business. From http://www.gsb.stanford.edu/news/headlines/vftt_kelleher.shtml. Trottman, M., & McCartney, S. (2004, July 26). Southwest's CEO resigns, citing personal reasons. *Wall Street Journal,* pp. A1, A2.

Chapter 12

Preview Case Sources

Barancik, S., & Hundley, K. (2005, April 25). A law firm's sexual harassment case: An inside story. *St. Petersburg Times.* From http://www.sptimes.com/2005/04/24/Business/A_law_firm_s_sexual_h.shtml. Trigaux, R. (2005, March 30). H&K's handling sets a troubling standard. *St. Petersburg Times.* From http://www.sptimes.com/ 2005/03/30/Columns/HK_s_handling_sets_a_.shtml.

Chapter Notes

1. Martin, S. (2005, April 5). Holland & Knight: One of the last sex harass suits for BigLaw. *Law.com Blog Network.* From http://legalblogwatch.typepad.com/legal_blog_watch/2005/ 04/ holland_knight_.html.
2. Yukl, G. (2009). *Leadership in organizations* (7th ed.). Upper Saddle River, NJ: Prentice Hall.
3. Yukl, G., Falbe, C. M., & Young, J. Y. (1993). Patterns of influence behavior for managers. *Group & Organization Management, 18,* 5–28.
4. Offermann, L. R. (1990). Power and leadership in organizations. *American Psychologist, 45,* 179–189.
5. Falbe, C. M., & Yukl, G. (1992). Consequences for managers of using single influence tactics and combinations of tactics. *Academy of Management Journal, 35,* 638–652.
6. Brinkley, C. (2001, September 7). In Las Vegas, casinos take a big gamble on the highest rollers. *Wall Street Journal,* pp. A1, A8.
7. Mergard, K. (2007, November 7). Perks of being a high roller or whale. *AssociatedContent.com.* From http://www.associatedcontent.com/article/439256/perks_of_being_a_high_roller_or_whale.html?cat=46.
8. Seifert, C. F., Yukl, G., & McDonald, R. A. (2003). Effects of multisource feedback and a feedback facilitator on the influence behavior of managers toward subordinates. *Journal of Applied Psychology, 88,* 561–569.
9. Podsakoff, P. M., & Schriesheim, C. A. (1985). Field studies of French and Raven's bases of power: Critique, re-analysis, and suggestions for future research. *Psychological Bulletin, 97,* 387–413.
10. Huber, V. L. (1981). The sources, uses, and conservation of managerial power. *Personnel, 51*(4), 62–67.
11. Kipnis, D., Schmidt, S. M., Swaffin-Smith, C., & Wilkinson, I. (1984, Winter). Patterns of managerial influence: Shotgun managers, tacticians, and bystanders. *Organizational Dynamics,* 58–67.
12. Stewart, T. (1999, November 6). CEOs see clout shifting. *Fortune,* p. 66.
13. Kahn, R. L., Wolfe, D. M., Quinn, R. P., Snoek, J. D., & Rosenthal, R. A. (1964). *Organizational stress: Studies in role conflict and ambiguity.* New York: Wiley.
14. See Note 13.
15. DeRue, D. S., Conlon, D. E., Moon, H., & Willaby, H. W. (2009). When is straightforwardness a liability in negotiations? The role of integrative potential and structural power. *Journal of Applied Psychology, 94,* 1032–1047.
16. Heathfield, S. (2006). Inspirational quotes for business: Empowerment and delegation. *About.com.* From http://humanresources.about.com/od/workrelationships/a/quotes_empower.htm.
17. See Note 16.
18. Thomas, K. W., & Velthouse, B. A. (1990). Cognitive elements of empowerment: An "interpretive" model of intrinsic task motivation. *Academy of Management Review, 15,* 666–681.
19. Arnold, J. A., Arad, S., Rhoades, J. A., & Drasgow, F. (in press). The empowering leadership questionnaire: The construction of a new scale for measuring leader behaviors. *Journal of Organizational Behavior.*
20. Ford, R. C., & Fottler, M. D. (1995). Empowerment: A matter of degree. *Academy of Management Executive, 9,* 21–29.
21. Dumaine, B. (1990, May 7). Who needs a boss? *Fortune,* pp. 52–54, 56, 58, 60.
22. Shipper, F., & Manz, C. C. (1991). Employee self-management without formally designated teams: An alternative road to empowerment. *Organizational Dynamics, 20*(3), 48–61.
23. National Union of Public and General Employees (2004). Provincial employees suffering most from downsizing. *NUPGE,* August 4, p. 23.

24. DuBrin, A. J. (1994). *Contemporary applied management* (4th ed.). Burr Ridge, IL: Irwin.

25. Patalon, W., III. (1992, June 14). Xerox's gateway to the world. *Rochester Democrat and Chronicle*, pp. 1F–2F.

26. Lesser, Y. (1992, May). From the bottom up: A toast to empowerment. *Human Resources Forum*, pp. 1–2.

27. Byham, W. C., & Cox, J. (1991). *ZAPP: The lightening of empowerment*. New York: Harmony.

28. Seibert, S. C., Silver, S. R., & Randolph, W. A. (2004). Taking empowerment to the next level: A multiple-level model of empowerment, performance, and satisfaction. *Academy of Management Journal, 47*, 332–349.

29. Triandis, H. A. (1995). *Individualism and collectivism*. Boulder, CO: Westview Press.

30. Robert, C., Probst, T. M., Martocchio, G., Drasgow, F., & Lawler, J. J. (2000) Empowerment and continuous improvement in the United States, Poland, and India: Predicting fit on the basis of the dimensions of power distance and individualism. *Journal of Applied Psychology, 85*, 643–658.

31. Kirkman, B. L., Rosen, B., Tesluk, P. E., & Gibson, C. B. (2004). The impact of team empowerment on virtual team performance: The moderating role of face-to-face interaction. *Academy of Management Journal, 47*, 175–192.

32. Gresov, C., & Stephens, C. (1993). The context of inter-unit influence attempts. *Administrative Science Quarterly, 38*, 252–276.

33. Pfeffer, J., & Salancik, G. (1978). *The external control of organizations*. New York: Harper & Row.

34. Salancik, G., & Pfeffer, J. (1974). The bases and uses of power in organizational decision-making. *Administrative Science Quarterly, 19*, 453–473.

35. Boeker, W. (1989). The development and institutionalization of subunit power in organizations. *Administrative Science Quarterly, 34*, 388–410.

36. Lawrence, P. R., & Lorsch, J. W. (1967). *Organization and environment*. Cambridge, MA: Harvard University Press.

37. Miles, R. H. (1980). *Macro organizational behavior*. Glenview, IL: Scott, Foresman.

38. Hickson, D. J., Astley, W. G., Butler, R. J., & Wilson, D. C. (1981). Organization as power. In L. L. Cummings & B. M. Staw (Eds.), *Research in organizational behavior* (Vol. 4, pp. 151–196). Greenwich, CT: JAI Press.

39. U.S. Equal Employment Opportunity Commission. (2006). Sexual harassment. From http://www.eeoc.gov/types/ sexual_harassment.html.

40. U.S. Equal Employment Opportunity Commission. (2010). Sexual harassment charges: EEOC & FEPAS combined: FY 1997–FY 2009. From http://www. eeoc.gov/eeoc/statistics/enforcement/sexual_ harassment.cfm.

41. HR World Editors. (2010). The top 20 sexual-harassment cases of all time. From http://www.hrworld.com/ features/top-20-sexual-harassment-cases-121307.

42. Roberts, B. S., & Mann, R. A. (2006). Sexual harassment in the workplace: A primer. University of Akron. From http://www3.uakron.edu/lawrev/ robert1.html.

43. U.S. Equal Employment Opportunity Commission. (2006). Questions & answers for small employers on employer liability for harassment by supervisors. From http://www.eeoc.gov/policy/docs/harassment-facts.html.

44. Myths about Sexual Harassment. (2002). University of California Women's Center. From http://www.sa.ucsb. edu/ women%27scenter/sexualharassment/ mythsaboutsexual.asp.

45. Ura, A. (2003, July/August). HR policy trends challenge small companies. Michigan Manufacturers Association. From http://images.google.com/imgres? imgurl=http://www.mma-net.org/content/images/ enterprise/hrtrend03b-big.jpg&imgrefurl=http://www. mma-net.org/publications_ent.asp%3FEntArticleID% 3D93&h=490&w=691&sz=32&hl=en&start=75&tbnid= D4oXfRfLSCdEGM:&tbnh=97&tbnw=137&prev=/ images%3Fq%3Dsexual%2Bharassment%2Bpolicy% 26start%3D60%26ndsp%3D20%26svnum%3D10% 26hl%3Den%26lr%3D%26sa%3DN.

46. Drory, A., & Romm, T. (1990). The definition of organizational politics: A review. *Human Relations, 43*, 1333–1354.

47. Ferris, G. R., & Kacmar, K. M. (1992). Perceptions of organizational politics. *Journal of Management, 18*, 93–136.

48. Rosen, R. H. (1991). *The healthy company*. New York: Jeremy P. Tarcher/Perigree (quote, p. 71).

49. Carter, N. M., Gartner, W. B., Shaver, K. G., & Gatewood, E. J. (2003). The career reasons of nascent entrepreneurs. *Journal of Business Venturing, 18*, 13–39.

50. Mulder, M., de Jong, R. D., Koppelaar, L., & Verhage, J. (1986). Power, situation, and leaders' effectiveness: An organizational field study. *Journal of Applied Psychology, 71*, 566–570.

51. Greenberg, J. (1990). Looking fair vs. being fair: Managing impressions of organizational justice. In B. M. Staw & L. L. Cummings (Eds.), *Research in organizational behavior* (Vol. 12, pp. 131–157). Greenwich, CT: JAI Press.

52. Boeker, W. (1992). Power and managerial dismissal: Scapegoating at the top. *Administrative Science Quarterly, 37*, 400–421.

53. Liden, R. C., & Mitchell, T. R. (1988). Ingratiatory behaviors in organizational settings. *Academy of Management Review, 13*, 572–587.

54. Biberman, G. (1985). Personality and characteristic work attitudes of persons with high, moderate, and low political tendencies. *Psychological Reports, 57*, 1303–1310.

55. Kirchmeyer, C. (1990). A profile of managers active in office politics. *Basic and Applied Social Psychology, 22*, 339–350.

56. Allen, R. W., Madison, D. L., Porter, L. W., Renwick, P. A., & Mayer, B. T. (1979). Organizational politics: Tactics and characteristics of its actions. *California Management Review, 22*, 77–83.

57. Ferris, G. R., Frink, D. D., Galang, M. C., Zhou, J., Kacmar, K. M., & Howard, J. L. (1996). Perceptions

of organizational politics: Prediction, stress-related implications, and outcomes. *Human Relations, 49,* 233–266.

58. Andrews, M. C., Kacmar, K. M., & Harris, K. J. (2009). Got political skill? The impact of justice on the importance of political skill for job performance. *Journal of Applied Psychology, 94,* 1427–1437.

59. See Note 57.

60. Wayne, S. J., & Ferris, G. R. (1990). Influence tactics, affect, and exchange quality in supervisor-subordinate interactions. *Journal of Applied Psychology, 75,* 487–499.

61. Bartol, K. M., & Martin, D. C. (1990). When politics pays: Factors influencing managerial compensation decisions. *Personnel Psychology, 43,* 599–614.

62. See Note 61.

63. Cropanzano, R. S., Howes, J. C., Grandey, A. A., & Toth, P. (1997). The relationships of organizational politics and support to work behaviors, attitudes, and stress. *Journal of Organizational Behavior, 18,* 159–181.

64. Kacmar, K. M., Bozeman, D. P., Carlson, D., & Anthony, W. P. (in press). A partial test of the perceptions of organizational politics model. *Human Relations.*

65. Randall, M. O., Cropanzano, R., Bormann, C. A., & Birjulin, A. (in press). Organizational politics and organizational support as predictors of work attitudes, job performance, and organizational citizenship behavior. *Journal of Organizational Behavior.*

66. Hochwarter, W. A., Witt, L. A., & Kacmar, K. M. (2000). Perceptions of organizational politics as a moderator of the relationship between conscientiousness and job performance. *Journal of Applied Psychology, 85,* 472–478.

Case in Point Sources

General Motors. (2006, April). Senior leadership: John F. Smith. From http://www.gm.com/company/investor_information/corp_gov/bios/smith_john.htm. Blumenstein, R. (1997, October 23). How the Smith boys grew up to be CEOs. *Wall Street Journal,* pp. B1, B12.

Chapter 13

Preview Case Sources

Paynter, B. (2010, March). Happy hour. *Fast Company,* p. 24. Evans, L. (2008, May 9). Houlihan's (2010). A little bio action. *Houlihans.com.* From http://houlihans.com/about.aspx. WOMMA WOMM-U: Jen Gulvik presents Houlihan's WOMM case study. *SearchMarketingGurus.com.* From http://www.searchmarketinggurus.com/search_marketing_gurus/2008/05/womma-womm-u-je.html.

Chapter Notes

1. Yukl, G. (2009). *Leadership in organizations* (7th ed.). Upper Saddle River, NJ: Prentice Hall. Lord, R. G. (2001). The nature of organizational leadership: Conclusions and implications. In S. J. Zaccaro & R. J. Klimoski (Eds.), *The nature of organizational leadership: Understanding the performance imperatives confronting today's leaders* (pp. 413–436). San Francisco, CA: Jossey-Bass.

2. House, R. J., & Podsakoff, P. M. (1995). Leadership effectiveness: Past perspectives and future directions for research. In J. Greenberg (Ed.), *Organizational behavior: The state of the science* (pp. 45–82). Hillsdale, NJ: Erlbaum.

3. Bennis, W. G. (2009). *On becoming a leader.* New York: Basic Books. Bennis, W. G., & Nanus, B. (1985). *Leaders: The strategies for taking charge.* New York: Harper & Row (quote, p. 4).

4. See Note 1.

5. Locke, E. A. (1991). *The essence of leadership.* New York: Lexington Books.

6. Cialdini, R. B. (1988). *Influence* (2nd ed.). Glenview, IL: Scott, Foresman.

7. Famous Quotes and Quotations. (2006). From http://www.famous-quotes-and-quotations.com/leadership-quotes.html.

8. Kotter, J. P. (1990). *A force for change: How leadership differs from management.* New York: The Free Press.

9. Geier, J. G. (1969). A trait approach to the study of leadership in small groups. *Journal of Communication, 17,* 316–323.

10. Kirkpatrick, S. A., & Locke, E. A. (1991). Leadership: Do traits matter? *Academy of Management Executive, 5,* 48–60 (quote, p. 58).

11. Barker, R. A. (2001). The nature of leadership. *Human Relations, 54,* 469–494.

12. House, R. J., Shane, S. A., & Herold, D. M. (1996). Rumors of the death of dispositional research are vastly exaggerated. *Academy of Management Review, 21,* 203–224.

13. See Note 9.

14. Chan, K-Y., & Drasgow, F. (2001). Toward a theory of individual differences and leadership: Understanding the motivation to lead. *Journal of Applied Psychology, 86,* 481–498.

15. Zaccaro, S. J., Foti, R. J., & Kenny, D. A. (1991). Self-monitoring and trait-based variance in leadership: An investigation of leader flexibility across multiple group situations. *Journal of Applied Psychology, 76,* 308–315.

16. Avolio, B. J., & Gardner, W. L. (2005). Authentic leadership development: Getting to the root of positive forms of leadership. *The Leadership Quarterly, 16,* 315–338.

17. Avolio, B. J., & Walumbwa, F. O. (2006). Authentic leadership: Moving HR leaders to a higher level. In J. Martoccio (Ed.), *Research in personnel and human resources management* (Vol. 25, pp. 273–304). San Diego, CA: Elsevier.

18. Chemers, M. M. (2001). Efficacy and effectiveness: Integrating models of leadership and intelligence. In R. E. Riggio & S. E. Murphy (Eds.), *Multiple intelligences and leadership* (pp. 139–160). Mahwah, NJ: Erlbaum.

19. Offerman, L. R., & Phan, L. U. (2001). Culturally intelligent leadership for a diverse world. In R. E. Riggio & S. E. Murphy (Eds.), *Multiple intelligences and leadership* (pp. 187–214). Mahwah, NJ: Erlbaum.

20. Anonymous. (1999, October 11). Molding global leaders. *Fortune*, p. 270.

21. Stein, N. (2000, October 2). Global most admired companies: Measuring people power. *Fortune*, pp. 273–288.

22. Bass, B. M. (1998). *Transformational leadership: Industry, military, and educational impact*. Mahwah, NJ: Erlbaum.

23. Turner, N., Barling, J., Epitropaki, O., Butcher, V., & Milner, C. (2002). Transformational leadership and moral reasoning. *Journal of Applied Psychology, 87*, 304–311.

24. Colvin, G. (1999, November 22). The ultimate manager. *Fortune*, pp. 185–187. Slater, R. (1999). *Jack Welch and the GE way*. New York: McGraw-Hill.

25. Tichy, N. M. (1993). *Control your destiny or someone else will*. New York: Doubleday Currency.

26. Stewart, T. A. (1998, March 2). America's most admired companies. *Fortune*, pp. 70–82.

27. Colvin, C. (2000, December 18). America's best and worst wealth creators. *Fortune*, pp. 207–208, 210, 212, 214, 216.

28. Judge, T. A., & Bono, J. E. (2000). Five-factor model of personality and transformational leadership. *Journal of Applied Psychology, 85*, 751–765.

29. Koh, W. L., Steers, R. M. & Terborg, J. R. (1995). The effects of transformational leadership on teacher attitudes and student performance in Singapore. *Journal of Organizational Behavior, 16*, 319–333.

30. Hater, J. J., & Bass, B. M. (1988). Superiors' evaluations and subordinates' perceptions of transformational and transactional leadership. *Journal of Applied Psychology, 73*, 695–702.

31. Hauser, M., & House, R. J. (2000). Lead through vision and values. In E. A. Locke (Ed.), *The Blackwell handbook of principles of organizational behavior* (pp. 257–273). Oxford, England: Blackwell.

32. Bass, B. M., Avolio, B. J., Jung, D. I., & Berson, Y. (2003). Predicting unit performance by assessing transformational and transactional leadership. *Journal of Applied Psychology, 88*, 207–218.

33. Sagie, A., Zaidman, N., Amichai-Hamburger, Y., Te'Eni, D., & Schwartz, D. G. (2002). An empirical assessment of the loose-tight leadership model: Quantitative and qualitative analyses. *Journal of Organizational Behavior, 23*, 303–320.

34. Muczyk, J. P., & Reimann, B. C. (1987). The case for directive leadership. *Academy of Management Review, 12*, 637–647.

35. Chen, C. C., & Meindl, J. R. (1991). The construction of leadership images in the popular press: The case of Donald Burr and People Express. *Administrative Science Quarterly, 36*, 521–551.

36. Likert, R. (1961). *New patterns in management*. New York: McGraw-Hill. Stogdill, R. M. (1963). *Manual for the leader behavior description questionnaire, form XII*. Columbus, OH: Ohio State University, Bureau of Business Research.

37. Weissenberg, P., & Kavanagh, M. H. (1972). The independence of initiating structure and consideration: A review of the evidence. *Personnel Psychology, 25*, 119–130.

38. Judge, T. A., Piccolo, R. F., & Ilies, R. (2004). The forgotten ones? The validity of consideration and initiating structure in leadership research. *Journal of Applied Psychology, 89*, 36–51.

39. Vroom, V. H. (1976). Leadership. In M. D. Dunnette (Ed.), *Handbook of industrial-organizational psychology* (pp. 1527–1552). Chicago, IL: Rand-McNally.

40. See Note 3.

41. Band, W. A. (1994). *Touchstones*. New York: Wiley (quote, p. 247).

42. Blake, R. R., & Mouton, J. J. (1969). *Building a dynamic corporation through grid organizational development*. Reading, MA: Addison-Wesley.

43. Lee, C. (1991). Followership: The essence of leadership. *Training, 28*, 27–35 (quote, p. 28).

44. Graen, G. B., & Wakabayashi, M. (1994). Cross-cultural leadership-making: Bridging American and Japanese diversity for team advantage. In H. C. Triandis, M. D. Dunnette, & L. M. Hough (Eds.), *Handbook of industrial and organizational psychology* (2nd ed., Vol. 4, pp. 415–466). Palo Alto, CA: Consulting Psychologists Press.

45. Phillips, A. S., & Bedian, A. G. (1994). Leader-follower exchange quality: The role of personal and interpersonal attributes. *Academy of Management Journal, 37*, 990–1001.

46. Dunegan, K. J., Duchon, D., & Uhl-Bien, M. (1992). Examining the link between leader-member exchange and subordinate performance: The role of task analyzability and variety as moderators. *Journal of Management, 18*, 59–76.

47. Duarte, N. T., Goodson, J. R., & Klich, N. R. (1993). How do I like thee? Let me appraise the ways. *Journal of Organizational Behavior, 14*, 239–249.

48. Deluga, R. J., & Perry, J. T. (1991). The relationship of subordinate upward influencing behaviour, satisfaction and perceived superior effectiveness with leader-member exchanges. *Journal of Occupational Psychology, 64*, 239–252.

49. Ferris, G. R. (1985). Role of leadership in the employee withdrawal process: A constructive replication. *Journal of Applied Psychology, 70*, 777–781.

50. Scandura, T. A., & Schriesheim, C. A. (1994). Leader-member exchange and supervisor career mentoring as complementary constructs in leadership research. *Academy of Management Journal, 37*, 1588–1602.

51. Sheard, A. G., & Kakabadse, A. P. (2001). Key roles of the leadership landscape. *Journal of Managerial Psychology, 17*, 129–144. Zenger, J. H., Musselwhite, E., Hurson, K., & Perrin, C. (1994). *Leading teams: Mastering the new role*. Homewood, IL: Business One Irwin.

52. See Note 51.

53. Fiedler, F. E. (1978). Contingency model and the leadership process. In L. Berkowitz (Ed.), *Advances in*

experimental social psychology (Vol. 11, pp. 60–112). New York: Academic Press.

54. Hersey, P., & Blanchard, K. H. (1988). *Management of organizational behavior.* Englewood Cliffs, NJ: Prentice Hall.

55. House, R. J., & Baetz, M. L. (1979). Leadership: Some empirical generalizations and new research directions. In B. M. Staw (Ed.), *Research in organizational behavior* (Vol. 1, pp. 341–424). Greenwich, CT: JAI Press.

56. Whitworth, L., House, H., Sandahl, P., & Kimsey-House, H. (1998). *Co-active coaching: New skills for coaching people toward success in work and life.* Palo Alto, CA: Davies-Black.

57. Halberstam, D. (2005). *The education of a coach.* New York: Hyperion. Wolfe, R. (1998). *The Packer way.* New York: St. Martin's. Holtz, L. (1998). *Winning everyday.* New York: Harper Business.

58. Bradley, Bill. (1998). *Values of the game.* New York: Artisan.

59. Milbank, D. (1990, March 5). Managers are sent to "charm schools" to discover how to polish up their acts. *Wall Street Journal,* pp. A14, B3.

60. Pernick, R. (2001). Creating a leadership development program: Nine essential tasks. *Public Personnel Management, 30,* 429–444.

61. Day, D. V. (2001). Leadership development: A review in context. *Leadership Quarterly, 11,* 581–613.

62. Atwater, L. E., Ostroff, C., Yammarino, F. J., & Fleenor, J. W. (1998). Self-other agreement: Does it really matter? *Personnel Psychology, 51,* 577–598.

63. London, M., & Smither, J. W. (1995). Can multi-source feedback change perceptions of goal accomplishments, self-evaluations, and performance related outcomes? Theory-based applications and directions for research. *Personnel Psychology, 48,* 803–839.

64. Thornton, G. C., III, & Rupp, D. E. (2005). *Assessment centers in human resources management: Strategies for prediction, diagnosis, and development.* Hillsdale, NJ: Erlbaum.

65. Walker, A. G., & Smither, J. W. (1999). A five-year study of upward feedback: What managers do with their results matters. *Personnel Psychology, 52,* 393–423.

66. Leung, T. K., & Wong, Y. H. (2001). *Guanxi: Relationship marketing in a Chinese context.* Binghamton, NY: Haworth Press. Luo, Y. (2000). *Guanxi and business.* River Edge, NJ: World Scientific.

67. Balfour, F., & Einhorn, B. (2002, February 4). The end of guanxi capitalism? *BusinessWeek,* pp. 122–123.

68. Wood, E., Whiteley, A., & Zhang, S. (2002). The cross model of guanxi usage in Chinese leadership. *Journal of Management Development, 21,* 263–271.

69. Olivero, G., Bane, D. K., & Kopellman, R. E. (1997). Executive coaching as a transfer of training tool: Effects of productivity in a public agency. *Public Personnel Management, 26,* 461–469.

70. Giber, D., Carter, L., & Goldsmith, M. (1999). *Linkage: Inc.'s best practices in leadership development handbook.* Lexington, MA: Linkage Press.

71. Marquardt, M. J., & Revans, R. (1999). *Action learning in action.* Palo Alto, CA: Davies-Black.

72. Pedler, M. (1997). Interpreting action learning. In J. Burgoyne & M. Reynolds (Eds.), *Management learning: Integrating perspectives in theory and practice* (pp. 248–264). London: Sage.

73. Dotlich, D. L., & Noel, J. L. (1998). *Action learning: How the world's top companies are recreating their leaders and themselves.* San Francisco, CA: Jossey-Bass.

74. See Note 73.

75. Ilies, R., Morgenson, F. R., & Nahrgang, J. D. (2005). Authentic leadership and eudaemonic well-being: Understanding leader-follower outcomes. *Leadership Quarterly, 16,* 373–394.

Case in Point Sources

Booker, C. (2010, January 3). Let's break the cycle of re-arrest and re-imprisonment. *Newark Star Ledger.* From http://blog.nj.com/njv_guest_blog/2010/01/ lets_break_the_cycle_of_re-arr.html. Gilgoff, D. (2009, October 22). America's best leaders, 2009: Cory Booker. *U.S. News & World Report.* From http://www. usnews.com/articles/news/best-leaders/2009/10/22/ cory-booker-newarks-mayor-fights-for-a-revival.html.

Chapter 14

Preview Case Sources

Kuang, C. (2010, March). Most innovative companies 2010—top 10 by industry: Transportation. *FastCompany.com.* From http://www.fastcompany.com/ mic/2010/industry/most-innovative-transportation-companies. Ha, P. (2009, November 2). The best travel gadgets of 2009: Zipcar app. *Time.com.* From http://www.time.com/time/specials/packages/article/0,2 8804,1933520_1933522_1933468,00.html. Inc. 500 (2009). No. 375: Zipcar. From http://www.inc.com/ inc5000/2009/company-profile.html?id=200903750. Aston, A. (2008, September 8). Growth galore, but profits are zip. *BusinessWeek,* p. 62. Frankel, A. (2008, April 15). Zipcar drives toward the future. *MSNBC.* From http://www.msnbc.msn.com/id/23747341. Block, D. (2008, April 22). Green car service zipping into the Bronx. *New York Daily News,* p. 22.

Chapter Notes

1. Schneider, B. (1990). *Organizational climate and culture.* San Francisco, CA: Jossey-Bass.

2. Schein, E. H. (1992). *Organizational culture and leadership: A dynamic view* (2nd ed.). San Francisco, CA: Jossey-Bass.

3. Knight, T. (2004, October). Build a strong foundation: High performance begins with culture. *CPA Leadership Report.* From http://www.cpareport.com/Newsletter% 20Articles/2004%20Articles/BuildaStrongFoundation_ Oct_2004.htm.

4. Consumer Reports (2010, February 22). Toyota reportedly worked with feds to save $199 million in recalls. *Cars Blog.* From http://blogs.consumerreports. org. Liker, J. (2008). *Toyota culture: The heart and soul of the Toyota way.* New York: McGraw-Hill.

5. Martin, J. (1996). *Cultures in organizations.* New York: Oxford University Press.

6. Perna, J. (2001, July 15). Reinventing how we do business. *Vital Speeches of the Day, 67*(19), 587–591.

7. The Disney Institute & Eisner, M. D. (2001). *Be our guest: Perfecting the art of customer service.* New York: Hyperion.

8. Barrett, C. (2006, January). Coleen's corner: Managers in training. *Spirit Magazine,* p. 12. From http://www.southwest.com/about_swa.

9. Nash, G. D. (1992). *A. P. Giannini and the Bank of America.* Norman, OK: University of Oklahoma Press.

10. Anonymous. (1999, April). Toxic shock? *Fast Company,* p. 38.

11. Rosen, R. H., & Berger, L. (1992). *Healthy company: Eight strategies to develop people, productivity, and profits.* New York: J. P. Tarcher.

12. Institute for Business, Technology, and Ethics. (2004). Eight traits of a healthy organizational culture. From http://www.ethix.org/8%20traits.pdf. Barry, L. L. (1999). *Discovering the soul of service: Nine drivers of sustainable business success.* New York: The Free Press.

13. Vlamis, A., & Smith, B. (2001). *Do you? Business the Yahoo! way.* New York: Capstone.

14. Garr, D. (2000). *IBM redux: Lou Gerstner and the business turnaround of the decade.* New York: HarperCollins.

15. Meridden, T. (2001). *Big shots: Business the Nokia way.* New York: Capstone.

16. Florea, G., & Phinney, G. (2001). *Barbie talks!: An expose of the first talking Barbie doll.* New York: Hyperion.

17. Tsui, A. S., Zhang, Z.-X., Wang, H., Xin, K. R., & Wu, J. B. (2006). Unpacking the relationship between CEO leadership behavior and organizational culture. *Leadership Quarterly, 17,* 113–137.

18. Freiberg, K., Freiberg, J., & Peters, T. (1998). *Nuts! Southwest Airlines' crazy recipe for business and personal success.* New York: Bantam Doubleday Dell.

19. Cameron, K. S., & Quinn, R. E. (1999). *Diagnosing and changing organizational culture: Based on the competing values framework.* Reading, MA: Addison-Wesley.

20. Kauffman, J. (2005). Lost in space: A critique of NASA's crisis communications in the Columbia disaster. *Public Relations Review, 31,* 263–275.

21. Welch, J. (2005). *Winning.* New York: HarperCollins.

22. Welch, J. (1995, February). Interview with Jack Welch. *Business Today.* From http://www.1000ventures.com/business_guide/mgmt_new-model_25lessons-welch.html.

23. Berrio, A. A. (2003). An organizational culture assessment using the competing values framework: A profile of Ohio State University extension. *Journal of Extension, 41*(2). From http://www.joe.org/joe/2003april/a3.shtml.

24. Baker, S., Crockett, R. O., & Gross, N. (1998, August 10). Can CEO Ollila keep the cellular superstar flying high? *BusinessWeek,* pp. 55–57, 59. From http://www.businessweek.com/1998/32/b3590001.htm.

25. Waterman, R. J., Jr. (1993). *Adhocracy.* New York: W. W. Norton.

26. Deering, A., Dilts, R., & Russell, J. (2003, Spring). Leadership cults and cultures. *Leader to Leader, 28,* 36–43.

27. Martin, J., Sitkin, S. B., & Boehm, M. (1985). Founders and the elusiveness of a cultural legacy. In P. J. Frost, L. F. Moore, M. R. Louis, C. C. Lundberg, & J. Martin (Eds.), *Organizational culture* (pp. 99–124). Beverly Hills, CA: Sage.

28. Dobrzynski, J. H. (1993, April 12). "I'm going to let the problems come to me." *BusinessWeek,* pp. 32–33.

29. Lemon, M., & Sahota, P. S. (2004). Organizational culture as a knowledge repository for increased innovative capacity. *Technovation, 24,* 484–498. Walsh, J. P., & Ungson, G. R. (1991). Organizational memory. *Academy of Management Review, 16,* 873–896.

30. Reitman, J. (1998). *Bad blood: Crisis in the American Red Cross.* New York: Pinnacle Books.

31. Ornstein, S. L. (1986). Organizational symbols: A study of their meanings and influences on perceived psychological climate. *Organizational Behavior and Human Decision Processes, 38,* 207–229.

32. Martin, J. (1982). Stories and scripts in organizational settings. In A. Hastorf & A. Isen (Eds.), *Cognitive social psychology* (pp. 255–306). New York: Elsevier-North Holland.

33. Ransdell, E. (2000, January–February). The Nike story? Just tell it. *Fast Company,* pp. 44, 46.

34. Carroll, P. (1993). *Big blues: The unmaking of IBM.* New York: Crown.

35. Branwyn, G. (1997). *Jargon watch: A pocket dictionary for the jitterati.* San Francisco, CA: Hardwired.

36. Neuhauser, P. C. (1993). *Corporate legends and lore: The power of storytelling as a management tool.* New York: McGraw-Hill (quote, p. 63).

37. Mars, Inc. (2006). The five principles. From http://www.mars.com/About_us/The_Five_Principles. Brenner, J. G. (1999). *The emperors of chocolate: Inside the secret world of Hershey and Mars.* New York: Random House.

38. Manley, W. W., II. (1991). *Executive's handbook of model business conduct codes.* Englewood Cliffs, NJ: Prentice Hall (quote, p. 5).

39. Walter, G. A. (1985). Culture collisions in mergers and acquisitions. In P. J. Frost, L. F. Moore, M. R. Louis, C. C. Lundberg, & J. Martin (Eds.), *Organizational culture* (pp. 301–314). Beverly Hills, CA: Sage.

40. Vlasic, B., & Stertz, B. A. (2001). *Taken for a ride: How Daimler-Benz drove off with Chrysler.* New York: Harper Business. Naughton, K. (2000, December 11). A mess of a merger. *Newsweek,* pp. 54–57. Elkind, P. (1998, November 9). A merger made in hell. *Fortune,* pp. 134–138, 140, 142, 144, 146, 149, 150. Burrough, B., & Helyar, J. (1990).

Barbarians at the gate. New York: Harper Collins. Muller, J. (1999, November 29). Lessons from a casualty of the culture wars. *BusinessWeek,* p. 198. Muller, J. (1999, November 15). The one-year itch at DaimlerChrysler. *BusinessWeek,* p. 42.

41. Skidmore, S. (2010, February 2). Cadbury shareholders approve Kraft deal. *USA Today.* From http://www.usatoday.com/money/industries/food/2010-02-02-cadbury-kraft_N.htm. Bowers, S. (2009, October 21). Cadbury warns of culture clash under Kraft. *Guardian.co.uk.* From http://www.guardian.co.uk/business/2009/oct/21/cadbury-kraft-sales-profits-job-losses.

42. Smith, B. W. (2005, May 3). *Corporate culture clashes thwart mergers and acquisitions.* Indianapolis, IN: Smith Weaver Smith. From http://www.smithweaversmith.com/corporate%20culture%20clash.htm.

43. Charan, R. (2006, April). Home Depot's blueprint for culture change. *Harvard Business Review,* pp. 60–70.

44. See Note 43 (quote, p. 64).

45. Now for sale, the Zappos culture. (2010, January 11). *BusinessWeek,* p. 57.

46. Fischer, I., & Frontczak, D. (1999, September). Culture club. *Business 2.0,* pp. 196–198.

47. Amabile, T. M. (1988). A model of creativity and innovation in organizations. In B. M. Staw & L. L. Cummings (Eds.), *Research in organizational behavior* (Vol. 10, pp. 123–167). Greenwich, CT: JAI Press.

48. Amabile, T. M., & Fisher, C. M. (2009). Stimulate creativity by fueling passion. In E. A. Locke (Ed.), *The Blackwell handbook of principles of organizational behavior* (2nd ed., pp. 481–497). Oxford, England: Blackwell.

49. Ethics Resource Center. (2009). *2009 national business ethics survey.* Arlington, VA: Author.

50. Seligson, A. L., & Choi, L. (2006). *Critical elements of an organizational ethical culture.* Washington, DC: Ethics Resource Center.

51. Runco, M. A. (1991). *Divergent thinking.* Westport, CT: Greenwood.

52. The Drucker Foundation, Hesselbein, F., & Johnston, R. (2002). *On creativity, innovation, and renewal: A leader-to-leader guide.* New York: Wiley.

53. See Note 50.

54. Kabanoff, B., & Rossiter, J. R. (1994). Recent developments in applied creativity. In C. Cooper & I. T. Robertson (Eds.), *International review of industrial and organizational psychology* (Vol. 9, pp. 283–324). London: Wiley.

55. Michalko, M. (1998, May). Thinking like a genius: Eight strategies used by the supercreative, from Aristotle and Einstein and Edison. *The Futurist,* pp. 21–25.

56. Kabanoff, B., & Bottiger, P. (1991). Effectiveness of creativity training and its reaction to selected personality factors. *Journal of Organizational Behavior, 12,* 235–248.

57. Muoio, A. (2000, January–February). Idea summit. *Fast Company,* pp. 151–156, 160, 162, 164 (quote, p. 152).

58. Gogoi, P. (2003). Thinking outside the cereal box. *BusinessWeek,* pp. 74–75.

59. Baer, M., & Oldham, G. R. (2006). The curvilinear relation between experienced creative time pressure and creativity: Moderating effects of openness to experience and support for creativity. *Journal of Applied Psychology, 91,* 963–970.

60. Amabile, T. M., Conti, R., Coon, H., Lazenby, J., & Herron, M. (1996). Assessing the work environment for creativity. *Academy of Management Journal, 39,* 1154–1184.

61. Oldham, G. R., & Cummings, A. (1996). Employee creativity: Personal and contextual factors at work. *Academy of Management Journal, 39,* 607–634.

62. Zhou, J. (2003). When the presence of creative coworkers is related to creativity: The role of supervisor close monitoring, developmental feedback, and creative personality. *Journal of Applied Psychology, 88,* 413–422.

63. Amabile, T. M., & Conti, R. (1999). Changes in the work environment for creativity during downsizing. *Academy of Management Journal, 42,* 630–640.

64. Dahle, C. (2000, January–February). Mind games. *Fast Company,* pp. 169–173, 176, 178–179.

65. Shalley, C. E. (1991). Effects of productivity goals, creativity goals, and personal discretion on individual creativity. *Journal of Applied Psychology, 76,* 179–185.

66. Sutton, R. I., & Hargadon, A. (1996). Brainstorming groups in context: Effectiveness in a product design firm. *Administrative Science Quarterly, 41,* 685–718 (quote, p. 702).

67. Zachary, P. C. (2000, July). Mighty is the mongrel. *Fast Company,* pp. 270–272, 276, 278, 280, 282, 284.

68. Zachary, G. P. (2000). *The global me: New cosmopolitans and the competitive edge.* New York: Public Affairs Books.

69. Casson, M. (1990). *Enterprise and competitiveness.* New York: Oxford University Press.

70. Busentiz, L. W., Gomez, C., & Spencer, J. W. (2000). Country institutional profiles: Unlocking entrepreneurial phenomena. *Academy of Management Journal, 43,* 994–1003.

71. Fast Company Staff. (2010. March). The world's 50 most innovative companies. *Fast Company,* pp. 53–97.

72. See Note 71 (quote, p. 66).

73. Christensen, C. M., & Raynor, M. E. (2003). *The innovator's solution.* Boston, MA: Harvard Business School.

74. Tucker, R. B. (2002). *Driving growth through innovation.* San Francisco, CA: Berrett-Koehler.

75. Von Hippel, E. (2005). *Democratizing innovation.* Cambridge, MA: MIT Press.

76. Davila, T., Epstein, M. J., & Shelton, R. (2006). *Making innovation work: How to manage it, measure it, and profit from it.* Upper Saddle River, NJ: Prentice Hall. Chakravorti, B. (2003). *The slow pace of fast change: Bringing innovations to market in a connected world.* Boston, MA: Harvard Business School Press. Chesbrough, H. W. (2003). *Open innovation: The new imperative for creating and profiting from technology.* Boston, MA: Harvard Business School Press.

77. Bernard, S. (2005, April 18). The perfect prescription: How the pill bottle was remade—sensibly and

beautifully. *New York.* From http://newyorkmetro.com/nymetro/health/features/11700/index.html.

78. See Note 75.

79. Magadley, W., & Kamal, B. (2009). Innovation labs: An examination into the use of physical spaces to enhance organizational creativity. *Creativity and Innovation Management, 18,* 315–325.

80. Smethurst, J. (2010). *Embedded collaboration: The Bell Canada story.* Walnut Creek, CA: Innovation Labs.

81. Davila, T., Epstein, M., & Shelton, R. (2005). *Making innovation work: How to manage it, measure it, and profit from it.* Upper Saddle River, NJ: Prentice Hall. Ricchiuto, J. (1997). *Collaborative creativity.* New York: Oakhill.

82. Hamel, G. (2000, June 21). Re-invent your company. *Fortune,* pp. 99–104, 106, 110, 112, 116, 118 (quote, p. 100).

83. Hamel, G. (2000). *Leading the revolution.* Boston, MA: Harvard Business School Press.

84. DiCarlo, L. (2004, October 30). IBM chief's $200 million bet on U.S. talent. *Forbes.* From http://www.innovateamerica.org/hot_topics/hot_topics.asp?id=21.

85. First National Bank. (2006). Rewarding innovation a key focus at FNB. From https://www.fnb.co.za/news/archive/2005/20051118innovation.html.

86. 3M. (2002). *A century of innovation: The 3M story.* Minneapolis, MN: Author. From http://multimedia.mmm.com/mws/mediawebserver.dyn?000000JHT4507Da0nDa000rvRlWH3e_W-.

Case in Point Sources

Hof, R. D. (2004, August 19). Voices of the innovators: Jeff Bezos: "Blind-Alley" explorer. *BusinessWeek Online.* From http://www.businessweek.com/bwdaily/dnflash/aug2004/nf20040819_7348_db_81.htm. Spector, R. (2000). *Amazon.com: Get big fast.* New York: HarperCollins. Schlegelmilch, B., Diamantopoulos, A., & Kreuz, P. (2003). Strategic innovation: The construct, its drivers and its strategic outcomes. *Journal of Strategic Marketing, 11*(2). From http://search.epnet.com.gateway.library.qut.edu.au/direct.asp?an=10779277&db=bsh.

Chapter 15

Preview Case Sources

Greene, T. (2010, March 5). Cloud security, cyber war loom over RSA conference. *InfoWorld.* From http://www.infoworld.com/d/cloud-computing/cloud-security-cyber-war-loom-over-rsa-conference-734. Cloud computing and the tech giants. (2009, October 15). *The Economist.* From http://www.economist.com/displaystory.cfm?story_id=14637206. McAfee. (2009, October 8). Press release: Verizon Business and McAfee form strategic alliance. From http://newsroom.mcafee.com/article_display.cfm?article_id=3579. Strategic alliance between McAfee and Verizon Business aims for the clouds. (2009, October 9). Twilight in the valley of the nerds. From http://nerdtwilight.wordpress.com/2009/10/08/strategic-alliance-between-mcafee-and-verizon-business-aims-for-the-clouds. Gubbins, E. (2009, June 3). Verizon debuts cloud computing service. *Connected Planet.* From http://connectedplanetonline.com/business_services/news/verizon-cloud-computing-0603.

Chapter Notes

1. Daft, R. L. (2007). *Essentials of organization theory and design* (9th ed.). Cincinnati, OH: Thomson South-Western.

2. Miller, D. (1987). The genesis of configuration. *Academy of Management Review, 12,* 686–701.

3. Galbraith, J. R. (1987). Organization design. In J. W. Lorsch (Ed.), *Handbook of organizational behavior* (pp. 343–357). Englewood Cliffs, NJ: Prentice Hall.

4. Hendricks, C. F. (1992). *The rightsizing remedy.* Homewood, IL: Business One Irwin.

5. Swoboda, F. (1990, May 28–June 3). For unions, maybe bitter was better. *Washington Post National Weekly Edition,* p. 20.

6. Urwick, L. F. (1956, May–June). The manager's span of control. Harvard Business Review, 34, pp. 39–47.

7. Speen, K. (1988, September 12). Caught in the middle. *BusinessWeek,* pp. 80–88.

8. Dalton, M. (1950). Conflicts between staff and line managerial officers. *American Sociological Review, 15,* 342–351.

9. Chandler, A. (1962). *Strategy and structure.* Cambridge, MA: MIT Press.

10. Navran, F. J. (2002). *Truth and trust: The first two victims of downsizing.* Athabaska, Alberta, Canada: Athabasca University Press. Mitchell, R. (1987, December 14). When Jack Welch takes over: A guide for the newly acquired. *BusinessWeek,* pp. 93–97.

11. Lawrence, P., & Lorsch, J. (1967). *Organization and environment.* Boston, MA: Harvard University Press.

12. Pitta, J. (1993, April 26). It had to be done and we did it. *Forbes,* pp. 148–152.

13. Merholz, P. (2002, April 30). The pendulum returns: Unifying the online presence of decentralized organizations. Adaptive Path Essay Archives. From http://www.adaptivepath.com/publications/essays/archives/000028.php.

14. Schminke, M., Ambrose, M. L., & Cropanzano, R. S. (2000). The effect of organizational structure on perceptions of procedural fairness. *Journal of Applied Psychology, 85,* 294–304.

15. Schminke, M., Cropanzano, R. S., & Rupp, D. E. (2002). Organizational structure and fairness perceptions: The moderating effects of organizational level. *Organizational Behavior and Human Decision Processes, 89,* 881–905.

16. Anders, G. (2003). *Perfect enough: Carly Fiorina and the reinvention of Hewlett-Packard.* Middlesex, England: Portfolio.

17. Hewlett-Packard: About us. (2003). From http://www.hp.com/hpinfo/abouthp.

18. Mee, J. F. (1964). Matrix organizations. *Business Horizons, 7*(2), 70–72.

19. Bartlett, C. A., & Ghoshal, S. (1990, May–June). Matrix management: Not a structure, a frame of mind. *Harvard Business Review, 68,* pp. 138–145.

20. See Note 19.

21. Davis, S. M., & Lawrence, P. R. (1977). *Matrix.* Reading, MA: Addison-Wesley.

22. Goggin, W. (1974, January–February). How the multi-dimensional structure works at Dow Corning. *Harvard Business Review, 56,* pp. 33–52.

23. Ford, R. C., & Randolph, W. A. (1992). Cross-functional structures: A review and integration of matrix organization and project management. *Journal of Management, 18,* 267–294.

24. See Note 23.

25. McGregor, D. (1960). *The human side of enterprise.* New York: McGraw-Hill.

26. Argyris, C. (1964). *Integrating the individual and the organization.* New York: Wiley.

27. Likert, R. (1961). *New patterns of management.* New York: McGraw-Hill.

28. Duncan, R. (1979, Winter). What is the right organization structure? *Organizational Dynamics,* pp. 59–69.

29. Burns, T., & Stalker, G. M. (1961). *The management of innovation.* London: Tavistock.

30. Deveney, K. (1986, October 13). Bag those fries, squirt that ketchup, fry that fish. *BusinessWeek,* pp. 57–61.

31. Kerr, P. (1985, May 11). Witch hazel still made the old-fashioned way. *New York Times,* pp. 27–28.

32. Morse, J. J., & Lorsch, J. W. (1970, May–June). Beyond Theory Y. *Harvard Business Review, 48,* pp. 61–68.

33. Mintzberg, H. (2009). *Managing.* San Francisco, CA: Berrett-Koehler. Mintzberg, H. (1983). *Structure in fives: Designing effective organizations.* Englewood Cliffs, NJ: Prentice Hall.

34. Livesay, H. C. (1979). *American made: Men who shaped the American economy.* Boston, MA: Little, Brown.

35. See Note 1.

36. Harrigan, K. R. (2003). *Vertical integration, outsourcing, and corporate strategy.* Frederick, MD: Beard Group.

37. Mohrman, S. A., Cohen, S. G., & Mohrman, A. M., Jr. (1997). *Designing team-based organizations.* San Francisco, CA: Jossey-Bass.

38. Chandler, A. D. (1969). *Strategy and structure: Chapters in the history of the American industrial enterprise.* Cambridge, MA: MIT Press (quote, p. 14).

39. Donaldson, L. (2009). Design structure to fit strategy. In E. A. Locke (Ed.), *Handbook of principles of organizational behavior* (pp. 407–424). Chichester, UK: Wiley.

40. See Note 39.

41. See Note 39.

42. Bryan, L. L., & Joyce, C. I. (2007). Better strategy through organizational design. *The McKinsey Quarterly, 2,* 21–29.

43. Walsh, B. (2010, June 14). On the edge. *Time,* pp. 30–37.

44. GE: Just your average everyday $60 billion family grocery store. (1994, May 2). *Industry Week,* pp. 13–18.

45. Dees, G. D., Rasheed, A. M. A., McLaughlin, K. J., & Priem, R. L. (1995). The new corporate architecture. *Academy of Management Executive, 9,* 7–18.

46. See Note 45.

47. Tully, S. (1993, February 3). The modular corporation. *Fortune,* pp. 106–108, 110.

48. Byrne, J. (1993, February 8). The virtual corporation. *BusinessWeek,* pp. 99–103.

49. Sherman, S. (1992, September 21). Are strategic alliances working? *Fortune,* pp. 77–78 (quote, p. 78).

50. Nakarmi, L., & Einhorn, B. (1993, June 7). Hyundai's gutsy gambit. *BusinessWeek,* p. 48.

51. Gerlach, M. L. (1993). *Alliance capitalism: The social organization of Japanese business.* Berkeley, CA: University of California Press.

52. Miyashita, K., & Russell, D. (1994). *Keiretsu: Inside the Japanese conglomerates.* New York: McGraw-Hill.

53. Kanter, R. M. (1994, July–August). Collaborative advantage: The art of alliances. *Harvard Business Review,* pp. 96–108.

54. See Note 53.

55. Fletcher, N. (1988, December 10). U.S., China form joint venture to manufacture helicopters. *Journal of Commerce,* p. 58.

56. Bransi, B. (1987, January 3). South Korea's carmakers count their blessings. *The Economist,* p. 45.

57. Newman, W. H. (1992). Focused joint ventures in transforming economies. *The Executive, 6,* 67–75.

58. Lewis, J. (1990). *Partnerships for profit: Structuring and managing strategic alliances.* New York: Free Press.

59. Albrinck, J., Irwin, G., Neilson, G., & Sasina, D. (2000, third quarter). From bricks to clicks: The four stages of e-volution. *Strategy and Business,* pp. 63–66, 68–72.

60. Vanhonacker, W. (1997, March–April). Entering China: An unconventional approach. *Harvard Business Review, 97,* 130–131, 134–136, 138–140.

61. Earley, P. C., & Erez, M. (1997). *The transplanted executive: Why you need to understand how workers in other countries see the world differently.* New York: Oxford University Press.

Case in Point Sources

Commercial Metals Company. (2010). The world of CMC. From http://www.cmc.com/World-Map.aspx. CNNMoney. (2006, March 21). Commercial Metals Company reports strongest second quarter in its history. From http://money.cnn.com/services/tickerheadlines/prn/200603210855PR_NEWS_USPR_DATU026.htm. Commercial Metals Company Web site: http://www.comercialmetals.com. *Commercial Metals Company 2010 Annual Report.* Dallas, Texas: Commercial Metals Company.

Chapter 16

Preview Case Sources

When Campbell was in the soup. (2010, March 4). *Gallup Management Journal.* From http://gmj.gallup.com/content/126278/Campbell-Soup.aspx. Saving

Campbell Soup Company. (2010, February 11). *Gallup Management Journal.* From http://gmj.gallup.com/content/125687/Saving-Campbell-Soup-Company.aspx. Campbell's Soup Company. (2010). Our company: Executive team. From http://www.campbellsoupcompany.com/bio_conant.asp.

Chapter Notes

1. Dawson, P. (2004). *Understanding organizational change: The contemporary experience of people at work.* Thousand Oaks, CA: Sage. Sherman, S. (1993, December 13). How will we live with the tumult? *Fortune,* pp. 123–125.

2. McKinsey & Company. (2006, April). An executive take on the top business trends: A McKinsey Global Survey. *McKinsey Quarterly.* From https://www.mckinseyquarterly.com/An_executive_take_on_the_top_business_trends__A_McKinsey_Global_Survey_1754.

3. Haveman, H. A. (1992). Between a rock and a hard place: Organizational change and performance under conditions of fundamental environmental transformation. *Administrative Science Quarterly, 37,* 48–75.

4. Smith, D. (1998, May). Invigorating change initiatives. *Management Review,* pp. 45–48.

5. Nystrom, P. C., & Starbuck, W. H. (1984, Spring). To avoid organizational crises, unlearn. *Organizational Dynamics,* 44–60.

6. Avedis Zildjian. (2010). Background: Every company has a story: Ours starts in 1623. From http://www.zildjian.com/EN-US/about/background.ad2.

7. Kanter, R. M. (1991, May–June). Transcending business boundaries: 12,000 world managers view change. *Harvard Business Review,* pp. 151–164.

8. Lexus. (2008, September 2). Lexus committed to sustainable transportation and business. From http://www.lexus.com/articles/print/2008/9/20080902_1.html.

9. Levy, A. (1986). Second-order planned change: Definition and conceptualization. *Organizational Dynamics, 16*(1), 4–20.

10. A master class in radical change. (1993, December 13). *Fortune,* pp. 82–84, 88, 90.

11. Woodyard, C. (2005, February 21). Multilingual staff can drive up auto sales. *USA Today.* From http://www.usatoday.com/money/autos/2005-02-21-ethnic-cars-usat_x.htm?POE=click-refer.

12. Bureau of Labor Statistics. (2010, March 5). News release: The employment situation, February 2010. From http://www.bls.gov/news.release/pdf/empsit.pdf.

13. Ethics Resource Center (2009). *2009 national business ethics survey: Ethics in the recession.* Arlington, VA: Author.

14. Cameron, E., & Green, M. (2004). Making sense of change management. London: Kogan Page. David, F. R. (1993). *Concepts of strategic management.* New York: Macmillan.

15. Mead, R. (1998). *International management* (2nd ed.). Malden, MA: Blackwell.

16. Taylor, B. (1995). The new strategic leadership—driving change, getting results. *Long Range Planning, 28*(5), 71–81.

17. Tripas, M., & Favetti, G. (2000). Capabilities, cognition, and inertia: Evidence from digital imaging. *Strategic Management Journal, 21,* 1147–1161.

18. Polaroid. (2010, January 5). Press release: Lady Gaga named creative director for specialty line of Polaroid imaging products. From http://www.polaroid.com/About/News/Press+Release:+Lady+Gaga+Named+Creative+Director+for+Specialty+Line+of+Polaroid+Imaging+Products/4339.

19. Spooner, J. G., & Kanellos, M. (2004, December 8). IBM sells PC group to Lenovo. *CNET News.* From http://news.com.com/IBM+sells+PC+group+to+Lenovo/2100-1042_3-5482284.html.

20. Bellis, M. (2006). Inventors of the modern computer. From http://inventors.about.com/library/weekly/aa031599.htm.

21. Kennedy, R. E., & Sharma, A. (2009). *The services shift: Seizing the ultimate offshore opportunity.* Upper Saddle River, NJ: Pearson Education.

22. Travis, L. (2004, December 15). *India offshore outsourcing frees up $30B domestically.* Boston, MA: AMR Research. From http://www.amrresearch.com/Content/View.asp?pmillid=17845.

23. Let's offshore the lawyers. (2006, September 18). *BusinessWeek.* From http://www.businessweek.com/magazine/content/06_38/b4001061.htm?chan=search.

24. Guptill, B., & McNee. B. (2005). *Outsourcing transformed: New models and methods.* Westport, CT: Saugatech Technology. From http://www.saugatech.com/170order.htm.

25. Christensen, H. K. (1994). Corporate strategy: Managing a set of businesses. In L. Fahley & R. M. Randall (Eds.), *The portable MBA in strategy* (pp. 53–83). New York: Wiley.

26. Markides, C. (1997, Spring). Strategic innovation. *Sloan Management Review,* 9–23.

27. Collis, D. J., & Montgomery, C. A. (1995, July–August). Competing on resources: Strategy in the 1990s. *Harvard Business Review, 73,* 118–128.

28. Dean, J. W., Jr., & Scharfman, M. (1996). Does decision process matter? A study of strategic decision-making effectiveness. *Academy of Management Journal, 29,* 368–396.

29. Porter, M. (1996, March 14). "It's time to grow up." *Far Eastern Economic Review,* pp. 1–2.

30. Lasserre, P., & Putti, J. (1990). *Business strategy and management: Text and cases for managers in Asia.* Singapore: Institute of Management.

31. Yoshimori, M. (1995). Whose company is it? The concept of the corporation in Japan and the West. *Long Range Planning, 28*(4), 33–34.

32. Goldstein, A. P. (2001). *Reducing resistance: Methods for enhancing openness to change.* Champaign, IL: Research Press. Judson, A. S. (1991). *Changing behavior in organizations: Minimizing resistance to change.* Cambridge, MA: Basil Blackwell.

33. Nadler, D. A. (1987). The effective management of organizational change. In J. W. Lorsch (Ed.), *Handbook of organizational behavior* (pp. 358–369). Englewood Cliffs, NJ: Prentice Hall.

34. Katz, D., & Kahn, R. L. (1978). *The social psychology of organizations* (2nd ed.). New York: Wiley.

35. Beer, M. (1980). *Organizational change and development: A systems view.* Glenview, IL: Scott, Foresman.

36. Wanberg, C., & Banas, J. T. (2000). Predictors and outcomes of openness to change in a reorganizing workplace. *Journal of Applied Psychology, 85,* 132–142.

37. Nadler, D. A. (1987). The effective management of organizational change. In J. W. Lorsch (Ed.), *Handbook of organizational behavior* (pp. 358–369). Englewood Cliffs, NJ: Prentice Hall.

38. Reich, R. B. (2000, October). Your job is change. *Fast Company,* pp. 140–148, 150, 152, 154, 156, 158.

39. Dutton, J. E., Ashford, S. J., O'Neill, R. M., & Lawrence, K. A. (2001). Moves that matter: Issue selling and organizational change. *Academy of Management Journal, 44,* 716–736.

40. Huey, J. (1993, April 5). Managing in the midst of chaos. *Fortune,* pp. 38–41, 44, 46, 48.

41. Senge, P. M. (1990). *The fifth discipline.* New York: Doubleday.

42. Kotter, J. P. (1995, March–April). Leading the change: Why transformation efforts fail. *Harvard Business Review,* pp. 59–67. Kotter, J. P., & Schlesinger, L. A. (1979, March–April). Choosing strategies for change. *Harvard Business Review,* pp. 106–114.

43. Collarelli, S. M. (1998). Psychological interventions in organizations. *American Psychologist, 53,* 1044–1056.

44. Pascale, R., Millemann, M., & Gioja, L. (1997, November–December). Changing the way we change. *Harvard Business Review,* pp. 127–139.

45. Whitney, D., & Sachau, C. (1998, Spring). Appreciative inquiry: An innovative process for organization change. *Employment Relations Today, 25,* pp. 11–21.

46. Bushe, G. R., & Coetzer, G. (1995). Appreciative inquiry as a team-developed intervention: A controlled experiment. *Journal of Applied Behavioral Science, 31,* 13–30.

47. Sugarman, H. C. (2006). The United States Navy: A case study in leadership development. From http://appreciativeinquiry.case.edu/uploads/Navy%20-%20mini%20case%20summary.doc.

48. See Note 47.

49. Porras, J. I., & Robertson, P. J. (1992). Organization development: Theory, practice, and research. In M. D. Dunnette & L. M. Hough (Eds.), *Handbook of industrial and organizational psychology* (2nd ed., Vol. 3, pp. 719–822). Palo Alto, CA: Consulting Psychologists Press.

50. The International Organization Development Code of Ethics. (2006). Organizational Development Network: Organization and human systems development credo. From http://hometown.aol.com/odinst/ethics.htm.

51. Jaeger, A. M. (1986). Organizational development and national culture: Where's the fit? *Academy of Management Review, 11,* 178–190.

52. White, L. P., & Wotten, K. C. (1983). Ethical dilemmas in various stages of organizational development. *Academy of Management Review, 8,* 690–697.

53. Kedia, B. L., & Bhagat, R. S. (1998). Cultural constraints on transfer of technology across nations: Implications for research in international and comparative management. *Academy of Management Review, 13,* 559–571.

54. Trepo, G. (1973, Autumn). Management style *a la française. European Business, 39,* 71–79.

55. Blunt, P. (1988). Cultural consequences for organization change in a southeast Asian state: Brunei. *Academy of Management Executive, 2,* 235–240.

Case in Point Sources

Tuna, C. (2009, June 9). A.G. Lafley's advice for future leaders. *Wall Street Journal.* From http://online.wsj.com/article/SB124451772932297029.html. Procter & Gamble (2010). Our heritage. From http://www.pg.com/en_US/company/heritage.shtml. Markels, A. (2006, October 22). Turning the tide at P&G. *U.S. News & World Report.* From http://www.usnews.com/usnews/news/articles/061022/30lafley.htm. Lafley, Alan. (2010, March 9). The Procter & Gamble Company. *BusinessWeek.* From http://investing.businessweek.com/businessweek/research/stocks/people/person.asp?personId=186141&ticker=PG:US.

Appendix 1

Appendix Notes

1. Colquitt, J. A., & Zapata-Phelan, C. P. (2007). Trends in theory building and theory testing: A five-decade study of the *Academy of Management Journal. Academy of Management Journal, 50,* 1281–1303.

2. Schwab, D. P. (1999). *Research methods for organizational studies.* Mahwah, NJ: Erlbaum.

3. Edwards, J. A. (2003). Measurement of OB constructs. In J. Greenberg (Ed.), *Organizational behavior: The state of the science* (2nd ed.). Mahwah, NJ: Erlbaum.

4. Greenberg, J., & Folger, R. (1988). *Controversial issues in social research methods.* New York: Springer-Verlag.

5. Eisenhardt, K. M. (1989). Building theories from case study research. *Academy of Management Review, 14,* 532–550.

Appendix 2

Appendix Notes

1. Meager, N. (1995). Occupations. In N. Nicholson (Ed.), *The Blackwell encyclopedic dictionary of organizational behavior* (pp. 352–354). Cambridge, MA: Blackwell.

2. Bureau of Labor Statistics. (2010). National occupational employment and wage statistics. From http://www.bls.gov/oes/2010/may/oes_nat.htm#b11-0000.

3. Driver, M. J. (1994). Careers: A review of personal and organizational research. In C. L. Cooper & I. T. Robertson (Eds.), *Key reviews in managerial psychology: Concepts and research for practice* (pp. 237–269). New York: Wiley.

4. Pepin, J. (2002, March). Burger meister: Ray Kroc. *Time 100 Polls*. From http://www.time.com/time/time100/builder/profile/kroc.html. Love, J. F. (1995). *Grinding it out*. New York: Bantam.

5. Holland, J. (1973). *Making vocational choices: A theory of careers*. Englewood Cliffs, NJ: Prentice Hall. Gottfredson, G. D., & Holland, J. L. (1990). A longitudinal test of the influence of congruence: Job satisfaction, competency utilization, and counterproductive behavior. *Journal of Consulting Psychology, 37,* 389–398.

6. Cluskey, G. R., & Vaux, A. (1997). Vocational misfit: Source of occupational stress among accountants. *Journal of Applied Business Research, 12,* 43–54.

7. Savickas, M. L., & Spokane, A. R. (1999). *Vocational interests: Meaning, measurement, and counseling use*. Palo Alto, CA: Davies Black.

8. Lawrence, B. (1995). Career anchor. In N. Nicholson (Ed.), *The Blackwell encyclopedic dictionary of organizational behavior* (pp. 44–45). Cambridge, MA: Blackwell.

9. Schein, E. H. (1978). *Career dynamics: Matching individual and organizational needs*. Reading, MA: Addison-Wesley.

10. Nicholson, N. (1995). Career plateauing. In N. Nicholson (Ed.), *The Blackwell encyclopedic dictionary of organizational behavior* (pp. 49–50). Cambridge, MA: Blackwell.

11. Branch, S. (1998, March 16). MBAs: What they really want. *Fortune*, p. 167.

12. Penna Sanders & Sidney Career Consulting. (2001, November). *Taking the plunge*. Research report available at www.pennasanderssidney.com/research/report-takingtheplunge.html.

13. Bolles, R. N. (2010). *What color is your parachute?* Berkeley, CA: Ten Speed Press.

14. See Note 13.

15. Hanisch, K. A. (1995). Retirement. In N. Nicholson (Ed.), *The Blackwell encyclopedic dictionary of organizational behavior* (pp. 490–491). Cambridge, MA: Blackwell.

16. Hanisch, K. A., & Hulin, C. L. (1990). Job attitudes and organizational withdrawal: An examination of retirement and other voluntary withdrawal behaviors. *Journal of Vocational Behavior, 37,* 60–78.

17. Hanisch, K. A. (91994). Reasons people retire and their relations to attitudinal and behavioral correlates in retirement. *Journal of Vocational Behavior, 45,* 1–16.

18. Forum for Investor Advice. (1999, July 26). Work 'til you drop. *BusinessWeek*, p. 8.

19. Decker, J. P. (1999, November 22). Why pro golfers can't wait to hit the big five-oh. *Fortune*, p. 76.

20. Thornton, E. (1999, August 9). No room at the top. *BusinessWeek*, p. 50.

21. Hirsch, W. (1995). Succession planning. In N. Nicholson (Ed.), *The Blackwell encyclopedic dictionary of organizational behavior* (pp. 544–54AII). Cambridge, MA: Blackwell.

22. Rothwell, W. J. (2000). *Effective succession planning: Ensuring leadership continuity and building talent from within*. New York: AMACOM.

23. Bianco, A., & Lavelle, L. (2000, December 11). The CEO trap. *BusinessWeek*, pp. 86–92.

24. Darwin, A. (2000). Critical reflections on mentoring in work settings. *Adult Education Quarterly, 50,* 197–211.

25. Ragubsm, B. R., & Scandura, T. A. (1999). Burden or blessing? Expected costs and benefits of being a mentor. *Journal of Organizational Behavior, 20,* 493–509.

26. Ragins, B. R., Cotton, J. L., & Miller, J. S. (2000). Marginal mentoring: The effects of type of mentor, quality of relationship, and program design on work and career attitudes. *Academy of Management Journal, 43,* 1179–1194.

27. Clutterbuck, D., & Ragins, B. R. (2002). *Mentoring and diversity: An international perspective*. Burlington, MA: Butterworth-Heinemann. Wickman, F., & Sjodin, T. (1997). *Mentoring*. Chicago, IL: Irwin.

Glossary

Numbers in parentheses correspond to the page numbers of the location of terms in text.

360-degree feedback The process of systematically giving and receiving feedback between individuals at various organizational levels. (98, 324, 469)

abilities Mental and physical capacities to perform various tasks. (130)

absenteeism The practice of staying away from the job when scheduled to work. (198)

abusive supervision A pattern of supervision in which a boss engages in sustained displays of hostile verbal and nonverbal behaviors. (404)

accommodative processing (bottom-up processing) A way of processing information in which people carefully observe what's going on around them so that they can respond to situations appropriately. (150)

achievement motivation (need for achievement) The strength of an individual's desire to excel—to succeed at difficult tasks and to do them better than others. (125)

action lab An OD intervention in which teams of participants work off-site to develop and implement new ways of solving organizational problems by focusing on the ineffectiveness of current methods. (579)

action learning A leadership development technique involving a continuous process of learning and reflection that is supported by colleagues and that emphasizes getting things done. (472)

action plan A carefully specified set of guidelines indicating exactly what needs to be done to attain desired results. (576)

active learning A collection of learner-centered techniques in which individuals are active participants in the learning process. (98)

acute stressor Stressors that bring some form of sudden change that threatens us either physically or psychologically, requiring people to make unwanted adjustments. (156)

ad hoc committee A temporary committee formed for a special purpose. (253)

additive tasks Types of group tasks in which the coordinated efforts of several people are added together to form the group's product. (264)

adhocracy (a) A form of organization that cuts across normal bureaucratic lines to capture opportunities, solve problems, and get results. (487)

adhocracy (b) A highly informal, organic organization in which specialists work in teams, coordinating with each other on various projects (e.g., many software development companies). (535)

adhocracy culture In the competing values framework, organizations that emphasize flexibility while also paying a great deal of attention to the external environment. (487)

administrative model A model of decision making that recognizes that people have imperfect views of problems, which limits the making of optimally rational-economic decisions. (349)

affective commitment The strength of a person's desire to work for an organization because he or she regards it positively and agrees with its goals and values. (203)

affective conflict A form of conflict resulting when people experience clashes of personality or interpersonal tension, resulting in frustration and anger. (391)

affective events theory (AET) The theory that identifies various factors that lead to people's emotional reactions on the job and how these reactions affect those individuals. (151)

affinity groups Informal collections of individuals who share a common identity with respect to such factors as race, ethnicity, or sexual preference. (188)

affirmative action laws Legislation designed to give employment opportunities to groups that have historically been underrepresented in the workforce, such as women and members of minority groups. (185)

agreeableness A tendency to be compassionate toward others; one of the Big Five personality dimensions. (119)

alternative dispute resolution (ADR) A set of procedures, such as *mediation* and *arbitration,* in which disputing parties work together with a neutral party who helps them settle their disagreements out of court. (395)

analytical model of the decision-making process A conceptualization of the eight steps through which individuals and groups make decisions: identify the problem, define objectives, make a predecision, generate alternatives, evaluate alternatives, make a choice, implement the choice, and follow up to determine whether the problem still exists. (334)

anger A heightened state of emotional arousal (e.g., increased heart rate, rapid breathing, flushed face, sweaty palms, etc.) fueled by cognitive interpretations of situations. (154)

anger management Systematic efforts to reduce people's emotional feelings of anger and the physiological arousal it causes. (155)

appreciative inquiry (AI) An OD intervention that focuses attention away from an organization's shortcoming, and toward its capabilities and its potential; based on the assumption that members of organizations already know the problems they face and that they stand to benefit more by focusing on what is possible. (578)

apprenticeship programs Formal training programs involving both on-the-job and classroom training usually over a long period, often used for training people in the skilled trades. (95)

arbitration A process in which a third party (known as an *arbitrator*) has the power to impose, or at least to recommend, the terms of an agreement between two or more conflicting parties. (395)

assessment centers Sessions in which a variety of techniques are used to determine how people behave under various standardized conditions. (469)

assimilative processing (top-down processing) A way of processing information in which people rely on the knowledge already at their disposal instead of taking in new information. (150)

asynchronous communication techniques Forms of communication in which senders and receivers must take turns sending and receiving messages. (303)

attitudes Relatively stable clusters of feelings, beliefs, and behavioral intentions toward a specific object, person, or institution. (178)

attribute framing effect The tendency for people to evaluate a characteristic more positively when it is presented in positive terms than when it is presented in negative terms. (354)

attribution The process through which individuals attempt to determine the causes behind others' behavior. (73)

authentic leaders Highly moral individuals who are confident, hopeful, optimistic, and resilient, and who are highly aware of the contexts in which they operate. (451)

autocratic (leadership style) A style of leadership in which a leader makes all decisions unilaterally. (455)

autocratic-delegation continuum model An approach to leadership recognizing that leaders allow followers to have different degrees of decision-making power, ranging from autocratic, through participative, to delegating. (455)

availability heuristic The tendency for people to base their judgments on information that is readily available to them although it may be potentially inaccurate, thereby adversely affecting decision quality. (355)

avoidance See *negative* reinforcement. (92)

avoidance goal orientation The desire to achieve success to avoid appearing incompetent and to avoid receiving negative evaluation from others. (127)

baby boom generation The generation of children born in the economic boom period following World War II. (18)

balanced contracts Psychological contracts that combine the open-ended, long-term features of relational psychological contracts with the well-specified reward-performance contingencies of transactional contracts. (378)

bargaining (negotiation) The process by which two or more parties in dispute with one another exchange offers, counteroffers, and concessions in an attempt to find a mutually acceptable agreement. (393)

basking in reflected glory The tendency for people to identify themselves with the successes of others such that those others' success becomes their own. (74)

behavioral component (of attitudes) Our predisposition to behave in a way consistent with our beliefs and feelings about an attitude object. (179)

behavioral sciences Fields such as psychology and sociology that seek knowledge of human behavior and society through the use of the scientific method. (4)

benevolence Disposition of people to be considerate and to demonstrate concern and support for others. (382)

Big Five dimensions of personality Five basic dimensions of personality that are related strongly to different forms of organization behavior. (119)

binding arbitration A form of arbitration in which the two sides agree in advance to accept the terms set by the arbitrator, whatever he or she may be. (396)

blogs (Web logs) Web pages in which people express their personal experiences and feelings; an Internet-based diary. (303)

bogie rumors Rumors that are based on people's fears and anxieties. (314)

bottom-line mentality The belief that an organization's financial success is the only thing that matters. (53)

boundaryless organization An organization in which chains of command are eliminated, spans of control are unlimited, and rigid departments give way to empowered teams. (543)

bounded discretion The tendency to restrict decision alternatives to those that fall within prevailing ethical standards. (350)

bounded rationality The major assumption of the administrative model—that organizational, social, and human limitations lead to the making of *satisficing*, rather than optimal decisions. (350)

brainstorming A technique designed to foster group productivity by encouraging interacting group members to express their ideas in a noncritical fashion. (362)

brown bag meetings Informal get-togethers over meals in which people discuss what's going on in their companies. (325)

bureaucracy An organizational design developed by Max Weber that attempts to make organizations operate efficiently by having a clear hierarchy of authority in which people are required to perform well-defined jobs. (11)

burnout A syndrome of emotional, physical, and mental exhaustion coupled with feelings of low self-esteem or low self-efficacy, resulting from prolonged exposure to intense stress, and the strain reactions following from them. (159)

business continuity plans Systematic sets of plans designed to help organizations get up and running again in the event of a disruption of some sort. (23)

cafeteria-style benefit plans Incentive systems in which employees have an opportunity to select the fringe benefits they want from a menu of available alternatives. (233)

calculus-based trust A form of trust based on deterrence; whenever people believe that another will behave as promised out of fear of getting punished for doing otherwise. (380)

career The evolving sequence of work experiences over time. (599)

career anchor A person's occupational self-concept based on his or her self-perceived talents, abilities, needs, and motives. (605)

career development interventions Systematic efforts to help manage people's careers while simultaneously helping the organizations in which they work. (608)

career plateau The point at which one's career has peaked and is unlikely to develop further. (607)

cascading model of emotional intelligence Conceptualization proposing that emotional intelligence influences job performance through a succession of abilities: the ability to perceive emotions, then to understand them, and then to regulate them; these abilities, in turn, are linked to personality variables, such as conscientiousness and neuroticism, and also to cognitive ability. (133)

case method A research technique in which a particular organization is thoroughly described and analyzed for purposes of understanding what went on in that setting. (598)

centrality The degree to which an organizational unit has a key impact on others because it has to be consulted and because its activities have immediate effects on an organization. (430)

centralization The tendency for just a few powerful individuals or groups to hold most of the decision-making power. (523)

ceremonies Celebrations of an organization's basic values and assumptions. (492)

channels of communication The pathways over which messages are transmitted (e.g., telephone lines, mail, etc.). (293)

charisma An attitude of enthusiasm and optimism that is contagious; an aura of leadership. (420)

child-care facilities Sites at or near company locations where parents can leave their children while they are working. (18)

chronic stressor The most extreme type of stressor, constant and unrelenting in nature, and having a long-term effect on the body, mind, and spirit. (156)

circumplex model of affect A theory of emotional behavior based on the degree to which emotions are pleasant or unpleasant and the degree to which they make one feel activated (i.e., feeling alert and engaged). (147)

clan culture In the competing values framework, an organization characterized by a strong internal focus along with a high degree of flexibility and discretion. (486)

classical organizational theory An early approach to the study of management that focused on the most efficient way to design organizations. (11, 530)

classroom training The process of teaching people how to do their jobs by explaining various job requirements and how to meet them. (94)

code of ethics A document describing what an organization stands for and the general rules of conduct expected of employees (e.g., to avoid conflicts of interest, to be honest, and so on). (56)

coercive power The individual power base derived from the capacity to administer punishment to others. (419)

cognitive appraisal A judgment about the stressfulness of a situation based on the extent to which someone perceives a stressor as threatening and is capable of coping with its demands. (157)

cognitive component (of attitudes) The things we believe about an attitude object, whether they are true or false. (178)

cognitive intelligence The ability to understand complex ideas, to adapt effectively to the environment, to learn from experience, to engage in various forms of reasoning, and to overcome obstacles with careful thought. (131)

cognitive moral development Differences among people in the capacity to engage in the kind of reasoning that enables them to make moral judgments. (52)

cohesiveness The strength of group members' desires to remain a part of their groups. (261)

collectivistic cultures Cultures in which people place high value on shared responsibility and the collective good of all. (266)

command group A group created by the connections between individuals who are a formal part of the organization (i.e., those who legitimately can give orders to others). (253)

communication The process by which a person, group, or organization (the sender) transmits some type of information (the message) to another person, group, or organization (the receiver). (293)

competing values framework A conceptualization of organizational culture that specifies that cultures of organizations differ with respect to two sets of opposite values: (1) valuing flexibility and discretion as opposed to stability, order, and control, and (2) valuing internal affairs as opposed to what's going on in the external environment. (485)

competition A pattern of behavior in which each person, group, or organization seeks to maximize its own gains at the expense of others. (387)

competitive advantage The benefits enjoyed by an organization to the extent that its customers perceive its products or services as being superior to the products or services of another organization. (566)

competitors People whose primary motive is doing better than others, beating them in open competition. (388)

compressed workweek The practice of working fewer days each week, but longer hours each day (e.g., four 10-hour days). (25)

computer-mediated communication Forms of communication that are aided by the use of computer technology (e.g., e-mail, instant messaging). (302)

computerized performance monitoring The process of using computers to monitor job performance. (264)

confirmation candidate A decision alternative considered for purposes of convincing oneself of the wisdom of selecting the *implicit favorite.* (356)

conflict A process in which one party perceives that another party has taken or will take actions that are incompatible with one's own interests. (391)

conglomerate A form of organizational diversification in which an organization (usually a very large, multinational one) adds an entirely unrelated business or product to its organizational design. (544)

conjunctive statements Statements that keep conversations going by connecting one speaker's remarks to another's. (326)

conscientiousness A tendency to show self-discipline, to strive for competence and achievement; one of the Big Five personality dimensions. (119)

consensus In *Kelley's theory of causal attribution,* information regarding the extent to which other people behave in the same manner as the person we're judging. (77)

consideration Actions by a leader that demonstrate concern with the welfare of subordinates, having a person-oriented style. (457)

consistency In *Kelley's theory of causal attribution,* information regarding the extent to which the person we're judging acts the same way at other times. (77)

constructive organizational deviance Actions that deviate from organizational norms but are consistent with societal norms. (397)

contingencies of reinforcement The various relationships between one's behavior and the consequences of that behavior—*positive reinforcement, negative reinforcement, punishment*, and *extinction.* (92)

contingency approach A perspective suggesting that organizational behavior is affected by a large number of interacting factors. How someone will behave is said to be contingent on many different variables at once. (8)

contingency approach to organizational design The contemporary approach that recognizes that no one approach to organizational design is best, but that the best design is the one that best fits with the existing environmental conditions. (531)

contingency theories of leader effectiveness Any of several theories that recognize that certain styles of leadership are more effective in some situations than others. (462)

contingent workforce People hired by organizations temporarily, to work as needed for finite periods of time. (27)

continuance commitment The strength of a person's desire to continue working for an organization because he or she needs to do so and cannot afford to do otherwise. (202)

conventional arbitration A form of arbitration in which an arbitrator can offer any package or terms he or she wishes. (396)

conventional level of moral reasoning In Kohlberg's theory of cognitive moral development, the level attained by most people, in which they judge right and wrong in terms of what is good for others and society as a whole. (53)

convergence hypothesis A biased approach to the study of management, which assumes that principles of good management are universal, and that ones that work well in the United States will apply equally well in other nations. (15)

cooperation A pattern of behavior in which assistance is mutual and two or more individuals, groups, or organizations work together toward shared goals for their mutual benefit. (386)

cooperators People who are concerned with maximizing joint outcomes, getting as much as possible for their team. (388)

coordination mechanisms Different ways of governing how things get done in an organization. (540)

core competency An organization's key capability, what it does best. (20)

core self-evaluation People's fundamental evaluations of themselves, their bottom-line conclusions about themselves. (122)

core task behavior (CTB) Formal behaviors that traditionally are recognized as part of a particular job. (384)

corporate ethics programs Formal, systematic efforts designed to promote ethics by making people sensitive to potentially unethical behavior and discouraging them from engaging in unethical acts. (56)

corporate hotlines Telephone lines staffed by corporate personnel ready to answer employees' questions, listen to their comments, and the like. (324)

corporate social responsibility Business practices that adhere to ethical values that comply with legal requirements, that demonstrate respect for individuals, and that promote the betterment of the community at large and the environment. (61)

corporate universities Centers devoted to handling a company's training needs on a full-time basis. (96)

correlation The extent to which two variables are related to each other. (592)

correlation coefficient A statistical index indicating the nature and extent to which two variables are related to each other. (593)

correspondent inferences Judgments about people's dispositions, their traits and characteristics, that correspond to what we have observed of their actions. (76)

counternorms Practices that are accepted within an organization despite the fact that they are contrary to the prevailing ethical standards of society at large. (54)

counterpower The capacity to neutralize another's influence attempts. (421)

creativity The process by which individuals or teams produce novel and useful ideas. (496)

creativity heuristics Rules that people follow to help them approach tasks in novel ways. (497)

cross-cultural training (CCT) A systematic way of preparing employees to live and work in another country. (95)

cross-functional teams Teams represented by people from different specialty areas within organizations. (272)

cross-training The practice of training team members in several different areas of expertise so that they are qualified to help their teammates by members performing a variety of tasks required for team success. (268)

cultural due diligence analysis Before a merger or acquisition is finalized, the process of analyzing the cultures of both organizations to ensure their compatibility. (493)

cultural intelligence The degree to which one is sensitive to the cultural differences between people. (451)

culture The set of values, customs, and beliefs that people have in common with other members of a social unit (e.g., a nation). (14)

culture clashes Problems resulting from attempts to merge two or more organizational cultures that are incompatible. (493)

culture shock The tendency for people to become confused and disoriented as they attempt to adjust to a new culture. (14)

culture-free IQ tests Tests that are unbiased because they do not give an advantage to members of any one particular group. (132)

cutting off reflected failure The tendency for people to avoid making failure part of their identities by dissociating themselves from individuals or teams that have lost. (74)

cyberloafing The practice of using a company's e-mail and/or Internet facilities for personal use. (400)

daily hassles Unpleasant or undesirable events that put people in bad moods. (152)

daily uplifts Pleasant or desirable events that put people in good moods. (152)

decentralization The extent to which authority and decision making are spread throughout all levels of an organization rather than being reserved for top management (centralization). (523)

decision making The process of making choices from among several alternatives. (334)

decision style Differences between people with respect to their orientations toward decisions. (342)

decision style model The conceptualization according to which people use one of four predominant decision styles: *directive, analytical, conceptual,* or *behavioral.* (342)

decision support systems (DSS) Computer programs in which information about organizational behavior is presented to decision makers in a manner that helps them structure their responses to decisions. (336)

decoding The process by which a receiver of messages transforms them back into the sender's ideas. (294)

defensive avoidance The tendency for decision makers to fail to solve problems because they go out of their way to avoid working on the problem at hand. (364)

delegation (leadership style) A style of leadership in which a leader allows employees to make their own decisions. (455)

Delphi technique A method of improving group decisions using the opinions of experts, which are solicited by mail and then compiled. The expert consensus of opinions is used to make a decision. (364)

departmentalization The process of breaking up organizations into coherent units. (524)

dependent variable A variable that is measured by the researcher, the one influenced by the *independent variable.* (596)

desk rage Lashing out at others in response to stressful encounters on the job. (165)

destructive criticism Negative feedback that angers the recipient instead of helping him or her do a better job. (392)

destructive organizational deviance A form of behavior that violates both organizational and societal norms. (397)

deviant organizational behavior Actions on the part of employees that intentionally violate the norms of organizations and/or the formal rules of society, resulting in negative consequences. (396)

direct report Someone in an organization, a subordinate, who must answer directly to a higher-level individual in that organization. (308)

discipline The process of systematically administering punishments. (101)

discrimination The behavior consistent with a prejudicial attitude; the act of treating someone negatively because of his or her membership in a specific group. (180)

disjunctive statements Statements that are disconnected from a previous statement, tending to bring conversations to a close. (326)

display rules Cultural norms about the appropriate ways to express emotions. (145)

displayed emotions Emotions that people show others, which may or may not be in line with their *felt emotions.* (154).

dispositional model of job satisfaction The conceptualization proposing that job satisfaction is a relatively stable disposition of an individual—that is, a characteristic that stays with people through situations. (192)

disruptive innovation A form of innovation that is so extreme in nature that it changes the market in which companies operate. (506)

distinctiveness In *Kelley's theory of causal attribution,* information regarding the extent to which a person behaves in the same manner in other contexts. (77)

distributive justice The form of organizational justice that focuses on people's beliefs that they have received fair amounts of valued work-related outcomes (e.g., pay, recognition, etc.). (38)

divergence hypothesis The approach to the study of management which recognizes that knowing how to manage most effectively requires clear understanding of the culture in which people work. (16)

divergent thinking The process of reframing familiar problems in unique ways. (496)

diversity management programs Programs in which employees are taught to celebrate the differences between people and in which organizations create supportive work environments for women and minorities. (186)

division of labor The practice of dividing work into specialized tasks that enable people to specialize in what they do best. (11, 521)

divisional structure The form used by many large organizations, in which separate autonomous units are created to deal with entire product lines, freeing top management to focus on larger scale, strategic decisions. (535)

dominant culture The distinctive, overarching "personality" of an organization. (484)

doomsday management The practice of introducing change by suggesting that an impending crisis is likely. (558)

downsizing The process of redesigning organizations so as to reduce the number of employees required to meet its objectives (also known as *rightsizing*). (20, 519)

downward communication Communication from people at higher organizational levels to those at lower organizational levels. (308)

drive theory of social facilitation The theory according to which the presence of others increases arousal, which increases people's tendencies to perform the dominant response. If that response is well learned, performance will improve. But if it is novel, performance will be impaired. (263)

e-mail (electronic mail) A system whereby people use personal computer terminals to send and receive messages between one another using the Internet. (304)

e-training Training based on disseminating information online, such as through the Internet or a company's internal intranet network. (96)

elder-care facilities Facilities at which employees at work can leave elderly relatives for whom they are responsible (such as parents and grandparents). (18)

emoticons (emotional icons) Symbols typed using characters such as commas, hyphens, and parentheses for purposes of expressing emotions in online communication. (305)

emotional contagion The tendency to mimic the emotional expressions of others, converging with them emotionally. (145)

emotional dissonance Inconsistencies between the emotions we feel and the emotions we express. (153)

emotional intelligence (EI) The ability to make accurate judgments of emotions and to use such knowledge to enhance the quality of one's thinking; skills involved include the ability to recognize and regulate our own emotions, to influence those of others, and to facilitate performance. (132)

emotional labor The psychological effort involved in holding back one's true emotions. (152)

emotional stability The tendency to see oneself as confident, secure, and steady (the opposite of *neuroticism,* one of the Big Five personality variables). (122)

emotions Overt reactions that express feelings about events. (145)

employee assistance programs (EAPs) Plans offered by employers that provide their employees with assistance for various personal problems (e.g., substance abuse, career planning, financial and legal problems). (167)

employee handbook A document describing to employees basic information about a company; a general reference regarding a company's background, the nature of its business, and its rules. (298)

employee surveys Questionnaires designed to assess how employees feel about their organizations. (325)

employee theft The taking of company property for personal use. (406)

employee withdrawal Actions, such as chronic absenteeism and voluntary turnover (i.e., quitting one's job), that enable employees to escape from adverse organizational situations. (195)

empowered decision making The practice of vesting power for making decisions in the hands of employees themselves. (341)

empowerment The passing of responsibility and authority from managers to lower-level employees. (423)

empowerment climate A relatively enduring atmosphere in the workplace that is supportive of empowerment. (425)

encoding The process by which an idea is transformed so that it can be transmitted to, and recognized by, a receiver (e.g., a written or spoken message). (293)

end-user innovation The form of innovation in which new ideas are inspired by the individuals who use a company's products. (506)

engagement A mutual commitment between employers and employees to do things to help one another achieve each other's goals and aspirations. (24)

episodic stressor The result of experiencing lots of acute stressors in a short period of time. (156)

equalizers People who are primarily interested in minimizing the differences between themselves and others. (388)

equitable payment The state in which one person's outcome to input ratios is equivalent to that of another person with whom this individual compares himself or herself. (226)

equity theory The theory stating that people strive to maintain ratios of their own outcomes (rewards) to their own inputs (contributions) that are equal to the outcome/input ratios of others with whom they compare themselves. (224)

escalation of commitment phenomenon The tendency for individuals to continue to support previously unsuccessful courses of action. (359)

ethical imperialism The belief that the ethical standards of one's own country should be imposed when doing business in other countries (the opposite of *ethical relativism*). (59)

ethical organizational culture Set of attitudes, behavioral norms, and expectations about what constitutes "doing the right thing" inside an organization. (495)

ethical relativism The belief that no culture's ethics are better than any other's and that there are no internationally acceptable standards of right and wrong (the opposite of *ethical imperialism*). (58)

ethics Standards of conduct that guide people's decisions and behavior (e.g., not stealing from others). (48)

ethics audit The practice of assessing an organization's ethical practices by actively investigating and documenting incidents of dubious ethical value, discussing them in an open and honest fashion, and developing a concrete plan to avoid such actions in the future. (56)

ethics committee A group composed of senior-level managers from various areas of an organization who assist an organization's CEO in making ethical decisions by developing and evaluating company-wide ethics policies. (57)

ethics hotlines (ethics helplines) Special telephone lines that employees can call to ask questions about ethical behavior and to report any ethical misdeeds they may have observed. (58)

ethics officer A high-ranking organizational official (e.g., the general counsel or vice president of ethics) who is expected to provide strategies for ensuring ethical conduct throughout an organization. (58)

ethnocentrism A bias toward one's own subgroup and against other subgroups. (283)

ethnorelativistic thinking Taking the perspective of another group and understanding how they see the world, including one's own group. (283)

evaluation apprehension The fear of being evaluated or judged by another person. (263)

evaluative component (of attitudes) Our liking or disliking of any particular person, item, or event. (178)

evening persons Individuals who feel most energetic and alert late in the day or at night. (129)

executive coaching A technique of leadership development that involves custom-tailored, one-on-one learning aimed at improving an individual leader's performance. (471)

executive training programs Sessions in which companies systematically attempt to develop their top leaders, either in specific skills or general managerial skills. (96)

expatriates (expats) People who are citizens of one country, but who live and work in another country. (14)

expectancy The belief that one's efforts will positively influence one's performance. (230)

expectancy theory The theory that asserts that motivation is based on people's beliefs about the probability that effort will lead to performance (*expectancy*), multiplied by the probability that performance will lead to reward (*instrumentality*), multiplied by the perceived value of the reward (*valence*). (230)

experimental method A research technique through which it is possible to determine cause–effect relationships between the variables of interest—that is, the extent to which one variable causes another. (594)

expert power The individual power base derived from an individual's recognized superior knowledge, skills or abilities in a certain area. (419)

exploitative mentality The belief that one's own immediate interests are more important than concern for others. (53)

external causes of behavior Explanations based on situations over which the individual has no control. (77)

extinction The process through which responses that are no longer reinforced tend to gradually diminish in strength. (92)

extraversion A tendency to seek stimulation and to enjoy the company of other people; one of the Big Five personality dimensions. (119)

fair process effect The tendency for people to better accept outcomes into which they have had some input in determining than when they have no such involvement. (43)

faultline A condition in which the key attributes of group members are correlated across group membership instead of cutting across group membership. (283)

Federal Sentencing Guidelines for Organizations Guidelines for federal judges to follow when imposing penalties on organizations (e.g., restitution, fines, etc.) found guilty of breaking federal laws. (50)

feedback (1) Knowledge about the impact of messages on receivers. (294) (2) Knowledge of the results of one's behavior. (98)

felt emotions The emotions people actually feel (which may differ from *displayed emotions*). (154)

final-offer arbitration A form of arbitration in which the arbitrator chooses between final offers made by the disputing parties themselves. (396)

first-impression error The tendency to base our judgments of others on our earlier impressions of them. (81)

first-order change Change that is continuous in nature and involves no major shifts in the way an organization operates. (558)

five-stage model of group formation The conceptualization claiming that groups develop in five stages—forming, storming, norming, performing, and adjourning. (255)

flextime programs Policies that give employees some discretion over when they can arrive and leave work, thereby making it easier to adapt their work schedules to the demands of their personal lives. (27)

flight response An automatic rapid escape from a dangerous situation. (157)

formal communication The sharing of messages regarding the official work of the organization. (307)

formal groups Groups that are created by the organization, intentionally designed to direct its members toward some organizational goal. (253)

formal status The prestige one has by virtue of his or her official position in an organization. (260)

framing The tendency for people to make different decisions based on how the problem is presented to them. (353)

friendship groups Informal groups that develop because their members are friends, often seeing each other outside of the organization. (253)

functional organization The type of departmentalization based on the activities or functions performed (e.g., sales, finance). (524)

fundamental attribution error The tendency to attribute others' actions to internal causes (e.g., their traits) while largely ignoring external factors that also may have influenced behavior. (79)

gain-sharing plans Incentive plans in which employees receive bonuses in proportion to their company's profitability. (206, 276)

gatekeepers People responsible for controlling the flow of information to others to keep them from becoming overloaded. (323)

generalized self-efficacy A person's beliefs about his or her capacity to perform specific tasks successfully. (122)

glass ceiling Invisible barriers that keep women from advancing as rapidly as men in certain fields. (183)

globalization The process of interconnecting the world's people with respect to the cultural, economic, political, technological, and environmental aspects of their lives. (13)

goal commitment The degree to which people accept and strive to attain goals. (219)

goal framing effect The tendency for people to be more strongly persuaded by information that is framed in negative terms than information that is framed in positive terms. (354)

goal setting The process of determining specific levels of performance for workers to attain and then striving to attain them. (218)

goal-setting theory A popular theory specifying that people are motivated to attain goals because doing so makes them feel successful. (219)

Golem effect A negative instance of the *self-fulfilling prophecy,* in which people holding low expectations of another tend to lower that individual's performance. (83)

grapevine An organization's unofficial channels of communication, through which informal information travels. (313)

great person theory The view that leaders possess special traits that set them apart from others, and that these traits are responsible for their assuming positions of power and authority. (450)

grid training A multistep process designed to cultivate within leaders a concern for people and a concern for production. (458)

group A collection of two or more interacting individuals who maintain stable patterns of relationships, share common goals, and perceive themselves as being a group. (251)

group decision support systems (GDSS) Interactive computer-based systems that combine communication, computer, and decision technologies to improve the effectiveness of group problem-solving meetings. (367)

group dynamics Factors governing a group's formation and development, structure, and interrelationships with individuals, other groups, and the organizations within which it exists. (251)

group structure The pattern of interrelationships between the individuals constituting a group; the guidelines of group behavior that make group functioning orderly and predictable. (257)

groupthink The tendency for members of highly cohesive groups to so strongly conform to group pressures regarding a certain decision that they fail to think critically, rejecting the potentially correcting influences of outsiders. (346)

group-value explanation (of organizational justice) The idea that people believe they are an important part of the organization when an organizational official takes the time to explain thoroughly to them the rationale behind a decision. (41)

growth need strength The personality variable describing the extent to which people have a high need for personal growth and development on the job. People who have high levels of growth need strength are most inclined to behave in accordance with the *job characteristics model.* (240)

guanxi In China, a person's network of personal and business connections. (470)

halo effect The tendency for our overall impressions of others to affect objective evaluations of their specific traits; perceiving high correlations between characteristics that may be unrelated. (79)

hangover effect The tendency for people's levels of satisfaction to drop over time from when a position is brand new to when one gains more experience with it. (196)

Hawthorne effect The tendency for people being studied to behave differently than they ordinarily would. (10)

Hawthorne studies The earliest systematic research in the field of OB, this work was performed to determine how the design of work environments affected performance. (9)

healthy organizational cultures Organizational cultures in which people feel that they are valued (opposite of toxic organizational cultures). (482)

heuristics Simple decision rules (rules of thumb) used to make quick decisions about complex problems. (See *availability heuristic* and *representativeness heuristic.*) (355)

hierarchy of authority The distinction between members of organizations with respect to the degree of authority they have; higher positions in an organization chart reflect higher degrees of formal authority. (518)

hierarchy culture In the competing values framework, a form of organizational culture in which organizations have an internal focus and emphasize stability and control. (485)

high-performance work systems Organizations that offer employees opportunities to participate in decision making, provide incentives for them to do so, and emphasize opportunities to develop skills. (200)

hindsight bias The tendency for people to perceive outcomes as more inevitable after they have occurred (i.e., in hindsight) than before they occurred (i.e., in foresight). (357)

Holland's hexagon A conceptualization specifying the occupations for which people are best suited based on which of six personality types most closely describe them. (603)

Holland's theory of vocational choice A theory that claims that people will perform best at occupations that match their traits and personalities. (603)

home-stretchers Rumors designed to reduce the degree of ambiguity in a situation by telling a story about something before it happens. (314)

honeymoon effect The tendency for people to enjoy high levels of satisfaction on new jobs that they have taken in response to dissatisfaction with their old jobs. (196)

honeymoon-hangover effect The tendency for the *honey-moon effect* to occur (i.e., for job satisfaction to increase as a dissatisfied person takes a new job) followed by the *hangover effect* (i.e., for the high levels of satisfaction associated with a new job to decline over time). (196)

horizontal stretch goals Stretch goals that challenge people to perform tasks that they have never done. (222)

hostile environment sexual harassment A form of sexual harassment in which individuals are subjected to negative, unwanted, or abusive conditions under which their ability to work effectively and comfortably is compromised. (432)

human relations movement A perspective on organizational behavior that rejects the primarily economic orientation of scientific management and recognizes, instead, the importance of social processes in work settings. (9)

HURIER model The conceptualization that describes effective listening as made up of the following six components: *h*earing, *u*nderstanding, *r*emembering, *i*nterpreting, *e*valuating, and *r*esponding. (322).

hypervigilance The state in which an individual frantically searches for quick solutions to problems, and goes from one idea to another out of a sense of desperation that one idea isn't working and that another needs to be considered before time runs out. (364)

hypotheses Logically derived, testable statements about the relationships between variables that follow from a theory. (590)

identification-based trust A form of trust based on accepting the wants and desires of another person. (380)

idiosyncratic work arrangements (i-deals) Uniquely customized agreements negotiated between individual employees and their employers with respect to employment terms benefiting each party. (28)

image theory A theory of decision making that recognizes that decisions are made in an automatic, intuitive fashion. According to the theory, people will adopt a course of action that best fits their individual principles, current goals, and plans for the future. (351)

implicit favorite One's preferred decision alternative, selected even before all options have been considered. (356)

impression management Efforts by individuals to improve how they appear to others. (86)

improvement teams Teams whose members are oriented primarily toward the mission of increasing the effectiveness of the processes used by the organization. (270)

incentive stock option (ISO) plans Corporate programs in which a company grants an employee the opportunity to purchase its stock at some future time at a specified price. (235)

incivility Demonstrating a lack of regard for others, denying them the respect they are due. (401)

inclusion Making people feel valued as worthwhile members of the organization. (186)

incremental innovation A slow-and-steady approach to innovation, in which companies exploit existing technology and operate under conditions in which uncertainty about the future is low. (506)

indecisiveness An individual difference variable reflecting the degree to which people approach decisions eagerly as opposed to wanting to put them off. (344)

independent variable A variable that is systematically manipulated by the experimenter so as to determine its effects on the behavior of interest (i.e., the *dependent variable*). (596)

individual differences The many ways in which individuals differ from each other. (110)

individualistic cultures National groups whose members place a high value on individual accomplishments and personal success. (266)

individualists People who care almost exclusively about maximizing their own gain and don't care whether others do better or worse than themselves. (388)

influence Attempts to affect another in a desired fashion, whether or not these are successful. (415)

informal communication The sharing of messages that are unrelated to the organization's official activities. (307).

informal communication network The informal connections between people; the pathways through which they share informal information. (312)

informal groups Groups that develop naturally among people, without any direction from the organization within which they operate. (253)

informal status The prestige accorded individuals with certain characteristics that are not formally recognized by the organization. (261)

informate The process by which workers manipulate objects by "inserting data" between themselves and those objects. (20)

information anxiety Pressure to store and process a great deal of information in our head and to keep up constantly with gathering it. (163)

information overload The feeling of being overwhelmed by more information than one can process. (304)

information power The extent to which a supervisor has power by virtue of the information available to him or her. (419)

informational justice People's perceptions of the fairness of the information used as the basis for making a decision. (41)

ingratiation The practice of cultivating someone's favor by agreeing with that individual. (437)

initiating structure (production centered) Activities by a leader designed to enhance productivity, having a task-oriented style. (457)

innovation The process of making changes to something already established by introducing something new; the successful implementation of creative ideas within an organization. (504)

innovation labs Physical facilities that are built specifically as venues for employees to use when attempting to develop innovative solutions. (508)

inputs People's contributions to their jobs, such as their experience, qualifications, or the amount of time worked. (225)

instant messaging The practice of communicating with another online by typing messages into boxes that pop up on the screen as needed. (305)

instrumental conditioning See *operant conditioning*. (91)

instrumentality An individual's beliefs regarding the likelihood of being rewarded in accord with his or her own level of performance. (230)

integrative agreement A type of solution to a conflict situation in which the parties consider joint benefits that go beyond a simple compromise. (395)

interactionist perspective The view that behavior is a result of a complex interplay between personality and situational factors. (112)

interest group A group of employees who come together to satisfy a common interest. (253)

internal causes of behavior Explanations based on actions for which the individual is responsible. (77)

interorganizational designs Plans by which two or more organizations come together. (543)

interpersonal behavior A variety of behaviors involving the ways in which people work with and against one another. (375)

interpersonal justice People's perceptions of the fairness of the manner in which they are treated by others (typically, authority figures). (41)

intranet A private Web site that can be accessed only by a company's employees. (298)

intraorganizational designs Designs that concentrate on the arrangement of units within one organization. (543)

intrinsic task motivation The motivation to do work because it is interesting, engaging, or challenging in a positive way. (497)

invalidating language Language that arouses negative feelings about one's self-worth. (326)

jargon The specialized language used by a particular group (e.g., people within a profession). (319)

job A predetermined set of activities one is expected to perform. (599)

job characteristics model An approach to job enrichment specifying that five core job dimensions (skill variety, task identity, task significance, autonomy, and job feedback) produce critical psychological states that lead to beneficial outcomes for individuals (e.g., high job satisfaction) and the organization (e.g., reduced turnover). (238)

job design An approach to motivation suggesting that jobs can be created so as to enhance people's interest in doing them. See *job enlargement, job enrichment,* and *the job characteristics model.* (236)

job enlargement The practice of expanding the content of a job to include more variety and a greater number of tasks at the same level. (236)

job enrichment The practice of giving employees a high degree of control over their work, from planning and organization, through implementing the jobs and evaluating the results. (237)

job satisfaction Positive or negative attitudes held by individuals toward their jobs. (190)

job sharing A form of regular part-time work in which two or more employees assume the duties of a single job, splitting its responsibilities, salary, and benefits in proportion to the time worked. (29)

joint ventures Strategic alliances in which several companies work together to fulfill opportunities that require one another's capabilities. (545)

Kelley's theory of causal attribution The approach suggesting that people will believe others' actions to be caused by internal or external factors based on three types of information: *consensus, consistency,* and *distinctiveness.* (77)

Kohlberg's theory of cognitive moral development The theory based on the idea that people develop over the years in their capacity to understand what is right and wrong. (52)

lateral communication Communication between individuals at the same organizational level. (310)

Law of Effect The tendency for behaviors leading to desirable consequences to be strengthened and those leading to undesirable consequences to be weakened. (91)

leader An individual within a group or an organization who wields the most influence over others. (447)

leader match The practice of matching leaders (based on their LPC scores) to the groups whose situations best match those in which they are expected to be most effective (according to LPC contingency theory). (464)

leader-member exchange (LMX) model A theory suggesting that leaders form different relations with various subordinates and that the nature of such dyadic exchanges can exert strong effects on subordinates' performance and satisfaction. (459)

leadership The process whereby one individual influences other group members toward the attainment of defined group or organizational goals. (447)

leadership development The practice of systematically training people to expand their capacity to function effectively in leadership roles. (468)

leadership motivation The desire to influence others, especially toward the attainment of shared goals. (451)

learning A relatively permanent change in behavior occurring as a result of experience. (91)

learning goal orientation The desire to perform well because it satisfies an interest in meeting a challenge and learning new skills. (127)

learning organization An organization that is successful at acquiring, cultivating, and applying knowledge that can be used to help it adapt to changes. (574)

legitimate power The individual power base derived from one's position in an organizational hierarchy; the accepted authority of one's position. (418)

line positions Positions in an organization in which people can make decisions related to doing basic work. (522)

linear career The type of career in which someone stays in a certain field and works his or her way up the occupational ladder, from low-level jobs to high-level jobs. (601)

locus of control The extent to which individuals feel that they are able to control things in a manner that affects them. (122)

LPC Short for "esteem for least preferred coworker"—a personality variable distinguishing between individuals with respect to their concern for people (high LPC) and their concern for production (low LPC). (463)

LPC contingency theory A theory suggesting that leader effectiveness is determined both by characteristics of leaders (their *LPC* scores) and by the level of situational control they are able to exert over subordinates. (463)

Machiavellianism A personality trait involving willingness to manipulate others for one's own purposes. (124)

machine bureaucracy An organizational form in which work is highly specialized, decision making is concentrated at the top, and the work environment is not prone to change (e.g., a government office). (535)

Madison Avenue mentality A way of viewing the world according to which people are more concerned about how things appear to others than how they really are—that is, the appearance of doing the right thing matters more than the actual behavior. (53)

management by objectives (MBO) The technique by which managers and their subordinates work together to set, and then strive to attain organizational goals. (576)

manufacturer innovation The traditional form of innovation in which an individual or organization develops an innovation for the purpose of selling it. (506)

market culture In the competing values framework, a form of organizational culture in which organizations are concerned with stability and control, and are external in their orientation. (486)

matrix organization The type of organization in which a product or project form is superimposed on a functional form. (527)

mechanistic organization An internal organizational structure that is stable in nature, where people perform jobs that do not change much over the years. (532)

media richness theory A conceptualization specifying that the effectiveness of any verbal medium depends on the extent to which it is appropriate for ambiguity of the message being sent. (299)

mediation The process in which a neutral party (known as a *mediator*) works together with two or more parties sides to reach a settlement to their conflict. (395)

meditation The process of learning to clear one's mind of external thoughts, often by repeating slowly and rhythmically a single syllable (known as a mantra). (168)

member assistance programs (MAPs) Plans offered by trade unions that provide their members with assistance for various personal problems (e.g., substance abuse, career planning, financial and legal problems). (167)

mentor A more experienced employee who guides a newer employee (see *protégé*) in learning about the job and organization. (611)

mentoring The process by which a more experienced employee (see *mentor*) advises, counsels, and otherwise enhances the professional development of a new employee (see *protégé*). (611)

middle line In Mintzberg's framework, managers who transfer information between the strategic apex and the operating core. (See *strategic apex* and *operating core*.) (533)

mission statement A document describing an organization's overall direction and general goals. (508)

mixed motives Contexts in which people have reasons both to cooperate and to compete. (387)

modular (networked) organizations Businesses that outsource noncore functions to other companies while focusing on their own core business. (543)

mood An unfocused, relatively mild feeling that exists as background to our daily experiences. (147)

mood congruence The tendency to recall positive things when you are in a good mood and to recall negative things when you are in a bad mood. (151)

moral values (morals) People's fundamental beliefs regarding what is right or wrong, good or bad. (48)

morning persons Individuals who feel most energetic and alert early in the day. (129)

motivating potential score (MPS) A mathematical index describing the degree to which a job is designed so as to motivate people, as suggested by the *job characteristics model*. It is computed on the basis of a questionnaire known as the Job Diagnostic Survey (JDS). The lower the MPS, the more the job may stand to benefit from redesign. (240)

motivation The set of processes that arouse, direct, and maintain human behavior toward attaining some goal. (214)

motivational fit approach The framework stipulating that motivation is enhanced by a good fit between the traits and skills of individuals and the requirements of the jobs they perform in their organizations. (216)

multifoci approach to justice A conceptualization of organizational justice recognizing that people take into account both individuals and larger units when assessing fairness. (38)

multinational enterprises (MNEs) Organizations that have significant operations spread throughout various nations but are headquartered in a single nation. (14)

multiple domains of intelligence Intelligence as measured in several different ways, such as cognitive intelligence (traditional measures of the ability to integrate and interpret information), emotional intelligence (the ability to be sensitive to one's own and others' emotions), and cultural intelligence (awareness of cultural differences between people). (451)

multiple regression A statistical technique through which it is possible to determine the extent to which each of several different variables contributes to predicting another variable (typically, where the variable being predicted is the behavior in question). (593)

MUM effect The reluctance to transmit bad news, shown either by not transmitting the message at all, or by delegating the task to someone else. (309)

mutual service consortia A type of strategic alliance in which two similar companies from the same or similar industries pool their resources to receive a benefit that would be too difficult or expensive for either to obtain alone. (544)

naturalistic observation A research technique in which people are systematically observed in situations of interest to the researcher. (598)

needs Forces that motivate people to satisfy states that they inherently require for biological and/or social reasons. (231)

negative affectivity The tendency to experience negative moods in a wide range of settings and under many different conditions. (121)

negative correlation A relationship between two variables such that more of one variable is associated with less of the other. (593)

negative reinforcement The process by which people learn to perform acts that lead to the removal of undesired events. (92)

neoclassical organizational theory An attempt to improve upon the classical organizational theory, claiming that economic effectiveness is not the only goal of organizational structure, but also employee satisfaction. (530)

networking A leadership development tool designed to help people make connections to others to whom they can turn for information and problem solving. (469)

neuroticism A tendency to experience unpleasant emotions easily; one of the Big Five personality dimensions. (119)

newsletters Regularly published internal documents, either hard copy or electronic in nature, describing information of interest to employees regarding an array of business and nonbusiness issues affecting them. (298)

noise Factors capable of distorting the clarity of messages at any point during the communication process. (294)

nominal group technique (NGT) A technique for improving group decisions in which small groups of individuals systematically present and discuss their ideas before privately voting on their preferred solution. The most preferred solution is accepted as the group's decision. (365)

nonpreferential affirmative action Efforts to get companies to conduct ongoing, conscious appraisals of their rules and procedures and to eliminate those that exclude women and members of minority groups without sufficient justification. (186)

nonprogrammed decisions Decisions made about a highly novel problem for which there is no prespecified course of action. (337)

nonsubstitutable The degree to which an organizational unit is the only one that can perform its particular duties. (430)

nonverbal communication The transmission of messages without the use of words (e.g., by gestures, the use of space). (297)

normative commitment The strength of a person's desire to continue working for an organization because he or she feels obligations from others to remain there. (202)

norms Generally agreed-upon informal rules that guide group members' behavior. (259)

objective tests Questionnaires and inventories designed to measure various aspects of personality. (115)

observational learning (modeling) The form of learning in which people acquire new behaviors by systematically observing the rewards and punishments given to others. (93)

obstructionism Attempts to impede another's job performance. (402)

OCB-I Acts of organizational citizenship directed at other individuals in the workplace (i.e., helping coworkers in ways that go beyond what is expected). (383)

OCB-O Acts of organizational citizenship directed at the organization itself (i.e., helping the company in ways that go beyond what is expected). (383)

occupation A coherent set of jobs. (599)

offshoring Short for *offshore outsourcing*, the practice of using outsourcing services of overseas companies. (564)

old boys' network A gender-segregated informal communication network composed of men with similar backgrounds. (312)

online surveys Questionnaires presented to people either via e-mail or on a Web site that are completed and returned to administrators by using the same electronic means. (591)

open systems Self-sustaining systems that transform input from the external environment into output, which the system then returns to the environment. (7)

openness to experience Personality variable that reflects the degree to which people are interested in things that are new and different and get excited by new ideas. (119, 499)

operant conditioning The form of learning in which people associate the consequences of their actions with the actions themselves. Behaviors with positive consequences are acquired; behaviors with negative consequences are avoided. (91)

operating core In Mintzberg's framework, employees who perform the basic work related to an organization's product or service. (533)

organic organization An internal organizational structure that changes frequently, making it likely that people will have to alter the nature of the jobs they perform over the years. (532)

organization A structured social system consisting of groups and individuals working together to meet some agreed-upon objectives. (3)

organization chart A diagram showing the formal structure of an organization, indicating who is to communicate with whom. (307)

organizational behavior (OB) The field that seeks to understand individual, group and organizational processes in the workplace. (3)

organizational behavior management (OB Mod) The practice of altering behavior in organizations by systematically administering rewards. (100)

organizational change Planned or unplanned transformations in an organization's structure, technology, and/or people. (554)

organizational citizenship behavior (OCB) An informal form of behavior in which people go beyond what is formally expected of them to contribute to the well-being of their organization and those in it. (383)

organizational commitment The extent to which an individual identifies and is involved with his or her organization and/or is unwilling to leave it (see *affective commitment, continuance commitment,* and *normative commitment*). (201)

organizational culture A cognitive framework consisting of attitudes, values, behavioral norms, and expectations shared by organization members; a set of basic assumptions shared by members of an organization. (481)

organizational demography The nature of the composition of a workforce with respect to various characteristics (e.g., age, gender, ethnic makeup, etc.). (179)

organizational design The process of coordinating the structural elements of organizations in the most appropriate manner. (529)

organizational development (OD) A set of social science techniques designed to plan change in work settings, for purposes of enhancing the personal development of individuals and improving the effectiveness of organizational functioning. (575)

organizational justice The study of people's perceptions of fairness in organizations. (37)

organizational memory Information from an organization's history that is stored through the recollections of events and their shared interpretations by key individuals in the organization who pass it along to others. (488)

organizational politics Unauthorized uses of power that enhance or protect one's own or one's group's personal interests. (435)

organizational structure The formally prescribed pattern of connections between the various units of an organization—reflecting, for example, reporting relationships, formal communication channels. (307, 518)

outcomes The rewards employees receive from their jobs, such as salary and recognition. (224)

outplacement programs Systematic efforts to find new jobs for employees who are laid off. (608)

outsourcing The process of eliminating those parts of organizations that focus on noncore sectors of the business (i.e., tasks that are peripheral to the organization), and hiring outside firms to perform these functions instead. (20, 564)

overload The condition in which a unit of an organization becomes overburdened with too much incoming information. (323)

overpayment inequity The condition, resulting in feelings of guilt, in which the ratio of one's outcomes to inputs is more than the corresponding ratio of another person with whom that person compares himself or herself. (225)

overt aggression Acts that are outwardly intended to harm other people or organizations. (402)

participant observation A qualitative research technique in which people systematically make observations of what goes on in a setting by becoming an insider, part of that setting itself. (598)

participation Active involvement in the process of learning; more active participation leads to more effective learning. (97)

participative leadership style A style of leadership in which a leader solicits opinions from subordinates before making decisions. (455).

path-goal theory A theory of leadership suggesting that subordinates will be motivated by a leader only to the extent they perceive this individual as helping them to attain valued goals. (466)

pay-for-performance A payment system in which employees are paid differentially, based on the quantity and quality of their performance. Pay-for-performance plans strengthen *instrumentality* beliefs. (234)

perceptual biases Predispositions that people have to misperceive others in various ways. (79)

performance appraisal The process of evaluating employees on various work-related dimensions. (89)

performance goal orientation The desire to perform well to demonstrate one's competence to others. (127)

person sensitivity bias The tendency for people to give too little credit to others when things are going poorly and too much credit when things are going well. (358)

person-job fit The extent to which the traits and abilities of individuals match the requirements of the jobs they must perform. (112, 603)

personal identity The characteristics that define a particular individual. (73)

personal power The power that one derives because of one's individual qualities or characteristics. (419)

personal support policies Widely varied practices that help employees meet the demands of their family lives, freeing them to concentrate on their work. (18)

personality The unique and relatively stable pattern of behavior, thoughts, and emotions shown by individuals. (111)

personalized power motivation The desire to dominate others. (451)

physical abilities People's capacities to engage in the physical tasks required to perform a job. (134)

pipe dreams Types of rumor that express people's wishes. (314)

podcast A prerecorded message distributed for playback on an MP3 player, such as Apple's iPod (i.e., an iPod broadcast). (303)

position power Power based on one's formal position in an organization. (417)

positive affectivity The tendency to experience positive moods and feelings in a wide range of settings and under many different conditions. (121)

positive correlation A relationship between two variables such that more of one variable is associated with more of the other. (592)

positive reinforcement The process by which people learn to perform behaviors that lead to the presentation of desired outcomes. (92)

postconventional level of moral reasoning In Kohlberg's theory of cognitive moral development, the level at which people judge what is right and wrong not solely in terms of their interpersonal and societal obligations, but in terms of complex philosophical principles of duty, justice, and rights. (53)

power The capacity to exert influence over others. (418)

practical intelligence Adeptness at solving the practical problems of everyday life. (131)

preconventional level of moral reasoning In Kohlberg's theory of cognitive moral development, the level at which people (e.g., young children and some adults) haven't yet developed the capacity to assume the perspective of others, leading them to interpret what is right solely with respect to themselves. (52)

predecision A decision about what process to follow in making a decision. (335)

predictive validity The extent to which the score achieved on a test administered to a person at one time predicts (i.e., is correlated with) some measure of his or her performance at some later time. (116)

preferential affirmative action The practice of hiring women and members of minority groups in proportion to their representation in the population near organizations. (186)

prejudice Negative attitudes toward the members of specific groups, based solely on the fact that they are members of those groups (e.g., based on age, race, ethnicity, sexual orientation). (179)

prescriptive norms Expectations within groups regarding what is supposed to be done. (259)

presenteeism The practice of showing up for work but being too sick to be able to work effectively. (167)

principles of learning The set of practices that make training effective, participation, repetition, transfer of training, and feedback. (See *transfer of training*.) (97)

procedural justice People's perceptions of the fairness of the procedures used to determine the outcomes they receive. (39)

process conflict A form of conflict resulting from differences of opinion regarding how work groups are going to operate, such as how various duties and resources will be allocated and with whom various responsibilities will reside. (391)

product organization The type of departmentalization based on the products (or product lines) produced. (526)

productive forgetting The ability to abandon unproductive ideas and temporarily put aside stubborn problems until new approaches can be considered. (497)

professional bureaucracy Organizations (e.g., hospitals and universities) in which there are lots of rules to follow, but employees are highly skilled and free to make decisions on their own. (535)

programmed decisions Highly routine decisions made according to preestablished organizational routines and procedures. (337)

progressive discipline The practice of gradually increasing the severity of punishments for employees who exhibit unacceptable job behavior. (101)

prosocial behavior The tendency for people to help others on the job, even when they will not personally benefit from assisting. (375)

proscriptive norms Expectations within groups regarding behaviors in which members are not supposed to engage. (259)

protégé An inexperienced employee who receives assistance from a more experienced employee (see *mentor*). (611)

psychological contract A person's beliefs about what is expected of another in a relationship. (376)

punctuated-equilibrium model The conceptualization of group development claiming that groups generally plan their activities during the first half of their time together, and then revise and implement their plans in the second half. (256)

punishment Decreasing undesirable behavior by following it with undesirable consequences. (92)

Pygmalion effect A positive instance of the *self-fulfilling prophecy,* in which people holding high expectations of another tend to improve that individual's performance. (82)

pyramid of corporate social responsibility The term used to describe an organization's four most basic forms of responsibility, in order from economic responsibility, to legal responsibility, to ethical responsibility, to philanthropic (i.e., charitable) responsibility. (61)

qualitative research A nonempirical type of research that relies on preserving the natural qualities of the situation being studied. (597)

quality circles (QCs) An approach to improving the quality of work life, in which small groups of volunteers meet regularly to identify and solve problems related to the work they perform and the conditions under which they work. (580)

quality of work life (QWL) Programs An OD technique designed to improve organizational functioning by humanizing the workplace, making it more democratic, and involving employees in decision making. (579)

queuing Lining up incoming information so it can be managed in an orderly fashion. (323)

quid pro quo sexual harassment A form of sexual harassment in which the harasser requires sexual favors in exchange for some tangible conditions, privileges, or terms of employment from a victim. (432)

radical innovation A form of innovation in which companies make quantum leaps; involves exploring new technology and operating under highly uncertain conditions. (506)

rational decisions Decisions that maximize the chance of attaining an individual's, group's, or organization's goals. (349)

rational-economic model The model of decision making according to which decision makers consider all possible alternatives to problems before selecting the optimal solution. (349)

rebound effect The tendency to think about something when you try intentionally not to think about it. (87)

reciprocity The tendency to treat others as they have treated us. (388)

recruitment ads Written documents prepared for the purpose of sharing information about the organization for purposes of soliciting new employees. (298)

referent power The individual power base derived from the degree to which one is liked and admired by others. (419)

relational contract A variety of psychological contract in which the parties have a long-term and widely defined relationship with a vast focus. (378)

relations-oriented role (socioemotional role) The activities of an individual in a group who is supportive and nurturing of other group members and who helps them feel goal. (259)

reliability The extent to which a test yields consistent scores on various occasions, and the extent to which all of its items measure the same underlying construct. (115)

religious intolerance Actions (e.g., personal ridicule, vandalism) taken against persons or groups based on their faith. (185)

repatriation The process of readjusting to one's own culture after spending time away from it. (14)

repetition The process of repeatedly performing a task so that it may be learned. (97)

reporting relationships Formal connections between people indicating who must answer to whom in an organization. (308)

representativeness heuristic The tendency to perceive others in stereotypical ways if they appear to be typical representatives of the category to which they belong. (355)

resiliency The extent to which one is able to "bounce back" from potentially stressful situations without being harmed by them. (158)

resistance to change The tendency for employees to be unwilling to go along with organizational changes, based on some combination of individual and organizational barriers. (568)

resource-dependency model The view that power resides within subunits that are able to control the greatest share of valued organizational resources. (427)

retirement The phase of people's lives in which they reach the end of their careers and stop working for their primary income. (610)

reward power The individual power base derived from an individual's capacity to administer valued rewards to others. (418)

rightsizing See *downsizing.* (20)

risky choice framing effect The tendency for people to avoid risks when situations are presented in a way that emphasizes positive gains, and to take risks when situations are presented in a way that emphasizes potential losses that may be suffered. (353)

role The typical behavior that characterizes a person in a specific social context. (257)

role ambiguity Confusion arising from uncertainty regarding exactly what one is expected to do as a role incumbent. (162, 258)

role conflict Incompatibilities between the various sets of obligations people face. (161)

role differentiation The tendency for various specialized roles to emerge as groups develop. (258)

role expectations The behaviors expected of someone in a particular role. (257)

role incumbent A person holding a particular role. (257)

role juggling The need to switch back and forth between the demands of work and family. (161)

RSS feed Information, usually news, delivered to Web sites on a real-time basis, as events occur. (303)

rumors Information with little basis in fact, often transmitted through informal channels. (See *grapevine.*) (314)

Sarbanes-Oxley Act (SOX) A law enacted to guard against future accounting scandals (such as occurred at Enron), by initiating reforms in the standards by which public companies report accounting data. (51)

satisficing decisions Decisions made by selecting the first minimally acceptable alternative as it becomes available. (350)

say-do matrix A way of differentiating systematically with respect to consistencies and inconsistencies in what people say and what they do. (320)

scapegoat Someone who is made to take the blame for someone else's failure or wrongdoing. (436)

scientific management An early approach to management and organizational behavior emphasizing the importance of designing jobs as efficiently as possible. (9)

scientific method The systematic process of gathering and assessing information that identifies and helps explain the relationships between variables. (588)

second-order change Radical change; major shifts involving many different levels of the organization and many different aspects of business. (558)

selective perception The tendency to focus on some aspects of the environment while ignoring others. (81)

self-conscious emotions Feelings that stem from within, such as shame, guilt, embarrassment, and pride. (146)

self-efficacy One's belief about having the capacity to perform a task. (219)

self-esteem The overall value one places on oneself as a person. (122)

self-fulfilling prophecy The tendency for someone's expectations about another to cause that person to behave in a manner consistent with those expectations. This can be either positive (see the *Pygmalion effect*) or negative (see the *Golem effect*) in nature. (81)

self-managed work teams (self-directed teams) Teams whose members are permitted to make key decisions about how their work is done. (270)

self-oriented role The activities of an individual in a group who focuses on his or her own good, often at the expense of others. (259)

semi-autonomous work groups Work groups in which employees get to share in the responsibility for decisions with their bosses and are jointly accountable for their work outcomes. (270)

sex-role stereotypes Narrow-minded beliefs about the qualities of women and men and the kinds of tasks for which each is most appropriately suited. (183)

sexual harassment Unwelcome sexual advances, requests for sexual favors, or other verbal or physical conduct of a sexual nature. (161, 431)

shared mental models The common understanding that develops between team members regarding how their team operates, including how people are expected to work together and what each particular person is expected to do at any given time. (268)

short-term successors Individuals who are considered suitable candidates, at least temporarily, to fill the position of someone who leaves his or her job unexpectedly. (611)

similar-to-me effect The tendency for people to perceive in a positive light others who are believed to be similar to themselves in any of several different ways. (80)

simple structure An organization characterized as being small and informal, with a single powerful individual, often the founding entrepreneur, who is in charge of everything. (535)

situational leadership theory A theory suggesting that the most effective style of leadership—either delegating, participating, selling, or telling—depends on the extent to which followers require guidance and direction, and emotional support. (465)

skill-based pay Paying employees not only on the basis of how well they perform but on the breadth of their skills as well. (278)

skills Dexterity at performing specific tasks, which has been acquired through training or experience. (130)

skip-level meetings Gatherings of employees with corporate superiors who are more than one level higher than themselves in an organizational hierarchy. (325)

snowball effect The tendency for people to share informal information with others with whom they come into contact. (312)

social chameleons Individuals who do whatever it takes to get others to like them. (437)

social dilemmas Situations in which each person can increase his or her individual gains by acting in a purely selfish manner, but if others also act selfishly, the outcomes experienced by all are reduced. (387)

social emotions People's feelings based on information external to themselves, such as pity, envy, jealousy, and scorn. (147)

social facilitation The tendency for the presence of others sometimes to enhance an individual's performance and at other times to impair it. (263)

social identity Who a person is, as defined in terms of his or her membership in various social groups. (73)

social identity theory A conceptualization recognizing that the way we perceive others and ourselves is based on both our unique characteristics (see *personal identity*) and our membership in various groups (see *social identity*). (73)

social impact theory The theory that explains social loafing in terms of the diffused responsibility for doing what is expected of each member of a group (see *social loafing*). The larger the size of a group, the less each member is influenced by the social forces acting on the group. (265)

social information processing model A conceptualization specifying that people adopt attitudes and behaviors in keeping with the cues provided by others with whom they come into contact. (194)

social loafing The tendency for group members to exert less individual effort on an additive task as the size of the group increases. (264)

social perception The process of combining, integrating, and interpreting information about others to gain an accurate understanding of them. (73)

social skills The capacity to interact effectively with others. (135)

social support The friendship and support of others, which help minimize reactions to stress. (163)

socialized power motivation Leaders' interest in cooperating with others, developing networks and coalitions, and generally working with subordinates rather than trying to control them. (451)

spam Unsolicited commercial e-mail messages. (294)

span of control The number of subordinates in an organization who are supervised by managers. (520)

spinoff An entirely new company that is separate from the original parent organization, one with its own identity, a new board of directors, and a different management team. (546)

spiral career The kind of career in which people evolve through a series of occupations, each of which requires new skills and that builds upon existing knowledge and skills. (602)

staff positions Positions in organizations in which people make recommendations to others, but are not themselves involved in making decisions concerning the organization's day-to-day operations. (522)

spam Uncolicited commercial e-mail messages. (294)

stakeholder Any individual or group in whose interest an organization is run. (566)

standing committees Committees that are permanent, existing over time. (253)

statements of principle Explicitly written statements describing the principle beliefs that guide an organization, helping to reinforce it's culture. (492)

status The relative prestige, social position, or rank given to groups or individuals by others. (260)

status symbols Objects reflecting the position of any individual within an organization's hierarchy of power. (260)

steady-state career The type of career in which there is a lifetime of employment in a single occupation. (600)

stepladder technique A technique for improving the quality of group decisions that minimizes the tendency for group members to be unwilling to present their ideas by adding new members to a group one at a time and requiring each to present his or her ideas independently to a group that already has discussed the problem at hand. (366)

stereotype A belief that all members of specific groups share certain traits and are prone to behave similarly as a result. (84, 180)

stereotype threat The uncomfortable feeling that people have when they run the risk of fulfilling a negative stereotype associated with a group to which they belong. (85)

stonewalling The practice of willingly hiding relevant information by being secretive and deceitful, which

occurs when organizations punish individuals who are open and honest and reward those who go along with unethical behavior. (54)

straightforwardness The tendency for people to behave in ways that are frank, sincere, and candid in their dealings with others. (422)

strain Deviations from normal states of human functioning resulting from prolonged exposure to stressful events. (158)

strategic alliance A type of organizational design in which two or more separate companies combine forces to develop and operate a specific business. (See *mutual service consortia, joint ventures*, and *value-chain partnerships*.) (544)

strategic apex In Mintzberg's framework, top-level executives responsible for running an entire organization. (533)

strategic communication The practice of presenting information about the company to broad, external audiences, such as the press. (311)

strategic contingencies model A view explaining power in terms of a subunit's capacity to control the activities of other subunits. A subunit's power is enhanced when (1) it can reduce the level of uncertainty experienced by other subunits, (2) it occupies a central position in the organization, and (3) its activities are nonsubstitutable. (430)

strategic decisions Nonprogrammed decisions typically made by high-level executives regarding the direction their organization should take to achieve its mission. (338)

strategic planning The process of formulating, implementing, and evaluating decisions that enable an organization to achieve its objectives. (562)

strategy Particular objectives a company has for the future and how it plans to focus its business activities so as to create and sustain value. (539)

stress The pattern of emotional and physiological reactions occurring in response to demands from within or outside an organization. See *stressor*. (156)

stress management programs Systematic efforts to train employees in a variety of techniques that they can use to become less adversely affected by stress. (167)

stressor Any demands, either physical or psychological in nature, encountered during the course of living. (156)

stretch goals Goals that are so difficult that they challenge people to rethink the way they work. (222)

strike The practice in which workers engage in a systematic stoppage of work designed as protest against one or more organizations believed to have treated them unfavorably. (229)

strong culture An organization in which there is widespread agreement with respect to the core elements of culture, making it possible for culture to exert major influences on the way people behave. (484)

structural inertia The organizational forces acting on employees, encouraging them to perform their jobs in certain ways, thereby making them resistant to change. (569)

subcultures Cultures existing within parts of organizations rather than entirely through them. (484)

substantive conflict A form of conflict that occurs when people have different viewpoints and opinions with respect to a decision they are making with others. (391)

succession planning A person's systematic attempt to identify possible holders of particular positions ahead of time as preparation for his or her departure. (611)

suggestion systems Formal mechanisms through which employees can present ideas to their companies. (324)

support for creativity The degree to which people believe that others in their workplaces are supportive of their efforts to come up with novel ideas. (500)

support staff In Mintzberg's framework, individuals who provide indirect support services to an organization. (534)

supportive communication Any communication that is accurate and honest, and that builds and enhances relationships instead of jeopardizing them. (325)

surveys Questionnaires in which people are asked to report how they feel about various aspects of themselves, their jobs, and organizations. (591)

survey feedback An OD technique in which questionnaires and interviews are used to collect information about issues of concern to an organization. This information is used the basis for planning organizational change. (577)

sustaining innovation A form of innovation that is incremental in nature; innovation that allows companies to approach their markets in the same manner as they have done in the past. (505)

swift trust Trust that occurs as a set of collective perceptions develops among members of temporary groups. (381)

symbols Material objects that connote meanings that extend beyond their intrinsic content. (490)

synchronous communication techniques Forms of communication in which the parties can send and receive messages at the same time. (303)

task force See *ad hoc committee*. (253)

task group A formal organizational group formed around some specific task. (253)

task-oriented role The activities of an individual in a group who, more than anyone else, helps the group reach its goal. (258)

team A group whose members have complementary skills and are committed to a common purpose or set of performance goals for which they hold themselves mutually accountable. (267)

team-based organizations Organizations in which autonomous work teams are organized in parallel fashion such that each performs many different steps in the work process. (537)

team building Formal efforts directed toward making teams more effective. (279)

team halo effect The tendency for people to credit teams for their successes but not to hold them accountable for their failures. (80)

technostructure In Mintzberg's framework, organizational specialists responsible for standardizing various aspects of an organization's activities. (534)

telecommuting (teleworking) The practice of using communications technology to perform work from remote locations, such as one's home. (21)

theory A set of statements about the interrelationships between concepts that allows us to predict and explain various processes and events. (589)

Theory X A traditional philosophy of management suggesting that most people are lazy and irresponsible, and will work hard only when forced to do so. (5)

Theory Y A philosophy of management suggesting that under the right circumstances, people are fully capable of working productively and accepting responsibility for their work. (6)

time-and-motion study A type of applied research designed to classify and streamline the individual movements needed to perform jobs with the intent of finding "the one best way" to perform them. (9)

time management The practice of taking control over how we spend time. (168)

time-out A brief delay in activities designed to reduce mounting tension. (170)

top-down decision making The practice of vesting decision-making power in the hands of superiors as opposed to lower-level employees. (341)

toxic organizational cultures Organizational cultures in which people feel that they are not valued (opposite of healthy organizational cultures). (482)

training The process of systematically teaching employees to acquire and improve job-related skills and knowledge. (94)

transactional contract A variety of psychological contract in which the parties have a brief and narrowly defined relationship that is primarily economic in focus. (377)

transfer of training The degree to which the skills learned during training sessions may be applied to performance of one's job. (98)

transformational leaders People who do things to revitalize and transform organizations or society. (452)

transitory career The type of career in which someone moves between many different unrelated positions, spending about one to four years in each. (602)

transparency The practice of making information about pay available openly instead of keeping it secret. (230)

triple bottom-line The contemporary notion that in addition to focusing on an organization's financial performance, officials also are interested in assur-ing that their companies are performing well with respect to promoting environmental quality and social justice. (57)

trust A person's degree of confidence in the words and actions of another. (379)

two-dimensional model of subordinate participation An approach to leadership that distinguishes between leaders who are *directive* or *permissive* toward subordinates, and the extent to which they are *participative* or *autocratic* in their decision making. (455)

uncertainty Lack of knowledge about the likelihood of certain events occurring in the future. (430)

unconflicted adherence The tendency for decision makers to stick to the first idea that comes to their minds without more deeply evaluating the consequences. (364)

unconflicted change The tendency for people to quickly change their minds and to adopt the first new idea to come along. (364)

underpayment inequity The condition, resulting in feelings of anger, in which the ratio of one's outcomes to inputs is less than the corresponding ratio of another person with whom one compares himself or herself. (225)

unfolding model of voluntary turnover A conceptualization that explains the cognitive processes through which people make decisions about quitting or staying on their jobs. (197)

unplanned changes Shifts in organizational activities due to forces that are external in nature, those beyond the organization's control. (558)

upward communication Communication from people at lower organizational levels to those at higher organizational levels. (309)

valence The value a person places on the rewards he or she expects to receive from an organization. (230)

validating language Language that makes people feel recognized and accepted for who they are. (326)

validity The extent to which a test actually measures what it claims to measure. (115)

value-chain partnerships Strategic alliances between companies in different industries that have complementary capabilities. (545)

value theory of job satisfaction A theory suggesting that job satisfaction depends primarily on the match between the outcomes individuals value in their jobs and their perceptions about the availability of such outcomes. (193)

verbal communication The transmission of messages using words, either written or spoken. (296)

verbal media Forms of communication involving the use of words (e.g., telephone messages, faxes, books, etc.). (297)

vertical integration The practice in which companies own their own suppliers and/or their own customers who purchase their products from them. (536)

vertical stretch goals Stretch goals that challenge people to achieve higher levels of success in current activities. (222)

video-mediated communication (VMC) Conferences in which people can hear and see each other using computers. (303)

virtual organization (a) A highly flexible, temporary organization formed by a group of companies that join forces to exploit a specific opportunity. (21)

virtual organizations (b) Organizations composed of a continually evolving network of companies linked together to share skills, costs, and access to markets. They form a partnership to capitalize on their existing talents, pursuing common objectives. (544)

virtual teams Teams that operate across space, time, and organizational boundaries, communicating with each other only through electronic technology. (273)

virtuous circle The tendency for companies that are successful financially to invest in social causes because they can afford to do so (i.e., they "do good by doing well") and for socially responsible companies to perform well financially (i.e., they "do well by doing good"). (64)

voluntary arbitration A form of arbitration in which the two sides retain the freedom to reject the agreement recommended by an arbitrator. (396)

voluntary reduced work time (V-time) programs Programs that allow employees to reduce the amount of time they work by a certain amount (typically 10 or 20 percent), with a proportional reduction in pay. (29)

voluntary turnover A form of employee withdrawal in which an individual resigns freely from his or her job. (195)

weak culture An organization in which there is limited agreement with respect to the core elements of culture, giving culture little influence on the way people behave. (484)

wedge drivers Rumors in which people intentionally say malicious things about someone with the intent of damaging that individual's reputation. (314)

wellness programs Company-wide programs in which employees receive training regarding things they can do to promote healthy lifestyles. (167)

whistle-blowing The disclosure by employees of illegal, immoral, or illegitimate practices by employers to people or organizations able to take action. (398)

win-win solutions Resolutions to conflicts in which both parties get what they want. (394)

work group inertia Forces within a work group that encourage employees to perform their jobs in certain ways, thereby making them resistant to change. (569)

work restructuring The process of changing the way jobs are done to make them more interesting to workers. (580)

work teams Teams whose members are concerned primarily with using the organization's resources to effectively create its results. (269)

work-related attitudes Attitudes relating to any aspect of work or work settings. (178)

workplace aggression Acts of verbal and physical abuse toward others in organizations, ranging from mild to severe. (401)

workplace bullying The repeated mistreatment of an individual at work in a manner that endangers his or her physical or mental health. (404)

Company Index

Name Index

A

Agassi, Shai, 250
Alexander the Great, 450
Alter, Karen, 250
Amabile, T. M., 498, 508
Amon, Carol, 173
Andrews, M. C., 438
Antonius, Marcus Aurelius, 157
Arango, Andres, 478
Argyris, Chris, 530
Armenakis, A. A., 284
Armstrong, Lance, 288
Ashford, S. J., 573
Atchinson, Tonya, 398
Austin, Nancy K., 322

B

Baer, M., 501
Baird, Eric, 120
Bakker, A. B., 159
Baldes, J., 220
Baldwin, Jerry, 141
Banas, J. T., 571
Barger, David, 184
Barling, J., 200
Bass, B. M., 454
Beach, L. R., 352
Beer, M., 570
Beersma, B., 389
Belichick, Bill, 467
Bell, B. S., 98
Benne, K. D., 259
Bennis,W. G., 449
Berkowitz, Seth, 478
Bethune, Gordon, 83–84
Bezos, Jeff, 510, 514–515
Binet, Alfred, 132
Birkenfeld, Bradley, 398, 399, 400
Blair, Jayson, 47
Blake, R. R., 459
Blanchard, K. H., 466
Blauwet, Cheri, 177
Bolles, R. N., 610
Bolt, Usain, 242
Booker, Cory, 477
Boswell, W. R., 196
Boudreau, J. W., 196
Boulgaides, J. D., 343, 370
Bowerman, Bill, 491
Bowker, Gordon, 141
Boyd, Zachary, 262
Bradley, Bill, 467
Braeden, Eric, 226
Bragg, T., 393
Brandon, David, 210–211
Brin, Sergy, 246–247
Brownell, J., 322
Browning, Elizabeth Barrett, 350
Buckingham, Martin, 174
Burns, Tony, 203
Burr, Don, 457
Bush, Bill, 398
Bush, George W., 358

C

Cameron, James, 21
Cameron, K. S., 486
Campion, M. A., 195
Capetola, Anthony, 395

Caplan, S. E., 307
Carroll, A. B., 61
Case, Steve, 480
Caudron, S., 280
Chase, Robin, 480
Chenault, Kenneth I., 110
Cherian, Joy, 185
Christensen, H. K., 565
Chung, M.-H., 130
Clark, Richard T., 189
Clinton, Bill, 433, 470
Coccolo, Dante, 289
Cole, David E., 444
Conant, Douglas R., 553
Conlon, D. E., 359
Contador, Alberto, 288
Coolidge, Calvin, 321

D

Dabos, G. E., 378
Daft, R. L., 297
Danielson, Antje, 480
Davila, T., 509
Day, Jennifer P., 399
Dean, Earl R., 372–373
Deci, E. L., 232
DeRue, D. S., 423
DeSimone, Livio D., 503
Disney, Walt, 488
Disraeli, Benjamin, 448
Donaghy, Tim, 173–174
Donaldson, L., 539, 540, 542
Donaldson, T., 59
Doyle, Patrick, 210
Drucker, Peter F., 284, 334, 576
Druversteyn, Kent, 49
Dulebohn, J. H., 42
Dunn, Patricia, 69
Dutton, J. E., 573

E

Edison, Thomas, 269, 503
Eichler, Todd, 587
Eisenhower, Dwight D., 448
Elizabeth I, Queen, 450
Ellerth, Kimberly, 433
Els, Ernie, 611
Essenfeld, Joe, 478

F

Fairbank, Richard D., 189
Favre, Brett, 345
Fayol, Henri, 11, 530
Feldman, D. C., 260
Felid, H. S., 284
Ferris, G. R., 136
Field, R. H. G., 335
Fisher, C. M., 498
Ford, Henry, 11, 60
Forgas, J., 150
Francesco, Anne Marie, 78, 96
Franklin, Benjamin, 149
Franklin, Nigel, 247

G

Gallinsky, E., 215
Gantenbein, D., 300
Garrett, Tim, 102
Gates, Bill, 195, 450, 488

Geller, E. S., 224
Gersick, C. J. G., 257
Giles, W. F., 284
Giuliani, R., 39
Godwin, Linda, 280
Goekel, Maryella, 70
Gold, Barry Allen, 78, 96
Goldstein, A. P., 569
Gong, Y., 204
Graham, J. L., 318
Grant, A. M., 241
Greenberg, J., 39, 46
Greene, A., 187
Gregoire, Michael, 2
Gulvik, Jen, 446

H

Hackman, J. R., 241, 273
Hamel, Gary, 510
Hammer, MC, 303
Hannan, Kathy, 247
Hardy, G. E., 199
Hastings, Reed, 460
Heggestad, E. D., 216
Henderson, Maxine, 433
Herman, Jenny, 174
Hersey, P., 466
Heyzer, Noeleen, 64
Highhouse, S., 117
Hill, Anita, 433
Hirschfeld, R. R., 284
Hodgson, J. D., 318
Hoglund, M., 444
Holtz, Lou, 467
Horvitz, Eric, 291
Huelsman, T. J., 148
Hulbert, Mary A., 418
Hurd, Mark, 69

I

Ibuka, Masaru, 429
Ilics, R., 193
Iverson, Jonathan Lee, 114
Iverson, R. D., 200

J

Jackson, Phil, 467
Jaeger, A. M., 582
James, LeBron, 372
Jansen, E., 55
Jensen, M. A., 255
Jenson, Lois, 433
Jobs, Steve, 269, 420
Johnson, Ronald, 174
Johnson, S. K., 385
Johnston, Kristen, 247
Jones, Paula, 433
Jordaan, Michael, 510
Jordan, M. H., 284
Jordan, Michael, 610
Joseph, D. L., 134
Judge, T. A., 193
Judson, A. S., 569

K

Kabanoff, B., 499
Kanfer, R. M., 216, 545
Kaplan, Mark, 184
Kaplinsky, Moshe, 250

Subject Index

Note: Page numbers with f indicate figures; those with t indicate tables.